S0-CCC-090

Magill's Cinema Annual 1998

Magill's Cinema Annual 1998

17th Edition
A Survey of the Films of 1997

Beth A. Fhaner, Editor

Devra M. Sladics, and Jeff Hermann,
Contributing Editors

Christine Tomassini and Michelle Banks, Associate Editors

A VideoHound® Reference

GALE

DETROIT • LONDON

Beth A. Fhaner, Editor
Devra M. Sladics and Jeff Hermann,
Contributing Editors
Christine Tomassini and Michelle Banks,
Associate Editors
Mary Beth Trimper, Production Director
Shanna Heilveil, Production Assistant
Cynthia Baldwin, Product Design Manager
Michelle S. DiMercurio, Art Director
Sherrell Hobbs, Macintosh Artist
Randy Bassett, Image Database Supervisor
Robert Duncan and Mikal Angari, Imaging Specialists
Pamela A. Hayes, Photography Coordinator
Jeffrey Muhr, Editorial Technical Services Specialist

∞™ The paper used in this publication meets the minimum requirements of American National Standard for Information Sciences—Permanence Paper for Printed Library Materials, ANSI Z39.48-1984.

This book is printed on recycled paper that meets Environmental Protection Agency standards.

Address after September 15, 1998:
27500 Drake Road
Farmington Hills, MI 48331-3535
A Cunning Canine® Production

ISBN 0-7876-1156-5
ISSN 0739-2141

Printed in the United States of America

Table of Contents

Preface

Magill's Cinema Annual 1998 continues the fine film reference tradition that defines the VideoHound series of entertainment industry products published by Gale Research. The seventeenth annual volume in a series that developed from the 21-volume core set, *Magill's Survey of Cinema*, the *Annual* was formerly published by Salem Press. Gale's fourth volume, as with the previous Salem volumes, contains essay-reviews of significant domestic and foreign films released in the United States during the preceding year.

The *Magill's* editorial staff at Gale, comprising the VideoHound team and a host of *Magill's* contributors, continues to provide the enhancements that were added to the Annual when Gale acquired the line. These features include:

- More essay-length reviews of significant films released during the year
- Photographs which accompany the reviews and illustrate the obituaries and Life Achievement Award sections
- Trivia and "fun facts" about the reviewed movies, their stars, the crew and production
- Quotes and dialogue "soundbites" from reviewed movies, or from stars and crew about the film
- More complete awards and nominations listings, including the American Academy Awards, Golden Globe, New York Critics Awards, Los Angeles Film Critics Awards, and others (see the User's Guide for more information on awards coverage)
- Box office grosses, including year-end and other significant totals
- Critics' and publicity taglines featured in film reviews and advertisements

In addition to these elements, the *Magill's Cinema Annual 1998* also features:

- A celebrity interview with actress Kim Basinger
- An essay reviewing the career and accomplishments of the recipient of the American Film Institute's Life Achievement Award presented each year to Hollywood luminaries. Director Robert Wise is the 1997 award recipient profiled in this volume.
- An obituaries section profiling major contributors to the film industry who died in 1997
- An annotated list of selected film books published in 1997
- Nine indexes: Director, Screenwriter, Cinematographer, Editor, Art Director, Music, Performer, Subject, and Title (now cumulative)

Compilation Methods

The *Magill's* editorial staff reviews a variety of entertainment industry publications, including trade magazines and newspapers, as well as online sources, on a daily and weekly basis to select significant films for review in *Magill's Cinema Annual*. *Magill's* staff and other contributing reviewers, including film scholars and university faculty, write the reviews included in the *Annual*.

Magill's Cinema Annual: ***A VideoHound Reference***

The *Magill's Survey of Cinema* series, now supplemented by the *Annual*, was honored with the Reference Book of the Year Award in Fine Arts by the American Library Association.

Gale Research, an award-winning publisher of reference products, is proud to offer *Magill's Cinema Annual* as part of its popular VideoHound product line, which includes *VideoHound's Golden Movie Retriever, The Video Sourcebook, VideoHound's Independent Film Guide, VideoHound's Soundtracks, VideoHound's Family Video Guide, VideoHound's Complete Guide to Cult Flicks and Trash Pics, VideoHound's Sci-Fi Experience, VideoHound's Video Premieres,* and many more. Other Gale film-related products include the *St. James Dictionary of Films and Filmmakers* and the *Contemporary Theatre, Film, and Television* series.

Acknowledgments

Thank you to Judy Hartman, GGS Information Services, for her typesetting expertise, and Jeff Muhr, Gale Research, for his technical assistance. A special thank you to Jim Olenski of Thomas Video (Clawson, MI) for making preview copies of videos available to our staff. The *Video-Hound* staff is thanked for its contributions to this project, especially Christine Tomassini, Michelle Banks, Jeff Hermann, Devra Sladics, and Carol Schwartz for their hard work and goodwill, as well as Marty Connors, Christa Brelin, and Julia Furtaw for their guidance and direction.

We most appreciate Bob Cosenza, the Kobal Collection, for his assistance in obtaining photographs.

Introduction

Just as 1996 was labeled the "year of the independents" in the film industry, 1997 saw the Hollywood studios returning to a position of prominence. Studio pictures dominated not only with audiences at the boxoffice, but with critics as well. It's heartening for moviegoers that the studios released so many movies of merit in 1997. These films served to remind us that Hollywood can still do a big picture and do it well. This was especially evident with the overwhelming success of James Cameron's *Titanic*, the megabudget blockbuster that was *the* movie event of the year.

Blessed by audiences and critics alike, Hollywood's biggest and most expensive movie ever made not only blew the competition out of the water at the boxoffice, but swept the Academy Awards as well. Nominated for 14 Oscars and winning 11, *Titanic* entered the Oscar record books, tying with the 1959 film *Ben Hur* for the most prizes given to one film. Director James ("I'm King of the World!") Cameron nabbed a trio of trophies for helming, producing (with Jon Landau), and also serving as one of the pic's editors. It was a fitting tribute to Cameron, who, as director, writer, producer, and editor, took a huge risk in combining his romantic fiction with a real-life tragedy. Cameron devoted years to bringing his vision of *Titanic* to the big screen. Besides building a replica of the *Titanic* 90 percent to scale in Rosarito Beach, Mexico, he also made the dive two and a half miles beneath the Atlantic Ocean to shoot the haunting, rusted ruins of the *Titanic*. Using robo-cameras to shoot inside the ship, Cameron was able to reproduce the original interiors down to the silverware, wallpaper, and carpeting. This attention to detail, along with the breathtaking visuals and superior digital effects, combined to make this sweeping epic one of the most thrilling movies ever experienced in the history of filmmaking. Cameron's extravaganza now stands as the highest grossing film of all time and (as of press time) is still going strong.

The brilliant *L.A. Confidential*, a noirish Hollywood drama focusing on police corruption in '50s Los Angeles, was another studio film that garnered several awards and was considered a cinematic highlight of 1997. Beautifully photographed and directed, *L.A. Confidential* was the overwhelming critics' choice as the best film of the year. Although *L.A. Confidential* had the misfortune of being released in the same year as *Titanic*, director Curtis Hanson didn't walk away from the Academy Awards empty-handed. Nominated for nine Academy Awards, *L.A.* copped two Oscars, including one for Hanson and Brian Helgeland for their adapted screenplay of James Ellroy's complex novel, and another one for supporting actress Kim Basinger for her portrayal of a Veronica Lake look-alike *femme fatale*. Hanson was also nominated as director and a producer of the film, putting him in the company of only a handful of men who have ever been nominated for these three prizes in one year; and among those who didn't win the triple crown were such distinguished filmmakers as Elia Kazan, Ingmar Bergman, and Stanley Kubrick. In this critic's opinion, *L.A. Confidential* was one of the few films of the year that warrants repeat viewing. It truly is a masterpiece—a very impressive accomplishment for Hanson, co-writer Helgeland, and its superior ensemble cast.

In yet another studio release, *As Good As It Gets* made a strong showing at the Oscars, winning both the best actor and actress prizes for Jack Nicholson and Helen Hunt, respectively. Although writer-director James L. Brooks missed out on a directing nomination for *As Good*, he can take heart in the fact that he now has helmed four actors to Oscar wins after directing only four films—an excellent batting average. With his *As Good* win, Nicholson marked his third Oscar, making him only the fourth actor to take home that many. Also of note, each time Nicholson's won, his female co-star also took home the golden statuette.

Other noteworthy cinematic achievements of 1997 included Canadian director Atom Egoyan's hypnotic tragedy *The Sweet Hereafter*, the delightful Japanese film *Shall We Dance?*; writer-director Victor Nunez's low-key story of a beekeeper, a comeback performance by Peter Fonda, in *Ulee's Gold*; Great Britain's sleeper hit comedy *The Full Monty*; Barry Levinson's outrageous political satire *Wag the Dog*; Dame Judi Dench's Oscar-nominated performance as Queen Victoria in the true-life romance *Mrs. Brown*; and Robert Duvall's personal project *The Apostle*, a years-in-the-making effort that he wrote, directed, and starred in.

One common theme throughout the year involved the risk-taking of many established directors. Several of our best directors, including Martin Scorsese, Steven Spielberg, Woody Allen, Francis Ford Coppola, Spike Lee, David Lynch, and many others stretched their creative boundaries and came out with works that seemed to not only inspire, but to challenge them as well. Scorsese explored new territory with *Kundun*, his epic spiritual biography of Tibet's Dalai Lama, as did Spielberg with his impressive and powerful drama *Amistad*, based on a real-life 1839 slave revolt. Clint Eastwood made the most offbeat film of his career with *Midnight in the Garden of Good and Evil*, and Francis Ford Coppola went mainstream with *John Grisham's The Rainmaker*. Even Woody Allen pushed the envelope with his raunchy, scathing look at marriage, adultery, and the literary life in *Deconstructing Harry*. And David Lynch, who's never been known as a conventional filmmaker, proved to be so daring with his latest film *Lost Highway* that many audiences refused to go along for the ride.

Another significant trend that clearly emerged in 1997 was the retro movie movement. The year was full of period films, such as *Austin Powers* with the swinging '60s, Ang Lee's superb drama *The Ice Storm* with its Watergate-era wife swapping, the '70s porn stars of *Boogie Nights*, as well as the '70s cop drama *Donnie Brasco*, not to mention *L.A. Confidential* (1950s), *Titanic* (1912), and Steven Spielberg's *Amistad* (1839). Even old movies found new theatrical life in 1997. George Lucas's classic *Star Wars* trilogy was rereleased and brought in over $138 million in boxoffice revenue—pretty impressive for a film (*Star Wars*) made in 1977. The enormously successful reissue of the *Star Wars* trilogy proved that nostalgia is an extremely powerful force among today's moviegoers. Many studios noted the *Star Wars* phenomenon and quickly took stock of their own libraries, hoping to cash in on other past cinematic treasures.

In addition to classic films, several careers were resurrected in 1997, as witnessed by Peter Fonda's understated lead performance in *Ulee's Gold*, Kim Basinger's Oscar-winning role in *L.A. Confidential*, Burt Reynolds's critically acclaimed turn in *Boogie Nights*, and Sylvester Stallone's effective performance in the riveting thriller *Cop Land*. In fact, Matt Damon (star of *John Grisham's The Rainmaker* and *Good Will Hunting*) was the only youngster nominated among the best actor awards this past year. All the other nominees had him beat by at least a few decades. Even Robert Forster, who starred as a world-weary bondsman in Quentin Tarantino's *Jackie Brown*, earned a supporting Oscar nomination and saw his long-dormant acting career revived. Tarantino also put Pam Grier (the star of such 1970s B-films as *Coffy* and *Foxy Brown*) back into the spotlight as the lead in *Jackie Brown*. Overall, 1997 was considered the year of the comeback for many experienced performers who had been gone too long.

Among new talent to surface this past year were the 27-year-old writer-director Paul Thomas Anderson, who created not only the dazzling *Boogie Nights*, but also made his feature debut with *Hard Eight*, a terrific character study of a small-time professional gambler; director Neil LaBute with his cold-hearted black comedy *In the Company of Men*; director Kasi Lemmons with her outstanding debut *Eve's Bayou*; and actors-screenwriters Matt Damon and Ben Affleck, who won Oscars for best original screenplay for their story of a blue-collar math prodigy in *Good Will Hunting*, and were immediately declared the new *It* boys of Hollywood. And although he's been acting for a while, Rupert Everett had the breakout performance of the summer playing a hilarious role opposite Julia Roberts in *My Best Friend's Wedding*. Expect to see a whole lot more up on the big screen from this talented group of actors and directors.

Sadly, the film industry also lost some beloved stars in 1997: the popular and much respected actor Jimmy Stewart, the Everyman of American cinema; Academy Award–winning director Fred Zinneman; maverick filmmaker Sam Fuller, revered by critics and the French as one of the greatest filmmakers of the postwar era; veteran character actor Burgess Meredith; legendary Japanese actor Toshiro Mifune, known for working extensively with director Akira Kurosawa; popular comedian Red Skelton; and bad boy actor Robert Mitchum, best known for his classic film noir roles. See the Obituaries section in the back of this book for profiles of these and other major contributors to the film industry who died in 1997.

As the silver screen fades out upon another year of moviemaking, the *Magill's* staff looks forward to preparing the 1999 *Annual*, for which additional changes and enhancements are planned. We invite your comments. Please direct all questions and suggestions to:

Beth A. Fhaner
Editor, *Magill's Cinema Annual*
Gale Research
835 Penobscot Bldg.
Detroit, MI 48226-4094
Phone: (313)961-2242
Toll-free: (800)776-6265
Fax: (313)961-6812

Contributing Reviewers

Michael Adams
Graduate School, City University of New York
Vivek Adarkar
Long Island University
Michael Betzold
Freelance Reviewer
David L. Boxerbaum
Freelance Reviewer
Beverley Bare Buehrer
Freelance Reviewer
Reni Celeste
University of Rochester
Robert F. Chicatelli
Freelance Reviewer
Peter N. Chumo II
Freelance Reviewer
J.M. Clark
99Xpress Magazine (Atlanta) Film Editor
Paul B. Cohen
L.A. Weekly Theatre Critic
Roberta Cruger
Freelance Reviewer
Bill Delaney
Freelance Reviewer
David Flanagin
Howard Payne University
G.E. Georges
Freelance Reviewer
Robert F. Green
Virginia Polytechnic Institute and State University
Jill Hamilton
Freelance Reviewer
Diane Hatch-Avis
Freelance Reviewer
Mary Hess
Freelance Reviewer
Glenn Hopp
Howard Payne University
David King
Freelance Reviewer
Patricia Kowal
Freelance Reviewer/Script Consultant
Leon Lewis
Appalachian State University
Nancy Matson
Freelance Reviewer
Karl Michalak
Freelance Reviewer
Robert Mitchell
University of Arizona
Lisa Paddock
Freelance Reviewer
Carl Rollyson
Baruch College, City University of New York
Jacqui Sadashige
University of Pennsylvania
Kirby Tepper
Freelance Reviewer
Hilary Weber
Freelance Reviewer
James M. Welsh
Salisbury State University

User's Guide

Alphabetization

Film titles and reviews are arranged on a word-by-word basis, including articles and prepositions. English leading articles (A, An, The) are ignored, as are foreign leading articles (El, Il, La, Las, Le, Les, Los). Other considerations:

- Acronyms appear alphabetically as if regular words.
- Common abbreviations in titles file as if they are spelled out, so *Mr. Magoo* will be found as if it was spelled *Mister Magoo.*
- Proper names in titles are alphabetized beginning with the individual's first name, for instance, *Jackie Brown* will be found under "J."
- Titles with numbers, for instance, *4 Little Girls*, are alphabetized as if the number were spelled out, in this case, "Four." When numeric titles gather in close proximity to each other, the titles will be arranged in a low-to-high numeric sequence.

Special Sections

List of Awards. An annual list of awards bestowed upon the year's films by ten international associations: Academy of Motion Picture Arts and Sciences, Directors Guild of America Award, Golden Globe Awards, Golden Palm Awards (Cannes International Film Festival), Los Angeles Film Critics Awards, National Board of Review Awards, National Society of Film Critics Awards, New York Film Critics Awards, and the Writer's Guild Awards.

Life Achievement Award. An essay reviewing the career and accomplishments of the recipient of the American Film Institute's Life Achievement Award presented each year to Hollywood luminaries. Director Robert Wise is the 1997 award recipient profiled in this volume.

Obituaries. Profiles of major contributors to the film industry who died in 1997.

Selected Film Books of 1997. An annotated list of selected film books published in 1997.

Indexes

Film titles and artists are arranged into eight indexes, allowing the reader to effectively approach a film from any one of several directions, including not only its credits but its subject matter.

Director, Screenwriter, Cinematographer, Editor, Music, Art Director, and *Performer Indexes* are arranged according to artists appearing in this volume, followed by a list of the films on which they worked.

Subject Index. Films may be categorized under several of the subject terms arranged alphabetically in this section.

Sample Review

Each *Magill's* review contains up to sixteen items of information. A fictionalized composite sample review containing all the elements of information which may be included in a full-length review follows the outline below. The circled number preceding each element in the sample review on page XV designates an item of information that is explained in the outline on the next page.

1 **Title:** Film title as it was released in the United States.

2 **Foreign or alternate title(s):** The film's original title or titles as released outside the United States, or alternate film title or titles. Foreign and alternate titles also appear in the Title Index to facilitate user access.

3 **Taglines:** Up to ten publicity or critical taglines for the film from advertisements or reviews.

4 **Box office information:** Year-end or other box office domestic revenues for the film.

5 **Film review or abstract:** A one-paragraph abstract or 750-1500-word signed review of the film, including brief plot summary, and for full-length reviews, an analytic overview of the film and its critical reception.

6 **Principal characters:** Up to 25 listings of the film's principal characters and the names of the actors who play them in the film. The names of actors who play themselves are cited twice (as character and actor).

7 **Country of origin:** The film's country or countries of origin if other than the United States.

8 **Release date:** The year of the film's first general release.

9 **Production information:** This section typically includes the name(s) of the film's producer(s), production company, and distributor, director(s), screenwriter(s), author(s) or creator(s) and the novel, play, short story, television show, motion picture, or other work, or character(s), that the film was based upon; cinematographer(s) (if the film is animated, this will be replaced with Animation or Animation Direction); editor(s); art director(s), production designer(s), set decorator(s) or set designer(s); music composer(s); and other credits such as visual effects, sound, casting, costume design, and song(s) and songwriter(s).

10 **MPAA rating:** The film's rating by the Motion Picture Association of America. If there is no rating given, the line will read, "no listing."

11 **Running time:** The film's running time in minutes.

12 **Reviewer byline:** The name of the reviewer who wrote the full-length review. A complete list of this volume's contributors appears in the "Contributing Reviewers" section which follows the Introduction.

13 **Reviews:** A list of up to 25 brief citations of major newspaper and journal reviews of the film, including publication title, date of review, and page number.

14 **Awards information:** Awards won by the film, followed by category and name of winning cast or crew member. Listings of the film's nominations follow the wins on a separate line for each award. Awards are arranged alphabetically. Information is listed for films which won or were nominated for the following awards: American Academy Awards, Australian Film Institute, British Academy of Film and Television Arts, Canadian Genie, Cannes Film Festival, Directors Guild of America, French Cesar, Golden Globe, Independent Spirit, Los Angeles Film Critics Association Awards, Montreal Film Festival, MTV Movie Awards, National Board of Review Awards, National Society of Film Critics Awards, New York Critics Awards, Sundance Film Festival, Toronto-City Awards, Writers Guild of America, and others.

15 **Film quotes:** Memorable dialogue directly from the film, attributed to the character who spoke it, or comment from cast or crew members or reviewers about the film.

16 **Film trivia:** Interesting tidbits about the film, its cast, or production crew.

2

1 The Gump Diaries (Los Diarios del Gump)

3 "Love means never having to say you're stupid."
—Movie tagline

"This was a really good movie. I liked it." —Joe Critic, *Daily News*

4 

Box Office Gross: $10 million (December 15, 1994)

CREDITS

6 **Jim Carroll:** Leonardo DiCaprio
Swifty: Bruno Kirby
Jim's Mother: Lorraine Bracco
Mickey: Mark Wahlberg

7 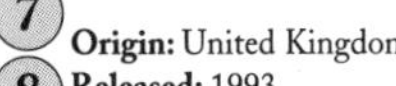

Origin: United Kingdom
8 **Released:** 1993
Production: Liz Heller, John Bard Manulis for New Line Cinema; released by Island Pictures 9
Direction: Scott Kalvert
Author: Bryan Goluboff; based on the novel by Jim Carroll
Cinematographer: David Phillips
Editing: Dana Congdon
Production design: Christopher Nowak
Set decoration: Harriet Zucker
Sound: William Sarokin
Costume design: David C. Robinson
Music: Graeme Revell
10 **MPAA rating:** R
11 **Running time:** 102 minutes

5 In writer/director Robert Zemeckis' *Back to the Future* trilogy (1985, 1989, 1990), Marty McFly (Michael J. Fox) and his scientist sidekick Doc Brown (Christopher Lloyd) journey backward and forward in time, attempting to smooth over some rough spots in their personal histories in order to remain true to their individual destinies. Throughout their time-travel adventures, Doc Brown insists that neither he nor Marty influence any major historical events, believing that to do so would result in catastrophic changes in humankind's ultimate destiny. By the end of the trilogy, however, Doc Brown has revised his thinking and tells Marty that, "Your future hasn't been written yet. No one's has. Your future is whatever you make it. So make it a good one."

In *Forrest Gump*, Zemeckis once again explores the theme of personal destiny and how an individual's life affects and is affected by his historical time period. This time, however, Zemeckis and screenwriter Eric Roth chronicle the life of a character who does nothing but meddle in the historical events of his time without even trying to do so. By the film's conclusion, however, it has become apparent that Zemeckis' main concern is something more than merely having fun with four decades of American history. In the process of re-creating significant moments in time, he has captured on celluloid something eternal and timeless—the soul of humanity personified by a nondescript simpleton from the deep South.

15 "The state of existence may be likened unto a receptacle containing cocoa-based confections, in that one may never predict that which one may receive." —Forrest Gump, from *The Gump Diaries*

The film begins following the flight of a seemingly insignificant feather as it floats down from the sky and brushes against various objects and people before finally coming to rest at the feet of Forrest Gump (Tom Hanks). Forrest, who is sitting on a bus-stop bench, reaches down and picks up the feather, smooths it out, then opens his traveling case and carefully places the feather between the pages of his favorite book, *Curious George*.

In this simple but hauntingly beautiful opening scene, the filmmakers illustrate the film's principal concern: Is life a series of random events over which a person has no control, or is there an underlying order to things that leads to the fulfillment of an individual's destiny? The rest of the film is a humorous and moving attempt to prove that, underlying the random, chaotic events that make up a person's life, there exists a benign and simple order.

Forrest sits on the bench throughout most of the film, talking about various events of his life to others who happen to sit down next to him. It does not take long, however, for the audience to realize that Forrest's seemingly random The action shifts to the mid-1950's with Forrest as a young boy (Michael Humphreys) being fitted with leg braces to correct a curvature in his spine. The action shifts to the mid-1950's to a in his spine. When the first U.S. Ping-Pong team to This of movie magic has not accomplished by special effects or computer-altered images, by something much more impressive and harder to achieve.

AWARDS AND NOMINATIONS

14 **Academy Awards 1994:** Best Film, Best Actor (Hanks), Best Special Effects, Best Cinematography
Nominations: Best Actress (Fields), Best Screenplay, Best Director (Zameckis)
Golden Globe Awards 1994: Best Film,
Nominations: Best Actor (Hanks), Best Supporting Actress (Wright), Best Music, Best Special Effects

chatter to a parade of strangers has a perfect chronological order to it. He tells his first story after looking down at the feet of his first bench partner and observing, "Mama always said that you can tell a lot about a person by the shoes they wear." Then, in a voice-over narration, Forrest begins the story of his life, first by telling about the first pair of shoes he can remember wearing.

16 

Hanks was the first actor since Spencer Tracy to win back-to-back Oscars for Best Actor. Hanks received the award in 1993 for his performance in *Philadelphia*. Tracy won Oscars in 1937 for *Captains Courageous* and in 1938 for *Boys Town*.

The action shifts to the mid-1950's with Forrest as a young boy (Michael Humphreys) being fitted with leg braces to correct a curvature in his spine. Despite this traumatic handicap, Forrest remains unaffected, thanks to his mother (Sally Field) who reminds him on more than one occasion that he is no different from anyone else. Although this and most of Mrs. Gump's other words of advice are in the form of hackneyed cliches, Forrest whose intelligence quotient is below normal, sincerely believes every one of them, namely because he instinctively knows they are sincere expressions of his mother's love and fierce devotion.

12 —*John Byline*

REVIEWS

13 Entertainment Weekly. July 15, 1994, p. 42.
The Hollywood Reporter. June 29, 1994, p. 7.
Los Angeles Times. July 6, 1994, p. F1.

Interview with Kim Basinger

Just two years shy of two full decades in the movie business, Kim Basinger's mercurial career has seen many peaks and valleys. In retrospect, one could describe her as a magnet for controversy. She has lived her life under the unforgiving, myopic public eye and has clearly gone in directions, both personally and professionally, that could be viewed as haphazard. After closer examination it becomes clear that Kim Basinger is a woman who is spirited yet focused and has arrived at her current station in life on sheer will and chutzpah. She has faults and frailties but has survived in a mercilessly shallow environment with her dignity fully intact. She is a master of marketing and self-promotion, and her savvy, trailblazing business acumen was firmly entrenched long before it came into vogue.

Her latest and arguably greatest professional accomplishment was recently winning the supporting actress Oscar for her performance in *L.A. Confidential*, the crime thriller many considered to be the best film of 1997. Her marriage to actor Alec Baldwin recently eclipsed the five-year mark, a stretch of time practically unheard of in La-La Land. The three-year gap between the dismal 1994 feature *Pret-a-Porter* and *L.A. Confidential* is the longest she's gone without appearing onscreen, causing virtually everyone to brand her *Confidential* role as a "comeback" performance. The expression "comeback" is a buzzword that has been bandied about so many times in the entertainment industry that its meaning has become frivolous.

After a string of brain-dead parts in mediocre projects, Basinger decided to hold out until something substantial was presented to her. She even initially passed on *L.A. Confidential* until director Curtis Hanson convinced her that it wasn't just another "hooker-with-a-heart-of-gold" role.

The remainder of Basinger's three-year hiatus was spent doting on her newborn baby girl, Ireland, and taking a high-profile role as a champion for assorted animal rights causes. With husband Alec's equally visible campaigning for the NEA, the Baldwin-Basinger marriage is among the most socially aware that Hollywood has ever seen. For the first time ever, it appears Basinger has struck a healthy balance between career and family; but it was a long time coming and not without assorted calamities that would cause other, less resilient individuals to surrender.

Although she had appeared in eight features previously, Basinger didn't make much of a lasting impression until *9 1/2 Weeks* made its auspicious debut in 1986. Often unfairly dismissed as soft-core pornography with attitude, *9 1/2 Weeks* became a culture-altering event. Basinger's portrayal of a woman discovering her repressed sexuality went beyond the merely physical and delved into psychological realms never before explored in a mainstream film. By doing as well as she did, Basinger raised the expectations of future roles to a level few would have been able to match. The overwhelming critical praise and commercial windfalls that came in the wake of *9 1/2 Weeks* raised Basinger to A-list status among Hollywood's leading ladies, and offers began pouring in. As is the case with such bountiful rewards, there is the often-accompanying downside. The bulk of the subsequent roles called for vacuous, sexually drenched, damsel-in-distress bimbos.

What followed was a series of sophomoric romantic thrillers and disastrous slapstick comedies that virtually erased the praises of *9 1/2 Weeks*. Needing once again to gain respect from scratch, Basinger regrouped and delivered a riveting presentation as the title character in *Nadine*. As a beautician in early '50s rural Texas, she witnesses a murder and, with the assistance of her estranged husband, tracks down the killer. Basinger expertly delivered several bits of offbeat, black humor that made it evident (with the right material and director) that she could do comedy.

Although she had a part in the worldwide success of *Batman*, her performance never rose much higher than glorified window-dressing. In 1991, after a two-year respite, Basinger began working on a new film that paired her with Baldwin, whom she would marry two years later. (She was previously wed to former make-up artist Ron Britton). *The Marrying Man* gave Basinger the opportunity to showcase her considerable singing abilities as Vicki Anderson, a Las Vegas lounge singer who just happens to be dating mob kingpin Bugsy Siegel.

In late 1992, Basinger met with writer-director Jennifer Lynch (daughter of legendary avant-garde auteur David Lynch) to discuss the lead role in a disturbing psychological drama. Lynch left the meeting with an oral agreement from Basinger to play the part of Helena, a woman who has all of her limbs surgically removed by a demented admirer. After further consideration, Basinger decided to turn down the role—not that uncommon an occurrence in Hollywood, but evidently financing for the film was contingent on

Basinger's participation, and Lynch's Main Line Productions wasn't pleased with her change of heart. Main Line decided to make an example out of Basinger; they sued her for $9 million and won.

To make matters worse, the string of films Basinger made right before and directly after the *Boxing Helena* fiasco (*Final Analysis*, *Cool World*, *Wayne's World 2*, *The Real McCoy*, *The Getaway*, and *Ready to Wear*) had brought her bankability down to an all-time low. Turning out a couple stinkers back-to-back is OK; six in a row can sound the death knell.

With *L.A. Confidential*, Basinger has, like the proverbial phoenix, risen from the ashes. At age 44, she possesses the same physical allure women half her age would kill for. Along with receiving not only an Oscar, but also Golden Globe and Screen Actors Guild Awards, Basinger garnered some long-overdue vindication. Somewhere beyond the sultry image that has been indelibly burned into the minds of movie fans for the last couple decades lies the soul of a very talented actress. The role of Lynn Bracken has also brought her what she has been looking for her entire life: respect for her work on her own, unconditional terms.

The following contains excerpts of an exclusive interview Basinger granted to Atlanta-based *Magill's* contributor J.M. Clark upon the theatrical release of *L.A. Confidential*.

What was it [writer-director] Curtis Hanson said that convinced you to take the Lynn Bracken role in *L.A. Confidential*?

I've never in my life sat across from any director and had them *tell* me I was going to take a role. He just said "You *are* Lynn Bracken." I took a moment and thought, well...that took some nerve. As it turns out, Curtis is a very charming and persuasive man; I fell in love with him the instant I met him. He asked me to read the script a second time. Frankly, I didn't get it on the first read; it's pretty heavy material. But what ultimately sold me was the dialogue. I had never read such great dialogue.

It's been rumored you turned him down initially. Is that true?

Yes, but not because I didn't like it. I had just had a baby and was not interested *at all* in going to work. I was really getting into that June and Ward [Cleaver] life. I just loved staying home with the baby; she was the one getting my full attention. None of the scripts I was being sent were getting the consideration they deserved. But I knew that it was in my best interest to get back into the swing of things and this was, by far, the best work I was being offered.

How do you feel about all of this talk regarding the Oscars?

I hope that you're talking about Curtis and the movie getting those Oscars. I could tell when we were doing our first read-through that we had stumbled on to something special. Usually when you're making a movie, you have a good idea what it's going to look like when it's done. But *Confidential* is so textured and richly detailed; I had no idea how the finished product would look. I first saw it while sitting next to Curtis at Cannes. I was in awe. Just speechless. That doesn't happen very often [laughs a self-deprecating laugh]. It's given me a newfound respect for directors—what they have to do day in, day out. It's tough work, especially with this kind of material. The way he handled everything on the set; with such grace and humor, it took away all the pressure. You get a director who stays cool and chances are you're going to see great things happen when the cameras role.

Of all the characters you've played, which one is the most like you?

I'd have to say "Nadine." Her sense of humor is what got her through everything in the end and that's been the one constant saving grace for me. If you don't have a sense of humor in this business, you're sunk.

Did you know early on that you wanted to act?

I was always a big fan of the movies. I was intrigued with the emotional impact they had on my father; emotions I rarely saw in real-life situations. I think when we're younger, we want our parents to be proud of us; we seek their approval. I think my father's love of the movies was the principal reason I chose acting.

What is the best thing about being married to Alec Baldwin?

I really lucked out there. The one thing that drew me to Alec was his deep moral and ethical fiber; something I hadn't seen elsewhere. He's very intelligent and intriguing and I've always been drawn to people who carry a deep passion for what they believe in.

How did your performance in *9 1/2 Weeks* affect your career?

I didn't know it at the time, but it turned out to be a very wise career choice; I'm very proud of that movie. It has a huge cult following, especially among women. I think it's still playing in a theater somewhere in Paris. From an acting perspective, I felt very compelled to do it; emotionally it was a very hard piece to do and that's where I wanted to go.

Any regrets regarding the appearance in *Playboy*?

It's not something I could or would want to do now, but no. No regrets. Success in this business is mostly an issue of timing and at the time, it was the right thing to do. Remember, I was promoting a James Bond film, it wasn't much of a stretch. I'm really not the kind of person who regrets things. Everything that's happened in my career, both good and bad, has taught me something and made me wiser. If you go through an experience and fail to learn anything, that's when you should think about regrets.

Thank you for that segue. What did you take away with you from the *Boxing Helena* debacle?

Somebody had to take a hit for that and again, timing was everything. Every single day in Hollywood, people are leaving movies because of conflicts of interest. Walking away from a role, for whatever the reason, rarely gets any notice in this town. Look at Travolta, he just went through it with [Roman] Polanski [with *The Double*]. He left because of artistic differences, just like me. In the end it was all about money. But unfortunately, they picked the wrong girl. Few people know that Madonna was [director Jennifer Lynch's] first choice but she walked away too, for the same reason as me and they were very angry. Madonna is very well protected in Hollywood because of all the money she generates, so they were afraid to go after her. She was the one with all the money, not me. It didn't matter; someone was going pay and I got stuck with the tab. But you know what? It didn't change one thing.

When did you first realize that you'd really made it?

When my daddy made a comment to me after seeing my picture on the cover of a magazine at a newsstand. When he acknowledged it, when it was seen through his eyes, that's when it registered. I could never measure it with other people. You get requests for autographs and pictures, but that stuff just comes with the territory. Strangely enough, you can tell whether or not you've made it when you go to Europe. It's true. Europeans are very honest that way. If they love you, they'll show it. If they don't, they won't lie to you, they'll tell you they hate you. They aren't as star-struck as Americans.

Is it true that you've got an album coming out?

Well, I did finish an album for Warner Bros., but I decided not to release it. I did it at the same time that I was recording the soundtrack for *The Marrying Man*. Standards in the morning, R&B at night. It's actually got some pretty good upbeat, urban contemporary material, but I don't think it's really indicative of me or where I'm at now.

Describe the time with Alec during the filming of *The Marrying Man*.

I loved it. A lot of people had a problem with the movie but I thought it turned out very well. No matter what anybody says, or what other people say went on, it's a great thing to have on film, something we can give to our daughter.

Did your Southern upbringing help or hurt you in Hollywood?

A lot of people have a preconceived notion that everyone from the South just fell off of a hay truck. I'm serious. If you're not from the Northeast, you're not a serious player and you must be out of it. But I'll tell you where the South has the North and the rest of the world beat hands down and that's with literature. Southern writers have more heart, more soul, more humor. They've got their finger on the pulse of life, period. I'd like to think that I have one real good book in me. I've already toyed with the idea of doing a children's book or two.

Any favorite writers?

Mark Twain and Truman Capote.

Has there been any improvement in the offers as a result of the critical reaction to *L.A. Confidential*?

Well, yes and no. I'm getting the same amount of offers as before and I do see some higher-brow dramatic pieces that I wouldn't have gotten before, but I'm still going to be more selective than I was in the past. Having a family will do that to you; you know, change your priorities. If I have to spend time away from [daughter] Ireland, it better be for a good reason. Like I said before, timing is everything and right now, things are good, but this is a fickle business. Getting the critical approval I've received is not something that I'm used to and I'm going to let it soak in. It feels nice. For a change.

Absolute Power

Absolute Power Corrupts Absolutely.—Movie tagline

"A tight, taut thriller with a twist."—Roger Ebert, *Chicago Sun-Times*

"An absolutely terrific thriller!"—Joel Siegel, *Good Morning America*

"Sleek and satisfying entertainment! Enlivened with suspense and bursts of sly, biting humor." —Kenneth Turan, *Los Angeles Times*

"Delightful. Eastwood is at his effortless, sly-boots best."—David Ansen, *Newsweek*

"A gripping thriller. Top-notch supporting players."—Leah Rozen, *People*

"A wickedly entertaining spine tingler!"—Peter Travers, *Rolling Stone*

"A sweet pleasure."—Richard Corliss, *Time*

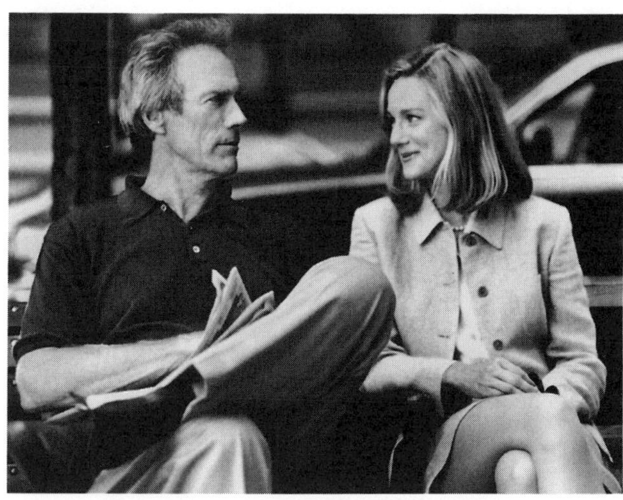

After witnessing the President commit a murder, master thief Luther Whitney confides in his estranged daughter Kate (Laura Linney) in the political thriller *Absolute Power*.

Box Office: $50,068,310

For the bulk of his extensive, stellar career, Clint Eastwood has been discounted as an emotionless, monotone, steely-eyed adventure star who alternated his productions between period westerns and bad action films. He started directing in 1971 (*Play Misty For Me*), but was never considered a true "artist" until *Unforgiven* won the Best Picture and Best Director Oscars in 1992. Eastwood turned 67 years old in 1997. His immensely loyal following is larger than ever and he has remained a box office behemoth for close to 40 years, a monumental achievement by anyone's standards. In an industry obsessed with youth, he defies the odds and can be counted on as one of a very small group of male actors who are old enough to receive social security *and* have the ability to open films based solely on their sex appeal quotient. No longer having the need (or desire) to prove anything to anybody, Eastwood handpicks the projects he wants to be involved with and nonchalantly refuses to play by anything resembling the normal Hollywood rules. His projects are routinely delivered to the studios under budget and usually before the due date. He employs the same basic crew he used on *Play Misty For Me*. He works extremely fast and often incorporates practice or off-takes into the final print. He doesn't ask actors to provide screen tests or personal interviews: he hires people based on gut instinct and the body of their previous work. The performers say he's a joy to work for but he won't suffer fools gladly.

In Baldacci's novel, Luther Whitney dies halfway through the book; also his hero, lawyer Jack Graham, is nowhere in the movie.

Absolute Power, the twentieth Eastwood-directed movie, goes where no mystery/espionage film has ever gone before. Luther Whitney (Eastwood), is a burglar of the upper-crust, who takes his time meticulously casing prospective victims. Luther is a war hero and has never been arrested for any crime. The film opens with a normal day in his otherwise unspectacular life. With sketch pad in hand, he sits in a museum and gently passes the day away doing pencil sketches of El Greco paintings. In the evening, he's seen alone in the dining room of his quiet, nondescript Washington, DC row house. He sits in a dark room while drinking fine wine and eating dinner off of china rather than out of styrofoam containers. He's a solitary man, but not necessarily lonely. He appreciates the finer things in life and has an erudite refinement, but is devoid of any haughty pretentiousness. Luther is patient and methodical. The homework he does preparing for his crimes virtually ensures his undetected escape.

Luther's current target is the home of wealthy socialite and philanthropist, Walter Sullivan (E.G. Marshall). After subduing a highly sophisticated alarm system, he makes his way upstairs to the master bedroom. The cache of riches is hidden in a safe room, accessible only by remote control and paneled with two-way mirrors. Luther liquidates immense amounts of cash and jewelry from the many drawers and bureaus. Just as he prepares to evacuate, a young lady enters the room with a gentlemen suitor in tow. He recognizes her from the many pictures in the hall as the lady of the house, Christy Sullivan (Melora Hardin). Christy is young enough to be her husband's grandchild. She and her guest are visibly intoxicated. In their stupor, they begin a fumbling romantic interlude until the man begins to get abusive. It's clear that Luther wants to help the woman but would risk his own capture by doing so. After many clothes are torn and much blood is drawn, Christy grabs a nearby letter opener and stabs the man in the arm. She raises the blade again but before she can drive it into the man's chest, two men wearing suits enter the room and put two bullets in her brain.

The lights in the room go up and in walks Gloria Russell (Judy Davis). After gasping at the carnage before her, she begins bellowing at the two goons, questioning how things could have gotten so far out of hand. In reply, Bill Burton (Scott Glenn) reminds her that rough sex is the man's typical modus operandi and the noises from the other side of the door were nothing out of the ordinary. Gloria looks at the lothario, now passed out on the bed, and nods back at Burton in feigned agreement as the trio begin to meticulously clean up the mess. All the while, Luther sits patiently, waiting for a window of escape. Now that the three stalwart handlers have the crime scene in order, they carry their employer out of the house and into a waiting limousine. In error, they leave the letter opener behind, which Luther grabs while exiting. He gets away, but only after a lengthy chase through the surrounding woods. Burton and his associate Tim Collin (Dennis Haysbert) are able to get a license plate number and, after reporting back to Gloria, all three feel confident that they can track the witness down and eliminate him before any further damage is done.

CREDITS

Luther Whitney: Clint Eastwood
President Alan Richmond: Gene Hackman
Seth Frank: Ed Harris
Kate Whitney: Laura Linney
Gloria Russell: Judy Davis
Tim Collin: Dennis Haysbert
Bill Burton: Scott Glenn
Walter Sullivan: E.G. Marshall
Christy Sullivan: Melora Hardin

Origin: USA
Released: 1997
Production: Clint Eastwood, Karen Spiegel for Castle Rock Entertainment and Malpaso; released by Columbia Pictures
Direction: Clint Eastwood
Screenplay: William Goldman; based on the novel by David Baldacci
Cinematography: Jack N. Green
Sound: Darin Knight
Editing: Joel Cox
Music: Lennie Niehaus
Production design: Henry Bumstead
Art direction: Jack Taylor
Set decoration: Dick Goddard, Anne D. McCulley
Stunt coordination: Buddy Van Horn
Casting: Phyllis Huffman
MPAA rating: R
Running Time: 120 minutes

At this point, barely 20 minutes into the film, Eastwood has already broken convention and shown us all of the bad guys. What he hasn't done, but is about to do, is drop the bomb and reveal the identity of the man everyone is protecting. He is Alan Richmond, current president of the United States. On the surface, it would appear that Eastwood and screenwriter William Goldman have now removed all of the suspense from the story (which is based on the 1996 best-seller by David Baldacci), but that isn't the case. Knowing that a philandering US president (played with slimy gusto by Gene Hackman) is behind a cover-up isn't hard to believe. Scandal seems to be part of the job description (just ask the current, real-life White House resident). Eastwood has now set up a four-way chess match between Luther, the presidency, the DC police (led by detective Seth Frank (Ed Harris), and grieving widower Sullivan. Because of his inexhaustible patience, cunning, and talent for getting in and out of precarious situations, Luther holds all of the cards. He knows everything, everyone else knows just bits and pieces. He has the real absolute power here.

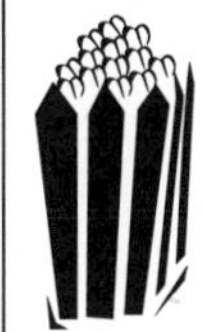

Luther to detective Frank: "Go down a rope in the middle of the night? If I could do that, I'd be a star at my AARP meetings."

The license plate number that everyone thought would lead them to Luther is no good; the vehicle he used was stolen. As Burton, Scott Glenn shows us a man who has grown weary of playing baby-sitter to a carnally obsessed chief executive. His better years are far behind him and the idea of tracking down and killing Luther doesn't particularly thrill him. The Secret Service was designed to protect the president, but not in this manner. The thought of eliminating Luther does, however, appeal to Collin, whose ice-water-in-the-veins, business-as-usual approach to murder is truly menacing. Haysbert's rendering of Collin as the nihilistic, reptilian button man is astounding. Collin seems to take particular pleasure in pursuing Luther's estranged lawyer daughter Kate (Laura Linney). The White House figures that stalking and intimidating Kate will draw Luther out of the woodwork. Their assumption is right and Kate does have a near death experience, but it gets them no closer to Luther. For her part, Davis milks the dedicated, Chief of Staff role for all it's worth. The Australian born Davis, easily one of the industry's most talented actresses, paints Russell as high-strung and career-driven, willing to do anything to save the nation's highest office from scandal. Luther clearly understands Russell's lust for power and later uses her to make a dig at Richmond.

Like Davis, Ed Harris is regularly handed supporting roles in high profile projects and is never less than riveting. After discovering a crime scene that's a little too neat, and finding a corpse in a position that defies logic, Frank determines that this wasn't simply a botched burglary. After checking the FBI files, he determines that only a very select few men could have gotten past the intricate security system and targets Luther as his number one suspect. He can't arrest or detain Luther without any evidence (and Luther has already arranged an ingenious alibi) so he instead decides to coyly and informally quiz him about the crime. Luther responds in kind to Frank's queries, not with any direct answers but in a rather couched, roundabout fashion that he hopes will push Frank in the right direction. Along the way, Eastwood pokes fun at Luther and himself by inferring that a man of such advanced age could never make the harrowing escape Frank suggests and with all of this excitement, he might even want to get his pacemaker checked.

Because of Sullivan's (understandable) thirst for wrathful, frontier justice, he hires all the right people to first bug police headquarters (which the White House has already done), then hunt down and assassinate his wife's killer (who he assumes is also the burglar). Luther eventually learns of the patriarchal relationship between Sullivan and Richmond and becomes incensed at the president's heartless and dishonest treatment of his alleged mentor. This is when Eastwood's trademark clenched teeth, "make-my-day" resolve is called to the forefront.

Director Eastwood's unique pattern of strategic, mental hopscotch is practiced throughout the entire length of the movie and concludes with an unconventional, poetic ending. As Luther, Eastwood the actor seems to be drawing comparisons to his own current station in life: a sly, successful, oft misunderstood, dedicated, artistic career man who is aging gracefully but stays young by always having something wickedly delightful going on behind that stoic, ruggedly handsome facade.

—J.M. Clark

REVIEWS

Chicago Tribune. February 14, 1997, p. 4.
Entertainment Weekly. February 14, 1997, p. 39.
Detroit News. February 14, 1997, p. 1D.
Los Angeles Times. February 14, 1997, p. F1.
New York Times. February 14, 1997, p. B1.
People. February 17, 1997, p. 19.
Rolling Stone. March 6, 1997, p. 75.
Sight and Sound. June, 1997, p. 44.
Time. February 24, 1997.
USA Today. February 14, 1997, p. 4D.
Variety. February 10, 1997, p. 62.
Village Voice. February 18, 1997, p. 75.

Addicted to Love

A comedy about getting off on getting even.
—Movie tagline

"Extremely funny. Meg Ryan is a dazzling delight. Matthew Broderick is irresistible."—Susan Granger, *American Movie Classics*

"A romance that's full of surprises."—Jeanne Wolf, *Jeanne Wolf's Hollywood*

"You won't see a funnier, more daring romantic comedy this year."—Jim Svejda, *KNX, CBS Radio*

"Funny, fresh, outrageous!"—Peter Travers, *Rolling Stone*

"Exhilarating romantic comedy. Meg Ryan gives one of her best performances. Matthew Broderick wins you over."—Barbara and Scott Siegel, *Siegel Entertainment Syndicate*

"A great date film."—Gene Siskel, *Siskel & Ebert*

Box Office: $34,673,095

Meg Ryan sheds her girl-next-door persona to play a hard-edged stalker in Griffin Dunne's black romantic comedy, *Addicted to Love.* While it is a welcome change from such maudlin roles as *Sleepless in Seattle* (1993) and *When Harry Met Sally* (1989), Ms. Ryan is left adrift with the weakest of co-stars, Matthew Broderick. The result is a total lack of chemistry between the two stars and proves to be the major undoing of this potentially wicked comedy about the lengths some jilted lovers will go to extract revenge.

Producers Bobby Newmyer and Jeffrey Silver first optioned the screenplay in 1989 intending it as a follow-up to their first movie, *sex, lies and videotape.*

When Midwestern astronomer Sam (Matthew Broderick) learns that his estranged fiancee Linda (Kelly Preston) has moved in with the sexy French chef, Anton (French film star Tcheky Karyo from *The Professional,* 1996), he puts his life on hold and goes to New York with the hope of winning her back. He entrenches himself into the dilapidated building across from the couple and, in some perverted attempt to convince himself that he is not a voyeur, Sam erects a camera obscura that allows him an indirect way to spy on the love of his life. Sam is hoping to be able to wait out Linda's fascination with this exotic foreigner and intends to be there when the inevitable big split occurs.

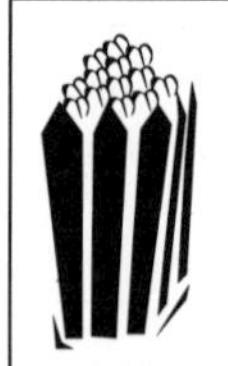

Maggie about Anton: "I don't want him back. I want him vaporized."

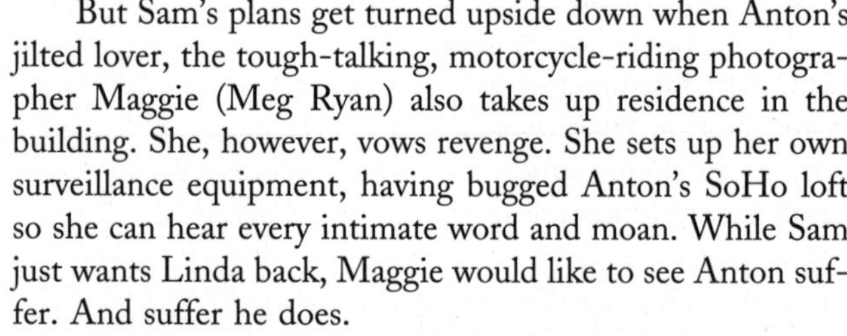

But Sam's plans get turned upside down when Anton's jilted lover, the tough-talking, motorcycle-riding photographer Maggie (Meg Ryan) also takes up residence in the building. She, however, vows revenge. She sets up her own surveillance equipment, having bugged Anton's SoHo loft so she can hear every intimate word and moan. While Sam just wants Linda back, Maggie would like to see Anton suffer. And suffer he does.

With Sam's help, Maggie ensures that Linda suspects Anton of cheating on her with another woman, as well as trying to destroy his restaurant with a few well-placed cockroaches in the meal of the arrogant newspaper food critic (played humorously by director Dunne's real-life father, writer Dominick Dunne.)

As one might imagine, Sam and Maggie do not like each other much at first. She views him as a passive wimp, while he has a hard time getting past her hard-edged demeanor. But as the conventions of the romantic comedy genre dictate, Sam and Maggie begin to fall in love as they watch their ex-lovers, projected on the wall like an elusive, unattainable movie image, drift farther and farther away.

While Maggie talks tough, deep down she is brokenhearted. She suspects that Anton never loved her, but merely viewed her as a way to secure his green card. As for Sam, he begins to learn things about the schoolmarm Linda that he never expected, such as, much to his shock, how rough she likes her sex.

Actor Griffin Dunne makes his feature-film directing debut with *Addicted to Love* and it seems obvious that he picked up more than a few tips from Martin Scorsese while filming the black comedy *After Hours* (1985). He previously directed the short film, *Duke of Groove,* which earned an Academy Award nomination, and with *Addicted to Love,* Dunne demonstrates a talent for recreating urban angst. It is unfortunate, however, that he softens the emotional blow with this material, no doubt succumbing to studio pressure for a happy ending.

Dunne makes terrific use of the camera obscura, a device through which reflected light can be projected onto a surface. He uses it in a multi-dimensional way, showing two distinct environments in a way that allows them to overlap in a way the split screen never could. Comparisons to Alfred Hitchcock's *Rear Window* (1954) were inevitable.

Undoubtedly the toughest obstacle *Addicted to Love* must overcome is the lack of chemistry between Meg Ryan and Matthew Broderick. Things are made even more difficult by the biggest fault to plague many of today's romantic comedies: it is hard to believe that any of these people would ever be attracted to one another.

Meg Ryan's last few comedies, *I.Q.* (1996) and *French Kiss* (1996), fared poorly at the box office, leading some critics to question whether the actress's sweet demeanor and Kewpie-doll looks have worn thin. Her attempts at redefining herself, however, are admirable; she manages an edge here that is effective—until Robert Gordon's script lets her down. (One wonders, however, if this softening of her character was the result of infamous test screening focus groups.) With her heavy eyeliner, spiky blonde hair with black roots, and black leather jacket, Ms. Ryan captures both the punk spirit and the bitterness of a scorned woman. Reviews for *Addicted to Love* were decidedly mixed.

—Patricia Kowal

REVIEWS

Boxoffice. July, 1997, p. 89.
Chicago Tribune. May 23, 1997, p. 5.
Detroit News. May 23, 1997, p. 3F.
Entertainment Weekly. May 30, 1997, p. 54.
The Hollywood Reporter. May 19, 1997, p. 7.
Los Angeles Times. May 23, 1997, p. F9.
New York Times. May 23, 1997, p. B14.
People. June 2, 1997, p. 21.
Rolling Stone. June 12, 1997.
San Francisco Chronicle. May 23, 1997, p. C3.
Sight and Sound. September, 1997, p. 36.
Time. June 2, 1997.
USA Today. May 23, 1997, p. 3D.
Variety. May 19, 1997, p. 49.
Village Voice. June 3, 1997, p. 74.

CREDITS

Maggie: Meg Ryan
Sam: Matthew Broderick
Linda Green: Kelly Preston
Anton Depeaux: Tcheky Karyo
Nana: Maureen Stapleton
Ed Green: Nesbitt Blaisdell
Prof. Wells: Remark Ramsay
Matheson: Dominick Dunne

Origin: USA
Released: 1997
Production: Jeffrey Silver and Bobby Newmyer for Outlaw Production; released by Warner Bros.
Direction: Griffin Dunne
Screenplay: Robert Gordon
Cinematography: Andrew Dunn
Editing: Elizabeth Kling
Production design: Robin Standefer
Costumes: Renee Ehrlich Kalfus
Art direction: Stephen Alesch
Music: Rachel Portman
Sound: Ed Novick
MPAA rating: R
Running Time: 100 minutes

Afterglow

"Luminously tender! Julie Christie has found the greatest role of her career! If it doesn't bring out the romantic in you, nothing will!"—Jay Carr, *Boston Globe*

"The most satisfying movie in years! Julie Christie gives her best performance since 1975's *Shampoo.* She's simply magical, and so is the movie."—Rene Rodriguez, *Miami Herald*

"Maybe there's a more ruefully beautiful screen actress than Julie Christie. But that's hard to imagine while watching her radiant performance in *Afterglow,* Alan Rudolph's sinuous romance!"—Janet Maslin, *New York Times*

"Alan Rudolph reaches new heights with his deeply moving *Afterglow*!"—Bob Campbell, *Newhouse Newspapers*

"A recklessly funny sexual roundelay! The movie plays like a great piece of jazz, it just soars. Nolte is magnificent!"—Dennis Dermody, *Paper Magazine*

"Christie is dazzling!"—Bruce Williamson, *Playboy*

"Poignant and wonderful! Christie's luminous performance deserves an Oscar nomination and reminds us why she was one of the queens of the '60s!"—John Powers, *Vogue*

Writer/director Alan Rudolph's *Afterglow* is an idiosyncratic look at two troubled marriages. Phyllis and Lucky Mann (Julie Christie and Nick Nolte) have been married for 24 years and live with the traumas and disappointments the years have brought. Marianne and Jeffrey Byron (Lara Flynn Boyle and Jonny Lee Miller) are a yuppie couple who seem to be off to a rocky start. True to the spirit of much of Rudolph's work, *Afterglow* centers on ambiguous characters searching for love and fulfillment and not always finding what they think they want. Set in Montreal, the film is by turns a funny sex farce of two couples switching partners and a serious drama of marital crisis and adultery. Balancing all of these elements is a tricky task, but Rudolph creates engaging situations for his characters, even if the Manns are far more compelling than their younger counterparts.

Robert Altman has also produced Alan Rudolph's *Welcome to L.A., Remember My Name,* and *Mrs. Parker and the Vicious Circle.*

There is a restlessness in each marriage. Marianne desperately wants to have a baby, but Jeffrey is immersed in his career and not interested in even having sex with her. Meanwhile, Lucky is a handyman who has affairs on the job, while Phyllis, a former B-movie actress, accepts this arrangement. When Lucky takes a job at the Byrons' apartment to create a child's room (for a baby who does not yet exist), the sex-starved Marianne is immediately attracted to him.

While there are obvious serious overtones to a story about marital crises, Rudolph injects a great deal of humor into the film. Marianne's flirtation with Lucky is sad in her desperation but also funny in the awkward way she tries to seduce him. Because Lucky once attempted to write poetry and has some appreciation for painting, she thinks he has the soul of an artist, which, compared to Jeffrey, he probably does. Lara Flynn Boyle meets the challenge of playing an airhead and delivering often banal lines without giving a flat performance.

At times, some of the jokes are heavy-handed, but they feed into the film's farcical aspects. When we first meet Lucky, he is doing some plumbing work with a wrench sticking up from his crotch, and there are other references to his phallic tools later in the film. As he works, he tells his female client, "I want you to turn me on"—referring to the water faucet—and soon is making his moves on her. There are also numerous puns on Lucky's name. He tells Marianne about the women he likes, the ones "that never sleep around but who feel like getting lucky." Later in the film, Jeffrey's business associate says that Jeffrey "must be lucky" to have Phyllis with him, to which Phyllis responds, "Oh, I find him very different from Lucky." Such banter may feel overly arch, but, as delivered by Nolte and Christie, it feeds into the world-weariness of characters who find wry humor in the funny details of life.

Phyllis, meanwhile, is having a mid-life crisis. Her old co-star has died and her thoughts turn to her mortality. "The hardest part of all," she tells Lucky, "is finding out too late that none of it lasts." She spends her time watching her old movies on videotape and clearly lives in the past, but she is not a garish Norma Desmond figure who is cut off from reality. Rather, she is a woman who has accepted a certain situation but seems to be growing weary of her lonely days while her husband is on the prowl. We eventually learn she has essentially chosen a sexless marriage ever since her husband's anger drove her daughter away when he found out she was not his.

Lucky and Marianne have an affair, and, when they meet at the bar in the Ritz-Carlton, Phyllis is there spying on them. Jeffrey also arrives to see what his wife is doing, but Lucky and Marianne are departing as he arrives. Jeffrey goes to the bar, where he flirts with Phyllis. The humor in his scenes with Phyllis stems from Jeffrey's attempt to be suave but not really having what it takes. When she tells him that his wife is doing the same thing her husband is doing, he gallantly tells her, "Well, I do hope they're enjoying themselves as much as we are" in an attempt to look sophisticated. Phyllis clinks his glass, gives him a half-amused look, and drolly responds, "I don't."

Indeed, Phyllis has the film's best lines, and Julie Christie makes the most of them. Her greatest scene is a monologue telling the poignant story of her infidelity many

CREDITS

Phyllis Mann: Julie Christie
Lucky Mann: Nick Nolte
Marianne Byron: Lara Flynn Boyle
Jeffrey Byron: Jonny Lee Miller

Origin: USA
Released: 1997
Production: Robert Altman for Moonstone Entertainment, Sand Castle 5, and Elysian Dreams; released by Sony Pictures Classics
Direction: Alan Rudolph
Screenplay: Alan Rudolph
Cinematography: Toyomichi Kurita
Editing: Suzy Elmiger
Music: Mark Isham
Production design: Francois Seguin
Costumes: Francois Barbeau
Art direction: Collin Niemi
MPAA rating: R
Running Time: 113 minutes

years ago and the heartbreak it brought when she finally told her husband and lost her daughter. Christie delivers the standout performance among the four principals and demonstrates a wide range in what could have been a stereotype of the aging movie star. She is beautiful and vulnerable, sardonic and witty, depressed and yet vital.

Why, then, does Phyllis spend a weekend with a neophyte like Jeffrey? After all, he is a shallow character who utters banalities like "As a matter of fact, I live up to the very edge of my charm" to seduce Phyllis. She may want to relive her youth, to experience what Lucky gets to do everyday. She may want to act again—her flirtation with Jeffrey allows her to play a role, to be the seductive older woman who can toy with the younger man. When Jeffrey attempts to introduce her to a business associate, she introduces herself by her screen name, "Hart," and boldly announces, "I'm his mistress," even though they have not slept together.

Jeffrey: "You're a movie star?"
Phyllis: "All the time."

Jeffrey is a very ambiguous character. He is a cold careerist who shuns his wife's advances and also acts a little nutty by periodically balancing on the ledge of his office building. What is Jeffrey's problem? We are presented with the possibility that Jeffrey may be a repressed homosexual. His beautiful wife does not arouse him sexually, and, when Phyllis finally seems willing to sleep with him, he walks out on her. Most interestingly, when his colleague at work, Donald (Jay Underwood) comes out of the closet, Jeffrey is visibly disturbed. As a result, Donald even quits his job; as he says good-bye to Jeffrey and exits through a hotel's revolving door, Phyllis is entering through the same door at the same moment, which visually suggests two opposing options, two possibilities for Jeffrey. The issue is never resolved, but the suggestion is tantalizing and gives some depth to an otherwise clichÈd character.

Near the end, the movie bogs down slightly in a series of confrontations. Phyllis and Jeffrey bump into Marianne and Lucky in a bar, and Jeffrey picks a fight with Lucky, who is thrown out. All leave and finally meet at the Byrons' apartment, where Phyllis learns of Marianne's pregnancy by Lucky before the men arrive and resume their fighting. These macho displays are funny in light of the fact that everyone is flawed and no one really has the moral high ground, but they also feel forced. A film anchored in character more than plot does not need a climactic confrontation, especially one that ends up not being very climactic and resolving nothing.

The ending is ambiguous—a trademark of the Rudolph sensibility. Lucky spots Phyllis's daughter, Cassie (Genevieve Bissonnettte), and begs her forgiveness. Marianne is pregnant but separated from Jeffrey. In the last scene, Phyllis is wailing on her bed, and Lucky comes in to try to comfort her. The camera moves to reveal Cassie standing in the next room. It is not clear if Phyllis has been reunited with her daughter and is crying from the reunion or if she is still upset over Marianne's pregnancy and has yet to see Cassie. Whatever the outcome, Rudolph leaves us with beguiling possibilities for his characters but no pat solutions.

Rudolph makes some creative stylistic choices throughout the film. Jeffrey and Marianne's apartment, for example, has an ultra-modern design—cold and sterile like their marriage. One of its key features is a remote control to turn on music, lights, etc., which does not always work properly. Jeffrey and Marianne are the typical yuppie couple who have money and surround themselves with the accoutrements of success but ultimately cannot control their environment like they want to.

Rudolph also uses his camera in fresh ways. On several occasions, Jeffrey is presented upside-down, and then the camera turns around slowly until he has been righted. Since Jeffrey is confused, the camera move reflects his inner character, his constant attempts to find stability and balance. Rudolph also punctuates scenes by presenting his characters in mirrors, as if to suggest how little we can really know of these people, how all we can get are reflections.

Alan Rudolph's *Afterglow* is an accomplished film that deftly mixes humor and drama, sex farce and a serious look at human relationships. As Owen Gleiberman wrote in his review in *Entertainment Weekly*, Rudolph "tickles your palate

AWARDS AND NOMINATIONS

Academy Awards 1997 Nominations: Actress (Christie)
Independent Spirit Awards 1997: Actress (Christie)
National Society of Film Critics 1997: Actress (Christie)
New York Film Critics Circle 1997: Actress (Christie)

REVIEWS

Boxoffice. February, 1998, p. 53.
Chicago Tribune. January 16, 1998, p. 5.
Detroit News. February 27, 1998, p. 1C.
Entertainment Weekly. January 16, 1998, p. 45.
Los Angeles Times. December 26, 1997, p. F8.
New York Times. December 25, 1997, p. E1.
People. January 12, 1998, p. 98.
Rolling Stone. January 22, 1998, p. 62.
Time. January 12, 1998.
USA Today. December 27, 1997, p. 3D.
Variety. May 19, 1997, p. 58.

with sultriness, with high-gloss farce, with seduction and tenderness and a heartache so piquant it's like pain melting into pleasure." In Lucky and especially Phyllis, Rudolph has created two memorable characters. If Marianne and Jeffrey are thinner creations, at least they bring out the vitality of the older couple. Like most of Rudolph's films, though, the sophisticated and ambiguous tone made it a tough sell at the box office, despite the near universal acclaim for Julie Christie's performance.

Peter N. Chumo II

Air Bud

He Sits. He Stays. He Shoots. He Scores. The Dog Is In The House.—Movie tagline

"Simply amazing!"—Alan Silverman, *Hollywood Bytes*

"Irresistible!"—*KNX/CBS Radio*

Box Office: $24,646,936

A sad and lonely new-boy-in-town, Josh Framm (Kevin Zegers), learns to win at basketball and life with the help of "Buddy," a stray golden retriever he befriends. After an incident at a birthday party where the dog's owner, Slappy the Clown (Michael Jeter), is sent flying into the cake when chasing the "mongrel" in pursuit of a ball—the animal is fired.

Josh discovers the dog hiding in the bushes while he secretly practices basketball in a deserted court of an abandoned churchyard. The runaway emerges to show his special skill with bouncing balls through the hoop. The thrilled 12-year-old brings his new pal home, asking his Mom to keep him as the excited dog repeats his knack for disaster and turns the house inside out, knocking over ladders and spilling paint. The mutt has two weeks.

Withdrawn since the death of his father, Josh comes alive with the dog's companionship, but despite his athletic skill, he can't bring himself to tryout for the basketball team. But when he accepts an assistant job he suffer taunts of "water boy" by a mean player. Attending to the team's laundry, Josh snoops around the school basement to uncover a New York Knicks jersey hanging inside the office of the engineer, Arthur Chaney (Bill Cobbs), who claims the basketball star died a long time ago.

Buddy died from cancer on February 10, 1998. His son, Buddy 2, will star in the *Air Bud* sequel.

Coach Chaney to players: "You take that dog. It doesn't give a rat's behind about his point average—he just likes to play the game!"

The practice Josh gains on his clandestine court with his four-legged partner gives him the confidence to try out again—and he succeeds. Buddy shows up and leaps into the Timberwolves game at the sight of a bouncing ball. Chaos breaks out, refs bump around, whistles blow and the crowd cheers. "Michael Wuff Jordan" (hence the Air Bud nickname, presumably) becomes the team mascot with half-time performances dunking baskets with the touch of his talented nose.

The coach, who spouts cliches like "win on the courts and you win at life," is discharged but conveniently replaced, at Josh's suggestion, by the janitor and covert former Knick. Chaney's Bill Cosby-esque meaningful lessons on teamwork and innovative Air Ball technique improve the team's scores. But when he takes Josh's nemesis out of a game, the boy's father takes the kid out of school.

Josh tries to dunk a shot in the last few seconds of a game, hoping to find the acceptance of his teammates, but misses. Coach Chaney explains he has to play from the heart—the way Buddy loves to play the game. The philosophy pays off. The Timberwolves turn around their losing streak and achieve local recognition and media attention. Buddy's former owner, Norm Snively or Slappy the Clown, catches his old sidekick's tricks on the TV and plans a scheme to cash-in.

The clown arrives to retrieve his property and book his mutt on beer commercials (Budweiser, perhaps). Josh rescues his pet from being chained up in the mud, and the chase scene that ensues results in Slappy's jalopy falling apart—brakes break, doors drop, the steering wheel flies off. But surprisingly, Josh liberates Buddy, leaving him in a field to avoid the sinister Snively snagging him back. It's heart-wrenching as the pooch attempts to swim across the lake to Josh.

CREDITS

Josh Framm: Kevin Zengers
Norm Snively: Michael Jeter
Jackie Framm: Wendy Makkena
Arthur Chaney: Bill Cobbs
Judge Cranfield: Eric Christmas
Larry Willingham: Brendan Fletcher
Buck Willingham: Norman Browning
Referee: Jay Brazeau
Coach Joe Barker: Stephen E. Miller
Principal Pepper: Nicola Cavendish

Origin: USA
Released: 1997
Production: Robert and William Vince for Keystone Pictures; released by Walt Disney Pictures
Direction: Charles Martin Smith
Screenplay: Paul Tamasy and Aaron Mendelsohn
Cinematography: Mike Southon
Editing: Alice Grace
Music: Brahm Wenger
Production design: Elizabeth Wilcox
Art direction: Eric Fraser
Set decoration: David Chiasson
Costumes: Jana Stern
Sound: Ruth Huddleston
Buddy's trainer: Kevin DiCicco
MPAA rating: G
Running Time: 97 minutes

The State Finals arrive and the nasty boy shows up on the rival Warriors team. The Timberwolves play poorly, then suffer two injuries and seem doomed until Air Bud finds Josh in time to join the game as K9, receiving a rousing reception. No rules exclude dogs and although he can't dribble, he dunks shot after shot with his special snout, bringing the score even, despite the struggle to "Cover the dog!" In the last few seconds, Josh experiences a slow-motion moment, absorbing Buddy's joy of playing, and slams a ball through the net to win the game.

Yet victory takes a twist when Slappy shows up again to seize custody of his celebrity canine. The coach intervenes for the judge, suggesting the dog decide his fate. Buddy's obvious choice underscores the message of triumph over adversity and the virtue of team spirit. The happy ending helps lift the gloominess of this sober story, despite the pup's appeal.

Not as slapstick or amusing as expected and with some leaps in logic—not including the dog's amazing abilities (as seen on "The David Letterman Show" and "America's Funniest Videos")—this Disney picture is nicely acted and decently directed. Parents will find *Air Bud* wholesome family fare, perhaps more than children may find it entertaining.

—Roberta Cruger

REVIEWS

Los Angeles Times. August 1, 1997, p. F14.
New York Times. August 1, 1997, p. C14.
USA Today. August 1, 1997, p. 3D.
Variety. August 4, 1997, p. 35.

Air Force One

The fate of the nation rests on the courage of one man.—Movie tagline

"Run to this movie! Ford is the perfect president, the best of the best roles of his career! This is it!"—Patty Spitler, *CBS-TV*

"A rare summer thriller! Tense and satisfying!" —Owen Gleiberman, *Entertainment Weekly*

"*A.F.O.* lands as the top summer thrill ride!" —Larry Ratliff, *Fox-TV*

"*A.F.O.* is a true winner! Gary Oldman is superb and Glenn Close is #1 as America's #2!"—Bill Zwecker, *NBC-TV*

"Breathtaking, gripping, nail-biting, edge-of-your-seat entertainment!"—Peter Travers, *Rolling Stone*

Box Office: $171,880,017

The silver screen has played host to many films based on premises or scenarios that may, on paper at least, sound far-fetched, outrageous, or even completely unbelievable, but it takes an intelligent script, believable performances, and skilled direction to turn an improbable premise into a credible, satisfying film. Many people would consider the goal underlying *Air Force One* to be one of those far-fetched premises, for the basic idea behind this film is to turn the president of the United States into an action hero. However, director Wolfgang Peterson (*Das Boot* [1981] and the more recent *In the Line of Fire* [1993]) manages to succeed in accomplishing this goal, supported by an excellent cast

Harrison Ford, as the President of the United States, has his combat skills put to the test after his plane is hijacked by Russian terrorists in the blockbuster hit *Air Force One.*

and a fast-paced, well-written story. Many plot elements of the film, particularly the action sequences, are not entirely original, bearing much resemblance to similar sequences in other action movies, and the ultimate resolution of the conflict is predictable (no one expects the hero of an action film, much less the president of the U.S., to lose), but overall *Air Force One* works well as a thoroughly engaging and emotionally intense moviegoing experience.

President James Marshall (Harrison Ford) is a conscientious man who stands by his principles instead of playing politics. After a United States strike force captures a neo-Soviet general who threatens to stop democracy in Russia, President Marshall delivers a speech in Moscow and pledges that he will not tolerate terrorism and that the United States "will never negotiate" with terrorists. It is "the right thing to do, and you know it," Marshall tells his National Security Advisor and Chief of Staff.

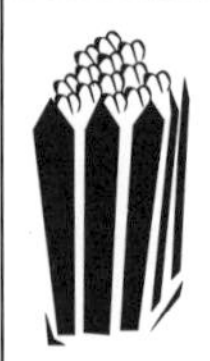

Ivan: "I would turn my back on God himself for Mother Russia."

As luck would have it, the president is promptly given the opportunity to test this policy when a group of Russian terrorists posing as news reporters hijacks Air Force One shortly after the plane leaves Moscow. To protect Marshall, security personnel rush him to an escape pod which is then ejected from the plane to carry him to safety. However, as the audience later learns, the president does not get into the pod but chooses to remain on board Air Force One. Believing Marshall has in fact escaped, the terrorists, led by Ivan Korshunov (Gary Oldman), contact Washington, D.C. and inform Vice President Kathryn Bennett (Glenn Close) that the president has been taken hostage. Korshunov demands the release of the Russian general Radek, believing that upon his release the general will gain widespread support and usher in a new age of glory for "Mother Russia." He then threatens to execute a hostage every half hour until his demand is met.

While Vice President Bennett, Defense Secretary Dean (Dean Stockwell), and others of the president's cabinet wrestle with the question of whether to give in to Korshunov's demands or sacrifice the lives of everyone on board the plane, President Marshall attempts to stop the terrorists. Using a cellular phone, he manages to communicate briefly with his staff at the White House, who are relieved to learn he is still alive. However, his contact with the White House is severed when the phone's batteries run out, so his struggle to thwart Korshunov becomes that of a lone man racing against the clock. Eventually Korshunov realizes there is someone on board trying to sabotage his plans. Assuming that this someone is a secret service agent, the Russian terrorist continues to follow through on his threat to kill innocent passengers. He then takes the president's wife (Wendy Crewson) and daughter (Liesel Matthews) hostage and threatens to kill them next.

Marshall finds and rescues the other passengers, who parachute from the cargo hold to safety, but the president himself is captured and taken to Korshunov. The terrorist threatens to kill his wife or daughter if he does not order the release of the Russian general, and finally the president gives in and gives the order. However, with heroic ingenuity and more than a little physical prowess, Marshall breaks free and pursues Korshunov to the cargo hold. There a physical struggle culminates in the terrorist's death as he tries to parachute away. The president then promptly sends out the order for General Radek to be taken into custody again. The story ends with a final action scene in which the president and his family are spirited to safety aboard a rescue aircraft, just moments before the crippled Air Force One dives into the ocean.

Harrison Ford, who has tackled similar action hero roles as Indiana Jones, Jack Ryan (*Patriot Games* [1992], *Clear and Present Danger* [1994]), and others, is superbly cast as the principled, determined president who finds himself forced to use his cunning to save the day. Many of Ford's successful roles have placed him in the position of an amiable Everyman—a decent, likeable character with whom the audience can identify—who is forced to become a hero, and President Marshall fits nicely into that same pattern. Ford's soft-spoken, ethical, resolute persona creates a presidential figure that earns respect and admiration, yet his character is also believable and very human, due in part to Ford's performance. As many critics have often noted, Harrison Ford is an actor whose portrayals rely as much on expression and behavior as on dialogue and action (his role as Dr. Kimble in 1993's *The Fugitive* is perhaps the clearest example of this). The actor's ability to say as much with his face as with words also works well here, as Marshall alone desperately strives to save his friends, family, and colleagues on the plane. During a scene in which Marshall must listen helplessly to the intercom as Korshunov shoots a female staff member, the president's face clearly registers his sorrow and frustration. One of the most effective scenes in the film occurs when Korshunov has captured Marshall and threatens to kill his family if he does not order the release of the Russian general. Ford's performance during this horrible dilemma, pitting his principles against the lives of his wife and daughter, is emotionally stirring and believable, as the president's teary-eyed, bloodied expression projects his love for his family.

Jurgen Prochnow, who starred in Petersen's *Das Boot,* has no dialogue in his cameo role.

Gary Oldman creates a villain that stands in appropriately sharp contrast to President Marshall, though he tries to tell Alice, the president's daughter, that there is actually little difference between the two men. Blindly nationalistic, willing without reserve to shed innocent blood for his "Mother Russia," Korshunov is an evil counterpart to Marshall—a man who, like the president, is determined to stand up for what he believes in. However, his devotion is a mad, violent one that puts the state ahead of individuals, whereas Marshall's democratic principles emphasize protection of life and individual freedom. Oldman's villain is genuinely terrifying, and the moment when he threatens to kill the president's wife or daughter is an intense, uncertain one, for he clearly demonstrates that he is willing to kill even a young girl.

The scenes in Washington, D.C. are also well-played and effectively propel the story along, owing to Glenn Close's strong performance as Vice President Bennett. Close lends credibility to her role as a woman whose principled determination resonates almost as loudly as that of the president. Bennett actually functions as the secondary hero in the story, as she must deal with the conflict aboard Air Force One as well as a conflict with Secretary of Defense Dean, who is at first willing to sacrifice the passengers of the airplane and later argues for certifying the president incapable of performing his duties. Bennett, however, clings to her trust in Marshall to the very end, and it is her strength in standing her ground that gives the president time to stop the terrorists.

There are plenty of dazzling special effects and action scenes in *Air Force One*, but fortunately they are accompanied by strong characterizations, an interesting story, and a dose of patriotic sentiment. While *Air Force One* is primarily an action movie that puts a few new spins on familiar material by turning the president of the United States into an Indiana Jones/Jack Ryan persona, the film also works on a more personal level. President Marshall is a well-drawn, sympathetic character who appeals to the audience not only because of his "Everyman" role but also because he instills a sense of pride in a public office that is often maligned. Underlying the action in the movie is an effective story of standing up for one's principles, and there is a sense of patriotic reassurance in the fact that the man who demonstrates this resolution holds the highest office in the land. The human elements of loyalty, trust, and love also motivate and round out characters such as Vice President Bennett, Grace Marshall, Alice Marshall, and others, and as a result the audience is led to genuinely admire and care for

CREDITS

President James Marshall: Harrison Ford
Ivan Korshunov: Gary Oldman
Vice President Kathryn Bennett: Glenn Close
Defense Secretary Walter Dean: Dean Stockwell
Grace Marshall: Wendy Crewson
Alice Marshall: Liesel Matthews
Major Caldwell: William H. Macy
Agent Gibbs: Xander Berkeley
Chief of Staff Lloyd Shepherd: Paul Guilfoyle
General Northwood: Bill Smitrovich
General Alexander Radek: Jurgen Prochnow

Origin: USA
Released: 1997
Production: Wolfgang Petersen, Gail Katz, Armyan Bernstein, Jon Shestack for Radiant and Beacon Pictures; released by Columbia Pictures
Direction: Wolfgang Petersen
Screenplay: Andrew W. Marlowe
Cinematography: Michael Ballhaus
Editing: Richard Francis-Bruce
Music: Jerry Goldsmith
Production design: William Sandell
Art direction: Carl Aldana, Carl Stensel
Costumes: Erica Edell Phillips
Sound: Keith A. Wester
Visual effects supervisor: Brad Kuehn
Stunt coordinator: Doug Coleman
MPAA rating: R
Running Time: 124 minutes

AWARDS AND NOMINATIONS

Academy Awards 1997 Nominations: Film Editing, Sound

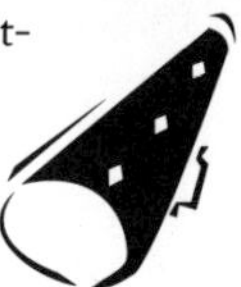

REVIEWS

Boxoffice. September, 1997, p. 119.
Chicago Tribune. July 25, 1997, p. 4.
Entertainment Weekly. July 25, 1997, p. 48.
Los Angeles Times. July 25, 1997, p. F1.
Movieline. June, 1997, p. 53.
New York Times. July 25, 1997, p. C1.
New Yorker. July 28, 1997, p. 77.
People. August 4, 1997, p. 19.
Rolling Stone. August 7, 1997, p. 67.
Sight and Sound. October, 1997, p. 42.
Time. July 28, 1997.
USA Today. July 25, 1997, p. 2D.
Variety. July 21, 1997, p. 37.
Village Voice. July 29, 1997, p. 71.

these people. Many elements of the story are not original, which is frequently true of action films, but *Air Force One* has its share of twists and turns as well as a compelling conflict involving strong characters. The film accomplishes quite effectively what many storytellers set out to do: breathe fresh life into an old subject. In the case of *Air Force One*, this accomplishment is all the more satisfying in that the premise of the story could have resulted in far less.

—David Flanagin

Albino Alligator

Deliberate sacrifice for deliberate gain.—Movie tagline

"A vividly intense crime story! Kevin Spacey's dynamic, deft directing draws astute performances from his top cast, led by Matt Dillon, Gary Sinise and Faye Dunaway."—Peter Travers, *Rolling Stone*

In 1995, Kevin Spacey firmly established himself as one of the most distinctive character actors of his generation with compelling performances in *Seven*, *Swimming With the Sharks*, and *The Usual Suspects*, winning an Academy Award for his unforgettable Keyzer Soze in the latter. This skill at portraying off-center, dangerous neurotics confirmed the promise he showed years earlier with his heroin-addicted gangster on the television series "Wiseguy". Spacey is the kind of eccentric actor with an eye for details who might also be a good director. *Albino Alligator*, his first film behind the camera, offers inconclusive evidence of his filmmaking talent.

Dova to himself in restroom mirror: "I should have settled down and gotten married."

Dova (Matt Dillon), his brother Milo (Gary Sinise), and Law (William Fichtner) are robbing a copper factory in New Orleans when alarms go off and they quickly flee the scene. At the same time, federal Alcohol, Tobacco, and Firearms agents have staked out a Canadian arms dealer nearby. Just as the arms dealer is making his move, the three robbers stray into the stakeout, running over one agent and killing two more when Law rams their car.

Dova, Law, and the injured Milo take refuge in a basement bar and hold as hostages its inhabitants: Dino (M. Emmet Walsh), the owner; Janet (Faye Dunaway), a barmaid; Jack (John Spencer), a barfly; Danny (Skeet Ulrich), a pool-shooting customer; and the mysterious Guy (Viggo Mortensen). Forces led by ATF agent G. D. Browning (Joe Mantegna) quickly surround the building, which has only one exit. The rest of the film consists of the hoodlums trying to decide what to do while the hostages cower.

The action, such as it is, consists mainly of bickering between the thugs. Dova, the leader, is neither as smart nor as ruthless as he thinks he is. Milo, the brains of the trio, makes his brother promise not to kill any more hostages after Law beats Dino to death when the barman draws a shotgun. Law, a sadistic brute, spends his time leering at Janet and looking forward to further violence. The film's title refers to a story recounted by Law of alligators sacrificing their albino brethren in order to set up a trap for their enemies. Much of the would-be tension results from wondering which hostage or hostages the criminals will let be killed so that they can escape by pretending to be hostages themselves. Comic relief is provided by Browning, who refuses to cooperate with a nosy television reporter (Melinda McGraw).

The screenplay by Christian Forte (son of singer/actor Fabian), owes a considerable debt to such similar gangster/hostage melodramas as *The Petrified Forest* (1936), *Key Largo* (1948), and *The Desperate Hours* (1955). The filmmakers acknowledge their debt to these films by having the bar decorated with posters of James Cagney in *G Men* (1935) and Humphrey Bogart in *Dead Reckoning* (1947). While Forte may indulge his script in the cliches of such films, he presents them unironically or as thudding banalities: Is the nerdy-looking Guy as harmless as he appears to be? What exactly is going on between Janet and Danny? Will Dova betray his brother? The answers to all these questions are as obvious and uninteresting as the questions themselves. Having the criminal the authorities have been after all along be one of the hostages is a tad too mechanical a coincidence, and the interfering reporter is an especially stale device.

First screenplay by 25-year-old Christian Forte, who's the son of pop idol Fabian.

The week *Albino Alligator* opened, the *New York Times* published an article by Betsy Sharkey dealing with actors turned directors. Sharkey notes that such filmmakers often neglect the technical or stylistic sides of their films in favor of the performances. Spacey establishes at the beginning that he wants to pay attention to the visual elements by using such touches as having the camera follow the yellow line down the highway as the robbers make their escape, a conceit which recalls 1940s B-movies and the techniques of David Lynch. Once inside Dino's, Spacey, cinematographer Mark Plummer, and editor Jay Cassidy adeptly vary the types of shots, if not the angles, in an attempt to prevent the proceedings from being too monotonous. While there are plenty of tracking shots and one 360-degree maneuver, Spacey, in love with his performers, overuses close-ups, robbing them of their emotional impact—a deficiency alarmingly too frequent in American films of the 1990s. When Guy is in his passive stage, Mortensen sits unmoving with his ankles collapsed. While the character might adopt such a posture to try to convince the bad guys that he is a wimp, it is also the type of attention-getting, actorish trick to which Spacey himself is prone.

Albino Alligator has a few unusual touches. The entire hostage drama is set in motion because one of the surveillance agents has had his cigarette lighter stolen by another agent, and when he spots some matches in the street, he crawls after them only to be killed. (Spacey takes a cue from Bryan Singer, his *Usual Suspects* director, by making only one violent incident truly graphic.) Also interesting are the reasons the mother-obsessed Law cannot shoot Janet, or make coffee, and how the hostage chosen to be the albino alligator dies is handled with some originality. Michael Brook's score is also distinctive in its blending of blues, jazz, and classical elements, especially during the opening credits.

For the most part, *Albino Alligator* is simply a grim, unexciting, claustrophobic hostage drama. While some reviewers praised the film for not resorting to stylized tough-guy dialogue as in *The Usual Suspects* or *Reservoir Dogs* (1992), it needs some such touch to enliven it. Forte provides what he considers to be four unexpected plot twists, but any half-alert viewer can too easily see at least three of them coming. Matters are not helped by Spacey making unimaginative directorial choices such as calling attention to Dino's shotgun hidden behind the bar, and repeating earlier scenes where Guy's identity is revealed to make certain the viewers get the point.

Such an underwritten project could have been salvaged with interesting casting, but for the most part, *Albino Alligator* fails here as well. Dillon can be an adequate actor in supporting roles, as in *To Die For* (1995), but he is too bland and too nice for Dova. The character should have some degree of cunning and maliciousness, but Dillon can convey only his confusion. Dunaway, a wonderful performer in such

CREDITS

Dova: Matt Dillon
Janet: Faye Dunaway
Milo: Gary Sinise
Law: William Fichtner
G. D. Browning: Joe Mantegna
Guy: Viggo Mortensen
Danny: Skeet Ulrich
Dino: M. Emmet Walsh
Jack: John Spencer
Marv: Frankie Faison
Jenny: Melinda McGraw

Origin: USA
Released: 1997
Production: Brad Krevoy, Steve Stabler, Brad Jenkel for Motion Picture Corporation of America; released by Miramax Films
Direction: Kevin Spacey
Screenplay: Christian Forte
Cinematography: Mark Plummer
Editing: Jay Cassidy
Production design: Nelson Coates
Art direction: Burton Rencher
Costumes: Isis Mussenden
Sound: Mark Weingarten
Music: Michael Brook
Makeup: Felicity Bowring, Kimberly Greene
Casting: David Rubin
MPAA rating: R
Running Time: 105 minutes

films as *Bonnie and Clyde* (1967), *Chinatown* (1974), and *Three Days of the Condor* (1975), has more presence than anyone else in the bar, but the part requires constant pleading and begging, forcing Dunaway to indulge herself in mannerisms. She is more effective in quieter moments, as in the film's supposedly surprise ending.

The vastly overrated Sinise, too often given to whining and tearful glances, is surprisingly effective as Milo, the most sympathetic character in Dino's, because he subdues his usual tricks. Fichtner, who plays a sleazy, well-dressed money launderer in *Heat* (1995), is equally convincing as a muscular, slimy, shabbily dressed sociopath. Fichtner's unusual line readings, most spoken in icy monotone, recall the stylized deliveries of Benicio del Toro in *The Usual Suspects* and *Basquiat* (1996). Both he and Dunaway offer fairly realistic versions of southern Louisiana accents with the occasionally slurred or swallowed words. (Except for these accents and the alligator metaphor, the film could be taking place in Omaha.) Fichtner is clearly having a good time playing this brutal mama's boy, and the wonderful Mantegna does the same with his short-tempered agent. When Browning agrees to be interviewed by the reporter, Mantegna twists and wiggles while she does her lead-in as if he can barely contain his contempt before releasing an expletive-drenched description of the events so far. While Mantegna may not have the range to play leads in films not written by David Mamet, he is perfect in supporting roles.

Kenneth Branagh, Clint Eastwood, and Mel Gibson have shown that actors can direct visually impressive, large-scale films, while others, notably Stanley Tucci and Campbell Scott with the nearly perfect *Big Night* (1996), have shown actors can achieve in directing smaller, more intimate films. *Albino Alligator* shows primarily that Spacey the director is a bad judge of screenplays.

—*Michael Adams*

REVIEWS

Boxoffice. November, 1996, p. 137.
Entertainment Weekly. January 31, 1997, p. 40.
Los Angeles Times. January 17, 1997, p. F4.
The New York Times. January 17, 1997, p. C10.
People. February 3, 1997, p. 20.
Rolling Stone. November 28, 1996, p. 142.
USA Today. January 17, 1997, p. D4.
Village Voice. January 21, 1997, p. 54.

Alien Resurrection

Witness the resurrection.—Movie tagline

"*Alien Resurrection* rocks! An operatic, juiced-up marvel that pulses with energy."—Leah Rozen, *People*

"A visual marvel!"—Peter Travers, *Rolling Stone*

"A startling blast of thrills, action and sheer stimulating imagination."—Dennis Cunningham, *WCBS-TV*

Box Office: $45,491,872

Ridley Scott's original *Alien* (1979) is considered by many to be a science fiction/horror classic, as is James Cameron's 1986 sequel *Aliens*. The original film was a dark, atmospheric picture that featured well-developed, interesting characters, haunting production design and cinematography, and a suspenseful story. *Aliens* was an even darker and more intense film, featuring another strong performance by Sigourney Weaver as Ellen Ripley as well as another cast of intriguing characters. However, with David Fincher's *Alien 3* (1992), many critics and fans of the movie series thought the *Alien* franchise may have run aground.

Ripley (Sigourney Weaver) is back in the fourth *Alien* by way of cloning, but shipmate Call (Winona Ryder) receives a greeting that signifies Ripley's genetic bond with her alien foes in *Alien: Resurrection.*

Regarded by critics and moviegoers alike as a failure, the third *Alien* offered little that was new and lacked the well-developed stories and characters that made the first two films above-average fare; to make things worse (in fans' eyes at least), the story killed off two very popular characters, including that of Ripley herself. The eventual decision to make a fourth *Alien* film was, in part, an attempt to revive (and, for some, to redeem) the once-lucrative series. During its opening week, *Alien Resurrection* was the highest grossing film at the box office, but that initial success quickly faded as audiences clearly reacted to the picture with disappointment. The failure of *Alien Resurrection* to generate the kind of success experienced by *Alien* and *Aliens* is understandable, because the film, like its immediate predecessor, fails to live up to the quality with which the series began.

Elgyn: "You wanna tell us what this is?" Ripley: "It's a queen. She'll breed. You'll die."

Alien told the story of a crew of space travelers, including Ellen Ripley, who discovered an abandoned spacecraft on a mysterious alien planet. On that ship they discovered an alien creature that reproduced by incubating its offspring in the bodies of other life forms. As the crew soon found out, the creatures were also ruthless, powerful killers. By the end of the story, only Ripley had survived. In *Aliens*, Ripley wakes up after 57 years of hibernation and returns with another crew to the planet where the original alien was found. There a human colony had been destroyed by the aliens; the only survivor was a young girl named Newt. At the end of this film, only Ripley and Newt survived. *Alien 3* took place on a prison planet and saw the death of both Newt and Ripley, who at the end of the film sacrificed her life in order to destroy a queen alien maturing inside her body.

In *Alien Resurrection*, two hundred years have passed since Ripley died. On board the spaceship USM Auriga, scientists working with the United Systems Military have cloned Ripley from a drop of blood; their purpose, however, is not simply to clone Ripley but to use the alien growing inside her (evidently it was somehow cloned as well) to breed more of the creatures for experimental investigation of their powerful genetic makeup. This cloned Ripley has retained all the memories of the woman who fought the aliens throughout the first three films, but evidence soon suggests that perhaps she is not entirely human. Her blood, like that of the aliens, is acidic, and she possesses seemingly superhuman physical strength. Unsure of whether the clone can be trusted, the military locks Ripley in a cell.

Soon a commercial freighter manned by a crew of ruffians arrives and docks with the Auriga; the freighter's crew includes young Call (Winona Ryder), who becomes fascinated with Ripley and expresses concern that the clone's allegiance may lie more with the aliens than with humanity. Eventually, the aliens who have been bred on the Auriga break loose and begin a bloody killing spree. Those of the military who are still alive evacuate the ship, but Ripley, Call, and the crew of the freighter are left behind. They soon discover that the vessel's auto-pilot has been activated and is taking the ship back to Earth.

The rest of the story involves Ripley and the others battling their way through the alien-infested ship to stop the Auriga's progress toward Earth by destroying it and to escape in the freighter. Along the way, Call reveals that she is actually an android and most of the rest of the freighter crew dies. Ripley also comes face-to-face with the queen alien that was bred in her body and discovers that it has produced a baby that is half-human and half-alien. Finally they reach the freighter and escape from the doomed Auriga, but they are not alone; the half-human alien manages to make its way on board. As the ship nears Earth, only Ripley, Call, and the half-breed offspring have survived. Ripley, who feels

CREDITS

Ellen Ripley: Sigourney Weaver
Annalee Call: Winona Ryder
Johner: Ron Perlman
Vriess: Dominique Pinon
Elgyn: Michael Wincott
General Perez: Dan Hedaya
Dr. Wren: J.E. Freeman
Purvis: Leland Orser
Gediman: Brad Dourif
Hillard: Kim Flowers

Origin: USA
Released: 1997
Production: Bill Badalato, Gordon Carroll, David Giler, and Walter Hill for Brandywine; released by 20th Century Fox
Direction: Jean-Pierre Jeunet
Screenplay: Joss Wheldon
Cinematography: Darius Khondji
Editing: Herve Schneid
Music: John Frizzell
Production design: Nigel Phelps
Art direction: Andrew Neskoromny
Set decoration: John M. Dwyer
Costumes: Bob Ringwood
Sound: Richard Bryce Goodman
Visual effects supervisor: Erik Henry
Alien effects design: Alec Gillis, Tom Woodruff
MPAA rating: R
Running Time: 108 minutes

some strange sort of maternal connection to the creature even though she knows it must be destroyed, regretfully sends it to a grisly death by breaking a small window in the ship's hull and watching as the vacuum of space sucks the alien's body through the small opening, ripping it to shreds. The story then ends as Ripley and Call, the sole survivors, return to Earth.

Although *Alien Resurrection* has its share of intense moments (a scene in which Ripley and her companions are pursued by aliens underwater is particularly suspenseful), the film overall seems to be more a strung-together collection of gory visual effects rather than a coherent story propelled by unnerving intensity. While the previous *Alien* films certainly included their fair share of gore as part of the horror-filled plots, it often seems that the gore itself is the focus of *Alien Resurrection*. There are also plot questions left unexplained, and some elements of the story are virtually incoherent. It is not clear, for example, how an alien was cloned along with Ripley, and the film never explains exactly how or why the queen alien produced a half-human offspring. The character of Ripley (or her clone) is an intriguing and fairly well-developed one, though she is not the Ripley seen in the first three films. Her attachment to the aliens, particularly the queen and its half-breed offspring, actually attempts to create a small degree of sympathy for the creatures, and the occasional ambiguity over Ripley's allegiance creates some suspense as to whether she will remain the "good guy." In addition, Ripley's strong persona commands the screen, but too often her dialogue is reduced to humorous, "tough" one-liners.

While *Alien Resurrection* includes it share of fascinating visual effects, intense moments, dark humor, and an interesting characterization in Ripley, the film does not meet the level of quality storytelling or filmmaking established in the first two *Alien* movies. Essentially, this fourth film is little more than average science fiction/horror movie fare, and its failure at the box office suggests that only a well-made picture comparable to *Alien* and *Aliens* may have a chance of "resurrecting" the series.

—David Flanagin

REVIEWS

Chicago Tribune. November 26, 1997, p. 1.
Cinemafantastique. April, 1998, p. 40.
Detroit News. November 26, 1997, p. E1.
Entertainment Weekly. December 5, 1997, p. 47.
Los Angeles Times. November 26, 1997, p. F1.
New York Times. November 26, 1997, p. E1.
Newsweek. June 9, 1997, p. 75.
People. December 1, 1997, p. 29.
Rolling Stone. December 11, 1997, p. 83.
Sight and Sound. December, 1997, p. 36.
Time. December 1, 1997.
USA Today. November 26, 1997, p. 9D.
Variety. November 17, 1997, p. 63.

Alive and Kicking; Indian Summer

Love is the ultimate kick.—Movie tagline

"A celebration of gay spirit and strength . . . Intellectually bracing and emotionally satisfying." —Bob Satuloff, *The Advocate*

"A striking performance from Jason Flemyng . . . Meckler creates a wonderful sense of a small company nearing the end of its tether and her actors reciprocate with an elan that makes sense of the message: Where there's Life, There is Hope."—Derek Malcolm, *The Guardian*

"Gracefully directed. Brilliantly scripted. Flemyng and Sher ignite the screen."—Stephen Farber, *Movieline*

"Exceptionally well-written!"—John Hartle, *Seattle Times*

Alive and Kicking, an English film that was a recent entry in Los Angeles' successful gay "Outfest" is a passionate, ebullient love story set in the world of professional dancers. Yet unlike the dance world shown in Herb Ross' *The Turning Point* this is an arena dominated by much more than scores and tours—this is a world that has been decimated by the AIDS plague. Yet this film, centering on an oddball, "Mutt and Jeff" love story between two unlikely lovers, Tonio, a handsome, preening HIV positive dancer, and Jack, a brooding AIDS counselor, draws the viewer in with its unabashed life-affirming viewpoint. Director Nancy Meckler (*Sister, My Sister*) infuses Martin Sherman's (*Bent*) screenplay with an "in-your-face" acknowledgment of the terrain one is about to cross and then surprises us with the level of drama and humor contained.

The film opens with the impending death of Ramon (Anthony Higgins), one of the lead dancers of a eclectic London dance troupe, from AIDS. Ramon is surrounded by friends and fellow dancers, one of whom, Tonio, has HIV positive status, but has not yet shown any signs of illness. Tonio is devastated by Ramon's approaching death, as he just last year buried his lover from AIDS. As Tonio, Millie (Diane Parish), a lesbian dancer from the troupe, and others rally around Ramon, they move through their actions with sad familiarity. No fewer than four of their star dancers have passed away from AIDS in the last few years.

Jack to Tonio: "Would you even look at me if you were healthy?"

At Ramon's funeral, the troupe faces what has become painfully obvious—they are sinking and sinking fast. Besides losing their dancers to AIDS, their once ethereal and witty founder and chief choreographer Luna (Dorothy Tutin) is rapidly losing her rational mind to Alzheimer's Disease. Tonio refuses to bow to such grim, dreary circumstances—this boy must dance, and dance he will. He applies himself to his craft with fierce discipline; dance is all he has ever wanted or known and despite the personal and professional facades crumbling around him, he steels himself to go on.

After a hard week's dancing, where do dancers go to blow off steam? To a disco, of course, and in the bobbing, sweaty crowd, Tonio bumps into Jack (Antony Sher). Jack bellies up to the bar and introduces himself to Tonio; he was at Ramon's funeral in a professional context—he was Ramon's AIDS counselor. Tonio is flip, glib and neither attracted to Jack, nor emotionally ready to hear any psychological talk. Nevertheless, Jack strikes a chord with him, and after exchanging witty, flirtatious banter all night, ends up having breakfast in a coffee shop. Although Jack chastises Tonio for his vain ways, it is obvious that Jack is smitten. Tonio brushes him off; Jack is short, stocky and bearded—a real Bob Hoskins type—but Tonio has no time for anyone less than gorgeous.

To the world Tonio radiates cocky charm, yet at night he stares at the urns on his mantle that contain both Ramon and his dead lovers' ashes. Eating gallons of ice cream is his only respite; he will do anything to keep from thinking about the past, the present or the frightening future. When Jack does ask Tonio out again, he seems like such a normal, stable fellow, that Tonio accepts.

The men have dinner and engage in small talk, which for a gay male couple in the 90's includes more than background, family, hopes and dreams; it includes the inevitable litany of friends, lovers and one's own health in regards to AIDS. Tonio tries to fend off Jack's advances; he is not ready, he has not dealt with Ramon, with his lover's death, and he is trying to focus on his life's work and passion. Yet Jack is dogged in his pursuit and the men engage in lovemaking that night. To her credit Meckler does not shy away from romanticizing the men's lovemaking—it is as torrid and realistic as you would find in any heterosexual love story.

Soon the men are a couple and predictably the issues and problems arise. It seems that all of Jack's compassion and dedication to his job as an AIDS counselor has its price—a serious drinking problem. He adores Tonio and is constantly trying to get him to open up and express his anger about his situation, the entire AIDS crisis, the frustrating bureaucracy of the government and medical establishment but Tonio is quite adept at blocking out anything but his next performance. This is a clash between two classic personality types, the giver and the taker and the story lies in the two personalities coming together to a space of giving, sharing and receiving. Were Tonio not sick and so emotionally low he would never be receptive to someone so flatly ordinary as Jack—a fact obvious to both of the men. On a vacation trip to Greece they have a brutal talk—Tonio rightly accuses Jack of loving him for his looks, and Jack acknowledges that he knows Tonio would never look at him in a perfect world. Director Meckler and the actors magnificently portray this cruel aspect of the gay male existence, where there is a high premium placed on youth and beauty.

One joyous aspect of this film is how it highlights the world of dance, and more specifically, the small spectrum of a dance troupe such as this one. This is a world seemingly untouched by high tech films with dinosaurs and computer

CREDITS

Tonio: Jason Flemyng
Jack: Antony Sher
Millie: Diane Parish
Luna: Dorothy Tutin
Ramon: Anthony Higgins

Origin: Great Britain
Released: 1997
Production: Martin Pope for Channel Four Films; released by First Look Pictures
Direction: Nancy Meckler
Screenplay: Martin Sherman
Cinematography: Chris Seager
Editing: Rodney Holland
Art direction: Phillip Robinson
Production design: Cecilia Brereton
Costumes: Monica Howe
Music: Peter Salem
Choreography: Liz Ranken
MPAA rating: R
Running Time: 100 minutes

graphics, fast cutting technology and the impersonality of the Internet. Dance is an intensely personal form of expression and these dancers live and breathe it. The parallels between Tonio's personal problems and the disintegration of the troupe are obvious and devastating—indeed, even Jack with his drinking problem, seems like the Rock of Gibraltar compared to Luna's ravings. When Jack's benders become unbearable, Tonio retreats even more into his dance.

The company is planning one final dance, "Indian Summer" and Tonio will dance the lead, a role that Ramon was to have done. The stress seems to be closing in on both men with a vengeance. Jack is virtually ripped apart from his job, feeling inept and part of the "AIDS Industry," unable to effect change nor comfort those he is assigned to. Tonio backs away from Jack and his drinking and takes solace with Millie, who has her own relationship problems.

But eventually, Jack and Tonio reconcile and their relationship progresses. Tonio tries to be there as much for Jack as Jack is for him. Tonio is practically salivating with nerves and excitement when opening night approaches for "Indian Summer." The unexpected happens though when he starts to feel ill and wakes up the next morning unable to move his legs. It's merely a temporary paralysis, but it seems to knock out any chance of Tonio dancing that week. Jack, Millie and the troupe rally round Tonio and he makes a decision—he will dance the lead, no matter what.

That night, supported (literally and figuratively) Tonio dances. It is a rousing, emotionally charged success. He collapses in Jack's arms, exhausted but triumphant. The picture ends when Tonio emerges weeks later from the hospital, limping with a partially paralyzed foot. He bursts forth with a renewed energy and, much to Jack's delight, a walloping case of "anger." Tonio vows to teach, to put forth love and devotion to his dance, and to keep his angry fires stoked against the "machine of AIDS." It has been said that the mates/spouses of AIDS victims almost universally stick by their partner to the very end, and it seems that this case will be no different. Whatever unusual or perverse situations drew Tonio and Jack together in the first place, they are now firmly ensconced as a couple.

As touching and direct as the film is, it is not without its faults. A scene in which Jack and Millie attempt to make love with each other (as an escape from their problems with their current partners) falls flat as a pancake, overbearing in its point and context. And whoever heard of a dance troupe that would mount fully-produced different productions as frequently as this one? The serious issue of Jack's drinking problem is never addressed, which is indeed strange. But most of the characterizations and dialogue ring true and powerful. Among the questions that hang over these characters heads, "What could our lives encompass, what could we possibly achieve in our lives if we didn't have to deal with this plague? How many ideas were lost, how many dances were lost, songs that weren't composed, novels left unwritten, due to AZT, loss of sight, hearing and delusions?" This large question hangs over this specific love story, and it explores both the questions and answers well.

—G.E. Georges

REVIEWS

Boxoffice. July, 1997, p. 88.
Detroit Free Press. October 3, 1997, p. 5D.
Entertainment Weekly. August 8, 1997, p. 56.
Los Angeles Times. July 25, 1997, p. F12.
Movieline. August, 1997, p. 38
New York Times. July 25, 1997, p. C14.
San Francisco Chronicle. August 22, 1997, p. D3.
San Francisco Examiner. August 22, 1997, p. C5.
Sight and Sound. July, 1997, p. 35.
Village Voice. July 29, 1997, p. 78.

All Over Me

In a world that expects you to fit in, sometimes you have to stand out.—Movie tagline

"Awash with riot grrrl irreverence and the urban foreboding of *Kids.*"—*Premiere Magazine*

"Astonishing, bursts onto the screen with white-hot energy!"—B. Ruby Rich, *Sundance Film Festival*

"Wonderful!"—Aaron Gell, *Time Out New York*

All Over Me is a project of sisters, director Alex Sichel and writer Sylvia Sichel. Unlike many movies that purport to be about teenagers, *All Over Me* tries to get under the skin of real teenagers. It is the kind of grittier, realistic movie that uses a regular, flawed, awkward teen to play the starring role instead of an Alicia Silverstone type. The result is more in the spirit of *Kids* than *Clueless.* The characters live in a bad section of town instead of Beverly Hills and their problems are about drugs and death and desperate passion instead of boys and cars. And, there's no prom or big game at the end.

The movie is set in Hell's Kitchen, a gritty, poor section of Manhattan. There, two girls, Claude (Alison Folland) and Ellen (Tara Subkoff) watch their friendship change. When the movie begins, both girls are as close as (non-sexual) best friends can be. They spend a lot of time in Claude's cramped room, sleep in the same bed and casually touch each other when they talk. Claude is a big, somewhat awkward girl who is finding out that she wants her friendship with Ellen to become something more. Ellen is a thin, bleached blonde who can't give Claude what she wants, but can't let her go either.

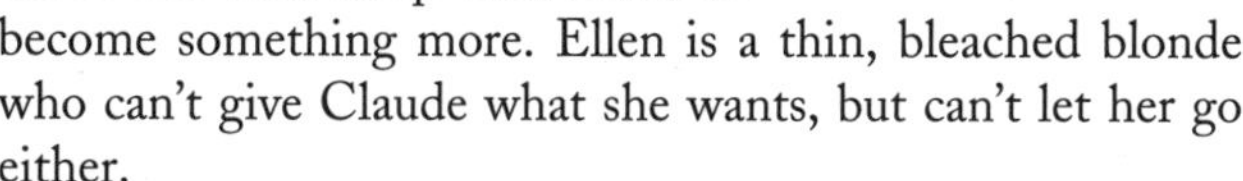

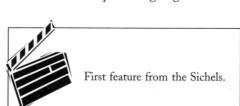

First feature from the Sichels.

Several forces are at work to change the girls' relationship. Ellen is spending time with her new boyfriend, Mark (Cole Hauser), the neighborhood tough guy. Claude is both jealous and worried about Ellen since Mark seems to be a violent and possessive jerk, who treats Ellen badly. Ellen is getting more into drugs and seems to be lurching uncontrollably toward a junkie lifestyle. At one point in a restaurant, Ellen nearly overdoses while Mark looks on unconcerned. Claude is the one who grabs Ellen, takes her to the bathroom and sticks her fingers down Ellen's throat to make her vomit. "You know I'm your dog," says Claude after Ellen starts showing signs of life. Later, back at the table with Mark, Ellen says, "Claude's my knight in shining armor." It's typical of Ellen to play Mark and Claude against each other. But no matter how helpful and loving Claude is, it's not going to matter. This is one incident that helps Claude realize that she is never going to win against Mark.

A second part of Claude's self-discovery is the arrival of new neighbor, Luke (Pat Briggs), in her building. Unlike Claude's man-obsessed mother (Ann Dowd), Luke helps Claude find out what she needs out of life. Luke is gay and he tells her about a lesbian club, pushing Claude more toward her own truth. Luke is also a musician and helps Claude remember how she and Ellen had dreamed of starting a band together. Claude also makes friends with Jesse (Wilson Cruz), her co-worker at a pizza place, who is in the process of coming out, paralleling her own journey.

Then Claude meets Lucy (Leisha Hailey) at the lesbian bar she's heard about from Luke. Lucy helps Claude see that she could have some sort of post-Ellen life, maybe even a better one. Lucy is a vibrant, pink-haired musician who is out of the closet. The two have an abortive date that ends when Claude shows her pain at not being able to decide between her old life with Ellen or the uncertain path with someone new. Claude puts on a Patti Smith record and blares "Pissing in the River." Claude sways and dances, crying with passion to the music. This naked moment and the unrelenting eye of the camera is reminiscent of Jennifer Jason Leigh's cathartic rendition of a Van Morrison song in *Georgia.* Lucy just lets Claude do what she needs to do.

The experiences of the characters and the decisions that Claude and Ellen have to make are enough to have an engaging movie, but the Sichels throw in an unnecessary "action" plot point involving a murder. It does help Claude clarify her position with Ellen once and for all, but there seems like there could be a better way to move the film along—something truer to the rest of the picture's tone.

What does ring true are the performances. Folland plays a somewhat similar role to the one she had in *To Die For,* that of a shy, vulnerable gay teen. Because her character can't say what she's thinking, Folland shows her feelings through subtle expressions and gestures. Folland's Claude seems like

CREDITS

Claude: Alison Folland
Ellen: Tara Subkoff
Mark: Cole Hauser
Jesse: Wilson Cruz
Lucy: Leisha Hailey
Luke: Pat Briggs
Anne: Ann Dowd

Origin: USA
Released: 1997
Production: Dolly Hall for Medusa Pictures; released by Fine Line Features
Direction: Alex Sichel
Screenplay: Sylvia Sichel
Cinematography: Joe DeSalvo
Editing: Sabine Hoffman
Music: Miki Navazio
Production design: Amy Beth Silver
Art direction: Kristen Vallow
Set decoration: Walter Bagnett
Sound: Jan Mclaughlin, Neil Seba
MPAA rating: R
Running Time: 90 minutes

AWARDS AND NOMINATIONS

Independent Spirit Awards 1997 Nominations:
Actress (Folland)

a real girl, dealing with problems in a believable way and facing life with fear and curiosity. Also good is Subkoff's Ellen, who has the sort of heavy-lidded, pale and thin look of a half-glamorous/half-doomed nightclub creature. She appears insistent on heading toward self-destruction. She won't accept Claude's love, but seems to enjoy knowing the power it has over Claude. Wilson Cruz, who played Ricky on the television show "My So-Called Life," is in similar territory here as the shy, sensitive gay teen who is just starting to come out.

All Over Me has a few cameos, but they're the kind that most people outside the indie music scene won't pick up on. And these performances are just as good as the major ones. Briggs, who plays gentle neighbor Luke, is also the lead singer of the band Psychotica. He has just the right touch of beatific wisdom for his mentor role and as the eventual martyr of the movie. Hailey, who's a member of the Murmurs, makes Lucy, Claude's possible new love interest, brave, together, and happy—about the opposite of Ellen. She's the kind of mature force that Claude could use in her life, if Claude can accept her.

The Hell's Kitchen setting adds a gritty sense to the film, but the story could take place anywhere. The smallness of the apartment that Claude shares with her hovering mother helps to throw the two together and makes their relationship seem more cramped, but it's not necessary that the apartment be small—hovering mothers and teenage daughters the world over can get in each other's way regardless of home size. The bleakness of the neighborhood does add a certain sense of hopelessness to the story. When Ellen starts getting into drugs, it seems almost inevitable. From her point of view, what other options does she really have?

A high point of the film is the soundtrack, featuring tunes from riot grrrl types like Ani DiFranco, Babes in Toyland, and Tuscadero. (Not everyone agrees—*Entertainment Weekly* called it "tuneless, depressive mope rock.") The music is as rough, passionate and girl-powered as the movie. Plus, it nicely reflects what Claude could become—a musician and strong woman.

All Over Me has a nice offhandedness to it. It gives the viewer the sense of just picking up with some teenagers and watching their lives for awhile. The moments are not huge and dramatic, they just happen, like real life. The film seems like a documentary with the Sichels keeping a nice distance from these kids and letting them tell their story.

—*Jill Hamilton*

REVIEWS

Boxoffice. February, 1997, p. 73.
Entertainment Weekly. May 2, 1997, p. 44.
Los Angeles Times. April 25, 1997, p. F6.
New York Times. April 25, 1997, p. C19.
San Francisco Chronicle. April 25, 1997, p. D3.
San Francisco Examiner. April 25, 1997, p. D3.
Variety. July 29, 1996, p. 59.
Village Voice. April 29, 1997, p. 71.

An American Werewolf in Paris

Things are about to get a little hairy—Movie tagline

Box Office: $13,858,476

Andy (Tom Everett Scott), Brad (Vince Vieluf) and Chris (Phil Buckman) are three young men on a "Daredevil Tour of Europe" as their t-shirts advertise. In this self-made tour they evidently accumulate various points for doing really stupid things. (There must also be a "sex tour" going on at the same time because the boys also talk about accumulating various sex points.) The daredevil part of the tour explains why the three are heading for Paris, because that's where Andy plans on amassing beaucoup points by bungee jumping off the Eiffel Tower.

Since the gendarmes would surely arrest them for such a stunt, the boys hide away on the famous French landmark until it closes. Then, as Andy prepares to jump, they discover they are not alone. Also getting ready to jump—but without a bungee cord—is Serafine (Julie Delpy). She is obviously troubled and has suicide is on her mind. Andy is instantly smitten by the sad, moonlit beauty, and when she jumps, he jumps after her. The only problem is, he has forgotten to tie his bungee to the tower. Thankfully his friends catch the rapidly uncoiling cord, and Andy grabs Serafine's leg just in time to gently deposit her on the ground. As he rebounds upward, all he has left of his mysterious Cinderella is her shoe.

The trip upward is not a gentle experience for Andy since he bashes his head on the observation deck's overhang, and after a period of unconsciousness, he awakes, head bandaged, in a Parisian hospital.

Andy now becomes obsessed in finding the beautiful woman—partly out of fear she'll try to commit suicide again and partly because he is bewitched by her. He next glimpses her in the hospital, dressed as a nurse and carrying a heart in a plastic bag. But he is again knocked out, this time by a suddenly opened door (and this klutzy guy's a daredevil?).

Brad to Andy: "The kind of girl who jumps off the Eiffel Tower has issues, man, major issues."

Eventually, with the help of his sidekicks, Andy finds Serafine's home. She is very evasive (and covered in blood—which she says is paint) and wants him to leave, but he finally manages to extract a commitment for a coffee date the next day. At the cafe, however, Andy soon realizes Serafine is anything but a typical mademoiselle. For one thing, she demonstrates a superhuman strength when she throws a very large bully halfway across the restaurant.

It also seems that Serafine is living with another man, Claude (Pierre Cosso), who, in a gesture of international friendship, invites Andy and his pals to a charity party to be held that night at the Club de la Lune. As it turns out, however, this wasn't as friendly an act as one might think. As it turns out Claude and his pals are werewolves, and these phony parties are just their way of luring people to a location where they can be confined and eaten. When Serafine learns that Andy is about to become haute cuisine for werewolves, she sets out to rescue him. Unfortunately, she's too late for Brad, and poor Andy only escapes after being injured by one of the party throwers.

Once again Andy blacks out only to wake up this time in a bed in Serafine's house. She tries to tell him that he is about to become a werewolf just as she herself is, but Andy isn't buying her sales pitch. Well, he wasn't until he finds himself eating very raw meat in a restaurant and talking to a very chewed up and very dead Brad. Hallucinations, it seems, are a part of the transformation process.

Now Andy has to figure out how to save himself as well as his friend Chris who has been captured by Claude and his band of merry werewolves, not to mention trying to give Serafine a less suicidal outlook on life.

At the beginning, *An American Werewolf in Paris* shows a lot of atmosphere and energy. From its gloomy, rain-soaked shots of a gothic cathedral (assumedly Notre Dame?) while equally gothic Omen-like music plays in the background, to its chilling first kill as a man in a lab coat is dragged back into a Paris sewer while the credits role, one is hyped for a good and spooky horror film. Unfortunately, about halfway through it degenerates into a less than formula grade B film.

For awhile, though, it does hold promise. And every now and then it offers sparks of humor and horror. For example, Andy's first kill as a werewolf involves a young American space queen named Amy (Julie Bowen) prone to giggling, skimpy clothes, bad French, and one-night stands. After being killed—near Jim Morrison's grave in the Pere-Lachaise Cemetery—Amy now "haunts" Andy just as Brad does. The scene of her trying to draw attention to Andy's location by whistling through her mauled punctured face is gross . . . but funny.

This mix of comedy and fright was what made John Landis' 1981 *An American Werewolf in London* such a success, but this time around the parts just don't fit together as well.

Although actor Tom Everett Scott tries valiantly to carry the film, it may be asking too much of one person.

CREDITS

Andy: Tom Everett Scott
Serafine: Julie Delpy
Brad: Vince Vieluf
Chris: Phil Buckman
Amy: Julie Bowen
Claude: Pierre Cosso
Dr. Pigot: Thierry Lhermitte
Inspector Leduc: Tom Novembre
Chief Bonnet: Maria Machado
Detective Ben Bou: Ben Salem Bouabdallah
Bouncer: Charles Maquignon

Origin: USA
Released: 1997
Production: Richard Claus for Cometstone Pictures, J&M Entertainment and Hollywood Pictures; released by Buena Vista Pictures
Direction: Anthony Waller
Screenplay: Tim Burns, Tom Stern and Anthony Waller; based on characters created by John Landis in *An American Werewolf in London*
Cinematography: Egon Werdin
Editing: Peter R. Adam
Production design: Matthias Kammermeier
Art direction: Hucky Hornberger
Set decoration: Andrea Schlimper
Costumes: Maria Schicker
Music: Wilbert Hirsch
Visual effects supervisor: John Grower, Bruce Walters
MPAA rating: R
Running Time: 100 minutes

First gaining notice in Tom Hanks' 1996 *That Thing You Do!*, Scott again proves that he is a winning presence. He is one of those personable nice guys (like Hanks) who can create likability for his character just by being cast in a role.

But there are more problems than assets in *An American Werewolf in Paris*. One is that normal werewolf "rules" don't seem to be adhered to while new ones make an all-too-convenient magical appearance. For example why do normal police bullets kill them? Aren't they supposed to be silver? And who invented the bit about eating the heart of the werewolf who infected you will cure you? Add a potion that allows the beasts to metamorphosize even when the moon isn't full, and it may be one more modification than the horror gods will allow.

Many famous locations, including the Eiffel Tower and the Pere-Lachaise Cemetery, were actually recreated on soundstages.

Another problem is that sometimes the characters, their actions, and the plot don't really make a lot of sense. Claude stole Serafine's blood so he could start a gang to purify the world of all its scum. But, if there appears to be any "scum" at Claude's parties, it's Claude and his fellow skinheads. Who does he seem to define as scum? American tourists! I know the French have a reputation of being rude to tourists but eating them is a new low.

Equally strange, when Andy kills the werewolf who created him by eating the heart, it seems to be implied that he has cured Serafine, too. But how can that be? And while the ending may tie things up neatly, it really makes little sense, and leaves many questions unanswered.

Perhaps even more disappointing, however, are the film's special effects. In the Landis film, watching the agony of David Naughton's tortured transformation contributed to our squeamishness and concern for the character. This time around the transformations are mostly computer generated and create little connection with the viewer. In fact, the final werewolves are unconvincing and look more as if they belong in some Nintendo computer game than in a film.

What's interesting about the production of *An American Werewolf in Paris* is that it was initially filmed in the summer of 1996 and set for an appropriate October (Halloween) release. However, it was only released in Britain in October. For the U.S., release was set for the highly inappropriate Christmas Day. Whose brilliant marketing idea was that? Probably the same guy who disregarded old werewolf rules and made up those that suited him.

—Beverley Bare Buehrer

REVIEWS

Cinemafantastique. November, 1997, p. 18.
Cinemafantastique. April, 1998, p. 59.
Entertainment Weekly. January 9, 1998, p. 47.
Hollywood Reporter. December 23, 1997, p. 17.
Sight and Sound. December, 1997, p. 37.
USA Today. December 24, 1997, p. 3D.
Variety. November 3, 1997, p. 99.

Amistad

Freedom is not given. It is our right at birth. But there are moments when it must be taken.
—Movie tagline

"A powerhouse film. Big in its passion, generosity and humanity. Don't let anyone tell you *Amistad* is a dry history lesson."—Jay Carr, *Boston Globe*

"Djimon Hounsou gives one of the year's great performances."—Peter Travers, *Rolling Stone*

"Two thumbs up. Anthony Hopkins is amazing."—*Siskel & Ebert*

"A superlative achievement - A shattering drama. No other contemporary director can surpass Steven Spielberg's amalgam of cinematic skills, resources, sensitivity, boldness, dramatic intuition, and good-heartedness."—Gene Shalit, *Today Show*

"Mystery, action thriller, courtroom drama, even comedy. What *Amistad* has going for it is sheer power."—Susan Wloszczyna, *USA Today*

"Absolutely unforgettable. A towering achievement. Surely one of the best films of the year."—Jeffrey Lyons, *WNBC-TV*

Box Office: $20,636,332

A forgotten passage in American history in the form of slave revolt leader Cinque (Djimon Hounsou pictured center) is portrayed in Steven Spielberg's *Amistad.*

Steven Spielberg's *Amistad* is the re-creation of a little-known event in American history—the 1839 mutiny of a group of Africans aboard the Spanish slave ship *La Amistad* and the consequent trials that concluded in the Supreme Court. While Spielberg, the most commercially successful director in history, is generally known for his fantasy and adventure films, he has tackled historical subject matter before in *Empire of the Sun* (1987) and most notably in the Oscar-winning *Schindler's List* (1993). *Amistad* lacks the sheer sweep and complexity of Spielberg's Holocaust epic but nonetheless is a moving, well-acted drama that contains some of the most powerful scenes of his career.

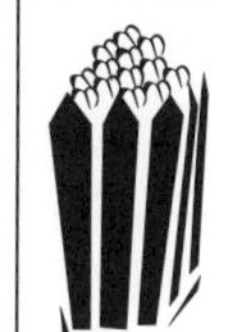

Adams to Joadson: "In a courtroom, whoever tells the best story wins."

The film opens brilliantly with the slave insurrection. We first see an extreme close-up of a man's anguished face and soon realize we are in the hold of the slave ship in the pitch-black of night as Cinque (Djimon Hounsou) frees himself from his shackles and leads his fellow captives in a bloody rebellion that wipes out most of the slave ship's crew. These opening scenes are swift and brutal; shot against the black sky, they are primal images of man rising up to claim his freedom.

Instead of returning to Africa, the surviving Spanish sailors trick the Africans and steer the ship to the American coast, where the Africans are arrested and put on trial in New Haven, Connecticut. Two abolitionists, Tappan (Stellan Skarsgärd) and the former slave Joadson (Morgan Freeman), take the case and win the aid of a real-estate lawyer, Roger Baldwin (Matthew McConaughey), who sees the case revolving around property rights. He argues that, if the Africans were not born into slavery, they must have been acquired illegally and should therefore be set free; the Africans' origin becomes the key issue of his case. The early court maneuvering then becomes a matter of different parties competing for rights to the Africans—the surviving Spanish sailors, the naval officers who salvaged the Amistad, and Queen Isabella II of Spain (Anna Paquin)—as the pro-slavery president, Martin Van Buren (Nigel Hawthorne), follows the case closely during his run for reelection.

These early scenes are effective in laying out the legal issues and the pre-Civil War tensions over slavery in a fairly clear, understandable manner, but at the same time the legal maneuvering is somewhat pedestrian. While the stakes are high because they involve human freedom, the overall proceedings are sluggish and seriously weaken the first part of the film. Instead of an epic story of the fight for freedom, we seem to be in a routine legal drama (with Matthew McConaughey even playing a period version of his role in 1996's *A Time To Kill*—the stereotypically inexperienced, young lawyer taking on more than he can handle).

The freshest aspect of the first part of the film is the Africans' perception of the New World and their bemused take on American customs. The prisoners think, for example, that abolitionists singing hymns outside their jail are entertainers. And of course there is the language barrier, which inhibits communication between the captives and their advocates until Tappan and Joadson finally wander the streets speaking the Africans' native Mende in an attempt to find a black person who knows the language.

When Baldwin finds papers from a Portuguese ship on board the Amistad, he knows that the Africans' journey started in West Africa—not Havana, as the Spanish sailors claim. He is able to make a strong case, but, when victory is within reach, Van Buren gets the judge removed and replaced with one thought to be more likely to rule against the Africans. Cinque takes the stand to tell his story, and we see a flashback depicting the capture of the Africans and their transatlantic crossing.

This sequence is among the most powerful in Spielberg's career in its unflinching illustration of the total dehumanization of slavery. He depicts the brutality and shock of the capture and the sheer horror and misery aboard a slave

AWARDS AND NOMINATIONS

Academy Awards 1997 Nominations: Supporting Actor (Hopkins), Cinematography, Costume Design, Original Dramatic Score
Golden Globe Awards 1998 Nominations: Best Drama, Drama Actor (Hounsou), Supporting Actor (Hopkins), Director (Spielberg)

ship; we see scenes of human beings mercilessly whipped and shot dead, huddled together in conditions befitting an animal, and even thrown overboard to accommodate the shortage of provisions. In one poignant moment, a woman simply slides overboard with a baby—it is a quietly tragic moment that suggests the extinction of hope under such harrowing circumstances. *Amistad* opens in total darkness with the slave insurrection, but the slave trade scenes are shot in the bright light of day, as if one sequence were the counterpart of the other; the mutiny must take place under cover of night, but the horrors of slavery that precipitated it take place for all the world to see.

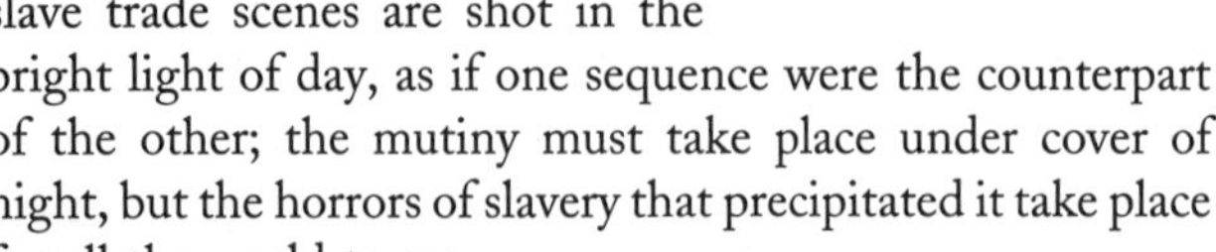

Producer Debbie Allen first started her quest to have the film made in 1984 after optioning William Owen's novel *Black Mutiny*.

Like the liquidation of the Jewish ghetto in *Schindler's List*, the Middle Passage scenes in *Amistad* are stark and unforgettable. Unfortunately, however, while the Nazi purge in *Schindler's List* led to a development of conscience in Schindler and thus was an integral part of the film, the slave trade scenes in *Amistad*, while a brilliant set piece, do not develop character in a significant way.

CREDITS

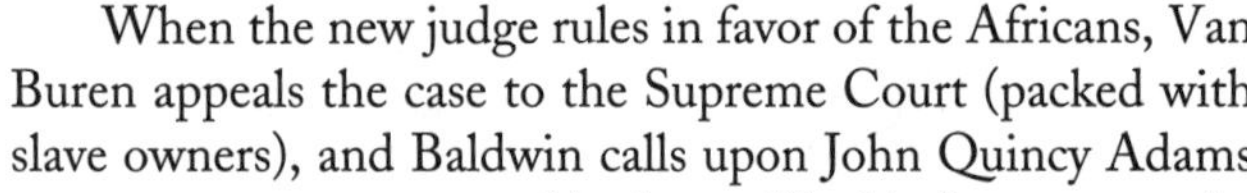

Cinque: Djimon Hounsou
Theodore Joadson: Morgan Freeman
John Quincy Adams: Anthony Hopkins
Roger Baldwin: Matthew McConaughey
Martin Van Buren: Nigel Hawthorne
Secretary Forsyth: David Paymer
Holabird: Pete Postlethwaite
Tappan: Stellan Skarsgärd
Queen Isabella: Anna Paquin

Origin: USA
Released: 1997
Production: Steven Spielberg and Debbie Allen for HBO Pictures; released by DreamWorks Pictures
Direction: Steven Spielberg
Screenplay: David Franzoni
Cinematography: Janusz Kaminski
Editing: Michael Kahn
Music: John Williams
Production design: Rick Carter
Art direction: Chris Burian, Mohr, Jim Teegarden, Tony Fanning
Set decoration: Rosemary Brandenburg
Costumes: Ruth E. Carter
Sound: Ronald Judkins, Robert Jackson
Visual effects supervisor: Scott Farrar
MPAA rating: R
Running Time: 152 minutes

When the new judge rules in favor of the Africans, Van Buren appeals the case to the Supreme Court (packed with slave owners), and Baldwin calls upon John Quincy Adams (Anthony Hopkins) to argue the case. In the first part of the film, Hopkins plays Adams as an old, almost doddering man, a former president passing time in the Congress when he is not tending his garden. Once unwilling to take up the case, he now agrees to go to the Supreme Court. He comes alive—and so does the movie.

A compelling relationship forms between Cinque and Adams; both are leaders of their people, but Adams is a former leader who has seen his time come and go and is now trying to prove himself in one last fight. In the preparation for the final case, Cinque is not a passive observer but rather an active participant (or at least as active as he can be given his status as a prisoner). He suggests legal strategy to Adams and even provides the inspiration for Adams's final plea. Cinque declares that he will "call into the past" to his ancestors and "beg them to come and help me . . . for at this moment I am the whole reason they have existed at all"—we can see this statement resonate with Adams, who, in the final argument before the Supreme Court, calls upon the country's ancestors and most especially his own.

Hopkins's performance, especially his eloquence and force of argument before the Supreme Court, elevates *Amistad*. What started out as a property-rights case becomes a plea for the final chapter in the American Revolution. Adams links Cinque to the heroes of the Revolution—quite simply, if Cinque were not black, he would be valorized for throwing off the shackles of his oppressors. Moreover, Adams links the nation's history to his own. John Quincy Adams lived in the shadow of his father, John Adams, one of the Founding Fathers, but in his speech he quite movingly embraces that past. Cinque's reverence for his ancestors transfers nicely to Adams's own situation. Busts of the country's founders encircle the edge of the court, and Adams passes each one and looks at his father's. With his father's image in the background, he declares, "Who we are is who we were"—a summation that puts the Africans' case into the larger context of American history. The slave rebellion, then, is not a betrayal of America but part of the American tradition itself.

Although Adams wins the case, the film ends on a bittersweet note. Cinque returns home only to find it no longer exists—his people are in Civil War, his family is gone, and his village has been destroyed—but the slave fortress at Sierra Leone, where Cinque and his comrades were held, is demolished.

In *Schindler's List*, a man of ambiguous character is able to save the lives of hundreds of Jews by using the system

against itself. Oskar Schindler is a greedy, flawed man who nonetheless outwits the Nazi leaders even as he is initially in some ways a reflection of them. This kind of complexity is missing in *Amistad*, which offers clear-cut good and bad and fairly straightforward motives all around. The basic set-up is simple, but within it strong characterizations emerge.

Hounsou is a charismatic force throughout the film. He speaks mostly Mende but is able to communicate quite vividly through his facial expressions and the power of his voice. One scene in which he disrupts the courtroom to demand his freedom is especially powerful in its raw emotion and impatience with the judicial system. Hopkins realistically portrays an old man who has accepted his status as a former president but is finally willing to fight for what is right. Even during his rousing closing remarks, we see the old man in the great orator as he takes little gasps of breath throughout his monologue.

Critical reaction to *Amistad* was generally positive. While there were some detractors like *Entertainment Weekly*'s Owen Gleiberman, who called the film "a courtroom drama of dull, soapbox ponderousness," *Time*'s Richard Schickel felt Spielberg examined "every aspect of his saga in rich detail." Ultimately, *Amistad* is an emotional experience tempered somewhat by the conventionality of its basic courtroom structure. Nonetheless, there are enough scenes of raw power and poignancy to make Amistad a rewarding experience.

—*Peter N. Chumo II*

REVIEWS

Boxoffice. November, 1997, p. 22.
Detroit Free Press. December 7, 1997, p. J1.
Entertainment Weekly. December 12, 1997, p. 54.
Los Angeles Times. March 28, 1997, p. F1.
Los Angeles Times. November 9, 1997, p. 8.
Los Angeles Times. December 10, 1997, p. F1.
New York Times. September 7, 1997.
New York Times. December 10, 1997, p. E1.
People. December 15, 1997, p. 19.
Rolling Stone. December 25, 1997, p. 172.
Sight and Sound. March, 1998, p. 36.
Time. December 15, 1997.
Variety. December 8, 1997, p. 110.
Village Voice. December 16, 1997, p. 71.
Washington Post. December 12, 1997, p. C1.

Anaconda

It will take your breath away.—Movie tagline

When you can't breathe, you can't scream. —Movie tagline

"Spine tingling! Utterly breathtaking! *Anaconda* is one film you won't forget, a superior thriller, unbelievably powerful!"—Ron Brewington, *American Urban Radio Networks*

"A thriller that gives you bumps bigger than golfballs."—Bobbie Wygant, *KXAS-TV*

"A creepy, crawly, guilty pleasure!"—Thelma Adams, *New York Post*

"Two thumbs up! This movie is fun!"—Roger Ebert, *Siskel & Ebert*

Box Office: $65,885,767

With *Anaconda*, it's painfully obvious that director Luis Llosa's goal was to create a high-tech, Amazonian version of *Jaws* (1975), when in actuality he has come up with an (unintentionally humorous) episode of "Gilligan's Island" on acid. It's typically par for the course for Llosa, whose 10 year career as a director has found him slogging through a series of sensationalized B-films. He's now made seven movies and seems blissfully content to explore only two subjects: hired guns and the Amazon Jungle. Of the former, he's churned out *Hour of the Assassin* [1987], *Crime Zone* [1988], *The Specialist* and *Sniper* [both from 1994]. Even his one previous shot at the big time from this genre (*The Specialist*) called on the dubious talents of two B-grade leads (Sylvester Stallone and Sharon Stone) who spent a great deal of time wrestling with each other in mildly erotic shower scenes. This is Llosa's third cinematic excursion down one of the world's most famous and mysterious rivers. Despite the inclusion of two high-profile sexy co-stars (Craig Sheffer and Sandra Bullock), *Fire In The Amazon* (1991) didn't even stir up enough interest to be released on video. Although the like-minded *800 Leagues Down The Amazon* (1993) was made available on video, it was adapted from a Jules Verne work and would have served everyone better if it had remained permanently shelved.

Give Llosa credit for one thing, the cast of *Anaconda* is as eclectic, racially balanced and politically correct as is possible in a feature film. But again, the characters and the vessel on which they travel seem to be nothing more than a sloppy re-working of the cast of the late '60s comedy series "Gilligan's Island."

The story opens with a group of documentarians who board a dilapidated flat-bottom boat (as fragile and unseaworthy as "GI's" SS Minnow) and head out, Huckleberry Finn-style, into the dark, murky South American jungle to film a shy, reclusive Indian tribe. Leading the group is Cale (Eric Stoltz in the "Professor" role), who is confined to bed, literally comatose and near death the entire time (he's stung by a creature while attempting to free the boat after it's been snagged by some underwater growth). A prime example of Llosa flexing his directorial acumen by regulating one of the few marquee actors in the project to a bed for the bulk of the picture.

Sarone describing an anaconda's attack: "It strikes, wraps around you, holds you tighter than your true love. And you get the privilege of hearing your bones break before the power of their embrace causes your veins to explode."

The anacondas are a mixture of computer graphics, animatronics, and some real snakes.

Cale's plucky girlfriend, Terri (a very unadorned Jennifer Lopez in the "Mary Ann" role), ends up taking the reigns as the quasi ship's captain. She gets assistance from camera man Danny (Ice Cube in the "Skipper" role), a blustery, fearless man who believes his urban, east L.A. upbringing has sufficiently prepared him to go toe-to-toe with the formidable title character. Having shown great promise in *Bottle Rocket* (1996), the young Owen Wilson (as the mumbling, malleable "Gilligan" character) slips into a severe case of the stupids. Once the lines have been drawn as the travellers take sides against one another, he waffles back and forth, jumping from one side of the fence to the other. When he's not getting pushed around, he's concentrating full-time on his libido along with his girlfriend, the scatterbrain Denise (Kari Wuhrer in the "Ginger" role). In one of the many scenes that finds their ship dry-docked, the pair ventures out into a dark, foreboding jungle for a midnight rendezvous.

In the role of the documentarian narrator Westbridge, the classically trained British actor Jonathan Hyde (in both the "Mr. and Mrs. Howell" roles) gets saddled with the most embarrassing and over-the-top character in the film. When he's not whining about the heat or browbeating the crew, he's hitting golf balls into a net (this could perhaps be Llosa's sly homage to "The Love Boat").

Having recently made a comeback of sorts, Oscar winner (*Coming Home*, [1978]) Jon Voight plays Paul, a shady river rat/poacher who hitches a ride with the film crew. His barely hidden real agenda is to trap the snake, a slithering computer-generated reptile. The casting of Voight (blonde, blue-eyed, WASP) as a lazy-eyed, gravel-throated Latin bad-ass is one of the great casting catastrophes of all-time, but not all that surprising. Although Voight's career is in resurgence, the roles he's taking are all within the frame-

CREDITS

Terri Flores: Jennifer Lopez
Danny Rich: Ice Cube
Paul Sarone: Jon Voight
Dr. Steven Cale: Eric Stoltz
Warren Westridge: Jonathan Hyde
Gary Dixon: Owen Wilson
Denise Kalberg: Kari Wuhrer

Origin: USA
Released: 1997
Production: Verna Harrah, Leonard Rabinowitz and Carole Little for CL Cinema Line Films Corporation; released by Columbia Pictures
Direction: Luis Llosa
Screenplay: Hans Bauer, Jim Cash, and Jack Epps, Jr.
Cinematography: Bill Butler
Editing: Michael R. Miller
Production design: Kirk M. Petruccelli
Art direction: Barry Chausid
Costumes: Roberto Carneioro
Music: Randy Edelman
Sound: Douglas B. Arnold
Animatronic effects: Walt Conti
Visual effects: John Nelson
MPAA rating: PG-13
Running Time: 89 minutes

REVIEWS

Chicago Tribune. April 11, 1997, p. 5.
Cinefantastique. April, 1997, p. 8.
The Detroit News. April 11, 1997, p. 3C.
Entertainment Weekly. April 18, 1997, p. 48.
Los Angeles Times. April 11, 1997, p. F4.
New York Times. April 11, 1997, p. B5.
The New Yorker. April 21, 1997, p. 96.
People. April 21, 1997, p. 23.
Sight and Sound. July, 1997, p. 35.
USA Today. April 11, 1997, p. 4D.
Variety. April 14, 1997, p. 91.
Village Voice. April 22, 1997, p. 82.

work of lackluster material (save for maybe *Mission: Impossible* [1996]). Like the Robert Shaw character in *Jaws*, he thinks he can tame an overpowering force of nature with sheer will, but eventually ends up playing an entree.

Anaconda is a travesty. It attempts to recapture the heart-pounding, "man vs. the elements" fear of *Jaws* and instead replaces it with exaggerated, computer-generated histrionics. Llosa's cookie-cutter action/adventure slop, totally lacking any noticeable originality, are the products of a filmmaker with very little say, albeit one who says it with thunderous, ear-splitting volume.

—J.M. Clark

Anastasia

Discover the adventure behind the greatest mystery of our time.—Movie tagline

"The family film event of the season."—Mike Cidoni, *ABC-TV*

"A new era has begun in magical animation." —Don Stotter, *Entertainment Time-Out*

"It's a musical, it's a mystery, it's a masterpiece."—Bonnie Churchill, *National News Syndicate*

"Enchanting! The animation and songs will astound you."—Jeffrey Lyons, *NBC-TV*

"An enchanting experience for both children and adults."—Michael Medved, *New York Post*

"Fantastic! An animated wonder. Take the kids."—Jim Ferguson, *Prevue Channel*

"Two thumbs up!"—*Siskel & Ebert*

"Magnificent!"—Gene Shalit, *Today Show*

Box Office: $50,246,584

Twentieth Century Fox's first feature-length animation obviously owes much to the Disney canon. Like many recent Disney films, *Anastasia* is a reworking of a familiar tale, complete with music, dancing, a spunky heroine, a reluctant hero, a disgusting villain, and cute animal sidekicks. The formula is a familiar one, but Fox has pulled off an upset, for *Anastasia* is better than most recent Disney fare. In fact, it may be the best cartoon musical since *Beauty and the Beast* (1991).

Bartok the bat: "Oh sure, blame the bat. What the heck, we're easy targets."

Mouse Inc. was so concerned about its upstart competition that it dusted off *The Little Mermaid* (1989), the film which launched the new genre of animated features, for re-release around Thanksgiving 1997 to go head-to-head, along with *Flubber*, against *Anastasia*. Disney had good reason to worry. *Anastasia*'s look is fresher and richer, its songs snappier and its characters more appealing than anything Disney has produced in years.

Filmmakers Don Bluth and Gary Goldman are veteran competitors to the Disney juggernaut. Director Bluth has had his own minor hits over the years—*An American Tail* (1986), *The Land Before Time* (1988) and *All Dogs Go to Heaven* (1989)— and failures as well, like *Thumbelina* (1994) and *A Troll in Central Park* (1994). Bluth's stories are usually lively, but the quality of his animation has taken a back seat to Disney. No longer. The Fox Animation Studios in Phoenix used state-of-the-art computer animation and wide-screen Cinemascope to create some breathtaking panoramas and thrilling action sequences in *Anastasia*. The faces of the characters are not as sharp or as subtle as Disney's best, but the rich backgrounds in *Anastasia* more than make up for that defect.

A remarkable sequence with a speeding train is quite possibly the most jaw-dropping in animation history. With the main characters fighting to stop a train car that is speeding down the tracks towards a collapsed bridge, the filmmakers employ lightning-fast editing, brilliant camera perspectives and dazzling computer graphics. All of *Anastasia* is filled with sweeping, rich landscapes and majestic and detailed interiors.

A willingness to take risks and bend the confines of the formula also distinguishes *Anastasia* from its competitors. Start with the clever sidekick, a Disney staple and now a mandatory part of animated features. The sidekick in *Anastasia* is Bartok, an albino bat with a Scandinavian accent, a deadpan delivery and an air of offended propriety. As enlivened by the voice of Hank Azaria,

Bartok provides plenty of rather twisted humor. Not only that, but he's in the service not of the heroes but of the villain, Rasputin, albeit somewhat reluctantly.

Rasputin (Christopher Lloyd) is himself a rather bizarre character. In this historically twisted version of the events of the Russian Revolution, he's a sorcerer who curses Czar Nicholas II and his family and incites the Russian people to riot. In truth, Rasputin was a faith healer who advised Nicholas to institute even more repressive measures against the Russian people and was murdered by members of the resistance.

Historical findings and DNA analysis have shown that the real Anastasia was killed along with her family in 1916.

In *Anastasia*, when the royal family is overthrown, Rasputin chases Anastasia and her grandmother but falls through the ice and drowns. We next meet him as a sort of underworld zombie demigod, dreaming with the fishes and the crustaceans in a watery cavern. His body is literally falling apart—mouth, eyes, hands, and head are all detachable and constantly getting away from him. It's a great concept for a villain, and saves Rasputin from becoming the cliche that the plot requires. It also gives Bartok plenty of opportunity for sarcastic commentary. Rasputin is a cross between Ursula the sea witch in *The Little Mermaid* and something from the mind of Tim Burton. It's fortunate that he's so surreal and comic, since he leaves something to be desired in the menace department: his powers are intermittent and undefined and depend a lot upon ghostly green ghoulish things emanating from what looks like a lava lamp.

Merchandising in these films is everything, but in *Anastasia*'s case it's not overwhelming saccharine. One toy figure given away in the fast-food tie-in is that of Bartok holding Rasputin's eyeball. That's a far cry from the usual white-bread fare, and illustrates the offbeat sensibilities of *Anastasia*'s creators.

Turning historical events upside down, *Anastasia* gets off on the wrong foot, but these liberties can be excused; after all, this is a cartoon, not a documentary. Once the story gets rolling, it's clear that the tale fits the times perfectly, with our post-Diana longing for brushes with monarchy and the contradictory demand that monarchs be accessible to commoners.

Anastasia (Meg Ryan), saved from her family's execution by the quick-thinking efforts of a kitchen boy named Dimitri (John Cusack), becomes an orphan who doesn't remember her past. Dimitri, himself ignorant of his past, becomes a con man auditioning St. Petersburg girls to play the part of Anastasia. He plans to take the winner to Paris to meet the dowager grandmother and claim her reward of 10 million rubles pledged to the person who can bring her Anastasia. Dimitri is aided by the avuncular Vladimir (Kelsey Grammer), a former aristocrat who's also on the make.

The plot is about an ex-princess discovering her past and regaining her confidence. In the process Dimitri gains his soul and his sense of values. Of course, the two are destined to fall in love, and so they are destined at first to clash. But a quartet of screenwriters carry the spats a lot further than is usually done. Anastasia is not just a run-of-the-mill headstrong, sassy type; she has a bit of a mean streak. When she awakens from a nap on a train car, stretches her arms, and accidently strikes Dimitri in the face, she discovers it's him and exclaims: "Good!" When they discover their mutual attraction, it's aboard a boat, as Vladimir is using Dimitri to teach Anastasia to dance. "You must let *him* lead," Vladimir tells Anastasia. Then, as they start getting starry-eyed, Vladimir sees trouble ahead, and says to himself: "I never should have let them dance."

While Disney heroines take pseudo-feminism only so far, Anastasia is the genuine article. She is not so swept away

CREDITS

Anastasia: Meg Ryan (voice)
Dimitri: John Cusack (voice)
Vladimir: Kelsey Grammer (voice)
Rasputin: Christopher Lloyd (voice)
Bartok: Hank Azaria (voice)
Sophie: Bernadette Peters (voice)
Dowager Empress Marie: Angela Lansbury (voice)
Young Anastasia: Kirsten Dunst (voice)

Origin: USA
Released: 1997
Production: Don Bluth and Gary Goldman for Fox Family Films; released by 20th Century Fox
Direction: Don Bluth, Gary Goldman
Screenplay: Susan Gauthier, Bruce Graham, Bob Tzudiker, and Noni White
Editing: Fiona Trayler
Music: David Newman
Songs: Lynn Ahrens (lyrics)
Songs: Stephen Flaherty (music)
MPAA rating: G
Running Time: 94 minutes

AWARDS AND NOMINATIONS

Academy Awards 1997 Nominations: Original Musical or Comedy Score, Song, ("Journey to the Past")
Golden Globe Awards 1998 Nominations: Song ("Journey to the Past"), Song ("Once Upon a December")

by Dimitri that she becomes putty in his arms; far from it. You can see an ending coming from miles away—Dimitri is going to rescue Anastasia from Rasputin, and by doing so finally earn Anastasia's love. But when the ending arrives and Dimitri comes to the rescue, it ends up being Anastasia who delivers the decisive blow to Rasputin and saves Dimitri from certain death. It is something of a much-belated turning point in the history of cinema melodrama (and these modern cartoons certainly qualify as melodrama). The damsel in distress, that staple of film plots since the days of the silents when the villains tied them to railroad tracks, finally is given the power to make her own choices and fight her own battles.

Regrettably, both Anastasia and Dimitri are loaded with modern-day looks, styles of talking and oodles of sarcasm. Bluth says the filmmakers got Anastasia's look by combining photos of Audrey Hepburn with cover girls from teen magazines, and modeled Dimitri also on contemporary teenage actors, adding a mop of unruly Hugh-Grant-type hair. The result is disconcerting, but no more so than Pocahontas looking like a rock star in Disney's *Pocahontas* (1995). Though Anastasia is too Western in appearance and too sassy in attitude to be a Russian orphan—she's Meg Ryan, not Julie Christie—Dimitri comes off a little more realistically. His moral confusion is appealing, and Cusack's halting manner of speech works wonders for the character's believability. He's genuinely a lost soul in need of redemption, but never comes off too wistful.

Angela Lansbury is perfectly suited to be Marie, the aristocratic Romanov matriarch. Some of the minor characters are delightful, especially Sophie (Bernadette Peters), a French advisor to Marie and Vladimir's love object; she's a big-bosomed, fun-loving hunk of Parisian pastry. There is also Pooka, the requisite cute dog, playing Anastasia's loyal pet, as a bone tossed to the very young in the family.

But the real stars of this film are among the army of 400 top animators who have created some delightful and astonishing and very adult tableaus: a golden-spired St. Petersburg, an enormous royal palace, a cavernous undersea world for Rasputin, an evening at the Parisian ballet. The sets and the choices of camera angles approach the realism of live action; they are enchanting. The songs, by Lynn Ahrens and Stephen Flaherty, are delightful, with "Once Upon a December" a sure hit ballad.

Anastasia is both firmly rooted in the cinematic tradition paved by Disney and also a departure, a step ahead. It is the first postmodern version of the traditional family blockbuster cartoon. The feel of the film makes its competitors look staid by comparison. The attitude is a little hipper, the mandatory moral lessons a little less contrived. This film is not a masterpiece—the plot is too pedestrian and inconsistent for that—but it is a refreshing change of pace in a genre that has become too worn and predictable. Its characters are fresh, its outlook pleasingly off-kilter yet within the mainstream of family fare. With *Anastasia*, fully marketed with spin-off dolls and games, Fox has opened a new era in animated feature films, one in which the Mouse empire no longer reigns supreme. The result can only be good for film if it forces everyone to take more risks.

—Michael Betzold

REVIEWS

Boxoffice. November, 1997, p. 24.
Boxoffice. January, 1998, p. 46.
Chicago Tribune. November 21, 1997, p. 5.
Entertainment Weekly. November 14, 1998, p. 58.
Los Angeles Times. November 21, 1997, p. F1.
New York Times. November 14, 1997, p. E22.
People. November 24, 1997, p. 19.
USA Today. November 14, 1997, p. 6D.
Variety. November 10, 1997, p. 39.
Village Voice. November 25, 1997, p. 96.

Angel Baby

In Love. In Deep.—Movie tagline

"A harrowingly impressive, one-of-a-kind love story. John Lynch and Jacqueline McKenzie are a striking, vital and brilliant couple."—Jay Carr, *Boston Globe*

"Heartbreakingly good! As perilous as it is intoxicating. Written and directed with great depth of feeling by Michael Rymer."—Janet Maslin, *New York Times*

Angel Baby stars John Lynch as Harry, and Jacqueline McKenzie as Kate, two psychiatric patients who fall in love. This extraordinary film manages to avoid virtually all the Hollywood cliches about the mentally ill and their caretakers. The lovers are not romanticized; society is not portrayed as a repressive place with no sympathy for romantics. Instead, *Angel Baby* provides a searing insight into damaged, fallible people trying to cope with illness and to lead normal lives.

Harry first spots Kate at a group therapy session. She

is sullen and withdrawn, and apparently unmoved by his expressions of interest in her. He announces to his brother Morris (Colin Friels) and his wife Louise (Deborra-Lee Furness) that he is in love. Morris and Louise are pleased, if somewhat worried—because Harry is just regaining his equilibrium after a suicide attempt and more than two years without a job. These facts emerge slowly as Morris takes the excruciating steps toward re-entering the world of work and adult responsibilities. One of the pleasures of this picture is the way the backgrounds of the characters gradually reveal themselves rather than being forced out through contrived dialogue early on.

First feature for director/writer Michael Rymer.

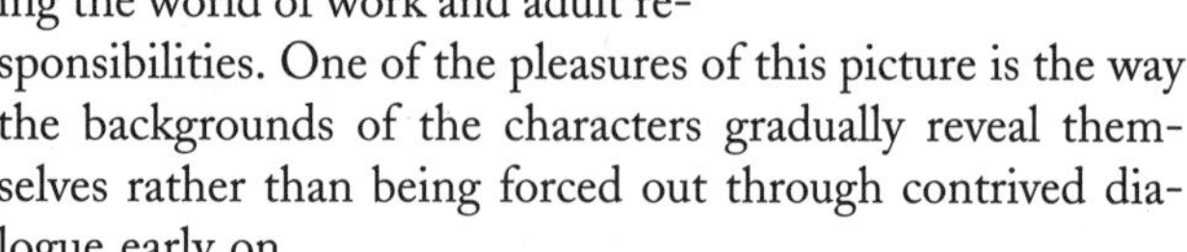

After the conversation with Morris and Louise, Harry determines to pursue Kate, following her when she leaves the clinic. She tries to lose him, but when he catches up with her, she warily begins to open up to him. She denies that she is like the others at the clinic, and Harry does nothing to challenge her—even when she insists that she is receiving messages from an angel via her daily viewings of "Wheel of Fortune." Harry becomes interested in her obsessions because he is obsessed with Kate. As for himself, he does not deny his self-destructiveness—showing Kate the scars from his slashed wrists.

Soon the couple become lovers. If Kate thinks she communicates with an angel, Harry thinks he has found one. During one exhilarating scene on a bridge Louise stands on a railing flapping her arms like wings and squawking like a bird. Harry joins her. They look ridiculous and wonderful—this couple loving each other literally on the edge of life and death. Watching them creates a wistful feeling. They have a purity of passion that is hard to sustain, and they know it. They want to settle down and be normal—just like Morris and Louise, who are quite ordinary people and yet charming and comfortable with themselves. Seldom has a movie presented ordinary people and middle-class life so attractively. Yet there is nothing sentimental about Morris and Louise; rather their stability becomes a treasured virtue set against Harry and Kate's precariousness. When the foursome sit down to dinner, and it becomes apparent that Kate does not know how to use silverware, no comment is made, but the pathos of Kate's fate—the concern about how such a vulnerable person will be able to manage a "normal" life—is palpable.

When Harry and Kate announce that they want to set up a home and that a baby is on the way, Morris and Louise are stunned. They can see that the couple is deeply in love, but how will they cope? Harry outlines their plans with passion. Morris gives Louise an anxious look, and she smiles, saying they will do everything they can to help Harry and Kate. Louise is not naive. Her face tells that the odds are against Harry and Kate, yet she cannot deprive them of their chance of happiness. It is never said, but Harry's moving out also means that Morris and Louise can resume a more normal life themselves. The film's down-to-earth observation of such domestic details is one of its quiet strengths. Harry will be missed, nevertheless, for he has been good with Morris and Louise's young son. When the boy is troubled by a poster of a rather malevolent-looking clown, Harry rolls up the frightening visage and tosses it out the window of the boy's room, delighting the surprised boy.

At the clinic, Harry and Kate have to brave a meeting with their psychiatrists, who are doubtful that the couple can take on the new responsibility of starting a new household and family. The scene could easily have turned into a rap against the bureaucratic control of individuals. On the contrary, the psychiatrists seem genuinely concerned, and it is the couple who will not—and are probably afraid to—acknowledge the terrible risks they are taking. Yet the psy-

CREDITS

Harry: John Lynch
Kate: Jacqueline McKenzie
Morris: Colin Friels
Louise: Deborra-Lee Furness

Origin: Australia
Released: 1995, 1997
Production: Timothy White, Jonathan Shteinman for Stamen/Meridian Films Production and Australian Film Finance Corporation; released by Cinepix Film Properties
Direction: Michael Rymer
Screenplay: Michael Rymer
Cinematography: Ellery Ryan
Editing: Dany Cooper
Music: John Clifford White
Production design: Chris Kennedy
Art direction: Hugh Bateup
Costumes: Kerri Mazzocco
Sound: John Phillips
MPAA rating: Unrated
Running Time: 105 minutes

AWARDS AND NOMINATIONS

Australian Film Institute 1995: Actor (Lynch), Actress (McKenzie), Cinematography, Director (Rymer), Film, Editing, Screenplay

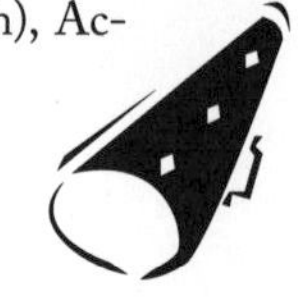

chiatrists concede Harry and Kate their right to embark on a normal life—only cautioning the couple to take their medication faithfully.

The first days on their own are euphoric for Harry and Kate. Their passionate lovemaking gives way to thoughts about the baby. Harry is worried that medication will harm their child, and he convinces Kate that they should stop taking their pills. The results are horrendous. Kate paces back and forth, her anxiety level rising every day. Harry cannot concentrate at work and is eventually fired. Kate is hospitalized and Harry returns to the clinic.

A forlorn Harry is told that the recovering Kate does not want to see him. When he finally gains admission to her hospital room, she is doped up and barely conscious. Unable to function without Kate and agonizing over her death-like condition, Harry hatches a plot to spirit her out of the hospital. He takes her to a half-finished high-rise and then pleads with his brother Morris to bring her medication. Divided between love for his brother and the certainty that Harry's abduction of Kate will end in another disaster, Morris strikes a bargain with Harry: Morris will get the medication if Harry agrees to call for medical help at the first sign that Kate is in trouble. It is a lunatic plan that Morris conceals from Louise. If there is any moment in *Angel Baby* that strains credulity, it is Morris's clandestine agreement with Harry. Yet Morris loves his brother so passionately that it is just conceivable that he would do what he knows is wrong. If he were to tell Louise, he would not be able to do it.

The film's denouement is wrenching. The angel baby is born in the hospital, but Harry's angel baby, Kate, dies. He returns to their bridge, where they perched like birds with soaring spirits—and also like fragile human beings about to be drowned in the elements of life. There Harry struggles to fly—to leave this world, or to remain in it? *Angel Baby* does not answer the question. How can the question be answered? For it is like a modern enactment of Hamlet's troubled question about existence.

As one reviewer notes, *Angel Baby* is hard to watch. A sense of doom pervades the film even as the characters seem most hopeful. Scene after scene is heartbreaking yet exhilarating—another version of the bridge scene. John Lynch plays Harry with beautiful abandon and sensitivity. Lynch's Harry is heroic; he is also foolish. Jacqueline McKenzie's performance may be even more extraordinary than Lynch's. Playing a demented misfit is not exactly the way to sustain a rich, complex performance. But the underside of Kate's denial that she is mentally disturbed is her dread that flushing the pills down the toilet will result in the mental storms that took her to the clinic. She is the one who begs Harry to get medication for her when she begins to realize that she cannot cope without it. There is a down-to-earth core in her character that keeps her from jumping off the bridge.

Angel Baby is director Michael Rymer's first film. It is an impressive debut that won seven Australian Film Institute Awards, including best film, best director, best actor, and best actress. Rymer also wrote the screenplay, which perhaps accounts for the subtle interplay between the words and camera angles. There is nothing fancy in Ellery Ryan's cinematography, but with such strong characters, it would be a mistake to do anything but allow their feelings to rise to the surface of the camera lens.

The perfect casting certainly contributes to the film's unity of effect. Reviewers have emphasized the balanced performances of Lynch and McKenzie, but the film itself would lose balance without the subtle support of Colin Friels and Deborra-Lee Furness. Watch Friels looking at Lynch as the two men talk about the child who has just been born; the intensity of Morris's love in that scene is every bit as riveting as the most passionate scenes between Harry and Kate, and that kind of brotherly love, in its quieter forms, has rarely been captured by the cinema.

—*Carl Rollyson*

REVIEWS

Boxoffice. April, 1996, p. 108.
Entertainment Weekly. February 21, 1997, p. 107.
Los Angeles Times. January 31, 1997, p. F4.
New York Times. January 24, 1997, p. C6.
Variety. September 4, 1995, p. 76.

Angel Dust

"*Silence of the Lambs* on acid!"—Michael Wilmington, *Chicago Tribune*

"Slick, quick, and drop-dead flashy!"—Andrew Sarris, *New York Observer*

"The best crime film to arrive onscreen since *The Usual Suspects*!"—Stephan Talty, *Time Out NY*

Angel Dust may seduce devotees of "The X Files" and "Millennium," the stylish, creepy productions created for the Fox network by Chris Carter. Director Sogo Ishil makes Tokyo look like a futuristic film noir, with gloomy backdrops and gleaming objects lit by flashlights. The probing points of light evoke that Chris Carter feeling that the truth is out there. Unfortunately, *Angel Dust* is not a television series, and as a feature length film its loose threads annoy rather than tantalize, since there will be no next episode, no constantly delayed sense that perhaps eventually the mystery will finally be revealed in one of those flashlight beams.

Nevertheless, *Angel Dust* is fascinating to watch. The visual style created by Norimichi Kasamatsu, director of photography, makes everyday things look threatening. A crowded subway car, the scene where several women have dropped dead—the casualties of poisons deftly injected into their necks—takes on a ghoulish atmosphere. A passenger whistles Dvorak's New World Symphony, which becomes the signal for murders in subsequent scenes. In an ironic sense, it is a new world, in which the Japanese—and perhaps all urban masses—feel menaced. The real-life chemical attacks of a Japanese sect seem to have inspired the film's evocation of crowds who seem almost to expect to be victimized.

Angel Dust toys with contemporary anxiety just like the 11 o'clock news, which purveys a story a night about how the things people take for granted—like the fillings in their teeth—may poison them. The killing is insidious, shadowy, and almost impossible to protect against. The film is so successful in working up this atmosphere of dread that every shot of faces in a crowd seems to reveal mass apprehension.

Setsuko Suma (Kaho Minami), a criminal psychologist, is assigned to solve the murder cases. She is very much on her own. Introduced to a room of male colleagues, her male boss feels it necessary to assure his colleagues that even though Setsuko is good looking, she is a superb investigator. In other words, she will not lose her cool; she can be relied on to be an honorary man.

But *Angel Dust* is not a feminist thriller, and men are not the enemy—as the film's ending (not to be given away here) clearly underscores. Indeed, Setsuko soon gives way to her emotions, suffering what amounts to a nervous breakdown. For her prime suspect is her former lover, Rei Aku (Takeshi Wakamatsu), a Svengali of a de-programmer who runs an institute named the Refreezing Psychorium. Although Aku is supposed to be rehabilitating cultists, he practices his own forms of mind control.

When Setsuko interviews Aku, he keeps turning the conversation into an analysis of her feelings. Reacting like a victim herself, she naturally suspects that what Aku does mentally to her, he has been doing, mentally and physically, to the women who have been murdered. They have been his passive victims. The more attracted Setsuko is to this thesis, the more passive she becomes—eventually groveling at Aku's feet. He gives her a good working over by making a tape that plays constantly on his television while he (apparently) watches her from another room. It is hard to say exactly where he is because the scene focuses on Setsuko and her responses to the television screen. The televised Aku is rather like Poe's raven, in that his repetitious speech seems calculated to draw out Setsuko's worst fears, so that like the narrator of Poe's poem, she ends up torturing herself.

To enjoy *Angel Dust* it is necessary to concede the film's premise: the psychological and the empirical—what people feel and see—cannot be disentangled. Asking matter-of-fact questions such as why Setsuko is not pulled off the case destroy the illusion. Similarly, the classic detective plot, in which

CREDITS

Setsuko Suma: Kaho Minami
Rei Aku: Takeshi Wakamatsu
Tomoo: Etshusi Toyokawa

Origin: Japan
Released: 1996
Production: Taro Maki, Kenzo Horikoshi and Eiji Izumi; released by Northern Arts Entertainment
Direction: Sogo Ishii
Screenplay: Yorozu Ikuta, Sogo Ishii
Cinematography: Norimichi Kasamatsu
Editing: Sogo Ishii, Hiroshi Matsuo
Music: Hiroyuki Nagashima
Production design: Tomoyuki Maruo
MPAA rating: Unrated
Running Time: 116 minutes

REVIEWS

New York Times. January 24, 1997, p. C20.

the detective may be threatened and even, momentarily, lose control of himself or herself, only to restore order, has to be abandoned. Rather like science fiction writer Stanislaw Lem in his novel, *The Investigation*, *Angel Dust* destroys generic expectations. The detective cannot be counted on to establish reality and to solve the mystery; rather he or she becomes part of it, and the mystery story becomes a species of autobiography. While a radical departure from generic expectations is refreshing, this exercise in thwarting the conventions seems for all its style to lack substance. For its conclusion is about as cliche ridden as a genre film can get; that is, it finally and simplistically yields up a villain.

—*Carl Rollyson*

The Apostle

The hardest soul to save was his own.—Movie tagline

Lust, Obsession, Revenge . . . Redemption. —Movie tagline

"Screen acting to cherish and remember. The defining role of Robert Duvall's career! Duvall has created as complete a person as the screen allows."—Kenneth Turan, *Los Angeles Times*

"An extraordinary performance."—Dave Kehr, *New York Daily News*

"An intense portrayal of a charismatic American original."—Thelma Adams, *New York Post*

"A film that can create a full, fiery portrait without reducing it to any kind of stereotype. Duvall delivers with volcanic, galvanizing energy."—Janet Maslin, *New York Times*

"A fascinating and fervent film! As passionate and complex a performance as Duvall has ever given."—David Ansen, *Newsweek*

"Two thumbs up. A triumph!"—Roger Ebert, *Siskel & Ebert*

"Nothing short of astonishing."—Jeffrey Lyons, *WNBC-TV*

In 1983, when their financing failed to materialize, director Sidney Lumet and playwright David Mamet abandoned a film project called *The Kingdom*. Actor Robert Duvall had been set to play one of two evangelists central to the story. Duvall was attracted to the idea of playing a Pentecostal preacher and decided to write his own script. He spent thirteen years unsuccessfully trying to interest Hollywood in the project. Eventually, he had to finance and direct the film himself (it is his directorial debut). Part of the problem for Hollywood may have been that *The Apostle* does not use the emotionalism of tent religion as a subject for humor. Rather than adopt the eye of scorn, Duvall chooses the eye of the realist, presenting his main character Sonny Dewey as a man who egocentrism and love of himself mixes with his genuine passion for God and for showing others the path to spiritual wholeness. Duvall documents Sonny's lifelong conversation with God with unsparing honesty. The resulting film is a riveting character study.

The Apostle E.F.: "I'm a genuwine, Holy Ghost, Jesus-filled preachin' machine this mornin'!"

The opening scene shows as well as any how taking such an unconventional approach to the subject of evangelicalism can produce some truly absorbing moments. Driving down a Texas highway with his mother (June Carter Cash), Sonny (Robert Duvall) stops at the debris of a serious car crash. He takes his Bible with him and trudges off the road, past the police, to one of the victims still trapped in his smoking car. Telling the barely conscious man that there are angels in the automobile, Sonny counsels him that a faith in God and Jesus Christ can assure his salvation. One of the highway cops orders Sonny back to his car; Sonny pushes him away with his leg while still holding the hand of the crash victim and continuing his pleading. When the victim assents with a squeeze of his hand, Sonny proclaims to the insistent cop, "I'd rather die and go to heaven than live to be 100 and go to hell!"

This scene has the rich tonal ambivalence of most of the motion picture: audience members suppress a laugh at the slapstick of Sonny pushing away the cop with his leg while at the same time they watch in fascination as he brings to this desperate man a sense of God's presence. As if in confirmation of Sonny's work, the film cuts away to the wrecked auto again after Sonny leaves, and the hand of the girl in the passenger seat who appeared to be dead now moves. About the accident Sonny had told his mother, "One may live and one may die," and this brief shot seemingly confirms the power of prayer.

The conflict of the film is simple and straightforward. Sonny awakens one night with a conviction that his wife Jessie (Farrah Fawcett) is with another man. Mumbling his thanks to God for the revelation, he gets his gun and goes off looking for her. He suspects correctly that she is in bed with the "puny-assed youth minister" to whose house Sonny drives in frustration. He throws a baseball through the bedroom window. Later, an emotionally spent Jessie reminds Sonny of his own past womanizing and asks for a divorce. As he paces the room and tries to change her mind, she quietly removes the bullets from the gun. The breakup of the marriage carries with it another danger: Jessie and the youth minister have started a movement to claim control of Sonny's church. Sonny's frustrations emerge in a nightlong tirade to God that seems to be part-prayer, part-soliloquy, part-scream-therapy: "I've always called you Jesus, and you always called me Sonny!" Neighbors complain about the noise, but Sonny's mother reassures them that all is well.

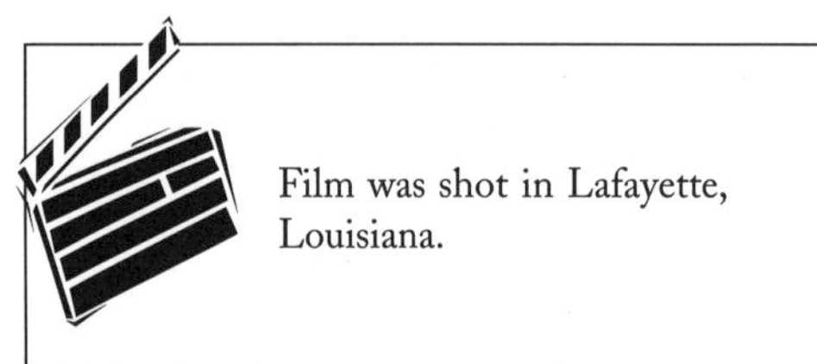

Film was shot in Lafayette, Louisiana.

A turning point arrives when Sonny, who is glimpsed taking a nip from a flask, confronts the youth minister at a child's softball game. Sonny hits his rival with a bat and strides away. When the youth minister lapses into a coma, Sonny leaves town. He sinks his Cadillac in a lake and rebaptizes himself. Now a self-proclaimed apostle called E.F., he travels to a small-town bayou in Louisiana, finds a retired local pastor (John Beasley), and starts a new church. The remainder of the film provides a gallery of scenes that documents Sonny's month-long success at building a congregation from scratch. Part of the growth comes from the coverage he gets from a local radio station. A secretary there named Toosie (Miranda Richardson) shyly accompanies this flamboyant local celebrity on two dates. Back in Texas, the authorities search for leads to track Sonny down.

Duvall usually keeps the camera at a noticeable distance. In this age of closeups, he favors shooting the performers from the waist or at three-quarter length. This medium camera setup was once the staple of American films, and the influential writers in the French film journal *Cahiers du Cinema* even referred to it as "the American shot." Such framing is close enough to the actors to register their facial expressions but far away enough to capture body English and physical proximity. When two actors share the same frame, as in the scene when Sonny tries to talk his wife out of leaving him, this medium two-shot faithfully records the subtext in their movements. Sonny tries to sit on the sofa with Jessie, and her suppressed jitters and nervous glances wordlessly convey in the same shot her fears for potential violence from her husband. This type of framing was also favored by Stanley Tucci, another actor who co-wrote and -directed the independent film *Big Night* (1997). Tucci explained how wider framing can place some welcome demands on the actors: "So many movies have all these closeups. It's all coverage. . . . Whereas the other way forces you. The script has to be tight. The blocking has to be right. The actors' intentions have to be clear."

This practice maintains the spontaneity of a single take, and it is not surprising that actors when they direct should prefer such a realistic approach. Other aspects of *The Apostle* also indicate an inclination toward realism: the leisurely narrative that documents key moments in Sonny's life rather than shapes the events of the plot into a highly patterned

CREDITS

The Apostle E.F./Euliss Dewey: Robert Duvall
Jessie Dewey: Farrah Fawcett
Toosie: Miranda Richardson
Horace: Todd Allen
Brother Blackwell: John Beasley
Mrs. Dewey Sr.: June Carter Cash
Troublemaker: Billy Bob Thornton
Joe: Billy Joe Shaver
Sam: Walton Goggins
Elmo: Rick Dial

Origin: USA
Released: 1997
Production: Rob Carliner for Butchers Run Films; released by October Films
Direction: Robert Duvall
Screenplay: Robert Duvall
Cinematography: Barry Markowitz
Editing: Steve Mack
Music: David Mansfield
Production design: Linda Burton
Art direction: Irfan Akdag
Costumes: Douglas Hall
Sound: Steve C. Aaron
MPAA rating: PG-13
Running Time: 148 minutes

AWARDS AND NOMINATIONS

Academy Awards 1997 Nominations: Actor (Duvall)
Independent Spirit Awards 1997: Feature, Director (Duvall), Actor (Duvall)
Nominations: Screenplay, Supporting Actress (Fawcett), Supporting Actress (Richardson)
Los Angeles Film Critics Association 1997: Actor (Duvall)
National Society of Film Critics 1997: Actor (Duvall)

storyline, the de-emphasis of editing in many scenes to preserve the richness of the actor's performance, the choice to shoot many interior scenes in lower light, giving the film's look an everydayness. In an interview in *Film Comment* magazine, Duvall admitted the importance of respecting the actor's performance when editing: "It's better to cut around things rather than into them." In contradiction to style-conscious filmmakers like Hitchcock, Duvall doubted that editing could create a good performance out of an assortment of takes: "Find it. If you don't have it, I don't think you can find it. A chef has to have good produce to make good food. Rearranging and mixing takes are legitimate cheating as long as it comes out somewhat pure. But when you have a good take, you try to stick with it, not out of laziness but out of clarity." Such a transparency of style usually requires a good deal of effort.

It is Duvall's acting that assumes the greatest importance in *The Apostle.* Gavin Smith titled his interview with Duvall in *Film Comment,* "America's Greatest Living Actor." In its de-emphasis of obvious cinematic devices, the camera operates primarily as a recording apparatus for Duvall's fascinating character study. His performance as Sonny works on a number of levels: he superficially captures the rhythms of the speech patterns and the strutting gait of tent preachers, but he also brings out underlying qualities like the hardness that can attack his wife's lover in one scene and in another can bring a racist redneck (Billy Bob Thornton) to repentance.

The final scene in the film gives an extended look at Sonny's preaching in a revival service. Having been tipped by Jessie, who picked up a reference to "E.F." amid scattered radio static, dozens of police cars arrive outside Sonny's church as he rises to preach. An officer enters the church and stands impassively in the back of the building while the service continues. Sonny then delivers the sermon that sums up his life, and he again reveals the traits that make his character so interesting—his frankness with God, his mix of pride and zeal in starting a church from nothing, his love of attention, and his genuine emotion in seeing others reconcile themselves to God. After the final altar call, Sonny walks out through the back door where the police gather around him. The sounds of continued congregational singing mingle with those of the officer reading Sonny his rights as he searches and handcuffs him. After a fade out, the closing credits crawl up the screen over shots of Sonny in prison garb preaching to his companions on a road gang as they clear away weeds.

This last shot and its hurried way of suggesting a resolution also indicates the difficulty Duvall had in deciding on a final cut for the film. One source quoted Duvall as saying, "The first cut was about four hours. I don't know why—we only had 115 pages in the script." By the time the movie debuted at the Toronto and New York film festivals, the improvisational excess had been cut out of a version then two and one half hours. October Films wanted a shorter version for national distribution, so editor Walter Murch trimmed another seventeen minutes. Although there is still ample attention given to Sonny, some of the supporting characters, especially Toosie, now drop out of the film a bit suddenly. The last third is not as tightly organized as the preceding portions.

The industry reaction to *The Apostle* at the film festivals was so positive that Duvall was able to regain from the sale of the distribution rights the five million dollars he spent making the movie as well as an additional million. His film appeals to audiences in its uncommon approach to the subject of religion and in its strong acting.

—*Glenn Hopp*

REVIEWS

Boxoffice. February, 1998, p. 55.
Entertainment Weekly. December 19, 1997, p. 52.
Entertainment Weekly. February 13, 1998, p. 24.
Film Comment. November-December, 1997 p. 30.
Hollywood Reporter. September 9, 1997, p. 6.
Los Angeles Times. December 17, 1998, p. F1.
New York Times. October 9, 1997, p. E5.
New Yorker. February 2, 1998, p. 81.
People. February 9, 1998, p. 19.
Rolling Stone. January 22, 1998, p. 62.
Variety. September 15, 1997, p. 69.
Village Voice. December 23, 1997, p. 84.

As Good As It Gets

A comedy from the heart that goes for the throat.—Movie tagline

"You're going to love this movie! Nicholson is unbelievable. Kinnear is terrific."—Joel Siegel, *Good Morning America*

"The best and funniest romantic comedy of the year! Magically written, directed and acted." —Kenneth Turan, *Los Angeles Times*

"Winning! Tart and warmly entertaining. Helen Hunt is irresistible."—Janet Maslin, *New York Times*

"Hugely entertaining! Comic gold. Nicholson is in top form."—Peter Travers, *Rolling Stone*

"Two thumbs up! Wonderful. One of the year's best pictures."—Gene Siskel, *Siskel & Ebert*

Romance novelist Melvin Udall (Jack Nicholson) tries to contain his offensive and erratic behavior long enough to charm waitress Carol (Helen Hunt) in the romantic comedy *As Good As It Gets.*

Box Office: $24,394,469

As Good As It Gets is a romantic comedy that pulls off a magic trick. Director/writer/producer James L. Brooks takes an unsympathetic, foul-mouthed curmudgeon with an obsessive-compulsive disorder and turns him into a romantic hero.

Jack Nicholson plays Melvin Udall, a misanthropic romance writer, who saves all his love for the characters in his novels. In real life he insults strangers and acquaintances alike with painfully bigoted remarks, while relishing the effect of his scathing diatribes. Udall is so offensive, he even picks on little dogs, throwing his neighbor's pet Verdell down the apartment garbage chute.

In *As Good As It Gets,* his compulsive behavior drives him to unwittingly preform two acts of kindness in his fanatical quest to keep the routine of his life in its proper order. Udall's life is an endless round of the same activities every day. One stop in his routine is having lunch at the same restaurant, at the same table, with the same waitress each noon, while gleefully indulging in spewing caustic vitriol at the other waitresses and diners.

One day he comes into the restaurant and finds that his waitress, Carol Connelly (Helen Hunt), has quit. She has a chronically asthmatic son, Spencer (Jesse James), and so she leaves her job in Manhattan to be closer to home in Brooklyn.

Udall, who needs to have the regularity of having the same waitress serve him, becomes so distraught by this disruption in his routine that he hires a specialist to cure her son in hopes that Carol will return to the restaurant. It works. But this act of kindness makes Carol so grateful that she mistakes Udall for a normal human being and, to his horror, she begins to treat him as one.

Simon to Melvin: "The best thing you have going for you is your willingness to humiliate yourself."

Meanwhile, his gay artist neighbor, Simon Bishop (Greg Kinnear), is robbed in his apartment and beaten so badly that he is laid up in the hospital for weeks. This leaves his dog, Verdell, in need of a temporary home. Simon's friend and art dealer, Frank Sachs (Cuba Gooding Jr.), foists the dog upon an intimidated Udall, who is so racist that he's too frightened to dispute with the man.

Verdell, who has taken the long ride down the garbage chute because of Udall, is at first wary of him, but soon warms up to the man. Stranger still, Udall also warms to the dog. When Simon gets out of the hospital, Udall returns Verdell to the artist, who is now penniless and despairing.

Udall, who has now included Verdell in his routine, and has even learned to love the little canine, invites Simon to stay at his apartment, with the underlying motive of having Verdell back in his life.

Together these two acts of kindness change Udall. Carol and Simon's gratitude spark an emotion in the self-centered curmudgeon that begins the painful process of humanizing him. As the film follows the fortunes of these three people, it also explores the affect compassion can play in changing a person.

When Brooks has these three interacting, the dialogue is smart and real, their relationship to one another is dynamic, and the plot and the characters are believable. But from the moment Udall becomes romantically involved with Carol, the credibility gap yawns wide.

Udall pulls two compliments out of his swamp of insults, and the no-nonsense Carol is swept off her feet. Brooks can make us like Udall, but it seems unlikely that as grounded a person as Carol appears to be, with a son to raise, would even consider getting involved with someone with such a cornucopia of issues.

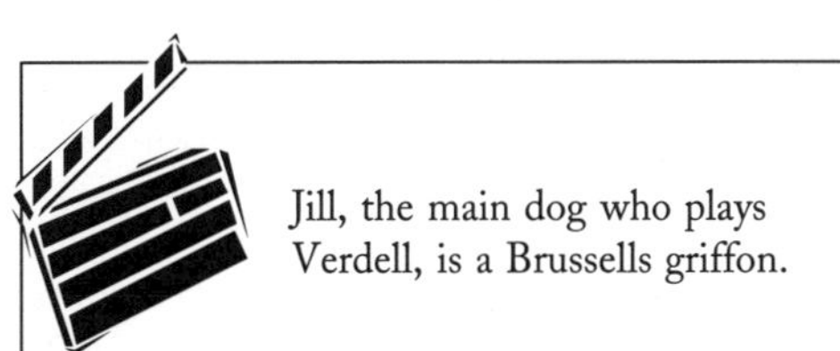

Jill, the main dog who plays Verdell, is a Brussells griffon.

Besides his cruel remarks, Udall doesn't step on cracks, can't bear to be touched, locks and unlocks his door in a complicated routine that includes light switches, and washes his hands with a number of new bars of soap, which he disposes of immediately. After Carol says, "All you do is make me feel bad about myself," the formulaic happy ending is really out of place.

But *As Good As It Gets* does succeed on a number of other levels. The dialogue is intelligent, the characters are compelling, and Udall's metamorphosis is a joy to watch. The film also gives a sympathetic, but not sugarcoated, view into the life of a person suffering from a mental disorder.

One of the best scenes is when a distraught Udall charges into his psychiatrist's office, demanding a session, and is turned away because he doesn't have an appointment. Udall stomps out and, to a waiting room full of startled patients, he asks, "What if this is as good as it gets?"

James L. Brooks has said about Melvin Udall, "There's something wrong with Melvin, but the nature of what is wrong with him is that he spends his life disguising what's wrong with him." Brooks, who directed *Terms of Endearment* (1983) and *Broadcast News* (1987), has once more explored the quirky unpredictability of relationships. But his dark-humored investigation of the troubled man could have delved deeper into Udall's character and motivations. By the time he gets us to love the man, Brooks leaves us wondering about who he really is.

Jack Nicholson deserves a lot of the credit for making Udall likeable. Not many actors could portray such an unsympathetic character and yet ultimately gain the sympathy of the viewer. Nicholson brought a vulnerability to this part that was the character's saving grace. A raised eyebrow, a dropped jaw, a forced smile—and we suddenly find ourselves liking the crusty fellow.

But Udall is not the only one going through a transformation. Simon's long battle to re-create himself after being broken and broke, is a wonderful example of feel-good cinema, although Kinnear's role can be cloyingly nice at times. His portrayal of Simon is best when he has a slight edge to him, but those moments are far too few. Simon is so nice that he comes to love a man who, in the past, has verbally abused him to the point that Simon was moved to call Udall a "horror of a human being."

Helen Hunt's portrayal of the down-to-earth but weary single mother, who is a little the worse for wear, showcases

CREDITS

Melvin Udall: Jack Nicholson
Carol Connelly: Helen Hunt
Simon Bishop: Greg Kinnear
Frank Sachs: Cuba Gooding Jr.
Vincent: Skeet Ulrich
Beverly: Shirley Knight
Jackie: Yeardley Smith
Nora: Lupe Ontiveros
Spencer Connelly: Jesse James

Origin: USA
Released: 1997
Production: James L. Brooks, Bridget Johnson, and Kristi Zea for Gracie Films; released by TriStar Pictures
Direction: James L. Brooks
Screenplay: James L. Brooks and Mark Andrus
Cinematography: John Bailey
Editing: Richard Marks
Music: Hans Zimmer
Production design: Bill Brzeski
Art direction: Philip Toolin
Costumes: Molly Maginnis
Sound: Jeff Wexler
Head animal trainer: Roger Schumacher
MPAA rating: PG-13
Running Time: 138 minutes

AWARDS AND NOMINATIONS

Academy Awards 1997: Actor (Nicholson), Actress (Hunt)
Nominations: Best Picture, Supporting Actor (Kinnear), Film Editing, Original Musical or Comedy Score, Original Screenplay
Broadcast Film Critics Association 1997: Actor (Nicholson)
Golden Globe Awards 1998: Best Musical/Comedy, Musical/Comedy Actress (Hunt), Musical/Comedy Actor (Nicholson)
Nominations: Director (Brooks), Screenplay
National Board of Review 1997: Actor (Nicholson), Supporting Actor (Kinnear)
Screen Actors Guild Awards 1997: Actor (Nicholson), Actress (Hunt)
Writers Guild of America 1997: Original Screenplay

her maturity as an actress. She brings realism, tempered with a drop of playfulness to the part, and her casual indifference becomes the perfect foil to Udall's self-satisfied eccentricity.

At one point, Holly Hunter, Ralph Fiennes, and Kevin Kline were all being considered for the film. But it is a tribute to Nicholson and Hunt that their performances were so original that it is difficult to imagine anyone else playing their roles.

Although the film is not as good as it gets, it works. The cast and writers succeed in proving what Simon believes: "You look at a person long enough you'll discover his humanity."

—Diane Hatch-Avis

REVIEWS

Boxoffice. February, 1998, p. 54.
Drama-Logue. January 8, 1998, p. 24.
Entertainment Weekly. January 9, 1998, p. 42.
Hollywood Reporter. December 10, 1997, p. 12.
Los Angeles Times. December 23, 1997, p. F1.
New York Times. December 23, 1997, p. E1.
New Yorker. January 5, 1997, p. 75.
The Outlook. December 23, 1997, p. D3.
People. January 12, 1998, p. 21.
Rolling Stone. January 22, 1998, p. 62.
Sight and Sound. March, 1998, p. 38.
Time. December 15, 1997.
Variety. December 15, 1997, p. 58.
Village Voice. December 30, 1997, p. 66.
Washington Post. December 23, 1997, p. D1.

The Assignment

"A surprise ending you won't forget!"—Ron Brewington, *American Urban Radio Networks*

"Powerful and exciting. The most engrossing spy thriller since *Day of the Jackal.*"—Jim Svejda, *CBS Radio*

"An intelligent and gripping thriller."—Roger Ebert, *Chicago Sun-Times*

"A terrific mystery that keeps you guessing." —Alan Silverman, *Hollywood Bytes*

"Intriguing and fast-paced!"—John Anderson, *Los Angeles Times*

"The best espionage thriller since *The Spy Who Came In from the Cold.*"—Paul Wunder, *WBAI Radio*

"A riveting thriller!"—Jeffrey Lyons, *WNBC-TV*

"Sexy, smart, scary, superb. It sizzles!"—Dr. Joy Browne, *WOR Radio Network*

The Assignment is an adequate thriller with a simple premise, a long and elaborate setup, and a rather flat ending. In Paris, 1974, the viewer sees a thirtyish Latin-looking man assume the disguise of a hippie and head to a cafe, where he asks for a light from an American (Donald Sutherland) who's having a coffee. The man then disappears inside the cafe, heads to the second level, and tosses a grenade. Many are killed but the American, Henry Fields, CIA counterterrorism, survives and informs the French that the terrorist act was committed by the infamous Illich Ramirez Sanchez AKA "Carlos the Jackal."

Jack to Ramirez: "Terrorism is, regrettably, a growth industry."

In Vienna, 1975, during a meeting of the O.P.E.C. ministers, Carlos and his terrorist group take the ministers hostage, demanding $20 million and a plane to Libya. Fields, who's in Vienna, is asked to travel to the airport and identify that the terrorist leader is indeed Carlos. He wants to assassinate Carlos at the airport but is prevented from doing so. Having been played for a fool twice by Carlos leaves Henry a very unhappy man.

Flash-forward 11 years to Jerusalem in 1986. A tourist is taking pictures in the marketplace where he's apparently recognized by a group of men, chased through the streets, captured, beaten, and thrown in jail. He's then taken to be interrogated by Amos (Ben Kingsley), a Mossad commander, who is happy to have caught Carlos the terrorist. But his very angry prisoner insists he's a U.S. naval officer, Annibal Ramirez (Aidan Quinn), assigned to the 6th Fleet and docked in Haifa. [Ramirez is the son of an Irish-American mother (explaining his blue eyes) and a Cuban father, which is a neat explanation for how the blue-eyed, Irish-American actor gets to play a Venezuelan terrorist]. This turns out to be true and as Amos says, "Oy."

Then at his home in Norfolk, Virginia, family man Ramirez is visited by Jack Shaw (whom we know as Henry Fields and why Sutherland's character has undergone a name change is unclear). Shaw wants to use Ramirez to get Carlos by turning the naval officer into the terrorist. He finally guilts Ramirez into agreeing and the two head off for Montreal and a very thorough training session, aided by Amos the Israeli. They try to drill into Ramirez all Carlos' survival skills and abilities as an efficient killer. As Amos warns Ramirez, Carlos will: "kill whomever he chooses. Ravish whomever he chooses. Take whatever he chooses. Do what he chooses." And Ramirez must learn to do the same.

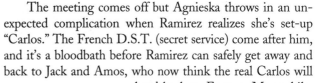

Carlos the Jackal was found guilty of murder and sentenced to life in prison in a 1997 Paris trial.

Months later (now it's early 1987), Jack finally informs Ramirez that the plan is to convince the KGB, who are sheltering Carlos, that he has turned traitor and spilled his guts to the CIA for a large wad of cash and a new identity, so that the KGB will finish Carlos off. Ramirez must use one of Carlos' ex-girlfriends, Agnieska (Liliana Komorowska), to set things in motion and she won't believe it's him unless he can convince her in the sack. So first, another former girlfriend, Carla (Celine Bonnier), will tutor Ramirez sexually. As Jack crudely puts it: "Don't think of this as cheating on your wife, look at it as f***ing for your flag." Oh yeah, Ramirez is also going to have to travel to Libya, where the real Carlos has one of his safe houses (the other is in East Berlin) to meet Agnieska.

CREDITS

Annibal Ramirez/Carlos: Aidan Quinn
Henry Fields/Jack Shaw: Donald Sutherland
Amos: Ben Kinglsey
Agnieska: Liliana Komorowska
Maura Ramirez: Claudia Ferri
Carla: Celine Bonnier
KGB Head Officer: Vlasta Vrana

Origin: Canada
Released: 1997
Production: Tom Berry and Franco Battista for Allegro Films; released by Triumph Films
Direction: Christian Duguay
Screenplay: Dan Gordon and Sabi H. Shabtai
Cinematography: David Franco
Editing: Yves Langlois
Music: Normand Corbeil
Production design: Michael Joy
Art direction: James Fox
Costumes: Ada Levin
Digital effects: Richard Ostiguy
Sound: Thierry Morlaas-Lurbe
MPAA rating: R
Running Time: 119 minutes

The meeting comes off but Agnieska throws in an unexpected complication when Ramirez realizes she's set-up "Carlos." The French D.S.T. (secret service) come after him, and it's a bloodbath before Ramirez can safely get away and back to Jack and Amos, who now think the real Carlos will head back to Europe. Meanwhile, Carlos has learned about Agnieska's betrayal (she's now under French protection in Paris) and sent an associate to kill her. In one of those grand coincidences that are there to spike the plot, Jack, Amos, and Ramirez are in the same airport as the killer who's just completed his job. The killer forces Ramirez into an airport bathroom when he realizes Ramirez isn't the real Carlos and Amos comes to the rescue: he kills the gunman but is killed himself.

Thanks to the debacle, Jack's superiors call a halt to the assignment and Ramirez heads back to Virginia, where he has trouble re-adjusting. But it doesn't matter because soon enough Jack shows up again. The plan is on, since Carlos has travelled to his other safe house in East Berlin and is probably planning a new terrorist operation. Now, it's back to convincing the KGB to get rid of Carlos. Ramirez and Jack manage a simple nighttime set-up that has the KGB invading Carlos' home but both Carlos and Ramirez are on the property at the same time. The real Carlos manages to shoot his way out of the KGB trap but runs into his double. They begin to fight and then Jack shows up to get revenge for being played for a fool. Can you figure out that'll he shoot the wrong man? Well, of course. Carlos manages to escape once again but Jack is pleased that the KGB will be certain to think that Carlos has betrayed everyone and sooner or later one of his "friends" will turn him in.

Ramirez recovers and is re-united with his family, their deaths are faked so Carlos won't take revenge, and Jack gets them all new identities and a tropical island home. But it's not quite end of story. There's a small hint in the end scene that involves a spider and a lit cigarette, which mirrors a scene at the beginning of the film with Carlos, that maybe Ramirez either isn't Ramirez or has assumed more of Carlos' brutal identity than is good for him. This is more annoying than intriguing. A crawl informs that the real Carlos the Jackal eventually found himself living in the Sudan, where he was arrested by the French in 1994 and flown to Paris to await trial.

This movie isn't unwatchable (Quinn, Sutherland, and Kingsley provide professional if unexceptional performances) but it's also nothing that hasn't been seen countless times before. Much of the middle part of the film is spent in turning a play-by-the-rules naval officer into an ice-cold terrorist but the repeated physical and mental trials Ramirez undergoes finally get tedious. The brief (and violent) sex scenes are supposed to show that Carlos has such a hold over his lovers that they'll do anything for him but they're gratuitous at best (at least Quinn is also shown nude so it's not just the actresses baring all). Much of the dialogue is predictable and predictably vulgar while the one exciting action sequence turns out to be Ramirez's escape from the French in Libya (occurring about three-quarters of the way into the film), with the ending tying things up except for leaving one thin thread to dangle annoyingly.

—*Christine Tomassini*

REVIEWS

Boxoffice. November, 1997, p. 124.
Entertainment Weekly. September 26, 1997, p. F14.
Los Angeles Times. September 26, 1997, p. F14.
New York Times. September 26, 1997, p. E20.
Variety. September 22, 1997, p. 40.
Village Voice. September 30, 1997, p. 84.

Austin Powers: International Man of Mystery

Debonair. Defiant. Defrosted.—Movie tagline

"A lot of fun!"—Gene Siskel, *CBS This Morning*

"*Austin Powers* is as witty a creation as the blissed-out Wayne Campbell!"—Owen Gleiberman, *Entertainment Weekly*

"A very, very funny movie!"—Joel Siegel, *Good Morning America*

"Hip! Funny! *Austin*'s hard to resist!"—Janet Maslin, *New York Times*

"Two thumbs up!"—*Siskel & Ebert*

Box Office: $53,883,989

Debonair and now defrosted, '60s spy Austin Powers (Mike Meyers) and his assistant, Vanessa (Elizabeth Hurley), try to foil the plans of Dr. Evil in the retro spy spoof *Austin Powers.*

Everyone from aging hippies to conservative talk-show hosts to producers of TV commercials have adopted or skewered the 1960s for their own purposes, but rarely has that culturally rich era looked quite so silly as in *Austin Powers: International Man of Mystery*, a thoroughly goofy send-up of the mod London scene of 30 years ago. This is the 1960s as seen through James Bond movies and old TV shows and as squeezed through the zaftig brain of Mike Myers, a 33-year-old comic until now best known for satirizing the 1980s in *Wayne's World.*

What such a relatively youngster is doing taking dead aim on the more vapid aspects of the 1960s is unclear, but he's certainly found an easy target. Perhaps the Liverpool origins of Myers' parents explain it; they moved to Canada when Mike was young, and he went on to Second City and Saturday Night Live fame. *Austin Powers* is an extended skit of the type SNL might have done in its prime.

Baby Boomers should find plenty to laugh and wince at in this film. Most depictions of the 1960s are pretentious, investing the times and its personalities with heavy significance. In contrast, Myers ridicules what was viewed as trendy and important then; he makes the hipsters of the era look tremendously lame in the light of today.

His mythical protagonist, Austin Powers, is a shallow, conceited geek with bad teeth and a tremendously inflated view of his sexual prowess, which is confirmed by the swooning admiration of mod bombshells. Powers is a photographer who snaps at purring, posing women when he's not chasing villains for British intelligence.

First-time director Jay Roach, who has a great deal of fun with the bizarre cinematic possibilities of Myers' script, introduces Powers as a hip secret agent in a giddy psychedelic dance number on the London streets. Powers, in thick-framed glasses, blue striped pants, pink polka-dotted shirt and flowered scarf, leads mod babes and bobbies through a Carnaby Street tableau, then hops into his Union-Jack-painted convertible on a spy caper at the Electric Psychedelic Pussycat Swingers' Club with his Emma-Peel-like sidekick, Mrs. Kensington (Mimi Rogers).

It's 1967, and Powers' nemesis, the evil Dr. Evil (also played by Myers) is going into cryogenic hibernation aboard an orbiting spaceship in the form of the fast-food Big Boy. (Myers even gets the product placements right for the era; Powers is seen drinking pink cans of Tab, a soda more popular then than now.) Evil vows to return "when free love no longer reigns and greed and corruption rule again."

Of course, that's the present, and both Evil and Powers are unfrozen in 1997. Powers has been locked in a "celebrity storage" vault with the frozen likes of Gary Coleman and Vanilla Ice. The basis for almost all the subsequent gags is that Powers' mind and libido are stuck in 1967 but his body has to contend with the much-changed world of 1997. Dr. Evil suffers the same dilemma.

CREDITS

Austin Powers/Dr. Evil: Mike Myers
Vanessa Kensington: Elizabeth Hurley
Basil Exposition: Michael York
Mrs. Kensington: Mimi Rogers
Number Two: Robert Wagner
Scott Evil: Seth Green
Alotta Fagina: Fabiana Udenio
Frau Farbissina: Mindy Sterling

Origin: USA
Released: 1997
Production: Suzanne Todd, Demi Moore, Jennifer Todd, Mike Myers for Movie Pictures, Eric's Boy; released by New Line Cinema
Direction: Jay Roach
Screenplay: Mike Myers
Cinematography: Peter Deming
Editing: Debra Neil-Fisher
Music: George S. Clinton
Costumes: Deena Appel
Production design: Cynthia Charette
Art direction: Daniel Olexiewicz
Sound: Mark Ulano
MPAA rating: PG-13
Running Time: 89 minutes

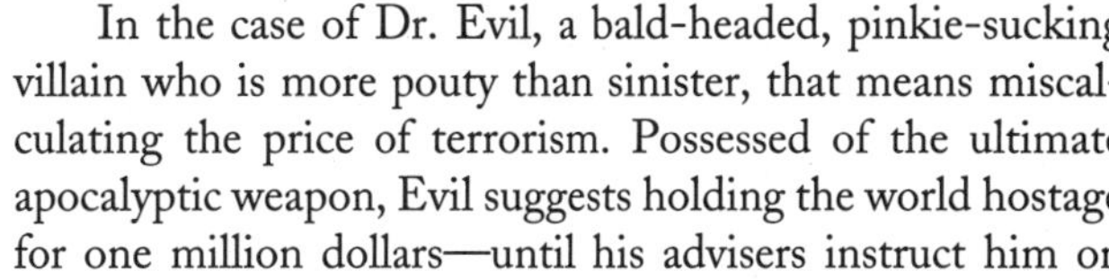

In the case of Dr. Evil, a bald-headed, pinkie-sucking villain who is more pouty than sinister, that means miscalculating the price of terrorism. Possessed of the ultimate apocalyptic weapon, Evil suggests holding the world hostage for one million dollars—until his advisers instruct him on inflationary realities. He also proposes holding the British Royal Family hostage by spreading rumors about Prince Charles' infidelity. And the terrorist network of his second-in-command, Number Two (Robert Wagner), has turned into a multinational conglomerate as legitimate as any other.

Austin to any woman: "Shall we shag now or shall we shag later?"

Evil also must contend with associates who carried out his pre-freezing instructions to create an offspring by artificial insemination. He meets his 20-something son, Scott Evil (played brilliantly by Seth Green), who is a slacker lacking his dad's terrorist ambitions, or any ambitions at all. In a Woody-Allen-like sequence, they attend a therapy group run by the uncredited Carrie Fisher, and Dr. Evil recounts his awful childhood in a truly bizarre monologue (he had his testicles shaved at 14 by a father who also "accused chestnuts of being lazy").

Powers has his own problems. Upon first awakening from the deep freeze, Powers discovers the Cold War is over and announces how glad he is that the capitalists have been defeated. He says he'll be alright as long as people are still having promiscuous sex with strangers and indulging in experimental mind-altering drugs without consequences. He can't figure out how to play a CD on his 45-rpm record player, and he is surprised to discover that Liberace turned out to be gay.

His biggest problem, though, is keeping it in his pants. He is flustered to discover that his sexy sidekick, Mrs. Kensington's daughter Vanessa (Elizabeth Hurley), finds his overrated charms a turn-off. Powers still exists in a world where groovy chicks melt at the sight of him beckoning from his circular, leopard-skin-topped rotating bed. He can't understand why any woman wouldn't want to "shag" him.

Some of the funniest bits in *Austin Powers* involve Myers' relentless ability to lampoon his own lead character's foolishness as a leading man. He does drive home the point that what was once considered sexy now is revolting. We have come a long way from the world of "What's New, Pussycat?"—a song that should have been in this film's soundtrack, but wasn't. Instead, we get Burt Bacharach songs, and a cameo by Bacharach himself.

Unfortunately, there's way too much lampooning of a long-discarded sexual mystique. And the comic situation is undermined by Vanessa Kensington's sudden and inexplicable shift from repulsion at Powers to attraction to him. Hurley's character becomes just an updated version of the groovy babes Powers used to "shag"; the film would have been a lot funnier if she had remained an appalled feminist.

Myers' humor is a strange mix of crude potty jokes and more sophisticated innuendos that only aging hippies will comprehend. Perhaps that's called marketing savvy, an attempt to lure both teenagers and their parents. His is also a show-stopping sort of comedy, which makes for a movie that often slows to a crawl to let the jokes simmer. In one scene, Dr. Evil and his sidekicks laugh the stereotypical villains' guffaw, then continue for several minutes until the laughter is replaced by uneasy silence. Dispatching a villainous underling down a hellhole with the push of a button, Dr. Evil must listen while the man cries out for help beneath a floor vent. This is daffy stuff that does not always go down smoothly, but at its best partakes of Monty Python sensibilities.

Burt Bacharach (Austin's a fan of his songs) does a cameo.

Myers has an ear for the language of the '60s, even inventing his own phrases like "shagadelic." His leering, grotesquely unattractive Powers character is actually less likeable than his Dr. Evil, who seems more befuddled than truly evil. It takes considerable comic courage to play dual rules that are both so unappealing, but Myers can't resist making himself the fool.

The weakness of the film's flimsy, almost non-existent plot dooms most of the movie to being a series of comic sketches. Some seem to have fallen victim to a clumsy editor's scissors. Myers' showdown with the voluptuous Alotta Fagina (Fabiana Udenio, in a spoof on the Bond character Pussy Galore) ends up with the two in a hot tub, the femme fatale about to move in for the kill, and then an abrupt cut to another sequence. It is also strange that Rogers gets high billing for a role that is hardly there, and Tom Arnold gets no billing for the one cameo involving toilet humor that succeeds brilliantly. *Powers* has the look and feel of a film that went through too many wringers before its release.

Fortunately, the humor revives in a boffo ending that features Powers out-seducing an army of robotic bimbos sent to waylay him and then being late for the ultimate showdown because he can't get an electric cart to turn around in a tight space. The most inventive sequences involve trick camera shots that parody how film censors hide forbidden body parts. In a comedy that hits and misses, Myers stretches his comic premise further than might be thought possible and shows an unfailing knack for invention. It would be fun to see him tackle a satire of a subject that can be less easily satirized than the London swingin' sixties culture. Myers has the ability to take on more substantial targets, but is more likely to try an Austin Powers sequel.

—*Michael Betzold*

REVIEWS

Boxoffice. July, 1997, p. 94.
Chicago Tribune. May 2, 1997, p. 5.
Entertainment Weekly. May 9, 1997, p. 56.
Los Angeles Times. May 2, 1997, p. F10.
New York Times. May 2, 1997, p. B7.
People. May 5, 1997, p. 22.
Sight and Sound. September, 1997, p. 37.
USA Today. May 2, 1997, p. 12D.
Variety. April 28, 1997, p. 99.
Village Voice. May 6, 1997, p. 94.

Bad Manners

Finally . . . a movie about a band.—Movie tagline

"*Bandwagon* recalls *Spinal Tap* and *The Commitments*."—David Poole, *Cover Magazine*

"A smart, funny film."—Jennifer Pierce Bar, *Elle Magazine*

"*Bandwagon* is one on-the-road movie worth the trip."—Andrea M. Duncan, *Vibe*

Bad Manners is a film adaptation of David Gilman's one-act play *Ghost in the Machine,* which debuted at Chicago's prestigious Steppenwolf Theater. Here, Jonathan Kaufer directs an impressive cast in a story of marital strife, jealousy and revenge set in Cambridge, Massachusetts, the prototypical academic town. Wes (David Strathairn) has just been passed over for tenure at a girls' finishing school, and must face the annoyingly earnest and sympathetic consolations of his successful wife, Nancy (Bonnie Bedelia). Nancy is quietly succeeding in her literature career, just as Wes seems to be stalling in his; their marriage strikes the right note of complacent, childless passion, a marriage of converging interests, not anything more than habit.

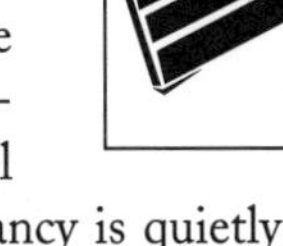

Saul Rubinek also starred in director Jonathan Kaufer's first feature, *Soup for One* (1982).

To add fuel to Wes' already simmering rage, Nancy's old college beau, Matt (Saul Rubinek) arrives in town with his smoldering, sexually provocative girlfriend Kim (Carillon Feeney.) A musicologist, Matt is in town to present his lecture at Harvard, a lecture that presents a little known theological quotation from the 15th century, which he will link to a modern Vietnamese composer. Matt is more than a little smarmy and pretentious, and he is aided and abetted in this endeavor by computer prodigy Kim, who helped Matt locate and nail down his evidence.

Although the warm and gracious Nancy is happy to see old flame Matt, she, like Wes, is somewhat put off by Matt and Kim's obnoxious sexual groping and pawing. To put it further, the blunt and tactless Kim also manages to make Nancy feel like Grandma Moses when she is, in actuality, only asking her advice. Feeney plays Kim as a sly seductress, agile with her mind, read to prey on this *Who's Afraid of Virginia Woolf* couple, while ascertaining information that will help her decide whether to land an academic job or head for the open job market.

After a night of good food and wine at a local restaurant, the next morning Wes discovers that he is missing $50 from his wallet. He and Nancy argue the fact, and Wes repeatedly brings up what he thinks is the only logical explanation—Kim has stolen the money. To pacify him Nancy sneaks into Kim and Matt's room and discovers $50 in Kim's makeup bag. Nancy takes the money, gives it to Wes, and runs to work, immediately regretting it. Kim later discovers her own missing money and tells Matt in private that she suspects Wes and Nancy. The couples pair up and off with one another, each revealing their desires and insecurities. Matt reveals to Nancy that he wonders why the sexy Kim is with a chubby middle-aged man such as himself, and expresses his fervent desire that his presentation will help him make his mark on the music world. Nancy ruefully admits that her marriage has its ups and downs, but is that so extraordinary?

That night the couples gather to drink and chat and Kim, ever the provocateur, eggs on both Nancy and Wes. Nancy and Matt retire, separately, and Kim and Wes meet up later to toss more sexual barbs at each other. The next day, Matt is called to task by the venerable Dr. Harper (Julie Harris); his theory is full of holes—she basically accuses

CREDITS

Wes: David Strathairn
Nancy: Bonnie Bedelia
Matt: Saul Rubinek
Kim: Caroleen Feeney
Dr. Harper: Julie Harris

Origin: USA
Released: 1997
Production: J. Todd Harris, Stephen Nemeth, and Alan Kaplan for Davis Entertainment Classics, Skyline Entertainment Partners and Wavecrest
Direction: Jonathan Kaufer
Screenplay: David Gilman; based on his play *Ghost in the Machine*
Cinematography: Denis Maloney
Editing: Robin Katz
Production design: Sharon Lomofsky
Set decoration: Susan Ogu
Music: Ira Newborn
Sound: Ben Patrick
Costumes: Katherine Jane Bryant
MPAA rating: Unrated
Running Time: 88 minutes

him of planting the quotation he so triumphantly points out.

When Matt confronts Kim about the veracity of her research, Wes and Nancy are drawn into the fray; soon the air is full of innuendo, accusations, hostility and mistrust. Questions are raised and the answers never quite settle; did Kim fabricate the evidence that Matt needed for his theory? Did Kim and Wes stray from the arms of their companions last night?—as Matt proclaims to Nancy—or were the sounds of passion Matt heard merely Kim masturbating, as Kim herself asserts? Did Kim steal from Wes? Enough is said to send Matt and Kim off separately, and to have Wes and Nancy enter a new, more uncertain phase of their relationship.

Author Gilman gives his characters a full range to explore; once the gloves are off, the actors rise to the occasion, particularly Strathairn and Bedelia. Bedelia shows the fire beneath her seemingly placid character; by the end of the film, the doubts about Wes that Kim has planted in Nancy's mind results in Nancy's determination to open herself up to affairs. In Wes, Strathairn follows in the classic "George" role from Edward Albee's *Who's Afraid of Virginia Woolf*, although Gilman ultimately refuses to allow Wes the rock-solid strength and control that Albee's George had.

When a waiter finds a fifty-dollar bill under the cushion that Wes sat on in the restaurant, questions still linger. Even if Kim didn't steal the money, did she sleep with Wes? Did she invent the evidence that Matt so desperately trusted her to get? Audiences will have to settle for these questions merely raised, and debate about each individual's imagined guilt or innocence all the way home.

—*G.E. Georges*

REVIEWS

Variety. June 9, 1997, p. 69.

Bandwagon

Bandwagon tells the story of four young men from a small southern college town who, like many others before them and many others to follow, form a band. They bicker, bond, express themselves, get girls, lose girls, attract a record label, and essentially grow up in the process.

Tony Ridge (Lee Holmes) has a menial office job, but dreams of playing his own music in a band that he fronts. Wynn Knapp (Kevin Corrigan) also has an aimless post-college existence, as do record store clerk Charlie Flagg (Matthew Hennessey) and mechanic Eric Ellwood (Steve Parlavecchio). Although the four are not really the closest of friends, they find themselves bound together by "band fever," a malaise that strikes young people in small towns such as Raleigh, Austin, Charlotte, or Athens. Charlie, the record store clerk, knows better than anyone how much the "chicks and babes" are drawn to musicians—and he wants a part of the action. Eric is chafing at his low-paying existence and welcomes the chance at big money. Wynn, an inscrutable loner, has his own reasons for joining the band, which he won't share with the others. Only Tony seems dedicated to the music.

Doug MacMillan, who plays manager Linus Tate, is the lead singer for the indie band The Connells.

After a series of stops and starts, the boys manage to pull together a series of songs that will allow them to play at a local hotspot. Every band has its oddities and this band is no exception. After a variety of band names are tried and abandoned, they decide on the formidable "Circus Monkey." When they play their first gig, they discover that Tony, the lead singer, cannot overcome his stage fright enough to play *to* the crowd—he must turn his back and play to the band instead. Fortunately, this quirk endears him to hordes of college girls.

Soon, their signature song, "It Couldn't Be Anne," brings enough attention to the band that it forces them to make their next move. Linus Tate (Doug MacMillan), a laconic, mysterious man of worldly intelligence and manner (at least to these boys) steps into their life and offers to shepherd them through every band's rite of passage—the tour.

Using a dilapidated van the guys push off, beginning a tour of frayed nerves, irritations and playdates. Soon, their separate oddities and idiosyncrasies send them to various corners of the van between gigs. The bad food, lack of sleep, lack of respect, and poverty only fade into the background when their song becomes a staple on college radio stations and they experience a minuscule amount of fame.

Conflict arises again when the infamous "Anne" (Lisa Keller) appears at one city to say hello to Tony. Despite his protestations of "art for art's sake," it comes out that Tony has been gunning for coed Anne's undying love all along. To add insult to injury, she thinks of Tony as only a chance acquaintance—a friend—and goes off for a date with skirt-chasing Charlie.

This event catapults the band into a soul-searching crisis, interrupted only by the vow to stay together and play for a major record label showcase. Concurrently, they are approached by two slick talent scouts, on the prowl for their record label, Rival Records. At first seduced by the image of fame, fortune, and unlimited women, the guys listen patiently. But when they weigh the options and listen to their hearts, they realize that they are not up to the soul-searing experience at hand—at least not with Rival Records. They turn in a kick-ass performance at the showcase, confident that whatever happens, they will write their own ticket.

Although this film features an engrossing and amusing story and is directed and acted well, the lack of recognizable names dooms this sweet film to the video shelves. Kevin Corrigan (Wynn) is the most recognizable face (the "ugly guy" from *Walking and Talking* (1996) and various television stints). The music is both catchy and well-composed, particularly "It Couldn't Be Anne," and would not be out of place on any real-life college station playlist. Writer/director Schultz has offered up a gentle story of earnest innocents, a road trip of great intentions, and a learning experience for all. Schultz will most certainly emerge again, for his characterizations ring true and satisfying.

—*G.E. Georges*

CREDITS

Wynn Knapp: Kevin Corrigan
Tony Ridge: Lee Holmes
Charlie Flagg: Matthew Hennessey
Eric Ellwood: Steve Parlavecchio
Linus Tate: Doug MacMillan
Anne: Lisa Keller
Dizz: Steph Robinson
Chester Mealy: Doug McCallie

Origin: USA
Released: 1996
Production: Alyson Poole and John Schultz for Palmlico Pictures and Lakeshore Entertainment; released by Cinepix Film Properties
Direction: John Schultz
Screenplay: John Schultz
Cinematography: Shawn Maurer
Editing: John Pace
Music: Greg Kendall
Production design: Irina Rivera
Costumes: Betzy Reisinger
Sound: Knox White
MPAA rating: Unrated
Running Time: 99 minutes

REVIEWS

Boxoffice. April, 1997, p. 188.
Los Angeles Times. September 12, 1997, p. F9.
New York Times. September 12, 1997, p. C13.
Variety. January 29, 1996, p. 62.
Village Voice. September 16, 1997, p. 89.

B.A.P.S.

Beverly Hills will never be the same.—Movie tagline

Box Office: $7,246,735

Actress Halle Berry sheds her dignified upper-crust skin to play a Georgia homegirl in Robert Townsend's uneven comedy, *B.A.P.S.* (an acronym for Black American Princesses). Little more than a Southern *Pretty Woman* (1990) meets *The Beverly Hillbillies* (1993), it is a modern-day fish-out-of-water fairy tale without a modicum of characterization. The film is more insulting than inspired and soon drifts into a tedium that neither actors nor director can survive.

Initially, *B.A.P.S.* is perversely entertaining, mostly on the strength of Ms. Berry's comedic performance and her willingness to go from ravishing to grotesque. Watching the usually demure and dignified actress don a tacky blonde wig, skin-tight vinyl and a jarringly hideous gold-capped tooth offers some laughs; unfortunately, once that cheap novelty wears off, the film has already slipped into a maudlin, sentimental mess.

It is curious that Ms. Berry would choose to play this type of cliched character. Arguably one of film's most glamorous women, the actress in the past has focused on less ethnically-defined roles. Perhaps *B.A.P.S.* is her attempt to prove to Hollywood that she is more than just a pretty face—or is it a desperate attempt to revive a faltering career?

Nisi (Halle Berry) and her best friend, Mickey (Natalie Desselle) are two Georgia waitresses looking for a way out of their dead-end, small-town existence. Nisi hopes to become a hair stylist, while Mickey dreams of opening a soul-food restaurant. Feeling trapped in a life that offers little chance of the kind of success that the women long for, the two say farewell to their slacker boyfriends and head off for Hollywood where Nisi plans to audition as a dancer for a music video. (Just one of many implausibilities presented by novice scribe Troy Beyer's formulaic script.)

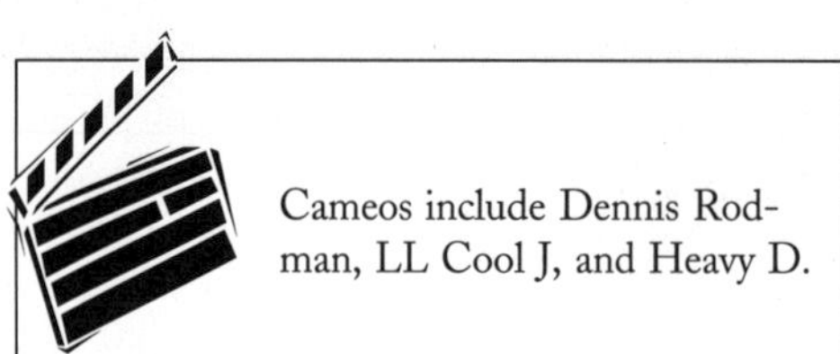

Cameos include Dennis Rodman, LL Cool J, and Heavy D.

Nisi, of course, blows the audition, but is immediately offered $10,000 to pose as the granddaughter of the long-lost love of the filthy rich Mr. Blakemore (Martin Landau). Lily was his family's black maid and the romance was quickly squelched. Now Blakemore is apparently on his last legs, dying of some unnamed disease, and his scheming nephew, Isaac (Jonathan Fried), intends to steal the old man's money by declaring him mentally incompetent once he falls for the engineered charade. Nisi and Mickey, however, believe that their job is to make Blakemore's final days on earth happy ones.

Of course Blakemore quickly falls under the spell of these two B.A.P.S. and before long he is chowing down on Mickey's soul food cooking and dancing the night away at a disco. There is the obligatory Rodeo Drive shopping spree, bidet jokes and culture clashes, as well as the stiff English butler (Ian Richardson) whom Mickey insists on calling "Alfred." And of course, there's the women's ultimate realization that money is not everything, and that honesty is indeed the best policy. For this they are richly rewarded when Blakemore leaves them a juicy inheritance that allows Nisi and Mickey to open their long-dreamed-of combination hair salon and restaurant.

First-time screenwriter Troy Beyer makes the fatal mistake of resolving the slight conflict that existed in the film long before the end. The bad guys are caught red-handed barely an hour into the story, leaving all involved to flounder around for another thirty minutes in search of a plot.

Director Robert Townsend first caught Hollywood's eye with the equally uneven *Hollywood Shuffle* (1987), a low-budget film that Townsend financed by maxing out his credit cards. His writing and directing career boasts the horrific *The Meteor Man* (1993), as well as the sentimental *The Five Heartbeats* (1991).

Martin Landau, Academy Award-winner for *Ed Wood* (1994), plays the role of the dying millionaire with a seriousness and intensity that drips with sentiment, leading one to wonder if Mr. Landau realized that *B.A.P.S.* was intended as a comedy. Natalie Desselle (*Set It Off*, 1997), on the other hand, turns the character of Mickey into a walking stereotype, all sass and vulgarity, chewing up the scenery with gusto. It is not a pretty sight.

The blame for propagating such vicious and demeaning cultural stereotypes squarely rests on all those involved. It is puzzling why African-American filmmakers continue to make films that portray their fellow men and women,

CREDITS

Nisi: Halle Berry
Mr. Blakemore: Martin Landau
Manley: Ian Richardson
Mickey: Natalie Desselle
Tracy: Troy Beyer
Antonio: Luigi Amodeo
Isaac: Jonathan Fried

Origin: USA
Released: 1997
Production: Mark Burg and Loretha C. Jones for Island Pictures; released by New Line Cinema
Direction: Robert Townsend
Screenplay: Troy Beyer
Cinematography: Bill Dill
Editing: Patrick Kennedy
Production design: Keith Brian Burns
Sound: Russell Williams II
Costumes: Ruth E. Carter
Music: Stanley Clarke
Makeup: Lalette Littlejohn
MPAA rating: PG-13
Running Time: 91 minutes

REVIEWS

Chicago Tribune. March 28, 1997, p. 5.
Detroit News. March 28, 1997.
Entertainment Weekly. April 11, 1997, p. 64.
Los Angeles Times. March 28, 1997, p. F25.
New York Times. March 28, 1997, p. B3.
People. April 14, 1997, p. 19.
Rochester Democrat and Chronicle. March 28, 1997.
San Francisco Chronicle. March 28, 1997, p. C3.
San Francisco Examiner. March 28, 1997, p. C1.
Sight and Sound. August, 1997, p. 38.
USA Today. March 28, 1997, p. 4D.
Variety. March 31, 1997, p. 86.
Village Voice. April 8, 1997, p. 90.

particularly Southerns, as buffoons, all garish, tasteless and loud, while at the same time lashing out at their white counterparts for similar transgressions. It is not surprising that *B.A.P.S.* performed so dismally at the box office, particularly when compared to the more positive role models provided by such films as *Soul Food* (1997), *love jones* (1997) and *Waiting to Exhale* (1996). One is forced to ask, what is the message of Townsend's and Beyer's film? Is it that the only way for two homegirls to succeed is by befriending an old rich white guy? It seems like the same old Cinderella tale that teaches young women that if you are charming and sincere, you will get what you want without working for it. What a sad commentary on both black culture and the Nineties.

—*Patricia Kowal*

Batman and Robin

"A lot of fun."—Joel Siegel, *Good Morning America*

"The best of the *Batman* movies! A super treat!"—Liz Smith, *L.A. Times Syndicate*

"Spectacular!"—Bobbie Wygant, *NBC-TV*

"Big. Bold. Lavish. Outlandish visual mischief."—Janet Maslin, *New York Times*

"Sizzling!"—Jules Peimer, *WKDM Radio*

"A blockbuster. Astonishing. Oscar-calibre special effects."—Jeffrey Lyons, *WNBC-TV*

Box Office: $107,325,195

Batman and Robin is the fourth in Warner Bros.' successful series based on Bob Kane's classic Batman comic strip, which wowed young readers when it first appeared in 1939 as a competitor to Superman. Warner's first three Batman films were *Batman* (1989), *Batman Returns* (1992), and *Batman Forever* (1995). The new caper stars Arnold Schwarzenegger as Mr. Freeze, a mad scientist whose experiments with refrigeration have led to his becoming a living ice man himself. (Movie critic Kenneth Turan of the *Los Angeles Times* called him "a walking Popsicle.") Freeze is after diamonds—the bigger the better. He intends to use them—somehow or other—to complete his cryogenic research. His immediate motive is to save his beloved wife, whom he is keeping frozen until he can find a way to cure her. Like many another mad scientist, including Dr. Frankenstein and Dr. Moreau, he started out with the best intentions but got a little carried away.

Batman to Robin after a tiff: "This is why Superman works alone."

The icy motif which dominates this production is not a bad gimmick, considering that the film was released as a summer blockbuster to theater audiences who might appreciate the cooling subliminal effect augmenting air-conditioning and ice-cold soda pop. Ice also provided screenwriter Akiva Goldsman with a way to eliminate death and bloodshed at a time when film violence is under heated criticism from parents, educators, church groups, psychologists, politicians, and many others. Freeze, after all, does not actually kill people; he only encases them in blocks of impressionistically sculpted ice with his bazooka-like freeze gun. Since the victims can—at least theoretically—be thawed out, they are not really murdered but only held in suspended animation. One of the victims is an English bulldog frozen in the act of urinating on a fire hydrant; after a time in that embarrassing position, the dog thaws out, shakes off the melting ice, and goes on his doggie way. This is a subtle way of suggesting that nobody is getting seriously hurt.

The real damage is inflicted on buildings, furnishings, and motor vehicles. At one point the frenzied Freeze turns Gotham City into an iceberg. Warner's has gone all-out with special effects—so much so that the actors seem dwarfed by the cascading real estate as well as drowned out by the soundtrack's foreboding musical overkill. Joe Morgenstern, who trashed the film in the *Wall Street Journal*, calling it a "gargantuan goon show," said that "'All right, everyone, chill!' is one of the few lines that survived the combined effect of [Schwarzenegger's] accent and the movie's monstrous amplification."

The film's other villainous character does not kill people either. Poison Ivy (Uma Thurman), who was transformed into a plant-woman by a laboratory mishap too awful to describe, only drugs them with her poisonous breath. This is another of the radical metamorphoses so common among Batman villains. She is a direct descendant of the heroine of Nathaniel Hawthorne's *Rappaccini's Daughter*.

Poison Ivy is out to depopulate the globe and turn it over to the plants.

The ecological theme is one of the contemporary hot-buttons the screenwriter pushes in hopes of lending this feature some redeeming social significance. Another is the theme of adolescent rebellion. She creates hostility between Batman (George Clooney) and Robin (Chris O'Donnell) by kissing each of them in turn. Under her spell, each thinks he is madly in love, ready to do her bidding. Robin is going through a rebellious phase anyway, and his rivalry with foster-father Bruce Wayne (aka Batman) pushes him over the edge.

Last role for actor/wrestler Jeep Swenson (Bane), who died at 40 in August, 1997.

The role of Batman/Wayne was played by Michael Keaton in the first two WB productions and then by Val Kilmer in *Batman Forever*. In *Batman and Robin* the part is played by George Clooney, who has risen to superstardom practically overnight without delivering any really memorable performances. Unlike the rest of the cast, Clooney has elected to play his role without the tongue-in-cheek, twinkle-in-the-eye expression that most actors affect when they want to let the audience know they are not really acting but only "acting." Clooney seems self-conscious and (to his credit) even a little embarrassed. Critic Mick La Salle of the *San Francisco Chronicle* called Clooney "smug, complacent, one-dimensional." Clooney knows he is incredibly good-looking with his dark eyebrows and cropped haircut and doesn't have to do much except to look grave, patient, wise, responsible and handsome. He has been called a new Cary Grant, but his acting style seems to have been modeled after that of brooding, potentially explosive Burt Lancaster. It is indicative of Clooney's still evolving artistic development that he has not yet found his own identity but is still being compared with Clark Gable, Mel Gibson, Cary Grant, and other matinee idols of past and present.

The filmmakers have introduced a young blonde called Batgirl in an effort to appeal to more young female viewers and potential purchasers of the Batman line of products sold in Warner's 150 stores and other retail outlets around the world. This complex character, who combines exuberant feminine sexuality with strictly tomboy interests, is played by luscious young Alicia Silverstone, a junior Marilyn Monroe/Goldie Hawn whose effervescent personality made a hit out of the teenybopper fashion extravaganza *Clueless* (1995). So the Dynamic Duo may become the Terrific Trio in future sequels if *Batman and Robin* manages to score an respectable gross.

Robin and Batgirl hit it off immediately because they both like to race motorcycles and risk their lives swinging from skyscrapers. Their love affair never goes very far, however, even though they are living under the same roof. Instead, Robin pursues Poison Ivy, who is obviously too old for him, as well as being out to break up his cozy relationship with an amazingly permissive foster father who just happens to be a billionaire.

The ongoing conflict between Batman and Robin, a major element of this film, sounds bogus. The Boy Wonder lives in a mansion, keeps his own hours, and owns a whole fleet of motorcycles. He does not work or go to school. Now he has a beautiful blonde as a live-in companion. His only complaint would seem to be that he has nothing to complain about. Kenneth Turan called Robin "the whiniest of heroes."

Barbara Wilson, who quickly becomes Batgirl when she finds out how much fun the boys are having, arrives from England to care for her uncle Alfred Pennyworth (Michael Gough). Alfred has been Bruce Wayne's butler for many years. He is part of the family. Now he is dying of some undiagnosed disease. Janet Maslin, who reviewed the film for the *New York Times*, suggested that all the concern about this minor character's health was intended to evoke a semblance of real human emotion. It is not until the very end that Bruce Wayne finds out that, ironically, his arch-enemy Freeze may have the cure. In keeping with the nonviolent camouflage of this violent film, Freeze is not killed, as he richly deserves, but rehabilitated.

Why do Batman, Robin and Batgirl wear masks? Is this supposed to frighten their enemies? Is there something Freudian involved? Or do masks somehow help the reader/viewer identify with the hero? The Lone Ranger wore a mask too. Superman did not wear a mask but kept his identity a secret. Most of the imitators of Superman, Batman and the Phantom wore masks. No doubt the easy answer is that all these crusaders are lawbreakers themselves. They are vigilantes taking the law into their own hands. Are they really such good role models for kids?

Even though *Batman and Robin* opened to mostly negative reviews, it was expected to make a profit on its estimated $100-million budget. Warner's had already received $50-million up front in guaranteed minimums from product licenses—T-shirts, costumes, character toys, plastic Batmobiles, lunch boxes, coffee mugs, wristwatches, etc. Schwarzenegger, hardly a brilliant actor, was paid a whopping $20-million plus a percentage of the revenues for starring as Freeze because of his popularity with European audiences. The international box-office revenue could actually surpass the domestic box-office revenue, and domestic video revenue for blockbusters such as this have become as important as box-office revenue. (It is hard to imagine what people in places like Africa, Asia and the Middle East make of a movie like *Batman and Robin*. Do some of them think this is the way people in America actually behave? Do they think that Batman, Robin and Batgirl are anything like the typical American family?)

Batman and Robin is more a conglomerate entity, "a huge international franchise," than a mere motion picture. The film was released at a time when Warner Bros. really needed a winner. They had been disappointed with returns on a string of recent releases, including *Joe's Apartment* (1996), *My Fellow Americans* (1996), *Mars Attacks!* (1996), *Vegas Vacation* (1997), *Murder at 1600* (1997), *Father's Day* (1997), *Michael Collins* (1996), and *Addicted to Love* (1997). Warner's co-chairmen Robert Daly and Terry Semel were banking on cash cow Batman to turn things around. They may be asking too much of a hero who, if he was in his thirties when he debuted in "Detective Comics," would now be a nonagenarian.

In spite of Joel Schumacher's competent direction and the professional expertise of production designer Barbara Ling, supervising art director Richard Holland, and visual effects specialist John Dykstra, *Batman and Robin* lacks soul. It feels too much like a meretricious commercial product manufactured by a hydra-headed corporation for viewers regarded only as mindless consumers. Unfortunately, this is becoming the case with too many American films.

—*Bill Delaney*

CREDITS

Batman/Bruce Wayne: George Clooney
Robin/Dick Grayson: Chris O'Donnell
Mr. Freeze/Dr. Victor Fries: Arnold Schwarzenegger
Poison Ivy/Dr. Pamela Isley: Uma Thurman
Batgirl/Barbara Wilson: Alicia Silverstone
Alfred Pennyworth: Michael Gough
Commissioner Gordon: Pat Hingle
Dr. Jason Woods: John Glover
Julie Madison: Elle Macpherson
Ms. B. Haven: Vivica A. Fox
Nora Fries: Vendela K. Thommessen
Bane: Jeep Swenson

Origin: USA
Released: 1997
Production: Peter Macgregor-Scott; released by Warner Bros.
Direction: Joel Schumacher
Screenplay: Akiva Goldsman; based on the characters created by Bob Kane and published by DC Comics
Cinematography: Stephen Goldblatt
Editing: Dennis Virkler
Music: Elliot Goldenthal
Production design: Barbara Ling
Art direction: Geoff Hubbard
Costumes: Ingrid Ferrin, Robert Turturice
Sound: Petur Hliddal
Visual effects: John Dykstra
MPAA rating: PG-13
Running Time: 130 minutes

REVIEWS

America Cinematographer. July, 1997, p. 34.
Chicago Tribune. June 20, 1997, p. 4.
Cinemafantastique. June, 1997, p. 8.
Entertainment Weekly. June 27, 1997, p. 93.
The Hollywood Reporter. June 16, 1997, p. 8.
Los Angeles Times. June 20, 1997, p. F1.
New York Times. June 20, 1997, p. B1.
People. June 30, 1997, p. 19.
San Francisco Chronicle. June 20, 1997, p. C1.
Sci-Fi Universe. July, 1997, p. 34.
Sight and Sound. August, 1997, p. 39.
USA Today. June 20, 1997, p. 4D.
Variety. June 16, 1997, p. 34.
Village Voice. July 1, 1997, p. 94.
Wall Street Journal. June 20, 1997, p. A16.

Bean

Bean, Bean, he's good for your heart. He's very funny, he's not too smart. The more you laugh, the better you feel. So go see Bean, he'll make you squeal.—Movie tagline

"Hands down the funniest picture in years! An all-ages blast!"—Michael Rechtshaffen, *The Baltimore Sun*

"*Bean* amounts to a hill of laughs!"—Jack Mathews, *Los Angeles Times*

"I started to laugh, and I couldn't stop!"—Thelma Adams, *New York Post*

"When it comes to laughs, *Bean* delivers!" —Lawrence Van Gelder, *New York Times*

Box Office: $44,875,484

Beloved Brit Mr. Bean comes to America in this overtly "Hollywood" comedy featuring Rowan Atkinson, star of England's television series, "Mr. Bean" and memorable as the neophyte minister in 1994's, *Four Weddings and a Funeral.* Atkinson, sometimes described as the British Jim Carrey because of his mastery of facial and bodily contortions, created the bumbling but lovable character, Bean, who rarely speaks. Although Atkinson's silent slapstick shtick is as satisfyingly goofy as ever, the meager excuse for a plot and lame subplots torpedo what could have been a triumphant big-screen debut for Bean. Politically correct writing with its misplaced morality has managed to take the zing out of Bean by toning down his mischievous behavior in order to redeem himself, presumably, in the eyes America and perhaps for its intended young audience.

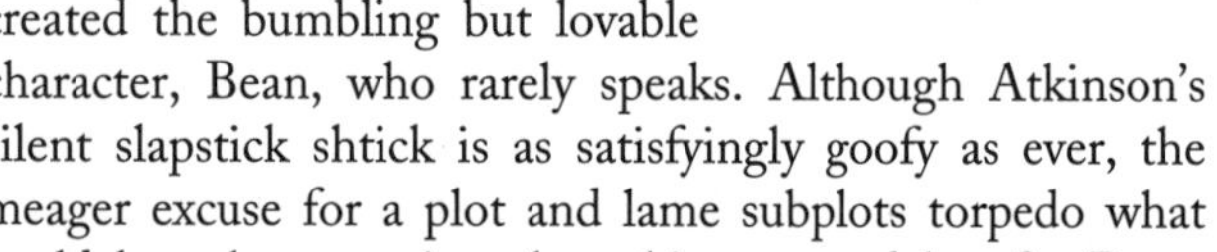

Alison on meeting houseguest Bean: "There are Martians who have been exiled from Mars for looking weird who look less weird than this guy."

Rowan Atkinson created the character of Mr. Bean in 1989 for a BBC TV series.

The amusingly inept Bean is the dimwitted security guard in a famous British museum and is the bane of the lives of the stuffy board of directors. It seems Bean is a favorite of the museum's curator who protects him from being fired, for some unexplained reason, so the frustrated board finds another way to rid themselves of him. The sale of the famous painting "Whistler's Mother" has been purchased by the Americans, and since they must send an art historian to Los Angeles to accompany the painting for a three month period, they, of course, unanimously vote for Mr. Bean. Meanwhile, in Los Angeles, L.A. museum curator, David Langley (Peter MacNicol), is sent word of the prestigious Bean's arrival and excitedly insists to his family that he stay with them for the duration.

The childlike Bean immediately wreaks havoc upon his arrival at the Los Angeles airport and winds up being interrogated by security who don't appreciate his James Bond impersonation. It's not long after that David and his family realize that Bean is a fraud, as well as a very strange guy. David's cantankerous wife Alison (Pamela Reed), son Kevin and daughter Jennifer (Tricia Vessey) do not appreciate this bizarre house guest and go to stay at Alison's mothers until Bean vacates. David, solely on his own now, is forced to keep the tireless Bean amused while keeping his real identity hidden from his boss at the museum (Harris Yulin).

The two men, naturally, get into all kinds of minor disasters. While entertaining David's boss, Bean tries to stuff a turkey which ends up over his head and eventually blows up in the microwave. When David takes Bean to an amusement park, the overzealous Bean rigs a ride in overdrive, sending people flying everywhere. Although some of these antics are classic Bean and entertaining, there are stretches which simply yawn endlessly on. It's also not made clear how Bean's albeit weird but good natured presence manages to single-handedly ruin David's marriage and alienate his children. Supporting actors are written as if they should be in an altogether different genre, especially Alison, whose dramatic threat to leave David for good seems unmotivated by the previous events and out of place in this wacky comedy.

The highlight of the film occurs after David and Bean go to the museum to view the painting which has finally arrived. In the tightly secured vault, Bean manages, in the stretch of a few hilarious minutes alone, to completely ruin the multimillion dollar masterpiece. To David's complete horror, Bean shows him his panicked attempt to undo the damage. Now with David's career and marriage in a shambles to Bean's credit, the two men proceed to the nearest bar to get drunk. Later that evening, Bean, desperate to mend things with David, speeds off to the museum on

CREDITS

Mr. Bean: Rowan Atkinson
David Langley: Peter MacNicol
Alison Langley: Pamela Reed
George Grierson: Harris Yulin
Gen. Newton: Burt Reynolds
Chairman: John Mills
Detective Brutus: Richard Gant
Jennifer Langley: Tricia Vesey
Kevin Langley: Andrew Lawrence

Origin: Great Britain
Released: 1997
Production: Tim Bevan , Eric Fellner, and Peter Bennett-Jones for Tiger Aspect Films and Working Title; released by Polygram Filmed Entertainment
Direction: Mel Smith
Screenplay: Richard Curtis, Robin Driscoll, and Rowan Atkinson
Cinematography: Francis Kenny
Editing: Chris Blunden
Music: Howard Goodall
Production design: Peter Larkin
Art direction: Kevin Constant
Sound: Robert Anderson
MPAA rating: PG-13
Running Time: 92 minutes

Kevin's skateboard where he overdoses the security guard's coffee with laxative, rushes in to where the painting is, and uses common household items and a poster of the painting to restore it. A more triumphant scene for Bean could not be found.

After an amusing cameo by Burt Reynolds as the gruff general who financed the purchase of the painting and Bean's winning speech at the unveiling, the film easily could (and probably should) have ended. However, an unfortunate and unlikely plot twist occurs and Bean is given a chance to redeem himself to David's family and *Bean* goes on uselessly for another fifteen minutes.

Beautifully designed sets, especially the elaborate museum set-up, are impressive and add to the overall visual impact and enjoyment of the film. If the visual is pleasing, the music, however, is one of the film's worst liabilities, especially a mangled rendition of the Beatles "Yesterday." Although *Bean*'s shining comic moments can't battle uneven pacing and script problems, it does make it worth seeing for those unfamiliar with the moronic Mister, however, die-hard "Beaniacs" may be disappointed.

—*Hilary Weber*

REVIEWS

Boxoffice. September, 1997, p. 114.
Detroit News. November 7, 1997, p. 3F.
Entertainment Weekly. November 14, 1997, p. 56.
Los Angeles Times. November 7, 1997, p. F12.
New York Times. November 7, 1997, p. E22.
New Yorker. November 24, 1997, p. 137.
People. November 17, 1997, p. 24.
Sight and Sound. August, 1997, p. 41.
USA Today. November 7, 1997, p. 8D.
Variety. June 30, 1997, p. 65.
Village Voice. November 18, 1997, p. 85.

Beaumarchais the Scoundrel; Beaumarchais L'Insolent

A most remarkable true story of love affairs, scandals and espionage.—Movie tagline

"Sumptuous, brilliant and wickedly funny, *Beaumarchais* is one of the year's best films."—Jim Svedja, *KNX/CBS Radio*

Who was Pierre Augustin Caron de Beaumarchais (1732-1799), the subject of director Edouard Molinaro's brilliant new film? He was an artist, author, and theatrical producer, an opponent of Louis XVI but also his emissary, and a flamboyant figure at odds with the French Parliament of 1773, inspired by his mentor, the fiercely critical Voltaire. Beaumarchais wrote two classic plays, *Le Barbier de Seville* (1773) and *Le Mariage de Figaro* (1778), the inspiration for Mozart's opera. The first is a comedy of intrigue not unlike the life Beaumarchais pursued. The film capitalizes on this playfully wicked aspect of the artist and man, driven by democratic principles but also by a love of controversy and fame for its own sake.

The Beaumarchais of history and of the film seems a contemporary figure. He knows how to manipulate public opinion. He would undoubtedly have been thrilled with the opportunities for protest in the America of the 1960s and the France of 1968, when the students struck. Like some of the sixties radicals, however, Beaumarchais was a bit of a flake—not nearly disciplined enough as a writer or a revolutionary.

Beaumarchais was the son of a watchmaker and his lower class origins made him especially sensitive to the sufferings of the people and the tyranny of people in power. His background also made him a target of aristocrats and patrons of art who tried to embarrass him with his humble origins. In one of the film's best scenes, a nobleman approaches Beaumarchais at court to ask him to fix his watch. It is an insult, of course. Beaumarchais sizes up his man and mildly remarks that yes he once knew how to fix watches but he has grown clumsy. The nobleman persists in foisting the watch on Beaumarchais who promptly drops it to the floor, casually reiterating that he has indeed grown clumsy.

Beaumarchais was litigious, and the film fully exploits courtroom scenes in which the playwright is able to display his histrionic talents. He soon sets up a dichotomy between himself and the judges, addressing the people in the courtroom as his audience and his only source of support.

But Beaumarchais was only partially successful at the law and in order to rehabilitate himself at court agreed to go on several secret missions for Louis XV and XVI. Even while Beaumarchais was in the service of the king (1770-1780), *Le Barbier de Seville* was banned from the stage. In 1774, his memoirs (critical of the state) were burned by Parliament. In 1778, *Le Mariage de Figaro* was suppressed on the grounds that it would corrupt the public morality, and Beaumarchais was put in prison.

Beaumarchais trod a precarious line between respectability and roguery. He always seemed on the verge of victory or defeat, a seesaw life that the film captures well not only in Fabrice Luchini's insouciance but in carefully crafted scenes—like the one in which Louis XV is not certain whether he can trust a man who is half-scoundrel and a dangerous satirist. In 1792 Beaumarchais was accused of treason against the Republic and his works were once again suppressed. Released the same year, he went into exile for four years and died shortly after returning to France.

Beaumarchais has been called an elegant period piece, a costume drama with wit. Certainly it does have a bit of the dash associated with the Hollywood swashbucklers of the 1930s, although it takes a far more jaundiced look at its hero's egocentricity than any Hollywood epic would essay. Some reviewers have complained that the story line is hard to follow, but this is not important, except to those souls who have to know at every moment exactly where they are. In the end, there is little mystery, though some background in the period's history enhances an understanding of the film's achievement.

Beaumarchais is a likeable rascal. Some reviewers tend not to take him seriously because of his character flaws and his opportunism. But he is an inviting personality because of his lack of pomposity. As Fabrice Luchini plays him, Beaumarchais realizes that he does not develop his talent for writing plays and that he succumbs all too easily to exhibitionism. The darker side of Beaumarchais—the way he uses people, especially women—is not ignored in the film. Indeed, Beaumarchais is unapologetic about his womanizing. Unlike the cinema's usual tendency to glamorize history into hagiography, *Beaumarchais* gives its hero a hard, if still appealing, look.

—*Carl Rollyson*

CREDITS

Beaumarchais: Fabrice Luchini
Marie-Therese: Sandrine Kiberlain
Gudin: Manuel Blanc
Prince de Conti: Michel Piccoli
Louis XV: Michel Serrault
Duc de Chaulnes: Jacques Weber
Sartine: Jean: **Francois Balmer**
Marion Menard: Florence Thomassin
Rosine: Isabelle Carre
Louis XVI: Dominique Besnehard

Origin: France
Released: 1996
Production: Charles Gassot for Telema, Studio Canal Plus, France 2 Cinema, and France 3 Cinema; released by New Yorker Films
Direction: Edouard Molinaro
Screenplay: Edouard Molinaro and Jean-Claude Brisville; based on an unpublished work by Sacha Guitry
Cinematography: Michael Epp
Editing: Veronique Parnet
Music: Jean-Claude Petit
Production design: Jean-Marc Kerdelhue
Costumes: Sylvie de Segonzac
Sound: Dominique Warnier
MPAA rating: Unrated
Running Time: 104 minutes

REVIEWS

Boxoffice. October, 1997, p. 36.
Los Angeles Times. October 24, 1997, p. F16.
New York Times. October 24, 1997, p. E12.
People. November 17, 1997, p. 25.
Sight and Sound. September, 1996, p. 9.
Variety. April 1, 1996, p. 56.
Village Voice. October 28, 1997, p. 88.

The Beautician and the Beast

Once upon a time . . . —Movie tagline

"Smartly funny. A hoot."—John Anderson, *Newsday*

"Hysterical! Easily a thousand laughs!"—Louise Palanker, *Premiere Radio*

Box Office: $11,438,337

In the charming romantic comedy, *The Beautician and the Beast,* comedienne Fran Drescher stays close to her patented television persona of the whining Jewish American princess with the nasal delivery. In this fish-out-of-water tale, Ms. Drescher exudes a great deal of charm opposite dashing former James Bond, Timothy Dalton.

Beautician Joy on teaching: "I used to give pedicures to women who wore plastic shoes in summer. What's a tougher gig than that?"

CREDITS

Joy Miller: Fran Drescher
Boris Pochenko: Timothy Dalton
Grushinsky: Ian McNeice
Kleist: Patrick Malahide
Katrina: Lisa Jakub
Jerry Miller: Michael Lerner
Judy Miller: Phyllis Newman
Karl: Adam LaVorgna
Masha: Heather DeLoach
Yuri: Kyle & Tyler Wilkerson
Alek: Timothy Dowling

Origin: USA
Released: 1997
Production: Howard W. Koch, Jr., Todd Graff for Koch Company and High School Sweethearts; released by Paramount Pictures
Direction: Ken Kwapis
Screenplay: Todd Graff
Cinematography: Peter Lyons Collister
Editing: Jon Poll
Production design: Rusty Smith
Art direction: Steve Cooper
Costumes: Barbara Tfank
Music: Cliff Eidelman
Sound: Richard Goodman
MPAA rating: PG
Running Time: 100 minutes

Joy Miller (Fran Drescher) has big dreams. A beautician by trade, the plucky Queens native is determined to rise above her working-class origins and is certain that her charm, wit and sheer willfulness will help her to succeed. When she saves not only her beauty school students but a slew of laboratory animals from an accidental fire caused by a lethal mixture of hairspray and a Bunsen burner, Joy makes the news—and garners the attention of Grushinsky (Ian McNeice), emissary from the former Communist Eastern European nation of Slovetzia. Sent by the tyrannical dictator, the widower Boris Pochenko (Timothy Dalton) to find a tutor to help westernize his three children, Grushinsky mistakes the beautiful woman with the voice like chalk on a blackboard for an exemplary academician and offers Joy the job. Having lost her dream job—doing makeup for the New York lottery—Joy immediately accepts the offer to be what she thinks is the Royal Beautician. The result is a classic comedy of errors, not very different from such television fare as "I Love Lucy."

Arriving in the tiny imaginary country of Slovetzia, Joy is unprepared for the larger-than-life "President for Life," the man known by his few living detractors as "Boris the Beast" and "Stalin without Charm." Pochenko begrudgingly acknowledges that he must attempt to democratize his country and vows to set an example for his citizens by having his own children learn the ways of the Western world. Joy refuses to allow Boris to break her up-beat spirit and as one might expect, romantic sparks soon fly as the spunky New Yorker goes about transforming this frog into her Prince Charming. Before long, Joy has the cantankerous and tempestuous Boris shaving off his mustache, switching from military uniform to Yves Saint Laurent, and hugging the peasants, much to the dismay of his prime minister, Kleist (Patrick Malahide). The Beast, of course, learns that he cannot live without this charming Jewish American princess with the proverbial heart of gold. The romantic subplot about Pochenko's daughter, Katrina (Lisa Jakub), and an young insurgent (Timothy Dowling), however, is limpid and appears mostly as an afterthought to flesh out the minimal story.

The script by actor (*Dominick and Eugene*, 1988) and writer (*Used People*, 1992) Todd Graff has modest intentions and offers few surprises. Instead, it plays to Fran Drescher's strengths, not the least of which is the acknowledgement of the absurd juxtaposition of beauty with a voice that defies explanation, as well as description. The direction by Ken Kwapis, formerly of HBO's scathingly funny satire, "The Larry Sanders Show", is adequate, yet ultimately uninspired. A seriousness overtakes the film in the last act and results in tonal problems that threaten to undercut the comedy.

British actor Timothy Dalton—the former Agent 007 from *The Living Daylights* (1987) and *License to Kill* (1989)—is not widely known for his comedic talents, despite his noteworthy performance as the villain in the ill-fated *The Rocketeer* (1991). Yet Mr. Dalton displays a surprising willingness to act buffoonish and proves himself quite adept at tongue-in-cheek delivery. The on-screen chemistry between the actor and Ms. Drescher helps to raise *The Beautician and the Beast* above its otherwise predictable storyline and trite premise.

Serving as both Executive Producer and story inspiration, Ms. Drescher's first attempt at filmic leading lady is reminiscent of such musicals as *The King and I* (1956), *The Sound of Music* (1965), and obviously, *The Beauty and the Beast* (1991). There are several hilarious moments in the film that lampoon everything from Eva Peron to John F. Kennedy, Jr.'s marriage. Ms. Drescher made her film debut in the seminal *Saturday Night Fever* (1977) opposite another sitcom break-away star, John Travolta.

While *The Beautician and the Beast* is pleasant enough entertainment, it offers little more than standard television sitcom fare. The film performed poorly at the box office and disappeared quickly amid mixed reviews.

—*Patricia Kowal*

REVIEWS

Boxoffice. April, 1997, p. 200.
Chicago Tribune. February 7, 1997, p. 5.
Entertainment Weekly. February 14, 1997, p. 42.
Los Angeles Times. February 7, 1997, p. F8.
New York Times. February 7, 1997, p. B12.
People. February 17, 1997, p. 20.
Variety. February 10, 1997, p. 63.
Village Voice. February 18, 1997, p. 84.

Bent

"Unforgettable! A brave, brilliantly effective movie."—Brandon Judell, *Detour*

"A chic and stunning visualization. Clive Owen and Lothaire Bluteau are superb."—Mary Corliss, *Film Comment*

"Powerful and extremely moving!"—Bob Satuloff, *Film Journal International*

"Sean Mathias' direction inspires actors to create towering portrayals."—Kevin Thomas, *Los Angeles Times*

"A film of rare power, passion and cinematic brilliance!"—Rex Reed, *New York Observer*

"*Bent* has the power to touch hearts and minds."—Allan Hunter, *Screen International at Cannes*

"Beautifully made, superbly acted, and immensely powerful."—Bill Bregoli, *Westwood One Radio Network*

Bent, a superbly acted and deftly directed (by Sean Mathias) film version of playwright Martin Sherman's 1979 hit, explores the relatively unknown plight of homosexuals who were incarcerated and killed by the Nazis during

CREDITS

Max: Clive Owen
Horst: Lothaire Bluteau
Rudy: Brian Webber
Uncle Freddie: Ian McKellen
Greta/George: Mick Jagger
Stormtrooper: Jude Law
Officer on Train: Rupert Graves

Origin: Great Britain
Released: 1997
Production: Michael Solinger and Dixie Linder for Channel Four Films; released by Goldwyn Entertainment Company
Direction: Sean Mathias
Screenplay: Martin Sherman; based on his play
Cinematography: George Arvanitis
Editing: Isabelle Lorente
Production design: Stephen Brimson Lewis
Music: Phillip Glass
Costumes: Stewart Meachem
MPAA rating: NC-17
Running Time: 109 minutes

WWII. Opening with a striking image of a sultry cabaret singer descending from the sky, singing the eerily prophetic "Streets of Berlin," said singer turns out to be none other than the club owner, drag queen Greta (Mick Jagger). Despite the bacchanalia raging within Greta's club, the atmosphere outside is turning ugly. It is June 30th, 1934, the "Night of the Long Knives," when homosexuals, including Nazi commander Ernst Rohm were killed via Hitler's orders.

The role of Max was first played on stage by Ian McKellen in London and Richard Gere in New York.

Partly due to destiny and partly due to Greta's duplicitous ways, playboy Max (Clive Owen) and his lover, Rudy (Brian Webber), come under scrutiny, with the Gestapo first raiding Greta's club and then breaking into Max and Rudy's loft the next morning, killing the German soldier Max had picked up the night before. Max and Rudy manage to escape and Max's gay, closeted Uncle Freddie (Ian McKellen) tries to help spirit them out of Germany, but the plan fails, and they are both captured and placed on a train to Dachau.

Horst to Max about Dachau: "Friendship lasts about 12 hours in this place."

On the train, Max is forced to deny any connection to Rudy and to assist in fatally beating him, watching as Rudy's body is thrown off. "This isn't happening" becomes his mantra, as his world falls apart. Max is befriended by Horst (Lothaire Bluteau), a gentle prisoner who wears a pink triangle, signifying that he is homosexual, while Max wrangles a yellow, "Jewish" triangle, thinking that he will get better treatment in the camps.

In the grim, industrial camp atmosphere, Max gets assigned the pointless task of hauling rocks from one side of the yard to another. He manages to get Horst assigned to work with him, and thus the men develop a friendship that blossoms into a love relationship. This is truly a "pure" platonic relationship, as the two men cannot even be seen conversing, much less embracing. Horst chides Max for not being true to his nature, for hiding his homosexuality; Max acknowledges this to be true, but he cannot come to terms with this yet—he sloughs off any character issues with his standard throwaway comment—"I'm a terrible person."

All events build to the inevitable tragic denouement, where Horst declares his love for Max and is ultimately killed. Max then dons Horst's pink triangle and throws himself on the electric fence.

There have been many Holocaust-themed projects, but none have dealt so directly with the homosexuals who also suffered at the hands of the Nazi regime as this play/film. The production design, the directing, and the acting are all lean and austere; there in no room for histrionics—the horror of this situation speaks for itself. In this particular setting, dealing with repressed and open homosexuality, the Nazis' uniforms (lately discovered to be designed by Hugo Boss) have never looked so sleek and sexy—a stark contrast to the grim and dusty prisoners.

All of the actors, from Jagger to McKellen to Bluteau shine in this sparely directed production, the film debut for celebrated British stage director Mathias. The subject of the Holocaust is never easy to endure, but all of these elements coalesce to form a moving tale.

—G.E. Georges

REVIEWS

Boxoffice. January, 1998, p. 45.
Entertainment Weekly. November 28, 1997, p. 55.
The Hollywood Reporter. November 25, 1997, p. 18.
Los Angeles Times. November 26, 1997, p. F8.
New York Times. November 26, 1997, p. E5.
Rolling Stone. December 11, 1997, p. 85.
San Francisco Chronicle. November 26, 1997, p. E8.
Sight and Sound. March, 1998, p. 39.
Variety. May 26, 1997, p. 66.
Village Voice. December 2, 1997, p. 84.

Beverly Hills Ninja

Kung Fool! *Beverly Hills Ninja* Master of Disaster.—Movie tagline

"Farley has a flawless talent for physical comedy. Farley fills the screen with charming likability and pratfall panache. It's a kick."—Todd Camp, *Fort Worth Star Telegram*

"Lively and funny. The slapstick and sight gags come thick and fast. Director Dennis Dugan and writers Mark Feldberg and Mitch Klebanoff keep everything light and bouncy."—Kenneth Turan, *Los Angeles Times*

"I laughed my head off. The funniest scenes would sound stupid, but on-screen they're hilarious. There's more laughs than you might expect."—Jeff Craig, *Sixty Second Preview*

Box Office: $31,480,418

No matter how hard he tries, ninja-in-training Haru (Chris Farley) can't seem to master the stealth-like movements of his peers in the comedy *Beverly Hills Ninja.*

Although no one goes to see *Beverly Hills Ninja* with the highest expectations, there are probably plenty of filmgoers that have come away disappointed. The film is a martial arts comedy, but there's not enough martial arts or comedy. The concept is that a Japanese martial arts group has a prophecy that one day a white child will come to their dojo and become the greatest ninja of them all. When a white baby washes ashore near the group's compound, the ninjas naturally think that this is their guy and they adopt him. The thing is, as Haru (Chris Farley) grows up, it becomes apparent that perhaps Haru is not the great ninja they were waiting for.

Sensei about Haru: "He's fat, a fool and an embarrassment to ninja everywhere."

The big joke, repeated over and over again, lest anyone miss it, is that Haru is a big klutz. In the first few minutes of the movie, Haru falls down, knocks down shelves, accidentally hits other people, etc . . . The filmmakers deem one bit of physical comedy so funny—Haru accidentally hitting his adopted ninja brother Gobei (Robin Shou) with a ninja tool—they repeat the same gag in several variations. What is barely funny the first time, becomes exponentially less funny with each new go-round.

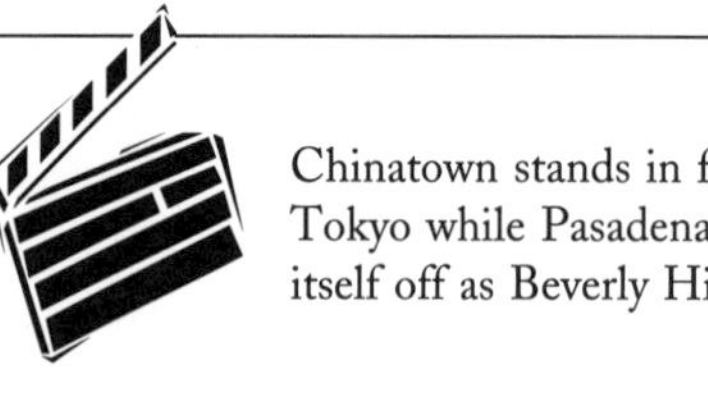

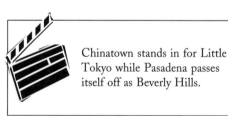

Chinatown stands in for Little Tokyo while Pasadena passes itself off as Beverly Hills.

Haru is launched into his adventure when the rest of the group are away from the compound and a beautiful woman, Alison Page (Nicollette Sheridan), comes seeking a ninja to help her find out if her boyfriend, Martin Tanley (Nathaniel Parker), is betraying her. Haru, after breaking the requisite amount of things before he sets off, finds out the boyfriend is a counterfeiter. He decides to follow Alison to Beverly Hills and to warn her of the danger she is in. Haru's Sensei (Soon-Tek Oh) hears of the plan and secretly sends the reluctant Gobei to tail Haru. Like a guardian angel, Gobei helps Haru without him knowing it. It's a clever device, since we never know what prop or which character is really Gobei in disguise.

Still, when the movie hits U.S. shores, it becomes much less interesting. At least when the setting is a Japanese ninja compound, there is an enjoyable travelogue-like aspect in seeing the scenery. Once in the U.S., the rest of the silly plot kicks in. Haru and the girl (really, she is just "the girl" whose main function is to run around looking pretty, yet distressed) try to foil the bad guys, while the bad guys try to foil them first.

Farley as a graceless ninja is an okay gag. The real gag is that Farley himself is surprisingly graceful. Critics who liked the movie (yes, there were a few) compared Farley to a lesser John Belushi and described his "hippo-ballet grace." Farley's gift for physical comedy is fully exploited—if a viewer wants to see Farley get hurt, this is the place to look.

CREDITS

Haru: Chris Farley
Alison Page: Nicollette Sheridan
Gobei: Robin Shou
Martin Tanley: Nathaniel Parker
Joey: Chris Rock
Sensei: Soon-Tek Oh

Origin: USA
Released: 1997
Production: Brad Krevoy, Steve Stabler, and Brad Jenkel for Motion Picture Corp. of America; released by TriStar Pictures
Direction: Dennis Dugan
Screenplay: Mark Feldberg and Mitch Kelbanoff
Cinematography: Arthur Albert
Editing: Jeff Gourson
Production design: Ninkey Dalton
Art direction: Christa Munro
Costumes: Mary Claire Hanan
Sound: Jonathan Stein
Martial Arts training: Master Jian-Hau Guo
Music: George S. Clinton
MPAA rating: PG-13
Running Time: 88 minutes

His other forte is being a big, fat man. Cashing in on that bit of talent, there's a recycled gag from a "Saturday Night Live" skit where Farley has to gyrate onstage in a strip club. (Memo to the writers: old gags=no fun.)

Another supposed hilarity focal point is a scene in a Japanese-style steak house where Farley plays it stereotypically Japanese, probably offending plenty of the audience, and fights the bad guys, using, ha-ha, fish. And speaking of racial stereotypes, what is comedian Chris Rock doing playing a shifty bellhop? It's not only offensive, but—knowing what an insightful player Rock can be—it's also disappointing.

Some good things about the movie? Well, it is very cartoony, and thus, maybe a good bet for the kids. The action is silly and the jokes are quick, visual, and easy to understand. Even Farley himself looks like a big cartoon character. But all in all, *Beverly Hills Ninja* has about enough comedy for a so-so "Saturday Night Live" skit.

—*Jill Hamilton*

REVIEWS

Boxoffice. March, 1997, p. 46.
Detroit Free Press. January 18, 1997, p. 2A.
Entertainment Weekly. January 31, 1997, p. 39.
Los Angeles Times. January 20, 1997, p. F4.
Variety. January 20, 1997, p. 45.

Bliss

Love is only the beginning.—Movie tagline

"*Bliss* is a sincere exploration of how the advanced study of sexual techniques can become a tool for eliminating obstacles of intimacy. Intriguing and exotic."—*Los Angeles Daily News*

"Original and daring."—*Playboy*

"*Bliss* emerges as the kind of film that no one can experience without engaging in deep thought and perhaps open talk. The three principals are so convincing that *Bliss* attains a higher level that parallels the teachings in the story."—*Toronto Sun*

Bliss is a preposterous movie about modern marital sex therapy lathered in New Age psychobabble and smothered with sanctimonious drivel. First-time writer-director Lance Young's film is essentially soft-corn pornography overlaid with a therapeutic gloss. Strained and didactic, the film never achieves bliss. It's preachy, overly serious, clinical and pretentious. This laughably scripted and ponderously plotted film is boring despite the game efforts of its three stars—Sheryl Lee, Craig Sheffer and Terence Stamp.

Lee and Sheffer play Maria and Joseph, a newly married yuppie couple with rather old-fashioned conflicts. She wants fancy houses, cars and a baby; he wants not to be interrupted by frequent calls from his wife while he's at work. Joseph's a construction supervisor or engineer; exactly what he does is not made clear. Apparently, Maria doesn't work, for reasons that are never explained.

Going into the marriage, as we learn from a conversation between the groom and his best man as they ride to the wedding, Joseph already knows Maria is compulsive about bugs and housecleaning, is prone to locking herself in her bedroom, and at times is suicidal. His friend Tanner (Casey Siemaszko), who is a prototypically insensitive male, counters: "All women are suicidal at times." Huh?

Maria's emotional problems are the center of marital therapy sessions with a subdued psychoanalyst named Alfred (Spalding Gray). For this couple, therapy is a matter of course, as much a part of marriage as wedding rings. But it's only when Maria confesses she has been faking her orgasms that Joseph comes unglued. His wife's suicidal tendencies are a trivial matter to Joseph compared to his inability to satisfy Maria sexually. *Bliss* shares in the worldview, popularized by talk-show sex therapists, that sexual function is the paramount concern in any relationship, and that proper technique in bed can cure whatever ails a couple.

Alfred, who seems well-intentioned but ineffectual, tells Joseph that Maria has a "borderline personality," a condition he says is incurable. Maria, it turns out, has been seeing a more daring therapist on the sly. Joseph discovers this fact while visiting a construction site where workers have trained a telescope on the uncurtained window of an apartment. There they see a man having sex with five or six different women a day, hour by hour. Joseph, of course, happens to sneak a peak just as Maria is entering the building.

Outraged, Joseph enters the apartment, which turns out to be the well-appointed "home office" of sex therapist Baltazar Vincenza. It's a name Woody Allen might have called a similar character, in jest, but Young is dead serious. Joseph discovers, by overhearing his wife's screams, that the doctor is treating her with rough sex. Joseph consults Alfred—therapists in this film function as the first recourse in every crisis. Alfred knows of Vincenza, who he says "operates on the edge of the law" but has never been closed down because no patients have complained. Right. If you can believe a world exists where a therapist has sex with scores of clients without consequence, then you deserve to endure *Bliss*.

Therapists should sue Young for making a film in which a therapist who has sex with his patients is made into an all-knowing god. Far from being punished as the criminal he is, Stamp's Baltazar is exalted as an all-knowing guru, a New Age superman. His success in avoiding the law implies that here is a man who knows how to satisfy women by giving them the kind of sex their partners cannot. The idea that this is the kind of "treatment" women need is repulsive, and undermines Young's later attempts to redeem the film as a pseudo-feminist look at childhood sexual abuse. Joseph initially is angry at Doctor Feelgood, but never threatens to call the cops. In an inexplicable plot twist, he quickly morphs from enraged cuckolded husband to devoted acolyte worshipping at the feet of the sex instructor.

Joseph asks Baltazar to teach him how to please Maria, and *Bliss* turns into an instructional sex tape that plays as if it had been cobbled together from reading sex tip articles in popular magazines. The haughty, insufferable Baltazar instructs Joseph on how to masturbate ("how can you love another if you don't love yourself?"), withhold ejaculation ("I will teach you how to *in*jaculate and thereby increase your sexual powers") and practice techniques such as "spooning" (non-sexual full-body holding) and massaging his mate's G-spot (Baltazar calls it the "sacred spot"). There are scenes of Joseph hanging upside down and practicing yoga, parading around in his underwear and learning how to admire his body, and telling passersby on the street that he loves himself at least three times a day. And Young presents all of this with a straight face.

Baltazar: "The goal of sex isn't orgasm, but ecstasy."

The sessions Baltazar conducts are as unorthodox in location as his subject matter. The guru is always doing something manly when Joseph comes by—practicing his violin, smoking a cigar, taking a sauna, or even fixing his classic car! They talk about orgasmic techniques while walking on a pier where people are fishing. Some of the scenes bring to mind the caustic satire of Woody Allen, but not even Allen could parody this film. No parody could be more laughable than *Bliss* itself. Stamp takes his ridiculous character completely seriously; he's a real hoot.

Despite its modernist pretensions about a new, more sensitive manhood, *Bliss* presents a premise as old as the hills. It's about a man learning to push the right buttons to satisfy his woman, with instructions by a vaguely exotic sexual sophisticate, illustrated profusely by gauzy shots of the couple in bed doing their homework. The formula gets a New Age makeover with the au courant notion that men need to downplay their obsession with orgasm in order to have really great sex. Joseph learns how to delay gratification to climb higher on Baltazar's ladder of sexual bliss, where Level Four is female orgasm, but Level Nine is tantric ecstacy. *Bliss* is about men learning how to play women like a violin, as deftly as Baltazar does—with exquisite sensitivity but firm command.

Bliss would be nothing but revisionist misogyny were it not for the film's final half-hour, in which Maria recovers her memories of past sexual abuse at the hands of her father. To work through her pain, she has to banish Joseph for a time, the better to effect a tearful reunion at the film's end. This part of the film is more tolerable, but it's noteworthy that the way in which Maria discovers her abusive past is by Joseph touching her sacred spot in a manner prescribed by Baltazar. Thus, in the view of *Bliss*, not only is the man who is wise in sexual technique able to cure his woman of frigidity, he also can instantly unlock the cure to "incurable" emotional problems.

Even on its own terms, *Bliss* makes no sense. Early on, Baltazar explains his extraordinary techniques to Joseph by saying Maria needs to keep acting out her patterns of past sexual abuse until she no longer asks to be abused. But he also confesses he has no idea what is causing her disfunction, and he has been unable to unlock her repressed memories by repeating the abuse. When he instructs Joseph, he doesn't tell her to abuse her, but instead to be gentle and forgiving. And when these techniques magically uncover Maria's horrible past and end up putting Joseph on the street, Baltazar tells Joseph his problem is that he's too obsessed with curing Maria of her problems. By any measure, Baltazar is a fraud, but nobody in the film does anything but worship him. He even is rewarded in the end with his own "real" girlfriend, a hot redheaded librarian.

Stamp throws himself into this material with sanctimonious gusto, and the result is a finely crafted but repelling performance. Sheffer, a veteran of a slew of B movies, looks suitably confused and frustrated—a poor ignorant slob who must suffer many indignities to become a knight. Lee, who cut her teeth on David Lynch's "Twin Peaks" TV series and learned how to do sex scenes in the "Red Shoe Diaries" soft-porn videos, manages a commendable performance playing the film's only believable character. Her bubbly seductiveness and intermittent spurts of crazed compulsiveness make for a recognizably disturbed woman in the first part of the film. At the end of the film, Lee is even more compelling as a sexual abuse survivor, and her performance alone salvages something from the wreckage of *Bliss*.

If Young had made a movie about a married couple confronting and overcoming past sexual abuse but left out the ludicrous Baltazar character, it would at least have been a honest look at a serious problem. But most of this movie is just an updated rehash of the leering soft-porn, no-plot quickies that parade across late-night cable channels, masquerading as legitimate movies. *Bliss* doesn't have a serviceable plot, its characters are mostly cardboard cut-outs, and its dialogue is ponderous and silly. It's bloated, self-important and ludicrous. And it's not even remotely erotic, unless your taste runs to the clinical. Eroticism requires real characters, real chemistry, and real tension, and *Bliss* has only fakery.

—Michael Betzold

CREDITS

Joseph: Craig Sheffer
Maria: Sheryl Lee
Baltazar: Terence Stamp
Tanner: Casey Siemaszko
Alfred: Spalding Gray
Redhead: Leigh Taylor Young
Eva: Lois Chiles

Origin: USA
Released: 1997
Production: Allyn Stewart for Triumph Films; released by Sony Pictures
Direction: Lance Young
Screenplay: Lance Young
Cinematography: Mike Malloy
Editing: Allan Lee
Music: Jan A.P. Kaczmarek
Production design: John Willett, David Lloyd Fischer
Art direction: William Heslup, Eric Norlin
Costumes: Jori Woodman
Sound: Michael McGee
MPAA rating: R
Running Time: 103 minutes

REVIEWS

Boxoffice. May, 1997, p. 54.
Entertainment Weekly. June 20, 1997, p. 46.
Los Angeles Times. June 6, 1997, p. F10.
New York Times. June 6, 1997, p. B18.
People. June 16, 1997, p. 24.
USA Today. June 5, 1997, p. 12D.
Variety. April 28, 1997, p. 100.
Village Voice. June 10, 1997, p. 74.

Blood and Wine

Stealing a fortune is easy. Getting away with it is murder.—Movie tagline

"A richly textured crime picture."—Roger Ebert, *Chicago Sun-Times*

"Devilishly good! Suspenseful, top-notch moviemaking. A cinematic pinot noir."—Michele Shapiro, *Glamour*

Box Office: $1,094,668

Film noir is a wonderful film genre in part because it lends itself so easily to style: sinister lighting—particularly in black-and-white films—tilted camera angles, alternately suspenseful and romantic music, tough dialogue, unexpected flashes of offbeat humor, doomed sexual attractions, and an overall mood of oppressive cynicism. The best works in this genre—*Laura* (1944), *Double Indemnity* (1944), *The Big Sleep* (1946), *Out of the Past* (1947), *Kiss Me Deadly* (1955), *The Killing* (1956), *Touch of Evil* (1958), *Chinatown* (1974), *Taxi Driver* (1976), *Body Heat* (1981), *The Last Seduction* (1994)—are memorable for striking a perfect balance between these elements. *Blood and Wine* has everything—with the notable exception of an appropriate musical score—it needs to be a worthy addition to the film noir tradition, including a good director and a good cast, but the elements do not blend as well as they should.

Vic to Alex: "The interesting thing about rich people is they're so cheap. They'll spend 1.3 million on a necklace, with diamonds the size of chocolates, then they'll lock it in a tin box from Sears."

Alex Gates (Jack Nicholson) is an unprosperous Miami wine merchant with a dissatisfied, boozing wife, Suzanne (Judy Davis), and a surly stepson, Jason (Stephen Dorff). Alex plans to run away from his failures and obligations by stealing a million-dollar diamond necklace from one of his customers and going to Paris with his mistress, Gabriella (Jennifer Lopez), also the nanny of the robbery target. Alex sets up the theft to be performed by a British safecracker, Vic (Michael Caine). Vic has a respiratory disease and longs for one last score to keep from dying in a county hospital. Getting caught and dying in prison would be even worse.

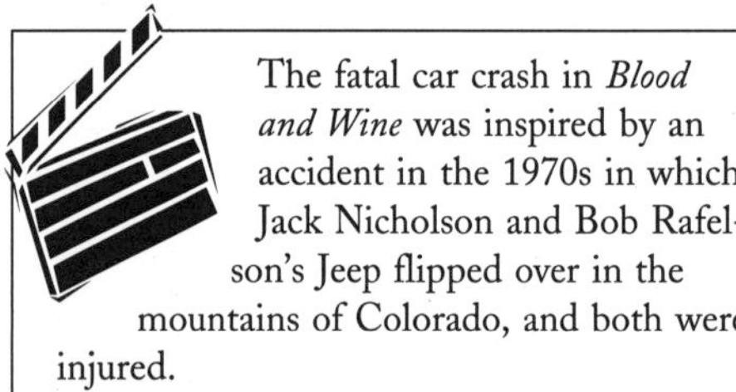

The fatal car crash in *Blood and Wine* was inspired by an accident in the 1970s in which Jack Nicholson and Bob Rafelson's Jeep flipped over in the mountains of Colorado, and both were injured.

Film noir characters hoping to run away from it all or planning one last caper are just asking for trouble, and these get all they deserve and more. The robbery itself goes well with Vic improvising through a couple of unexpected hang-ups. Then Suzanne catches the careless Alex about to leave her and hits him with a cane until he is unconscious. She and Jason flee to a friend's houseboat in Key Largo, unaware that they are also taking the necklace. When they find it and discover how valuable it is, they become almost as greedy as the thieves. When Alex and the uncontrollably violent Vic track them down, matters become even more complicated. A further divisive element is introduced when Jason falls for Gabriella, not knowing she is involved with his stepfather.

Blood and Wine deserves a more satisfying ending in which everyone is punished to different degrees, but there is nothing unexpected or memorable about the film's conclusion. Things end as they might in real life, out of stupidity and sentimentality, but the sloppiness of real life is what draws viewers to the pessimistic escapism of film noir in the first place. Director Bob Rafelson, upon whose story the screenplay by Nick Villiers and Alison Cross is based, delivers mostly good performances and throws in the occasional odd camera angle—reminiscent of Orson Welles' *Touch of Evil*—but the film's pacing is off. Rafelson and editor Steven Cohen seem to end some scenes a bit abruptly and make awkward transitions between others. As a result, the film never establishes any rhythm, any sense that the filmmakers are in control.

In a long but spotty career, Rafelson has directed one great film, *Five Easy Pieces* (1970), two good films, *Black Widow* (1987) and *Mountains of the Moon* (1990), one excruciatingly bad film, *Man Trouble* (1992), and a handful of others of mixed quality. While *The King of Marvin Gardens* (1972) and *Man Trouble* have superficial noirish tendencies, *Blood and Wine* is the director's third pure film noir, after *The Postman Always Rings Twice* (1981) and *Black Widow*. While Rafelson's version of James M. Cain's classic crime novel is sluggishly paced and pretentiously arty, *Black Widow* finds the right blending of cynicism, suspense, and dark humor that *The Postman Always Rings Twice* and *Blood and Wine* lack.

A degree of the sense of style Rafelson's latest film needs could have been provided with a fitting score. Films noir are greatly augmented by music that conveys both the tension and romance inherent in the genre, as with Miklos Rozsa's score for *Double Indemnity*, Jerry Goldsmith's for *Chinatown*, Bernard Herrmann's for *Taxi Driver*, or John Barry's for *Body Heat*. Michal Lorenc's music for *Blood and Wine*, unfortunately, is its weakest component, as mechanical and derivative as that of a made-for-television potboiler.

Blood and Wine does, however, have production design by Richard Sylbert, the greatest contemporary artist in his field: *The Manchurian Candidate* (1962), *The Graduate* (1967), *Rosemary's Baby* (1968), *Chinatown*, *Reds* (1981), *Dick Tracy* (1990). Sylbert makes the estate of the necklace's owners ostentatious without being tacky, the Gates home messily lived in, and Jason's fishing boat as dilapidated as possible and still be seaworthy. Sylbert and costume designer Lindy Hemming provide one of the film's best touches by making the necklace itself the trashiest trinket imaginable, a tawdry token of the characters' values. When she finds it, Suzanne is right to assume it is paste because nothing so vulgar should be valuable. By believing in the worth society has assigned the necklace, the protagonists allow themselves to be destroyed.

Dorff, a young actor in the Brad Pitt-Ethan Hawke-Christian Slater mold, has little to do as Jason except look angry or out of his depth. Rafelson even resorts to a self-reference by having Dorff carry on an angry outburst in the cab of his pickup, recalling Nicholson's famous pounding of his car's steering wheel in *Five Easy Pieces*. Dorff's very similar explosion only calls attention to the fact that he is far from being the charismatic actor Nicholson was and still can be. Davis, a great actress in desperate need of better roles, gives perhaps her quietest performance in an American film, resisting the camp flourishes in which she indulges in *Absolute Power* (1997). Lopez, a young actress of considerable potential, does the best she can in what is little more than the sultry-sexpot-thrown-in-for-seasoning role. The screenwriters could have made *Blood and Wine* more interesting by having Gabriella clearly prefer the world-weary Alex to the younger, more upstanding Jason. That Rafelson, Villiers, and Cross may think they may have done exactly this is indicative of another of the film's problems.

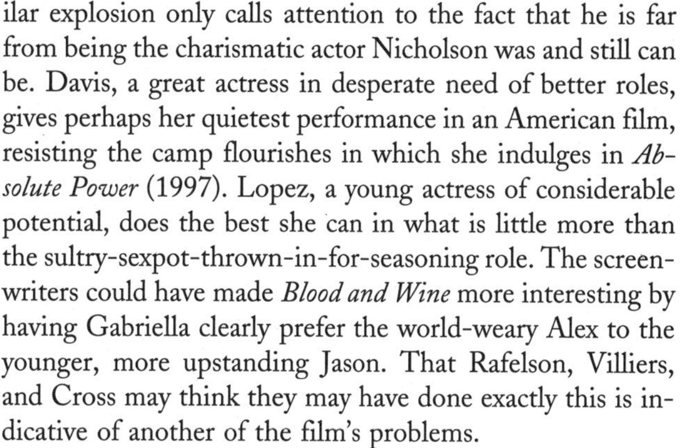

What makes *Blood and Wine* worth seeing despite its deficiencies, however, are the performances of Nicholson and Caine. Nicholson has not been this natural since his cameo in *Broadcast News* (1987). Holding his patented raised-eyebrow leer in check, Nicholson creates a complex character who thinks he can control his destiny while his life is increasingly spinning into chaos. Alex is an unscrupulous man who can easily seem normal and pleasant because his brand of evil is so banal. When his humanity begins leaking out, as with his initial concern for his wife's welfare when her car, pursued by Vic and Alex, overturns, his true nature quickly asserts itself as he begins desperately looking for the necklace. Alex, who once sold neckties at Saks Fifth Avenue, considers himself a dandy yet wears the kind of ugly shirts and ties affected by someone with a sense of style but a limited one. Hemming, again as with the necklace, makes Alex's surface reflect his interior.

Caine, one of the greatest and most likable film actors, has seemingly been a victim of the Oscar jinx since winning an Academy Award for *Hannah and Her Sisters* (1986), with his film work since then steadily declining to a point at which he must co-star with the Muppets—*The Muppets' Christmas Carol* (1992)—and with Steven Seagal—*On Deadly Ground* (1994). Caine reinvigorates himself with *Blood and Wine*, making Vic a memorable villain by seeming so harmless on

CREDITS

Alex Gates: Jack Nicholson
Vic: Michael Caine
Jason: Stephen Dorff
Suzanne Gates: Judy Davis
Gabriella: Jennifer Lopez
Henry: Harold Perrineau, Jr.
Mike: Mike Starr

Origin: USA
Released: 1997
Production: Jeremy Thomas for Blood and Wine Productions and Recorded Picture Company; released by Fox Searchlight Pictures
Direction: Bob Rafelson
Screenplay: Nick Villiers, Alison Cross
Cinematography: Newton Thomas Sigel
Editing: Steven Cohen
Production design: Richard Sylbert
Art direction: William Kemper Wright
Costume design: Lindy Hemming
Sound: Peter J. Devlin
Music: Michal Lorenc
MPAA rating: R
Running Time: 101 minutes

REVIEWS

Boxoffice. March, 1997, p. 73.
Chicago Tribune. February 21, 1997, p. 5.
Entertainment Weekly. February 21/28, 1997, p. 106.
Interview. February, 1997, p. 74.
Los Angeles Times. February 21, 1997, p. F16.
New York. February 24, 1997, p. 122.
The New York Times. February 21, 1997, p. C15.
The New Yorker. February 17, 1997, p. 92.
People Weekly. February 24, 1997, p. 19.
Rolling Stone. March 6, 1997, p. 78.
Sight and Sound. March, 1997, p. 41.
USA Today. February 21, 1997, p. D4.
Variety. September 30, 1996, p. 181.
The Village Voice. February 25, 1997, p. 70.
Vogue. February, 1997, p. 140.

the surface. Overweight and sweaty, Vic constantly smokes even though he can barely breathe. He apparently has no energy yet can erupt into violence at the least slight. Caine, who has always been a very physical actor, uses his awkward bulk here to suggest leadenness when waiting for something to do and danger when provoked. He and Nicholson combine on the film's best bit of business when Alex wets his hands in a seedy washroom only for Vic, impervious to even the basic needs of others, blocks his path to the drying towels. More such moments could have made *Blood and Wine* a truly memorable film.

—Michael Adams

Boogie Nights

The life of a dreamer, the days of a business and the nights in between.—Movie tagline

"*Boogie Nights* is a sprawling masterpiece of a movie. Its raw energy, its untidy morality, and its shocking juxtaposition of violence and comedy will wake up an audience. This is a reminder that movies can rattle and surprise." —Roger Ebert, *Chicago Sun-Times*

"*Boogie Nights* is the most sensational act of moviemaking so far this year. It's a movie that may well leave Quentin Tarantino and Martin Scorsese drop-jawed with envy!"—Owen Gleiberman, *Entertainment Weekly*

"Everything about *Boogie Nights* is unexpected! Paul Thomas Anderson sees a lot of good stories in this particular naked city, and he wants to tell them, with enormous flair!"—Janet Maslin, *New York Times*

"The most invigorating, deeply entertaining American movie this year so far!"—David Ansen *Newsweek*

"*Boogie Nights* is a chunk of movie dynamite! A hilarious and harrowing spectacle! It's another fireball in a time capsule!"—Peter Travers, *Rolling Stone*

"*Boogie Nights* is *GoodFellas* meets *Pulp Fiction.*"—Richard Corliss, *Time*

Box Office: $23,696,805

The critical and box-office successes of *The English Patient* (1996) and *Titanic* (1997) appear to signal the return of the epic in contemporary cinema. Both audiences and critics alike have proved more than willing to sit through lengthy films that take on weighty subjects. Positioned amidst such films is Paul Thomas Anderson's *Boogie Nights,* two-and-a-half-hours chronicling nearly a decade in the adult film industry. Like *The English Patient* and *Titanic,* which approach large-scale events by examining their effects on private individuals, *Boogie Nights* tracks a shift in the American zeitgeist by following the lives of several porn-industry workers as they spiral downward from the glittering innocence of the disco era into the heartless commodification of the Reagan years.

Adult movie producer/director Jack Horner (Burt Reynolds) and his latest discovery Dirk Diggler (Mark Wahlberg) take the porn industry by storm in *Boogie Nights.*

The much-touted opening shot sets the scene both thematically and stylistically. The camera swoops into a dance club, negotiates its way through the crowded scene, and takes the audience for a spin around the dance floor to the exhilarating sounds of "Best of My Love." As the camera winds its way through the club, it pauses momentarily on the major players who will, through the course of the film, come to form a makeshift family within the adult-film industry. Despite his subject matter, Anderson handles the nudity in *Boogie Nights* with admirable restraint, and this focuses attention on the characters and their stories. By introducing his characters against the background of popular American culture and not within the world of porn, Anderson immediately establishes a central truth of his film. Despite their occupations and lifestyles, individuals like Jack Horner (Burt Reynolds, in a deservedly praised performance), a visionary director who dreams of making porn that is "true and right and dramatic," and his leading star Amber Waves (Julianne Moore) are, in many ways, ordinary people.

Jack about Eddie: "I got a feeling beneath those jeans something wonderful is waiting to get out."

Anderson makes this point most clearly through the character of Eddie Adams (Mark Wahlberg), a dishwasher whose prodigious member transforms him into Dirk Diggler, pornography's great white hope. When we first meet Eddie he is an ordinary 17-year-old living with his parents in Southern California. His bedroom is covered with posters of Bruce Lee and Cheryl Tiegs. Despite a troubled family life, Eddie maintains the belief that "everyone's blessed with one special thing." Wahlberg, like the other members of the ensemble cast, puts in a strong performance. He imbues Eddie with a boyish eagerness that draws the audience to his story. As a result, Eddie's rocket to stardom reads like a twisted variation on the American dream. Likewise, his subsequent fall into cocaine-addicted desperation becomes an emblematic loss of innocence for the culture at large. Eddie's decline is mirrored by the other characters. Maternal porn queen Amber fails to gain custody of her own child, she and fellow porn actress and surrogate daughter Rollergirl (Heather Graham) descend into drug-addicted hysteria, and the entire industry loses its sense of integrity as the ease and efficiency of video technology render "true and right" pornography obsolete.

The 27-year-old director made a 30-minute mockumentary *Dirk Diggler* at 17, inspired by porn star John Holmes, which eventually became *Boogie Nights.*

Anderson negotiates the balance between character and context deftly. To a certain extent, Eddie and Amber embody characters and play out narratives that we have seen before. And for this reason, the film's scrupulous reproduction of seventies fashion, decor, and music sometimes seems like exquisite window dressing on another update of *A Star is Born.* Yet the over-the-top nature of these characters' lives, combined with a tantalizing peek into the world of adult-film, allows Anderson to paint his story in bold strokes. Gleefully displaying stylistic borrowings from Martin Scorsese, Quentin Tarantino, and MTV, *Boogie Nights* moves at a frenetic pace, jumping from near tragedy to black humor in one shot—while the music never stops. More significantly, *Boogie Nights* suggests that no amount of drugs, wealth, or sex can protect anyone from the larger forces that effect widespread cultural change. History, it would seem,

CREDITS

Eddie Adams/Dirk Diggler: Mark Wahlberg
Jack Horner: Burt Reynolds
Amber Waves: Julianne Moore
Reed Rothchild: John C. Reilly
Rollergirl: Heather Graham
Buck Swope: Don Cheadle
Little Bill: William H. Macy
Rahad Jackson: Alfred Molina
Maurice T. Rodriguez: Luis Guzman
Scotty: Philip Seymour Hoffman
Floyd Gondolli: Philip Baker Hall
The Colonel: Robert Ridgely

Origin: USA
Released: 1997
Production: Lloyd Levin, Paul Thomas Anderson, John Lyons, and Joanne Sellar for Ghoulardi Film Company; released by New Line Cinema
Direction: Paul Thomas Anderson
Screenplay: Paul Thomas Anderson
Cinematography: Robert Elswit
Editing: Dylan Tichenor
Music: Michael Penn
Production design: Bob Ziembicki
Art direction: Ted Berner
Set decoration: Sandy Struth
Costumes: Mark Bridges
Sound: Stephen Halbert
MPAA rating: R
Running Time: 152 minutes

AWARDS AND NOMINATIONS

Academy Awards 1997 Nominations: Supporting Actor (Reynolds), Supporting Actress (Moore), Original Screenplay
BAFTA 1997 Nominations: Original Screenplay, Supporting Actor (Reynolds)
Golden Globe Awards 1998: Supporting Actor (Reynolds)
Nominations: Supporting Actress (Moore)
Los Angeles Film Critics Association 1997: Supporting Actor (Reynolds), Supporting Actress (Moore)
National Society of Film Critics 1997: Supporting Actor (Reynolds), Supporting Actress (Moore)
New York Film Critics Circle 1997: Supporting Actor (Reynolds)

happens everywhere, and its progress may be tracked in the oddest places and among socially marginalized individuals.

Like most acts of nostalgia, *Boogie Nights* engages in creative misremembering. The seventies appear to have been the high point of recent American history. A childlike attitude marks the characters' approach to their own self-indulgence in the earlier scenes. But film turns to video, Melanie's jangly "Brand New Key" gives way to the orchestrated excess of Night Ranger's "Sister Christian," and the climate changes. The seventies take on the youthful exuberance of the experiments in mind-altering substances and "free love" associated with the sixties—but without the darkening presence of the Vietnam War. In this way Anderson's poignant fable invites us to forget that the seventies were also the era of "blaxploitation" films like *Get Christie Love!* (1974) and *Mandingo* (1975), and that AIDS was breeding just a few steps off the dance floor. Although history happens everywhere, *Boogie Nights* inadvertently makes clear that its representation will change as surely as "video killed the radio star."

—*Jacqui Sadashige*

REVIEWS

Boxoffice. November, 1997, p. 121.
Chicago Tribune. October 17, 1997, p. 5.
Details. September, 1997, p. 123.
Entertainment Weekly. April 25, 1997, p. 26.
Entertainment Weekly. October 17, 1997, p. 39.
Los Angeles Times. October 17, 1997, p. F1.
New York Times. October 8, 1997, p. E1.
People. October 20, 1997, p. 21.
Rolling Stone. October 16, 1997, p. 113.
Sight and Sound. January, 1998, p. 36.
Time. October 6, 1997.
USA Today. October 10, 1997, p. 1D.
Variety. September 15, 1997, p. 68.
Village Voice. October 14, 1997, p. 85.
Washington Post Weekend. October 17, 1997, p. 32.

Booty Call

Some guys will do anything for a little something.—Movie tagline

"*Booty Call* is the year's first fall-down, bust-a-gut-laughing comedy."—Jim Svejda, *KNX/CBS Radio*

"Sassy, brassy and full of mischief. Down-dirty hilarious in spots."—Bob Strauss, *Los Angeles Daily News*

"Two thumbs up. Very funny."—*Siskel & Ebert*

"An outrageously funny look at the war between the sexes."—Paul Wunder, *WBAI Radio*

Box Office: $20,066,917

When a film alerts an audience to its sexual content with such a conspicuous title, odds are that you shouldn't really expect great things from it. But not all of *Booty Call* is cinematic garbage. Its flimsy plot is somewhat redeemed by the presence of its lead stars, faced with the daunting task of giving credibility to such a childish premise, which involves two men in search of the perfect contraceptive in order to have sex with their dates. They succeed in making the film slightly entertaining only by their talents as comedic actors.

The film wastes no time in setting its feeble storyline into motion as two inseparable buddies, Rushon (Tommy Davidson) and Bunz (Jamie Foxx), are about to partake in a double date. By their walk and talk, Rushon and Bunz are opposites. Their differences are further reinforced by their physical appearance. Rushon dresses in professional attire and seems very friendly and mature. Bunz, as he is introduced playing cards on the street corner, looks (with short-braided cornrows) and acts the part of a streetwise con artist with the emotional development of an adolescent. Before they reach their destination, Bunz and Rushon engage in a sometimes funny banter focusing on their opinions and views of the opposite sex. As a witness to a public argument between a man and his female companion, Bunz becomes even more convinced that long-term relationships with women are a mistake and stresses his reliance on one-night stands or "booty calls." To Bunz, they are not just simplistic, but the only option available to avoid disastrous relationships. Another one of Bunz's fears arises when we learn that he's been set up on a blind date with Rushon's girlfriend's best friend. Unlike Bunz, Rushon has an ongoing relationship with Nikki, but all is not bliss, since Rushon has not had sexual intercourse with her. This fact is cause for Bunz to playfully tease Rushon. Rushon seems smitten by Nikki, but Bunz can't comprehend a feeling other than mere sexual gratification. Feeling his manhood questioned and tired of Bunz's accusations of romantic flaccidity, Rushon decides to bet Bunz that he will consummate his relationship with Nikki within the next 24 hours.

Intercutting Bunz and Rushon's conversation is the introduction of Nikki (Tamala Jones) and her girlfriend Lysterine (Vivica A. Fox). They are the female equivalent of Rushon and Bunz in temperament and demeanor. Nikki is demure, timid, and personable. Her friend Lysterine has no shortage of self-esteem and prides herself as an independent woman. She is not shy when it comes to showing off her attractiveness, even if it is for a blind date. As Nikki dresses in a simple blouse and pants outfit and worries about showing too much cleavage, Lysterine wears a skimpy satin miniskirt and button-down top that is tied in the front. Through their conversation, it is clearly established that Nikki cares about her relationship with Rushon and doesn't want a night of wanton sex to ruin what two months has accumulated. In between comments, Lysterine questions Nikki about her blind date. Nikki quells her fears by saying he's a nice guy. Her words were not enough, for once Lysterine gets a glimpse of Bunz in the Chinese restaurant they are to dine in, she immediately makes a beeline for the exit. Nikki chases after her and is only berated by Lysterine for setting her up with a "gutter rat" named Bunz. Nikki assures her that this double date is not a prerequisite to anything but dinner and begs Lysterine to stay for her sake. Lysterine reluctantly agrees.

Knowing that Bunz is definitely not her type, the animosity between Lysterine and Bunz is established and some of the more funnier moments of the film occur as the two trade insults. Lysterine whips out her American Express Gold card and informs Bunz that she could "buy and sell" him. In rebuttal, Bunz takes out his only credit card which is a gold gas card. It doesn't do him any good since Bunz doesn't even have a car. Lysterine's loathing of Bunz doesn't prevent him from attempting to sweet-talk her into some sexual activity. Lysterine only looks on in disgust. Meanwhile, the two lovebirds Rushon and Nikki couldn't be happier by the sight of each other. The depth of his emotional commitment to Nikki is demonstrated as he offers her his last shrimp from dinner.

After the dinner date, the foursome moves on to shoot pool, dance, and play cards at Nikki's. The action eventually turns to sex, with the bulk of lewd humor taking place as viewer interest wanes. The second portion of the film is set into motion and it becomes the film's weaker half. *Booty Call* looses its energy and humor at the expense of taste and logic. Much of its humor starts out risque and you're apt to smile and admire its daring. But due to a lack of sophistication on director Jeff Pollack and the screenwriters part, the jokes are stretched to the point of tastelessness. The smile slowly becomes a scowl. Lysterine soon develops a kinky and lustful attraction toward Bunz and Nikki is ready to physically commit to Rushon, with one exception, they must practice safe sex by using condoms. Having his one and only condom eaten by Nikki's dog, Rushon and Bunz are sent out late at night in Chinatown in search of contraceptives. Their search for the perfect condom resorts to three separate trips to party stores that truly wear on one's patience. The store owners are Middle Eastern immigrants and the film resorts to petty stereotypes as the they grow suspicious of two black men entering their store late at night. The film's lack of imagination is portrayed by the explicit comments made by the store owners towards Rushon and Bunz as they accuse them of being homosexuals. The film's finale includes Rushon getting accidentally shot and being mistaken for a patient about to be castrated. The immaturity of the filmmakers has blossomed and the comedic material here becomes nothing more than a badly-executed episode on a Fox network television show.

All four lead characters started out on television, and it's obvious that the two male leads, Davidson and Foxx, are comfortable with the raunchy material. Both are stand-up comedians and were regulars on the hit comedy show "In Living Color." The show often walked a thin line between tasteful and tackiness, but the talent of Davidson and Foxx remained intact. Davidson is an energetic comic with a knack for dancing and singing in his concerts, but here, he is adequately cast as the laid-back friend to Foxx's more irrational and wild character. In a sequence that once again borders on the issue of taste, Lysterine informs Bunz that she gets really excited when a man can perform imitations. Well, it just so happens that Foxx is a gifted comedian who

CREDITS

Bunz: Jamie Foxx
Rushon: Tommy Davidson
Lysterine: Vivica A. Fox
Nikki: Tamala Jones
Akmed: Art Malik
Chan: Gedde Watanabe

Origin: USA
Released: 1997
Production: John Morrissey for Turman/Morrissey Company; released by Columbia Pictures
Direction: Jeff Pollack
Screenplay: Takashi Bufford and Bootsie
Cinematography: Ron Orieux
Editing: Christopher Greenbury
Music: Robert Folk
Production design: Sandra Kybartas
Art direction: Armano Sgrignuoli
Sound: Douglas Ganton
Costumes: Vicki Graef
MPAA rating: R
Running Time: 77 minutes

can perform meticulous impersonations of such people as Jesse Jackson and Martin Luther King Jr. Some viewers will be appalled by hearing such men of power describe certain sexual acts while others will laugh at its gall. One positive aspect of the film is that Rushon and Bunz's friendship is made more believable by the history that Davidson and Foxx shared.

Vivica A. Fox started out on the soap opera "The Young and The Restless," but became well-known thanks to a supporting role in the mega-box office hit *Independence Day* (1996) as Will Smith's love interest. Tamala Jones is the relative newcomer with a role on the short-lived series "Dangerous Minds." Despite these actresses lack of past comedic roles and the inferior material they're given to work with, they are competent enough to stand up against the pros.

Booty Call was the subject of public outcries, mainly from the African American communities around the country. Upon its release, the posters enraged leaders in these areas for its close-up view of an African American woman's backside with the film's title placed over it. Community leaders demanded that billboards and ads for the film be taken down due to its insulting image of African American women. Meetings were called and rallies were held which pressured the film studio to change the movie poster to a shot of the four lead characters around the title. Some even went so far as to discourage people from seeing the film. But such a title attracts a kind of audience that a flyer or picket sign will have little or no effect on. In fact, if you are going to see a movie with such a title, you pretty much deserve what you get. In the case of *Booty Call*, you'll get a few laughs and a somewhat limited viewpoint on the battle between the sexes.

—Michelle Banks

REVIEWS

Chicago Sun-Times. February 22, 1997.
Chicago Tribune. February 26, 1997, p. 10.
Entertainment Weekly. March 17, 1997, p. 59.
Los Angeles Times. February 26, 1997, p. F10.
Sight and Sound. December, 1997, p. 39.
USA Today. February 26, 1997, p. 3D
Variety. February 24, 1997, p. 75.
Village Voice. March 11, 1997, p. 74.

Box of Moonlight

Some people have a hard time unwinding.—Movie tagline

Leap before you look.—Movie tagline

"A shining summer gem!"—Bill Diehl, *ABC Radio*

"One of the best independent films of the year!"—Derek Malcolm, *The Guardian*

"Smart! Funny! Perfect!"—Richard Raynor, *Harper's Bazaar*

"Relentlessly wacky!"—Jami Bernard, *New York Daily News*

"Sexy . . . Seductive . . . Amazingly fresh!"—Janet Maslin, *New York Times*

"Two thumbs up!"—*Siskel & Ebert*

Box Office: $795,128

Box of Moonlight is a whimsical fable about how the rejuvenative powers of stopping to smell the roses will kick start your life. Al Fountain (John Turturro) is a humorless clock-watcher, an electrical engineer who is overseeing a turbine installation project near his Chicago home. He calls his wife every night at 8PM on the dot, he humorlessly and grimly grills his son Bobby (Alexander Goodwin) on his multiplication tables. Al is just as rigid and unyielding in his pursuit of squeezing every drop of manpower out of every day; he thinks nothing of breaking up a good-natured stickball game at 4:45 PM, urging his men to press on for another 15 minutes. Director Tom DiCillo (*Johnny Suede* 1992, *Living in Oblivion*, 1994) deftly captures the drone-like nature of Al; we have all had the misfortune of knowing, if not actually working for, someone like him.

Naturally, this does not endear him to his blue-collar crew, led by lead man Soapy (Ray Aranha). Despite Soapy's best attempts to integrate Al into a bit of friendly camaraderie, Al can't fit in—he's just too stiff. Yet, under his officious veneer, Al would like nothing more than to join the guys for a beer or a game of cards. One night Soapy invites Al to the nightly game, and Al's eyes literally bug out with repressed excitement. He informs his wife Deb (Annie Corley) during his nightly call that he is about to roll down the hall and join "the guys." She encourages him, pushing him to enjoy this bit of "normalcy." Unfortunately, as Al rounds the corner to Soapy's room, he hears the guys moan about the possibility of him actually joining the game; they bemoan his stiffness, ridicule his attitude and, most painful of all to Al—actually feel sorry for him.

Al returns to his room, stunned and in pain. He shows no sign of hearing their conversations the next day, although he is tempted to reveal his hurt feelings to Soapy. But everyone is soon distracted by another turn of events: the turbine project has been terminated and everyone is sent home early with a bonus. Al takes this opportunity to have some thinking time to himself and tells Deb that he will see her as planned in five days. He also discovers a horror that has been known to bring grown men and women to their knees in horror—his first grey hair!

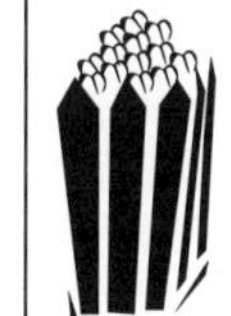

The Kid to Al: "It's not where you're going but how you get there."

Renting a car from the grumpy proprietress at Circle Car Rental, Al sets out to find a happy childhood memory; Lake Splashee, where he swam and dove with his family and friends. Even though he is supposedly "carefree and aimless" Al still engages in clock-watcher tendencies; he often looks at his watch, notes the time and spouts a pithy witticism about life. In his wonderfully rustic hotel (vibrant, quirky production design by Therese DePrez) Al calls Deb, but still doesn't tell her of his changed plans.

After learning from the equally quirky desk clerk ("I loved that lake—me and my brothers drowned a cat there") that the lake is called Splatchee, not Splashy, Al sets out. He has begun to have a series of disturbing images—things seem to go "backward" for him; coffee and water flow backwards from cups into pitchers, children ride backwards on their bicycles. Al tries to shake these images from mind.

Rounding a curb he nearly crashes into a marooned old car that belongs to the Kid (Sam Rockwell). Kid, a good-natured, long-haired survivalist type dressed in a Davy Crockett outfit, begs Al to help him fix his car. After Al determines the problem, Kid convinces him to hook the cars together, drive to Kid's home and then in the morning deliver him to a service station. Against his better judgment, Al agrees. Kid delivers Al to an unbelievable home—an open-aired, trailer—sans walls and roof, populated by purloined lawn jockeys and gnomes, strung with Christmas lights and vintage junk of all kinds. Kid, as he proudly proclaims, is in "salvage." When Al calls his wife promptly at 8PM, Kid informs him to make it snappy—he's tapped into someone else's line. Al is disgusted and outraged by someone who lives this way and gives Kid a tongue-lashing on the responsible nature of adults in the modern world. But Kid just shrugs him off—he's happy to breakfast on Oreos and milk and steal Humpty Dumpty gnomes from suburban front lawns to survive.

Al accompanies Kid to the local garage where, as they wait for service, they run into Wick, a wacked-out burn victim who thinks everyone is taunting his misfortune by flicking lit matches at him. On the way home, Kid stops in a local tomato field, where he entices Al into munching on fresh tomatoes, and ultimately starts a raucous tomato fight with him. Al actually cuts loose for a minute, until the owner calls the cops. Kid rises to the occasion by creating a diversion (releasing the brake on the cop car, thus causing it to roll into the tomato field), allowing he and Al to scamper away.

Al now informs Kid that the "fun" is over and he intends to leave—but where are his keys? They look back in the tomato field, but no luck. Kid takes Al to a deserted quarry for a swim and tries to cheer him up. Kid is the type who relishes life, eats it up, grabs what is in front of him and exhorts those around him to do the same. Al looks at him as if he is from another planet, but his steely resolve is beginning to melt.

The more Al learns about Kid, the more he marvels at his determination to fly under society's radar; Kid hasn't paid taxes, hasn't paid bills—as the Kid himself puts it—he's almost "off the grid"—and he couldn't be happier about it. Al marvels at such an individual. He still is having backward visions, but he is relaxing a little bit more. He finds himself feeling amused and slightly protective of Kid—yet he can't help bursting his bubble by telling him that professional wrestling is rigged.

The next day Al decides to arrange for extra car keys to be delivered to Kid's trailer. Kid drags him to see something before he leaves—a "secret, government nuclear facility" which is in reality Al's dismantled turbine factory. After Al assures Kid that this building is harmless, they go on a joyous, destructive rampage, shooting out windows and smashing paint cans. Al sees the factory for the soul-sucking endeavor that it really was—and he doesn't dissuade Kid from his idea that he was not the "blow-hard boss." As Al and the Kid loll about in the hayfields, telling their deep, dark secrets the Kid becomes incensed when he hears a sad story about Al's childhood. It seems that Al's father did not act quickly enough to save Al's favorite pet, who had eaten some poison; by the time that they made it to the vet, the dog had died. "Your Dad's an Asshole!!," Kid screams, then stomps off. Al stares at him; Kid taps into feelings that Al himself did not even know he possessed.

When Al goes to pickup his keys from Circle Car Rental he makes a snap decision—he will have the keys delivered in two days, rather than leave right now. Something is hap-

AWARDS AND NOMINATIONS

Independent Spirit Awards 1997 Nominations:
Actor (Turturro)

pening to him—he doesn't know what or why, but he decides to go with the flow for the first time of his life. From here on, they engage in a series of ordinary activities that somehow become adventures to Kid. A trip to the supermarket ends up in front of a billboard which is throbbing with the image of the Virgin Mary (ensconced in a tattered visage of a hamburger bun). The Kid shows Al how to capture moonlight in an ornate wooden box.

When the two men stumble upon Floatie (Catherine Keener) and her sister Purlene (Lisa Blount) at the quarry, Kid's hormones kick into overdrive. His exuberant nature overrides his lack of sophistication—but hell, these women are no sophisticates either. Al is bashful, but drawn to the spectacle of these trailer-trash queens. They all jump in the water and the experience, recorded in slow motion languor, reminds one of the days before adults worried about time, taxes, and jobs. The two women end up at the Kid's the next day for a 4th of July barbecue. When Kid tells Al that Floatie is attracted to him, Al reacts in a self-righteous manner, and informs him that he is happily married. The foursome interact throughout the night; Kid comes on strong to Purlene and Floatie steals glances at Al—she is obviously smitten. When Kid sets off fireworks at the end of the night, the evening takes on a surreal quality. A bonfire is built and all four semi-strip to dance a free, joyous bacchanal around the flames, losing inhibitions along the way. Al finds himself drawn to Floatie and, despite his initial misgivings, makes love with her. He finds beauty in her awkwardness and weirdness, her oddness attracts him.

Al awakens the next morning a changed man; he confesses to Kid that ever since he saw a grey hair on his head, he has unconsciously been trying to "turn back time," that now he realizes that he has been seeing things backwards for a reason. A "red flag" reality check, if you will.

The next morning, Al's delivered his keys and takes off towards home, with the gift of the carved wooden box under his arm as a gift from the Kid. Once home, he reacts warmly to his wife, and embraces his son without even quizzing him on his math. He smiles to himself when Deb opens the wooden box and finds the original car keys Al lost hidden in a secret compartment; Al has indeed been changed forever by this chance encounter with his cosmic opposite.

—*G.E. Georges*

CREDITS

Al Fountain: John Turturro
Kid: Sam Rockwell
Floatie Dupre: Catherine Keener
Purlene Dupre: Lisa Blount
Deb Fountain: Annie Corley
Bobby Fountain: Alexander Goodwin
Soapy: Ray Aranha
Wick: Dermot Mulroney

Origin: USA
Released: 1997
Production: Marcus Viscidi and Thomas A. Bliss for Lemon Sky, Lakeshore Entertainment, and Largo Entertainment; released by Trimark Pictures
Direction: Tom DiCillo
Screenplay: Tom DiCillo
Cinematography: Paul Ryan
Editing: Camilla Toniolo
Music: Jim Farmer
Production design: Terese DePrez
Costumes: Ellen Lutter
Art direction: Steve Brennan
Set decoration: Nick Evans
Sound: Mathew Price
MPAA rating: R
Running Time: 107 minutes

REVIEWS

American Cinematographer. July, 1997, p. 66.
Entertainment Weekly. August 1 1997, p. 45.
Los Angeles Times. August 1, 1997, p. F16.
New York Times. July 25, 1997, p. C3.
New Yorker. August 4, 1997, p. 78.
People. August 11, 1997, p. 20.
Sight and Sound. May, 1997, p. 38.
USA Today. August 7, 1997, p. 3D.
Village Voice. July 29, 1997, p. 78.

The Boxer

Love is always worth fighting for.—Movie tagline

Nothing could keep them apart.—Movie tagline

"Powerful. Daniel Day-Lewis and Emily Watson are brilliant."—Sara Edwards, *NBC News Channel*

"Beautifully and sensitively acted, skillfully directed and written by Jim Sheridan."—Rex Reed, *New York Observer*

"A haunting love story."—Peter Travers, *Rolling Stone*

"Passionate. One of the year's best! Passionate, provocative and profoundly moving."—Paul Wunder, *WBAI Radio*

Just released from prison, Danny Flynn (Daniel Day-Lewis) reunites with his love Maggie (Emily Watson), but finds his freedom jeopardized when he can't break from his destructive past in *The Boxer*.

The Boxer begins with stark footage of Danny Flynn (Daniel Day-Lewis) shadow-boxing in a hooded sweatshirt in the yard of a British prison the day he is to be released for good behavior. He has served time because of his involvement with the Irish Republican Army, and though he regrets his involvement and the 14 years of his life lost in prison, where he refused to associate with other I.R.A. prisoners, he never betrayed the cause and never informed on his mates.

All Danny wants to do is to go "home" to his old neighborhood in Belfast, become a professional boxer, and train youngsters interested in the sport. His old trainer Ike Weir (Ken Stott) has his doubts because Danny is now 32 years old, but before long the two of them are back on track for a match between Danny and a fighter from Scotland. Maggie (Emily Watson), the girl Danny left behind, got married while Danny was serving his time and now has a son, Liam (14-year-old Ciaran Fitzgerald); Maggie's husband, whom she no longer loves, is serving time in prison for political terrorism, but the neighborhood code requires Maggie to be faithful, regardless of her feelings toward Danny, who obviously loves her. Maggie's father, I.R.A. leader Joe Hamill (Brian Cox) believes in the code but he is not so willing to enforce it as strictly as one of his lieutenants, Harry (Gerard McSorley), who hates Danny for other reasons, for Danny knows that Harry is a hateful, miserable coward and has protected Harry's secret in prison.

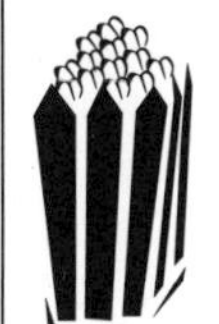

Danny to Maggie: "I've lived with you alone in silence for 14 years. You know, it's hard to talk to the real you."

Joe Hamill negotiates a cease fire with the British and is willing to work toward a peaceful settlement on the condition that the British will release all political prisoners. Harry wants to continue the bombings, however; he wants war, not peace. Danny alienates Harry further when he finds a satchel of explosives hidden in the gym and pitches it in the river. Danny is also bringing Protestants and Catholics together through their interest in boxing. While Danny boxes the Scot on the Protestant side of Belfast, Harry rigs a car bomb that explodes a British police car, killing an officer and violating the truce.

Meanwhile young Liam has seen Danny visit his mother and fears Danny will take his mother away from him, so he and his friends burn down Danny's gym. Defeated, Danny goes to England to box because Maggie has asked him to leave. Danny is successful in London, but when pitted against a Nigerian who is clearly no match for him, Danny refuses to finish the fight since he does not want to kill his opponent. Watching this fight back in Northern Ireland on television, Harry claims Danny is a quitter, but the audience knows better. When Danny's trainer Ike stands up to Harry and accuses him of being a coward, Harry simply puts a bullet in Ike's head. Young Liam is devastated by Ike's death, and Danny is furious when he learns about it. By this time Liam has accepted Danny, and Danny goes to Maggie's father to be up front with him and declare his intentions. Harry, of course, wants Danny executed, and the power struggle between Harry and his chief at the end yields interesting and surprising results.

This film has been described as the third increment of director Jim Sheridan's Irish "trilogy," but viewers need to be convinced of that. Since *The Boxer* is concerned with the "Troubles," as the Irish refer to the civil war that has divided their country; this gives the film something in common with *In the Name of the Father* (1993), which Sheridan directed, produced, and co-wrote with Belfast native Terry George. But the first film in this alleged "trilogy" is said to be *My Left Foot* (1990), in which Daniel Day-Lewis played the writer and artist Christie Brown, who struggled against being handicapped by cerebral palsy and managed to become something of a celebrity. Although the artist's biography was twisted and shaped into a sentimentalized film narrative, Day-Lewis won an Academy Award for Best Actor and earned yet another Oscar nomination for *In the Name of the Father* portraying another "true story" of a man unjustly imprisoned for fifteen years.

Daniel Day-Lewis and Jim Sheridan previously worked together on *My Left Foot* and *In the Name of the Father.*

Day-Lewis' performance in *The Boxer* is certainly worthy of another Oscar nomination. This film never strikes a false note. Even when it seems headed towards pure blarney, when "Danny Boy" is sung before one of Flynn's boxing matches, Jim Sheridan knows that the music is purposefully maudlin and manipulative, and has the British authorities orchestrating it for public-relations purposes. *New York Times* sports columnist Ira Berkow did question the way Danny stopped fighting the battered Nigerian in the London bout: "a true pro would know how to continue and win the fight without seriously damaging his opponent," Berkow noted, but Danny in the film does not have enough experience to qualify as a "true pro." At the heart of this film is a non-political fighter who abhors violence but is made to survive in terribly violent circumstances. Even Joe Hamill, wonderfully played by Brian Cox, is weary of the killing and wants to put an end to it.

Writer-director Sheridan told the *New York Times* that the film was based on the life-story of Barry McGuigan, the Irish World Featherweight Champion who trained Day-Lewis for his role for over two years. McGuigan served as captain of the Irish Olympic Boxing Team at the 1980 Moscow Games. After turning professional, he won both the European and British titles in 1983. In 1985 he was named WBA World Featherweight Champion and WBA Boxer of the Year. The fight scenes are convincingly realistic no doubt because McGuigan was on board as Boxing Consultant for the film.

Though Emily Watson was born and raised in London, she manages to pass for Irish and plays her role with impressive dignity. Janet Maslin praised her in the *New York Times* for the way she "beautifully conveys all of Maggie's melting ambivalence about a man who has been gone 14 years." Just as Emily Watson passes for Irish, Dublin passes for Belfast. The *New York Times* praised the film for its "stirring" performances. Other reviews were mixed, however. Mike Clark wrote in *USA Today* that the film's "suppression of a romantic payoff—while making dramatic sense—somewhat diminishes its emotional power, given the leads' obvious chemistry in their scenes together." *Time* critic Richard Corliss criticized the film for the way it "renounces political nuance for emotional bullying and old Hollywood-style blarney," but added that Day-Lewis nearly makes this "gritty fantasy plausible" by his "laser stare and world-class rope skipping" and "his very devotion to the project." Lisa Schwarzbaum wrote for *Entertainment Weekly* that *The Boxer* "teaches that the path to a peaceful resolution of an old, old conflict can be covered only in steps as tiny and alert as a fighter's practiced footwork." She praised the film for its "moderate stance" and for its "innately likable" principals. All critics were willing to give Day-Lewis his due, and most also praised the "magical" Emily Watson. The supporting performances by Ken Stott, Brian Cox, and Gerard McSorley are also particularly effective. The performers make the dialogue effective, as when Maggie tells her father: "I'm the prisoner here. You and your politics have made sure of that." Janet Maslin found the characters "well-drawn" in this "fine, galvanizing film" that frames the question of the Troubles "starkly while avoiding easy answers, although the central metaphors of boxing and prison powerfully reflect a wider awareness of Belfast's plight."

Examining the current state of Irish culture, Alan Riding noted in the *New York Times* that "with no tradition of its own to tap, Irish filmmaking has its roots in Irish writers," such as novelist Neil Jordan and playwright Jim Sheridan. Sheridan told Bernard Weinraub of the *New York Times* that he wanted to tell "a human universal story that cuts through politics," as his love story of forbidden romance in fact manages to do. He first considered simply an Irish reworking of the Romeo and Juliet idea, but the older lovers

AWARDS AND NOMINATIONS

Golden Globe Awards 1998 Nominations: Best Drama, Drama Actor (Day-Lewis), Director (Sheridan)

CREDITS

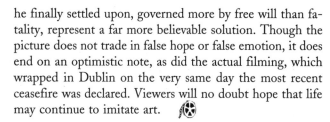

Danny Flynn: Daniel Day-Lewis
Maggie: Emily Watson
Harry: Gerard McSorley
Joe Hamill: Brian Cox
Liam: Ciaran Fitzgerald
Ike Weir: Ken Stott
Patsy: Eleanor Methven
Sean: David McBlain
Matt Maguire: Kenneth Cranham

Origin: Ireland, Great Britain
Released: 1997
Production: Jim Sheridan and Arthur Lappin for Hell's Kitchen; released by Universal Pictures
Direction: Jim Sheridan
Screenplay: Jim Sheridan and Terry George
Cinematography: Chris Menges
Editing: Gerry Hambling
Music: Gavin Friday, Maurice Seezer
Production design: Brian Morris
Art direction: Fiona Daly, Richard Earl
Costumes: Joan Bergin
Sound: Kieran Horgan
Boxing consultant: Barry McGuigan
MPAA rating: R
Running Time: 107 minutes

he finally settled upon, governed more by free will than fatality, represent a far more believable solution. Though the picture does not trade in false hope or false emotion, it does end on an optimistic note, as did the actual filming, which wrapped in Dublin on the very same day the most recent ceasefire was declared. Viewers will no doubt hope that life may continue to imitate art.

—*James M. Welsh*

REVIEWS

Boxoffice. February, 1998, p. 52.
Detroit News. January 9, 1998, p. C1.
Entertainment Weekly. January 16, 1998, p. 42.
Los Angeles Times. December 31, 1997, p. F1.
New York Times. September 14, 1997.
New York Times. December 21, 1997, Sec. 2, p. 1.
New York Times. December 31, 1997, p. E1.
New York Times. January 2, 1998, p. B7.
New York Times. January 4, 1998, Sec.2, p. 11.
People. January 19, 1998, p. 17.
Rolling Stone. January 22, 1998, p. 62.
Sight and Sound. March, 1998, p. 41.
Time. January 12, 1998, p. 84.
USA Today. December 31, 1998, p. D1.
Variety. December 22, 1997, p. 59.
Village Voice. January 6, 1998, p. 66.
Washington Post. January 9, 1998, p. D1.

Boyfriends

"A queer *Big Chill* for the nineties!"—*Miami New Times*

"A perceptive comedy of modern gay manners [with] freewheeling sexual behavior."—Stephen Holden, *The New York Times*

Boyfriends marks the feature film debut of the British writing and directing team of Neil Hunter and Tom Hunsinger. Made for a mere $25,000 and shot in just eighteen days, the film grew out of interviews that Hunter and Hunsinger conducted with roughly one hundred actors. After asking these interviewees about their lives, lifestyles, and fantasy lives, the writer-directors arrived at a sextet of characters that illustrate in brief the spectrum of modern gay life.

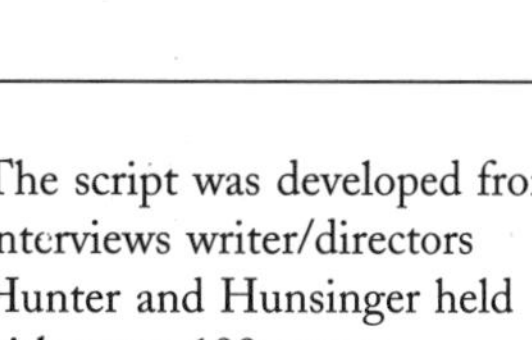

The script was developed from interviews writer/directors Hunter and Hunsinger held with some 100 actors.

As *Boyfriends* opens, we are introduced to the three couples who will absorb most of our attention for the next eighty-one minutes. The first consists of ill-humored Ben (Mark Sands) and highly domestic Paul (James Dreyfus). The two have lived together for five years and are plainly on the verge of a break-up. Paul even goes so far as to accuse Ben of trying to kill his favorite plant by blowing cigarette smoke on it: plainly Paul sees some analogy between his role and that of the plant in the domestic dynamic. Next we meet uptight, insecure Matt (Michael Urwin) who is serving an anniversary breakfast to his handsome, fey actor boyfriend, Owen (Andrew Ableson). After three months of dating, Matt wants Owen to commit to the relationship and set up housekeeping together. Lastly we encounter Will (David Coffey), an older social worker, and Adam (Darren

Petrucci), a Cockney boy he counselled some years earlier and slept with just the night before.

Hunter and Hunsinger create a microcosm of gay life by bringing these three disparate couples together for a weekend. The pretext for the get-together is a birthday party for Paul, which is being held over the course of a weekend at a country home once owned by Paul's brother, now dead. The English country house weekend is, of course, a well-worn plot device, and Hunter and Hunsinger honor its many conventions. Still, as the couples break apart and then regroup, the directors manage to prevent the formula from going stale. Not all of the performances are strong, but there is enough freshness in the improvised dialogue and unique cast of characters to prevent filmgoers from constantly predicting what comes next.

By the time they arrive at the country house, Paul and Ben have agreed to split up. Owen, who has been trying to squirm out of his involvement with Matt, manages to find a couple of willing alternative partners to help him break the connection. First, during an outing in the woods, Owen encounters an attractive stranger with whom he has quick, anonymous sex. The stranger turns out to be James (Michael McGrath), Paul's dead brother's former lover and the current owner of the country house, to which he has unexpectedly returned. Later that evening, Adam, whose short attention span strays from the much older Will to Owen, provides another excuse for Owen to break with Matt. Poor, self-conscious Matt fails dismally when Owen and Matt attempt to include him in three-way sex.

Borrowing a page out of another weekend country house idyll, *The Big Chill* (1983), Hunter and Hunsinger focus on the restlessness and anxiety that beset the three couples by having Paul ask the others acerbic questions while recording their responses on videotape. Presumably much of the improvised dialogue of these interviews mirrors what the directors themselves found when they were casting their film. Despite differences in affect and articulation, there is a great deal of emphasis on love, commitment, and compatibility.

The night of his birthday party, it seemed funny and ironic that the misanthropic Paul should be given two books on making gay relationships work. The next morning, however, the relevance of these how-to manuals to his life—and to those of the others—is revealed. During a walk at the beach, Paul discloses that a large part of his dissatisfaction with Ben has grown out of his infatuation with a man, Owen, whom he met at his brother's funeral. And Owen, who has seemed until then the embodiment of promiscuity, in turn reveals his romantic nature when he confesses his love to Paul. Perhaps he goes on too long, though. After Owen explains that he only stayed with Matt because he hoped that Matt's friendship with Paul might provide him with another chance encounter with the true object of his affections, Paul has second thoughts. Realizing that his relationship with Ben is the truer, more significant one, Paul rejects Owen's entreaties, and he and Ben agree to work things out.

Will and Adam reconcile, too. After chastising Adam for hitting on all his friends, Will accepts his apologies, and the two drive back to London together. Along the way they pick up Owen, the only one left out in the cold. After learning of Owen's many deceptions, Matt has thrown him out of his car and out of his life. In the end, *Boyfriends* seems to stand for the proposition that in modern gay society, loyalty and honesty outweigh romance and purely sensual appeal.

—Lisa Paddock

CREDITS

Paul: James Dreyfus
Ben: Mark Sands
Owen: Andrew Ableson
Will: David Coffey
Matt: Michael Urwin
Adam: Darren Petrucci
James: Michael McGrath
Mark: Russell Higgs

Origin: Great Britain
Released: 1996
Production: Neil Hunter and Tom Hunsinger; released by First Run Features
Direction: Neil Hunter, Tom Hunsinger
Screenplay: Neil Hunter and Tom Hunsinger
Cinematography: Richard Tisdall
Editing: John Trumper
Art direction: James Dearlove
Set decoration: Elise Napier
MPAA rating: Unrated
Running Time: 82 minutes

REVIEWS

New York Times. February 14, 1997, p. B12.
Sight and Sound. July, 1996, p. 39.
Variety. March 25, 1996, p. 69.
Village Voice. February 25, 1997, p. 72.

Brassed Off

Fed up with the system. Ticked off at the establishment. And mad about . . . each other.—Movie tagline

"Inspiring . . . One of the best films of the year!"—Jim Svejda, *CBS-Radio*

"A rousing crowd-pleaser!"—Amy Dawes, *LA Daily News*

"Two thumbs up!"—*Siskel & Ebert*

"Everyone I've recommended this film to leaves the theatre smiling!"—Jeffrey Lyons, *WNBC-TV*

Box Office: $2,589,188

B*rassed Off* is a film that is, at times, warmly engrossing, whimsical, and charming and, although it occasionally ventures into overly-emotional territory, it ultimately scores high in flat-out entertainment value. Although the characters may be familiar, the actors and their performances are so heartfelt that the uneven pitch of the storyline can be forgiven.

Phil: "I love the band—we all do—but there's other things in life that are more important."
Danny: "Not in my book."

Taking a drastic turn from his last directorial outing, *Blame It On the Bellboy,* writer/director Mark Herman shows a Yorkshire village, Grimley, at an important crossroads in 1992. Grimley has fallen on hard times, and the Thatcher government is gearing up to hand down a crucial decision; soon the town's miners (some of whom are second and third generation) will get to vote on whether to keep the mine open, or take a government buy-out (in Thatcher-ite terms "redundancy"). Like many towns of this ilk, the townspeople gather in the pubs to commiserate, plot, plan or complain. Grimley also has a first-rate brass band—or rather, it used to be first rate until members became so worried about their jobs, paychecks and families that the band itself seems frivolous and an unnecessary luxury.

The actual Grimethorpe Colliery Brass Band supplied the soundtrack and musician extras.

To everyone but Danny (Pete Postlethwaite), that is. Danny, a retired miner, is their strict, no-nonsense bandleader, the man who has led the Grimley Colliery Band for years and years, and who is all but oblivious to the town's economic problems. Danny rules his band with such an iron-fist that even his friends and stalwart band members Harry (Jim Carter) and Greasely (Kenneth Colley) cannot work up the courage to resign. Danny is so self-absorbed that he doesn't even notice how his son Phil's (Stephen Tompkinson) life is in shambles; his wife Sandra (Melanie Hill) is at her wit's end with their dwindling finances and cannot believe that Phil is still humoring his father with the band's activities.

At band practice the men are shocked to see a lovely woman enter with her flugelhorn. She is Gloria (Tara Fitzgerald), who was raised in Grimley, but left years ago. This makes Andy (Ewan McGregor) extremely happy; he had a terrific crush on Gloria and has never really shaken her from his system. Despite initial misgivings, the men welcome Gloria into the band. After all, they are about to enter a few competitions—wouldn't a pretty girl be a welcome addition?

Although the town may be in a downward spiral, band members surreptitiously decide to hang on just a bit longer to help Danny through the last lap of the competition. In perfect "Honeymooners" style, Harry and Greasely lustily chat up Gloria; that is, until their wives catch wind of the new female flugelhorn player and decide to tag along as "cheerleaders." Andy and Gloria circle each other—their attraction is still evident. What Andy doesn't know is that Gloria has been recruited by the British Coal Board and is secretly amassing statistics to present as evidence as to whether the mine can turn around and be profitable. Gloria keeps mum about her job; she deftly skirts any questions about why she has come home after all these years.

When the band plays in the next level of competition, it is an unmitigated disaster; the members drink, jostle each other and can barely remember the simplest of tunes. Danny is disgusted and tells the members off; he implores them to keep the Grimley Colliery Band tradition going and not to let it die. Danny is so truly blind to his band members' circumstances that he seems personally wounded when Harry and thc others tell him that they are in dire straits. But Danny has a secret of his own; he is suffering from black lung disease, from his own years spent in the mines. The band, literally and figuratively, is the only thing that is keeping Danny alive. Its members look on, horrified, as Danny collapses in the street, coughing up blood.

Phil places his father in the hospital and watches as his own life falls deeper into chaos. His wife Sandra cannot bear watching repo men carry out any more furniture, or bear up under the charity of friends, while enduring her husband's blind devotion to the band. Herman handles these family-in-crisis scenes with compassion and honesty; Sandra is in an untenable position—she is watching her spouse flounder, and loose his grip with his own reality. Phil finally admits to his dad that he and Sandra are separated, and she has taken the kids with her. Although Danny has already heard this piece of news from the town gossips, he is heartbroken to see his son this way.

Meanwhile, Andy and Gloria have consummated their flirtation; neither of them can really believe that they are in each other's orbit once again and they are trying to sort out their feelings. Andy is shocked, therefore, to see Gloria emerging from the British Coal Board office. As shocked as he is, the rest of the gang are furious and bitter. Gloria, once the "golden girl-savior" of the band, is now regarded as a traitor to both the band and her own heritage in the town.

Despite the turmoil in the band they manage to sweep the preliminaries, ending up in the finals that will be held at London's Albert Hall. The band serenades Danny in his hospital room, a mournful "Danny Boy," that is the emotional high-point of the film.

The town is broken apart when the majority of the miners vote to accept the government's buy-out; it is a crushing blow to the men who want to stay, and to the dozens of townspeople who have sat outside the mine and protested the redundancy for months. Gloria is revolted by her boss' decision; when she approaches her superior and demands to know why her positive research about the mine was not taken more seriously, she is laughed out of his office. She is disgusted at the way she was suckered, and angry that she unwittingly contributed to the mine's closing.

Gloria and Andy stop seeing each other, succumbing to the pressures surrounding her. Phil is so desperate to earn some money that he stoops to dressing up as a clown at wealthy children's birthday parties. His composure breaks at one party and he launches into a diatribe that is as heartbreaking and woeful as it is frightening to the children. Phil finally tries to hang himself from a girder at the mine. He doesn't succeed, but his father looks up from his hospital bed to see his son's enormous purple-and-red clown feet being wheeled past. Father and son finally have a real, sitdown talk; Danny is shaken to the core by the naked emotion and pain that Phil is experiencing. Suddenly, the band doesn't seem so important.

Andy, Harry, and Greasely commiserate at the local pub. While they all agree that it would be the right and proper thing to follow through with the competition finals—both for Danny's sake and for the general respect of the town—where would they come up with the hefty entrance fee? All are surprised, none more than Andy, when Gloria shows up with the money. She explains that it was the least she could do; besides the competition is extremely important to her too.

The band heads to London. They play as they never have before, a stirring and moving rendition of "The William Tell Overture," which brings down the house. Danny appears, weakened but ecstatic, just in time to see his beloved Colliery Band win the most coveted prize in the land. Danny holds the prize cup in his hand—and declines. He declines on behalf of all his colleagues, friends and family members who have ben cast off, laid off, and jerked around—generally made to feel worthless and to use the government's own phrase "redundant." It is a moving, stirring, emotional speech. Gloria and Andy reconcile and decide to face their mutual unemployment together.

CREDITS

Danny: Pete Postlethwaite
Gloria: Tara Fitzgerald
Andy: Ewan McGregor
Harry: Jim Carter
Jim: Philip Jackson
Phil: Stephen Tompkinson
Ernie: Peter Martin
Greasely: Kenneth Colley
Sandra: Melanie Hill

Origin: Great Britain
Released: 1996
Production: Steve Abbott for Prominent Features, Channel Four Films; released by Miramax Films
Direction: Mark Herman
Screenplay: Mark Herman
Cinematography: Andy Collins
Editing: Michael Ellis
Music: Trevor Jones
Production design: Don Taylor
Art direction: Felicity Joll
Costumes: Amy Roberts
Sound: Peter Lindsay
Brass band music coordinator: John Anderson
MPAA rating: R
Running Time: 107 minutes

REVIEWS

Boxoffice. March, 1997, p. 47.
Detroit News. May 31, 1997, p. C1.
Entertainment Weekly. May 30, 1997, p. 54.
Los Angeles Times. May 23, 1997, p. F9.
New York Times. May 23, 1997, p. B21.
New Yorker. May 26, 1997, p. 88.
People. June 6, 1997, p. 21.
Sight and Sound. November, 1996, p. 44.
USA Today. May 23, 1997, p. 3D.
Variety. October 28, 1996, p. 71.
Village Voice. May 27, 1997, p. 22.

As the credits roll, information scrolls by that informs the audience as to the number of mines and towns that have been "downsized" and made "redundant" over the past few years. As indicated before, director Herman hovers on overly emotional scenes that play on at too high a pitch, but he is aided by his superlative acting ensemble. Stephen Tompkinson, as Phil, particularly shines in his role of a man stretched to his absolute limit. Pete Postlethwaite is, as usual, wonderfully expressive, sympathetic, and irritating—all at the same time.

—G.E. Georges

Breakdown

A cross-country trip. An unexpected breakdown. The trap has been set.—Movie tagline

It could happen to you.—Movie tagline

"This film delivers!"—Roger Ebert, *Chicago Sun-Times*

"*Breakdown* is a first-class movie thriller, technically awesome and outrageously exciting. The best high-tech nail-biter since *Speed*."—Michael Wilmington, *Chicago Tribune*

"A tense, beautifully crafted, edge-of-your-seat thriller."—Jack Mathews, *Los Angeles Times*

"Packs a punch! A tough, vigorous exercise in pure action. Kurt Russell makes a fit and handsome action hero."—Janet Maslin, *New York Times*

"A high-octane thriller! Will keep you entertained and on the edge of your seat."—Leah Rozen, *People*

"Fresh and exciting!"—Mike Clark, *USA Today*

"An eighteen-wheeler of an action thriller. *Breakdown* carries the freight and then some."—Joe Morgenstern, *The Wall Street Journal*

Box Office: $50,159,144

To four scruffy outlaws of the rural Southwest, a man and woman driving down a desert highway in a Jeep Grand Cherokee with Massachusetts plates must have money to burn. In fact, they may be worse off economically than their pursuers. That's only one of the many ironic elements masterfully woven into the straight-ahead thriller *Breakdown*, a film that effortlessly comments on the American dream while providing plenty of heartfelt emotion and heart-stopping action.

In this exquisitely tense thriller, Jeff Taylor (Kurt Russell) and his wife Amy (Kathleen Quinlan) are urban yuppies who look like easy and profitable marks to the quartet of rednecks who waylay them. But writer-director Jonathan Mostow's brilliant script is like a shattered mirror, and neither the Taylors nor their pursuers are exactly what they seem.

As they drive down the road, we learn that the Taylors are changing jobs, are short on cash and are up to their necks in car payments and, one can safely assume, credit-card debt. Their professions aren't revealed, but it hardly matters. Like millions of Americans, they're struggling against a downsizing corporate culture that makes their upper-middle-class affectations mere window dressing for a deeper malaise. The Southwestern country boys, who salve their own dead-end lives with hatred for the likes of the Taylors and the liberal, snobbish lifestyle they symbolize, may have more assets than their prey. Once you grasp this insight, *Breakdown* becomes more than the year's most taut and effective suspense drama. It's a no-nonsense terror ride, but it's also a trenchant comment on the way that distinct cultural groups fight for the spoils of a bankrupt American dream while failing utterly to see their commonality.

Mostow's script, played out across the barren landscape of the high desert, places the breakneck, close-quarters action and almost choking emotion of the high-powered plot against the background of an implacable landscape, as if nature itself is an unfeeling enemy. It evokes the old Westerns where Native American "savages" ambush the wagon trains of poor white settlers; it's the rootless preying on the restless. And everything about this remarkable film jangles the nerves of our rootlessness and restlessness.

Amy, as they drive across the desert: "This could be the worst decision we ever made."

Like all masterful films, *Breakdown* never stops to reveal its purpose, but keeps the viewer's mind churning through an absorbing plot with plenty of twists and surprises. For Jeff Taylor, the Everyman protagonist, and thus for the audience, what happens is like a series of Pandora's boxes, each unleashing a more horrifying new danger. At the end, the heroes and the audience are drained rather than elated, yet another testament to the authenticity of this extraordinary movie, which serves up melodramatic action without ever wallowing in cheap histrionics and sentimentalism.

Writer/director Jonathan Mostow got the idea for the film when he and his wife were driving from Los Angeles to Las Vegas.

For Jeff Taylor, it's a trial by fire: a tough, relentless, unsparing measure of his mettle. At film's start, Russell's character doesn't look up to the task. He seems lazy, flaccid, easily distracted. Then, as his predicament becomes clear and he realizes his wife has been abducted, he seems overwhelmed first by fear, then anger. He soon is made to realize he must improvise and fight to survive, and he has no choice but to become more than he ever has been. This forced transformation into a man of unshakable courage and resourcefulness rings true, an amazing accomplishment for both Mostow and Russell, an actor who uses understatement to wondrous effect.

Even in the moments of his most breathtaking bravery, Russell's Taylor is awfully human. On a desperate, daredevil ride on the undercarriage of the villain's truck, his only weapon, a gun, falls out of his pocket. Trying to make his escape from the outlaws' lair, he cannot find the keys to several potential escape vehicles and doesn't know how to jump-start them. Though his cunning increases as his trial intensifies, he never completely loses his naivete.

The film to which *Breakdown* harkens most pointedly is *Deliverance* (1972). Like the latter, it's a story of city folk who are trapped out of their element in the American wilds. The natives they meet are cunning and amoral. There is even an imbecilic hick, but this time, he is not what he seems. And here, unlike in *Deliverance*, the enemy is surprisingly sophisticated. Mostow gives his rural villains the upper hand technologically. Taylor's cell phone doesn't work when he tries to call for help, but the murderous thieves communicate by cell phones, have seemingly unlimited surveillance technology and resources, and frequently outwit their more educated opponent.

Heightening the irony, near film's end Taylor must battle the gang at its hideout, a barn on the big homestead of Red Barr (J.T. Walsh), the cunning ringleader. Barr has a wife, a son, and an apparently successful life of crime disguised behind his job as a trucker. The rural setting might be different, but in other respects Barr has the kind of life to which the Taylors might aspire.

As it is, the Taylors can only dream of success. Reading a donut wrapper that promises a $90,000 prize to a sweepstakes winner, Amy Taylor fantasizes about how the money will solve their problems. It's remarkable how the donut package figures into the plot, as the Taylors discover how to use their captors' inflated notion of their Yankee wealth to fool them. One of the most satisfying things about this extremely satisfying film is how long it takes for the opponents to see beneath their initial impressions and learn the true measure of each other.

The story is simple yet masterful in its unweaving of the captors' web. Unlike many suspense thrillers where the action is jacked up, *Breakdown* is logical throughout, down to the killers' motivations. The film opens with Jeff Taylor narrowly averting an accident when a pick-up trucks pulls out in front of him on a desert road. At a gas station, the truck's driver, wearing a black shirt and a white cowboy hat, berates Taylor. Then, down the road, the Taylors' car breaks down, the cowboy drives past, then turns around and waits up the road, and a big 18-wheeler pulls up. The driver seems friendly and offers to help by taking them to a diner down the road where they can call for a tow truck.

Jeff's refusal of the offer seems stupid. Amy argues, logically enough, that it's hot, it's the middle of nowhere, and no other help is likely to be forthcoming. Jeff doesn't want to leave the car and all their belongings out in the middle of nowhere, so he stays. Amy walks into the truck, and into the trap.

What follows is Kafkaesque and mesmerizing. At the diner, a greasy spoon populated by menacing-looking locals, everyone swears they haven't seen Jeff's wife. When Jeff runs down the trucker on the road and a cop pulls up, the driver is alone and swears he's never seen Jeff or his wife. The trooper lets the trucker leave, and suggests Jeff go back to town and see his deputy.

As Jeff, with increasing despair, studies a wall full of pictures of missing women and children, the deputy douses his remaining hopes with discouraging words. Mostow's close-ups of the grainy photos of the disappeared are chilling, and Russell's grimaces are those of a man pierced to his heart. When, back at the diner, a seemingly retarded boy tips him off to his wife's whereabouts and says the police are in on the kidnapping plot, Jeff's separation from the civilized world he knew and relied on is complete, and he is on his own.

The rest of the film is harrowing and exhilarating by turns, as Jeff and his nemeses exchange positions of relative advantage, though it's Jeff who's always battling the longest odds. Throughout, the pacing is superb and the acting flawless. Walsh, who's played similar villains before, most notably in *Red Rock West* (1995), here displays sheer malevolence beneath his civilized facade. Billy (Jack Noseworthy), the other polished performer in the outlaw troupe, is chilling in his own smart-aleck way. Quinlan is fine in her limited role. Russell is brilliant and utterly believable.

Breakdown has the sharpness of a razor blade and the tenacity of water torture. Yet it is also a picture about the

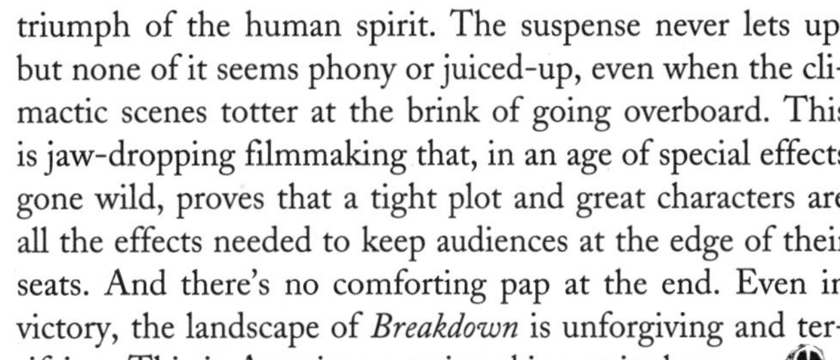

triumph of the human spirit. The suspense never lets up, but none of it seems phony or juiced-up, even when the climactic scenes totter at the brink of going overboard. This is jaw-dropping filmmaking that, in an age of special effects gone wild, proves that a tight plot and great characters are all the effects needed to keep audiences at the edge of their seats. And there's no comforting pap at the end. Even in victory, the landscape of *Breakdown* is unforgiving and terrifying. This is American moviemaking at its best.

—Michael Betzold

CREDITS

Jeff Taylor: Kurt Russell
Red Barr: J.T. Walsh
Amy Taylor: Kathleen Quinlan
Earl: M.C. Gainey
Billy: Jack Noseworthy
Sheriff Boyd: Rex Linn

Origin: USA
Released: 1997
Production: Martha De Laurentiis, Dino De Laurentiis for Spelling Films; released by Paramount Pictures
Direction: Jonathan Mostow
Screenplay: Jonathan Mostow and Sam Montgomery
Cinematography: Doug Milsome
Editing: Kevin Stitt
Music: Basil Poledouris
Production design: Victoria Paul
Art direction: Lee Mayman
Costumes: Terry Dresbach
Sound: Felipe Borrero
Stunt coordinator: Jim Arnett, Pat Romano
MPAA rating: R
Running Time: 93 minutes

REVIEWS

Boxoffice. July, 1997, p. 93.
Chicago Tribune. May 2, 1997, p. 4.
Entertainment Weekly. May 9, 1997, p. 54.
Los Angeles Times. May 2, 1997, p. F1.
New York Times. May 2, 1997, p. B10.
People. May 12, 1997, p. 23.
Sight and Sound. March, 1998, p. 42.
USA Today. May 2, 1997, p. 12D.
Variety. April 28, 1997, p. 99.

Breaking Up

When the sex is great. When the passion is intense. When the love is this strong. It's time for . . . *Breaking Up.*—Movie tagline

Breaking Up, the late year, low-budget film directed by Robert Greenwald is a stunningly embarrassing example of just how bad a Hollywood production can get. This travesty, based on the play by Michael Cristofer, takes an intimate look at a couple falling out of love. It is monumentally downbeat which, in and of itself, isn't a bad thing. Tragedies (especially those making their debut on the stage) have a place in modern cinema, although the audience for such productions is rapidly shrinking. One glance at the paltry boxoffice numbers for the critically acclaimed *Leaving Las Vegas* (1995) will confirm this: the masses want happy endings. Real life offers up enough bad news, they don't want to have to pay money to get depressed. But often times, a good shot of the blues is what we need to make us appreciate the good times even more. *Breaking Up* is not a good shot of anything, save for a 90-minute waste of your time.

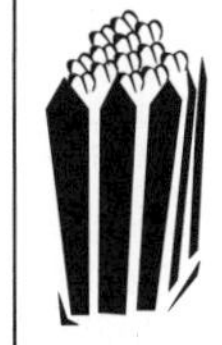

Monica on their relationship: "It's a failure, but it's ours."

The foundation is certainly sound. Greenwald had previously helmed the comedy *Sweet Hearts Dance* (1988), the Marlee Matlin thriller *Hear No Evil* (1993), the 1980 musical *Xanadu* and the Emmy-nominated television miniseries "A Woman Of Independent Means" starring Sally Field. Cristofer won both the Pulitzer and Tony Awards for *The Shadow Box* later made into a 1980 feature directed by Paul Newman and starring Joanne Woodward. His credits also include screen adaptations of the novels *The Witches Of Eastwick* (1987), *The Bonfire of the Vanities* (1990), and *Mr. Jones* (1993). The behind-the-camera talent was in good order and much can be said for the onscreen talent as well. Australian actor Russell Crowe, who made such a strong showing in *L.A. Con-*

fidential (1997), has made great strides in American productions in a relatively short amount of time. Mexican actress Salma Hayek, once the queen of soap operas in her native land, has had a tougher transition. Having already been cast in roles that accentuate her ample physical attributes, Hayek wants to be taken as a serious actress but doesn't seem able to pull it off. It's clear she is sorely miscast here, but her role is in no way the only thing wrong with the production.

Crowe plays Steve, a photographer who thinks his commercial shots of fruit are tantamount to high art. He's in the midst of an on-again, mostly off-again relationship with teacher Monica (Hayek). Greenwald and Cristofer's first and most detrimental problem is not showing Steve and Monica in happier times. We're given no background information about their relationship, thus no reason to want them to resolve their problems and get back together. Even the included flashback scenes, which could have explained "the good times", merely rehash and amplify the "bad times." Cristofer is obviously a talented writer and knows the adaptation process well. Often times, however, adapting one's own work can prove to be a losing proposition.

Breaking Up has the look and feel of little more than a home video of a play. Greenwald gets cute with some basic filming techniques (split screen, black-and-white film, grainy and discolored stock) that attempt to add some variety and texture but just end up being an annoyance. The track record of adapting stage plays to the screen is dismal at best. Cristofer's work might have been better served by using someone else's perspective for the screen version of his play. Also working against the film is the lack of any supporting players. Crowe and Hayek have the only two speaking parts and spend the entire time spouting hand-wringing, teeth-gnashing, finger-pointing drivel at each other; there's no break in the action. Such combative, whiny material needs a balance and the only diversion offered is that old movie standby—hot sex. When they're not fighting, they're having sex. Crowe and Hayek have done their best work when playing characters that are slightly off-kilter. Romantic entanglement that makes halfhearted stabs at satirical comedy isn't either of their strong suits. Greenwald's annoyingly blurred, muted tones only draw unwanted attention to the bellicose dialogue, shoddy appearance, and miscast female lead. This adds up to little more than cinematic static. "Breaking up is hard to do," a man once said. It's definitely hard to do right.

CREDITS

Steve: Russell Crowe
Monica: Salma Hayek

Origin: USA
Released: 1997
Production: Robert Greenwald and George Moffly for New Regency; released by Warner Bros.
Direction: Robert Greenwald
Screenplay: Michael Cristofer
Cinematography: Mauro Flore
Editing: Suzanne Hines
Music: Mark Mothersbaugh
Production design: Terrence Foster
Set decoration: Karen E. Burnett
Costumes: Kelly Vitric
Sound: Felipe Borrero
MPAA rating: R
Running Time: 90 minutes

REVIEWS

Boxoffice. September, 1997, p. 114
Hollywood Reporter. June 10, 1997, p. 10.
Sight and Sound. March, 1998, p. 43.
Variety. June 23, 1997, p. 95.

Broken English

Sometimes when you make love you make war.—Movie tagline

"Bold! hard-hitting!"—Jay Carr, *Boston Globe*

"Wild! Combustible! Sexy!"—Daphne Davis, *Movies & Videos*

"An impassioned offbeat film . . . portrayed with astonishing naturalness by Alexsandra Vujcic."—Janet Maslin, *New York Times*

"Extremely powerful! The performances are riveting! Aleksandra Vujcic is a bright new star!"—Jeffrey Lyons, *Sneak Previews*

"Absorbing!"—Mike Clark, *USA Today*

"A bright, energetic and moving romance! Unique and refreshingly different."—Paul Wunder, *WBAI Radio*

"Explosive!"—Dr. Joy Browne, *WOR Radio*

New Zealand director Gregor Nicholas' impassioned interracial love story, *Broken English*, is essentially a modern day *Romeo and Juliet*, a cross-cultural tale of forbidden love where the Capulets are from war-torn Croatia and the Montagues are of the New Zealand earth. Set in a fresh environment where feelings of displacement run rampant amid a melting pot powder keg, this theme of ethnic clashes is very similar to producer Robin Schole's *Once Were Warriors* (1994).

Nina about living in a war zone: "I had my own shelter. I had the shelter of my mind, which I carry with me wherever I go."

Broken English begins with a compelling voice-over from Nina, purportedly written by the film's star Aleksandra Vujcic, as she strolls through her war-torn homeland: "I have shelter of my mind, which I carry with me wherever I go." What starts out as a compelling cultural dialogue, however, quickly lapses into a trite melodrama with an all-too-predictable storyline. The film's one saving grace is the intensity and alluring sensuality of the talented cast.

Like her character Aleksandra Vujcic emigrated from Croatia to New Zealand. Casting director Fiona Edgar spotted her in a bar and offered Vujcic her first acting job.

Aleksandra Vujcic, whom makes her acting debut as Nina, was discovered in an Auckland bar. Having emigrated from Croatia to New Zealand just over a year earlier, Vujcic was working as a receptionist when her big break came. She initially had no particular ambitions to act; but once she committed to Nicholas' project, she brought with her both a blitheness and tempestuousness that combines with an unbridled sexuality and an entrancing emotional clarity.

Nina is the hot-blooded and rebellious apple of her daddy's eye. Ivan (the dynamic Rade Serbedzija of *Before the Rain* [1994] and *The Saint* [1997]) is a volatile and fiercely proud man whose violent streak and macho possessiveness has Nina chafing at the bit for a little freedom. Stubbornly nationalistic and reluctant to assimilate into what he calls "this place at the bottom of the earth," Ivan seethes at the news reports documenting the injustices against his ravaged homeland. He transfers his anger to his festive Polynesian neighbors and explodes at the slightest affront.

When Nina jumps hedonistically into a passionate affair with Eddie (*Once Were Warriors*'s Julian Arahanga), the sexy new cook at the restaurant where she is a waitress, it triggers a violent family maelstrom. When he catches his one daughter having sex in the back of his friend's Jaguar, Ivan and his obedient son, Darko (Marton Csokas), demolish the car. He would prefer that no one even date his beautiful Nina—especially some swarthy Maori like Eddie. Ivan orders Nina to stay away from Eddie, but that just strengthens her disobedient resolve. Like a fairy tale princess in an ivory tower, Nina is literally boarded up in her bedroom just prior to the big confrontation scene between Ivan and Eddie. Seems one interracial grandchild—from his eldest daughter—is enough for Ivan and he will not tolerate another.

To complicate matters further, Nina, in a desperate attempt to gain her financial freedom, agrees to a "green card" wedding to the fiance (Yang Li) of a Chinese political refugee (Jing Zhao) as arranged by the owner of the restaurant where they all work. Since Nina's mother is a New Zealand native, Nina is a naturalized citizen. It is a mere plot device to get Nina out of her tyrannical father's hands and into Eddie's apartment, so the Chinese couple can then move in and talk about making their own "little kiwi."

The story quickly disintegrates into a raging melodrama. Eddie is forced to cart around some kind of tree that is a Maori symbol of family ancestry, while mouthing platitudes like, "My family's in this dirt." For her part, Nina is saddled with lines like "You're out of control" to her father and "They'll hurt you real bad, Eddie!" As expected, the couple is threatened to be torn apart by their own respective inability to understand the other's cultural roots. When pres-

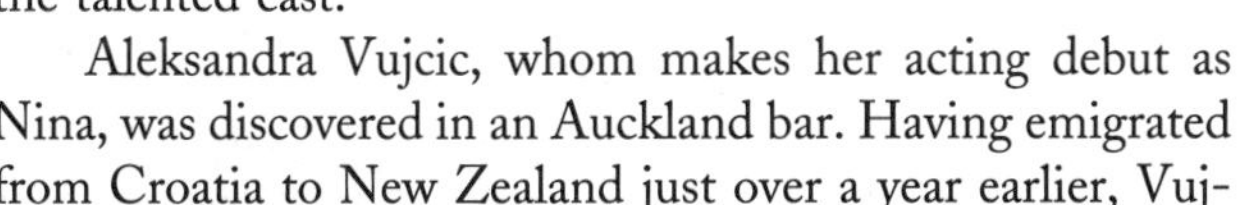

CREDITS

Nina: Aleksandra Vujcic
Eddie: Julian Arahanga
Ivan: Rade Serbedzija
Darko: Marton Csokas
Clara: Jing Zhao
Wu: Yang Li
Mira: Madeline McNamara

Origin: New Zealand
Released: 1996
Production: Robin Scholes for Communicado and Village Roadshow; released by Sony Pictures Classics
Direction: Gregor Nicholas
Screenplay: Gregor Nicholas, Johanna Pigott and Jim Salter
Cinematography: John Toon
Editing: David Coulson
Music: Murray Grindlay, Murray McNabb
Production design: Michael Kane
Art direction: Clive Memmott
Costumes: Glenis Foster
Sound: Tony Johnson
MPAA rating: NC-17
Running Time: 92 minutes

sured by Eddie to refrain from her sexy interaction with her relatives and family friends, Nina just shrugs. "Can't change nothing about who I am, you know."

The film's title comes from the influx of multi-national immigrants into New Zealand and the resultant dilution of the country's predominately British roots. The film's energy and impetus is derived from the engendered racial tension that often arises when disparate cultures are thrown together in a melting pot.

Broken English received an NC-17 rating from the MPAA in Hollywood for its "explicit sex scenes." Director Nicholas was told that he should have shot the sex from the waist up and alleges that one board member remarked, "We can't expose the youth of America to buttock-thrusting of this type." To be honest, there is nothing here that has not been seen before and while there is no explicit depiction of genitals, one of the more acrobatic sex scenes apparently was a bit too realistic for the rating board's comfort. Once again proving that violence is okay, but fervent passion apparently has no place in American cinema.

—Patricia Kowal

REVIEWS

Boxoffice. April, 1997, p. 200.
Chicago Sun Times. June 13, 1997.
Los Angeles Times. May 2, 1997, p. F18.
The New Yorker. May 12, 1997, p. 106.
New York Times. May 2, 1997, p. B16.
People. May 19, 1997, p. 22.
San Francisco Chronicle. May 23, 1997, p. C3.
San Francisco Examiner. May 23, 1997, p. C5.
Sight and Sound. August, 1997, p. 42.
USA Today. May 1, 1997, p. 3D.
Variety. September 16, 1996, p. 71.
Village Voice. May 6, 1997, p. 92.

A Brother's Kiss

Only make promises you can keep.—Movie tagline

"Intense!"—Dwight Brown, *Emerge Magazine*

"One of the most compelling debut films of the year."—Anne Marie O'Connor, *Mademoiselle*

"Chinlund is electrifying."—Dennis Dermody, *Paper*

"Nick Chinlund . . . gives a performance that is so electric that his star power, alone, could light up a marquee."—Barbara & Scott Siegel, *Siegel Entertainment Syndicate*

"Thrilling performances . . . A definite winner this season."—Tracii McGregor, *The Source*

"A compelling story. Chinlund delivers an intense, moving performance."—Chiedo Nkwocha, *Vibe*

In the late eighties, writer/director Seth Zvi Rosenfeld was told by actor Michael Raynor, with whom he'd grown up in East Harlem, that fellow actor Nick Chinlund, who was from the same neighborhood, was looking to commission a play he could act in that was based on their common interests. (It's not biographical.) So Rosenfeld wrote a one-acter, *A Brother's Kiss,* that successfully debuted off-Broadway in 1989, starring Chinlund and Raynor. The screenplay was developed as part of the Sundance Filmmaker's Lab, eventually leading to this low-budget, feature film debut for Rosenfeld.

CREDITS

Lex: Nick Chinlund
Mick: Michael Raynor
Doreen: Cathy Moriarty
Debbie: Rosie Perez
Missy: Marisa Tomei
Lefty Louie: John Leguizamo
Stingy: Michael Rapaport
Vic: Talent Harris
Young Lex: Justin Pierce
Young Mick: Joshua Danowsky
Doper: Adrian Pasdar

Origin: USA
Released: 1997
Production: Bob Potter and E. Bennett Walsh for Rosenfunk Pictures; released by First Look Pictures
Direction: Seth Zvi Rosenfeld
Screenplay: Seth Zvi Rosenfeld; based on his play
Cinematography: Fortunato Procopio
Editing: Donna Stern
Music: Frank London
Production design: Roger Fortune
Art direction: Rona Taylor
Costumes: Carolyn Greco
Sound: Jan McLaughlin
MPAA rating: R
Running Time: 92 minutes

It's a familiar kitchen-sink/gritty-street story but the talent shows through. In 1979, teenaged Lex (Justin Pierce) and his little brother Mick (Joshua Danowsky) are growing up with their loving-but-alcoholic, single mother, Doreen (Cathy Moriarty), in a tough neighborhood where being white is to be a minority. Lex dreams of being a basketball star, Mick is the quiet younger bro who wants to join the police force, and both boys know to survive on the streets is to watch out for each other. And that everything can change in an instant.

A late-night excursion through Central Park turns into a lasting nightmare. The boys are hassled by an off-duty cop, who sexually assaults Mick. Lex stabs the man and winds up in reform school. When the film picks up the duo in the present, the emotionally-damaged brothers are two sides of the same coin.

Lex (Nick Chinlund) is a charismatic-but-desperate screw-up. He's in a disintegrating marriage to the neighborhood girl, Debbie (Rosie Perez), he's gotten pregnant, but has gone from trying to support his family through menial jobs to selling cocaine for local dealer Lefty Louie (John Leguizamo). The problem is Lex is also addicted to the product he sells and is in trouble with said dealer. Mick (Michael Raynor) has indeed become a cop and settled into a structured routine. The unspoken-of sexual trauma has left him withdrawn and unable to get close to anyone. Except for Lex. If Lex once protected Mick, Mick now returns the favor, responding to his brother's phone calls, desperately trying to help him.

But of course what's always been clear in the film is that Mick can't. Lex, who had so many childhood dreams, however unrealistic, is on an inevitable downward path and even his brother's fiercest desire can't change that. You know there's no escape and it's a reflection of Chinlund's strong presence that, however badly Lex has behaved, you still wish there was someway he could be saved, and a reflection of Raynor's strength that you wish his Mick could do it.

REVIEWS

Boxoffice. April, 1997, p. 201.
Entertainment Weekly. May 9, 1997, p. 57.
Filmmaker. Spring, 1997, p. 52.
Hollywood Reporter. July 21, 1997, p. 9.
Los Angeles Times. July 18, 1997, p. F10.
New York Times. April 25, 1997, p. C15.
Variety. July 28, 1997, p. 58.
Village Voice. April 29, 1997, p. 76.

Buddy

Welcome to a family that will make yours seem tame.—Movie tagline

"The perfect family movie for the summer!" —Maria Salas, *CBS-Telenoticias*

"The top banana of family fun!"—Patty Spitler, *CBS-TV*

"Pure magic!"—John Anderson, *Los Angeles Times*

"You cannot help but be won over by *Buddy*. It's a great kids movie."—Holly Millea, *Premiere Magazine*

"A truly delightful family movie!"—Gene Shalit, *Today Show*

"Charming family entertainment."—Paul Wunder, *WBAI Radio*

Box Office: $10,111,239

Films about animals usually seek some middle ground between obvious comedy and easy pathos. While there are many good films focusing on animals, including *Lassie Come Home* (1943), *National Velvet* (1944), *Rhubarb* (1951), *The Incredible Journey* (1963), *The Three Lives of Thomasina* (1963), *Ring of Bright Water* (1969), *The Black Stallion* (1980), and *Fly Away Home* (1996), only *Babe* (1995) approaches greatness because of its filmmakers' ability to combine sentiment with wit, originality, and style, factors too often missing from films aimed primarily at children, as most animal films inevitably must. The best use of animals in films occurs in allowing them to aid in revealing depths in the human characters, as with the dog in Vittorio de Sica's *Umberto D* (1952). Writer-director Caroline Thompson attempts something along these lines in *Buddy* but fails because her quest for pathos forces her to focus too much on the title character and not enough on the humans in his life.

Based on an autobiographical book by Gertrude Davies Lintz, *Buddy* depicts the true story of the wealthy Lintz (Rene Russo) and her physician husband, Bill (Robbie

Coltrane), living in the 1930s on an estate whose house and grounds are overrun with dogs, cats, horses, geese, raccoons, chimpanzees, a hedgehog, a parrot, and other creatures. Trudy's dogs have won numerous competitions, but her real challenge comes from trying to raise apes as if they were humans. After proving her then-revolutionary—according to the film—theories with Maggie and Joe, the chimpanzees, she acquires a dying infant gorilla from a Philadelphia zoo. The fate of the gorilla's mother is unclear, as is why the zoo contacts Trudy since the keeper is shocked when she takes the baby away. Such problems of clarity, motivation, and tone are the film's main flaws.

Trudy to Buddy: "I don't just belong to you, you know. Well, maybe I do."

After nursing to health the baby she names Buddy, Trudy decides to raise him in captivity, despite Bill's doubts resulting from the gorilla's ever-increasing size and naturally wild temperament. Any viewer who has ever seen any film or television program about well-intentioned humans daring to treat a wild beast as a pet or substitute child knows what will happen. Add predictability to the problems Thompson is unable to overcome. Buddy sees Trudy as his mother, panics when she is not near, becomes civilized up to a point, and grows increasingly depressed. When Buddy and the chimps are taken to be displayed at the Chicago World's Fair, the mischievous Maggie releases him from his cage, and he goes on a mild rampage. Back home, he turns on his beloved Trudy and knocks her down. Finally admitting she has been wrong, Trudy establishes a large natural habitat at the zoo in Philadelphia and unites Buddy with his kind.

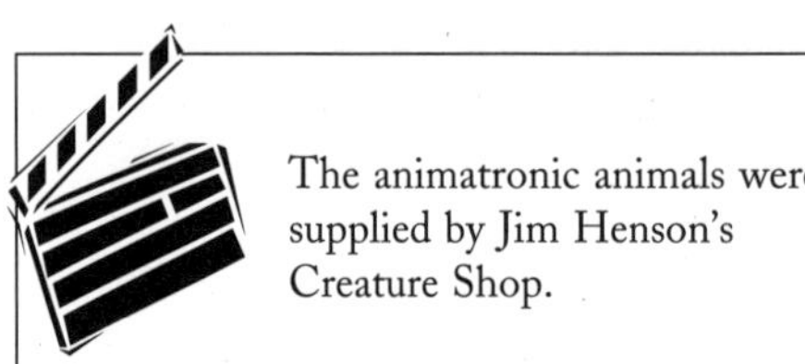

The animatronic animals were supplied by Jim Henson's Creature Shop.

The real Buddy was not so fortunate. Thompson's Buddy is a composite of two Lintz apes: Buddy and Massa. While Massa did live at the Philadelphia Zoo until he died at fifty-four, Buddy was sold to the Ringling Brothers and Barnum and Bailey Circus, spending eleven years displayed in a cage before dying. Thompson's sanitized, if half-truthful, ending, in which woman and gorilla are seemingly wiser and better off for their experiences, leaves the viewer shrugging about what point the filmmakers have been trying to make.

The film's schizophrenic nature leaves it uncertain about whether it is a children's film or a drama for adults, a moral lesson about the mistreatment of animals or a cutesy diversion about apes in pants and dresses. Thompson seems to be trying to show the dangers of treating animals as if they were human, of ignoring their true natures, but if it is wrong to make animals wear clothing, why does she present so many scenes in which human-like behavior is supposed to be funny? Trudy dresses up Maggie and Joe and takes them to see a film in a theater. Buddy and the chimps sit at table to dine with the Lintzes. Maggie rides a horse, and Joe roller skates with a kitten in his pants pocket. To demonstrate what Trudy has been able to achieve with teaching the chimpanzees, they perform various vaudeville routines on stage at the World's Fair. Thompson both shows the folly of such actions and milks them for laughs.

While *Buddy* does have a few genuinely amusing moments, as with the ability of Trudy's parrot to imitate any voice or sound it hears and the ensuing befuddlement of the housekeeper (Irma P. Hall), much of the film is likely to be disturbing for children. Not only is the adult Buddy severely depressed and angered by his circumstances, but the infant gorilla is truly terrified by anything new it encounters. Young Buddy's greatest fear occurs during a slapstick scene in which Maggie has set loose most of the animals on the Lintz estate as Thompson once again brings humorous proceedings to an awkward halt.

Buddy shares with *Babe* the technological achievements of Jim Henson's Creature Shop. The emotions of the baby Buddy, actually an animatronic puppet, are quite convincing, and the adult Buddy is mostly believable even though he is a fake gorilla inhabited at various times by nine performers and whose voice is created by three additional actors. The primary actor performing Buddy is Peter Elliott, who has created several ape parts in several films beginning with *Greystoke: The Legend of Tarzan, Lord of the Apes* (1984). The movements of Elliott and his fellow ape impersonators are credible whether Buddy is cleaning the kitchen floor, serving hors d'oeuvres, running in terror, or hulking in ennui. A greater range of facial displays, however, would have helped in creating a more memorable character.

The film's human performers fare less well. Several reviews claimed *Buddy* shows Russo's limitations since this is the first film in which she has had the lead and it is a failure. Russo has shown her comic skills in several films, most notably *Get Shorty* (1995) and *Tin Cup* (1996), but Thompson rarely calls upon her to do anything other than laugh throatily or smile tenderly at the animals' behavior. Coltrane has shown considerable comic and dramatic range in several films and particularly in his British television series "Cracker", in which he does some of the best acting in the history of the medium. As Bill Lintz, all he is allowed is showing patience and mild amusement at Trudy's eccentricities and the animals' antics. As the animals' trainer/babysitter, the great comic actor Alan Cumming, so good in *Circle of Friends* (1995) and *Emma* (1996), has little to do but showcase his dimples.

Despite its flaws, *Buddy* does succeed in proving that Thompson is a true auteur with consistent themes in her work. She has written or cowritten the screenplays for *Edward Scissorhands* (1990), *The Addams Family* (1991), *Homeward Bound: The Incredible Journey* (1993), *Tim Burton's the Nightmare Before Christmas* (1993), and *The Secret Garden* (1993), and she wrote and directed *Black Beauty* (1994), with Cumming providing the voice-over for the title character. More than an affinity for animals and the way they interact with and are misunderstood by humans, Thompson shows in her films an identification with misunderstood outsiders. Buddy is nothing less than Edward Scissorhands with fur.

Though Thompson gives her actors few opportunities, the technical work in *Buddy* shines, particularly the production design of David Nichols and Daniel Lomino, the art direction of Roland Rosenkranz and Thomas Fichter, the set decoration of Linda Spheeris, and the costume design of Colleen Attwood. *Buddy* is a joy to look at because of the sets and costumes. The bright color scheme, in which reds and yellows predominate, is at least partly inspired by the children's books of William Joyce who worked with Thompson on adapting Lintz' book. The chimpanzees' bedrooms are highlighted with charming animal decorations recalling the bright nostalgic style of such Joyce books as *George Shrinks* (1985) and *Bently & Egg* (1992). Trudy's elaborate but tasteful dresses suggest the period, and because Buddy grows to associate Trudy with red and often must be calmed by red cloth, this color is used ironically to suggest both the comfort the gorilla seeks and the danger he poses. These craftsmen fail only in being unable to disguise that the Lintz estate in Brooklyn (whose exact location is never mentioned in the film) is clearly in southern California.

Russo has said in interviews that she was attracted to *Buddy* for the opportunity to play an outrageously eccentric Auntie Mame type of character, but Thompson, unfortunately, forgot to provide any such flamboyance. It is easy to see how *Buddy* could have worked if it had focused on what drove Gertrude Lintz into turning her home into a menagerie and how this behavior affected her marriage and her relations with society in general. Buddy's plight is moving, but it is not enough to carry the film.

—Michael Adams

CREDITS

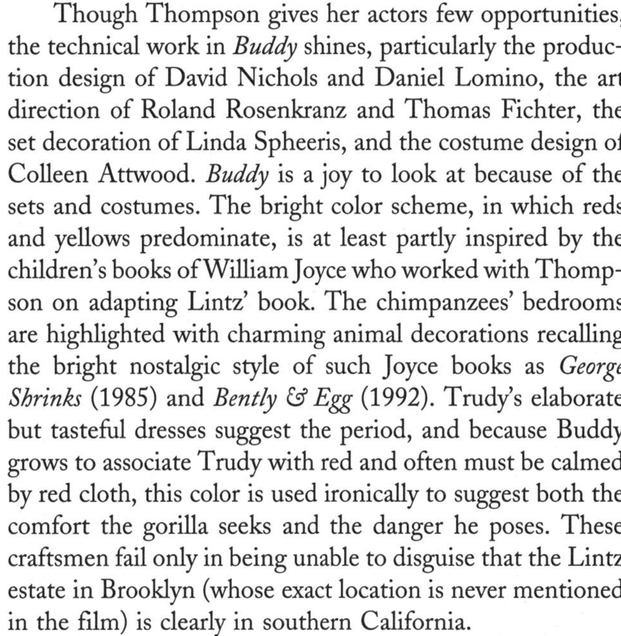

Gertrude Lintz: Rene Russo
Bill Lintz: Robbie Coltrane
Dick: Alan Cumming
Emma: Irma P. Hall
Professor Spatz: Paul Reubens

Origin: USA
Released: 1997
Production: Steve Nicolaides, Fred Fuchs for American Zoetrope, Jim Henson Pictures; released by Columbia Pictures
Direction: Caroline Thompson
Screenplay: Caroline Thompson; based on the book *Animals Are My Hobby* by Gertrude Davies Lintz
Cinematography: Steve Mason
Editing: Jonathan Shaw
Production design: David Nichols, Daniel Lomino
Art direction: Roland Rosenkranz, Thomas Fichter
Set decoration: Linda Spheeris
Costumes: Colleen Attwood
Music: Elmer Bernstein
Sound: Robert Eber
Special effects: Dennis Petersen
Casting: Carrie Frazier
MPAA rating: PG-13
Running Time: 84 minutes

REVIEWS

Boxoffice/ July, 1997, p. 89.
Chicago Tribune. June 6, 1997, p. 5.
Christian Science Monitor. June 6, 1997, p. 12.
Entertainment Weekly. June 6, 1997, p. 44.
The Hollywood Reporter. June 2, 1997, p. 5.
Los Angeles Times. June 6, 1997, p. F6.
Movieline. June, 1997, p. 52.
The New York Times. June 6, 1997, p. C12.
People. June 16, 1997, p. 21.
USA Today. June 6, 1997, p. D4.
Variety. June 6, 1997, p. 69.

Cafe Society

The shocking true story of the fall of high society.—Movie tagline

"Frank Whaley finally scores a leading role suited to his wonderfully off-kilter charm." —Maureen Callahan, *New York Magazine*

"Raymond De Felitta's nifty sleeper of a film is the rare '50s period piece that gets it right. *Cafe Society* is filmed in a style that exudes tawdry glamour."—Stephen Holden, *New York Times*

"The amount of love that went into this production could fuel Hollywood's assembly line for half a decade. Writer-director De Felitta is a skilled visualist."—Stephen Talty, *Time Out*

Cafe Society is the very slow-moving tale of a vanished post-war, New York City society where having fun is all that matters. Based on a true story that took place in 1952, writer/director De Felitta's feature film debut is set in the nightclub world of martinis, manhattans, sidecars, and other cocktails, lounge music, cigarettes, tuxedos, and pretty girls in evening gowns and furs. One of these nightclubs is the (fictitious) El Casbah where press agent Ray Davioni (John Spencer) likes to hold court.

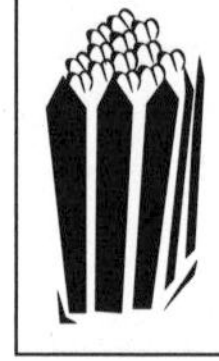

Ray about Pat: "She's new to cafe society. Nescafe, we call that."

And one night, handsome John Francis Joseph "Jack" Kale (Peter Gallagher) makes himself at home at the bar. Ray assumes Jack is an out-of-work actor but nobody's really what they seem, except for 23-year-old porno-collecting playboy and oleomargarine heir, Mickey Jelke (Whaley). Mickey's got "nightclubitis," he likes to go slumming—drinking too much, partying, and generally enjoying the lowlife. He's friends with Ray and knows he has a sideline as a pimp but then one of Mickey's dearest companions, Erica Steele (Anna Thomson), is also New York's favorite society madam.

While Jack gets acquainted with Ray, Mickey's eyes are drawn to hard-edged beauty Pat Ward (Lara Flynn Boyle, doing her best low-and-breathy bad girl voice), who walks into the club on the arm of a much-older man. Soon it's Mickey sitting at her table, buying her drinks and feeding her lines, even as Ray tells Jack that there's less to Pat than meets the eye. Jack manages to snag one of Ray's girlie pictures from his black book and checks out the photographer, where he stumbles across a racy picture of Pat, who's really Sandra from Avenue D. Meanwhile, Mickey and Pat have quickly become a romantic twosome.

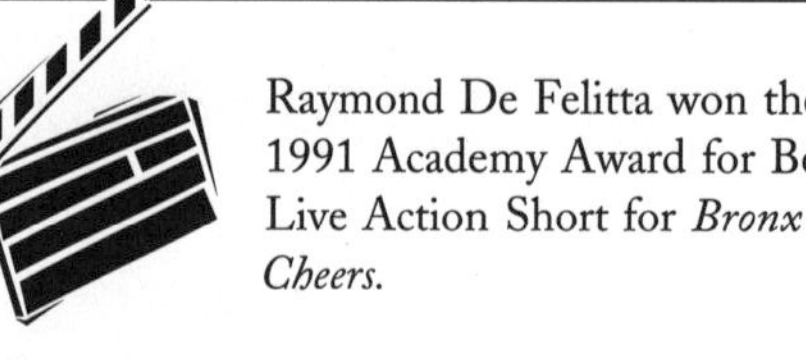

Raymond De Felitta won the 1991 Academy Award for Best Live Action Short for *Bronx Cheers.*

Jack gets in Mickey's good graces after helping him out of a nightclub fight but also lets Pat know that he knows she's not the society girl she professes to be. But then Jack is actually an undercover cop working for the New York City Vice Squad, investigating prostitution rings in high society. The problem is Jack's beginning to enjoy Mickey's hedonistic world and wild parties, where Mickey states: "Welcome to Cafe Society. Where the elite meet to eat–each other."

Another nightclub evening finds Jack and a inebriated Pat being introduced to Mickey's very disapproving mother (Kelly Bishop). Pat's just told Mrs. Jelke that Mickey's proposed to her (they've known each other two weeks) and the matriarch makes it clear to her son that his trust fund money is about to be cut off.

Since 1952 is an election year, the boys at city hall want a nice juicy scandal that will get lots of headlines—like a naughty vice ring the cops can bust, so the politicos can trumpet about their moral guardianship and cleaning up society. Jack seduces Erica-the-madam at one of Mickey's parties and gets her call book but it's clear that nothing can be tied to Mickey. He's merely a "benevolent patron to a bunch of slightly deviant individuals." But this doesn't stop Jack's superiors from going after him since the idle rich are so easy to hate.

During another drunken revel at Mickey's apartment, Jack gives Pat's girlie photo to Ray, who blackmails her into servicing a guest and then makes certain Mickey discovers them. So, when Mickey's trust fund money is frozen, he gives Pat an engagement ring and then tells her in order to get the money to get married and live the life she's become accustomed to, she'll have to "work" for awhile.

Pat goes to Jack's apartment and let's him know what's about to happen. Knowing that this will make his case, Jack doesn't discourage Pat from going through with Mickey's plan. Later, when Pat wants to quit, she and Mickey get into an argument and he makes it clear he's not going to marry her. Pat goes to cry on Jack's shoulder, saying she's not what he thinks and he finally lets her know he's a cop. A hysterical Pat tries to overdose on pills but Jack rescues her and tells her that he expects her to testify against Mickey, who's been arrested as a pimp on some questionable evidence.

Soon, the media has turned Mickey into the city's leading vice lord, instead of the patsy he truly is. As Mickey tells his lawyer (Richard B. Schull): "I'm not a vice lord. I'm not the head of some ring. I'm a pervert." Pat's the star witness against him, a headline-grabber dubbed "the golden girl of vice," who's willing to play along with whatever's suggested, playing the injured party—a poor, innocent girl lead astray by an uncaring trust fund baby who'd promised to marry her. She tries laying a guilt trip on Jack by suggesting that he convinced her to go through with Mickey's idea, but Jack feels guilty enough about Mickey, whom he truly liked and who he knows is being railroaded.

When it comes time for disenchanted Jack to give his testimony in court, he deliberately blows it, saying he ensnared Mickey to get headlines for the department. But as Mickey tells Jack at their last meeting, outside a nightclub, his testimony was too little too late and Mickey knows he's going to be convicted and go to prison as the scapegoat for some would-be moral crusade.

Everyone looks just swellegant in their satin gowns and black tie, swilling liquor and smoking with abandon. Too bad the film wasn't a little more abandoned. Everything's obvious from the beginning—Mickey's a rich boy with more money than brains and unfortunate taste in women, Pat's too knowing (she acts like a good-time girl even before she turns pro), and both Jack's enjoyment of Mickey's world and self-disgust at his betrayal of it is a paint-by-numbers scenario. The film also tends to stop dead during several similar drunken party scenes that are accompanied by various renditions of the song "Remind Me."

An end crawl lets the viewer know what happened to some of the principals—none ended up well—except for the character of Jack, who must be one of the infamous some-names-and-incidents-have-been-changed ilk.

—Christine Tomassini

CREDITS

Mickey Jelke: Frank Whaley
Jack Kale: Peter Gallagher
Pat Ward: Lara Flynn Boyle
Ray Davioni: John Spencer
Erica Steele: Anna Thomson
Anthony Liebler: Paul Guilfoyle
Segal: Richard P. Schull
Frank: Christopher Murney
J. Roland Sala: David Patrick Kelly
Mrs. Jelke: Kelly Bishop
Diane Harris: Cynthia Watros

Origin: USA
Released: 1995, 1997
Production: Steve Alexander and Elan Sassoon for Skyline Entertainment, Daylight Productions, and The Shooting Gallery; released by Cineville
Direction: Raymond De Felitta
Screenplay: Raymond De Felitta
Cinematography: Michael Mayers
Editing: Suzy Elmiger
Music: Chris Guardino
Production design: Markus Canter, Stuart Canter
Set decoration: Betsy Alton
Costumes: Juliet Polcsa
MPAA rating: R
Running Time: 104 minutes

REVIEWS

Chicago Tribune. August 7, 1997, p. 6.
New York Times. July 18, 1997, p. C16.

Career Girls

To know where you're going, you have to remember where you've been.—Movie tagline

"It'll make you cry, even as you laugh out loud."—Jeanie Pyun, *Mademoiselle*

"Brilliant! An antidote to all the dinosaurs, aliens and superheroes."—*Marie Claire*

"A masterpiece! Brilliant, insightful, funny and utterly charming."—Paul Wunder, *WBAI Radio*

Box Office: $2,632,149

Career Girls, written and directed by Mike Leigh, features the sharp dialogue and social commentary that graces his other films—notably *Life is Sweet*, *High Hopes*, and *Secrets and Lies*. Life is hard for Leigh's characters, and they never indulge in the luxury of sentimentalizing their fate. They are honest to the point of cruelty, and their humor is savage. With Leigh's films gaining more and more attention, he provides a welcome antidote to most mainstream filmmaking. Even when his characters make it, they never forget how much crudity and suffering underpins an affluent society. As Hannah (Katrin Cartlidge) says while surveying a posh Thameside apartment: "I suppose on a clear day you can see the class struggle from here."

Hannah, flat-hunting: "I suppose on a clear day, you can see the class struggle from here."

Hannah wants a better view, actually, but she does not blink at the stiff moral as well as economic price exacted by seeking a better life. The alternative, however, is the rather bleak, if supportive, life she shared with Annie (Lynda Steadman) when they were college students. Insecure and angry, Hannah lashed out at loutish men but also at the vulnerable Annie, who could not look people in the eye and suffered from a facial rash, which Hannah sneeringly compares to tangoing with a cheese grater. Annie retreats to her room in tears. A repentant Hannah tries to make it up to Annie, and the two do eventually become fast friends. Annie admires Hannah's independence; Hannah identifies with Annie's struggle to stand on her own.

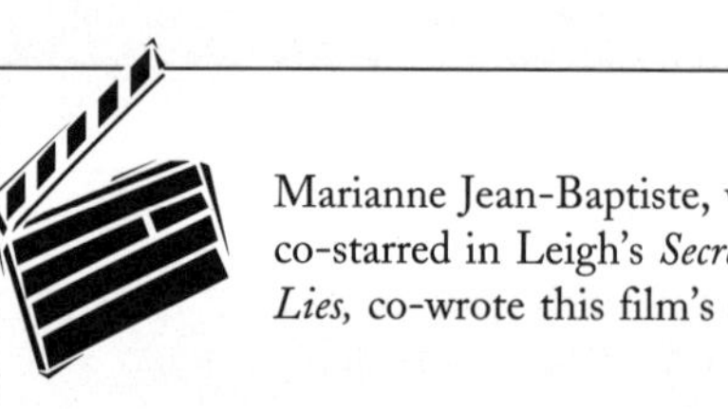

Marianne Jean-Baptiste, who co-starred in Leigh's *Secrets & Lies*, co-wrote this film's score.

The story of these career girls—who are meeting after a six-year separation—is constantly broken-up by flashbacks which show the similarities and differences between then and now. Then Hannah spoke in virtual code, with jabbing staccato gestures and speeches, practically turning herself into a verbal machine gun and retreating into stupid adolescent games. One such example is her transformation of *Wuthering Heights* into a fortune-telling book, in which Hannah and her friends express a wish/query and then pat the novel, randomly opening a page and alighting on a word that must be interpreted as an answer. It is silly but symbolic, of course, to fondle this great romantic work about the questing self.

Six years later Hannah has calmed down. She is doing well in her career, rents a nice apartment, and no longer plays adolescent games. But she is still Hannah with the sharp tongue, and her years with Annie figure as a foundation for her character. Similarly, Annie has matured, her facial rash has disappeared, and she has little trouble looking people in the eye, but she is not content with her career and unsure of her next step. Although she became a psychology major in order to learn how to deal with people, she finds herself pushing paper most of the time. Admiring Hannah's success, Annie contemplates a move to London, which would certainly signal her full emergence as a competitive member of society.

As if to emphasize what is at stake for these career girls, Leigh takes them on a tour of London, hunting for a flat Hannah would like to buy—a sign that she has made it. One thing about Annie has not changed: she carefully studies every move Hannah makes. Is Annie in love with Hannah? Is there a suppressed lesbianism at work here? Perhaps. But it is beside the point. The males who show various flats to Hannah and Annie assume that the women are lovers, but then that says more about the men than it does about the women—both of whom are attracted (and repulsed) by males but show no sign of a sexual interest in women.

Hannah and Annie have quite an interesting discussion at the end of the day. Annie says quite directly, and for the first time, how much she admires Hannah's independence. Hannah is not so impressed with herself. She takes her hard-edged self-confidence as an armor she has had to don because of her hopeless alcoholic mother and her early recognition that she would have to fend for herself. What Hannah likes about Annie is her sensitivity and vulnerability. Annie experiences more, Hannah implies, by letting the world get to her. Annie is not so sure and suggests that together she and Han-

CREDITS

Hannah: Katrin Cartlidge
Annie: Lynda Steadman
Claire: Kate Byers
Ricky: Mark Benton
Adrian: Joe Tucker

Origin: Great Britain
Released: 1997
Production: Simon Channing-Williams for Channel Four Films and Thin Man; released by October Films
Direction: Mike Leigh
Screenplay: Mike Leigh
Cinematography: Dick Pope
Editing: Robin Sales
Music: Marianne Jean-Baptiste, Tony Remy
Production design: Eve Stewart
Costumes: Eve Stewart
Art direction: Helen Scott
Sound: George Richards
MPAA rating: R
Running Time: 87 minutes

nah would make the perfect woman. This scene is indicative of Leigh's work at its best—when he is able to balance psychological development with social commentary and the personal with the political. Hannah and Annie are examples of career girls, to be sure, but they are also irreducibly and uniquely themselves.

—*Carl Rollyson*

REVIEWS

Boxoffice. August, 1997, p. 44.
Entertainment Weekly. August 8, 1997, p. 52.
New York Times. August 8, 1997, p. C3.
People. August 18, 1997, p. 21.
Rolling Stone. August 21, 1997, p. 116.
Sight and Sound. September, 1997, p. 38.
Time. August 11, 1997.
USA Today. August 7, 1997, p. 3D.
Variety. August 8, 1997, p. C3.
Village Voice. August 12, 1997, p. 67.

Cats Don't Dance

For a bunch of funny friends trying to break into show business . . . it's a jungle out there!—Movie tagline

"Perfect family entertainment!"—Leo Quinones, *KHS-FM*

"The freshest, funniest, animated feature since *Aladdin.* A sidesplitting four paws up triumph."—Jim Svejda, *KNX Radio*

"*Cats Don't Dance* is the cleverest animated feature to come along in many years."—Charles Solomon, *Los Angeles Times*

"*Cats Don't Dance* is the cat's meow!"—Larry Worth, *New York Post*

Box Office: $3,588,602

Only a great story can elevate an animated movie to a point where it truly does appeal to "all ages". More typically these films fail in their lofty ambition to have multi-generational appeal and instead receive a lukewarm reception in all quarters. Then they suffer the fate of all generic, uninspired G-rated movies: they become default activities for families with young children, leaving the accompanying parents wishing they had taken the kids to the beach instead.

Cats Don't Dance is such a film. It's by no means the worst of this category. No child will run screaming from the theater during the second reel; nor will these same children grow up and look back on this film with nostalgia. It will just be one of many throwaway experiences of a young child, on par with a fall in the schoolyard, a dispute with a sibling, or lunch.

The story opens with Danny the Cat (voice of "Quantum Leap"'s Scott Bakula), an aspiring film star, leaving his hick town of Kokoma to make it big in the doggy-dog world of Hollywood. He carries a banner declaring his destination (spelled "Hollywud," in an attempt to infuse his character with personality. I guess cats can't spell, either).

Danny arrives in California and is visibly dazzled. Who can blame him. One of the few pluses of this film is that it's set in Hollywood in the 1930s, and the sight of the old Chinese Theater, Brown Derby, and a *Gone With The Wind* marquee is enough to inspire nostalgia even in people who weren't born until years after this period.

The love interest, Sawyer (voice of Jasmine Guy, Natalie Cole for the singing parts), another cat, is introduced immediately to the viewers (though not yet to Danny). Unknowingly, he knocks her into a fountain, slams the door into her, etc, in a series of cliché-ridden mishaps. This sets up an obvious obstacle for Danny to overcome before Sawyer discovers he really is the one for her.

Danny arrives in the big city with a checklist of goals, each a necessary step on the road to fame and fortune. His first step is to get an agent. So he goes to an animal agent where Sawyer is coincidentally employed as a secretary. In the agent's lobby Danny meets the pack of jaded animal actors that will form his posse. These include Tillie the hippo (Kathy Najimy), T.W. the turtle (Don Knotts), and Cranston the goat (Hal Holbrook). The animals are skeptical and somewhat put off by Danny's enthusiasm and expectations for stardom. Their years of professional disappointment have taught them the ugly truth: It's *people* who become famous, not animals. Doesn't he get it?

Natalie Cole provides the singing voice for Sawyer the cat.

But, of course, he doesn't get it. When he gets his first big break—to appear in child legend Darla Dimple's new vehicle, Lil Ark Angel—he milks it for all it's worth. Though he only has one line, "Meow", he takes the occasion as his cue to exhibit all his song and dance talents. Darla, whose vicious temper keeps the cast and crew constantly on edge, doesn't enjoy Danny's performance at all. Feeling threatened by Danny's attempt to steal the spotlight, she calls in her much larger than life bodyguard, Max (voice of Mark Dindal), to put Danny in his place. Darla declares, "I hate animals . . . especially that one."

This incident doesn't diminish Danny's belief in himself and his other trod-upon friends. He schemes to have an all-animal performance for the studio head, L.B. Mammoth (voice of George Kennedy). Unfortunately, he makes the naïve mistake of accepting Darla's offer of help with his plan, which she offers up with the condition that he tell no one about her generosity. She foils their audition, creating a flood which washes them right off the lot.

This prompts a brief period of soul-searching for Danny, as we might have guessed, which ends with his renewed strength to go on, as we also might have guessed. His revelation has no real cause, but then it's so predictable that it raises no real questions.

Danny and his friends ultimately triumph. They perform a surprise audition at Darla's premiere, wow the audience, and embarrass Darla. The studio head sees them for the talented bunch they really are, and they presumably all go on to big contracts and top billing.

It is no mystery to me why this cast of animals had such a hard time winning over L.B. Mammoth. If they had a little more spark and talent, he would have noticed them a long time ago.

—Nancy Matson

CREDITS

Danny: Scott Bakula (voice)
Sawyer: Jasmine Guy (voice)
Darla Dimple: Ashley Peldon (voice)
Tillie: Kathy Najimy (voice)
Wollie: John Rhys-Davies (voice)
L.B. Mammoth: George Kennedy (voice)
Flanigan: Rene Auberjonois (voice)
Cranston: Hal Holbrook (voice)
T.W.: Don Knotts (voice)

Origin: USA
Released: 1997
Production: David Kirschner and Paul Gertz for Turner Feature Animation; released by Warner Bros.
Direction: Mark Dindal
Screenplay: Robert Gannaway, Cliff Ruby, Elana Lesser, and Theresa Pettengill
Editing: Dan Molina
Music: Steve Goldstein
Songs: Randy Newman
Art direction: Brian McEntee
MPAA rating: G
Running Time: 75 minutes

REVIEWS

Detroit News. March 26, 1997, p. E1.
New York Times. March 26, 1997, p. B6.
People. April 7, 1997, p. 22.
San Francisco Chronicle. March 26, 1997, p. E2.
USA Today. March 28, 1997, p. 4D.
Variety. March 24, 1997, p. 34.

Chasing Amy

Finally, a comedy that tells it like it feels.—Movie tagline

Sex is easy. Love is hard.—Movie tagline

"Full of truth and explosive comedy! Completely original"—Roger Ebert, *Chicago Sun-Times*

"Freewheeling and often very funny!"—Janet Maslin, *New York Times*

"A blast of gleeful provocation! Comic nirvana."—Peter Travers, *Rolling Stone*

"A true movie rarity . . . Funny, smart and truthful. Kevin Smith is an original."—Richard Schickel, *Time*

"The funniest, most honest sex-comedy I've ever seen!"—Amy Taubin, *Village Voice*

Holden (Ben Affleck) thinks he has found the perfect woman in Alyssa (Joey Lauren Adams) in the comedy *Chasing Amy.*

Box Office: $12,027,147

Writer-director Kevin Smith seems to have grown up some. The young filmmaker who made the very funny and well-written *Clerks* (1994), (winner of major awards at both the Cannes and Sundance Film Festivals), and the big-budget flop *Mallrats* (1995), returns to the smaller scale in his latest release. This time though, the conversations have turned from the joys of pornography and the intricacies of *Star Wars* (1977), to the previously unexplored world of relationships. *Chasing Amy* still has much of the low-grade humor of Smith's previous films (and most of it is still very funny), but adds a bigger dose of character depth to what many are calling his first "real" movie.

Holden to Alyssa: "I love you, and not in a friendly way."

The end credit dedication states: "To the critics who hated our last flick - all is forgiven."

Holden and Banky (Ben Affleck and Jason Lee; both of whom appeared in *Mallrats*, a creation Smith later apologized for) are best friends who, now in their mid-20s, find themselves fairly successful comic book artists (one writes, the other "colors"). Aside from steady jobs, one gets the feeling that their lifestyles haven't changed much since they were pre-teens. Their apartment is a messy bedroom of a home, and comic books and sex still dominate their conversations. The routine of bachelor living, however, becomes threatened when Holden falls for Alyssa Jones (Joey Lauren Adams), a fellow comic book writer who appears to be the answer to a question that Holden didn't even know he was capable of asking. But a problem exists: Alyssa is gay. Unable to control his feelings for her, Holden falls in love anyway. Initially angered by Holden's confession, Alyssa too begins to question her feelings and assumptions and ultimately falls for him as well. Thus begins the turmoil.

Most of the writing up to this point is quite good, and, as with *Clerks*, you get the feeling that you're watching something genuine. The lifestyles may not be familiar, or even respectable to you, but the feelings the characters are experiencing probably are. Smith, who has been praised for his writing abilities, has a knack for infusing a base sense of honesty into his characters and their dialogue (even if the conversations are peppered with expletives). Like a lot of great writer-directors, he has a knack for relating his surroundings to an audience.

AWARDS AND NOMINATIONS

Golden Globe Awards 1998 Nominations: Musical/Comedy Actress (Adams)
Independent Spirit Awards 1997: Screenplay, Supporting Actor (Lee)
Nominations: Feature

As the two become a couple—much to the dismay of their peers—Holden is struck with some unusually strong insecurities over Alyssa's sexual history (not her lesbianism, of course, but her varied heterosexual experiences) that quickly become such a bone of contention that it threatens to split them apart.

While the writing is still good and Smith's attention to his characters continues to be strong, from here on in the film becomes frustrating to watch. How can a grown man (he is approaching 30 after all), capable of seemingly sincere love and commitment, let such a juvenile hang-up go to such extremes? As the relationship dwindles you can't help but feel disappointed, both in Holden and in the film. Some might call what transpires honesty, but it seems more like inconsistency. Insecurities are universal, but extreme reactions need interpretation. In the end, without any other explanation, immaturity seems the only answer. I don't think that's the feeling the director wanted audiences walking away with.

—*Jeffrey Herman*

CREDITS

Holden McNeil: Ben Affleck
Alyssa Jones: Joey Lauren Adams
Banky Edwards: Jason Lee
Hooper: Dwight Ewell
Jay: Jason Mewes
Silent Bob: Kevin Smith

Origin: USA
Released: 1997
Production: Scott Mosier for View Askew; released by Miramax Films
Direction: Kevin Smith
Screenplay: Kevin Smith
Cinematography: David Klein
Editing: Kevin Smith, Scott Mosier
Production design: Robert Holtzman
Set decoration: Susanna McCarthy
Costumes: Derrick Tseng
Sound: William Kozy
MPAA rating: R
Running Time: 105 minutes

REVIEWS

Boxoffice. April, 1997, p. 176.
Detroit News. April 11, 1997, p. 3C.
Entertainment Weekly. April 4, 1997, p. 64.
Entertainment Weekly. April 11, 1997, p. 25.
Filmmaker. Spring, 1997, p. 40.
Los Angeles Times. April 11, 1997, p. F12.
New York Times. April 4, 1997, p. B3.
New Yorker. April 7, 1997, p. 97.
Rolling Stone. April 17, 1997, p. 86.
Sight and Sound. November, 1997, p. 36.
Time. April 7, 1997.
USA Today. April 11, 1997, p. 4D.
Variety. February 3, 1997, p. 46.
Village Voice. April 8, 1997, p. 79.

A Chef in Love

"Intoxicating!"—Marshall Fine, *Gannett News Service*

"*A Chef in Love* earns a four star rating for being a lusty food and love comedy par excellence." —Daphne Davis, *Movies and Video*

"A mouth-watering movie about cuisine, love and intrigue."—Thelma Adams, *New York Post*

"Deliciously sentimental."—Jack Mathews, *Newsday*

"You can gorge yourself on the scrumptious cinematography; not just table after table of steaming delicacies but riotous shots of fleshy delights that rival the great food-as-sex scenes on film. Pierre Richard gives a bravura performance. Nino Kirtadze sizzles as Cecilia. Open hearted. Full of humor."—Francine Russo, *Village Voice*

"A magnificent feast for the eyes and the mind. Lush, intriguing and highly entertaining!"—Paul Wunder, *WBAI Radio*

Box Office: $697,504

Food, like sex, in films becomes imbued with a reality that far outweighs the fiction it is intended to serve. We thus have a sub-genre of films that have made food, and its preparation, integral to their plots: *Babette's Feast* (1987) from Denmark, *Tampopo* (1986) from Japan and *Eat Drink Man Woman* (1994) from Taiwan, to name just the more notable international examples. Where Nana Djordjadze's *A*

Chef in Love differs from its predecessors is that it is more about cooking as a repository of cultural identity, than about the consumption of food.

Again, unlike its earlier counterparts, the film opens as far from the subject closest to its heart as it possibly could. Inside, a Parisian art gallery, Anton (Jean-Yves Gautier), a young art dealer, is arranging an exhibit reflecting life in the Republic of Georgia before it came under Soviet domination. As if through the workings of synchronicity, he is approached by the elderly Marcelle (Micheline Presle) who, as a fellow Georgian, lures him with an unpublished manuscript about the secret life of her uncle, the famous chef Pascal Ichac, renowned for his book, *1001 Recipes of a Chef in Love*. Anton is quick to recall how his mother, the Princess Cecilia, use that very cookbook as her Bible. What Anton learns to his surprise, however, is that his mother had had an affair with Pascal before she married the man he has always assumed to be his father. As if to get the sordid end of that relationship out of the way, the film shows Anton's stepfather, Zigmund (Teimour Kahmhadze) murdering Cecilia (Nino Kirtadze, a Julie Hagerty look-alike) in a jealous rage by bludgeoning her to death.

Pascal: "Communism will disappear; good cooking, never."

As Anton shuffles through Pascal's papers, the film is now free to focus on the joyous affair between Cecilia and Pascal, in no particular chronological order. Thus, we first glimpse Pascal (Pierre Richard), half-undressed, leading Cecilia in her nightie, out into a moonlit night. With bottles of wine in their hands, they appear to embody the very essence of sybarite excess. Then, as the film at last opens out to reveal the Georgia of the 1920s, we find its peasant lifestyle, ripe with sensual indulgence, functioning as an objective correlative for Pascal's Gallic passion. We see Cecilia squeezing bright blue grapes in ecstatic delight, as a laughing Pascal embraces her from behind. Then, at a family picnic, as elderly Georgians toast to a long and good life, Pascal, his arm around Cecilia, watches them, as if enraptured. It becomes clear then that Cecilia's rival for Pascal's love will be Georgia itself, and its gourmet traditions.

The film was inspired by a real French chef who had a restaurant in Tbilisi in the 1920s.

As the film reverts back to Marcelle's apartment in Paris, we learn that Marcelle is a culinary photographer. Presumably, her health prevents her from enjoying the succulent dishes she prepares. As Anton feasts at her table, she invites him to move in and translate Pascal's papers. Despite his commitment to his exhibit, Anton accepts. This bonhomie suffusing the film's present pervades the segments of Pascal's life that now come alive. We see his fortuitous first meeting with Cecilia, the two in a compartment by themselves on a train bound for Tbilisi. Then follows his jaunt as an operatic tenor, mercifully cut short by a bitter stage feud. We then see Pascal and Cecilia chugging along the scenic Georgian countryside in her vintage auto. At a lookout point, Pascal, behind a camera on a tripod, declaims, "What a bizarre country! Each time I'm in a pretty landscape, there's a church or feast!" He then picks Cecilia up with one arm, the tripod with the other and cries out: "Here we come!"

Ironically, it is at a wayside inn that very day that Pascal meets for the first time the man who will prove to be his bitter enemy, and who will eventually marry and murder Cecilia. When we first see him, however, Zigmund is a mere obsequious cook-cum-helper. When Pascal finds that the innkeeper has cheated them of a fresh suckling pig, he takes Cecilia by the hand and storms out. It is only when Zigmund makes an overture to Cecilia in a native dialect that Pascal erupts in rage. Putting a gun to Zigmund's head, Pascal has him deliver the live pig into the back seat of the car. Zigmund then retrieves a hidden revolver, runs across and down a hillside in time to meet the car, and shoots the pig dead. After which, he scampers away. Pascal, visibly shaken by this act of elemental vengeance, can only console an unnerved Cecilia, both woefully ignorant of the turn their lives have taken.

It is here, when the film shifts back to Anton, that its dramatic structure begins to creak. Nothing that happens to Anton—his shock at learning more and more about his two fathers notwithstanding—can match the events that gather Pascal and Cecilia into their historical sweep. By the same token, the film's burdensome need to switch back and forth leaves little time for it to portray Pascal in relation to anything but his cooking. This apparent lapse on the filmmaker's part can, in a sense, be justified, since cooking gradually becomes Pascal's whole life.

At a command performance of the ballet, Pascal's vocational sense of smell allows him to detect a terrorist's bomb under the President's seat. In the first of many ironic twists, the bomb expert who defuses the device turns out to be none other than Zigmund. Later, at a picnic held in Pascal's honor, the President wholeheartedly supports Pascal's plan to open a French restaurant in Tbilisi. "But why not in Paris or Nice?" the President asks. "I fell in love with Georgia, Mr. President," Pascal is quick to answer. As the chief guest, Pascal drinks from the horn of plenty, cheered on to consume all its wine in a single swig, while Zigmund watches from a distance. That afternoon, as their paths cross, away from the President and his entourage, Pascal accuses Zigmund of planting the bomb, claiming he could smell the powder on his hands. As if to confirm the allegation, Zigmund knocks Pascal down with a blow to the stomach, then escapes.

With the President's patronage, Pascal's restaurant is inaugurated with all due pomp. As Pascal modestly points to the table he has laid, the camera swoops over the mouth-watering dishes: the roasted turkey and game hens, a whole fish in cream sauce, monumental cakes surrounded with fruits and cheeses. Even so, all that pales before our eyes, as Pascal's wildest imaginings achieve fruition under his supervision, making his restaurant world-famous. A haunting melodic theme, played by a live ensemble, underscores Cecilia's silent longing, as shè wanders by herself through Pascal's dream come true, feeling incomplete as a woman.

A rift we could have long foreseen now becomes apparent. Not that it hinders the all too busy Pascal. What his success is unable to withstand however, is the simultaneous thrust of history. As the Red Army rides into Tbilisi, Pascal refuses to abandon his restaurant and make a fresh start elsewhere. What follows is an ideological tug-of-war between Pascal, as the lone believer in the power of his cuisine and the crude might of the Red oppressors. The scales appear to be unfairly balanced when Zigmund reappears as a Red military officer.

CREDITS

Pascal Ichac: Pierre Richard
Marcelle Ichac: Micheline Presle
Cecilia Abachidze: Nino Kirtadze
Zigmund Gogoladze: Teimour Kahmhadze

Origin: Republic of Georgia
Released: 1996
Production: Marc Ruscart; released by Sony Pictures Classics
Direction: Nana Djordjadze
Screenplay: Irakli Kvirikadze
Cinematography: Guiorgui Beridze
Editing: Vassela Martschewski, Guili Grigoriani
Music: Goran Bregovic
Production design: Vaktang Rouroua, Teimour Chmaladze
MPAA rating: PG-13
Running Time: 100 minutes

Since we already know the end of the story, Pascal's persecution and eventual banishment come as no surprise. Zigmund, who has been harboring a passion for Cecilia since he first saw her with Pascal at the inn, now uses his political clout to marry her, though she is pregnant with the child who will become Anton. Pascal, after a comic attempt to get back at the Reds via food poisoning, is confined to a garret atop what was once his restaurant, where he puts down his recipes that will one day comprise his famous cookbook. Till the last, he keeps talking to his herbal plants, as if they were his friends. Until one morning, Zigmund, relishing the prospect of putting an end to Pascal's life, finds to his dismay that he has starved to death.

In Paris, as Anton enjoys the dishes Marcelle has prepared from the master chef's immortal recipes, Pascal's prophecy, from the depths of his disempowerment, continues to haunt the audience, and give the film its political thrust: "Communism will disappear one day. Fine cooking won't."

"As cinematic banquets go," writes Stephen Holden in the *New York Times*, "*A Chef in Love* is not quite as satisfying as *Babette's Feast* or *Big Night* (1996). Its culinary metaphors are a little too overbearing and its storytelling a bit too fragmentary." Even so, he describes the film as "a voluptuous celebration of abundance . . . in which attitudes toward food carry moral and philosophic weight." Noting Pierre Richard's "bravura performance, from triumph to mad defiance" and the "scrumptious cinematography," Francine Russo in *The Village Voice* calls the film "open-hearted" and "full of humor." Understandably, Deborah Young in *Variety* zeroes in on what she sees as the film's major drawback, the way its story "meanders from Tbilisi to Paris and back without hitting its emotional target."

A Chef in Love bagged an Oscar nomination for Best Foreign Language Film, and was showcased at Cannes as part of the Director's Fortnight.

—*Vivek Adarkar*

REVIEWS

Boxoffice. May 1997, p. 57.
Los Angeles Times. April 23, 1997, p. F2.
Los Angeles Times. April 24, 1997, p. 8.
New York Times. April 20, 1997, p. H22.
New York Times. April 25, 1997, p. C3.
Newsday. April 25, 1997, p.
Variety. June 3, 1996, p.
Village Voice. April 29, 1997, p. 78.

Children of the Revolution

A red comedy about the ultimate party animals.—Movie tagline

"Irreverently funny! A zany comedy . . . with sheer chutzpah and a first-rate cast."—Janet Maslin, *The New York Times*

"A dizzyingly original comedy!"—Leah Rozen, *People*

Box Office: $845,391

In *Children of the Revolution* writer and director Peter Duncan follows the life of Joan Fraser (Judy Davis), a fiery yet naive communist activist who works unceasingly for the cause.

Combining drama and black comedy with PBS-type interviews and even a bit of vaudeville shtick, Duncan has created a multifaceted exploration of the politics of power.

The film opens in 1951, at a time when Prime Minister Menzies demanded a national referendum to outlaw communism in Australia. Fraser tries to convince her friends to march on Parliament in protest, but her tiny band of halfhearted revolutionaries are horrified at the very thought.

Geoffrey Rush of *Shine* (1996) fame, plays Zachary, a member of the group whose interest in communism centers more around Fraser than it does around the Manifesto. He asks her to marry him, but she is so involved with politics that she does not even consider the offer.

It soon becomes apparent that Joan is not just obsessed with political reform. She is also obsessed with Stalin. For years she has written long, enthusiastic and sometimes heartrending missives to him, in which she expounds her devotion to the cause and her hope that one day Stalin might write back to her.

The letters are being read, but not by Stalin. They are being read by Australian intelligence, who are watching her movements. Joan returns home one evening to find a government agent, David Hoyle (Sam Neill), sitting in her living room. He tells her that they are following her, but this warning only strengthens Joan's resolve to fight harder for the revolution.

When her letters finally reach Moscow, they are read by Stalin's personal secretaries, who are brought to tears by Fraser's fervor. Stalin, who has never read the letters, chances upon a photo Joan has sent him and decides to entertain the young woman in Moscow.

Communist party member, Joan Fraser (Judy Davis), arranges for a one-night stand with Josef Stalin, becomes pregnant, and raises her son to follow in Stalin's footsteps. But her plan backfires in the satire *Children of the Revolution.*

Joan on Mikhail Gorbachev: "Take off his wig and makeup and he's Ronald McDonald. And Ronald McDonald is the devil."

When Joan arrives, she is escorted by a Lieutenant Colonel of the KGB who takes her to Stalin. Joan is alarmed when she recognizes the KGB agent as David Hoyle, the same Australian agent who has been following her in Sydney. It seems that Hoyle or "Nine," as he is called, is a sort of spy for hire.

David brings Joan to an elegant dining room where Stalin wines, dines, and seduces her. Their passion turns out to be a bit too much for Stalin, and he dies in the throes. Frightened and in shock, Joan runs to Nine and tells him that she has killed Stalin, He tries to console her, and they also make love.

In the morning when Stalin is found dead and everyone figures out what happened, instead of a firing squad, Joan is greeted with flowers and champagne from Khrushchev and his buddies and sent back to Australia.

She returns to Australia pregnant and marries her old friend and admirer Zachary. Together they raise her son Joe (Richard Roxburgh), and as he grows he follows in his mother's footsteps, attending demonstrations and spouting communist propaganda by rote.

AWARDS AND NOMINATIONS

Australian Film Institute 1996: Actress (Davis), Production design, Costumes

Nominations: Best Film, Director (Duncan)

After getting arrested time after time for demonstrating, Joe develops a passion for prisons instead of revolution, and finally ends up doing time for avoiding the draft. While he is in jail, his bunk mate, an historian, sets him straight about Stalin, telling him that he was responsible for the death of millions of people.

After a violent incident in prison, Joe is scarred badly on his upper lip and grows a moustache to hide it, revealing an uncanny likeness to Stalin. And that likeness is not limited only to his looks. When Joe is released, he becomes a prison worker and after a forceful speech, Joe initiates a policemen's strike. His success during the strike catapults him to the position of president of the Law Enforcement Alliance, and he begins to wield his power and to destroy his enemies.

The film's plot reflects the faith of Peter Duncan's grandfather, who was a steadfast member of the Communist Party, despite all evidence of political problems, until his death in 1979.

The film is unconvincing as an argument for biological determinism, but it is an interesting portrayal of the idealist as the dupe of the more insidious undercurrents of power.

Davis plays straight man to the film's other characters, who play their parts with full-blown satire. But her earnest sincerity is perfect for the part, bringing a deeper credibility to her role as a true believer. As the film dances playfully with the horrors of abusive power, Davis's character storms through it all, blind to everything except her devotion to the cause, and, in the end, her ignorance makes her the most dangerous of all the characters.

Sam Neill is outstanding as David Hoyle/Nine, the spy who doesn't much care who he works for. He is the most intelligent of all the characters and also the most complex, bringing an unpredictability to the plot that is fascinating.

An outstanding feature of the film is Roger Ford's production design, which is so expressive that changes in the sets reflect the emotional changes taking place within the characters. An example of Ford's magic is Joe's office. As Joe becomes more power hungry and more isolated, his office becomes larger and larger, until finally his office looks just like the modern version of the mausoleum where Stalin once worked.

Children of the Revolution, with its suicides, assassinations, and genocide, might sound a little dreary. But Duncan adds a light touch to his subject, incorporating a kind of wacky humor throughout. In one very camp scene, Khrushchev and his cronies dance and sing "I Get a Kick Out of You," looking for all the world like a cross between The Supremes and the Three Stooges.

Although at times one wonders where the film is taking us, its unconventional switching from realism to theatrics pays off in the end. In *Children of the Revolution,* first-time writer/director Peter Duncan has given us a provocative tale of innocence and evil.

—Diane Hatch-Avis

CREDITS

Joan Fraser: Judy Davis
David Hoyle: Sam Neill
Joe Welch: Richard Roxburgh
Zachary Welch: Geoffrey Rush
Anna: Rachel Griffiths
Joseph Stalin: F. Murray Abraham
Barry: Russell Kiefel
Wilkie: John Gaden

Origin: Australia
Released: 1996
Production: Tristram Miall for Rev Kids and Australian Film Finance Corporation; released by Miramax Films
Direction: Peter Duncan
Screenplay: Peter Duncan
Cinematography: Martin McGrath
Editing: Simon Martin
Music: Nigel Westlake
Production design: Roger Ford
Art direction: Laurie Faen
Costumes: Terry Ryan
Sound: Guntis Sics
MPAA rating: R
Running Time: 101 minutes

REVIEWS

Boxoffice. May, 1997, p. 57.
Entertainment Today. May 2, 1997, p. 12.
Entertainment Weekly. May 9, 1997, p. 58.
The Hollywood Reporter. May 1, 1997, p. 8.
Los Angeles Times. May 1, 1997.
New Times. May 1, 1997, p. 24.
New York Times. April 27, 1997, p. H25.
New York Times. May 1, 1997, p. C18.
The New Yorker. May 5, 1997, p. 104.
People. May 5, 1997, p. 24.
Variety. August 5, 1996, p. 49.

City of Industry

Wanting a man dead can be reason enough to live.—Movie tagline

"A deliciously dark thriller that serves up suspense, surprises and terrific performances."—Jeanne Wolf, *Jeanne Wolf's Hollywood*

"John Irvin delivers a taut, tense, edge of your seat thriller."—Bonnie Churchill, *National News Syndicate*

Box Office: $1,568,258

Crime films and Westerns have many similarities with the two genres often borrowing from each other. It is no surprise when Akira Kurosawa transforms Dashiell Hammett's *Red Harvest* (1929) into his samurai film *Yojimbo* (1961), when Sergio Leone turns Kurosawa's film into the western *Per Un Pugno Di Dollar* (1964; *A Fistful of Dollars*), and when Walter Hill goes back to Kurosawa, bypassing Hammett, to make his gangster film *Last Man Standing* (1996). *City of Industry* is on the surface a fairly standard film noir, but it is also a variation on a standard Western plot: thieves fall out, one ruthlessly steals the loot, and a survivor of the treachery tracks down the betrayer with the help of a beautiful woman. While the film is watchable and competently made, it ignores any possibility of having fun with its mixed genres, going instead for straight-ahead action.

Jorge Montana (Wade Dominquez) plans to pull one last job before going off to prison. He needs the money for his wife, Rachel (Famke Janssen), and their children, but he also enjoys the criminal life. The leader of the Los Angeles gang is Jorge's friend Lee Egan (Timothy Hutton) who enlists Skip Kovich (Stephen Dorff) as getaway driver. The group is completed by Lee's older brother, Roy (Harvey Keitel). (Hutton and Keitel may be the most unlikely screen brothers since John Wayne, Dean Martin, Earl Holliman, and Michael Anderson, Jr. in 1965's *The Sons of Katie Elder*.)

The robbery of a swanky Palm Springs jewelry boutique goes smoothly, especially since Jorge has broken into the security company's computer system to make it seem as if all of its clients' alarms are going off simultaneously. By the time the four gather to discuss the dispersal of the gems, Skip has grown greedy and kills Lee and Jorge with Roy narrowly escaping. Skip's decision to start shooting after Roy goes to the bathroom is one of the few missteps in *City of Industry*'s efficiency.

After recovering from the first of several sets of wounds, Roy tells Rachel she is a widow and begins seeking her help in finding Skip. The wily Skip pays an African-American gang from whom he has bought guns to protect him, and when Harvey (an ill-at-ease Elliott Gould), a loan shark to whom he is in debt, begins putting pressure on him, Skip convinces Harvey to lend him some of the Chinese hoodlums in his employ to ferret out Roy. The revenge theme of the film's second half makes its western roots more obvious as Roy and Skip drift toward their eventual showdown.

City of Industry needs some unusual touches to make it stand out from the plethora of similar crime films released in recent years. While some may praise the film for the honesty of its simplicity, for not giving in to imposing fashionable Quentin Tarantinoesque flourishes on this material (as Terrence Rafferty did in *The New Yorker*), it needs something to enliven it. Having blacks and Asians protect the white punk Skip is an effort at being different, as may be the casting of Gould as an unlikely crime boss, but screenwriter-producer Ken Solarz, with his first produced script, provides too little impetus for the film to rise above its cliches. The audience knows well before the characters that Roy and Rachel will bond and that Skip will sacrifice his girlfriend to his greed.

After making the magnificent 1979 television adaptation of John le Carre's *Tinker Tailor Soldier Spy*, director John Irvin has worked in a variety of genres with mixed results. These films have ranged from bad—*Raw Deal* (1986) and *Next of Kin* (1989), both comic-book gangster yarns—to adequate—the sexy horror film *Ghost Story* (1981), the sentimental jockey-with-cancer tale *Champions* (1984), the realistic Vietnam drama *Hamburger Hill* (1987)—to good—the mercenary film *The Dogs of War* (1980); *Turtle Diary*, in which lonely Londoners find fulfillment; the Irish village saga *Widow's Peak* (1994); and *A Month By the Lake* (1995), his best film, a story of thwarted middle-aged romance. In these films, Irvin has demonstrated a feeling for gritty violence, alienation, the need for revenge, and the nuances of loneliness, all of which come into play in *City of Industry*.

Director John Irvin on his intentions: "I wanted to make it suspenseful rather than a bash-'em-up movie. It's more complex than just brute force and firepower."

Irvin and production designer Michael Novotny do a wonderful job of creating an archetypal noir landscape, envisioning Los Angeles as an anonymous industrial wasteland where crime and betrayal seem the norm. Irvin's unevenness, unfortunately, is also on display. The robbery sequence is extremely well done. Irvin and Solarz show just enough of the planning to make what transpires logical, and Irvin and editor Mark Conte provide just the right amount of tension as the heist is carried out professionally with a minimum of showiness. The best touch is when Skip drives the getaway car slowly to a traffic light and the thieves sit there calmly while police cars with sirens roaring swirl around them in confusion, not knowing where to go since dozens of alarms are sounding.

In contrast is the sloppiness of Roy's escape from the murderous Skip. Lee has rented a trailer where they hide out after the robbery, and when Roy flees Skip's shots, a convoy of recreational vehicles just happens to separate them. Even clumsier direction occurs when Roy checks into a seedy motel and Irvin's camera lingers ominously on a propane tank so that the audience will know it will explode later. When it does, however, the motel manager peeks out his window at the violence and simply returns to watching television. *City of Industry* has a few such stylistic touches but not enough.

Solarz clearly intends to create a lean tale of existential alienation along the lines of such French imitations of American film noir as Jean-Pierre Melville's *Bob Le Flambeur* (1955) and *Le Samourai* (1967). He does this mainly by making Roy a taciturn loner about whom the audience knows nothing but that he is Lee's brother and is drawn to Rachel. The plot of *City of Industry*, whose title is never explained and means nothing, is essentially that Roy is beaten or wounded, grimaces, recovers, and goes on to the next step in his quest for revenge. The excess of these punishments recalls the beatings inflicted on the Marlon Brando characters in *One-Eyed Jacks* (1961) and *The Chase* (1966), with Roy's stoic resolve also strongly reminiscent of Clint Eastwood's Man with No Name in Leone's westerns.

Keitel has played such understated characters effectively in the past, most notably in *The Piano* (1993), but from *Mean Streets* (1973) to *Smoke* (1995), he is at his best when his characters try to find the language to express their complex emotions. While he does not so much embody Roy as he endures him, Keitel's strong presence and quiet authority lend the film considerable weight it would otherwise lack.

In *Blood and Wine*, another underachieving film noir released just a few weeks before *City of Industry*, Dorff also plays a young jewel thief, but that character was naive. Skip is viciously brutal, even shooting his girlfriend without hesitation when a thug employs her as a shield. Dorff has a flair for flamboyant characters, as with his transvestite in *I Shot Andy Warhol* (1996), and he clearly enjoys Skip's malevolence.

Skip's character is established by Irvin and cinematographer Thomas Burstyn when he first appears on the screen with his spiky blond hair and driving his ostentatiously huge convertible. The tilted shot makes Skip appear to be a creature arriving in his spaceship to conquer our world. The film might have had greater resonance as film noir if Skip had prevailed. Instead, it has a sentimental ending resembling that of *Dogs of War*.

Some of the drippiness of this ending is subdued by the performance of Janssen as Rachel. Almost unrecognizable as the same person who plays Xenia Onatopp, the *Goldeneye* (1995) villainess who crushes her victims between her legs, Janssen takes a token sensitive-woman-among-all-these-hard-asses role and gives Rachel a touching depth by being the only performer to display any complicated emotions: unease at Jorge's continuing his life of crime, grief at his death, distrust of and then affection for Roy. (In a western, Rachel would be a rancher's earthy widow, hardened by her experiences but eager to respond to the kindness of a rugged stranger.) Even deglamorized, Janssen seems a bit too stylish to be convincing as a low-life criminal's pink-collar wife, but she provides *City of Industry* with a welcome breath of reality amid all the noir posturing.

CREDITS

Roy Egan: Harvey Keitel
Skip Kovich: Stephen Dorff
Rachel Montana: Famke Janssen
Lee Egan: Timothy Hutton
Jorge Montana: Wade Dominquez
Keshaun Brown: Reno Wilson
Odell: Michael Jai White
Harvey: Elliott Gould

Origin: USA
Released: 1997
Production: Evzen Kolar and Ken Solarz for Largo Entertainment; released by Orion Pictures
Direction: John Irvin
Screenplay: Ken Solarz
Cinematography: Thomas Burstyn
Editing: Mark Conte
Production design: Michael Novotny
Costumes: Eduardo Castro
Music: Stephen Endelman
Sound: Walter Hoylman
Casting: Cathy Henderson
MPAA rating: R
Running Time: 97 minutes

REVIEWS

Chicago Tribune. March 14, 1997, p. 5.
Entertainment Weekly. March 28, 1997, p. 52.
Los Angeles Times. March 14, 1997, p. F6.
New York Times. March 14, 1997, p. B19.
The New Yorker. March 24, 1997, p. 84.
Sight and Sound. August, 1997, p. 44.
USA Today. March 13, 1997, p. 8D.
Variety. March 3, 1997, p. 67.
Village Voice. March 18, 1997, p. 76.

Irvin's main virtue as a director may be his ability to elicit strong yet sensitive performances from women: Glenda Jackson in *Turtle Diary*, Natasha Richardson and Mia Farrow in *Widow's Peak*, and, especially, the magnificent Vanessa Redgrave in *A Month By the Lake*. Janssen's work is hardly in that league, but Irvin allows her to show she has considerably more to offer than most former Bond femmes.

—*Michael Adams*

Commandments

He's getting even . . . by breaking all the rules.—Movie tagline

" . . . a fun, amusing and unpredictable romantic comedy."—Lawrence Van Gelder, *The New York Times*

"Delightful, witty and funny!"—Jeffrey Lyons, *WNBC-TV*

Writer-director Daniel Taplitz makes his film debut with the uneven black comedy, *Commandments*. While based on a promising premise, the film is softened with romantic elements that undercut the power of its potential and is further undone by its inconsistent tone.

Aidan Quinn stars as Seth Warner, a modern day Job who loses nearly everything in his life. One day he is a happy New York doctor, the next his pregnant wife (Joanna Going) vanishes below the water while Seth snoozes on the beach. Before long Seth loses his job to a heartless and hypocritical boss and his house to a tornado that spares everything else on the block. Can Seth's loss of faith be far behind? Perched atop a roof, the rain pelting down around him, the bitter Seth screams to the heavens, "I don't believe in God," while his cynical brother-in-law, Harry Luce (Anthony LaPaglia) tries to dissuade him from suicide. God seems to intervene once again, however, when Seth is struck by lightening.

Harry: "I break five or six commandments every day before lunch."

He does not die—that would be too easy on him—but in yet another of God's tests, his cute little dog loses his leg. His life unraveling at an astonishing rate, Seth moves in with his wife's comely sister, Rachel (Courteney Cox), a high-powered lawyer, and her philandering, crime journalist husband, Harry. Figuring there is only one way to get God's attention, Seth vows to break each of the Ten Commandments.

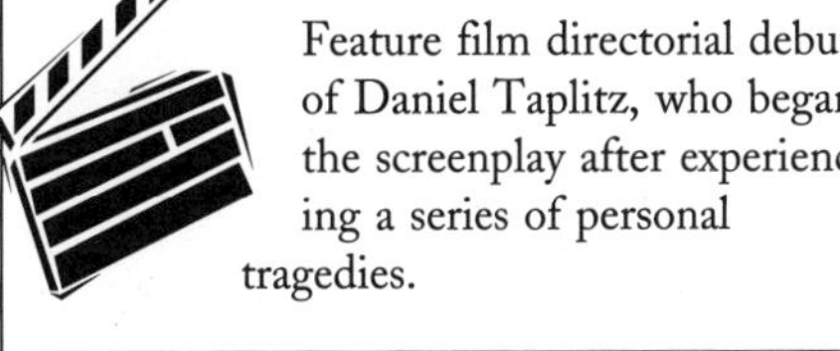

Feature film directorial debut of Daniel Taplitz, who began the screenplay after experiencing a series of personal tragedies.

Things roll along easily, with such Commandments dealing with the worship of false idols even proving to be somewhat fun to break. When Seth comes to the part of Thou Shalt Not Kill, however, writer Taplitz seems content to gloss over the more complex issues—preferring instead to concentrate his efforts on adultery. It is convenient that Rachel is as miserable in her marriage as Seth is currently in his life.

Commandments is an ambitious project that fails on almost every level, perhaps by virtue of attempting too much in too short of time. While it deserves to be commended for its willingness to tackle such complex themes, the film falls by the way of Michael Tolkin's challenging foray into religious fanaticism, *The Rapture* (1991). While the philosophical and theological issues of the existence of God and the reasons behind man's suffering have held our attention for centuries, it is difficult to fashion such themes so directly into an entertaining and compelling story for a feature film. Other films have been more successful in addressing these issues by weaving them below the surface of a less dogmatic tale.

Commandment's inability to maintain a consistent tone throughout often leaves the viewer wondering just how serious to take the film. The connections to the Old Testament biblical Book of Job are obvious, but the ending—a blatant variation of the tale of Jonah and the whale—is particularly perplexing and so ludicrous its meaning remains obscure. At one point Seth philosophizes that if God is willing but unable to stop man's earthly suffering that makes Him unworthy of our worship; if God's able but unwilling to intervene, He's malicious. As film critic Mick LaSalle from the *San Francisco Chronicle* suggested in his review, this might be an obvious starting point for the film, but hardly a profound conclusion. Furthermore, events within the story need to build to some sort of cathartic resolution. With *Commandments*, we are left to ponder the ways in which Harry's commitment of adultery differs from Rachel's. Is it because Seth is in some way deemed more worthy than Harry's mistress? How can this be if God loves all people equally? The writer continually gets himself in trouble with such issues, demonstrating the precarious nature of trying to fashion a film out of such weighty issues.

The cinematographer, Slawomir Idziak, who photographed the "Thou Shalt Not Kill" part of Krzysztof Kieslowski's *The Decalogue*, succeeds in giving *Commandments* a mysteriously complex look. The film is beautiful to look at, but the performances, unfortunately fail to rise the material to the level of the visuals. It is not that the actors do not commit to their roles; they do. But the characters are consistently thinly drawn, particularly Courteney Cox's Rachel. Anthony LaPaglia has the most fun on-screen with the fervent sinner Harry.

Following in the aftermath of the darker and more exploitive *Seven* (1996), this film can only be seen as a lightweight attempt to mine similar territory, unfortunately, in a far less compelling and intriguing story. Reviews for the film were fairly consistent in their negative vein.

—Patricia Kowal

CREDITS

Seth Warner: Aidan Quinn
Rachel Luce: Courteney Cox
Harry Luce: Anthony LaPaglia
Rudy Warner: Louis Zorich
Melissa Murphy: Pamela Gray
Gordon Bloom: Jack Gilpin
Karen Warner: Joanna Going

Origin: USA
Released: 1997
Production: Michael Chinich, Daniel Goldberg and Joe Medjuck for Northern Lights Entertainment; released by Gramercy Pictures
Direction: Daniel Taplitz
Screenplay: Daniel Taplitz
Cinematography: Slavomir Idziak
Editing: Michael Jablow
Production design: Robin Standefer
Art direction: Stephen Alesch
Costumes: John A. Dunn
Music: Joseph Vitarelli
MPAA rating: R
Running Time: 87 minutes

REVIEWS

Boxoffice. April, 1997, p. 184.
Chicago Tribune. May 9, 1997, p. 5.
Entertainment Weekly. May 16, 1997, p. 86.
The Hollywood Reporter. January 28, 1997, p. 10.
Los Angeles Times. May 2, 1997, p. F14.
New York Times. May 2, 1997, p. B36.
People. May 12, 1997, p. 24.
San Francisco Chronicle. May 2, 1997, p. C3.
San Francisco Examiner. May 2, 1997, p. C3.
USA Today. May 1, 1997, p. 3D.
Variety. January 27, 1997, p. 82.
Village Voice. May 6, 1997, p. 86.

Con Air

They were deadly on the ground. Now they have wings.—Movie tagline
"Two thumbs up!"—*Siskel & Ebert*

Box Office: $101,117,573

Every Summer Hollywood unleashes a torrent of action/adventure fare designed to appeal to the lowest common denominator. These pictures are crafted with the accent on vibrant visuals and thunderous auditory stimulation. Producers of these projects try to avoid stories that might tax too much of the audiences attention span. Summer is when the studios make the *real* money. Some studios actually channel their mid-year profits into their more prestigious, Oscar-seeking fall projects that never seem to snare the behemoth numbers enjoyed by their warm-weather brethren.

In 1996, producers Jerry Bruckheimer and Don Simpson presented *The Rock*, one of the more cerebral crowd pleasers of the year that featured not one but two Oscar-winning actors in the lead roles. Simpson and Bruckheimer had assembled a respectable roster of films. They were responsible for *Flashdance* [1983], *Beverly Hills Cop* [1984], *Top Gun* [1986], *Days Of Thunder* [1990], and 1995's *Bad Boys*, *Dangerous Minds* and *Crimson Tide*. None of the pictures won any major awards, but they all finished in the black and con-

Cameron Poe (Nicolas Cage) ducks for cover amid gunplay and explosions in the action adventure *Con Air.*

tained above average smarts. The partnership ended abruptly with Simpson's untimely death in early 1996. *The Rock* was already in the can and it wouldn't be until his next feature that anyone would be able to tell whether or not Bruckheimer could achieve further sterling success on his own. When *Con Air* was announced, it caught the eye of more than one ardent film fan. As a rule, action flicks are only as good as their villains and *Con Air* was blessed in that regard. It featured a handful of respected actors, virtually all of them playing bad guys with an abundance of pyrotechnics and an overflow of testosterone. As predicted, the casting decisions paid off well at the box-office, but it brought into question Bruckheimer's abilities as a solo act. If it weren't for the A-list cast, it would have been wretched. As it is, the final product is a failure. Confidently rote and occasionally inspiring in places, but a failure nonetheless.

"I told him to put the bunny back in the box."—Poe after dispatching a con who's touched his daughter's present, a stuffed rabbit.

The movie opens as Desert Storm veteran Cameron Poe (Nicolas Cage) is returning home to his pregnant wife Tricia (Monica Potter) in Alabama. During a barroom brawl where he's defending his own life as well as his wife's honor, Poe kills a drunk redneck who had harassed him earlier. During the subsequent trial, the presiding judge tells Poe that the skills learned in the service make him a lethal weapon and he cannot be regarded as a "normal" person. Please. Poe refuses to cop a plea and begins to serve out the bulk of his sentence in a maximum security facility. This all takes place before the opening credits.

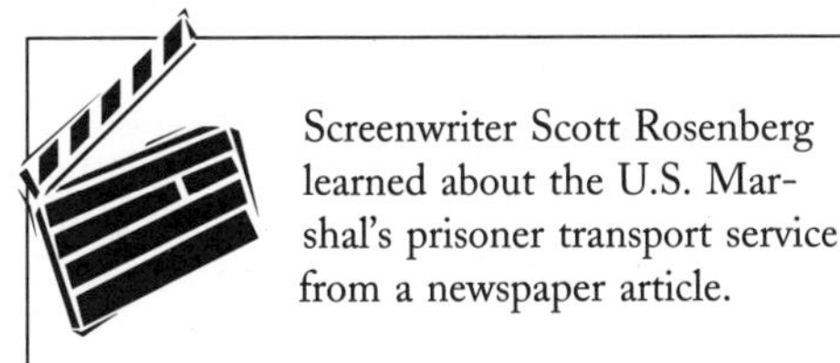

Screenwriter Scott Rosenberg learned about the U.S. Marshal's prisoner transport service from a newspaper article.

Several years later, the now long-haired Poe is being paroled on the birthday of the daughter he's never seen. He will be transported home by a plane from originating in California. (Why would a man convicted of murder in Alabama serve his sentence in California? This is just the start of a laundry list of illogical, only-in-the-movies irony). The US Marshals are including Poe with other prisoners who are the absolute dregs of society. Among them are Cyrus "The Virus" Grissom (John Malkovich), Diamond Dog (Ving Rhames) and Garland Greene, a blatant Hannibal Lecter clone played with dead-pan grace by Steve Buscemi. Other prisoners carry such distinguished names as Swamp Thing, Baby-O, Johnny 23, Pinball and Sally Can't Dance, a gay cross-dresser. As you know, every prison block needs a homosexual transvestite. Shortly after the plane takes off, the inmates (led by Grissom, who earned two doctorate degrees while incarcerated) overpower the guards and hijack the vessel in the hopes of reaching freedom in a non-extraditional South American country.

The prisoners must make a pit-stop in Carson City, Nevada, where some of the passengers will get off and others will board. This is the first of several opportunities Poe is presented with to get out of danger and reunite with his wife and daughter. He instead sticks around to save the lives of a few innocents. While on the ground, Poe stumbles across the convey hired by Grissom to take the troupe to South America. With more of his "lethal weapon" talents he takes them out but soon finds himself staring down the wrong end of a gun pointed at him by US Marshall Vince Larkin (John Cusack). With yet another chance to get away, Poe tells Larkin he's going to jump back into the fray in order to "save the day." The cliches are now being delivered ever more rapidly and even when read by high-octane talent like Cage, they result in exaggerated rolling of the eyes or embarrassing unintended laughter.

Cusack escapes *Con Air* relatively unscathed, which in itself is a minor miracle. His role here was sandwiched between three other '97 stints; *Grosse Pointe Blank, Anastasia* and *Midnight In The Garden Of Good & Evil* [all reviewed in this issue]. It was a banner year for Cusack, who has long been a favorite of fans and critics alike. He has smoothly graduated from awkward teen roles to more heady adult performances. Romantic leading man offers should be just around the corner.

Malloy, Larkin's legal counterpart on the ground is given an histrionic interpretation by Irish actor Colm Meaney who gives new meaning to the term "over-the-top." The best that can be said for Meaney's performance is that you can't tell that he's Irish. He screams and bellows at every turn, providing the film with the requisite, fumbling, love-to-hate-'em character. His Malloy provides an unrelenting thorn in the side for Larkin who tends to use more methodical and logical methods.

After a confrontation with what appears to be half of the entire United States armed forces, the convicts are again airborne, this time heading for Las Vegas (?!), which is, of course, the next best thing to South America. While including indie staple Buscemi might have added some nominal prestige value, he's given very little in the way of actual dialogue. A previous scene on the ground shows Greene having tea in an empty swimming pool with a little girl who lives by the abandoned airfield. A wholly believable premise indeed. Nothing happens between Greene and the girl, which makes one wonder why would director Simon West set up such a passage between an ominous, ogling, foreboding criminal and an innocent, unsuspecting child without any sort of payoff, good or bad? It makes no sense. West had never made a feature film before; his previous experience is comprised of television commercials and music videos.

One of Bruckheimer's more glaring errors was handing over the reigns to such an obvious greenhorn. Nevertheless, it was West's background with video production that allowed him to choreograph the film's funniest scene. Shortly after the second take-off, the Lynyrd Skynyrd song "Sweet Home Alabama" starts. An appropriate choice considering the Poe's home state and state of mind. With the effeminate Sally Can't Dance character leading them, this group of hardened criminals breaks into a routine that would be right at home in any one of a number of the nation's premier leather bars. Keenly observing the ludicrous nature of what he's witnessing, Buscemi turns to Cage and asks him to "define irony." Not really expecting a reply, he answers his own question with the Buscemi-like retort: "A bunch of idiots dancing on a plane to a song made famous by a band that died in a plane crash." Finally, a line worthy of the actors.

The plane begins its descent on the main Vegas strip and winds up crashing into the front of a casino. The production notes indicated that the real Sands Hotel was going to be remodeled and the ownership granted Bruckheimer and company the pleasure of starting the demolition process with a real crash. Here, Poe has his final opportunity to walk away in one piece, but a truly superfluous action movie like this would be incomplete without the tacked-on false ending. Poe sees his nemesis Grissom escaping on the ladder of a fire truck and takes off in hot pursuit. The fire truck provides the final insult, twisting and turning down various Vegas streets until Grissom meets his end. With no more fires to extinguish himself, Poe turns to his family with a recently salvaged stuffed animal in hand to greet his wife and daughter. The film finally shows mercy and fades to black.

While there are tons of explosive action scenes and patches of irreverent, snappy humor, there's nothing here that hasn't been seen in every other shoot-em-up, exaggerated, brain-numbing blockbuster that has preceded it. Cage and Malkovich play out the requisite cat-and-mouse rou-

CREDITS

Cameron Poe: Nicolas Cage
Vince Larkin: John Cusack
Cyrus Grissom: John Malkovich
Garland Greene: Steve Buscemi
Diamond Dog: Ving Rhames
Duncan Malloy: Colm Meany
Baby-O: Mykelti Williamson
Pinball: Dave Chapelle
Swamp Thing: M.C. Gainey
Sally Can't Dance: Renoly
Johnny 23: Danny Trejo
Billy Bedlam: Nick Chinlund
Sally Bishop: Rachel Ticoin
Tricia Poe: Monica Potter
Casey Poe: Landry Allbright

Origin: USA
Released: 1997
Production: Jerry Bruckheimer for Touchstone Pictures; released by Buena Vista
Direction: Simon West
Screenplay: Scott Rosenberg
Cinematography: David Tattersall
Editing: Chris Lebenzon, Steve Mirkovich, Glen Scantlebury
Music: Mark Mancina, Trevor Rabin
Art direction: Edward T. McAvoy
Costumes: Bobbie Read
Sound: Arthur, Arthur Rochester
Visual effects supervisor: David Goldberg
Stunt coordinator: Kenny Bates, Steve Picerni
MPAA rating: R
Running Time: 115 minutes

REVIEWS

Chicago Tribune. June 6, 1997, p. 4.
Entertainment Weekly. June 13, 1997, p. 38.
Hollywood Reporter. June 3, 1997, p. 10.
Los Angeles Times. June 6, 1997, p. F1.
New York Times. June 6, 1997, p. B1.
New Yorker. June 9, 1997, p. 107.
Newsweek. June 9, 1997, p. 74.
People. June 16, 1997, p. 21.
Rolling Stone. July 10, 1997, p. 31.
Sight and Sound. July, 1997, p. 37.
Time. June 9, 1997.
USA Today. June 6, 1997, p. 4D.
Variety. June 2, 1997, p. 53.

tine while Buscemi, Rhames and Cusack attempt to contribute a modicum of texture and depth. Bruckheimer is sure to continue down the action/adventure path that has proven to be such a lucrative cash cow. Perhaps the spirit of Don Simpson can help guide him into picking a higher quality project the next time out.

—J.M. Clark

AWARDS AND NOMINATIONS

Academy Awards 1997 Nominations: Song ("How Do I Live"), Sound

Conspiracy Theory

Jerry Fletcher sees conspiracies everywhere. One has turned out to be true. Now his enemies want him dead. And she's the only one he can trust.—Movie tagline

"Winning performances from Mel Gibson and Julia Roberts! Gibson gives one of the most rawly emotional performances of his career." —Marshall Fine, *Gannett News Service*

"Thriller, romance and comedy all in one intriguing film."—Jami Bernard, *New York Daily News*

"*Conspiracy Theory* is a tantalizing thriller packed with pleasures. Mel Gibson has never been more impressive!"—Gene Shalit, *Today*

"Thunderously entertaining and feverishly paced!"—Joe Morgenstern, *Wall Street Journal*

"Full of non-stop action! *Conspiracy Theory* is a perfect blend of drama, comedy and originality."—Kathryn Kinley, *WPIX-TV, New York*

Box Office: $76,118,990

Conspiracy Theory reunites producer Joel Silver, director Richard Donner, and star Mel Gibson, three of the creative talents of the successful *Lethal Weapon* series. According to reports about the preproduction meetings, they enjoyed each other's company so much during their earlier films that they initiated *Conspiracy Theory* primarily out of a desire to continue a pleasant association. Julia Roberts was similarly recruited and cajoled into joining the project. The resulting film shows both the strengths and the weaknesses of such a fun-first approach to moviemaking. The celebrity personalities add color and charisma, but the obligatory scenes of many big-budget movies eventually simplify the script and keep the second half of the film from equalling the first.

Jerry Fletcher (Mel Gibson), a New York cab driver, maintains a running banter with both his passengers and himself about an endless string of conspiracies. The Vietnam War was fought over a bet Howard Hughes lost to Aristotle Onassis. The fluoride in tap water weakens the will. The new hundred dollar bills carry a secret tracking device. Space shuttle launches and earthquakes suggest a mysterious correlation and alarming portents: If the President should visit a city on a fault line when a shuttle lifts off, are there grounds for suspecting a geological assassination attempt? When Jerry sees the sparks from a streetside welder, he reels as if about to lose consciousness. "I got some problems," he says.

One of them seems to involve Alice Sutton (Julia Roberts), an attorney at the Justice Department. Jerry drives at night to Alice's apartment and gazes at her while she works on her treadmill and listens to a Walkman. With binoculars he can scrutinize the movement of her lips as she sings, and he is able to tune his car radio to the same station Alice hears on her Walkman. She exercises unaware that in the street below he is serenading her in his car. At work the next day, Alice tries yet again to get her boss to order some wiretaps in the unsolved case of her father's murder. She then spots Jerry in the building and refers to him as "a restraining order waiting to happen." It develops that they first met months ago—six months and eleven days, Jerry later tells her—when he rescued her from muggers. He has occasionally brought his theories to her at work. Now, Jerry shyly asks Alice to dinner, but she politely refuses.

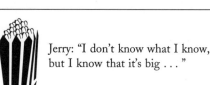

Jerry: "I don't know what I know, but I know that it's big . . . "

An unexpected brush with danger for Jerry makes Alice wonder if she has too quickly dismissed him as a crank. A character known only as Dr. Jonas (Patrick Stewart), a government psychiatrist, orders agents to abduct Jerry. Jonas threatens Jerry with an ominous syringe of "gravy for the brain," but Jerry bites off a chunk of Jonas's nose, frees himself, and manages to get to Alice before he is subdued and hospitalized by other government agents. Alice visits Jerry and he pleads with her to switch his chart with that of another patient. When she returns the next morning, this other patient has unexpectedly died. In the hospital cafeteria, Dr. Jonas, now outfitted with a prominent nose bandage, tries to warn Alice about the danger Jerry poses. Meanwhile, Jerry begins an elaborate escape from the hospital in which he profusely apologizes every time he smashes someone into unconsciousness with his bed railing. He hides in Alice's car, and they eventually travel to his apartment so that he can show her his conspiracy newsletter, which he mails off regularly to his five subscribers.

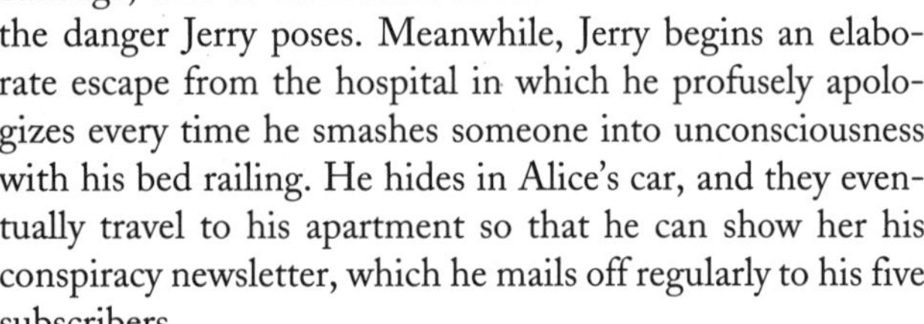
Mel Gibson previously worked with Joel Silver and Richard Donner on the three *Lethal Weapon* films.

Jerry's apartment is one of the triumphs of the motion picture's production design. Its steel walls, floors, and ceilings reflect Jerry's paranoid need for the security of fireproofing. A bank of file cabinets crowds the front door and further depersonalizes the setting. Jerry has seemingly taken note of every suspicious occurrence in his life and squirreled them away into the slate gray drawers stretching into the tunnel of his apartment. To him, apparently, nothing is a coincidence. Stacks of old magazines and newspapers totter everywhere. He has padlocked even the refrigerator door; the desk where he writes his newsletter occupies the center of this labyrinthine bunker. The exteriors for these scenes were shot on Thompson Street in Manhattan's Soho district to evoke the nostalgia of an older New York, but the interiors were designed by Academy Award-winning production designer Paul Sylbert. "Jerry's apartment is a rat's nest," says Sylbert. "He saves everything. When you enter his apartment, it's the first time you see how disturbed and terribly frightened he is. It's an introduction to his mind."

A tear gas attack at the apartment confirms that even a paranoid like Jerry can have enemies. Alice and Jerry flee but she separates from him when she sees that he has adorned his wall with a collage of her pictures. As Jerry goes to purchase yet another copy of *The Catcher in the Rye*, government agents close in. The middle scenes of the film suffer from a number of chase sequences that fail to develop plot or character. Roger Ebert, reviewing the film for the *Chicago Sun-Times*, made the excellent point that "very few action sequences work. Most of them bring movies to a lurching halt. *Conspiracy Theory* is never more interesting than when Gibson is spinning his bizarre theories, and never more boring than when secret agents are rappelling down ropes from helicopters hovering over New York streets. There have been so many action sequences in so many movies that we have lost the capacity for surprise."

The turning point of the film occurs when Alice begins to investigate the five subscribers to Jerry's newsletter and learns that one by one they are turning up dead. She tracks down the last subscriber, a Henry Finch, and discovers that both Dr. Jonas and Jerry have been involved with CIA mind-control projects—"science sanctioned by the government"—a plan reminiscent of *The Manchurian Candidate* (1962). The climax of the film reunites Alice with Jerry and involves a chase to the Connecticut house where years ago Alice's father died.

Although Brian Helgeland's script does not dwell much on character, the principal stars use their familiar screen personas effectively. *Conspiracy Theory* is an excellent example of how personality stars can add to an otherwise ordinary film. Mel Gibson succeeds at balancing Jerry's paranoia with a caring and witty side. He has a running speech about "Geronimo," which is his name for the exhilaration of genuine love and the way it can "give you wings." Gibson's performance makes Jerry likable. Julia Roberts, whom Gibson calls "the queen of subtext," uses her talent for fleshing out underwritten characters on the role of Alice, which seems to have been thought of as nothing more than a Grieving Daughter. Patrick Stewart adds polish and urbanity to the role of Dr. Jonas.

Another strength of the film is the photography of the early scenes. As Jerry drives his cab at night, the photographic style disorients and unhinges, like the perspective of this cab driver pushed to the edge by the chaos of modern life. These scenes are shot with a long lens and a narrow focus. Such a style gives a sense of fragmentation and eeriness to the shots of workmen soldering broken water pipes, the kaleidoscope of streetlights, and the shimmer of water. Cinematographer John Schwartzman describes the look that director Richard Donner sought: "He . . . wanted lots of reflection, which confuse the characters about what is real and what is not." Schwartzman also reported that Warner Bros. allowed him to use a specially processed film, "a combination that is black and white and color. It's beautiful and expensive—about two times more than usual."

The film encounters some problems when it shifts its focus from depicting the rantings of Jerry Fletcher to explaining how one of his theories seems to have actually hit home. After establishing a rich atmosphere and a quirky character, the filmmakers stumble in resolving their story. Part of the problem may result from the roster of big names associated with the project, any one of whom had enough clout to make a viewpoint heard. Julia Roberts, for example, kept pushing the film toward a more romantic emphasis, the element that is perhaps the least effective. The filmmakers test-marketed two endings to preview audiences and chose the "less pure" one, in the words of the director. As the completed film now plays, the implications of the last scene clearly prepare for a sequel. Such decision making, of course, reflects the profit-driven nature of Hollywood and the willingness to compromise quality for the sake of the box office. However, when producer Joel Silver says, "If I could find a way to make sequels without doing the first one, I'd do them all the time," he may be providing, intentionally or unintentionally, the most telling comment of all. *Conspiracy Theory*, like so many big-budget films, was constructed not so much to provide even light entertainment as to start the hum of a self-sustaining cash machine.

—*Glenn Hopp*

CREDITS

Jerry Fletcher: Mel Gibson
Alice Sutton: Julia Roberts
Dr. Jonas: Patrick Stewart
Agent Lowry: Cylk Cozart

Origin: USA
Released: 1997
Production: Joel Silver and Richard Donner for Shuler Donner/Donner Prods. and Silver Pictures; released by Warner Bros.
Direction: Richard Donner
Screenplay: Brian Helgeland
Cinematography: John Schwartzman
Editing: Frank J. Urioste, Kevin Stitt
Music: Carter Burwell
Production design: Paul Sylbert
Art direction: Gregory William Bolton, Chris Shriver
Costumes: Ha Nguyen
Sound: Tim Cooney, James Sabat
MPAA rating: R
Running Time: 135 minutes

REVIEWS

Boxoffice. October, 1997, p. 43.
Chicago Tribune. August 8, 1997, p. 4.
Entertainment Weekly. August 15, 1997, p. 48.
Movieline. June, 1997, p. 54.
New York Times. August 8, 1997, p. C1.
New Yorker. August 18, 1997, p. 78.
Newsweek. August 11, 1997, p. 72.
People. August 18, 1997, p. 21.
Rolling Stone. August 21, 1997, p. 115.
Sight and Sound. September, 1997, p. 39.
Time. August 18, 1997.
USA Today. August 6, 1997, p. 1D.
USA Today. August 8, 1997, p. D1.
Variety. August 4, 1997, p. 34.
Village Voice. August 19, 1997, p. 81.

Conspirators of Pleasure; Spiklenci Slasti

Conspirators of Pleasure is an exercise in metaphor, reality, live action, and animation. A thinly veiled allegory about political, sexual, and sociological repression in the Czech Republic, Svankmajer uses a mixture of animation, exaggerated sound effects, and ridiculously obscene close-ups to both ridicule and personify human desire and repression. Six people receive mysterious missives in the mail, with a one word message—"Sunday."

Six characters begin individual journeys that will unite them a week later in their desire for pleasure. Mr. Pivonka (Petr Meissel) surreptitiously buys *Playboy* magazines from a News Vendor (Jiri Labus). When Pivonka received his message, he immediately begins to create his own "pleasure" setup. He kills a chicken and begins to paste its feathers on a huge papier-mache chicken head. He spies on the obese landlady Mrs. Loubalova (Gabriela Wilhelmova) next door and sneaks into her apartment and steals her clothing when she's out preparing her own sexual feast.

The News Vendor himself is involved in an equally bizarre situation; he has jerry-rigged bits and pieces of left-over metals and scraps to form a kind of all-embracing "hugging machine." He is obsessed with a beautiful blonde Newscaster (Ana Veltinska) who has her own problems. She cannot get her husband, the Police Commissioner (Pavel Novy), to pay attention to her. She resorts to lavishing all her love on a huge fish that she keeps alive in a large basin in her bedroom. At times she even brings the fish into work, immersing her toes in the same water while conducting her newscasts.

The reason the Police Commissioner is so busy is that between crime investigations he is searching the town for fluffy things—feathers and fur. He snatches them from hats, coats, and other items, and stores them in his workroom—to which he denies his wife access. Finally, Mrs. Malkova (Barbora Hrzanova), the postwoman who brought everyone their "Sunday" invitations, engages in her own preparation;

she rips apart loaves of bread and rolls the dough into dozens of tiny, hard little balls.

Svankmajer shows the lengths all the characters will go to achieve their bliss—they do everything but interact with other humans, which is, precisely the point of this treaty. These characters live in an industrialized, pleasure-devoid society where they rarely interact at all, much less in a satisfying manner basic to most civilization. All the characters bring a zeal to their mission that is lacking in their everyday life.

CREDITS

Mr. Pivonka: Petr Meissel
Mrs. Loubalova: Gabriela Wilhelmova
News Vendor: Jiri Labus
Mrs. Malkova: Barbora Hrzanova
Newscaster: Ana Veltinska
Police Commissioner: Pavel Novy

Origin: Czech Republic
Released: 1996
Production: Jaromir Kallista for Athanor; released by Zeitgeist
Direction: Jan Svankmajer
Screenplay: Jan Svankmajer
Cinematography: Miroslav Spala
Editing: Marie Zemanova
Puppet designer: Eva Svankmajerova
Animators: Bedrich Glaser, Martin Kublak
Costumes: Ruzena Blahova
Art direction: Eva Svankmajerova, Jan Svankmajer
MPAA rating: Unrated
Running Time: 83 minutes

In the climax (no pun intended) all of the pleasure-seekers achieve their nirvana—or do they? Mrs. Malkova sucks the hard little balls of bread up her nose, theoretically into her brain, and then rests back, exalting in the experience. The Police Commissioner lays on a hard bed, yet caresses himself with all the feathers and fur he has gathered. The News Vendor plays tapes of his beloved Newscaster and allows himself to be embraced via his contraption, dreaming that it is she that is loving him. At home, the Newscaster is consoling herself with her fish. Mrs. Loubalova engages in a strange, pseudo-sexual dance with a dummy in an abandoned building, while Mr. Pivonka puts on his huge chicken head and does likewise in a field.

Metaphors for repression—social and sexual—abound, and Svankmajer lets his characters' extreme behavior speak volumes. No one speaks a word in the movie—only raucous, ungodly sound effects accompany every action. These people are so desensitized and separated from each other that they don't even realize it. They live in a vast, mechanized society that undervalues the individual, so given any opportunity to break free warrants this kind of behavior. This is very specialized filmmaking, not for everyone—heavy on the metaphors, overwhelming in the allegories—with never a subtle moment in the entire film.

—*G.E. Georges*

REVIEWS

Cinemafantastique. December, 1997, p. 51.
Detroit Free Press. March 1, 1998, p. 7H.
Los Angeles Times. September 19, 1997, p. F17.

Contact

A message from deep space. Who will be the first to go? A journey to the heart of the universe.—Movie tagline

"The smartest and most absorbing story about extraterrestrial intelligence since *Close Encounters of the Third Kind.*"—Roger Ebert, *Chicago Sun-Times*

"Two thumbs up!"—*Siskel & Ebert*

"*Contact* is dazzling and utterly amazing."—Susan Granger, *SSG Syndicate*

"The season's first superb major motion picture. Jodie Foster gives it everything she's got—which is plenty. *Contact* is gripping and stunning."
—Gene Shalit, *Today*

"One of the best movies of the decade."—Arch Campbell, *WRC-TV*

Box Office: $100,920,329

Astronomer Ellie Arroway (Jodie Foster) has just spent the night with divinity school dropout Palmer Joss (Matthew McConaughey). She became attracted to him when he unknowingly answered her question about the possibility of

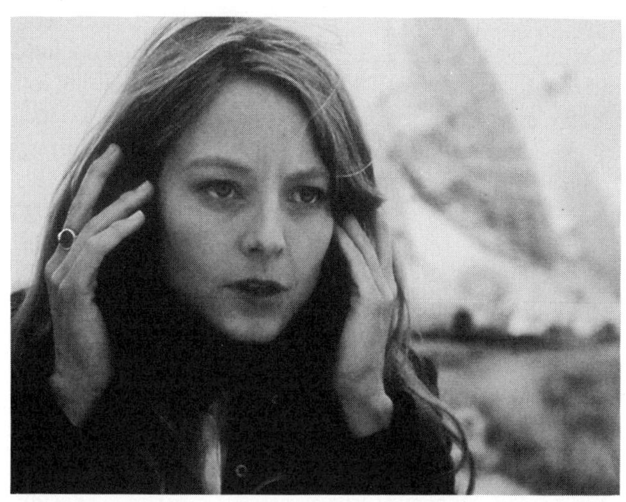

Dedicated astronomer Dr. Eleanor Arroway (Jodie Foster) listens for intelligent life in the universe. Her eventful discovery leads to a wondrous journey through the cosmos in *Contact*.

life in space with the same words her father (David Morse), who died when Ellie was nine, had used: "If it's just us, it seems like an awful waste of space." After he has talked to Ellie about his belief in God and now watches her prepare to rush back to her telescope, Palmer asks, "How can I reach you?" *Contact* is essentially an exploration of that question in its many emotional, spiritual, and astronomical possibilities.

The film is based on the 1985 best-selling novel by Carl Sagan, which was originally conceived in 1979 as a film idea. As the project passed through many hands—in one big change toward the end of preproduction, director George Miller was replaced with Robert Zemeckis—the script somehow managed to maintain its basic fairness with ideas. The screenplay credits list Sagan (who died in December 1996 during filming), his widow Ann Druyan, and Michael Goldenberg. The greatest strength of the film is the evenhanded way it pursues the urgent questions of belief—in science as an extension of human curiosity, in life beyond earth, in God.

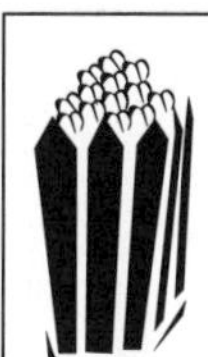

Ellie Arroway: "For as long as I can remember, I've been searching for some reason why we're here—what are we doing here, who are we? If this is a chance to find out even just a little part of that answer, I think it's worth a human life, don't you?"

Ellie finds that the project she rushes back to after Palmer asks her his question has just been shut down by her boss, Dr. David Drumlin (Tom Skerritt). Ellie works for SETI (the Search for Extra-Terrestrial Intelligence), and she intends to establish listening stations to monitor sounds from space. Her fundraising efforts to continue her work take her to a trio of corporate leaders who scorn the notion that other life forms exist. Ellie's anger has mounted over the thirteen months of failed efforts to raise money, and she lets out her frustrations in a tirade at these faceless CEOs. Her passionate work has evidently caught the eye of someone, however, since she later receives approval for her program in an anonymous phone call from the representative of an unknown benefactor. Ellie later finds that it is the reclusive billionaire, S.R. Hadden (John Hurt).

Four years pass before the listening dishes that Ellie has mounted pick up a blip of something that might turn out to be more than static. The mysterious sound is traced to the galaxy Vega, twenty-six light years away. As a government security advisor, Michael Kitz (James Woods), arrives to monitor developments, the scientists decode the sound by recognizing its use of prime numbers. This elaborate decoding eventually leads to the discovery of over 63,000 encrypted pages of data for what appears to be a transportation device to send someone to Vega. Kitz wants to militarize the project as people all over the world become fascinated by the message from outer space. The suspenseful development of the film gains much of its drama by showing the impact such an event would have at both the societal and the personal levels. In one scene, the previously unpopulated listening outpost transforms into a makeshift community of drifters and soul-searchers—crackpot preachers, skinhead Nazis, Elvis impersonators singing "Viva Las Vega"—who have all been drawn to the enormous dishes that have picked up some sliver of meaning from deep space. This brief scene, like others in the film, nicely captures the desperation and the hunger of modern life.

Ellie Arroway is the best-drawn character in the film and one of the real strengths of the motion picture. She reveals her intelligence in both the flashback scenes with her father as they toy with her short-wave radio and in the scenes of her as an adult. Jodie Foster, one of the screen's most intelligent actresses, makes Ellie appealing for her relentless intelligence, curiosity, and honesty. The best example of her integrity appears when a passenger is selected to travel to Vega. Ellie competes with Drumlin, who gives the selection committee a vague "cherished belief" speech about his spiritual views. Ellie responds honestly about her agnosticism, saying "there is no data either way" when asked about spiritual beliefs. She loses out in her refusal to tailor her answers to fit the committee's expectations.

The film itself handles with equal honesty the question of belief and refuses to stack the deck for either side. Although Ellie remains a doubter, Palmer Joss tries to advance the cause of faith. In one scene he asks her if she loved her

AWARDS AND NOMINATIONS

Academy Awards 1997 Nominations: Sound
Golden Globe Awards 1998 Nominations:
Drama Actress (Foster)

father. "Yes," she says. "Prove it," he replies as an answer to her remarks about the lack of proofs for the existence of God. As the film moves toward its conclusion, questions of belief and skepticism remain at the heart of the developing story. An act of sabotage allows Ellie to replace Drumlin in a second attempt to reach Vega. When her sphere zooms through a time-space "worm-hole" to whatever awaits on Vega, she sees such beauty that she can only respond, "They should have sent a poet." To the onlookers at the site, however, her capsule simply drops into its safety net. Ellie insists that she traveled to Vega, and the audience is shown her experiences twenty-six light years away. The technicians counter that the entire event lasted only a matter of seconds. Did she experience what she says she did? This ambiguous conclusion beautifully resolves the plot so that faith and healthy doubt might find a way to reinforce one another.

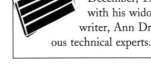

The filmmakers consulted with Carl Sagan until his death in December, 1996, as well as with his widow and co-story writer, Ann Druyan, and numerous technical experts.

Few films try as hard as *Contact* to establish a sense of authenticity. Director Robert Zemeckis peoples many scenes with the talking heads of real media figures all playing themselves. CNN, a subsidiary of Time-Warner, whose Warner Bros. produced and released the film, contributes a number of these figures: Larry King, Leon Harris, Tabitha Soren, Geraldine Ferraro, Bobbie Battista, Robert Novak, Bernard Shaw. In addition, Geraldo Rivera is glimpsed hosting a talk show, and Jay Leno appears in a clip from a monologue. However, this strategy never really becomes anything more than a distraction, and it may actually weaken the credibility of the film. The most intrusive example by far is the footage from President Clinton's 1996 press conference about the Mars probe, which has been taken out of context and blended with background shots of James Woods and Angela Bassett. "I swear to God it was like it was scripted for this movie," Zemeckis bragged over this *Forrest Gump*-like special effect. "When he said the line, 'We will continue to listen closely to what it has to say,' I almost died." Such a technique may ultimately reflect a dismissive attitude toward the audience. The giggles in the theater during these scenes suggest that audiences recognize the contrivance of real journalists playing themselves, and many will remember the small controversy at the time of the film's release concerning the distortion of the President's words. The filmmakers therefore risk seeming on the one hand to desire their viewers to think about serious subjects like the struggle between science and faith and on the other to distract from that desire with such manipulative cinematic devices.

Other weaknesses may be traced to the bloat that usually accompanies a big-budget production. To protect the estimated $90 million-dollar investment budgeted for *Contact*, the filmmakers introduce an intermittent love story between Ellie and Palmer Joss. Studios seem to see this as a way of broadening the film's appeal: a certain segment of the audience, they seem to assume, wants a love story, and so a romance begins even if the subject of the film does not justify it or, as is the case with *Contact*, even if the two leads have absolutely no chemistry together on screen. Both the surplus of famous names and the gratuitous love plot needlessly distract from a thoughtful premise that is often well developed.

The stereotypical depiction of supporting characters is another point often faulted by reviewers. The character of Palmer Joss comes off as a bland composite of New Age spiritualists. Matthew McConaughey's unexciting performance contributes to this drawback. Dr. David Drumlin is the scientist-villain who first eliminates the funding for Ellie's research and then grabs the credit for her discovery. S.R. Hadden is clearly based on the eccentricities of Howard Hughes. Rob Lowe's appearance as Richard Rank, a Ralph Reed-like spokesman for the religious right, is the one clever example of casting against the stereotype. James Woods simply reprises the villain roles he has played in other films. Supporting characters, of course, often need to be nothing more than one clear personality trait,

CREDITS

Ellie Arroway: Jodie Foster
Palmer Joss: Matthew McConaughey
Michael Kitz: James Woods
S.R. Hadden: John Hurt
David Drumlin: Tom Skerritt
Kent: William Fichtner
Rachel Constantine: Angela Bassett
Richard Rank: Rob Lowe
Joseph: Jake Busey
Ted Arroway: David Morse
Young Ellie: Jena Malone

Origin: USA
Released: 1997
Production: Robert Zemeckis, Steve Starkey for South Side Amusement Company; released by Warner Bros.
Direction: Robert Zemeckis
Screenplay: James V. Hart, Michael Goldenberg; based on the novel by Carl Sagan
Cinematography: Don Burgess
Editing: Arthur Schmidt
Music: Alan Silvestri
Production design: Ed Verreaux
Art direction: Lawrence A. Hubbs, Bruce Crone
Costumes: Joanna Johnston
Sound: William B. Kaplan
MPAA rating: PG
Running Time: 150 minutes

REVIEWS

American Cinematographer. July, 1997, p. 52.
Boxoffice. September, 1997, p. 123.
Chicago Tribune. July 11, 1997, p. 4.
Cinemafantastique. April, 1997, p. 5.
Cinemafantastique. July, 1997, p. 12.
Entertainment Weekly. July 18, 1997, p. 50.
The Hollywood Reporter. July 7, 1997, p. 5.
Los Angeles Times. July 11, 1997, p. F1.
Movieline. June, 1997, p. 54.
New Yorker. July 21, 1997, p. 81.
People. July 21, 1997, p. 17.
Rolling Stone. August 7, 1997, p. 68.
Sight and Sound. October, 1997, p. 44.
USA Today. July 11, 1997, p. 8D.
Variety. July 14, 1997, p. 43.
Village Voice. July 22, 1997, p. 65.
Washington Post Weekend. July 11, 1997, p. 37.

but some of the figures here become cartoonish. The biggest irony of the film may be that the scriptwriters were more interested in treating complexly the ideas of science and faith than in giving credibility to many of the supporting characters who espouse those ideas. With the exception of Ellie Arroway, who seems to be based on Sagan, the ideas in *Contact* are always more interesting than the characters.

Ultimately, however, these weaknesses matter less than the strengths. *Contact* is never more effective than when the political, scientific, and spiritual implications of the Vega message unfold almost as fast as new developments occur. The fairness with which the screenwriters present their ideas and the way the film encourages its audience to think are quite rare in a Hollywood production. The ambiguity and subtlety of the ending also merit respect. *Contact* finally implies that a desperate world might find solace if it confronts the infinitudes of space and doubt with a touch of the poet.

—Glenn Hopp

Cop Land

No one is above the law.—Movie tagline

"One of the most entertaining films of the year!"—Gene Siskel, *Chicago Tribune*

"One of the smartest movies of the year!"—David Sterritt, *The Christian Science Monitor*

"A knock-your-socks-off thriller!"—Larry King, *CNN*

"A rich thriller! An acting showcase with top-flight performances. Sylvester Stallone is a wonder!"—Jack Garner, *Gannett News Service*

"Dazzling . . . a film that is as good as its cast!"—Janet Maslin, *The New York Times*

"A remarkable film!"—Peter Travers, *Rolling Stone*

"Virtuoso acting from its big-name cast!" —Richard Corliss, *Time*

"An outstanding film! A high-voltage movie with a haymaker cast!"—Gene Shalit, *Today Show*

Box Office: $44,906,632

Cop Land, a film about police brutality, is about as timely a movie as Sylvester Stallone has ever made. It tells the story of rogue cops behaving badly and setting themselves up before the law. A few days before this film's release, Abner Louima, a Haitian immigrant, was beaten, tortured, and "sodomized" by at least two and perhaps as many as five New York policemen. The good news was that the New York City crime rate was down by 50%, but at the cost, perhaps, of police misconduct and brutality. Amnesty International has traced a pattern of police brutality in the city. Surprisingly, reviewers did not put *Cop Land* in the context of these current headlines, probably because reviews had already been written and filed after advanced press screenings and before the incident. The same "blue wall of silence" that was apparent in New York is also an issue in the film. A brutal attack had taken place, involving those who were culpable and those who knew about but did not report the beating.

Sylvester Stallone has finally managed to reinvent himself in a movie role that goes beyond caricature and beyond silliness. He first achieved stardom through his portrayal of Rocky Balboa as an archetypal American Everyman testing the national myth of success through hard work and determination, but the sequels to the original *Rocky* (1977) became merely slicker imitations of the raw and brutal first concept, and the character was not able to develop in interesting ways. Likewise the John Rambo of *First Blood* (1982) was originally a psychotic veteran pushed beyond the limits of sanity by a sheriff who could not understand how dangerous Rambo was. The later Rambo pictures, like the later Rocky pictures, were cartoonish and attempted to improve the original by enhancing production values rather than by delving into character.

In *Cop Land* Stallone manages to out-Rocky Rocky. Stallone plays Freddy Heflin, a sheriff in (fictional) Garrison, New Jersey, just across the river from Manhattan. Garrison is called "Cop Land" because it is dominated by Ray Donlan (Harvey Keitel), a New York police officer who has turned it into a colony of dirty cops who have sold out to the Mafia and have obtained mortgages through Mafia-controlled banking operations. The Mob helps them, and they help the Mob by looking the other way and ignoring drug deals in their precinct.

Tilden to Heflin: "I see a man waiting for something to do."

Freddy, who is deaf in one ear and apparently past his prime, doesn't have a clue about how corrupt his friends and neighbors are, or maybe he just doesn't want to know. There is not much ordinary crime to worry about in Garrison, since typical criminal lowlifes are afraid to go there. The cops, after all, are armed and dangerous, on duty or off, as Freddy discovers.

Freddy, first seen drunk at a bar the cops frequent, once dreamed of becoming a NYPD officer but could not make the force because his hearing was impaired as a consequence of saving the life of Liz Randone (Annabella Sciorra), after her car crashed over a bridge and into the river. She later married one of the neighborhood cops, who treats her like dirt and is unfaithful. Obviously, Freddy still loves her. The point of this backstory is that Freddy is a hero, even though he now seems to be a slob.

The film begins with rookie police officer Murray Babitch (Michael Rapaport) driving home to Garrison over the George Washington Bridge. He is sideswiped by a car driven by two black teenagers who seem to be armed. The accident escalates and Babitch shoots and kills them, but officers investigating the shooting find no weapon in the car. Babitch's uncle is Ray Donlan, who makes it appear that Babitch has jumped from the bridge, but this is merely a diversion to get Murray out of a tight spot.

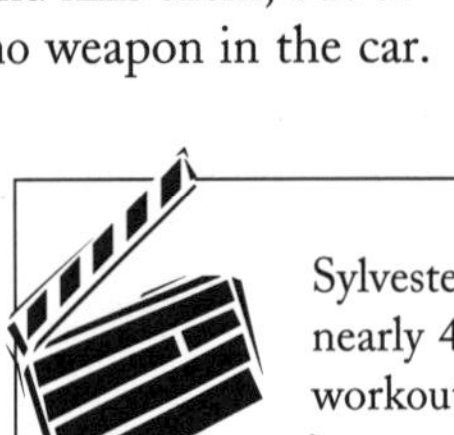

Sylvester Stallone gained nearly 40 pounds and quit his workouts to play the lumbering, overweight sheriff.

Murray is hidden in the back seat of Ray's car and taken to Garrison, where he goes into hiding. Later on, because of political pressure over the killing of the two black youths, Ray is ordered killed by the Mafia to provide the body—Murray's body—that was never found in the river. Ray's wife warns Murray that he is to be sacrificed, and he escapes.

Freddy knows that Murray is not dead. Tipped by Internal Affairs investigator Moe Tilden (Robert De Niro) that Garrison is run by corrupt cops over whom Tilden has no control (since they live in New Jersey), Freddy decides to save Murray's life by turning him in, but to do so, he has to get Murray out of Garrison past Ray and his armed friends.

Freddy seems to be a stupid, alcoholic patsy, but he is courageous and finally determined to do the right thing when it becomes apparent that the police are taking the law into their own hands. The last half of *Cop Land* is like a Western, as the sheriff attempts to clean up the town. Sensing a no-win situation when Freddy decides to go up against Ray, Deputy Cindy Betts (Janeane Garofalo) requests a transfer to upstate New York. When Deputy Bill Geisler (Noah Emmerich) tells Freddy his wife is pregnant just before Freddy attempts to take Murray across the river to New York, Freddy echoes Marshal Kane's parting words to his cowardly deputy in *High Noon* (1952)—"Go on home, Herb." Freddy will have to fight his own battles, apparently, although at the last minute officer Gary Figgis (Ray Liotta) gives him some unexpected but essential back-up.

In fact, writer-director James Mangold admits to mixing elements of the classic Western with his 1970s police action-drama. *Cop Land* is a morality play. The characters are faced with a moral dilemma: The choice of doing the right thing, of upholding the law, or of protecting their friends and loyalty to their community. This choice is not an easy one for Freddy, but it's one that he has to make in order to protect his own self-respect and dignity. It is the responsibility of the sheriff to uphold the law and clean up the town. Garrison, New Jersey, thus becomes Dodge City, with Freddy as the sheriff whose job it is to clean up the town.

Cop Land is none the less a prestige picture, loaded with talent. As the unusually demanding Gary Arnold noted in his *Washington Times* review, Stallone "deferred an eight-figure salary to play the protagonist" and also put on nearly 40 pounds in order to make the character appear convincing. Ordinarily Stallone could command up to $20 million for a starring role, but this time he agreed to work for scale because, as he told *USA Today*, "It was time to put something in the bank of the soul." Stallone's box-office staying power as an action-hero is indisputable, but at the age of 51 the actor is overdue for an image makeover.

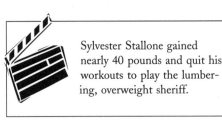

Stallone's earlier attempts to remold his image were not at all successful, but *Cop Land* could do the trick. He is no longer young enough to play Rocky, and the end of the Cold War also brought an end to the Rambo series. *Cop Land* allows him to act his age, at least, and gives him a character that has far more depth than other recent roles, such as the cartoonish *Judge Dredd* (1996). But most important, *Cop Land* gives him an opportunity to act. It would perhaps be wrong to suppose that behind every star there is an actor trying to escape, but in this picture Stallone does act, more convincingly than he has done in the last several years. *Cop Land* is not only his best acting role since *Rocky*; it is arguably the best performance of his career.

The stand-out performances in this picture are not those of Robert De Niro and Harvey Keitel; they act out their hostilities with expert precision, but both of them are in supporting roles. Stallone lumbers through the picture holding his own against such gifted competition. The only actor whose presence nearly matches Stallone is Ray Liotta, a cokehead cop who seems to be a loser but ultimately and unexpectedly has the integrity to support Freddy.

It's been so long since Sylvester Stallone has had a really worthy role that one is surprised and astonished to find this decent and likable actor in a role matching his early potential after all these years. This is not merely another star turn as a predictable action hero. Freddy Heflin is smaller, not larger, than life, a man whose life has been beset by failure and frustration. Stallone is able to humanize the character and play him perfectly to scale. His performance makes the film worth seeing.

—James M. Welsh

CREDITS

Freddy Heflin: Sylvester Stallone
Ray Donlan: Harvey Keitel
Gary Figgis: Ray Liotta
Moe Tilden: Robert De Niro
Joey Randone: Peter Berg
Deputy Cindy Betts: Janeane Garofalo
Jack Rucker: Robert Patrick
Murray Babitch: Michael Rapaport
Liz Randone: Annabella Sciorra
Deputy Bill Geisler: Noah Emmerich
Rose Donlan: Cathy Moriarty

Origin: USA
Released: 1997
Production: Cary Woods, Cathy Konrad, Ezra Swerdlow for Woods Entertainment; released by Miramax Films
Direction: James Mangold
Screenplay: James Mangold
Cinematography: Eric Edwards
Editing: Craig McKay
Music: Howard Shore
Production design: Lester Cohen
Art direction: Wing Lee
Set decoration: Karin Weisel
Costumes: Ellen Lutter
Sound: Allan Byer
Stunt coordinator: Jerry Hewitt
MPAA rating: R
Running Time: 105

REVIEWS

The Baltimore Sun. August 15, 1997, p. E1.
Boxoffice. September, 1997, p. 116.
Chicago Tribune. August 15, 1997, p. 4.
Entertainment Weekly. August 15, 1997, p. 44.
The Hollywood Reporter. August 11, 1997, p. 8.
Los Angeles Times. August 15, 1997, p. F14.
The New York Times. August 15, 1997, p.B3.
The New Yorker. August 18, 1997, p. 77.
Newsweek. August 25, 1997, p. 73.
People. August 25, 1997, p. 23.
Rolling Stone. September 4, 1997, p. 73.
Sight and Sound. December, 1997, p. 41.
Time. August 11, 1997, p. 70.
USA Today. August 15, 1997, p. D1.
Variety. August 11, 1997, p. 56.
The Washington Post. August 15, 1997, p. G1.
Washington Post Metropolitan Times. August 15, 1997, p. C15.
Washington Post Weekend. August 15, 1997, p. 32.

Cosi

Alone they were lost. Together they were magic.—Movie tagline

"A wonderfully original and very funny film! You're bound to fall in love with this cast."
—*Jeanne Wolf's Hollywood*

"Uproarious!"—*Los Angeles Times*

"Spunky and satisfying! Toni Collette and Rachel Griffiths are aces."—*Miami Herald*

"Irresistible and hilarious!"—*Sixty Second Preview*

Cosi is about inmates in a mental asylum who put on a production of Mozart's *Cosi Fan Tutti*. Film buffs may immediately conjure up images of *King of Hearts* or *One Flew Over the Cuckoo's Nest*, in which the patients are shown more sympathetically than the asylum's staff. Such films are irreverent, subversive, and rather sentimental—finding in the madness a decency and humanity that their sane and conventional keepers are sorely lacking. This dissenting view of the world, in which mental illness is equated with romantic nonconformity, was fashionable in the 1960s and 1970s, and was given professional polish by psychiatrists such as R.D. Laing. But the cultural winds have shifted in the 1990s, making a replay of the schizophrenic as tormented genius jejune. Psychological disturbance may still be treated with psychotherapy of various kinds, but drugs are preferred because they attack the biological basis of most personality disorders. Indeed, all forms of Freudian therapy have come under massive attack in recent years as Freud and his followers have been condemned for overlooking human physiology. In other words, a movie audience of the 1990s is less likely to identify with characters who don't take their medicine—like Jack Nicholson, who tucks his pill under his tongue in *Cuckoo's Nest*—and to regard the idea of putting on an opera for therapeutic purposes as rather quaint, if not misguided.

Cosi admirably adapts to the changing zeitgeist, however, by presenting a nuanced portrait of the sane and the insane. The asylum director and his staff are well meaning, if vague about how acting will help their troubled charges. They want to do good as well as put on a good show for the government administrator they report to. Their major failing, not surprisingly, is lack of imagination. They do not know what to say to two applicants applying for the theater director's job.

Cosi portrays the staff/patient dynamic not as an us against them proposition but rather as a continuum, a broad range of human behaviors that can veer to extremes. Lewis (Ben Mendelsohn), is an out-of-work director hired to put together some kind of theatrical production. He has gotten the job by default, since his rival for the position is too eccentric looking—not the picture of conventional health his employers prefer. But Lewis has no idea what to do and no experience with the mentally ill. He has lied about his resume to get the job, and he is there largely because he has been goaded into seeking employment by his law student girlfriend, Lucy (Rachel Griffiths).

Immediately out of his depth, Lewis is bowled over by Roy (Barry Otto), a histrionic and manic inmate who assembles a casting call and confidently announces to his fellows that they will be performing Mozart's opera. No one knows the work except for Roy. No one has singing experience. Their pianist, Zac (Colin Hay) is comatose much of the time. The audition process is itself a farce, with very few of the hopeful exhibiting any talent whatsoever. The erstwhile cast includes Henry (Paul Chubb) a virtual catatonic, who keeps trying to bolt out of the theater; Doug (David Wenham) a thuggish pyromaniac, who threatens Lewis and nearly jabs his cigarettes into the director's face; Cherry (Jacki Weaver) a nymphomaniac, Ruth (Pamela Rabe) a suicidal recluse, who advises Lewis on the best way to slash his wrists; and Julie (Toni Collette) a drug addict, who misses rehearsals for appointments with her psychiatrist.

> Director Mark Joffe: "It's a film about how important it is not to be sour or negative about the things life offers you because you never know what they can turn into."

Lewis is depressed. Even worse, Lewis is inept. The institution's security guard, Errol Grier (Colin Friels), tries to help Lewis, providing clear, common sense advice. Essentially Errol counsels Lewis to make do: forget how ridiculous a full dress performance of the opera would be. Concentrate on putting on a show, building a story, developing character relationships, and make the music grow out of what emerges from the chemistry of this motley ensemble.

Slowly Lewis stumbles into his role as director. He begins to study the opera's text and to construct models of stage sets. He takes his cast to a performance of a play put on by his friend Nick (Aden Young), a self-important ac-

AWARDS AND NOMINATIONS

Australian Film Institute 1996: Supporting Actress (Collette), Adapted Screenplay
Nominations: Supporting Actor (Otto)

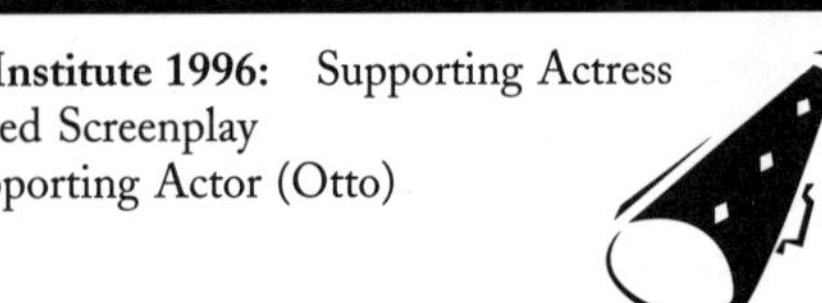

tor/director whom Lewis thinks can help him and his cast. Actually Nick is a bombastic fool who is after Lucy. Nick has moved in on Lucy and Lewis after a tiff with his girlfriend. As Lewis later realizes, Nick is hardly more than a parasite. Nick, the cynic, carries on a running commentary on the unfaithfulness of women that is also the theme of Mozart's opera. Lewis resists Nick's subversive personality even as he admires Nick's bravado. Gradually the opera and Lewis's life seem to merge, and he suspects that Lucy has sought succor elsewhere as Lewis becomes obsessed with his inmates. Indeed Nick has bet Lewis $50 that Lucy has been unfaithful, and Lewis suspects that Nick has won his bet by seducing Lucy himself.

Picture is dedicated to actor Bruno Lawrence, who started the role of Errol Grier but who was unable to continue when diagnosed with a terminal illness.

The opera of everyday, then, rivals the opera of the stage. And what makes Lewis's suspicions of Lucy all the more convincing to him is that he has become attracted to Julie. She is the one inmate who can really sing—as he discovers one day when he hears her passionate voice coming out of the shadows of what she supposes is an empty theater. Toni Collette makes a ravishing Julie. She is warm and flirtatious and down to earth. She has a drug problem, but it does not rob her of her humanity. She is afraid of returning to the world outside the asylum, yet she clearly does not belong there. Her voice fills the theater so powerfully that Lewis glimpses a kind of intensity lacking in his own life.

Although they kiss and obviously have feelings for each other, neither Lewis nor Julie pursue an affair. It is hard to say why. Certainly Lewis is still in love with Lucy, and Julie seems to sense that. She is not well and Lewis would be taking advantage of her even if she would be willing to become his lover. But something else is represented here that is rare in contemporary film. It is simply the story of two adults acknowledging a powerful attraction to each other and not acting on it—respecting each other's feelings and circumstances in a way that reflects well on their integrity. When Lewis later tries to apologize for kissing Julie in a romantic moment, she smiles by way of acknowledging their attraction, suggesting also that the kiss was a natural occurrence—not one that either party has to feel guilty about or transform into a major event.

Cosi is a comic contrivance that must observe conventions—such as a happy ending. But there is so much realism and wit in its character development that it is able to blend the farcical and the factual without any sense of incongruity, or that the film is forcing emotion. Take, for example, the finale—the actual performance of the opera. Much goes wrong. Roy gets stage fright and claims he cannot remember his lines. He has fooled Lewis into believing that he has had significant stage experience. But Roy confesses he never got any closer to the stage than as a janitor in a theater. Lewis overcomes Roy's qualms by pretending to panic, by telling Roy what he wants to hear—that the whole production depends on him. Then there is Zac who has been grumbling about doing an opera through rehearsals and in a near comatose state falls into a pit below stage stopping the performance and bewildering the audience until Julie steps forward to sing an impromptu solo. She sings with such yearning and authenticity that the audience believes that what has been spontaneous has actually been cunningly planned. Julie's star turn is pure fantasy, yet it works—for both the cast and the audience, who want to make believe.

Thus the rather naive premise that a theatrical production will be good therapy for the patients is vindicated. They do get to act-out their fears and desires—but in the same way that all people do who are drawn to become actors or audiences. No one is cured by art, but everyone is able to

CREDITS

Lewis: Ben Mendelsohn
Roy: Barry Otto
Julie: Toni Collette
Lucy: Rachel Griffiths
Nick: Aden Young
Errol Grier: Colin Friels
Jeff Kirner: Tony Llewellyn-Jones
Henry: Paul Chubb
Ruth: Pamela Rabe
Cherry: Jacki Weaver
Doug: David Wenham
Zac: Colin Hay
Auditioner: Greta Scacchi (cameo)
Auditioner: Paul Mercurio (cameo)

Origin: Australia
Released: 1995, 1997
Production: Richard Brennan, Timothy White for Smiley Films, Meridien Films, and Australian Film Finance Corporation; released by Miramax Films
Direction: Mark Joffe
Screenplay: Louis Nowra; based on his play
Cinematography: Ellery Ryan
Editing: Nicholas Beauman
Music: Stephen Endelman
Production design: Chris Kennedy
Art direction: Hugh Bateup
Costumes: Tess Schofield
MPAA rating: R
Running Time: 100 minutes

conceive of a happy ending, to—yes—contrive one. As in *Some Like It Hot*, the greatest of screen farces, artifice and actuality keep commenting on each other, renewing Shakespeare's metaphor of the world as a stage. *Cosi* is not as great a film as *Some Like It Hot*, but it shares that masterpiece's sense that the greatest comedies contain the world of tragedy within them.

—*Carl Rollyson*

REVIEWS

Boxoffice. April, 1997, p. 198.
Los Angeles Times. April 11, 1997, p. F6.
New York Times. April 11, 1997, p. B10.
Variety. March 25, 1996, p. 67.
Village Voice. April 15, 1997, p. 76.

Crash

Love in the dying moments of the twentieth century.—Movie tagline

In a society driven to extremes, two people met by accident.—Movie tagline

"Sleek and emotional . . . this movie is bumper-to-bumper sex!"—Jack Mathews, *Newsday*

"Cronenberg has made the hydrogen bomb of shock movies. It's the apotheosis of auto eroticism."—Jack Kroll, *Newsweek*

"A brave, unprecedented movie, *Crash* is a classic!"—Georgia Brown, *Village Voice*

Box Office: $2,101,043

It would seem only appropriate for director David Cronenberg, master of visceral horror, to bring to the screen J.G. Ballard's notorious cult classic novel *Crash*, an adventure into the ecstasies of the head-on collision between the automobile and the body. David Cronenberg is after all a filmmaker who has founded his career on the ambition to represent the strange borders of the desiring body as it comes into contact with the reflexivity of technological representation. He has charted important territory in such films as *Videodrome* (1982), *Dead Ringers* (1988), and *Naked Lunch* (1991). Once again it appears that his subject is more interesting than his film. Besides being poorly cast, neither the characters nor the themes are adequately developed enough to provoke any interest, and this fascinating material becomes simply boring. Receiving an NC-17 rating and the Cannes special jury prize for daring and audacity, the film fails to deliver the promises implied by both, provoking neither the sexual arousal nor the intellectual curiosity its subject deserves.

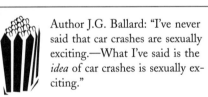

> Author J.G. Ballard: "I've never said that car crashes are sexually exciting.—What I've said is the *idea* of car crashes is sexually exciting."

The film's protagonist, James Ballard (James Spader), is a TV producer who shares an open marriage with his wife Catherine (Deborah Kara Unger). The film opens with a nude image of Catherine being pleasured from behind by a lover while leaning against the wing of a jet, her breast resting on the metal. When Ballard causes a car crash that kills a man and injures the man's wife, he develops a fetish for automotive violence. While recovering from his injuries in the hospital he makes the acquaintance of Vaughan, a scar covered mad scientist who harbors an obsessive passion for photographing the visceral details of automotive crashes, the union of metal and flesh. In the novel Vaughan's larger project is to die in a head-on collision with Elizabeth Taylor, the object of his and society's dreams and desires. Considering the changing meaning of this contemporary figure, Cronenberg chooses to eliminate this project, focusing instead on Vaughan's passion for recreating as spectacle the car crashes of American mythologies such as James Dean and Jayne Mansfield. Unfortunately the complexity of the project and the character of Vaughan are reduced by this omission.

In the hospital Ballard also comes into contact with Dr. Helen Remington, the injured wife of the man he killed. After their release they become sexually involved and together begin to explore the new erotic possibilities emerging in the aftermath of their trauma. They are both driven to seek out the twisted remains of their cars in a junk yard, to consummate their desires inside an assortment of rental cars, and to nearly recreate their accident in a car identical to the one driven by Ballard in the accident. Their interest also leads them into the hornet's nest of the mad Vaughan, who is something of a guru to a group of torn, wounded bodies racked by obsessive violent fantasies—a group whose greatest pleasures include masturbating together in front of a television screen depicting the collisions of crash test dummies.

One day Ballard and Helen attend Vaughan's staged spectacle of the famous James Dean crash. Vaughan's passion for the transcendent seconds preceding and culminating in the irreversible moment of fate is utterly convincing and mesmerizing. Chaos ensues after the collision with the police arriving to break up the illegal event and the stunt man suffering a head injury and being rushed away to Vaughan's lair. It is here that Ballard and Helen first meet Vaughan's other disciples, including Vaughan's ideal woman, the sensuous crippled Gabrielle (Roseanne Arquette), the victim of a convertible car crash that left her legs ripped into wounds resembling the female genitalia, all held together with metal braces and wrapped in black leather attire, her miniskirt exposing her obscene orifices. It is also here that Ballard is first presented to Vaughan's photo album of trauma images, which includes the gory details of Gabrielle's crash as well as images of her gradual reconstruction and recovery. To his surprise the second half of the album contains images of Ballard's own crash, his days in recovery in the hospital, and his ensuing sexual encounters with Helen inside an assortment of automobiles.

Crash was awarded a Special Jury Prize at the 1996 Cannes Film festival for "originality, daring, and audacity."

Gradually the group expands to include Ballard's wife Catherine, who has been developing her own automotive fetish and who becomes equally fascinated with the scarred figure of Vaughan. Catherine and Ballard begin to fantasize over Vaughan in bed, and she helps stimulate Ballard's emerging homoerotic desires which he will eventually realize inside the oily interior of Vaughan's battered black Lincoln. Vaughan expresses his interest in Catherine by trying to collide his big American automobile, which has taken on a demonic quality, into her tiny vulnerable sports convertible. In one such race toward disaster, with the aroused and terrified Ballard following helplessly in pursuit, Vaughan accidentally drives off a viaduct, meeting his own strangely anti-climatic encounter with death. In the aftermath of his death, Ballard and Catherine set off along the highways searching for disaster and death. Catherine crashes first, and is thrown from her car onto the grassy slope beside the highway. Ballard rushes to her side and with just a touch of disappointment and arousal finds her still alive. They both look ahead eagerly to the next time, when maybe they will find the closure they seek, the ultimate satisfaction of desire which only bodily death can provide. In the novel Ballard recalls Catherine saying "that she would never be satisfied until every conceivable act of copulation in the world had at last taken place." This tale marries that metaphysical ambition to modernity in the form of the automobile disaster.

Other than the deletion of Elizabeth Taylor, the film is committed to a close reading of the plot structure of the novel, perhaps even to a fault since in many respects the novel does not lend itself to a literal translation into images. Despite the visual nature of the obsession, much of the strength of the novel lay in the first person portrayal of the workings of the narrator's mind as he mentally explores the potential of the flesh. For example, in the novel Ballard takes pleasure in assaulting the dignity of each person with whom he comes into contact by pondering the details of their genitalia, wondering what their lips look like around their husband's penis, wondering if there is fecal matter around their anus, meat in their teeth, semen on their dashboards. On the other hand, Cronenberg fails to capitalize adequately on the novel's visual metaphors, from the geometry of the body to the architecture of the automobile, from bodily fluids to radiator fluids, from orgasm to collision. Cronenberg might have had better access to Ballard's interior drama had his visual expression been less traditional. Perhaps the greatest discrepancy and failure of the film is in its insistence on turning a traditional lens on untraditional content.

The dominant theme of *Crash* is the strange entanglement of the animate and the inanimate which transpires across two paradoxical longings: to turn life into death, completion, and static form, and to turn death into life, growth,

CREDITS

James Ballard: James Spader
Catherine Ballard: Deborah Unger
Helen Remington: Holly Hunter
Vaughan: Elias Koteas
Gabrielle: Rosanna Arquette
Colin Seagrave: Peter MacNeil

Origin: Canada
Released: 1996
Production: David Cronenberg for Alliance Communications; released by Fine Line Features
Direction: David Cronenberg
Screenplay: David Cronenberg; based on the novel by J.G. Ballard
Cinematography: Peter Suschitzky
Editing: Ronald Sanders
Music: Howard Shore
Production design: Carol Spier
Art direction: Tamara Deverell
Sound: David Lee
Costumes: Denise Cronenberg
Stunt coordination: Ted Hanlan
Casting: Deirdre Bowen
MPAA rating: NC-17
Running Time: 98 minutes

and movement. These longings are read over the landscape of the developing reign of technology, where modern culture becomes inseparable from the new host of machines that service its economy. Central to this theme is the problem of reflexivity in modern machine and media culture, which manifests itself as the impossibility of locating the real amongst a field of dreams, myths, and newspaper blurbs. The gender dynamics are also central. In the novel Ballard had explored Catherine's interest in aviation and the independence she expressed by flying with her lovers over her husband's inert body confined in their domestic interior. He had also explored the authority vested in Helen's medical profession, and the relationship she bore to the body as scientist. In the novel the homoerotic scene also plays a key role in James' sexual development centering on the notion of transgression. Cronenberg is, on one hand, wise to downplay these elements, lest the philosophical issues be obscured by the current interest to read every phenomenon strictly in terms of gender politics. On the other hand, the film develops neither the metaphysical content of the story nor the concrete terms on which these problems are played out between bodies. Ultimately some very serious material is reduced here to its most predictable and sensational level.

—*Reni Celeste*

AWARDS AND NOMINATIONS

Genie Awards 1996: Cinematography, Director (Cronenberg), Editing, Adapted Screenplay
Nominations: Film, Sound

REVIEWS

Boxoffice. July, 1996, p. 86.
Chicago Tribune. March 21, 1997, p. 5.
Entertainment Weekly. March 28, 1997, p. 51.
Los Angeles Times. March 21, 1997, p. F10.
New York Times. March 19, 1997, p. B9.
New York Times. March 21, 1997, p. B3.
The New Yorker. March 31, 1997, p. 106.
People. March 24, 1997, p. 20.
Rolling Stone. April 17, 1997, p. 85.
Time. March 24, 1997.
USA Today. March 19, 1997, p. 5D.
USA Today. March 21, 1997, p. 4D.
Variety. May 20, 1996, p. 30.
Village Voice. March 25, 1997, p. 78.

Critical Care

At Memorial Hospital no one ever dies . . . until their insurance runs out.—Movie tagline

"One of the best recent films by a master whose credits include *Network* and *The Verdict* . . . sharp-edged, smart and darkly funny . . . one of the most clever films of the season."—Roger Ebert, *Chicago Sun-Times*

"Sidney Lumet shakes things up and draws some blood . . . Lumet's hand with actors is as unerring as ever."—Michael Wilmington, *Chicago Tribune*

"Kyra Sedgwick's strongest performance yet." —David Noh, *Film Journal*

"Splendid performances by James Spader, Helen Mirren and especially Albert Brooks."—Stephen Farber, *Movieline*

"A timely, dark comedy . . . biting and topical . . . it recalls Lumet's brilliant *Network*."—Bruce Williamson, *Playboy*

"Provocative, daring and unusual."—Jeffrey Lyons, *WNBC-TV*

Critical Care is a dark comedy set in the antiseptic atmosphere of a futuristic intensive care unit, where state-of-the-art technology keeps the terminally ill alive interminably. The film attempts to question the morality of a health care system that is so far removed from simple humanity that the decisions regarding a patient's life or death center more around his medical insurance than on his condition.

Sidney Lumet directed *Critical Care* with a cast that boasts top boxoffice talent, all of whom took a cut in pay to work on the film. James Spader, who starred in *sex, lies and videotape* (1989), plays Dr. Werner Ernst, a second-year resident in a large metropolitan hospital.

Ernst works in the critical care unit where victims of accidents, illness, and old age are being kept alive on machines and ventilators, with pacemakers to jolt them back from "that dark night." The film opens as head nurse Stella

(Helen Mirren) makes her rounds in barren rooms full of such high-tech equipment that at first the set looks like a space station out of *2001* (1968).

The dying lie silently immobile on plastic air mattresses, entangled in nets of tubes and wires, as computers monitor the thin thread of life that lingers on within them. *Critical Care* chronicles Ernst's awakening to the real purpose of medicine as he becomes aware of the suffering of bed five, a patient who has been so dehumanized that even his name has been replaced by a number.

Dr. Ernst about a patient: "I have lettuce in my refrigerator with a better chance of becoming conscious than this guy."

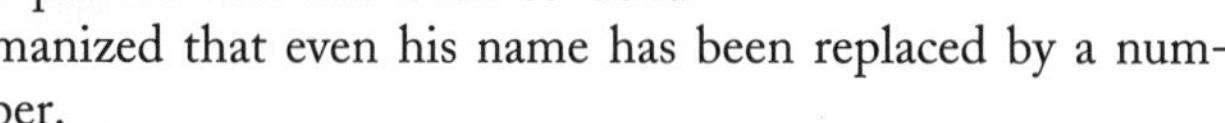

But the ambitious Dr. Ernst is not interested in his patients, so much as he is interested in himself. He is being groomed for a position with the world-renown Dr. Hofstader (Philip Bosco) who is on the cutting edge of the "future of medicine." Hofstader's laboratory is a room full of computers where doctors field queries from hospitals all over the world.

Dr. Hofstader explains to Ernst the theory behind their computer modeling of patient diseases. "Seeing patients is a waste of time," he tells Ernst, "We like to think of patients as information that can be digitized . . . then we can build computer models for surgeons to practice on that are identical with any patient."

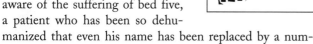

First screenplay from veteran TV producer Steven S. Schwartz.

But career success is not the only thing on Ernst's mind. He has only recently realized how seductive his M.D. status has made him to women, and his dalliances are about to get him into serious trouble.

When bed five's beautiful daughter Felicia Potter (Kyra Sedgwick) drops by, Ernst comforts the distraught woman, who is upset that her father is being kept alive after months of being in a coma. The hospital wants her to give permission for yet another operation on her father so that they can insert a feeding tube directly into his stomach.

Ernst makes a date with Felicia, in order to discuss her father's condition. But Felicia's motives turn out to be less than pure, and she seduces the young doctor in an attempt to get him to admit that her father is in a "persistent vegetative state." She succeeds in getting him to say it on tape, and when her lawyer gets an injunction against the doctors to perform any more lifesaving procedures on her father, Felicia blackmails Ernst.

At first, she tries to get him to tell the judge that her father is a vegetable and then she tries to blackmail him to pull the plug on her father. At the center of the conflict is a trust fund of $10 million that, in the event of bed five's death within the next three weeks, will go to Felicia. If he survives past that period, the money will go to her half-sister, Connie (Margo Martindale).

With so much at stake, lawyers from both daughters, insurance companies, and the hospital are all called in to decide bed five's fate. The only interested party that is missing, Ernst realizes, is the patient himself, and his interests are being grossly overlooked.

Ernst goes to bed five's doctor, Dr. Butz (Albert Brooks), an aged alcoholic who is forever paging Ernst then forgetting why, to discuss bed five's future, or lack thereof. Butz, in a moment of candor, explains to Ernst that as long as bed five has catastrophic insurance, they will continue to perform procedures on the man.

Butz tells him that he gets a cut from every procedure, and they netted $112,000 from him during that last month alone. He can't understand why Ernst would even think of letting this cash cow go. When Ernst questions the need to let him continue to suffer, Butz tells him there is no other way for bed five. But he confides that he has found a way to avoid ever suffering the same fate. Butz tells Ernst that he has something even better than a living will. He has no insurance at all. No doctor on earth would torture him in some bed without insurance, he says.

Meanwhile, nurse Stella, the resigned yet loving floor nurse, tends to the patient in bed two (Jeffrey Wright), a 23-year-old who has rejected two kidney transplants and now functions through a machine. His parents refuse to let him go, so he is brought back from near death over and over again. All bed two wants is to die.

In the delirium of fever, he is visited by the Furnaceman (Wallace Shawn), who calls himself the "devil's little helper" and tries to convince bed two to join him in his hell, which he promises is better than the one bed two is in now. Bed two, whose endless pain has robbed him of his faith, suffers on and on until nurse Stella, in a moment of compassion, unplugs his machine and lets him die.

At the moment of death, bed two loses the fetters of the mass of tubes that tied him to the bed and leaves the tortured world of the half-dead, ascending to heaven on a ray of white light to "be with God."

AWARDS AND NOMINATIONS

Independent Spirit Awards 1997 Nominations:
Debut Screenplay

Dealing with the moral and political issues surrounding the health care system, with questions about the right-to-die, and even touching on the purpose of life itself, *Critical Care* proves to be too ambitious. The sheer breadth and range of the film dilutes its impact. The film has a wealth of talent, playing roles that range from caricature to realism to fantasy, but the segments are so diverse that the actors don't seem to be acting in the same film.

Helen Mirren, who plays the head nurse, is known best for her role in the BBC production of *Prime Suspect* and her portrayal of Queen Charlotte in *The Madness of King George* (1994). Through the character of Stella, with her unique mixture of compassion and cynicism, Mirren brings a hint of realism to the film that doesn't mesh with the other more comedic performances.

Kyra Sedgwick plays the soulless Felicia Potter with an almost comic book humor that contrasts well with Ernst's dry disposition. James Spader, as Dr. Ernst, is convincing as the ambitious yet unmoved doctor who is changed forever when he gives up the battle to save lives at any cost and learns to accept death as a natural part of life.

Although Jeffrey Wright, of *Basquiat* (1996) fame, gives a wonderful performance as the long-suffering patient in bed two, his feverish hallucinations with the Furnaceman tend to lessen the impact of his supposed suffering. While Albert Brooks, as the buffoonish Dr. Butz, gives us some hard truths in the form of impeccably timed one-liners, his aging makeup distracts from his performance.

A highly stylized film, *Critical Care* uses color coordination to imbue the film with a sense of sterility and dehumanization. Lumet said: "I wanted a look that was abstract—almost science fiction—yet absolutely accurate medically." Production designer Philip Rosenberg gave him that look, with icy aqua and white "pods," where the patients sleep, set in a circle around the central nurse's station. Only after Ernst's epiphany, when he walks out of the hospital into the light of day, do we see real-life colors, paralleling the doctor's new perspective of reality.

But in the end, the sets and the jokes and the fantasy segments work so well in portraying the dehumanization of the patients, that the patients are dehumanized. It becomes almost impossible to connect the earthy emotions of compassion and empathy with the lifeless forms floating on plastic air mattresses in the sterile pods, where the thread of life is more animated on the computer screen than in the bodies of the dying.

The pace of the film lags in places, and the dialogue is sometimes a trifle too quietly reverential to be understood clearly, but the film's message is as clear as the white light when bed two ascends. The message is clear, and yet we remain untouched.

—Diane Hatch-Avis

CREDITS

Dr. Werner Ernst: James Spader
Felicia Potter: Kyra Sedgwick
Stella: Helen Mirren
Connie Potter: Margo Martindale
Dr. Butz: Albert Brooks
Bed Two: Jeffrey Wright
Furnaceman: Wallace Shawn
Nun: Anne Bancroft
Dr. Hofstader: Philip Bosco
Robert Payne: Edward Herrmann
Wilson: Colm Feore

Origin: USA
Released: 1997
Production: Steven S. Schwartz and Sidney Lumet for Village Roadshow and ASQA Film Partnership; released by Live Entertainment
Direction: Sidney Lumet
Screenplay: Steven S. Schwartz; based on the book by Richard Dooling
Cinematography: David Watkin
Editing: Tom Swartwout
Music: Michael Convertino
Production design: Philip Rosenberg
Art direction: Dennis Davenport
Set design: Gord White
Costumes: Dona Granata
Sound: Bruce Cartwardine
MPAA rating: R
Running Time: 107 minutes

REVIEWS

Boston Globe. October 31, 1997.
Boxoffice. December, 1997.
Entertainment Weekly. November 14, 1997, p. 58.
Hollywood Reporter. October 13, 1997, p. 5.
LA Weekly. October 31, 1997.
Los Angeles Times. October 31, 1997, p. F20.
New York Times. October 31, 1997, p. E20.
People. November 10, 1997, p. 26.
Variety. October 13, 1997, p. 84.
Village Voice. November 4, 1997, p. 79.

Dangerous Ground

What he wants is revenge. What he gets is the fight of his life.—Movie tagline

Box Office: $5,303,931

Dangerous Ground is a sort of private detective story set in post-apartheid South Africa. Filmed on location in Johannesburg, Soweto, Sun City, and Coffee Bay, it stars popular gangsta-rapper Ice Cube as Vusi, who returns to his homeland after living for many years in America. Vusi was forced to flee South Africa at the age of 13 because, as shown in grainy black and white flashbacks, he was already heavily involved in the native resistance movement and his life was in danger. Now as a thoroughly Americanized, 25-year-old man he returns to his homeland to attend his father's funeral. As the oldest male member of his family he is expected to officiate at certain ceremonies, which include killing a bull with a Zulu-type spear and drinking its blood. He has become so citified, so Westernized, so alienated from his people's traditions that he finds it impossible to commit such a distasteful deed. He is shamed in front of the gathering of relatives, friends, and tribal affiliates by having to stand by while his younger brother Ernest (Sechaba Morojele) snatches the spear and performs the execution in his stead.

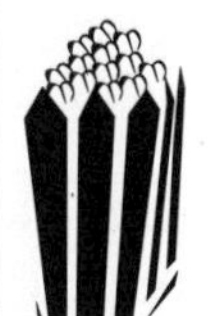

Vusi: "You can't fall into the same trap that the black Americans did in the '70s. They got free, then they got high. Drugs have taken over where apartheid left off."

Vusi finds little in his native land to appeal to him anymore. He is anxious to get through with his filial obligations and catch the earliest possible flight back to San Francisco, where he is a drug counselor and graduate student. Throughout the film his departure is delayed by one circumstance after another. Fist, his mother begs him to go to Johannesburg to find out what has happened to the prodigal Steven (Eric Miyeni), another of his younger brothers. Vusi very reluctantly agrees to do so; he cannot bear to hurt his bereaved mother any further, and he already feels a need to make up for his humiliating loss of face during the bull sacrifice.

The plot bears a strong resemblance to that of *The Third Man* (1949), in which Holly Martins (Joseph Cotton) is forced into the role of amateur detective in a strange, war torn city. Martins' quest for information about his friend Harry Lime (Orson Welles) led him all over bomb-gutted postwar Vienna, providing the audience with a guided tour of that nearly extinguished city. Vusi's quest for his missing brother takes him and the audience all over post-apartheid Johannesburg, where the population seems as demoralized as the defeated Austrians. Like Martins, Vusi keeps blundering into situations that imperil his own life and the lives of others. Like Martins, Vusi is always on the point of going home to America but never quite making it to the plane.

Liberation has been a mixed blessing for the black Africans. Many expected that liberation would immediately bring them the kind of prosperity they had always seen white people enjoying. Their imaginations had been shaped by American movies. They expected to have luxury cars, beautiful clothes, spacious homes, private swimming pools, and all the other luxuries that seemed commonplace in capitalist society. Instead they are living in a disintegrating society where crime is rampant.

Vusi is introduced to the terrible reality of modern South Africa when an armed band of drug-crazed black thugs stop him in broad daylight and not only steal his rented car but strip him of his trendy American clothing. He cannot understand why brothers are doing this to another brother. His hysterically laughing assailants are indifferent to such a concept. To them all men are created equal and are equally victimizable. There is an apocalyptic feeling about *Dangerous Ground* that is enhanced by the relentless beat and menacing lyrics of the rap music on the film's soundtrack. People seem to be living for the day, knowing that the end of the world is close at hand. The mood is often reminiscent of such nihilistic films as *Mad Max* (1980) and *Escape from New York* (1981).

Vusi's quest for Steven eventually leads him to Steven's white girlfriend Karin (Elizabeth Hurley). She is a streetwise crack-addict who makes her living as a nude exotic dancer in a desegregated dive. Like Anna (Alida Valli) in *The Third Man,* Karin serves as a guide to the blundering, bewildered American hero. Right from the start Vusi makes it clear that he has no use for whites and no sexual interest in white women. The film is not overtly anti-white but seems to suggest that black troubles are directly correlated with acceptance of white values. Vusi's hostile attitude does not enhance audience sympathy, since without Karin he would be lost in an urban jungle 10,000 miles from home.

Together Vusi and Karin learn why Steven has gone underground. He is a crack addict. He has blown $15,000 that belongs to the powerful and totally ruthless drug lord Muki (Ving Rhames). Muki has put out a contract on Steven and is confident that it is only a matter of time before the execution will be carried out. Muki is more concerned about his image than about the money. His enterprise is based on force and terror and he cannot afford to let one of his flunkies steal from him and get away with it. Steven is a living symbol of the new South Africa. His cheap, gaudy, Western-style clothing, his flashy junk jewelry, and his conked hair reveal the meretricious values he has assimilated. Karin's loyalty to such an obvious loser makes her stand out as the most admirable character in the film.

It takes Vusi a long time to understand what is going on. As he sees it, the liberated black Africans are going the way of too many African-Americans. He sermonizes to Steven about the need for black South Africans to learn self-discipline and responsibility. The format of the story, however, undercuts the message because the totally demoralized Steven is obviously a lost cause. He is so far gone into drugs, gambling, and wild night life that there is no hope of bringing him back to his senses.

The arrogant Muki agrees to let Steven off the hook if Vusi will pay his debt. Muki takes it for granted that any American would have no trouble raising $15,000, but Vusi has to stretch his credit to the limit to get the money sent to him from California. After accepting the payoff, Muki, surrounded by heavily armed bodyguards, coldly and deliberately shoots Steven and orders Vusi, Karin, and Vusi's other brother Ernest thrown out.

This leads to a revenge wind-up in which Muki's luxurious penthouse is shredded by bullets and redecorated with blood. In one of the more striking scenes a naked woman is torn to pieces by machine gun bullets in a pool-sized bathtub. One by one the heavily armed members of the mini-army surrounding the drug lord are eliminated. Naturally the viewer is expecting the ultimate confrontation to be with Muki, who remains so serene throughout all the bloodletting that one would suspect that, like Tony Montana (Al Pacino) in *Scarface* (1983), he has been sampling too much of his own merchandise. This shotgun ending may please the younger members of the audience but reveals that *Dangerous Ground* has little to say and nowhere to go. Critics have deplored the fact that South African filmmaker Darrell James Roodt, who did such an outstanding job with *Cry, the Beloved Country* (1995), should have gotten involved in what *Variety* reviewer Joe Leydon accurately describes as "a retread of a 1970s blaxploitation drama."

The main interest in *Dangerous Ground* was in its star, Ice Cube, who was praised for his performance as embittered ex-con Doughboy in *Boyz N the Hood* (1991), and seemed to have a promising future as an actor. But *Dangerous Ground* was dangerous ground indeed for his budding film career. He seems stiff, awkward, and out of his depth. Throughout the film Ice Cube wears the same angry frown featured on the movie posters. His part as Vusi would seem to call for a sophisticated black man showing a lot of country bumpkins how things are done in the tough American inner cities. But what actually happens is just the opposite: everybody leads him around by the nose—his mother, his brothers, Karin, and Muki. Everybody seems more hip than Vusi until the last few minutes when he takes charge and leads the implausibly reckless assault on Muki's stronghold.

The viewer is left with the impression that South Africa has even more troubles than the United States. The situation in modern South Africa resembles that of the American South after the Civil War. The blacks are free, but the economy is shattered and there are too many people in need. South Africa, like many of the other former African colonies, seems destined to undergo a period of political and economic chaos before it may possibly emerge as a transformed, unified, viable new nation. The injustice and violence it has already experienced may be nothing compared to what the future holds in store.

—Bill Delaney

CREDITS

Vusi: Ice Cube
Karin: Elizabeth Hurley
Muki: Ving Rhames
Steven: Eric Miyeni
Ernest: Sechaba Morajele

Origin: USA
Released: 1997
Production: Gillian Gorfil, Darrell James Roodt; released by New Line Cinema
Direction: Darrell James Roodt
Screenplay: Darrell James Roodt and Greg Latter
Cinematography: Paul Gilpin
Editing: David Heitner
Music: Stanley Clarke
Production design: Dimitri Repanis
Art direction: Emilia Roux
Costumes: Ruy Filipe
Sound: Mark Phillips
MPAA rating: R
Running Time: 95 minutes

REVIEWS

Boxoffice. April, 1997, p. 199.
Chicago Tribune. February 13, 1997, p. 6.
Los Angeles Times. February 12, 1997, p. B9.
New York Times. February 12, 1997, p. F6.
Sight and Sound. June, 1997, p. 97.
USA Today. February 13, 1997, p. 4D.
Variety. February 17, 1997, p. 70.
Village Voice. February 25, 1997, p. 70.

Dante's Peak

Whatever you do, don't look back!—Movie tagline

"Hold on to your seat!"—Ron Brewington, *American Urban Radio Networks*

"One hell of a ride!"—Tom Brown, *KDNL*

"Heart-pounding, run for your life thrills."—Sara Edwards, *NBC News Channel*

"Unforgettable. The impact is truly awesome." —Michael Medved, *New York Post*

"An action blasting ride that rocks."—Kyle Osborne, *Newschannel 8*

"Spectacular, mind blowing special effects."—Sam Hallenbeck, *WTVT*

Harry Dalton (Pierce Brosnan) and town mayor Rachel Wando (Linda Hamilton) are faced with a major catastrophe when a once dormant volcano erupts in the disaster film *Dante's Peak.*

Box Office: $67,175,940

Although there is no explicit reference to Italian poet Dante Alighieri (who wrote of the circles of hell in his *The Divine Comedy*), the exploding volcano, the spume of lava, and the fireballs rocketing from the summit at the opening of this motion picture certainly puts one in mind of a devilish inferno. Over brooding and ultimately turbulent orchestra music, two people are seen fleeing a catastrophe. One is Harry Dalton (Pierce Brosnan); the other is his wife Marianne, who is killed by a ball of molten lava that plunges through the roof of their vehicle.

Harry: "I move around a lot, wherever there's a volcano with an attitude."

Four years have passed and Harry, a volcanologist, takes a trip to the picturesque town of Dante's Peak. Seismic activity suggests a problem he feels needs checking out at once, despite his being overdue for a vacation.

Dante's Peak is a settlement of some 7,000 souls, nestling beneath an idyllic snow-clad mountain. Racing the clock, the town's mayor Rachel Wando (Linda Hamilton) finishes dressing and drives her truck to a town gathering where she receives, on behalf of her community, an award proclaiming it to be the second best place to live in the United States under 20,000 people. Up on the slopes, however, a skinny-dipping couple are boiled to death in suddenly scalding hot springs.

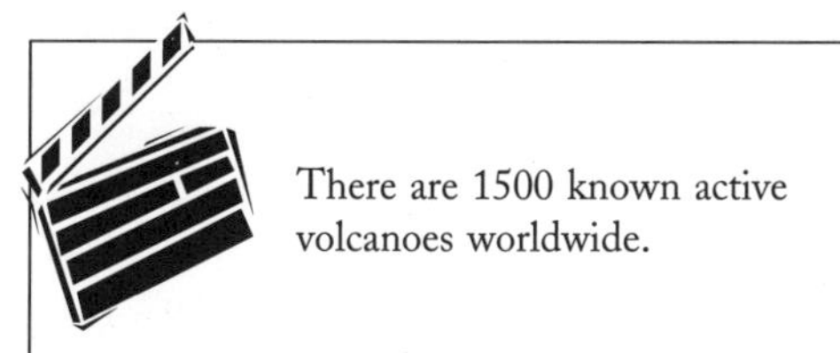

There are 1500 known active volcanoes worldwide.

Harry and Rachel's first meeting does not disguise the immediate chemistry between the two, but at this point, our volcano expert is more concerned with the acidic chemistry of the peak's water. With Rachel's two kids in tow, young Graham (Jeremy Foley) whom Rachel has to pull out from playing with his pals in a dangerous, abandoned mine, and the more obedient Lauren (Jamie Renee Smith), the party heads up the mountain. After collecting Grandma Ruth (Elizabeth Hoffman) from her expansive log-cabin on a lake, the kids prepare for a dip in the springs, until Harry performs his first act of heroism and catches Graham as he's about to vault into the deadly water. The boiled bodies of the couple are then discovered.

A town council is summoned to discuss the warning signs; they worry about scaring off Blair Industries, a company about to inject eighteen million dollars into the local economy. Harry pushes for the declaration of a state of alert, but is overruled by his boss, Dr. Paul Dreyfus (Charles Hallahan), whose arrival reverses the mood of the meeting. Dreyfus promises to bring in a team, forecasts there to be nothing to be worried about, and orders Harry to take his vacation. But Harry won't leave.

A helicopter reconnaissance over the peak reveals no unusual activity. Rachel, who runs a coffee shop in addition to her mayoral duties (and who supplies free drinks to the team each morning), plucks up her courage and invites Harry over for dinner. On the porch after the meal, and when her children are tucked up in bed, the two reflect on their past romances and lives. Rachel's former husband maintains no contact with his children and hasn't for years; Harry shares the tragic loss of his Marianne—and one senses nobody has come near to taking her place since her death.

Back at work, the team has a robot lowered into the volcano's rim to pursue further scientific investigation. But when it malfunctions, one of the crew members follows to make repairs. A tremor sends rocks flying, and Harry descends to aid his stricken colleague. Both need a helicopter winch to rescue them.

More convinced than ever of the clear and present danger, Harry presses for Dante's Peak to be put on alert, but Paul continues to resist, ordering his team to depart the following morning. In what looks like being their final evening together, Harry and Rachel stroll back to her house, and on a bridge, their kiss is interrupted by a nosy friend. In her kitchen, another kiss is precluded by Lauren's need for a drink. When Rachel turns on her kitchen tap, the water is horribly brown. A drive to the community's water supply demonstrates the impending crisis: sulphur dioxide is contaminating the water.

During a town meeting in which a call for calm goes out, more tremors shake the auditorium. The National Guard has been summoned but will not arrive until the next morning. As the ground under feet shifts, and as ceiling panels falls, panic ensues. Plumes of black smoke from the peak and the subsequent shock waves force buildings to their knees. Cars skid and crash as people flee in terror. Harry and Rachel are forced to drive across the river to make progress past the jammed roads, and are virtually submerged at one point. Emerging from the water, they eventually reach Rachel's home, whereupon they discover that their kids have taken their mother's truck to rescue their stubborn grandmother; she has refused to leave her mountain-hugging home.

Under blizzards of ash, and enveloping darkness, the family reunites at Mirror Lake, and Ruth is finally convinced to abandon her house. With the roads impassible, the party takes a boat across the silent water, now bloated with dead fish. The acid in the water erodes the boat and Ruth wades in to force the vessel to shore—in effect sacrificing herself, although she makes it some way through the forest before expiring. Meanwhile, the scientific party finally abandons Dante's Peak, but Dr. Dreyfus is caught on a bridge being washed away by a raging river, and he is lost. Back on the road further down the mountain, Harry commandeers another truck and ends ups trying to outrun the volcano's onslaught, seeking the mine in a desperate attempt at shelter.

But they are not out of danger, and Harry—separated from Rachel and her family rescuing a sophisticated homing device he'd brought—is buried under rubble. But at least the group can be located, and a search party saves them. To cheers and applause, the couple at last embrace, and the customary Hollywood ending mutes the obliterated lives of the inhabitants of the town called Dante's Peak.

Brilliant special effects propel this film (and, no doubt, pumped up the budget). Although one knows from the beginning that the volcano will explode, the resounding force of this natural disaster is vividly evoked. The blue-gray phantasmagoric envelope into which Dante's Peak slips is memorable.

John Frizzel's music provides a turbulent accompaniment to the action, and has even a touch of lyricism when the helicopter flies over the volcano. Crisp editing by Howard Smith, Conrad Buff and Tina Hirsch ensures that the inevitable disaster doesn't seem too long in coming. For this, director Roger Donaldson takes credit as well. He keeps a steady hand of proceedings and contributed to the human dimensions of this action movie's script.

For a *Los Angeles Times* article, Donaldson revealed that he was committed to accuracy. "The whole second half of the movie is nonstop disaster," he commented. "The only people who've seen it before are those who've seen the real thing." And most of those folks are not here to tell the tale. Tim Appelo's piece in the *Times* also explains that Donaldson wanted to elaborate upon screenwriter Les Bohem's "effect-conscious script." One way the director did so was by strengthening the Dalton-Wando romance.

Also writing in the *Los Angeles Times*, a not terribly impressed Kenneth Turan makes the point that "*Dante's Peak*

CREDITS

Harry Dalton: Pierce Brosnan
Rachel Wando: Linda Hamilton
Paul Dreyfus: Charles Hallahan
Greg: Grant Heslov
Ruth: Elizabeth Hoffman
Lauren Wando: Jamie Renee Smith

Origin: USA
Released: 1997
Production: Gale Anne Hurd and Joseph M. Singer for Pacific Western; released by Universal Pictures
Direction: Roger Donaldson
Screenplay: Leslie Bohem
Cinematography: Andrzej Barkowiak
Editing: Howard Smith, Conrad Buff, Tina Hirsch
Music: John Frizzell
Production design: Dennis Washington
Art direction: Tom Targownik Taylor, Francis J. Pezza
Costumes: Isis Mussenden
Sound: Dave Macmillan
Visual effects: Patrick McClung
Special effects: Roy Arbogast
MPAA rating: PG-13
Running Time: 108 minutes

treats its volcanic eruption as if it were a mass murderer . . . the potential victims in Bohem's predictable script are blithely oblivious to the danger they're facing." The volcano does kill a sizeable portion of the town's population, yet is it not true that it is human nature to wear blinkers? If people did not do that, why would so many people, Turan included, continue to live, for example, in earthquake-threatened southern California?

Donaldson builds suspense and the love story so that the prelude to the catastrophe is neither superfluous nor sagging. Andrzej Bartowiak's cinematography excels in the many shades and colors of the film. As for the two stars, both, happily, have charm. Pierce Brosnan is an actor always at ease in his roles—albeit roles that don't appear to stretch him tremendously—while Linda Hamilton's Rachel combines an inner strength with a vulnerability sure to appeal to red-blooded men. They give a human quality to an effective story testifying that natural forces, not mankind, control this planet.

—Paul B. Cohen

REVIEWS

Boxoffice. April, 1997, p. 201.
Chicago Tribune. February 7, 1997, p. 4.
Detroit News. February 7, 1997, p. D1.
Entertainment Weekly. February 14, 1997, p. 41.
Los Angeles Times. August 19, 1996, p. F2.
Los Angeles Times. February 7, 1997, p. F1.
New York Times. February 7, 1997, p. B1.
People. February 17, 1997, p. 19.
Time. February 17, 1997.
USA Today. February 7, 1997, p. 4D.
Variety. February 10, 1997, p. 62.
Village Voice. February 18, 1997, p. 80.

The Daytrippers

It's a family affair.—Movie tagline

What a day. What a trip.—Movie tagline

"Do yourself a favor - see *Daytrippers.* An irresistible charmer, sparkling with wit and humor."—Bill Diehl, *ABC Radio*

"Smart and charmingly neurotic. *The Daytrippers* reinvents an American classic."—Dwight Garner, *Harper's Bazaar*

"Smart, funny and poignant. A treasure worth unearthing!"—Juan Morales, *Detour*

"Savvy and delightful."—Jami Bernard, *New York Daily News*

"Splendid! Greg Mottola makes one of the most accomplished, original debuts since *sex, lies & videotape.*"—Michael Medved, *New York Post*

"Wonderful! Spirited, expertly acted, generous and funny. The journey is worth the ride."—Janet Maslin, *New York Times*

"A terrific gem! Hilarious, distinctive . . . extremely funny. Fellini meets Woody Allen."—Jeff Craig, *Sixty Second Preview*

"Hilarious! A wonderful new comedy."—John Powers, *Vogue*

Box Office: $2,099,677

Greg Mottola's *The Daytrippers* constructs, at its core, an ideal image of a smug suburban family. The film's congeniality seems to have been calculated to work like a mirror in relation to the limited audience the filmmaker must have had in mind. Until, that is, the mirror, in which we have been watching our own attitudes reflected, shatters before our eyes. Ironically, its frame still holds, so that no one is allowed to escape. Like the family in the film, we are forced to contemplate the truth in the fragments.

Such a structural substratum allows the film an edge over its low-budget rivals, and could explain its success as among the year's surprise hits. Both a sprightly comedy as well as a serious family melodrama, the film can choose to be foolishly romantic as well as seductively intellectual. Thirty-two year old Mottola, a recent alumnus of Columbia University's graduate-level film program, must have paid close attention through all those screenings of Jean Renoir. Like the characters in Renoir's *A Day in the Country* (1946), the Malones set off from their Long Island home for a daylong outing, except in the opposite direction. It is the bohemian quarter of New York City that will mark their eventual destination.

We are introduced to them at a sunny breakfast table. Ruling the roost is the domineering Rita (Anne Meara) with her hand in everything from the morning's early-bird shopping, dutifully undertaken by the henpecked Jim (Pat McNamara), to the careless hairdo of her attractive but recalcitrant daughter, Jo (Parker Posey), home from college. Enjoying the mother-daughter tussle is Carl (Live Schreiber) who, as Jo's boyfriend, is gobbling down what is heaped on his plate while secretly priding himself on the surreptitious sex he has just enjoyed with Jo. Only poor Jim is absent, as if banished to perform the garage chores.

Intruding like a catalyst into this state of domestic equilibrium is the beautiful Eliza (Hope Davis), the family's other daughter, married to Louis (Stanley Tucci), and set up with a suburban home of her own. Eliza has come to consult her mother about an all too common, yet nevertheless unsettling, predicament. While gathering her husband's clothes for washing, she has stumbled upon a love poem that has opened a chasm she never suspected. But what are families for, the film seems to ask, if not for all to take on the troubles of one?

Rita about facing Louis: "It's very easy to lie on the phone."

So, after allowing the erudite Carl to clue them in on the literary allusions used by the writer of the note, the family has to come to a decision. Worse, the mystery lover's medieval romantic stance has everyone doubting if the note was meant for Eliza's husband in the first place. "I should just call him and ask him what this is," Eliza thinks aloud. "No! No," Rita overrules with matriarchal wisdom. "It's very easy to lie on the phone! You can't see the eyes!" Masking her urge to manipulate with an air of moral support, she suggests they all drive Eliza into the city so that she can confront her husband, eye to eye. Eliza's dilemma thus provides the film with its narrative goal, thereby making it clear to the other characters, and us, that there really is nothing else to worry about. The film can thus stretch itself around this nodal point. We thus become ready to enjoy ourselves at Eliza's expense, as it were.

As with characters out of Chekhov, the conversation in the family station wagon on the way to the city serves more to isolate than unite. First, Jo idly comments on the "hideous" office buildings along the highway. "Architecture is dead," Carl declares. "The Europeans may have been imperialists but they know how to make a building." Rita nods from the front seat, more out of admiration for Carl than in agreement, then says to Jo, "Did you hear about Mr. Andrew having an affair with a tenth-grader?" Eliza, who has been trying to convince herself that nothing is wrong, says about her husband, "He works for a publishing company. He's got all kinds of stuff in his briefcase. That note could belong to anyone."

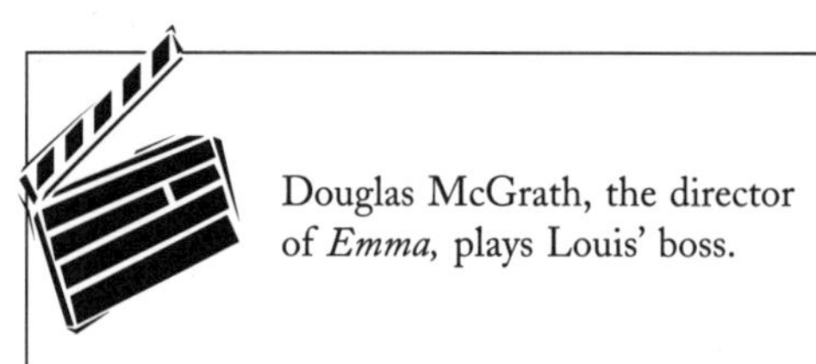

Douglas McGrath, the director of *Emma,* plays Louis' boss.

At her husband's office, Chap (Douglas McGrath), his boss, tells her that he has given Louis the rest of the day off, but that she is certain to find him at a book party that evening. Not content to rest till then, Rita, despite Eliza's halfhearted protest, snoops around Louis' desk and uncovers a set of snapshots. These lead the family to an address in Lower Manhattan, but Eliza is hesitant to ring the bell. The family remains frozen in their station wagon until Jim spots Louis emerge onto the street with a lithe dark-haired female companion. As the two get into a cab, Rita orders Jim to give chase. Unused to such activity, Jim lets the cab slip out of view while halting at an amber light. Undaunted, Rita gets out and gives chase on foot until she finally collapses on the sidewalk.

This allows the film to digress by introducing Ronnie (Andy Brown), a graduate student, who is harboring his deadbeat dad, the middle-aged, Leon (Paul Herman). When Ronnie is approached in the street by a desperate Carl, he provides the comfort of his couch for Rita to gather herself. This momentary kindness gives way to an extended sequence during which Rita prepares soup for everyone and the two families, one healthy, the other dysfunctional, share a convivial lunch.

The book party, we learn, is in honor of as frizzy-haired female novelist whose latest work is based on her relationship with her stepfather, "a cross between a Fred MacMurray and a Pol Pot." However, it is here that the film appears to espouse a romantic ideal. Jo strikes an immediate rapport with Eddie (Campbell Scott, son of George C.), a handsome young novelist about to have his work published. Later, Jo sneaks back into the party by herself in the guise of retrieving her handbag. Eddie then takes her onto the balcony where the two share a brief but torrid kiss.

Eliza meanwhile checks with her answering machine at home and finds a message from Louis saying that he has been delayed at a book party she knows he never attended. Shattered, she and the family are thrown into a somber silence as they drive back to the place where they last saw Louis. There, against the dark, deserted streets of arty Soho, the film stages its climactic encounter as it erupts into raw melodrama. It is also the only place the writer-director betrays a lack of confidence in the dramatic impact of his material. Totally unconvincing attempt on Jo's part to contact Eddie results in a confrontation between her, Carl and Rita, intended to presage the moment of truth between Eliza and Louis.

This time, as Eliza boldly rings the bell by herself, she finds a party in progress. On the roof, she sees a drunk Louis kissing Sandy (F. Evanson), his male lover. As she charges out, shocked, Louis follows her down and into the street. Louis himself is taken aback at the sight of the family around the station wagon, and demands to speak to his wife in private, a right he is eventually granted after Jim squashes Rita's desire to whisk Eliza away. All Eliza wants, it seems, are a few direct answers. Louis, on his part, while admitting to a year-long homosexual affair with Sandy, is not prepared to categorize his sexual desire. "I don't know what it is!" Louis screams. "I don't know! I'm confused and you have to help me find out!"

Louis' puzzling but heartfelt admission sets the tone for the winding down of passions and the eventual painful reconciliation. On a closing note, the film's ironic symmetry, accentuated by a simple melody played on an acoustic guitar, leads us to think back to the contentment shared by Eliza and Louis in the very opening scenes, a rose-tinted mirror now splintered.

Critics seem to have rooted for the film unanimously, some preferring it to its slick Hollywood counterpart, the previous year's *Flirting with Disaster*. According to Henry Cabot Beck of *The Star-Ledger*, what makes the film unique "is its willingness to not step outside the boundaries of the family drama." The film is "willing to be charming and noisy," Beck goes on, "like a real family, and remain true to its characters. That alone indicates the presence of a director with unusual patience and presence of mind." The venerable Stanley Kauffmann, writing in *The New Republic*, describes Mottola's style as "bright, funny, seemingly casual" while admitting that this debut feature "has some of the larky yet perceptive quality of the French New Wave."

The Daytrippers was awarded the Grand Jury Prize at the Slamdance Film Festival of 1996, and later showcased as part of the Critics' Week at Cannes. In addition, the film scored numerous other festival awards, including the Audience Award at both the Deauville and Athens Film Festivals.

—*Vivek Adarkar*

CREDITS

Eliza: Hope Davis
Jim Malone: Pat McNamara
Rita Malone: Anne Meara
Jo: Parker Posey
Carl: Liev Schreiber
Louis: Stanley Tucci
Eddie: Campbell Scott
Libby: Marcia Gay Harden
Ronnie: Andy Brown

Origin: USA
Released: 1996
Production: Nancy Tenenbaum and Steven Soderbergh; released by Columbia Pictures
Direction: Greg Mottola
Screenplay: Greg Mottola
Cinematography: John Inwood
Editing: Anne McCabe
Production design: Bonnie J. Brinkley
Costume: Barbara Presar
Sound: David Powers
MPAA rating: R
Running Time: 90 minutes

REVIEWS

Boxoffice. August, 1996, p. 53.
Entertainment Weekly. March 14, 1997, p. 60.
Los Angeles Times. March 21, 1997, p. F2.
New Republic. March 10, 1997.
New York Post. March 5, 1997.
New York Times. March 7, 1997, p. B27.
New Yorker. March 24, 1997, p. 85.
Newsweek. March 31, 1997, p. 75.
People. March 24, 1997, p. 22.
Star-Ledger. March 5, 1997.
Variety. March 18, 1996, p. 48.
Village Voice. March 11, 1997, p. 78.

Deconstructing Harry

Harry Block wrote a bestseller about his best friends. Now, his best friends are about to become his worst enemies.—Movie tagline

"Hilarious!"—Peter Travers, *Rolling Stone*

"A triumph! *Deconstructing Harry* is among the most uproarious comedies in memory. A work of comic genius!"—Gene Shalit, *Today Show*

"One of the year's best pictures!"—Jeffrey Lyons, *WNBC*

Box Office: $2,536,881

Woody Allen stars as a writer who makes enemies out of his friends after writing a scathing autobiography in *Deconstructing Harry*.

Woody Allen has occasionally flagellated himself in interviews for making charming, pleasant comedies rather than the harsher films, like those of his idol, Ingmar Bergman, he sometimes envisions. The immensely talented actor-writer-director has, of course, made a few non-comedies, such as *Interiors* (1978), *September* (1987), and *Another Woman* (1988), but far from displaying the insight into male-female relations seen in his best films, these dismal efforts have been labored and obvious, the work of someone who has seen all the great European films but is unable to communicate what he has learned. They are examples of what the Allen character in *Annie Hall* (1977) terms "heavyosity." Allen's sensibility is closer to the bright humanism of Eric Rohmer and Francois Truffaut than to Bergman's dark brooding anyway, though *Deconstructing Harry* has superficial similarities to Bergman's one farce, *For Att Inte Talla Om All Dessa Kvinnor* (*All These Women*; 1964).

Doris: "You have no values. Your whole life, it's nihilism, it's cynicism, it's sarcasm and orgasm." Harry: "You know, in France, I could run on that slogan and win."

The best way for Allen to release the obvious anger he feels over the way people demean each other and themselves is through humor, and he does that in *Deconstructing Harry*, the darkest of his comedies. While Allen may not be guilty of some of the things he has been accused of since his private life unfortunately became controversial, he has been guilty, especially since *Annie Hall*, of pandering to his core audience: upper-middle-class, educated, urban whites. Unlike the typical Allen film, however, *Deconstructing Harry* features excessive profanity (more in almost any one scene than in all his previous films) and even nudity, an Allen first. The departure is necessary since Allen is portraying, instead of the nebbish he has played so many variations on, for the first time a real bastard, who even abuses pills and alcohol. The film is also notable for offering Allen's first significant African-American character—though she is a prostitute—and for ignoring the many glories that are Manhattan.

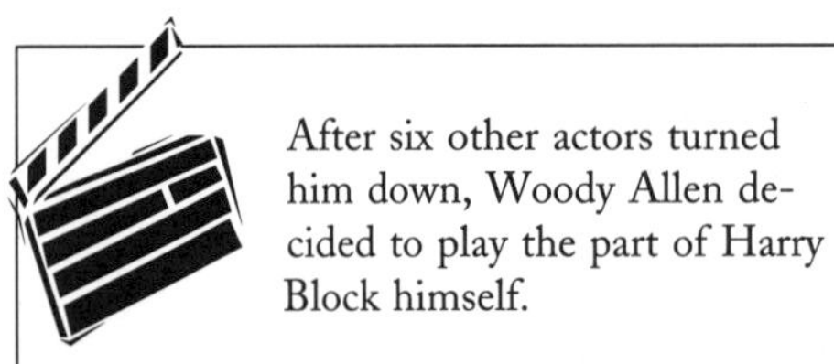

After six other actors turned him down, Woody Allen decided to play the part of Harry Block himself.

Harry Block (Woody Allen) is a successful writer who transfers the events of his life into fiction, outraging his former sister-in-law, Lucy (Judy Davis), who is certain her sister, Jane (Amy Irving), will recognize Harry's treatment of their adulterous affair. *Deconstructing Harry* alternates between events in Harry's life from the past and in the present with dramatizations of his fictional versions. The film opens with the Harry-Jane affair as Ken (Richard Benjamin) and Leslie (Julia Louis-Dreyfus) have sex at a family gathering with their mates nearby and in front of a blind grandmother.

Harry's tempestuous marriage to Joan (Kirstie Alley), his former psychiatrist and the mother of their son, Hilly (Eric Lloyd), ends because of his infidelity, and Joan refuses to let him be alone with Hilly. Harry's sister, Doris (Caroline Aaron), whose husband, Burt (Eric Bogosian), has conservative religious values, berates her atheistic brother for being a self-hating Jew for the way he caricatures Jews in his fiction. This charge, along with the sexual content of his work, makes Harry resemble Philip Roth, whose ex-wife, Claire Bloom, has appeared in two Allen films.

The other major threads of the narrative focus on Harry's love for a young woman, Fay (Elizabeth Shue), who has left him for one of Harry's best friends, Larry (Billy Crystal), also a writer, and on Harry's being honored by the university that expelled him years earlier. In the last half of the film, Harry slowly makes his way to this Upstate New York institution accompanied by the prostitute, Cookie Williams (Hazelle Goodman), he engages the night before; a friend, Richard (Bob Balaban), with a heart condition; and Hilly, whom Harry kidnaps from the boy's school. This picaresque journey features a confrontation with Doris, fantasy encounters in which such characters as Ken offer Harry advice, and another fantasy in which Harry visits Hell and finds Larry in charge.

While the profanity, nudity, and general unWoodylike behavior of the protagonist make *Deconstructing Harry* a departure for Allen, in many other ways, the film is typical of his work. The appearance of literary characters in the real world recalls one of Allen's best short stories, "The Kugelmass Episode," in which a professor has an affair with the heroine of Gustave Flaubert's *Madame Bovary* (1857), as well as Allen's *The Purple Rose of Cairo* (1985), in which a character in a film steps off the screen and into the life of the protagonist. The writer interacting with his characters also resembles the scenes in which the Allen character revisits his past in *Annie Hall*, and the scene in which Harry and Cookie become invisible so that they can hear what Doris really thinks about her brother recalls *Alice* (1990), which has a similar fantasy structure. The end of *Annie Hall* features a scene in which the protagonist's ill-fated romance with the title character has been recreated in a play, and the brief dramatizations of Harry's stories are similar to the sketches in *Everything You Always Wanted to Know About Sex But Were Afraid to Ask* (1972).

Not all the dramatizations are drawn directly from Harry's life. One deals with an elderly woman's discovery that her husband murdered his first wife and children and ate them. (This is one of the stories Doris attacks as mocking Jews.) Another depicts a film actor (Robin Williams) who suddenly becomes out of focus in real life. But the best present Harry's selfish interpretations of the events of his life. Allen draws a strong contrast between the Harry-Joan marriage and Harry's fictional view of it. In the story, Paul Epstein (Stanley Tucci), is a pleasant, passive husband who grows increasingly bemused as his wife, Helen (Demi Moore), becomes more and more an Orthodox Jew after the birth of their son. She not only prays before meals but over Paul's penis before they have sexual relations.

In real life, Joan is outraged that not only has Harry been unfaithful but that he has done so with one of her patients. The story exaggerates, for wonderful comic effect, the wife's devotion to her religion while ignoring the husband's sins. The comic high point of this consistently funny film is Joan's inability to break off her argument over Harry's unfaithfulness even when a patient shows up. (Her office is in their apartment.) At first, she leaves the consulting room to shout at Harry, but finally, she begins wailing at him in front of the flustered, embarrassed man. This scene displays Allen's superb skills at comic writing and pacing.

AWARDS AND NOMINATIONS

Academy Awards 1997 Nominations: Original Screenplay

CREDITS

Harry Block: Woody Allen
Cookie Williams: Hazelle Goodman
Larry: Billy Crystal
Fay: Elizabeth Shue
Joan: Kirstie Alley
Hilly Block: Eric Lloyd
Lucy: Judy Davis
Jane: Amy Irving
Doris: Caroline Aaron
Burt: Eric Bogosian
Richard: Bob Balaban
Beth Kramer: Mariel Hemingway
Paul Epstein: Stanley Tucci
Helen Epstein: Demi Moore
Ken: Richard Benjamin
Leslie: Julia Louis-Dreyfus
Harvey Stern: Tobey Maguire
Mel: Robin Williams
Grace: Julie Kavner

Origin: USA
Released: 1997
Production: Jean Doumanian for Sweetland Films; released by Fine Line Features
Direction: Woody Allen
Screenplay: Woody Allen
Cinematography: Carlo DiPalma
Editing: Susan E. Morse
Production design: Santo Loquasto
Art direction: Tom Warren
Set decoration: Elaine O'Donnell
Costumes: Suzy Benzinger
Sound: Les Lazarowitz
MPAA rating: R
Running Time: 95 minutes

Allen excels at creating memorable exaggeratedly neurotic women, usually played by Diane Keaton, Diane Wiest, or Judy Davis. *Deconstructing Harry* offers two such characters with Davis and Alley playing variations on wronged women who lose control in venting their anger at Harry. Davis, who does her best work with Allen, as in *Alice* and *Husbands and Wives* (1992), is a delight with her over-the-top mannerisms. Davis acts with her entire body, but Alley, who has never been particularly effective in a film, allows her face to collapse slowly into a distorted mask of exasperation and pain. Alley's progressively losing control is wonderful.

Moore, often justifiably attacked for being humorless, presents, as the fictional version of Joan, a much more subtle comic portrait of a woman desperate to impose some sort of order on her life. She and Tucci, as Harry's slick, smug reimagining of himself, play off each other quite well. Crystal, always better in smaller parts, as in *Hamlet* (1996), is effective as Harry's oily rival.

Deconstructing Harry, as a title, would seem to be acknowledging Allen's wide audience among academics, those most likely to be familiar with the theory of textual analysis evolved by French philosopher Jacques Derrida. (Allen wanted to entitle the film "The Meanest Man in the World," apparently to make his intentions even clearer.) The title is fitting in the sense that the film attempts to analyze Harry's character. It is ironic that while deconstructionists may ignore artists' lives to concentrate on a close reading of their works, Allen asks that Harry's fiction be seen primarily as lies constructed to justify his despicable behavior. The film ends with Harry's characters applauding him in a way that his friends, family, and lovers could never do. That he can be comfortable only with his creations confirms his failure as a human being, yet the resulting sadness makes him sympathetic despite himself.

Harry does not seem to be the total monster everyone says he is—and as Doris' secret affection for him makes clear. Part of the problem is his being played by Woody Allen, an immensely likable performer. Allen seems to delight in Harry's lies and deceptions, and this joy softens the character to a degree. Harry never quite becomes the anti-hero Allen apparently intended. Even with this weakness, however, *Deconstructing Harry* is funnier than any of his films since *Manhattan Murder Mystery* (1993) and more inventive than any since *Hannah and Her Sisters* (1986). Allen attempts this type of examination of the artist as selfish jerk in *Stardust Memories* (1980) without realizing such a portrait would be invigorated, not diminished, by humor and sympathetic characters. His portrait of Harry Block corrects that failing.

—Michael Adams

REVIEWS

Boxoffice. January, 1998, p. 45.
Entertainment Weekly. December 19, 1997, p. 54.
Los Angeles Times. December 12, 1997, p. F1.
New York. December 22, 1997, p. 134.
New York Times. December 12, 1997, p. B1.
Newsweek. December 22, 1997, p. 85.
People. December 22, 1997, p. 21.
Time. December 22, 1997, p. 82.
USA Today. December 12, 1997, p. D14.
Variety. September 1, 1997, p. 74.

Deep Crimson; Profundo Carmesi

Arturo Ripstein's *Deep Crimson* proves that filmic pretense can operate on two levels: the make-believe comprising the fiction we are enjoying, and the film itself attempting to deceive us with its own perspective. It is to the credit of this mature director that he is bold enough to remain loyal to his cinematic vision, so that his seemingly incongruous stance towards his characters functions as a stylistic correlative for the chasm between the Old World dignity and ritual animating their lives and the legacy of colonialism pervading the severe Mexican landscape to which they appear inextricably bound. Thus, it is through this dichotomy, organic to the film's content, and the director's rendition of it, that the film can best be described.

In the Mexico of the late 1940s, Coral (Regina Orozco), a plump but darkly attractive nurse, finds sustenance for her harried life in the fantasy worlds evoked by popular music, trashy romance fiction and, most important, her obsessive adulation of Charles Boyer. While preparing to start her day, she plants a kiss with her fingers on Boyer's photograph beside her dressing table mirror, dons her nurse's whites, then grabs at her two young kids and pulls them out the door.

That evening, while attending at home to the aging Don Dimos (Giovanni Florido), an emaciated figure confined to a wheelchair, Coral's anxieties about her age and figure become apparent. Before administering his injection, she attempts to arouse him with talk of the affair between Boyer and Hedy Lamarr, then unbuttons her uniform and flaunts her protuberance in his face. When he proves unresponsive, she takes his limp hand and places it on a breast. Her precocious daughter, as if unable to bear the humiliation, interrupts the love play. In frustration, Coral then screams at her kids: "I'm fat from looking after you! And fed up!" Soon after, while kissing her daughter good night, she is stricken by guilt and makes the sign of the cross in repentance. By establishing the tug-of-war between the desires and pressures in Coral's life, the film thus sets the stage for the melodramatic upheaval about to overturn her existence.

Nicholas to Coral: "Providence brought us together, or maybe the devil."

Coral's prayers seem to be answered when she spots a personal at the back of a pulp magazine. A Spanish gentleman, who claims to look like Charles Boyer, is seeking a woman "to share sentiments." Since he has not specified looks, Coral thinks herself to be the object of his desire, and sends off a letter, enclosing a photo taken in her younger, much slimmer, days. To accentuate the irony, Coral's words of self-description, spoken in her voice, are superimposed over the action of Nicolas (Daniel Gimenez Cacho), a handsome but bald charmer, trying on toupees, seated in front of his dressing table mirror, much as we saw Coral in the film's opening scene. With Coral's letter in hand, Nicolas chooses the hairpiece that makes him look the most like Charles Boyer. Unlike Coral however, and her romantic fantasies, Nicolas' aspirations are rooted in fact: as a schemer after the fortunes of widows, he has meticulously maintained a file on such women.

When Nicolas comes calling, Coral's first glimpse of him is as a silhouette, much like a cameo against the glass of her front door, a debonair profile in an overcoat and fedora. Despite her overflowing but awkward generosity, Nicolas cuts short the visit. In desperation, Coral asks if he has been repelled by her breath and body odor, which she explains are the result of working with formaldehyde at the morgue. "The body is a temple made for love," Nicolas comforts her. As if melting from his flattery, Coral drops the phonograph record of romantic music she is holding, which breaks into pieces, like her hopes. "I'll save them as a souvenir of the Spanish gentleman," she says, as Nicolas slithers out the door.

Based on the 1949 true crime story about "Lonely Hearts Killers" Martha Beck and Ray Fernandez.

Late that night, as she lies sprawled in her housecoat, drinking by herself, she is surprised by Nicolas, who presents her with a rose and a copy of the record he feels responsible for breaking. "In Spain, Quixote taught us to look upon our Dulcineas with the eyes of the soul," he declares. Then adds, "no matter what their physical appearance." Her passion stirred once again, this time beyond control, Coral grabs at the lapels of his overcoat and kisses him, while pushing him into her bedroom. The film then strikes up a musical love theme of its own, as the camera tracks along the pallid walls of Coral's dwelling, and glides up to the two in bed after their lovemaking. As if wanting us to empathize with Coral's sense of fulfillment, the love theme continues as Nicolas sneaks to the dressing table, where he reaches for Coral's purse and removes a folded wad of bills from her change pouch. Once home, he marks Coral's card as a rejection, and files it away in a shoebox.

What should have ended within the bounds of normalcy, instead gathers the momentum of an uncontrollable force of nature, as Coral throws all civilized custom to the winds in her mad pursuit of Nicolas. Now it is Nicolas' turn to be surprised as Coral arrives in the rain with her two kids and a suitcase, intending to move in. Nicolas first apologizes for the petty theft, which Coral is quick to forgive. Then, in his most gentlemanly manner, he admits that he cannot be a father to her children. When all pleading fails, Coral makes a shocking choice. The next morning, she takes both kids by the hand and, in a harrowingly poignant scene, leaves them in front of a mission entrance.

A changed woman, Coral now boldly breaks into Nicolas' place, and even into his file on widows. When he returns, Nicolas is shocked at her cruelty towards her children, and incensed at her ransacking his papers. Dropping all gentlemanly pretense, he spits out verbal abuse and calls her insane, Coral then hits back by revealing her nurse's knowledge about insulin and diabetic coma, and how the forged prescriptions she has found show that Nicolas murdered his wife. "But only I know," she adds, resolved to be a part of his life, even if by blackmail.

The film accentuates new resolve with a second musical love theme sprightlier than the first. "I'll pretend to be your sister," she says, kneeling before Nicolas. "I'll select the prospects." This turning point, in what had begun to look like an unlikely romance, now lays bare an underbelly of sinister design, requiring the film itself to switch its viewpoint on the characters, which it doesn't do. After portraying Coral's natural human passion, with which we can identify, the film expects us to view the inhuman acts of evil that follow as an extension of that passion. In so doing, it risks alienating a good part of its audience.

Moreover, as Coral and Nicolas embark on their enterprise of deceit, which soon turns murderous, the culmination of each episodic sequence, the killing of yet another widow, cannot help but appear signposted. This drags the film's dramatic quotient down to the sensationalistic level of its American counterpart, *The Honeymoon Killers* (1970), and its many variants.

The hunt for prospects, which takes Coral and Nicolas from one arid town to another, is livened by notable cameos:

Julieta Egurrola, as a vivacious flirt seeking an escape from her gypsy lover; the beautiful Marisa Paredes as a lonely Spanish widow, bereft of her children, finding solace in missionary work; Veronica Merchant as a slim, attractive single mother, saddled by her late husband with an auto repair shop and whose daughter reminds Coral of her own. During each encounter, Coral is forced to play the hanger-on, except in the case of the single mother. As Coral is forced to bide her time in the nearby town, we see Nicolas give vent to his true sexual passion. Each murder is cleanly executed, except for the last, which involves drowning the little girl in a bathtub, an act that makes Coral relive the guilt of abandoning her own daughter. Between each murder, Coral forces Nicolas into ungainly sex, while forcing him to admit that he loves her.

It is after the last widow, however, that Nicolas appears unable to live with the guilt. Presumably, the film would like us to believe, because he has been spurred by nothing more than greed. After he confesses to the authorities, it is a matter of days before the couple are executed on a barren field, while made to run for their lives like dogs. As Coral and Nicolas lie dead in a puddle, holding each other's hand, she is wearing the deep crimson dress which has come to embody the extension of her womanly desire. As the camera pulls back, the second musical love theme is now played in a dance tempo, as if in celebration of an undying love.

As would be expected, the film's raw honesty has not escaped its reviewers. Richard Corliss, writing in *Time*, calls it a "poisonous, beautifully acted tragicomedy (which) exerts a cold fascination." Understandably, Thelma Adams in the *New York Post* finds that "as the story becomes increasingly sordid and, finally downright sick, we have become accomplices in unanticipated atrocities." *Deep Crimson* received its U.S. premiere at the 1997 New York Film Festival.

—*Vivek Adarkar*

CREDITS

Coral Fabre: Regina Orozco
Nicolas Estrella: Daniel Gimenez Cacho
Irene Gallardo: Marisa Paredes
Widow Ruelas: Patricia Reyes Espindola
Julieta Egurrola: Juanita Narton

Origin: Mexico
Released: 1996
Production: Miguel Necoechea and Paolo Barbachano; released by New Yorker Films
Direction: Arturo Ripstein
Screenplay: Paz Alicia Garciadiego
Cinematography: Guillermo Granillo
Editing: Rafael Castanedo
Music: David Mansfield
Sound: Carlos Faruolo, Antonio Betancourt
Production design: Marcarena Folanche, Marisa Pecanins, Monica Chirinos
MPAA rating: Unrated
Running Time: 114 minutes

REVIEWS

Chicago Tribune. January 16, 1997, p. 7.
Detroit News. November 14, 1997, p. 3F.
Los Angeles Times. October 31, 1997, p. F22.
New York Post. October 6, 1997.
New York Times. October 6, 1997, p. E5.
Sight and Sound. September, 1997, p. 40.
Time. October 20, 1997.
Village Voice. October 14, 1997, p. 85.

Def Jam's How to Be a Player

Are you a player?—Movie tagline

"You can't get too snooty when the subject is booty!"—Michael Medved, *New York Post*

Box Office: $14,010,363

The word "player" in *Def Jam's How to Be a Player* has multiple shades of meaning. In Robert Altman's acclaimed *The Player* (1992) the term denoted a highly paid, highly influential insider in a glamour industry. In Def Jam's African-American rap film, however, it means all that plus spending most of one's time at play and playing one woman against another. It means being a playboy and living in the lap of luxury without having to work. Griffin Mill (Tim Robbins) in Altman's movie was making lots of money but never seemed to be having any fun. Drayton Jackson (Bill Bellamy of "MTV Jams"), on the other hand, goes through life bouncing to happy music and surrounded by adoring beauties.

Dray lives in a high-rent split-level Los Angeles apartment and has a wardrobe as extensive as that of any Hollywood movie star. He has so many women pursuing him that he can hardly keep their names and appointments straight.

He is the envy of his three unsophisticated buddies: Kilo (Jermaine Hopkins), Spootie (A.J. Johnson), and David (Pierre). They dog his heels throughout the film, studying him in action and listening to his unflattering observations about the opposite sex. It is this thread of cynical advice that gives this "how-to" film its title. Some of the hero's moxie rubs off on his disciples. They will never be as successful as Dray, however, because they lack his brains, magnetism, and testosterone.

Dray's advice to his friends: "Never beg on no answering machine."

The term "player" as used in this film also means being a pimp and living off women. Very little of this sort of private enterprise is depicted, however, perhaps for fear of totally alienating female viewers (who should be alienated enough by the film's unmitigated male chauvinism already). Dray's attitude may be "love 'em and leave 'em," but it is not overtly "love 'em and exploit 'em." No doubt a couple of his more affluent mistresses (one of whom is married to a very rough customer who makes every tryst an adventure) give Dray money—but never on camera. His apartment, his clothes, his beautiful car, his dizzying round of partying, all must be subsidized by something—but the viewer is left to imagine the mundane financial details.

Max Julien, who plays Uncle Fred, starred in 1973's *The Mack,* a poster of which Dray has in his apartment as inspiration.

The story is hardly original. Griffin Mill of *The Player,* who knew every plot line backwards and forwards, would have recognized it immediately and cited some of its previous guises. Alec Guinness, for example, led a double life in *Captain's Paradise* (1963). What with inflation and everything, our modern hero Dray Jackson is leading a septuple life and even trying to add to his harem. The threat to his own paradise comes in the form of his sister Jenny (Natalie Desselle), a militant feminist who resents the way he uses women. She and her foxy, not-so-militant friend Katrina (Mari Morrow) are conducting a case study of Dray for their anthropology class when they discover evidence of his infidelity in his boudoir. They decide to upset his apple cart by inviting all seven of his mistresses to an upcoming party in Malibu. They anticipate plenty of female fireworks. You can fool some women some of the time and some women all of the time, but you cannot fool all of the women all of the time—especially when they get together and compare notes. Even though Dray collects panties as trophies, and even though many of his girlfriends display the very feminine trait of curiosity, Dray has managed to keep each believing she is his one and only.

Bill Bellamy looks like Eddie Murphy and has borrowed many of Murphy's mannerisms. Like Murphy, Dray's forte is staying cool under pressure and jiving his way out of every sticky situation. The viewer could easily be beguiled into thinking he was watching an Eddie Murphy feature, were it not for the low-budget production values. *Variety* reviewer Todd McCarthy observed accurately: "Clunky opening couple of reels look just like TV on the bigscreen."

The lavish Malibu party itself (what playwright and screenwriters used to call the "obligatory scene") is a disappointment. There is such a thing, after all, as being too cool. "The comic potential of the occasion," as *New York Times* critic Lawrence Van Gelder concluded, "eludes the skills of the director, Lionel C. Martin, and the writers, Mark Brown and Demetria Johnson." Even though Dray keeps running into girlfriends—even in the hallway and the bathroom—he never loses his grin. Not only that, but he pursues an eighth and even a ninth woman between one contretemps and the next. Perversely, instead of empathizing with the hero, the male viewer finds himself hoping Dray will get caught. Instead, it is sister Jenny who has to acknowledge defeat in the end.

CREDITS

Drayton Jackson: Bill Bennett
Jenny Jackson: Natalie Desselle
Lisa: Lark Voorhies
Katrina: Mari Morrow
David: Pierre
Kilo: Jermaine Hopkins
Spootie: A.J. Johnson
Uncle Fred: Max Julien
Robin: Beverly Johnson

Origin: USA
Released: 1997
Production: Mark Burg, Todd Baker, Russell Simmons, and Preston Holmes for Outlaw Productions and Island Pictures; released by Polygram Filmed Entertainment
Direction: Lionel C. Martin
Screenplay: Mark Brown and Demetria Johnson
Cinematography: Ross Berryman
Editing: William Young
Music: Darren Floyd
Production design: Bruce Curtis
Set decoration: Claire Kaufman
Costumes: Mimi Melgaard
Sound: Mathew Markey
MPAA rating: R
Running Time: 93 minutes

REVIEWS

Boxoffice. September, 1997, p. 117.
Hollywood Reporter. August 6, 1997, p. 8.
New York Times. August 7, 1997, p. C16.
Sight and Sound. January, 1998, p. 37.
Variety. August 11, 1997, p. 58.

The smorgasbord of feminine pulchritude and the infectious songs are the best ingredients in this lightweight farce. The list of music credits at the end is almost as long as the other credits combined. *How to Be a Player* should enjoy some shelf line at the video outlets because of its music and dancing—as long as female viewers do not take its exploitative message too seriously.

—*Bill Delaney*

The Delta

The distance between two men is . . . *The Delta*—Movie tagline

"Dazzling."—Gary Morris, *Bay Area Reporter*

"Flawless."—Kevin Thomas, *Los Angeles Times*

"The most substantive independent film in many years."—Armond White, *NY Press*

"Hypnotic."—Dennis Dermody, *Paper*

The Delta opens abruptly on a night scene in a rural park. The only illumination comes from headlights of a few cruising cars whose headlights twinkle in the hot, humid air. The viewer keeps expecting to see a few opening credits or at least the title, but no printed words are superimposed until the story abruptly ends and closing credits roll. The effect is a little like finding that a videotape has not been completely rewound. Apparently, writer-director Ira Sachs' intention was to make his film as much like *cinema verite* as possible. The viewer is never quite sure whether he is watching drama or documentary. This blending of drama and documentary is the outstanding characteristic of *The Delta.* It strongly resembles *Kids* (1995), even though *Kids* was shot in the middle of a big city and *The Delta* was shot mostly out in the boondocks.

Memphis-born writer/director Ira Sachs makes his feature debut as do Shayne Gray and Thang Chan, neither of whom had acted before.

How viewers will react to *The Delta* will depend on their age group. Younger viewers may see it as a slice of the life they are quite familiar with. Parents may be shocked to see the kind of behavior that goes on among their sons and daughters when they are not around. The oldest generation—if any of them go to such films—will have their suspicions confirmed that the human race is going to the dogs. The behavior of young people in suburban Memphis seems no different from that of young people in New York City. They have gotten their manners and ideas from rock and rap and whatever else they listen to on their headphones, their car radios, and in the seclusion of their bedrooms.

As was the case in *Kids*, there are a few characters in *The Delta* whose identities and problems emerge in sharper focus against a backdrop of teenagers doing exactly what they do in everyday life but doing it in front of a camera. One of the three principals is Lincoln Bloom (played by Shayne Gray, who resembles the young Matt Dillon). Lincoln, a white, middle-class teenager, is trying to be a heterosexual but feels drawn to the underground world of homosexuality like a moth to a flame. He cruises the dimly lighted park, picking up strange men in his car or being picked up by them. The "zipperless" sexual contacts are mostly simulated by groping hands and facial expressions suggesting passion and orgasm. When Lincoln returns to his white, suburban, middle-class world, the viewer understands why this mixed-up youth, like a teenage Dr. Jekyll, must keep his Mr. Hyde persona carefully concealed.

Lincoln has a beautiful white girlfriend named Monica (Rachel Zan Huss), who smokes pot, drinks, and engages in premarital sex, but might be considered almost straitlaced by her peers. Monica represents the safe, conventional lifestyle that Lincoln is unwilling to give up. In time the couple might marry, have children, buy a big white neo-colonial house of their own, join the country club, and live the American Dream. This is obviously what Monica wants and what she sees in her future. She does not understand Lincoln or why he should not want to go along with such a scenario.

The third principal character in *The Delta* is by far the most interesting. His name is Minh Nguyen but he goes by the street name of John. The role is played by Thang Chang, who was born for it. All of the actors have to do a certain amount of ad-libbing, but Chang is the only one who seems completely comfortable and natural doing it. John has no conflict about homosexuality. He has not only accepted the fact that he is gay but has made it his profession. He picks up men in bars and charges them for sex. He is a product of the Vietnam War. His mother was Vietnamese and his father an African American G.I.

Although John seems vivacious, happy-go-lucky and easily approachable, this young drifter has a grudge against the whole world for making him what he is and then leaving him to fend for himself in an impossible situation. The film ends as abruptly as it began after John entices a black customer to a lonely setting and commits a cold-blooded, premeditated murder. He kills in such a competent manner that he is obviously no amateur. This is a shocking revelation of his depravity. The fact that his customer is black suggests that the root of his anger goes down to his feelings about a father he never knew. Evidently his sexual preference is the warped result of an unrequited, unconscious yearning for a father's love. If Lincoln is a little like Dr. Jekyll, then John is a little like Mary Shelley's Frankenstein monster who went on a killing spree because he blamed all mankind for his condition.

The viewer will remember John long after he has forgotten Lincoln and Monica. John is older than Lincoln by about ten years—but older in terms of experience by considerably more. John understands everything the tongue-tied Lincoln is going through and thinks he can help him by drawing him completely into the homosexual underworld. Although John is worldly wise, he does not understand the world he is asking Lincoln to give up. He cannot understand it because he has never had any part of such comfort, security, and social acceptance. The two men attract each other because they are opposites. Homosexuality makes strange bedfellows. It is the contrast between their characters and by implication between their backgrounds that forms the dynamic of the film. Monica, the third ingredient in the concoction, is more of a symbol than a character. She is so lily-white that she seems made of marble—and almost as cold.

Critics have pointed out that the production values of this low-budget motion picture, shot on 16mm film, leave much to be desired. The only reason *The Delta* has received so much word-of-mouth publicity is that its contemporary social significance could make it a cult classic. White Americans feel themselves losing their cultural and numerical superiority. Lincoln has good reason to be afraid of John. John is not only beckoning him to give up his tenuous hold on heterosexuality but to relinquish the birthright that automatically entitles the youth to the whole white middle-class package of college, profession, marriage, children, suburban home, country club, and membership in the Republican Party. John does not understand that his love for Lincoln is a love for everything that this mixed-racial immigrant, the product and symbol of a shameful war, can never have. *The Delta* is as much about social classes as about homosexuality. Lincoln does not understand that his attraction to John is not merely physical but an attraction to the freedom the rootless, homeless older man enjoys—freedom from social and family pressure, freedom of conscience, freedom of sexual expression, freedom from dissimulation and chronic anxiety.

Symbolizing all this, John persuades Lincoln to borrow the immaculate white family cabin cruiser without permission and steal off down the Mississippi on an excursion which critics have compared to the river journey of Huck and Jim in Mark Twain's *Huckleberry Finn*. Far from home on the vast, bleak Mississippi Delta, stripped of their clothes, John and Lincoln enjoy complete emotional and physical freedom. But the idyll has to end. Lincoln has already been too strongly conditioned. He feels compelled to resume his alter-identity as an ordinary middle-class kid, abandoning John to his dirty, dangerous world of multiracial bars, pool halls, and X-rated video arcades.

Critics in New York and Los Angeles praised this film, which opened to limited engagements in only those two cities. Kevin Thomas of the *Los Angeles Times* wrote: "Sachs has created . . . an achingly poignant portrait of alienation and longing so evocative that it is poetic in its impact." Stephen Holden of the *New York Times* could hardly have summed it up better when he wrote in his review: "*The Delta* has the grainy look and elliptical narrative style of a home movie featuring nonactors. But this quasi-documentary approach, with dialogue that feels largely improvised, lends the story a certain authenticity." The abrupt and melodramatic ending was a major target of complaint. Emanuel Levy, who saw the film at the Toronto Film Festival, wrote in *Variety*:

CREDITS

Lincoln Bloom: Shayne Gray
John: Thang Chan
Monica: Rachel Zan Huss
Colonius Davis: Ricky Little

Origin: USA
Released: 1996
Production: Margot Bridger; released by Strand Releasing
Direction: Ira Sachs
Screenplay: Ira Sachs
Cinematography: Benjamin P. Speth
Editing: Alfonso Goncalves
Music: Michael Rohatyn
Production designer: Bernhard Blythe
Costumes: Stevan Lazich
Art director: Ying Ling Wong
MPAA rating: Unrated
Running Time: 85 minutes

"The ending, which shows no results or growth emanating from the bond between the two young men, doesn't ring true and leaves the impression that the scripter didn't know how to resolve his tale."

The Delta has a strong impact, considering all its defects. Many of the scenes are shot with a hand-held camera in near darkness, yet the hot, humid, cricket-serenaded ambiance of summer in the South is effectively captured. Benjamin P. Speth, director of photography, deserves as much praise for his work under difficult conditions as does Ira Sachs for managing a group of inexperienced young actors. Thang Chan, who has never appeared in a film before, is an interesting personality and a natural actor who nearly steals the show. It has been said that low-budget films made by dedicated young beginners will be responsible for most of the important cinematic development of the future. *The Delta* is a good example.

—Bill Delaney

REVIEWS

Los Angeles Times. August 15, 1997, p. F4.
New York Times. August 15, 1997, p. B14.
Variety. December 16, 1996, p. 83.
Village Voice. August 19, 1997, p. 90.

The Designated Mourner

"Shawn's brilliant drama . . . delivers an extraordinary punch . . . "—David Sterritt, *Christian Science Monitor*

"A cerebral ticking bomb. Brilliant. Haunting."—Richard Rayner, *Harper's Bazaar*

"Inspiring. A cinematic experience in which words replace images."—Oren Moreman, *Interview*

"Insidiously superb. Compelling. Engrossing." —Stanley Kauffmann, *New Republic*

"Magnificently acted. Exquisitely written." —Stephen Holden, *New York Times*

Like an ill-fitting new shoe, *The Designated Mourner* demands a lot from us before we can feel at ease with it. In its quirky minimalist fashion, the David Hare film, which reverently transposes Wallace Shawn's play onto the screen, locks itself into a darkened space no larger than a prison cell, which we soon realize is not a physical setting at all, but rather a spatial continuum.

> Jack: "I understood that my self was just a pile of bric-a-brac—just everything my life had quite by chance piled up—everything I'd seen or heard or experienced—meticulously, pointlessly piled up and saved, a heap of nothing."

Once the film's formal eccentricity reveals itself, we have a choice: either walk out, or abandon our expectation of being able to settle back and watch a story being acted out for our benefit. This is because the film's dramatic structure remains that of the revelatory flashback, revolving around the story that is literally told by Jack (Mike Nichols), the film's eponymous lead, who treats us, the film's audience, as if we were at a tribal gathering by a fireside. Jack, through Nichols' illuminating portrayal, comes across as an amiable, introspective middle-aged libertine. The film's other two leads—his wife Judy (Miranda Richardson), an elite attractive liberal, and her father, Howard (David de Keyser), an aging poet, once nationally honored but soon disgraced by a repressive government—come alive in a dimension apart, as if evoked by Jack. Thus, unless we, like tribals, are prepared to make the effort of imagining the interwoven experiences being recounted by all three, sitting through this film can be torture.

At the very start, Jack mockingly informs us: "A very special little world has died" and that he is its designated mourner. "It's an important custom in many groups and tribes," he goes on. "Someone is assigned to grieve, to wail and light the public ritual fire, when there's no one else." This circumscription allows Jack's story to eschew all codes of realism, so that its setting remains a mythic, unidentified time and place. When the film switches to Judy, after Jack casually refers to her, her mood is earnest and serious. Oblivious to Jack's scoffing, Judy relates her own vision of pain, of how its customary use as a means of political oppression cannot match its intensity when it is produced by love. Similarly, Howard is introduced through Jack's half-mocking words as "someone we can all revere." We then see Howard, silent and self-absorbed, buried in his reading. "This complex man," Jack begins, "who responded most sensitively to the most obscure verses and also to the cries of the miserable and downtrodden, virtually at the same time, and all without leaving his breakfast table."

It soon becomes clear that at the core of what all three have to tell us is the phenomenon of repression, both outer and inner. For Jack, it takes on a sexual tinge, as no amount of deviant behavior can help him cast off the yoke of impotence, until he is finally forced to abandon his carnal pursuits for the pleasure of the evening breeze. For Judy, it is her persecution as a political prisoner that leads her to experience an inner liberation. For Howard, all his intellectual deliberations lead him to the epiphany that what he has been repressing within himself all along is a confrontation with the moment of his death.

Shot in three days during the play's premiere London run.

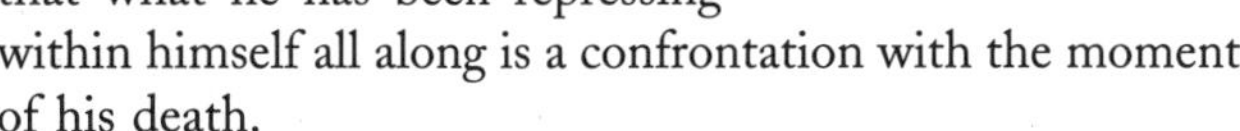

All said, *The Designated Mourner* does succeed in utilizing its unique form and dramatic structure to question the very antinomy on which it has built its edifice. We are repaid for our effort at paying close attention to its predominantly verbal discourse by a fresh perspective on repression, especially as practiced by power-hungry governments. Like Jack, we are forced to ponder the paradox that maybe there isn't anything worth repressing.

The film, by espousing a tribal ethos, distances itself from the cultural and social institutions that continue to circumscribe our lives, and "our special little worlds." As we are forced to contemplate its austere form, *The Designated Mourner* ironically ends up telling us more about the films we are conditioned to enjoy, than about its mysterious self.

"By keeping you at a distance from the horrors to which the characters allude," writes Stephen Holden of the film in *The New York Times*, "it prevents your emotions from blocking out its subversive ideas." One of the film's rare treats, according to Holden, is "the thrill of (its) language that has the concentration of poetry." Like most of his fellow reviewers, Andrew Sarris in *The New York Observer* cannot help but be impressed by Mike Nichols' performance. He however wryly notes that "Nichols profits from a rhetorical bias in the script at least as old as John Milton's *Paradise Lost* in which the devil gets all the good lines." *The Designated Mourner* marks an unique collaboration between two noted playwrights, one working as scenarist, the other as director.

—Vivek Adarkar

CREDITS

Jack: Mike Nichols
Judy: Miranda Richardson
Howard: David de Keyser

Origin: Great Britain
Released: 1997
Production: Donna Grey and David Hare for Greenpoint Film and BBC Films; released by First Look Pictures
Direction: David Hare
Screenplay: Wallace Shawn; based on his play
Cinematography: Oliver Stapleton
Editing: George Akers
Music: Richard Hartley
Production design: Bob Crowley
Art direction: John Ralph
Sound: Clive Winter
MPAA rating: R
Running Time: 94 minutes

REVIEWS

Boxoffice. May, 1997, p. 56.
Entertainment Weekly. May 16, 1997, p. 89.
Los Angeles Times. June 6, 1997, p. F14.
New York Observer. May 5, 1997.
New York Times. May 2, 1997, p. B7.
Variety. March 10, 1997, p. 81.
Village Voice. May 6, 1997, p. 94.
Wall Street Journal. June 6, 1997.

The Devil's Advocate

The newest attorney at the world's most powerful law firm has never lost a case. But he's about to lose his soul. *Devil's Advocate* Evil has its winning ways.—Movie tagline

"*Devil's Advocate* is loads of fun—a one-two punch of solid craft and playful spirit that's hard to resist!"—Eleanor Ringel, *Atlanta Journal*

"Pacino has one hell-of-a-good time. Reeves is remarkably good."—Terry Lawson, *Detroit Free Press*

"A stylish and watchable hoot!"—Kenneth Turan, *Los Angeles Times*

"Provocative, dazzling, clever! Al Pacino is devilishly delicious."—Joanna Langfield, *The Movie Minute*

"A sinfully guilty pleasure! Pacino has never seemed to enjoy a role more than this one!" —Thelma Adams, *New York Post*

"Seductive and cleverly entertaining! Pacino has great, wily fun."—Janet Maslin, *New York Times*

"Pacino hasn't had such fun in years. Charlize Theron says *star* with every breath she takes!" —Jack Kroll, *Newsweek*

"Pacino gives new meaning to *The Boss from Hell!*"—Tonya Pendleton, *Philadelphia Inquirer*

"*Devil's Advocate* is a devilishly good supernatural thriller!"—Peter Howell, *The Toronto Star*

John Milton (Al Pacino) is the head of the world's most powerful law firm. He also happens to be the Devil in disguise who fires things up in *The Devil's Advocate*.

Box Office: $58,994,812

Taylor Hackford's *The Devil's Advocate* at first seems to have borrowed its plot gimmick from John Grisham's 1991 novel *The Firm*, in which Harvard hotshot lawyer Mitchell McDeere took a job with a very wealthy Memphis tax firm, only to discover that their dealings were crooked and under investigation by the FBI. He sells his soul and gets into a peck of trouble. In fact, however, the screenplay for *The Devil's Advocate* by Jonathan Lemkin and Tony Gilroy was based on another novel, this one by Andrew Neiderman. Director Taylor Hackford had earlier worked with Tony Gilroy on the Stephen King vehicle *Dolores Claiborne* in 1995.

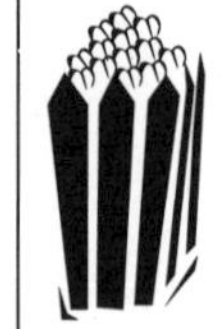

Milton to Kevin: "I'm just warming my hands on your talent."

In *The Devil's Advocate*, young hotshot Florida defense attorney Kevin Lomax (Keanu Reeves) is so brilliant that he has never lost a case, but as the film begins he seems headed for his first setback as he attempts to defend a teacher accused of child molestation. A teenaged girl has just testified in such a say that it is clear that his client is probably guilty. Lomax has a moral crisis as he attempts to compose himself in the courthouse washroom during a recess. In order to destroy the victim's credibility, he will have to destroy her on the witness stand in order to establish reasonable doubt. This he proceeds to do in order to protect his perfect record, even though he knows his client is guilty as sin because, well, that is what lawyers do.

Immediately after the trial Lomax is approached by a very smooth New York attorney (Ruben Santiago-Hudson), who offers him a job with the firm from hell, Milton, Chadwick & Waters, a firm that has powerful clients all over the world. Having demonstrated his willingness to override truth and justice, Lomax and his wife Mary Ann (Charlize Theron) decide to go to New York, where they are dazzled and tempted by the sinister John Milton (Al Pacino), who offers Kevin not only a job, but a luxury apartment owned by the firm. Chadwick and Waters are never seen or heard from in the film.

What Lomax does not immediately realize is that by joining this firm, he is entering into an unholy pact with the devil himself. His first assignment is to defend a scary, drug-dealing, voodoo witch doctor (Delroy Lindo), who is decidedly creepy, but Kevin is not especially bothered by this, or anything, for that matter. His next client is Alexander Cullen (Craig T. Nelson, an Emmy Award-winner for his starring role on the ABC television series "Coach"), a wealthy real-estate developer accused of three brutal murders. While Kevin becomes involved in this case, Mary Ann is soon disillusioned by her role as trophy wife; she has no friends other than the materialistic and hedonistic wives of Kevin's colleagues, and while her husband works long hours, she is left in the company of these bizarre creatures. Ultimately she eventually is seduced and ravished by the Devil, goes crazy, and dies.

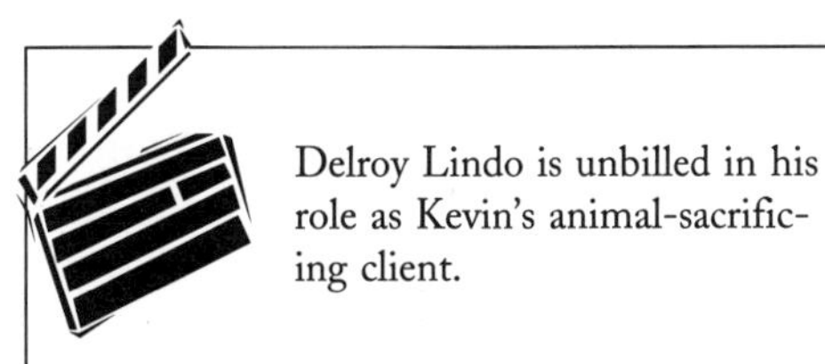

Delroy Lindo is unbilled in his role as Kevin's animal-sacrificing client.

The film gets increasingly allegorical and less realistic after Lomax goes to New York. Kevin's mother (Judith Ivey), an intensely religious woman, pays him a visit from Florida but is so frightened by John Milton that she beats a hasty retreat to Gainesville. Kevin later discovers that his mother had been to New York once before, when she was young and foolish, and that she had met John Milton and been seduced by him. It turns out that Milton was Kevin's father, and that explains Milton's intense interest in him. Milton wants to get Mary Ann out of the way so as to mate Kevin with Christabella (Connie Nielson), another partner in the firm, who happens to be Kevin's half-sister. Out of this unholy and unnatural union, the Anti-Christ will be born and will bring about the end of the world—unless Kevin asserts his free will. Or maybe the whole thing was simply a nightmare or a bad dream? If Kevin could do it all over again, would the film end differently?

The film goes on too long and has rather too many false endings, but it is carried by Keanu Reeves in the first hour, who is on target as the lawyer who loses his innocence and is in danger of being cast into darkness, and, especially, by Al Pacino in the second hour, who plays the hell out of his role as a fast-talking and deviously slick satanic con-man. As Stephen Hunter noted in his *Washington Post* review, the film is "preposterously entertaining," but it is also effectively creepy. The real John Milton (1608-1674), the author of *Paradise Lost* and *Paradise Regained*, knew that Satan, the fallen angel, the Prince of Darkness, was a fascinating character that threatens to take on heroic proportions. The fact that Pacino's character is named after the Puritan poet who wrote the last epic poem in English, is a sort of cheesy-comic tribute to Milton.

The story is too awkwardly split between the real world and the supernatural, as several reviewers noticed, without lodging too loud a protest. Todd McCarthy remarked in his *Variety* review that this "supernatural potboiler" strains "to be taken seriously." Reviewing the film for the *Washington Times*, Gary Arnold called the name of Pacino's character an "erudite misnomer" and considered Pacino's performance "the hammiest satanic caricature in recent memory." Janet Maslin of the *New York Times* was far more tolerant of this foolishness, however, and dismissed the naming of the character as a "gratifyingly light touch." She was also highly amused that the receptionist at Milton's law firm was named Caprice.

Stephen Hunter of the *Washington Post* simply could not contain his enthusiasm for Pacino's extravagances: "Polymorphous perversity in clothes by Armani," he wrote, a "Devil of too much testosterone and too little conscience, wildly seductive to both men (who emulate) and women (who succumb)." The screenplay feeds Pacino the best lines, such as "Vanity is definitely my favorite sin," and "Look at me, underestimated from Day One!" Like hell!

In fact, Pacino is simply outrageous in his excess, and so is the film, the sheer perversity of which seemed to disarm most of the critics. Reviewing the film for *Entertainment Weekly*, for example, Owen Gleiberman conceded that this was "probably Pacino's finest bad performance since *Scarface* [1983]," but was finally won over by a film that was "at once silly, overwrought, and almost embarrassingly entertaining." He also praised Charlize Theron for bringing so "much conviction to material this luridly outlandish." Gary Arnold noted in the *Washington Times* that the days "are probably numbered for directors who can think of nothing more suitable for Miss Theron than torture and dementia." What could this actress do "with a real role?"

Todd McCarthy praised Rick Baker's demon creations and Richard Greenberg's visual effects, which bring to life a hedonistic mural in Milton's office in one particularly seductive sequence. Bruno Rubeo's production design offers at least one in-joke, when the film uses Donald Trump's actual apartment as a set. For Todd McCarthy cameos by Don King and others were dismissed as "needless distractions," but Janet Maslin was amused to recognize Senator Alfonse D'Amato as a guest at one of Milton's wicked parties. Hell of a party, hell of a guy. The real John Milton knew that evil could be fascinating as well as seductive.

Though he may be named for John Milton, Pacino's

CREDITS

Kevin Lomax: Keanu Reeves
John Milton: Al Pacino
Mary Ann Lomax: Charlize Theron
Eddie Barzoon: Jeffrey Jones
Mrs. Lomax: Judith Ivey
Christabella: Connie Neilsen
Alexander Cullen: Craig T. Nelson
Jackie Heath: Tamara Tunie
Leamon Heath: Ruben Santiago-Hudson
Barbara: Heather Matarazzo

Origin: USA
Released: 1997
Production: Arnon Milchan, Arnold Kopelson, Anne Kopelson for Regency Enterprises; released by Warner Bros.
Direction: Taylor Hackford
Screenplay: Jonathan Lemkin and Tony Gilroy; based on the novel by Andrew Neiderman
Cinematography: Andrzej Bartkowiak
Editing: Mark Warner
Music: James Newton Howard
Production design: Bruno Rubeo
Art direction: Dennis Bradford
Set decoration: Roberta Holinko
Costumes: Judianna Makovsky
Sound: Tod A. Maitland
Demon design: Rick Baker
Visual effects design: Richard Greenberg
Visual effects supervisor: Stephanie Powell
MPAA rating: R
Running Time: 144 minutes

lines are never really Miltonic. Instead, they are Mametic, as the actor cracks wise wickedly in the style of David Mamet's Ricky Roma from *Glengarry Glen Ross* (1992), one of the defining roles of Pacino's film career. His verbal display is awesome and ultimately leaves Keanu Reeves sputtering in the wings. But the co-star's wooden acting serves as an effective complement to Pacino's flamboyance, as Gleiberman contended: "it's balsa-wood acting—light and airy and easy to watch." Even though he may be "intoxicated by his own hamminess" in this role, Pacino makes darkness visible in his portrayal of Milton. In fact, he is so radioactive-toxic that he glows in the dark. Pacino upstages and outclasses everyone else in the film, and, though far overdone, his astonishing performance makes the film worth seeing.

—*James M. Welsh*

REVIEWS

Boxoffice. December, 1997, p. 50.
Chicago Tribune. October 17, 1997, p. 4.
Entertainment Weekly. October 24, 1997, p. 40.
Los Angeles Times. October 17, 1997, p. F10.
New York Times. October 17, 1997, p. B12.
People. October 27, 1997, p. 20.
Premiere. November, 1997, p. 24.
Sight and Sound. January, 1998, p. 38.
Variety. October 13, 1997, p.77.
The Washington Post. October 17, 1997, p. D1.
Washington Post Weekend. October 17, 1997, p. 33.
Washington Times Metropolitan Times. October 17, 1997, p. C16.

The Devil's Own

One man trapped by destiny, and another bound by duty. They're about to discover what they're willing to fight, and to die for.—Movie tagline

"First rate! This taut thriller explodes. Superb performances by Brad Pitt and Harrison Ford."—Jeanne Wolf, *Jeanne Wolf's Hollywood*

"Dynamic and suspenseful!"—Bobbie Wygant, *KXAS-TV/NBC*

"Both Pitt and Ford bring a heavy-duty emotional investment to their roles. I admired their performances."—David Ansen, *Newsweek*

"It's a real treat to watch! Ford and Pitt are in top form!"—Gene Siskel, *Siskel & Ebert*

"This is really a good character-driven suspense drama. Director Pakula develops his story patiently, without letting its tensions unravel." —Richard Schickel, *Time*

"Powerful and exciting! Ford and Pitt are superb in this highly entertaining thriller!"—Paul Wunder, *WBAI*

"Harrison Ford and Brad Pitt deliver!"—Pat Collins, *WWOR-TV*

Box Office: $42,885,593

A month before *The Devil's Own* was to be launched, Brad Pitt almost torpedoed it with just a few lines of interview. In the February 3, 1997 issue of *Newsweek* he is quoted as saying, "It was the most irresponsible bit of filmmaking—if you can even call it that—that I've ever seen. I couldn't believe it. I don't know why anyone would want to continue making that movie. We had nothing. The movie was the complete victim of this drowning studio head [Mark Canton] who said, 'I don't care. We're making it. I don't care what you have. Shoot something'."

Of course, realizing the incredible publicity faux pas he had committed, Pitt later claimed his comments were about the early stages of filming and *not* about the final product. But when added to the gossip about out-of-control expenses (the budget supposedly soared from $60 to $90 million) and contentious egos on the set between Pitt and his co-superstar, Harrison Ford, one might not be blamed for entering the theater with more than a few misgivings. Thankfully, there is little in the final product that reflects any behind-the-scenes problems, real or rumored.

Frankie to Tom: "You pick up a gun, sooner or later someone gets a bullet. Big boys' rules."

The plot of *The Devil's Own* involves "The Troubles" in Ireland imported to American soil. The Irish problems go back centuries and can trace their roots to Irish nationalists vs. English colonizers, but over those hundreds of years it has turned into a war of vengeance infused with religious underpinnings. However, this is not a history lesson. In fact, Britain and the Irish Unionists are mere shadow figures. The main character's hatred is given no historical context, only a personal one. The focus of the film is to take the concerns of this one example of the many historical hatreds which are still playing themselves out today and elevating them into the realm of ethics, humanity, and justice in general.

When Francis "Frankie" McGuire (Brad Pitt) was a mere lad, he witnessed his father's execution by masked men as he sat down for dinner with his family. A scaring event for any boy but in the setting of the Irish Troubles, it becomes a sacred mission to obtain revenge. And so Frankie becomes one of Britain's ten-most-wanted criminals as he terrorizes his way to fame working with the Irish Republican Army. After one particularly violent event, Frankie has to go into hiding, and what better place to hide in plain site than in a police officer's home? And while he's at it, why not make it a police officer who lives in America so that Frankie can also purchase a few stinger missiles while he's "visiting" the land of opportunity and the NRA.

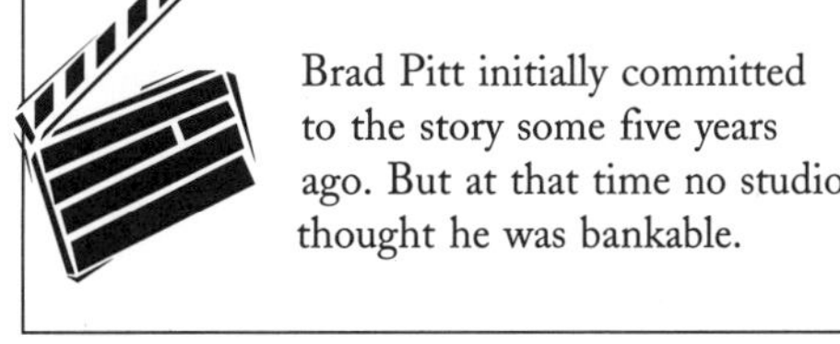

Brad Pitt initially committed to the story some five years ago. But at that time no studio thought he was bankable.

Using IRA connections with a State Court Judge, Frankie gets himself a new identity, Rory Devaney, a green card, a phony construction job, and a room with the Judge's friend, Tom O'Meara (Harrison Ford), an Irish-American cop who's glad to have a man from the old sod to join his family of four women (one wife and three daughters). Tom is one of those rare breeds of film cops: he has never abused his power or taken a bribe and only fired his gun four times in 23 years. He is ethical above and beyond the call of duty and actually becomes physically ill when he is put in the position of having to lie to protect his fellow police officer Edwin Diaz (Ruben Blades).

Since Tom has no idea as to Rory's true identity, it doesn't take long for Tom to accept the young man as the son he never had, and for Rory to think of the decent cop as the father he lost so early in life. But living with the virtuous Tom in the diversely ethnic, and seemingly idyllic, neighborhood on Staten Island also brings out a sad recognition within Rory of what life "could" be like without a constant search for revenge and the violence it engenders.

Tom despises violence; Rory accepts it as a normal part of life. Although he is a police officer, Tom has never lived with the day-to-day brutality that Rory has. In fact, Tom, like many Americans, only has the most vague notion of what it means to be Irish. (When he serves Rory his first dinner, it is corned beef and cabbage. Rory finds it tasty, but has no idea what it is.)

As the two men form their bonds, Rory continues on his mission to purchase missiles. He finds a supplier in a bar owner/arms dealer, Billy Burke (Treat Williams). Burke obtains the missiles, but when an IRA leader back home is killed, Rory puts the deal on hold. Burke, however, is not happy with the idea of keeping the contraband and not being paid the money he is owed. So Burke sends some of his goons to Tom's house to look for Rory's money. When Tom and his wife interrupt the thieves, the violence of Rory's life enters the sanctity of Tom's home with its own form of vengeance.

Now Tom discovers the true identity of his house guest. He feels betrayed, but also realizes the British agents who have come to arrest Rory will probably kill him. Tom must now attempt to prevent the missiles from getting to Ireland and creating more violence, bring his "friend" to justice, and not get either of them killed in the process.

Like the Troubles in Ireland, *The Devil's Own* is filled with moral ambiguities. Tom may be naive in his lack of understanding of the realities of Irish life, but Rory has been fanaticized into a similar blindness. So, of these two A-list superstars, who is the hero? Between the coddled American and the extremist liberator, between the British and the Irish, between the Protestants and the Catholics, between the orange and the green, between violence and submission, which side is in the right?

With this moral dilemma as its background, *The Devil's Own* contributes plenty of fodder for the debate, but also provides enough cinematic entertainment that not even Pitt's *Newsweek* comments can sink it. Audiences are not only given the usual action film chases, gunfights, and intrigue, but also ethical quandaries to think about and interesting characters to see them through.

While Ford's Tom may be a little too perfect, he almost has to be to be a valid foil for Rory's zealousness. Similarly, Pitt's Rory may glamorize the life and goals of the IRA a bit too much, but if he were portrayed as a complete villain it would undermine the moral ambiguities of the Irish situation.

Although the characters have their share of flaws (moral perfection for Tom, allure for Rory), there is no denying the powerful and convincing portrayals done by both Ford and Pitt. We want to live in the safety and decency of Tom's family, and we are seduced by Rory's humor and charm. This film belongs to the two actors; all other players are mere foils for their story and their actions.

Thankfully director Alan Pakula (*All the President's Men*, *Sophie's Choice*) knows that even though the film is an action/thriller, it is really the story of two men and the moral predicaments of their lives. Pakula allows the film to belong to Ford and Pitt instead of focusing on explosions and chases.

The Devil's Own may not approach the problems of Ireland with as much intelligence or historical accuracy as *Cal*, *In the Name of the Father* or the more recent *Michael Collins*, but it is an absorbing thriller that refuses to be overwhelmed by stunts and action or to resort to black-and-white heroes and villains. We are given something to watch and something to think about. Just what is justice? Duty? Honor? Do the ends justify even violent means? In the capable hands of Pakula, Pitt and Ford we can come to understand—maybe even sympathize with—both sides, even though we know neither side has the monopoly on the truth. There are no simple solutions for the complex problems and long-standing hatreds of Ireland; there can be no happy endings for a film that is as ambiguous as is life.

—*Beverley Bare Buehrer*

CREDITS

Tom O'Meara: Harrison Ford
Rory Devaney/Francis "Frankie" McGuire: Brad Pitt
Sheila O'Meara: Margaret Colin
Edwin Diaz: Ruben Blades
Billy Burke: Treat Williams
Peter Fitzsimmons: George Hearn
Chief Jim Kelly: Mitchell Ryan
Megan Doherty: Natascha McElhone
Sean Phelan: Paul Ronan
Harry Sloan: Simon Jones
Bridget O'Meara: Julia Stiles
Morgan O'Meara: Ashley Carin
Annie O'Meara: Kelly Singer

Origin: USA
Released: 1996
Production: Lawrence Gordon, Robert F. Colesberry; released by Columbia Pictures
Direction: Alan J. Pakula
Screenplay: David Aaron Cohen, Vincent Patrick and Kevin Jarre
Cinematography: Gordon Willis
Editing: Tom Rolf, Dennis Virkler
Production design: Jane Musky
Art direction: Robert Guerra
Set decoration: Leslie Bloom
Costume design: Bernie Pollack
Music: James Horner
MPAA rating: R
Running Time: 110 minutes

REVIEWS

Boxoffice. May, 1997, p. 62.
Chicago Tribune. March 26, 1997, p. 1.
Entertainment Weekly. March 21, 1997, p. 49.
Los Angeles Times. March 26, 1997, p. F1.
Newsweek. March 31, 1997, p. 75.
New York Times. March 26, 1997, p. B1.
The New Yorker. April 7, 1997, p. 96.
People. March 31, 1997, p. 21.
Rolling Stone. April 17, 1997, p. 83.
Sight and Sound. June, 1997, p. 50.
Time. March 31, 1997.
USA Today. March 26, 1997, p. 4D.
Variety. March 24, 1997, p. 33.
Village Voice. April 1, 1997, p. 72.

Diary of a Seducer; Le Journal d'un Seducteur

"Quirky & intense!"—Janet Maslin, *New York Times*
"Wonderful!"—Richard Corliss, *Time*
"Delirious."—Amy Taubin, *Village Voice*

Diary of a Seducer is the title of a nineteenth century classic by Soren Kierkegaard, the Danish philosopher, heralded as a forerunner of Sartre and other existentialists. It is also the playful title of writer-director Daniele Dubroux's film about various sets of lovers—all of whom are inspired or tormented by Kierkegaard's book. Although he is not known for humor, Dubroux nevertheless manages to turn the lugubrious Kierkegaard's material into a modern comedy.

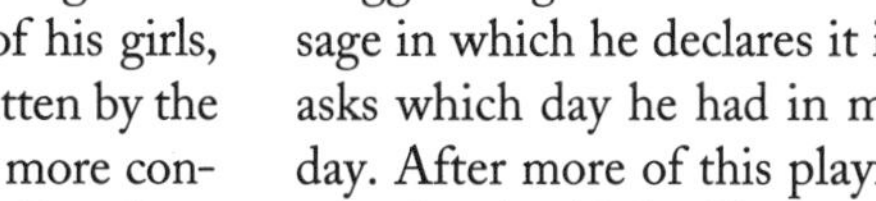

Daniele Dubroux: "To be seduced is interesting because it involves an odd kind of alchemy, a sort of hypnosis, a sort of spell, in which you lose your critical sense, you lower your guard."

Gregoire Moreau (Melvil Poupaud) is the lean, dark, and rather taciturn philosophy student who lends his Kierkegaard to women who are seduced by—what exactly? Gregoire is hardly a Don Juan. He earnestly explains to one of his girls, Claire (Chiara Mastroianni), that the book was written by the philosopher in his esthetic phase, in which he was more concerned with passion and beauty than with ethics. But Gregoire remains fairly aloof and secretive. The virginal Claire has to chase him. And the film creates no sense that Gregoire is particularly manipulative or playing hard to get. Indeed, one of the film's frustrations is that the character—and Melvil Poupaud's acting—contains so little affect. He almost seems like a neutral party in this libidinal world that resembles a Shakespearean comedy more than an existentialist movie.

Perhaps a close reading of Kierkegaard would explain why Dubroux finds him fit material for a farce. But the moviegoer not up on Kierkegaard may be bored by one scene after another in which eccentric characters appear to act without much motivation, other than responding to the basic premise that Kierkegaard's book turns them on.

Claire's therapist Hubert (Hubert Saint Macary) becomes obsessed with Claire, Gregoire, and Kierkegaard's book. Why? Claire is attractive enough, but before Hubert hears about Claire's involvement with Gregoire he does not show any particular attraction to her. Of course, that may be the point: here is an unusual film that insists that ideas and books count, that people can be aroused by philosophy, that the cerebral and the erotic are symbiotic.

It seems quaint and very French to say that people can be turned on by words. But this is what seems to happen when one of Claire's male pursuers, Sebastien (Mathieu Amalric) succeeds not with Claire (who is smitten with Gregoire) but with Claire's mother, Anne, played by writer-director Dubroux. Sebastien's tale of confused sexuality bores Claire. She does not want to hear about his homo/heterosexual encounters. She does not find it amusing that he wears makeup and tries on women's clothing. But Anne, apparently overworked and without a man in her life, is charmed by Sebastien's rather histrionic and clumsy efforts at seduction. During a country idyll in a boat Claire, near the shore, overhears him ask her mother whether he can touch her breasts. Claire shakes her head in a mixture of amusement and disgust, but the enchanted Anne only laughs and cries out that his hands are cold.

Sebastien has been keeping his own diary, plotting his attack on Claire but also fomenting an alternative strategy for Anne. When Anne discovers the diary and begins to recite portions of it to Sebastien, he is embarrassed but gamely tries to defend himself and also to explain that he is exaggerating his reactions. Anne confronts him with a passage in which he declares it is about time to seduce her. She asks which day he had in mind. He says perhaps that very day. After more of this playful palaver Sebastien asks Anne what he should do. She responds that perhaps he should do as he writes.

CREDITS

Claire Conti: Chiara Mastroianni
Gregoire Moreau: Melvil Poupaud
Sebastien: Mathieu Amalric
Anne: Daniele Dubroux
Hubert Markus: Hubert Saint Macary
Hugo: Jean-Pierre Leaud
Diane: Micheline Presle

Origin: France
Released: 1995, 1997
Production: Philippe Saal for Gemini Films; released by Leisure Time Features
Direction: Daniele Dubroux
Screenplay: Daniele Dubroux
Cinematography: Laurent Machuel
Editing: Jean-Francois Naudon
Music: Jean-Marie Senia
Costumes: Anne Schotte
Production design: Patrick Durand
Sound: Henri Maikoff
MPAA rating: Unrated
Running Time: 95 minutes

There are no real sex scenes in this film. It is all about the lover's pursuit and the grand passion. Jean-Pierre Leaud makes a flamboyant appearance as Hugo, who is absolutely obsessed with Gregoire's grandmother, Diane (Micheline Presle), a handsome lady past her prime but still beautiful enough, Hugo insists, to play Madame Bovary. But Diane remains elusive and Hugo waves a gun around threatening to shoot himself.

There are a few scenes with a dead body that Claire helps Gregoire to dispose of. It is better not to try explaining how these scenes fit into the plot, since there is no plot, really. And there is one other act of violence in this otherwise low-key, quirky comedy. It has its moments of fun, but it is hard to see what it all adds up to, except the cliched notions about human desire and the madness that can inflict the lover, who can wind up, like Bottom, in love with a horse's head—or some other less attractive part of the human or animal anatomy.

—*Carl Rollyson*

REVIEWS

Boxoffice. September, 1996, p. 115.
Hollywood Reporter. July 24, 1997, p. 7.
Los Angeles Times. July 25, 1997, p. F6.
New York Times. April 27, 1997, p. H15.
Variety. December 11, 1995, p. 87.
Village Voice. May 6, 1997, p. 86.

Different for Girls

He's not half the man she used to be.—Movie tagline

"Fast, funny, sexy."—Michael Wilmington, *Chicago Tribune*

"Rupert Graves [shows] ferocious energy and sizzling sex appeal."—Stephen Farber, *Movieline*

"*Tootsie* with surgical reality."—Michael Musto, *Village Voice*

Different for Girls is perhaps the first sex-change comedy/drama that is well-written, beautifully acted and skillfully directed, and manages to achieve a satisfying sense of realism, warmth, and poignancy. In fact, it transcends any smirkiness about its admittedly titillating subject and shows a wonderful—if offbeat—love story.

The films opens with Kim Foyle (Steven Mackintosh) in a London cab which smashes into a motorbike messenger, Paul Prentice (Rupert Graves). As Paul dusts himself off, both he and Kim realize that they went to public school together fifteen years ago. Only at that time, Kim was "Karl." It seems that not only were they acquaintances, but Paul often came to the effeminate Karl's defense from school bullies.

Their lives couldn't be more different now—and not just because of Karl's recent surgery. Kim has settled into a comfortable, respectable existence; she has a job writing copy for a greeting card company and lives in a beautifully decorated apartment. Paul, on the other hand, barely ekes out a living as a motorcycle messenger, lives hand-to-mouth, and still possesses the anti-authoritarian attitude of an adolescent. They catch up on their lives over a few awkward drinks. They both seem to be attracted to one another, but Kim is cautious about proceeding; she knows that she is often labeled a "freak" before she is labeled a "woman." Paul is essentially an extremely confused individual; even his girlfriend Angela (Nisha K. Nayar) cannot figure him out.

One night Kim has Paul over to dinner and talk turns to explicit detail about Kim's body and the changes therein from the operation and hormone treatments—rounded hips, buttocks, smoother limbs, and budding breasts. When a horrified Paul realizes that he has an erection, he runs from her apartment and into the street. Kim tries to calm him and they are both arrested for disturbing the peace. The police who arrest them think that Paul and Kim are a gay couple and harass Kim on the way to the station. Paul then leaps to Kim's defense and gets into real trouble. When Paul is released on bail, he begs Kim to agree to testify for him in the upcoming trial.

Paul, about to be kissed: "Whoa, I'm straight."
Kim: "So am I."

Kim is horrified by all of this; her life for the last few years has been nothing but scrutiny—she just can't bear anymore questions. She retreats to her sister's home and hides from Paul's insistent calls. Meanwhile, it is plainly obvious to Angela that Paul is not mature enough to be in a relationship and she breaks off with him. Through much soul-searching, Kim comes to the conclusion that she should help Paul, and it is her testimony about the policeman's abuse that gets Paul cleared of all the charges.

That night Paul comes to Kim's apartment to thank her. By this time, both of their respective defenses have been broken down and they make love. It is a revelation to both. Kim is overcome that she has found someone who accepts and loves her, and Paul has truly grown up from an irresponsible boy to a "man." He muses out loud to Kim that if only he could make some quick cash, he could pay off all of his debts and they could start their lives together. Quick cut to a sleazy tabloid: "My night of love with Kim/Karl." Despite the shock, Kim gave Paul permission to go to the press with the story. Besides providing Paul with money, it announces to the world that they are a couple and everyone else can go "sod off."

In almost every way this is a very conventional love story. A man and a woman meeting later in life and trading on each other's strengths and weaknesses to grow and change is a time-honored, traditional storyline. If it wasn't for issues of surgery and hormones, this could be viewed as a conventional love story, handed down through the ages. The fact that there is such an unusual twist merely enhances the character history and makes their final embrace all the sweeter.

—*G.E. Georges*

CREDITS

Paul Prentice: Rupert Graves
Kim Foyle: Steven Mackintosh
Jean: Saskia Reeves
Neil: Neil Dudgeon
Pamela: Miriam Margolyes
Alison: Charlotte Coleman
Angela: Nisha K. Nayar

Origin: Great Britain
Released: 1995, 1997
Production: John Chapman for X Pictures; released by First Look Pictures
Direction: Richard Spence
Screenplay: Tony Marchant
Cinematography: Sean Van Hales
Editing: David Gamble
Production design: Grenville Horner
Art direction: Melanie Allen
Music: Stephen Warbeck
Costumes: Susannah Buxton
Makeup: Fae Hammond
MPAA rating: R
Running Time: 101 minutes

REVIEWS

Boxoffice. March, 1997, p. 38.
Detroit Free Press. February 22, 1998, p. 8H.
Entertainment Weekly. September 26, 1997, p. 56.
Los Angeles Times. September 12, 1997, p. F6.
New York Times. September 12, 1997, p. C8.
People. September 29, 1998, p. 19.
San Francisco Chronicle. September 12, 1997, p. C3.
Variety. February 5, 1996, p. 63.
Village Voice. September 16, 1997, p. 100.

The Disappearance of Garcia Lorca; Lorca; Death In Granada

"A very powerful movie, Andy Garcia's performance is extraordinary."—Alex Kaham, *KMEX*
"An exceptional film with extraordinary performances."—Angel Prada, *La Voz Libre*
"An illuminating film!"—Rex Reed, *New York Observer*
"Two thumbs up."—*Siskel & Ebert*
"Powerful and passionate!"—Jeffrey Lyons, *WNBC-TV*

Spain's greatest poet-playwright, Federico Garcia Lorca (1898-1936), became a martyr to the Spanish Republic when he was murdered in the early stages of Francisco Franco's fascist revolt. Lorca's passionate writing and his intense, joyous personality made his loss especially poignant. Also a fine musician, he became the symbol of the artist who dies for democracy.

Exactly how Lorca died and who was responsible for having him shot has been the subject of endless speculation. The events leading to his last days haunt the history of his country and bemuse devotees of modern literature. How does a man of such glorious spirit go to his death? Why did Lorca put himself in harm's way, returning to his home, where he could expect the fascist forces to find him? And what is Lorca's legacy to modern Spain—seemingly recovered from decades of fascist rule—and once again a progressive and democratic country? Who is left who remembers those evil days? Can the truth of Lorca's death finally be discovered and told?

The Disappearance of Garcia Lorca aims to explore these

questions and to convey the fearless and humane life of the man and the artist. Indeed, it capitalizes on the myth of Lorca, in that it presents him as the embodiment of a life lived as art. In Lorca's case, there seems to be no discrepancy between the private and public life, no division between the democratic man and artist. The solidarity he expresses with humanity in his poems and plays is expressed as well in his return home to be with his friends and family, who are persecuted by the fascists.

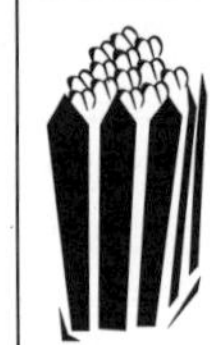

Ricardo on meeting Garcia Lorca: "That night I learned that poetry could be an act of violence."

Andy Garcia plays Lorca with the requisite flair and sensitivity. He makes Lorca's braving of fascist thugs credible. Garcia's Lorca is a man of destiny who cannot spare a moment to worry about his own death. He lives the words of his plays. He is anything but naive. He knows how much danger he is in, and he wants to live. But he can only live on his terms. Garcia portrays a character who never stops believing that he can influence events and protect his people.

Film was originally released in Spain under the title *Death In Granada* with a 142 minute running time.

The film's premise is that Lorca's death disturbs not only his supporters but also his killers. They did not find it easy to murder him, and they could not forget the dignity he maintained even in his last moments. In his death, they took their own sorry measure—their willingness to connive with an evil regime and to survive in a craven period.

As the title suggests, *The Disappearance of Garcia Lorca,* is plotted as a mystery story. A young reporter, Ricardo Fernandez (Esai Morales), whose family has lived in exile in Puerto Rico, returns to investigate Lorca's death. He grew up idolizing the writer, and he senses that the story of Lorca's last days might finally be uncovered. Thus the film becomes a story within a story. As Fernandez penetrates to the heart of the mystery, he finds that friends of his family are implicated in Lorca's death, and that there is a conspiracy to prevent him from learning the truth. Indeed, Fernandez himself is threatened with violence, but like his hero Lorca, he fearlessly forges ahead.

The idea that Fernandez's so-called helpers are also his enemies makes perfect sense in the context of the Spanish Civil War, which had its collaborators and double agents, and its fascists who become latter-day supporters of the Lorca myth. Everyone in Spain, regardless of what side they were on, can now more or less safely mourn their poet's loss—even if they contributed to Lorca's murder.

But the inherent tension and tragedy of Lorca's story is dissipated by the parallel plot of Fernandez's search. Fernandez is given the obligatory love interest—and of course he falls in love with a fascist colonel's daughter. Will the irrepressible Fernandez also suffer Lorca's fate? The parallel is too obvious, and it sentimentalizes Lorca's significance. The film loses energy in the flabby conversations between Fernandez and his sidekick taxi driver, played by Giancarlo Giannini. The rest of the supporting cast, however, provide suitably sinister performances, including Jeroen Krabbe as the fascist colonel and Miguel Ferrer as a fascist thug. Perhaps the most complex character, played slyly by Edward James Olmos, is a wily politician, entangled in Lorca's death and now a publisher of his writing.

—*Carl Rollyson*

CREDITS

Federico Garcia Lorca: Andy Garcia
Ricardo: Esai Morales
Lozano: Edward James Olmos
Col. Aguirre: Jeroen Krabbe
Maria Eugenia: Marcela Wallerstein
Centeno: Miguel Ferrer
Cab Driver: Giancarlo Giannini

Origin: Spain
Released: 1996
Production: Enrique Cerezo and Marcos Zurinaga for Miramar Films; released by Triumph Films
Direction: Marcos Zurinaga
Screenplay: Marcos Zurinaga, Juan Antonio Romos, and Neil Cohen; based on the books *The Assassination of Garcia Lorca* and *Federico Garcia Lorca: A Life* by Ian Gibson
Cinematography: Juan Ruiz-Anchia
Editing: Carole Kravetz
Music: Mark McKenzie
Art direction: Gil Parrondo
Costumes: Leon Revuelta
Sound: Antonio Bloch
MPAA rating: R
Running Time: 108 minutes

REVIEWS

Boxoffice. September, 1997, p. 115.
Los Angeles Times. September 12, 1997, p. F16.
New York Times. September 12, 1997, p. C5.
San Francisco Chronicle. September 12, 1997, p. C3.
San Francisco Examiner. September 12, 1997, p. C3.
Variety. March 10, 1997, p. 80.
Village Voice. September 16, 1997, p. 100.

Donnie Brasco

In 1978, the U.S. government waged a war against organized crime. One man was left behind the lines.—Movie tagline

"A wonderfully tense, clever and moving gangland thriller."—Owen Gleiberman, *Entertainment Weekly*

"A great film!"—Joel Siegel, *Good Morning America*

"This is Depp's coming-of-age role, and he's terrific. Pacino reminds us how great he can be when he loses himself inside a character."—David Ansen, *Newsweek*

"Al Pacino and Johnny Depp are a match made in acting heaven!"—Peter Travers, *Rolling Stone*

"Two thumbs up!"—*Siskel & Ebert*

"Smart and suspenseful!"—Richard Schickel, *Time*

"A killer gangster picture!"—Gene Shalit, *Today Show*

"Johnny Depp comes up with his most winning performance yet."—Susan Wloszcyna, *USA Today*

"*Donnie Brasco* ia an *A,* and may rightfully take its place beside the best films of this genre."—Pat Collins, *WWOR-TV*

Box Office: $41,993,313

Most films about the Mafia depict these gangsters as larger-than-life figures, as in Francis Ford Coppola's operatic treatment of the mob in three films beginning with *The Godfather* (1972), or as vicious thugs, as in Martin Scorsese's gritty *Mean Streets* (1973), *Goodfellas* (1990), and *Casino* (1995). Other filmmakers have taken approaches to the Mafia ranging from an almost documentary style to pure melodrama. Director Mike Newell and screenwriter approach their Mafia story in *Donnie Brasco* much like Sidney Lumet does in his police dramas *Serpico* (1973) and *Prince of the City* (1981), by emphasizing realism and character study. Together with an excellent cast, they have created an instant classic crime film, full of violence, emotion, and memorable moments.

Donnie Brasco is based on the experiences of Joseph D. Pistone, an FBI agent who was undercover in the Mafia from 1976 to 1981. Using the cover name Donnie Brasco, Pistone (Johnny Depp), spends two years establishing a reputation as a fence for stolen jewelry before being taken on as a protégé by Lefty Ruggiero (Al Pacino), a lower-level Brooklyn gangster who has killed twenty-six people. Pistone impresses Lefty by being even more vicious than the hit man in scaring a club owner who owes Lefty money. One of the many pleasures of *Donnie Brasco* is seeing how increasingly the hero enjoys being a tough guy much more than being a federal agent.

Loyalty to his job or to the mob confronts undercover agent Donnie Brasco (Johnny Depp) as he befriends aging henchman Lefty (Al Pacino) in the true crime drama *Donnie Brasco.*

The film is a careful study of mob behavior, but even more, it painstakingly paints a portrait of two memorable characters. Lefty's son is a disappointment, a drug addict who nearly dies of an overdose, and the protégé slowly becomes the gangster's surrogate son. Likewise, Pistone grows to care about this man he is betraying and whose death he is ensuring. Pistone sees in Lefty, whose entire life is obsessed with being a wise guy, as having loyalty, integrity, and strength of character missing in his law-enforcement colleagues. A supervising agent (Gerry Becker) constantly on Pistone's back is the closest the film comes to having a villain.

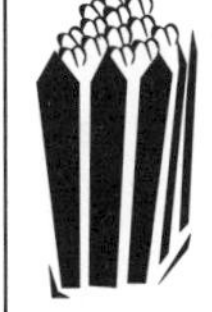

Lefty to Donnie: "My family, my children, my mother can hold her head up in any neighborhood in this city when she walks down the block, see. In all the five boroughs, I'm known. I'm known all over the f**king world. Anybody—ask anybody about Lefty from Mulberry Street. Fuggedaboudit."

Lefty's son is not the only disappointment in the hit man's life. Lefty himself has not advanced through the mob ranks as he had hoped. When a chance for promotion comes along, the younger Sonny Black (Michael Madsen) is chosen instead. This slight is aggravated when Sonny seems to be wooing Pistone away from Lefty.

When the gang goes to Miami to set up a gambling operation with an elaborate nightclub as the front—all as part of an FBI sting operation—someone informs the police, and suspicions among the wise guys increase. In the film's most violent sequence, Sonny's crew retaliates against a higher-up who has betrayed them, and Lefty brutally executes Nicky (Bruno Kirby), the clown of the group, for holding out on them. The FBI have meanwhile become increasingly uneasy about the difficult-to-control Pistone who seems to be taking his cover role too seriously, and after the revenge shootout, the authorities decide to bring in Pistone against his will and for his own good.

The real Lefty Ruggiero was not executed by the Mafia. He was released from prison because of terminal cancer and died at 67.

Attanasio, who wrote *Quiz Show* (1994) and is one of the creators, along with producer Barry Levinson, of the television series "Homicide", pays close attention to the details of mob life. The FBI agents become confused over what gangster goes with which nickname since these names are so similar, and they have Pistone explain all the possible meanings of "forgetaboutit," the mob's pet expression.

As in such instances, the film's almost anthropological approach to its subject is often employed for comic effect. When Pistone visits Lefty on Christmas and presents him with cash as a gift, he receives the same gift in the same way. Lefty then borrows back his gift to Pistone. One of the ironies of *Donnie Brasco* is that Lefty and his kind, unlike Coppola's and Scorsese's relative high rollers, make very little money from their criminal activities, occasionally resorting to stealing parking meters and tickets to a Chaka Khan concert.

Pistone's dilemma of betraying those who trust and even love him is intensified by keeping secret the existence of his wife and three daughters and by trying to steal moments with them to keep up the pretense that he is still a husband and father. Almost all his encounters with Maggie (Anne Heche) end in arguments, and he takes to sneaking quietly into his home like a burglar to observe his family. Maggie forces him to meet with a psychobabbling marriage counselor and starts divorce proceedings, but Pistone chooses loyalty to Lefty over his family. (The real-life Pistones remain married.)

Donnie Brasco ends with closing credits revealing that over two-thousand criminals were indicted and over one thousand convicted because of Pistone's work and that the Mafia has placed a $500,000 bounty on his head. The true purpose and consequences of his work, however, mean relatively little in the context of the film which is more interested in exposing the mundane side of the mob and in exploring character. In support of the latter, Depp and Pacino deliver wonderful performances.

Pistone is the first true adult role for Depp, previously little more than a too-sensitive adolescent. Depp conveys the conflicts raging within Pistone by contorting his body with nervous tension during the lawman's visits to Maggie, ready to explode at the least sign of discord. Newell and Attanasio provide plenty of assistance to the actor's interpretation, having Pistone, obsessed with order when away from the mob, rearrange the contents of the kitchen shelves.

Pistone knows he is destroying his family, his friends, and himself, and Depp does little to soften this portrait. When the gangsters go to a Japanese restaurant and are asked to remove their shoes, Pistone refuses since he is concealing a tape recorder in his boot. He improvises a story about his father being killed in World War II and refuses to obey the commands of the people who robbed him of a normal childhood. When Sonny and the gang begin viciously beating the poor maitre d', Pistone is horrified, then realizes he must take part, and becomes angry at his victim when he injures his hand slugging the man. Depp expertly conveys both Pistone's fear and his disgust at the discovery of what he is capable of. The actor's finest moment comes at the end of the film when the FBI presents Pistone with a medal and a $500 check for his five years of agony, and Depp silently expresses the horror of a man seemingly unable to live with himself.

Pistone's emotion over causing his friend's death is moving because of Depp's performance and also because of the emotional investment Pacino has made in this character. Though Lefty is a simple man whose greatest pleasure is watching wildlife documentaries, Pacino makes him both an everyman—without ever sentimentalizing him in obvious ways—and a tragic figure. Though the character and Pacino's performance resemble his work on stage in David Mamet's *American Buffalo*, Lefty is more sympathetic and pathetic than Mamet's low-life loser. When a major Florida hoodlum (Val Avery) brushes Lefty off, Pacino seemingly shrinks to half his size.

Pacino's weakness for shouting is absent as he relishes the character's quieter moments. Pacino's greatest moment comes when Lefty is summoned to his death, and he carefully places his wallet, wristwatch, and rings in a drawer. This is one of the most poignant moments in any American film, and the performance may be this great actor's best.

AWARDS AND NOMINATIONS

Academy Awards 1997 Nominations: Adapted Screenplay

Donnie Brasco also confirms Newell's stature as a director. Many reviewers of the film wondered how the man who made the British comedies *Enchanted April* (1992) and *Four Weddings and a Funeral* (1994) could make such a gripping American crime drama, but in addition to these charming, highly entertaining films, Newell has also done some darker work. *Dance with a Stranger* (1985) examines the self-destructive life of the last woman executed for murder in the United Kingdom, and *The Good Father* (1986) looks at an angry working-class man's quest for revenge after his wife leaves him. Newell also combines charming and somber elements in *Into the West* (1993), depicting two young Irish gypsies' flight from squalor into fantasy.

Donnie Brasco is both a moving and an entertaining film because of how Newell and Attanasio have structured the film's shifts between light moments, realistic looks at the inner workings of the Mafia, and scenes emphasizing character. Newell and editor Jon Gregory pace the film extremely well, and the director trusts the story and characters to carry the film, resisting stylistic flourishes except for an evocative shot of a car moving through the city toward its destiny that recalls Scorsese's *Taxi Driver* (1975).

Since Newell has elicited great performances from his actors before, most notably Miranda Richardson in *Dance with a Stranger* and Anthony Hopkins in *The Good Father*, he must also receive some credit for the work of Pacino and Depp. In giving the film positive reviews on their television program, Gene Siskel and Roger Ebert did not even mention Newell. *Donnie Brasco* shows that the director, who also did not receive sufficient credit for the success of *Four Weddings and a Funeral*, can be taken for granted no longer.

—Michael Adams

CREDITS

Lefty Ruggiero: Al Pacino
Joseph Pistone/Donnie Brasco: Johnny Depp
Sonny Black: Michael Madsen
Nicky: Bruno Kirby
Paulie: James Russo
Maggie Pistone: Anne Heche
Tim Curley: Zeljko Ivanek
Dean Blandford: Gerry Becker
Annette: Ronnie Farer
Richie Gazzo: Rocco Sisto
Bruno: Brian Tarantina
Sonny Red: Robert Miano
Trafficante: Val Avery

Origin: USA
Released: 1997
Production: Mark Johnson, Barry Levinson, Louis DiGiaimo and Gail Mutrux for Baltimore Pictures and Mandalay Entertainment; released by TriStar Pictures
Direction: Mike Newell
Screenplay: Paul Attanasio; based on *Donnie Brasco: My Undercover Life in the Mafia* by Joseph D. Pistone and Richard Woodley
Cinematography: Peter Sova
Editing: Jon Gregory
Production design: Donald Graham Burt
Art direction: Jefferson Sage
Set decoration: Leslie Pope
Costumes: Aude Bronson-Howard, David Robinson
Music: Patrick Doyle
Sound: Tod A. Maitland
Casting: Louis DiGiaimo, Brett Goldstein
MPAA rating: R
Running Time: 121 minutes

REVIEWS

Christian Science Monitor. February 28, 1997, p. 12.
Entertainment Weekly. March 7, 1997, p. 44.
Interview. March, 1997, p. 116.
The Nation. March 31, 1997, p. 35.
The New York Times. February 28, 1997, p. B1.
The New Yorker. March 17, 1997, p. 121.
Newsweek. March 3, 1997, p. 69.
People. March 3, 1997, p. 19.
Rolling Stone. March 20, 1997, p. 89.
Sight and Sound. May, 1997, p. 40.
USA Today. February 28, 1997, p. D1.
Variety. February 24, 1997, p. 75.

Double Team

They don't play by the rules.—Movie tagline

"Hell-raising, non-stop action! Van Damme and Rodman make a great super-action team!"—Ron Brewington, *American Urban Radio Networks*

"An enjoyably decadent spectacle . . . the movie has more sheer personality than any previous Van Damme outing."—Owen Gleiberman, *Entertainment Weekly*

"Terrifically entertaining."—Dave Kehr, *New York Daily News*

Box Office: $11,438,337

The most interesting aspect of *Double Team* was the debut of professional basketball's bad boy Dennis Rodman, who plays a black marketeer/undercover CIA agent named Yaz. Many people were wondering whether Rodman could make the transition from basketball court to silver screen. His debut was neither a great success nor a total disaster. The best that can be said of him is that he did a fairly good job of acting for a basketball player. His was a role that might have been played by the volatile Wesley Snipes—but Dennis Rodman is no Wesley Snipes. Rodman has only one deadpan expression which mirrors the already familiar deadpan expression of his partner, Belgian karate champion Jean-Claude Van Damme, who plays a CIA agent named Quinn. They are the double team referred to in the title.

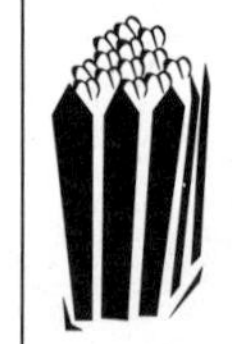

Quinn to Yaz about his colorful coif: "Who does your hair, Siegfried or Roy?"

The plot is very hard to follow. This is partly the fault of script writers Don Jakoby and Paul Mones and partly the fault of the direction by Hong Kong action master Taul Hark, who predictably was more interested in action and spectacle than continuity or character development. *Double Team* is somewhat like a basketball game in which there are several basketballs, an unlimited number of players, and a court littered with banana peels. Quinn, another one of those world-weary former secret agents who is dragged back out of retirement, is ordered to bring back his arch-enemy Stavros (Mickey Rourke) dead or alive, preferably dead. Stavros is a modern-day Professor Moriarty who currently specializes in terrorism for hire. He knows everything there is to know about explosives. The film probably contains more explosions than any since *Apocalypse Now* (1979). Neither the good guy Van Damme, nor bad guy Stavros, nor in-between guy Yaz cares about what these explosions do to innocent bystanders.

Tsui Hark has directed more than 50 Hong Kong films; this is his American feature debut.

Quinn has set up an elaborate trap for Stavros at an amusement park. But Stavros is too foxy to get suckered. One of the many fatalities in the shoot-out is Stavros' beloved little son. After this the MacGuffin changes and the hunter becomes the hunted. Stavros wants revenge—and Van Damme is especially vulnerable because he has a pregnant wife waiting at home at the peaceful Riviera villa where he had hoped to enjoy his early retirement. Yet another plot twist is provided by the fact that Quinn is being chased by his own employers after escaping from an escape-proof island where disaffected agents end up when the world thinks they are dead.

It is never quite clear how Yaz gets involved with Quinn. Yaz is a cold-blooded dealer in high-powered guns. Yet he closes up shop and goes along with Quinn to a number of scenic European locales where they are inevitably shot at or blown high into the air. Once again the MacGuffin changes. Now it is Quinn's pregnant wife who is the object of all the conflict. Stavros kidnaps her and threatens to murder her and her unborn child. Ultimately the child, a son, is born in spite of all the rough handling undergone by the mother, and the infant becomes the new MacGuffin.

The climax comes at the Coliseum in Rome. It has withstood over two thousand years of exposure, earthquakes, and warfare, but it is no match for Quinn, Yaz, and Stavros. Quinn is forced to meet Stavros out in the center of the arena, where they face off like a couple of ancient gladiators, with Quinn's newborn son in between them asleep in a basket. Stavros is not a model of good sportsmanship. He has the ancient grandstand packed with his heavily armed henchmen. He has planted land mines all over the floor of the stadium, and just to add a touch of color he has brought in a hungry Bengal tiger which intends to do to Quinn what the lions used to do to Christians on this same blood-soaked soil.

Rodman's role is always peripheral. In this showdown he is mainly occupied with grabbing the baby and handling him the way he handles the basketball on the court. The baby passes from hand to hand so often that the viewer is

CREDITS

Jack Quinn: Jean-Claude Van Damme
Yaz: Dennis Rodman
Stavros: Mickey Rourke
Goldsmythe: Paul Freeman
Kath: Natacha Lindinger
Dr. Maria Trifioli: Valeria Cavalli
Brandon: Jay Benedict
Dieter Staal: Rob Diem

Origin: USA
Released: 1997
Production: Moshe Diamant for One Story Pictures and Mandalay Entertainment; released by Columbia Pictures
Direction: Tsui Hark
Screenplay: Don Jakoby and Paul Mones
Cinematography: Peter Pau
Editing: Bill Pankow
Music: Gary Chang
Production design: Marek Dobrowolski
Art direction: Damien Lanfranchi
Set decoration: Christian Calviera
Costumes: Magali Guidasci
Sound: Daniel Brisseau
Special effects supervisor: Bruno Van Zeebroeck
Visual effects supervisor: Joe Bauer
Stunt coordinator: Charles Picerni
MPAA rating: R
Running Time: 91 minutes

bewildered. In the meantime Van Damme and a surprisingly muscular Rourke are fighting it out karate-style among the hidden land mines. When one of these mines finally goes off it starts a chain reaction more spectacular than anything Caligula or Nero could have dreamt of in their days of glory. The venerable Roman Coliseum is apparently blown to bits by the special effects team, who are undoubtedly the hardest working members of the entire crew.

Double Team was not taken seriously by most reviewers because the three stars did not take the film seriously themselves. It was another one of those campy buddy adventure films in the spirit of legendary box-office loser *Hudson Hawk* (1991), which starred Bruce Willis and Danny Aiello as a couple of smart alecks who were indifferent to danger because they knew they were only making a movie for gullible teenagers. Reviewer Janet Maslin of the *New York Times* called *Double Team* a "flashy, cheesy, overheated ... cartoonish adventure."

—*Bill Delaney*

REVIEWS

Boxoffice. February, 1997, p. 40.
Chicago Tribune. April 4, 1997, p. 5.
Entertainment Weekly. April 11, 1997, p. 58.
Los Angeles Times. April 4, 1997, p. F16.
New York Times. April 4, 1997, p. C7.
People. April 21, 1997, p. 23.
USA Today. April 4, 1997, p. 4D.
Variety. April 7, 1997, p. 43.

Dream With the Fishes

"This is a revelation! Fantastical vignettes that keep defying your assumptions!"—Oliver Jones, *Details*

"A surprisingly affecting film!"—Marshall Fine, *Gannett News Service*

"Throws you back to the late '70s, to the dark and glorious days ... A buddy movie that keeps you guessing. David Arquette is excellent!"—Richard Rayner, *Harpers Bazaar*

"Shows an uncommon tenderness!"—Graham Fuller, *Interview*

"Sharply etched, nicely offbeat debut feature.... A lean and distinctive visual style."—Janet Maslin, *New York Times*

"An affecting comedy about voyeurism, LSD and nude bowling. David Arquette gives a fine performance."—Dennis Dermody, *Paper Magazine*

Dream With the Fishes is a buddy film about two unlikely companions whose relationship is built on the shaky foundation of suspicion, anger and desperation. This first feature by screenwriter Finn Taylor (*Pontiac Moon*, 1994) is an offbeat and refreshing black comedy most welcome in a summer full of mainstream fare.

David Arquette (best known as the naive but lovable Deputy Dewey of *Scream* [1996] and *Scream 2* [1997] fame) stars as Terry, a voyeur so socially disconnected that he's decided to end it all with a leap from the Oakland Bay Bridge.

There he is distracted by Nick (Brad Hunt), who steps forth not to stop him, but to tell him that pills would be a better way to go. Nick, who is terminally ill, offers to help fulfill Terry's death wish if Terry will finance Nick's final days and some of his lifelong fantasies.

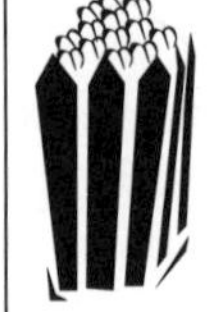

Nick asks suicidal Terry for his watch before he kills himself: "Since you're going to be dead in a few minutes anyway, what use will it be to you?"

Terry agrees to this arrangement and together they embark in search of adventure. Among Nick's many aspirations are a nude bowling game with hookers; dropping acid while driving; a visit to an aquarium; naked armed robbery; and a trip to Nick's hometown, where he has some unfinished business with an old girlfriend and an abusive father.

Finn Taylor's film is partially autobiographical, dealing with the relationship between Taylor and a close friend who was dying.

Eventually, Nick and Terry begin to lend each other moral support as their relationship grows, but never in the way that we're accustomed to seeing with mainstream films. Taylor always keeps the audience off balance as he leaves many questions hanging and credible twists coming right up to the end.

CREDITS

Terry: David Arquette
Nick: Brad Hunt
Liz: Kathryn Erbe
Aunt Elise: Cathy Moriarty
Nick's father: J.E. Freeman
Nick's mother: Allyce Beasley

Origin: USA
Released: 1997
Production: Johnny Wow and Mitchell Stein for 3 Ring Circus Films; released by Sony Pictures Classics
Direction: Finn Taylor
Screenplay: Finn Taylor
Cinematography: Barry Stone
Editing: Nick LeCompte
Music: Tito Larriva
Music supervisor: Charles Raggio
Production design: Justin McCartney
MPAA rating: R
Running Time: 97 minutes

The performances in this film are all excellent. Both Arquette and Hunt do commendable jobs in fleshing out their characters. Arquette's portrayal of Terry, the lonely and pathetic lost soul who's forced to connect with another human being, is amazingly subtle. And Hunt delivers a standout performance as the more charismatic and erratic Nick. Supporting work is equally strong with roles by Kathryn Erbe as Nick's long-suffering girlfriend, and Cathy Moriarty, as his Aunt Elise, a blowsy ex-stripper.

Dream With the Fishes pays homage to '70s films (like *Dealing* [1971], *The Last Detail* [1973]), and *California Split* [1974]) with unapologetic substance abuse, retro costumes, and characters who drop out of the mainstream on their way to enlightenment. Taylor gives the picture a stark and distinctive visual style and the film stock itself was processed to further imitate the grainy, color-saturated look of '70s cinema. As Dennis Harvey comments in *Variety*, "Taylor orchestrates a breezy, like-mindedly subversive tribute to that period's maverick films sans excessive derivation, nailing every *outre* and heartfelt story nuance."

At times funny and other times heartrending, *Dream With the Fishes* is ultimately a tale of unlikely friendship held together by a shared humanity. Critical reaction to this well written and humorous film was mostly positive, although it didn't generate much at the box office. Hopefully, this original and profound comedy will find a much-deserved audience on video.

—*Beth Fhaner*

REVIEWS

Boxoffice. June, 1997, p. 52.
Los Angeles Times. June 20, 1997, p. F8.
New York Times. June 20, 1997, p. B20.
People. July 1, 1997, p. 20.
San Francisco Chronicle. July 11, 1997, p. D3.
San Francisco Examiner. July 11, 1997, p. C7.
Variety. January 27, 1997, p. 76.

Drunks

All they want is another shot . . . —Movie tagline
"A powerhouse!"—*Boston Herald*
"Dianne Wiest, Faye Dunaway and Parker Posey give dead-on performances."—*Buzz Magazine*
"Tragic and . . . hilarious."—*Filmmaker Magazine*
"Lewis delivers a brilliant dramatic performance!"—*Knight-Ridder Newspapers*
"In this gravity there is also grace."—*New York Magazine*
"A strong group of actors . . . deliver intense performances."—*San Francisco Examiner*
"Star-studded cast . . . stellar performances!" —*Village Voice*

Adapted by Gary Lennon from his stageplay *Blackout*, *Drunks* is a series of monologues interspersed with the escalating odyssey of a recovering alcoholic hell-bent on breaking his sobriety. The film, which first aired on Showtime, has a paper-thin storyline combined with the gross miscasting of comedian Richard Lewis at the dramatic center. The result is a stage-bound piece that offers little more than an opportunity for a group of talented actors to show off their wares.

Drunks records the events of one singular evening at an Alcoholics Anonymous meeting in the basement of a New York church. As coffee is made and chairs are placed, the twitchy Jim Epstein (Richard Lewis) is itching to get high. A recovering alcoholic and heroin addict, Jim is called upon to present his story to the group and reveals that his now-deceased wife insisted that he clean up before she would agree to marry him. He did, but since her death from a brain aneurysm, sobriety seems unnecessary and talking dredges up unbearable pain. Jim bolts from the meeting headlong into a night-long debauchery of sex, drugs and booze.

Covering just about every ethic group and social status, the other participants take their turns recounting their own woeful tales of the evils of alcohol and drug abuse. A neurotic woman (the always peculiar Amanda Plummer) frets about her domineering mother's up-coming visit. An African-American father (the late Howard E. Rollins, Jr.) recounts how he sent his young son through the windshield of the car when he suffered a blackout. Newcomer Fanni Green portrays an inner-city woman trying to cope with AIDS, and a younger brother's foray into heroin use.

Actress Faye Dunaway (who broke into the Big Time with 1967's trend-setting *Bonnie and Clyde*) gives a refreshingly restrained performance as a middle-class mother struggling with temptation at the prospect of losing custody of her shoplifting son. But it is Academy Award-winning Diane Wiest (*Bullets Over Broadway*, 1994) who is the most memorable as a successful doctor who has replaced her addiction to painkillers with long hours of work. Parker Posey, however, does her standard party girl routine as a football groupie who longs to be the reincarnation of singer/junkie Janis Joplin, and Spalding Grey gets saddled with the most obviously scripted piece as the WASPish alcoholic-in-denial who claims to have stumbled onto the meeting while looking for choir practice.

Richard Lewis, making his dramatic acting debut, is arguably the film's weakest link—and it is a costly casting miscalculation. The comedian's portrayal of the free-falling, self-loathing Jim is undoubtedly sincere, but Lewis's lack of acting technique leads him to resort to a bizarre and inadvertently funny Jewish Al Pacino impersonation.

Ultimately, *Drunks* reminds us that it is "One Day at a

CREDITS

Jim: Richard Lewis
Becky: Faye Dunaway
Rachel: Diane Wiest
Debbie: Parker Posey
Shelley: Amanda Plummer
Joseph: Howard E. Rollins Jr.
Louis: Spalding Gray
Helen: Calista Flockhart
Marty: George Martin
Tanya: Anna Thomson
Melanie: Lisa Harris

Origin: USA
Released: 1995, 1997
Production: Burtt Harris and Shireen Meistrich for Kardana Films, Seagoat Films and the Shooting Gallery; released by BMG Independents
Direction: Peter Cohn
Screenplay: Gary Lennon; based on his play *Blackout*
Cinematography: Peter Hawkins
Editing: Hughes Winborne
Production design: Michael Shaw
Art direction: Daniel Goldfield
Costumes: Kim Marie Druce
Music: Joe Delia
Sound: Andrew Moran
MPAA rating: R
Running Time: 90 minutes

Time" for those in the program. While it avoids taking on a preachy tone and offers no pat quick-fix solutions, neither does it offer any deep insights or revelations. While it may be comforting to fellow AA members and may offer support and encouragement for those still struggling with their own addictions, the film proves to be tedious for those of us blessed with non-addictive personalities.

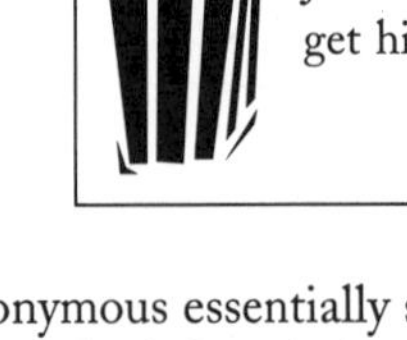

Jim to the group: "I just want to get high!"

In its own way, Alcoholics Anonymous essentially substitutes one addiction for another. While definitely less destructive than a drunken stupor, AA meetings, with their perpetual dramas and endless storytelling, seem to provide a fix for the lost souls seeking redemption.

Drunks has a voyeuristic feel to it. Since Alcoholics Anonymous insists on confidentiality among its members, the film's eavesdropping on a meeting-in-progress seems like a betrayal of trust, the ultimate attempt to benefit from other people's pain. On top of it all, the ruminations on why alcoholics drink is just not that interesting. In fact, it is downright boring to watch these folks wallow in self-pity as they bare their souls. For a film that attempts to be so life-affirming and revealing, *Drunks* has surprisingly little to say. Other critics, however, such as the *New York Times'* Janet Maslin were quite smitten with both the film and Mr. Lewis' performance.

—*Patricia Kowal*

REVIEWS

New York Times. March 14, 1997, p. B20.
San Francisco Chronicle. August 15, 1997, p. C3.
San Francisco Examiner. August 15, 1997, p. C7.
Variety. September 11, 1995, p. 106.
Village Voice. March 18, 1997, p. 80.

The Edge

They were fighting over a woman until the plane went down. Now, their only chance for survival is each other.—Movie tagline

"Incredibly tense and super scary. This classic outdoor adventure is driven by superb performances by Hopkins and Baldwin."—Jeanne Wolf, *Jeanne Wolf's Hollywood*

"Wild edge-of-your-seat entertainment. Anthony Hopkins and Alec Baldwin make David Mamet's screenplay erupt on screen." —Larry Ratliff, *KABB-TV*

"Hopkins and Baldwin go at each other with gusto in a gripping con game that is something rare these days: an action thriller that relies more on smarts than special effects to keep an audience on edge."—Peter Travers, *Rolling Stone*

"An action film that celebrates not brute force but survival of the smartest."—Richard Corliss, *Time*

Box Office: $27,828,527

Surviving a plane crash in the Alaskan wilderness, Charles Morse (Anthony Hopkins) and Robert Greene (Alec Baldwin) find themselves battling a vicious Kodiak bear in *The Edge*.

A film about men lost in the wilderness combatting nature and each other would seem to hold little interest for contemporary audiences, but when the star is Anthony Hopkins and the screenwriter is David Mamet, such a film rises above genre expectations. Directed expertly by Lee Tamahori, *The Edge* is one of the best action films of the 1990's and features one of the greatest animal performances ever.

Famed billionaire Charles Morse (Anthony Hopkins) accompanies his wife, Mickey (Elle Macpherson), a model, on a fashion shoot in a northern wilderness. (The film was made in the Canadian Rockies.) Mickey has such a friendly relationship with macho photographer Bob Green (Alec Baldwin) that Charles suspects they may be more than friends. When a male model (David Lindstedt) becomes ill, Bob gets the brilliant idea of using a local Indian (Gordon Tootoosis) as a replacement. Flying north of the lodge where the group is staying to the Indian's camp, Charles and Bob's plane crashes, leaving them and Bob's assistant, Stephen (Harold Perrineau), stranded with little hope of rescue.

Charles to Robert: "So, how are you planning to kill me off?"

Mamet stacks the decks against survival as well as he can. The trio lose most of their supplies in the crash, are insufficiently dressed for the coming snow, and have only Charles' hunting knife, just given to him by Bob as a birthday present, as a weapon/tool. To complicate their chances even further is the considerable threat posed by a huge, fearless, rampaging bear (Bart). Charles has just read a survival guide entitled *Lost in the Wilds* and tries to use what he has learned, but an improvised compass fails to lead the trio in the right direction. Soon, they are chased by the bear, Stephen cuts his leg badly, and their chances continue to deteriorate.

The central conflict in *The Edge* is that Bob, though a fashion photographer, is a real man, that Charles is a wimp, and that the two are pitted against each other as much as they are against nature. With so cliched a dilemma, the outcome is fairly obvious, but the delight of *The Edge* is how Mamet, Tamahori, and their cast, especially Hopkins, can play variations on the situations seen in dozens of such survival films. The suspense comes from the audience not being certain about Bob's motives. Just before the plane crashes, Charles asks his adversary how he plans to kill the billionaire. Which is the greater threat, the film asks, man or nature? Mamet, who has examined the lengths people will go to cheat others and fool themselves in such plays as *American Buffalo* (1976), *Glengarry Glen Ross* (1984), and *Speed-the-Plow* (1988) and such films as *House of Games* (1987) and *Homicide* (1991), creates characters capable of any duplicity or act of violence.

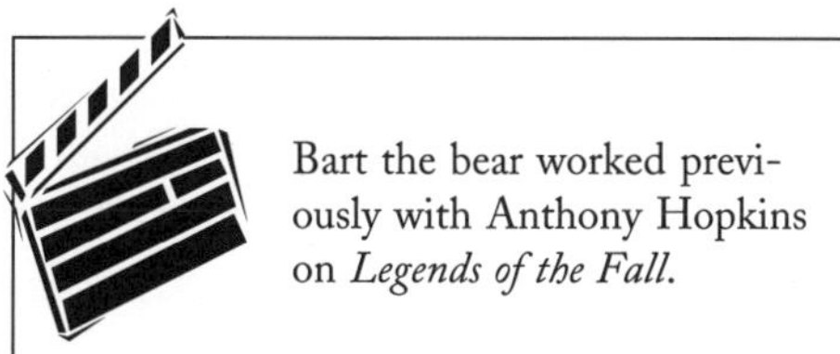

Bart the bear worked previously with Anthony Hopkins on *Legends of the Fall.*

Charles resembles the Robert Redford character in *Three Days of the Condor* (1975) in his ability to improvise solutions to problems based on what he has read. Charles seems to know something about everything, a fact tested early in the film by the lodge keeper (L. Q. Jones) who challenges him to identify what is on the other side of a Cree oar depicting a panther, and Charles knows that it is a rabbit smoking a cigar, a symbol of the triumph of wiliness over naked aggression and a metaphor for the rich man's battles with the bear and the photographer. Several reviews have compared *The Edge* to such films as *Deliverance* (1972) and *Jaws* (1975), but its true forerunner is *Lawrence of Arabia* (1962). Charles Morse, like T. E. Lawrence, is a cultured, civilized man who enjoys testing himself in a potentially fatal ordeal and triumphs because of his intellect.

The macho posturing in *The Edge* skirts a very thin line between seriousness and parody. In their efforts first to evade and then to kill the bear, Charles and Bob experience male bonding in the extreme though they remain distrustful antagonists. That Charles concludes he would rather have the friendship of the man trying to kill him than possess his beautiful young wife is typical of Mamet's approach to such situations. The a-woman's-just-a-woman-but-a-pal's-a-pal mentality seen in hundreds of Hollywood films—prototypically in Howard Hawks' gloriously loony *Only Angels Have Wings* (1939)—is often too silly to be taken seriously, but when the director and actors give it the straightforward treatment it receives here, as if *The Edge* was the first film to deal with a Hemingwayesque quest for masculine identity, it works. (The film owes a considerable debt to Hemingway's short story "The Short, Happy Life of Francis Macomber.")

Tamahori made his reputation with *Once Were Warriors* (1994), a highly praised if overwrought treatment of spousal abuse in a Maori ghetto in the director's native New Zealand. In the attention given him for that film, Tamahori identified himself not as an art-house filmmaker but as a devout fan of Hollywood genre films, especially those made by Robert Aldrich, Sam Peckinpah, and Don Siegel. His first American film, *Mulholland Falls* (1996), is an attempt to explore the film noir style associated with Aldrich and Siegel but fails as a result of a sketchy screenplay. Mamet's script for *The Edge*, however, gives Tamahori the opportunity to play with genre conventions, particularly those of his favorite: the western.

The Edge establishes Tamahori as an auteur in the tradition of the directors he admires who impose their personalities upon their material. All three of his films examine spiritual emptiness, the nature of manhood, and the loss of something irreplaceable—love, respect, self-esteem, a sense of order. Like Nick Nolte's detective in *Mulholland Falls*, Charles is thrown into unusual circumstances he thinks he can control and learns about his true self by making mistakes. The real Charles lurking within his gentlemanly, bookish exterior has a primitive side that both delights and saddens the hero.

Tamahori and cinematographer Donald M. McAlpine present the wilderness as a smoky, gloomy place that stoically mocks the protagonists' efforts to understand it. The best-staged sequences are the confrontations with the bear which are probably the most realistic human-bear battles ever filmed. McAlpine, whose credits include *Breaker Morant* (1980), uses a telescopic lens that distorts the bear to make him seem even closer to his enemies.

Bart, the 1,400-pound trained bear portraying the menacing force, is a revelation. Twenty-year-old Bart has been with trainers Doug and Lynne Seus since he was a cub and has appeared in several films, including *The Clan of the Cave Bear* (1985) and *The Bear* (1989), in which he stars. The bear works only with one stuntman, Doug Seus himself, but because of Tamahori's staging and Neil Travis' brilliant editing, he seems to be right on top of the actors. (Sometimes the bear is a man in a bear suit.) The most thrilling and frightening scene occurs when Charles hangs precariously from a log across a chasm as the bear paws at him. In most films, the fakery resulting from editing and special effects would be obvious, but in this instance, Bart truly seems to be clawing viciously inches from Hopkins. He does not seem to a trained bear at play but an authentically malevolent creature. Tamahori's calling Bart the John Wayne of bears is well-deserved praise. The creation of a sense of genuine threat from the bear is essential if all the film's elements are to coalesce.

CREDITS

Charles Morse: Anthony Hopkins
Bob Green: Alec Baldwin
Mickey Morse: Elle Macpherson
Stephen: Harold Perrineau
Styles: L. Q. Jones
Ginny: Kathleen Wilhoite
James: David Lindstedt
Amphibian pilot: Larry Musser
Jack Hawk: Gordon Tootoosis
Bear: Bart the bear

Origin: USA
Released: 1997
Production: Art Linson for Knickerbocker Films; released by 20th Century Fox
Direction: Lee Tamahori
Screenplay: David Mamet
Cinematography: Donald M. McAlpine
Editing: Neil Travis
Production design: Wolf Kroeger
Art direction: Richard Harrison
Set decoration: Janice Blackie-Goodine
Costumes: Julie Weiss
Sound: Eric J. Batut
Music: Jerry Goldsmith
Special effects: Mike Vezina, Kent Houston
MPAA rating: R
Running Time: 121 minutes

The other notable supporting performance comes from Jones, veteran of several Peckinpah films, including *Ride the High Country* (1962) and *The Wild Bunch* (1969). Even more grizzled than usual because of the scars adorning his face, Jones plays, in the film's mythic context, the type of figure whose early ominous warnings come into play during the course of the film. Jones also directed the cult survival-in-a-post-apocalyptic-wilderness film *A Boy and His Dog* (1975), whose subject and musings about masculinity may have influenced *The Edge*.

Baldwin is a good actor whose roles never seem to challenge him sufficiently. His work in *The Edge*, however, is his best since his small role as the vicious company man in the disappointing adaptation of Mamet's *Glengarry Glen Ross* (1992). Baldwin shines when Bob mocks the pallid world they have left far behind and when he does a double take as he discovers that an apparently nineteenth-century photograph of an Indian is actually a recent picture taken by the lodge keeper. Baldwin's shocked expression indicates Bob's awareness of the shallowness of his own art.

One of the many virtues of Mamet as both a playwright and screenwriter is his ability to create situations and dialogue that allow actors to play off each other rather than perform in narcissistic isolation. Both the excellence of Mamet's screenplay and Hopkins' genius encourage Baldwin's talents to shine. Hopkins continues his amazing streak of excellent-to-great performances in the 1990's. The actor has said in several interviews that at this stage in his career he prefers working in action roles rather than the quieter parts he has undertaken in the oh-so-civilized James Ivory-Ishmael Merchant films. Hopkins is one of the best ever at being able to portray both strong and weak characters, and his Charles is both. He remains calm when Bob and Stephen panic because of his confidence in his ability to find a way

REVIEWS

Boxoffice. October, 1997, p. 42.
Chicago Tribune. September 26, 1997, p. 5.
Detroit Free Press. September 26, 1997, p. 6C.
Entertainment Weekly. October 3, 1997, p. 54.
Film Comment. September-October, 1997, p. 26.
Los Angeles Times. September 26, 1997, p. F4.
Mademoiselle. October, 1997, p. 130.
New York. October 6, 1997, p. 66.
The New York Times. September 26, 1997, p. E10.
Newsweek. October 6, 1997, p. 73.
People. October 6, 1997, p. 25.
Rolling Stone. October 16, 1997, p. 116.
Time. September 29, 1997, p. 100.
USA Today. September 26, 1997, p. D6.
Variety. September 8, 1997, p. 75.
Village Voice. September 30, 1997, p. 84.
Vogue. October, 1997, p. 220.
Washington Post Weekend. September 26, 1997, p. 49.

out of their predicament. The audience knows they will kill the bear because Hopkins makes Charles' resolve to survive believable when it could easily be cartoonish. Hopkins' equally conveys Charles' insecurities. Despite his wealth and brilliance, he worries that his life is meaningless. The contradictions raging within Charles, his love-hate for both his wife and her lover, could easily have made for a confusing or unsympathetic character, but Hopkins, the master, brings it off wonderfully. It is significant that the actor told *Entertainment Weekly* that the role is the closest he has ever come to playing himself. The film's memorable final shot shows what should be a triumphant Charles revealing himself to be a soul more lost than ever he was in the wilderness.

—*Michael Adams*

The Education of Little Tree

"A wonderful and delightful film. *Little Tree* is not just a family film, but a film for everyone."
—Brian Sebastian, *Movie Reviews & More*

"A magical journey you'll long remember."
—Bonnie Churchill, *National News Syndicate*

"A heart-warming, though-provoking film."—Jeff Craig, *Sixty Second Preview*

In 1935, poor orphaned Little Tree (Joseph Ashton) is sent to live with his mother's parents in the Smokey Mountains of Tennessee. Little Tree is schooled by his sage Cherokee Gramma (Tantoo Cardinal from *Dances with Wolves*, 1990) and his white Granpa (James Cromwell, the farmer who hammed it up in the lovable *Babe*, 1995) in the folkloric tribal wisdom the Cherokee call "The Way."

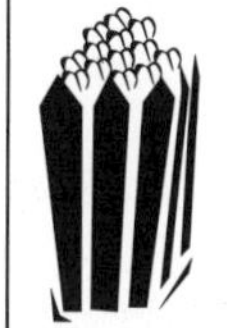

Granpa to Little Tree: "White man put up a flag, says, 'This stands for my right to have more.'"

Screenwriter Richard Friedenberg (*A River Runs Through It*, 1992) makes his feature directorial debut in this stylish adaptation of the much-loved children's classic by Forrest Carter. The result is a top-notch children's film in the league of *A Little Princess* (1995), *The Secret of Roan Inish* (1994), and *The Secret Garden* (1993).

In this rite-of-passage film, Little Tree suffers through the school of hard knocks, overcoming injustice and intolerance to reclaim the integrity of his heritage. The film accurately portrays the American Indian experience that has slowly eroded over time. This sentimental family fare chronicles Little Tree's journey to his ancestral roots as it delivers important reminders about ethnic diversity, education, and family values.

Carter's book caused a literary scandal when it was first published as an autobiography but was later listed as fiction when it was revealed that the author's real name was Asa Carter and he once had ties to the Ku Klux Klan.

During the Great Depression, Little Tree suffers the tragic loss of both parents. Avoiding the clutches of his aunt, he chooses to live with his racially mixed grandparents, Indian Gramma and Scotch-Irish Granpa. Living in a rustic cabin high in the majestic mountains, Little Tree is lovingly home-schooled by his new family.

Spiritual guidance comes in the form of Willow John (Graham Greene), a mystic medicine man who reinforces pride in Little Tree's Indian heritage. He relates one of the worst trials of the Cherokee, the infamous Trail of Tears. Due to a gold strike, in 1835 President Martin Van Buren ordered a federally enforced relocation of the Cherokee nation from Georgia to western frontiers. The movie depicts the American Indians ongoing struggle with racism, bigotry, and devaluation of the culture.

Granpa has adopted his wife's ethnic heritage after a long, loving marriage. True to his Scottish heritage, Granpa carries on the tradition of making moonshine whiskey, the family's only source of income. He passes along the brewing art to Little Tree and they use Indian wiles to escape the long arm of the law while delivering contraband to market. Little Tree's newfound experiences include learning a snakebite remedy, attending church, befriending an impoverished white girl in town, and getting conned out of his hard earned money.

Eventually his aunt, a Bible-toting busybody, raises the roof with authorities and he's off to a state institution. At the harsh Gap Indian School, the boy is robbed of his Indian name and subjected to cruel racism at the hands of school officials. An honest reply to a teacher's question results in old-fashioned discipline. He is further punished by being locked in an attic un-

CREDITS

Little Tree: Joseph Ashton
Granpa: James Cromwell
Gramma: Tantoo Cardinal
Willow John: Graham Greene

Origin: USA
Released: 1997
Production: Jake Eberts for Allied Films and Lightmotive; released by Paramount Pictures
Direction: Richard Friedenberg
Screenplay: Richard Friedenberg; based on the novel by Forrest Carter
Cinematography: Anastas N. Michos
Editing: Wayne Wahrman
Music: Mark Isham
Production design: Dan Bishop
Costumes: Renee April
Art direction: Peter Stratford
Sound: Claude Hazanavicius
MPAA rating: PG
Running Time: 112 minutes

til he admits he was wrong. Director Friedenberg has carried over 1930s values intact and this somewhat brutal approach is out of sync with today's commercial fare.

The Education of Little Tree mixes lush landscapes with serene country charms. Filmed in the wilds of the Canadian bush, Mark Isham's score evokes broad sweeping vistas. As a rough-hewn mountain man, Cromwell exudes quiet strength, while Cardinal is the essence of dignity. Protagonist Joseph Ashton turns in a fine performance, chronicling the troubled times of Little Tree's life. Overall, *The Education of Little Tree* is an important branch of American history.

—*Hilary Weber* and *Magdalen Weber*

REVIEWS

Boxoffice. February, 1998, p. 53.
Entertainment Weekly. January 16, 1998, p. 50.
New York Times. December 17, 1997, p. E1.
People. December 15, 1997, p. 20.
USA Today. February 12, 1998, p. 3D.
Variety. December 22, 1997, p. 60.

8 Heads in a Duffel Bag

He's got two days to deliver this bag, or more heads are gonna roll.—Movie tagline

Box Office: $3,602,884

A group of thugs give associate Tommy Spinelli (Joe Pesci) 24 hours to deliver their rivals' heads to the mob boss as proof that they're dead . . . or heads will roll. He loses his heads, of course, and through a series of madcap mishaps, the chase is on to recover the noggins.

Tommy flies off to San Diego, sneaking his carryall past security only to have the oversized bag carted off to the cargo hold. A fellow passenger, Charlie (Andy Comeau), unwittingly snags the wrong luggage and drives to Mexico for a holiday with his fiancee, Laurie (Kristy Swanson), and her parents. When Tommy discovers his bag is switched, he panics, desperately tries to track it down, showing up at Charlie's fraternity.

Charlie on Mexico: "They have no laws down here. They'll turn us into tacos!"

Meanwhile at a Baja California resort, Mrs. Bennett (Dyan Cannon), the mother of Charlie's girlfriend, is the first to accidently find the heads in the bag. She flips out, finally agreeing with her husband's disapproval over the young medical student, but her frantic behavior looks like she's more drunk than terrified. Then, when Charlie comes face-to-face with the heads instead of his clothes, he bounces them around his room like hot potatoes, seeming more befuddled than shocked.

He reveals his creepy dilemma to an unsympathetic Laurie, which adds to her reasons to end their relationship. After she composes her hysteria, they try to toss the heads in the trash, but hide them in his room instead, losing one to the laundry.

Charlie's roommates, Steve (Todd Louiso) and Ernie (David Spade), can't provide a vacation location, but that doesn't stop Tommy from terrorizing them in a variety of slapstick torture and wisecrack responses.

While Charlie and Laurie bury the heads in the desert, they're confronted by banditos who steal Dick's Jeep when the cops arrive. Laurie conveniently suggests they send the heads to Steve—for no apparent reason, except that it coincidentally saves his friend's life when they call. Tommy makes arrangements for exchanging the satchels.

Returning to San Diego for the trade, Charlie mysteriously drags along Laurie and her parents, but because the car is gone, they must fly. Two of the heads curiously show up on the ex-ray in Mr. Bennett's suitcase. When the news of his arrest makes it to TV in the States, the mobsters happen to recognize the faces of the men they killed.

The eight heads were named Hugo, Marty, Jamal, Little Joey, Frank, Isaiah, Benito, and Stu.

To replace the head missing in the washing machine, Ernie suggests snatching frozen body parts from the cryonics lab on campus. To complicate the situation further, Tommy insists on a look-alike for the dead head, though he doesn't know if it's Hugo, Marty, Stu, Little Joey or Frank, so he snags a bunch.

Changing plans, Tommy heads directly to the hotel, but Charlie takes off for the border after recovering the stolen Jeep at a rental agency. Tommy tracks them all down on the road but soon notices his mob associates spying from a distance. Charlie secretly joins forces with the hood, coming up with a master plan that works to everyone's end.

Tommy heads in the opposite direction with the gangsters following. A wild series of events ensue, more chaotic than screwball, with the entire group (except for Dad, who's still in jail) ending up together at the airport chasing after the satchel of skulls. Through a complicated "sleight of bag," Charlie leads the bad guys along and with the extra cryonic heads sets them up to take the fall with the authorities. Not only does his idea get Laurie's father off the hook and redeem himself with her parents, but it allows Tommy to slip through security and onto the departing flight holding the bag—of heads.

"A mindless comedy" is the all-too-true-tagline. From the producers of *Dumb & Dumber* (1994), this may be the dumbest, unless this twist on dark humor is considered entertaining. It seems redundant to call this a ridiculous story, with an absurd premise that's more preposterous than funny or farcical. The bumbling crook is a typical role for Pesci, and everyone else is fodder for his performance—which appears more nasty than zany. Although full of ludicrous gags, only Spade's facetious brand of humor stands out in the attempts at hilarity. It's all one big chase scene but nobody's running.

—*Roberta Cruger*

CREDITS

Tommy Spinelli: Joe Pesci
Charlie Pritchett: Andy Comeau
Laurie Bennett: Kristy Swanson
Ernie Lipscomb: David Spade
Dick Bennett: George Hamilton
Annette Bennett: Dyan Cannon
Steve: Todd Louiso

Origin: USA
Released: 1997
Production: Brad Krevoy, Steve Stabler and John Bertolli for Rank Film Distributors; released by Orion Pictures
Direction: Tom Schulman
Screenplay: Tom Schulman
Cinematography: Adam Holender
Editing: David Holden
Music: Andrew Gross
Production design: Paul Peters
Art direction: Thomas P. Walkins
Costumes: Sanja Milkovic Hyas
Special makeup effects: Greg Cannom
Sound: Ed White
MPAA rating: R
Running Time: 95 minutes

REVIEWS

Detroit News. April 18, 1997, p. C3.
Entertainment Weekly. April 25, 1997, p. 50.
Los Angeles Times. April 18, 1997, p. F2.
Los Angeles Times. April 23, 1997, p. F3.
New York Times. April 18, 1997, p. C10.
People. April 28, 1997, p. 19.
Sight and Sound. December, 1997, p. 42.
USA Today. April 15, 1997, p. 1D.
USA Today. April 18, 1997, p. 3D.
Variety. April 21, 1997, p. 59.

The Eighth Day; Le Huitieme Jour

What a difference a day makes . . . —Movie tagline

"A daring and extraordinary film with a stunning pull-the-rug-out-from-under-you climax."—Kevin Thomas, *The Los Angeles Times*

"Unabashedly big-hearted. Touching and surprisingly fresh."—Janet Maslin, *The New York Times*

The Eighth Day contains one fresh performance and a tired, sentimental story. Harry (Daniel Auteuil) is a hard driving corporate salesman—or rather, he is the specialist executives bring in to stimulate their sales force. Harry has a pat routine about the way the customer should be treated and how the salesman must always present himself as a winner. He is relentlessly upbeat, and his pitch never varies. The trouble is that he has become a prisoner of his pitch. His wife has left him, and he is estranged from his children. In one particularly painful scene, his two young daughters show up at the train station and wait hours for their father to arrive. They are seen re-entering another train as Harry just misses them—rushing to the tracks having just remembered to pick them up.

Director Van Dormael is a former circus clown and children's theater director.

Harry realizes that his devotion to work has destroyed his family life. What is more, that work is depicted as trivial and mindlessly repetitive. Each morning, Harry performs the same routine: checking his tie in the mirror, eating his toast, and fuming in traffic jams on the way to work. Clearly, Harry has to change, yet he does not know how to get out of his rut. He is trapped in what used to be called the "rat race."

Daniel Auteuil performs his part according to specifications. It is hard to fault an actor who is given a stereotype, although occasionally a truly gifted actor is able to invest a cliche with new life. Auteuil does not manage this miracle, settling instead for alternating between manic and morose moods. He flickers to life in a few scenes with his co-star.

Life changes for Harry when he has an accident. On a dark road his car hits a dog, and when he stops he discovers Georges (Pascal Duquenne). Georges has Down's Syndrome and has run away from an institution, where he was put after his mother's death. Harry conscientiously tries to give Georges a lift home, but he learns that like himself, Georges has no home, really. This "odd couple" become an on-the-road team who conjure up every corny scene imaginable about misfits and a conformist society.

The exuberant Georges makes Harry experience what it really means to live, to experience nature and simple expressions of love and comradeship. This treacle provokes the memory of Oscar Wilde's remark that one would have to have a heart of stone not to laugh at the death of Little Nell. Like the most preposterous, sentimental Dickens story, *The Eighth Day* jerks tears. If not for Pascal Duquenne, the film would be unwatchable, because it never stops trying to manipulate emotions in the most obvious ways. But Duquenne is refreshing, especially because he does not act the victim. On the contrary, he seeks control over his own life—not merely running away but interesting himself in helping others. He can also be selfish and manipulative. He has a playful sense of himself—practicing, for example, menacing noises that he knows will frighten others and help him to get his way.

The film's title refers to Georges's charming, if unorthodox, story of how the world was created. In his catalogue of what God made, Georges puts in the things he likes, making of God a rather arbitrary but also fetching image of Georges himself. The eighth day is also, of course, a

Harry: Daniel Auteuil
Georges: Pascal Duquenne
Julie: Miou-Miou
Fabienne: Fabienne Loriaux
Nathalie: Michele Maes
Julie's mother: Helene Roussel

Origin: France, Belgium
Released: 1995, 1997
Production: Philippe Godeau; released by Gramercy
Direction: Jaco Van Dormael
Screenplay: Jaco Van Dormael
Cinematography: Walther Van Ende
Editing: Susana Rossberg
Music: Piere Van Dormael
Art direction: Hubert Pouille
Costume design: Yan Tax
Sound: Dominique Warnier, Francois Groult, Bruno Tarriere
MPAA rating: Unrated
Running Time: 114 minutes

reference to Harry's effort to re-create his own life, to find another day that is different from a work schedule that dominates his whole week.

Georges has a wistful quality attributable both to Duquenne's acting and to director/writer Jaco van Dormael's script. It is Georges who recommends that he and Harry take another moment to enjoy reclining on the forest grass. "A nice minute for us," Georges says with extraordinary delicacy and tact. Both in the writing and in the acting Georges lifts this otherwise trite film out of a rut as deeply grooved as Harry's career.

AWARDS AND NOMINATIONS

Cesar Awards 1997 Nominations: Actor (Auteuil)

Of course, society has no place for poets like Georges, and there is no solution for Harry, although the film pretends that by jettisoning his corporate identity he will find a new lease on life (to use a cliche appropriate to this film). Reviewers usually complain that Hollywood rips off good ideas from foreign films. In this case, the French have raided Hollywood, producing—as more than one reviewer has noted—a retread of *Rain Man*.

—*Carl Rollyson*

REVIEWS

Boxoffice. July, 1996, p. 87.
Los Angeles Times. March 7, 1997, p. F16.
New York Times. March 7, 1997, p. B23.
Sight and Sound. November, 1996, p. 48.
USA Today. March 13, 1997, p. 8D.
Variety. May 20, 1996, p. 37.
Village Voice. March 11, 1997, p. 80.

The Empire Strikes Back; Star Wars, Episode V: The Empire Strikes Back

The Adventure Continues . . . —Movie tagline

Box Office: $67,597,806

George Lucas told Oprah Winfrey on television that he reissued the Star Wars Trilogy in a 20th Anniversary "Special Edition" for the fun of it, and there was no reason to doubt him. After all, the man has made a fortune out of Industrial Light & Magic, and one could suppose that he made the trilogy in the first place for pure entertainment, despite the conscious plotting and deliberate mythic framework. Lucky for him, entertainment sells. The merchandising of the "Special Edition" was carefully calculated to build, renew, and sustain audience interest. A great deal of work, money, and ingenuity went into sprucing up *Star Wars* and much was made of the digital enhancement of images and sound, and the "new" footage that was added to make it "special."

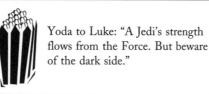

Yoda to Luke: "A Jedi's strength flows from the Force. But beware of the dark side."

In *The Empire Strikes Back* (1980), the second increment of the series directed by Irvin Kershner, Lucas worked to make Cloud City look better, but the main interest here is not so much in Cloud City and its master, Lando Calrissian (Billy Dee Williams), as in the teachings of Jedi Master Yoda, Luke Skywalker's mentor, Zen with ears (speaking through the voice of Frank Oz) enlarged to gather cosmic wisdom, and "new" information about Darth Vader (David Prowse, with the voice of James Earl Jones). The story goes on, and so does the gimmickry—the Imperial Walkers attacking Rebel Headquarters on the frozen planet Hoth, for example, to get this show in the road that leads to the asteroid belt, a monstrous space worm, and even more visual enhancements. The timing of the sequel was perfect. Three weeks after its opening *Star Wars* had already grossed $100 million and the hype for the sequel was so powerful that by then everyone seemed convinced that the "special edition" was special indeed, and that the whole thing had to be seen.

If the appeal of *Star Wars* was all action-adventure and ethereal dogfights (Janet Maslin thought the attack on the

Death Star was absolutely Freudian, since the Rebel fighters appear to be spermatozoa attempting to fertilize a giant egg) and hardware (the Imperial Troopers are as robotic, dehumanized and faceless as Sergei Eisenstein's Teutonic Knights in *Alexander Nevsky* [1938]), Irving Kershner's sequel is more mythic and human, even if Yoda is a Jim Henson animatronic puppet creation. Here a romance develops between Princess Leia (Carrie Fisher of the majestic hairdo) and Han Solo (Harrison Ford), who gets carbonized. The fresh-faced farmboy Luke Skywalker from *Star Wars* is more weathered and worn here, since the actor Mark Hamill survived an automobile accident between the completion of *Star Wars* and the shooting of *The Empire Strikes Back* that required reconstructive surgery on his face. Hence, he seems more mature when he encounters Yoda on the jungle planet Dagobah.

The action starts on the ice-planet Hoth, with the Empire striking back by attacking the Rebel Federation base. The Emperor wants Luke under his control and wants him converted to the dark side, for the Emperor fears the power of the Force, which Luke may be able to recover. Darth Vader has his own reasons for wanting Luke on his side and is obsessed with finding him. Luke has his own problems, meanwhile, when he is captured by a shaggy, carnivorous cave monster. Luke manages to escape but nearly freezes to death before Han Solo comes to his rescue. By then the Empire has landed and sent its Imperial Walkers to attack the Rebel base, though all of the Rebel leaders eventually manage to escape.

The Princess escapes with Solo, Chewbacca, and C-3PO on the Millennium Falcon to Cloud City, ruled by the scoundrel Lando Calrissian, one of Solo's reprobate friends. Luke takes R2-D2 and heads for another planet, on the advice of a spiritual visitation from Ben Kenobi instructing him to seek out the Jedi Master Yoda. Luke is surprised to find that Yoda is an ancient, diminutive gnome but soon learns to respect him and goes into training in order to master the Force. By telepathic means Luke discovers that Solo and the Princess are in grave danger and decides to go to their rescue, even though Yoda warns him that he needs further instruction before he can go mano-a-mano against Darth Vader.

Unbeknownst to Solo, Darth Vader gets to Cloud City before the Millennium Falcon, and our heroes are walking into a trap. Consequently, the Rebels are captured and tortured. Because Vader made a deal with a bounty hunter, Solo is freeze-dried in carbon and sent to Jabba the Hutt. Luke arrives and finds himself in combat with Darth Vader, who makes an astonishing revelation about Luke's father; but Luke refuses to give in to his fear or his hatred and rejects Vader's offer to join him on the dark side. Luke gives Vader a hand, so to speak, after a forceful battle with light sabers; he escapes but nearly falls out of Cloud City while attempting to get away.

Lando soon discovers that Vader will double-cross him and organizes an escape with the Princess, Chewbacca, R2-D2 and C-3PO on the Millennium Falcon, but first they swing back to pick up Luke, who has been left hanging. They are pursued into the asteroid belt, where the Falcon hides within a cave on a huge asteroid, not exactly a safe haven, since they soon find themselves in the belly of a beast, but they eventually escape from all threats to journey on into the next sequel in order to rescue frozen Han Solo.

The screenplay for *The Empire Strikes Back* was developed from the original story Lucas sketched out by Leigh Brackett and Lawrence Kasdan, who went on to become a popular director in his own right. Stephen Hunter of the *Baltimore Sun* criticized the screenplay for lacking "an overarching narrative situation" and described it as "a holding action," a cliffhanger sequel that would allow Lucas time to figure out how to end the Trilogy in the third installment, *The Return of the Jedi.* Lisa Schwarzbaum of *Entertainment Weekly* was far more positive (and on target), praising the storytelling for its "zingy balance of drama, humor, and Deep Thoughts," however, and praising the sequel as "the best of the *Star Wars* trilogy reissue."

Leonard Maltin reflects a critical consensus that still stands when he praises *The Empire Strikes Back* as a "smashing" sequel that "manages to top the original in its embellishment of [the] leading characters' personalities." But not all reviewers were so impressed. Stephen Hunter complained in the *Baltimore Sun*, for example, that the embellishment was at times silly: even "the supremely annoying C-3PO is doing ancient British music hall shtick," if, indeed, this robotic tin man can have a "personality." During the three-year interval between *Star Wars* and its sequel, Lucas invested his profits wisely in Industrial Light & Magic, an investment that paid off when *The Empire Strikes Back* won a special Oscar for its special effects. The film further perfects the escapist formula, a formula powerful enough to knock over a serious film like John Singleton's *Rosewood* and to challenge and surpass Clint Eastwood's *Absolute Power* in 1997. The power of the Force was still supremely potent, even if the opening of the revised sequel did not match the overwhelming success of *Star Wars.*

A commonplace of popular culture is that movies reflect back the values and the anxieties of the society that produced them. The Evil Empire of President Ronald Reagan's political rhetoric would immediately call to mind vivid images of Darth Vader's Empire and his boast that "Resistance is futile." The Rebels demonstrate that good people can find the Force to resist tyranny and Evil effectively. For Janet Maslin of the *New York Times*, Yoda's comic wisdom "lauded New Age gentleness and the power of positive thinking," a faith that the Good will conquer, even if the Empire strikes back, a belief in one's self and one's instincts and inner "forces." Maslin saw the arrogance

CREDITS

Luke Skywalker: Mark Hamill
Han Solo: Harrison Ford
Princess Leia: Carrie Fisher
Lando Calrissian: Billy Dee Williams
C-3PO: Anthony Daniels
R2-D2: Keny Baker
Darth Vader: David Prowse
Darth Vader: James Earl Jones (voice)
Yoda: Frank Oz (voice)
Chewbacca: Peter Mayhew
Ben (Obi-wan) Kenobi: Alec Guinness

Origin: USA
Released: 1980, 1997
Production: Gary Kurtz for Lucasfilm Ltd.; released by 20th Century Fox
Direction: Irvin Kershner
Screenplay: Leigh Brackett, Lawrence Kasdan
Cinematography: Peter Suschitzky
Editing: Paul Hirsch
Music: John Williams
Production design: Norman Reynolds
Costumes: John Mollo
MPAA rating: PG
Running Time: 124 minutes

of Darth Vader as prefiguring corporate raiders and symbolizing the "prototypical captain of industry at the height of corporate power," the "Master of the Universe" syndrome that Tom Wolff so effectively satirized in his novel, *The Bonfire of the Vanities*. This film extols individual initiative, but it also seems to anticipate and encapsulate the awfulness of the 1980s, a decade of selfishness, corporate greed and the lust for power, giving the Trilogy sociological as well as mythic significance. In many ways the film speaks to and across generations. Apparently, the current generation is still listening attentively and willing to embrace the Trilogy.

—*James M. Welsh*

REVIEWS

The Baltimore Sun. February 21, 1997, p. E1.
Entertainment Weekly. March 7, 1997, p. 47.
The New York Times. February 21, 1997, P. C3.
The Philadelphia Inquirer Weekend. February 21, 1997, p. 4.
The Washington Times Metropolitan Times. February 21, 1997, p. C16.

The End of Violence

Nothing lasts forever.—Movie tagline
"Brilliant!"—*New York Times*
"One of the five best movies of the year."—Gene Siskel, *Siskel & Ebert*

Wim Wenders' treatise on Hollywood and technology is familiar ground, and unlike his most interesting films which explore the mythical and urban geography of cities (Berlin in *Wings of Desire* (1988) and *Faraway, So Close*! (1993) and the quirky *Tokyo-Ga* (1985), *The End of Violence* fails to convince us that we are really entering into the spiritually empty territory of Lotus Land. Beautiful as all Wenders films are, with stunning photography and carefully evocative sets (one scene is a painstaking reconstruction of Edward Hopper's "Nighthawks"), this film is chockablock with ill-defined characters who interact uneasily, if at all.

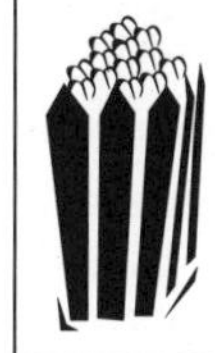

Max: "Paranoia is our number one export. Everybody needs an enemy."

The fundamental problem with this film lies in its galaxy of consciously cartoon-like supporting characters, which is only enhanced by Wenders' casting of well-known television actors like Peter Horton ("Thirtysomething") as an empty-suit studio exec, or, particularly, Daniel Benzali ("Murder One"), the ominously vigilant boss of Ray Bering (Gabriel Byrne), the reclusive scientist who is the focus of *The End of Violence*'s paranoid center. This is fun for awhile, as you realize that really is the late, cranky old director Sam Fuller (like the late Nicholas Ray, a hero of Wenders) playing Ray's aged father, but this game of who's who swiftly drains away energy as well as credibility. The two turns of Peter Falk and his television alter-ego Columbo in *Wings of Desire* and *Faraway, So Close!* were playful and charming because Falk is a big presence, an international star made instantly recognizable by syndication. To see Peter Falk in Berlin made perfect sense and no sense, a deft touch by a director at the top of his form. The deadly serious, metaphysically dense monologues that worked so well in *Wings of Desire* seem off here, probably because they are out of character for most of the cast.

Wim Wenders re-edited and remixed his film after it premiered at the 1997 Cannes Film Festival.

Bill Pullman plays his now-familiar sleazy operator (most notably as Linda Fiorentino's spouse and nemesis in *The Last Seduction* (1994). Mike Max is a producer who has made a fortune making action films, the latest of which is *Seeds of Violence*. He orchestrates his life on a cell phone and by laptop with his decent and loyal assistant Claire (Rosalind Chao), who is most often seen as a face on a computer screen. Nothing penetrates his self-involvement, not even wife Paige phoning him poolside from their living room to announce she is finally leaving him. He is more worried about the possible legal ramifications of an accident to a stuntwoman, Cat (Traci Lind). When Max is carjacked by two bumbling criminals who would be at home in a Coen film, he is plunged into a netherworld and vanishes from the Hollywood scene with only two dead kidnappers left behind. For the rest of the film he is like a living ghost, just out of sight of his wife and associates. As he observes them, he is pursued by police and by questions raised by a mysterious e-mail message. His send-up of the kings of action pictures works well enough, but Pullman's rather limited in his ability to convincingly portray virtue. His transformation into a moral man is never plausible, even though Wenders places him among "the people"—as he hides in plain sight among the Mexican gardeners manicuring his Malibu home.

Wenders displays his characteristic belief in the goodness of the laboring classes, but his earnest appreciation of their kindness is uncomfortable and stereotypical. His depiction of Los Angeles's racially complex makeup is one of the most glaring faults of the film. The director stumbles badly here—the black gangsta rapper Six (K. Todd Freeman) is the most egregious example. His smooth-talking stud is ridiculous and offensive. Another error is a half-silly, half-serious poetry reading that is meant to showcase some serious emotion, but stalls the film. Virtually any scene with the film's most pointless character, the young detective Doc (Lorin Dean, on Max's trail, more or less), does the same—his romance with Cat adds up to zero. One scene with Mike Max and Cat (who proves to be a loyal friend to her old boss) has more charge than their entire courtship.

Andie MacDowell's angst is pretty but shallow. Only later does her Paige begin to make sense—a sort of steely "widow" determined to seize the opportunity to best her now contrite and newly reformed husband. Having achieved a transference of power as Mike Max walks away from his wife and empire, Paige's languid personality is enervated. Suddenly she is the wheeler-dealer, the player. As Mike Max wanes, Paige steps into his life and shuts the door against his reentry. Echoes of great films (Sturges' *Sullivan's Travels* (1941) and Antonioni's *Blow-Up* (1966) and also a mediocre one (Lawrence Kasdan's *Grand Canyon* (1991), which a few critics noted as uncomfortably similar in plot) haunt *The End of Violence*. Wenders loves the man-on-the-run trope, and he clearly enjoys affecting a noir-ish look and attitude here, albeit very tongue in cheek. There is too little tension to propel the film, so it fails as a thriller (not a little due to the diffuse story line and vague characters).

What does work in *The End of Violence* is the visual—there is a surfeit of visual beauty, which remains with you after the jumbled plot fades. Several stunning scenes deserve special notice. The observatory is an electronic beehive, humming eerily as a bank of glowing screens dwarf the scientist who remains riveted to the images of everyday life. Into his solitude comes a silent woman and her inquisitive child, and he resents them. But Ray is more vulnerable than he appears—he finally succumbs to his hunger for human contact more than any desire for the sphinx-like housekeeper Matilda. Inside the observatory and away from the screens, Matilda stands with her naked back marked by the scars inflicted by her torturers in Guatemala. As Ray caresses her, a spinning sphere of some remote planet is projected on the wall. The camera lingers on Ray's loneliness and rightly so, because Byrne has a depth none of the other actors possess. Here is the romantic in Wenders, who has similarly represented the expressive Bruno Ganz and Otto Sander as angels who yearned to be human. His eyes say more about the despair Ray feels than any of his on camera musings.

Ray's connection to Mike Max is his anguished computer communication about the sinister government enterprise he is trapped in, high above the city. Surveillance cameras watch us all and promise the impossible: the end of violence. What Ray saw in his isolated observatory seals his doom, a martyr of conscience. Technology is a necessary evil, especially in an increasingly jumpy LA where the Hol-

AWARDS AND NOMINATIONS

Independent Spirit Awards 1997 Nominations:
Director (Wenders)

lywood sweet life is interrupted by riots and carjacking, perhaps the worst fate an Angeleno could imagine.

Wenders plays up the lush oceanside estate of Mike Max, gorgeous blue sea and sky playing a backdrop to the sultry posing of Andie MacDowell. Paige is lovely and stoic, swimming underwater in a spectacular seaside pool, driving a sportscar through a night lit by Hollywood neon, and looking more and more like a woman used to the pleasures of power. Intercut with her vaguely unhappy countenance is a scene where Mike tries to sleep in his hideaway with the Mexican family, and perhaps thinking of Paige, visits a roost of birds. This one sequence is particularly effective because it illustrates their marriage quietly ebbing away. Unfortunately, that elegant and understated moment is undercut by the final showdown between Paige, now thoroughly inhabiting her producer persona, and Mike, who hopes for a kiss and is instead held off as she coolly brandishes a gun. The new Paige negotiates the terms of Mike's survival—cash up front to disappear again. Her lover Six calls to her from the bedroom and she lies easily that nothing is wrong. And nothing is wrong for Paige.

Wim Wenders' films always have excellent scores, and this one doesn't disappoint—Ry Cooder's in top form. Also featured are Michael Stipe, Tom Waits, and Bono among others. Pascal Rabaud's cinematography is exquisite, suffused with all the brilliant colors of this city of dreams. Nicholas Klein's ambitious and earnest script has moments of lucidity and humor, but all the subplots perilously stitched together never amount to much.

It isn't impossible to see what Wim Wenders intended to do—all his favorite themes are laid out like a road map. The little boy who loved to watch the energy of Berlin from a window high above the street is an artist with a camera watching us in our everyday struggles, and he deplores the depravity and destruction of urban life just as he is drawn to film it. Always the watcher—helpless to intervene, able only to observe. To interfere is inevitably to risk destruction. *The End of Violence* is Wim Wenders without his characteristic poetry, a poetry perhaps best expressed in his own German language and milieu. Making American popular films may be as crass as he depicts it (and probably far worse), but his critique of film violence is hopelessly muddled and falls flat. Wenders fared far better with *Paris, Texas* (1984), so perhaps his great American film is still in the future.

—*Mary Hess*

CREDITS

Michael Max: Wim Wenders
Paige Max: Andie MacDowell
Ray Bering: Gabriel Byrne
Doc: Loren Dean
Cat Daniel: Traci Lind
Phelps: Daniel Benzali
Matilda: Marisol Padilla Sanchez
Claire: Rosalind Chao
Six: K. Todd Freeman
Ray's father: Sam Fuller

Origin: USA, Germany, France
Released: 1997
Production: Deepak Nayar, Wim Wenders, and Nicholas Klein for CIBY Pictures, Road Movies, and Kintop Pictures; released by MGM
Direction: Wim Wenders
Screenplay: Nicholas Klein
Cinematography: Pascal Rabaud
Editing: Peter Przygodda
Music: Ry Cooder
Production design: Patricia Norris
Set decoration: Leslie Morales
MPAA rating: R
Running Time: 123 minutes

REVIEWS

Boxoffice. August, 1997, p. 45.
Entertainment Weekly. September 19, 1997, p. 58.
Hollywood Reporter. May 12, 1997, p. 6.
Los Angeles Times. September 12, 1997, p. F8.
New York Times. September 7, 1997, p. H70.
New York Times. September 12, 1997, p. C5.
People. September 22, 1997, p. 23.
Sight and Sound. January, 1998, p. 34.
USA Today. September 12, 1997, p. 2D.
Village Voice. September 16, 1997, p. 94.

Event Horizon

Infinite Space. Infinite Terror.—Movie tagline

"*Event Horizon* will scare the living daylights out of you! Intelligent, visually awesome and dramatically satisfying."—Colin MacLean, *CBS Newsworld*

"An electrifying marriage of science fiction, suspense and classic horror. Leads us to a realm we've never seen before."—Mark Montgomery, *Sci-Fi Channel*

"Be prepared to be scared!"—John Platt, *Sci-Fi Buzz*

Box Office: $26,673,242

In the year 2040, the deep space research vessel "Event Horizon" was launched to explore the boundaries of the solar system. Unfortunately, she disappeared without a trace as she passed Neptune on her way to Alpha Centuri. The official line is that she exploded, but seven years later, a rescue beacon has been detected near Neptune. A rescue beacon from the "Event Horizon."

Now it is the job of the search and rescue ship the "Lewis and Clark" to find the ship, salvage it, and rescue anyone still alive. The "Lewis and Clark" is helmed by a no-nonsense, seasoned professional, Captain Miller (Laurence Fishburne). He is aided in his mission by his tight-knit crew: navigator Starck (Joely Richardson), emergency technicians Peters (Kathleen Quinlan) and Cooper (Richard T. Jones), engineer Justin (Jack Noseworthy), doctor D.J. (Jason Isaacs) and pilot Smith (Sean Pertwee).

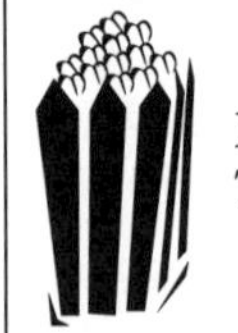

Miller: "What are you telling me? That the ship is alive?"

But also attached to the mission is Dr. Weir (Sam Neill), the engineer who developed the "Event Horizon's" top secret, untested engine: a gravity drive that creates an artificial black hole, folding space, and thereby allowing the ship to make faster-than-light travel. According to Dr. Weir, when the "Event Horizon" engaged the engine for the first time, it disappeared. But now it's back, and sending out a rescue beacon containing hellish screams and a message that seems to be Latin for "save me."

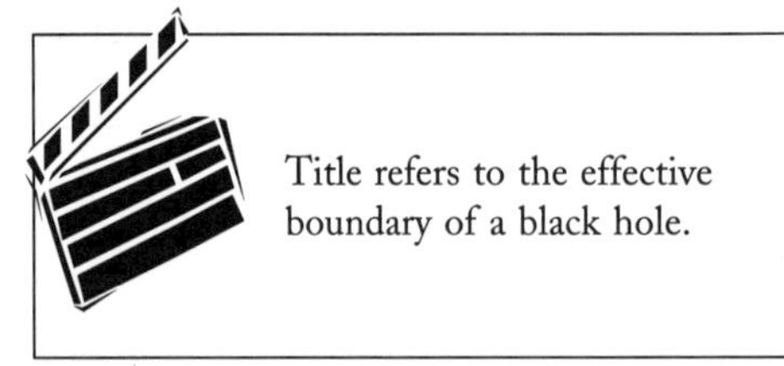

Title refers to the effective boundary of a black hole.

When the "Lewis and Clark" finally reaches the "Event Horizon" the crew scans the ship and finds traces of life forms all over the ship, but nothing specific. As crew members explore it, odd things begin to happen. Engineer Justin finds the gravity drive which appears to have a liquid center. When he touches it, he is sucked in only to return later incoherently rambling, "It shows you things—horrible things—the dark inside me from the other place. I won't go back there!" Then he lapses into a coma before he can give his crewmates more helpful information.

Soon other crew members are having what appear to be incredibly realistic hallucinations. Peters sees the child she left on earth, terribly mangled. Miller sees the burning body of a man he had to leave behind on a previous space mission that ended in disaster. And Weir sees his deceased wife committing suicide.

The longer the crew remains on the "Event Horizon," the weirder—and the more deadly—things get. Is anyone still alive? Who sent the message? Where has the ship been? And what is terrorizing the crew members of the "Lewis and Clark?"

The premise of *Event Horizon* is an intriguing one. Black holes, collapsed stars where gravity is so intense that nothing, not even light, can escape, certainly are one of the mysteries of the universe. (By the way an event horizon is the point of no return for matter that is being sucked into the gravity vortex of a black hole.) But what exactly is on the other side of a black hole? Can it be some kind of passage through time and space? Or, as this film suggests, can it lead to an entirely new dimensions? Dimensions that may be better left unexplored?

In the process of examining this premise, *Event Horizon*, is a festival of special effects, and they, inevitably become one of the film's stars. Fortunately, from zero-gravity space walks to model space craft, *Event Horizon* does a commendable job of making fantasy reality.

Even the actors do a laudable job of trying to bring realism to the unreal. Right from the start we know that this crew has been together for awhile, that they care about each other, and that they are true professionals. These are good actors, doing the best they can with the script they've been given. (Although it is doubtful that Fishburne's Miller, who reflects resolve through stiffness, will turn him into an action hero . . . but when one thinks about it, Stallone and Schwarzenegger have their share of stiff action heroes! And there's always stiffer-than-life Steven Seagal!)

The problem with *Event Horizon* is the script. Philip Eisner has made his screenwriting debut with this film, but he has taken a fascinating premise and muddled it with some cheap frights, an inexplicable conclusion, and some illogical actions. Too often after being led through a suspenseful scene we are rewarded with nothing more than a startling tap on the shoulder. And when it comes to explaining the entire plot of the film, it is being done by someone who has never been through a black hole. So how does he know what's on the other side? He's already shown himself to be a bit more than loony, is he now supposed to be possessed by the ship? And why is there a really rough ride as they approach the ghost space ship and then complete calm when they reach her? But perhaps silliest of all, on a ship where CO2 is about to reach lethal levels, why would crew members light up cigarettes? In fact, what are cigarettes doing in the oxygen-enriched atmosphere of space travel? Heck, what are cigarettes doing in our future? Are we still that stupid? The screenwriter thinks so.

Event Horizon also shows itself to be the inheritor of many previous films, some of them science fiction and some of them horror. The idea of something in space creating hallucinations was seen in *Solaris*, a much better psychological/science fiction film. The working ship "Lewis and Clark" has a gritty look, a lot like that of the "Nostromo" in *Alien*, a much superior horror in space film. The idea of a building/ship that is possessed plays out a lot like *The Shining*, a much more exceptional horror film (even if Kubrick wasn't true to the Stephen King novel.) But the most obvious "homage" of all is that the room that houses the gravity engine—and one especially gruesome murder—all look as if they had been lifted out of the *Hellraiser* films. The engine itself appears to be a cross between this year's *Contact* space travel machine (a coincidence?) and the puzzle box used in *Hellraiser* (a rip off?). One would not be surprised to find Pinhead at the controls of the "Event Horizon."

These slightly distracting tributes to previous films could be overlooked if they weren't so obvious, but when they're set in an inept script that causes viewers to detach themselves from the action, it becomes a fatal mistake for a horror/science fiction film which desperately needs to maintain the suspension of disbelief in its viewers to be successful.

—Beverley Bare Buehrer

CREDITS

Miller: Laurence Fishburne
Weir: Sam Neill
Peters: Kathleen Quinlan
Starck: Joely Richardson
Cooper: Richard T. Jones
Justin: Jack Noseworthy
D.J.: Jason Isaacs
Smith: Sean Pertwee
Kilpack: Peter Marinker
Claire: Holley Chant
Denny: Barclay Wright
Burning Man: Noah Huntley
Rescue Technician: Robert Jezek

Origin: USA
Released: 1997
Production: Lawrence Gordon, Lloyd Levin and Jeremy Bolt for Golar and Impact Pictures; released by Paramount Pictures
Direction: Paul Anderson
Screenplay: Philip Eisner
Cinematography: Adrian Biddle
Editing: Martin Hunter
Production design: Joseph Bennett
Art direction: Malcolm Middleton
Set decoration: Crispian Sallis
Costumes: John Mollo
Music: Michael Kamen
Visual effects supervisor: Richard Yuricich
MPAA rating: R
Running Time: 95 minutes

REVIEWS

Cinescape. May/June, 1997, p. 47.
Entertainment Weekly. September 5, 1997, p. 55.
New York Times. August 15, 1997, p. C16.
People. September 1, 1997, p. 21.
USA Today. August 15, 1997, p. 3D.
Variety. August 18, 1997, p. 30.

Eve's Bayou

"*Eve's Bayou* will restore your faith in movies. SEE IT!"—Eleanor Ringel, *Atlanta Journal Constitution*

"One of the very best films of the year! If it is not nominated for Academy Awards then the Academy is not paying attention."—Roger Ebert, *Chicago Sun-Times*

"Mesmerizing! Ripe with desires, disappointment and the mysterious scent of sex."—Lisa Schwarzbaum, *Entertainment Weekly*

"An inspired achievement! One of the year's best!"—Kevin Thomas, *Los Angeles Times*

"Intoxicatingly vivid! Remarkable! Exceptional!"—Leah Rozen, *People*

"Piercingly alive . . . the poise and passion leaves one grateful, exhausted and nourished."—Richard Corliss, *Time*

"Miracles occasionally do happen, but until the next one, *Eve's Bayou* will have to do."—Stephen Hunter, *Washington Post*

Box Office: $13,357,623

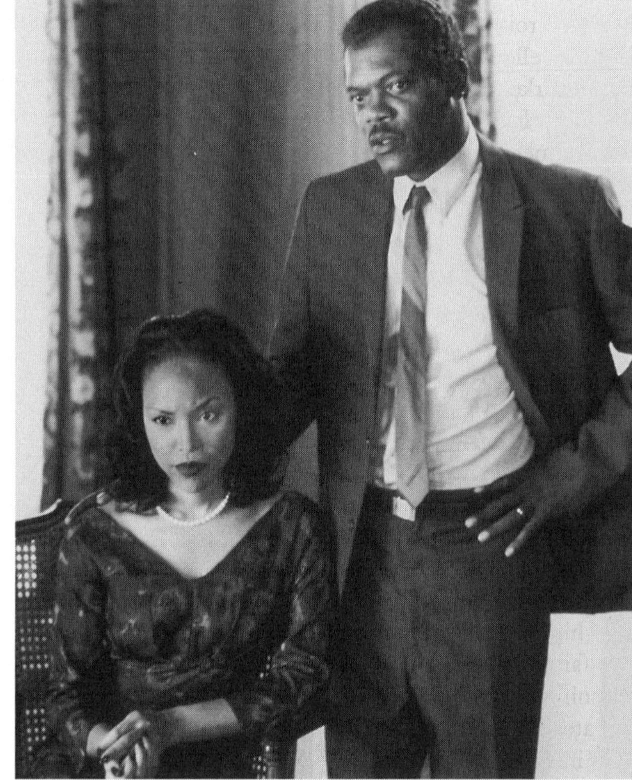

The once tranquil Batiste household headed by Louis and Roz (Samuel L. Jackson and Lynn Whitfield) runs into turmoil when Louis's philandering ways catch up to him in the atmospheric drama *Eve's Bayou.*

Eve's Bayou, a vivid portrait of Southern life in the early 1960s highlighting a prosperous black family in a small Louisiana backwoods town, is the dynamic directing debut of Kasi Lemmons. Lemmons (who also wrote the script) fashions a strong portrait of a group of women who exhibit amazing strength and spirit, but find themselves vulnerable to an elusive factor in their life—the husband and father of the clan.

The movie starts off with a powerful narration by Eve Batiste (Jurnee Smollett): "I was 10 years old the summer I killed my father" and this statement is an apt metaphor for the power and mysticism that embraces the Batiste women. Eve lives with her family in the small Louisiana town of Eve's Bayou, where they are the direct descendants of "Eve" herself, a slave woman who saved the life of a wealthy white planter, Jean-Louis Batiste. Eve's father Louis (Samuel L. Jackson) is the town's popular doctor, who brought his beautiful wife Roz to Eve's Bayou, where they produced Cisely (Megan Good) who is 14-years-old, Eve, and Po (Jake Smollett), a little brother who is 6-years-old. On the surface the Batiste family enjoys the good life—a fine house, shiny cars, beautiful dresses, and a sunny outlook for the future. Yet Louis is a loquacious charmer who dallies with both patients and old girlfriends. When suspicious minds mention this to him, he is the very picture of devotion to his wife and family.

Louis: "To a certain type of woman, I am a hero. I need to be a hero."

Family dysfunctions roil beneath the surface, waiting to explode. At a family party Eve simmers with jealousy as Louis dances only with Cisely. Later that night, Eve catches her father with a neighborhood woman, Matty (Lisa Nicole Carson), and is thoroughly shaken by the event. Louis is such a smooth operator that he doesn't even worry about what his daughter saw. But Eve does tell Cisely, who pretends to not believe it. However, it is evident that Cisely does believe it, and it breaks her heart.

Eve begins to spend a lot of time with Mozelle (Debi Morgan), her father's sister who operates as a fortune-teller out of her home. Mozelle is something of a "black widow" character, having just buried her third husband. Like many psychics and psychiatrists, she can help others but a cloudy veil hangs over her own life—"Sometimes I feel like I've lost so much I have to find new things to lose—and all I know is, there must be a divine point to all of it and it's just over my head . . . " Mozelle's confidence is further shaken when she and Roz talk to Elzora (Diahann Carroll), a rumpled, eccentric fortune-teller who hangs out at the local marketplace. In a matter of minutes, Elzora wrecks havoc in the women's lives: she places a curse on Mozelle, telling her that she will *never* find personal happiness, and instills a fear in Roz to "watch her children, keep them close." Panicked, Roz goes home and dictates to her three children that, until further notice, they will not leave the house—for anything!

Vondie Curtis Hall, who plays the artistic Julian, is the husband of writer/director Kasi Lemmons.

Understandably, the Batiste children chafe under this rule and tempers flare. Precocious Eve even mouths off to her mother, intimating that Louis is running around behind her back. Mozelle steps in and takes Eve away. Although Mozelle is barren, she considers Eve to be practically her own child and, after slapping some respectful sense into her, she lets her watch her receive psychic clients. Thus, an important theme of *Eve's Bayou* unravels; the very real relationship between the women of this family and their spiritual faith, their respect for black and white magic alike. The stunning cinematography of Amy Vincent beautifully illuminates this shadowy and magical terrain; when Mozelle goes into a trance and "sees" her visions, the shapes flow and meld together in a hauntingly beautiful manner.

Eve finds herself at a crossroads; she is bright enough to know that something is very amiss with her father and his behavior (Louis is so cocky that he dallies with a comely patient even as he has Eve along with him for the day), but, like most children her age, she worships her father and thinks he can do no wrong. Like her sister, Cisely also harbors resentment against her mother and unbridled affection towards her father. But Cisely is approaching womanhood herself: her affection is tempered by her sexual awakening as she feels the palpable tension in the house.

The fortune-teller's prophecy rings true when a bus fells another child in the neighborhood. The Batiste children are finally free! Unbelievably, it seems as if Mozelle's curse is about to be lifted as well, when handsome stranger Julian (Vondie Curtis-Hall) arrives on her doorstep, seeking the whereabouts of his missing wife. A romance blossoms, giving Mozelle the strength and courage to believe in love again. Julian seems completely unfazed by Mozelle's track record with men, a fact that pleases and astonishes her.

But while Mozelle's love life is pleasantly shaping up, the relationships in Louis and Roz' home are straining to the breaking point. Eve approaches Elzora and begs the fortune-teller to give her a "curse" to kill someone. At first Elzora refuses to take the passionate ramblings of a 10-year-old seriously. But Eve impresses upon her that this "someone" who must be killed, is "harming my family." Eve sets about snatching hairs from her father's hairbrush to give to Elzora; her ferocity is both amusing and frightening. But Eve sets her father's death in motion in a way that even she couldn't have foreseen. She deliberately taunts Matty's husband with tidbits about Louis and Matty spending time together.

Cisley is also having problems with her father as evidenced by an incident that crosses the line of father-daughter propriety. Since Cisely is obviously distraught, Louis and Roz offer her the chance to go away for a while—and to their surprise, Cisely accepts. Roz has no idea of what has happened to her daughter, but she is heartbroken that Cisely is breaking away from her. Before she goes away, Cisely tells Eve about the improper advance her father made on her, and Eve is horrified. Mozelle picks up on something between the two sisters, but they will not tell her anything.

The next night Eve seeks out her father and finds him in the local bar, drinking and smooching with Matty. She successfully pulls Louis away from Matty just as Matty's husband

CREDITS

Eve Batiste: Jurnee Smollett
Cisely: Megan Good
Louis: Samuel L. Jackson
Roz: Lynn Whitfield
Mozelle: Debi Morgan
Poe: Jake Smollett
Elzora: Diahann Carroll
Gran Mere: Ethel Ayler
Julian Grayraven: Vondie Curtis Hall
Narrator: Tamara Tunie

Origin: USA
Released: 1997
Production: Caldecott Chubb and Samuel L. Jackson; released by Trimark Pictures
Direction: Kasi Lemmons
Screenplay: Kasi Lemmons
Cinematography: Amy Vincent
Editing: Terilyn A. Shropshire
Production design: Jeff Howard
Costumes: Karyn Wagner
Music: Terence Blanchard
Art direction: Adele Plauche
Sound: Benjamin A. Patrick
Set decoration: Joanne Schmidt
MPAA rating: R
Running Time: 109 minutes

shows up. A confrontation ensues and even though Louis and Eve walk away safely, Louis cannot leave well enough alone. Louis taunts Matty's husband and is shot point-blank.

Shocked, the Batiste women huddle together for comfort. Eve finds a letter that her father has written to Mozelle, defending himself against "improper behavior" with Cisely—behavior that Mozelle must have somehow "divined." Eve confronts her sister with her father's version, whereupon Cisely breaks down and confesses that she is so upset that she can't remember correctly. The sisters cling together, secure in the knowledge that they have each other to weather the mysterious and difficult years ahead.

Director Lemmons' film is populated entirely with African-Americans, set in an affluent neighborhood in a time that was not kind to other black Americans. She has achieved a world that is rife with voodoo and magic, rather than prejudice and racism, and has successfully given her characters rich inner lives that are reflected onscreen. Beautifully acted, directed, and realized on the screen, *Eve's Bayou* is an auspicious debut and earmarks the emergence of a truly original filmmaker.

—*G.E. Georges*

AWARDS AND NOMINATIONS

Independent Spirit Awards 1997: First Feature, Supporting Actress (Morgan)

REVIEWS

Boxoffice. November, 1997, p. 124.
Entertainment Weekly. November 7, 1997, p. 59.
Los Angeles Times. November 7, 1997, p. F16.
New York Times. November 7, 1997, p. E14.
People. November 10, 1997, p. 23.
Rolling Stone. November 27, 1997, p. 116.
Time. October 13, 1997.
USA Today. November 7, 1997, p. 8D.
Variety. September 8, 1997, p. 80.
Village Voice. November 11, 1997, p. 82.

Excess Baggage

A crash course in kidnapping, car thefts and other rituals of dating.—Movie tagline

"Funny, sexy, hot and cool!"—Maria Salas, *CBS-TV*

"Two thumbs up."—*Siskel & Ebert*

"Alicia Silverstone is funny and believable with a bold performance!"—Jeff Craig, *Sixty Second Preview*

Box Office: $14,355,189

"It's time to take out the trash," as the Arnold Schwarzenegger character said in *Last Action Hero* (1993), a dumb movie with a sense of humor. *Excess Baggage* is another dumb movie without a sense of humor, featuring characters who are far less than lovable or endearing. They're all trash, in fact, even Emily T. Hope, the pouty, spoiled heroine played by Alicia Silverstone, who has worked hard at being perky and cute, but gets stuck in an awful role here. The only thing that sorts her out from the rest of the trash is that her father is a mega-millionaire with a heart of flint. It's hard to feel sympathy for her.

Emily: "All I ever wanted was a father who loved me."

Emily Hope, the Silverstone heroine, seems to be both hopeless and clueless in this stupidly contrived picture. To get the attention of her workaholic, self-absorbed, rich-but-sleazy father, Alexander (Jack Thompson), she decides to kidnap herself to see if daddy will pay a million dollar ransom. Presumably, she just wants to be noticed, and loved. Working with a mechanically disguised voice on her cell phone and impersonating a kidnapper, she instructs her father to drop a briefcase containing a million dollars from a bridge onto a passing barge. After the drop has been made, she binds her ankles with duct tape, gags herself, puts on handcuffs, and locks herself in the trunk of her BMW, after telling her father (and the police) where she can be found. But, as she explains in a voice-over as the film begins, there was no way to anticipate what would happen before the police could get to her.

This dumb plot is further complicated when professional car thief Vincent Roche (Benicio Del Toro) steals her Beamer before the police can arrive to rescue her. Vincent realizes that something is awry when he notices that several police cars are in hot pursuit of him, but he manages to lose them. After he gets to a warehouse filled with hot cars, he hears a thumping in the trunk, opens it, and finds the "excess baggage." She is a tough little tramp, who fights like Batgirl, but he manages to overpower and get her handcuffed, then tries to figure out what to do next, which must have also been a real challenge for the scriptwriter, too.

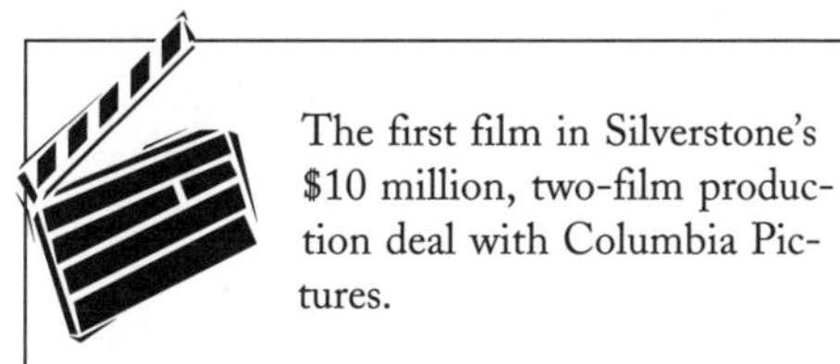

The first film in Silverstone's $10 million, two-film production deal with Columbia Pictures.

Vincent doesn't want to hurt her, however, and agrees to drop her outside the city; but as the BMW is leaving the warehouse garage, chain-smoking Emily flips a lit cigarette out the car window. It lands in a trash bin and starts a fire that later burns down the warehouse, destroying its contents. Fortunately, Vincent has taken along a bag containing $200,000 that belongs to two thugs, Stick and Gus (Nicholas Turturro from "NYPD Blue" and Michael Bowen), who have paid for cars that were destroyed in the fire. The police are after Vincent as the presumed kidnapper. At first the thugs just want to recover their money, but after they find out who Emily is, they decide to hold her hostage and demand a million dollars. Finally, Emily's "Uncle" Ray (Christopher Walken), a sort of bodyguard and "fixer" for her father, is after both Vincent and Emily, with instructions to rescue her and kill him.

The hoods are dumb and dangerous, but Uncle Ray takes care of them, and the police quickly trace the hostage call the hoods have forced Emily to make to her father to ask for even more money. The father seems more concerned about a business trip he should be making to Brussels. He is impatient: he wants Vincent out of the way, but Emily intercedes for his life, and Ray, respecting her wishes, decides to spare him. Viewers are supposed to believe that Emily and Vincent have fallen in love as a consequence of their two-day ordeal, even though there is no real chemistry between them. Ray hides Vincent in the trunk of his car, where Emily joins him with a bottle of wine at the film's end. In a final stupid gesture, they get into the trunk and close the lid. The baggage is packed and the case closed, if anyone cares, and few will.

The movie was intended as an Alicia Silverstone vehicle, part of a deal she managed to negotiate after the success of *Clueless*, a teen comedy written and directed by Amy Heckerling in 1995. *Clueless* was a perfect match. Heckerling had helped to shape the teenpix genre years before with her acclaimed comedy *Fast Times at Ridgemont High* in 1982. Silverstone had appeared in a few made-for-television movies and had played Fred Savage's dream date on television's "The Wonder Years" to that time, but her main claim to fame had been her appearances in several Aerosmith music videos, one of which was proclaimed the Best Video of All Time on MTV.

Her breakthrough picture, however, was *Clueless*, which made her a celebrity at the age of 18. "A Star Is Made" proclaimed the title of a cover story published about her in *Entertainment Weekly* to celebrate the success of *Clueless*. Silverstone was also to grace the covers of *Rolling Stone* and *Seventeen*. When interviewed by James Ryan for the *New York Times*, she was hoping to capture the role of Juliet against Leonardo DiCaprio in Baz Luhrmann's *Romeo and Juliet* (1996), but that role finally went to Claire Danes. Switching from teen comedy to teen tragedy would have been a good career move, but *Excess Baggage* is a far cry from Shakespeare. It is remarkable for its wasted talent.

Christopher Walken, who plays Emily's devoted but dangerous Uncle Ray, could be "a wonderful prince of darkness in the right movie," Jane Horwitz noted in *The Washington Post*, but this is not the right movie. Del Toro, who played Fred Fenster in *The Usual Suspects* (1995) had better presence in that ensemble homage to Raymond Chandler than he does in *Excess Baggage* in a leading role. Though he makes an appealingly "scuzzy naïf" (though not an especially endearing one), as Horwitz noted, "he's got to play second fiddle to a potboiler of a script, and Silverstone's pudgy posturing," and this is "not a pretty sight."

In brief, then, this was not a very smart move in image modification for Silverstone, who was also co-producer on the picture. It lacks the sensibility and charm of *Clueless* (1995), which had a far better script going for it since it was an updated Jane Austen spin-off. Jane Horwitz conjectured that this "failed attempt at quirky romantic comedy" would not attract the teen fans of Alicia Silverstone, but, rather, "leave them disappointed." Although the "issue of parental indifference, real or imagined, may resonate with some teens," she added, it is "not given much emotional depth." In fact, there is absolutely no emotional depth in this cold and cynical picture.

The reviews were miserable. Reviewing the movie for *Entertainment Weekly*, for example, Lisa Schwarzbaum criticized this "slow-moving, sour, sloppily assembled teen drama" for not allowing Silverstone to endow her predicament with "any emotional interest." In the *New York Times* Stephen Holden protested that the screenplay refused to give Silverstone "a single funny line" and objected to Marco Brambilla's "sluggish" direction.

Silverstone succeeded as a supporting player in *Batman and Robin*, released earlier in the summer and grossing over $100 million by the time *Excess Baggage* was released, but

Excess Baggage was her own project, marketed on the basis of her lead. It was, as James Sterngold explained in the *New York Times*, "the first of two films produced under a $10 million deal Columbia signed with Ms. Silverstone" after the success of *Clueless*. Columbia was so eager to sign Silverstone that it empowered her to choose, develop, and produce, but, according to the *New York Times*, "many in the industry questioned the wisdom of giving a production deal to a teen-ager who, despite obvious talent, was new to the business." After the devastating reviews, Columbia was reportedly rethinking its position and whether or not to finance the second movie, paying Silverstone $5 million "to keep her happy." An unnamed source at SONY Pictures speculated that "the company was likely to proceed with the second film if for no other reason than to avoid scaring off other actors interested in such deals."

Director Marco Brambilla, said to have been "discovered" by Ridley Scott in 1989, made his feature film debut with *Demolition Man*, starring Sylvester Stallone and Wesley Snipes in 1993. *Demolition Man* was another brainless vehicle, but it had its moments of dumb fun. *Excess Baggage* isn't much fun at all, but the characters do have a certain talent for getting out of locked automobile trunks. That is not a very stunning endorsement, however.

—*James M. Welsh*

CREDITS

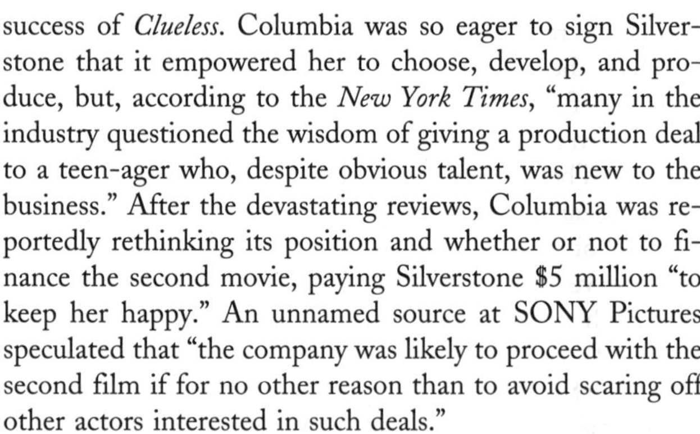

Emily: Alicia Silverstone
Vincent: Benicio Del Toro
Alexander: Jack Thompson
Ray: Christopher Walken
Greg: Harry Connick Jr.
Stick: Nicholas Turturro
Gus: Michael Bowen
Detective Sims: Robert Wisden
Detective Barnaby: Leland Orser
Louise: Sally Kirkland

Origin: USA
Released: 1997
Production: Bill Borden and Carolyn Kessler for First Kiss; released by Columbia Pictures
Direction: Marco Brambilla
Screenplay: Max D. Adams, Dick Clement, and Ian La Fresnais
Cinematography: Jean Yves Escoffier
Editing: Steve Rivkin
Music: John Lurie
Production design: Missy Stewart
Art direction: Richard Hudolin
Set decoration: Elizabeth Wilcox
Costumes: Beatrix Aruna Pasztor
Sound: Eric J. Batut
Stunt coordinator: Betty Thomas
MPAA rating: PG-13
Running Time: 98 minutes

REVIEWS

Boxoffice. November, 1997, p. 134.
Chicago Tribune. August 29, 1997, p. 5.
Entertainment Weekly. September 5, 1997, p.51.
Los Angeles Times. August 29, 1997, p. F14.
The New York Times. August 29, 1997, p. B10.
The New York Times. October 3, 1997, p. B7.
People. September 15, 1997, p. 28.
Sight and Sound. November, 1997, p. 11.
Variety. September 1, 1997, p. 75.
Village Voice. September 2, 1997, p. 78.
Washington Post Weekend. September 5, 1997, p. 42.

Eye of God

The leap of faith nearly killed her.—Movie tagline

"The performances are excellent. It spins a powerful spell."—*New York Daily News*

"Powerful, stunning!"—*New York Magazine*

"A reminder of the illuminating power of exquisitely meticulous acting. Every detail feels absolutely right."—*The New York Times*

"Two thumbs up!"—*Siskel & Ebert*

"It will win your heart before breaking it."—*Time Out*

"A real magic trick of a movie!"—*Village Voice*

There is a good deal about *Eye of God* that a reviewer should not give away. This superb suspenseful movie, tautly written and directed, with superb performances by all of the actors, is a probing exploration of life's mystery. The film begins with a reflective voice-over by Hal Holbrook, who plays the town sheriff. He dwells on his perplexity over the biblical story of Abraham and Isaac, of a father willing to sacrifice his son according to the Lord's dictates. The sheriff never says so, but he clearly has a problem with the idea of sacrifice. Why do such events have to occur? How can one have such faith in a God-ordered universe?

Ainsley: "Yes. Just children. That's all we are, Lord, if you're out there at all. Children. Your children. Boys and girls. Forgive us."

The sheriff's musings apply to his story about Ainsley Dupree (Martha Plimpton), a lonely but hopeful young woman in a small Oklahoma town who marries a recently released convict, Jack (Kevin Anderson). They have corresponded but never met. When Ainsley sees Jack for the first time, she wants to flee, but the charming Jack coaxes her into trying out a new life with him. This story unfolds, however, against the backdrop of a crime. Fourteen-year-old Tommy Spencer (Nick Stahl) has been found near a small river covered in blood. Soon it is determined that the blood is someone else's. But Tommy, in a state of shock, cannot talk, and it takes all of the sheriff's patience to slowly piece together the events that led to a horrible murder.

Martha Plimpton is the daughter of actors Keith Carradine and Shelly Plimpton.

CREDITS

Ainsley: Martha Plimpton
Jack: Kevin Anderson
Sheriff Sam Rogers: Hal Holbrook
Tom: Nick Stahl
Sprague: Richard Jenkins
Dorothy: Maggie Moore
Claire Spencer: Mary Kay Place

Origin: USA
Released: 1997
Production: Michael Nelson, Wendy Ettinger for Cyclone Film and Minnow Pictures; released by Castle Hill Productions, Inc.
Direction: Tim Blake Nelson
Screenplay: Tim Blake Nelson; based on his play
Cinematography: Russell Lee Fine
Editing: Kate Sanford
Music: David Van Tiegham
Production design: Patrick Geary
Art direction: Richard Williams
Costumes: Jill O'Hannesson
Sound: Mack Melson
MPAA rating: R
Running Time: 84 minutes

As the sheriff gingerly questions Tommy, the film flashes back to the evolving relationship between Ainsley and Jack. A sober Jack who has found God wants to take things slowly. He refuses to have sex until they are properly married. Ainsley is the eager one. For she does not share his rock-solid Christian convictions, though she does desire the home and family that Jack craves. They marry. Jack finds a job—quite a feat in this economically depressed town. Ainsley loses her job at the local burger place which is shutting down. Jack pressures her to go to church with him. She consents out of love for him, though she confesses her doubt that there is a God.

Ainsley has always worked and is troubled by her inactivity. After only five months of marriage he is already tense about the fact that she has not gotten pregnant. When she takes to hanging out at the local gasoline station (one of her haunts since she was old enough to go out by herself) Jack demands that she stay home. She consents, but she feels frustrated. Then she becomes pregnant. Jack is overjoyed, but Ainsley is depressed. She tells him that she feels empty inside. She cannot live couped up in the house. Jack won't listen. When she tries again to tell him about her feelings, he attacks her, strangling her and making her gasp out the words that she will have his baby.

Jack's violence frightens Ainsley. It comes as quite a shock to a woman who has been curious about the crime that led to Jack's incarceration. Before his attack on her, she said she would stay with him no matter what he had done, and Jack's only response is that he is a different man from the one who committed the crime. But his attack comes just after Ainsley has learned from Jack's parole officer about his crime. It is so similar to his attack on her that she determines to leave him.

The remainder of the film sorts out (through the sheriff's investigation) the details of the crime that Tommy Spencer witnessed. Something is wrong with Tommy, though what it is is not made clear until the film's final scenes. The sheriff senses that Tommy is as much a victim of a crime as is the person who is pulled out of the river near where Tommy was found. But like life itself, the connections the sheriff makes are based on hindsight. He cannot prevent the horrible crime that Tommy witnesses, and the sheriff cannot understand the meaning of the murder until after it is committed. Thus the use of flashbacks is integral to the film's meaning. Life is understood only in retrospect.

What makes *Eye of God* so compelling is its ability to explore the profoundest questions about human existence

REVIEWS

Boxoffice. December, 1997, p. 50.
Entertainment Weekly. October 31, 1997, p. 80.
Los Angeles Times. October 31, 1997, p. F20.
New York Times. October 17, 1997, p. E12.
People. October 27, 1997, p. 20.
Variety. January 27, 1997, p. 77.
Village Voice. October 21, 1997, p. 94.
Washington Post Weekend. November 14, 1997, p. 50.

without ever seeming portentous or manipulative. The questions are not imposed on the film's plot but rather arise out of the very telling of the story—making the biblical beginning and the ending in a small Oklahoma town all of a piece.

—*Carl Rollyson*

Face/Off

In order to trap him, he must become him.
—Movie tagline

"An absolute blast! John Woo's finest film since *The Killer.*"—Mike Cidoni, *ABC-TV*

"An explosive movie that will keep you at the edge of your seat! Cage and Travolta are magnificent!"—Maria Salas, *CBS-TV*

"Finally with *Face/Off* there's something new and genuinely interesting to watch in an action film: the performances."—Susan Stark, *Detroit News*

"A delicious inside-out double reverse movie that's as outrageous . . . as anyone could want."—Kenneth Turan, *Los Angeles Times*

"A summer movie extraordinaire; imaginative, crazily funny and, even more surprising, oddly moving."—David Ansen, *Newsweek*

"A complete and total blast!"—Leah Rozen, *People*

"This, you gotta see! Exciting and then some with an off-the-wall humor that allows Travolta and Cage to really let it rip. There is no resisting *Face/Off.*"—Peter Travers, *Rolling Stone*

"Two thumbs up!"—*Siskel & Ebert*

"This isn't just a thrill ride, it's a rocket into the thrilling past when directors could scare you with how much emotion they packed into a movie. For once a movie knows how to use its stars. John Woo's smartest American thriller. A white-knuckle action film for all seasons."
—Richard Corliss, *Time*

Box Office: $112,276,146

Face/Off is more than just the title of this John Woo film. Faces do come off as terrorist Castor Troy (Nicholas Cage) and FBI agent Sean Archer switch identities to bring the other man down.

It takes a long time to build a successful career. Sometimes you have people who are blessed and rise above what came before, going on to reach plateaus their first life had never promised. Meet actor John Travolta. Rising from the ashes not once, but twice, Travolta has defied logic and positioned himself as one of the industry's top-notch leading men.

Legendary Hong Kong director John Woo has a career that, in many ways, parallels Travolta's. Although the 50-year-old, Chinese-born auteur has churned out more than 30 films in his homeland, he is virtually unknown in the United States. His first American film, the commercial and critical flop *Hard Target* (1993) with Jean-Claude Van Damme, nearly broke his will and sent him back to Hong Kong. Accustomed to always having the final cut, Woo wasn't prepared for the studio to take his work and edit it down to suit an American audience. In interviews during the *Face/Off* promotional tour, Woo still carried with him a noticeable trace of disenchantment during his first brush with the Hollywood hit machine. What the public saw wasn't what he had intended which could be why it was received so poorly. Here is a man who wrote his own ticket for of a quarter century, working in a field he obviously loves. Why would he give up almost iron-clad security by ripping his artistic foundation up by the roots and transplanting himself in a land that had never heard of him?

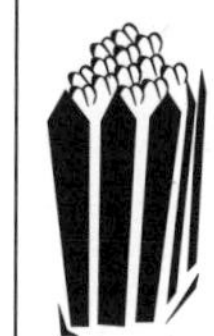

Archer imposter about his "wife:"—"Lies, distrust, mixed messages. This is turning into a real marriage."

After dusting himself off from the *Hard Target* debacle, Woo was able to wrestle back most of the control he'd become accustomed to and began work on a new project with an actor he'd long admired. In *Broken Arrow* (1995), Woo cast Travolta as a psychotic pilot who attempts the theft of nuclear warheads. Woo took a major gamble when he took one of the industry's most beloved figures and turned him into a terrorist. Travolta has rarely played a villain and even his stint as the assassin Vincent Vega in *Pulp Fiction* (1994) was viewed as more of a protagonist character. Woo explained his decision by adding just a smidgen of Eastern philosophy in his response, "It takes a kind man to play a believable villain." Although *Broken Arrow* received mixed critical reviews, the public loved what they saw. It went on to be one of the top grossers of the year. More importantly, it saw Woo recapturing the breakneck, free-for-all style that had made him so unique.

With *Face/Off*, Woo and Travolta are paired together once more and the director takes his 'kind man' philosophy a step further. To effectively play off Travolta, Woo needed someone who had roughly the same physical characteristics, a graceful way of movement and a performer who could be convincing as both a hero and a villain. Enter Nicolas Cage. Having recently been awarded his much deserved Oscar for his portrayal of a suicidal alcoholic in *Leaving Las Vegas* (1995), Cage finally began receiving the worldwide acclaim that had eluded him for most of his career. Possessing not only an emotional range that can run the gamut, Cage has an innate comic sensibility and can more than handle the exhaustive physical demands of action/adventure projects.

With one of shrewdest castings in recent memory complete, Woo takes what is arguably two of the top box-office draws in the business and pits them against each other in the smartest, tautest, action film of the year. This cat and mouse crime thriller, complete with all of the trademark Woo tongue-in-cheek humor and exaggerated pyrotechnics, is admittedly heavy on testosterone but is effectively counterbalanced with a love triangle and a touching subplot about parents coping with the loss of a child. Woo has taken a threadbare genre (good vs. evil) and came up with a story that wisely points out that good and evil lurks within all of us. Not only did Travolta and Cage imitate each other's characters but their counterpart's acting techniques as well.

As the film opens, FBI agent Sean Archer (Travolta) is seen on a merry-go-round with his toddler son, Mikey. Castor Troy (Cage) has Archer in the crosshair of his high powered rifle and with one shot, nails his target. Going through Sean, the bullet instead kills Mikey, starting a multi-year feud between the two men. Troy is a maniacally diabolical terrorist who has no conscience and carries with him a long laundry list of previous offenses. Jump ahead six years. During an airport standoff, Sean finally apprehends Castor who is nearly killed in the process. The FBI victory is short-lived when it is learned that Castor has planted a bomb somewhere in Los Angeles that is set to get off within 72 hours. In order to find out exactly where it is, Sean must infiltrate a prison and ferret the information out of Castor's brother, Pollux (Alessandro Nivola). It would be unfair to reveal the method used to disguise Sean as Castor, but suffice to say, it's far more intricate than your run-of-the-mill plastic surgery and will definitely shock and disturb some viewers.

Because of the cloak-and-dagger nature of Archer's mission, only two of his associates know of the identity switch. Archer's short stay in the prison is extended after Troy wakes from his coma and has the surgical procedure performer on him. With his transformation complete, Troy (as Archer) gets his brother out of jail and leaves Sean to rot in his cell. Castor then murders Archer's associates and the doctor, the only people aware of the switch. Not even Archer's wife Eve (Joan Allen) is aware of what's going on.

On the surface, the casting of the plain-Jane Allen may have seemed inappropriate. The classically trained Allen doesn't spring to mind as the first choice for a female love-interest in an action flick. After a lengthy career in the theater, the Tony award-winning Allen made the switch to film and has since been typecast in roles where she plays the demure, accommodating, and supportive woman. They have all been great performances in superb projects, among them *Tucker: The Man & His Dream* (1988), *In Country* (1989), *Without Warning: The James Brady Story* (1991), *Searching For Bobby Fischer* (1993), *Nixon* (1995), *The Crucible* (1996) and *The Ice Storm* (reviewed in this issue). With two Oscar nominations already to her credit, Allen has been given something of a left-handed compliment by casting directors. She's great at what she does, but nobody seems willing to

AWARDS AND NOMINATIONS

Academy Awards 1997 Nominations: Sound Effects Editing

let her try something different. Allen's ability to show inner-strength and resolve while still maintaining a tight-lipped facade is no mean feat. She is the one stable character in *Face/Off*, keeping the entire production grounded in reality.

Ironically, the part of Sasha, Castor's love interest, was given to Gina Gershon, another actress with a theater background whose film credits follow a distinct pattern and are the polar opposition of Allen's. While Allen was an original member of Chicago's famed Steppenwolf Company, Gershon was cutting her teeth with New York's Naked Angels. Known mostly for her performance as the demanding prima donna in *Showgirls* (1995), Gershon's turns in *Bound* (1996) and *This World, Then The Fireworks* (reviewed in this issue) have continued the trend that began with *Pretty In Pink* from 1986. Gershon almost invariably dons the sex-kitten pose but does so in a manner that is atypical in Hollywood. Her characters have a lot on the ball and are, for the most part, caring and vulnerable beneath their hardened veneer. Despite her limited screen time, Gershon's role is pivotal to the film's conclusion.

If there is any noticeable fault in the film, it is with the concluding scenes. The duels between Archer and Troy started shortly before the two-hour mark and continue to the end, some 30 minutes later. Woo's propensity to go over-the-top goes unchecked here and showing restraint along with some judicious editing would have given this part of the movie a bigger emotional impact. But this is an action movie and, as it almost always does, poignancy takes a backseat. Like the rest of Woo's back catalogue, it is brimming with carnage, but is still relatively tame by today's standards and unlike other efforts of this ilk, the violence serves a purpose. In a Summer that provided so few surprises, Woo superbly mixed brawn and brains and came up with a refreshing and daring piece of work.

—J. M. Clark

CREDITS

Sean Archer: John Travolta
Castor Troy: Nicolas Cage
Eve Archer: Joan Allen
Pollux Troy: Alessandro Nivola
Sasha Hassler: Gina Gershon
Jamie Archer: Dominique Swain
Dietrick Hassler: Nick Cassavetes
Lazzaro: Harve Presnell

Origin: USA
Released: 1997
Production: David Permut, Barrie M. Osborne, Terence Chang, Christopher Godsick for WCG Entertainment; released by Paramount Pictures
Direction: John Woo
Screenplay: Micke Werb and Michael Colleary
Cinematography: Oliver Wood
Editing: Christian Wagner, Steven Kemper
Music: John Powell
Production design: Neil Spisak
Art direction: Steve Arnold
Costumes: Ellen Mirojnick
Special makeup effects: Kevin Yagher
Stunt coordinator: Brian Smrz
MPAA rating: R
Running Time: 138 minutes

REVIEWS

Boxoffice. August, 1997, p. 49.
Chicago Tribune. June 27, 1997, p. 4.
Entertainment Weekly. July 11, 1997, p. 42.
The Hollywood Reporter. June 23, 1997, p. 8.
Los Angeles Times. June 27, 1997, p. F1.
Movieline. June, 1997, p. 54.
New York Times. June 27, 1997, p. C1.
New Yorker. July 14, 1997, p. 84.
People. July 7, 1997, p. 19.
Rolling Stone. July 10, 1997, p. 30.
USA Today. June 27, 1997, p. D1.
Variety. June 23, 1997, p. 93.
Village Voice. July 8, 1997, p. 69.

Fairy Tale: A True Story

"A movie of intelligence, heart and imagination. One of the year's most special surprises."—Marshall Fine, *Gannett Newspapers*

"An instant children's classic for adults. The movie fervently believes in its fairy folk, and renders them to gossamer perfection."—Graham Fuller, *Interview Magazine*

"True movie magic!"—Janet Weeks, *Los Angeles Daily News*

"One of the year's best films. An audacious richly original classic. Breathtakingly beautiful."—Michael Medved, *New York Post*

"An enchanting film."—Stephen Holden, *The New York Times*

"A richly atmospheric film, one convincing in its period and history."—John Anderson, *Newsday*

"Two thumbs up!"—*Siskel & Ebert*

"A beguiling fantasy. The photography is gorgeous, the fairies endearing."—Joe Morgenstern, *The Wall Street Journal*

Box Office: $13,918,220

Fairy Tale: A True Story is "true" in more ways than one. Fairies truly exist for children who believe in them. And the story is "true" for adults because it is based on fact. In 1917 two young English girls created a sensation by producing a number of photographs of themselves apparently surrounded by fairies. The pictures had been taken with simple cameras and the girls had no previous experience with photography. Eventually their claim was reported in British newspapers and magazines. This produced the famous Cottingley Fairies controversy, not unlike the controversy over Charles Darwin's theory of the origin of species through natural selection. If fairies really existed, then angels probably existed too; and if angels existed, then God must exist, and the claims of traditional religion must be true.

Conan Doyle to Houdini: "There is a point where learning teaches you nothing."

As the film demonstrates, this was a time when the British desperately wanted something to believe in. World War I was raging. British boys were being maimed and slaughtered by German cannons and machine guns. Aboard a train packed with wounded soldiers, 10-year-old Frances Griffiths (Elizabeth Earl) is returning to England from Africa to stay with her uncle and aunt. Her mother is dead and her father has been reported missing in action. She quickly becomes fast friends with her 12-year-old cousin Elsie (Florence Hoath), who has a secret dell that she is convinced is inhabited by fairies. The beautiful cinematography features the green rolling hills of West Yorkshire with ancient stone walls and flocks of grazing sheep. If fairies existed anywhere, they would have to exist near Elsie's pretty little brook shaded by English oaks. And sure enough, they do!

The producers have tried to enhance the marketability of their film by hiring a couple of name actors. Sir Arthur Conan Doyle, a believer in spiritualism, is played by Peter O'Toole with what *New York Times* critic Stephen Holden called "a grandly drooping patrician sadness." Internationally famous American magician/escape artist Harry Houdini is played by the ubiquitous Harvey Keitel. Houdini, a faker who exposes fakes, particularly dislikes spiritualists who claim to communicate with the dead. Houdini invites the girls to one of his sell-out performances and afterwards enters into their conspiracy. He confesses that his own famous feats are nothing but trickery but pointedly warns that a magician should never reveal how he creates his illusions.

Houdini's advice is heeded by the magicians who made *Fairy Tale: A True Story.* It is easy to guess how they created some of their effects but nearly impossible to explain others. It is as if the filmmakers are paying a sort of homage to the two Yorkshire girls who were their predecessors in playing photographic tricks. There are some scenes at the end of the film in which the girls' home is invaded by a whole army of fairies. Reviewer Susan Wloszczyna of *USA Today,* who was not terribly impressed, said they looked like "an armada of human dragonflies in Shakespearean drag." These are obviously human beings with transparent wings attached, but they fly and hover in a most convincing way.

By far the best parts of the film are the scenes featuring "real" fairies. They have double pairs of wings like biplanes, which make them very maneuverable. In fact, their very maneuverability keeps the viewer from getting a good look at them. They tend to dive, soar, and then zoom out of the camera shot. Technically-minded adults will be distracted from the story by wondering how the scenes were shot. In some cases they are obviously little dolls being whisked around on invisible threads; but in other cases they are real boys and girls. It would seem that fairies have to be children and are demoted to elves, gnomes, brownies, and other pedestrian-type spirits when they get older.

The film never makes it clear that the girls were perpetrating a hoax. In one scene a nosy reporter named John Ferret (Tim McInnerny) breaks into their home and finds cutouts of fairy drawings that he arranges in front of enlarged photos of the girls. He is sure they had hit upon this method of producing their pictures without using the easily detectable method of double exposure. The same technique has been used more recently in flying-saucer hoaxes. Hollywood has been using a more sophisticated method for many years with so-called "process shots." Live actors are photographed in front of footage projected on a screen behind them. What is amazing is that such a hoax could have been perpetrated by young children with photography still in its infancy. But the ambiguous *Fairy Tale* immediately cancels out Ferret's discovery by having the ghost of Elsie's brother, killed in the war, appear in the room and terrorize the snooper.

The Cottingley Fairies story is also the basis for the 1997 British film *Photographing Fairies* from director Nick Willing and taken from the novel by Steve Szilagyi.

The British press welcomes the girls' story as a refreshing contrast to all the gloomy war news. Reporters descend on Elsie's secret garden, followed by sightseers in the jolting, backfiring motor vehicles of the period. Many intruders are carrying butterfly nets, hoping to capture a fairy on the wing and bring it home to keep in a cage. There is an impressive scene in which fairies, elves, gnomes, pixies, and other little people are evacuating the desecrated garden like civilians fleeing an invading army.

The Cottingley Fairies hoax would have been short-lived if the famous Sir Arthur Conan Doyle had not been taken in by it. The girls solemnly assure him that fairies are real. They truly believe this much of their story. It is ironic that the creator of the super-rational detective Sherlock Holmes, who believed in nothing but facts, should have fallen prey to spiritualists and other charlatans. Conan Doyle was an excellent example of the person who believes in something because he wants to believe. He wrote his friend Houdini that he had "two photos, one of a goblin, the other of four fairies in a Yorkshire wood . . . The fairies are about eight inches high. In one there is a single goblin dancing. In the other four, beautiful, luminous creatures. Yes, it is a revelation." Conan Doyle reported the discovery of the Cottingley Fairies in the *Strand* magazine and in 1920 published a book titled *The Coming of the Fairies.*

The children who come to the theater to see fairies have a tendency to do acrobatics and practice yoga contortions in their seats when the story reverts to the "adult mode." The kids cannot understand the ambiguous relationship between the fairies and the scenes of khaki-clad soldiers coming back bandaged and limping from the battlefields of France. The relationship is a little hard for even adults to appreciate. The suggestion is that the girls were able to perpetrate their hoax because the British were traumatized by the deaths of a generation of loved ones and wanted a metaphysical explanation for the cruelties of reality. The contrast between the whimsical little children's tale, resembling James Barrie's story of Peter Pan, and the scenes of suffering, grief and separation is almost too severe.

Even the adults prefer the complex story's "child mode" because most of them are watching with one or more kids. The adults want to share vicariously in childish awe and delight and not to be watching a different story in another dimension like people shooting craps in Las Vegas while their kids are playing video games in protective custody. *Fairy Tale* is not destined to be a big hit in spite of its fine acting, impressive technical abracadabra, excellent recreation of the period, and other outstanding production values. Ty Burr of *Entertainment Weekly* hit the nail on the head when he complained that the film was "too heady for small fry and too sticky for grown-ups."

Throughout the film, Frances is anxiously awaiting a letter from her missing dad. Adults are aware that "missing" is too often synonymous with "blown to unidentifiable bits and buried in an unmarked grave." They are hoping against hope that Frances will not have to suffer the same kind of emo-

CREDITS

Elsie Wright: Florence Hoath
Frances Griffiths: Elizabeth Earl
Arthur Wright: Paul McGann
Polly Wright: Phoebe Nicholls
Sir Arthur Conan Doyle: Peter O'Toole
Harry Houdini: Harvey Keitel
E.L. Gardner: Bill Nighy
Harry Briggs: Bob Peck
John Ferret: Tim McInnerny
Frances' father: Mel Gibson

Origin: USA
Released: 1997
Production: Wendy Finerman and Bruce Davey for Icon Productions; released by Paramount Pictures
Direction: Charles Sturridge
Screenplay: Ernie Contreras
Cinematography: Michael Coulter
Editing: Peter Coulson
Music: Zbigniew Preisner
Production design: Michael Howells
Costumes: Shirley Russell
Sound: John Midgley
Visual effects supervisor: Tim Webber
MPAA rating: PG
Running Time: 99 minutes

tional blow that devastated Ingemar Johansson (Anton Glanzelius) in *My Life As a Dog* (1985). *Fairy Tale* ends on a happy note when Frances's father (a cameo by Mel Gibson) returns unharmed and sweeps her up into his arms. The father's safe return is associated with the girls' belief in fairies. Just as the fairies exist because the girls believe in them, so the father returns safely because Frances has steadfastly believed he would. All the little people return from exile at the same time and flock into the girls' home in a grand finale, which should amaze children and leave grown-ups asking, "How in the heck did they *do* that?"

The two English girls, Elizabeth Earl and Florence Hoath, are outstanding. Either one can steal a scene from old pros Keitel and O'Toole with one arm tied behind her back. The girls brighten the screen with their youthful charm and grace. In their billowing dresses, they look like the Tenniel illustrations of Lewis Carroll's *Alice's Adventures in Wonderland* (1865). The actual Elsie and Frances had made a solemn pact to keep their secret forever and ever. But forever is a long time. In 1983, when the real Frances was 76 and the real Elsie was 82, they finally confessed that the fairies were cutouts propped up with hatpins. Kindly, gullible Sir Arthur Conan Doyle was not around to be disenchanted by the news: he had been dead for over 50 years.

—*Bill Delaney*

REVIEWS

Boxoffice. October, 1997, p. 37.
Cinemafantastique. November, 1997, p. 118.
Cinemafantastique. December, 1997, p. 48.
Entertainment Weekly. October 31, 1997, p. 79.
Los Angeles Times. October 24, 1997, p. F10.
Movieline. December, 1997, p. 50.
New York Times. October 24, 1997, p. B12.
People. November 3, 1997, p. 22.
Sight and Sound. March, 1998, p. 45.
USA Today. October 24, 1997, p. 6D.
Variety. September 22, 1997, p. 40.
Village Voice. October 28, 1997, p. 84.
Wall Street Journal. October 24, 1997, p. A20.

Fall

Sometimes the girl in your heart isn't the girl in your dreams.—Movie tagline

"Poetically lyrical, *Fall* examines the surprisingly moving and remarkably tender sides of erotic craving."—Kathleen McInnis, *Moviemaker*

"By far Eric Schaeffer's best film!"—*The New Times*

Written, directed and co-produced by Eric Schaeffer, *Fall* stars the filmmaker's favorite leading man—himself. The film is yet another vanity project that allows the narcissistic actor the opportunity to surround himself with beautiful women who cannot help but fall—please note how cleverly the title reflects the story content—for his trademarked, self-declared charismatic intellectual with the artist's poetic soul.

Michael Shiver (Eric Schaeffer) is a cocky young New York City taxicab driver who spends his time spouting drivel and dropping clues of his intellectual prowess as he drives through Manhattan's Upper West Side. (One suspects that Schaeffer sees himself as some sort of Robert De Niro in the making, a charismatic rather than ominous Travis Bickle.)

One day he picks up a beautiful woman as his fare. She turns out to be the rich and brainy supermodel, Sarah Easton (played by real-life model Amanda DeCadenet). Michael is immediately smitten by this vision of loveliness, but the married Sarah spends at least a nanosecond being uninterested before engaging in a passionate affair.

When Sarah is not catering to all of Michael's sexual fantasies—including anal sex with a strapped-on dildo—or being moved to tears by his profound poetry, the two engage in numerous discussions about God as they sit on the floor, feasting on take-out food. (It is hard not to scoff when Sarah later complains to her husband (Rudolph Martin), "Why do we always have to go to the fanciest restaurants? Why can't we just get Chinese food and sit on the floor and talk about God?")

There is very little in Schaeffer's latest offering that has not already been covered in his low-budget debut, *My Life in Turnaround* (1994), or last year's equally-as-tedious romantic comedy, *If Lucy Fell* (1996). The possible exception might be the additional number of steamy sex scenes, no doubt designed to demonstrate the star's virility and irresistibility.

Schaeffer desperately tries to convince us of his character's charm and wit by surrounding him with female friends who are quick to come to his defense in any situation that might be construed as sexist. One even goes so far as to remark that Michael "deserves some kind of award" for his ability to orally stimulate his beautiful supermodel to multiple sexual orgasms.

CREDITS

Michael Shiver: Eric Schaeffer
Sarah Easton: Amanda DeCadenet
Phillipe: Rudolph Martin
Robin: Francie Swift
Sally: Lisa Vidal
Joan Alterman: Roberta Maxwell
Scasse: Jose Yenque
Zsarko: Josip Kuchan

Origin: USA
Released: 1997
Production: Eric Schaeffer and Terrence Michael for Five Minutes Before the Miracle; released by Capella International
Direction: Eric Schaeffer
Screenplay: Eric Schaeffer
Cinematography: Joe De Salvo
Editing: Thom Zinney
Production design: Michael Shaw
Costumes: Kim Marie Druce
Music: Amanda Kravat
MPAA rating: Unrated
Running Time: 91 minutes

Fall suffers from a decided lack of dramatic tension. It is so easy for Michael to woe and win the girl, while the character of Phillippe does not pose much of a threat, leaving no real antagonist against whom our protagonist can "do battle." It is far too convenient to have Sarah and Phillippe be in a sexless marriage, and to have the husband later confess to infidelity, which allows our leading lady to be guilt-free over her own adulterous behavior. It is perfectly okay for audiences to know that the cab driver will prevail in the end, but it always helps if there is some tension and self-doubt on the main character's part. Storytelling is, after all, a dramatic art.

Fall is a remarkably self-indulgent project for someone who, to date, has accomplished so little. Eric Schaeffer is nothing if not self-confident. But it is important to remember that there is a difference between self-confidence and narcissism. The young filmmaker would benefit from an expansion of his narrative repertoire beyond this sort of smug vanity project. This Beauty-and-the-Beast tale has become shopworn, even by the master of self-parody, Woody Allen.

—*Patricia Kowal*

REVIEWS

Boxoffice. April, 1997, p. 184.
Los Angeles Times. June 27, 1997, p. F8.
New York Times. June 21, 1997, p. 15.
Variety. June 30, 1997, p. 66.
Village Voice. July 1, 1997, p. 96.

Farmer and Chase

Crime was their passion . . . passion was their crime!—Movie tagline

"Reminiscent of the emergence of Quentin Tarantino!"—*San Francisco Chronicle*

Farmer and Chase marks the inauspicious debut of writer/director Michael Seitzman. Although there are a few entertaining scenes in this love story/crime drama, and Ben Gazzara as Farmer plays a credible criminal—at least in the film's first half—the cliches abound and the characters are torpidly written. Seitzman's premise—what does an old stick-up man do when his partner is shot?—might have passed scrutiny if the dialogue or the scene setups had some new twist to them.

Farmer has had a flawless twenty-year career. He has never scored with a big heist, but the work has been steady, and his longtime partner, Ollie (Steven Anthony Jones), assures him that they can be proud of their record. They have a good laugh over the costumes they've worn and the hazardous situations they have negotiated without a hitch. But Farmer knows the work has been low-grade, and there is not much to be proud of. He has no illusions about petty crime. It has made him a living, but he is nothing more than a journeyman in his trade. He is also tired. One more caper with Ollie, and they are going to call it quits. When their store holdup goes wrong, and Ollie is shot and killed, a shaken Farmer returns home, telling his son Chase (Todd Field) of this terrible ending to his career in crime.

Chase has been begging his father for a crack at the world of crime. Farmer has dismissed his son's pleas, pointing out that he does not have the nerve to be a criminal. Farmer reminds Chase of the fight he ducked as a kid, and when Farmer has Chase pull over the car to rob a convenience store, Chase balks. Yet a desperate Farmer eventually yields to his son's pestering and proceeds to toughen him up through a series of fighting lessons out in the back country.

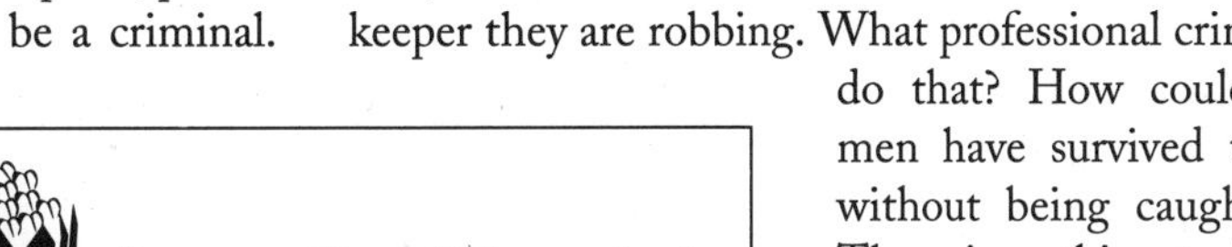
Farmer to Chase: "Women cloud yer judgment!"

The only actor worth watching is Gazzara. His demeanor as a tired, bored criminal is convincing. And he is right: Chase is poor material, mooning over a young, stupid girl, Hillary (played with almost no nuance by Lara Flynn Boyle), and lacking in the guts to look after himself. The only motivation for Farmer's sudden turnabout embrace of his son as a partner is Farmer's loneliness and desperation. He has lost his partner, and he loves his ne'er-do-well son. He has to recreate his occupation to save himself.

But Farmer's character steadily loses credibility as soon as he makes his decision to train Chase. Farmer becomes a dispenser of blowhard advice, a has-been who has lost contact with reality. The trouble actually begins earlier in the film, when Farmer and Ollie turn their backs on the shopkeeper they are robbing. What professional criminals would do that? How could these two men have survived twenty years without being caught or killed? There is nothing to indicate that they are losing their edge. Rather, they are made to turn their backs because the plot requires it.

Farmer and Chase is a factitious film. Not only does Farmer improbably turn to Chase, he decides that after twenty years of middling success he will go for a big job: a bank robbery. Yet from the start it is clear that Chase does not have the stomach for it, and that he is not prepared to use violence. Once in the bank, things go predictably wrong. Farmer is quite willing to begin killing hostages to show the police that he means business. Chase stands up to Farmer, demonstrating for the nth time that he has flunked crime school.

What is worse is that in the last scenes Gazzara destroys the crusty old character of the film's early scenes. Farmer is just a thug without even an honest sense of himself and what he is really capable of. The script gives Gazzara no help. He has to mouth incredible lines while Chase's moronic girlfriend tries to make friends with the bank hostages.

Perhaps *Farmer and Chase* could have been made as a black comedy, or as a shrewd study of the pettiness of petty crime, but the characters' lines are written and delivered in earnest, as if the audience should care about what happens to these pathetic people. Without style or wit, *Farmer and Chase* just peters out, leaving the viewer yearning for *Dog Day Afternoon*, that classic film of a bank robbery gone wrong.

—*Carl Rollyson*

CREDITS

Chase: Todd Field
Farmer: Ben Gazzara
Hillary: Lara Flynn Boyle
Ollie: Steven Anthony Jones

Origin: USA
Released: 1995, 1997
Production: Scott Kalmbach, Julie Costanzo, Michael Seitzman for Red Sky Films; released by Arrow Releasing
Direction: Michael Seitzman
Screenplay: Michael Seitzman
Cinematography: Michael Maley
Editing: Doug Werby
Music: Tony Saunders
Production design: Doug Freeman
MPAA rating: Unrated
Running Time: 97 minutes

REVIEWS

New York Times. February 7, 1997, p. B23.
Variety. October 16, 1995, p. 97.

Fast, Cheap & Out of Control

"Excellent!"—Kenneth Turan, *Los Angeles Times*
"Exhilarating, funny & quite moving!"—Karen Durbin, *Mirabella*
"Strange & wonderful! The bizarre at its best!"—Janet Maslin, *New York Times*
"A tour de force!"—Harlan Jacobson, *USA Today*

Box Office: $776,967

Whereas a fiction film cannot hold our interest without making known its narrative thrust, Errol Morris' *Fast, Cheap & Out of Control* proves that a documentary can grip us without the filmmaker conveying a specific message.

By presenting four remarkable individuals—a wild animal trainer (Dave Hoover), a robotics scientist (Rodney Brooks), a mole-rat specialist (Ray Mendez), and a topiary gardener (George Mendonca)—talking to us about their work, it is left to us to decide what all those fascinating details and personal insights gained in the field have to do with the film's title, or our own aspirations, or simply, with the price of eggs.

Errol Morris: "If you just keep your eyes open, you can find the most extraordinary stories in the most ordinary places."

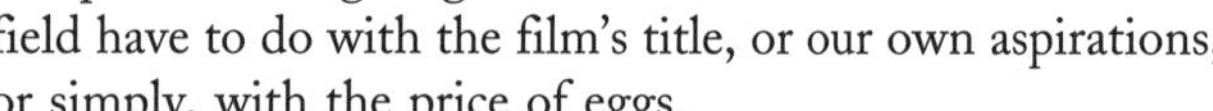

What makes the film a true gem as a film of fact is that it also makes clear that the four are, in a sense, having a filmic conversation with the invisible filmmaker. Thus, what they have to say can, within the modality of the film documentary, evoke a response from him, who is free to interact by interjecting their talk with images from his celluloid arsenal. This not only allows the film to cast off the all too common curse of having to present a visually sterile succession of talking-heads, but also to generate curious ironies its four subjects could never have suspected.

In keeping with the challenge to the viewer's intellect posed by his earlier documentary, *A Brief History of Time* (1992), Morris' talk-cinema looks determined to give any thinking man a run for his money. *Fast, Cheap,* for example, forces us to make sense of what its subjects are saying, by relating it to what Morris as filmmaker seems to be saying. Initially, what emerges as most admirable about all four subjects is their sense of direction about their life's work.

"A lot of kids want to be firemen, cowboys, whatever," Hoover confides, "but I wanted to be a wild animal trainer." The film underscores Hoover's ambition by cutting to excerpts from the jungle serials of his childhood.

As we see Mendonca trimming a hedge, surrounded by his creations, the beautiful giraffes, elephants and bears his hands have shaped over the years, he recounts in a voiceover of how he was first hired by the estate to clean up after the hurricane of 1938. Then, in a matter-of-fact tone belying the superhuman diligence involved, he adds that he just stuck around to do "what had to be done."

We then learn how from the time Mendez was a teenage entomologist, he had been taught that mammals would never be like insects, that our society and theirs were radically different. It was only in his thirties that he came upon the African mole-rat. As he tells it, his face glows with fresh excitement: "A friend of mine called me in the middle of the night and he said to me, 'Ray, they've found 'em! And they have a society just like termites!'"

Over giant close-ups of biotechnological apparatuses in operation, Brooks then tells us: "I liked to build stuff. In my childhood days, I used to build electronic things in a little tin shed in the backyard." He then addresses the camera. "But I had this tremendous feeling of satisfaction," he confides, then widens his eyes for emphasis, "when I switched the things on, the lights flashed and the machines came to life!"

It is to the filmmaker's credit that he makes us share the thrill of being involved in endeavors commensurate with one's innate skills, especially in increasingly technocratic times, when most of the thinkers amongst us have to pay our rents through cyberlabor that threatens to render all effort anonymous.

No wonder then that the four, through their respective callings, stumble upon some profound truth, inaccessible through any other means, that provides moral sustenance for them, and us. Typical is Brooks' credo: "I like to look at what everyone is doing, find some common thing they are all assuming implicitly but they don't even realize they're assuming, and then negate that thing."

After bestowing equal importance on the accomplishments of all four, the film, aided by a touching musical score, evokes a sense of transience in relation to the all too human striving we have been watching. Mendonca, we realize, after spending five years transforming a hedge into the likeness of a bear, stands to have his work destroyed by insects.

AWARDS AND NOMINATIONS

National Board of Review 1997: Documentary
National Society of Film Critics 1997: Documentary
New York Film Critics Circle 1997: Documentary

With devilish glee, the film cuts to a cartoon snippet showing the representation of insects as benign and lovable.

While the first image we see after the Main Title is that of a fluttering American flag, the political dimension underlying the film's subjects matter gets short shrift. Drowned in the moody lyricism of the film's closing moments is the affirmation of freedom, seemingly taken for granted, that has allowed the four to pursue their goals with maniacal dedication.

Critics seem to have hailed the film as coming from a singularly innovative documentarist. David Ansen in *Newsweek* believes that the filmmaker's "nonfiction films don't pretend to be 'capturing' reality: they're probing and poking at it, like a doctor looking for a surface aberration that will reveal an inner secret."

Fast, Cheap & Out of Control has fared outstandingly well at the box office, after being showcased at the New York Film Festival.

—Vivek Adarkar

CREDITS

Wild Animal Trainer: Dave Hoover
Topiary Gardener: George Mendonca
Mole-Rat Specialist: Ray Mendez
Robot Scientist: Rodney Brooks

Origin: USA
Released: 1997
Production: Errol Morris for Fourth Floor Productions; released by Sony Pictures Classics
Direction: Errol Morris
Cinematography: Robert Richardson
Editing: Karen Schmeer, Shondra Merrill
Music: Caleb Sampson
Production design: Ted Basaloukos
Set decoration: Scott Doonan
Sound: Steve Nemes, Fred Burnham
MPAA rating: PG
Running Time: 80 minutes

REVIEWS

Boxoffice. April, 1997, p. 181.
Chicago Tribune. November 14, 1997, p. 5.
Entertainment Weekly. October 24, 1997, p. 46.
Los Angeles Times. October 3, 1997, p. F19.
Los Angeles Times. October 17, 1997, p. F1.
New York Times. September 30, 1997, p. E5.
Newsweek. October 20, 1997.
People. October 27, 1997, p. 20.
People. November 10, 1997, p. 25.
Time. October 27, 1997.
USA Today. October 7, 1997, p. 3D.
Variety. January 27, 1997, p. 79.

Fathers' Day

The reason why some animals eat their young.
—Movie tagline

"As good as comedy can get."—Larry King, *CNN*

"Big Laughs! Great laughs! A lot of laughs!"
—Joel Siegel, *Good Morning America*

"An irresistible comic team."—Janet Maslin, *New York Times*

"Uproarious! Its hearty laughter has plenty of heart!"—Gene Shalit, *Today Show*

"Riotously funny! Williams and Crystal are brilliant together."—Jeffrey Lyons, *WNBC-TV*

"The mother of all comedy events! Williams and Crystal are hilarious in their first movie together."—Pat Collins, *WWOR-TV*

Box Office: $28,681,080

Besides the Statue of Liberty, France has also given us the plots for a number of film comedies. In some cases, the statue has been more amusing. Recent examples of French films to get the Hollywood treatment include last year's *The Birdcage*, which was based on 1978's *La Cage Aux Folles*, and this year's *Jungle 2 Jungle*, a remake of 1994's *Un Indien Dans La Ville*. Now there is *Fathers' Day*, the latest offering from Ivan Reitman, who this year produced Howard Stern's *Private Parts* and has directed such films as *Dave* (1993), *Ghostbusters* (1984) and three Arnold Schwarzenegger comedies in the late 1980's and early 1990's. Before it lost its accent, the film was entitled *Les Comperes*, a 1983 hit which starred Gerard Depardieu and Pierre Richard, a deft and daft comedy team which also succeeded in *La Chevre* (1981) and *Les Fugitifs* (1986). (This last film, incidently, was remade in the U.S. as *The Three Fugitives* in 1989.) In Reitman's *Fathers' Day*, Billy Crystal steps into the Depardieu role and Robin Williams replaces Richard. As neither Crystal nor Williams are known for a lack of humor and energy, their version is surprisingly flat and anemic.

The basic plot is simple: a teenage boy runs away after an argument with his father, and his desperate mother gets help in finding the boy from two old flames by telling each of them that he is the boy's biological father. The film begins with a quasi-music video for Paul McCartney's latest single, entitled "Young Boy." A montage of photographs shows young Scott (Charlie Hofheimer) over the years and leads up to a scene of the fight with his father (Bruce Greenwood). While the angry adult is sure that the boy will return shortly on his own, the teen's mother, Colette, (Nastassja Kinski) is not so sure, and hatches a desperate plan to ensure that her son is found. She shows up in the back of a courtroom and startles old boyfriend Jack Lawrence (Crystal), a lawyer who has not seen her in sixteen years. Colette shocks him further when she informs him that he has a son—who is now missing. Although somewhat skeptical, Jack, who is childless and thrice-married, does the responsible thing and goes to find his newfound son. Also on the boy's trail is Dale Putley (Williams), a loony loser who is in the midst of a suicide attempt when Colette calls. (For the first part of the conversation, he attempts to speak to her with the gun still stuck in his mouth.) Jack and Dale soon meet and team up, thinking they are looking for two different boys who have run away with a girl named Niki and a group of other teens who are following an area rock band from town to town. When each man shows a photo of his son to the girlfriend's mother, they are baffled and then angered to see that they are holding identical snapshots. Jack and Dale call Colette, and she tells them that she actually does not know which man is Scott's real father. Mollified, the two continue their search.

Dale's response to Jack's desire to use force to get information: "How Joe Pesci of you!"

While looking for Scott, Jack and Dale get to know each other. Jack is a confident and successful attorney who is now happily married to Carrie (Julia Louis-Dreyfus of TV's "Seinfeld"), has a blinding hatred for mimes and an inability to properly digest cheese. He met Colette at a ball game. Neurotic, aging hippie Dale teaches English as a third language at the local Jewish Community Center and writes experimental poetry and plays on the side, including a musical with numbers like "Hello, Doctor? It's Still Swollen!" While driving, he sometimes passes out due to anxiety and is continuously positive that he has just run over someone. His first sexual experience was a traumatic one with his high school drama teacher, and he met Colette in a Berkeley photography class which led to his taking nude pictures of her. After overhearing Colette on the phone, Scott's father sets out to tell his son that he loves him, but his trip is aborted due to problems with his car and an unanchored port-o-potty. Meanwhile, the two supposed fathers find Scott at a club in Sacramento. Before passing out, the tipsy teen pukes on Jack. ("At least we know he ate," says Dale, reassuringly.) Each man proceeds to point to the way Scott's toes overlap or the way his hair curls upward as indisputable proof that he is the father. After Scott comes to in the shower in one of the film's more entertaining sequences, Dale and Jack awkwardly explain things to the boy, who soon flees to Reno. After the men locate him there, Scott is rejected by his girlfriend, engages in a heart-to-heart with his prospective fathers, and is chased by angry drug dealers who want money he took from them. To escape, Scott has no choice but to flee in Jack's car, and Jack, misunderstanding, gives up on the teen. In a touching moment, Dale tells Jack that, while Jack has a wife and successful career which "fill up areas" in his life, "I need this kid." Carrie makes her husband realize that he should also continue the search, and soon the bad guys are routed and Scott is brought home. There, Scott has a warm reunion with his loving parents, and Colette admits to her husband and son that she only told Dale and Jack that they could be Scott's father because she wanted help in finding him. In the end, the boy tries to make Jack and Dale happy by telling each one separately that he is the true father. Jack sees through it, chuckles, and looks forward to actually having a child of his own with his wife. Dale is thrilled, leaves Scott in his parents' capable hands, and picks up a woman on the way to the airport.

Mel Gibson appears in an unbilled cameo as a punk tattoo artist with assorted body piercings.

Despite the fact that Crystal and Williams vigorously promoted the film on television (including NBC's blockbuster "Friends," which, like *Fathers' Day*, is a property of Time-Warner), the film received a lukewarm reception, taking in a relatively weak $28.6 million in two and a half months before disappearing from *Variety*'s list of the sixty top-grossing films. Both stars, as well as Reitman and producer Joel Silver (the *Lethal Weapon* and *Die Hard* films), greatly admired *Les Comperes* and were excited about the prospect of remaking it. Silver has said that he knew translating the original for American consumption would be an easy task with the right people on board. Unfortunately, something was, indeed, lost in that translation. While Francis Veber, who wrote and directed *Les Comperes*, served as executive producer for *Fathers' Day*, the script was given the Hollywood treatment by talented screenwriters Lowell Ganz and Babaloo Mandel, who penned Crystal's *City Slickers* (1991) and *Forget Paris* (1995). Their *Fathers' Day*, however, is not as funny as you would expect with the people involved. It is certainly not as clever or charming as the film it was based on, which *Variety* re-

CREDITS

Dale Putney: Robin Williams
Jack Lawrence: Billy Crystal
Scott Andrews: Charlie Hofheimer
Collette Andrews: Nastassja Kinski
Carrie Lawrence: Julia Louis-Dreyfus
Bob Andrews: Bruce Greenwood
Lee: Jared Harris
Shirley Trainor: Patti D'Arbanville

Origin: USA
Released: 1997
Production: Joel Silver and Ivan Reitman for Silver Pictures and Northern Lights Entertainment; released by Warner Bros.
Direction: Ivan Reitman
Screenplay: Lowell Ganz and Babaloo Mandel; based on the film *Les Comperes* by Francis Veber
Cinematography: Stephen H. Burum
Editing: Sheldon Kahn, Wendy Greene Bricmont
Music: James Newton Howard
Production design: Thomas Sanders
Art direction: Daniel T. Dorrance
Costumes: Rita Ryack
Sound: Gene S. Cantamessa, Clark King
MPAA rating: PG-13
Running Time: 98 minutes

ferred to as "brisk, amusing and warm-hearted . . . the film has rhythm, color and feeling." While it is sometimes painfully clear where Reitman and company expected big laughs, most of the film's scenes fall uncomfortably flat, generating only mild amusement. When Bruce Greenwood tumbling down the side of a hill in a portable toilet gets some of the biggest laughs in the theater, something is wrong with the material given the two comedic powerhouses in the lead roles. Considering its raw materials, this *Fathers' Day* gives surprisingly little reason to celebrate.

—*David L. Boxerbaum*

REVIEWS

Boxoffice. July, 1997, p. 92.
Chicago Tribune. May 9, 1997, p. 5.
Entertainment Weekly. May 23, 1997, p. 39.
Hollywood Reporter. March 5, 1997, p. 5.
Los Angeles Times. May 9, 1997, p. F1.
New York. May 26, 1997, p. 66.
New York Times. May 9, 1997, p. C3.
New Yorker. May 19, 1997, p. 96.
People. May 19, 1997, p. 21.
Sight and Sound. October, 1997, p. 48.
USA Today. May 9, 1997, p. 13D.
Variety. May 5, 1997, p. 67.
Wall Street Journal. May 9, 1997, p. A16.
Washington Post. May 9, 1997, p. D7.

Female Perversions

It's all about power.—Movie tagline
"Tantalizing! Enormously provocative."—Stephen Farber, *Movieline*
"Stunning! Highly erotic!"—*San Francisco Bay Times*

Box Office: $967,203

Female Perversions is not what the title implies. Far from pornography, this is an effort to make a film out of a feminist neo-Freudian treatise by Louise Kaplan ("Female Perversions: The Temptations of Emma Bovary") on the restraints of gender roles. A scholarly polemic is not a fertile place from which to grow a screenplay, however, and the script by director Susan Streitfeld and Julie Herbert is strained. Despite some elegantly rendered scenes and intriguing concepts, *Female Perversions* falls flat on its face, a victim of its own clumsy and heavy-handed pretensions.

The only discernible plot of the film has possibilities, though it proves limited. Razor-sharp, ambitious, and attractive attorney Eve Stephens (Tilda Swinton) is on the verge of being appointed to a vacancy on the California Court of Appeals. A dedicated careerist, she wants badly to be a judge. But her plans are endangered when, on the eve of her interview with the governor, her sister Maddie (Amy Madigan) is arrested for shoplifting.

In appearance and temperament, Maddie is Eve's opposite, though they prove to be two sides of the same familial coin. Maddie, like Eve, is simultaneously on the verge of a nervous breakdown and a career breakthrough. She is studying for her final defense of her doctoral thesis, which is about a Mexican village where women wield power. But when Eve goes to Maddie's desert home to defend her, she discovers that her sister is a kleptomaniac.

A reasonable assumption by viewers would be that Maddie's transgressions might damage Eve's ambitions. That seems to be borne out when, in Eve's make-or-break interview, the governor starts asking Eve questions about her sister. In these days of close scrutiny of political officeholders, any governor presumably would know of a prospective appointee's familial skeletons in the closet, especially any sisters who possess arrest records and are currently facing charges. But *Female Perversions* does not stoop to follow the logical plot devices of conventional films, and the potential issue of public revelation of private matters evaporates. Eve believes she has blown the interview, but only because she is not married or engaged and thus does not embody sufficient family values. She does blame her sister, but only because Maddie has stolen her lucky power suit and Eve has to wear an inferior outfit to meet the governor.

Madelyn: "I steal to stop me from killing myself."

The makers of *Female Perversions* are interested in dramatic tension of the inner, psychological kind. The film is more a character study than a drama, and it is peopled with stereotypes—or archetypes, if you prefer to subscribe to the script's high-brow pretensions. The primary tension of the film is within the tortured psyche of Eve. Behind her velvet, extremely competent exterior is a morass of self-doubt and self-loathing.

Eve, as is obvious from her name, is meant to be a sort of prototypical modern woman. She is torn between her drive for success and the demands of femininity. Director Streitfeld uses devices which hammer audiences over the head to make sure we understand Eve's demons. Practicing her signature as a judge, she hallucinates that she is being throttled by a man who calls her vulgar, lewd and disgusting, so we can understand that the image of women as degraded sex objects constantly punctures Eve's attempts to succeed in a man's world. Later, when she erupts in a profane torrent of lawyerly abuse—making threats on behalf of her client— she imagines being scolded by a maternal figure who berates her for being a domineering bitch.

Thus, while on the surface Everywoman Eve is in charge, in fact she is at the mercy of the demons which the filmmakers contend are plaguing every woman who seeks to break out of her gender constraints. It's a strident and perhaps outdated point of view, which gives *Female Perversions* the feel of a film of the 1960s rather than the 1990s. While it is undeniable that any professional woman has such inner voices tugging to keep her in line with old notions of traditional femininity, the question that remains is why for Eve these voices rage so strongly that they threaten to destroy her utterly.

The answer that is proposed is that Eve is restricted by "female perversions." The suggestion is that her power is constantly constrained by her meticulous attention to makeup, dress, voice, and manner. This is unsatisfactory in several respects. For one, the world of the 1990s and the film itself are populated by other successful women—a young psychiatrist, Renee (Karen Sillas), and an attorney who is being groomed to succeed Eve (Paulina Porizkova),—all of whom seem to have their heads on straight. And, Eve herself is succeeding in her world—she is brilliant and powerful and sexy, all at the same time, and she is about to be rewarded with a position of power. Far from denying her sexuality in order to climb the ladder of success, she is comfortable enough with it to seduce both a male lover (Clancy Brown) and the doctor with an office down the hall (Sillas) with equal fervor. Eve clearly is capable enough to be a judge, despite her self-doubts. The insistent drumbeat of *Female Perversions*—the idea that cosmetics and obsession with appearance undermine power—is didactic and implausible.

The film's explanation to why Eve is so befuddled lies in murky flashbacks —mostly occurring while Eve has sex—that suggest Oedipal motivations stemming from Eve's observations of her father rejecting her mother's sexual advances. These dreams coincide with images of Eve balancing on a tightrope, the rope pulled taut by figures wearing the masks of king and queen. While these sequences are intriguingly photographed, they are annoyingly simplistic. Eve Stephens would never argue a court case in as obvious and silly a fashion as Streitfeld argues the film's psychological thesis.

Also annoyingly pedestrian are the Godard-like devices that pop up in the first part of the film: polemical messages on TV sets, park benches, phone booths, and even Eve's pillowcase. "Perversion keeps despair, anxiety, and depression at bay," announces a typical one. Startlingly clumsy, these messages spell out the thesis of the film, and seem to indicate a director who's not confident enough in her plot to let audiences decipher the point of the movie on their own. After awhile, these messages disappear, as if Streitfeld had thought better of the device.

Rising exquisitely above all this murky mess is the luminous, striking Swinton. In *Orlando* (1992), her other major role, she was androgyny personified. Here, she plies the opposite end of the spectrum of gender, attending constantly to shoring up the various facades of femininity. Even in casual clothes, she is constantly aware of her appearance. Her whole life is sculpted, dressed up, calculated to impress. Swinton's performance—hot and cool, raging and muted—is so complex and so finely tuned it almost salvages the film. And Madigan, playing her usual tomboy type, is nicely muted for a change.

Unfortunately, many of the film's minor characters are cardboard figures. They obviously exist to portray various warring aspects of the female personality. The stereotypes include a cynical sexpot, Annunciata (Frances Fisher), who uses men for her own satisfaction; Emma (Laila Robins), an hysterical woman desperate for love and marriage; and Emma's tomboyish, confused daughter Edwina (Dale Shugar), who is struggling with puberty and menstruation. When this trio gets together with Eve for a weird encounter in a motel room, Streitfeld seems to be striving for a David Lynch effect, but the scene ends up laughable, with Annunciata performing a striptease among mannequins while giving lessons on seduction and Emma uttering the most implausible line of many implausible lines in the film. "Archetypal?" she casually inquires during the course of a conversation about gender roles.

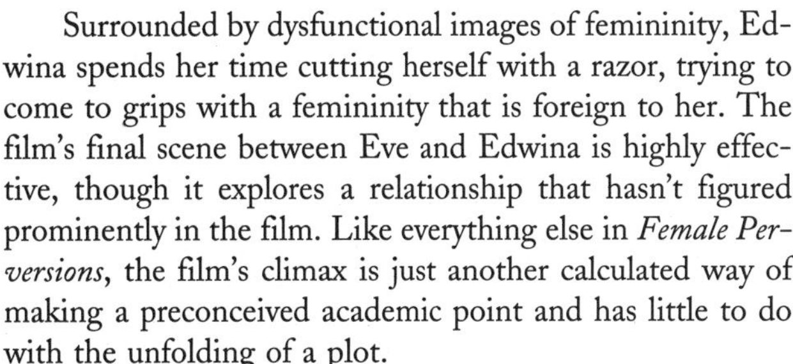

Surrounded by dysfunctional images of femininity, Edwina spends her time cutting herself with a razor, trying to come to grips with a femininity that is foreign to her. The film's final scene between Eve and Edwina is highly effective, though it explores a relationship that hasn't figured prominently in the film. Like everything else in *Female Perversions*, the film's climax is just another calculated way of making a preconceived academic point and has little to do with the unfolding of a plot.

The main problem with *Female Perversions* is that when its archetypes interact, nothing interesting happens. The film is all interior, but the interior isn't at all subtle and not very profound. It's a stuffy, muddled film.

But there are some startling, successful images and scenes. Among them is Eve's prickly encounter with a gas-station attendant who offends her by offering to pump her gas. It's a neat synopsis of the confused state of everyday relationships between men and women in the post-feminist world. Also effective is a scene showing Eve making a complex legal argument while the men in the courtroom dress her down with their eyes; Streitfeld makes the camera itself into a leering voyeur. And Eve's seduction of Renee in a hammock is a delicately steamy and believable lesbian encounter. It's not that Streitfeld doesn't know how to mount a fascinating scene. It's obvious from the intriguing images in *Female Perversions* that this director has talent. She just keeps stumbling over a script that is more like a textbook than a movie.

—Michael Betzold

CREDITS

Eve: Tilda Swinton
Madelyn: Amy Madigan
Renee: Karen Sillas
Emma: Laila Robins
John: Clancy Brown
Annunciata: Frances Fisher
Langley: Paulina Porizkova
Ed: Dale Shuger
Margot: Lisa Jane Persky
Jake: John Diehl

Origin: USA
Released: 1996
Production: Mindy Affrime for MAP Films and Trans Atlantic Entertainment; released by October Films
Direction: Susan Streitfeld
Screenplay: Susan Streitfeld and Julie Hebert; based on the book *Female Perversions: The Temptations of Emma Bovary* by Louise J. Kaplan
Cinematography: Teresa Medina
Editing: Curtiss Clayton, Leo Trombetta
Music: Debbie Wiseman
Production design: Missy Stewart
Costumes: Angela Billows
MPAA rating: R
Running Time: 119 minutes

REVIEWS

Boxoffice. November, 1996, p. 140.
Detroit Free Press. January 25, 1998, p. 8G.
Film Threat. January, 1997, p. 53.
Los Angeles Times. April 25, 1997, p. F10.
New York Times. April 25, 1997, p. C8.
Sight and Sound. May, 1997, p. 43.
Variety. January 29, 1996, p. 65.
Village Voice. April 29, 1997, p. 82.

Fierce Creatures

Don't pet them.—Movie tagline

"Untamed laughs! An outrageous comedy."—Sara Edwards, *NBC News Channel*

"Non-stop fun, a must-see comedy."—Jim Ferguson, *Prevue Channel*

"Wildly, outrageously, fiercely funny!"—Paul Wunder, *WBAI*

"Absolute, off-the-wall lunacy! Unrelentingly funny!"—Jeffrey Lyons, *WNBC*

Box Office: $9,381,260

Corporate downsizing takes on a whole new dimension when a multinational conglomerate headquartered in Atlanta gains control of a small English zoo. The new owner, the Murdoch-esque Rod McCain (Kevin Kline), demands a 20% return on all his capital investments, so he brings in Hong Kong executive Rollo Lee (John Cleese) to raise the profit level of the zoo. Lee attempts to do this by enacting a plan to satisfy the public's demands for excitement, danger, risk, and violence. "I want a lethal weapon in every cage," he announces to the zoo's keepers. "What do we do with the other ones?" one keeper asks, worried about all the soft and cuddly animals in the zoo. "Simply get rid of them," Rollo cold-bloodedly replies.

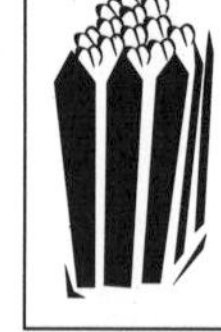

When asked if he has any experience with animals, Rollo Lee answers, "Well, I've eaten them, haven't I?"

At first the keepers (among whom are Michael Palin, Ronnie Corbett, and Cleese's own daughter Cynthia) try to revamp the characters of their favorite animals hoping Rollo will change his mind if they change a few cage signs: "The meerkat is known as the piranha of the desert! It can strip a corpse clean in three minutes!" However, the animals' cute antics betray their keepers' attempts at good-intentioned character assassination. The keepers then decide that if Rollo wants to enforce the laws of the corporate jungle within Marwood Zoo, he'll just have to get rid of the animals himself. Consequently they plop five of the zoo's cuddliest inhabitants (coati, lemur, baby ostrich, baby wallaby, and mara) on Rollo's desk and walk out knowing no one could possibly kill them. However, in the distance they hear five gunshots and when they run to find Rollo, he's patting dirt onto five tiny graves.

One of the scenes cut from the final version of *Fierce Creatures* was that in which Kevin Kline played a third role, his mother.

Enter into the picture Willa Weston (Jamie Lee Curtis), a high-powered executive just hired by McCain's Octopus Inc. to run a radio network. But, when she shows up for work on her first day, Rod has already sold the station. With the help of Rod's worthless, unloved and embezzling son Vince (also Kevin Kline), Willa convinces Rod to give her control of the newly acquired zoo. However, the smitten Vince, who can't help drooling over Willa (whose business suits can be found in a Victoria's Secret catalogue), also convinces his father to send him along to help.

When Willa and Vince arrive with their own ideas about how to run the zoo, they immediately demote Rollo and give him a new office. . . . an outdoor animal cage. Thus humiliated, the only two things Rollo has going for him are that the zoo keepers flock to his side when they find out he has not really killed their animals but has secreted them in his own apartment, and the fact that Willa has mistakenly come to believe that Rollo is quite a ladies' man, and this has piqued her curiosity.

Meanwhile, Vince is busy enacting his own plan to make the zoo as profitable as possible: sponsorship. Soon the zoo keepers (who have great names like Cub Felines, Sydney Small Mammals, Reggie Sealions, Gerry Ungulates, Hugh Primates, etc.) are wearing colorful safari suits blanketed with corporate logos, animals become the "property" of one celebrity or another (Bruce Springsteen's turtle), and even the animals are pressed into service as walking billboards (the Absolutetiger).

As Willa, Rollo, and the zoo keepers join forces to save the zoo animals, they make an interesting discovery: Vince has again been syphoning off funds from his father's businesses and has pocketed all the money his tacky sponsorship campaign has brought in. Rod quickly becomes fed up with his son, and the unprofitable zoo, and plans to turn Marwood into a golf course. Now how will the animals be saved?

Fierce Creatures reunites the four leads (Cleese, Curtis, Kline, and Palin) from 1988's *A Fish Called Wanda*, the second most successful British film ever made, which took in more than $200 million in worldwide box office receipts and garnered three Oscar nominations (supporting actor, screenplay and director), winning one for Kevin Kline as best supporting actor. However, this is not a sequel. Instead, everyone involved is calling *Fierce Creatures* an "equal."

Actor/producer/writer Cleese thought briefly about making a *Wanda 2*, but decided, as most critics have come to realize, that sequels are usually failures. However, as Cleese said, "If you've got a really good team, why not work together again?" Why not, indeed? What he didn't know at the time was that it would take eight years, two directors, several rewrites, some last-minute reshoots, and many delays before the *Wanda* team could be enjoyed by audiences again. (In fact, for a while, this "equal" was even being called Dead Fish 2.)

Rather than just do another story about *Wanda*'s incompetent thieves, Cleese was inspired by visits to a wildlife preserve in Jersey, England, and by a pre-Monty Python sketch written by Palin and fellow Python alum Terry Jones about a zoo with only scary animals. So, in 1992 Cleese and Iain Johnstone, a *London Sunday Times* film critic and first-time screenwriter, began to write the script that would become *Fierce Creatures.*

Finally, in the summer of 1995, the script was filmed. But when Universal screened it for a test audience, their reaction was less than enthusiastic. (They liked most of the film but hated the ending—Rollo and Vince were both gored to death by a rhino.) Everyone agreed a rewrite and a reshoot was needed, but there was just one hitch: Michael Palin had just set off on one of his BBC/PBS Around the World jaunts—this time around the Pacific Rim—and wouldn't be back for eight months. Although Universal suggested shooting an ending without his character, Cleese refused, and *Fierce Creatures* was put on hold, missing its original release date.

In the meantime, Cleese and Johnstone worked on a revised conclusion with the help of an uncredited William Goldman who lives in the same building in Manhattan as Cleese. When Michael Palin was finally available for reshoots, Cleese was faced with another problem. The film's original director, Robert Young, was already working on his next movie, *Jane Eyre.* Into the breech stepped Australian director Fred Schepisi (*Roxanne*, *A Cry in the Dark*, *Six Degrees of Separation*), who was preparing to direct Cleese and Robin Williams in *Don Quixote.* Schepisi also brought along his cinematographer, Ian Baker, to replace Adrian Biddle who was also not available. Finally, after three weeks of reshoots, the film was in the can. It was worth the wait. *Fierce Creatures* is a gently funny film with a well-written story that manages to be superseded by some of the most interesting characters a comedy could ask for.

In one respect, Rollo is vintage John Cleese. He starts out as the typically stiff and stuffy Cleese character undone by his own pompousness, but here we're allowed a glimpse of the heart below the facade. Watching him try to carry on a phone conversation as he is overrun by five fugitive cuddlies, or listening as he commits one Freudian slip after another in the presence of Curtis' Willa is a real treat.

Curtis again proves herself most adept at playing a woman with brains and sex appeal, and at playing her with more than a dash of humor. Getting to the heart of her character, Curtis calls Willa a corporate slut. It's an apt description, until her character discovers the beauty of the animals in her charge, that is.

To Michael Palin went the role that was most different from that which he had in *Wanda.* In the first film he could barely get out a line of dialogue for the stutter given his character. Here, however, Palin's zookeeper in charge of insects, Bugsy Malone, never shuts up—to hilarious effect.

But it's Kline who once again walks off with the film. Playing dual roles (just as he did in *Dave*) and with minimum make-up, Kline once again proves his mastery of the actor's craft, playing both the belching, macho, unfeeling Rod and the drooling, inept, narcissistic Vince.

CREDITS

Rollo Lee: John Cleese
Willa Weston: Jamie Lee Curtis
Vince McCain/Rod McCain: Kevin Kline
Adrian "Bugsy" Malone: Michael Palin
Reggie Sealions: Ronnie Corbett
Cub Felines: Carey Lowell
Sydney Small Mammals: Robert Lindsay
Neville Coltrane: Bille Brown
Gerry Ungulates: Derek Griffiths
Pip Small Mammals: Cynthia Cleese
Hugh Primates: Richard Ridings
Di Amin: Maria Aitken

Origin: USA
Released: 1997
Production: Michael Shamberg and John Cleese for Fish Productions/Jersey Films; released by Universal Pictures
Direction: Robert Young, Fred Schepisi
Screenplay: John Cleese, Iain Johnstone
Cinematography: Adrian Biddle
Editing: Robert Gibson
Production design: Roger Murray-Leach
Art direction: David Allday, Kevin Phipps
Set decoration: Brian Read, Stephanie McMillan, Peter Howitt
Costumes: Hazel Pethig
Music: Jerry Goldsmith
Animal consultant: Rona Brown
Chief animal trainer: Jim Clubb
Sound: Chris Munro
MPAA rating: PG-13
Running Time: 93 minutes

REVIEWS

Boxoffice. March, 1997, p. 44.
Chicago Tribune. January 24, 1997.
Entertainment Weekly. January 24, 1997, p. 38.
The Hollywood Reporter. January 21, 1997, p. 12.
Los Angeles Times. January 24, 1997.
New York Times. January 24, 1997, p. C5.
New Yorker. February 3, 1997, p. 85.
People. January 27, 1997, p. 21.
Premiere. January, 1996, p. 30.
Sight and Sound. March, 1997, p. 46.
Time. January 27, 1997.
USA Today. January 24, 1997, p. 3D.
Variety. January 20, 1997, p. 44.

Place this entertaining crew in a good story and in a setting that's positively inspired (a whole zoo was created by production designer Roger Murray-Leach on Pinewood Studio's back lot) and the result is a farce that has energy, silliness, warmth, and a lot of laughs. There may not be a lot of thigh-slapping guffaws in *Fierce Creatures*, but it has plenty of cute animals, silly costumes, and sight gags for the kids, and double entendres, social commentary, and plot twists to keep the adults interested.

—*Beverley Bare Buehrer*

The Fifth Element

It must be found. There is no future without it.—Movie tagline

"A futuristic, eye-popping adventure! It's like nothing you've ever seen before with knock-out special effects."—Bill Diehl, *ABC Radio Network*

"The thrill ride of the decade!"—Taylor Baldwin, *CBS-TV*

"Wildly imaginative, but even better, it's funny."—Leonard Maltin, *Entertainment Tonight*

"A jaw-dropping, mind-blowing epic. Astonishingly ingenious, exuberantly exciting and brazenly hilarious!"—Joe Leydon, *NBC-TV*

"An entertaining blast! Stunning visual effects and eye-popping costuming."—Jami Bernard, *New York Daily News*

"Eye-popping images. Jovovich is a sexy sensation. Willis is the life of the party. The movie is a visual knockout. Besson's film has the lunatic poetry of a really fun dream."—Peter Travers, *Rolling Stone*

"Two thumbs up!"—*Siskel & Ebert*

"High-voltage fun! Your eyes are always thrilled!"—Desson Howe, *Washington Post*

Box Office: $63,820,180

One of the very first overpriced and overproduced intended blockbusters of the 1997 summer season was *The Fifth Element*, a science-fiction extravaganza that reputedly

Bruce Willis finds himself in a predicament with this alien army in the futuristic *The Fifth Element.*

cost $90 million to make. The money invested certainly shows in the film's visual design that puts all the emphasis on a continuing and dazzling spectacle serving cardboard characters caught up in a plot that makes no sense whatsoever. The film was conjured out of the childish imagination of French boy-wonder Luc Besson who wrote the first draft for the story at the age of 16, but viewers should not be misled by the Gaumont logo that appears in the credits, or the fact that this picture opened the Cannes Film Festival. This would-be blockbuster released by Columbia Pictures has all the expected "elements" of an overdone Hollywood summer spectacle—peculiar alien creatures, fashion-plate costumes by Jean-Paul Gaultier, a nonsensical story, often impressive but ultimately meaningless special effects, and, of course, Bruce Willis, praised by one reviewer for his "muscular intensity and droll, sardonic energy." Willis is cast as an American Everyman destined to help save the planet.

The film starts with a flashback to 1914 that recalls *Raiders of the Lost Ark* (1981) and involves a visitation by friendly aliens called Mondoshawans (Janet Maslin of *The New York Times* accurately described them as looking like "half-hubcaps with tiny insect heads") to a temple in Egypt. This prologue explains the "elements," represented by four stone tablets and a magical key. According to the fabricated mythic framework, planet Earth is visited every 5,000 years by an "evil" death star that these friendly aliens help to ward off by some sort of metaphysical device involving the four elements (earth, air, fire, and water) represented by the carved stones. The "fifth element" comes 300 years later in the person of a "supreme being." The next visitation is scheduled for the year 2214, the main time-frame for the movie.

> Leeloo: "Everything you create, you use to destroy."
> Korben: "Yeah, we call it human nature."

The "fifth element" turns out to be a space chic fashion model named Leeloo (Milla Jovovich), a so-called "perfect being" whose mission it is to save the planet, but she needs help. Her helpmates are a gentle monk named Cornelius (British actor Ian Holm is much too good for this silly role, but that's show business) and a cab driver named Korben Dallas (Bruce Willis). By the year 2214, taxicabs are airborne, and Leeloo, escaping from the laboratory that revived her, drops into Korben's taxi. Korben eludes the police who are in pursuit of Leeloo and takes her to his apartment. Though he can hardly understand her when she jabbers on about a "big badda-boom," he agrees to help her in her quest. Cornelius turns up to help explain the dilemma and clarify the problem, so far as clarification is possible. All the "elements" must be combined in order to ward off the "evil" threat of the fireball death-star, described by critic Nigel Floyd as "a giant sphere of anti-energy that threatens to consume every living organism in the universe."

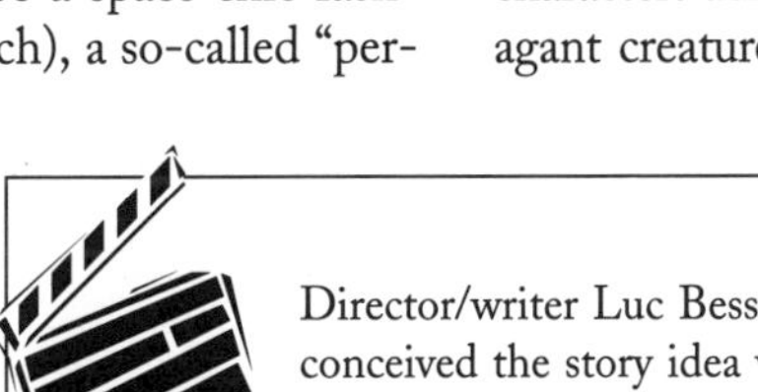

Director/writer Luc Besson conceived the story idea when he was 16.

Gary Oldman plays an extravagant villain named Zorg, whose motives are never clearly explained, probably because they do not make sense and cannot be explained. For some reason he seems intent upon assuring the destruction of Earth, though how that would be to his advantage, no one can say. He just seems committed to evil deeds and devices. Chris Tucker plays an even more extravagant flaming creature named Ruby Rhod, a talk-show host and celebrity parasite who joins the others as an entertainer on a space cruise called Fhloston Paradise. His function is never explained but is obviously intended as a bizarre comic diversion to fill up empty spaces in the plot. Rhod appears to be a Dennis Rodman clone whose flamboyance and babbling presence is extremely irritating, though intended, no doubt, to be amusing. Chris Tucker is a stand-up comedian turned actor here, to ill effect. Owen Gleiberman described his "super-freak entertainment queen" as being "like Rodman, Little Richard, RuPaul, and Urkel stirred up in the same cocktail shaker—a vision of the human soul baptized in media. He's so much he's too much, just like the movie." Gary Arnold, adding Stepin Fetchit and Willie Best to Rhod's amalgam, concluded that Tucker wears out "his welcome on very short acquaintance." If Ruby Rhod is the face of the future, then maybe a "big badda-boom" would be an appropriate solution.

Leeloo's mission to save the planet is made action-adventure plausible once she is given Bruce Willis as a sidekick. At least Willis and Ian Holm give the movie what little down-to-earth ballast it is allowed. They are at least quasi-realistic characters adrift in a population of freaks, aliens, and extravagant creatures. Gary Oldman's Zorg is constantly over the top, as is his costuming and make-up. He is a sort of split personality. Half of his head is punk-normal, the other half is encased in a transparent plastic dome, for no reason, other than to astonish. Zorg is commander-in-chief of an army of alien mercenaries called Mangalores, who are up to no good.

This is a deceptive picture that seems to be more international than it in fact is. Gary Oldman was born in South London (New Cross) and came to cinema via London's Royal Court Theatre. Ian Holm is another well regarded British actor, once associated with the Royal Shakespeare Company and a fine Polonius in Franco Zeffirelli's filmed *Hamlet* (1990). Milla Jovovich was born in Kiev and emigrated with her family to Sacramento from her native Ukraine in 1975. Producer Patrice Ledoux holds a Doctorate of Literature from the University of Paris. Cinematographer Thierry Arbogast is French, as is costume designer Jean-Paul Gaultier, and writer-director Luc Besson, born in Paris in 1959. But the spirit of this gaudy thing is absolutely American. It is nothing more than a Bruce Willis action-

AWARDS AND NOMINATIONS

Academy Awards 1997 Nominations: Sound Effects Editing
BAFTA 1997 Nominations: Special effects
Cesar Awards 1998: Director (Besson), Cinematography
Nominations: Best Film

adventure extravaganza set in a peculiarly imagined future.

The Fifth Element was selected to open the Cannes Film Festival in May, marking the 50th anniversary of the Festival, which Owen Gleiberman of *Entertainment Weekly* found "the most garish of ironies," since this movie "represents the annihilation of everything Cannes has stood for." The futuristic design of this extravaganza makes the spectacle work as spectacle, but there is no intelligent substance here. Plot logic falters constantly. Gary Oldman described the project as "*Star Wars* on acid." Leeloo is surely an astonishing humanoid creature whose attempts to learn English are sometimes amusing, an inarticulate wonder who is sometimes cute and other times downright spooky. At least she represents an original concept in a film that is otherwise derivative and packed with sci-fi clichés. The film's screenplay by Besson and Robert Mark Kamen, based on the story Besson himself cooked up, borrows shamelessly from other, better pictures: *Star Trek* (1979), *Star Wars* (1977), *Blade Runner* (1982), *Total Recall* (1990), *Die Hard* (1988), and *Stargate* (1994).

To give Besson credit, the film's special effects are often astonishing. The film's visual design created by Mark Stetson's Digital Domain's special visual effects team and influenced by the work of "two legendary French comicbook artists, Moebius and Jean-Claude Mézières," according to Nigel Floyd of *Sight and Sound*, sets new standards for science fiction cinema. The three-dimensional city of the future visualized in *The Fifth Element* and the police chase when Dallas rescues Leeloo offer eye-popping wonders. An-

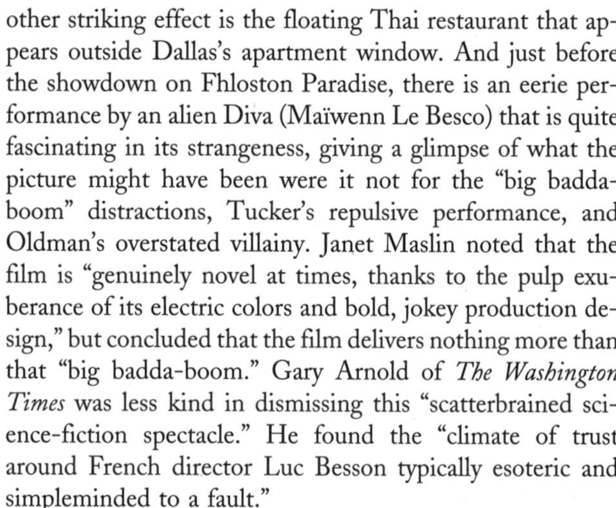

other striking effect is the floating Thai restaurant that appears outside Dallas's apartment window. And just before the showdown on Fhloston Paradise, there is an eerie performance by an alien Diva (Maïwenn Le Besco) that is quite fascinating in its strangeness, giving a glimpse of what the picture might have been were it not for the "big badda-boom" distractions, Tucker's repulsive performance, and Oldman's overstated villainy. Janet Maslin noted that the film is "genuinely novel at times, thanks to the pulp exuberance of its electric colors and bold, jokey production design," but concluded that the film delivers nothing more than that "big badda-boom." Gary Arnold of *The Washington Times* was less kind in dismissing this "scatterbrained science-fiction spectacle." He found the "climate of trust around French director Luc Besson typically esoteric and simpleminded to a fault."

Luc Besson became an international success as a result of *La Femme Nikita* (1991), about a drug-addicted woman conditioned to become a government assassin. This was followed by *The Professional* (1994), in which Jean Reno played a hit-man who protects a young girl whose family has been assassinated. Gary Oldman played a renegade government agent in *The Professional*, which earned Besson Cesar nominations for best director and best picture. *The Professional* was an odd love story, stylishly done, with a questionable premise. The same could be said of *The Fifth Element*, the first sci-fi time-waster of the summer season.

Describing his work habits for the Columbia Pictures press-release, Besson wrote "on my first draft I never think of realistic needs—I just put down on paper everything that I'd love to see. I just like to go for it, and I consider the serious questions later." *The Fifth Element* shows ample evidence that the writer-director went for it, but, unfortunately, he never got around to dealing with "the serious questions" in any kind of coherent way. The film is too extravagant and jokey for its own good.

—*James M. Welsh*

CREDITS

Korben Dallas: Bruce Willis
Leeloo: Milla Jovovich
Zorg: Gary Oldman
Cornelius: Ian Holm
Ruby Rhod: Chris Tucker
Billy: Luke Perry
General Munro: Brion James

Origin: France
Released: 1997
Production: Patrice Ledoux for Gaumont; released by Columbia Pictures
Direction: Luc Besson
Screenplay: Luc Besson, Robert Mark Kamen
Cinematography: Thierry Arbogast
Editing: Sylvie Landra
Music: Eric Serra
Costumes: Jean-Paul Gaultier
Production design: Dan Weil
Special visual effects supervisor: Mark Stetson
MPAA rating: PG-13
Running Time: 105 minutes

REVIEWS

Boxoffice. July, 1997, p. 91.
Chicago Tribune. May 9, 1997, p. 4.
Cinescape. May/June, 1997, p. 21.
Entertainment Weekly. May 16, 1997, p. 84.
The Hollywood Reporter. May 7, 1997, p. 12.
Los Angeles Times. May 9, 1997, p. F1.
The New York Times. May 9, 1997, p. B3.
People. May 19, 1997, p. 21.
Rolling Stone. May 29, 1997, p. 55.
Sight and Sound. June, 1997, p. 6.
USA Today. May 9, 1997, p. 13D.
Variety. May 12, 1997, p. 63.
Village Voice. May 20, 1997, p. 71.
The Washington Times Metropolitan Times. May 9, 1997, p. C16.

Fire Down Below

Beneath a land of wealth and beauty hides a secret that could kill millions. Undercover has never run so deep.—Movie tagline

Box Office: $16,254,149

Fire Down Below is another Steven Seagal film that offers up yet another, soft-spoken, tightly-wound hero, friend to the environment and underdog who lashes out with expert kicks and punches when he has no other recourse. Produced by Seagal as a vehicle to highlight both his passion for preserving the environment and whooping ass, this film brings another love of Seagal's to the forefront—country music. As hard as it is to believe, Seagal plays guitar and croons a tune in this film.

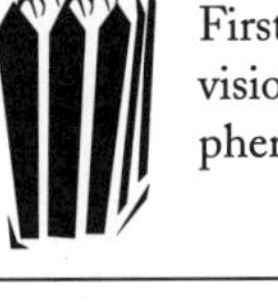

First feature film for veteran television director and cinematographer Felix Enrique Alcala.

EPA agent Jack Taggart (Steven Seagal) arrives in a small Kentucky town in Appalachia that has apparently swallowed up three previous EPA agents who dispatched there on a tip that there was a mysterious "disease" polluting the waters and making the locals sick. Jack enters the town under the guise of a do-gooder needing rehab, and he is put up by the local preacher (Levon Helm). Only the preacher knows Jack's real identity, so Jack is left attempting to wheedle information out of people while fixing their fence posts or repairing their front steps. Besides Jack's obvious passion for his job and the environment, Jack is determined to avenge the EPA agents' death—one of them was a good friend.

Appalachia folks are a suspicious sort, so soon Jack is the object of a lot of gossip and none-too-subtle harassment by the local goons—even the sheriff himself. Jack gravitates towards two people that seem slightly less hostile than the others, Cotton (Harry Dean Stanton) and Sarah (Marg Helgenberger). Jack notices that the rest of the townspeople shun Sarah, but she keeps to herself on the outskirts of town, raising bees and honey. Through back issues of the local newspaper, Jack gathers that Sarah was accused of killing her father when she was 16 years old, but later acquitted. When Earl (Stephen Lang), Sarah's brother appears, Sarah becomes nervous, visibly agitated. Earl works in the local mine, and tries to deflect Jack's inquires about its reported nocturnal activities. After Jack leaves the brother and sister, Earl threatens Sarah with thinly-veiled violence—both physical and sexual.

It doesn't take long for Jack to suspect that someone is dumping chemicals in the mine; besides the random rashes and sickness that the children exhibit, there is a slow-burning fire underground. By this time, the entire town is aware of Jack's presence, and Orin Jr. (Brad Hunt), the flunky son of wealthy, bullying, sleazy businessman Orin Sr. (Kris Kristofferson) reports to dad that the hulking, soft-spoken stranger is inquiring about issues that come too close to their "operation." Orin Sr. stops making money and cavorting with scantily-clad secretaries long enough to order the sheriff to "take care" of Jack. Jack is attacked by local boys, and makes short work of them through flashy kicks and karate chops. When Cotton reveals himself to be the anonymous letter writer that tipped off the EPA, he and Jack vow to help save the town and the people themselves. Unfortunately, Cotton is then beaten up by Orin Jr. and his pals.

Incensed, Jack interrupts Sunday church services and makes an impassioned plea to the locals; he begs them to consider their land, their heritage and the future of their children.

CREDITS

Jack Taggart: Steven Seagal
Sarah Kellogg: Marg Helgenberger
Earl: Stephen Lang
Orin Sr.: Kris Kristofferson
Orin Jr.: Brad Hunt
Cotton: Harry Dean Stanton
Reverend Goodall: Levon Helm
Sheriff Lloyd: Ed Bruce
Ken Adams: Randy Travis
Pratt: Richard Masur

Origin: USA
Released: 1997
Production: Steven Seagal and Julius Nasso; released by Warner Bros.
Direction: Felix Enriquez Alcala
Screenplay: Jeb Stuart and Philip Morton
Cinematography: Tom Houghton
Editing: Robert A. Ferretti
Music: Nick Glennie-Smith
Production design: Joe Alves
Costumes: Rosanna Norton
Sound: Charles Wilborn
Stunt coordinator: Bobby Brown
MPAA rating: R
Running Time: 95 minutes

His plea is met with fearful stares from frightened people. Jack and Sarah spend more time together; she is drawn to his quiet strength, he is drawn to her warmth and graciousness. Sarah confides that she knows there are shenanigans going on at the mines, and gives Jack detailed mine maps that were her late father's.

The town gathers for a musical get-together, and Jack demonstrates his rudimentary guitar/singing style. Orin Sr. appears and tries to bribe Jack to back away from his town. Jack refuses. The local tough guys once again try to crush Jack, but he easily overcomes them. Earl appears and confesses to Jack that his instincts are correct; there is a huge, profitable dumping operation at the mine. In fact, Earl offers to lead Jack to the exact spot where a dump will occur later that night.

When Sarah commends Earl for doing the right thing and assisting Jack in helping their town, he smugly informs her that he is going to lure Jack to his death, and when he returns, things are going to go back to the way they used to be between them. He then locks her in a closet. Jack arrives at the mine and is immediately attacked by Earl and his comrades. Jack manages to decimate them, set off an explosion and escape the mine. He rescues Sarah, and, with her testimony, manages to put away Orin Sr. for a very long time. Jack and Sarah vow to stay together.

The cinematography by Tom Houghton is first-rate, the supporting cast is excellent (a raft of country stars—from Levon Helm to Randy Travis make appearances), but nothing can detract from Seagal's lack of spark and charisma. His acting style consists of enunciating so softly that one strains to hear the dialogue, then exploding into violence, and in an action film of this genre, a magnetic leading character is a must.

—*G.E. Georges*

REVIEWS

Boxoffice. November, 1997, p. 133.
Detroit Free Press. September 6, 1997, p. 2A.
Entertainment Weekly. September 19, 1997, p. 60.
Los Angeles Times. September 8, 1997, p. F6.
New York Times. September 6, 1997, p. 18.
Variety. September 8, 1997, p. 76.

Flipping

Money. Betrayal. Murder. L.A. is still the place to be.—Movie tagline

"A major thunderclap of a movie—scary, powerful, electric. Go see it!"—Rod Lurie, *KMPC Radio*

"A taut, fast moving narrative."—Emanuel Levy, *Variety*

"An excellent cast brings a new vitality to roles we're quite familiar with, giving Joe Pesci and his boys a run for their money as the most regular-guy killers around!"—Frank Ruscetti, *Village Voice*

Flipping has been compared to the work of Quentin Tarantino and other stylish directors of criminal comedy dramas. Certainly writer/director Gene Mitchell, who also stars as Shot, an unstable gunman, creates characters with some of Tarantino's dash and merciless exposure of their stupidities. But there is a plaintive earnestness in the core plot of the film that makes *Flipping* stand out. There is also a sexual twist: Billy (David Proval) is a cop who has fallen in love with his snitch Michael (David Amos).

Billy narrates this film noir. Small, wiry, and intense, Billy has apparently spent his career among lowlifes. He does not seem to have much of a life outside his job. And he takes his work home with him when the handsome Michael becomes his lover. But this aspect of the story unfolds gradually through a series of flashbacks. In the foreground is Billy's effort to control Michael, to keep him from becoming implicating in the murder of his gangster boss, Leo Richards, played with consummate *savoir faire* by Keith David. Michael has already messed up on another case, and this time he is under strict orders from Billy not to do any of the shooting.

The Billy/Michael liaison is entirely unknown to the crew Michael works with. They are preoccupied with pleasing their boss Leo, who has already broken Shot's hand for irresponsibly lending Leo's money without asking Leo's permission. Shot is incorrigible. Although he recovers Leo's money—in a gruesome confrontation with the gambler in a parking lot—Shot immediately begins asking Leo for a cut of the money. Leo is enraged but then he settles down, offering his henchmen the possibility of making real money by killing his chief rival.

Leo's crew is suspicious. As Michael points out, Leo will get rid of them as soon as his rival is out of the way. Leo won't want any evidence of what he planned. So Michael proposes that they do the job for Leo and then kill Leo. These small-time thugs are aghast but desperate.

Michael coaxes Hooker (Shant Benjamin) to actually pull the trigger on Leo. Hooker is plainly terrified. The job is better suited to Shot—or to Michael. But that is the point, Michael insists, the obedient, conscientious Hooker is the last person Leo would suspect.

This plan does work—up to a point. But it gets accomplished as a farce, especially since it has evolved out of the very night on which Hooker is getting married. The wedding party has already been interrupted once because Shot has insisted on going after the gambler he lent Leo's money to. Now the rest of the night is spent in getting rid of Leo and his rival.

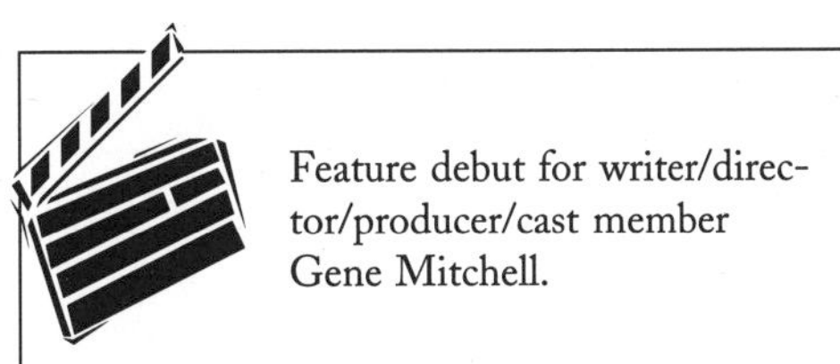

Feature debut for writer/director/producer/cast member Gene Mitchell.

CREDITS

Michael Moore: David Amos
Billy White: David Proval
Shot: Gene Mitchell
Hooker: Shant Benjamin
Joey: Barry Primus
Dennis: Paul Klar
Chuckie: Tony Burton
C.J.: Mike Starr
Leo Richards: Keith David

Origin: USA
Released: 1996
Production: Gene Mitchell, David Amos for Mon Frere Motion Pictures; released by Dove Entertainment
Direction: Gene Mitchell
Screenplay: Gene Mitchell
Cinematography: Phil Parmet
Editing: Kevin Krasny
Production design: Diane Hughes
Costumes: Nadine Reimer
Sound: Benjamin Patrick
MPAA rating: R
Running Time: 102 minutes

Billy shows up at the wedding to check up on Michael. At this point, the relationship between the two men is not entirely clear. Just how involved are they? As the plot against Leo progresses, the flashbacks to the affair between Billy and Michael make their connection clearer. Billy, it turns out, is just as obsessive and reckless as the criminals he pursues. He allows nothing to get in the way of his passions. And Michael is actually the one controlling the action—trying to placate Billy and to manipulate his crew.

It is Michael's drive for power that dooms both his affair with Billy and his career as a criminal. Overly ambitious, he cannot control the explosive elements of his life. Billy, on the other hand, has lost all perspective. He only cares about Michael and is in despair when he sees how Michael has messed up the plan to expose these criminals.

The pleasure of *Flipping* derives from the working out of the plot and the flashbacks, and it would be a shame to ruin that pleasure by bald plot summary. Suffice it to say, that when Billy has to step in to save Michael, it is too late, and Billy turns his anger and sense of betrayal against his lover, the criminal he cannot control, the man he cannot keep in his bed. This aspect of the film, which one critic has called a "gimmick," seems the very thing that makes *Flipping* distinctive. On the one hand, it is impossible to empathize with these characters, and yet on the other hand, their culture and the cop who tries to destroy it even as he becomes implicated in it, yield a fascinating study set apart from even the most unconventional crime dramas.

—Carl Rollyson

REVIEWS

Los Angeles Times. February 21, 1997, p. F15.
New York Times. March 7, 1997, p. B7.
Variety. January 22, 1996, p. 100.
Village Voice. March 11, 1997, p. 78.

Flubber

"*Flubber* is a knee-slapping, rib-tickling, side-splitting, gut-busting laugh-a-thon!"—Louis B. Hobson, *Calgary Sun*

"Robin Williams is at his zaniest."—Jeanne Wolf, *Jeanne Wolf's Hollywood*

"It's the best Robin Wiliams since *Mrs. Doubtfire.*"—Brian Sebastian, *Movie Reviews and More*

"Outrageously funny!"—Paul Wunder, *WBAI Radio*

Box Office: $77,217,495

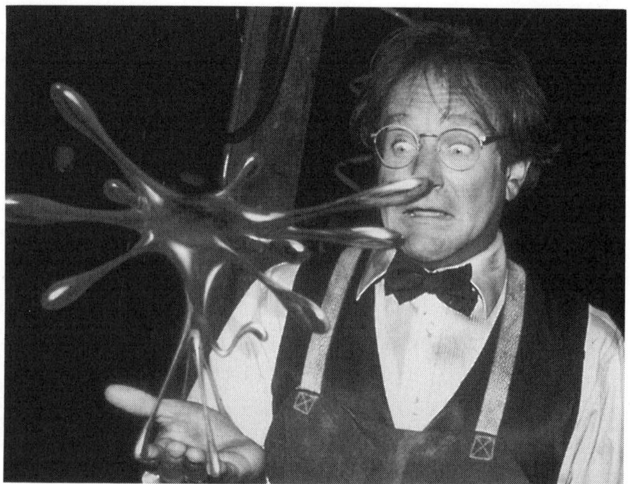

Disney remakes its 1961 classic, *The Absent-Minded Professor,* with Robin Williams as the inventor of a green elastic substance called *Flubber.*

With the comic talent of Robin Williams and the laughable potential of a glob of rubbery green goo, you'd think *Flubber* would be an easy hit. Instead, it's a dismal failure, not nearly as delightful as the silly original, *The Absent-Minded Professor* (1961), which starred Fred MacMurray. Neither Williams nor the flubber itself gets a chance to do much in this remake from the Disney studios.

The trouble with updating a comic script based on a scientific fantasy of the early 1960s is that science, technology and the moviemaking art can do so much more now. Flubber—flying rubber—was a high concept back then; now it's ho-hum. This updated version of flubber is so fluid and talented it can dance, laugh, duplicate itself and change shape with infinite grace. Blame the folks at Industrial Light and Magic, who got a license to run wild from director Les Mayfield. With the script meandering aimlessly, the film pauses for a nonsensical dance routine featuring the flubber in a Busby Berkeley tribute that will leave the kids in the audience puzzled. It's mildly entertaining but meaningless.

Philip Brainard to fiancee Sara Jean: "I love you on a subatomic level!"

The flubber of 1997 has become much more than a chemistry class experiment gone awry. With the aid of computer animation, it has become yet another cinematic gob of green stuff that can do and become virtually anything. It's a benign version of the green slime in *Ghostbusters* and the gelatinous green gremlins in *Anastasia.* Screenwriter John Hughes—an industry unto himself with his success from the *Home Alone* series—can't leave well enough alone. With Hughes as co-writer and co-producer, flubber has become cute and squeaky as well. It looks and acts like a trained seal. In this case, more is less. Because the animators can make it do anything at all, the moviemakers don't seem to know exactly what to do with the flubber. Their idea of inventiveness is to have Williams's Professor Philip Brainard spray it on golf balls and bowling balls which keep conking out a pair of goofy, bumbling goons—exactly the same characters Hughes has used in the *Home Alone* series.

The filmmakers have so little faith in the substance the film is named for that they give most of their creative ideas and good lines to another non-human character. It's a cute, sassy, sarcastic little flying computer/household appliance/personal secretary for Brainard. Weebo, which looks like a miniature flying saucer and acts like Tinkerbell, hogs more camera time than the flubber. It speaks with a coy feminine voice (supplied by Jodi Benson) and has an annoying habit of displaying old film clips—many of them from Disney—on a pop-up screen. These clips announce the emotion of the moment; when something is scary, up pops a cartoon character covering its eyes. This feature is amusing at first but soon becomes insulting. It's obviously being used too much as a sort of product endorsement for the Disney canon. And it leaves a disturbing gloss of irony over the picture, demonstrating that every act, every feeling and every situation can be cross-referenced to another snippet from the entertainment universe.

Weebo serves as Brainard's constant companion, functioning as the equivalent of one of those little animal cartoon sidekicks that are mandatory in Disney films. (There's another computerized appliance, too, but it mostly vacuums.) When the plot calls for Brainard to be reconciled with his love interest, Sara Jane Reynolds (Marcia Gay

Harden), Weebo acts as matchmaker, awakening Sara in her bedroom and showing her its videotape of Brainard declaring his love. When the bad guys steal the flubber despite Weebo's brave resistance, Brainard returns to find the computer-robot smashed and battered. There's a long, embarrassing scene in which Weebo "dies" as Williams, tears cascading down his cheeks, holds her and mourns. When a movie has to milk sympathy from an audience by having a computer "die," there's serious trouble. Brainard and Sara sit and bewail Weebo while they should be out chasing whomever stole the flubber. Of course, Weebo is so smart it figured out a way to give birth to a sportier model, so all the tears are wasted.

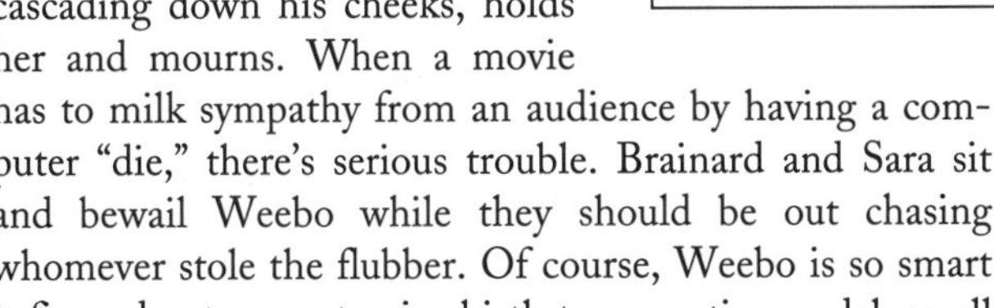
Nancy Olson, who played Sara Jean in the 1961 film, has a cameo.

The biggest problem with *Flubber* is a surprising one: Williams isn't funny. He's taken his manic act down to such a low-key level that his characterizations are at most mildly amusing. The plot, which has Williams trying to win back the affections of Sara after forgetting to show up at their wedding three times, centers around the professor as a poor, loveable, pathetic incompetent. Instead of the crazy, inventive, hyperkinetic Williams, *Flubber* offers up a warm, fuzzy and bland Williams. The plot cries out for a character with a few screws loose, and who else but Williams would you cast for such a part? But Brainard, even with Williams, is more befuddled than screwy. In the end Brainard confesses that the only reason he's so absent-minded is that he's smitten with Sara. He's just a lovesick puppy.

The best scenes in *Flubber* are the ones borrowed from the original, when the professor's Thunderbird uses flubber to fly among the clouds. Brainard also hatches a scheme to win back Sara's affection by engineering a win for the college's hapless basketball team. With flubber sprayed on tacks on the bottom of their shoes, the short, fat, glasses-wearing nerds become super-Jordans, defeating the college of Brainard's oily rival, Wilson Croft (Christopher McDonald). This is great goofy fun, but it turns out to be inconsequential. The basketball triumph is supposed to skewer Croft, who's been stealing not only Brainard's ideas but also his girlfriend. But, betraying the purposelessness of the plot, the game doesn't alter anything. Afterward, Sara is still mad at Brainard and Croft still has the upper hand.

The film's lame plot has Medford College going bankrupt, and Brainard trying to prove to Sara, a college president who acts distinctly unpresidential, that his invention of flubber can save the day. Interference comes not only from Croft, but from a rich and ruthless tycoon, Bennett Hoenicker (played smoothly by Raymond Barry) whose slacker son (Wil Wheaton) has gotten a poor mark in Brainard's chemistry class and been kicked off the basketball team. Hoenicker schemes to buy, and then steal, the flubber. All this plays mostly like filler.

The few laughs comes when Williams tiptoes out of his shell. At one point, he rambles on about his love for Sara, professing: "I love you at the subatomic level." At another point, he stumbles into an art class with nude models and starts teaching physics, oblivious to the fact that he's in the wrong classroom. These bits are the closest *Flubber* comes to real humor. Another serviceable concept has a young child who is afraid of things coming in his bedroom window, being constantly assured by his father there is nothing to fear, yet continually seeing bizarre occurrences outside his window—first the flubber, then Brainard in his flying car, then other flubber-induced marvels.

For the most part, though, Mayfield and Hughes flub a golden opportunity for a hit movie. Williams should be funnier than Fred MacMurray, and a 1997 flubber should

CREDITS

Professor Philip Brainard: Robin Williams
Sara Jean Reynolds: Marcia Gay Harden
Wilson Croft: Christopher McDonald
Chester Hoenicker: Raymond Barry
Smith: Clancy Brown
Wesson: Ted Levine
Bennett Hoenicker: Wil Wheaton
Martha George: Edie McClurg
Weebo: Jodi Benson (voice)
Flubber: Scott Martin Gershin (voice)
Weebette: Julie Morrison (voice)

Origin: USA
Released: 1997
Production: John Hughes and Ricardo Mestres for Great Oaks and Walt Disney Pictures; released by Buena Vista
Direction: Les Mayfield
Screenplay: John Hughes and Bill Walsh
Cinematography: Dean Cundey
Editing: Harvey Rosenstock, Michael A. Stevenson
Music: Danny Elfman
Production design: Andrew McAlpine
Art direction: James E. Tocci
Costumes: April Ferry
Sound: Agamemnon Andrianos
Visual effects supervisors: Peter Crosman, Tom Bertino, Douglas Hans Smith
MPAA rating: PG-13
Running Time: 93 minutes

REVIEWS

Chicago Tribune. November 26, 1997, p. 1.
Cinemafantastique. December, 1997, p. 10.
Detroit News. November 26, 1997, p. 8E.
Entertainment Weekly. December 5, 1997, p. 50.
Los Angeles Times. November 26, 1997, p. F6.
New York Times. November 26, 1997, p. E8.
Sight and Sound. March, 1998, p. 47.
USA Today. November 26, 1997, p. 9D.
Variety. November 24, 1997, p. 63.

be funnier than a 1960 flubber. Instead, too many special effects, and too much restraint on Williams' antic personality, ruin the show. Gizmos and gadgets don't make a good movie; a good story, and a willingness to be a little loony at times, do. *Flubber* has plenty of the high tech and none of the necessary craziness.

—*Michael Betzold*

Fools Rush In

What if finding the love of your life meant changing the life that you loved?—Movie tagline

An impulsive love story.—Movie tagline

"A sweet and funny comedy that will warm your heart."—Jeanne Wolf, *Jeanne Wolf's Hollywood*

"It has magic, glamour and romance. It also represents a major breakthrough for its stars Matthew Perry and radiantly beautiful Salma Hayek."—Kevin Thomas, *Los Angeles Times*

"Fresh and vibrant with a great big heart, *Fools Rush In* is the perfect date movie for anyone who still believes in love."—Rex Reed, *New York Observer*

"One of the most endearing, delightful love stories in years."—Jeffrey Lyons, *WNBC-TV*

Box Office: $29,481,428

Matthew Perry, TV's final "Friend" to take his turn on the big screen, stars as one of the titular fools, along with Salma Hayek, in this troublesome mix of drama and romantic comedy. Based on the true story of producer Doug Draizin and co-producer Anna Marie Davis, the story takes the traditional theme of a classic odd couple who meet, marry in a flash, then get to know each other with disastrous results. Although there is a slightly new spin on this premise and the leads are both charismatic and likable, the shift in tone from comedy to drama takes away much of the movie's potential charm. Somewhat admirable attempts to inject spirituality into a formulaic genre end up making the movie play like a watered-down, wanna-be version of the Mexican film *Like Water For Chocolate* (1993).

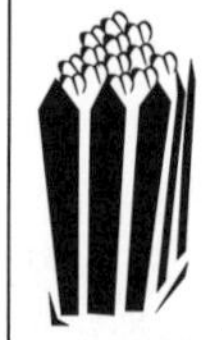

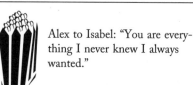

Alex to Isabel: "You are everything I never knew I always wanted."

Manhattan WASP Alex Whitman (Perry) is sent to Las Vegas to oversee construction of one in a chain of nightclubs. While in line at a bathroom in a Mexican restaurant, he portentously meets Isabel Fuentes (Hayek), a local girl, who works in a casino but dreams of becoming a photographer. The two share a one night stand, and when Isabel leaves early the next morning, Alex doesn't see her again for three months. When she does re-enter his life, it's to tell the career-minded bachelor that he's the unwitting father of her soon-to-be-child. Yes, she's having his baby, she tells him, but the strong-willed spitfire expects nothing more from him.

Startled, a feeling of responsibility is awakened in the perennially randy Alex, and he is suddenly curious to learn more about the beautiful stranger who will be the mother of his child. Isabel takes him to meet her very extended family, and soon Alex is won over by the amiable and earthy people so unlike his own rather cold and reserved relatives. Relishing the glow of the dinner and needing a change in his life, Alex impulsively decides that the thing to do is to get married—immediately—a la Vegas, complete with an Elvis impersonator in attendance.

Initially, the unlikely duo's minor conflicts are merely quaint or humorous. Isabel's father and brothers, who upon learning of the shotgun wedding, threaten Alex at his job site with a baseball bat. Isabel's family then redecorates Alex's starkly modern apartment as a post-wedding present in bright yellows, oranges, and reds, complete with a large wooden crucifix hanging on the wall. And later, Isabel's brothers take city-boy Alex to the desert, get him annihilated, and bring him home to his wife with a bum full of cactus quills. When the two families finally meet, they only agree on one thing, that their children should not have gotten married, while Alex's mother (Jill Clayburgh) proceeds to get bombed on margaritas.

It soon becomes apparent, however, that the couple's culture clash threatens their tenuous connection. Alex has also forgotten to mention, until well after the nuptials, that he actually lives in New York and is here temporarily. Isabel cannot dream of leaving her close family behind. Both begin to have serious doubts about the union—especially Alex, who, not wanting to slow down his fast-track career, begins to withdraw emotionally. Despite efforts on Isabel's part to draw him out and get him to talk, he remains distant and unsure of what he has gotten himself into. This more serious tone takes over the remainder of the film.

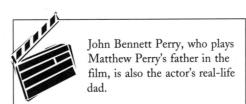

John Bennett Perry, who plays Matthew Perry's father in the film, is also the actor's real-life dad.

The film's attempts to portray these different cultures often lead to stereotypical characters and situations. Isabel's overbearing Catholic father and obnoxiously rowdy brothers are terribly cliched. Ditto for Alex' racist father and neurotic mother (although Clayburgh gives a stand-out performance here). Hayek, in her first starring role, is probably the film's best asset, portraying Isabel with a multi-faceted nature and exuding an authentic and natural comedic flair. Perry plays Alex capably, but with little evidence of the character's inner struggles. Supporting roles are standard, except Siobhan Fallon who, as Isabel's best friend Lanie, shines sarcastically in her brief appearance.

In the real-life story, Davis and Draizin divorced but remain friends and business associates. Some of this reality is reflected, but the genuinely truthful moments in this film get lost in the attempts at broad comedy. The genuinely comedic moments, likewise, are few and far between. Technically, the film is highly proficient and easily makes the stereotypically decadent Las Vegas look like a beautiful, untouched oasis.

—Hilary Weber

CREDITS

Alex Whitman: Matthew Perry
Isabel Fuentes: Salma Hayek
Jeff: Jon Tenney
Chuy: Carlos Gomez
Tomas: Tomas Milian
Lanie: Siobhan Fallon
Richard: John Bennett Perry
Nan: Jill Clayburgh

Origin: USA
Released: 1997
Production: Doug Draizin; released by Columbia Pictures
Direction: Andy Tennant
Screenplay: Katherine Reback
Cinematography: Robbie Greenberg
Editing: Roger Bondelli
Music: Alan Silvestri
Production design: Edward Pisoni
Art direction: David Crank
Set design: Evelyne Barbier
Set decoration: Leslie Morales
Costumes: Kimberly A. Tillman
Sound: Peter J. Devlin
MPAA rating: PG-13
Running Time: 108 minutes

REVIEWS

Boxoffice. April, 1997, p. 199.
Detroit News. February 14, 1997, p. 3D.
Entertainment Weekly. February 14, 1997, p. 42.
Los Angeles Times. February 14, 1997, p. F6.
New York Times. February 14, 1997, p. B14.
People. February 24, 1997, p. 19.
Sight and Sound. October, 1997, p. 50.
USA Today. February 14, 1997, p. 4D.
Variety. February 17, 1997, p. 69.
Washington Post Weekend. February 14, 1997, p. 68.

For Ever Mozart

"A lot of laughs."—Jeanne Wolf, *Jeanne Wolf's Hollywood*

"Hilarious."—Bobbie Wygant, *KXAS*

"A terrific comedy team!"—Jeffrey Lyons, *WNBC*

"Tim Allen and Kirstie Alley make a dynamic duo. *Witness* on acid!"—Mike Cidoni, *WOKR*

Box Office: $20,173,220

In *For Ever Mozart*, the latest film by famed French New Wave auteur Jean-Luc Godard, a veteran film director attempts to cast his latest project, one inspired by Spanish novelist Juan Goytisolo's observation that "the history of the 1990s in Europe is a rehearsal, with slight symphonic variations, of the cowardice and chaos of the 1930s."

For Ever Mozart is, in large part, a philosophical treatise on the inability of films to alter the course of historical events nor to redeem the horrors of war. (According to *Los Angeles Times* critic Kevin Thomas, Godard publicly denounced Steven Spielberg for having made *Schindler's List* in 1993.) Redemption, according to Godard, is best left to the other arts. What interested the filmmaker more was how the medium could be transformed from a mere audio-visual communique to a self-sustained, and sometimes esoteric, language of its own. Godard once remarked that "cinema replaces our gaze with a world in harmony with our desires"—a quote that is repeated in *For Ever Mozart*.

The Bosnian War provides the catalyst for the film's first part. A group of actors accompany the director (Vicky Messica) to the former Yugoslavia where they intend to film a performance of the Alfred de Musset comedy, *One Must Not Play at Love*. Naive arrogance fuels their belief that a few hours of theatre will provide some cultural respite from the fighting and the bloodshed.

When the troupe—which includes the director's daughter Camille (Madeleine Assas)—actually arrives in Sarajevo, however, they do not receive the kind of reception they had anticipated. The violence envelopes them, they are arrested, tortured, forced to dig their own graves, then shot to death.

It is the second half of *For Ever Mozart* that is perhaps the most evocative, for it deals with films as art in the age of the big-budget Hollywood blockbuster. When the Bosnian film is finally released and the potential patrons learn of the plot—and the lack of nudity—most head off to see *Terminator 4* instead; moviegoers apparently prefer not having to "work" at their entertainment.

As expected, *For Ever Mozart* is visually striking, crisply edited and contains the requisite Godard trademark references to the cinema, literature and music. Godard also continues to examine the filmmaking process and the ignominy often attached to "serious" films.

Godard has always had a passionate romance with the cinema; he loved watching, writing about, and making films. He was one of the founding fathers of the French New Wave; his 1959 film *Breathless* broke all the filmic rules and revolutionized the cinema. It was audaciously inventive and controversial, and Godard reveled in the medium's potential. As fellow cineaste Francois Truffaut often said, "Vive le cinema!"

But now in the late 1990s, one cannot help but wonder if film as an art has perhaps reached its outer limits. Have filmmakers like Martin Scorsese, Oliver Stone, and the Coen Brothers (to name a few) manipulated film into as many permutations and configurations as possible? The French New Wave strived to keep its viewers off balance; it took our pre-conceived notions about what film should be and turned them upside-down and inside-out. Today's filmmakers, like Quentin Tarantino, seem to equate the shock value of shattering societal taboos with artistic groundbreaking merit.

CREDITS

Camille: Madeleine Assa
Jerome: Frederic Pierrot
Dzamila: Ghalia Lacroix
Vicky Vitalis, the Director: Vicky Messica
The Great Writer: Harry Cleven

Origin: France, Switzerland
Released: 1996
Production: Ruth Waldburger and Alain Sarde for Avventura Films/Peripheria Vega Film AG; released by New Yorker Films
Direction: Jean-Luc Godard
Screenplay: Jean-Luc Godard
Cinematography: Christophe Pollock, Katell Dijan, Jean-Pierre Fedrizzi
Editing: Jean-Luc Godard
Production design: Ivan Niclass
Costumes: Marina Zuliani
Music: David Darling, Ketil Bjornstad, Ben Harper, Gyorgi Kurtag
Sound: Francois Musy, Olivier Burgaud
MPAA rating: Unrated
Running Time: 84 minutes

While over the years his films may have become increasingly inaccessible from a conventional narrative approach, Jean-Luc Godard can still dazzle us with his visual virtuosity. *For Ever Mozart* may not be his most evocative film, but at the age of sixty-seven, Godard continues to refuse to surrender to the cinematic status quo. Film historian Royal S. Brown once wrote of Godard's body of work, "each film is a chapter in an amazingly broad intellectual and aesthetic autobiography." Vive Jean-Luc Godard!

—Patricia Kowal

REVIEWS

Detroit Free Press. March 15, 1998, p. 7F.
Los Angeles Times. September 26, 1997, p. F21.
The New Yorker. July 14, 1997, p. 85.
New York Times. July 4, 1997, p. C4.
Time. August 4, 1997.
Variety. September 16, 1996, p. 70.

For Richer or Poorer

Some critics reviewing *For Richer or Poorer* commented that Tim Allen and Kirstie Alley, the stars of the movie, were good. It was the plot that was the problem. Other reviews said that the story was fine, but ruined by Allen and Alley. Guess what? They're both partially right. It's both the story and the acting that's wrong with this film.

We first meet Brad Sexton (Tim Allen) and wife Caroline (Kirstie Alley) at their huge 10th anniversary party. The two are kissy-face, rich Manhattanites, sort of a darker-haired Ivana and Donald Trump. (Lest we miss any Trump association, the party is set in the Trump Plaza Hotel and Marla Maples shows up as one of Alley's best friends.) Allen is making the tasteless, overblown party even more tasteless by using the captive audience to hawk his latest cockamamie real estate venture, the Holy Land theme park.

After Brad accidentally sets a local judge's dress on fire (an example of the type of humor in this flick), the anniversary couple heads home to their sumptuous high-rise apartment and starts one heck of a fight. After retreating to their separate bedrooms, the two come back out to the foyer for another round. The result? D-I-V-O-R-C-E. Caroline asks for one and Brad acquiesces. For once, they can agree on something.

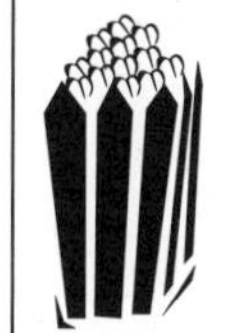

Brad threatens an unruly plowhorse: "Be submissive or be adhesive."

At the same time, the couple's accountant, Bob Lachman (Wayne Knight, aka Newman on TV's "Seinfeld"), has a meeting with the IRS. It seems he has been bilking the couple out of big money. Instead of having his indiscretions revealed at the forthcoming audit, Bob skips town. At first, Brad and Caroline think that their accounts are frozen because of each other's devious divorce moves, but Brad quickly discovers what's really going on when he finds a couple of rabid IRS agents on his tail (including comedian Larry Miller as a crazed, vigilante-type).

Brad reacts by fleeing, and by an insanely improbable coincidence, he and Caroline wind up in a cab speeding somewhere, anywhere out of town. Like the movie *Witness* (1985), which this film bears more than a passing resemblance to, they end up in an Amish community. Overhearing some local townspeople talking about some soon-to-be-visiting cousins, Brad comes up with a plan to impersonate these Amish relations. Soon, Brad and Caroline show up on the doorstep of the sweet, docile Yoder family, headed by Samuel (Jay O. Sanders) and Levinia (Megan Cavanagh).

This is the humor conceit of the film. Spoiled rich New Yorkers try to deal with Amish life in Intercourse, Pennsylvania. Caroline can't stand waking up before 5 a.m., cooking casseroles that contain organ meats, and not having a cigarette. And Brad has to fake knowledge of plowing fields and taming a huge, unruly horse named Big John. Is all this funny? Not really.

Between the Sexton's big city airs and complete lack of knowledge about Amish customs, the Yoders would have to be very slow-witted not to pick up on the ruse. But the Sextons explain any and all mistakes away by saying they're from a "more liberal" group.

Or maybe it's the audience that's presumed to be slow-witted. At one point, Caroline makes a compliment on an intricate quilt, only to find out that "she" (the real cousin, that is) made it. A few scenes later, Caroline is called upon to demonstrate her fine sewing skills to a group of local women. Caroline naturally sews her quilt to her sleeves—an action typical of what the writers would like us to consider funny. Oddly, though, later in the film when Caroline discovers her true calling as a fashion designer (shades of Alley's TV series "Veronica's Closet") , her lack of sewing ability is not mentioned at all. And not only is it not mentioned, but Caroline can suddenly sew so well that she can make—by hand, no less—all the clothes for a big Amish fashion show. (This scene is also not as funny as it sounds—or could be.)

Just being an unfunny comedy is one thing, but this film goes one worse. It gets sentimental. Just like Harrison Ford in *Witness,* the two become charmed by Amish life and begin to realize the value of hard work and nature. With all these good vibes going around, the Sextons even begin to fall in love again.

There's nothing that bad about romance, exactly, but a romance involving Allen and Alley is a different thing. It's one thing to see Allen kiss his TV wife on the small screen but to see him 20-feet tall, in a big movie kiss close-up with Alley is not a particularly appealing sight. Of course, some may disagree.

At least Allen and Alley seem to be trying in this film. They bring a sitcom professionalism to their work and are certainly competent in their roles. But Alley is annoying, especially early in the film as a screechy, spoiled, rich city girl. Her unlikable character is almost too unlikable, so much so that who would want to watch such a whiny brat? And Allen, without his "Home Improvement" shtick to fall back on, is bland and just sort of . . . there. He mugs gamely, but doesn't have the presence to be a romantic leading man.

As the heads of the Yoder household, Sanders and Cavanagh are round-faced and full of salt of the earth words of wisdom. Sanders is understated as the kindly male figure with a bad haircut and Cavanagh brings a pleasant, stable quality to her role as a devoted servant of God and family.

One surprise performance is Marla Maples' as Cynthia, one of Caroline's ultra-blonde, rich ladies-who-lunch type of friends. Maples seems natural and at ease in the role, although it's not like she's making a big stretch from her real life as an ex-wife of The Donald.

What's good about this film is the chance to look at how another culture lives. It's nice to get a glimpse of the Amish day-to-day life and learn a few things about Amish customs (such as only married Amish men wear beards). Like the Sextons, it's easy to get seduced by the gentle Amish way of life.

That, and the settings are the best part of this film. The Amish farmland (filmed in Pennsylvania) is lovely, with old, picturesque barns and a classic, simply decorated farmhouse. It's just as fun to check out the Sexton's pretentious big city apartment, with its giant screen TVs, water sculptures, and wildly lush and expensive furniture.

Despite the panoramic vistas and the lingering shots over the beautiful rolling farmland, the film still looks and feels like a sitcom, with Bryan Spicer having directed such previous cartoonish work as the based-on-TV-shows movies *Mighty Morphin Power Rangers: The Movie* and *McHale's Navy*. The problem with *For Richer or Poorer* is that it's trying to pass itself off as a romantic comedy but it's neither sufficiently romantic or comedic. It fails on both fronts and for the film to work, it would have to get at least one of them right.

—Jill Hamilton

CREDITS

Brad Sexton: Tim Allen
Caroline Sexton: Kirstie Alley
Samuel Yoder: Jay O. Sanders
Phil Kleinman: Michael Lerner
Bob Lachman: Wayne Knight
Derek Lester: Larry Miller
Levinia Yoder: Megan Cavanagh
Frank Hall: Miguel A Nunez Jr.
Henner Lapp: John Pyper-Ferguson
Cynthia: Marla Maples
Rebecca Yoder: Carrie Preston

Origin: USA
Released: 1997
Production: Sid, Bill, and Jon Sheinberg for The Bubble Factory; released by Universal Pictures
Direction: Bryan Spicer
Screenplay: Jana Howington and Steve Lukanic
Cinematography: Buzz Feitshans IV
Editing: Russell Denove
Music: Randy Edelman
Production design: Stephen Hendrickson
Art direction: Bob Shaw
Set decoration: Beth Kushnick
Costumes: Abigail Murray
Sound: Jim Sabat
MPAA rating: PG-13
Running Time: 115 minutes

REVIEWS

New York Times. December 12, 1997, p. E16.
San Francisco Chronicle. December 12, 1997, p. C3.
San Francisco Examiner. December 12, 1997, p. B3.
USA Today. December 12, 1997, p. 14D.
Variety. December 9, 1997, p. 111.
Village Voice. December 23, 1997, p. 79.
Washington Post. December 12, 1997, p. C8.

For Roseanna; Roseanna's Grave

A romantic comedy about the things we do for love.—Movie tagline

A romantic comedy about getting what you want out of life . . . if it's the last thing you do.—Movie tagline

"A charming, whimsical romance."—John Anderson, *Newsday*

"Two thumbs up!"—*Siskel & Ebert*

"An exhilarating comedy with a spectacularly charismatic cast."—Laura Wise, *Time Out New York*

Storytelling is the core element in the making of any film—at least it should be. Foreign films seem to approach this process in a more simplistic fashion than do many American films. Certainly, more so than the current crop of 1997 summer, action-adventure blockbusters such as *Batman and Robin*, *Con Air*, *Face/Off*, *Contact*, and *Air Force One*. This genre of film primarily attempts to raise the adrenalin level of an audience to a fever pitch, much the same as a roller-coaster ride in an amusement park. The box-office receipts for many of these films seem to support this statement. So, it is of interest when a smaller, independent film, such as Fine Line Features' *For Roseanna* chooses a re-release in the summer in many major cities across the United States. It was originally released at the 12th Annual Santa Barbara Film Festival in March '97.

There are other interesting facts about *For Roseanna* (originally titled "Roseanna's Grave"). The producers felt that having 'Grave' in the title would be too ominous for many filmgoers. Although *Roseanna* aspires to be an authentic Italian folktale, it actually has a cast of at least four nationalities playing Italians. Also, it is the first major screen outing for veteran American writer Saul Turtletaub whose writing credits include two vintage T.V. series, the Jackie Gleason and the Carol Burnett shows. It seems curious that an American television comedy scribe would select a project about a shortage of burial plots in a small Italian village for his first feature film.

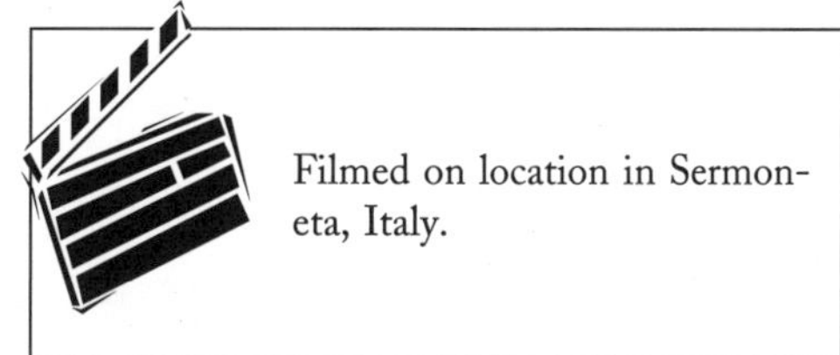

Filmed on location in Sermoneta, Italy.

The film unfolds in a quaint and picturesque Italian village. Of course, it is populated by an assortment of "colorful" characters who all speak with an eclectic array of Italian accents. In the center of this human antipasto are Roseanna, played by American Mercedes Ruehl and Marcello, played by Frenchman Jean Reno. There is a twofold problem—the first being Roseanna's deteriorating health and the second being the shortage of burial plots in the local cemetery. Since Roseanna wishes to be buried next to the couple's deceased daughter, Marcello tries everything in his power to keep the townsfolk healthy. Although touched by his motive, Roseanna protests to Marcello, "you can't keep everyone in the town alive." The only other alternative to this dilemma is to acquire more land. It just so happens that a wealthy man named Capestro (Luigi Deberti) owns a large amount of property close to the cemetery. It also just happens that Capestro is an arch rival of Marcello's and, unbeknownst to Marcello, a former lover of Roseanna's. In spite of Marcello's impassioned pleas, Capestro won't budge.

Meanwhile, the other group of characters are having problems of their own. Iaccoponi (Trevor Peacock), a man of dubious reputation, is about to be released after serving a long prison term. He's heading back to the village to collect a large sum of money that he had entrusted to the local banker, Rossi (Roberto Della Casa). The problem is that Rossi spent a large portion of the loot on his younger, somewhat mercenary mistress. This scenario weaves a complicated concoction of events where both men end up shaking hands with the Grim Reaper. Two more burial plots gone—poor Marcello! However, due to his ingenuity, the corpses never quite make it to the already crowded cemetery. As if these events weren't enough, Roseanna's sister, Cecilia, played by Polly Walker (*The Restoration* [1994]), is being pursued by handsome lawyer, Antonio (the late Mark Frankel). Roseanna, in her concern for her husband after her death, wants Cecilia to consider marrying widower Marcello. Cecilia doesn't seem to respond to this suggestion well at all and the plot thickens. Jennifer Vandever of the *Village Voice* stated, " . . . the film starts to feel like a wacky Italian version of 'Knots Landing'". *People* magazine added, " . . . the movie's plot eventually overstrains to amuse." Perhaps the film would have been served better had there only been one writer instead of three. Besides Turtletaub, Dick Clement and Dan LeFrenais also scripted.

The centerpiece of all these going-ons is, of course, Roseanna. Mercedes Ruehl is a gifted and truthful actress. In 1991, she was awarded an Academy Award as best supporting actress in Terry Gilliam's offbeat film *The Fisher King*. In it, she played Jeff Bridges' patient but forceful girlfriend. She also displayed her comic ability, delighting audiences in Jonathan Demme's 1988 mobster spoof, *Married to the Mob*. She's understated and believable and never falls into the Italian stereotype. The difficulty lies in believing that she's sick since she looks healthy and robust. The only indication of ill-health is an intermittent cough.

French actor Jean Reno is also convincing as the Italian husband, Marcello, who runs a popular trattoria. American filmgoers are most familiar with Reno's work from his appearances in such films as *The Professional* (1994), *French Kiss* (1995), and the remake of the popular television series, *Mission Impossible* (1996). Reno instills an honest charm to his portrayal of Marcello but lacks an intrinsic charisma that would have greatly enhanced the chemistry between him and Roseanna. In *Weekly Variety*, reviewer Todd McCarthy commented that "Marcello Mastroianni would have been the perfect actor for the role, Marcello, two or three decades back." Actually to further heighten audience interest, Sophia Loren would have made an exciting Roseanna. However, although both Ruehl and Reno may not have the star power or glamour of a Loren and Mastroianni, they did effectively convey a genuine and caring bond between them as husband and wife.

For Roseanna has one major ingredient going for it and that is the scenic wonder of Italy. Henry Braham's widescreen lensing utilized the country's beauty to its best advantage. This gave the film the bonus element of escapism—the feeling of being transported to a simpler way of life. This aspect should offer a pleasant alternative to the audience member who is fed up with the explosions, murder and mayhem of the summer movie menu.

To his credit, the director, Paul Weiland, keeps the action moving at an accelerated pace. Perhaps, had there not been so much happening, the film's rather unusual subject would have seemed morbid and unfunny. It failed when it crossed the line into tasteless slapstick. As an example, there is one scene in particular where Marcello is arguing with a doctor over a dying man on a respirator while they take turns plugging it in and out. This is one of the film's low points.

There are some enjoyable, if not spectacular parts to *Roseanna*. Yes, it has a sweet charm about it and the international cast was uniformly good. Trevor Jones' musical score was pleasant and appropriate although precariously too close to that of *Il Postino*'s (1994). As always, Italy was enchanting. But there was something missing—it somehow lacked a vitality of spirit that many foreign films possess. There is a magical quality to such films as *Cinema Paradiso* (1988), *Like Water For Chocolate* (1992) and *Il Postino* (1994). They all managed to create an illusion of romance and mystery.

No matter how beautiful the background or how talented the cast, the story seems weak and uninteresting. This is the central problem as to why the other elements don't add up to a great film. It is possible to be amused by it and laugh at its funnier moments. However, it is very much like eating Chinese rather than Italian. When you leave the theater after seeing *For Roseanna*, you're hungry in a half-hour. This certainly is no way to feel after spending almost two hours in Italy.

—Rob Chicatelli

CREDITS

Marcello: Jean Reno
Roseanna: Mercedes Ruehl
Cecilia: Polly Walker
Antonio: Mark Frankel
Father Bramilia: Giuseppe Cederna

Origin: USA
Released: 1997
Production: Paul Trijbits, Alison Owen and Dario Paloni for Hungry Eye and Spelling Films; released by Fine Line Features
Direction: Paul Weiland
Screenplay: Saul Turteltaub
Cinematography: Henry Braham
Editing: Martin Walsh
Music: Trevor Jones
Production design: Rod McLean
Art direction: Livia Borgognoni
Set decoration: Judy Farr
Costumes: Annie Hardinge
MPAA rating: PG-13
Running Time: 99 minutes

REVIEWS

Boxoffice. April, 1997, p. 191.
Entertainment Weekly. June 27, 1997, p. 96.
Los Angeles Times. July 2, 1997, p. F10.
New York Times. June 20, 1997, p. B18.
People. July 7, 1997, p. 19.
Sight and Sound. August, 1997, p. 53.
Variety. March 17, 1997, p. 53.
Village Voice. June 24, 1997, p. 84.

4 Little Girls

"Remarkable!"—Janet Maslin, *The New York Times*
"Two thumbs up!"—*Siskel & Ebert*

4 *Little Girls*, director Spike Lee's superb documentary for HBO, explores the traumatic events of thirty-four years ago, when four African-American girls, ages eleven to fourteen, were killed in the basement of a bombed Birmingham church. Needless to say, Lee's topic has particular relevance today, when scores of African-American churches have again become targets of arsonists and when the extent to which the Civil Rights campaigns of the late 1950s and early 1960s have succeeded is open to question.

Lee is an outspoken critic of American society's lack of progress on the race issue. In this film, however, he eschews both preaching and an adversarial stance. His subject is so dramatic in itself and the characters who played a part in it are so compelling that he hardly needs to emphasize points or to editorialize. Indeed, at one point he assures one of his interviewees that "this is not 60 Minutes," and unlike Mike Wallace Lee is not seeking to embarrass or to goad his subjects. In fact, he is rarely on camera—only when the nature of his question is important do we see or hear him. For the most part, the friends of relatives of the four dead girls are allowed to tell their stories simply and apparently without much interruption.

Even so many years later emotions run high—although most of the people interviewed remember the tragedy with sadness, not anger or outrage. The father of one child is an impressive photographer. His calm measured words and his appreciation of his photographs underscore the humanity and intelligence of people who had to put up with racial prejudice and violence when they tried to assert their human rights.

Lee also conducts remarkable interviews with the lawyer who defended Ku Klux Klansman, Robert Chambliss (convicted in 1977 of bombing the church and sentenced to life in prison), and with Alabama governor George Wallace. Chambliss's lawyer is mild spoken and appears reasonable, yet it is what he does not say about his client or his community that is disturbing. Listening to him one would think there was hardly a racial problem in Birmingham and the rest of the South. His very blandness about injustice is shocking. Even more startling is the interview with Wallace, who appears quite infirm and inarticulate. Wallace excuses his standing in the way of Federal marshals who were escorting black students into the University of Alabama, affirming that he was simply representing the values of his generation. In an extraordinary scene he even produces an African-American factotum, explaining that this man goes with him everywhere. Wallace reiterates he would not travel without his man—apparently not realizing how much he sounds like a slavemaster saluting his darky. The factotum just stands there. What can he say? What can he be thinking? News reports indicate that Governor Wallace and his representatives were unhappy about his appearance in the film and tried to get Lee to remove or to edit the sequence differently. As several books and articles have pointed out, Wallace has been trying to rehabilitate himself for many years, and apparently the opportunity to do so again in the Lee film proved irresistible. Yet Wallace damns himself without any comment from Lee.

The Justice Department has reopened the probe into the bombing, with new leads to possible accomplices to the convicted bomber.

The film presents a rich array of vintage photographs, period music, and paraphernalia from an era of protest marches and folk songs about oppression. As one review puts it, the bombing was a galvanizing event in America, one that, in Walter Cronkite's words in the film, focused the country's attention on the tyranny of racial prejudice.

In addition to the commentary on the martyred girls and their families, there are extraordinary reminiscences by African-American leaders who fearlessly walked through hostile white crowds and insisted on their rights. Others who were merely observers in the great confrontation between Bull Connor, the vicious chief of police who set his dogs on Civil Rights demonstrators, convey a "man in the street" impression of parlous times. One matter-of-fact African-American observer notes that Connor was simply

CREDITS

Origin: USA
Released: 1997
Production: Spike Lee and Sam Pollard for 40 Acres & a Mule Filmworks; released by HBO
Direction: Spike Lee
Cinematography: Ellen Kuras
Editing: Sam Pollard
Music: Terence Blanchard
Sound: J.T. Takagi
MPAA rating: Unrated
Running Time: 102 minutes

"crazy," and though that word is often used to short-circuit thinking about human beings and complex issues, in this case the comment seems apt. Judged by any decent standard of behavior, Connor and his ilk have to be judged insane.

Reviewers has used words such as graceful and dignified to convey the mood of Lee's film. Unlike Lee's semi-documentary, *Get on the Bus,* which has a hortatory tone, *4 Little Girls* is subdued. It has a pensive quality and the assured pace of a documentary steeped in history.

—*Carl Rollyson*

REVIEWS

Chicago Tribune. October 24, 1997, p. 5.
The Hollywood Reporter. July 11, 1997, p. 12.
Los Angeles Times. October 24, 1997, p. F4.
People. August 11, 1997, p. 87.
San Francisco Chronicle. October 10, 1997, p. C3.
San Francisco Examiner. October 10, 1997, p. C3.
Variety. July 21, 1997, p. 38.

Free Willy 3: The Rescue

A new friend. A new threat. A new adventure that will capture your heart.—Movie tagline

Box Office: $3,512,593

In 1993 audiences were introduced to Jesse (Jason James Richter), a street kid whose life is turned around by his friendship with Willy, a killer whale trapped in an tourist sea park. Since then, the real Willy has become a cause celebre with animal activists, a sequel has been released, and Richter has grown up.

Now we have a third installment of the series which still features the original Willy (droopy dorsal fin and all), a post-pubescent Richter, and a new child actor to interphase with the whale and young audiences.

In *Free Willy 3: The Rescue,* Jesse now has a job as an assistant on a whaling research ship whose crew includes Randolph (August Schellenberg), the sage native American from the two previous films, and an oceanographer Drew (Annie Corley).

Now playing the role of the young lad who befriends Willy is ten-year-old Max (Vincent Berry). Max is sailing on his father's (Patrick Kilpatrick) salmon fishing ship for the first time, only to discover that his father illegally hunts whales for the underground Norwegian, Russian and Japanese markets.

Of course the prime target of Max's father's hunting is Willy, set free in previous films and who now has a pregnant girlfriend. When Jesse creates an electronic call which he uses to find Willy along the Northwestern Pacific coast, the whaler's discover it and use it to attract Willy to their harpoons. It doesn't take long for Jesse to figure out what Max's father is up to, but proving it is another matter.

Although we hate what Max's dad is doing, at least the movie doesn't paint him as a bad man. Instead he is portrayed as a loving father who is just trying to make a living. The film does attempt to lay out the moral grounds against whale hunting, but it is an unconvincing discussion between Max and his father that falls flat and won't change anyone's mind. Instead, the movie relies on Max's father coming to know Willy personally and reaching an intuitive epiphany about whales.

Producer Jennie Lew Tugend on whaling: "Whales are extremely intelligent mammals and the idea that we would slaughter them for food and sell them as a delicacy just seems reprehensible."

In some respects this is *Free Willy 3*'s best (and worst) aspect. The failure to present a clear, morally defensible theory on why whales should be treated any differently than cows is its weakest point. Max eats hamburgers without a thought, but maybe if he met the cow and roamed the meadow with it he wouldn't. Is that the extent of the rationalization for exempting Willy from exploitation? Someone else's personal experience is not necessarily a particularly convincing argument.

Principal photography took place in Howe Sound and Pitt Lake, British Columbia.

However, on the other hand, personal experience can be moving when depicted captivatingly. It can cause an emotional conversion instead of a logical one. Luckily, as weak as *Free Willy 3* is in rational debate, it is stronger in portraying the majesty of whales in the wild—

CREDITS

Jesse: Jason James Richter
Randolph Johnson: August Schellenberg
Drew: Annie Corley
Max Wesley: Vincent Berry
John Wesley: Patrick Kilpatrick
Mary Wesley: Tasha Simms
Sanderson: Peter Lacroix

Origin: USA
Released: 1997
Production: Jennie Lew Tugend for Regency Enterprises and Shuler Donner/Donner Productions; released by Warner Bros.
Direction: Sam Pillsbury
Screenplay: John Mattson
Cinematography: Tobias Schliessler
Editing: Margie Goodspeed
Music: Cliff Eidelman
Production design: Brent Thomas
Art direction: Douglasann Menchions
Costumes: Maya Mani
Sound: Rick Patton
Whale design/effects supervisor: Walt Conti
MPAA rating: PG
Running Time: 86 minutes

a more persuasive location than that sea tank in the first film.

Also in this third installment's favor is the beautiful photography which puts Willy and his family in their best light. According to the film's production notes, Willy is "a combination of wildlife photography, special effects, computer imaging and digital composition," but it is often difficult to tell where the real Willy ends and the special effects begin. However, after hearing about the plight of the original Willy (Kieko) most viewers would rather the filmmakers just use convincing replacements than exploit the real thing all over again.

Free Willy 3 is a much better film than the second one, and it is more realistic and thoughtful than the first. And with the introduction of a new youngster (both human and whale), there's a strong likelihood that there will be a fourth.

—*Beverley Bare Buehrer*

REVIEWS

Boxoffice. October, 1997, p. 43.
Chicago Tribune. August 8, 1997, p. 5.
New York Times. August 8, 1997, p. C8.
Variety. August 11, 1997, p. 57.

The Full Monty

Six men, With nothing to lose. Who dared to go . . . *The Full Monty.*—Movie tagline

The year's most revealing comedy.—Movie tagline

"A total pleasure!"—Lisa Henricksson, *GQ*

"Irresistible . . . hilarious! This summer at the movies has been no laughing matter. Not until *The Full Monty!*"—Janet Maslin, *The New York Times*

"Enchantingly funny! Crowd-pleasing!"—David Ansen, *Newsweek*

"Two thumbs up, way up! One of the most entertaining movies of the year!"—Gene Siskel, *Siskel & Ebert*

"A comic delight! Such pure joy is utterly contagious!"—Susan Wloszczyna, *USA Today*

Box Office: $35,015,019

When six steelworkers in Sheffield are laid off they form a male striptease act, which serves as the unusual premise for *The Full Monty*. Inspired by the local women paying to watch Chippendale dancers, Gaz (Robert Carlyle, who played psychopathic Begbie in *Trainspotting*, 1995) concocts the scheme to get off the dole in this popular British comedy. A wired and wiry lovable rogue, he persuades his pals to join him in this outrageous plan, managing to literally and figuratively pull it all off.

What distinguishes this group of least-likely candidates for a male version of *Striptease* (1996) isn't just their unappealing bodies and lack of good looks—it's that they offer something startling special by going "the full monty"—or totally nude.

According to a mock 25-year-old promotional film, this Yorkshire city is on the move—ironically, today it's a post-industrial town with scads of out-of-work men hanging out on financial assistance. At the job center, Gaz and his buddy Dave (Mark Addy) play cards with other former workers, bemoaning their obsolescence—they're "scrap," dinosaurs.

Encouraged by lines of adoring lasses lined up at a male strip club, Gaz devises the plan, recruiting his skeptical companions with the prospect of quick cash results. "Folks won't laugh when you have a grand in your pocket." It's his harebrained solution to afford child support payments his ex-wife demands for visitation rights.

Helping a fellow fix his broken-down car, Dave discovers a hose connected from the exhaust pipe to the interior. He and Gaz befriend the suicidal Lomper (Steve Huison)—"Don't tell us we're not your mates, we just saved your life," Gaz blurts as he enlists the "pasty, pigeon-chested" bloke for his floor show. Demonstrating his dancing chops to the Hot Chocolate tune "You Sexy Thing," Gaz flings off his t-shirt, tangling it on a lit cigarette dangled from his lips, flubbing his performance to the line "I believe in miracles." His young son, Nathan (William Snape), walks off mortified with dad in pursuit.

In search of a choreographer they attempt to solicit their former foreman Gerald (Tom Wilkinson) at a dance class. Gerald snubs these losers—dancers have coordination, fitness and grace, he claims—and busily sends off resumes from the unemployment office. After the crew sabotages his job interview, distracting him from outside the window with a line-up of prancing gnomes from his garden, an honest confrontation follows. Gaz takes it to heart, but continues his strategy and finally enlists his old supervisor's services.

The men hold auditions, in which a pathetic string of hopefuls try out, barely able to disrobe, much less exhibit style. A grey-headed chap, Horse (Paul Barber), struts his stuff, impressing them with the Funky Chicken. The line-up fills out with a sixth member when a young hunk, Guy (Hugo Speer), clumsily attempts to imitate Donald O'Connor tapping up the wall—but really stands out at the cattle call after simply unzipping his jeans. The film audience is discreetly spared the view, unlike Nathan, who's been cueing songs for participants.

Dave filches a copy of *Flashdance* (1983) for rehearsals at Gerald's and critiques Jennifer Beals' welding technique instead of her moves. Gerald, who postponed telling his wife

AWARDS AND NOMINATIONS

Academy Awards 1997: Original Musical or Comedy Score
Nominations: Best Picture, Director (Cattaneo), Original Screenplay
BAFTA 1997 Nominations: Best Film, Best British Film, Director (Cattaneo), Original Screenplay, Actor (Carlyle), Supporting Actress (Sharp), Supporting Actor (Addy), Supporting Actor (Wilkinson), Music, Editing, Sound
Golden Globe Awards 1998 Nominations: Best Musical/Comedy
Screen Actors Guild Awards 1997: Best Cast

Gaz (Robert Carlyle) and his pals take desperate measures to earn money by becoming male strippers who go all the way in the surprise hit comedy *The Full Monty*.

that he's unemployed for the last six months, finds repo men ready to remove the couple's belongings. However, they're greeted by the blushing team in briefs and back off. As Tom Gliatto in *People* explained, "There's something going on here about disempowered men trying to reclaim their masculinity by exposing themselves."

In revealing skin, their insecurities show. This caper isn't merely for economic reasons—they have ulterior motives also. Dave's wife is disturbed by his impotence and he's ashamed of his extra weight, especially with the prospect of standing naked before spectators. Horse is nervous about his size. Gaz wants custody rights. Depressed Lomper wants friends. They all have something at stake but nothing to lose.

Lomper's mother dies, underlining his sense of loss until he shares an intimate exchange with Guy. At his mother's funeral, Lomper plays trumpet with a horn section in a sweet tribute. His new cronies lend support and his new attraction holds his hand. On seeing the two together, Dave mumbles "Nowt so queer as folks," (translated "Nothing so odd as folks"). The audience gets a giggle from the pun, although slang and heavy Northern English accents regrettably hamper grasping every joke.

Despite second thoughts, such as Gerald's stuffy sense of propriety, a moment of reckoning happens in line waiting for their checks at the unemployment office. As "Hot Stuff" blasts through the intercom speakers, the troupe's heads nod rhythmically, shoulders turn in time, hips sway and feet step, subtly synchronized to Donna Summer's song.

Horse on his dancing: " . . . me break-dancing days is probably over, but there's always the funky chicken."

As their debut nears, the men engage in exercises, including soccer, to build stamina for the routine and try to improve their physiques for the approaching scrutiny. Taunted by a couple of women who read their poster, "Hot Metal—We Dare To Be Bare," Gaz boldly accepts the challenge to go all the way when they proclaim that would be worth the look. What was a risque lark until now seems imminently risky. Dave backs off to take a job after desperate attempts to lose his potbelly prove futile.

Feature film debut for director Peter Cattaneo and screenwriter Simon Beaufoy.

The rest of the revue practices in front of female members of Horse's family, including his mum. They show a bemused but uncensorious eye as the gawky group awkwardly performs until the pounding Gary Glitter music summons the police. When the dancers are arrested for indecency and plastered across headlines—"Steel Strippers Exposed"—the mishap draws predictable responses from Gerald's wife and Gaz's ex, but unexpected, even appreciative glances from others, like Lomper's brass band, which breaks into the bawdy "Stripper" theme. Nathan offers Gaz his savings to pay the club rental because he believes in his dad.

Dave's wife discovers his discarded leather G-string and prepares to leave, assuming his inability to perform in bed is because of an affair with another. When he apologizes, admitting the dancing intrigue, he's surprised by her encouraging reaction to rejoin his partners performing on stage.

The 10,000 pounds that Chippendale boys rake in seems a possible take for Gaz's guys when the night arrives with a packed house of cheering, leering women—and men. The co-ed audience sends the ringleader into abject fear of complete humiliation, and he refuses to step on stage. Dressed in security guard uniforms, his showmen go on, including Dave—his wife hooting from her table—announcing their "for one night only" expose.

To the strains of Tom Jones wailing Randy Newman's "You Can Take Your Clothes Off," ties and belts fly. The crowd howls. Using his dad's tactics, Nathan orders Gaz out of the dressing room—"They're cheering because of you"—in time to rip off their shirts. Next come the velcroed pants in a hysterical bump-and-grind, compared to the lusty act of buff professional boys. Ignoring the song's line "you can leave your hat on," they cover their thongs with their caps and in the last shot—from a rear view behind the stage—they toss it all off.

"Hats off! Roaringly funny. An exuberant charmer," said *Rolling Stone*'s Peter Travers. Other critics agree: "Crowd pleasing!" says Janet Maslin (*New York Times*), "A smart, funny gem!" per *US Magazine*, "Two thumbs up, way up!" according to Siskel and Ebert.

The Full Monty isn't about a strip act as much as it involves six unlucky men transformed from the indignity of losing a job to gaining a sense of self-worth, overcoming their shortcomings—from overweight and overaged to inhibited, lonely and irresponsible. "The audience roots for them to succeed, even if it's just a striptease," writes Ruth Stein (*San Francisco Chronicle*). The film's raucous humor focuses on the embarrassment of being exposed. Susan Wloszczyna in *USA Today* states "More than *Showgirls* (1995) with hair on its chest, it's an engrossing study of the male ego stripped bare."

Hardly erotic material, *The Full Monty* speaks to our own dread of undressing in public. It's not about sexual pol-

CREDITS

Gaz: Robert Carlyle
Gerald: Tom Wilkinson
Dave: Mark Addy
Lomper: Steve Huison
Horse: Paul Barber
Guy: Hugo Speer
Jean: Lesley Sharp
Mandy: Emily Woof
Nathan: William Snape

Origin: Great Britain
Released: 1997
Production: Uberto Pasolini for Redwave Films; released by Fox Searchlight Pictures
Direction: Peter Cattaneo
Screenplay: Simon Beaufoy
Cinematography: John De Borman
Editing: David Freeman, Nick More
Music: Anne Dudley
Production design: Max Gottlieb
Costumes: Jill Taylor
Sound: Alistair Crocker
MPAA rating: R
Running Time: 90 minutes

itics exactly, though they catch themselves examining women's bodies in a girlie magazine, self-consciously noticing the tables turned and witnessing their own vulnerability. The subject is handled with unpretentious sincerity, the amusement from clever lines and goofy mishaps surrounding the silly escapade and the meaning from the pathos of endearing characters' lives. The superb acting brings the story alive.

If an American version results from the success of this UK film, it's likely to be lewd, lascivious, and vulgar instead of delightful good fun with nary a naughty touch and the many touching moments that increase its inoffensive quality. Desson Howe of the *Washington Post* states screenwriter Simon Beaufoy and director Peter Cattaneo "handle this potentially racy material with an engaging balance of good taste and outright slapstick."

Apparently the term "Full Monty" is a gambling reference associated with Monte Carlo, card games and racehorses certain to win—sure bets. It's said of the Monte Carlo car rally that decent driving helps but masterly planning increases your chances—and once started, it's tough to stop. The analogy is apt in the context of this film.

—*Roberta Cruger*

REVIEWS

Boxoffice. April, 1997, p. 178.
Chicago Tribune. August 27, 1997, p. 1.
Detroit News. September 12, 1997, p. 3C.
Entertainment Weekly. August 22, 1997, p. 109.
The Hollywood Reporter. August 12, 1997, p. 9.
Los Angeles Times. August 13, 1997, p. F5.
Movieline. August, 1997, p. 38.
People. August 25, 1997, p. 24.
Rolling Stone. August 21, 1997, p. 118.
Sight and Sound. September, 1997, p. 43.
Time. August 25, 1997.
USA Today. August 13, 1997, p. 3D.
Variety. August 11, 1997, p. 57.
Village Voice. August 19, 1997, p. 81.

Gabbeh

Iranian director Mohsen Makhmalbaf has made mostly political films that have earned him nothing but trouble from the repressive government of his native Iran. *Gabbeh,* his 13th film and the first to receive theatrical release in America, was also banned for a time in his homeland, for reasons difficult for Westerners to fathom. If there is political allegory in this content-skimpy tapestry about a doomed love in a nomadic tribe, it is subtle indeed.

Judging only from *Gabbeh,* Makhmalbaf might be placed in the category of directors who believe a film can get by on visuals alone. This lushly photographed, splendidly rendered picture is narratively deprived. Its simple story revolves around a young woman's desire, against her father's wishes, to marry a mysterious man on horseback. But Makhmalbaf proves as diffident with the story as he is meticulous with his carefully crafted images. The result is a film that veers dangerously close to travelogue material. Its length of just over an hour seems to pass in twice that time.

Director Makhmalbaf's previous films include *Marriage of the Blessed, Time of Love, Nights of Zayandehroud,* and *Salam Cinema.*

Gabbeh is not just boring and repetitive, it is needlessly opaque. Unlike India's Satyajiyt Ray and other directors who can elicit universal human dilemmas from the specifics of an unfamiliar culture, Makhmalbaf doesn't provide Western audiences with many tools to understand the seemingly timeless culture he is chronicling. The project began as a documentary look at the Ghashgai tribe, who are most noted for their finely embroidered woolen rugs, called gabbeh. It veered off into a fable that has pretensions to high mystery but is actually quite pedestrian in plot and scope.

Gabbeh is not only the name of the film and the carpets that appear throughout the movie and serve as its storyboards, it is also the name of the young beauty (Shaghayegh Djodat), dressed in bright blue robes, who is the film's central character. We meet her as a bickering old couple stumble down to a stream to wash their bright blue gabbeh, which depicts a pair of people on horseback. As the old woman, also dressed in blue, steps onto the rug in the water, she is joined by Gabbeh, who appears magically out of nowhere.

As the film progresses, Gabbeh tells the story of her long wait for the chance to marry the mysterious horseman. First her father says she must wait for her uncle to return, then for her uncle to marry, then for her mother to give birth. At each turn, Gabbeh displays her sorrow and anger as if the events she is narrating were actually happening in the present. The old woman and man (Rogheih and Hossein Moharami) respond with advice and entreaties. Also, the old man is smitten with Gabbeh and wants to replace his wife with her. The man talks in a staccato, sing-sing voice as if oddly possessed.

Throughout the film, young Gabbeh and the old woman appear and disappear as the gabbeh is washed in the stream. Sometimes they are both present, sometimes only one is. Makhmalbaf plays with vanishing and reappearing images of the two women as if he were toying with the audience, dangling before them a great mystery. But the narrative trick he is employing is transparent and soon becomes tiresome. At film's end, Makhmalbaf makes it clear what all but the most inattentive viewer should figure out right from the beginning; that the old woman and man are Gabbeh and her horseman decades later.

It should be noted that the Moharamis are married in real life. Only the elegantly beautiful Djodat is a professional actor. The rest of the cast are members of the Ghashgai tribe. Their performances are authentic, if unremarkable.

Also wearisome are Makhmalbaf's other two conceits: the device of using the gabbeh carpets as allegories for the film's events and characters, and his use of color as a metaphor for life and nature. The directorial stance resembles that of a simplistic Fellini. The filmmaker seems to feel his devices are precious, because he keeps repeating them. But his methods are obvious and fail to cover up for the limpid plot.

The film's other main character is Gabbeh's uncle (Abbas Sayahi), an itinerant schoolteacher who is able to reach out his hand and pluck colors from the natural world around him for his lessons. The uncle obviously represents some mystic strain in Iranian culture, but what else he stands for is fuzzy to non-Iranians. Guided by a dream that he will find his wife by a stream singing like a canary, he keeps searching until he finds the prophecy fulfilled.

There's also a sequence in which Gabbeh is placed in charge of her younger sister and loses her when she follows a stray goat on a treacherous mountainside path. It seems totally disconnected to the rest of the film. Events seem only to mark time until Gabbeh's longing for her horseman is fulfilled. As the tribe journeys from one fantastic landscape to another, crossing barren stretches, snowy mountains, wide rivers, and marshy meadows, the horseman is seen only at a distance, howling like a wolf. And Gabbeh, a rug on her shoulder, is shown looking off wistfully into the distance, again and again and again. When she finally runs out of patience waiting for her father's approval, her escape comes without warning, as does a sudden tragic climax, which is quickly revealed to be misleading.

Ironically, while Makhmalbaf in tedious fashion keeps pronouncing that "Life is color" and illustrating his point with the vividness of the gabbehs and the landscapes, the film itself grows colder and colder. If life is full of warmth and exuberance, as *Gabbeh* repeatedly suggests, Makhmalbaf seems either reluctant or incapable of showing those qualities in human terms. Gabbeh's father, mother, and lover rarely appear in the film, so there is no dramatic or romantic tension built up among them. Though they are vividly dressed, the characters might as well be stick figures. And the reasons for the father's reluctance to approve Gabbeh's marriage are never explained. What this is all supposed to represent is a mystery. The result is that Western audiences view an allegory that is meaningless to them, and are simply left to admire the film's beauty.

And beautiful it is. The camera devours a land that is as stark, rich and seemingly limitless as anything ever shown on the screen. The stretches of southeastern Iran where the tribe roam make the western United States look tame and tired in comparison. The yellows of wheat fields, the deep blues of the sky, the pale green of grasslands, and the pristine white of the snowy mountains comprise a sumptuous palette for cameraman Mahmoud Kalari. And the members of the tribes wear strikingly vivid clothes and weave colorful carpets. In one breathtaking scene, hundreds of the gabbehs are spread out across a rocky riverside area, gifts for the newlywed uncle and his bride.

CREDITS

Gabbeh: Shaghayeh Djodat
Old Man: Hossein Moharami
Rogheih: Rogheih Morarami
Uncle: Abbas Sayahi

Origin: Iran
Released: 1995
Production: Khalil Daroudchi and Khalil Mahmoudi for Sanayeh Dasti and MK2 Productions; released by New Yorker Films
Direction: Mohsen Makhmalbaf
Screenplay: Mohsen Makhmalbaf
Cinematography: Mahmoud Kalari
Editing: Mohsen Makhmalbaf
Music: Hossein Alizadeh
Sound: Mojtaba Mirtahasebi
MPAA rating: Unrated
Running Time: 75 minutes

REVIEWS

Boxoffice. March, 1997, p. 41.
Entertainment Weekly. July 25, 1997, p. 54.
Nation. June 30, 1997, p. 35.
New Republic. July 7, 1997, p. 26.
New York Times. October 10, 1997, p. C24.
Sight and Sound. December, 1996, p. 47.
Time. June 16, 1997, p. 76.
Variety. May 20, 1996, p. 33.

Gabbeh shouts out that the world and its people are full of the color of life. But the movie itself is lifeless because the characters are little more than parts of the landscape who rarely interact in any but the most stilted manner. While Makhmalbaf repeatedly shoots water flowing over the gabbehs, suggesting the stream of life, his film doesn't flow at all, but merely lurches from one astounding panorama to the next. What the director has made is not as much a motion picture as a series of moving paintings. As visual art, the product is stunning. As film, it's dreadfully dull.

—Michael Betzold

The Game

Players wanted.—Movie tagline

"Michael Douglas is terrific!"—Joel Siegel, *Good Morning America*

"A must-see thriller . . . A true 10!"—Bill Zwecker, *NBC-TV, Chicago*

"A masterpiece. The most original and outstanding movie you're likely to see this year." —Paul Wunder, *WBAI Radio*

Box Office: $48,294,305

What kind of birthday present do you get the man who has everything? If he's a bitter, lonely, workaholic, divorcee like Nicholas Van Orton (Michael Douglas), try waking him up with a series of jarring, life-threatening scenarios. That will revive his senses. Van Orton resides in San Francisco inside a huge palatial estate, guarded by ominous iron gates that scream, "stay-out!" He wakes up every morning to the latest financial news, goes through the motions getting dressed and in stilted silence, eats the breakfast prepared for him by his long-time housekeeper, Ilsa (Carroll Baker). As he returns home late in the evening, Ilsa retires to her adjoining cottage and Nick sinks deep into self pity.

Conrad to Nicholas: "It'll make you have fun. You know what that is. You've seen other people have it."

The beginning of David Fincher's riveting new thriller opens with well-crafted home movies that go far to explain Nick's regimentation. He lives in the same house where he grew up, amidst a life of extreme wealth and doting privilege. The young Nick is shown standing with his late father and both individuals look constrained and distant. His father was a man who believed that being a good provider would prove an adequate substitute for authentic love and affection. Nick learned early on that emotions are better kept to one's self and that the dogged, unwavering pursuit of riches should be every mans' main concern.

Though divorced for over two years, his remarried ex-wife calls to wish him a happy birthday, which he greets with indifference and petty sarcasm, although it's clear he still loves her. Ilsa has prepared his birthday dinner: a burger with fries and a chocolate cupcake with a singular candle that he washes down with expensive champagne. Van Orton has immense wealth and power, unquestionable status and respect, yet this is a man with absolutely no soul. During his Oscar-winning performance in *Wall Street* [1987], Douglas' Gordon Gecko gleefully barked "greed is good." Here, he's not so sure. There's a lot of Gecko in Van Orton, but absent is any glimpse of the shallow, chest-pounding bluster. This man needs a cathartic jolt and his brother Conrad (Sean Penn) is just the man to give it to him.

Conrad is as much an extrovert as his brother is introverted. In those previously seen home movies, he's an infant cradled in his brothers' arms and at one time, they were close. While Nick evolved into the stoic business mogul, Conrad became a drugged-out playboy who eventually bottomed-out, subsequently requiring extensive psychotherapy. As these two polar opposite, deeply wounded brothers share lunch, the now "well-adjusted" Conrad gives Nick his birthday present. A gift of adventurous escapism, something of a daring thrill-ride Club-Med for the soul. Conrad has already gone through the program and heartily extols its virtues. Nick looks at the modestly-designed gift certificate where the words "Consumer Recreation Services" appear in the center. He gives Conrad some halfhearted lip service, saying he'll look into it and files the card away in his suit jacket, never intending to follow through. With his curiosity getting the best of him, he visits the company's nearby offices and after some mild pressure from a salesman (James Rebhorn), signs up for the program. The CRS staff puts him through a lengthy regimen of physical and psychological evaluations and a few days later he's informed that he didn't have what it takes to handle the intensity of "the game." Feeling mildly insulted but also slightly relieved, Nick settles back into his normal daily routine.

Director David Fincher was the perfect man to helm this project. His two previous efforts, *Alien 3* [1992] and *Seven* [1995] were unnerving ventures that used a dark palate to paint a sense of endless dread and ennui that never sacrificed their gritty narratives for the sake of a Hollywood ending. While *Alien 3* failed to live up to the mammoth box-office expectations set by its predecessors, the truly unsettling *Seven* hit a collective raw-nerve with critics and audiences alike and established Fincher as a fringe, Gothic visionary. He's definitely not playing by the rules and seems very content to avoid the neat, happy, predictable Hollywood hit machine. The stark, realistic fatalism from *Seven* permeates into this project. He is obviously a fan of all that has come before and draws a great deal of inspiration for *The Game* from Alfred Hitchcock; *Vertigo* [1958] in particular. Like the James Stewart character, Douglas's Nick is basically a loner. Both men have an inquisitive nature and share an unquenchable thirst for the truth, despite any obvious threats to their own well-being. Both are on the trail of a mysterious woman who will lead them to that truth, which is nothing that they (or we) expect. They both appear to prefer the negative aspects of those truths rather than accepting the safer confines of the day-to-day. Unlike other directors (Brian DePalma in particular) whose ideas of homage to The Master is direct imitation, Fincher actually captures the mundane, everyday fears Hitchcock searched for and almost always found. Fincher also incorporates several bits of sarcastic humor into the narrative. Without them, the audience would jump out of its skin.

Echoes of the 1973 western cult classic *Westworld*, which put people in harms way when they thought they were in the middle of a an eccentric, offbeat vacation are also present. The characters played by James Brolin and Richard Benjamin aren't prepared for the game (a robot played with frightening precision by the late Yul Brynner) to become the hunter. Nick's initial rejection by CRS makes all of the freak mishaps that begin shortly thereafter seem like plain bad karma. Testing his survivalist instincts, psychological resolve and sanity, nothing is what it appears to be. The challenges of his professional life that fuel his miserable existence are suddenly taken from him. In their stead are the basic challenges of simply staying alive. At this point, he's not sure whether Conrad's bizarre gift has gone awry or whether it was merely a carefully crafted method for one underachieving sibling to exact some twisted revenge on his over-achieving, patronizing brother.

The beauty of Fincher's sense of timing and keen understanding of the mystery genre is what makes him a very welcomed, talented film crafter. Like he did in *Seven*, he never reveals the significant details too soon. He also gets the most out of his supporting cast, painting them with the same depth and complexity of the lead. Released just two weeks after his gritty *She's So Lovely*, Sean Penn once again proves that he is clearly the most talented actor of his generation. Although his is the first name to appear under the title, he essentially has only three scenes but steals the attention away from Douglas every time (strange as it may sound, this role was originally given to Jodie Foster). Armin Mueller-Stahl is given an even smaller role as a book publisher who heads a division of the Van Orton empire. His mere handful of dialogue speaks volumes. It's clear he was an indispensable facet of the success of *Shine* [1996]. The supporting actor Oscar nomination he received as a result was well deserved. As the slick but understated salesman who convinces Nick to enroll in the CRS program, James Rebhorn waffles back-and-forth between friend and foe to Nick. His guilt or innocence in the conspiracy isn't known until the last minute.

Having broken on the scene in 1991 that began with a series of thankless, forgettable, sex kitten roles, Deborah Unger seemed destined to a career of obscurity. Her role here could change that. She appears as Claire, a waitress who starts Nick's dominos tumbling when she spills a tray

CREDITS

Nicholas Van Orton: Michael Douglas
Conrad: Sean Penn
Christine: Deborah Kara Unger
Jim Feingold: James Rebhorn
Samuel Sutherland: Peter Donat
Ilsa: Carroll Baker
Elizabeth: Anna Katarina
Anson Baer: Armin Mueller-Stahl

Origin: USA
Released: 1997
Production: Steve Golin and Cean Chaffin for Propaganda Films; released by Polygram Films
Direction: David Fincher
Screenplay: John Brancato and Michael Ferris
Cinematography: Harris Savides
Editing: James Haygood
Music: Howard Shore
Production design: Jeffrey Beecroft
Art direction: Steven Saklad
Set design: Alan Kaye
Set decoration: Jackie Carr
Costumes: Michael Kaplan
Sound: Willie Burton
Visual effects supervisor: Kevin Haug
MPAA rating: R
Running Time: 128 minutes

of drinks on him. Like Kim Novak in *Vertigo*, Unger is distant and aloof; an off-putting ice queen who becomes the obsessional object of the leading man's attentions. Her mixture of menace and allure are the perfect vehicle to keep Douglas' Nick in hot pursuit.

Despite advancing in years, Douglas doesn't seem the worse for wear in taking on a role that would tax the stamina of an actor half his age. His previous appearances in other more scandalous features (*Fatal Attraction* [1987], *Basic Instinct* [1992] and *Disclosure* [1994]) went far in establishing him as a leading man whose age proved to be irrelevant to the role. Co-starring with women who were significantly younger than he, strangely enough increased his believability (and in the process, provided those projects with a modicum of class). This role requires his participation in almost every scene. Never do we think he can't handle it and even when he's at his most ornery, we feel a definite connection with his plight.

The one glaring fault with *The Game*, the kind that often mars thrillers of this ilk, is the false ending. While the first ending puts the viewer through an emotional ringer and sufficiently wraps everything up, the second, very unnecessary trail-off ending not only discounts the impact of the build-up, it fades to black and begins rolling the credits on a whimper. If Fincher had chopped off the last five minutes, *The Game* would have been a genuine classic. As it stands now, it's still a gut-wrenching roller-coaster ride that will get your blood and imagine racing.

—*J.M. Clark*

REVIEWS

Chicago Tribune. September 12, 1997, p. 4.
Detroit News. September 12, 1997, p. C1.
Entertainment Weekly. September 12, 1997, p. 109.
Los Angeles Times. September 12, 1997, p. F1.
New York Times. September 12, 1997, p. C1.
People. September 22, 1997, p. 23.
Rolling Stone. October 2, 1997, p. 60.
Sight and Sound. November, 1997, p. 41.
Time. September 22, 1997.
USA Today. September 12, 1997, p. 1D.
Variety. September 8, 1997, p. 75.

Gang Related

The best place to hide is behind a badge.—Movie tagline

"Surprise after dramatic surprise!"—Greg Procaccino, *ABC-TV*

"Gritty, smart and tough! One more example that the late Tupac Shakur was a brilliant actor."—Dan DiNicola, *CBS-TV*

"A high flying hit for James Belushi!"—Don Stotter, *Entertainment Time Out*

Box Office: $5,896,713

Gang Related concerns the nefarious activities of two renegade cops who see their lucrative scam dissolve before their eyes—endangering both of them. From writer-director Jim Kouf (*Stakeout*, 1987), *Gang Related* tells the story of two cops, Davinci (Jim Belushi) and Rodriguez (Tupac Shakur), who twist the judicial system to benefit themselves—and then, predictably, watch the system turn the screws on them.

Rap star Tupac Shakur's last film.

Davinci and Rodriguez have carefully honed a plan that has provided well for them over the last few years. They pretend to be drug dealers, sell drugs to criminals, then kill the criminals and pocket both the money and the drugs. Conveniently the first cops on the scene, they pronounce the crime to be "gang-related" and chalk the entire incident up to another crime from the "scum" on the streets. Repeating this stunt over and over has barely helped stem Rodriguez' gambling problem and provided a nest egg for Davinci, who longs to retire to Hawaii. Using Cynthia (Lela Rochon), Davinci's girlfriend as bait, the two cops rationalize their way out of any morality and accountability for their actions. Only Rodriguez expresses remorse and wonders when their luck will run out. He will not have to wait long to find out.

One night, after another seemingly "usual" gang related incident, Davinci and Rodriguez are shocked to be called to the murder scene—especially when the victim turns out to be an undercover DEA agent. As both their local police force and the federal branch turn the heat up under the cops to help find the killers, Davinci spins a treacherous web of lies and excuses. To obtain a gun as evidence they steal a gun from the police weapons room, effectively screwing up the District Attorney's heretofore certain conviction of a heinous criminal.

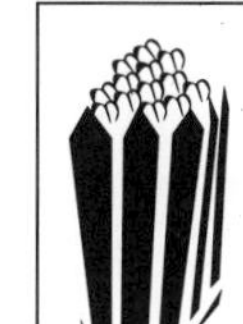

Davinci: "We're gonna find the killers." Rodriguez: "We *are* the killers."

Davinci puts the fingerprints of William, a skid-row alcoholic on the gun, and presents him as the missing killer. Although William can't remember anything about his past, and has so little sense of self that he goes along with the information that Davinci plants in his head, Davinci soon finds out that he has chosen the proverbial "wrong man" as their dupe. For when William is clean shaven and sober, and his picture is broadcast over the news, formidable lawyer Arthur Baylor (James Earl Jones) shows up to speak with William. It seems that William is actually a wealthy doctor, missing and presumed dead for years and Arthur is the family's oldest friend and lawyer.

Cynthia, as part of Davinci's scam, is called to the trial to identify and incriminate William. But Cynthia chokes on the stand when she recognizes William as a bum she frequently encountered in her neighborhood. Davinci's love, lust, and affection for Cynthia turns menacing and fearing for her safety, she flees underground.

Kouf has assembled a wonderful cast and an interesting premise. But by the time James Earl Jones appears on the scene, the storyline has disintegrated into a series of "can you believe it"?! coincidences that pile one upon another. Acting is uniformly good all around, particularly Quaid, who demonstrates a deep sadness when he reveals the history behind the reason that he dropped his medical career and took to life on the streets. Belushi, with his selfish, "take no prisoners" attitude regarding his checkbook, is a perfect counterpart to the more interior, thoughtful Shakur. Cinematographer Brian J. Reynolds (*Guarding Tess* [1994]), TV's "NYPD Blue") infuses scenes with beautifully layered textures, and former Grateful Dead drummer Mickey Hart provides the score.

—G.E. Georges

CREDITS

Davinci: James Belushi
Rodriguez: Tupac Shakur
Cynthia: Lela Rochon
William: Dennis Quaid
Arthur Baylor: James Earl Jones
Elliot Goff: David Paymer
Helen Eden: Wendy Crewson
Richard Simms: Gary Cole

Origin: USA
Released: 1997
Production: John Bertolli, Brad Krevoy, and Steven Stabler for Orion Pictures; released by MGM
Direction: Jim Kouf
Screenplay: Jim Kouf
Cinematography: Brian H. Reynolds
Editing: Todd C. Ramsay
Music: Mickey Hart
Production design: Charles Breen
Costumes: Shari Feldman
Set decoration: Stephanie Ziemer
Sound: David B. Chornow
MPAA rating: R
Running Time: 122 minutes

REVIEWS

Boxoffice. December, 1997, p. 52.
Chicago Tribune. October 8, 1997, p. 1.
Entertainment Weekly. October 17, 1997, p. 46.
Los Angeles Times. October 8, 1997, p. F4.
New York Times. October 8, 1997, p. E3.
People. October 27, 1997, p. 19.
Variety. October 6, 1997, p. 54.
Village Voice. October 14, 1997, p. 94.

Gattaca

There is no gene for the human spirit.—Movie tagline

"Gripping, fascinating and suspenseful! A real thriller!"—Ron Brewington, *American Urban Radio Networks*

"Timely, intelligent and visually potent!"—*Boston Globe*

"This is one of the smartest and most provocative of science fiction films, a thriller with ideas."—*Chicago Sun-Times*

"First-time writer/director Andrew Niccol's movie is a mix of high-tech thriller and impassioned drama."—*Chicago Tribune*

"A handsome and fully imagined work. An impressively fine-tuned first feature from Andrew Niccol. Uma Thurman grows more bewitching with each role."—*The New York Times*

"Visually stunning and smartly conceived, Uma Thurman is radiant!"—Bruce C. Steele, *Out Magazine*

"Streamlined visuals and a provocative plot. Andrew Niccol scores an impressive debut."—*People*

"Smart and provocative. Ethan Hawke gives a riveting performance."—Veronica Mixon, *The Philadelphia Inquirer*

Box Office: $12,284,471

Gattaca tells a cautionary tale about the future when science, technology, big business, and government have created a sterile, regimented civilization devoted to colonization of outer space. So many spaceships are blasting off each day that nobody notices, except for young Vincent Freeman (Ethan Hawke), a janitor at Gattaca Corporation, the futuristic equivalent of the Kennedy Space Center at Cape Canaveral. Vincent yearns to be an astronaut but was born an "In-Valid" (his misguided parents conceived him "the old-fashioned way"). His inferior genetic makeup disqualifies him for any good jobs. His resentment has made him a loner and a renegade, not unlike Bernard Marx, the hero of Aldous Huxley's utopian novel *Brave New World* (1932), who was born in a bottle like everybody else but was thought to have had alcohol accidentally added to his blood-surrogate.

Vincent: "They used to say that 'a child conceived in love is a child of happiness.' They don't say that anymore."

Deemed inferior because of his birth, Vincent Freeman (Ethan Hawke) assumes a more "perfect" identity in the sci-fi drama *Gattaca.*

Vincent's brother Anton (Loren Dean) was engineered with perfect genes and is therefore eligible to receive all the prerogatives of the upper class, including the best education and choice of careers. He is a yuppie of the future. Though handicapped by a defective heart, Vincent wants to prove he is as good as Anton. Their favorite mode of competition is swimming side by side out into the ocean until one "chickens out."

Too much is made of their sibling rivalry. Its only real plot function is to explain Vincent's obsession with personal achievement. Most people who are genetically "in-valid" are resigned to accepting underclass status. They do all the dirty work, and many find no work at all. Tomorrow's homeless look no different from today's and are treated the same. But Vincent refuses to accept second-class status. His motivation drives the story—although many viewers might feel it would be better to be a vagrant or a flunky than the kind of hyper-conformist zombie who gets the cushy job and the fat salary.

Opportunity knocks. Vincent meets German (Tony Shalhoub), an underworld character who sells false identities to the genetically inferior. German introduces Vincent to Eugene (Jude Law), a handsome elitist destined to be a space engineer until an accident confined him to a wheelchair. Eugene is willing to let Vincent assume his identity for a price. Vincent must support him in the luxury to which he has always been accustomed and also pay German 25% of the big yuppie income he will receive as an astronaut.

Gattaca is carefully guarded. No one is allowed access to the sensitive areas without proper I.D., which involves taking a tiny bloody sample from each worker's finger on a daily basis. The futuristic equipment can identify anyone instantaneously through analyzing DNA. The smallest quantity is all it takes—an eyelash, a hair, a few skin scales, even the trace of saliva left in glue after someone licks an envelope. Vincent's problem is to circumvent all the identification safeguards.

Title refers to the genetic sequence guanine, adenine, thymine, and cytosine that exists in every human being.

Candidates for space assignments begin at desk jobs. Following Vincent to work, the viewer sees how he is fooling the equipment. He has a flesh-colored cover on his index finger that contains drops of Eugene's blood. On days when Vincent expects the security staff to be taking urine and larger blood samples, he comes to work with plastic bags of Eugene's bodily fluids strapped to his body. He has to get up early, bathe, shave, dress, and report to work on time with a body so immaculate that there is no chance of an eyelash or particle of dead skin falling off and giving him away. Not only that, but his morning preparations include making sure he has the correct blood and urine samples.

Jude Law, as Vincent's patron and permanent houseguest, is charming. With his upper-class English drawl, he resembles such actors as James Mason, Leslie Howard, and Rex Harrison who often played English aristocrats. Mick La Salle of the *San Francisco Chronicle* called Law "the acting discovery of *Gattaca.*" If Vincent is stressed out at work, he can hardly unwind when he gets home. Confined to a wheelchair, with little to do all day, Eugene has a tendency to hit the bottle. And any alcohol he ingests could show up in Vincent's blood or urine samples.

Vincent meets an attractive young woman at work, but instead of the kind of comfort and compassion a man would like to get from female companionship, Irene (Uma Thurman) only adds to his stress. Irene is, ironically, a "Valid" with a heart defect that also prevents her from going into space. She is interested in Vincent because he is good-looking and upwardly mobile, but she wonders why he sometimes acts so funny. She spies on him. On one occasion she retrieves a single hair from the comb on his desk and runs a DNA test. Vincent has foreseen that possibility, however, and has planted one of Eugene's hairs in the comb.

Director Joseph, Vincent's boss, is played by Gore Vidal, who has had a few previous outings as an actor but is better known as an author and talk-show personality. Detective Hugo is played by another familiar figure, Alan Arkin. When a murder occurs, Hugo erroneously deduces that the victim was killed by an In-Valid to prevent exposure. An exhaustive search is conducted in an effort to find the intruder hiding in their midst. High-tech equipment is brought to hunt for any telltale eyelash, flake of skin, or trace of saliva. Surprise urine and blood tests have the entire staff lines up for hours, wreaking havoc with Director Joseph's rigorous schedule.

Nobody in this brave new world of the future protests against invasion of their privacy or violation of their civil rights; they line up like sheep. Viewers can only imagine what they will be doing on Titan (Saturn's largest moon) , but it does not look as if they will be having a whole lot of fun. Vincent manages to duck and dodge and fake his way through all the traps, but the stress is taking a physical toll. At this point writer/director Andrew Niccol's script begins to bear a strong resemblance to *No Way Out* (1987), which starred Kevin Costner as a naval officer suspected of murder, a thriller which itself was a remake of the noir classic *The Big Clock* (1948), starring Ray Milland.

Gattaca is something of an anomaly, a science-fiction film without the customary special effects—no intricate mile-long space vehicles, no dogfights with laser weapons. When the astronauts take off for outer space, there are no blinding flashes, no shuddering passenger seats, no facial contortions inside space helmets; the space travelers look like weary businessmen entering an elevator. Instead of wearing futuristic outfits, men wear dark double-breasted suits that suggest a revival of 1920s fashions. Arkin himself wears the kind of raincoat that Humphrey Bogart wore in *The Big Sleep* (1946) and a fedora with the brim turned down all around. Anyone who comes to *Gattaca* expecting a whiz-bang spectacular will be disappointed. As critic Emanuel Levy wrote in *Variety*: "Lacking bankable stars and spectacular special effects, this well-produced, character-driven film should receive solid, if not sensational, response from educated viewers, with potent results overseas and in ancillary venues," suggesting that, like a lot of modern films, it will do better on video that at the multiplex.

As Detective Hugo's bloodhounds draw closer, Vincent and Irene become bonded. She realizes he is the fugitive when she sees him knock out a plainclothesman who stops him for questioning. There is minimal sex in the film. The ambitious female of the future does not seem

AWARDS AND NOMINATIONS

Academy Awards 1997 Nominations: Art Direction

Golden Globe Awards 1998 Nominations: Original Score

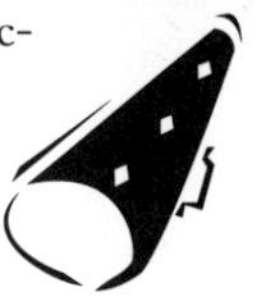

made for cuddling. Vincent's proletarian virility, his refreshing anti-establishmentarian attitude, and the excitement of the chase, however, melt her a little. *Gattaca* raised some questions, as well as a few eyebrows. Joe Morgenstern gave his *Wall Street Journal* review a Freudian spin but thinking the real emotional relationship was between Vincent and Eugene rather than between Vincent and Irene. Morgenstern called *Gattaca* "a crypto-gay romance in a not-too-distant future when it's OK once again to exchange bodily fluids."

It is touch and go until the spaceship is on the launching pad and the brainwashed, look-alike passengers are filing aboard to do whatever men can do on Titan in double-breasted suits. Then Vincent flunks the final blood test. He may not only miss the flight but spend the rest of his life orbiting the earth in some futuristic hoosegow.

In an epigraph to *Brave New World,* Huxley quotes Nicolas Berdiaeff as suggesting what might be the thesis of all such cautionary sci-fi tales as *Gattaca:* "The time will come when thinking people will look for ways to avoid utopias and to return to a non-utopian society, less 'perfect' and more free." Amen to that!

—Bill Delaney

CREDITS

Vincent/Jerome: Ethan Hawke
Irene: Uma Thurman
Jerome/Eugene: Jude Law
Director Joseph: Gore Vidal
Detective Hugo: Alan Arkin
Anton: Loren Dean
Lamar: Xander Berkeley
Marie: Jayne Brook
Antonio: Elias Koteas
German: Tony Shalhoub
Caesar: Ernest Borgnine

Origin: USA
Released: 1997
Production: Danny DeVito, Michael Shamberg, and Stacey Sher for Jersey Films; released by Columbia Pictures
Direction: Andrew Niccol
Screenplay: Andrew Niccol
Cinematography: Slawomir Idziak
Editing: Lisa Zeno Churgin
Music: Michael Nyman
Production design: Jan Roelfs
Art direction: Sarah Knowles
Set decoration: Nancy Nye
Costumes: Colleen Atwood
Sound: Stephan Von Hasse-Mihalik
Special effects: Gary D'Amico
MPAA rating: PG-13
Running Time: 112 minutes

REVIEWS

Boxoffice. November, 1997, p. 122.
Chicago Tribune. October 24, 1997, p. 4.
Cinemafantastique. November, 1997, p. 10.
Entertainment Weekly. October 31, 1997, p. 76.
Los Angeles Times. October 24, 1997, p. F6.
New York Times. October 24, 1997, p. E18.
People. November 3, 1997, p. 21.
San Francisco Chronicle. October 24, 1997, p. C3.
Sight and Sound. March, 1998, p. 48.
USA Today. October 24, 1997, p. 6D.
Variety. September 15, 1997, p. 70.
Village Voice. October 28, 1997, p. 84.
Wall Street Journal. October 24, 1997, p. A20.

Gentlemen Don't Eat Poets; The Grotesque; Grave Indiscretions

Obsession, seduction, murder . . . and it's only the butler's first week on the job.—Movie tagline

"Sting's terrific, poised and stylishly seductive . . . A lascivious delight of a movie . . . lip-lickingly kinky and joyously odd."—Rex Reed, *New York Observer*

The year is 1949, when a new butler, Fledge (Sting) comes to Crook House, once one of England's stately homes, now a disintegrating rock pile. The lord of the manor is Sir Hugo Coal (Alan Bates), who is far more interested in his collection of old bones than in the luscious body of his wife, the American-born Lady Harriet Coal (Theresa Russell). Enter Fledge, who quickly beds Lady Harriet *and* Sir Hugo, shaking up the status quo considerably. It soon becomes apparent that Fledge, who dresses like an aristocrat, represents the rising British lower classes, poised to take over from the decaying landed gentry.

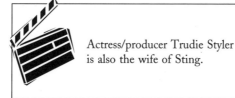

Actress/producer Trudie Styler is also the wife of Sting.

Sting plays Fledge with arched eyebrows and sinister overtones. We begin to see just how sinister a figure Fledge is when his ambitions are threatened by a young poet, Sidney Giblet (Steven Mackintosh), who wants to marry Sir Hugo's only daughter, the lovely Cleo (Lena Headey). Fortunately for Fledge, his interests coincide at this point with those of Sir Hugo, who is violently opposed to Giblet. After Giblet observes Fledge seducing Lady Harriet and confronts the butler with this knowledge, Fledge seduces him, and the poet is seen no more.

At this point, *Gentlemen Don't Eat Poets*, which started out as what critic Rex Reed calls a "comedy of bad manners," metamorphoses into a murder mystery, in which Giblet—as his name implies—becomes more than food for thought. Who is to blame for the disappearance of young Giblet? Is it the cunning arriviste Fledge, or is it George Lecky (Jim Carter), the gamekeeper who is Sir Hugo's most loyal employee? After Giblet's body is discovered, having been dismembered and gnawed on by pigs, George comes under suspicion, even though he claims that his half-witted pig farmer brother, John (Chris Barnes), discovered Giblet's corpse when he disturbed someone trying to bury it. The unfortunate George is hanged, but Cleo remains unconvinced of his guilt. Rifling through Fledge's belongings, she comes across newspaper clippings describing the mysterious death of Fledge's former employer. Cleo shares her discovery with her father, but in confronting the butler, Sir Hugo is felled by a stroke. It is up to Cleo to avenge the murder of her betrothed, whom she suspects Fledge's drunken wife (played by Sting's real-life wife, Trudie Styler) has just served up to the family as an especially strong-tasting ham. Reading up on her witchcraft, she distills a poison from the skin excretions of the family's pet toad, with which she anoints Fledge's after-dinner pipe. As the incapacitated Lord Hugo impotently watches Fledge dance with Lady Harriet and presumably retire with her to the connubial bed—the one-time servant's ambitions fully realized—our eyes remain focused on the deadly pipe. Gentlemen don't eat poets, but Fledge is no gentleman and is about to receive his comeuppance.

The screenplay for *Gentlemen Don't Eat Poets* was adapted by Patrick McGrath from his darkly comic novel, *The Grotesque*

CREDITS

Sir Hugo Coal: Alan Bates
Fledge: Sting
Lady Harriet Coal: Theresa Russell
Cleo Coal: Lena Headey
Sidney Giblet: Steven Mackintosh
Doris: Trudie Styler
Mrs. Giblet: Anna Massey
Harbottle: Timothy Kightley
George Lecky: Jim Carter
Inspector Limp: James Fleet

Origin: Great Britain
Released: 1995, 1997
Production: Trudie Styler for J&M Entertainment and Xingu Films; released by Live Entertainment
Direction: John Paul Davidson
Screenplay: Patrick McGrath; based on his novel
Cinematography: Andrew Dunn
Editing: Tariq Anwar
Music: Anne Dudlem
Production design: Jan Roelfs
Costumes: Colleen Atwood
Sound: Chris Atwood
MPAA rating: R
Running Time: 98 minutes

(1996), and it seems to have lost something in translation. British class warfare is sketched in broad strokes, reflected in the names of the characters, which include not just Sidney Giblet, but the ineffectual Inspector Limp (James Fleet), who investigates Giblet's murder, and Lavinia Freebody (Maria Aitken), who arrives at Crook House in the aftermath of the murder with the poet's grieving mother, Mrs. Giblet (Anna Massey). The storytelling itself becomes rather grotesque, as we watch Sir Hugo fall asleep with a book titled *Extinct Animals* resting on his chest and, after his stroke, hear him referred to as a "vegetable" just as a huge platter of cabbage appears at the table.

In the pivotal role of Sir Hugo, Alan Bates wildly overacts—himself becoming the gamy ham we are obliged to digest. Sting does manage to convey an impression of sinister ambition, but he, too, delivers a character without any real shading or nuance. To be fair, the screenplay does not allow much character development, but when the satiric send-up of upper class decay devolves into a whodunit, some change of pace seems in order. In the end, *Gentlemen Don't Eat Poets* promises more than it delivers: it is neither a true satire nor a compelling—or even very interesting—mystery. It compares unfavorably with other examples of the distinctive British genre of the Gothic absurd, the most recent of which, *Cold Comfort Farm* (1996), is both more charming and more surprising.

—*Lisa Paddock*

REVIEWS

Entertainment Weekly. March 28, 1997, p. 52.
Los Angeles Times. March 14, 1997, p. F12.
New York Times. March 7, 1997, p. B7.
Sight and Sound. August, 1996, p. 50.
Variety. September 25, 1995, p. 95.
Village Voice. March 11, 1997, p. 74.

George of the Jungle

"One of the funniest films that I have seen in a long time!"—Jimmy Carter, *Nashville Network*

"Everyone will love this wild and funny ride!" —Don Stotter, *WDZL-TV*

"The most fun you will have in the movies this summer!"—Bill Bregoli, *Westwood One Radio*

"Howlingly funny!"—Roger Moore, *Winston Salem Journal*

"A comedy smash!"—Bill Zwecker, *WMAQ-TV, Chicago*

"Watch out! Here comes the surprise smash of the summer!"—Mike Cidoni, *WOKR-TV, Rochester*

Box Office: $105,239,073

Based on the enormously popular Jay Ward cartoon of the 1960's, Walt Disney's *George of the Jungle* is a fully satisfying, live-action cartoon in its own right. Containing talking apes, idiotic henchmen, stuffy heiresses, and a good-hearted, muscle-bound lead, this film perfectly captures the spirit of the original subject with the added dimension of modern special effects.

Baby George, as we are shown from the amusing cartoon preface, wandered away from a plane crash and was subsequently raised by friendly apes in the jungle habitat known as Bukuvu. His education and "socializing," as it were, came from Ape (voiced by John Cleese), a simian given to reading philosophy books and painting the afternoons away. George has been sighted by natives and poachers alike and goes by the legend "White Ape." George, as the booming voice of the Narrator (Keith Scott) informs us, grows up into a handsome young man (Brendan Fraser), but is cursed with a good-natured goofiness that hinders his sense of direction and often sends him flying into trees.

Enter heiress Ursula Stanhope (Leslie Mann) on a educational safari. Petite, blonde and hungry for adventure, Ursula is somewhat dismayed when her stuffy fiancee Lyle Van de Groot (Thomas Haden Church) unexpectedly joins her. Lyle is so pompous that his African guides constantly carp and undermine his actions. Ursula and George "meet cute" (in the classic tradition of Tarzan rescuing Jane) when he saves her from certain death by swooping up and away from a hungry lion. George is awed by this blonde beauty and brings her home to Ape—whereupon she promptly faints dead away at the prospect of a talking Ape.

George has feelings that he has never experienced before, and he imposes upon Ape to school him in impressing and wooing a woman. When Ursula recovers and begins to enjoy her surroundings, she is amused and touched by George's "simian-like" approaches to romance. George rolls out the "green" carpet for her, entrancing her with his peaceful jungle family, including his pet elephant, Shep, who larks-albeit heavily-through the trees like a dog (a real-life elephant who shimmies and shakes thanks to the digital masters at Dream Quest Images). Meanwhile, Lyle overcomes his cowardice enough to search for Ursula, aided by his guides Max (Greg Cuttwell) and Thor (Abraham Benrubi), who are scheming to capture "the great White Ape" for sale and profit.

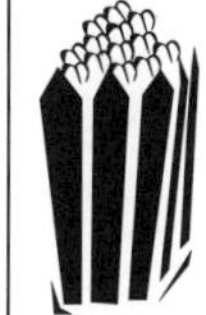

Theme song: "George, George, George-of-the-jungle, strong as he can be! George, George, George-of-the-jungle, watch out for that tree!"

In a twist that defines Lyle's lily-livered nature even further, George sustains minor injuries, which inspires Ursula to fly him home to San Francisco to care for him. In classic "fish-out-of-water" manner, director Sam Weisman contrasts George's earnest, sincere nature with Ursula's snotty, high echelon environment—her mother Beatrice (Holland Taylor) and father Arthur (John Bennett Perry), and her neurotic, man-hungry best friend Betsy (Kelly Miller). George embarks upon a series of misadventures in the city that sparkle with wit; George clothed in Armani, George picks up nouvelle cuisine, George climbs the Golden Gate Bridge, accompanied by dozens of news crews.

The animated TV series "George of the Jungle," ran on Saturday mornings from 1967-1970.

The film is imbued (by both the narrator and the characters' dialogue themselves) with a sense of whimsy and self-awareness that never descends into smugness, and manages to draw in both children and adults alike. In fact, when Ursula boards a tugboat to chase down George on the Golden Gate Bridge, her journey is accompanied by a swell of "Don't Rain On My Parade."

Meanwhile, Thor and Max manage to capture Ape (after seeing him play chess) and prepare to ship him back to the States to sell him as a Las Vegas attraction. George learns of this and panics; his decision to return to the jungle to rescue Ape couldn't come at a better time, as he is learning firsthand about snootiness from Ursula's parents, particularly her mother. George arrives in the jungle and quickly uses his physical prowess to track down Thor and Max. Relying on his buddies—the jungle animals—George thwarts the poachers and frees his mentor, Ape.

Ursula is faced with the prospect of satisfying her parents by marrying Lyle, or following her heart by letting George know how much she really cares for him. She surprises even herself by racing to George's side in Africa. The film ends with a jubilant jungle wedding, complete with an exotic leopard-skin wedding dress, tribal music and the surrounding animals serving as the wedding party. Ursula declares her own independence by choosing her own mate—and George finds his own version of "Jane." Screenwriters Olsen (*The 'Burbs*) and Wells (*The Truth About Cats and Dogs*) infuse this story with a light touch, never smug, only hip enough to make the audience feel included, that they "get the joke" in this gentle tale.

—G.E. Georges

CREDITS

George: Brendan Fraser
Ursula Stanhope: Leslie Mann
Lyle Van de Groot: Thomas Haden Church
Ape: John Cleese (voice)
Kwame: Richard Roundtree
Max: Greg Cruttwell
Thor: Abraham Benrubi
Beatrice Stanhope: Holland Taylor
Arthur Stanhope: John Bennett Perry
Betsy: Kelly Miller
Narrator: Keith Scott

Origin: USA
Released: 1997
Production: David Hoberman, Jordan Kerner, and Jon Avnet for Mandeville Films and Walt Disney Pictures; released by Buena Vista
Direction: Sam Weisman
Screenplay: Dana Olsen and Audrey Wells; based on characters developed by Jay Ward
Cinematography: Thomas Ackerman
Editing: Stuart Pappe, Roger Bondelli
Music: Marc Shaiman
Production design: Stephen Marsh
Art direction: David Haber, Mark Zuelzke
Costumes: Lisa Jensen
Visual effects supervisor: Tim Landry
MPAA rating: PG
Running Time: 91 minutes

REVIEWS

Boxoffice. August, 1997, p. 48.
Chicago Tribune. July 16, 1997, p. 2.
Cinemafantastique. July, 1997, p. 8.
Detroit Free Press. July 16, 1997.
Entertainment Weekly. July 25, 1997, p. 53.
The Hollywood Reporter. July 14, 1997, p. 5.
Los Angeles Times. July 16, 1997, p. F5.
New York Times. July 16, 1997, p. C18.
People. July 28, 1997, p. 21.
Sight and Sound. January, 1998, p. 43.
USA Today. July 16, 1997, p. 3D.
Variety. July 14, 1997, p. 43.
Washington Post Weekend. July 18, 1997, p. 41.

G.I. Jane

Failure is not an option.—Movie tagline
"Two thumbs up!"—*Siskel & Ebert*
"The most powerful motion picture of the summer!"—Steve Arvin, *UPI Radio*
"Intelligent, provocative, and highly entertaining."—Paul Wunder, *WBAI Radio*
"Demi Moore gives the performance of her career."—Jeffrey Lyons, *WNBC-TV*

Box Office: $48,169,156

G.I. Jane opened at the right time to guarantee maximum attention. Every day there were new reports of sexual abuse in the military. Not only that, but there had been glaring exposure of troubles at The Citadel, where female applicants were being accepted under pressure from the federal government and male cadets were using mental and physical abuse to make them drop out. Then along came the highly publicized case of beautiful blonde bomber pilot Kelly Flinn, being drummed out of the Air Force for committing adultery, an offense customarily hushed up when it involved a male officer.

Women have made progress in the military. They have gained acceptance in non-combat roles, but there has been heated objection to allowing women to fight. There have been as many excuses for excluding women from combat as male imaginations have been able to invent. Women weren't as strong as men, weren't as brave as men, weren't as aggressive as men, and so on. Furthermore, men were so instinctively protective and so downright chivalrous that in a combat situation they would spend their time worrying about their female comrades in arms.

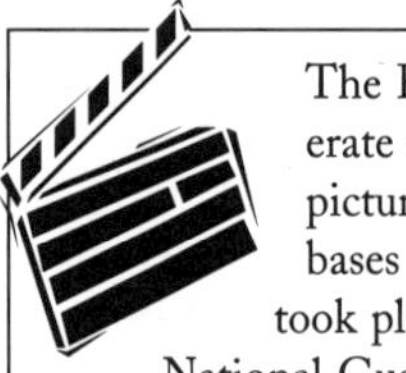

The Pentagon refused to cooperate with the making of the picture, barring use of Naval bases and personnel. Filming took place at Camp Blanding, a National Guard site in Florida.

Then of course there was the sex angle. How could you mix young women and young men in the same unit without having a whole lot of shaking going on? Comrades in arms might really become comrades in arms. This was a can of worms the producers of *G.I. Jane* decided not to open. Their story is only intended to show that women can be as tough as men and can serve in combat as effectively.

Demi Moore as Lieutenant Jordan O'Neil is not subjected to sexual harassment. There is no peekaboo, no hanky-panky, no innuendo, no groping, no attempted rape. One might almost think these men were unaware that one of their buddies was equipped with a gorgeous set of curves and didn't have to shave every day. One of these strange young warriors actually protests against having a beautiful young woman sleeping right in the next bunk. War is hell!

Lieutenant O'Neil is being used as a pawn by Texas Senator Lillian DeHaven (Anne Bancroft), senior member of the arms committee. This tough-talking lady is playing a deep game. It turns out that she was never really interested in proving that a woman could pass through "the most intensive military training known to man." The government is closing military bases all over the country in response to the collapse of the Soviet Empire and pressure to balance the federal budget. Senator DeHaven is mainly interested in insuring her political popularity. Knowing full well that the top brass—all cigar-smoking males—do not want women in combat roles, she is willing to offer a trade-off. She will approve their man as the new secretary of the Navy. She will let them sabotage her highly publicized test case by making things so tough for G.I. Jane that the young woman will throw in the towel. They in turn will guarantee that none of the military bases to be closed will be located in her home state of Texas.

The writers have given O'Neil a boyfriend, mainly in order to make it clear that she is not a lesbian. Publicity-conscious Senator DeHaven was careful about selecting a test subject who was feminine and photogenic. She did not want an Amazon who took steroids and had questionable chromosomes. When O'Neil and Royce (Jason Beghe) first appear together they are sitting face-to-face in a bathtub. This is an effective cinematic way of establishing that O'Neil is definitely heterosexual, while at the same time the argument between the two naked lovers can spell out the basic conflict.

Royce, a Naval officer, cannot understand why any woman would want to spend eight weeks of torture with a lot of macho men. The men are trying to prove their masculinity. They are bound to resent the presence of a woman. If she can do what they can do, it will make what they can do less impressive. They want to prove they are supermen—but what is O'Neil trying to prove? While sitting naked in the bathtub she explains that she wants to climb the ladder of promotion to the highest possible rung, and she knows that the only way to do so is by getting combat experience. Otherwise she will be confined to a desk job and end up retiring as a junior officer.

Most of the story concerns the rigorous SEALs training program which only forty percent of male candidates survive. The Navy obviously cooperated wholeheartedly with the filmmakers, providing them with everything from helicopters to aircraft carriers in exchange for valuable publicity. SEAL trainees get more rigorous training than even Marine recruits. Most viewers will wonder how anyone, male or female, could get through the Hell Week that is dramatized on the screen—or would want to. These gung-ho young athletes are kept awake day and night, subjected to endless drilling, inhuman physical demands, and terrifying obstacle courses involving machine guns with live ammunition and exploding land mines, always accompanied by verbal abuse. They are covered in muck and half-drowned in the ocean. Much of the time they are cold and hungry. They sometimes wolf down food retrieved from garbage cans.

The objective, as they are constantly reminded by priggish, sadistic Master Chief John Urgayle (Viggo Mortensen), is to make the weaklings drop out. Urgayle makes Sergeant Markoff (Brian Donlevy) of the classic Foreign Legion film *Beau Geste* (1939) look like Mother Teresa—but the boys love him. Even O'Neil grows to love him, but not before she knocks out a couple of his teeth and kicks him in a very sensitive place. Screenwriters Danielle Alexandra and David Twohy tried to make this stereotypical drill sergeant a three-dimensional character by having him read and quote poetry. O'Neil is strongly motivated to succeed. Urgayle is just as strongly motivated to make her quit. This is the core of the story, reminiscent of the conflict between Zack Mayo (Richard Gere) and Sergeant Emil Foley (Louis Gossett, Jr.) in *An Officer and a Gentleman* (1982).

The final stage of the training program is called S.E.R.E. ("survival, evasion, resistance and escape"). The conditions are meant to simulate what might be inflicted on commandos who fell into enemy hands. O'Neil and her companions end up in wooden tiger cages. One by one they are taken off to be interrogated with verbal and physical abuse. These repellant scenes immediately call to mind the harrowing episode in *The Deer Hunter* (1978) in which two American soldiers are forced to play Russian Roulette while their friend is nearly drowning in the cage in the river.

The SEALs are what used to be called commandos. Their main function is to mount clandestine amphibious operations. *G.I. Jane* culminates with such an operation against the hostile nation of Libya. O'Neil and her comrades are assigned to a rescue mission. They are spotted by a Libyan patrol unit and all hell breaks loose. Master Chief Urgayle, leading the operation, is badly wounded. Who should decide to brave a hail of enemy bullets to rescue him but his arch-enemy Lieutenant O'Neil? Like many military films of the past, *G.I. Jane* ends with everybody at dress parade shaking hands and passing out medals. O'Neil gets her coveted SEAL insignia along with the others who have managed to survive the training course and the Libyan debacle. Urgayle acknowledges not only his gratitude to the brave young woman for saving his life but also his respect for her as a fellow warrior.

Critics had mixed feelings about this film, although they recognized its technical merits. The direction by Ridley Scott is first-class. Cinematographer Hugh Johnson's nighttime and daytime photography is the film's outstanding feature. Demi Moore does a fine job in a role that was tailormade for her. The supporting cast is excellent, especially Mortensen and old pro Anne Bancroft. Nevertheless, there is something not entirely satisfying about this production. It does not seem to prove its case that women belong in combat but only that one exceptionally motivated and exceptionally athletic young woman can perform as well as equally motivated and equally athletic young men. It is a triumph for Lieutenant O'Neil but not for women in general.

Films like *G.I. Jane* and *Courage Under Fire* (1996) raise more questions than they answer. Can the military ever really become as gender-blind as it has supposedly become color-blind? The idea of having men and women serving together in the military as complete equals is nothing new. It was recommended 2400 years ago by Plato. He even suggested that it would be a good idea to have young male and female soldiers wrestle in the nude—something American military recruiters haven't thought of yet. Is this feminization of the military (which seems to correspond to the feminization of police forces and prisons) a sign of the times? Will armies of the future be like those envisioned in *Things to Come*

CREDITS

Lt. Jordan O'Neil: Demi Moore
Master Chief John Urgayle: Viggo Mortensen
Sen. Lillian DeHaven: Anne Bancroft
Royce: Jason Beghe
C.O. Salem: Scott Wilson
Blondell: Lucinda Jenney

Origin: USA
Released: 1997
Production: Roger Birnbaum, Demi Moore and Suzanne Todd for Scott Free and Largo Entertainment; released by Hollywood Pictures
Direction: Ridley Scott
Screenplay: David Twohy and Danielle Alexandra
Cinematography: Hugh Johnson
Editing: Pietro Scalia
Music: Trevor Jones
Production design: Arthur Max
Art direction: Richard Johnson
Set design: Thomas Minton
Costumes: Marilyn Vance
Stunt coordinator: Phil Neilson
MPAA rating: R
Running Time: 124 minutes

(1936), based on the H.G. Wells story in which he envisioned the use of "peace gas" rather than bullets and bombs? Has the U.S. become such an almighty superpower that it has to use gentleness, compassion and persuasion to avoid bad press?

Perhaps the biggest question is this. Is the public being insidiously conditioned to accept the idea of drafting women should the U.S. become involved in another really big war? Will women someday wake up to discover that, whether they like it or not, their courageous sisters like G.I. Jane have won them the right to have arms and legs blown off, to kill and be killed, to wear dog tags and be treated like dogs, just like men?

—Bill Delaney

REVIEWS

Boxoffice. September, 1997, p. 116.
Chicago Tribune. August 22, 1997, p. 4.
Entertainment Weekly. August 22, 1997, p. 105.
Los Angeles Times. August 22, 1997, p. F1.
New York Times. August 22, 1997, p. B1.
People. August 25, 1997, p. 23.
Rolling Stone. September 4, 1997, p. 74.
Sight and Sound. November, 1997, p. 42.
Time. August 25, 1997.
USA Today. August 22, 1997, p. 7D.
Variety. August 11, 1997, p. 56.
Village Voice. August 26, 1997, p. 73.

Going All the Way

In love and life there's only one way to go.—Movie tagline

"A classic, filmed with wit and flair."—Graham Fuller, *Interview*

"Ben Affleck gives a terrifically engaging performance."—Stephen Farber, *Movieline*

"Wonderfully entertaining! A moving, funny and utterly charming tale of youth and self-discovery, beautifully set in the turbulent fifties."—Paul Wunder, *WBAI Radio*

As Norman Rockwell-type drawings roll over the opening credits of *Going All the Way*, the soundtrack plays "A White Sportcoat and a Pink Carnation," depicting the wholesome image of life in the '50s. This film follows the awakening of two young men who become unlikely friends when traveling home on the train after the Korean war.

Although these soldiers ran with opposite crowds in high school—Sonny Burns (Jeremy Davies) was an introverted photographer for the paper, and Gunner Casselman (Ben Affleck) was a popular athlete—they learn they have more in common now. Gabbing about Buddhism and Communism, they smoke and drink until arriving in Indianapolis.

Sonny: "I don't believe in God. I don't even like the guy."

Sonny is met by his overbearing, religious parents, while an attractive woman picks Gunner up at the station. Sonny's childhood sweetheart welcomes him back with a cake and a smile, but he's overwhelmed with the reception. At the "perfect" breakfast table, his terminally cheery mother (Jill Clayburgh) serves him pie as his father hounds him about finding a job with a retirement plan.

Despite his mother's admonition "If you lie down with dogs, you come up with fleas," Sonny meets up with his new friend for some deep dialogue, soul-searching and pursuit of women. Being befriended by a self-assured guy gives the shy and sheltered Sonny a look into an enticing lifestyle, fueling him strength to stand up to his repressive environment.

Gunner puts off his marriage-seeking girlfriend when he falls for a sophisticated art student who's both sexy and smart. But his mother (Lesley Ann Warren)—the voluptuous woman who met him at the train station—remarks on how he can't be serious about the Jewish girl. Sonny's mother foists a prisoner who found God onto him, but he rejects the proselytizer, stating he'll find his own way. The young men refuse to conform to a world they see filled with hypocrisy under a perfect surface.

Sonny sends his girlfriend mixed messages, standing her up when he meets his fantasy woman. Suddenly he comes out of himself, entertaining to impress the woman, but his performance is less successful sexually, and the shame shatters his dream and his new self-image. He tears home half-naked, the voices in his head building to a cacophony, and tries to commit suicide.

Gunner plans the escape to New York. Driving in the rain, Sonny falls asleep at the wheel and crashes the car. Af-

CREDITS

Sonny Burns: Jeremy Davies
Gunner Casselman: Ben Affleck
Buddy Porter: Amy Locane
Gale Ann Thayer: Rose McGowan
Marty Picker: Rachel Weisz
Alma Burns: Jill Clayburgh
Nina Casselman: Lesley Ann Warren

Origin: USA
Released: 1997
Production: Tom Gorai and Sigurjon Sighvatsson for Lakeshore Entertainment; released by Polygram Filmed Entertainment
Direction: Mark Pellington
Screenplay: Dan Wakefield; based on his novel
Cinematography: Bobby Bukowski
Editing: Leo Trombetta
Music: Tomandandy
Production design: Therese Deprez
Costumes: Arianne Phillips
MPAA rating: R
Running Time: 110 minutes

ter a long recuperation, he's trapped back at home. When he discovers his parent's hid Gunner's postcards, he hops a train to meet his friend instead of meeting his folks at his "favorite" restaurant.

Although critics call this a coming-of-age film, perhaps because of the prolonged naivete of the era, and the term, "Going All the Way" may be outmoded for sex among young adults now, the experience of seeking our own values is always relevant, as is the loss of innocence. The film authentically captures a decade when life seemed more simple. It's beautifully shot and superbly acted, and the interesting period music evokes the emerging changes the characters experience.

—*Roberta Cruger*

REVIEWS

Entertainment Weekly. October 10, 1997, p. 70.
Los Angeles Times. September 19, 1997, p. F9.
New York Times. September 19, 1997, p. E14.
San Francisco Chronicle. October 10, 1997.
San Francisco Examiner. October 10, 1997.
USA Today. October 7, 1997, p. 3D.
Village Voice. September 25, 1997, p. 90.

Gone Fishin'

Even the fish are laughing!—Movie tagline

Box Office: $19,745,922

Every time lifelong friends Joe (Joe Pesci) and Gus (Danny Glover) take their annual fishing trip, something goes wrong. One year it ended in the hospital, another in jail, and once, when they were boys, they caused a major metropolitan blackout.

A similar problem seems to have plagued *Gone Fishin*'s filmmakers. Once they started this film, nothing went right. Not only was it jolted by a stunt accident during production that resulted in a woman's death, but the final product is one of the year's unfunniest comedies.

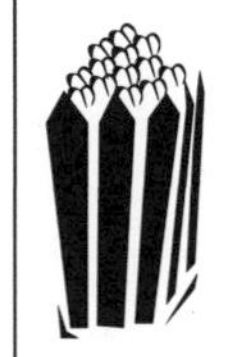

Dekker: "These guys are a two-man disaster area."

The basic story has Joe and Gus entering a contest that wins them a free fishing trip to the Everglades, As can be expected, everything goes wrong for these working-class dimwits. First off their car is stolen by con man Dekker Massey (Nick Brimble) who, while escaping, sends their boat crashing into the restaurant where they are eating. Dekker, it appears, has a history of marrying and then stealing from 43 women, one of whom he stabbed to death. Evidently one of the women he robbed was the mother of Rita (Rosanna Arquette) who is now chasing him with the help of her friend Angie (Lynn Whitfield). So, when Rita and Angie find out Dekker has stolen Joe and Gus' car and later see the boys pushing their boat down the road, they offer them a lift.

Of course, things continue to go wrong. Gus' poor knot-tying abilities soon has the boat coming loose from Rita's car then careening down the road with Gus and Joe as passengers. Even when they manage to stop by throwing the anchor around a tree, they find themselves trapped on railroad tracks with—you guessed it—a train bearing down on them. As they push their boat free, the anchor latches onto the train and Joe and Gus watch as their boat rumbles down the track into the sunset.

Eventually Joe and Gus come into possession of evidence that links Dekker to his crimes—a bloody knife they soon lose—which dashes their dream of collecting the $100,000 reward. Then they find a map showing where Dekker has hidden his millions in stolen jewelry and cash . . . only to lose it, too.

Continuing on their luckless way they manage to blow up a gas station, weave their new boat through a fishing tournament, crash the boat, get a flat tire, get hit by lightning, and burn down a first-class hotel.

Incredible as it may seem, these two disaster-prone idiots are usually totally oblivious to the chaos they cause. And even if they do, in some remote corner of their minds, recognize their calamity-causing ways, they naively insist on always looking on the bright side of things.

Unfortunately, virtually every catastrophe caused by Gus and Joe is telegraphed well in advance. When Gus reads about alligators, we know they'll meet one. When Joe complains about Gus' sleepwalking or knot-tying abilities, we know they, too, soon will cause problems. And if a plot point isn't telegraphed, it's totally illogical. Give them a new boat and no driving lessons, and the boat owner is just as responsible for the inevitable crash as are Joe and Gus. And can these guys really be so stupid that they not only don't call the police when they find the bloody knife, but continue to act alone when they find the map. And why on earth would a murderous villain not kill Joe and Gus when he easily has the opportunity to erase two annoying witnesses to his crimes?

It's bad enough that the filmmakers give us such an unfunny, predictable story, but they also give us unfunny characters. Gus and Joe are idiots of such depth that one could easily believe the title of the film was *Dumb and Dumber, Part 2*. The scriptwriters have tried to make Joe and Gus likable (which, I suppose they are), but they are such morons that they are incredibly irritating. It becomes positively annoying listening to their endless chatter as they discuss their inane plans.

This film was distributed with no advance screenings for the press—typically a sign that even the studio knows it has a bomb on its hands. In fact, the film is such a disaster one can't help but wonder if Gus and Joe had a hand in making it.

—Beverley Bare Buehrer

CREDITS

Joe Waters: Joe Pesci
Gus Green: Danny Glover
Rita: Rosanna Arquette
Angie: Lynn Whitfield
Billy (Catch) Pooler: Willie Nelson
Dekker Massey: Nick Brimble
Phil Beasly: Gary Grubbs
Donna Waters: Carol Kane
Cookie Green: Edythe Davis

Origin: USA
Released: 1997
Production: Roger Birnbaum and Julie Bergman Sender for Caravan Pictures and Hollywood Pictures; distributed by Buena Vista
Direction: Christopher Cain
Screenplay: Jill Mazurzky Cody and Jeffrey Abrams
Cinematography: Dean Semler
Editing: Jack Hofstra
Production design: Lawrence Miller
Art direction: Michael Rizzo, Phil Dagort
Set decoration: Cloudia
Costumes: Lizzy Gardiner
Music: Randy Edelman
MPAA rating: PG
Running Time: 94 minutes

REVIEWS

Chicago Tribune. June 2, 1997, p. 8.
Entertainment Weekly. June 13, 1997, p. 42.
Los Angeles Times. June 2, 1997, p. F3.
New York Times. May 31, 1997, p. 10.
People. June 16, 1997, p. 24.
Variety. June 2, 1997, p. 60.

Good Burger

A comedy with everything on it.—Movie tagline

"A fun film for kids of all ages."—John Pascuzzi, *CBS-TV*

"*Good Burger* rocks with good fun and rolls with a lot of laughs!"—Joanna Levenglick, *Kids News Network*

"A very funny movie! Delicious entertainment for the whole family."—Jeff Craig, *Sixty Second Preview*

"A fresh, funny, super-sized kid's comedy."—Ken Fox, *TV Guide*

"Kids will squeal with delight at this laugh-out-loud comedy!"—Paul Wunder, *WBAI-FM*

Box Office: $23,712,993

Animated burgers plead "Don't sell us, we love you!" in the opening to this story of an old-fashioned burger joint's triumph over the greedy commercialized restaurant industry—a spin-off sketch from Nickelodeon's kid's comedy series "All That." Ed (Kel Mitchell) leaps up from his dream and into the shower, still in uniform—due to his dedicated obsession with employer Good Burger. "Welcome to Good Burger, home of the good burger, can I take your order?" The mouthful slides off his tongue sincerely. Roller-blading to work, he creates a series of calamities typical of this film's plot twists.

Angry customer: "I'm reporting your name to the manager."
Ed: "The manager already knows my name."

It's the last day of school and Dexter Reed (Kenan Thompson, Kel's co-hort from "All That" and "Kenan & Kel") races around in his Mom's car without a license, bragging about the fun ahead all summer. Swerving to avoid Ed, he slams into his teacher's auto. A '70s throwback, the irate teacher (Sinbad) allows Dexter to pay for damages. Instead of hanging at the beach, Dexter gets a job at Mondo Burger, the flashy fast-food spot looming over Good Burger.

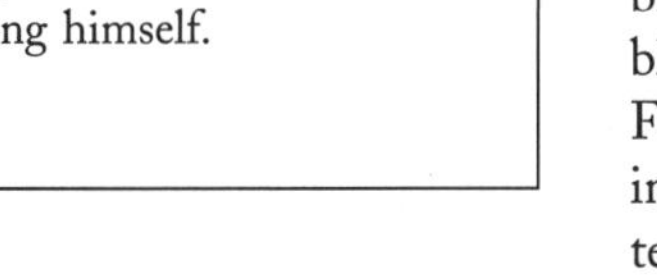

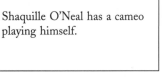

Shaquille O'Neal has a cameo playing himself.

Dexter promptly loses his job and drowns his sorrow in milk shakes at the competitors. He becomes their delivery boy but since he can't drive, he must endure Ed behind the wheel of the wacky Burgermobile. It's an odd group—Fizz, Spatch, a 77-year-old played by Abe Vigoda, and pretty Monique (Shar Jackson), whom Dexter tries to charm.

Meanwhile, Kurt, nasty ruler of the evil Mondo Burger, plots to put the rival in the grinder. The grand opening, a snazzy event with live band, limos and lines, successfully puts the lights out on Good Burger.

However, Dexter seizes an opportunity when Ed pulls out a jar of his homemade special sauce. The delicious dressing is an instant hit and the place is packed again. Ed is offered 10 cents per burger by owner Mr. Baily (Dan Schneider, co-writer and co-producer. His fellow actor from the "Head of the Class" show is director Brian Robbins.) Dexter snags a chunk of Ed's bonus since it was his idea—but the contract only gives innocent Ed a 20% morsel. The partners seal their bond together on the roof, where Dexter shares the sad story of his childhood. Ed is touched by his new pal's tale. Dexter thinks Ed is just touched.

Good Burger's reign over Mondo infuriates creepy Kurt, who devises his next maneuver to take a bite out of his opponent's business—a delicious dish—Roxanne. She arrives at Ed's counter claiming to want him, not lunch, breathily announcing "You're hot!" Smiling simpleton Ed agrees that he works up a sweat working, letting out a goofy chuckle. A few tacos short of a combo plate, he brings buddy Dexter and Monique on the date.

Miniature golf is a disaster. Ed's swing leaves Roxanne in casts and crutches, and her attempts to obtain his sauce recipe go in vain. Monique confesses that if Ed thinks the world of Dexter, he must be a great guy since Ed is the sweetest . . . but her opinion changes after she learns the real split in their financial arrangement.

Ed and Dexter sneak into the Mondo kitchen to discover the now triple-sized burger contains a drop of "triampathol" to make the meat mysteriously grow. The spies are kidnapped and put in an insane asylum while the menacing Mondos poison Ed's sauce. Abe spots them, and also gets tossed in the bin, only to warn of the latest trouble. George Clinton sings "Do Fries Go With the Shake" as the inmates do a dance routine, an entertaining diversion for the guy's escape in the O'Beese Brothers ice cream truck for a madcap chase scene.

The heroes rescue customers from the tainted Good Burger in time and infiltrate Mondo to seize evidence. Ed dumps the triampathol into the grinder and as the burg-

CREDITS

Ed: Kel Mitchell
Dexter Reed: Kenan Thompson
Mr. Wheat: Sinbad
Otis: Abe Vigoda
Monique: Shar Jackson
Mr. Bailey: Dan Schneider
Kurt Bozwell: Jan Schweiterman

Origin: USA
Released: 1997
Production: Mike Tollin and Brian Robbins for Nickelodeon Movies; released by Paramount Pictures
Direction: Brian Robbins
Screenplay: Dan Schneider, Kevin Kopelow, Heather Seifert
Cinematography: Mac Ahlberg
Editing: Anita Brandt-Burgoyne
Music: Stewart Copeland
Production design: Steven Jordan
Art direction: Robert J. Bacon
Costumes: Natasha Landau
Sound: Veda Campbell
MPAA rating: PG
Running Time: 95 minutes

ers cook along the conveyor belt they transform into gigantic ground rounds, exploding the home of the bad burger. Kurt and his cronies are arrested for using illegal food additives as Ed articulates a complex discourse on the process of his clever strategy—changing Dexter's opinion of his buddy.

This anti-food chain film amuses parents and their giggling 7-to-11-year-olds, the prime audience for this ridiculous romp in silly and wholesome fun. More than a deterrent from munching McDonald's, it's a lesson in true friendship, fairness and not judging a burger by its buns. Despite standard gags and foolish antics, if you swallow the premise, *Good Burger* is a harmless take on food fights.

—*Roberta Cruger*

REVIEWS

Boxoffice. September, 1997, p. 119.
The Hollywood Reporter. July 21, 1997, p. 8.
Los Angeles Times. July 25, 1997, p. F14.
New York Times. July 25, 1997, p. C10.
People. August 4, 1997, p. 20.
Sight and Sound. March, 1998, p. 49.
USA Today. July 25, 1997, p. 6D.
Variety. July 28, 1997, p. 57.

Good Will Hunting

Wildly charismatic. Impossibly brilliant. Totally rebellious. For the first 20 years of his life, Will Hunting has called the shots. Now he's about to meet his match.—Movie tagline

"One of the best films of the year! This is one of those movies you'll want everybody you know to see—You will love it!"—Joel Siegel, *Good Morning America*

"Smart and touching with a very warm heart! *Good Will Hunting* is passionately acted by Robin Williams and Matt Damon!"—Janet Maslin, *New York Times*

"Rich, funny and sensationally appealing!"—David Ansen, *Newsweek*

"A winner! Heartfelt and riotously funny!"—Peter Stack, *San Francisco Chronicle*

"Two big thumbs up!"—*Siskel & Ebert*

"Astonishing and thrilling entertainment! Matt Damon delivers the year's best performance while Robin Williams gives the finest performance of his career. *Good Will Hunting* gives movies a good name!"—Joe Morgenstern, *Wall Street Journal*

Box Office: $4,370,528

Friends since childhood, Matt Damon and Ben Affleck each scored individual filmic triumphs in 1997. Affleck starred in Kevin Smith's highly original, offbeat romantic comedy, *Chasing Amy*, and Damon made his first starring appearance in Francis Ford Coppola's adaptation of *John Grisham's The Rainmaker.* As a writing team, they saw their original script called *Good Will Hunting* turned into a critically-acclaimed year-end release directed by Gus Van Sant. *Good Will Hunting* is a character-driven film about a gifted but troubled young man named Will Hunting, who must face the psychological scars of his past and break free of the day-to-day existence that is stunting his growth. The basic formula is not new, but the characters themselves are fresh, and the relationships between Will and the various people who help him are quite compelling.

Damon himself makes his acting breakthrough as Will, a cocky, smart-mouthed kid who works as a janitor at the Massachusetts Institute of Technology and spends his free time hanging out with his lifelong friends, especially Chuckie, played by Affleck. Will is a tough, working-class orphan, in some ways a streetwise punk, who also happens to be a mathematics genius. Damon invests his character with the ambiguity of a person who realizes he has talent and wants to use it but also knows that that talent will separate him from the people he has known all of his life.

Psychiatrist Sean Maguire (Robin Williams) wants to reveal the brilliant mind beneath the anger of young Will Hunting (Matt Damon) in the drama *Good Will Hunting*.

A math professor at the university, Gerry Lambeau (Stellan Skarsgård), gives his students a challenging math problem to solve, and Will solves it anonymously. When he does this a second time, he is discovered and taken under the wing of Gerry, who sees Will as the next Einstein. The problem is that Will is arrested for a street fight (just the latest in a series of arrests), and, in order to get Will released, Gerry must get him to see a therapist. Will goes to several, all of whom cannot cope with his wiseacre persona. Finally, Will visits Sean (Robin Williams), who, like Will, is from South Boston and something of an underachiever, and, because of their similar backgrounds, may be able to break through Will's defenses.

Will as he hugs Sean: "Does this violate the doctor/patient relationship?" Sean: "Only if you grab my ass."

Through their sessions, Sean and Will form a contentious, if finally healing bond. Sean is still in mourning for the wife he lost to cancer years earlier, and Will very quickly touches a nerve when he raises the subject with Sean in their first session together—Will in essence tries to make Sean the patient and psychoanalyze him—and pushes him to the point where Sean grabs Will by the throat for not respecting his departed wife.

In their second session, Sean turns the tables and confronts Will with his lack of real-life experience. Will has read voraciously on many subjects and remembers all he has learned, but he has never experienced anything real. Williams delivers a quietly powerful monologue in which the stakes are laid out—Will can rely on his intellect to push people away but must explore his heart to become a man. (One reason for Will's lack of experience is the insularity of his world—it is safer to hang out after work in bars with lifelong friends in a kind of extended adolescence than to take a chance on the larger world.)

The heroic therapist who helps a troubled young man heal the scars of his past is not an original concept (1980's *Ordinary People* provides perhaps the prototype for this kind of relationship). However, given the general formula, Damon and Williams interact wonderfully, and Williams gives an incredibly strong performance, perhaps the best of his career. It is tempting to compare his work to his roles in *Dead Poets Society* (1989) and *Awakenings* (1990), in which he plays a high-school teacher and a doctor respectively. While his therapist in *Good Will Hunting* has certain affinities with these mentor-like roles, Sean is a deeper character and does not rely on Williams's usual funny-man shtick that even crept into *Dead Poets Society*. In *Good Will Hunting*, we feel the weight of age in Williams's character; Sean has experienced a great loss, and we see the toll it has taken on him. In his somewhat scruffy look and often subdued manner, he seems worn down by life, and yet he is still able to grow along with Will and make a new start by film's end.

AWARDS AND NOMINATIONS

Academy Awards 1997: Supporting Actor (Williams), Original Screenplay
Nominations: Best Picture, Actor (Damon), Supporting Actress (Driver), Director (Van Sant), Film Editing, Original Dramatic Score, Song ("Miss Misery")
Broadcast Film Critics Association 1997: Original Screenplay
Golden Globe Awards 1998: Original Screenplay
Nominations: Best Drama, Drama Actor (Damon), Supporting Actor (Williams)
Screen Actors Guild 1997: Supporting Actor (Williams)

In a change-of-pace scene for Sean, he enthusiastically describes a famous Boston Red Sox victory in a World Series game that he had tickets to see with some friends. The larger lesson of the story, though, involves taking a chance on love, for it turns out that Sean missed the game with his friends because that night he met the woman who would later become his wife; it is a funny, stirring story of true love that is meant to serve as an example for Will in his own romantic life.

Script started out in 1992 as a short story written by Harvard student Matt Damon for a creative writing class.

Indeed, the great love Sean has for his late wife becomes an example for Will. He impresses a Harvard student named Skylar (Minnie Driver) in a bar one night when he wins a battle of wits with a college student, and soon Will and Skylar develop a tentative romance. She brings out his romantic side, but, as an orphan, Will is insecure about his background compared to a rich pre-med student (he even lies to her about having a huge family). Class issues are interwoven into the film; Will and his pals basically live a blue-collar existence, while Skylar (the name itself has an upper-class ring to it) is rich and British. They share several tender scenes together, and their relationship develops nicely, but Will finally is too scared to take a chance on love. She eventually asks Will to travel to California with her, but he turns her down and even tells her he does not love her. Their relationship is heartbreaking because they have genuine chemistry together, and yet Skylar cannot break through the defenses that Will has erected.

As the film progresses, a battle for Will emerges between Sean and Gerry. Gerry wants Will to put his gifts to good use right away and sets him up with job interviews, while Sean believes Will may not yet be ready. The rivalry between the mentors in Will's life goes way back to when they were students together. Gerry went on to a distinguished, award-winning university career, while Sean teaches at a community college. Gerry seems to think Sean wasted his opportunities and does not want Will to do the same.

Obviously we are meant to side with Sean, but it is to the film's credit that Gerry does not become a villain trying to exploit Will. He may be somewhat condescending to Sean and jealous of Will's genius, but he genuinely does want Will to use his full potential; he just may not be going about it the right way. An early scene in which they bond over solving a difficult math problem shows Gerry bringing out the best in Will. We see Will's sense of accomplishment in being able to use his talent, just as we later see the pain that talent can bring when it threatens to separate him from his very roots.

Nonetheless, the greatest push Will receives comes from within his own circle. In a powerful scene that underscores the affection Chuckie feels for Will, Chuckie chastises him for not using his gifts and even suggests it would be a betrayal of their friendship if he did not take advantage of his opportunities and leave South Boston for the larger world. "You owe it to me," he tells him in an effort to show Will what his success means to him. But when Chuckie reveals that he always comes to Will's home with the secret hope that maybe he has already left without saying good-bye, the film falls into some heavy-handed foreshadowing.

This climactic scene does come but not soon enough, and, as a result, *Good Will Hunting* flags a little near the end. Having rejected Skylar and remaining ambivalent about the many job offers he has received, Will and indeed the film itself remain in a holding pattern until the big "cure," which consists of Will coming to grips with his foster father beating him as a little boy—a plot device that comes out of nowhere just to give the film a dramatic finish—and learning that Sean too was abused as a youngster. Will cries and shares a hug with Sean in a climax that is well-acted but feels clichéd (the tough kid finally letting down his guard and showing his vulnerability) for a film that mostly avoids such melodrama.

In a fairly predictable finish, Will rejects the job offers he has received to pave his own way, and the conclusion finds Will driving cross-country to try to win Skylar back. Nonetheless, the last shot of a car going down the open road is a fitting summation suggesting that Will has

CREDITS

Will Hunting: Matt Damon
Sean McGuire: Robin Williams
Chuckie: Ben Affleck
Skylar: Minnie Driver
Lambeau: Stellan Skarsgard
Morgan: Casey Affleck
Billy: Cole Hauser

Origin: USA
Released: 1997
Production: Lawrence Bender; released by Miramax Films
Direction: Gus Van Sant
Screenplay: Ben Affleck and Matt Damon
Cinematography: Jean Yves Escoffier
Editing: Pietro Scalia
Music: Danny Elfman
Production design: Melissa Stewart
Costumes: Betrix Aruna Pasztor
MPAA rating: R
Running Time: 126 minutes

his future ahead of him and that it really could go anywhere.

Good Will Hunting is a touching, often funny story of a troubled boy becoming a man, realizing his potential, and finally breaking free of his provincial life. Except for its melodramatic flourishes near the end, Damon and Affleck's screenplay rings true in evoking the working-class South Boston milieu and making it come alive with fresh characters we genuinely like and care about.

—*Peter N. Chumo II*

REVIEWS

Boxoffice. January, 1998, p. 45.
Entertainment Weekly. December 5, 1997, p. 52.
New York Times. November 20, 1997, p. E1.
New York Times. December 5, 1997, p. E10.
People. December 15, 1997, p. 20.
Rolling Stone. December 25, 1997, p. 175.
Sight and Sound. March, 1998, p. 50.
USA Today. December 5, 1997, p. 1D.
Variety. December 1, 1997, p. 73.
Village Voice. December 9, 1997, p. 69.

Gravesend

4 kids. 3 bodies. 2 fights. 1 night. No $#!*.—Movie tagline

" . . . Fascinating. Riveting cinema . . ."—Jeffrey Lyons, *WNBC-TV*

The English Patient's virtual sweep of the 1996 Academy Awards marked the first time in a long while a film made outside of a major Hollywood studio claimed the brass ring. With the exception of *Jerry Maguire*, the majors were shut out in '96, leading many to hail it "the year of the independents." Miramax, the studio that produced *The English Patient*, has run with its renegade upstart attitude and has managed to find a niche in the fickle American marketplace without sacrificing its artistic edge. Recognized as the leader of the independent movement, Miramax's persistence finally paid off with *The English Patient.*

Strangely enough, the first wave of 1997 independent releases met with critical backlash and dismal boxoffice results. Even the word "independent," when used in this context is a misnomer; Miramax and its many burgeoning contemporaries are all owned or overseen by market-savvy media behemoths such as Disney, Time-Warner, Turner, and Polygram. Besides the prestige factor involved in owning an "art-house" label, these (mostly) silent financiers pony up a minimal investment, thereby expecting little in return. Most importantly, the producers and directors of independent projects are given free rein artistically. Many hard-core film fans feel that once an indie studio loses its autonomy, it must answer, in some form or fashion, to corporate concerns. All this "business" dulls the artistry. Thus indies are independent no more. Luckily for the adventurous types, the next wave of revolutionaries is churning out films that recapture the independent spirit. They've been anointed the new "guerrilla" filmmakers.

Narrator: "Zane wasn't well liked; we were his friends and we didn't like him."

Sal Stabile attended NYU for two years before running out of tuition funds. The death of his grandmother left him with a $5,000 inheritance and rather than go back to school, he decided to sink it into *Gravesend.* At a New Year's Eve party, he met Joseph dell'Olio, a former New York City cop turned cinematographer, who he recruited to be his DP. He met one of his leads at a restaurant (the guy was working as a waiter; go figure!) and the remainder of his cast came from ads placed in *Back Stage.* Although he now had a cast in place, he had no script. He threw the story volley over to the actors who basically ad-libbed everything. As any aspiring filmmaker knows, $5,000 won't get you very far no matter how inventive your techniques may be. For one scene at a corner market, Stabile merely asked the owner if he could use his store. Obviously, the notoriety and vanity factors weighed heavily on the man's mind while he was deciding whether to say yes or no. The recognition factor again worked in Stabile's favor when he needed extras for several fight scenes. Not only did he find ample volunteers, he soon discovered that when he instructed non-professional Brooklyn boys to stage a fight scene, they didn't hold back. The ensuing fisticuffs not only looked authentic, they were often all too real. No phony Sharks and Jets here. In many ways, Stabile's film plays out like a documentary. It could have just as easily been titled "A Night In Brooklyn." While making the festival circuit, rumors of Stabile illegally tapping into New York City street lights for a power supply ran rampant.

Gravesend made its debut (in rough cut form) at the Hamptons Film Festival. Many attending patrons were so impressed, they collectively put up $60,000 for Stabile to fine-tune the film. After playing at the Seattle Film Festival, *Daily Variety* reviewed the film which opened a floodgate of national attention. Soon enough, many publications (including *The New Yorker*) began writing stories heralding Stabile's "can-do" methods. Island Records soon latched onto the project, securing rights to the film's soundtrack and acting as the distributor. The crowning achievement was receiving the endorsement of iconoclast Oliver Stone, who slapped his moniker along with the word "presents" at the top of the credits. This virtually insured Stabile a never ending supply of interested, inquisitive audiences wherever the film played.

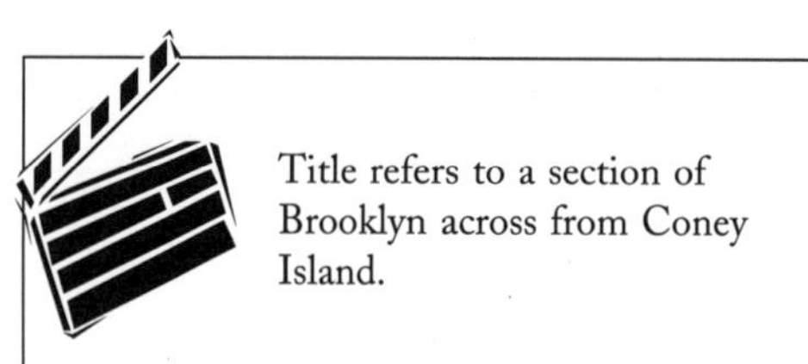

Title refers to a section of Brooklyn across from Coney Island.

Equally harrowing and hilarious, Stabile's film follows four lay-about Brooklynites through one long, often desperate Saturday night. Chicken (Tom Malloy), Zane (Tony Tucci), and Mikey (Thomas Brandise) meet at Ray's (Michael Parducci) basement, stare at each other until boredom sets in, tempers flare, voices escalate, and Ray's brother Sean (Mark Quinn) instructs everyone to leave. After the trading of insults, the impulsive Zane brandishes a pistol and shoots Sean. Teetering back and forth on whether to call the authorities or dump the body, Zane convinces the other three to opt for the latter. A series of comic errors ensues as the boys must come up with the cash to pay off a local crime boss who can make the necessary arrangements needed to solve their problem. As the evening crawls along, the four accomplices turn a possible scuffle into a Mathematics contest, argue about who really is the host of TV's "20/20" and join in unison to sing along with Louis Armstrong's "It's A Wonderful World." Zane's often hair-trigger responses to sticky situations is balanced by an ability to sweet-talk his way out of other potentially deadly scenarios. Zane saves the group from detrimental confrontations with a tow truck driver and an undercover cop with his gift of gab. Stabile ends his film on a relatively shocking note which stays true to the nature of the rough New York streets and could be upsetting to many viewers.

Stabile follows in the footsteps of many now (commercially) successful, former guerrillas. Richard Linklater's $23,000 *Slacker* (1991) led to other higher budget, subsequent, like-minded releases. Robert Rodriguez' $7,000 *El Mariachi* (1993) paved the way for three more projects with fellow maverick Quentin Tarantino including *Desperado* (1995), the sequel to *El Mariachi* that left many feeling he'd lost his edge. Kevin Smith's $7,000 *Clerks* (1994), led to a multi-picture deal with Miramax. *Clerk*'s quasi-sequel, *Mallrats* (1995) also suffered the dreaded sophomore slump. In an ironic twist, Stabile has since been given a two-picture deal with DreamWorks. In an effort to keep Stabile in close check, DreamWorks partner Steven Speilberg has put a $1.5 million cap on those two projects. Speilberg doesn't want his golden guerrilla to turn into a sideshow monkey. Give the young buck enough rope but not enough to hang himself. It's a smart decision.

—*J.M. Clark*

CREDITS

Zane: Tony Tucci
Ray: Michael Parducci
Chicken: Tom Malloy
Mikey: Thomas Brandise
Mark: Sean Quinn
JoJo the Junkie: Macky Aquilino
Narrator: Salvatore Stabile

Origin: USA
Released: 1997
Production: Salvatore Stabile; released by Island Digital Media
Direction: Salvatore Stabile
Screenplay: Salvatore Stabile
Cinematography: Joseph Dell'Olio
Editing: Mireanda Davin
Music: Bill Laswell
MPAA rating: R
Running Time: 85 minutes

REVIEWS

Boxoffice. September, 1997, p. 120.
Detroit Free Press. September 21, 1997, p. 8G.
Hollywood Reporter. September 16, 1997, p. 8.
Los Angeles Times. September 19, 1997, p. F12.
New York Times. September 5, 1997, p. C5.
New Yorker. September 15, 1997, p. 94.
People. September 15, 1997, p. 29.
Village Voice. September 9, 1997, p. 81.

Gray's Anatomy

Gray's Anatomy is the third installment of actor/monologuist Spalding Gray's autobiography. Of course, put that way there is the presumption that he is telling the truth about himself. And like all autobiographies, Gray's is open to question. For one thing, he is a performer, using himself as material. The material is real and yet as soon as he presents it, it becomes another story for the purposes of a film. The sly Gray, however, complicates the matter of veracity further when he remarks that the real people he becomes involved with may suspect that he is turning their stories into another quest for material. He is fictionalizing them, yet in a film which is by definition a made-up thing, Gray's authenticity is bolstered precisely by calling attention to his story-making powers and that they arise out of reality, rather than being opposed to it.

Director Steven Soderbergh fruitfully extends Gray's playing with the reality/fiction nexus by beginning the film with several interviews with people who have suffered from eye problems—the malady that will be the subject of Gray's monologue. These people are not actors. The no-frills black-and-white photography emphasizes their documentary value. They tell horrendous stories without Gray's curiously suave/neurotic delivery. A woman is embarrassed to report that she mistakenly used super glue instead of eye drops, but she does not explain how such an absurd event could have occurred. Rather she relates her anxiety and the choices she faced: she could either have her eyelids surgically opened or wait several days until the glue dissolved. She elected the latter course and all was well. What is curious about her story is that it is believable precisely because it is told without any particular skill or wish to entertain. It is not a boring story because its content is arresting. How awful to be faced with such a terrifying yet also ridiculous situation. Other eye tragedies are told with even greater flatness of voice and paucity of gesture. The woodenness of these interviews is so striking that Gray's neurotic need to shape a story out of his own ailment—and the film's insistence on making a saga of his neurotic need—are brought into high and hilarious relief.

On the one hand, the interviews suggest that everyone has a story to tell. On the other hand, most stories of maladies prove to be incredibly banal—like the mechanic who matter-of-factly explains how he pulled a piece of metal out of his eye and blinded himself. His stoic and stolid narrative is in its own way stunning, the perfect foil to Gray's frenzied search for a cure to his "macular pucker," a draining away of fluid in the eye that threatens to blind him.

Gray: "I don't want medicine. I want magic and miracles."

Gray's previous two films, *Swimming to Cambodia* and *Monster in a Box* are brilliant monologues, but they lack his third film's cinematic form, which comments on his craziness even as he is speaking about it. Soderbergh does follow a pattern set by previous directors, though, in his use of reverse camera angles, so that Gray seems to be turning toward different members of the audience, just as one would in a conversation with more than one person. This relatively simple technique gives the film an intimate feel, as if Gray is not addressing an audience (no audience is present in the filming) but a few individuals. He could be a friend talking to other friends.

And what do friends talk about? Certainly ones that are approaching or who have surpassed fifty are concerned with their health. This is the time when various kinds of degeneration become apparent—when the fiftyish want referrals to specialists and when they seek out alternative forms of medicine when the traditional practitioners let them down. This is the period Gray calls the "Bermuda triangle" of health, a phrase his relative has coined to convey her theory that between fifty and fifty-three the individual confronts a health crisis that will determine whether or not he or she survives.

Gray's own crisis begins when he notices that his vision is blurry in one eye. He is working on a novel, and he does not want to interrupt his concentration or to contemplate the idea that there may be something really wrong with his eye. Several months later, however, the problem remains and a trip to an ophthalmologist confirms that he has a "macular pucker," a kind of bunching up of tissue where fluid has drained out of his eye. There is only a one per cent chance that the condition will correct itself—according to the officious specialist who calls Gray "Gary"—and who recommends a $10,000 operation. An unnerved Gray immediately thinks of his friends who have had disastrous experiences in New York hospitals. At the very least he wants a second opinion. He consults a kinder, gentler specialist (recommended by a friend). Whereas the previous specialist said he had to "scrape" Gray's eye to correct the condition, the second one calls it "peeling," a more soothing concept to Gray. Still, Gray is hoping for some alternative to the knife. Is the operation urgent? No, the specialist replies. They can monitor the condition for a while before making the decision on an operation. And Gray is free to seek alternative solutions? he asks the specialist. Certainly, the specialist says gently, and then he can perform the operation.

Of course, both these specialists exist only in Gray's monologue—that is to say, there may have been doctors just like the ones he describes, but they have become Gray's characters performed with his trademark changes of voice and expression. Gray mocks the doctors as he mocks himself. If he is a neurotic, they seem altogether too confident about their modern specializations. Things go wrong, Gray knows, everyone knows.

This third Gray film approaches the complexity of a modern self-reflexive novel, in which the narrator interrogates his own narrative, raising questions about his grasp of reality, and of what reality means when it has to be filtered through many points of view. Only the most unimaginative minds—which includes some of the documentary interviewees in the film—can treat Gray's woes as merely those of a nutty New Yorker. Not that any of these interviewees comments on Gray directly, except to say that they would not have consulted a psychic surgeon or participated in a Indian sweat lodge ceremony or gone to a nutritional ophthalmologist as Gray has done. Their reactions are hilarious because they levelly consider these alternatives and say in deadpan voices that such alternative cures do not appeal to them.

But if the film is having fun with these rationalists who would only seek conventional treatment, it is also skewering Gray, whose shaky grasp on his identity is wonderfully revealed when he is picked up by two Hasidim who think he is a homeless person in need of work. They drive him to their temple in Brooklyn where he does some clean-up work, performing so well that a neighbor wants to hire him. Gray, who has never been to the Williamsburg section of Brooklyn, seems enchanted with the Hasidim and plays his role so well that he dickers with them, holding out for ten dollars instead of the eight they offer him for his work. Again, it is to be wondered if this incident occurred—or at the least if Gray is embellishing it. Further doubt is cast on the incident when he describes himself walking across the Brooklyn Bridge from Williamsburg—an impossible feat. No matter. Gray himself has already conceded that he is a storyteller. He selects/invents details that conform to the story's shape.

Quite aside from the fiction/fact tension of the film, there are Gray's musings about disease, which include the pet theories of lay men and women, the pontifications of doctors, and the spiritual and psychic healing services of alternative practitioners. Here Gray is tapping into the superstition and professionalism that pervades the culture's discussion of health. When he starts to blame himself for his illness, thinking he is being punished for an inflated ego, readers of Susan Sontag's classic *Illness as Metaphor* will want to rise up and say a disease is a disease is a disease. It is not caused by some kind of psychic or moral sin. But that would end the film—and Gray's exploration of the sneaking feeling of the ill that they are somehow to blame for their sickness.

All this talk of disease, however, is remarkably entertaining. Gray is never less than amusing. A great talker, he can make just about anything interesting because he filters it through an exquisitely perceptive and ironic sensibility. As Henry James said, the artist must be granted his subject matter. It is how he treats it that counts, and with Gray, style is nearly all. Perfectly titled, *Gray's Anatomy* shows him to be in fine form.

—*Carl Rollyson*

CREDITS

Origin: USA
Released: 1996
Production: John Hardy for Bait and Switch Inc. and BBC Films; released by Northern Arts Entertainment
Direction: Steven Soderbergh
Screenplay: Spalding Gray
Cinematography: Elliot Davis
Editing: Susan Littenberg
Music: Cliff Martinez
Production design: Adele Plauche
MPAA rating: Unrated
Running Time: 80 minutes

REVIEWS

Boxoffice. April, 1997, p. 196.
New York Times. March 20, 1997, p. B3.
Variety. September 16, 1996, p. 68.
Village Voice. March 25, 1997, p. 78.

Gridlock'd

Life is a traffic jam.—Movie tagline

"A shockingly funny film!"—Paul Chambers, *CNN Radio*

"A vibrantly gritty comedy. Roth and Shakur seem feverishly alive."—Owen Gleiberman, *Entertainment Weekly*

"Roth is hilarious."—Jami Bernard, *New York Daily News*

"Fiercely funny! Tupac Shakur's best and most appealing performance."—Peter Travers, *Rolling Stone*

Box Office: $5,573,929

In the 1970 film *Catch-22*, screenwriter Buck Henry performed an amazing feat by adapting Joseph Heller's scathing novel that examines the insanity and futile nature of war. Although the film featured an eclectic all-star cast, the story focused on a fighter pilot played by relative unknown Alan Arkin. The armed services required Yossarian (Arkin) to perform a certain number of successful bombing missions before he could receive his discharge. Desperately longing to finish his duty and return home, the pilot expeditiously performed his duties so well, his superior officers kept raising his mission number, making it impossible for him to receive his discharge. In effect, he was being punished for performing his job too well. Directed by Mike Nichols, this project was a war film in only the loosest sense of the word. The film soon became an allegory for the common man's inability to successfully win the game by sticking to the rules.

Spoon: "When gettin' high becomes a job, what's the point?"

Adhering to the rules is what Jonathan Pryce's Sam Lowry did all too well in Terry Gilliam's *Brazil* (1985). A tiny cog in a huge, faceless colonnade, Lowry performed his duties with the type of dulling precision employers only dream about. Lowry did so well at work because he simply had no life beyond his dead-end career. Once he had found love, or at least the prospect of love, his previously high rate of efficiency plummeted. He also fell quickly out of favor with his employer.

As director Vondie Curtis-Hall's brilliant new film opens, three musicians are sitting around a table on New Year's Eve. There is Spoon (Tupac Shakur) the bassist, Stretch (Tim Roth) who plays keyboards and the singer, Cookie (Thandie Newton). They play beatnik-influenced, atmospheric, avant-garde jazz in nightclubs and all three are serious heroin addicts. While Spoon and Stretch share wandering insights into penis enlargement, Cookie is in the early stages of overdosing. Unable to find a cab or an ambulance willing to venture into their neighborhood (a crime-riddled area of Detroit), the two men carry Cookie to the closest hospital emergency room. The unwavering receiving nurse (Elizabeth Pena) doesn't much care whether Cookie dies or not, she needs the paperwork filled out properly before she will lift a finger. Spoon then explodes—angering the nurse even further. Luckily for Spoon and Cookie, a doctor who actually adheres to his Hippocratic oath is within earshot. After several hours of waiting, the men are told that Cookie has a mere 50/50 chance of survival.

With his girlfriend at death's doorstep, Spoon takes a time-out for some personal reflection regarding his own lifestyle. He sees himself as man who has been lucky but believes (like all good things do) his luck will eventually run out. Heroin no longer gets him high, it merely prevents him from getting sick. Whether Cookie pulls through or not, that's it. He's going to "kick." Not wanting to go through the experience alone, he begins the arduous task of coercing Stretch to do the same. After a few fits and starts, Stretch comes around and decides to join his partner on the road to sobriety.

Spoon and Stretch head downtown to begin what will be a long series of searches, rebuffs and wild-goose chases. At their first stop, a rehab house, they are informed by a fellow junkie that they can forget applying for benefits without a Medicaid card. However, if they take an HIV test, their paperwork could be expedited sooner. Stretch is visibly nonplused and ready to throw in the towel. Undaunted, Spoon forges onward. They take the test and are told, not only will their tests be ready the next day, they will receive $40.00 each for their trouble. They will still need to wait a week or so to get their benefit card. As anyone who has ever had an addiction knows, the first week away from their particular poison is always the hardest. After that week, it's mostly just a mental battle. If they're going to wait, they might as well get a fix to kill the time. The vicious circle has begun.

Next stop, St. James outpatient clinic. After waiting all day to be interviewed, they find out the clinic now only handles alcohol dependency. The welfare office is the next stop on the tour. The goal: a temporary Medicaid card. The caveat: you can't get the Medicaid card unless you're already on welfare. In other words, you can't get government assistance unless you're already receiving another form of government assistance. Rush jobs are only given consideration in a medical emergency. Two musicians wanting to get their act together and going straight just won't qualify. Spoon, a major charmer when he wants to be, gets a new name at yet another location who might be able to help them.

When they arrive at their suppliers' home, they find them both murdered. Unfazed, Spoon and Stretch riddle the already strewn-about apartment and proceed to shoot up while their friends' bodies grow stiff and cold. Comfortably numb and the proud new owners of three ounces of heroin, Spoon and Stretch exit and make the acquaintance of two police officers who are investigating the gun shots. One of them (played by director John Sayles) decides to get a little rough, throwing Stretch up against the wall, dislodging his stash. The police eventually go their way, oblivious to the contraband at their feet. Our heroes make one more narrow escape.

John Sayles, who directed Vondie Curtis Hall in *Passion Fish,* makes an appearance as Cop #1.

Like mice in a maze looking for cheese, Spoon and Stretch trudge onward, looking for their Holy Grail in the form of a Medicaid card. They are at the mercy of government employees who whittle the time away, performing their jobs with a minimum amount of effort and following a hackneyed procedure to the letter. Spoon and Stretch soon find out that they are the suspects in the dealers' murder, causing their search to grow even more impossible.

Having made a handful of cookie-cutter urban/gang/drug related pictures prior to *Gridlock'd*, the late Tupac Shakur finally made his mark as a serious actor with this effort. Unlike Stretch, Spoon is a man who is sure about his decision to get his life in order. He is the leader, his friend merely follows. Shakur showed immense maturity for such a young man. His delivery of dramatic and comedic material is top-notch. Unlike many other musicians who have tried their hand at acting, he seems unaware of the camera and possessed a rare, natural quality. He is gone now and the inevitable "what if" scenarios have run rampant since his death. It's a safe bet that he could have gone far in an industry in need of young, serious, talented African-American actors.

Roth, an acting chameleon, shows why he is without peer as the premier character performer of his age. He could have gone Hollywood after his Oscar-nominated turn in *Rob Roy* (1995), but has opted to keep his edge and has remained a fringe player, taking on roles that make him a better actor. He has kept the vision that draws individuals to this craft in the first place.

Is director Curtis-Hall (who also plays a drug kingpin in the film) telling us that going straight is just too much trouble and being bad is good? Is he pointing out just how out of hand the government bureaucracy has gotten? Sticking to policy regarding paperwork and procedure but losing touch with the human element in the process is not what the welfare state was designed for. This exploration also gives credence to the notion that all drugs should be legalized. Spoon and Stretch could care less about the legal consequences of their lifestyle, but they eventually see the physical and emotional downside.

If illicit, mind-altering chemicals were suddenly made available to the general public, would the country go drug crazy? Highly unlikely. The majority of the adult population (and many of the nation's young people) are fully aware of the drawbacks of drug addiction. For the time being, alcohol and tobacco products are legal, but the numbers of people using both decreases every year. If the government wants to rid itself of a drug epidemic, they should take control and curtail its use with basic education. Attempting to stop the import of narcotics has proven to be a futile venture. If a person wants to get high, no amount of attempted prevention will stop them. It's time the government began facing reality. Throw this baby out with the bathwater. It's clear that these antiquated methods will not work in modern day society.

Many have (quite understandably) compared Curtis-Hall's work with *Trainspotting* (1995). While heroin is the common bond in both, *Trainspotting* featured many dream sequences that detracted somewhat from the reality it was

CREDITS

Stretch: Tim Roth
Spoon: Tupac Shakur
Cookie: Thandie Newton
Mr. Woodson: Charles Fleischer
Blind Man: Howard Hesseman
Supervisor: James Pickens Jr.

Origin: USA
Released: 1997
Production: Damian Jones, Paul Webster, and Erica Huggins for Interscope Communications; released by Polygram Filmed Entertainment
Direction: Vondie Curtis Hall
Screenplay: Vondie Curtis Hall
Cinematography: Bill Pope
Editing: Christopher Koefoed
Music: Stewart Copeland
Production design: Dan Bishop
Art direction: Scott Plauche
Costumes: Marie France
Sound: Craig Woods
Set decoration: Kristen Toscano Messina
MPAA rating: R
Running Time: 91 minutes

trying to portray. Curtis-Hall's picture is devoid of such sequences and remains grounded in a stark, gritty, everyday mood that any audience can easily relate to, whether they have addictions or not. After the film is over, it's clear that the drug angle was secondary. Frustration with government monoliths and fighting irrational rules is what he's striving to make clear. He takes two layabout slackers who live in a cesspool and are constantly looking for a free ride and makes them the good guys. Curtis-Hall is telling us that America is still the greatest country in the world. It got to be that way because of a constant need for change and modification. As long as its citizens continue to attempt to fine-tune its inner workings, it will remain great.

—J.M. Clark

REVIEWS

Boxoffice. February, 1997, p. 57.
Chicago Tribune. January 29, 1997, p. 1.
Entertainment Weekly. January 31, 1997, p. 38.
Film Threat. January, 1997, p. 52.
Los Angeles Times. January 29, 1997, p. F1.
New York Times. January 29, 1997, p. C12.
People. February 10, 1997, p. 21.
Rolling Stone. February 6, 1997, p. 53.
Time. February 3, 1997.
USA Today. January 29, 1997, p. 4D.
Variety. January 20, 1997, p. 45.
Village Voice. February 4, 1997, p. 70.

Grizzly Mountain

"Strongly recommended for the entire family."—*The Dove Foundation*

"Enchanting and adventurous."—*The Family Channel*

"Absolutely terrific . . . thoroughly enjoyable."—Elayne Blythe, *The Film Advisory Board*

"Breathtaking!"—*The National Enquirer*

No one seemed to have noticed but *Grizzly Mountain* quietly slipped into theaters in November. After an inauspicious run of playing to tiny crowds in various movie houses, it slipped out just as quietly.

Why the bad run? For one thing, it was competing around the time of the powerhouse battle between 20th Century Fox's entry in the animation field *Anastasia* and the Disney re-release of *The Little Mermaid.* With an ad budget that probably couldn't pay the catering bill for the other two movies, poor old *Grizzly Mountain* didn't stand a chance.

First movie for Haggerty in four years, after his recovery from a near-fatal motorcycle accident.

Of course it didn't help that *Grizzly Mountain* was not an especially good movie. Not only did audiences stay away but critics hated it too. The *New York Times* called it "dull and unimaginative." Critics Inc. was even harsher, saying it "is so deadly dull that it will cause narcolepsy in parents throughout the land."

The idea is essentially a rehash of the old "Grizzly Adams" television show. Dan Haggerty reprises his role as the big, bearded wise old mountain man (though a disclaimer at the beginning of the film informs us that *Grizzly Mountain* and "Grizzly Adams" are in no way related.) How are the two not related? Well, in "Grizzly Adams," Haggerty's mountain man was named "Grizzly Adams," in *Grizzly Mountain*, his name is Jeremiah. So, as you can see, the two are quite different.

The plot centers around dad Bill Marks, a developer, (Don Borza), who is surveying the lovely Grizzly Mountain so he can figure out where he's going to put all the condos and mini-malls. He takes his wife, Karen, (Marguerite Hickey) and kids—Nicole (Nicole Lund), Dylan (Dylan Haggerty) and Megan (Megan Haggerty)—along so he can show them the joys of nature before they're destroyed by all the new development. (Megan and Dylan are Haggerty's real-life kids.)

As luck would have it, Nicole and her younger brother, Dylan, wander off and find themselves at a cave. They go in and, after a show of special effects worthy only of community access television, find themselves back in 1870.

There they meet the kind and gentle Jeremiah. Jeremiah is battling the local bad guys, including an evil mayor (Ed Bell) and Betty, the resident scheming woman (Kim Morgan Green), who want to tunnel through the mountain to build a railroad.

The kids band together with Jeremiah, the local Native American tribe and a host of nice animals, including Jack the Bear and Thor the Eagle, to defeat the bad guys. And everyone has a role to play. The animals either look scary (the bear) or deliver messages (the eagle), Jeremiah dispenses extra folk wisdom for the occasion and Dylan, following in the wisdom of *Home Alone* (1990), uses his toys to help defeat the baddies. (It helps that his toys are 20th century toys, meaning much havoc can be raised with a walkie-talkie or computer war game.)

There are a lot of good things about *Grizzly Mountain.* For instance, there's nothing wrong with the ideas behind the movie. The messages—that nature is good, we should respect native peoples, that greed shouldn't rule our lives—are all fine and admirable. Dan Haggerty's Jeremiah, if not a brash, new character, is certainly a solid, reassuring presence. And the mountain scenery is gorgeous.

But there is also a lot that to fault with this movie. The aforementioned special effects are, in a word, lame. Actually, the whole film has a low-budget, unfinished feel. There are more than a few scene transitions where the sound just cuts off abruptly. The acting is similarly spotty. Haggerty's Jeremiah is good and the kids Dylan and Nicole Lund's Nicole are as good as kid actors in family films generally get. But a trio of bad guy lackeys who are supposed to be comic relief are just heinous. Their antics, like bumping into each other and falling down, would only be funny to, maybe, a four-year-old.

There is nothing really seriously objectionable about *Grizzly Mountain.* It's just that it's seems like no one behind the movie really cared enough about it to make it above average. And if they didn't care about the movie, why should the audience?

—Jill Hamilton

CREDITS

Jeremiah: Dan Haggerty
Dylan: Dylan Haggerty
Nicole: Nicole Lund
Betty: Kim Morgan Greene
Boss Man Burt: Perry Stephens
Marshall Jackson: Martin Kove
Bill Marks: Don Borza
Karen Marks: Marguerite Hickey

Origin: USA
Released: 1997
Production: Anthony Dalesandro and Peter White for Mega Communications; released by Legacy
Direction: Jeremy Haft
Screenplay: Jeremy Haft and Peter White
Cinematography: Andy Parke
Editing: Richard Westover, Anthony Dalesandro
Music: Jon McCallum
Production design: Joe Schilling
Art direction: Christine Schulman
Set design: Patrick Danz
Costumes: Diane Hansen
MPAA rating: G
Running Time: 96 minutes

REVIEWS

Boxoffice. January, 1998, p. 48.
Los Angeles Times. October 31, 1997, p. F22.
Variety. November 3, 1997, p. 100.

Grosse Pointe Blank

A comedy about a hit man, a high school reunion, and the girl he left behind.—Movie tagline

"One of the most refreshing films so far this season!"—Dolores Barclay, *Associated Press*

"Charming, uproarious and startlingly original!"—Jim Svejda, *CBS Radio/KNX*

"This year's most daring and ambitious movie!"—Dennis Cunningham, *CBS-TV*

"A zingy, deadpan-hilarious comedy!"—Lisa Schwarzbaum, *Entertainment Weekly*

"A wild at heart comedy that believes in living dangerously!"—Kenneth Turan, *Los Angeles Times*

"Bright and surprising!"—Janet Maslin, *The New York Times*

"A bright burst of action and comedy! Cusack is brutally funny!"—Peter Travers, *Rolling Stone*

Box Office: $28,084,357

One of the interesting things about *Grosse Pointe Blank* is that it takes three fairly familiar plot ideas and, by braiding them together, manages to make the common uncommon. Story one involves the angst of someone who returns home after ten years to attend their high school reunion. The second is the old story of boy loves girl, boy abandons girl and disappears, boy reappears in girl's life to reclaim her love. Story three is a midlife crisis where the hero realizes he no longer enjoys his chosen profession. Now, make the man who is attending his reunion, returning to his long-lost-love, and hating his job as a professional hit man, and one has just the ingredient to make three relatively trite story ideas unique—and more than a little quirky—when combined.

To the musical strains of "I Can See Clearly Now," Martin Blank (John Cusack) peers through the sites of his high-powered rifle. His target appears to be a businessman on the street below, but in reality it is another hit man who is disguised as a bicycle messenger. After dispatching the messenger, Martin begins disassembling his rifle only to realize yet a third hit man disguised as a doorman has killed the businessman anyway.

Immediately Martin gets on the phone to his secretary-office manager Marcella (Joan Cusack), who finds out the doorman was Martin's rival assassin, Grocer (Dan Aykroyd). Since the fall of Berlin, the hit man market has been flooded. Grocer wants Martin to join a "club" in which they could pool their talents, work less, and make more money. Martin, however, is not inclined to work for Grocer. He likes his independence, but his freelancing is a threat to Grocer's plans.

As good as Martin is at his job, however, he is becoming more and more disillusioned about it. So, he takes his confusions—and a recurring dream about his high school love, Debi (Minnie Driver) to a therapist, Dr. Oatman (Alan Arkin), who keeps trying to get rid of Martin as a patient because he's terrified of him.

When Martin's next hit goes awry and what should have looked like an accidental death now involves bullets, Martin's employers want him to make up for the mistake by doing a job in Grosse Pointe, Michigan . . . Martin's hometown . . . where Debi still lives . . . and where his 10-year high school reunion is being held. Now the love, the reunion, and the professional crisis story all fall together.

While driving around in Grosse Pointe, Martin's car radio pulls in a very familiar voice. Debi, the high school love Martin had stood up on prom night, is a disc jockey on the local radio station. Martin quickly finds her doing her job in the store-front station's window and when he goes inside to say hi, she immediately puts him on the air and asks her listeners to phone in and give her advice on what she should do with him.

Martin: "I'm not married, don't have any kids, and I'd blow your head off if somebody paid me enough."

Most of the film's exterior scenes were shot not in Grosse Pointe but in Pasadena, California.

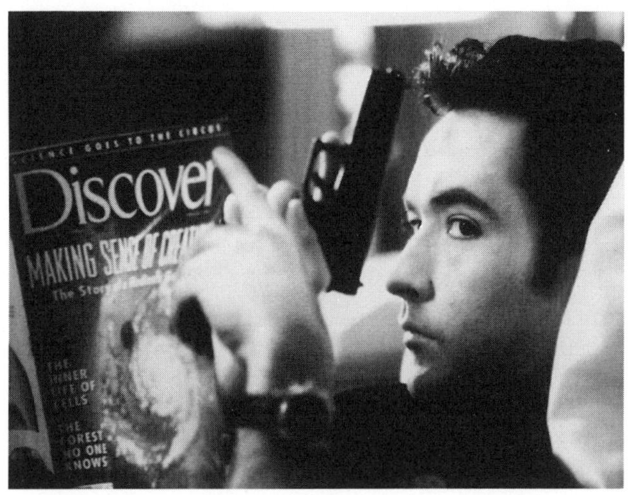

The decision to attend his ten year high school reunion troubles professional hitman Martin Blank (John Cusack) in the black comedy *Grosse Pointe Blank.*

Later, as he wanders the town, Martin runs into his old friend Paul Spericki (Jeremy Piven) who's now a successful real estate salesman. But Paul's not the only person he recognizes. He soon realizes he's being followed by two CIA spooks and a ghoul (another hit man). The CIA agents are there because Grocer is setting Martin up. As soon as he does the job he's supposed to be in town for, the CIA will arrest him and Grocer will be lighter one competitor.

So, who is Martin's target? Will he perform this last hit or change professions? Will he be arrested by the CIA spooks or killed by the ghoul? Will Debi take him back? And what will he answer at the reunion when his classmates ask him what he does for a living?

Actually, the answer to this last question is another key to the film's success. What will Martin say? He's the best in his craft, but his craft happens to be assassin. In fact, as he practices his reunion small talk in his hotel room mirror Martin says, "I'm not married, don't have any kids, and I'd blow your head off if somebody paid me enough." Not exactly the profession one brags about in suburban America. But, the three times he's asked what he does, he always tells the truth. His questioners' responses? Debi asks if he has a dental plan, Paul asks if it required any post graduate work, and Debi's father in complete deadpan says, "Good for you, it's a growth industry."

These exchanges are typical of the wry, off-kilter black humor that permeates *Grosse Pointe Blank.* There's not much to be taken seriously here, and that's just fine. When Martin goes to see his mother, he finds his house has been torn down and an Ultimart convenience store built on the site. In a state of anger and confusion, Martin immediately calls his therapist. "You can never go home again, Oatman, but you can shop there."

The scenes within the Ultimart are a combination of 1994's *Clerks* (1994) and *Pulp Fiction* (indeed a cardboard cutout of the later decorates the video section of the store in homage). Like the rest of the film, even the violence is not to be taken seriously. When the ghoul and Martin become involved in a store-shattering gun fight, it goes on behind the back of the teenage clerk who is so engrossed in a video game while wearing music-blasting earphones that he is oblivious to the produce and products flying in shards over his shoulders. Only when Martin finds a bomb cooking in the microwave does he grab the clerk and drag him out the door.

It is a sharp script co-written by Cusack and his old friends Steve Pink, D.V. DeVincentis and Tom Jankiewicz. The first two, along with Cusack founded the Chicago theater company New Crime Productions—and have bit parts in the film as security guard Terry Rostand and Dan Koretzky.

Of course this is not the limit of Cusack's nepotism. The film's cast also includes family members other than sister Joan as Marcella: sister Ann plays the tipsy Amy while brother Bill plays a waiter. Even Jeremy Piven (Paul) is a friend from Cusack's early Evanston, Illinois days. However, this casting of friends and family is yet another factor working in the film's favor.

Sister Joan, with the largest bit part, is over-the-top funny as the diligent office manager who can rip apart an errant arms supplier on one phone line while providing a soup recipe to a friend on the other.

Joan's Marcella is typical of how even the smaller parts in the film are given plenty of character. Alan Arkin is delightful as the psychiatrist who is terrified of the patient who won't go away, kills without conscience, and knows where the doc lives. No professional wall of objectivity here, and Arkin knows how to do a lot with the gems he is given by the writers.

Similarly good is Dan Aykroyd as the rival assassin who tries to make a club out of what are inherently a secretive and elusive bunch of members. It is one of Aykroyd's best roles in years.

Equally enjoying the ride is Minnie Driver who doesn't play Debi as a spurned, angry shell of a woman, but instead can match Martin volley for volley in their verbal sparing. Driver easily delivers her retorts and keeps Martin on his toes as punishment with believable ease. Their friendship—if not their love—is immediately and easily rekindled. Their intelligence and affection is apparent. We want her to forgive Martin and we want Martin to change his ways.

This kind of wry, dark comedy could become labored and artificial except that here it becomes pure gold because of the irresistible onscreen talents of John Cusack. He is one

CREDITS

Martin Q. Blank: John Cusack
Debi Newberry: Minnie Driver
Dr. Oatman: Alan Arkin
Grocer: Dan Aykroyd
Marcella: Joan Cusack
Lardner: Hank Azaria
McCullers: K. Todd Freeman
Mr. Newberry: Mitchell Ryan
Paul Spericki: Jeremy Piven
Bob Destepello: Michael Cudlitz
Felix: Benny Urquidez
Ultimart Carl: Duffy Taylor
Arlene: Audrey Kissel
Ken: Carlos Jacott
Amy: Ann Cusack
Mrs. Blank: Barbara Harris

Origin: USA
Released: 1997
Production: Susan Arnold, Donna Arkoff Roth and Roger Birnbaum for Hollywood Pictures, Caravan Pictures and New Crime Productions; released by Buena Vista
Direction: George Armitage
Screenplay: Tom Jankiewicz, D.V. DeVincentis, Steve Pink, John Cusack
Cinematography: Jamie Anderson
Editing: Brian Berdan
Production design: Stephen Altman
Art direction: Scott Meehan
Set decoration: Chris Spellman
Costumes: Eugenie Bafaloukos
Music: Joe Strummer
Sound: Arthur Rochester
MPAA rating: R
Running Time: 106 minutes

REVIEWS

Boxoffice. May, 1997, p. 58.
Chicago Tribune. April 11, 1997, p. 4.
Detroit News. April 11, 1997, p. C1.
Entertainment Weekly. April 11, 1997, p. 60.
Los Angeles Times. April 11, 1997, p. F1.
New York Times. April 11, 1997, p. B8.
New Yorker. April 21, 1997, p. 97.
People. April 14, 1997, p. 16.
Rolling Stone. May 1, 1997, p. 57.
Sight and Sound. August, 1997, p. 45.
Time. April 28, 1997.
USA Today. April 11, 1997, p. 4D.
Variety. March 31, 1997, p. 85.

of those rare actors who can play dead-on serious (*The Grifters*, 1990) or dead-pan comic (*The Sure Thing*, 1985). Here he is in fine form: outrageously charming, endearingly reticent, and facilely delivering funny lines from below warily furrowed brows. He may be an ace hit man, but, darn it all, he comes across as such a decent guy!

Grosse Pointe Blank's whimsical plot, quirky characters and sharp dialogue are well used by a bright cast that knows how to wink at an audience. Cusack, as not only actor, but also co-producer and co-writer, has delivered an entertaining and cleverly original product.

—*Beverley Bare Buehrer*

Guantanamera

From the directors of *Strawberry and Chocolate* comes a road story with a Cuban twist.—Movie tagline

"Funny and colorful!"—Dave Kehr, *Daily News*

"Deft and artful! A lilting melody. Passion, pleasure and playful sensuality abound."—Rod Dreher, *Ft. Lauderdale Sun Sentinel*

"Lovely! Graceful! A beautiful film!"—Thelma Adams, *New York Post*

"Vibrant! A breezy sexual odyssey about love and breaking the rules."—Bruce Williamson, *Playboy*

"An absolutely unqualified delight!"—Jeffrey Lyons, *WNBC*

Box Office: $808,432

Guantanamera is the last film of Tomas Gutierrez Alea, who died in 1996. He is the renowned director of *Death of a Bureaucrat*, *Memories of Underdevelopment*, and *Strawberry and Chocolate*. *Guantanamera* is Cuba's most popular song, and it is not hard to see why. Not only does its buoyant melody help drive the action of this comedy, there are chords of darker feelings in the song that suggest the film's laughter is provoked by the struggle and the absurdity of life in contemporary Cuba—and probably by the absurdity of life itself.

Take Adolpho (Carlos Cruz). He is an ambitious, high-strung government bureaucrat intent on using the funeral of his wife Georgina's aunt Yoyita (Conchita Brando) to further his reputation as an efficient administrator. He thinks he has found a way to convey the body to its burial sight and economize on the amount of precious petrol the government allots for such events. In terms of common sense and humanity his plans are ludicrous, but in terms of the system he serves, they make good sense. The awful and ridiculous spectacle of Castro's communism is evident in nearly every scene of this film. He is never mentioned, but it is clear that his people make whatever corrupt accommodations are necessary in order to survive. There seem to be very few true believers in the system itself.

But because the film so clearly focuses on human foibles and on personalities, politics, as such, is not the issue. There is not an expose of the failures of communism but a portrayal of the way people manage to survive under the current regime. In that sense, *Guantanamera* has universal applicability. Everyone—no matter what kind of government rules them—has to make accommodations to political realities. If anything, the Cubans in this film have a healthy regard for themselves and do not feel particularly oppressed. Only someone like Adolpho can be termed a villain because he has sacrificed nearly all his humanity to getting ahead in the system.

The other characters in the film are beyond ideology. Adolpho's wife, Georgina (Mirtha Ibarra) had been a university economics professor and once a committed Communist. She has clearly lost her fervor—as well as her job—and now reluctantly supports Adolpho's drive to success. She has to watch what she wears (Adolpho does not like her to wear even modestly low-cut dresses), and play the loyal partner even when Adolpho's smug and intolerant behavior mortifies her.

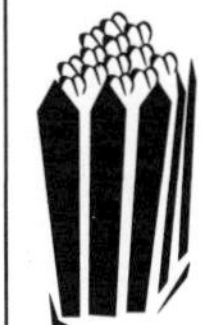

Mirtha Ibarra: "When this movie came out in Europe, they thought it was a comedy of the absurd. But it's not. It is a comedy drawn from reality, an X-ray of the island of Cuba."

Georgina is longing for passion. She once gave that passion to Communism and had a student who was impressed less with lessons than with her person. He wrote her a note expressing his love for her, and she has treasured his tribute even though he disappeared from her life shortly after he wrote the note. She meets him once again on the trip to bury Yoyita. Now he is a truck driver with a lover in every stop along the way—although he too is bothered by the emptiness of his life and is galvanized by his chance encounter with Georgina on the road.

What should these two people do who obviously have this passion for each other. Georgina feels she must respect her marriage vows, even though her former student/lover pursues her. But she changes her mind when Adolpho insults Candido (Raul Eguren), who accompanies Adolpho and Georgina on their trip to bury Yoyita. The gentle Candido has loved Yoyita through many years of separation (she left Cuba to follow a singing career abroad). Just when they are reunited at a reception in honor of Yoyita's return to Cuba, when they confess to never having stopped loving each other, Yoyita keels over and dies. This sense of a passion never fulfilled haunts Candido and Georgina. She despises her husband for insulting Candido, who asks that the car radio playing festive music be turned off. Later Georgina overhears Adolpho ridiculing Candido's fifty-year passion for Yoyita. She no longer can evade the realization that her husband has lost all fellow feeling and thinks only of himself.

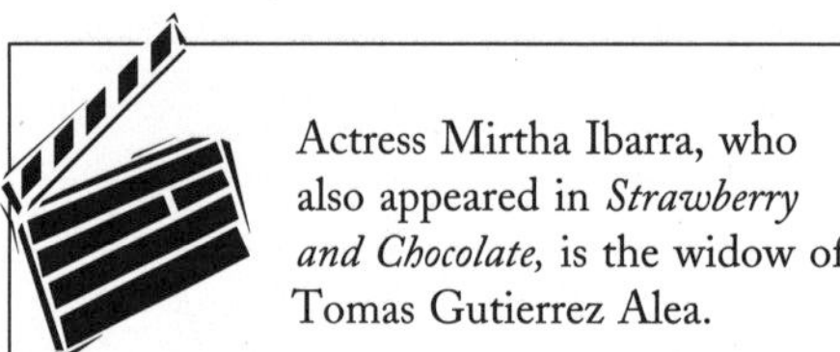

Actress Mirtha Ibarra, who also appeared in *Strawberry and Chocolate*, is the widow of Tomas Gutierrez Alea.

It can be argued that this is what the Cuban revolution has now amounted to: the inhuman ambitions of functionaries. That judgment may be too broad based for such an essentially lighthearted film, which resembles the journey of the Bundren family in *As I Lay Dying*. *Guantanamera* is not as dark a fable as William Faulkner's novel, but like that great work, it is a searching examination of what is owed to the living and the dead and of what it means to be fully human.

—Carl Rollyson

CREDITS

Adolfo: Carlos Cruz
Georgina: Mirtha Ibarra
Candido: Raul Eguren
Mariano: Jorge Perugorria
Iku: Suset Perez Malberti
Yoyita: Conchita Brando
Tony: Luis Alberto Garcia

Origin: Cuba
Released: 1995, 1997
Production: Gerardo Herrer; released by Cinepix Film Properties
Direction: Tomas Gutierrez Alea, Juan Carlos Tabio
Screenplay: Eliseo Alberto Diego, Tomas Gutierrez Alea, and Juan Carlos Tabio
Cinematography: Hans Burmann
Editing: Carmen Frias
Music: Jose Nieto
Production design: Frank Cabrera
MPAA rating: Unrated
Running Time: 101 minutes

REVIEWS

Boxoffice. April, 1997, p. 188.
Los Angeles Times. August 1, 1997, p. F12.
New York Times. July 20, 1997, p. H11.
New York Times. July 25, 1997, p. C12.
People. August 4, 1997, p. 20.
Sight and Sound. October, 1996, p. 40.
Village Voice. July 29, 1997, p. 71.

Gummo

"Shocking, funny, horrifying, and heartfelt. You'll be glued to the screen!"—Ingrid Sischy, *Interview*

Harmony Korine, the scribe behind Larry Clark's faux sexual expose *Kids* (1995) makes his directing debut with *Gummo*, a jumble of images that depicts the antisocial behavior of juveniles in an economically and physically devastated town in Ohio. The film will either garner praise from viewers who admire the 23-year-old filmmaker for his audaciousness, or more likely, will offend those who are bound to find his treatment of most of the characters as degrading and exploitive.

Xenia, a real-life suburb of Dayton that never recovered from the tornado that ravaged the town in the Seventies, is the setting for this relatively plotless series of vignettes of disillusioned and socially immoral teenagers. By choosing the unconventional narrative, Korine appears to be fashioning himself after the great filmmakers of the French New Wave, a film movement that followed, and more importantly, re-interpreted American Film Noir. Jean-Luc Godard, in particular, was fond of experimenting with film form, as witnessed in *Alphaville* (1965). But the thing that separates Godard from Korine most explicitly is that the French filmmaker's decisions were informed, while Korine's seem random. Godard was fully versed in the "rules" of filmmaking and when he chose to break them, he did so with conscious determination. Korine's work in *Gummo*, on the other hand, is ill-informed and juvenile, despite his strong visual sense and some impressive work by cinematographer Jean-Yves Escoffier (*Good Will Hunting*, 1997). Korine seems more interested in shocking the viewer, not necessarily out of its societal complacency by triggering outrage and offering solutions, but merely to accumulate the most offensive and demeaning scenes possible—a kind of perverse one-upmanship.

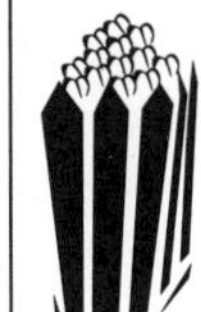

Harmony Korine: "The script is like a kit for a model, and the fun is in making things up off the script, taking things a little further and being spontaneous."

Although the film is set in Xenia, Ohio, it was filmed in the suburbs of Nashville, Tennessee.

What some viewers may find the most repugnant in *Gummo* is the representation of the physically and mentally-challenged as freaks, carnival sideshow attractions with enlarged heads and mutant features. (It is a pity that the Elephant Man died before Korine had a chance to similarly exploit him.) Some reviewers felt that Korine had managed to remain neutral in its depiction of the degradations inflicted on the characters; that is arguable. Korine reserves the most appalling and demeaning treatment for the female characters. A mentally challenged young woman is pimped into prostitution by her own husband. It is difficult not to react to Korine's capacity for cruelty when he persuades a young woman with Downs Syndrome to shave off her eyebrows for no reason but the filmmaker's amusement. While other actors—some professional, most amateur—made the conscious decision to participate in what *Newsday*'s John Anderson succinctly described as "this kind of smug decadence and spiritual bankruptcy," the Downs Syndrome woman more than likely was incapable of comprehending the film's obscene exploitation of her mental condition.

These individual scenes are loosely held together by a pair of demented friends (Jacob Reynolds and Nick Sutton) who earn money for prostitutes and glue-sniffing by killing cats and selling them to a local butcher who in turn supplies a Chinese restaurant. (Dog-lovers are not spared, either; there is a shot of a canine impaled on a rooftop antenna.) Further insults include the killing of a comatose grandmother on a respirator that is presented as a merciful deed—one can only speculate that Korine's message here is that these nihilistic teens can relate to human suffering—as well as gay-bashing, racial bigotry, misogyny and teenaged anomie. Korine appears as a drunk who makes a pass at a gay black encephalitic dwarf, played by a real-life friend. Nick Sutton, who plays one of the central characters, was sought out by the filmmaker following Sutton's appearance on a tabloid-style television talk show.

Director-writer Harmony Korine could possibly have been forgiven for his cruel filmic representations if they were used to underscore an editorial outrage. But Korine seems content to merely alienate further an audience that has already been satiated with tales of glorified youthful insignificance and growing anomie. *Gummo* fails as any true social document; it may very well have been titled "Korine's Freak Show."

—Patricia Kowal

CREDITS

Solomon: Jacob Reynolds
Tummler: Nick Sutton
Bunny Boy: Jacob Sewell
Darby: Darby Dougherty
Cole: Max Perlich
Dot: Chloe Sevigny
Helen: Carisa Bara
Solomon's Mom: Linda Manz

Origin: USA
Released: 1997
Production: Cary Woods for Independent Pictures; released by Fine Line Features
Direction: Harmony Korine
Screenplay: Harmony Korine
Cinematography: Jean-Yves Escoffier
Editing: Christopher Tellefsen
Production design: David Doernberg
Costumes: Chloe Sevigny
Music supervisor: Randall Poster
MPAA rating: R
Running Time: 95 minutes

REVIEWS

Boxoffice. November, 1997, p. 125.
Entertainment Weekly. October 31, 1997, p. 80.
Los Angeles Times. October 17, 1997, p. F6.
New York Times. October 17, 1997, p. E12.
Variety. September 8, 1997, p. 80.
Village Voice. October 21, 1997, p. 96.

Happy Together; Cheun Gwong Tsa Sit

"For stylistic magic . . . nothing surpasses the poetic grunge of *Happy Together.*"—David Ansen, *Newsweek*

"Dazzling quicksilver . . . a time jumping seductive portrait."—Todd McCarthy, *Premiere*

"Luscious . . . intimate . . . edgy. A dazzling story with a gorgeously garish palette."—Richard Corliss, *Time*

Wong Kar-Wai's *Happy Together* demonstrates that a film from an Oriental culture may need to be grasped as much in terms of its paradigms, as through the forward movement of its narrative.

The above was made clear at the New York Film Festival press conference where the Hong Kong director declared that though his film was about the love between two men, it could well be about the love between two women, or between a man and a woman, "or between a man and a tree." Logically, then, the homosexual attachment between his two young males, Lai (Tony Leung Chiu-Wai) and Ho (Leslie Cheung Kwok-Wing), has to be seen as representing all sexuality.

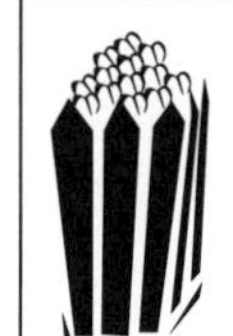

Lai: "Turns out that normal people are all the same."

Adrift in the seedy part of Buenos Aires, Lai and Ho, who could serve as mirror images of each other, redeem their sexual lust with an overpowering desire to visit the famous Iguazu Falls. Before they have even started on their journey, the film presents the waterfall in all its scenic glory, underscored by a lilting rendition of the Latin standard, "Cucurrucucu Paloma." By so doing, the Falls evoke the paradigm of a consummation wished for, but never reached, by those in the throes of unrepressed sex.

The literal translation of the Chinese title, taken from a poem, is "Spring Brilliance Suddenly Pours Out."

True enough, Lai and Ho fight and break up on the way to their hallowed destination. We soon find that their desire for each other, which extends to wanting each other both as friends and sexual partners, is allowed only momentary bursts of reciprocity. Inexplicably, for most of the film, when Lai desires Ho, the latter rejects him, and vice versa. Thus, despite the film's title and all its surface dazzle, *Happy Together* remains arduous viewing, since the film eventually turns out to be more about unrequited love, than about any romantic ideal.

Worse, perhaps conditioned by the codes of realism, we look for reasons why two such good-looking young men should turn away from women, but we are offered not a semblance of a clue. Instead, we are meant to empathize with the downward spiral that each of their lives takes, after being spurned by the other.

Lai's descent, which initially involves working as a doorman for a tango bar, turns him into a stalker when he accidentally spots Ho, who has now become an elite homosexual playboy. In a voice-over, Lai confesses that, unable to bear the frustration, he wants to return to Hong Kong, but lacks the resources. Lai's sexual passion thus becomes intermingled with, and diluted by, his more practical goal. When he does get together with Ho, at the latter's behest, he is confused and helpless, as the two are unable to get it on. The occasion however, allows Lai to voice his resentment. "I had no regrets till I met you!" he screams at a listless Ho, who lies sprawled on his hotel bed. Lai then adds: "Now my regrets could kill me!"

Their seesaw relationship now has Ho pursuing Lai. When Ho lands up at Lai's rooming house, injured and bleeding, Lai nurses him back to health. The film, which had hitherto depicted their affair in black-and-white, now breaks into color. Yet, despite moments of stray tenderness—such as the two doing the tango in the empty community kitchen—distrust seemingly leads Ho to walk off, after Lai refuses to return his passport. It's a fight as childish as any on TV's "The Newlywed Game."

Each of the two are then sucked into their private hells. Lai, pursuing his goal of wanting to return to Hong Kong, labors at two menial jobs a day, and strikes up a lasting friendship with Chang (Chang Chen), an amiable heterosexual co-worker. When the urge strikes him, Lai cruises the usual places, from men's rooms to porn houses, but is unable to follow through after bodily contact. Unlike him, Ho, who remains bound to

AWARDS AND NOMINATIONS

Cannes Film Festival 1997: Director (Kar-Wai)
Independent Spirit Awards 1997 Nominations: Foreign Film

Buenos Aires, continues seeking one-night stands with male strangers.

At the film's climax, Ho breaks down and weeps while looking at a rotating lampshade with a painting of the Iguazu Falls, while Lai, on his way back to Hong Kong, gets to stand below the majesty of the real thing, the spray trickling down his face like tears.

CREDITS

Lai Yiu-Fai: Tony Leung
Ho Po-Wing: Leslie Cheung
Chang: Chang Chen

Origin: Hong Kong
Released: 1997
Production: Wong Kar-Wai for Jet Tone and Block 2 Pictures; released by Kino International
Direction: Wong Kar-Wai
Screenplay: Wong Kar-Wai
Cinematography: Christopher Doyle
Editing: William Chang, Wong Ming-lam
Production design: William Chang
Music: Danny Chung
MPAA rating: Unrated
Running Time: 97 minutes

Critics, for the most part, seem to have been receptive to the film's visual style and its youthful subject matter. "The film's greatest asset," writes Jan Stuart in *The Advocate*, "is the dazzling palette of Australian cinematographer Chris Doyle" who, according to Stuart, "drapes the lovers in a ravishing gauze of melancholy." Armond White concludes his detailed appreciation of the film in *The New York Press* by noting that its director's "presentation of romantic sacrifice and friendship has high irony and mysterious depth." For White, the film manages to blend "images, emotion and cultural disparity into the movies' sweetest, most aching tune of regret."

—*Vivek Adarkar*

REVIEWS

The Advocate. November 11, 1997.
Boxoffice. September, 1997, p. 111.
Los Angeles Times. October 31, 1997, p. F9.
New York Observer. October 20, 1997.
New York Press. October 15, 1997.
New York Times. October 10, 1997, p. E10.
Sight and Sound. May, 1997, p. 14.
Time. October 27, 1997.
Variety. May 19, 1997, p. 50.
Village Voice. October 21, 1997, p. 85.

Hard Eight

When good luck is a longshot, you have to hedge your bets.—Movie tagline

"The dialogue and acting are sheer pleasure." —Roger Ebert, *Chicago Sun-Times*

"Gwyneth Paltrow in her best role yet."—John Anderson, *Los Angeles Times*

"Intelligent and engaging, *Hard Eight* is worth betting on."—Ann Marie O'Connor, *Mademoiselle*

"Two thumbs up! Terrific performances by Philip Baker Hall and Gwyneth Paltrow."—*Siskel & Ebert*

There is a pervasive existentialism that envelops *Hard Eight*, the impressive debut film from writer/director Paul Thomas Anderson. Seemingly drawn to the seamier side of life, Anderson would go on to explore the world of adult pornography in the critically-acclaimed *Boogie Night* (1997). This time he weaves a noirish tale of salvation, redemption and warped honor in the world of small-time Nevada gamblers.

Hard Eight is a deceptively simple tale. While on the surface it appears to be minimally plotted, the film is an intriguing thriller disguised as a moody character study. It is subtle, yet compelling in the way it modulates its protagonist's enigma with the development of all of its characters.

Outside a diner in the Nevada desert, a restrained and quiet older man befriends a young, downtrodden vagrant. Over coffee and a cigarette, John (John C. Reilly) explains that he had gone to Reno with hopes of winning enough money to pay his mother's funeral, but walked away empty-

AWARDS AND NOMINATIONS

Independent Spirit Awards 1997 Nominations: First Feature, Actor (Hall), Debut Screenplay, Supporting Actor (Jackson), Cinematography

handed. Sydney (Philip Baker Hall) poses the question, "If I were to give you fifty dollars, what would you do with it?" John is suspicious, but allows Sydney to drive him back to Reno.

Sydney, a professional small-time gambler working the Nevada casino circuit, shows John how to gamble in a precise, but convoluted way so as to secure free hotel accommodations for the night. John is too smitten with winning to question the motives behind Sydney's benevolence. This mysterious father-figure is an enigma, and it is the unraveling of this mystery that propels the film.

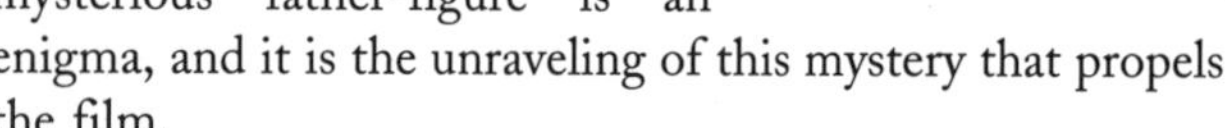

> Sydney's offended reply to Clementine's sexual question: "Never ask a question like that unless you already know the answer."

Two years later, John has fully embraced his role in this mentor-protege relationship. He idolizes Sydney to the point of emulating the older man's dress and drink preferences. But two outsiders are about to enter their lives who will disrupt the equilibrium: Clementine (Gwyneth Paltrow), a dimwitted cocktail waitress who moonlights as a prostitute, and Jimmy (Samuel L. Jackson), a vulgar casino security guard looking for the big score. Soon, Sydney finds himself summoned into a messy situation involving John and Clementine's impetus foray into matrimony and kidnapping that can only spell disaster.

CREDITS

John: John C. Reilly
Clementine: Gwyneth Paltrow
Jimmy: Samuel L. Jackson
Sydney: Philip Baker Hall
Hostage: F. William Parker
Craps Player: Philip Seymour Hoffman

Origin: USA
Released: 1996
Production: Robert Jones and John Lyons for Green Parrot, Trinity, and Rysher Entertainment; released by Goldwyn Entertainment Company
Direction: Paul Thomas Anderson
Screenplay: Paul Thomas Anderson
Cinematography: Robert Elswit
Editing: Barbara Tulliver
Production design: Nancy Deren
Art direction: Michael Krantz
Set design: David A. Koneff
Costumes: Mark Bridges
Music: Jon Brion, Michael Penn
MPAA rating: R
Running Time: 101 minutes

Hard Eight takes its title from a gambling term that refers to an eight rolled with a four on each of the dice. Going for the long-shot return on a bet proves to be one of the few weaknesses in the otherwise impeccably controlled Sydney's persona.

Philip Baker Hall is one of those fine character actors who powerfully inhabits supporting roles, yet finds name-recognition elusive. He gained critical recognition, however, for his portrayal of Richard Nixon in Robert Altman's *Secret Honor* (1984), a filmed version of Hall's one-man stage show. *Hard Eight* is ultimately Sydney's story and Hall, with his ravaged face, plays the mystery man without a hint of vulnerability. His restraint accentuates Sydney's underlying menace.

The acting in *Hard Eight* is uniformly impressive and unmistakably unsentimental. John C. Reilly is effective as the down-on-his-luck protege, while accomplished actor—and Quentin Tarantino favorite—Samuel L. Jackson (*Pulp Fiction*, [1994], *Jackie Brown* [1997]) has never been scarier. Shot some two years prior to its release, *Hard Eight* was trapped in purgatory when its distributor went bankrupt. In the interim, actress Gwyneth Paltrow gave a captivating performance as the charming matchmaker in *Emma* (1997), which unfortunately tended to overshadow her top-notch work in Anderson's film.

Hard Eight is a moody, slow-moving piece punctuated by bursts of violence that is controlled as it unravels the mystery behind Sydney's benevolence. The characters are not easy to like, but they are interesting. Unlike Martin Scorsese's *Casino* (1996), this film is about the small-time casino fringe-dwellers, not the showy high-rollers. Anderson displays a deft hand at diligently sustaining the suspense, leading to generally favorable—and often effusive—reviews from the critics.

—Patricia Kowal

REVIEWS

Boxoffice. August, 1996, p. 55.
Chicago Sun-Times.. February 28, 1997.
Chicago Tribune. February 28, 1997.
Entertainment Weekly. March 14, 1997, p. 60
Los Angeles Times. February 28, 1997, p. F1.
New York Times. February 28, 1997.
San Francisco Chronicle. February 28, 1997, p. D3.
Sight and Sound. January, 1998, p. 44.
Toronto Sun. February 28, 1997.
USA Today. March 13, 1997, p. 8D.
Washington Post. February 28, 1997.

Head Above Water

A comedy about keeping your ex-lover a secret, your husband in the dark and your *Head Above Water*—Movie tagline

Murder just became a water sport.—Movie tagline

Indecisiveness about tone is a fatal flaw for a filmmaker. Director Jim Wilson doesn't seem to know quite what to make of the strange script for *Head Above Water*, and neither will viewers. If this bizarre story about a woman and three men going at each other on an island is supposed to be a black comedy, it's neither comic enough nor black enough. Wilson stages it like a lighthearted, tongue-in-cheek romp, but the film is sunk by a script that's too heavy for farce and too thin for drama.

Nathalie on marrying George, a judge: "He helped me with my little addictions, calmed my nerves and sentenced me to only two years' probation."

Nathalie (Cameron Diaz) is a former drug-abusing, free-living delinquent rescued and sobered up by George (Harvey Keitel), a judge who is twice her age. In a voice-over at the movie's start, Nathalie explains how George sentenced her to two years probation, then married her. They are vacationing on a remote island off the coast of Maine, in Nathalie's spacious family summer home. Living nearby is the caretaker, a hunk named Lance (Craig Sheffer) who has been Nathalie's friend since childhood. Immediately it's obvious that there's more potential to their lifelong platonic relationship.

In her narrative, Nathalie explains she's "never had any luck with men." George and Lance shove off on an overnight fishing trip, and Nathalie notes it will be the first night she and her husband will spend separately. Then her narrative voice disappears for the rest of the film, an early indication of how much this movie lurches from one style to another.

As George and Lance depart, another man, wearing a white linen suit, is rowing a stolen dinghy toward the island. Nathalie, alone, is at loose ends and obviously a little neurotic. Then the man in the white suit surprises her. He is Kent (Billy Zane), her alcoholic ex-boyfriend. Nathalie doesn't exactly reject his advances, dressing fairly provocatively and making only perfunctory requests for him to leave, and a drunken night ends with an ambiguous scene of the two falling together onto a sofa.

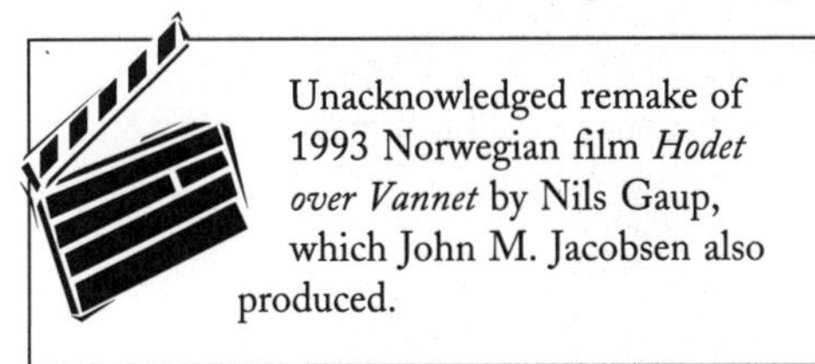

Unacknowledged remake of 1993 Norwegian film *Hodet over Vannet* by Nils Gaup, which John M. Jacobsen also produced.

The next scene has Nathalie awakening on a couch and finding Kent on the bed, naked and dead, of an apparent heart attack. With George and Lance coming ashore, Nathalie shoves the corpse down a cellar door under the dining-room floor. As George discovers evidence of Kent's visit, Nathalie inexplicably confesses to George what has happened, insisting she and Kent did not have sex.

It dawns on George that he would be a prime murder suspect, and his career ruined, if they return the corpse to mainland authorities. The film abruptly shifts into a get-rid-of-the-body comedy, with George and Nathalie trying to hide their actions from Lance. Through some ephemeral plot twists, the script has George and Nathalie becoming increasingly suspicious of and exasperated with each other. George hits the bottle—he also has a barely throttled substance-abuse problem—and the patient father-husband turns into a paranoid, violent psychopath. Nathalie, who comes to believe that George actually planned Kent's death by leaving poison in a vodka bottle for him to drink, flees to Lance for help, and discovers Lance wants more than friendship. This comes as no surprise to viewers, since Lance has been spending most of the film painting and sculpting figures of Nathalie.

As suspicions and alliances shift among the three remaining figures, the film suddenly turns gruesomely violent, with death by gunshot, grisly dissection of a corpse, and a ludicrous Rube Goldberg climax involving a chain saw, a bucket of cement, a toppling gazebo, an impaling, and the arrival of a clueless policeman. The final scene, involving the cop and a misplaced bottle of poison, is clever, but it's far too late by then to save the film.

Neither Wilson nor the principal actors adopt a consistent attitude toward the quirky material. That's partly because the script itself, adapted by Theresa Marie from a 1993 Norwegian screenplay, doesn't provide nearly enough in the way of motivation or character development for anyone to take the plot seriously, and it doesn't have enough humor to work as a comedy. Wilson should have taken the film toward satire or drama, but instead he treats the material like other directors treat Agatha Christie stories, with a wry, detached attitude. But this is no intricate mystery, and the plot can't stand on its own.

It's surprising that *Head Above Water* swam at all after its 1993 same-titled Norwegian predecessor sank so quickly. A remake of a flop makes no sense, especially one with such strange casting as this. The new version, which saw a very limited theatrical run before going to video, was apparently intended as a vehicle for rising star Diaz. It would have helped had she been surrounded by more intriguing male actors. Zane is zesty and bizarre enough, but he gets killed-off early. Sheffer is rather wooden, and Keitel, in a rare departure, plays his judge in much too restrained a fashion, even after George goes off the deep end.

It's hard to imagine why Keitel's George turns murderous. Nothing about his performance suggests the kind of passionate love and hate for Nathalie that would explain his actions. He's merely jealous and fatherly. There are no sparks between Keitel and Diaz, either in love or war. They are totally mismatched.

Diaz gives her character a game try, but Nathalie seems more befuddled than calculating, more ditzy than seductive. This script cries out for a femme fatale whose spidery intrigues catch all three men in her net. Instead, Diaz plays Nathalie as a hapless, clueless, spoiled brat who seems completely unaware of her effect on those around her. For the sake of Diaz's promising career, hopefully *Head Above Water* will stay submerged, and Diaz will go on to better things.

Apart from Zane, the three principals don't have the wry, sardonic qualities necessary to make this work as the farce Wilson wants it to be. The actors and Wilson play the material much too straightforward, without any sense of how to make the characters work. An incessantly tinkling, lightweight musical score by Christopher Young doesn't help. Wilson, who directed only a couple of forgettable films in the mid-1980s (*Stacy's Knights*, *Smart Alec*) and has made more of an impact as a producer (*Dances with Wolves*), never takes charge.

With veteran weirdo Keitel and promising ingenue Diaz, a deft director might have taken *Head Above Water* out of the shallows of parlor-room charades and into darker, more promising waters. Unfortunately, the script's twists and turns depend on relatively minor revelations. There are too many moments that fall flat. In one long scene, George and Nathalie try to dump Kent's corpse into deep water, but Lance tags along on the boat. George pushes him off and Nathalie jumps in, playfully frolicking in the water to distract Lance's attention, but George is unable to dump the body. The whole sequence is pointless.

Everything about *Head Above Water* is puzzling. The casting is all wrong. Keitel's special talents are wasted, as are Diaz's physical charms. The mayhem seems random and inconsequential. It is revealing that a movie with implied extramarital sex, drug abuse, dismemberment of corpses, murder, and gruesome death earned a PG-13 rating. The film seems to be targeted at no one in particular. There are few laughs and no horror, no suspense and no insight, just a series of scenes that manage barely to keep their head above water.

—Michael Betzold

CREDITS

George: Harvey Keitel
Nathalie: Cameron Diaz
Lance: Craig Sheffer
Kent: Billy Zane
Policeman: Shay Duffin

Origin: USA
Released: 1997
Production: Jim Wilson and John M. Jacobsen for Tig Productions and Majestic Films; released by Fine Line Features
Direction: Jim Wilson
Screenplay: Theresa Marie
Cinematography: Richard Bowen
Editing: Michael R. Miller
Music: Christopher Young
Production design: Jeffrey Beecroft
Art direction: Joseph P. Lucky
Costumes: Colleen Atwood
Sound: Richard Bryce Goodman
MPAA rating: PG-13
Running Time: 92 minutes

REVIEWS

New York Times. June 25, 1997, p. C15.
Sight and Sound. September, 1997, p. 44.
Variety. November 11, 1996, p. 58.

Hercules

"The most entertaining movie of the year!"—Jeffrey Gantz, *Boston Phoenix*

"This summer's best movie!"—Terry Lawson, *Detroit Free Press*

"Wall-to-wall fun!"—Bob Strauss, *Los Angeles Daily News*

"A triumph! The surest bet this summer for family entertainment!"—Jack Mathews, *Newsday*

"*Hercules* is the ultimate action hero!"—Peter Plagens, *Newsweek*

"Non-stop hilarity!"—Carrie Rickey, *Philadelphia Inquirer*

"It rocks!"—Peter Travers, *Rolling Stone*

Greek mythology supplies the material for Disney's 35th animated feature *Hercules*.

Box Office: $99,080,340

After reaching a peak with *The Lion King* in 1994, the box office revenues of Disney's animated features dropped for the third year in a row with the release of *Hercules*. While the film performed well at the box office, earning just under $100 million, its take was less than that of 1996's *The Hunchback of Notre Dame*, whose darker and more "adult" tone and style may have trimmed down its audience somewhat. Interestingly, *Hercules* is much more similar in tone to the upbeat, witty 1992 feature *Aladdin* than to the thought-provoking, "mature" *Hunchback*. Yet, in comparison to both those earlier productions, *Hercules* stands proudly on its own as an enjoyable, humorous, and multi-layered film that should appeal to both children and adults.

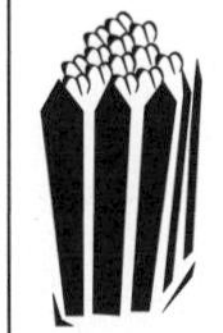

Hades: "We dance, we schmooze, we kiss, we carry on, we go home happy. Come on, what do you say?"

As one might expect, Disney's approach in adapting mythology is consistent with all its previous adaptations of familiar fairy tales and books, including *The Hunchback of Notre Dame*. The "Disney-fied" version of *Hercules* rewrites the original myth by eliminating its darker elements, filling it with fun musical numbers, giving it a happy ending, and weaving into its story a useful moral theme, in this case involving heroism. The lesson to be learned in *Hercules* is that "a true hero isn't measured by the size of his strength, but the strength of his heart," a theme more typical of Walt Disney than of Greek mythology. Yet the synthesis of Disney's brand of storytelling and the mythology of ancient Greece manages to work quite well.

When Hercules is born to Zeus (voice of Rip Torn) and Hera (voice of Samantha Eggar), he immediately becomes the target of the resentful god of the underworld, Hades (voice of James Woods), who would like nothing better than to overthrow Zeus and conquer Mt. Olympus. Hades sends his bumbling minions Pain (voice of Bobcat Goldthwait) and Panic (voice of Matt Frewer) to kidnap Hercules, feed him a potion that will make him mortal, and finally kill him. However, a drop of the potion is accidentally spilled, and as a result Hercules loses his immortality but retains his godlike strength. Unable to live on Mt. Olympus with the gods, Hercules grows up on earth under the care of human parents. Because his superhuman strength often makes him unintentionally dangerous, young Hercules is shunned and feared by society. Despite his attempts at fitting in among normal humans, he never feels he belongs. In search of answers, he travels to the temple of Zeus, where the ruler of the gods appears and tells his son of his true origins. Zeus then explains to Hercules that he may become immortal again and return to Olympus if he can prove himself a true hero.

Hercules seeks out a trainer of heroes, the satyr Philoctetes (voice of Danny DeVito), who goes by the name "Phil." After the satyr teaches "Herc" the skills of a warrior, the two of them travel to the city of Thebes, where Herc intends to prove himself a hero. There the townspeople scoff when he claims to be a hero, until at last he demonstrates his abilities by defeating the multi-headed Hydra, sent by Hades to wreak havoc and kill Hercules. With this victory, Herc suddenly finds himself hailed as a hero by the people of Thebes. His popularity grows to rival that of any present-day movie or athletic star.

Meanwhile, Hades decides to use other methods to destroy his enemy: "Maybe I haven't been throwing the right curves at him," he says to himself. The lord of the underworld calls upon the beautiful but world-weary and cynical Megara (voice of Susan Egan) to charm Hercules and find out if he has any weaknesses. Meg had sold her soul to Hades to save a man she loved, but the man ultimately left her, and now she has no choice but to do the evil god's bidding. However, as she gets to know Herc, she finds she has fallen in love with him, and Herc in return falls in love with her. Realizing the two have fallen for each other, Hades makes a deal with Hercules: if Hercules will give up his strength for twenty-four hours, Hades promises to release Meg from his grip. Eager to save the woman he loves, Hercules agrees, and suddenly his superhuman strength leaves him.

This is Disney's 35th full-length animated feature.

Thrilled that his plan worked, Hades releases the Titans, ancient enemies of Zeus, from their age-old prison, and they begin an assault on Mount Olympus. Though robbed of his godlike power, Hercules does everything he can to stop the Titans, but his valiant effort accomplishes very little, and he is nearly killed by a giant Cyclops. In the chaos, a pillar falls on Meg and kills her, whereupon her spirit travels to the underworld. Desperate to save her, Hercules travels to Hades' domain, where he tames the giant two-headed dog Cerberus and makes his way to the evil god himself. Hercules offers to trade places with Meg, and Hades gleefully agrees. However, as Hercules dives into the river of the dead and swims toward Meg's spirit, his immortality returns. Now a god once again, Herc saves Meg, returning her spirit to her body.

Zeus and the other gods welcome Hercules back to Mount Olympus, and the former explains why Herc regained his immortality. "You were willing to give your life for this woman," Zeus says, adding that a true hero is measured by the strength of his heart, not by the size of his strength. Although he has gained the immortality he sought, Herc realizes that he has found true happiness with Meg, and he tells his father he wishes to remain human so that he may stay with the woman he loves. "I finally know where I belong," he explains.

The theme of home and belonging is played out well in the character of Hercules, a likable sort of guy whose awkward differences from everyone else cast him in the unenviable role of a lonely outsider. His quest for acceptance and belonging is a familiar story and a familiar experience for many people, which makes his Superman-like character more personal and accessible. Likewise, the character's occasional clumsiness, energetic eagerness, and naivetè make him more human and more endearing, qualities that could easily be lacking in a story about a mythological hero. Herc's kindness and bright optimism in the face of the social rejection he experienced as a youth encourage the audience to root for him when he sings, "I will find my way / I can go the distance / I'll be there someday / If I can be strong / I know every mile / Will be worth my while / I could go most anywhere / to feel like I belong."

Meg's character, on the other hand, contrasts interestingly with Hercules. Whereas Herc is naive and optimistic, Meg is a woman who has experienced too much disappointment in life to let her guard down easily. She was jilted by a man for whom she gave up her freedom and her soul, and now she is used as a pawn by an egotistical god. Unwilling to be hurt again, she asserts as much independence as she can even though her soul belongs to Hades. Initially she tries to resist acknowledging the attraction she feels to Hercules, but she is unable to deny her feelings. The conflict within her, a mature one that may be more understandable to the adult audience, comes to the fore in a fun, self-examining pop song entitled "I Won't Say": "I thought my heart had learned its lesson / It feels so good when you start out / My head is screaming get a grip, girl / Unless you're dying to cry your heart out." The song ends with a sort of resolution that reveals what the audience already knows to be true: "At least out loud, I won't say I'm in love," Meg sings in a near-whisper. Ultimately, it is Herc's kindness, trust, and naivetè that draws Meg to him, and her journey toward trust is a kind of character development normally reserved for live-action films.

As a villain, Hades functions more as a comic character than a menacing, scary foe. Many critics have compared him to the genie (voice by Robin Williams) of 1992's *Aladdin*, due in part to the character's many humorous and seemingly spontaneous one-liners. With lines like "Let's get ready to rumble!" and "Two thumbs way, way up for our leading lady," Hades elicits more smiles and laughter than fear. While the lord of the underworld does pose a genuine threat, he—like most other aspects of the film—is never taken too seriously. As a result, his character gains a certain likability one might not expect from a mythical being of Evil.

Likability, fun, and lack of seriousness seem to be key words in describing the overall tone of *Hercules*. One of the

AWARDS AND NOMINATIONS

Academy Awards 1997 Nominations: Song ("Go the Distance")

Golden Globe Awards 1998 Nominations: Song ("Go the Distance")

most enjoyable elements of the film is the way it refuses to take itself too seriously by incorporating many references not only to popular culture but to itself as well. After Herc becomes a hero and star to the people of Thebes, children are seen wearing "Air-Herc" tennis shoes, reminiscent of actual products popularized by their ties to famous athletes. One particular shot reveals "The Hercules Store," which of course brings to mind the existence of Disney's own chain of retail stores. When Herc goes to Zeus and tells his father he has become a hero, he tries to prove his point by showing the god that he has been made into an action figure, the humor of which lies not only in real-life action figures based on popular characters or people but in the fact that Disney Hercules figures have actually been produced as tie-ins for the movie. Other references to the animated world of Walt Disney appear throughout the movie, such as when Hades welcomes Hercules to the underworld with the words, "It's a small underworld after all." With these kinds of postmodern self-acknowledgments, *Hercules* incorporates into its fun story line a humorous yet sophisticated appreciation of its own status as a work of art and as a consumer product. Thus, *Hercules* becomes not only a story about belonging, heroism, and goodness but also a lighthearted reflection on itself.

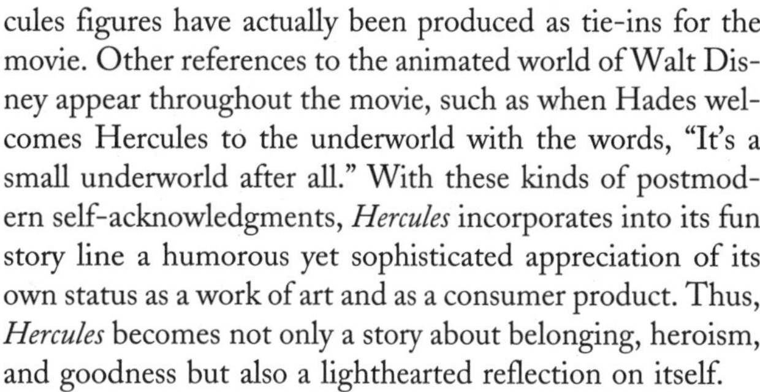

In keeping with the upbeat, fun-filled tone of the movie, the animation in *Hercules* is colorful and detailed but not as realistic as the artistry found in *The Hunchback of Notre Dame*, *Pocahontas*, or *Beauty and the Beast*. Many scenes such as Herc's battle with the Hydra, animated in part through computer imagery, are rich in depth and detail, but the characters and scenery are more "cartoonish" and stylized than those of most recent Disney films. However, this is not a weakness, because the caricature-like characters and the pastel-colored backgrounds are in keeping with the atmosphere of the movie and help maintain its consistency. From the delightful characters, themes, and self-references to the upbeat songs and colorful animation, *Hercules* works as a successful, well-rounded fairy tale that merits favorable comparison to its classic Disney predecessors.

—David Flanagin

CREDITS

Hercules: Tate Donovan (voice)
Phil: Danny DeVito (voice)
Hades: James Woods (voice)
Meg: Susan Egan (voice)
Pain: Bobcat Goldthwait (voice)
Panic: Matt Frewer (voice)
Zeus: Rip Torn (voice)
Hera: Samantha Eggar (voice)
Alcemene: Barbara Barrie (voice)
Amphitryon: Hal Holbrook (voice)
Hermes: Paul Shaffer (voice)
Narrator: Charlton Heston

Origin: USA
Released: 1997
Production: Alice Dewey, John Musker, Ron Clements for Walt Disney Pictures; released by Buena Vista
Direction: John Musker, Ron Clements
Screenplay: John Musker, Ron Clements, Bob Shaw, Donald McEnery, Irene Mecchi
Music: Alan Menken
Lyrics: David Zippel
Production design: Gerald Scarfe
Art direction: Andy Gaskill
Story animation supervisor: Barry Johnson
MPAA rating: G
Running Time: 92 minutes

REVIEWS

Boxoffice. July, 1997, p. 12.
Boxoffice. August, 1997, p. 49.
Chicago Tribune. June 20, 1997, p. 5.
Cinemafantastique. May, 1997, p. 14.
Cinemafantastique. June, 1997, p. 14.
Entertainment Weekly. June 27, 1997, p. 91.
The Hollywood Reporter. June 13, 1997, p. 14.
New York Times. June 13, 1997, p. B1.
People. June 30, 1997, p. 19.
Sci-Fi Universe. July, 1997, p. 28.
Sight and Sound. October, 1997, p. 52.
Time. June 23, 1997.
USA Today. June 13, 1997, p. 1D.
Variety. June 28, 1997, p. 94.
Village Voice. July 1, 1997, p. 89.

Hijacking Hollywood

The difference between success and failure . . . is pulling off the perfect crime.—Movie tagline

Hijacking Hollywood might very well be entitled "Revenge of the Abused and Poorly Paid." It tells the story of Kevin Conroy (Henry Thomas), a bright-eyed, bushy-tailed young man from Detroit who wings into Hollywood after winning a string of local, small filmmaking prizes. Through the connection of an aunt, he lands a job as a production assistant to Michael Lawrence (Mark Metcalf). Lawrence, who was formerly married to Kevin's aunt, snidely abuses him from the minute they meet. Kevin is assigned to work under the wing of Russel (Scott Thompson), the ass-kissing toady Production manager of Lawrence's latest epic *Moby Dick II: Ahab's Revenge*. Kevin finds that he is now relegated to running personal errands, delivering supplies, picking up cans of undeveloped film from the airport and delivering it to the lab, and basically satisfying the whims of mercurial Russell.

Kevin needs to find a nice place to live, and find it quick. He finds a place, but "nice" is hardly the correct adjective—small, cramped and poorly located would be better descriptors. He meets fast-talking Tad (writer-director Neil Mandt), who informs Kevin that he is a producer with many things "in development"—this apartment is merely a "temporary" situation. Although Kevin is taken aback by Tad and the place, he really has no place to go and decides to move in.

Neil Mandt used his credit cards and money from his mother's retirement fund to finance his movie.

Soft-spoken Kevin confesses to Tad that he really wants to direct his own movie, a low-budget project entitled *3 Days in a Salt Mine*, but he feels inadequate in this crowded town of big-time producers. To his surprise, Tad lets him in on the "big secret"—practically everyone is a producer with something "in development"—join the crowd! Kevin takes this all in stride. His life takes a wonderful turn when he is picked up by Sarah, an attractive older woman, who takes him to her home and ravishes him all night. The delightful memory fades the next day when Kevin discovers that she is the nymphomaniac wife of his boss, Michael. Hereafter, he can barely avoid her tentacles when he picks up mail from their home.

Just when Kevin can't take the pointless abuse anymore, he hits upon a "surefire" idea to raise money for his film and release him from his own private purgatory with Russell. Kevin explains to Tad that the most expensive part of a film is trusted to a lowly production assistant, who carries it to and from the airport. Kevin and Tad decide to "kidnap" the can of film that holds the most elaborate and expensive shots and hold it hostage for $150,000.

Tad's ransom call to Russell wipes the perpetual smirk off of Russell's face. Lawrence is called in to mediate and soon, despite Tad's best efforts, Russell and Lawrence nab Kevin with the cans of film. It is only through the most brash and ballsy negotiating of Tad that the boys find themselves on the set of *3 Days in a Salt Mine*—with Kevin directing and Tad lining up financing for their next movie (by ransoming other cans of film, of course).

Despite the good gimmick at the center of this film, it never lives up to other "Hollywood" movies such as *The Big Picture* (1989), *The Player* (1992) or even the hilarious character piece *Swingers* (1996). The production values are mediocre at best, and although Thompson fires off some zingers, the rest of the dialogue drags more often than not. Thomas, a veteran of the entire gamut of the filmmaking spectrum (from the behemoth *E.T.* (1982) to smaller, quirky independents such as 1998's *Niagra, Niagra*) exhibits stalwart professionalism in his role, but he mainly plays straight man to the deliciously evil Thompson and the out-of-control Mandt. Thompson, known for his stint in the Canadian comedy group "Kids in the Hall" and a supporting role in

CREDITS

Kevin Conroy: Henry Thomas
Russell: Scott Thompson
Michael Lawrence: Mark Metcalf
Tad Sheen: Neil Mandt
Sarah Lawrence: Nicole Gian

Origin: USA
Released: 1997
Production: Neil Mandt, for Broken Twig Productions; released by Curb Entertainment
Direction: Neil Mandt
Screenplay: Neil Mandt and Jim Rossow
Cinematography: Anton Floquet
Editing: Charlie Webber
Production design: Todd Cherniawsky
Art direction: Linda Louise Sheets
Costumes: Micheline Michel
Music: Erik Lundmark
Sound: Lawrence Freed
MPAA rating: Unrated
Running Time: 91 minutes

HBO's acclaimed series "Larry Sanders" steals the show with his portrayal of Russell, the line producer/manager who knows enough to delegate, but not enough to produce.

—*G.E. Georges*

REVIEWS

Boxoffice. September, 1997, p. 124.
Los Angeles Times. July 18, 1997.
Variety. July 14, 1997, p. 45.

Hollow Reed

Another secret from the producers of *The Crying Game.*—Movie tagline

"Powerful."—Justin Wyatt, *Detour*

"Excellent! Intelligent. First rate. Loaded with a deeply involving, increasingly harrowing suspense. Martin Donovan is a marvel of versatility."—Kevin Thomas, *Los Angeles Times*

"Wrenching and hypnotic."—Rex Reed, *New York Observer*

"Powerful and unsettling. A suspense thriller . . . Exceptional performances. *Hollow Reed* gets under the skins of its major characters in a way that movies seldom do."—Stephen Holden, *New York Times*

"Hot and tender! Compelling! Ian Hart and Martin Donovan take it to another level."—Amy Taubin, *Village Voice*

"Swiftly paced and completely gripping."—Stephen Hunter, *Washington Post*

"Heartfelt. A first rate film."—Jeffrey Lyons, *WNBC-TV*

Hollow Reed is a hard film to watch. You know something's wrong, at first you don't know what, when you find out, it's chilling, and in the end there's still a lingering tragedy to the entire situation.

Oliver "Ollie" Wyatt (Sam Bould) is a pale, quiet, nine-year-old who doesn't seem very happy. He's first seen running through the park, desperately trying to reach his father's flat. His father is Dr. Martyn Wyatt (Martin Donovan), a middle-class, 40ish general practitioner living with his twentysomething lover, Tom (Ian Hart). Martyn immediately takes Ollie to the hospital, where you can see he's badly cut above one eye. Ollie says some boys beat him up. His mother, Hannah (Joely Richardson) and her lover, Frank (Jason Flemyng), arrive to take Ollie home. Ollie tells his mother he was out on his bike (at night without permission) and some boys tried to steal it from him. She warns him that "terrible things can happen to a child." When Martyn discerns the discrepancies in Ollie's story, he begins to brood but tries to reassure Ollie that his son doesn't have to lie to him and "can tell me anything."

Martyn to Tom about Oliver: "I want you both. But I'm afraid I'll louse it up and lose you both."

Hannah's a nurse who works a lot at night, leaving Ollie in Frank's care. It's soon apparent that Frank, handsome and hard-working though he may be, is also volatile and a harsh disciplinarian. When he catches Ollie drinking out of the juice carton, which the boy then spills, he quickly loses his temper, hitting Oliver and grabbing his hand, all the while telling him that "there's a right way and a wrong way of doing everything" and that "You bring it on yourself, Ollie, you really do."

The next day the school calls Martyn about Ollie's hand and when Martyn is told by another doctor that the hand has been crushed and it couldn't have been an accident (which is what Ollie claims), he comes to the obvious conclusion that Ollie's being abused and by Frank. Hannah's the one with custody and Martyn is not allowed even overnight visits. He goes to his lawyer to change the custody agreement and informs Hannah that Frank is abusing Oliver, which she naturally does not believe. Hannah promptly tells Frank. Martyn again tries to reason with Hannah, you can see the obvious pain still between them, urging her to tell Frank to move out and that there's worse things than being alone. Martyn is also worried about how his living arrangements will affect his custody chances and he asks a furious Tom to move out temporarily.

Trusting Hannah once again leaves Ollie in Frank's company, only this time she unexpectedly returns, catching Frank hitting Oliver, and promptly throws him out. She asks her scared son why he never told her, he replies solemnly "I thought you liked him." Frank returns that evening and the two adults share what turns into a tearful reconciliation scene. Though some critics found it impossible to believe that the obviously educated Hannah would so quickly forgive her son's abuser, director Angela Pope films it so as to make it all too likely. Frank is lost and contrite, complaining that Oliver wants only his father and he could never get the boy to like him; that his own father slapped him and where's the harm—all to Frank completely believable statements. (It's also clear that Frank is rabidly homophobic and wants Oliver to stay away from his father so the boy will be "normal".) The devastated Hannah moans "I can't believe I got it so wrong again" and she's clearly still demeaned that her husband left her for a man, completely undermining her self-confidence. It may not sound valid but it plays true.

Film was shown at the 1996 Sundance Film Festival under the title *Believe Me.*

When Ollie sees Frank's car the next morning, Hannah tries to reassure him that nothing bad will ever happen again. Martyn and Tom also reconcile and Tom moves back in. A first custody hearing leaves "unresolved issues" and the case is remanded to the High Court. One problem is the frightened Oliver refusing to tell the child welfare workers what's been happening to him. There's a lot of miscommunication between Oliver and various adults. After a talk with Oliver, Martyn is led to believe that Hannah always knew about Frank's abuse. Later, Martyn's continual suggestions to Oliver that he should tell the authorities about Frank lead Oliver to inadvertently suggest to the custody judge that Martyn told him to say Frank hit him so that the boy could come to live with him, which he wants to do. The custody hearing is itself an ugly bit of soft-voiced business, with each barrister doing their best to impugn the other defendant's morals—Martyn being, in particular, subjected to pointedly embarrassing questions about his homosexual lifestyle.

Martyn has told Oliver that he will pick him up at school after the hearing is over. When Hannah and Frank come instead, it's clear to Ollie that his father has lost the hearing and he runs away. While Hannah, Martyn, and Tom search the neighborhood, Frank waits at home, where Oliver happens to be hiding in the garage. He takes a chisel and attempts to stab Frank; Martyn hears them screaming and comes in, getting into a vicious brawl with Frank that carries out into the front yard where Oliver is watching in horror. What seems to be most of the neighborhood is soon watching, including Hannah, who finally realizes that Frank is violent and not going to change. Ollie goes to live with Martyn and Tom, and Hannah comes to their flat to try and reconcile with her son. Both she and Martyn realize it will be a long time before Oliver can come to terms with any of what's happened to him.

The performances are all wonderful. American Martin Donovan may be best known for his deadpan, slow burn performances in a number of films by director Hal Hartley. His slightly English-accented doctor is anxious, outraged, humiliated, and torn between his love for his son and his love for Tom. Versatile Ian Hart (*Backbeat*, *Land and Freedom*, *Nothing Personal*) plays Tom as a young man comfortable with his identity—unlike his older lover. He's hurt that Martyn could wish to hide him and their relationship away though he's understanding of the situation. Skinny, soft-voiced Sam Bould as Oliver is a heartbreaker. He wants both his parents to be happy, he wants to live with his father, but he also doesn't want to leave his mother—he's a child caught in the middle of an impossible situation, left unprotected by the very people who should be shielding him. Tall and attractive Jason Flemyng may be a particular revelation for those who know him primarily from his role as the bumptious Dr. David Neil in the Scottish TV series "Doctor Finlay." His abuser is no wild-eyed villain but a man reacting to a disruptive child the only way he knows how—probably the same abusive way he himself was raised. Joely Richardson comes by her acting genes naturally—she's the daughter of actress Vanessa Redgrave and the late director, Tony Richardson, and the sister of actress Natasha Richardson. Her character is willful and fragile, loving and angry.

CREDITS

Martyn Wyatt: Martin Donovan
Hannah Wyatt: Joely Richardson
Oliver Wyatt: Sam Bould
Tom Dixon: Ian Hart
Frank Donally: Jason Flemyng
Judge: Edward Hardwicke
Hannah's Barrister: Douglas Hodge
Martyn's Barrister: Annette Badland

Origin: Great Britain
Released: 1995, 1997
Production: Elizabeth Karlsen for Scala, Senator Film, and Channel Four Films; released by Cinepix Film Properties
Direction: Angela Pope
Screenplay: Paula Milne
Cinematography: Remi Adefarasin
Editing: Sue Wyatt
Music: Anne Dudley
Production design: Stuart Walker
Costumes: Pam Downe
Sound: John Pritchard
MPAA rating: Unrated
Running Time: 106 minutes

Though Hannah's character may have her caring moments, it's clear Pope is leading the viewer to side with Martyn, who gets points for re-committing to his lover (Tom's quick to forgive) and apparently accepting himself. The script also leaves some niggling questions—it's not clear how long Martyn and Hannah have been divorced, whether it happened when Oliver was a baby or if he was old enough to realize something between his parents was off. (Hannah still seems mighty bitter if the marriage has been over for a while.) There's also no way of knowing how long either Hannah and Frank or Martyn and Tom have been together or how long Frank's abuse of Oliver has been going on and whether at the end Hannah relinquished custody voluntarily or was forced to do so. You can hardly say you enjoy a film that centers on child abuse but it's a heartfelt and unsettling production.

—*Christine Tomassini*

REVIEWS

Boxoffice. April, 1997, p. 189.
Chicago Tribune. September 24, 1997, p. 6.
Hollywood Reporter. April 22, 1997, p. 7.
Los Angeles Times. May 2, 1997, p. F21.
New York Times. April 18, 1997, p. C4.
People. April 28, 1997, p. 20.
Sight and Sound. September, 1996, p. 45.
Variety. February 5, 1996, p. 62.
Village Voice. April 22, 1997, p. 77.

Home Alone 3

It's bad news for the bad guys . . . Again.—Movie tagline

There's a new kid on the block.—Movie tagline

"Better and more entertaining than the first two. Funnier and gentler, with a real charmer for a hero."—Roger Ebert, *Chicago Sun-Times*

"Big laughs! A real kid-pleaser."—Joel Siegel, *Good Morning America*

"One of the season's more pleasant surprises. Alex D. Linz is terrific—wholesome, smart and charming."—Michael Medved, *New York Post*

"The family film surprise of the year! A new family, new bad guys and hilarious new twists."—Jim Ferguson, *Prevue Channel*

Box Office: $19,173,063

When a movie is called *Home Alone 3,* no one is going to see it expecting any originality. And on that count, writer John Hughes doesn't disappoint. He makes sure that seeing this installment of *Home Alone* is as safe and predictable as walking into any McDonald's in the nation and getting the same expected cheeseburger.

First-time director Raja Gosnell is a veteran film editor who worked with John Hughes on *Home Alone* and *Home Alone 2.*

It's not like it's any big secret that *Home Alone 3* is a wee bit derivative. Even the ads for the movie tout, "It's not just a comedy, it's a tradition." Meaning, basically, "It's not just a comedy sequel, it's a comedy with all the same jokes as the original."

All the usual *Home Alone* elements are there. A boy is home alone. He has to foil bad guys. He does. Whoops. Hope that didn't spoil it for you. At the end, it's every kid's fantasy—the police commend him, his mom apologizes for not really listening, and, least believably, even his bratty older sister says admiringly, "You're a hero."

This time out Alex's (Alex D. Linz, Michelle Pfeiffer's son in *One Fine Day*) parents don't accidentally ditch him, like poor Macaulay Culkin's negligent parents did in the earlier pics. In this film, the kid playing the Culkin role has chicken pox and working parents who keep having to step out to take care of business. They probably could be cited by Child Welfare for repeatedly leaving the poor kid alone, even after he's called the police twice—but that would be a dramatic TV movie-of-the-week.

Left alone in his big house in a Chicago suburb, the ever-resourceful Alex spies out his window and sees some bad guys (and one bad gal) breaking into neighborhood houses. It seems that there is some business with a microchip they're looking for and, well, it really doesn't matter what the plot specifics are. The real point is that the bad guys (and gal) end up trying to break into Alex's house and he has to stop them. Alex first turns to adults to solve his problem but soon realizes that the adults are unaware of what's going on and/or unwilling to believe him. So he has to handle it himself. Covered with chicken pox, no less. (Not only does he seem to suffer no ill effects from his pox—not even itching—but the more unattractive dots on his face disappear soon after his diagnosis.)

CREDITS

Alex Pruitt: Alex D. Linz
Beaupre: Olek Krupa
Alice: Rya Kihlstedt
Jernigan: Lenny Von Dohlen
Unger: David Thornton
Karen: Haviland Morris
Jack: Kevin Kilner
Mrs. Hess: Marian Seldes
Stan: Seth Smith
Molly: Scarlett Johannson
Agent Stuckey: Christopher Curry
Police Captain: Baxter Harris

Origin: USA
Released: 1997
Production: John Hughes and Hilton Green; released by 20th Century Fox
Direction: Raja Gosnell
Screenplay: John Hughes
Cinematography: Julio Macat
Editing: Bruce Green, Malcolm Campbell, David Rennie
Music: Nick Glennie-Smith
Production design: Henry Bumstead
Art direction: Jack G. Taylor, Jr.
Costumes: Jodie Tillen
Sound: Jose Antonio Garcia
Stunt coordinators: R.A. Rondell, Freddie Hice
MPAA rating: PG
Running Time: 102 minutes

Armed with an intelligence far beyond his (or anyone's) years, Alex sets up a series of booby traps for the bad people. He puts a variety of his toys into action, including a remote control car, a robot and even his pet rat, Dorris. The second half of the movie, or the big pay-off, is basically that the crooks set off these traps and we see them get hurt. Big audience fave at one screening: men fall in icy pool, two people run into each other and bump heads, and the ever-popular man-get-hits-in-the-crotch-with-a-stick.

As the villains, Olek Krupa, Rya Kihlstedt, Lenny Von Dohlen, and David Thornton are interchangeable. As the kid, Linz is fine and sports the appropriate kid actor bowl haircut. His acting isn't great. Sometimes it seems that he's speaking lines of dialogue instead of just speaking. But maybe that's the fault of the script. For example, when he comforts his mother about leaving him alone with the words, "It's okay. It's not you, it's the times," you can almost see John Hughes at his computer typing out the script.

Or maybe it would be more accurate to say that Hughes was "hacking" out the script. With this third installment of *Home Alone* it's getting harder and harder to remember that once Hughes used to write smart, funny films like *The Breakfast Club* (1985) and *Sixteen Candles* (1984). Now it seems like he's not even trying anymore. Or rather, not trying for anything except a quick paycheck. And that's a shame.

—*Jill Hamilton*

REVIEWS

Entertainment Weekly. December 19, 1997, p. 51.
San Francisco Chronicle. December 12, 1997, p. C3.
Sight and Sound. January, 1998, p. 44.
USA Today. December 12, 1997, p. 14D.
Variety. December 8, 1997, p. 112.

Hoodlum

They had it all. It cost them everything.—Movie tagline

"Rousing . . . spectacular star power!"—Michael Medved, *New York Post*

"Fishburne is as coolly ruthless as Al Pacino's Michael Corleone in *The Godfather*. Mr. Roth's Schultz is a compelling enigma . . ."—Stephen Holden, *New York Times*

"*Hoodlum* is filmmaking on a grand scale . . . thrilling!"—Amy Taubin, *Village Voice*

Box Office: $23,495,622

Hoodlum is a period piece set in Harlem during the Great Depression and based very loosely on fact. It is an expensive production reminiscent of films like *The Godfather* (1972), *The Godfather, Part 2* (1974), *The Sting* (1973), *Ragtime* (1981), *The Cotton Club* (1984), and *Billy Bathgate* (1991). A great deal of thought and money went into sets and costuming. Laurence Fishburne's tailor-made suits and sports clothes are as beautifully cut as those of Robert Redford in *The Great Gatsby* (1974). Money was lavished on such matters as hiring and costuming extras as well as renting dozens of 1930's-vintage cars and trucks complete with drivers. *Hoodlum* is a visually impressive film. It is most successful as a slice of American history. It often succeeds in beguiling the audience into believing they have been transported back into the mid-1930s, when Harlem was in the grip of the worst economic depression this country had ever experienced.

African Americans had it worse during the Great Depression than any other group. Even in good times there were nothing but menial jobs available to black men and women crowded into rat- and roach-infested Northern urban ghettos. In those days most of them played "The Numbers," a supposedly illegal lottery in which the odds against winning were 999 to one but the payoff was substantially less. People could play for as little as ten cents. It was said that the Numbers provided employment for 2,000 people in the New York ghetto, most of them runners collecting tiny bets and scribbling out markers. The Numbers game, since replaced by state lotteries, not only gave its players the hope of winning money but also gave them something to think about and talk about in a cheerless environment. In several scenes the camera pans across men counting piles of pennies, nickels, real silver dimes, quarters and half-dollars, showing graphically that the food money and the rent money are riding on little people's dreams. There are also stacks of crumpled currency of small denominations, including many two-dollars bills, which were widely used in those days but seldom seen anymore.

Gangster Bumpy Johnson (Laurence Fishburne) seeks Lucky Luciano's (Andy Garcia) advice in ending a gangland war in Harlem in *Hoodlum.*

Attracted by all those coins and greenbacks, legendary mobster Dutch Schultz (Tim Roth) is moving in on the Harlem numbers racket. His chief opponent is "The Queen," Stephanie St. Clair (Cicely Tyson), an intelligent woman who sometimes speaks French and aspires rather pathetically to white upper-class culture and refinement. She is not psychologically prepared to cope with the kind of gangster tactics Dutch Schultz is introducing to Harlem. The Dutchman's men beat up her runners, kill them if necessary, and warn her loyal customers that it would be better for their health to place their numbers bets with the Dutchman. The script takes pains to manipulate audience sympathy by establishing that the Queen runs an honest book while Schultz is as ruthless with his customers as he is with his competitors. When too many people have picked the right number, Schultz's men simply refuse to pay off.

Bumpy on his career: "The numbers provide jobs for over 2,000 colored folks right here in Harlem alone. It's the only homegrown business we got."

At this crucial time in Harlem history, Ellsworth "Bumpy" Johnson (Laurence Fishburne), soon to become known as "the Godfather of Harlem," is released from prison. He has promised the Bible-reading warden to go straight but obviously has no respect for the Bible or for religion. Like the Queen, Bumpy has genteel tastes. He writes poetry, plays chess, and reads books. (Kenneth Turan of the *Los Angeles Times* called him "a one-man Harlem Renaissance.") Because of their common interests, Bumpy immediately becomes the Queen's right-hand man. In one shocking scene her limousine is attacked by Schultz's minions while they are on their way to attend the opera. The dead bodies fill up an entire intersection, but Bumpy saves the Queen. Later when she is framed and sent to prison, Bumpy finds himself in sole command.

Bumpy's taste for refinement attracts him to Francine Hughes (Vanessa Williams), a beautiful, well-educated African American woman who comes to Harlem to crusade for Marcus Garvey's United Negro Improvement Association. Their relationship resembles that between Michael Corleone (Al Pacino) and his WASP wife Kay (Diane Keaton) in *The Godfather* saga, and Bumpy's character evolution throughout the film seems patterned after Michael Corleone's as well. Francine falls in love with Bumpy because of his good looks, dignity, and sensitivity, but she falls out of love when she realizes that his vendetta with Dutch Schultz is turning him into a cold-blooded monster. After she walks out of their palatial home—with Bumpy hurling insults, jewelry and lingerie after her in a scene reminiscent of the break-up between Charles Foster Kane and wife Susan in *Citizen Kane* (1941)—Bumpy proceeds steadily downhill. He becomes increasingly ruthless, escalating the reprisals against Schultz & Co.

The story is sometimes hard to follow because so many different factions are involved. First there are the African Americans, represented by Bumpy and his close friend Illinois Gordon (Chi McBride). Next there is Dutch Schultz and his legion of thugs. Then there are the Italians represented by Lucky Luciano (Andy Garcia). And there are two elements of crooked government represented by Captain Jerrod Foley (Richard Bradford) and Thomas E. Dewey (William Atherton), then state prosecutor and later to become governor of New York. Viewers may be shocked to see Thomas E. Dewey, who twice ran for president against Franklin D. Roosevelt, depicted as a cynically corrupt politician working hand in glove with the Italian Mafia.

Laurence Fishburne played the character of "Bumpy Rhodes," actually Johnson, in 1984's crime/musical *The Cotton Club.*

In the 1930s, African Americans were confined to ghettos in all the big cities. It was all right for white mobsters to invade Harlem, but unthinkable for black mobsters to move into white neighborhoods. This is the "brilliancy" that chess-player Bumpy comes up with; it is based on the premise that the best defense is a strong offense. Everyone but the psychopathic Dutch Schultz is alarmed by this development. Pretending to be delivering yeast, Bumpy and Illinois drive a whole truckload of dynamite into Schultz's big downtown brewery and create a glorious multi-level, multi-stage explosion. Probably no one in the 1930s ever saw an explosion like those Hollywood's technicians can produce today. Unfortunately, such technical effects have a way of awakening viewers from the illusion of visiting the past and reminding them they are still in the 1990s.

This supreme act of defiance does exactly what Bumpy expects. He has succeeded at the age-old practice the Romans called "Divide and conquer." His audacity makes Dewey and Luciano realize that the gang war cannot be confined to Harlem. Dutch Schultz is intransigent, to say the least. He is a little man with delusions of grandeur. Luciano arranges to have him bumped off by one of the Dutchman's own men. This apparently authentic incident, which takes place while Schultz is relieving himself in the men's room, is one of the most effective scenes in the film.

With Schultz's death, Bumpy has won the war—but he realizes he has lost everything in the process. Illinois, his best friend, was one of the many victims. Bumpy's abrupt spiritual transformation at the very end of the film would seem to correspond to the agonies of conscience that afflict Michael Corleone throughout *The Godfather, Part 3* (1990) and made that film less appealing than the first two episodes. Michael Corleone's remorse does not ring true, and Bumpy's does not ring true either. Corleone, however, had three long films, covering many years from youth to late middle age, in which to experience his spiritual development, whereas Bumpy's happens practically overnight like a bad case of the flu. Bumpy's is symbolized by his entering a church to attend the funeral of one of his numbers runners.

Laurence Fishburne, who was also one of the film's executive co-producers, is on screen most of the time, often in very close closeups. He is a good actor who recently had the title role in a film version of Shakespeare's *Othello* (1995); however, he seems handicapped in the one-dimensional role of Bumpy Johnson. There is really very little character development comparable to the portrayal of Michael Corleone by Al Pacino, who may be a better actor. Bumpy is first seen as an ice-cold loner who keeps his own counsel and is pretty much the same when the story ends. Fishburne is continually upstaged by Tim Roth who has the really choice part in the film as the volatile Dutch Schultz.

Critics have pointed out that screenplay author Chris Brancato's story contains many elements that might be called homages to Francis Ford Coppola's classic *Godfather* trilogy. Among them is the murder of a high-ranking police officer. Bumpy catches Captain Foley literally with his pants down and kills him as dispassionately as Michael Corleone committed the dual murders in the memorable Italian restaurant scene in *The Godfather.*

The critical response to *Hoodlum* was not enthusiastic, in spite of the acknowledgement of the film's good acting,

CREDITS

Ellsworth "Bumpy" Johnson: Laurence Fishburne
Dutch Schultz: Tim Roth
Lucky Luciano: Andy Garcia
Francine Hughes: Vanessa L. Williams
Stephanie St. Clair: Cicely Tyson
Illinois Gordon: Chi McBride
Thomas E. Dewey: William Atherton

Origin: USA
Released: 1997
Production: Frank Mancuso Jr. for United Artists Pictures; released by MGM
Direction: Bill Duke
Screenplay: Chris Brancato
Cinematography: Frank Tidy
Editing: Harry Keramidas
Music: Elmer Bernstein
Production design: Charles Bennett
Art direction: Gary Baugh
Costumes: Richard Bruno
Choreography: Otis Sallid
Sound: Curt Frisk
MPAA rating: R
Running Time: 130 minutes

good direction, good photography, and generally first-class production values. *Entertainment Weekly*, which samples responses to new releases across the country, gave *Hoodlum* (which it called a "Godfather wannabe") a composite rating of only a C+. Using guarded language, *Variety* critic Leonard Klady wrote: "The material has limited international appeal but should hit a bull's-eye in domestic ancillaries." In other words, the film should do very well with African American audiences but is unlikely to be a mega-hit because it looks too much like high-grade, big-budget blaxploitation.

—*Bill Delaney*

REVIEWS

Boxoffice. November, 1997, p. 135.
Chicago Tribune. August 27, 1997, p. 1.
Entertainment Weekly. September 12, 1997, p. 115.
Los Angeles Times. August 27, 1997, p. F8.
New York Times. August 27, 1997, p. B3.
People. September 8, 1997, p. 18.
San Francisco Chronicle. August 27, 1997, p. E4.
USA Today. August 27, 1997, p. 2D.
Variety. September 1, 1997, p. 75.
Village Voice. September 2, 1997, p. 73.
Washington Post. August 27, 1997, p. D1.

Hotel de Love

A comedy for the romantically confused.—Movie tagline

"Sexy . . . wickedly funny."—Ted Casablanca, *E! Online*

"Just like *Four Weddings and a Funeral* this movie will charm you and set your heart aflutter."—Jeanne Wolf, *Jeanne Wolf's Hollywood*

"Entertaining, moving and an utterly charming love story."—Paul Wunder, *WBAI Radio*

Take a candy-coated romantic comedy about two brothers in love with the same girl set against an equally confectionery backdrop of the titular kitschy love nest, complete with a lounge singer who continually cranks out goofy love songs of the '60s, '70s, and '80s. Add a charming and attractive cast and all this works to create a delightful first time effort for writer/director Craig Rosenberg.

Shy, 17-year-old Stephen Dunne (Simon Bossell) is at a typical teen party when suddenly, he is overwhelmed by a sense of kismet and, in a flash of light, turns to see the woman of his dreams on the dance floor. However, Stephen's more suave, fraternal twin brother Rick (Aden Young) is the Johnny-on-the-spot as he quickly moves in on the beautiful British Melissa (Saffron Burrows) before Stephen realizes what's happening. Rick and Melissa are soon a hot and heavy item, while Stephen is forced to watch the cooing duo in action. Not for long, however, as Melissa must go abroad for school, with the still devoted Rick promising to write constantly.

Fast-forward ten years, to the present, where the still single brothers have embarked upon their careers: Stephen as a successful but lonely stockbroker and Rick, who manages the Hotel de Love, which caters to newlyweds with gaudy theme rooms that include Love in the Outback and Subterranean Seduction. Both the boys have a skewed sense of romantic love, embedded in them by their upbringing by two constantly bickering parents. Stephen, who gives his observations in voice-over throughout the picture, is a hopeless romantic who thinks he can mathematically figure his chances of finding love by surveying couples at the airport. Cynical of love, Rick has a girlfriend, fortune teller Alison Leigh (Pippa Grandison), but is unable to commit.

Rick: "See, men and women can never be completely honest with each other or else the social fabric will break down."

Checking in with her nerdy fiancé to inadvertently create total chaos in all their lives, is the boys' old flame, Melissa. Stephen, in a humorous about-face, decides to pursue her, this time around, with all the vigor he can muster. What ensues becomes a farce, with the once sweet, but now scary, stalker-like Stephen popping his head around every corner and literally shouting out his feelings of love for a quite bewildered Melissa. Rick, as well, realizes he still has strong feelings for Melissa himself, and quickly dumps Alison to become available should she want him back. Alison, in turn, finds herself falling for wacky Stephen, and while helping him win over Melissa, manages to let him know she is no slouch herself. As for Melissa, although she claims to love her milquetoast boyfriend, his lackluster presence suggests he will quickly be discarded, and it is only a matter of which brother will win her heart.

To complement the action going on with the brothers is the subplot concerning their parents (Julia Blake and Ray Barrett), who are renewing their wedding vows. Equally farcical, the two seem more on the verge of divorce than a second marriage, as they argue, scream, slam doors, and throw things at each others. Things heat up, however, as Mrs. Dunne starts receiving mash notes from an anonymous admirer who signs the notes "Lord Byron."

The witty dialogue and fast pacing of the film add to the engaging plot which keeps you involved, wondering who will end up with each other in the end, without having to sit through a lot of emotionally overwrought love scenes. Characters, both male and female, are thankfully well-written and developed. Rick, a cad who could easily wind up seeming like the bad guy, is instead able to show his sensitive side, spouting horribly written, but nonetheless touching poetry he wrote to Melissa but never had the courage to send. Melissa, besides being extremely beautiful, is also very intelligent and strong. Alison, who at once seems like a classic manhunter out to trap Stephen, quickly points out she is no longer willing to let men, like ex-Rick, rule her life and resumes her once-forgotten dream of a long-term trip to Barcelona. Stephen, too, learns much about real-life relationships and is able to combine his romantic ideal with a little reality. Even the battling Dunnes are allowed to transform and become better people.

Better than your average romantic comedy, this lighthearted Australian effort easily offers more unique and varied distractions. Visually, Rosenberg made a film that looks equally as good as its writing, acting, and distinctive soundtrack.

—Hilary Weber

CREDITS

Stephen: Simon Bossell
Rick: Aden Young
Melissa: Saffron Burrows
Alison: Pippa Grandison
Jack: Ray Barrett
Edith: Julia Blake

Origin: Australia
Released: 1996
Production: Michael Lake and David Parker for Village Roadshow and Pratt Films; released by Live Entertainment
Direction: Craig Rosenberg
Screenplay: Craig Rosenberg
Cinematography: Steve Windon
Editing: Bill Murphy
Music: Christine Woodruff
Production design: Simon Dobbin
Costumes: Bruce Finlayson
Sound: Gary Wilkins
MPAA rating: R
Running Time: 93 minutes

REVIEWS

Boxoffice. November, 1996, p. 137.
Los Angeles Times. February 7, 1997, p. F10.
New York Times. February 7, 1997, p. B10.
Variety. September 23, 1996, p. 127.

The House of Yes

She's elegant, glamorous and well bred. When you've got it all, you can get away with murder.—Movie tagline

"Bitingly funny! A daring film with real brilliance and a simply astonishing performance by Parker Posey!"—Vince Passaro, *Marie Claire*

"Parker Posey performs with memorable star presence and shocking intensity!"—Janet Maslin, *New York Times*

"A brilliant film! How good is Parker Posey? We're talking possible Oscar nomination!"—Mick LaSalle, *San Francisco Chronicle*

Box Office: $671,753

Like *The Myth of Fingerprints* (1997), Mark Waters' directorial debut *The House of Yes* is another entry in the dysfunctional, home-for-the-holidays genre, only this movie is one creepy black comedy. Adapted from Wendy MacLeod's acclaimed, hit stage play, this shocking tale of family secrets is both perversely funny and fearless.

Anything can happen (and does) in the gothic fun house of the privileged Pascal family. Marty Pascal (Josh Hamilton), along with fiancee Lesly (Tori Spelling), is returning home from college to his family's suburban D.C. mansion for the Thanksgiving holiday. It also happens to be the 20th anniversary of JFK's assassination, which holds an extra meaning for the Pascal family. Eagerly awaiting Marty's arrival is his beautiful and certifiably nutty twin sister, the so-called Jackie-O (Parker Posey), who has a fixation on her brother, as the result of the siblings' history of incest.

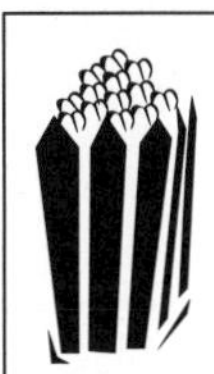

Jackie-O: "Love is for tiny people with tiny lives."

The glamorous, Kennedy-obsessed Jackie-O still lusts after her brother and is immediately jealous of Lesly, a donut-shop waitress from a modest upbringing, who represents some degree of normalcy to Marty. Threatened by the arrival of his fiancee, Jackie-O starts scheming to get Lesly out of the house and Marty back into her clutches. Meanwhile, brother Anthony (Freddie Prinze Jr.), a recent college dropout, plans to seduce the clueless Lesly and simultaneously lose his virginity. Overseeing all of this bizarre behavior is their eccentric and sharp-tongued mother played by Genevieve Bujold. We are warned that this is not going to be any ordinary Thanksgiving dinner when Mrs. Pascal tells her children: "I'm going to go baste the turkey and hide the kitchen knives."

In 1990, Wendy MacLeod's work was named "Best New Play" by *LA Weekly.*

The film opens with vintage clips of Jackie Kennedy's televised White House tour intercut with home movies of a young Jackie-O Pascal, dressed like the former First Lady in a pink suit and pillbox hat, guiding viewers around her family's stately home. Jackie-O thinks she *is* Jackie Kennedy or at least Jackie Kennedy on the day of her husband's assassination. This delusion is further carried out by one of the twins' favorite activities since childhood: re-enacting the Kennedy assassination with a gun and real bullets. It just so happens that, on Nov. 22, 1963, at the same time the nation's President was assassinated in Dallas, the twins' father mysteriously disappeared and this linking of events is blamed for the family's deep-rooted dementia.

The wicked repartee in *The House of Yes* compensates for the fact that the film often comes across as stagey and stilted (the downside of adapting a play to the screen). The writing is smart and snappy—the arch dialogue carrying this drawing-room comedy gone haywire. Jackie-O's brilliant wit is evidenced as she casually tosses off one epigram after another. When asked what a gun is doing in the house, she replies: "Just being gunlike. Gun-esque. Gun-onic."

Indie-film darling Parker Posey (*Sleep With Me* 1994, *Kicking and Screaming* 1995, *The Doom Generation* 1995) is perfectly cast as the glamorous yet twisted Jackie-O. Posey's performance is the highlight of the film—she far outshines the other actors with her dead-on portrayal of a unstable young woman about to go over the edge. Her camp-aristocratic hauteur is a hoot and you'll never see a more stylish nut-case than Posey's Jackie-O. Because of her prolific presence at the 1997 Sundance Film Festival, where three of the hottest films (including *The House of Yes* all featured Posey, she was awarded the festival's Special Recognition for Acting Award.

Spelling (of TV's "Beverly Hills, 90210") is credible as the slightly dizzy Lesly, although one has to wonder why she's dressed in these frumpy, Laura Ashley-style outfits. (We know she's the odd man out—she doesn't need to wear these ugly getups to further illustrate the point.) Hamilton and Prinze are both competent, though a bit bland, in their roles as the Pascal brothers. And internationally acclaimed actress Bujold brings just the right mix of haughtiness and fierceness to her turn as the Pascal family matriarch.

The title of the film refers to a place without boundaries, where anything and everything is permissible. Playwright MacLeod was reportedly inspired to write the story after seeing "We Are Living in a House of Yes" scrawled in the bathroom of a wealthy family's house outside of Washington, D.C. In the press kit for the movie, MacLeod says: "The play is about people who have never been said no to.

CREDITS

Jackie-O: Parker Posey
Marty: Josh Hamilton
Lesly: Tori Spelling
Anthony: Freddie Prinze Jr.
Mrs. Pascal: Genevieve Bujold

Origin: USA
Released: 1997
Production: Beau Flynn and Stefan Simchowitz for Bandeira Entertainment; released by Miramax Films
Direction: Mark Waters
Screenplay: Mark Waters; based on the play by Wendy MacLeod
Cinematography: Mike Spiller
Editing: Pamela Martin
Music: Rolfe Kent
Production design: Patrick Sherman
Costumes: Ed Giguere
Art direction: Andrew Cahn
MPAA rating: R
Running Time: 87 minutes

It's about an insularity I see in the upper classes, people who have cut themselves off from the rest of the world and are living by the rules they've invented."

An audience fave at Sundance, *The House of Yes* failed to attract much interest at the box office. Hopefully, sophisticated, urban audiences will discover this contemporary black comedy on video. Critical reaction to the film was mixed, although praise for Posey's performance was unanimous. Overall, *The House of Yes* is an impressive debut for Waters—proving he's a filmmaker to watch.

—*Beth Fhaner*

REVIEWS

Boxoffice. April, 1997, p. 180.
Entertainment Weekly. October 17, 1997, p. 44.
Los Angeles Times. October 10, 1997, p. F10.
New York Times. October 10, 1997, p. E10.
People. October 20, 1997, p. 21.
Rolling Stone. October 30, 1997, p. 73.
Time online. October 20, 1997.
USA Today. October 10, 1997, p. 4D.
Variety. January 27, 1997, p. 73.
Village Voice. October 14, 1997, p.85.

Hugo Pool

The right kind of strange.—Movie tagline

"A zany seat-of-your-pants spoof of Hollywood narcissism and family dysfunction."—Stephen Holden, *New York Times*

"A cultish comedy about as crazy as anything since Downey's *Greaser's Palace*!"—Bruce Williamson, *Playboy*

"Alyssa Milano is a revelation . . . tough, energetic and charming."—James Berardinelli, *Reel News*

"Sean Penn is deliciously daft . . . and Patrick Dempsey performs wonders with a smile."—Barbara & Scott Siegel, *Siegel Entertainment Syndicate*

"Outrageous and continually inventive, you never know what to expect next!"—Jeffrey Lyons, *WNBC-TV*

After a six-year hiatus, director Robert Downey, Sr. is back at the helm of a "wacky" day-in-the-life comedy that he co-wrote with his wife, Laura. She died in 1994 of ALS—commonly known as Lou Gehrig's Disease—at the age of 36. *Hugo Pool* is obviously intended to promote awareness of this degenerative disease that attacks the nervous system and leads to paralysis and death. But do not expect Downey to succumb to any maudlin movie-of-the-week expression of grief—it simply is not his style.

Robert Downey made his directing debut in 1965 with *Chafed Elbows*. He is perhaps best known for his films, the irreverent but dated *Putney-Swope* (1969) and *Greaser's Place* (1972), which featured a seven-year-old Robert Downey, Jr. as a mutilated child. Downey Sr. is considered by many to be one of America's truly original independent filmmakers, having never buckled under demands for commercial success. That said, be forewarned that his films—which Downey readily acknowledged would never make any money—are without a doubt an acquired taste.

Hugo Pool is a day-in-the-life of a levelheaded young Beverly Hills pool cleaner named Hugo Dugay (Alyssa Milano). As she attempts to service some forty clients in one day, she also receives an illegal demand from a threatening mobster named Chic Chicalini (the ludicrously miscast Richard Lewis) to fill his swimming pool during a Los Angeles drought. Hugo has little choice but to enlist the aid of her estranged and highly dysfunctional parents, Minerva (Cathy Moriarty) and Henry (Malcolm McDowell). Mom has a serious gambling addiction, while Dad prefers to shoot heroin with a hand puppet. (Best not to ask . . .)

While Minerva agrees to work with Hugo in exchange for enough money to settle her debt with her repulsive bookie, Henry is dispatched to the Colorado River to extract enough water to fill Chico's pool. In his sixth outing for his father, Robert Downey, Jr. is the deranged film director who is charged with murdering an actor for overacting. Sean Penn makes an appearance as the mysterious hitchhiker with the blue suede shoes (which the actor got to keep as part of his compensation for doing the film). And last, but certainly not least—he is the film's romantic interest —is Floyd Galen (Patrick Dempsey), a young man stricken with ALS. Floyd functions as a "travelling angel," a character whose mission it is to get the other people in the story to voluntarily change their wicked, wicked ways. And as expected, Floyd is the character who is treated with the most respect.

Actress Alyssa Milano spends the entire movie scantily clad in short shorts and a tank top—and Downey does not let one gratuitous shot of her well-endowed body escape the camera's gaze. Ms. Milano may be exploited, but the award for overacting in a feature film goes virtually uncontested to the director's son. If it were the intention here of Robert

CREDITS

Hugo Dugay: Alyssa Milano
Floyd Gaylen: Patrick Dempsey
Henry: Malcolm McDowell
Franz Mazur: Robert Downey, Jr.
Minerva: Cathy Moriarty
Chick Chicalini: Richard Lewis
Mysterious Hitchhiker: Sean Penn
Old Man: Bert Remsen
Irwin: Chuck Barris

Origin: USA
Released: 1997
Production: Barbara Ligeti for Nomadic Pictures; released by BMG Independents
Direction: Robert Downey, Sr.
Screenplay: Robert Downey, Sr. and Laura Ernst Downey
Cinematography: Joseph Montgomery
Editing: Joe D'Augustine
Production design: Lauren Gabor
Costumes: Hilary Lawson, Jocelyn F. Wright
Music: Danilo Perez
MPAA rating: R
Running Time: 92 minutes

Downey, Jr. to parody his own well-publicized, real-life substance abuse problem, it is neither admirable nor amusing. His inability to refrain from illicit drug use resulted in the eventual arrest and conviction of one of Hollywood's most talented, yet unpredictably uneven actors.

Hugo Pool is a comedy that tries so hard to be funny that it ends up not being funny at all. One could even say that it is horrifically unfunny. While it is noble of Downey to want to draw attention to the tragedy of ALS, and probably therapeutic to do it in an irreverent way, it is important to remember that good intentions do not a movie make. At least not a particularly good one.

—*Patricia Kowal*

REVIEWS

Entertainment Weekly. December 12, 1997, p. 56.
Los Angeles Times. December 12, 1997, p. F12.
New York Times. December 12, 1997, p. E26.
Variety. February 10, 1997, p. 66.
Village Voice. December 16, 1997, p. 78.

I Know What You Did Last Summer

If you're going to bury the truth, make sure it stays buried.—Movie tagline

Someone knows their secret, someone knows they're scared, and someone knows what they did last summer.—Movie tagline

"It's scarier than *Scream*! You'll be hooked for life!"—John Stanley, *ABC-TV*

"A wild terror ride!"—Ron Brewington, *American Urban Radio Networks*

"An edge-of-your-seat thriller!"—Linda Sue Stotter, *Entertainment Time-Out*

"Don't miss this sensational thriller!"—Jeanne Wolf, *Jeanne Wolf's Hollywood*

Box Office: $70,287,258

Teen slasher flicks had their heyday in the 1980's with films like the Friday the 13th series and the Halloween volumes. But by the 1990's, after (very) numerous installments and increasingly poor quality, it seemed as though teen slasher flicks were, yes, dead.

Then came last year's *Scream* which sold a bunch of movie tickets and helped make slasher flicks a viable genre again. And by the time *I Know What You Did Last Summer* came out in October, 1997, it went to number one in ticket sales in the first week and set a box office record for an October opening.

Why are slashers films suddenly popular now after being maligned for so many years? Well, for one, there's a whole new crop of young-un's who apparently need to be scared. Just as every generation of pre-teen girls needs a singing star to swoon over, every generation of teens seems to need their own version of Freddy Krueger or Jason Voorhees or Michael Myers.

Also, today's slasher flicks are very self-aware. Sure, they are basically teens-getting-cornered-and-killed-in-ever-differing-ways but today's slasher flicks know that's what they are. And they know that the audience knows that too. *Scream* referred incessantly to horror films of the past, and *I Know What You Did Last Summer* knows a bit of history, too. In one scene, the hometown beauty queen Helen (Sarah Michelle Gellar) refers to Jodie Foster in *The Silence of the*

Lambs, and even the TV series "Murder, She Wrote." "Don't you think we should have some sort of plan? Angela Lansbury always had a plan," she says as she and her smart, sensible friend Julie, (Jennifer Love Hewitt) prepare to enter a scary house. But any similarities between *Scream* and *I Know What You Did Last Summer* probably have less to do with any kind of giant movements in film styles than the fact that they were both written by Kevin Williamson. (Williamson's script for *I Know* is a reworking of the 1973 Lois Duncan young adult novel.)

Screenwriter Kevin Williamson: "It's about secrets and how they can kill us."

The premise itself is a reference to a past slasher story, albeit a really old one. It's based on the old ghost story about an escaped mental patient with a hook for a hand who, depending on the version, goes around terrorizing two young teens who are out "parking." The story comes into play early in *I Know What You Did Last Summer*, when our four teens heroes—the two women, plus rich jock Barry (Ryan Phillippe) and nice guy Ray (Freddie Prinze Jr.)—sit around on the beach at night telling the story. *I Know What You Did Last Summer* shows it's smart about its horror tale lessons when Helen explains the old story as being obviously about the dangers of premarital sex. And the hook? "A phallic symbol," she says surely.

For a teen slasher flick, the plot is deeper than most. (Although considering that the plot of most films of this genre is "kids hang out and then get killed," that's not saying all that much.) In *I Know* the four kids are celebrating the fourth of July after their high school graduation. Julie is going off to school; Helen, who has just won a beauty contest, is going to New York to become an actress; Barry is going to school to become a football player and Ray is staying behind to work on the fishing boats in their quaint North Carolina town. After talking about the future, making out a bit and telling some ghost stories, they head home. Ray drives Barry's dad's fancy car home because Barry has had too much to drink. As they go down the dark, winding ocean road they hit something with the car. It's a man!

Filmed on location in Southport, North Carolina, close to Kevin Williamson's boyhood home of Oriental.

After much fighting and debate, aggressive Barry tries to convince everyone that they should dump the body into the ocean, thus saving their collective behinds. Julie, especially, is hesitant but finally agrees. But, as the four try to dump the body in the ocean, the dead guy moves. He's not dead! They finish the job (maybe) and toss him into the ocean, making a solemn pact that they will never discuss the episode again.

Cut to the next summer. The terrible secret has taken its toll on everyone. Julie returns from school haggard and sullen but things get even worse when she takes a look at a letter she's received. It says "I know what you did last summer." She goes to tell the others and finds Helen slumming in a retail job, Ray working the docks and Barry as jerky as ever.

Things go downhill from there when it becomes apparent that someone is out to get them. A scary figure in a fisherman's hat and slicker tries to run over Barry. A couple of townspeople get killed by various gory methods involving a big hook—kind of like the hook mentioned in the opening ghost story. Who could be doing these things? Is it the dead man's spooky backwoods sister (Anne Heche)? The dead man himself? Their nerdy school friend (Johnny Galecki from TV's "Roseanne")? Or could it be one of them?

From there, the film turns into half mystery and half regular teen slasher flick. The slasher part seems up to par with enough people getting killed in interesting manners. The mystery part is more shaky. Various plot elements don't make much sense and even the killer's motive is unclear. So don't bother trying to figure out whodunit because it doesn't really matter.

What makes this movie better than most are the performances. The film bothers to take the time to flesh out these characters and it serves the movie well. Gellar as Helen does a nice job going from one year's confident blonde town beauty queen to the next year's down-and-out hometown girl whose dreams have not worked out. Phillippe's jock Barry is a pumped up, testosterone knucklehead who's quick to use his fists to solve any and all problems. Prinze is the sensitive guy in his role as Helen's rejected sweetheart but also acts suspicious enough that it seems possible that he may be . . . the killer.

But the stand-out performance is Hewitt's. The TV series' "Party of Five" actress gets a meaty role, especially for the kind of film she's in. Helen is a rarity in a horror film—a woman who's beautiful and also not a ninny. She is smart, resourceful and can fend for herself against the killer.

In general, *I Know* is less sexist than most of its ilk. (Although one review lauded the actresses in the film by saying their performances were "upstaging even their own spilling cleavages.") Besides Hewitt's strong female character, the movie lacks the weird, creepy sexual tinge to killing that some other movies have. When women in this film get killed, they aren't wearing lingerie or bathing suits and that somehow seems good. Even the fact that Anne Heche's character is a suspect in the murder—if not a step forward for women, exactly—at least implies that a woman could do the job.

As for the villain, he or she is no Freddy Krueger. This particular killer has no special powers and even his/her look is kind of lame. The killer's costume consists of a black fisherman's hat and rain slicker that looks sort of like a low-budget Darth Vader. And at one point in the film, the killer is not wearing the killer costume and doesn't seem nearly as menacing as just a plain old person.

Besides using good actors, director Jim Gillespie also is skilled at choosing good music. The film opens up with Type O Negative's harsh and dreary version of the Seals and Crofts' classic "Summer Breeze." The ominous tone of the song is just right for this movie about a summer gone wrong. And any movie that has Southern Culture on the Skids playing the house band at a beach party has something right going for it.

Besides putting its attractive teens in danger, *I Know What You Did Last Summer* shares another thing with its 1980's slasher flick ancestors—sequel potential. The ending of *I Know* leaves little doubt that the filmmakers are itching for another one, if not a whole series.

—*Jill Hamilton*

CREDITS

Julie James: Jennifer Love Hewitt
Helen Shivers: Sarah Michelle Gellar
Barry Cox: Ryan Phillippe
Ray Bronson: Freddie Prinze Jr.
Benjamin Willis: Muse Wats
Melissa Egan: Anne Heche
Elsa Shivers: Bridgette Wilson
Max: Johnny Galecki

Origin: USA
Released: 1997
Production: Neil H. Moritz, Erik Feig, and Stokely Chaffin for Mandalay Entertainment; released by Columbia Pictures
Direction: Jim Gillespie
Screenplay: Kevin Williamson; based on the novel by Lois Duncan
Cinematography: Denis Crossan
Editing: Steve Mirkovich
Music: John Debney
Production design: Gary Wissner
Art direction: John J. Rutchland III
Costumes: Catherine Afair
Sound: Carl Rudisill
Stunt coordinator: Freddie Hice
MPAA rating: R
Running Time: 101 minutes

REVIEWS

Entertainment Weekly. October 24, 1997, p. 44.
Los Angeles Times. October 17, 1997, p. F16.
New York Times. October 17, 1997, p. E14.
People. November 3, 1997, p. 22.
Sight and Sound. January, 1998, p. 45.
Variety. October 13, 1997, p. 78.
Village Voice. October 28, 1997, p. 88.
Washington Post Weekend. October 17, 1997, p. 33.

I Love You, I Love You Not

"Excellent, moving performances by Moreau and Danes."—Christine James, *Boxoffice.*

"An intelligent and powerful portrait of self-discovery and of a girl's first love."—Cynthia Lucia, *Cineaste*

I Love You, I Love You Not, the words of the lover who plucks the petals of a daisy, wondering whether the beloved returns the lover's passion are spoken by Daisy (Claire Danes), a high school girl enraptured with Ethan (Jude Law), the blonde lacrosse star that every female student longs for. Danes played a similar role in the superb television series, "My So-Called Life." She is a splendid actress with perennial freshness, her daisy-like quality.

But *I Love You, I Love You Not* is about more than adolescent angst. Daisy is Jewish and intense. She keeps her feelings bottled up inside of her, and she makes her schoolmates uncomfortable. When the boys tease her, she remains broodingly silent—which only goads them into ridiculing her. She wants to be "normal," but unlike the other students, she is not only a loner but a great reader. She is provoked into an angry speech when one of the boys calls Tess in *Tess of the D'Urbervilles*, a whore. Not only does Daisy defend

Tess, she excoriates the boy for his insensitivity. Of course, he has been especially crude because he knows it is the only way to get a rise out of Daisy.

This scene suggests what is wrong with *I Love You, I Love You Not*. Unlike "My So-Called Life," the film takes itself entirely too seriously. Yes, Daisy has a point. Yes, her values are admirable. But the fact that she cannot talk with her peers is a problem that is never explored. There is more to life than treasuring *Anna Karenina* (the novel Daisy is reading), and part of Daisy's problem is that she takes herself too seriously. Danes is too good of an actress to make Daisy tiresome, but the film's script settles entirely too easily for a cliched presentation of how high school is a vulgar place for the high-minded teenager. In "My So-Called Life," Danes's character was self-critical as well as hard on her family and friends. In *I Love You, I Love You Not*, she is never allowed to examine her high-strung nature.

Original production was a two-character, 20-minute play, directed by Hopkins, at the Ensemble Studio Theater.

The film tries to insulate itself from such criticism by making Daisy's grandmother Nana (Jeanne Moreau), a Holocaust survivor. Daisy knows about tragedy, about prejudice, and about all the human suffering that her affluent peers have been insulated from. When another Holocaust survivor comes to school and gives a talk (with slides) about her experience, Daisy's anguish increases—particularly when her classmates ask stupid questions such as did the Holocaust survivor ever meet Hitler. Certainly, Daisy can be excused for not wanting to consort with such insensitive types, though her unwillingness to articulate her feelings certainly makes it easier for them to remain in ignorance.

Daisy does seem to make a breakthrough when Ethan realizes that not only does she want him but that she is something special. He is attracted to her sad eyes, to her romantic poetry, to—in short—everything about her that makes her different from the other girls he has dated. Ethan injects energy and sunshine into Daisy's life, and she is dazzled by this golden boy—a dream too good to be true. And of course it is. For Ethan is superficial—also funny and articulate—but fundamentally only interested in being liked and popular. He jettisons Daisy when he realizes that his interest in her is costing him friends and subjecting him to criticism. He cannot take disapproval.

Daisy confides the story of this up-and-down saga to Nana (Jeanne Moreau). Daisy's parents are never there. They think she reads too much, and that she takes a "tone" with them that makes it hard for them to understand her. Both Daisy and Nana ridicule these parents—who are as superficial, apparently, as the classmates Daisy has to put up with. But Daisy and Nana do have a "tone" that is off-putting. They are shown embracing ad nauseam. Jeanne Moreau seems to be specializing these days in salt-of-earth women who are there to remind the audience of the fundamental human values. Of course, her attitudes cannot be questioned because she is a Holocaust survivor. This cheapening of the Holocaust's significance reveals the moral vulgarity of the film. It does little good to idealize Daisy's moral superiority. It is a position that leads nowhere. The Daisy-Nana relationship is supposed to be heartwarming, and certainly other reviewers have been moved by it, yet it is a claustrophobic union that Nana recognizes when she gently but firmly pushes Daisy away from her and sends her back into the world.

—Carl Rollyson

CREDITS

Nana: Jeanne Moreau
Daisy: Claire Danes
Ethan: Jude Law
Angel of Death: Robert Sean Leonard

Origin: USA
Released: 1997
Production: Joe Caracciolao Jr., John Fiedler, Amrk Tarlov for Polar Entertainment; released by Avalanche Releasing
Direction: Billy Hopkins
Screenplay: Wendy Kesselman; based on her play
Cinematography: Maryse Alberti
Editing: Paul Karasik, Jim Clark
Music: Gil Goldstein
Production design: Bill Barclay, Gudrun Roscher
Costumes: Sabine Boebbis, Candice Donnelly
MPAA rating: Unrated
Running Time: 92 minutes

REVIEWS

Boxoffice. December, 1997.
Los Angeles Times. October 31, 1997, p. F16.
New York Times. October 31, 1997, p. E12.
Variety. November 10, 1997, p. 41.
Village Voice. November 4, 1997, p. 84.

The Ice Storm

It was 1973 and the climate was changing.—Movie tagline

"Oscar bound . . . The best work yet by the director of *Sense and Sensibility.*"—Roger Ebert, *Chicago Sun-Times*

"One of the most persuasive and intelligent films of 1997, funny and haunting. Sensitive writing . . . and terrific performances."—Rex Reed, *The New York Observer*

"A beautifully acted drama [that] takes a cool, disturbing look at ties that fail to bind. [Ang Lee] creates a social and cultural web here as he did in *Sense and Sensibility*, despite a vastly different milieu."—Janet Maslin, *The New York Times*

"A certain Oscar contender."—Jack Mathews, *Newsday*

"One of the year's best."—Peter Travers, *Rolling Stone*

"Another insightful look at family and generational strains by Taiwanese director Ang Lee . . . James Schamus' script is constructed with studious care, attentiveness to dramatic unities and an eye to cultural detail."—Todd McCarthy, *Variety*

"A funny, moving portrait of family life. The quintessential American story."—John Powers, *Vogue*

Box Office: $7,085,724

At one point in *The Ice Storm*, Ben Hood (Kevin Kline), who is having an affair with his neighbor Janey Carver (Sigourney Weaver) meets her at her house and mentions that his wife Elena (Joan Allen) might be suspecting something: "I've been working a lot lately, and —No, that's not it. I guess we've just been on the verge of saying something, whatever it is, just saying something to each other. On the verge." *The Ice Storm* itself is a movie on the verge. Its leisurely pace, indirect plotting, interest in detail all postpone and minimize a dramatic climax and clear sense of resolution. But director Ang Lee and screenwriter James Schamus could have found no better method for depicting the "yearning and loss" of bored suburbanites over a Thanksgiving weekend in 1973 Connecticut.

Janey to her lover Ben: "Ben, you're boring me. I already have a husband."

Ben Hood (Kevin Kline) and Janey Carver's (Sigourney Weaver) adultery becomes one of many incidents that cause two families' crises in Ang Lee's *The Ice Storm.*

The fragments the film serves up about its characters define them as drifting, lifeless people. Their refusal to take part in any self-examination is part of what keeps them always on the verge. Many of the early scenes are presented as invitations for the characters to confront the issues they would rather avoid. The film begins as Ben and Elena's son Paul (Tobey Maguire) takes the train home to New Canaan from boarding school for his Thanksgiving weekend. As his parents prepare to attend a dinner at the home of Janey and Jim Carver (Jamey Sheridan), Paul's fourteen-year-old sister Wendy (Christina Ricci) heckles President Nixon on television. Wendy goes to school with the Carvers' sons Sandy (Adam Hann-Byrd) and Mikey (Elijah Wood). She and Sandy play in the school band.

Both generations struggle with the boredom of their routines. Most of the scattered scenes document the listlessness of the characters rather than develop into tightly structured plotlines. Wendy shoplifts a package of Twinkies from a five and dime; later she meets Mikey Carver in the deep, leaf-scattered end of an empty swimming pool. They both remove their chewing gum, stick the wads behind their ears, and begin to make out. Her mother Elena, who had spotted Wendy peddling by on her bicycle after school, meets Philip Edwards, the minister of a nontraditional congregation who seems to Elena to be flirting with her. Later Elena herself shoplifts a lipstick. Also that afternoon, Ben and Janey make love in the guest room at the Carvers' house. While still in bed, Ben automatically begins complaining that one of his competitors at work secretly takes golf lessons to humiliate him on the course. "Ben," Janey interrupts him suddenly with an edge in her voice. "You're boring me. I have a husband. I don't particularly feel the need for another."

Such dead-end attempts to dispel the boredom of affluent suburbia fill the middle scenes of the film. After school on Wednesday, Sandy wedges m-80s into his gliders one by one and watches them fly off and explode. Janey hears the fireworks and scolds her son; she permits him, however, to play with the whip his uncle brought him from Mexico, and Sandy maliciously snaps the blooms off the roses on the patio. He later finds himself reaching the bathroom door at the same time as Wendy, who has come by after school to watch television with Mikey. She asks Sandy how he upset his mother as they both stand casually in the bathroom. "I'll show you mine if you show me yours," Wendy says provocatively. Sandy, who is younger, is eager to accept this offer, but he panics and cries out, bringing Janey, who this time lectures Wendy.

Filmed on location in New Canaan, Connecticut.

The hollowness of the home life clarifies somewhat when Paul arrives from the train station. He greets his sister by asking, "How are the parental units functioning these days?" Wendy tells her brother that their parents have dropped out of couples therapy. "You think they're headed for the dustbin of history," Paul asks her, referring to divorce court. The brief Thanksgiving dinner at the Hoods the next day is tinted with the same cynicism. Ben asks Wendy to say the blessing. "Dear Lord," this fourteen-year-old prays, "thank you for this Thanksgiving holiday, and for all the material possessions that we have and enjoy, and for letting us white people kill all the Indians—and steal their tribal lands and stuff ourselves like pigs—while children in Africa and Asia are napalmed."

The day after the holiday brings more tension to the surface. Ben steals away to meet Janey at her house during the afternoon, but she says she is out of birth control and drives off, leaving him there. Ben waits but Janey does not return. He idles away time in the Carver house wondering about his lover's indifference. He then hears noises in the basement and discovers Wendy stretched out on the floor fully clothed but wearing a Nixon mask and Mikey quickly getting to his feet and pulling up his jeans. Ben, like Janey earlier, delivers a stern lecture on propriety and takes Wendy home. On the way he lets slip a telling comment, "Look, kiddo, don't worry about it. I really don't care that much—It's just that you develop a sense when you get older, if things are going to work out or if they won't, and sometimes it's not worth the mess."

That evening in reporting to Elena about the scene with Wendy, Ben fails to account for his own presence in the Carver house. Elena has suspected the affair, and her anger mounts as Paul goes off to catch the train to the city. He plans to meet Libbets Casey (Katie Holmes), a girl he likes from school. Though the television forecaster predicts a winter storm, Ben and Elena prepare to put in a brief appearance at a party. As they arrive, Dot Halford (Allison Janney) welcomes them shaking a serving bowl half-filled with car keys. Participation in the late-night key party—an optional excursion into wife-swapping—makes Ben and Elena pause. Finally, Elena angrily grabs Ben's keys and throws them toward Dot who adds them to the bowl.

The emotional and physical storms worsen as the evening progresses. Ang Lee and James Schamus have structured the strands of the narrative so that most of the characters approach or confront some sort of decision about themselves. When Janey chooses the keys of a teenager (Glenn Fitzgerald) brought to the party by his mother, Ben's jealousy and anger get the better of him. Elena, the last to choose, is left with the keys of Jim Carver, and they tentatively walk out to his car on the glass-like ice for their obligatory, passionless try at adultery. Wendy goes to the Carver house where she and Sandy continue their adolescent explorations into the curious adult world of drinking and sex. Mikey explores the frozen outside world, sliding down a deserted, ice-coated street. He sits on a metal guardrail as the ice-caked branches of a tree collapse on some power lines. The severed cables land against the guardrail; later Mikey's electrocuted body is found by Ben on his drive home. He tenderly brings the boy to Jim and Janey's house. The storm, like the gray fall and winter landscapes that appear throughout the movie, forms a sterile landscape for the paralyzed emotions of the characters.

Nineteen seventy-three, the year in which the film is set, has been jokingly called by director Ang Lee "America's most 'embarrassing' year, with Nixon, polyester, the admitting of defeat in Vietnam, stagflation, the energy crisis." In the final scene of *The Ice Storm*, Ben, Elena, and Wendy get to the train station to greet Paul after his return from Libbets Casey's apartment. The family walks to the car communicating through glances, tears, sighs, and smiles and then

AWARDS AND NOMINATIONS

BAFTA 1997 Nominations: Adapted Screenplay, Supporting Actress (Weaver)
Golden Globe Awards 1998 Nominations: Supporting Actress (Weaver)

silently drives home. Such an emotionally indirect conclusion fits the tone of the film perfectly. In his remarks in the published shooting script, writer James Schamus describes the ending as "a kind of embarrassment of forgiveness."

CREDITS

Ben Hood: Kevin Kline
Elena Hood: Joan Allen
Janey Carver: Sigourney Weaver
Jim Carver: Jamey Sheridan
George Clair: Henry Czerny
Sandy Carver: Adam Hann-Byrd
Paul Hood: Tobey Maguire
Wendy Hood: Christina Ricci
Mikey Carver: Elijah Wood
Francis Davenport: David Krumholtz
Libbey Casey: Katie Holmes
Philip Edwards: Michael Cumpsty

Origin: USA
Released: 1997
Production: Ted Hope, James Schamus, and Ang Lee for Good Machine; released by Fox Searchlight Pictures
Direction: Ang Lee
Screenplay: James Schamus; based on the novel by Rick Moody
Cinematography: Frederick Elmes
Editing: Tim Squyres
Music: Mychael Danna
Production design: Mark Friedberg
Art direction: Bob Shaw
Set decoration: Stephanie Carroll
Costumes: Carol Oditz
Sound: Drew Kunin
MPAA rating: R
Running Time: 112 minutes

Although *The Ice Storm* enjoyed many favorable, enthusiastic reviews, its slow, analytical, even undramatic pace is one that many audiences will have to adjust to. Its practice of looking at its characters from the outside rather than the inside applies perfectly to characters who shun introspection and verbalize few insights about themselves or their world. Paul's closing narration, which was written and added as a voice-over during the editing of the film, articulates the feeling that this mood-conscious motion picture captures: "When you think about it, it's not easy to keep from just wandering out of life. It's like someone is always leaving the door open to the next world, and if you aren't paying attention, you could just walk through it. And then you've died. That's why sometimes in your dreams it's like you're standing in that doorway and the dying people and the newborn people pass you by and brush up against you as they come in and out of the world during the night. You get spun around, and in the morning it takes quite a while to find your way back into the world." *The Ice Storm* dramatizes the interactions of a handful of people on the verge of finding their way back into the world.

—*Glenn Hopp*

REVIEWS

Boxoffice. July, 1997, p. 81.
Entertainment Weekly. October 3, 1997, p. 57.
Hollywood Reporter. May 13, 1997, p. 7.
Los Angeles Times. October 17, 1997, p. F8.
New York Times. September 26, 1997, p. E1.
People. October 13, 1997, p. 19.
Rolling Stone. October 16, 1997, p. 113.
Variety. May 19, 1997, p. 49.
Washington Post Weekend. October 17, 1997, p. 32.

I'm Not Rappaport

"In *I'm Not Rappaport* Walter Matthau has one of the richest characters of his career."—Stephen Holden, *New York Times*

"Walter Matthau has never been funnier. Ossie Davis is perfect. A marvelously odd couple."—Andy Seiler, *USA Today*

Whereas insightful and supple verbiage by a character can transfix an audience in a theatre, his or her same conversational flow in a film will often fail to hold the viewer's attention. For a film needs a wider vision than a play; it requires kinetic energy, and a sense of panorama. Such is the case in *I'm Not Rappaport*, adapted for the screen and directed by Herb Gardner from his award-winning play of the same name. Although *Rappaport* ultimately fails to satisfy as a motion picture, it has merits.

Gardner chooses to open proceedings in the early years of the century, when union leader Feigenbaum (Ron Rifkin) is carefully leading the crowd to a vote to go on strike. He is interrupted by Clara Lemlich (Elina Lowensohn) who, in a mixture of Yiddish and English, rouses the assembled to call for action and pledge solidarity. The camera focusses on a child, hypnotized by the political theater.

Clara: "Everybody else got a two wheeler when they turned ten, I got a paperback copy of *Das Kapital.*"

Gardner cuts to the mid-1980s. A crowd of demonstrators calling for industrial action has gathered near a senior citizens' home, and a man in a beret, calling himself Berkeley (Walter Matthau) is trying to incite his "comrades." Unfortunately, his comrades are listless old folks. A never-say-die Communist, Berkeley stands for the masses, however apathetic they may be. He enjoys more success rabble-rousing in a store, arbitrarily lowering prices for customers as a representative of the "United Consumers' Protection Agency," and he hands out a card which has his daughter Clara's (Amy Irving) phone number on it.

Midge (Ossie Davis) attends to an old-fashioned boiler until finishing work each day, whereupon he goes to Central Park to peruse his newspaper. He is joined by Berkeley, who wants to continue their previous day's conversation. Midge is less inclined to do so, feeling he has been subjected to three days of nonstop jaw-jaw already. So Berkeley, whose names eventually turns out to be Nat Moyer, spins out a story of being a deep cover spy recruited by the Cubans. For Nat is an endless fantasist, and usually succeeds in drawing even the most reluctant audience into his web of stories. Midge too is caught, even as he protests that Nat "ain't even friendly with the truth."

Indeed, Nat makes "alterations" with the truth: He lets out here, lets in there. "I was one person for 80 years," he retorts. "Why not a hundred for the next 5?"

Unbidden, Nat enrolls himself as an aide for Midge's meeting with Danforth (Boyd Gaines), an affable man who turns out to be the representative of the building in which both he and Midge live; Midge resides there for free in exchange for attending the complex boiler system. Before the meeting, Nat offers a joint, and the two men smoke together. "Even your children will become amusing," cracks Nat. They fall into reveries of past loves as they watch a girl, Laurie (Martha Plimpton), sketch them. She, in turn, is being watched by the Cowboy (Craig T. Nelson); she owes him money. To impress her, and under the influence of the marijuana, the men sing and dance, and Midge agrees to go along with Nat's version of "I'm not Rappaport," an old-time comedy routine that reflects Nat's ever-changing personae.

Herb Gardner's 1986 play won the Tony Award, the Outer Circle Critics Award, and the John Gassner Award.

When Danforth carefully offers a severance package, Midge is about to accept when Nat, briefcase in hand, shows up as Midge's lawyer, Reeseman. In this guise, he is a wonderfully persuasive orator, flowing with hyperbole, and bowling the well-meaning Danforth over with threats of lawsuits. A defeated Danforth promises to talk to the tenants' committee about Midge's position.

A bewildered Midge isn't at all pleased with Nat's impromptu tactics, since he had resigned himself to accepting the severance package. And who the hell is Reeseman? Nat replies, "Reeseman is the name of my surgeon. Eight years they trained his hands to take my wallet." When Midge tries to protest Nat's behavior, the maverick's response is, "You use who you need for the occasion." As we will see, shifting identities won't always work for Nat.

Indeed, Nat comes out the loser in a confrontation with the park thug, and is thrown to the ground in the ensuing tussle. The next day, he returns to the park with a walker, reporting, however, only a slight ankle strain. His daughter Clara, named after the young union agitator who so impressed Nat as a boy, finds him at last. The only child of Nat's four offspring who cares about him, she tries to make it clear that he cannot go on with his charades: they physically endanger him. She also fears for his mental stability; but Nat will have none of it.

After her father rejects her three options, Clara declares that she has no other choice than to take legal action to gain custody over him for his own good. Maneuvering, Nat weaves a story of an illegitimate child born to him and Hana Perlman, a woman the younger Nat once idolized. According to the tale, their daughter had grown up in Israel, but is in the U.S. to fetch him. A confused Clara does not know what to believe.

Meanwhile, Laurie is injured by the impatient Cowboy. The two old men want to help, and Nat asks what she is doing on Friday, the day he has "set" for Clara to meet her half-sister from Israel. And Nat has a plan to aid Laurie.

With a nervous Midge at his side, Nat rides like a mafia boss to meet with the Cowboy and set Laurie free from debt, but he has underestimated the dealer's resilience. The Cowboy sees through Nat's veiled threats as the transparencies they are, eventually rousing Midge to draw a knife taken from the Central Park hood. The following scene depicts a wind-whipped Central Park—a 'pathetic fallacy' in which the characters' moods are reflected by the weather—and we see Midge with his own walker now. He has been in the hospital for over a month, but thankfully will recover from his injuries.

Nat reports that he has told Clara the truth about her fictional half-sister, and that he has bowed to her will. Laurie never showed up at the Friday meeting, but how could she? Her fate remains unknown. Nat says that he is now a regular at a senior center and spends weekends with Clara, and reveals at last his real name, Nat Moyer, to Midge. He was a waiter for 41 years, except for the time he was a Hollywood mogul. The film trails off feebly with Midge falling again for one of Nat's tales.

The film is a marvelous showcase for the talents of Matthau and Davis, and this is recognized in a glowing review by Jack Mathews in the *Los Angeles Times.* Calling the movie a "gem," Mathews writes that "the great strength of *I'm Not Rappaport*, on stage and on the screen, is what takes place on the park bench." He rightly identifies the weakness of what he calls the "drug rescue operation. . . . In a film otherwise grounded in realism, the idea is preposterous." Stephen Holden, writing in the *New York Times*, is less fulsome in praise. He attacks the scheme to help Laurie out, and makes a sharp point about Gardner's dialogue. It "aspires to be a down-to-earth New York's vaudevillian echo of Samuel Beckett's metaphysical musings," but in fact, it shifts between "forced whimsy and a treacly sentimentality."

Holden feels that Ossie Davis has an underwritten role, "little more than Nat's handy comic foil." Although Midge is overshadowed by Nat, Davis has enough material to build a solid and dignified performance as the perennial underdog. The irony is that Matthau's Nat was always an underdog too, or perhaps an underachiever. As he states flatly at the end of the film: "I was no one at all. That's the truth."

One of the virtues of Gardner's languid film are the performances. Gaines is an earnest man bewildered by Nat, while Amy Irving brings vulnerability and also a determination to her role as Nat's sorely-tried loyal daughter. The scene in which she tackles her father has pathos and steel. Most of all, Walter Matthau is brilliant in what is, admittedly, a showy role. The character of Nat Moyer, and his personality permutations, seems ideal for this Hollywood veteran, but that's not to say that it would be an easy role for anyone to play. Matthau inhabits Moyer with intelligence, charm and resourcefulness.

As a whole, *I'm Not Rappaport* is disappointing and too long. Static and stagey, it could stand to lose at least thirty minutes. And yet Gardner's text is clever and sometimes perceptive, and his one-liners demonstrate virtuosity. Matthau's accomplished work and snatches of wit raise this film just above the level of forgettable mediocrity.

—Paul B. Cohen

CREDITS

Nat Moyer: Walter Matthau
Midge Carter: Ossie Davis
Clara Gelber: Amy Irving
Laurie Campbell: Martha Plimpton
The Cowboy: Craig T. Nelson
Pete Danforth: Boyd Gaines
J.C.: Guillermo Diaz
Clara Lemlich: Elina Lowensohn
Feigenbaum: Ron Rifkin

Origin: USA
Released: 1996
Production: John Penotti and John Starke for Greenstreet; released by Gramercy Pictures
Direction: Herb Gardner
Screenplay: Herb Gardner; based on his play
Cinematography: Adam Holender
Editing: Wendy Stanzler, Emily Paine
Music: Gerry Mulligan
Production design: Mark Friedberg
Art direction: Ginger Tougas
Costumes: Jennifer Von Mayrhauser
Sound: James Sabat
MPAA rating: PG-13
Running Time: 135 minutes

REVIEWS

Boxoffice. December, 1996, p. 46.
Chicago Tribune. January 24, 1997, p. 5.
Los Angeles Times. December 24, 1996, p. F12.
New York Times. December 26, 1996, p. C25.
Rolling Stone. December 28, 1996, p. 143.
Variety. January 23, 1997, p. 41.
Village Voice. December 31, 1996, p. 59.

In & Out

An out-and-out comedy.—Movie tagline

"The funniest movie of the year!"—Bob Parker, *CNN Headline News*

"An out-and-out masterpiece! A terrific comedy."—Dave Kehr, *New York Daily News*

"A riotously funny, screwball comedy for the '90s!"—Jack Mathews, *Newsday*

"A comedy knockout! Hilarious!"—Peter Travers, *Rolling Stone*

"Two thumbs up! *In & Out* is hilarious!"—*Siskel & Ebert*

"*In & Out* is out-and-out fun!"—Richard Corliss, *Time*

"The season's first hit that's funny to the core!"—Gene Shalit, *Today*

Box Office: $63,093,944

When Tom Hanks gave his acceptance speech for winning the Best Actor Oscar for 1993's *Philadelphia* about a gay lawyer with AIDS who is fired from his job, among the obligatory list of thankees was his high school teacher whom he then announced is also gay. This was no problem for Hanks' teacher who lives an openly gay life, but what if he weren't? From that seed of an idea, screenwriter Paul Rudnick (*Addams Family Values*, *Jeffrey*) has created the audience-pleasing comedy *In & Out*.

"Will you be going into show business?"—Frank to his son upon hearing he is gay.

In *In & Out* the actor giving the acceptance speech is Cameron Drake (Matt Dillon), a Brad Pittesque newcomer who wins for his second film, *To Serve and Protect*, about a soldier coming to terms with his homosexuality. But when Drake thanks his high school teacher Howard Brackett (Kevin Kline) and announces "he's gay!" it comes as a surprise not only to the small town of Greenleaf, Indiana where he lives, but also to Howard and his fiancee Emily (Joan Cusack). As his parents immediately appear on his doorstep, Howard reassures them that not only isn't he out of the closet, he wasn't even in it.

Oh sure, Howard dresses well, he's neat and clean, wears a prissy little bow tie, teaches romantic poetry, is still unmarried after 40, and loves Barbra Streisand, but gay . . . ? Hey, he can't possibly be gay, he's getting married in a few days. OK, so he's been engaged for three years and the relationship is still unconsummated, but Howard can't possibly be gay, can he?

After being pronounced gay on national television, high school teacher Howard Brackett (Kevin Kline) finds it difficult to convince family, friends, and gay news reporter Peter Malloy (Tom Selleck) otherwise in the comedy *In & Out*.

Drake's announcement has another repercussion: it sets off a feeding frenzy amongst the entertainment press who now swoop down on provincial little Greenleaf like crows on roadkill. One especially aggressive reporter is Peter Malloy (Tom Selleck) who seems to have more than a story in mind. Peter is gay, and he wants to be the reporter to do Howard's coming-out story, despite the fact that Howard keeps assuring him there is no story.

Unfortunately, all this conspires to put Howard on the defensive. Emily refuses to believe she's waited three years and lost untold pounds to Richard Simmons tapes only to face the

AWARDS AND NOMINATIONS

Academy Awards 1997 Nominations: Supporting Actress (Cusack)

Broadcast Film Critics Association 1997: Supporting Actress (Cusack)

Golden Globe Awards 1998 Nominations: Musical/Comedy Actor (Kline), Supporting Actress (Cusack)

New York Film Critics Circle 1997: Supporting Actress (Cusack)

possibility of no wedding at this point in her life. Howard's parents give him the benefit of the doubt, but even his mother, Bernice (Debbie Reynolds), demands that the wedding take place: "I need some beauty, some music and some place cards before I die—It's like heroin," she dictates. Even his students suddenly re-examine their feelings about their teacher: "He's smart and well dressed and very clean. It doesn't look good," they pronounce. But the worst doubts come from Howard's apprehensive principal Mr. Halliwell (Bob Newhart) who has a great deal of difficulty just stammering out the word homosexual, heaven only knows what he'd do if Howard was one.

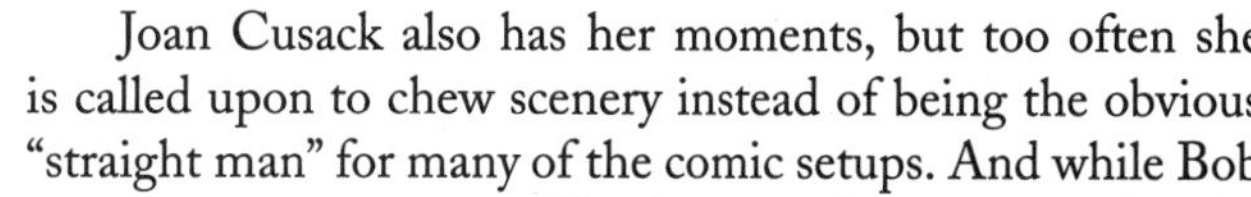

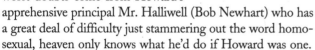

The movie's Oscar ceremony was partially filmed at Manhattan's Lincoln Center with some 3,000 extras and hosted by Glenn Close.

To tell more of the plot would unfairly diffuse the comic tension of this lighthearted film, and there are scenes a plenty to tickle one's funny bone—with special kudos to Cameron Drake's film within a film. What are we to think when the guys throw Howard a bachelor party and the obligatory stag films are replaced with an uncut version of *Funny Girl*. No, it's not a snide swipe at the town rumors, they honestly love Barbra since Howard threw a Streisand film festival the previous year.

But by far, the gem of the film is Howard's reactions to a self-help tape titled "Be a Man—Exploring your Masculinity." As he is instructed on manly vocabulary ("Yo," "Hot damn"), manly dress ("untuck one side of your shirt"), and manly acts ("real men don't dance, real men have bad backs") Kline delivers a tour-de-farce of laugh-inducing antics. As the tape exudes disco music and demands that he not dance, sway or even tap his foot, Howard tries his best, but finally succumbs to the tempting beat and just lets himself go, the tape be damned.

Reminiscent of the gusto he displayed in *The Pirates of Penzance*, Kline's winning and skillful performance is precisely what carries *In & Out* out of the shallows and into the deeper waters of laughs. He is an immensely likable actor who, while still being quite accomplished in dramas (*The Big Chill*, *Sophie's Choice*), seems to delight in his comic roles (*Dave*, *Silverado*, *Soapdish*, and winning a Best Supporting Actor Oscar for *A Fish Called Wanda*).

Kline is not the only actor having a good time on the screen here. Tom Selleck is delightfully roguish as he weasels his way into Howard's life. Just as Kline masterfully plays Howard as sexually ambiguous, Selleck plays Peter Malloy as both dogged newshound and sympathetic comrade, and we have no trouble believing them both.

While Matt Dillon's part isn't a big one, he steals the scenes he does have. From his anorexic supermodel girlfriend (Shalom Harlow) who hasn't the brains to figure out a rotary phone dial to his semi-articulate "I'm cool" attitude, Dillon is the perfect parody of the latest batch of Hollywood young studs.

Joan Cusack also has her moments, but too often she is called upon to chew scenery instead of being the obvious "straight man" for many of the comic setups. And while Bob Newhart may be stereotyped as the typical provincial homophobe, there's no denying the humor that can be found in his self-imposed discomfort.

Writer Rudnick (who also writes under the nom de word processor Libby Gelman-Waxner in *Premiere* magazine) may not have made *In & Out* a hard-hitting film about the perils and pleasures of being gay, but he has delivered a lighthearted comedy that only the most ignorant gay-basher could complain about. Combined with the light touch of director Frank Oz (*Dirty Rotten Scoundrels*) most viewers are more

CREDITS

Howard Brackett: Kevin Kline
Emily Montgomery: Joan Cusack
Peter Malloy: Tom Selleck
Bernice Brackett: Debbie Reynolds
Frank Brackett: Wilford Brimley
Cameron Drake: Matt Dillon
Tom Halliwell: Bob Newhart
Walter Brackett: Gregory Jbara
Sonya: Shalom Harlow
Ava Blazer: Deborah Rush
Ed Kenrow: Lewis J. Stadlen
Trina Paxton: J. Smith-Cameron
Aunt Becky: Kate McGregor-Stewart
Jack: Shawn Hatosy
Mike: Zak Orth
Vicky: Lauren Ambrose
Meredith: Alexandra Holden

Origin: USA
Released: 1997
Production: Scott Rudin for Spelling Films; released by Paramount Pictures
Direction: Frank Oz
Screenplay: Paul Rudnick
Cinematography: Rob Hahn
Editing: Dan Hanley, John Jympson
Production design: Ken Adam
Art direction: Charles V. Beal
Set decoration: Leslie A. Pope
Costumes: Ann Roth
Sound: Danny Michael
Music: Marc Shaiman
MPAA rating: PG-13
Running Time: 92 minutes

than willing to overlook obvious plot devices such as the clichéd small town homophobia or the idea that a man over forty has never examined his own sexuality.

The film exudes bonhomie and tolerance with an ending right out of an old Frank Capra film, but nowadays that can be a welcome change to car chases and explosions, sex and violence or even lame comedies featuring simpletons.

—Beverley Barc Buehrer

REVIEWS

Boxoffice. October, 1997, p. 37.
Chicago Tribune. September 19, 1997, p. 5.
Details. September, 1997, p. 74.
Detroit News. September 19, 1997, p. 3F.
Entertainment Weekly. September 26, 1997, p. 50.
Los Angeles Times. September 19, 1997, p. F19.
Movieline. June, 1997, p. 52.
New York Times. September 11, 1997, p. C7.
New York Times. September 19, 1997, p. E12.
People. September 22, 1997, p. 23.
Premiere. September, 1997, p. 41.
Rolling Stone. October 2, 1997, p. 62.
Time. September 22, 1997.
USA Today. September 19, 1997, p. 1D.
Variety. September 15, 1997, p. 68.
Village Voice. September 23, 1997, p. 94.

In Love and War

In war they found each other . . . In each other they found love—Movie tagline

"Spend two hours falling in love!"—Diane Kaminsky, *CBS-TV*

"A sweeping romance."—Jami Bernard, *New York Daily News*

"Bullock and O'Donnell in one of the more impassioned and believable love scenes in recent years!"—Michael Medved, *The New York Post*

"Richard Attenborough outdoes himself with *In Love and War.* The early romantic saga is letter perfect!"—Larry King, *USA Today*

Box Office: $14,481,231

In Love and War is based on the love story of novelist Ernest Hemingway and Agnes von Kurowsky, the nurse who cared for him after he was shot in the leg in Northern Italy, serving in the Red Cross during World War I. Hemingway drew on his own experience for the acclaimed novel, *A Farewell to Arms* (1929), which has been filmed twice—in 1932 with Helen Hayes and Gary Cooper, and in 1957 with Jennifer Jones and Rock Hudson. Hemingway's novels—as opposed to his short stories—have not worn well, and the movies have made his work seem even more sentimental, which is quite a turnabout for this macho writer who pioneered the clipped, understated speech that seemed proof positive against mushy prose. With Hemingway under attack for his male chauvinism, and a slew of biographies exposing his preening, showboat, side, the prospect of *In Love and War* evokes disgust in some, and just plain boredom in others. Only the most devoted of Hemingway fans, it might be supposed, would really welcome a filming of this oft-told tale.

The surprise is that director Richard Attenborough and his fine cast have produced not merely an engaging but also a probing film. It can be enjoyed by those who know next to nothing about Hemingway; it can repay the attention of those who think they know everything there is to know about Ernest Hemingway. Because the film ends rather abruptly—as did the relationship between Hemingway and von Kurowsky—it lacks a satisfying artistic shape. Yet the relationship ends because it fundamentally changed Hemingway, and those who do know his biography will be fascinated to see how the film manages to suggest what will become of the man in the later stages of his life.

Chris O'Donnell revels in playing the brash Hemingway, always referred to as the "kid." He is charming and imaginative, and underneath his bullying there is a sensitive man who can be easily hurt. Hemingway thinks he can win the older von Kurowsky with a combination of sweet-talking and overbearing behavior. Because he is a kid, she tolerates him and is even amused by his antics. He is used to getting his way. His energy is attractive. He wants to take the world by storm. But von Kurowsky, played beautifully by Sandra Bullock, is wary. Although she conspires with Hemingway's determination to survive, to keep his leg—which an Italian doctor wants to amputate—she realizes that he is hardly mature enough to be her husband.

Hemingway believes in the romantic notion that love can conquer all. It can break down the barriers between men and women; it can erase the ten year gap in age between himself and his beloved. But Hemingway's form of love is manipulative and possessive, and von Kurowsky, who has already escaped at least one suitor, resists. When Hemingway tries to get rid of a competitor, a fellow Red Cross worker, von Kurowsky makes sure that Henry Villard (Mackenzie Astin, who is a fine understated contrast to O'Donnell) comes along on the carriage ride that Hemingway has engineered. A furious Hemingway quarrels with Villard and tries to destroy Villard's interest in von Kurowsky by saying he has slept with her. An embarrassed and furious von Kurowsky slaps Hemingway, who is reduced to a pathetic whining state, lamenting that he has destroyed von Kurowsky's love for him.

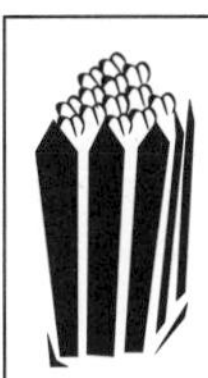

Ernest to Agnes: "You love me, you just don't know it yet."

Advised by an older nurse to think of her time with Hemingway as a "fling," von Kurowsky agrees at the end of the war to come to Venice, where the Italian doctor who has been courting her is establishing a hospital. She seems about to accept the doctor's proposal. Then in a key scene, the charming doctor pays her a florid compliment, and von Kurowsky is disappointed. Life with the doctor will obviously be a tame, boring affair. She misses Hemingway's dynamic personality.

The trouble is that von Kurowsky has written Hemingway about her impending marriage to the doctor, breaking her reluctant promise to marry Hemingway. An enraged, sulking Hemingway retreats to his family's cottage in Walloon Lake, Michigan. When von Kurowsky shows up, he is subdued and resentful. Although she tells him she loves him, he cannot forgive her for the eight months he spent suffering over her. It would not be the same now, he tells her. He has changed. She is the one who has changed him. And he implies, though he does not say, that he cannot forgive her. Von Kurowsky leaves saying that she will always love him.

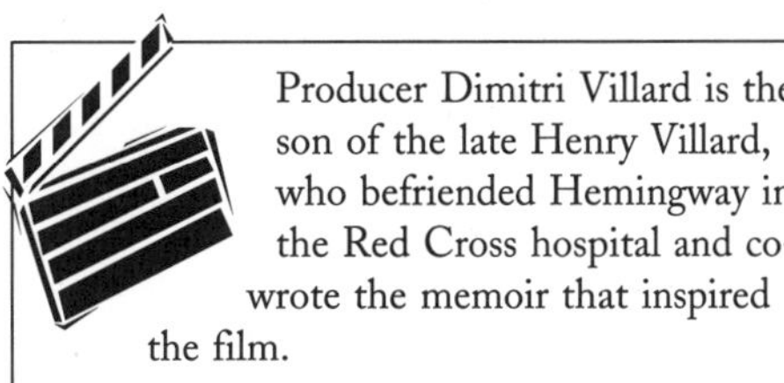

Producer Dimitri Villard is the son of the late Henry Villard, who befriended Hemingway in the Red Cross hospital and co-wrote the memoir that inspired the film.

This final scene is followed by brief capsule-like statements explaining that von Kurowsky continued her work with the Red Cross and died in her early nineties, and that Hemingway never saw her again and committed suicide in 1961. These facts have an emotional weight that such bald summaries rarely carry. For it is clear that Hemingway was embittered by his experience and was not changed for the better. Though von Kurowsky continued to love him, a marriage would have been disastrous. How could a woman who had so much to give to the world surrender herself to this brilliant but brutal tyrant?

All of Hemingway's later petulance and cruelty is evident in the last scene with von Kurowsky. He is going to make her pay for hurting him. He will make the world pay for his disillusionment. In this respect, the film is far less sentimental than Hemingway's novelized version of his relationship with von Kurowsky. In *A Farewell to Arms*, Fredric Henry and his love Catherine, share a love that is broken only by her death in childbirth. It is an ending that evades the much darker truth of the Hemingway-von Kurowsky affair. It is an ending that refuses to deal with what happens after the first infatuation, and with how couples learn to live with as well as love each other.

Attenborough is the first director to give full credit to Hemingway's charm and courage while revealing the fundamental immaturity of his outlook. It is not an anti-Hemingway film, however. When Hemingway begins to embroider his heroic exploit of carrying a wounded man to safety, Villard calls him on it. But it is clear that Hemingway's storytelling ability is part of what makes him likeable and even admirable. He is not a fraud or just on an ego trip; rather his stories about himself are an evocation of the human spirit, an indomitability that impresses Villard and von Kurowsky.

What Villard realizes is that Hemingway required something else. He needed a grounding in reality that von Kurowsky could have given him. But he would also have had to recognize limits on his ability to command other people. When he fancies marrying her and taking her back to Michigan, he tells her during an outing in the country near a lake that he will catch the fish and that she will clean them. Von Kurowsky demurs. She is not going to clean fish. Hemingway, still limping from his wounds, jumps into the lake and feigns drowning, stopping only when von Kurowsky promises to clean all the fish he catches. She laughs at his boyish bullying, but the scene turns ugly when he makes that comment to Villard about sleeping with her. In other words, whether in jest or in seriousness, Hemingway had to dominate. In marriage, he would have given von Kurowsky no space to be herself, to be the women who served in the Red Cross so long and so faithfully.

In Love and War succeeds because the script gives equal weight to von Kurowsky and the other supporting characters—all of whom serve to advise her and to confirm her own doubts about the "kid." As Hemingway, O'Donnell is almost never allowed to dominate the screen. As a physical type, he lacks some of Hemingway's robust size—perhaps a wise decision, since the point of the film is Hemingway's gradual realization that he will be thwarted and that he is not quite big enough to get everything he wants. Sometimes losing is inevitable. There is a moving scene in which one of his comrades—his face and body destroyed beyond repair—commits suicide. It is a bitter truth that Hemingway acknowledges but cannot incorporate into his own personality until the last moments of his life.

Undoubtedly, some audiences may be disappointed by this film's restrained passion. There are no nude scenes—not even in the brothel, the only place Hemingway can find for a tryst with von Kurowsky. Richard Attenborough, director of *Gandhi* and *Chaplin*, is noted for his almost Victorian understatement. But what would explicitness add to this movie? It is much more affecting to watch the young Ernest Hemingway lightly caress von Kurowsky's ankle and finger the material of her nurse's uniform. Attenborough realizes that suggestiveness can work better than explicitness. Anyway, there are far too many contemporary films that insist on scenes where the woman bears all and the man is photographed only above the waist. *In Love and War* has no truck with this double standard, presenting instead a fresh portrayal of an old story.

—Carl Rollyson

CREDITS

Agnes von Kurowsky: Sandra Bullock
Ernest Hemingway: Chris O'Donnell
Henry Villard: Mackenzie Astin
Domenico Caracciolo: Emilio Bonucci
Elsie MacDonald: Ingrid Lacey

Origin: USA
Released: 1996
Production: Dimitri Villard, Richard Attenborough; released by New Line Cinema
Direction: Richard Attenborough
Screenplay: Allan Scott, Clancy Sigal, Anna Hamilton Phelan; based on the memoir *Hemingway in Love and War* by Henry S. Villard and James Nagel
Cinematography: Roger Pratt
Editing: Lesley Walker
Music: George Fenton
Production design: Stuart Craig
Art direction: John King, Michael Lamont
Set decoration: Stephanie McMillan
Costumes: Penny Rose
Sound: Simon Kaye, Jonathan Bates, Gerry Humphreys
MPAA rating: PG-13
Running Time: 115 minutes

REVIEWS

Boxoffice. February, 1997, p. 64.
Chicago Tribune. August 19, 1996, p. 1.
Chicago Tribune. January 24, 1997, p. 5.
Entertainment Weekly. February 7, 1997, p. 50.
Los Angeles Times. December 18, 1996, p. F1.
New York Times. January 24, 1997, p. C5.
New York Times. January 26, 1997, p. H24.
The New Yorker. February 3, 1997, p. 84.
People. February 3, 1997, p. 17.
Sight and Sound. March, 1997, p. 50.
Time. February 3, 1997.
USA Today. January 24, 1997, p. 3D.
Variety. December 23, 1996, p. 41.
Village Voice. February 4, 1997, p. 70.
Washington Post. January 24, 1997, p. 30.

In the Company of Men

"A riveting film . . . reminded me of *sex, lies and videotape.* Neil LaBute makes corporate encounters feel like thriller confrontations."—Owen Gleiberman, *Entertainment Weekly*

"A tremendously gutsy first feature. An unflinching, sharply written film."—Janet Maslin, *The New York Times*

"Disturbing and controversial!"—David Ansen, *Newsweek*

"This is a movie event! A brilliant black comedy! By far the best film at Sundance! This is sure to be one of the best pictures of the year!"—Peter Travers, *Rolling Stone*

"Two thumbs up, way up!"—*Siskel & Ebert*

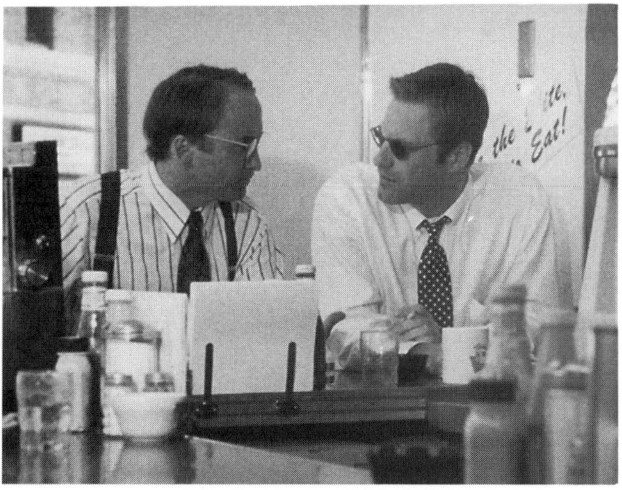

Junior executives Chad (Aaron Echart) and Howard (Matt Malloy) exact revenge on an unsuspecting female co-worker in order to soothe their own bitterness in *In the Company of Men.*

Box Office: $2,990,135

Although it initially seems to concern the subject of romance, Neil LaBute's *In the Company of Men* is anything but a love story.

Chad (Aaron Eckhart), an upwardly-mobile, white-collar drone, has a long list of complaints against the women in his life. It doesn't take much to set him off on his standard rant, in which he characterizes women as voracious, castrating bitches who are only out for what they can get, and who regularly take advantage of the hard-working, deeply oppressed men who are desperately trying to work their way up the corporate ladder.

Chad's soliloquies about his romantic disappointments, which he naturally assumes are endlessly fascinating to his contemporaries, are usually delivered in the corporate washroom. (In one of the film's great sustained in-jokes, this location becomes a kind of shrine. The gleaming, marbled bathroom is elevated to the level of a confessional, a place where ridiculously self-involved executives go to vent their rage and bemoan their earth-shattering personal difficulties.)

Chad: "She'll be reaching for the sleeping pills within a week. And we'll be laughing about this for the rest of our lives."

Chad's latest complaint concerns his most recent girlfriend, Suzanne (Emily Cline), who has unceremoniously dumped him after a courtship of several months. Although this breakup takes place offscreen, it comes as no particular surprise, given what we see of Chad's general behavior. For all his protestations about the mistreatment he has endured at the hands of women, it is clear that he is the author of his own misery.

Enter Howard (Matt Malloy), a similarly ambitious young executive who happens to be half a notch above Chad on the heavily-clawed office totem pole. Howard has been similarly disappointed in matters of romance. He does not appear to be quite as overtly malicious as Chad, but he nonetheless reacts with adolescent glee when Chad devises an elaborate plan to exact revenge on all women who have ever done either of them a bad turn. Chad decides that this would be "very therapeutic" for both men, and Howard willingly plays along.

Chad's principal character trait is a burning, almost psychopathic hatred, not only of women but of people in general, one which he expresses at every possible turn. Howard is ultimately the more softhearted of the two, but he is secretly fascinated by, and initially longs to emulate, Chad's freewheeling displays of misogyny.

Chad and Howard seek to get even with all women by selecting one suitably naive, defenseless woman, courting her simultaneously, then dumping her at the last minute. In short order, both men are assigned to spend several weeks out of town on an unspecified business project. The limited duration of their stay gives them a perfect time frame in which to select their prey, exact as much damage as possible and nimbly escape the ensuing fallout.

For awhile, everything proceeds according to plan. Working together, the men consider and then dismiss a number of prospective victims. They finally set their sights on Christine (Stacy Edwards), a beautiful, hearing-impaired woman who performs word-processing tasks in their office. Perceived as a defenseless social outsider because of her hearing loss, Christine is so thrilled to be the object of not one, but two desirable men's attention that she loses track of her better judgment and willingly pursues affairs with both Chad and Howard.

Director LaBute had a $25,000 shooting budget and filming lasted only 11 days.

Chad is a corporate Ted Bundy, a compulsive womanizer whose bedroom eyes and winning smile belie a welter of evil intentions. His deeply exaggerated misanthropy is chilling, but these moments are somehow less alarming than the artificial displays of kindness which he puts on in order to win Christine's trust. Chad is quite a creep, indeed, never more so than when he has switched into his contrived "nice-guy" mode. He repeatedly sends love notes and flowers to Christine, his intended victim, and pretends to be kind and chivalrous even as he plots her destruction.

But Chad has a higher goal, which is not only to "win" but to obliterate his enemies. He is a preternaturally energetic villain, never so busy that he cannot stop to take advantage of an opportunity to exert his dominance over others on the fiercely competitive office scene. Even as the plot to destroy Christine continues to unfold, Chad remains true to his primary objective: he keeps an eagle eye out for possible opponents who may arise from other sectors of the workplace.

Chad is a great believer in the pre-emptive strike. When a minor mishap involving the handling of an office document gives him an opportunity to demonstrate his power over a young, black subordinate, Chad proceeds to humiliate this man in the most graphic way imaginable. (The scene is supposed to illustrate Chad's unending need to advance himself by subjugating others, but given the particular method which Chad uses to belittle this co-worker, something even more sinister is implied. The scene has a peculiar homoerotic subtext which director LaBute may or may not have intended, and which he leaves strangely unexplored.)

Howard's cruelties toward Christine vary in degree, but not in kind, from those which are inflicted upon her by Chad. Howard may also be described as a heel, but Chad is the more aggressive of the two, and is ultimately made of more caustic stuff. Unlike his callously manipulative officemate, Howard is undone by his inability to disregard the pangs of a bad conscience, which set in shortly after he begins his contrived "affair" with Christine.

At this point, *In the Company of Men* borrows a plot device from Christopher Hampton's film adaptation of *Dangerous Liaisons* (1988). Howard's role in the elaborate intrigue involving Christine backfires in a time-honored and seemingly predictable way. Having been assigned the task of setting her up for a great fall, he makes the huge tactical mistake of falling in love with her. The eventual revelation of the men's nefarious plot has the desired effect of driving her into a state of despair and mortification, but this only paves the way for Chad's higher purpose—a still greater act of vengeance in which Howard, not Christine, is the principal target.

Initially, Christine blames herself for entering into a potentially explosive situation—"I let it go too far," she says—but even she manages to gain some measure of comeuppance in the final reel. The introduction of true love into the men's diabolical equation is most damaging to Howard, the secretly love-starved but shortsighted buffoon who ends up being just another one of Chad's victims.

In the Company of Men belongs to a long line of films that purport to expose the seamy underside of corporate life. Most of these are morality tales in which a brazenly ambitious central figure is tempted by, and then succumbs to, the allure of corruption and the tawdry glamour of the business world, only to undergo a redeeming moral transformation at the last minute. Billy Wilder's *The Apartment* (1960) is a classic example of this genre. Oliver Stone's *Wall Street* (1987) provides a more up-to-date rumination on these themes, but adopts a slightly different point of view, focusing upon Gordon Gekko (Michael Douglas), a particularly noxious corporate greaseball who gleefully toys with the mind of a younger subordinate (played by Charlie Sheen), all in the name of power-mongering. *Wall Street* was acclaimed in its time as a perfect evocation of '80s-era corporate blood lust; *In the Company of Men* makes Stone's film seem as innocuous as a children's movie.

Lower-echelon white-collar workers of both sexes will recognize all too well the singularly poisonous view of the world that is put forth in this film. Despite its inherent depravity, or perhaps precisely because of it, *In the Company of Men* is an actor's field day: Aaron Eckhart is demonically good as Chad, the unscrupulous white-collar shark who will stop at nothing to get what he wants. All smooth moves and disarming smiles, he stunningly evokes everything that is rotten about late-20th century corporate culture. Matt Malloy, as Howard, merits an occasional glimmer of sympathy, if only because he also falls prey to Chad's elaborate machinations.

In the Company of Men is not likely to qualify as anyone's idea of a fun night out. To view the film, and subsequently ponder its deeper meaning, is a vaguely distasteful

AWARDS AND NOMINATIONS

Independent Spirit Awrds 1997: Debut Screenplay, Debut Performance (Eckhart)
Nominations: First Feature, Actress (Edwards)
Sundance Film Festival 1997: Filmmakers' Trophy

CREDITS

Chad: Aaron Eckhart
Christine: Stacy Edwards
Howard: Matt Malloy
John: Mark Rector
Intern: Jason Dixie
Suzanne: Emily Cline

Origin: USA
Released: 1997
Production: Mark Archer and Stephen Pevner for Fair and Square Productions and Atlantis Entertainment; released by Sony Pictures Classics
Direction: Neil LaBute
Screenplay: Neil LaBute
Cinematography: Tony Hettinger
Editing: Joel Plotch
Music: Ken Williams, Karel Roessingh
Production design: Julia Henkel
Sound: Tony Moskal, George Moskal
MPAA rating: R
Running Time: 93 minutes

experience, which is perhaps the director's intention. The film is sleekly presented, and will no doubt augur well for the future career of director/writer LaBute, but he has produced a resoundingly cold movie, very detached in tone and disquieting to watch. The effect is ultimately rather revolting, like being rolled in all the world's filth.

—*Karl Michalak*

REVIEWS

Boxoffice. April, 1997, p. 181.
Detroit News. September 5, 1997, p. 3D.
Entertainment Weekly. August 1, 1997, p. 47.
Entertainment Weekly. August 15, 1997, p. 14.
Los Angeles Times. August 1, 1997, p. F6.
New York Times. March 28, 1997, p. B3.
New York Times. July 27, 1997, p. H11.
People. August 11, 1997, p. 19.
Rolling Stone. August 21, 1997, p. 116.
Time. August 18, 1997.
USA Today. July 31, 1997, p. 3D.
Variety. January 27, 1997, p. 73.
Village Voice. August 5, 1997, p. 67.

The Innocent Sleep

"Suspense grips the film and never lets go!"—*London Review*
"A solid, old fashioned thriller!"—*Variety*
"A compelling, powerful thriller!"—Jeffrey Lyons, *WNC-TV*

Yet another first-time director falls victim to the pitfalls of predictable plotting, stereotypical characters, and cliche-driven filmmaking. Scott Michell's thriller, *The Innocent Sleep*, is up to its knees in cliches and tired genre conventions, and the result is an old-fashioned, and as *Sight and Sound* film critic Geoffrey Macnah so aptly described it, "a very British thriller" in the spirit of formulaic Edgar Wallace crime dramas.

The Innocent Sleep's title is an oblique nod to Shakespeare's *MacBeth.* The story is based on a true-life incident in 1982 in which Italian banker Roberto Calvi was found hanging from the Tower Bridge over London's Thames River. Although his death was initially presumed to be a suicide, further investigation revealed a complex international conspiracy.

Talented British actor Rupert Graves (1997's *Intimate Relations* and *Mrs. Dalloway*, 1998) is Alan Terry, a drunken transient living in London's seedy homeless haven, Cardboard City. Forced to surrender his usual sleeping quarters to a maniacal bully, Alan beds down for the night near the Thames River. He inadvertently witnesses the execution-style murder of a man by a trio of British thugs, orchestrated by the suave Adolfo Cavani (Franco Nero).

Convinced by his fellow derelict friend George (Graham Crowden) to report the crime to the police, Alan is shocked to discover that one of the murderers is in fact the officer in charge of the investigation, Detective Inspector Matheson (Michael Gambon from Peter Greenaway's *The Cook, the Thief, His Wife & Her Lover*, 1989). Alan is soon on the run from the corrupt and homicidal cop and with nowhere else to turn, tells his story to a feisty, chain-smoking American journalist working in England, Billie Hayman (Annabella Sciorra). She just happens to be friends with derelict George who, it seems, was once a respected reporter himself until some mysterious (and unexplained) event brought him down.

No sooner does Alan begin to trust Billie when he stumbles across a video tape of an interview that Billie did in which she espouses support for pressuring reporters to reveal the names of a story's sources. Fearing that Billie might value her career more than his life, Alan heads out on his own. The remainder of the story deals with the burning question of how will Alan get himself out of this sticky wicket. Will Billie get to Alan in time to save him? And, which character will die in the inevitable showdown between Alan and the nefarious Matheson?

In fact, a lot is left unexplained. There is a scene where Alan seeks refuge in Billie's apartment and is told that there are some men's clothes hanging in the closet that he can change into; no further details are revealed. We never learn why the American journalist is working in London—we can only surmise that it had to do with the guy with the clothes in the closet.

The most surprising omission from this particular bag of genre conventions is the lack of any kind of sexual tension between Alan and Billie, and that results in an inescapable emotional distance that could leave the audience feeling quite apathetic towards their plight. The dramatic tension of *The Innocent Sleep* rests squarely on the definable and easily recognizable plot machinations and not in character development. Few, if any, of the characters created by writer Ray Villis are anything more than requisite thriller stereotypes. Gambon's Matheson is simply evil incarnate, while intriguing Annabella Sciorra (*Copland*, 1997) struggles to find the core essence of the tough-as-nails, sketchly-drawn reporter.

The odd thing about *The Innocent Sleep* is that despite its hackneyed material, it is not necessarily as amateurish an effort as one might expect from a novice director. The film is shot evocatively with plenty of blue-hued filters by cinematographer Alan Dunlop, and director Scott Michell displays a firm grasp of Hitchcockian tricks-of-the-trade. The musical score, however, is overblown, with operatic arias—a piece specifically composed for the film is performed by Lesley Garrett of the English National Opera—that tend to infuse the film with an alienating and unearned self-importance. Reviews were mixed.

—Patricia Kowal

CREDITS

Alan Terry: Rupert Graves
Billie Hayman: Annabella Sciorra
Det. Inspector Matheson: Michael Gambon
Adolfo Cavani: Franco Nero
George: Grahm Crowden
James: John Hannah

Origin: Great Britain
Released: 1995, 1997
Production: Scott Michell and Matthew Vaughn for Timedial Films; released by Castle Hill Productions
Direction: Scott Michell
Screenplay: Ray Villis
Cinematography: Alan Dunlop
Editing: Derek Trigg
Production design: Eve Mavrakis
Art direction: Bowesy
Costumes: Stephanie Collie
Music: Mark Ayres
MPAA rating: R
Running Time: 110 minutes

REVIEWS

Boxoffice. June, 1996, p. 57.
Los Angeles Times. June 27, 1997, p. F14.
New York Times. June 27, 1997, p. C12.
Sight and Sound. February, 1996, p. 44.

Intimate Relations

In the spring of 1956, in a quaint little town, a crime took place that shocked a nation. This is the true story.—Movie tagline

A mother. A daughter. A lodger. Relationships can be murder.—Movie tagline

"Shocking! Rips the lid off small-town life to reveal the shocking secrets underneath!"—*Details*

"Sharp! A sharp black comedy!"—*Interview*

"Delicious! A deliciously twisted sex-and-murder tale!"—*Premiere*

"The story that follows is inspired by true events," writer-director Philip Goodhew informs his audience as the film begins. "In the spring of 1956, in this quaint little English town [the film was shot on location in Abergavenny, Cymru (Wales), though the 'true events' happened elsewhere] a crime took place that shocked the nation," according to Fox Searchlight Pictures promotional copy; but that "crime" is not committed until the final reel, and until it happens, the story seems to be merely a bizarre comedy of errors that turns into a bedroom farce. The conclusion certainly comes as a shock, even though the events that transpire are carefully foreshadowed.

Harold Guppy (Rupert Graves) returns to Britain after having worked as a merchant seaman and goes to visit his brother Maurice (Les Dennis), who is married to Iris (Elizabeth McKechnie), a decidedly unfriendly sister-in-law who wants nothing to do with Harold. It is clear that Harold, the black sheep of the family who had been a hyperactive problem child and for that reason was sent to reform school, is not welcome to stay. When he finds a room to rent in town, the plot begins to take its crazy trajectory.

Marjorie Beasley (Julie Walters, the star of Willy Russell's filmed stageplay *Educating Rita*, whose performance earned a Best Actress Oscar nomination in 1983) has a room vacant and accepts Harold as a lodger. She is unhappily married to a one-legged veteran, Stanley (Matthew Walker), whom she ignores sexually, pretending that Stanley's handicap is an impediment to their sex life, though she clearly ignores Stanley's frequent advances. Stanley has his own room. Marjorie sleeps with her 13-year-old daughter Joyce (Laura Sadler). Harold gets the spare bedroom.

Marjorie: "It's not a lie. It's a deception."

At first Marjorie simply wants to mother Harold, who is good-natured and friendly to both Stanley and Joyce. Approaching fifty and sexually repressed at toxic levels, Marjorie clearly has more intimate plans for Harold and is soon visiting his bedroom on a regular basis. Joyce, of course, is aware that her mother is not sleeping in her room, so she joins her mother in Harold's room, mainly for the company. This bizarre *ménage à trois* incredibly goes unnoticed by Stanley through the winter and into the spring, but he probably just doesn't want to know. Joyce blackmails both her mother and Harold by threatening to tell her father about their relationship. Finally, she demands that Harold spend the night with her at a hotel, and the next morning her mother is enraged. When Joyce is then sent to live with her aunt Deirdre (Holly Aird), she tells her aunt about what has been going on at home, and the aunt then tells Stanley.

After a blow-up with Stanley, Harold enlists in the army, but Marjorie keeps writing to him and offers to pay the £30 necessary to get him released from service. Harold has meanwhile proposed marriage to a girl named Jean (Annie Keller), but Marjorie manipulates him out of the service and back into her arms. Harold has not forgot Jean, however, and resolves to leave Marjorie and go to Yorkshire to marry Jean. Before he can escape, unfortunately, Marjorie talks him into one last picnic and one last fling. After Harold, Joyce, and her mother have driven out into the countryside, Marjorie sends Joyce to pick flowers to get her out of the way. When Joyce returns and discovers them making love, she goes berserk and attacks her mother with a hatchet, wounding her in the neck.

The madness spreads. Marjorie then attacks Harold with a knife, and in the scuffle, Joyce, too, is mortally wounded. Sitting desolate on the car's running board, Harold drives the knife into his stomach, but he survives and is last seen in a prison hospital. Rupert Graves is excellent as Harold, who attempts to hold onto his own dignity and decency but is finally the victim of circumstances that are quite beyond his control. The acting is consistently strong. Julie Walters is somehow able to make Marjorie believable, despite the character's many contradictions. She seems to hold the moral high ground at the laundry where she works when a younger worker, Pamela (Amanda Holden), gets pregnant and loses her job as a consequence, without a breath of protest from Marjorie, who has lectured her against indiscretions. No one in this film is more seductive than Marjorie, yet she does not seem to recognize her hypocrisy. As Harold tells her at one point, failing to find quite the right word, "You're a bloody hippo!" And that pretty well describes her. Since Marjorie appears to be quite mad, the comedy turns pathetic when Marjorie turns murderous. In an earlier bout with the knife she had wounded Harold's hand, anticipating her behavior at the end, but there is no foreshadowing for Joyce's attack on her mother. In the actual "events" that transpired, Harold had to pay the consequences, but the film makes him appear to be rather too innocent.

Stranger than fiction? Well, that's the problem, given the unexpectedly nasty turn of events. "Ninety-nine percent of the facts are accurate," writer-director Goodhew claims, however: "I changed all the names and combined some of the events, but the language is spot-on," but how would he know on the basis of newspaper accounts?

The story is based on the life of a 33-year-old young man and the family he lodged with in Poole, Dorset, a provincial town in the south of England. The names have been fictionalized, but the facts are these: In 1956, after two years of living with the "Beasley" family, "Joyce" and her mother "Marjorie" were found axed to death in a New Forest Woodland glade, and "Harold" was arrested at the scene of the crime and charged with the murders. At the trial he pleaded not guilty and claimed it was "Joyce" who hit her mother with the axe, and that is the story the screenplay develops. He was found guilty and sentenced to hang, but he was spared the noose two hours before execution, judged to be a paranoid schizophrenic, and transported to Broadmoor, a high-security hospital. Paroled in 1971, "Harold" got married and raised six children, but in 1982 he was convicted of a knifing and theft and returned to jail. Released on paroled again in 1993, he was later convicted of indecently assaulting two schoolgirls, aged 12 and 13. At the time of the film's release, "Harold" at the age of 74 was still serving time in prison. This is hardly the profile of a comic figure, or a misguided innocent, but the filmed story is given a satiric spin. In the film "Harold" is presented as an innocent, exploited and manipulated by "Marjorie's" obscene lust. One wonders about the alleged 99% accuracy of the screenplay.

Philip Goodhew grew up in the city of Chester and took a degree in drama at Manchester University, where he met the actress Elizabeth McKechnie, who plays Iris Guppy in the film. He went on to work as an actor, theater director, and producer, first at the Royal Exchange Theatre in Manchester, then in London. Goodhew worked for an industrial film production company, Milestone Pictures, wrote and directed several shorts, and then formed Boxer Films in March of 1995 with producer Angela Hart, a graduate of London University. He appears to be finding himself as a writer-director, and this is evident in the peculiar shifts in mood and tone of *Intimate Relations*. He chose to shoot the film in the South of Wales because his mother's family had lived there, and it seemed to him that Abergavenny had not changed much since the 1950s.

"The situation is so preposterous that it's funny," Goodhew claimed, but it is made more preposterous than it should be by the treatment. Julie Walters is an accomplished comic actress, but Marjorie is not exactly a comic figure. She is a bad mother and an unfaithful wife and potentially monstrous, and even the best comic acting cannot gloss over these flaws. The problem is in the design and structure of the screenplay, which reduces such a character as Marjorie to a caricature, to be laughed at, perhaps, for her hypocrisy, but ultimately to be pitied. To see her daughter die at the age of 14 is simply ghastly. The real "Harold's" wife claimed he admitted to having killed "Joyce" because "she was a witness and could not be trusted to keep quiet." Perhaps the "truth" of the situation will never be known, but it is certainly not the same as what is suggested by the film.

The title comes from a journalistic euphemism. During the 1950s, Goodhew explains, "sex was always termed 'intimate relations.'" The writer-director was "fascinated by the use of the wrong words and catch-phrases to hide emotions," the pride involved in using such clichés as "the less we know, the better off we are," and the "single-minded wish of people then to completely deny the truth." This is an odd example of a comedy gone wrong that moved rather quickly into video markets. The writer-director of this offbeat film apparently aspires to be a British David Lynch, exposing the corrupt and indecent heart of provincial society. The concept is bizarre and misguided, but the acting is often quite effective.

—*James M. Welsh*

CREDITS

Marjorie Beasley: Julie Walters
Harold Guppy: Rupert Graves
Joyce: Laura Sadler
Stanley: Matthew Walker
Dierdre: Holly Aird
Maurice: Les Dennis
Iris: Liz McKechnie

Origin: Great Britain, Canada
Released: 1995, 1997
Production: Angela Hart, Lisa Hope, and John Slan for HandMade Films Ltd., Boxer Films, and Paragon Entertainment Corporation; released by Fox Searchlight
Direction: Philip Goodhew
Screenplay: Philip Goodhew
Cinematography: Andres Garreton
Editing: Pia Di Ciaula
Music: Lawrence Shrag
Production design: Caroline Greville-Morris
Costumes: John Hibbs
Sound: Keith Tunney
MPAA rating: R
Running Time: 98 minutes

REVIEWS

Los Angeles Times. September 19, 1997, p. F16.
New York Times. September 19, 1997, p. E22.
New Yorker. September 15, 1997, p. 93.
Sight and Sound. July, 1997, p. 42.
Village Voice. September 23, 1997, p. 90.

Inventing the Abbotts

When you want it all, but can't have it. There's only one way to handle life . . . invent it.—Movie tagline

"A new American classic in the tradition of *American Graffiti*. Sensational!"—Mike Cidoni, *ABC-TV, Rochester*

"Tremendous warmth, beauty and humor. An all-American smash."—Don Stotter, *Entertainment Time-Out*

"Exemplary acting. Joaquin Phoenix is terrific."—Peter Travers, *Rolling Stone*

"The most emotional, dramatic roller-coaster ride in years."—Larry Ratliff, *San Antonio Express News*

Working-class Doug Holt (Joaquin Phoenix) and socialite Pamela Abbott (Liv Tyler) find love despite their socio-economic differences in the coming-of-age story *Inventing the Abbotts.*

Box Office: $5,936,344

Coming-of-age films have remained popular from the 1950s to the present, from *A Summer Place* (1959) to *Porky's* (1981), from *Where the Boys Are* (1960) to *Fast Times at Ridgemont High* (1982), from *Rebel Without a Cause* (1955) to *Buffy, the Vampire Slayer* (1992), from *The Graduate* (1967) to *Sixteen Candles* (1984), from *The Sterile Cuckoo* (1969) to *Ferris Bueller's Day Off* (1986), from *To Sir with Love* (1967) to last year's *Romeo and Juliet*, from *East of Eden* (1955) to *Summer of '42* and *The Last Picture Show* (1971), and from *Peyton Place* (1957) to this year's *Inventing the Abbotts.* Varying widely in terms of dramatic intensity and the frankness with which sexuality is handled, these films nonetheless vary little from the mantra that adults and teens cannot and do not speak the same language and that, as a result, young people have to (or get to, as the case may be) relive the parents' mistakes.

In perhaps the newest of the genre, *Inventing the Abbotts*, two handsome brothers, Doug (Joaquin Phoenix) and Jacey (Billy Crudup) Holt are variously entranced and repulsed, wooed and spurned, by the local small-town "royalty," the Abbott sisters: Eleanor (Jennifer Connelly), Alice (Joanna Going) and Pamela (Liv Tyler). Beyond dealing with the unidentifiable or unnameable urges of adolescence, the Holt brothers must also wrestle with the class system in their town that will ensure that, while the Abbott girls may dabble with Holts, they will not marry them. In an era in which overt sexuality is punished with banishment and reserve with boredom and loss, only the thoughtful appear to survive.

Pamela to Doug: "Alice is the good one, Eleanor is the bad one, and I'm the one who gets off the hook."

While little is new in *Inventing the Abbotts*, in a genre such as coming-of-age films, originality is hardly the measure of worth. Instead, what matters is that the actors and actresses are intensely lovely, are intensely loved, and/or in love, and are intensely rewarded or punished for their actions. By this gauge, *Inventing the Abbotts* clearly succeeds. Each of the Abbott girls has long chestnut locks that shimmer by the candlelight of the Abbotts's lawn parties. Virtually indistinguishable in coloring and attractiveness, the three carve niches by behavior: Alice is ladylike and responsible, Eleanor is rebellious and promiscuous, and Pamela (the youngest) is thoughtful, sensitive and pliant. As much of the film's action occurs at night or inside, viewers may lament of ever distinguishing between the sisters until she acts. For instance, while viewers may be unsure which of the Abbott sisters is with Jacey in the garage, once the activity (i.e., sex) is clear, the identity is equally obvious: Eleanor.

Beyond the tensions created by class distinctions and gender, the film also explores the relationships between the siblings. Whereas Jacey sets about conquering each of the Abbott sisters in turn, Doug is reluctant to respond to Pam's affectionate attentions. Whereas Jacey is angry and voracious, Doug is sensitive and ponderous. An early scene is particularly graphic in portraying the differences between the brothers. Each is preparing for the Abbott's lawn party. Jacey is smooth, 1950s classic chic, while Doug is painting on pretend sideburns (a la Elvis), much to his brother's chagrin, his mother's surprise, and Pam's delight.

Another feature of the coming-of-age films is the chasm between the young people and the adults, often cast in terms of teens and their parents. In this film, the parental characters are flat for the largest portion of the film. For instance, Helen Holt (Kathy Baker) is the long-suffering school teacher, widow, mom, whose apron is clearly in place, a faded rose, but a rose nonetheless. Lloyd Abbott (Will Patton), as the patriarch of the Abbott clan, is combative, crude, defensive, a commoner who rose to the rank of "king" by marriage. In viewing his mother and Mr. Abbott, Jacey sees betrayal of his deceased father. He imagines his mother not only handed over the father's prized invention (full suspension file drawer), but also her virtue. Driven by anger, he sets out to defile or destroy each Abbott. Conversely, Mrs. Holt and Mr. Abbott have a gentle understanding between them (which no doubt led to the rumors), which the film's slow turns show to be friendship, pity, and plain kindness. One of the lessons the young learn in this film is that measuring others by their own behavior and values is often hurtful, wasteful and, finally, incorrect. Another important lesson, amazingly enough, is to beware who they judge, as they are destined to make the same errors, fall prey to the same hungers, and become the same adult.

The formula is at work in *Inventing the Abbotts*, but to write this film off as nothing more than that would be to sell it short. Director Pat O'Connor (an Irishman, whose *Company of Friends* won kudos) has managed to paint what feels to be an accurate picture of the Midwest in the late 1950s. While the film has a chiaroscuro quality about it, nonetheless it conveys the feel of a world on the edge of modernism, of the contemporary, of chaos. This is the world of old-fashioned aprons and new-fangled push-up bras, voluptuous 1950s cars and high-powered Ivy League educations, chaste kisses and alcoholism, premarital sex and saddle shoes. Director O'Connor has captured the unrest through this variety of small details, and if one feature of the film stands out, it is this *mise en scene*.

Stormy, dark, full of passion, *Inventing the Abbotts* reflects its characters. Short of original, but reassuringly formulaic, this film will fascinate and reward viewers themselves wrestling with the coming of an age.

—Roberta F. Green

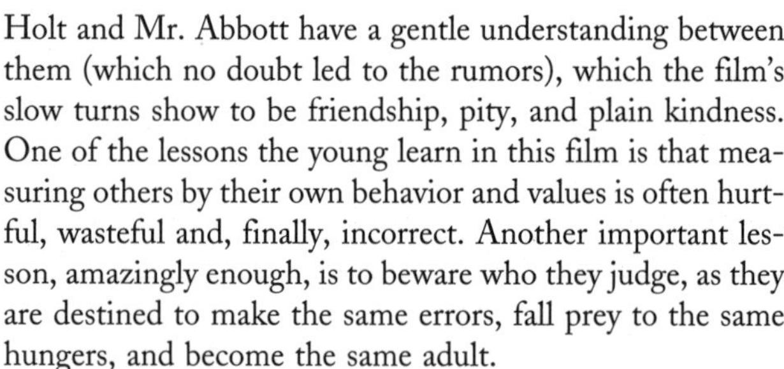

CREDITS

Doug Holt: Joaquin Phoenix
Jacey Holt: Billy Crudup
Pamela Abbott: Liv Tyler
Lloyd Abbott: Will Patton
Helen Holt: Kathy Baker
Eleanor Abbott: Jennifer Connelly
Alice Abbott: Joanna Going
Joan Abbott: Barbara Williams

Origin: USA
Released: 1997
Production: Ron Howard, Brian Glaser, and Janet Meyers for Imagine Entertainment; released by 20th Century Fox
Direction: Pat O'Connor
Screenplay: Ken Hixon; based on the story by Sue Miller
Cinematography: Kenneth MacMillan
Editing: Ray Lovejoy
Production design: Gary Futkoff
Art direction: William V. Ryder
Set decoration: Kathryn Peters
Costumes: Aggie Guerard Rodgers
Sound: John Patrick Pritchett
MPAA rating: R
Running Time: 110 minutes

REVIEWS

Chicago Tribune. April 4, 1997, p. 5.
Detroit News. April 4, 1997, p. 3D.
Entertainment Weekly. April 4, 1997, p. 62.
Los Angeles Times. April 4, 1997, p. F2.
New York Times. April 4, 1997, p. B3.
People. April 7, 1997, p. 19.
Rolling Stone. April 13, 1997, p. 86.
Sight and Sound. November, 1997, p. 43.
Time. April 7, 1997.
USA Today. April 4, 1997, p. 4D.
Variety. March 17, 1997, p. 52.
Village Voice. April 8, 1997, p. 79.

Irma Vep

"Fresh and hilarious!"—Ella Taylor, *Atlantic Monthly*

"A deliciously knowing comedy about the insanity of shooting a film."—Phillip Lopate, *Film Comment*

"A flash of cinematic brilliance! One of the most playful French movies in years."—Thelma Adams, *New York Post*

"Super cool!"—Michael Atkinson, *Village Voice*

Director Olivier Assayas serves up frothy French fare with *Irma Vep* (an anagram for vampire), starring Hong Kong actioner Maggie Cheung as the title super-vixen. This pointed satire is an edgy reprise of classics like Truffaut's *Day for Night* (1973), Wim Wender's *The State of Things* (1982), and Tom DiCillo's *Living in Oblivion* (1994), with the film acquiring instant cachet by using Truffaut/Godard regular Jean-Pierre Leaud as the burnt-out New Wave director Rene Vidal. Vidal's latest would-be production is a remake of the classic 1915 silent French vampire serial, *Les Vampires.*

Maggie Cheung: "Desire. It's what we make films with."

Catching the movie *Heroic Trio* in Marrakesh, director Vidal decides only Maggie Cheung (who plays herself) can become the black latex-clad arch-villain Irma Vep in his update of the Louis Feuillades classic. Irma, originally played by French icon Musidora, is the ringleader of a gang of thieves who terrorize Paris by night. Cheung shows up on the set straight after a 12-hour flight, speaks no French, and lands in the middle of a chaotic low-budget production nightmare. Soon the bewildered vamp is entangled in a web of infighting, gossip, and frustration. Nervous director Vidal can't control the set and wanders around whispering profound nonsense, "Is not because it's silent that you muss play more," he says to Cheung, "You muss play less."

Maggie is enthusiastic and professional, somewhat confused by the infighting of her colleagues. Getting fitted for her rubber catsuit, her hyper costumer Zoe (Nathalie Richard) gets a yen for the gorgeous Cheung. "You want to play with her, to touch her. She's like a plastic toy," she raves to the executive producer's wife. Of course, Zoe's confidante Mirielle (Bulle Ogier) sounds off to the unsuspecting star, "Do you like girls?"

Assuming her film persona one night, Maggie slinks down her hotel corridor and sneaks into a room, stealing worthless coustume jewelry from a naked woman arguing on the phone with her lover, which Cheung promptly throws away. After screening disastrous rushes, imperious Rene storms out proclaiming the footage worthless. Later the police are called to the director's house following a domestic dispute and the project looks finished. Rene suffers a breakdown and another world-weary auteur, Jose Mirano (Castel), is called in to replace him.

Bon vivant Castel and Leaud take good-natured jabs at French cinema, while one hilarious bit involves a journalist obsessed with Arnold Schwarzenegger and John Woo, who enthusiastically trashes French film as snobbish and passe. In an overblown, purist gesture, Cheung is fired by Mirano for not being "French" enough. In the impressionistic finale, we view Rene's discarded footage—a heart-wrenching canvas of emotion.

The film is largely an homage to Cheung (who later became involved with director Assayas), a splendid actress as well as action star. Her standard get-up features an S&M-style hood with cutouts only for her large luminous eyes, her body a study of shadow and light. Cheung who partnered with Jackie Chan in *Police Story* and *Supercop* (1992),

CREDITS

Maggie Cheung: Maggie Cheung (herself)
Rene Vidal: Jean-Pierre Leaud
Zoe: Nathalie Richard
Journalist: Antoine Basler
Laure: Nathalie Boutefeu
Desormeaux: Alex Descas
American Woman: Arsinee Khanjian
Mireille: Bulle Ogier
Jose Mirano: Lou Castel
Maitre: Dominique Faysse

Origin: France
Released: 1996
Production: Georges Benayoun for Dacia Films; released by Zeitgeist Films
Direction: Olivier Assayas
Screenplay: Olivier Assayas
Cinematography: Eric Gautier
Editing: Luc Barnier
Costumes: Francoise Clavel
Art direction: Francois-Renaud Labarthe
Sound: William Flageollet
MPAA rating: Unrated
Running Time: 96 minutes

was directed by Wong Kar-Wai (*Chungking Express*, 1995) and appeared in a slew of films in her home country. *Vep* marks her international debut.

This tour de farce was written in 10 days, shot in a few weeks and fueled by ad-libs. Not a performance film, it's more style than substance. Shot in Super 16, the characters seem *au natural*, resulting in a loose documentary style. *Irma Vep* is a surreal study of reality, fantasy, identity, and the follies of filmmaking. A layered parody, the film juxtaposes ponderous French cinema with Hong Kong action and Hollywood excess. The film is a cry for cinematic lost innocence, a forgotten commercial dominance, and the urge to recycle past film into a relevant statement.

—*Hilary Weber* and *Sarah Weber*

REVIEWS

Hollywood Reporter. October 1, 1996, p. 16.
Los Angeles Times. May 16, 1997, p. F12.
San Francisco Chronicle. August 8, 1997.
San Francisco Examiner. August 8, 1997.
Sight and Sound. March, 1997, p. 51.
Variety. May 20, 1996, p. 35.
Village Voice. May 6, 1997, p. 79.
Washington Post Weekend. June 13, 1997, p. 42.

The Jackal

The Jackal is loose.—Movie tagline

"Willis is chilling, Gere is powerful."—Jeanne Wolf, *Jeanne Wolf's Hollywood*

"A powerful action thriller."—Jim Ferguson, *Prevue Channel*

"*The Jackal* is a terrific thriller! A riveting international game of cat and mouse!"—Bill Zwecker, *WMAQ*

"One of the best movies of the year."—Kim Canavan, *WTVT*

Box Office: $52,612,515

The Jackal is technically a remake, but an odd one that distances itself from its ultimate source, Frederick Forsyth's best-selling novel *The Day of the Jackal*, which is not even mentioned in this film's somewhat irritating title-sequence that offers a fractured black-and-white newsreel survey of the Soviet century, from the Romanovs to Lenin and the Revolution to Stalin to the present. Instead, Kenneth Ross's screenplay for Fred Zinnemann's 1973 film adaptation of the novel is listed as the source for Chuck Pfarrer's reinvented screenplay; but the term "freely adapted" would be more accurate here, since *Jackal* has nothing to do with the Algerian crisis or with an assassination attempt on the life of French President Charles De Gaulle. Since that would be ancient history for today's movie generation, a new and updated story is invented for the new film directed by Michael Caton-Jones. The only history lesson this film offers is its postmodern survey of Russia compressed down to the opening minutes of the title sequence.

The story proper begins in Moscow, where the Russian military, assisted by FBI deputy director Carter Preston (Sidney Poitier), raids a Moscow discothéque and kill an arrogant mobster who believes the new Russia is so corrupt that he can buy his way out of any situation. Infuriated by this killing, the mobster's brother, Terek Murad (David Hayman), calls a meeting in Helsinki, buries a battle-axe in the head of another gangster he believes should have protected his brother ("against 30 armed soldiers I could do nothing," the younger man protests before he is struck from behind), and sets up a contract with the Jackal (Bruce Willis), a professional assassin, to murder a highly-placed American official so as to avenge his brother's death. The pricetag is $70 million. No problem. The identity of the target is kept a secret until the end, though authorities suspect it is the Director of the FBI, which gets that agency's attention immediately.

From this point on the film turns into a relatively conventional techno-thriller as the Jackal orders sophisticated weaponry from Poland to be shipped to Montreal and assumes a number of disguises to smuggle this weaponry into the United States from Canada. The FBI knows that dirty work is afoot, as Carter Preston works with Major Valentina Koslova (Diane Venora) to track the Jackal down. The problem is that they have no idea what he looks like, so they contact IRA operative Declan Mulqueen (Richard Gere), who is serving time for terrorist activities in a high-security American prison. Declan first tells them to shove off, but he agrees to help when he discovers his former lover Isabella (Mathilda May), a former Basque terrorist now living undercover as a housewife in Phoebusville, Virginia, may also be involved and in danger. Declan has a score to settle with the Jackal, who wounded Isabella when she was pregnant with Declan's baby, which was stillborn as a consequence. Declan both wants to protect Isabella and nail the Jackal, but that is not easily done.

Willis plays the Jackal as a ruthless, cold-blooded killer. When a sleazy munitions engineer (Jack Black) attempts to cheat him in Canada, he uses the exuberant cad for target practice when he tests his computerized weaponry, after first shooting at a pumpkin with a face drawn on it, suspended from a tree. (In the original *Day of the Jackal* a melon was used for less sophisticated weaponry.) If the trajectory is a bit off, so is the dealer's right arm, as he is forced to stand there holding a pack of cigarettes, after the pumpkin has been demolished. Later on the Jackal strikes up a friendship with a homosexual bureaucrat (Stephen Spinella) in a gay bar in Washington, D.C. After flirting with the man, he gets access to the bureaucrat's upscale apartment, then calmly shoots him between courses of Korean take-out food in the man's kitchen.

Murad on putting an axe through a betrayer's head: "I took no joy in that."

The Jackal comes to Isabella's house to kill her, but Isabella has by then been taken to a safe house. Instead, when the Jackal turns up, there is a firefight with Major Koslova and two FBI operatives, who are killed. Koslova is fatally wounded, but before she dies, she delivers a message to Declan from the Jackal, who wants Declan to know "You can't protect your women." From that cryptic message, Declan figures out that the Jackal's target is in fact the First Lady (Tess Harper), scheduled to dedicate a children's cancer wing at a D.C. hospital.

The finale involves the long anticipated assassination attempt, followed by a chase sequence through the District of Columbia Metro system (those who know the system will be disoriented, however, since the sequence was shot in Montreal, not Washington). Despite the Jackal's boast, Declan has by then demonstrated that he can save some of "his women," and the film goes on to demonstrate that one of his women may even be capable of saving him in the current era of the affirmative-action heroine. The film ends with an exchange between Declan and Carter Preston that recalls the ending of *The Rock* (1996), when the Sean Connery character is invited to take a walk into the sunset.

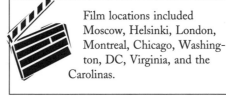

Film locations included Moscow, Helsinki, London, Montreal, Chicago, Washington, DC, Virginia, and the Carolinas.

British director Caton-Jones remade William Wyler's World War II documentary *Memphis Belle* (1944) as his second feature in 1990, so it figures that he could also be trusted to do a workmanlike treatment of this updated remake of Zinnemann's minor classic. "I had no desire to tamper with a classic," Michael Caton-Jones told the *Washington Post* (November 9), speaking of Zinnemann's 1973 film, "but it was an opportunity to do a picture on a really big canvas. We'd shoot it all over the world. I'd be able to utilize all my cinematic techniques."

As Stephen Hunter pointed out in his *Washington Post* review, the French detective Lebel (Michel Lonsdale) of the original story is split into the three characters played by Gere, Denora, and Poitier. The original film lacked stars of that order but had the advantage of an experienced director at the top of his form. For Caton-Jones the remake was merely "a job of work, not a passion of life," and not a personal film, but can an excellent film be made impersonally, without passion?

Caton-Jones would understandably distance himself from the superior Zinnemann original, but reviewers certainly remembered it. The Jackal as played by Edward Fox was portrayed as "Forsyth had imagined him, as an English gentleman of military bearing," Stephen Hunter protested in the *Washington Post,* whereas the Bruce Willis character is a nondescript American with no discernible background. Hunter found Gere's Irish terrorist "completely twitty," but in fact Gere gives one of the best performances of his career and is even capable of handling an Irish brogue convincingly. It is amusing, moreover, to see Gere's charm falling flat with the formidable Russian lady officer. When he attempts to warm up to her and asks her first name, she tells him that her name is "Major." Later, in a moment of weakness, she tells him her name is Valentina. An odd kind of chemistry is carefully developed here.

The screenplay was written by an ex-Navy SEAL military adviser, and then rewritten by others, "not to be a better story," Desson Howe pointed out in his *Washington Post Weekend* review, but to make the stars look better. The problem is, as Ann Hornaday pointed out in the *Baltimore Sun,* "star power can't make up for sophistication," and "action doesn't have to be bigger to be better."

This reinvented techno-thriller is in fact a "B" picture made with an "A" budget and an expensive cast, which offers quite a few surprises as the picture lopes along to its relatively tame conclusion. The Bruce Willis character is constructed mainly of cardboard, hardly more interesting than the multiple wigs he wears, but it is fun to watch him run his paces through multiple disguises, and, as expected, this brutal villain does die hard. Sidney Poitier is probably getting a little too old for action movies (can a 73-year-old actor be capable of heroic

CREDITS

The Jackal: Bruce Willis
Declan Mulqueen: Richard Gere
Carter Preston: Sidney Poitier
Valentina Koslova: Diane Venora
The First Lady: Tess Harper
Witherspoon: J.K. Simmons
Isabella: Mathilda May
Douglas: Stephen Spinella
Donald Brown: John Cunningham
Lamont: Jack Black
Terek Murad: David Hayman

Origin: USA
Released: 1997
Production: James Jacks, Sean Daniel, Michael Caton-Jones, and Kevin Jarre for Alphaville and Mutual Film Company; released by Universal Pictures
Direction: Michael Caton-Jones
Screenplay: Chuck Pfarrer; based on the motion picture screenplay *The Day of the Jackal* by Kenneth Ross
Cinematography: Karl Walter Lindenlaub
Editing: Jim Clark
Music: Carter Burwell
Production design: Michael White
Art direction: Ricky Eyres, John Fenner
Costumes: Albert Wolsky
Sound: Daivd John
MPAA rating: R
Running Time: 124 minutes

leaping?), but he limps along appropriately to the conclusion, as does the film. Richard Gere brings some interest—some growth and development—to his role, however, as does Diane Venora in her grumpy Russian way, but despite these performances, for some critics *The Jackal* barked like a dog. It's a high-budget, high-tech B-killer/thriller at heart, often preposterous in its design and dialogue, but expertly filmed, and generally amusing and entertaining.

—*James M. Welsh*

REVIEWS

The Baltimore Sun. November 14, 1997, p. E1.
Boxoffice. January, 1998, p. 47.
Chicago Tribune. November 14, 1997, p. 4.
Entertainment Weekly. November 23, 1997, p. 91.
Los Angeles Times. November 14, 1997, p. F12.
The New York Times. November 14, 1997, p. B19.
People. November 24, 1997, p. 19.
Rolling Stone. December 11, 1997, p. 85.
USA Today. November 14, 1997, p. D6.
Variety. November 10, 1997, p. 39.
Village Voice. November 25, 1997, p. 96.
The Washington Post. November 9, 1997, p. G10.
The Washington Post. November 14, 1997, p. D1.
Washington Post Weekend. November 14, 1997, p. 50.
The Washington Times Metropolitan Times. November 14, 1997, p. C14.

Jackie Brown

Six players on the trail of a half million in cash. There's only one question . . . Who's playing who?—Movie tagline

"One of the year's best films! *Jackie Brown* is filled with Oscar-worthy performances!"—Roger Ebert, *Chicago Sun-Times*

"A stylish, absorbing thriller with superb, Oscar-caliber performances!"—Jeffrey Lyons, *NBC-TV*

"Truly joyous entertainment! Outrageous and exhilaratingly clever!"—Andrew Sarris, *New York Observer*

"A knockout! Loaded with action and laughs!"—Peter Travers, *Rolling Stone*

"Two thumbs up!"—*Siskel & Ebert*

Box Office: $17,201,953

After the explosive originality of *Reservoir Dogs* (1992) and, especially, *Pulp Fiction* (1994) and having to wait three years for his third film as writer-director, reviewers and audiences may be excused for slight disappointment in Quentin Tarantino's *Jackie Brown.* While his first two films are filled with qualities, including graphic violence, unique narrative structure, unusual humor, and distinctive dialogue, that call attention to their youthful creator's exuberance, *Jackie Brown* is much more conventional, the work of a confident, maturing filmmaker who does not feel compelled to show off unnecessarily or to try to top himself. On its own terms, it is almost as good as its predecessors.

Adapted from Elmore Leonard's 1992 novel *Rum Punch*, *Jackie Brown* recounts a complicated series of double and triple crosses. Jackie Brown (Pam Grier), a forty-four-year-old flight attendant, is arrested by Los Angeles policeman Mark Dargus (Michael Bowen) and Bureau of Alcohol, Tobacco, and Firearms agent Ray Nicolette (Michael Keaton) for smuggling money into the United States from Mexico. Gunrunner Ordell Robbie (Samuel L. Jackson) funnels the cash from his sales into Mexico where a Mr. Walker (never seen) looks after it as Jackie sneaks small amounts back to Ordell. Nicolette desperately wants to arrest Ordell, and Jackie, who already has a criminal record, agrees to help entrap him.

Knowing that Ordell will kill her to keep her quiet, Jackie tells him what is going on and comes up with a plan to double cross Nicolette. She also becomes friends with Max Cherry, the bail bondsman Ordell hires to get her out of jail, and they conspire to cross everyone else. Ordell wants all his money, over half a million, from Mr. Walker, and Jackie and Max plan to steal it while convincing Nicolette that she is smuggling only $50,000.

This plot, which may be too elusive for the typical filmgoer, is obviously not what drew Tarantino to Leonard's novel. Tarantino's previous films show the influence of Leonard, whose writing is notable for his strong sense of place—most of his books take place in Detroit or Miami—attention to detail, focus on mood and character, and colorful dialogue. These same characteristics, added to an overpowering obsession with popular culture, flavor Tarantino's films.

> Jackie, trying to convince Max to steal the money: "It wouldn't even be missed." Max: "Half a million dollars will always be missed."

Leonard painstakingly creates a mood and slowly builds his characters, providing only enough plot to keep things moving, and in *Jackie Brown*, Tarantino attempts to duplicate this style. Many reviewers have complained that the film is too slow and, for its slender subject, too long, but Tarantino achieves the effect he intended. What the characters do is considerably less important than who they are. Tarantino makes at least three of them more rounded than the protagonists of most crime films.

Jackie, who makes only $16,000 a year working for a fourth-rate airline, knows that she must take advantage of every opportunity if she is to survive in a world that holds aging African-American women with murky pasts in low regard. The triumph of the film is how Grier and Tarantino make credible Jackie's progression from seemingly beaten victim to triumphant manipulator who outsmarts everyone. Max is just as worn-out as Jackie, having handled fifteen-thousand clients and seen the scum of the earth in closeup. While Ordell can be charming and funny, he is essentially a predator, an evil, vicious man who gets off on being a bad guy.

To avoid prison, stewardess Jackie Brown (Pam Grier) cooperates with the police to entrap her gun-running boss and decides to make the set-up more rewarding for herself in Quentin Tarantino's *Jackie Brown*.

The other characters are less well developed. Nicolette is a cocky cop who is not as sharp as he thinks he is. Ordell's slow-witted sidekick Louis (Robert De Niro) is, well, slow-witted. Ordell criticizes his friend Melanie (Bridget Fonda) for having no ambition, and she answers that all she wants to do is get high and watch television. *Jackie Brown* can be criticized for having someone as concerned with control as Ordell surrounding himself with losers like these (and three additional Ordell cohorts are on the same low level), but one of the points of Leonard's depiction of the crime scene is that such people are bumblers who succeed only through luck. Tarantino captures this milieu perfectly.

Tarantino makes two major changes from *Rum Punch*. Switching the setting from south Florida to his native Los Angeles (where his previous films also take place) is to be expected, for the filmmaker loves exploring the world he knows. *Jackie Brown*, set in such communities as Compton, Hawthorne, Hermosa Beach, and Torrance, continues Tarantino's portrait of Los Angeles as a loose-knit series of seedy shops, garish bars, bland diners, and empty streets. To this mix, he adds the essence of Southern California: the enormous shopping mall. Much of the last third of *Jackie*

AWARDS AND NOMINATIONS

Academy Awards 1997 Nominations: Supporting Actor (Forster)
Golden Globe Awards 1998 Nominations: Musical/Comedy Actress (Grier), Musical/Comedy Actor (Jackson)

Brown takes place in what a screen card identifies as the world's largest indoor mall, a site Ordell chooses for Jackie to drop off his money. Tarantino creates an ironic contrast between the sordid world of his protagonists and the omnivorous middle-class consumer culture represented the mall's cookie-cutter shops.

Lawrence Bender has also produced partner Tarantino's films *Reservoir Dogs, Pulp Fiction,* and *From Dusk Till Dawn.*

The other major change is the heroine's race. Tarantino's thralldom with African-American culture is even more pronounced here than in his previous films. Jackie's race makes her not only more of an outsider but cooler as well. She may have tacky art on the walls of her apartment, but she has an extensive jazz/rhythm and blues record collection she holds onto because of the effort that went into its creation. She unintentionally courts the smitten Max by introducing him to the Delfonics.

A main reason for making Jackie black is to restore 1970s blaxploitation goddess Grier to a leading role. (Tarantino adores the 1970s, filling the film with funk from the period.) Grier is an icon to many for portraying strong women who kick ass in such films as *Coffy* (1973) and *Foxy Brown* (1974). Her career has waned since the 1970s, and Tarantino clearly intends to resurrect it. This role is a showcase for her since the character is equally resourceful and vulnerable. Grier, a likable but limited performer, creates a good balance between these qualities.

Jackson is a great actor whose versatility has not received sufficient recognition. Both his appearance and his acting style vary considerably from film to film. Jackson gives his best performance as the philosophical hit man in *Pulp Fiction*, but his Ordell only vaguely resembles that character. While the curly hair Jackson affected in *Pulp Fiction* gave the hit man an otherworldly quality, Ordell's oriental goatee and ponytail fit his image of himself as sexy and threatening. Jackson makes Ordell friendly and joking one moment and glacially cold the next, a true psychopath. Like all great film actors, Jackson is at his best when he has no dialogue. Ordell tricks an employee who poses a threat into hiding in a car's trunk. As Ordell gets into the car to drive to the place where he intends to shoot the man, Jackson brilliantly shows how the character slips into an icy resolve to psych himself up to murder. While *Jackie Brown* is generally low-keyed and comic, the two scenes in which Ordell murders friends are quite chilling.

De Niro, who moves easily from bright, loquacious characters, as in *Wag the Dog* (1997), to morons like Louis, does nothing new here, but he has his moments. De Niro is at his best in conveying the sexual restlessness of a man just released after four years in prison. Louis sits in a rocking chair while Ordell's plump friend Simone (Hattie Winston) does her Diana Ross imitation for him. De Niro rocks in time both to the music and to Louis' erupting libido, continuing with a glazed expression even after Simone has left the room.

Keaton, better in comic parts, adequately portrays Nicolette's unjustifiably smug self-assurance, but the role is underwritten. The extraordinarily limited Fonda may nevertheless be a perfect choice to play Melanie since the character is vacuous and annoying. One good Tarantino touch has Melanie and Louis watching Susan George and Fonda's father, Peter, in *Dirty Mary, Crazy Larry* (1974). Those familiar with the fates of these characters will sense some portentous foreshadowing.

By far the best performance is that of Forster, another Tarantino reclamation project. After *Reflections in a Golden Eye* (1967), *The Stalking Moon* (1968), and, especially, *Medium Cool* (1969), Forster seemed headed for stardom. Nothing happened, however, and he drifted off into mostly forgettable B films, with the minor classic *Alligator* (1981)

CREDITS

Jackie Brown: Pam Grier
Ordell Robbie: Samuel L. Jackson
Louis Gara: Robert De Niro
Max Cherry: Robert Forster
Melanie: Bridget Fonda
Ray Nicolette: Michael Keaton
Mark Dargus: Michael Bowen
Beaumont Livingston: Chris Tucker
Winston: Tommy "Tiny" Lister, Jr.
Sheronda: Lisa Gay Hamilton
Simone: Hattie Winston
Judge: Sid Haig

Origin: USA
Released: 1997
Production: Lawrence Bender for A Band Apart; released by Miramax Films
Direction: Quentin Tarantino
Screenplay: Quentin Tarantino; based on the novel *Rum Punch* by Elmore Leonard
Cinematography: Guillermo Navaro
Editing: Sally Menke
Production design: David Wasco
Art direction: Daniel Bradford
Set decoration: Sandy Reynolds-Wasco
Costumes: Mary Claire Hannan
Sound: Mark Ulano
Set design: Mariko Braswell
MPAA rating: R
Running Time: 154 minutes

being an exception. The younger Forster was perhaps too stoic to make much of an impression, but age sometimes brings new depth, as it has with Peter Fonda, Dennis Hopper, and Dean Stockwell. Forster perfectly embodies the world weariness of Max, a sensitive man who has allowed a callous to form over his emotions. With intense, alert eyes staring out of a weathered face, Forster conveys Max's confusion and pleasure over his growing feelings for Jackie. The film's best scenes are those between the two, especially the one in which they discuss the effects of aging on his hair and her hips. *Jackie Brown* works best as a meditation on middle age.

Jackie Brown has several Tarantinoesque touches. The style is generally conservative and deliberate, like that of his idol Jean-Luc Godard, but he uses a split screen effectively once and repeats a climactic scene from three points of view. The film's drab cinematography may be intentional, another homage to blaxploitation perhaps, but it is ugly to look at. While the slow pace can be justified as fitting the characters, there are many shots that could easily be excised. When Ordell meets Jackie at a bar, he is shown driving up, parking, getting out, and walking to the door for one apparent reason. A good film, *Jackie Brown* could have been easily edited into a even better one.

—*Michael Adams*

REVIEWS

Boxoffice. November, 1997, p. 26.
Boxoffice. February, 1998, p. 53.
Entertainment Weekly. January 9, 1998, p. 40.
Maclean's. December 29, 1997, p. 103.
The New York Times. December 24, 1997, p. B5.
The New Yorker. January 12, 1998, p. 83.
Newsweek. December 22, 1997, p. 86.
People. January 12, 1998, p. 21.
Rolling Stone. January 22, 1998, p. 61.
Time. December 22, 1997, p. 80.
USA Today. December 24, 1997, p. D3.
Variety. December 22, 1997, p. 57.
Village Voice. December 30, 1997, p. 61.

Jackie Chan's First Strike; Jing cha gu shi IV: Jian dan ren wu; Police Story 4: First Strike

Jackie Chan fights for America in his biggest action film ever.—Movie tagline

"Nobody's action movies are more fun than Jackie Chan's!"—Jay Carr, *Boston Globe*

"Jackie Chan's the world's top action star!"—Roger Ebert, *Chicago Sun-Times*

"Chan, who does his own amazing stunt work, is the Gene Kelly of martial arts sequences!"—Gene Siskel, *Chicago Tribune*

"You'll be dazzled and delighted at its high-flying panache!"—Terry Lawson, *Detroit Free Press*

Box Office: $15,318,863

In this remarkably witless movie Jackie Chan is a Hong Kong cop sent to Ukraine to investigate a shady lady who seems linked to the Russian Mafia and the black market in nuclear arms. Why? Because he has been so helpful to the C.I.A. in Hong Kong he is recruited to help the C.I.A. worldwide. At first Jackie can't tell if he is dealing with the K.G.B. (or what's left of it) or the Mafia, not that it seems to matter much, since anyone vaguely Russian seems to be crooked and sinister. The function of these Evil Empire types is to make things difficult for Jackie, to chase him on snowmobiles, to let him do his stunts. Stanley Tong, who directed, also was responsible for action sequences and stunt coordination.

Jackie's fans expect stunts galore, but also goofy comedy, so every dilemma has a comic twist. In the frozen Ukraine on his snowmobile, Jackie does not have a jacket, only a silly hat that has the face of a baby seal. In addition, as all the reviewers noticed, this film attempts to spoof the excesses of the James Bond formula. As Jackie spies on his adversaries at a ski lodge, a whole army of white-suited thugs with automatic weapons emerges on snowmobiles from under the snow to chase him. The snowmobile propels him to a helicopter, then Jackie drops from the helicopter into a frozen lake. Of course, he survives this ordeal and is taken to Moscow, then sent by submarine to sunny Australia, where he ends up in a posh penthouse in Brisbane, and his own pet koala bear. Everything that happens is given a cute spin.

What is Jackie after in Australia? Nuclear material that is hidden in a shark tank in an "Oceanarium," put there by a young woman named Annie (Chen Chun Wu) on instructions from her brother Tsui (Jackson Lou). All of Jackie's foes seem to be double agents. Jackie is blamed for the death of Annie's father, so he has to establish his innocence. Her father is a sort of Chinese godfather in Chinatown, and his funeral parade puts Jackie on ten-foot stilts in yet another strange disguise. This gives Jackie a chance to demonstrate his martial arts skills with a distinctive handicap.

"Relax, have fun."—Uncle Bill to Jackie before sending him to the Ukraine.

The idiotic and discombobulated plot has a single purpose—to keep Jackie in motion, with or without his clothes on. Only occasionally does the plot threaten to turn serious, as when the Chinatown ganglord dies, but goofy antics always intercede. In one of the film's best sequences, Jackie has to escape from his high-rise penthouse by going out on a window ledge, working his way down to the next story below, then entering another apartment through a window. In another action sequence Jackie fights off a gang of thugs using a stepladder as his only weapon. Jackie is famous for doing his own stunts, so the film ends with outtakes of stunts that went wrong, documenting the fact that Jackie does not use a stunt double.

First Strike is a martial-arts romp done entirely for kicks.

CREDITS

Jackie: Jackie Chan
Jackson Tsui: Jackson Lou
Annie Tsui: Annie Wu
Uncle Bill: Bill Tung
Col. Gregor Yegorov: Yuri Petrov

Origin: Hong Kong
Released: 1996
Production: Barbie Tung for Golden Harvest; released by New Line Cinema
Direction: Stanley Tong
Screenplay: Stanley Tong, Nick Tramontane, Greg Mallot, Tong Kay-Meng
Cinematography: Jingle Ma
Editing: Peter Cheng, Uau Chi-Wai
Music: Nathan Wang
Art direction: Oliver Wong
Costumes: Money Cheng, Wendy Law
Sound: Gary Wilkins, Gretchen Thornburn
MPAA rating: PG-13
Running Time: 110 minutes

Stephen Hunter of the *Baltimore Sun* pointed out that the plots of Jackie's earlier Hong Kong police films "actually made sense." Stephen Holden of the *New York Times* claimed, however, that this silly plot involving the C.I.A., the Russian Mafia, and a stolen nuclear warhead was not "much dumber than any number of recent Hollywood action-adventure yarns in which former K.G.B. members are the bad guys." Holden considered the film a "more comfortable blend of Hong Kong martial-arts antics and glitzy Hollywood action-adventure" than Jackie's last picture, *Rumble in the Bronx* (1996).

Jackie Chan's persona recalls earlier comedians Douglas Fairbanks and Buster Keaton in the way comic action is mingled with acrobatic stunts. The surreal effect of this picture also recalls the silent cinema in which a distinctive logic tended to govern comic situations. Anything could happen in silent comedy in a world in which sound was suspended. Jackie is an astonishing Kamikaze comic-stuntman clown-hero whose world is not governed by sense, logic or language. Combining this surreal framework with the Bond gimmicks makes for an amusing comic spectacle. Stephen Hunter was impressed by the way J. Peter Robinson's pounding sound track "echoes the twangy bustle of John Barry's scores for the 007 movies." Carrie Rickey of *The Philadelphia Inquirer* stretched to find some deeper significance as Jackie "is being pulled between a corrupt former Communist regime and a corrupt clan of capitalist Chinese, which may be symbolic of Hong Kong as the ideological midpoint between Peking and Taipei." Maybe, but one should not expect a political lesson or message here, merely a clown acting up to combine laughs with far-fetched thrills. The film is a harmless and sometimes amusing diversion and about as bloodless an action adventure as can be found.

—*James M. Welsh*

REVIEWS

The Baltimore Sun. January 11, 1997, p. D1.
Boxoffice. March, 1997, p. 46.
Chicago Tribune. January 10, 1997, p. 5.
The Hollywood Reporter. April 16, 1996, p. I4.
Los Angeles Times. January 10, 1997, p. F2.
The New York Times. January 10, 1997, p. C3.
The Philadelphia Inquirer Weekend. January 10, 1997, p. 4.
USA Today. January 10, 1997, p. D4.
Variety. May 6, 1996, p. 86.
Village Voice. January 21, 1997, p. 70.

Jerusalem

"Bille August's epic boasts visual sweep and emotional depth . . ."—Stephen Farber, *Movieline*

"An epic romance of sweeping proportions. Intense, moving and brilliantly directed. If you liked *The English Patient*, *Jerusalem* is a must."—Paul Wunder, *WBAI Radio*

Director Bille August chronicles the religious pilgrimage of a radical sect of Swedish Christians in his powerfully evocative film, *Jerusalem*. The small group of agrarians moved from a remote village in the Swedish Dales to Palestine in the Nineteenth Century to await the Second Coming of Christ.

Based on the Nobel Prize-winning novel of the same name by Selma Lagerlof, *Jerusalem* is a gut-wrenching experience, guaranteed to elicit tears from even the most stoical viewer. (One is hard-pressed to think of another film that is so emotionally intense and so powerfully sad.) It is a devastating tale of love, faith and religious fervor; and like Chinese's *A Mongolian Tale* (1997), August's film is also about the vagaries of fate, or perhaps the Divine Plan of God.

As his father lies dying, the young Ingmar Ingmarsson vows to someday take his place as the leader of the small Swedish parish. The young boy is sent to live with the local schoolteacher and her young daughter, Gertrude.

Time passes and Ingmar (Ulf Friberg) and Gertrud (Maria Bonnevie) are grown and engaged to be married. But when he is cheated out of his rightful inheritance by his conniving brother-in-law, Ingmar leaves Gertrud behind to work at the family's sawmill some distance away. With Ingmar gone, the townspeople hunger for a new spiritual leader, and their prayers seem to be answered with the arrival of a charismatic evangelist, Hellgum (Sven-Bertil Taube).

Hellgum easily convinces some of the villagers to join his cult, and to surrender their life savings. Ingmar's sister Karin (Pernilla August) is among those who eagerly hands over the family farm in exchange for the promise of salvation. When Ingmar returns, he finds a stranger ensconced in his family's home and his fiancee under the spell of this self-proclaimed messiah who intends to lead his people to Palestine, where they will build a new Jerusalem.

Ingmar's world is devastated by the presence of Hellgum. Desperate to reclaim his land, he agrees to an arranged marriage, shattering Gertrud's heart. When a member of the cult dies after Hellgum refuses to obtain outside medical intervention for the woman, Hellgum is ordered out of the community. Gertrud is among the many who leave Sweden and follow Hellgum to the Promised Land.

The cast is primarily comprised of actors who are not that well-known to audiences outside of Scandinavia; but all are impeccable. Only the accomplished actors Max von Sydow (*Hannah and Her Sisters*, 1986) and Olympia Dukakis (*Moonstruck*, 1987) may be recognizable to most American filmgoers. Both appear in the film's second half as leaders of the gender-segregated religious colony in Palestine. Dukakis is Mother, the matriarchal head; Von Sydow, the Vicar. Both actors masterfully layer their characters with a range of repressed emotions, subtly and steadily revealing their suffering. In fact, all of the actors of *Jerusalem* are uniformly gifted.

The film's characters do not engage in lengthy diatribes; they are more reticent, like rural people tend to be. As a result, August's film relies heavily on the visuals to convey much of the emotion. The rich landscape of Sweden is contrasted with the arid and rocky terrain of Palestine, a perfect reflection of the characters' spiritual transitions.

Jerusalem is a complicated story that ultimately proves to be emotionally draining. Not only does the film run for over three hours, in part due to the languorous pace of the narrative, but it resonates long after the film has ended. Di-

CREDITS

Gertrud: Maria Bonnevie
Ingmar: Ulf Friberg
Barbro: Lena Endre
Karin: Pernilla August
Hellgum: Sven-Bertil Taube
Tim: Reine Brynolfsson
Mother: Olympia Dukakis
Vicar: Max von Sydow

Origin: Sweden
Released: 1996
Production: Ingrid Dahlberg for SVT Drama; released by First Look Pictures
Direction: Bille August
Screenplay: Bille August; based on the novel by Selma Lagerlof
Cinematography: Jorgen Persson
Editing: Janus Billeskov Jansen
Production design: Anna Asp
Costumes: Ann-Margaret Fyhregaard
Music: Stefan Nilsson
Sound: Paul Jyrala, Niels Arild Nielsen
MPAA rating: PG-13
Running Time: 168 minutes

rector Bille August (*Smilla's Sense of Snow*, 1997) slowly and methodically conveys the details of these farmers' lives, first in Sweden, then in Palestine, and the result is a hauntingly beautiful film. Despite the overwhelming sadness of *Jerusalem*, August still manages a relatively happy ending—perhaps his own version of salvation.

—Patricia Kowal

REVIEWS

Boxoffice. February, 1997, p. 58.
Los Angeles Times. March 7, 1997, p. F2.
Toronto Sun. April 18, 1997.
Variety. September 23, 1996, p. 126.

John Grisham's The Rainmaker; The Rainmaker

They were totally unqualified to try the case of a lifetime . . . but every underdog has his day.—Movie tagline

"Brilliant, just brilliant! A great ensemble cast! A fantastic motion picture experience!"—Ron Brewington, *American Urban Radio Networks*

"Francis Ford Coppola captures all the best of John Grisham with superb performances by an all-star cast. . . . Danny DeVito is devilishly funny and Matt Damon shines as a leading man."—Jeanne Wolf, *Jeanne Wolf's Hollywood*

"A stunning film! Francis Ford Coppola and a stellar cast have created the best film adaptation of a John Grisham novel ever!"—Paul Clinton, *Turner Entertainment Report*

"Director Coppola's best film since *The Godfather*. Engrossing and entertaining. A modern-day classic."—Earl Dittman, *Tune-In Publications*

Box Office: $43,622,262

John Grisham's The Rainmaker is a classic David and Goliath tale about a young lawyer who takes on the giant insurance company Great Benefit and wins the case. But the film is also much more. It is a poignant and humorous drama that takes us into the heart and mind of a young lawyer, Rudy Baylor (Matt Damon), as he springboards into the legal profession on a history-making case. The film follows Baylor on his journey from idealism all the way to disillusionment, and he covers all that ground in the space of one trial. His first.

Deck to Rudy: "There's nothing more thrilling than nailing an insurance company."

As a law student at Memphis State University, Baylor worked his way through law school at a local student watering hole. When he needed money, his boss introduced him to Bruiser Stone (Mickey Rourke), a sleazy lawyer who is also the owner of various bars and strip joints all over Memphis.

Baylor is given a job chasing ambulances and works on a commission basis. His mentor is Dick Schifflet (Danny DeVito), a self-proclaimed "para-lawyer" who has flunked his bar exam numerous times. Schifflet's genius is his ability to circumvent the more conventional and more legal methods of practicing law to get things done. Baylor watches as Schifflet shows him the ropes, sneaking into hospital rooms and bullying bedridden accident patients into taking on lawsuits. But soon it is Baylor's turn.

Bruiser tells him to go to the hospital and sign up a badly battered wife, Kelly Riker (Claire Danes), to file suit against her husband (Andrew Shue). He watches her from afar, but hesitates to approach her. When he does finally get to know her, instead of trying to get Kelly to file a lawsuit, Rudy does his best to get her away from the man who has threatened to kill her.

Legally, Baylor is more concerned with a couple of cases that he has brought to Bruiser's law firm from a law workshop at the University, than he is with chasing ambulances. One is an elderly widow called Miss Birdie (Teresa Wright), who wants to change her will. The other is the case of a young man named Donny Ray Black (Johnny Whitworth) who is suing his insurance company to pay for treatment of his leukemia.

After a doctor recommended a bone marrow transplant to save Donny Ray's life, Black's insurance company, Great Benefit, denied treatment over and over again. As the boy's health worsens, Baylor sues the insurance company to get money for the transplant. Meanwhile, Bruiser's office is padlocked by the FBI while he's investigated for jury tampering, and he and his partner escape to an undisclosed tropical paradise to avoid prosecution.

Left on their own, Baylor and Schifflet go into business for themselves, and the novice lawyer takes on his first case against a team of high-price lawyers representing the multi-million dollar insurance company who hold Donny Ray Black's policy. But when Donny Ray dies before the case goes to court, the parents (Mary Kay Place and Red West) file suit against the company for punitive damages.

Author Michael Herr, who wrote Rudy's voice-over narration, also wrote the narration on Coppola's film *Apocalypse Now.*

What transforms this somewhat predictable story into an engrossing drama is the acting. Director Francis Ford Coppola has assembled a talented cast of players who, in even the smallest roles, give stellar performances.

Matt Damon brings a charming vulnerability to the part of Rudy Baylor, whose humor, earnestness, and innate goodness make him the son every mother would love. But it is Damon's subtle touch that brings an intelligence to the part. He brings all these qualities together in one heartrending scene where Baylor waits silently by Donny Ray's deathbed and muses with sad irony, "This is how the uninsured die."

Damon gives credibility to the evolution of a character who, at the beginning of the trial, hopes to emulate the trial lawyers of the civil rights era and ends the trial totally disillusioned with the legal system.

Danny DeVito plays the street-smart scam artist, Deck Schifflet, with an edgy intensity that is both funny and endearing. Mary Kay Place is Dot Black, the mother of the dying Donny Ray. She portrays the chain-smoking, blue-collar mother in such an understated way that her suffering can only be glimpsed from beneath her thin veneer of toughness that gets thinner as her son gets closer to death.

Another memorable performance is by Virginia Madsen, who plays Jackie Lemancyzk, a former claims adjuster with Great Benefit, who has been given hush money to keep silent about the case. She gives a wonderful performance of a woman walking the fine line between emotional disintegration and salvation. Madsen brings a graceful intensity to the part, which, though small, leaves an indelible impression.

Jon Voight plays the insurance company's smooth and condescending lead lawyer Leo F. Drummond with the appropriate amount of villainy. Though Drummond is easy to hate, his character is flawed in its utter lack of humanity, contrasting starkly with the other fully-fleshed out characters in the film.

Wilfred Keeley, the CEO of Great Benefit, is played by Roy Scheider. In a brief but emotionally eloquent scene, Scheider plays a powerful CEO who comes to the witness stand confident and secure in the protection his money and his team of lawyers affords him. But he leaves the stand as a man who knows his life is just about to fall down around his ears.

Although the film has its share of visually stagnant courtroom scenes, one scene stands out for its brilliant use of imagery. Shortly before Donny Ray's death, the lawyers from both sides come together at the Black's house for a filmed deposition. But with the makeshift sickbed in the tiny living room, there is no room for all the lawyers. So they move Donny Ray outside to tape his deposition in the backyard. There, against the stark backdrop of bare autumn trees against a steel grey sky, an old junked car sits rusting and silent as curious neighborhood children line up along the fence to listen. The image of the insurance lawyers sitting outside in

CREDITS

Rudy Baylor: Matt Damon
Deck Schifflet: Danny DeVito
Leo F. Drummond: Jon Voight
Kelly Riker: Claire Danes
Dot Black: Mary Kay Place
Bruiser Stone: Mickey Rourke
Jackie Lemancyzk: Virginia Madsen
Judge Harvey Hale: Dean Stockwell
Miss Birdie: Teresa Wright
Donny Ray Black: Johnny Whitworth
Buddy Black: Red West
Wilfred Keeley: Roy Scheider
Cliff Riker: Andrew Shue
Judge Tyrone Kipler: Danny Glover

Origin: USA
Released: 1997
Production: Michael Douglas and Steven Reuther for Constellation Films and American Zoetrope; released by Paramount Pictures
Direction: Francis Ford Coppola
Screenplay: Francis Ford Coppola; based on the novel by John Grisham
Cinematography: John Toll
Editing: Barry Malkin
Music: Elmer Bernstein
Production design: Howard Cummings
Art direction: Robert Shaw, Jeffrey McDonald
Set decoration: Barbara Munch
Set design: Scott Murphy
Costumes: Aggie Guerard Rodgers
Sound: Nelson Stoll
MPAA rating: PG-13
Running Time: 135 minutes

expensive three-piece suits before the hollow-eyed leukemia victim creates the visual impact of a flock of black crows waiting by a dying animal.

Images are successfully used in other instances in the film, notably in Bruiser's law office, where a huge aquarium full of live sharks is placed humorously behind the lawyer's desk, a fitting analogy to Bruiser's legal methods.

Although the stories of the elderly widow and the battered wife give insight into Baylor's character, they seem to aimlessly circle the main plot, randomly intruding on the real action. It is Baylor's earnest battle to maintain his integrity and his humanity, while attempting to win the case, that is the real story in *The Rainmaker.* And it is his inevitable conclusion that neither integrity nor humanity can be sustained for long in the world of law.

Although this is a feel-good story about good winning over evil, and justice over greed, John Grisham has also shed light on a real issue of our time. Baylor's disillusionment with the legal system is based on what a lawyer must do and become in order to win a case.

At the end of the film, Baylor talks about how every lawyer at one point in a case feels himself crossing a line. And if he crosses it enough that line disappears. This makes Baylor's victory bittersweet and leaves the viewer wondering if there isn't a better path to justice.

—*Diane Hatch-Avis*

AWARDS AND NOMINATIONS

Golden Globe Awards 1998 Nominations: Supporting Actor (Voight)

REVIEWS

Chicago Tribune. November 21, 1997, p. 4.
Entertainment Today. November 14, 1997, p. 18.
Entertainment Weekly. November 21, 1997, p. 100.
Hollywood Reporter. November 14, 1997, p. 8.
Los Angeles Times. November 21, 1997, p. F2.
The Nation. December 22, 1997, p. 35.
New York Times. November 21, 1997, p. E18.
People. December 1, 1997, p. 31.
Rolling Stone. December 11, 1997, p. 85.
USA Today November 21, 1997, p. 9D.
Variety. November 17, 1997, p. 63.
Village Voice. November 25, 1997, p. 96.
Washington Post Weekend. November 21, 1997, p. 50.

johns

"*johns* is a gritty portrayal of friendship and survival."—*Film Threat*

" . . . edgy and unsparing . . ."—Justine Elias, *Interview*

"*Midnight Cowboy* for the '90s."—Kevin Thomas, *Los Angeles Times*

"A morality tale for our time with very strong performances."—Joy Browne, *WOR Radio*

Writer-director Scott Silver gives us yet another glimpse of the sordid life of young male street hustlers in Los Angeles in the lower-case *johns.* Despite a compassionate portrayal of two lost souls, the film ultimately is a thinly-veiled, sensationalist morality tale in which a sinner must be punished by the end.

John: "People come and go and the only thing that doesn't change is the boulevard."

Silver, whose background is in television documentaries, claims to have spent months of research, accompanying hustlers on the street and paying twenty dollars for each of their stories. The result is an independent first feature that has pretensions of tragic poetry while actually reading more like an immature bashing of the gay lifestyle.

johns treads unimaginatively into waters that have already been dredged by far more original filmmakers. John Schlesinger took home the Academy Award for his direction of 1969's Best Picture, *Midnight Cowboy*—an emotionally devastating character study starring Jon Voight and Dustin Hoffman as two unlikely friends in the seamiest side of New York City. Twenty-two years later, director Gus Van Sant gave us the cult favorite, *My Own Private Idaho* (1991) with River Phoenix and Keanu Reeves turning tricks in the Pacific Northwest. Van Sant's film starts out promising, but fails miserably with its ill-conceived gay variant of Shakespeare's *Henry IV.*

Those viewers familiar with *My Own Private Idaho* may

recall that Van Sant ends his story with a shot of some faceless stranger stealing the shoes off the young street hustler played by Phoenix as he lay unconscious, curled up on the ground. In *johns* Silver borrows this imagery, in what one would hope is an intentional homage to Van Sant; Asleep in a park, John (David Arquette), the young hustler, has his "lucky sneakers" stolen by, you guessed it, a faceless stranger. Silver, however, uses this event not as a summation, but as a starting point for his woeful tale.

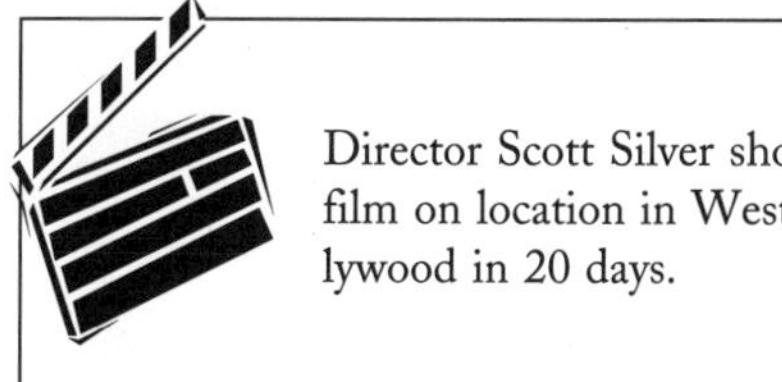

Director Scott Silver shot the film on location in West Hollywood in 20 days.

Unfortunately for John, stuffed inside those lucky shoes was the money he owes from dealing drugs for the nefarious Jimmy the Warlock (Terrence Dashon Howard). John had dreamed of using the money to bankroll a night's stay at a posh hotel to commemorate his twenty-first birthday, which just happens to fall on Christmas Day. Jimmy wants his money, John wants a room. As the clock ticks steadily towards the hour of reckoning, John is aided on the street by the sweetly optimistic and innocent Donner (Lukas Haas).

As in *My Own Private Idaho*, Donner is an acknowledged homosexual who has been disowned by his parents; John professes to be straight. He has a girlfriend (Alanna Ubach in shrill Rosie Perez mode), and insists that he hustles solely for the money. While John orients Donner to the harsh reality of life on the streets, Donner falls hopelessly in love with his mentor. John may dream of room service and cable TV at the Park Plaza, but Donner hopes to rescue John by taking him to Branson, Missouri and a Renaissance-Fair amusement park called Camelot.

Apart from his forced allegorical use of the name John, Silver over-indulges in overt religious symbolism and imagery. John the hustler is clearly Silver's Christ-figure, complete with a modern version of a crown-of-thorns. Solemn church music invades, John's birthday is Christmas Day, and there is even the mysterious Homeless John (*Dead Presidents'* Keith David) who could very well be the film's latter-day John the Baptist.

David Arquette (the sheriff in *Scream*, 1996) gives the kind of twitchy performance that actor Michael Rapaport (*Cop Land*, 1997) specializes in: all superficial physicality with very little emotional depth. In contrast, Lukas Haas imbues his doomed, romantic character with a deep sensitivity and painful innocence that is touching, yet heart-wrenching. Haas, best known as the young child in the Amish thriller *Witness* (1985), was most recently seen in Woody Allen's musical, *Everyone Says I Love You* (1996).

—*Patricia Kowal*

CREDITS

John: David Arquette
Donner: Lukas Haas
Homeless John: Keith David
John Cardoza: Arliss Howard
Manny Gould: Elliott Gould
Jimmy the Warlock: Terrence Dashon Howard
Nikki: Alanna Ubach
Mikey: Wilson Cruz

Origin: USA
Released: 1996
Production: Beau Flynn and Stefan Simchowitz for Bandeira Entertainment; released by First Look Pictures
Direction: Scott Silver
Screenplay: Scott Silver
Cinematography: Tom Richmond
Editing: Dorian Harris
Production design: Amy Beth Silver
Art direction: William P. Paine
Costumes: Sarah Jane Slotnick
Music: Charles Brown, Danny Caron
Sound: Andrew DeCristofaro
MPAA rating: R
Running Time: 96 minutes

REVIEWS

Boxoffice. April, 1996, p. 109.
Chicago Sun-Times. May 16, 1997.
Chicago Tribune. May 16, 1997.
Film Threat. January, 1997, p. 54.
New York Times. January 31, 1997.
Los Angeles Times. January 3, 1997, p. F6.
San Francisco Chronicle. January 31, 1997, p. D3.
San Francisco Examiner. January 31, 1997, p. C3.
Sight and Sound. June, 1997, p. 53.
Variety. January 29, 1996, p. 63.
Village Voice. February 4, 1997, p. 70.

Julian Po

Into a town with no future comes a man with a past.—Movie tagline

Julian Po is a charming, whimsical story of a thirty-year-old bookkeeper who has taken to the road with a tape recorder. Having failed to write his autobiography, he still feels compelled to leave some kind of witness to his life. Where is he going? Why would he be walking along country roads with a big leather suitcase? If he has decided to bum around, why not get more casual clothing and a backpack? What is this curious fellow up to, really?

These are the kinds of questions that occur to people in a town that Garrison Keillor would say time forgot. No one visits this unnamed town, and therefore the community thinks their visitor is up to no good. The town's one police car follows Po everywhere. Kids dog his every step. Everyone watches him drink coffee in a local cafe. The owner of the ramshackle hotel Po stays in keeps tabs on him.

Po, played by Christian Slater with his usual offhand allure, is not giving away his game. With time on their hands, townspeople speculate that he is a drug dealer—or worse, a murderer. But who would he murder? It all gets too much for them, and they corner him in the cafe. The beset upon Po is astonished by their frenzied questions. He explains that his car broke down and that he has entered town by accident. But they want a confession, and he finally blurts out that the person he is going to kill is himself! Well, it is his interrogators turn to be stunned. What to make of this unexpected reply?

The original 40-page novella by Yugoslavian author Branimir Scepanovic has been expanded by Wade and the location changed from Montenegro to the Catskills.

Recovering from their shock, they treat Po as a kind of wonder. No one tries very hard to pump this stranger about his reasons for choosing suicide. No, it is the fact that he has made such a choice and announces it to the world that impresses them. They admire his initiative. They even seem to envy him his choice. Watching and waiting for the moment he will do himself in also becomes a sport for certain town members. An elderly lady sets up a table on the street and takes bets on when Po will end it all. The boys who follow Po around bet every day that that day Po will kill himself. That way, as one boy explains to Po, they can't lose.

Po's first reactions are frustration and annoyance. No one will leave him alone. The local haberdasher outfits Po in a new suit so as to look good at his death. Three women offers themselves to Po. Most of these characters are likeable, if stunted or stifled in some way. Not much happens in this town. There is very little outlet for the imagination. Po provides an opportunity for them to act out their fantasies. The barber, for example, not only cuts Po's hair for free, he shaves him as well. With straight razor in hand, the barber asks Po if he would like the barber to help him die. The barber has been studying anatomy books and he assures Po that slitting someone's throat, done properly, will be over in a moment, with the victim feeling nothing at all. A frightened Po bolts from the barber's chair.

Like Po, these townspeople feel disappointed about their lives. They have been waiting for something to happen. A beautiful young girl, Sarah, played wistfully by Robin Tunney, makes love to Po, telling him that he is the man she has been waiting for all her life. Po is overwhelmed. He has already rejected the perfectly named Lilah (Allison Janney), who wants to bed Po as part of a cure for her middle-aged blahs, and he has ignored the yearning glances of Lucy (Cherry Jones) the hotel maid, a wonderfully expressive woman, even though she is both deaf and dumb. Sarah is like a fin-de-siecle fantasy figure. For her, Po represents a romance with death. She is seeking the perfect love in whose consummation she will find her own annihilation. Po is easily seduced—not realizing that Sarah means exactly what she says, and that she has chosen Po because he has so forthrightly expressed his own death wish.

Julian Po has to be enjoyed as a fantasy, for could any town in the United States still be as innocent and off the beaten track as the one in this movie? *Julian Poe* has to be regarded as a metaphor, a kind of pastoral poem that is meant by its very remoteness from reality to stimulate reveries about what life is like today, about how hard it is to make clear-cut decisions, to make a statement that everyone hears, to do exactly what the individual wants to do with his life. Po seems admirable precisely because he wants to confront his own failure to be himself. When he begins to have second thoughts about ending his life, the disappointed townspeople attempt to force him to make good on his word.

The film's ending is enigmatic. What should be the denouement—Po's death—is not shown, although he walks out of his hotel room with the townspeople just like a man going to his execution. The final scene is effective not only for preserving some of the mystery of Po's life, but for enjoining the viewer to revisit earlier scenes, to think about how a life has led to the final scene.

Look upon *Julian Po* as a kind of parable. It is not so much a comment on America today as on life itself. The story could happen virtually anywhere, and that is perhaps why the town is not named. What Po is disappointed about also does not matter very much because this is not a psychological film. Learning about Po's childhood or his job is not the point. It would not explain his depression.

In fact, screenwriter and director Alan Wade has adapted a 40-page novella by Yugoslavian author Branimir Scepanovic, adding characters and changing the location from Montenegro to the Catskills. Both are mountainous regions, though obviously the remote terrain of Scepanovic's land gives a realistic edge to the story that *Julian Po* cannot emulate. Nevertheless, the movie's origins in another culture suggests its universal, allegorical quality. The town has a sheriff, a barber, a haberdasher, a hotel owner—a one of each character that is reminiscent of a medieval mystery play.

Wade's work has been compared to the surrealism of David Lynch, though Wade does not have the manic quality that marks so much of *Twin Peaks*, for example. There

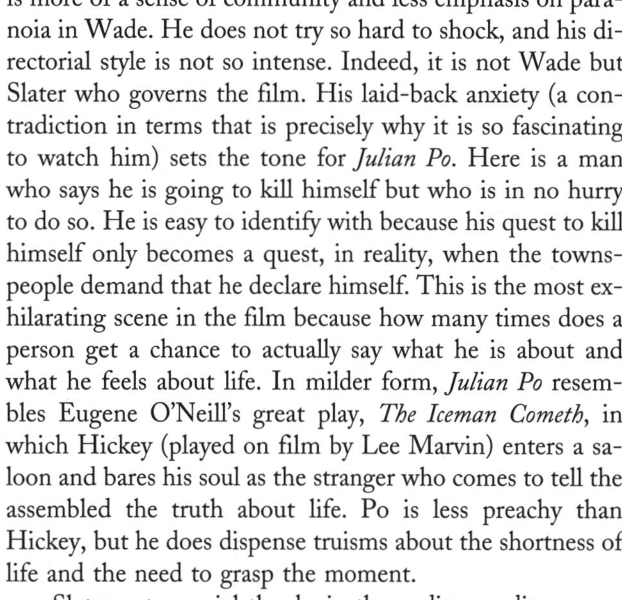

is more of a sense of community and less emphasis on paranoia in Wade. He does not try so hard to shock, and his directorial style is not so intense. Indeed, it is not Wade but Slater who governs the film. His laid-back anxiety (a contradiction in terms that is precisely why it is so fascinating to watch him) sets the tone for *Julian Po*. Here is a man who says he is going to kill himself but who is in no hurry to do so. He is easy to identify with because his quest to kill himself only becomes a quest, in reality, when the townspeople demand that he declare himself. This is the most exhilarating scene in the film because how many times does a person get a chance to actually say what he is about and what he feels about life. In milder form, *Julian Po* resembles Eugene O'Neill's great play, *The Iceman Cometh*, in which Hickey (played on film by Lee Marvin) enters a saloon and bares his soul as the stranger who comes to tell the assembled the truth about life. Po is less preachy than Hickey, but he does dispense truisms about the shortness of life and the need to grasp the moment.

Slater gets special thanks in the ending credits—most likely for two reasons. Without his participation such a small, independent film could not be made at all. But the final tribute to him is also a recognition that he was just the right actor for the part, for his understated acting makes him a kind of everyman. Few actors today have Slater's kind of low-key star power. When Slater has stumbled in other films, it is because too much of a wise-guy sarcasm surfaces, so that he seems to be playing himself, not his part. But in *Julian Po*, Slater always remains in the service of his role, and what writer-director would not be thankful for that kind of dedication, which reveals an honest humility that is far more appealing than the bravado that seems endemic in so many contemporary American films.

Julian Po has not been a commercial success in the movie houses, but it may yet have a successful life on video. The small scale of the story is suitable to smaller screens. The movie has a domestic, intimate feel that does not profit that much from being blown up to larger-than-life size in a multiplex. And it contains home truths that make it an ideal video rental.

—Carl Rollyson

CREDITS

Julian Po: Christian Slater
Sara: Robin Tunney
Vern: Michael Parks
Lucy: Cherry Jones
Sheriff: Frankie R. Faison
Mayor: Harve Presnell
Lilah: Allison Janney
Darlene: LaTanya Richardson
Potter: Zeljko Ivanek

Origin: USA
Released: 1997
Production: Joseph Pierson and Jon Glascoe for Cypress Films and Mindel/Shaw Productions; released by Fine Line Features
Direction: Alan Wade
Screenplay: Alan Wade; based on the novella *La Mort de Monsieur Golouga* by Branimir Scepanovic
Cinematography: Bernd Heinl
Editing: Jeffrey Wolf
Music: Patrick Williams
Production design: Stephen McCabe
Set decoration: Susan Goulder
Costumes: Juliet Polcsa
Sound: Scott Breindel
MPAA rating: PG-13
Running Time: 78 minutes

REVIEWS

Boxoffice. November, 1997, p. 133.
Variety. September 29, 1997, p. 63.

Jungle 2 Jungle

Get a little savage.—Movie tagline
"Delightful!"—Mose Persico, *CFCF-12, Montreal*
"The perfect family film!"—Jim Svejda, *KNX/CBS Radio*
"Funny!"—Frank Barron, *Satellite Entertainment*

Box Office: $59,927,618

When a Wall Street trader seeks a divorce from his estranged wife living in the Amazon, he discovers he has a son who's grown up in the jungle. This remake of a French film, *Un Indien dans la Ville*, is the standard fish-out-of-water comedy and is a typically tall tale—swapping the cliche loincloth, war paint, feathers and bare feet in Venezuela's rain forest for the island of Manhattan's jungle.

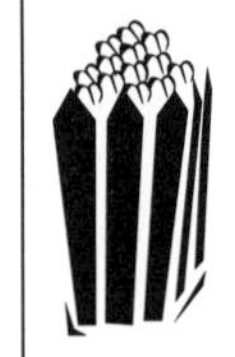

Michael on seeing the jungle: "Oh my god, it's Gilligan's Island."

On the frenzied floor of the stock exchange, Michael Crawford (Tim Allen) plays a hunch, buying 51,000 tons of coffee futures, leaving it in the capable hands of financial analyst Richard Kempster (Martin Short). Crawford takes off for a flight to obtain a divorce from his wife—who left him for "Gilligan's Island"—as his business associate's blood pressure rises.

After a trying trip along a river with pecking piranhas, Crawford finds his wife, Patrice (JoBeth Williams), in a remote village, administering to a pig in labor. She's the settlement's doctor, who explains why she left him—when he installed his fifth phone line. He hooks up his laptop computer to continue his coffee deal long-distance, barely listening to her announce they have a 13-year-old son. When it finally hits him, a shocked Crawford meets his progeny, Mimi-Siku (Sam Huntington), forgetting his sales transaction requires a confirmation.

Tim Allen reunited with the director and creative team responsible for his previous Disney hit, *The Santa Clause.*

Bonding briefly with his son, he's impressed with the youngster's prowess with a poison blowdart, and then discovers the child also speaks English. Crawford promises to take Mimi-Siku to New York when he becomes a man—not realizing the custom of the tribe—the boy's initiation into manhood is happening that night. The chief assigns the young man the task of bringing back fire from the Statue of Liberty's torch.

Back in New York City, Crawford's partner hasn't sold the coffee, the price is dropping and the boss is yelling. Waiting in the office lobby, the boy, still clothed in jungle gear, releases his pet tarantula, which runs to attack the screamer (the creature's natural reaction). Crawford manages to save his employer, and get the kid and spider out of the building.

Off to meet his fashion designer fiancee, Charlotte (Lolita Davidovich), Crawford finds a film crew covering their pre-wedding activities and she learns of the existence of his wild child. At their dinner party that evening, Mimi-Siku considers eating the cat, but satisfies his hunger on its food, sending the girlfriend into paroxysms. Crawford assures her they'll soon return to normal—"being entirely wrapped up in ourselves"—a rare moment of awareness in his chronically agitated state. He then shoots himself in the foot with his son's poison blowdart.

Mimi-Siku escapes the apartment to explore the city without his unavailable father, and locates the Statue of Liberty. Climbing to the crown he realizes the fire is not retrievable. When Crawford retrieves his son, they have a chat and share a meaningful moment dancing in Central Park to a street band.

Kempster finds a buyer for the coffee—a Russian mobster—and makes the black market sale, despite Crawford's uncertainty. Meanwhile, Crawford attempts to snag time for his offended fiancee, dropping his jungle boy at Kempster's house with his pretty young daughter. Mimi-Siku naively creates trouble, barbecuing expensive exotic fish and falling for the girl.

The price of coffee drops and the Russians seek revenge. Kempster takes back the certificates. Then the coffee price rises and the Russians arrive at the Kempster homestead out for blood again. With his tarantula and poison blowdarts, Mimi-Siku saves the day, outwitting the thugs and dazzling everyone with his resourceful daring. Although sad to leave the girl and fail the chief, he's still homesick and returns home with a Statue of Liberty cigarette lighter from his new-found dad.

In a turn of events, Crawford's girlfriend can't make time for him in her busy schedule with the filmmakers and he finally sees the light. While watching coffee prices rise further on Wall Street, he shoots a fly on his boss's back with a dart—officially allowing him into his son's

CREDITS

Michael Cromwell: Tim Allen
Mimi-Siku: Sam Huntington
Richard Kempster: Martin Short
Dr. Patricia Cromwell: JoBeth Williams
Charlotte: Lolita Davidovich
Alexei Jovanovic: David Ogden Stiers
George Langston: Bob Dishy
Jan Kempster: Valerie Mahaffey
Karen Kempster: LeeLee Sobieski

Origin: USA
Released: 1997
Production: Brian Reilly for Walt Disney Pictures and TF1 International; released by Buena Vista
Direction: John Pasquin
Screenplay: Bruce A. Evans and Raynold Gideon; based on the film *Un Indien dans la Ville*
Cinematography: Tony Pierce-Roberts
Editing: Michael A. Stevenson
Music: Michael Convertino
Production design: Stuart Wurtzel
Art direction: Timothy Galvin
Costumes: Carol Ramsey
Sound: Allan Byer
Animal supervisor: Jules Sylvester
MPAA rating: PG
Running Time: 105 minutes

tribe. A family reunion in the village includes a surprise visit from the Kempsters, along with their lovely daughter.

This contrived comedy about a primitive child out of place in modern life predictably shows the absurdity and shallowness of the financial and fashion worlds, and their insufferable intolerance of the supposedly unsophisticated foreigner. The *Crocodile Dundee* meets *Tarzan* theme has been done to death and this attempt is no improvement. The good actors are misused for such broad humor. Strictly for youngsters, who may be forgiving of the dopey dads and enjoy a laugh at their expense.

—*Roberta Cruger*

REVIEWS

Detroit News. March 7, 1997, p. D1.
Entertainment Weekly. March 21, 1997, p. 53.
Los Angeles Times. March 7, 1997, p. F8.
New York Times. March 7, 1997, p. B3.
People. March 24, 1997, p. 19.
Sight and Sound. June, 1997, p. 54.
USA Today. March 7, 1997, p. 4D.
Variety. March 10, 1997, p. 79.

Kama Sutra: A Tale of Love

In a world ruled by pleasure, love is the ultimate seduction.—Movie tagline

Passion. Pleasure. Power.—Movie tagline

"Richly sensual."—Douglas S. Barasch, *Elle*

"Ravishing . . . wonderfully sexy."—Kathleen Murphy, *Film Comment*

"Stunningly beautiful!"—Stephen Rebello, *Movieline*

"A beautifully and artfully crafted love story from Mira Nair."—Daphne Davis, *Movies & Video*

"Luminous. Exotic. Alluring."—Janet Maslin, *New York Times*

"Drop dead beautiful, amazingly sexy!"—Bruce Williamson, *Playboy*

Box Office: $4,208,640

Although raised together, mutual jealousy causes servant Maya (Indira Varma) to ruin Princess Tara's (Sarita Choundhury) royal wedding night in the seductive *Kama Sutra: A Tale of Love.*

Indian director Mira Nair took the idea for her latest movie, *Kama Sutra: A Tale of Love*, from a short story, Waiida Tabassum's "Hand-Me-Downs." Tabassum's tale, says Nair, is "a diabolical story about a girl avenging the humiliations she suffers at the hands of a rich friend by seducing the girl's husband on her wedding night." This story line is the basis for the first fifteen minutes of Nair's film, which sets the melodramatic plot in motion.

Raj Singh: "You must hate me." Tara: "I don't love you enough to hate you."

Set in sixteenth-century India, *Kama Sutra* focuses on the interconnected lives of servant girl Maya (Indira Varma) and Princess Tara (Sarita Choudhury). The two grow up together, and although both are great beauties, Maya blossoms into a sensual beauty, while Tara becomes an inhibited, jealous harridan. When Tara meets her husband-to-be, King Raj (Naveen Andrews), she watches as his interest shifts from her to Maya. In a rage, Tara publicly humiliates her best friend and servant, spitting on Maya. Maya avenges herself on Tara by seducing Raj on their wedding night.

Director Mira Nair ran into problems with India's censors over the film's explicit sexual scenes and nudity and had to appeal to India's Supreme Court for a compromise solution.

Nair has called her movie "Shakespearean" in its reach, but after the first fifteen minutes of running time, *Kama Sutra* loses any vestiges of myth or archetype, becoming more like a Harlequin romance. Tara, of course, soon finds out about Maya's betrayal, branding Maya a whore and banishing her from the court. Maya wanders briefly in the countryside, where she soon bumps into Jai (Ramon Tikaram), a hunk who also happens to be a sculptor. The two have a brief love affair, but Jai, who sees in Maya the inspiration for his masterwork, a sculpture of a Hindu goddess, declares that he cannot have Maya act both as his mistress and his muse. At his recommendation, Maya takes up training in the Kama Sutra, the third-century Indian guide to sexual and spiritual love, at a school for courtesans run by the venerable Rasa Devi (Rekha).

When Raj Singh learns that Maya has received her training, he installs her at court as his chief courtesan. This move causes both Tara's and Jai's jealousy to surface. While Maya uses some of her tricks to soothe the distraught Tara, Jai and Raj (who has by now become a dissolute opium addict) battle it out for Maya's favors. Jai wins the battle but loses the war: he is condemned to death, which is achieved by the picturesque means of having an elephant walk over him.

Nair seems to have set out to make a modern fable set in a place far away and in a time long ago. Somehow, all of the disparate elements never gel. Her goal, she has said, was to make a film about female sexuality as empowerment, a film "about sexual politics, not sexual positions." But grafting a modern, Western message onto an ancient Indian text simply results in a weird melange of trite yet anachronistic set pieces. What does work is the languid camera work: *Kama Sutra*, filmed on location in Khajuraho, a village in central India known for its erotic temple carvings, and in Amber, near Jaipur, is a feast for the eyes. The set design and costumes are gorgeous, and so are the principle players. Especially noteworthy is Indira Varma, an actress new to Western audiences. Despite the fact that the script (by Nair and Helena Kriel) calls on her to say and do a number of quite silly things, Varma manages to bring off her portrayal of Maya with dignity and grace.

One suspects that Mira Nair was simply stretching too far to find an audience with *Kama Sutra*. Although her first two films, *Salaam Bombay*, which was nominated for an Oscar in 1988, and *Mississippi Masala* (1992), were moderately successful, her third feature film, *The Perez Family* (1995), bombed. Unable to get studio backing for her next work, Nair went back to India to make *Kama Sutra* and to raise money from European distributors by pledging her own future earnings as collateral. Once back in her home

CREDITS

Maya: Indira Varma
Tara: Sarita Choudhury
Jai: Ramon Tikaram
Raj Singh: Naveen Andrews
Rasa: Devi Rekha

Origin: India
Released: 1996
Production: Lydia Dean Pilcher and Mira Nair for Mirabai Films; released by Trimark Pictures
Direction: Mira Nair
Screenplay: Mira Nair and Helena Kriel
Cinematography: Declan Quinn
Editing: Kristina Boden
Music: Mychael Danna
Production design: Mark Friedberg
Art direction: Nitin Desai
Set decoration: Stephanie Carroll
Costumes: Eduardo Castro
Sound: Drew Kunin
MPAA rating: Unrated
Running Time: 114 minutes

land, she had to contend with demands for bribes from bureaucrats and the Indian film ratings board, which adheres to a strictly non-Western code that bans all nudity and sexual contact—even kissing. Finally, after appealing to the Indian Supreme Court, Nair worked out a compromise that allowed her to show brief flashes of nudity.

In the U.S., *Kama Sutra* was released unrated, although the MPAA only asked her to make four cuts in order to receive an "R" rating. Nair was simply too weary from making compromises, from attempting to please everybody. Her film, unfortunately, bears the scars of her prolonged effort. *Kama Sutra: A Tale of Love* promises far more than it delivers. By playing to the lowest common denominator, Nair has produced a product that is trite rather than erotic, limited instead of universal in its appeal.

—*Lisa Paddock*

AWARDS AND NOMINATIONS

Independent Spirit Awards 1997: Cinematography

REVIEWS

Boxoffice. February, 1997, p. 42.
Detroit News. March 7, 1997, p. 3D.
Entertainment Weekly. March 21, 1997, p. 55.
The Hollywood Reporter. September 17, 1997, p. 13.
Los Angeles Times. February 28, 1997, p. F12.
People. March 17, 1997, p. 21.
Sight and Sound. July, 1997, p. 43.
Variety. October 21, 1996, p. 86.

Keys to Tulsa

Murder. Blackmail. Deceit. . . . There's no place like home.—Movie tagline

" . . . a swirling, saucy mix of Southwestern intrigue."—*The Hollywood Reporter*

Whether you love him or hate him, the influence of writer/director Quentin Tarantino on the movie business cannot be overestimated. A self-professed film junkie who received his education while working in a California video store, Tarantino has, in the short span of five years, changed the landscape of filmmaking in the '90s. Although his first effort *Reservoir Dogs* [1992], failed to make any significant dents in the box-office, it has garnered one of the most loyal cult followings in movie history. Many found its extreme violence to be off-putting, but few can deny the magnitude of its visceral imprint.

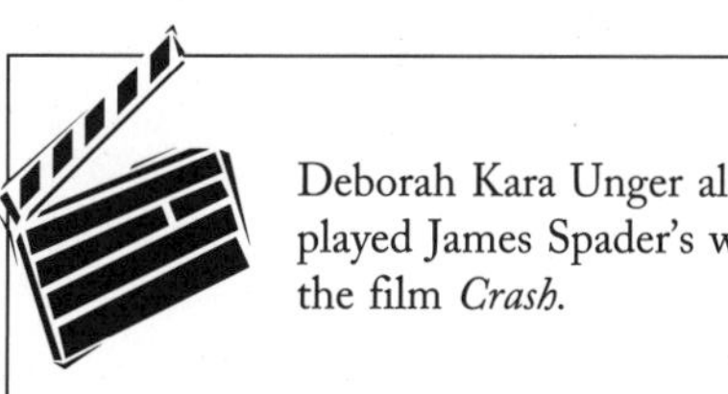

Deborah Kara Unger also played James Spader's wife in the film *Crash.*

With his 1994 project, *Pulp Fiction*, Tarantino did what few independent filmmakers could ever hope to achieve: appeal to the masses (and The Academy Of Motion Pictures Arts & Sciences) without sacrificing his artistic vision one iota. Unflinching graphic violence coupled with vignettes of drug abuse, sadomasochism, deviant homosexuality, drug abuse, armed robbery, gambling and sports fixing all surrounded with misogyny and (some say) overtly derogatory racial in-jokes. Plus, it was pieced together out of sequence and cast without one (at the time) actor who could open the film.

Just as all successful films often do; the ones launched into the commercial stratosphere, *Pulp Fiction* spawned a well-spring of lustful, rabid imitators, some good (*Things To Do In Denver When You're Dead* [1995], *2 Days In The Valley* [1996]), most others not worth mentioning. Try as it might, *Keys To Tulsa* wants to be Tarantino in the worst way but falls short on too many levels to be considered a success. It is however, a glorious failure that has many shining moments and a handful of uncharacteristically shining performances along the way. Unfortunately, the one key performance that matters the most is the least impressive.

The project is long on bizarre, colorful characters but short on any kind of cohesive, interesting plot. The film opens with Richter Boudreau (Eric Stoltz) returning home (from where or why, we're never told) to his rundown Oklahoma hovel where he halfheartedly resumes his job as a film critic at the local paper. Richter spends most of his time chasing girls and drinking, it's no wonder he gets very little actual work done. In the film's first scene, Stoltz shares an awkward romantic moment with sultry siren Cameron Diaz, who plays Trudy, a shallow gold digger. The fumbling love tryst quickly turns tepid after the lights go out (due to an unpaid electric bill) and Trudy suddenly realizes Richter's pockets aren't very deep after all. We never see her again. With the lithe chanteuse Diaz disposed of in the blink of an eye, Richter sets about re-establishing relations with assorted friends, family and lovers and eventually, almost unwittingly becomes the primary conduit in a murder/blackmail conspiracy.

Richter's been sorely missed by his friends. They're strong willed and he's weak and malleable. He trudges from one associate to another as they either bemoan their existence, missing what used to be or mold him to serve their own depraved needs. With one exception. The first stop during his homecoming tour includes a visit with his mother Cynthia played with acerbic zeal by Mary Tyler Moore. With this role as a multiple divorcee and seasoned social climber, Moore seems more determined than ever to shake her rock-solid, All-American image. Though nowhere near as good as the neurotic Manhattan grandmother in 1996's *Flirting With Disaster*, she gives further evidence that her talent is far from sweet and one-dimensional. She, too, is sorely underused.

The crux of the story centers around Richter's relationship between Ronnie Stover (James Spader), his wife Vicky Michaels Stover (Deborah Kara Unger) and Vicky's brother Keith (Michael Rooker). Spader is hard to recognize; he's dyed his hair jet black, grown his sideburns long and speaks in an affected draw that recalls the older Elvis. The Elvis-fixated Ronnie and the perpetually coquettish Vicky's formerly high society lifestyle has given way to insolvency. They now spend their time scratching, clawing and slithering their way through Tulsa's upper crust in order to keep their heads above water. Slater's Ronnie plays dumb but in actuality has a beat on what everybody else is thinking. Old flames Richter and Vicky start rekindling their tumultuous relationship, erroneously assuming that Ronnie won't notice, something they end up paying for in the long run. Ronnie used to run with Keith, an overbearing grown-up child who's doing his best to liquidate what's left of his once vast resources. Keith has a self-destructive streak a mile long and despises his sister. He puts up with her to accommodate Richter, but he's obviously not playing with a full deck.

While Richter is making time with Vicky, Ronnie is romancing Cherry (Joanna Going), a stripper who was the witness to a crime that involves a member of Tulsa's high-society and a black hooker. Going, who played the prissy, uptight debutante in *Inventing The Abbots* (1997) turns in her best performance yet as Cherry, who immediately takes a shine to Richter. Beyond his blackmail scheme, Ronnie doesn't have much use for Cherry and the feeling seems mutual. Cherry, it seems, also came from a privileged background but took a wrong turn somewhere. In many ways, she's still an innocent and makes a spiritual connection with Richter only to find out too late why she's being kept on such a short leash. Sensing his friends' weakness for flesh, Ronnie makes sure Richter and Cherry spend a lot of time together. Ronnie's ultimate goal is to use Richter's desperate need for money and inability to say no to enable him to make his "big score."

Where Tarantino and his vast array of admirers and imitators use the sprawling ennui of southern California, rookie director Leslie Grief draws on the trailer-park dwelling mentality of a rural boom town. The paper-thin level of the plot would seem more at home on a sleazy, prime-time Fox soap-opera. The crime of passion on everyone's lips isn't even hinted at until the midway point and by the end of the picture, the audience hasn't even been given an opportunity to relate to either the victim or the perpetrator. Hence, no developed sympathy or empathy for either.

As first features go, Grief could have done far worse. A major script overhaul and a little more assured direction could have risen this fragmentary, hazy tale into an offbeat, sexually-charged, political thriller classic. As uneven as it is, the cast appears to have had a fiendishly great time performing. Polygram, the distributor of *Keys To Tulsa* wasn't

CREDITS

Richter Boudreau: Eric Stoltz
Trudy: Cameron Diaz
Louise: Randy Graff
Vicky Stover: Deborah Kara Unger
Ronnie Stover: James Spader
Cynthia Bourdreau: Mary Tyler Moore
Harmon Shaw: James Coburn
Keith Michaels: Michael Rooker
Chip Carlson: Peter Strauss
Cherry: Joanna Going

Origin: USA
Released: 1997
Production: Leslie Greif and Harley Peyton for ITC Entertainment and Polygram Filmed Entertainment; released by Gramercy Pictures
Direction: Leslie Greif
Screenplay: Harley Peyton; based on the novel by Brian Fair Berkey
Cinematography: Robert Fraisse
Editing: Eric L. Beason, Louis F. Cioffi, Michael R. Miller
Music: Stephen Endelman
Production design: Derek R. Hill
Art direction: Greg Smith
Set decoration: Phil Shirey
Costumes: Marie France
Sound: David O. Daniels
MPAA rating: R
Running Time: 113 minutes

sure whether to give this project a theatrical release or send it direct-to-video. As a rule, films with a roster of talent this deep don't think twice about a wide or even limited release. The project was finished for well over a year before it saw the light of day in a theatre and again, as a rule, delaying any film for that long for any reason is too much of an artistic and commercial red flag.

Tarantino's arrival on the scene in the mid '90s gave the film industry a necessary jolt both artistically and financially. Though *Reservoir Dogs* garnered a bit of attention, *Pulp Fiction* received an unexpected windfall and caught the eye of many Hollywood executives who discovered an entirely new genre to mine. It was one where style is just as important to substance. In the case of *Keys To Tulsa*, with too much of the former and not enough of the latter, the results turned out to be merely average.

—*J.M. Clark*

REVIEWS

Boxoffice. May, 1997, p. 59.
Los Angeles Times. April 11, 1997, p. F19.
San Francisco Chronicle. April 11, 1997, p. D3.
San Francisco Examiner. April 11, 1997, p. D8.
Variety. April 7, 1997, p. 42.

Kicked in the Head

A raucous new comedy about life on the edge.—Movie tagline

"A stellar supporting cast! James Woods is the biggest kick!"—Thelma Adams, *New York Post*

A young man on an existential quest for the meaning of life stumbles along on a series of comical misadventures that lead him into the arms of an attractive older woman. Twenty-something slacker Redmond (Kevin Corrigan) claims he's on a spiritual search for truth, yet his two-bit hustler Uncle Sam (James Woods) aptly calls it a self-destructive period. Newsreel footage of the Hindenburg zeppelin voyage is a recurring image, apparently symbolic of the doom Redmond feels is imminent on his journey.

Director/co-writer Matthew Harrison: "It has to be New York. I couldn't have set this story in any other city—the mix of people that come through Redmond's life could only be found here."

Uncle Sam steals some sunglasses and a car, kicking the dog out from the passenger seat. He drives over to see "teenager," as he calls his nephew, who is evicted from his New York City apartment, which has mysteriously caught fire. Fast-talking Sam hands him a bundle to deliver at a subway station, and counsels him to call his Mom.

Clutching the plastic sack, Redmond watches a stewardess, Megan (Linda Fiorentino), crying on the train. He leaps out the doors after her, but is perfunctorily rejected. A gruff guy shoves his face at Redmond, warning him about the trouble his uncle is in, and just before snatching the parcel, another thug approaches and a shootout ensues. Neither grab the bag and Redmond is left holding it.

He crashes at a friend's place on the condition he's not involved with Uncle Sam, the "vortex of disaster." Stretch (Michael Rapaport) is a loose cannon, whose beer distribution business isn't on the up-and-up. Redmond says he's just trying to get his bearings while he researches a book. It's actually a journal of mediocre musings, poetic ramblings and sophomoric observations with lines like "hope becomes a rope dangling around my neck." Soon he's doing the drugs he botched delivering.

Over Chinese dinner, Redmond reads his fortune cookie—"Your attendant godling has lost her way"—which he believes refers to the flight attendant he's obsessing over. But Stretch insists he needs a job, offering him one with his shaky operation. Redmond laments that jobs are only for money and a place to go, as a car drives by with a gang shooting holes in Stretch's kegs.

Sam suddenly arrives, upset the cocaine never reached its destination—yet Redmond lies, insisting he made the connection. He's taken to wacky racketeer Jack (Burt Young), who says being a lowlife loser is a family trait and issues a veiled threat. In the meantime, the dumped dog from the car has been tied to a shopping cart and roams the streets, as lost as Redmond.

While shopping for a stuffed monkey for the fantasy stewardess, Redmond is approached by old girlfriend Happy (Lili Taylor). She wants to know if he's left her because he's not interested or is it a cry for help because he's crazy. His behavior indicates both are true. He's off to Stretch's party, where a neurotic carries on insipidly about the "core of love," suggesting Redmond do something insane if he's really in love. Another shootout occurs when the street gang shows up, then more tirades about nothing and more flashes to the Hindenburg blast.

Redmond arrives at the airport to present his gift to his dream woman. Ready to summarily dismiss him again, Megan gives in after Redmond reveals he believes she's his angel "attendant godling" who's forgotten her mission to restore his sight. She recognizes her weakness for boys in trouble and takes him home, missing her flight. Come the morning, she kicks him out.

CREDITS

Redmond: Kevin Corrigan
Megan: Linda Fiorentino
Stretch: Michael Rapaport
Happy: Lili Taylor
Uncle Sam: James Woods
Jack: Burt Young
Borko: Olek Krupa

Origin: USA
Released: 1997
Production: Barbara De Fina; released by October Films
Direction: Matthew Harrison
Screenplay: Matthew Harrison and Kevin Corrigan
Cinematography: John Thomas, Howard Krupa
Editing: Michael Berenbaum
Music: Stephen Endelman
Production design: Kevin Thompson
Costumes: Nina Canter
Sound: Jan McLaughlin
Set decoration: Ford Wheeler
MPAA rating: R
Running Time: 97 minutes

Jack's sidekick kidnaps Happy, motivating Redmond to finally take responsibility and hand over the drugs. Jack releases the girl, and tells them to "amscray." Sam, who's already schemed up another scam, is his own undoing when hit by a van swerving to avoid the runaway pooch. Redmond heads to the airport to reach out to his godling but when she ignores him, he gobbles a container of pills snatched from her house and runs screaming for her attention. As Megan attends to him at the bathroom toilet, tears stream down her face, and the Hindenburg travels in reverse, the fiery explosion extinguished.

Kicked in the Head is a modern tale, intended for so-called Generation-Xers, its circular plot line and outrageous absurdities a pale imitation of Quentin Tarantino's work. The indulgent script, a collaboration between director Matthew Harrison and actor Kevin Corrigan, is self-consciously clever. It's an edgy first attempt and not without interesting ideas and quirky characters—except for the pathetic protagonist.

The strong cast is wasted talent, best summed up by Roger Ebert in the *Chicago Sun-Times*: "you wish the story was about the supporting actors." Redmond's lack of direction is echoed in the meandering story and the self-fulfilling pointlessness of the film, as the title suggests.

—Roberta Cruger

REVIEWS

Detroit Free Press. September 28, 1997, p. 8H.
Los Angeles Times. September 26, 1997, p. F25.
New York Times. September 26, 1997, p. E10.
Variety. May 26, 1997, p. 70.
Village Voice. September 30, 1997, p. 86.

Kiss Me, Guido

When he answered the ad for a roommate he thought that "GWM" meant . . . "Guy With Money?"—Movie tagline

"Abounds in good-hearted humor adding up to a perfectly pleasant summer diversion. Scotti is flat-out terrific."—Kevin Thomas, *The Los Angeles Times*

"Fresh, clever and very funny!"—Jeffrey Lyons, *NBC-TV*

"*Kiss Me, Guido* has a playful comic ingenuity of its own."—Janet Maslin, *The New York Times*

"Exuberant! Sharply written characters and well-acted."—Edward Guthmann, *San Francisco Chronicle*

"A pleasant cross between *Moonstruck* and *The Birdcage*."—Andrew Johnston, *Time Out New York*

Box Office: $1,918,497

Of the four positive blurbs in an ad for *Kiss Me, Guido,* two of them contain the word "pleasant." That's about right for the movie—it's not great, it's not terrible, it's light, mildly funny, and, yes, pleasant. That critics reacted so blandly to the film is notable because this is a film that could have easily been offensive. Its whole premise depends almost entirely upon the generous use of stereotypes.

Warren to Frankie: "You're such a 'Guido'."

What kind of stereotypes? For one, the "Guido" of the title is pizza-maker Frankie Zito (Nick Scotti). "Guido" is slang for Italian guys from the Bronx. Like a modern-day version of Tony Manero of *Saturday Night Fever,* Frankie has a love of gold chains and the oeuvre of Al Pacino, Joe Pesci, Sylvester Stallone, and Robert De Niro. Calling Italian guys "Guidos" is touchy enough, but first time writer/director Tony Vitale decides to tackle stereotypes about gay men too. It's dangerous territory but the characters work and it's a testament to Vitale's skill in playing with prejudices.

In the film, we enter the life of Frankie at a moment of dissatisfaction. He's not happy with making pizza in the old neighborhood and would like to try his hand at acting (he's constantly quoting lines from his acting heroes). His plans become much more immediate when he catches his money-borrowing, girl-chasing, sleazy brother Pino (Anthony DeSando) in a very compromising position with Frankie's girlfriend.

Frankie spots a *Village Voice* ad for a Greenwich Village apartment. The ad terms are "Actors preferably" and "GWM," that is, Gay White Male. Frankie decides that GWM means Guy With Money. After suffering through various complications, Frankie ends up having to take the apartment with gay actor and choreographer, Warren (Anthony Barrile). Neither Warren nor Frankie is happy with the arrangement, but by the end of the movie, maybe, just maybe, they will learn to get along.

It's a set-up that's ripe for a lot of fun, but *Kiss Me, Guido* isn't a lot of fun, just a moderate amount of fun. A couple of scenes go in the right direction. In one, Warren and his showy, bleached-blonde friend Terry (Craig Chester) have to teach Frankie how to walk across the room like a gay man for an acting role. Terry flings his arms into the air and does his most queenly walk across the apartment. Frankie's lame attempts to temper his macho strut are some of the best moments in the film and play good-naturedly with stereotypes.

It's fun watching Frankie interact with Warren's theatre friends, like Warren's playwright ex, Dakota (Christopher Lawford), and his new flame, an actor (David Deblinger) so pretentious he now goes by an unpronounceable symbol rather than an actual name. There's a scene where Frankie, hoping to snag an acting part, meets these two at an outdoor cafe for espresso. Frankie is completely out of his depth and reacts as the semi-dopey innocent that he is. Frankie's freshness at seeing the Greenwich Village theatre life gives the audience a new perspective on the scene as well.

Writer/director Vitale exploits the differences between the two cultures when Frankie comes upon Warren curled up on the sofa watching *The Sound of Music.* "She did that before *Pretty Woman,* right?" says Frankie, confusing Julie Andrews and Julia Roberts. It's a nice moment, but just that, nice. It seems Vitale could have gone further and had more fun with the scene.

The performances in *Kiss Me, Guido* range from serviceable to quite good. Barrile is in the serviceable category as Frankie's low-key gay roomie who's searching for love. He plays the part blandly, but maybe that's the point—to have a gay character who's just a regular, even kind of boring, guy. As Frankie, Scotti has the role of the gorgeous young innocent in the film. Looks-wise, he's got it down. Scotti, who has a role on TV's "The Young and the Restless" and is also a model, is tall, dark and chiseled. He's also got the Bronx accent down (Scotti was born in Queens) and struts around like a good young Italian stallion. He plays Frankie as a mildly dense, yet ultimately sweet person.

As Frankie's brother, Pino, DeSando is the ultimate Guido. He wears shiny warm-up suits with gold chains, has a mirrored ball in his car (which is American, old and huge), and in his muscle-bearing tank tops, is constantly alert, like an animal waiting to pounce, looking for ways to take advantage of every situation. DeSando gets some of the funniest moments in the film in a side story involving Warren's sex-starved landlady, Meryl (Molly Price), where Pino gets some comeuppance.

But the best role is Chester's as the diva-like Terry. Terry is bitchy, full of life and flamboyant as he helps the unlucky-in-love Warren. By now the witty, gay friend has become a cliché, but Terry is such a fun character that it's hard to care. The other characters are quite . . . pleasant. In their slight roles as pretentious fops, Lawford and Deblinger are fine as Warren's ex Dakota and his actor/lover.

To his credit, Vitale brings the stereotypes of his characters out into the open and treats them with good humor. He seems to have a familiarity with and fondness for the settings and people in the film and this comes through in his affectionate portrayals. Vitale doesn't paint either the guidos or the gays as being superior to the other. Neither group is without moments of ridiculousness and each can learn something from the other. Vitale never gets preachy. The characters do learn about each other, but there aren't any teary group hugs or anything like that.

CREDITS

Frankie: Nick Scotti
Warren: Anthony Barrile
Pino: Anthony DeSando
Terry: Craig Chester
Joey Chips: Dominick Lombardozzi
Meryl: Molly Price
Dakota: Christopher Lawford
Actor: David Deblinger

Origin: USA
Released: 1997
Production: Ira Deutchman and Christine Vachon for Redeemable Features, Capitol Films, Kardana Films, and Swinsky Films; released by Paramount Pictures
Direction: Tony Vitale
Screenplay: Tony Vitale
Cinematography: Claudia Raschke
Editing: Alexander Hall
Production design: Jeffrey Rathaus
Costumes: Victoria Farrell
MPAA rating: R
Running Time: 91 minutes

Kiss Me, Guido, has the elements of a classic farce. There are misunderstandings (the GWM thing), mistaken identity (Frankie's mom thinks he might be gay), twists of fate (an opportune broken ankle), and facades (at one point, Frankie has to pretend to be Warren's new boyfriend). But to be a really great farce, it would have to go further. Nothing really outrageous happens. Still, for his first feature, Vitale has come up with something light, mildly funny, and well, pleasant.

—*Jill Hamilton*

REVIEWS

Boxoffice. September, 1997, p. 121.
Entertainment Weekly. August 1, 1997, p. 50.
Los Angeles Times. July 18, 1997, p. F16.
New York Times. July 18, 1997, p. C5.
People. July 28, 1997, p. 22.
San Francisco Chronicle. July 18, 1997, p. D3.
San Francisco Examiner. July 18, 1997, p. D8.
Sight and Sound. December, 1997, p. 44.
Variety. January 27, 1997, p. 76.

Kiss or Kill

The ultimate romantic getaway.—Movie tagline

"Tantalizing! Writer-director Bill Bennett keeps smartly surprising us."—Jay Carr, *Boston Globe*

"A wild sun drenched film noir!"—Robert Hoffler, *Buzz*

"A smart well-plotted thriller with a recklessly sexy performance by Frances O'Connor."—Lisa Henricksson, *GQ*

"Utterly fresh and invigorating! A refreshing change from the cliche of outlaw lovers."—Stephen Holden, *New York Times*

"A sizzling tour de force!"—Bruce Williamson, *Playboy*

"A racy thriller! Frances O'Connor really packs a wallop as a charismatic spitfire."—Jill Bernstein, *Premiere*

Box Office: $795,243

These two lovers play a deadly cat and mouse game when they blackmail a local sport's hero in the Australian film *Kiss or Kill.*

If you ignore the clunky, confusing and uninspired title (which was actually lifted from a Dylan Thomas poem), you'll unearth a low-budget, quirky, Australian love story—all fleshed out with attempted rape, pedophilia, extortion, and murder. Writer-director Bill Bennett pinches bits and pieces from other romantic, white trash/road pictures (*Natural Born Killers* [1994], *Bonnie & Clyde* [1967], *Dirty Mary Crazy Larry* [1974], *Raising Arizona* [1987], *Wild At Heart* [1990]) along the way but with some widely skewed camera angles and jittery editing techniques, he creates a unique picture that pulls off a near impossible feat. His two romantic leads have virtually no conscience and no concern for anyone but themselves. Either or both could be a sociopathic killer and all we want to do is wrap our arms around them, take them home, and nurse them through this tiny rough spot in their lives. We cheer their blind devotion to each other. Creating likable characters with disgusting, abhorrent characteristics is not easy and Bennett succeeds in never letting the audience forget that they're watching a love story.

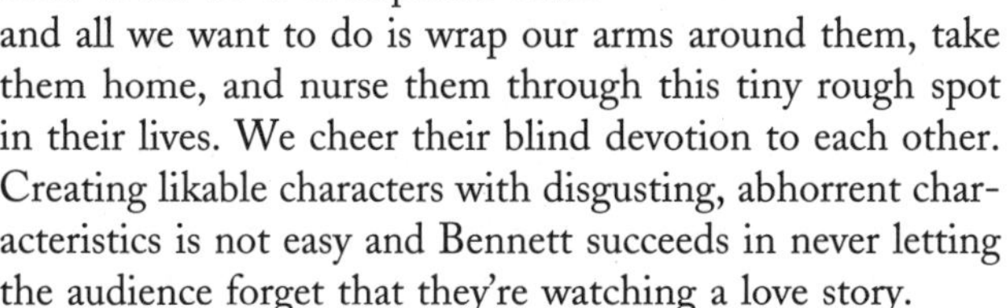

Frances O'Connor and Matt Day were also featured in *Love and Other Catastrophes.*

Matt Day and Frances O'Connor are Al and Nikki, two small-time grifters who specialize in plying married business men with liquor and the prospect of fleeting sex. Once they've been properly loosened up, the victims are attacked in their own hotel rooms and relieved of their valuables. Soon after one of Nikki's drunk and amorous gentlemen expires, the pair surreptitiously discover a video in the victim's briefcase that shows former rugby superstar, Zipper Doyle (Barry Langrishe), in a number of repugnant bedroom "vignettes." Quite by accident, Al and Nikki come to one rather obvious conclusion: it would be infinitely more lucrative to blackmail a nationally known (and respected) sports legend then to continue risking life and limb by scamming traveling, middle-aged business types.

With two very wily detectives, an ominous stranger and Zipper himself chasing them, Al and Nikki hit the road, leaving even more bodies in their wake. Despite being in each other's presence nearly 24 hours a day, Al and Nikki begin suspecting each other of the dastardly deeds that take place in their close company. Bennett calls the lovers (and business partners) to task by having them doubt the other's motives and irrational actions. They are seemingly in pursuit of the same goal; why would the other risk capture and sabotage everything without their partner's knowledge and consent? Much in the same manner of the Coen Brothers' *Blood Simple* [1985], Bennett creates an air of palpable paranoia that causes the guilty parties to begin stewing in their own juices.

The performances by Day and O'Connor are astounding. Having teamed up earlier in the year on *Love & Other Catastrophes* (1997), they both possess that wide-eyed, fresh-faced appearance that makes it easy for them to succeed in assorted confidence scams. While Bennett does little to explain anything from Al's past, Nikki's is examined in vividly disturbing detail. In a flashback sequence, Nikki the toddler is seen playing with her mother in relative tranquillity. Her mother answers a call at the door and is set on fire by a man, one we can assume has been jilted. This goes far to explain Nikki's inherit distrust of men. If only Bennett had given us a similar look into Al's past, his image of the tainted lovers would have been complete. The proclivity to overact or slip into self-parody in a situation like this is high; Day and O'Connor must retain a sense of danger and manic disregard without losing their teetering grasp on reality. Successful cinematic anti-heroes must have everyday, seemingly mundane traits with whom members of the mainstream populous can readily identify. Day and O'Connor keep the picture firmly grounded.

Kiss Or Kill is far removed from anything resembling mainstream cinema but still manages to deliver bits and pieces of romance, comedy, action/adventure, and film noir.

AWARDS AND NOMINATIONS

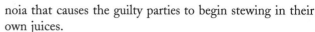

Australian Film Institute 1997: Best Film, Director (Bennett), Supporting Actor (Gilbert), Editing, Sound
Nominations: Original Screenplay, Cinematography, Costumes, Actress (O'Connor), Actor (Day)

CREDITS

Nikki Davis: Frances O'Connor
Al Fletcher: Matt Day
Detective Hummer: Chris Haywood
Adler Jones: Barry Otto
Stan: Max Cullen
Detective Crean: Andrew S. Gilbert
Zipper Doyle: Barry Langrishe

Origin: Australia
Released: 1997
Production: Bill Bennett and Jennifer Bennett for Australian Film Fiance Corporation; released by October Films
Direction: Bill Bennett
Screenplay: Bill Bennett
Cinematography: Malcolm McCulloch
Editing: Henry Dangar
Production design: Andrew Plummer
Costumes: Ruth de la Lande
Sound: Wayne Pashley, Toivo Lember
MPAA rating: R
Running Time: 95 minutes

It is an amalgamation of styles that will most certainly rub many the wrong way. It shows two lovers who battle their own dreary pasts, keep (often deadly) secrets from each other, and break the law in order to keep their heads above water. Bennett never once lets up with the level of doubt. Up to and including the last frame, we're never sure who the real killer is, who has the hidden agenda or who might crack under the mounting pressure. Bennett's twisted little love story is a double-edged sword; it has the capacity to make you feel warm and fuzzy all over while still managing to dig deep, making your skin crawl.

—*J.M. Clark*

REVIEWS

Boxoffice. November, 1997, p. 119.
Entertainment Weekly. November 21, 1997, p. 102.
GQ. November, 1997, p. 135.
Los Angeles Times. November 14, 1997, p. F16.
New York Times. October 2, 1997, p. E5.
People. November 24, 1997, p. 20.
Variety. June 30, 1997, p. 66.
Village Voice. November 18, 1997, p. 85.

Kiss the Girls

A detective is searching for a deadly collector. His only hope is the woman who got away.—Movie tagline

"*Kiss the Girls* is a taut, riveting thriller!"—Sam Hallenbeck, *FIX-TV*

"*Kiss* is a rollicking roller-coaster ride of thrills and chills."—Anne Marie O'Connor, *Mademoiselle*

"A thriller with intelligence. Judd and Freeman give remarkable performances."—Jim Ferguson, *Prevue Channel*

Box Office: $59,685,118

The job of a police forensic psychologist is to get into the mind of whoever you're studying. If it's a woman who has just killed her husband and is about to kill herself, the forensic psychologist must deduce that her husband was a drunken brute and the wife's killing him was justified. If it's a serial kidnapper who sometimes kills, the forensic psychologist must determine the "whys" of the criminal's behavior. It's all logical and analytical work . . . until one villain makes it personal.

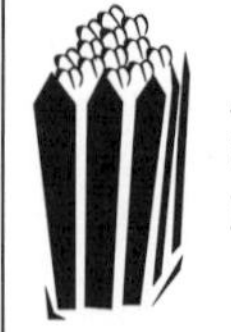

Alex Cross: "I don't think killing is his ulterior motive. He's a collector."

Dr. Alex Cross (Morgan Freeman) is that forensic psychologist who is forced to turn his deductive abilities on a case involving his own niece Naomi (Gina Ravera). Naomi has been missing for four days so Alex goes to Durham, N.C. to help in the search. He soon finds out, however, that Naomi is not the only missing girl. In fact, she's just one of eight missing women. And they have common characteristics: beautiful, bright, talented, independent, extraordinary.

Working with the local authorities, Nick Ruskin (Cary Elwes) and Davey Sikes (Alex McArthur), one of the girls is soon discovered . . . dead. She's the second one found tied to a tree in the dense Durham woods by a killer who calls himself Casanova. For Alex the question becomes why has Casanova killed these two of the eight girls he has kidnapped and can he discover who the killer is before Naomi is found tied to a tree?

Not long after Alex's arrival, another woman is abducted. Kate McTiernan (Ashley Judd) is a local doctor with a penchant for kick boxing. One night her rural home is invaded and Kate drugged. When she awakens, she finds herself in a subterranean cell where her kidnapper presents himself disguised in a mask and telling her not to call out or try to escape. Kate, however, is nobody's puppet and she immediately makes contact with the other women Casanova has incarcerated in the cells below ground. She also violates his no-escape rule by making a run for it. She races through the woods and is forced to jump off a cliff into a river. Her escape is successful, but she is injured and traumatized.

It doesn't take long for Alex to interview Kate and learn that Naomi is alive. He also begins to piece together information about the man who is collecting these self-reliant women with the goal of making them subservient to his own whims. Clues eventually lead the pair to a plastic surgeon in California where an eerily similar series of kidnappings undertaken by someone called "The Gentleman Caller" is also taking place. Are The Gentleman Caller and Casanova the same man? Or are they co-conspirators, competing with each other in a sick little game?

There is one thing that is absolutely certain about this dark suspense film, it would have been nowhere near as good as it is without the commanding presence of Morgan Freeman. A superb actor who brings dignity and intelligence to every part he plays, Freeman is always a pleasure to watch as he infuses his characters with believability. Along with his sense of conviction and integrity, Freeman can also infuse kindness into his characters with just a look. Taken all together, it's a powerful package that can make even the most mundane story immensely watchable.

The Alex Cross character is also featured in the novels *Along Came A Spider*, *Jack & Jill*, and *Cat & Mouse.*

Proving to be equally as strong as a screen presence is Ashley Judd. She will never be the damsel who dithers in distress and cowers in the corner until her knight in shining armor arrives to rescue her. Her characters, too, are endowed with intelligence and power just because she is playing the role.

If there is a weakness to *Kiss the Girls*, it is in the exploitive story. Comparisons to a previous Freeman film, *Seven*, will legitimately raise the "rip off" banner for some viewers. Yes, both focus on police who are on the path of an elusive and kinky serial killer who "bonds" with his pursuers and sends them cryptic messages, but *Kiss the Girls* is not the same movie.

Adapted from the best-selling novel by James Patterson (the second featuring Dr. Alex Cross), *Kiss the Girls* too often fails to weave all the threads of its story neatly together, especially the California strand of the story. As a final insult, it is fairly easy to guess who Casanova is and yet, at the same time, we feel cheated when we're proved correct.

Directed by Gary Fleder (*Things to Do in Denver When You're Dead*), *Kiss the Girls* has its share of problems (and more than its share of detracting critics), but the intelligent performances of Judd and Freeman make this a better film than one might be led to believe by the reviews.

—Beverley Bare Buehrer

CREDITS

Alex Cross: Morgan Freeman
Kate McTiernan: Ashley Judd
Nick Ruskin: Cary Elwes
Davey Sikes: Alex McArthur
Will Rudolph: Tony Goldwyn
Kyle Craig: Jay O. Sanders
Sampson: Bill Nunn
Dr. Wick Sachs: William Converse-Roberts
Chief Hatfield: Brian Cox
Seth Samuel: Richard T. Jones
Henry Castillo: Jeremy Piven
Naomi Cross: Gina Ravera

Origin: USA
Released: 1997
Production: David Brown and Joe Wizan for Rysher Entertainment; released by Paramount Pictures
Direction: Gary Fleder
Screenplay: David Klass; based on the novel by James Patterson
Cinematography: Aaron Schneider
Editing: William Steinkamp, Harvey Rosenstock
Production design: Nelson Coates
Art direction: Joseph Hodges
Set decoration: Linda Lee Sutton
Costumes: Abigail Murray
Sound: Lee Orloff
Music: Mark Isham
MPAA rating: R
Running Time: 120 minutes

REVIEWS

Detroit Free Press. October 3, 1997, p. 5D.
Entertainment Weekly. October 10, 1997, p. 67.
Los Angeles Times. October 3, 1997, p. F12.
New York Times. October 3, 1997, p. E14.
People. October 13, 1997, p. 19.
Rolling Stone. October 30, 1997, p. 73.
Sight and Sound. March, 1998, p. 51.
Variety. September 15, 1997, p. 69.
Washington Post Weekend. October 3, 1997, p. 18.

Kissed

"A film to really die for."—Brandon Judell, *Detour*

"Daring and brilliant."—Henry Beck, *Newhouse News*

"*Kissed* is a remarkable achievement, offering an understanding of matters unthinkable that will haunt you for a good long time."—Peter Travers, *Rolling Stone*

"Eerily gripping."—John Powers, *Vogue*

From early childhood, Sandra (Molly Parker) is obsessed with dead bodies. She and a playmate engage in rituals to bury dead birds and the young Sandra (Natasha Morley) anoints herself lovingly with a bloody carcass of a chipmunk. By the time she is a teenager, her fascination with death has her working at what could only be described as nirvana: a funeral parlor. It is here that Sandra (now played by Molly Parker) transcends the boundaries into sexual perversion and becomes a full-fledged necrophiliac.

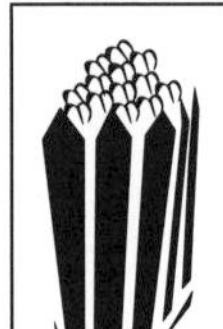

Sandra: "Crossing over was glorious and overwhelming. It was absolutely addictive."

Canadian filmmaker Lynne Stopkewich caused quite a stir at the Toronto Film Festival when her feature debut, *Kissed*, was screened. Adapted from the short story that appeared in an anthology of women's erotica, "We So Seldom Look on Love" by fellow Canadian Barbara Gowdy, it is a tale of a young, attractive woman who attempts to convey her passion for necrophilia. Told primarily through voice-over narration, as well as some symbolic visual interpretations, *Kissed* is as much a tale of spirituality as it is of sexuality.

Working for her father (Tim Dixon) at the family floral shop, Sandra makes a delivery to the Wallis Funeral home and knows instantly that this is where she belongs. When Mr. Wallis (Jay Brazeau) demonstrates the fine art of embalming, Sandra stares transfixed, her face a mixture of repulsion and fascination.

After her first erotic experience atop one of the funeral parlor's dead clientele, Sandra embraces what she feels is her true calling. When she meets a handsome young medical student, Matt (Peter Outerbridge) at the local diner, he becomes fascinated with her fascination. And when he learns of her sexual proclivities, he finds himself sexually excited by Sandra and becomes her first—and only—living, breathing lover.

But Sandra is unable to find sexual satisfaction with Matt and jealousy begins to eat away at him when he discovers that Sandra is still seeking ecstasy from the handsome young men who lie stone-cold on the slabs at Wallis Funeral Home (where, strangely enough, the funeral director himself has a fondness for the boyish corpses).

There is an undercurrent of sly humor that runs through *Kissed*. But director Lynne Stopkewich carefully threads the fine line between acknowledging that this is far from normal behavior and that of overt mockery. The story is surprisingly restrained and respectful.

Ms. Stopkewich is not explicit in the depiction of the sexual acts, choosing instead to portray the emotional content, rather than the physical. The scenes have a poetic and otherworldly feel to them, while the mechanics of exactly how Sandra is able to "excite" her dead companions into "active participation" remains a bit of a mystery.

Molly Parker gives a powerful performance as the young necrophiliac. She imbues her character with an eerie warmth and charm and her haunting interpretation helps to smooth over the obvious potentially alienating quirks in her character.

The dialogue is too often laden with such poetic and girlish metaphors as "It's like looking into the sun without going blind" or "It's like diving into a lake: sudden cold, then silence." But director Stopkewich displays her skill when she manages to make another character look even more perverse than Sandra. Matt, his jealousy towards Sandra's other lovers growing out of control, dresses up in a suit and paints his face in ghoulish makeup. Sandra is puzzled, until he lies prone on the bed and crosses his arms over his chest. Sandra is appalled—and so are we.

What makes this scene so important is that we, the audience, have accepted that Sandra's affection for the dead is genuine. It is not mere sexual perversion, it is more. She talks of "crossing over" as she draws her parallels between sexual orgasm and death, and she coos lovingly as she strokes the men's hands and faces, "You're so cold. That's okay." When she first has sex in the mortuary, it seems like the natural extension of her feelings, albeit extreme.

While some viewers may find the subject material offensive and in poor taste, *Kissed* is powerful in its ability to humanize such an offbeat main character as Sandra. Director Stopkewich maintains a tone that is consistently non-judg-

AWARDS AND NOMINATIONS

Genie Awards 1997: Actress (Parker)

CREDITS

Sandra Larson: Molly Parker
Matt: Peter Outerbridge
Mr. Wallis: Jay Brazeau
Young Sandra: Natasha Morley
Carol: Jessie Winter Mudie
Jan: James Timmons

Origin: Canada
Released: 1996
Production: Dean English and Lynne Stopkewich for Boneyard Film and British Columbia Film; released by Goldwyn Entertainment Company
Direction: Lynne Stopkewich
Screenplay: Angus Fraser and Lynne Stopkewich; based on the short story "We So Seldom Look on Love" by Barbara Gowdy
Cinematography: Greg Middleton
Editing: John Pozer, Peter Roeck, Lynne Stopkewich
Production design: Eric McNab
Sound: Marti Richa, Susan Taylor
Music: Don MacDonald
MPAA rating: Unrated
Running Time: 80 minutes

mental and compassionate, never succumbing to the potential exploitation of Sandra, never allowing the focus to shift away from the emotional experience. While Ms. Stopkewich may have erred on the poetic and impressionistic side, the casting of Molly Parker, with her beatific calm, saves the film from sinking under the weight of the material. Reviews for the film were understandably mixed, while comparisons to David Cronenberg's kinky *Crash* (1997) were inevitable.

—*Patricia Kowal*

REVIEWS

Boxoffice. November, 1996, p. 134.
Chicago Sun-Times. April 25, 1997.
Chicago Tribune. May 16, 1997.
Cinemafantastique. May, 1997, p. 56.
Entertainment Weekly. April 25, 1997, p. 48.
Filmmaker. Spring, 1997, p. 35.
Los Angeles Times. April 18, 1997, p. F6.
New York Times. April 18, 1997, p. C18.
Rolling Stone. May 1, 1997, p. 58.
San Francisco Chronicle. April 18, 1997, p. D3.
San Francisco Examiner. April 18, 1997, p. D3.
Sight and Sound. January, 1998, p. 47.
USA Today. May 1, 1997, p. 3D.
Variety. September 16, 1996, p. 69.

Kolya

The perfect grouch is about to meet his match - a five-year-old kid named *Kolya.*—Movie tagline

"A can't-miss crowd-pleaser!"—Kevin Thomas, *Los Angeles Times*

"Radiant . . . A gem of a film!"—Janet Maslin, *New York Times*

"A triumph!"—Bruce Williamson, *Playboy*

"I loved *Kolya* for helping to keep my love of film alive!"—Joe Morgenstern, *The Wall Street Journal*

Box Office: $5,792,325

It is not too surprising that the Czech production *Kolya*, a story about a reluctant stepfather and an adorable abandoned five-year-old, would be a popular hit in the Czech

Winner of the 1996 Oscar for best foreign film, *Kolya* tells the story of how five-year-old Kolya (Andrej Chalimon) melts the heart of bitter concert cellist Frantisek Louka (Zdenek Sverak).

Republic. Less predictably, *Kolya* has proven to be a favorite of film critics worldwide. Director Jan Sverak has managed the enviable feat of appealing to such a broad spectrum of viewers by making *Kolya* a many-layered treat, not only pairing an irresistible orphan with a middle-aged grouch, but mixing pathos with the political.

Five-year-old Andrej Chalimon was discovered in a Russian kindergarten a month before filming was scheduled to start.

For starters, *Kolya* is set in Prague in 1988, when the Soviets were on the verge of losing their grip on Eastern Europe. (In order to achieve the right look, the director was obliged to "dirty up" the Czech capital by parking fifteen-year-old cars on leaf and litter strewn streets.) As the middle-aged confirmed bachelor father, Frantisek Louka, Jan Sverak cast his father, the noted Czech actor, Zdenek Sverak. Louka ia a formerly famous musician, a cellist who once played with the Czech Philharmonic and now is reduced to freelancing at events such as ill-attended cremations. If *Kolya* were meant to be a real tearjerker, Louka would have lost his position because of political dissent. But director Sverak adopted a light touch, reducing the musician's rebellion to a offhand but offensive remark accidentally overheard by a bureaucrat who saw to it that Louka was fired. As *Kolya* opens, Louka is getting by—but just barely. He needs, more than anything else, the funds to buy a car that will enable him to get around to his various far-flung gigs.

A friend proposes a solution: a Russian woman who needs papers in order to stay in Czechoslovakia will pay handsomely for a marriage of convenience. Louka reluctantly agrees, but as soon as the formalities are over, the woman flees to East Germany to join her lover. In her wake, she leaves behind five-year-old Kolya (Andrej Chalimon) who, after his elderly aunt dies, is virtually abandoned. He shows up on Louka's doorstep with untied shoelaces, a runny nose, and a tiny suitcase. He speaks only Russian, and refuses to speak to Louka (who speaks no Russian) or even to shake his hand.

For his part, Louka is equally reluctant to take up the relationship. He knows nothing of children and cares even less, and the one person in the world to whom he is truly devoted, his aged mother, hates Russians. Louka is stuck: if he reveals the true nature of his liaison with the boy's mother, he will be in even more hot water with the authorities. Nonetheless, he is so desperate to maintain the equilibrium of his existence that he does try to fob Kolya off on the state child welfare agency. Red tape, naturally, thwarts this maneuver, and the boy stays on.

Louka does his best to carry on with his old life, but Kolya's presence obliges him to make some accommodations. A confirmed seducer of other men's wives (he wants, above all things, to avoid commitment), Louka's interactions with these lovers undergo considerable alteration. When Kolya becomes disconsolate, Louka telephones one of these mistresses so that she can tell the boy a bedtime story in his own language. And when Kolya is sick, Louka calls on yet another lover to nurse the boy back to health.

This is not to say that Kolya deprives Louka of a sex life. *Kolya* is very much a European film, and the same habits of stealth and irony that enabled the Czechs to live so long under Soviet rule provide Louka with the means of coping with his own Russian invasion. In short, the boy and the bachelor reach an accommodation.

Meanwhile, in the background to this central action, the Soviets are beginning to lose their hold on Czechoslovakia, but Louka is becoming so caught up in his own domestic drama that he seems almost not to notice. Visiting his mother in the countryside, Louka becomes alarmed when Kolya strikes up a conversation with some members of the Red Army whose tank is parked outside. Absorbed with the effort of keeping up a front, Louka fails to understand that the Russians are evacuating; his only concern is that Kolya's true identity will be discovered, an eventuality that could deprive Louka of his money, his liberty and, of course, the boy.

It is this last, of course, that begins to assume the utmost importance in Louka's life. We are treated to scenes such as one in which Louka and Kolya get separated in the subway, only to be emotionally reunited. Under a less adept director, such scenes would seem obligatory and manipulative. But Sverak manages to keep his film from being inundated with sentiment, while at the same time entertaining a theme of personal versus political freedom with such finesse that it never becomes strident.

In the end, of course, the Czechs undergo their Velvet Revolution, and as a consequence, Kolya's mother is able to return to Prague and reclaim her son. Louka does not blame her, and neither does the film. It is a bittersweet ending for Louka, but he has learned something profound about himself, and when we last glimpse him, he has resumed his proper place in society. As the Czech Philharmonic plays the national epic, Smetana's "Ma vlast" ("My Fatherland"), Louka plays his part, once again a member of the orchestra. The ease with which the Czechs picked up the threads of their lives after the fall of the Berlin Wall helps to prevent this finale from seeming too pat.

AWARDS AND NOMINATIONS

Academy Awards 1996: Foreign Language Film
Golden Globe Awards 1997: Foreign Language Film

Kolya is itself the product of a father-son collaboration. Jan Sverak, looking for an acting vehicle for his father, lighted on the idea for *Kolya* after talking to his friend Paul Taussig, who had written a synopsis about a relationship between a librarian and a young boy. The elder Sverak then wrote the screenplay for the film, transforming many of the elements of the original story in order to accommodate his own grizzled but virile image. The success of *Kolya*, however, would still rest on the slight shoulders of a boy barely past the age of toilet training. Casting the title character proved difficult. Even after hiring a Russian casting company and making five trips with his father to Russia, Jan Sverak still had no Kolya. The production found Andrej Chalimon only after the director instructed his scouts to look for the biggest troublemakers in the Russian kindergartens they visited.

Andrej Chalimon was an inspired choice. Like Kolya, he spoke no Czech, and like Kolya, he was adorable. He had to learn to act, of course, and he did so admirably, summoning up tears on queue when filming a heart-tugging scene in which the until then nearly speechless Kolya pretends to talk with his absent "Babushka" over a handheld shower which the boy employs as a telephone. Once he learned how to cry on-screen, Andrej began to inquire each morning if the day's shooting would require more tears. His Kolya is, indeed, a somber little boy, a waif who appears to be just as reluctant as Louka is to enter into a relationship with a foreigner. All smiles in the company of Russian soldiers who speak his language, Kolya spends much of the time he is with Louka staring mutely out of the window. And in the course of being lugged around by Louka—from crematorium to assignation—Kolya learns some peculiar lessons from his surrogate parent, a point brought home when Louka opens one of the makeshift coffins that Kolya plays with only to discover inside a pair of black lace panties. This discovery is both amusing and terribly sad—it is one of the events that forces Louka to reevaluate his life.

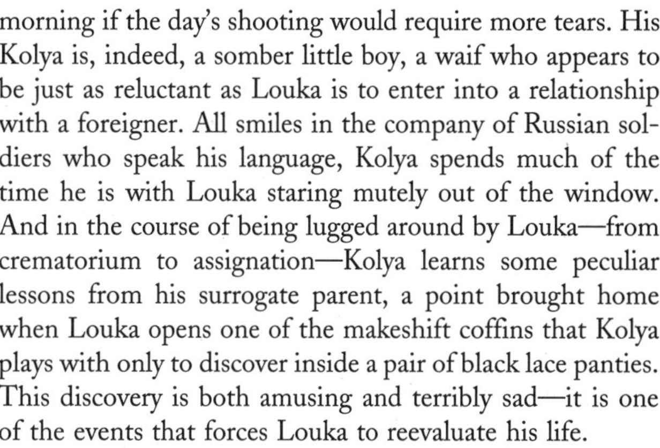

As played by Zdenek Sverak, Louka is at first a self-centered individual who is set in his ways and who has learned all manner of techniques for getting around authority and preserving his own personal status quo. Beset with a momentary urge for company, he rings up one married female acquaintance after another in hopes of finding one who is alone for the evening. Such escapades represent all he knows of freedom—and all he wants to know. Like his native land, he had learned to distrust the larger world, and his attitude towards life is one of irony, even cynicism. But like many of his countrymen, his mistrust of others has not hardened into rigid rejectionism. Even as he chastises his ward for being like all other "expansionist" Russians, he bends down to tie the little boy's shoelace. When national liberation comes, Louka has evolved to the point where he has learned to love someone other than himself. Forced to part with Kolya, he has nevertheless gained a portion of magnanimity that allows him to let the little boy go and embrace life instead.

—*Lisa Paddock*

CREDITS

Frantisek Louka: Zdenek Sverak
Kolya: Andrej Chalimon
Klara: Libuse Safrankova
Mr. Broz: Ondrez Vetchy
Mother: Stella Zazvorkvova

Origin: Czech Republic
Released: 1996
Production: Eric Abraham and Jan Sverak; released by Miramax Films
Direction: Jan Sverak
Screenplay: Zdenek Sverak
Cinematography: Vladimir Smutny
Editing: Alois Fisarek
Music: Ondrej Soukup
Production design: Milos Kohout
MPAA rating: PG-13
Running Time: 110 minutes

REVIEWS

Boxoffice. December, 1996, p. 50.
Chicago Tribune. January 31, 1997, p. 5.
Entertainment Weekly. March 7, 1997, p. 50.
Los Angeles Times. January 24, 1997, p. F1.
New York Times. January 19, 1997, p. H35.
New York Times. January 24, 1997, p. C3.
People. April 4, 1997, p. 19.
Sight and Sound. May, 1997, p. 46.
USA Today. February 13, 1997, p. 4D.
Village Voice. January 28, 1997, p. 68.

Kull the Conqueror

Courage conquers all.—Movie tagline

"Exciting, fun and sexy."—Marise Nazzaro, *Entertainment Asylum*

"Fun . . . fantasy-adventure."—Kevin Thomas, *Newsday*

"Visually engaging. Kevin Sorbo is dashing."—Peter Stack, *San Francisco Chronicle*

"*Kull* is cool."—Liz Braun, *The Toronto Sun*

Box Office: $6,108,763

Call *Kull,* as lead actor Kevin Sorbo does, 'Conan Lite.' If you're a fan of pulp writer extraordinaire Robert E. Howard you will know that Kull will indeed father Conan, as Howard fathered their brutal barbarian world in his fiction. Unlike the early '80s Conan movies, however, the PG-13 rating for this film keeps the gore to a minimum (no lopped limbs or spurting blood, though Kull does a lot of damage with that two-headed axe). Film opens with a brief explanation that the god Valka defeated Akivasha, the red witch of Acheron, but left an eternal flame burning as a reminder of her godless times. Acheron is now the kingdom of Valusia, where the low-caste Kull is literally battling for a place in the elite dragon guard of Taligaro (Thomas Ian Griffith), the king's commander. The fight scenes (which usually have the hunky Sorbo bare-chested) are accompanied by a *very annoying* and cliched heavy metal guitar soundtrack. The fight between the rivals is halted by a messenger announcing that current Valusian king, Borna (Sven Ole Thorsen), has taken to slaughtering his would-be heirs to the throne. When the king provokes Kull into a sword fight, Kull delivers a fatal blow but the mad monarch bequeaths his throne to the barbarian with his dying breath.

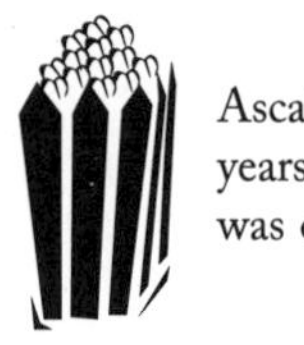

Ascalante: "Your bride is 3,000 years-old." Kull: "She told me she was only 19."

Raffaella De Laurentiis also produced 1981's *Conan the Barbarian* and its 1984 sequel *Conan the Destroyer. Kull the Conqueror* was initially developed in 1989 as a second Conan sequel.

Naturally this does not go over well with the ruling nobility, including Taligaro, who expected to inherit himself. Taligaro hooks up with a wizard to re-animate the evil spirit of Akivasha (Tia Carrere), who wants to make Acheron rise again. Meanwhile, Kull's enjoying some of the perks of kingship, including the attentions of slave girl Zareta (Karina Lombard), who's also a fortune-teller and once predicted for Kull that he would be king at the hands of a king. Now her cards foretell a dangerous quest and Kull's betrayal by a kiss. The betrayal comes swiftly—passed off as nobility Akivasha mesmerizes Kull into marriage and a kiss in their marriage bed leaves Kull seemingly lifeless. But taken by Kull's physical charms, Akivasha has Kull imprisoned in her temple instead and a substitute body readied for the royal funeral (the jealous Akivasha even manages to accuse Zareta of murder, thus getting rid of her rival for the big lug's affections).

Kull escapes, hooks up with Valka's priest Ascalante (Litefoot), who's conveniently Zareta's brother, rescues the girl, and the trio head off (via pirate ship) for Valka's Isle of Ice. Ascalante's told Kull that only the breath of Valka can defeat the fiery sorceress. Akivasha sends Taligaro and his men after them. Zareta's cards have told her that "the cause is the carrier" and it turns out that only she can enter Valka's icy temple without immediately being turned into a Popsicle. Since one woman was the reason for Valusia's trouble only another can provide the means of its salvation. Literally breathing in Valka's spirit, Zareta turns into an ice maiden (contrasting with Akivasha's fire demon) but Taligaro makes the scene, kills Ascalante, grabs Zareta, and after battling Kull once again, traps the hunk in Valka's ice chamber.

Back at Valusia, Akivasha has entered her eternal flame to regain her demon form. Taligaro believes that if he can shove Zareta in there with her, Valka's icy breath will extinguish the flame and destroy Akivasha. But when he tries, nothing happens. Kull (having naturally escaped the ice chamber) arrives to fight Taligaro, this time defeating him with his trusty two-headed axe, which is "how a barbarian fights." Since Zareta's predicted all along that the fate of the kingdom rests within a kiss, she kisses Kull, transferring Valka's breath into him. Akivasha, now in oozing demon form, is demanding a kiss from her 'husband,' Kull obliges, and destroys the demon, her flame, and any chance for Acheron to rise again. Kull's restored to power

CREDITS

Kull: Kevin Sorbo
Akivasha: Tia Carrere
Taligaro: Thomas Ian Griffith
Ascalante: Litefoot
Zareta: Karina Lombard
Tu: Roy Brocksmith
Juba: Harvey Fierstein
Enaros: Edward Tudor-Pole
Ducalon: Douglas Henshall
King Borna: Sven Ole Thorsen

Origin: USA
Released: 1997
Production: Raffaella De Laurentiis; released by Universal Pictures
Direction: John Nicolella
Screenplay: Charles Edward Pogue; based on the characters created by Robert E. Howard
Cinematography: Rodney Charters
Editing: Dallas Puett
Music: Joel Goldsmith
Production design: Benjamin Fernandez
Art direction: Pier-Luigi Basile
Costumes: Thomas Casterline, Sibylle Ulsamer
Sound: Reinhard Stergar
Special effects supervisor: Kit West
Visual effects supervisor: Richard Malzahn
Makeup effects: Giannetto de Rossi
Fight coordinators: Jerry Poteet, Fran Joseph
Stunt coordinator: Paul Weston
MPAA rating: PG-13
Running Time: 95 minutes

in Valusia, takes Zareta as his bride, and declares "By this axe, I rule."

Filmed on the same ruggedly beautiful locations in Slovakia and Croatia as producer Raffaella De Laurentiis' previous film *Dragonheart, Kull the Conqueror* is a not-unworthy entry to the sword-and-sorcery genre. Not as campy (or as anachronistic) as Sorbo's "Hercules: The Legendary Journeys" TV series, the movie still provides its share of humor and the fight scenes are generally impressive. Some mild profanity, some sexual suggestiveness (Kull does a certain amount of bed-rolling), and women's costumes that consist primarily of cleavage and/or diaphanous drapery, may not make this a film for the *entire* family but for young teens and above it's not an unpleasant way to spend an hour-and-a-half.

—*Christine Tomassini*

REVIEWS

Chicago Tribune. August 29, 1997, p. 5.
Cinemafantastique. September, 1997, p. 10.
Entertainment Weekly. September 12, 1997, p. 114.
Los Angeles Times. August 29, 1997, p. F12.
Los Angeles Times Online. September 4, 1997.
New York Times. August 29, 1997, p. C12.
People. September 15, 1997, p. 27.
San Francisco Examiner. August 29, 1997, p. D3.
USA Today. August 29, 1997, p. 3D.
Variety. August 25, 1997, p. 73.

Kundun

The destiny of a people lives in the heart of a boy.—Movie tagline

"If it's ravishing filmmaking you want, search no further than *Kundun*."—David Ansen, *Newsweek*

"Two thumbs up!"—*Siskel & Ebert*

"This is rapture in pictures."—Richard Corliss, *Time*

"A remarkable achievement!"—Mike Clark, *USA Today*

Kundun (pronounced koon-doon) opened Christmas Day in New York and Los Angeles in order to be eligible for 1997's Academy Awards and other honors. The film had received international publicity because the Chinese government tried to get it suppressed. *Kundun* depicts Communist China as a ruthless force determined to stamp out every vestige of a superior culture and turn Tibet into a colony.

Unable to get the American government to persuade the Walt Disney Company to shelve the film, the Chinese tried hinting directly to company heads that it might jeopardize penetration of the potentially lucrative Chinese market. The Disney response was firm—if not exactly courageous. "We have an agreement to distribute the film," read their terse public response, "and we will honor it." The media praised Disney's refusal to kowtow. A United Features Syndicate cartoon showed Mickey Mouse blocking a line of enormous Red Chinese tanks, recalling the student who confronted the tanks during the 1989 uprising. Disney's top brass, however, may have been motivated by more pragmatic considerations than belief in "mouse power" or sympathy for an underdog.

> Martin Scorsese: "I began to realize I wanted to make films that depict the culture of the people. You get that in *Mean Streets,* you get it in *GoodFellas,* and I believe you get it in *Kundun.*"

Kundun is something of an anomaly, an American feature film without American actors or actresses. The cast is composed almost entirely of Tibetan nonprofessionals. The only prominent American is Martin Scorsese, who directed such films as *Mean Streets* (1973), *Taxi Driver* (1976), *Raging Bull* (1980), *The Last Temptation of Christ* (1988), *GoodFellas* (1990), *The Age of Innocence* (1993), and *Casino* (1995). Disney may have been testing the commercial possibilities of what might be called "runaway productions." If such "American" films as *Kundun* were to become popular, they could generate greater returns on investment. Disney might find it feasible to subsidize and distribute similar ambitious, state-of-the-art films without having to woo increasingly expensive, increasingly temperamental superstars or deal with the powerful Hollywood guilds and unions.

Critical response in New York and Los Angeles was mixed. The film seems more like a travelogue than a dramatic epic. Emanuel Levy of *Variety* concluded that it "emerges as a movie that's hypnotic without being truly compelling, sensuously stunning but not illuminating." Viewers feel as if they are watching a foreign film with dubbed-in English, although the Tibetans are speaking their own lines with varying degrees of competency. There is a strong contrast between ultra-religious Tibet and atheistic, Marxist-Leninist China. Unfortunately, filmmakers dealing with religion never succeed in presenting anything but externalities because in motion pictures the camera is king.

The camera lavishes attention on exotic costumes, ancient temples and monasteries, idols, altars, candelabra, burning incense, ceremonial gongs, parades, and, of course, snowcapped mountains. (Although viewers are convinced they have been transported to Tibet, the film was actually shot in Morocco with a second unit shooting supplementary footage in British Columbia and Idaho). As far as Buddhist doctrine itself is concerned, little comes across except that Tibetan Buddhists are very interested in peace.

The screenplay by Melissa Mathison, whose credits include *E.T.: The Extra-Terrestrial* (1982) and *The Indian In the Cupboard* (1995), is based on the life story of the 14th Dalai Lama, who formed a government-in-exile in Dharmsala, India and won the Nobel Peace Prize in 1989. In the opening scenes a band of monks is scouring the country to find the child in whose body the 13th Dalai Lama has been reincarnated. They resemble the Three Wise Men in the New Testament who are following a star to Bethlehem. The monks believe they have found the reincarnated Dalai Lama when they stop in a village near the Chinese border and meet Tenzin Gyatso (Tenzin Yeshi Paichang), a cute two-year-old who has an unusually aristocratic bearing and seems to possess knowledge of previous incarnations. A cynic might think this precocious lad reads body language. When subjected to a test involving choosing the 13th Dalai Lama's personal possessions from among a group of objects on the kitchen table, he seems to let his hovering hand be guided by facial expressions and scarcely perceptible movements of the elderly monk administering the test. The event has a fairy-tale quality. Tenzin's amazed family members are suddenly elevated from poverty to privileged social status. The year is 1937. China is a divided land trying to fight off Japanese invaders. Tibet is totally isolationist, as it has been since time immemorial.

Then at the age of five the new Dalai Lama (now played by Tulka Jamyang Kunga Tenzin) is taken off to the capital city of Lhassa to be educated for the all-powerful position he will occupy in this ancient theocracy. Up to this point the story is engrossing because the audience feels sympathy for a little boy being torn from his family to be raised by strangers. Viewers are touched by scenes in which the small child, dressed in golden splendor and perched on a throne far too big for him, adjusts to his omnipotent but terribly lonely status. He is only an extreme example of the many little boys who for centuries have been taken from their families to be raised as Buddhist monks in various parts of Asia. As with almost any biography, the narrative is episodic because people's lives are episodic.

There is virtually no dramatic conflict until the boy reaches maturity and is faced with the menace of Commu-

AWARDS AND NOMINATIONS

Academy Awards 1997 Nominations: Art Direction, Cinematography, Costume Design, Original Dramatic Score
Golden Globe Awards 1998 Nominations: Original Score
Los Angeles Film Critics Association 1997: Music
National Society of Films Critics 1997: Cinematography
New York Film Critics Circle 1997: Cinematography

nist China, personified by Chairman Mao (Robert Lin). The film keeps the viewer somewhat abreast of events taking place in the outside world by scenes in which the boy, whom the monks address as Kundun (or "ocean of wisdom"), is shown watching newsreel footage and later watching television. This is a cinematic way of insinuating that the 14th Dalai Lama is different from his predecessors. He is becoming more modern, more democratic.

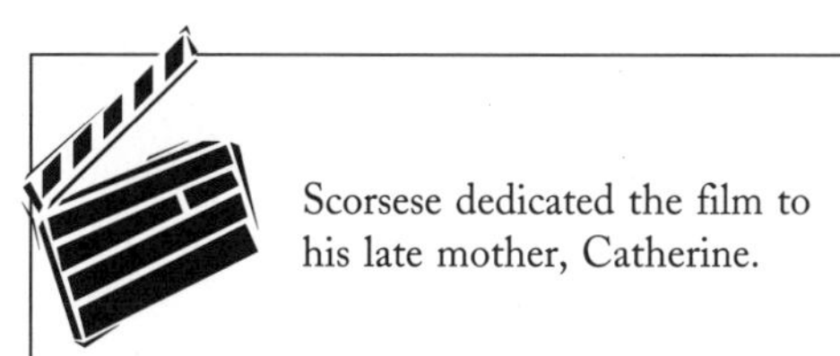

Scorsese dedicated the film to his late mother, Catherine.

As a grown man the Dalai Lama is portrayed by Tenzin Thuthob Tsarong. By this time the Dalai Lama has lost his boyish playfulness as well as his boyish charm. His steel-rimmed spectacles remind viewers that he has spent much of his life absorbing knowledge about the modern world through books as well as through audio-visual media. His years of indoctrination, along with the veneration he has received as a near deity, have made him reserved and autocratic. Because he is regarded as an "ocean of wisdom," the whole burden of coping with a gigantic, expansionistic neighbor falls on his young shoulders. The seasoned American moviegoer might mentally equate Kundun with a Native American tribal chief faced with the onslaught of land-hungry Europeans. (The Dalai Lama has been informed that overpopulated China is sending forty thousand "settlers" to take up permanent residence. These will be the first wave of intruders destined to turn native Tibetans into second-class citizens in their own homeland.)

Kundun appeals to Europe and America for diplomatic intervention. But he gets as little practical support as Emperor Haile Salassie did in 1934 when he appealed to the League of Nations for help against Benito Mussolini's ruthless invasion of Ethiopia. The war-weary West would prefer to have China expand its revolutionary energies against an impotent, landlocked neighbor rather than against a more strategically sensitive neighbor.

The contrast between ancient Tibet and modern Communist China is graphically presented when "His Holiness" is flown to Beijing for a personal meeting with Chairman Mao. This appears to be the first time he has flown in an airplane or set foot outside his native land. He still has hopes of persuading Mao to allow the Tibetans some measure of autonomy, but the oily Mao shows the brutal face behind the smiling mask. Towards the end of their interview the fanatical dictator says bluntly, "Religion is poison. Religion is 'the opiate of the people.'"

During their meetings, Kundun repeatedly reminds Mao that he and his theocratic government are making efforts to "modernize." He never elaborates on their progress in that direction. This concept of reform seems to be the real purpose in highlighting the Dalai Lama's lifelong interest in the outside world. The informed viewer will remember, however, that Tibet was hardly a Shangri La for the peasant majority who lived in abject ignorance and near slavery to the Buddhist theocracy. *Kundun* as *Los Angeles Times* reviewer Kenneth Turan observed, "has an inherent drawback because it is an *authorized* biography."

Crowds of monks and humble citizens beg the Dalai Lama not to leave Tibet. He stays as long as humanly possible but eventually realizes that Mao intends to use him as a puppet and keep him a prisoner in his own land. The drama intensifies as the camera shows waves of Chinese soldiers marching into the bleak, impoverished land. One striking pull-away helicopter shot gradually reveals hundreds of slaughtered monks forming a numinous pattern resembling the intricate mandalas of multicolored sand shown throughout the film. Escape to India is beginning to seem impossible because the young ruler is closely watched and the horseback journey over dizzying mountain trails is perilous.

By this point the twenty-five-year-old Dalai Lama has developed supernatural powers. Whether he actually was the

CREDITS

Dalai Lama (adult): Tenzin Thuthob Tsarong
Dalai Lama (age 12): Gyurme Tethong
Dalai Lama (age 5): Tulku Jamyang Kunga Tenzin
Dalai Lama (age 2): Tenzin Yeshi Paichang
Mother: Tencho Gyalpo
Father: Tsewang Migyur Khangsar
Chairman Mao: Robert Lin

Origin: USA
Released: 1997
Production: Barbara De Fina for Cappa/De Fina; released by Touchstone Pictures
Direction: Martin Scorsese
Screenplay: Melissa Mathison; based on the life story of the Dalai Lama
Cinematography: Roger Deakins
Editing: Thelma Schoonmaker
Music: Philip Glass
Production design: Dante Ferretti
Costumes: Dante Ferretti
Art direction: Franco Ceraolo, Massimo Razzi
Set decoration: Francesca Lo Schiavo
Sound: Clive Winter
Visual effects supervisor: Jeffrey Burks
MPAA rating: PG-13
Running Time: 134 minutes

reincarnation of the 13th Dalai Lama, or whether his years of training, meditating, solitude, and reverential treatment have transformed him, he has become a visionary. He can see into the future. As one example, when he reaches the Indian border he turns to look at the men who have escorted him and sees them all slumped dead in their saddles, the horses' manes soaked in their riders' blood. The viewer understands that the Dalai Lama is seeing them as they will look after they ride back into Tibet and encounter their Chinese pursuers.

Although critics faulted *Kundun* as drama, they were nearly unanimous in praising it as spectacle. *New York Times* critic Stephen Holden wrote: "The movie is a triumph for the cinematographer Roger Deakins, who has given it the look of an illuminated manuscript." Holden also joined in praising the highly effective musical score by avant-garde composer Philip Glass. *Variety* critic Emanuel Levy wrote: "It's a tribute to Glass' glorious achievement that it's impossible to evaluate *Kundun* without acknowledging the unforgettable spell of his music."

—*Bill Delaney*

REVIEWS

Boxoffice. January, 1998, p. 16.
Boxoffice. February, 1998, p. 54.
Chicago Tribune. January 16, 1998, p. 4.
Detroit News. January 16, 1998, p. 1D.
Entertainment Weekly. January 9, 1998, p. 45.
Los Angeles Times. December 24, 1997, p. F1.
New York Times. December 24, 1997, p. E1.
People. December 22, 1997, p. 22.
Rolling Stone. January 22, 1998, p. 62.
Time. December 22, 1997.
Variety. December 15, 1997, p. 57.
Village Voice. December 30, 1997, p. 61.

L.A. Confidential

Everything is suspect . . . Everyone is for sale . . . And nothing is what it seems.—Movie tagline

"Curtis Hanson's electrifying thriller *L.A. Confidential* brings the thrill of corruption cracklingly alive."—Owen Gleiberman, *Entertainment Weekly*

"The best storytelling since *Chinatown.* Terrific entertainment."—David Thompson, *Esquire*

"One of the best films of the year. A thrilling, gripping, expertly written, superbly directed piece about police corruption and the ways of the flesh."—Jeffrey Wells, *L.A. Times Syndicate*

"*L.A. Confidential* is riveting - a dangerous and intoxicating tale of big trouble in paradise."—Kenneth Turan, *Los Angeles Times*

"Smashing, jazzy and stylish. *L.A. Confidential* has a surprise in every scene."—Rex Reed, *New York Observer*

"Gangbusters! *L.A. Confidential* is a shrewd, elegant film with a flawless ensemble cast and style to burn."—Janet Maslin, *The New York Times*

"*L.A. Confidential* is a stylish thriller. Director Curtis Hanson brings James Ellroy's novel of cops and corruption to rancid, racy life."—David Ansen, *Newsweek*

"Crime busting, police corruption and show business! *L.A. Confidential* is a sizzling drama that seldom lets up!"—Bruce Williamson, *Playboy*

"The most vibrant crime drama since *Pulp Fiction. L.A. Confidential* is smart, funny, twisted and ultra-cool!"—Jeff Craig, *Sixty Second Preview*

"*L.A. Confidential* is a thrilling, utterly compelling cop yarn that's the most successful since *Chinatown.*"—John Powers, *Vogue*

Box Office: $37,557,100

Film noir resonates with many viewers—and especially with filmmakers—because of the ways it mingles thematic substance with visual style, romance with violence, attempting to explain the inexplicable: the nature of corruption. Noir qualities appear in fiction, especially that of masters like Raymond Chandler, but are more difficult to convey because of the inability to display color, shadows, economy of gesture, moody music, and all the other elements that make the genre, when done well, so cinematically resplendent.

The contemporary writer who perhaps best captures noir in his prose is James Ellroy, a crime novelist obsessed with the details of the recent past, especially Los Angeles in the 1950s. Ellroy is extremely adept at evoking the paranoia of conspiracies: See his brilliant take on the John F. Kennedy assassination in his 1995 novel *American Tabloid.* Ellroy's 1990 novel *L.A. Confidential* is a magnificent achievement, perhaps the most satisfying crime fiction since Chandler and Dashiell Hammett were in their prime, with the writer juggling what he has identified as eight major plots, bringing together all the seemingly unrelated elements at the end with mathematical precision. The novel's complexity would seem to defy adaptation to the screen, but writer-director Curtis Hanson and his cowriter Brian Helgeland have made *L.A. Confidential* into an almost perfect entertainment.

Set in Los Angeles in 1952-1953, the film centers around three homicide detectives. Jack Vincennes (Kevin Spacey) stands in flamboyant contrast to the other two. Well dressed, debonair, Jack is the Dean Martin of cops. Technical advisor to the television series "Badge of Honor," clearly inspired by "Dragnet," Jack also gets tips from sleazy Sid Hudgens (Danny DeVito), editor of *Hush-Hush*, a tabloid inspired by the notorious 1950s scandal sheet *Confidential.* Sid delights in exposing Communists, lesbians, and narcotics users in the entertainment industry, and Jack helps out by arresting pathetic perpetrators, such as two would-be stars (Matt Reynolds and Shawnee Free Jones) caught smoking marijuana on Christmas Eve in the full glare of Sid's camera. Bud White (Russell Crowe) is much more straightforward. Obsessed by arresting men who abuse women because he witnessed his father batter his mother to death, Bud too easily loses his considerable temper, as when he, his partner, Dick Stensland (Graham Beckel), and others assault some Hispanic suspects on this same Christmas Eve. This incident occurs despite the best efforts of rookie homicide officer Ed Exley (Guy Pearce). Ed is a Boy Scout compared to Jack and Bud, and much of *L.A. Confidential* is about his education into the complex corruption of law enforcement as practiced in Los Angeles.

The very complicated plot centers around solving the murders of six people, including Stensland, at the Nite Owl Coffee Shop. Some young African Americans are seen nearby at the time, and the police blame them for the shootings. Bud rescues a young woman (Marisol Padilla Sanchez) the suspects had been holding captive and sexually assaulting, and her evidence links them to the murders. After the three suspects escape from jail, Ed tracks them down and kills them in a shootout, much to the delight of his captain, Dudley Smith (James Cromwell). Ed, however, is not convinced of the guilt of the men he has killed.

One of the Nite Owl victims is Susan Lefferts (Amber Smith), a prostitute employed by Pierce Patchett (David Strathairn), a wealthy man involved in all sorts of illegal and semi-legal enterprises, including using plastic surgery to make his hookers resemble movie stars. Investigating Patchett's possible connection to the Nite Owl

Antagonistic police detectives Ed Exley (Guy Pearce) and Bud White (Russell Crowe) must put their differences aside in order to expose police corruption and solve a brutal murder in the highly acclaimed film noir drama *L.A. Confidential.*

Sid Hudgens: "Remember, dear readers, you heard it here first, off the record, on the QT, and very *Hush-Hush.*"

case, Bud falls in love with Lynn Bracken (Kim Basinger), Patchett's version of Veronica Lake. A seemingly unrelated subplot involves the murders of the henchman of Los Angeles crime boss Mickey Cohen (Paul Guilfoyle), currently in San Quentin for tax evasion. As Jack, Bud, and Ed delve deeper into this murky morass, the possible involvement of the district attorney (Ron Rifkin) and their fellow cops is revealed.

Hanson and Helgeland have done an excellent job of sorting through Ellroy's overlapping plots to create a unified narrative. Among the elements they have discarded are Ed's ill-fated romance with the rape victim and the involvement of his father, a retired heroic police detective with a dark secret, in Patchett's schemes. The screenwriters invent the unsolved murder of the senior Exley as a motivation for Ed's heroics. Such changes simplify Ellroy's intentions, as does the more upbeat ending, but are necessary if the film is to have a reasonable running time and is to be comprehensible to the average viewer.

While Hanson and Helgeland's efforts serve almost as a textbook example of film adaptation of a complex novel, the $40 million *L.A. Confidential* still did not perform as well at the box office as might be expected of a highly entertaining film receiving mostly rave reviews. Perhaps the plot is still too complicated for a mass audience, though such a difficulty did not keep viewers away from the equally demanding *Pulp Fiction* (1994) and *The Usual Suspects* (1995). (Ironically, the same fate befell another complicated film written by Helgeland, *The Conspiracy Theory*, earlier in 1997.)

Nothing in Hanson's earlier work indicates he is capable of the directorial skill he displays in *L.A. Confidential.* Previously, Hanson directed one surprise hit, *The Hand that Rocks the Cradle* (1992), an unpleasant psychological thriller. His best film has been *The Bedroom Window* (1987), a divertingly adequate Hitchcock imitation, and he also wrote *The Silent Partner* (1978), a minor cult film in which a straightforward crime takes unusual twists. While Hanson's credits label him a competent genre filmmaker, he is also something of a film scholar, having edited the magazine *Cinema* in the late 1960s. In fact, his article about *Bonnie and Clyde* (1967) inspired a petty thief named James Ellroy to steal so that he could see Arthur Penn's masterpiece, as the novelist recounts in his introduction to the published screenplay for *L.A. Confidential.*

To attune his cast and crew to the film noir rhythms of 1950s L.A., writer-director Curtis Hanson showed some of his favorite films from the period: *In a Lonely Place* (1950), *The Bad and the Beautiful* (1952), *Private Hell 36* (1954), *The Killing* (1956), *The Lineup* (1958), and the film he says is closest in spirit, *Kiss Me Deadly* (1955).

Hanson's own masterpiece—and it is that—overpowers the viewer with its sheer professionalism. As several reviews observed, this is slick Hollywood studio product at its best. All the elements of casting, acting, cinematography, production design, editing, and music combine to create a powerful entertainment. Hanson's contribution as director, with obvious assistance from editor Peter Honess, includes the film's pacing. The beating of the Hispanics is shot and cut to emphasize both the vulnerability of the victims, trapped in a small space filled with angry policemen, and Ed's desperate helplessness at being unable to stop his colleagues. The arrest of the Nite Owl suspects, Ed's hunting them down, and a final shootout between good cops and bad cops are each brilliantly staged set pieces, visceral action at its best. Cinematographer Dante Spinotti, whose credits include *Heat* (1995), another masterful L.A. crime film, shoots the night scenes in an atmospheric noir style, full of shadows and reflecting lights, and gives the few daylight scenes an unnaturally harsh glow. Production designer Jeannie Oppewall provides the film with a 1950s feel without resorting to obvious artifacts.

Underscoring all these achievements is one of the best scores by the veteran composer Jerry Goldsmith, his music commenting subtly on the desperate, violent, and occasionally romantic goings-on. The use of a solo trumpet seems to be a self homage to Goldsmith's masterwork, *Chinatown* (1974). The use of popular music of the period, sung by Chet Baker, Betty Hutton, Kay Starr, Lee Wiley, and, of course, Dean Martin, add texture and a bit of irony to the dark proceedings.

Spacey's Jack Vincennes could easily have been a one-note performance, but the actor realizes the character's smoothness is a barrier against the obscene world he encounters daily, a milieu he is repelled by but cannot live without. Spacey is brilliant in portraying Jack's reactions to the discovery of a corpse he is partially responsible for and to the revelation of the identity of the film's major villain. DeVito is also quite good at depicting Sid's delight in his unscrupulous work. Having Sid cockily narrate the film's opening to set the time and place is a wonderful touch. The loquacious Dudley Smith, an apparent stereotype of a veteran detective down to the thick Irish brogue, is at the other extreme from James Cromwell's best-known role: the taciturn farmer in *Babe* (1995). Basinger's tough-but-vulnerable prostitute is more than a bit of a cliché, but this underrated actress, aided by Ruth Myers' glamorous costumes, makes Lynn Bracken a compelling, if fuzzily motivated, character.

The biggest gamble in *L.A. Confidential* is the casting of two little-known foreign actors as Bud and Ed. New Zealander Crowe has been waiting for a role like this since his dishwasher in *Proof* (1992) showed his considerable potential. Despite the too-obvious psychological motivation he is given, Bud White is the film's most complex character: both a crusader and a bully, a tender lover and an impulsive brute. Crowe ably encompasses these contradictions, displaying sufficient sensitivity to complement the character's rowdy physicality. (If the film had been made in the 1950s, Aldo Ray would have played the part.) Han-

AWARDS AND NOMINATIONS

Academy Awards 1997: Supporting Actress (Basinger), Adapted Screenplay
Nominations: Best Picture, Director (Hanson), Art Direction, Cinematography, Film Editing, Original Dramatic Score
BAFTA 1997 Nominations: Best Film, Director (Hanson), Adapted Screenplay, Actress (Basinger), Actor (Spacey), Music, Cinematography, Production design, Costumes, Editing, Sound, Make-up/Hair
Broadcast Film Critics Association 1997: Film, Adapted Screenplay
Golden Globe Awards 1998: Supporting Actress (Basinger)
Nominations: Best Drama, Director (Hanson), Screenplay, Original Score
Los Angeles Film Critics Association 1997: Film, Director (Hanson), Screenplay, Cinematography
National Board of Review 1997: Film, Director (Hanson)
National Society of Film Critics 1997: Film, Director (Hanson), Screenplay
New York Film Critics Circle 1997: Film, Director (Hanson), Screenplay
Screen Actors Guild Awards 1997: Supporting Actress (Basinger)
Writers Guild of America 1997: Adapted Screenplay

son has Bud and Lynn attend a showing of *Roman Holiday* (1953) to hint at the romantic illusions to which the couple aspire and to emphasize the deep gulf between the world of make-believe and that of detectives and prostitutes.

An even bigger gamble is the casting of Pearce, whose only role known to American audiences, as one of the drag performers in *The Adventures of Priscilla, Queen of the Desert* (1995), is a world away from a 1950s police detective. Australian Pearce, like Crowe, has considerable presence, but the part is tricky because of Ed's almost prissy naivete. Hanson and Helgeland help keep the character's humanity in view by poking fun at Ed's inability to appear coplike while wearing his eyeglasses and with a comic scene in which Ed mistakes the real Lana Turner (Brenda Bakke) for a prostitute made up to resemble her. Pearce is at his best in showing Ed's disgust at having to kill the Nite Owl suspects and his resolve when the villain taunts him.

Like Ellroy, Hanson is a native of Los Angeles who thoroughly understands how the city can be symbols of both glamour and corruption, sex and violence. *L.A. Confidential* is a worthy addition to the great Los Angeles film noir tradition that includes *Double Indemnity* (1944), *The Big Sleep* (1946), *Kiss Me Deadly* (1955), and *Chinatown*.

—*Michael Adams*

CREDITS

Ed Exley: Guy Pearce
Bud White: Russell Crowe
Jack Vincennes: Kevin Spacey
Lynn Bracken: Kim Basinger
Sid Hudgens: Danny DeVito
Dudley Smith: James Cromwell
Pierce Patchett: David Strathairn
Ellis Lowe: Ron Rifkin
Mickey Cohen: Paul Guilfoyle
Dick Stensland: Graham Beckel
Police chief: John Mahon
Brett Chase: Matt McCoy
Johnny Stompanato: Paolo Seganti
Susan Lefferts: Amber Smith
Buzz Meeks: Darrell Sandeen
Matt Reynolds: Simon Baker Denny
Tammy Jordan: Shawnee Free Jones
Mrs. Lefferts: Gwenda Deacon
Inez Soto: Marisol Padilla Sanchez
Lana Turner: Brenda Bakke

Origin: USA
Released: 1997
Production: Curtis Hanson, Arnon Milchan, and Michael Nathanson for Regency Enterprises; released by Warner Brothers
Direction: Curtis Hanson
Screenplay: Brian Helgeland and Curtis Hanson; based on the novel by James Ellroy
Cinematography: Dante Spinotti
Editing: Peter Honess
Production design: Jeannine Oppewall
Art direction: Bill Arnold
Set decoration: Jay R. Hart
Costumes: Ruth Myers
Music: Jerry Goldsmith
Sound: Kirk Francis
MPAA rating: R
Running Time: 137 minutes

REVIEWS

Boxoffice. August, 1997, p. 45.
Boxoffice. September, 1997, p. 18.
Chicago Tribune. September 19, 1997, p. 4.
Detroit Free Press. September 19, 1997, p. D1.
Detroit News. September 19, 1997, p. F1.
Entertainment Weekly. September 19, 1997, p. 54.
Esquire. October, 1997, p. 50.
The Hollywood Reporter. May 15, 1997, p. 5.
The New York Times. September 19, 1997, p. E1.
The New Yorker. September 22, 1997, p. 141.
Newsweek. September 22, 1997, p. 83.
People. September 29, 1997, p. 19.
Playboy. October, 1997, p. 19.
Rolling Stone. October 2, 1997, p. 59.
Sight and Sound. November, 1997, p. 6.
Sight and Sound. November, 1997, p. 45.
Time. September 15, 1997, p. 100.
USA Today. September 19, 1997, p. D1.
Variety. May 19, 1997, p. 48.
Village Voice. September 23, 1997, p. 85.

The Last Time I Committed Suicide

"A hip, slick and cool close-up on the beat generation. Thomas Jane is one cool cat."—Gayle Murphy, *ABC Entertainment News*

Stephen Kay's first film, the audacious *The Last Time I Committed Suicide*, generated a great deal of buzz when it premiered at the Sundance Film Festival. Kay based his screenplay on a not-so-famous letter called the "Great Sex Letter" that Beat icon Neal Cassady wrote to Jack Kerouac, detailing his sexual exploits during a brief, but turbulent period in the mid-1940s.

From Neal Cassady's letter to Jack Kerouac: "As you know, this was not the last time I committed suicide. And so love goes. And so life goes. And so I go. You carry on my brother."

Twenty-year-old Neal Cassady (Thomas Jane) is unnerved by the suicide attempt of his beautiful, but troubled lover, Joan (Claire Forlani from *Basquiat*, [1996]) and despite his concern, he finds it increasingly difficult to visit her in the hospital. Before long, he stops going all together.

In his hometown of Denver, Cassady worked nights at a Goodyear tire plant and spent his days drinking and carousing with a thirty-two-year-old loser named Harry (Keanu Reeves). Through a wicked twist of fate, Cassady is reunited with the fragile Joan and he swears his gratitude for this second chance at love. But when he attempts to make the short trip across town to retrieve his suit for a job interview the next morning, Cassady finds himself unable to break the ties of spiritual wanderlust that would bind him forever.

Harry convinces Cassady to share some Christmas cheer with him and begs the younger man to place a call on his behalf to the under-aged, but precocious Cherry Mary (Gretchen Mol). But when the teenager's puritanical and vindictive mother (Christie Rose) sends the police to rendezvous with the two men, Cassady finds himself in jail—and his second chance at happiness with Joan slips away like sands in an hourglass.

Cassady was haunted by dreams of a life of domestic bliss, a bourgeois existence replete with the house with "the picket fence and the honey at home." He could not shake the notion that this was the life he should want, the one to which he should aspire. Yet it was not the life he necessarily needed. Disappointingly, however, the film does little to convey Cassady's hunger, his need to strike out on a different path.

Writer/director Stephen Kay has structured a tale that is very light on dramatic impetus. What it does capture, however, is the restlessness and general boredom that was characteristic of the leading intellectuals who would later be known as the Beats. Unfortunately, the young actor cast as Neal Cassady, Thomas Jane, lacks the sexual prowess needed to make us understand the appeal of the enigmatic Cassady. Here he comes off as a flighty punk who is unable to accept responsibility and it is hard to comprehend the power he seemed to have over women.

Perhaps it is not possible to fully understand the allure of Neal Cassady. He travelled the country in the Sixties with the Merry Pranksters and in 1968, after an intense night of drinking, Cassady died at the age of 42 when he passed out in his t-shirt and jeans on a cold night in a Mexican trainyard. Despite his literary ambitions, Cassady would never be published during his lifetime; but Kerouac would later immortalize Cassady as Dean Moriarty in his famous book, *On the Road.*

The Last Time I Committed Suicide has a beautiful and haunting look to it, thanks to the stunning visuals of Bobby Bukowski's camera work. The film's energy comes primarily from a jazzy, hopped-up be-bop score that includes works

CREDITS

Neal: Thomas Jane
Harry: Keanu Reeves
Captain: Tom Bower
Ben: Adrien Brody
Joan: Claire Forlani
Lizzy: Marg Helgenberger
Lew: Joe Doe
Cherry Mary: Gretchen Mol

Origin: USA
Released: 1997
Production: Edward Bates and Louise Rosner for Kushner-Locke Co. and Tapestry Films; released by Roxie Releasing
Direction: Stephen Kay
Screenplay: Stephen Kay; based on a letter by Neal Cassady
Cinematography: Bobby Bukowski
Editing: Dorian Harris
Production design: Amy Ancona
Costumes: Denise Wingate
Sound: Leonard Marcel
Music: Tyler Bates
MPAA rating: R
Running Time: 95 minutes

from Thelonious Monk and Charlie Parker, as well as from some first-rate editing from Dorian Harris that helps to create a spontaneous stream-of-consciousness feel that characterized Beat literature.

Keanu Reeves' performance as the drunken loser Harry is one of the film's strengths. Bloated and vulnerable, Reeves taps into something deep in the character, resulting in a powerful and sensitive portrayal of a man unable to stop his descent. The only disappointment is that Reeves was not cast as Beat writer Jack Kerouac, a role the thirty-something actor, with his Hollywood ennui and scattered intellectualism, seems destined to play. *The Last Time I Committed Suicide* is reported to be the project that Keanu Reeves chose to do instead of the twelve million paycheck offered for *Speed 2: Cruise Control* (1997).

While not totally successful, *The Last Time I Committed Suicide* is nonetheless much more effective at capturing the energy of the Beats than previous films, such as *Heart Beat* (1980), which starred Nick Nolte, John Heard and Sissy Spacek.

—Patricia Kowal

REVIEWS

Boxoffice. September, 1997, p. 122.
Chicago Tribune. August 22, 1997.
The Hollywood Reporter. June 20, 1997, p. 12.
Los Angeles Times. June 20, 1997, p. F12.
New York Times. June 20, 1997, p. B16.
San Francisco Chronicle. July 2, 1997, p. E5.
San Francisco Examiner. July 2, 1997, p. C3.
Variety. January 27, 1997, p. 77.

Latin Boys Go to Hell

"Erotic! . . . A send-up of gay Latino angst and passion!"—*Los Angeles Gay & Lesbian Film Festival*
"Steamy! . . . Smart and entertaining!"—*San Francisco Gay & Lesbian Film Festival*

Latin Boys Go to Hell is a campy romp of a film, both destined and doomed to midnight shows by its bad acting, direction, and melodramatic storyline. Based on a novel by Andre Salas, directed by Ela Troyano, it tries to follow in the melodramatic footsteps created by Douglas Sirk, *West Side Story,* and not least of all, the oeuvre of director Pedro Almodovar. It tells the story of two cousins in New York City, Justin (Irwin Ossa), a shy, awkward boy, and Angel (John Bryant Davila), a troubled teen who comes from Chicago to live with Justin and his family.

First feature for Ela Troyano, whose short films include *Once Upon a Time in the Bronx* and *Carmelita Tropicana.*

When Justin is first introduced, he is working for a photographer who is expressing her talents through an exhibit that shall later be titled "Latin Boys Go to Hell." It features scantily-clad, buffed young men engaged in a variety of erotic poses—with flowers, statues, and religious artifacts. Director Troyano uses this world—gay Latino Club life, religious imagery—to frame the hopes, dreams, restrictions and daily melodramas that propel and anchor her characters. Justin seems unaware or unwilling to face up to the fact that he is gay—or at the very least curious. He spends his nights at the local disco, where he is harassed and groped by Carlos (Mike Ruiz), an aggressive, handsome, openly gay man. Carlos' actions are not the least bit appreciated by his boyfriend Braulio (Alexis Artiles); they have a passionate spat—one in a series of flamboyant, public fights. Carlos is a flirty cad who convinces Braulio that he only has eyes for him, while Justin helplessly looks on, unable to convince the crowd that he didn't encourage Carlos' actions.

Justin is a romantic, confused young man, given to watching a popular Spanish soap opera titled "Dos Vidas" ("Two Lives") with religious devotion (as does Braulio, with more lethal repercussions). His boring existence is uprooted when his cousin Angel arrives from Chicago to stay indefinitely with Justin's family. Where Justin is shy and tentative, Angel is confident and assured. When the two boys go to the local disco, Angel is immediately smitten with Andrea (Jenifer Lee Simard), who, coincidentally, is Braulio's best friend. At first Andrea is not interested but she is impressed by Angel's sincerity and they strike up a conversation. They make a date to go out.

Justin and Carlos meet days later; Justin surprises even himself when he ends up at Carlos' apartment. After they have sex, Carlos exhibits brutish insensitivity towards Justin, despite the fact that Justin was a virgin. Justin flees the apartment, completely freaked out. Carlos later hooks up with Braulio, and deflects any jealous inquiries by pulling him quickly into bed.

Justin finds comfort with Angel, who surreptitiously offers his support to Justin when he suspects that his young cousin may be gay. Meanwhile, Angel pursues Andrea with gentle conversation and attention; he is certainly a breath of fresh air from the buffoons that she usually encounters. It becomes obvious that Justin is attracted to Angel, but the feelings are so overwhelming that he doesn't know what to do with them.

Carlos' constant cheating catches up with him and Braulio breaks it off. Andrea is concerned about her friend; he is so in love with Carlos that she cannot believe he has completely severed all ties with him. Braulio assures her that he is fine, but she can see that he is very disturbed. Andrea is puzzled; she wants to help Braulio, but she doesn't know how to break through to him. Even when Carlos turns up dead from a vicious stabbing, Braulio seems oblivious. Their crowd buzzes about who could have killed Carlos, and Braulio's cool detachment will soon reveal his guilt in the matter.

Finally, the party to celebrate the opening of "Latin Boys Go to Hell" arrives. The entire crowd arranges to go—most everyone is dressed up in some macabre costume—and it seems that a wild party will ensue. But Braulio arrives in quite a state—he is obviously cracking. In a dramatic confrontation on the rooftop, reminiscent of *West Side Story,* Braulio lets loose with a gun—and Andrea and Angel tragically die.

Like the archetype loner that comes to town and changes lives, Angel has left an indelible mark on his cousin, Justin. Although he was supposedly a troubled teen, Angel pursued Andrea with a gentleness heretofore unseen by the local girls, and he was unwaveringly sweet and receptive to Justin's angst. He was indeed, an "Angel."

Although filled with the ingredients for an affecting film, its downfall comes from the ill-developed characterizations. Carlos and Braulio are stereotypes with no layering to make them believable; the one relationship that should have been delved into, Angel and Justin's, is left unexplored. Ham-handed acting highlights Troyano's weak directing skills, and ultimately brings a hysterical tone to the film.

—*G.E. Georges*

CREDITS

Braulio: Alexis Artiles
Luz: Rebecca Summer Burgos
Carlos: Mike Ruiz
Angel: John Bryant Davila
Rodrigo: Umberto Gonzalez
Andrea: Jenifer Lee Simard

Origin: USA
Released: 1997
Production: Jurgen Bruning; released by Strand Releasing
Direction: Ela Troyano
Screenplay: Ela Troyano and Andre Salas; based on the novel by Salas
Cinematography: James Carman
Editing: Brian A. Kates
Music: Ari Gold
Production design: Uzi Parnes
Sound: Kristian Petersen
MPAA rating: Unrated
Running Time: 86 minutes

REVIEWS

Filmmaker. Summer, 1997, p. 44.
New York Times. September 12, 1997, p. C14.
Sight and Sound. December, 1997, p. 45.
Village Voice. September 16, 1997, p. 89.

Leave It to Beaver

The Beav is back.—Movie tagline

"Great fun. Funny and touching."—Gary Schendel, *KGTV*

"Family fun."—Bonnie Churchill, *National News Syndicate*

"Enormously funny."—Louise Patanker, *Premiere Radio*

Box Office: $10,915,025

The film version of the popular '50s television show on the all-American family, *Leave It to Beaver* has the Beaver (Cameron Finely) getting into various mishaps while looking for his stolen bicycle.

The television series "Leave it to Beaver" appeared from 1957 to 1963. Joe Connelly and Bob Moser, who had written for the "Amos and Andy" television show (1951-1953), wrote a pilot episode based on some of the everyday problems of their own children. Although "Leave it to Beaver", according to A. C. Nielsen rankings, never finished any season among the top twenty-five shows, its 234 episodes have found their greatest popularity in syndication, where the program has become a symbol for the innocence and happiness of pre-Vietnam, pre-Watergate America. Perhaps the biggest challenge for filmmakers adapting the series into a feature film lies in the choice of whether to update the material to the 1990s.

Writers Brian Levant and Lon Diamond, along with director Andy Cadiff, have decided to do so, but they also have sought to retain much of the freshness and charm of the original series. By wanting to have it both ways, they string a very difficult tightrope for themselves. The film is set in a Mayfield, Ohio, that has "evolved"—as the publicity for the film states—"beyond the original '50s and '60s version." In effect, what this balancing act means is that Levant and Diamond develop two storylines in their script that focus on the problems of Beaver (Cameron Finley) and his brother Wally (Erik von Detten) but also occasionally inject an extraneous scene, some throwaway lines, or slapstick comedy in an attempt to appeal to more contemporary tastes. The uneven results suggest that a wiser direction might have been to concentrate more completely on nostalgia and innocence.

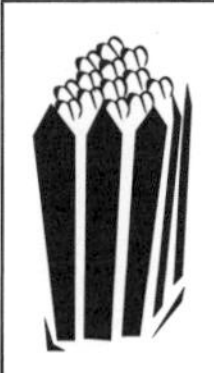

Ward: "June, you're vacuuming in pearls. You know what that does to me."

The two storylines concern a stolen bike and a stolen girlfriend. Beaver longs for a new bicycle, and smug Eddie Haskell (Adam Zolotin), who is presented in the film as in the TV show as a sort of early adolescent Frank Sinatra, advises him on how to manipulate his father Ward (Christopher McDonald). Beaver tells Ward that he will go out for the pee-wee football team. This appeals, as Eddie had suspected, to Ward's arrested fantasies of athletic success. At his birthday party, Beaver is rewarded with a new computer and a new bicycle, but soon one of the neighborhood kids talks Beaver into letting him ride the bike. While Beaver watches in horror, this stranger quickly pedals off.

In the related plot, Wally and his classmate Karen (Erika Christensen) feel an attraction for each other even though Eddie has already asked Wally to help him get to know Karen. Wally tries to be a faithful friend to Eddie. When Karen calls to invite Wally to a party, he coaxes her to invite Eddie as well. At the party the kids play spin the bottle, and the luck of the spin sends Karen and Wally off for their first kiss. Eddie eventually accepts losing Karen to Wally, but at a skating rink Karen spots a good-looking boy who used to live across the street. Suddenly Wally seems less interesting. Both brothers struggle to overcome their losses. Beaver becomes a greater liability to the football team; Wally pines for Karen from afar as she shows off her new boyfriend. When the film explores the feelings of the brothers, it produces its best effects. The audience can recall the seemingly innocent days of childhood and enjoy the nostalgia of a time when the world's biggest problems involved bikes and boyfriends.

After the scene at the skating rink, Beaver spots his bicycle again. The thief sits complacently at a sidewalk table across from an advertizing billboard with a giant coffee cup. He dares Beaver to climb up and look into the cup and promises to return his bike if he does. This scene was adapted by writers Levant and Diamond from one of the television episodes. Of course, Beaver attempts the climb. Predictably, he peeks over the rim and topples into the cup. Firetrucks, police, and newscrews arrive on the scene for the big rescue as night falls. Standing below with June (Janine Turner), Ward realizes that he has pushed Beaver too hard to excel at football, and he himself climbs up the firemen's ladder to be the first one to talk to his son as most of Mayfield looks on below. Ward concedes that he had forgotten what it felt like to be a little boy. Beaver sees that he can please his dad just by being himself. To complete the happy endings, at Mayfield's final football game, Karen and Wally reunite.

Barbara Billingsley, who plays Aunt Martha, is best-known as the original June Cleaver in the 1957-63 TV show, where Ken Osmond played the young Eddie Haskell.

The charm of the developing stories of the brothers is interrupted at times by the writers' clumsy efforts at slapstick. A running joke about the driver of a pie truck getting smeared with his own merchandise quickly wears thin. Similarly, Ward and June's gift of a new computer becomes one of the early illustrations of Beaver's knack for finding trouble. While Ward sits downstairs calmly reading the paper, the computer dangles out of the boys' second-floor window, and Beaver bravely clutches onto the cord trying to reel in one of his birthday presents.

Other elements show the scriptwriters' attempt to keep one foot of the story in the contemporary world. Throwaway lines by different characters remind the audience none too subtly that Larry Mondello (E.J. De La Pena) is on Ritalin and that Eddie thinks June is "a babe." When Beaver's classmates talk about their summers, the oral reports these eight-year-olds deliver discuss the death of grandparents and the separation of parents. In one extraneous scene, Ward embraces June from behind and murmurs, "Oh, June, you're vacuuming in pearls. You know what that does to me." She smiles serenely and answers, "Stick around. Later, I'll slip into a pair of oven mitts." The most jarring example is the scene in which Ward and June take Beaver to a psychiatrist for some family therapy at the request of his teacher Miss Landers (Grace Phillips). The low-keyed lighting, the canted shots of the Cleavers packed together timidly on the couch, and the nervousness of the Beaver all make this scene more like something out of Kafka than a family comedy. Such intrusive material is not developed enough, as in the two *Brady Bunch* movies, to give the film a consistently satirical edge; rather, these moments come off as signs of indecision. The screenwriters seemingly do not have enough trust in the nostalgic appeal of the story to allow it to carry the weight of the film.

The cinematic style, however, does feature some effective formalist touches and contributes nicely to a few scenes. At Karen's party, for example, as the spinning bottle turns in the center of the table, the camera momentarily adopts its rotating point of view and shows the expectant faces of the boys passing by. The dating montage of Wally and Karen is succinct and lyrical. In another example, director Andy Cadiff captures Beaver's loneliness after one difficult football practice by shooting him from high overhead, showing the little boy standing all alone on the deserted field weighted down by his pads.

Fans who are familiar with the television series will recognize a number of performers in cameo roles. Barbara Billingsly, who played June in the original show, appears at Beaver's birthday party as his Aunt Martha. Ken Osmond,

CREDITS

Ward Cleaver: Christopher McDonald
June Cleaver: Janine Turner
Theodore (Beaver) Cleaver: Cameron Finley
Wally Cleaver: Erik von Detten
Eddie Haskell: Adam Zolotin
Aunt Martha: Barbara Billingsley
Eddie Sr.: Ken Osmond
Karen: Erika Christensen

Origin: USA
Released: 1997
Production: Robert Simmonds; released by Universal Pictures
Direction: Andy Cardiff
Screenplay: Brian Levant and Lon Diamond; based on the TV series created by Bob Mosher and Joe Connelly
Cinematography: Thomas Del Ruth
Editing: Alan Heim
Music: Randy Edelman
Production design: Perry Andelin Blake
Art direction: Peg McClellan
Costumes: Jean Pierre Dorleac
Sound: Thomas Brandau
MPAA rating: PG
Running Time: 88 minutes

the Eddie Haskell of television, plays Eddie, Sr. in the film. Appearing as one of Ward's business associates is Frank Bank, the Lumpy Rutherford of the series.

The performances of the starring cast are effective in roles that are all rather undemanding. Cameron Finley succeeds as the Beaver in a part that requires that he say his lines naturally and look cute. He delivers well lines like this, spoken to Ward, who has shown up with a book at Beaver's bedside: "If a guy's old enough to play football, then he's too old to be read to. If a guy's too old to be read to, then he's probably too old to be kissed goodnight to." Finley's casting was the result of a national talent search that auditioned over 5,000 boys in seven cities. Erik von Detten and Erika Christensen are good at suggesting the trepidation of young love felt by Wally and Karen. Alan Rachins, as Fred Rutherford, Ward's boss, may have had his part cut down during editing since he appears very briefly in only two scenes. Janine Turner as June Cleaver wisely does not try to imitate Barbara Billingsly, and she brings to the part a youthful freshness. Of the entire cast, Christopher McDonald looks the most uncomfortable. As Ward, he conveys better the father's early aloofness toward his sons than his later warmth. McDonald and Turner also do not seem entirely convincing as a couple.

Although co-screenwriter Brian Levant referred to the film as a "kind of a stained glass window that we pieced together," a few cracks may show through. The efforts to mix in slapstick and some awkward contemporary touches weaken the story of two brothers trying to overcome the normal setbacks of childhood.

—Glenn Hopp

REVIEWS

Boxoffice. October, 1997, p. 43.
Los Angeles Times. August 22, 1997, p. F2.
New York Times. August 22, 1997, p. C8.
People. September 1, 1997, p. 21.
USA Today. August 22, 1997, p. 7D.
Variety. August 18, 1997, p. 33.

Leo Tolstoy's Anna Karenina; Anna Karenina

The classic novel. The timeless love story.—Movie tagline

In a world of power and privilege, one woman dared to obey her heart.—Movie tagline

"It captures a tumultuous array of human emotions. Recalls the golden age."—David Sterritt, *Christian Science Monitor*

"A classic drama that touches the heart. A feast for the eyes."—Bonnie Churchill, *National News Syndicate*

"Lush, opulent."—Paul Wunder, *WBAI Radio*

"Romantic. An exquisite looking movie."—Jeffrey Lyons, *WNBC-TV*

Box Office: $858,553

As one more entry in Hollywood's growing trend of retelling familiar stories, this latest adaptation of Tolstoy's classic novel illustrates much of what can go wrong in attempting, even with noble intentions, to translate a powerful literary work into a good film. *Leo Tolstoy's Anna Karenina* leaves one with the impression that director Bernard Rose and the film's cast genuinely hoped to create a beautiful work of cinematic art that is faithful, both dramatically and thematically, to the revered original text, but instead it seems the filmmakers have concentrated on the cinematic artistry and somehow in the process lost the story.

Like the novel, *Anna Karenina* follows the parallel stories of two lives, those of Anna Karenina herself (Sophie Marceau) and Constantin Levin (Alfred Molina), the latter of whom acts as an occasional narrator for the story. The film begins from Levin's point of view, dramatizing a nightmare in which he finds himself running from a pack of wolves and then falling into a well. "The fear of dying without ever having known love was greater than the fear of death itself," Levin's voice tells us. "I know now that I was not alone in the horror of this darkness. So too was the fear of Anna Karenina." Then the film shifts to Levin's story as he arrives in Moscow with the intentions of proposing to young Ekaterina "Kitty" Scherbatsky (Mia Kirshner). Though he fears he is too old and plain for her, Levin asks Kitty to marry him, but she turns him down. Soon Levin realizes this is because Kitty has eyes for Count Alexi Vronsky (Sean Bean).

Meanwhile, Anna Karenina arrives in Moscow to encourage reconciliation between her adulterous brother Stiva (Danny Huston) and his wife Dolly (Saskia Wickham). Anna meets Vronsky, they are clearly attracted to each other, and several scenes later the two meet again at a ball and enjoy a dance that makes it painfully clear to young Kitty that she has lost the count's attentions. During a train stop on her way home to St. Petersburg, Anna finds that she has been followed by Vronsky, who declares his feelings for her. Initially, Anna at least verbally tries to discourage Vronsky, but her resistance does not last long after he follows her home and continues to express his desire for her. Shortly after their affair begins, rumors about Anna's indiscretions reach the ears of her husband, Alexi Karenin (James Fox). Seemingly unaware of what her "indiscretions" may actually involve, Karenin warns her that their lives have been joined by God and can only be severed by a crime.

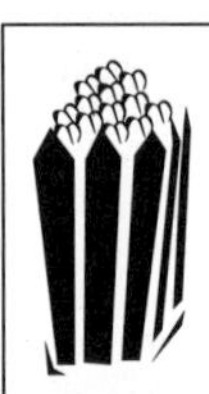

Anna to Karenin about Vronsky: "I'm his mistress and I love him; I'm desperately unhappy."

Soon Anna reveals to Vronsky that she is pregnant with his child. Alexi tells her to leave her husband, but Anna is reluctant because she does not want to leave their son. Finally, Anna confesses to Karenin that she is Vronsky's mistress. First he reacts by trying to force himself on her and telling her never to see her lover again, hoping they can simply ignore the affair and continue living their lives, but after learning of Anna's pregnancy Karenin offers her a divorce, with the condition that their son will not live with her.

Meanwhile, Levin finds contentment in his work back home in the country. He then meets Kitty again, who has recovered from a sickness induced by her depression over losing Vronsky. The two fall in love, marry, and begin a happy life together. Levin's discovery of true love and his growing happiness contrasts with the unhappiness developing in Anna's life. After nearly dying from pregnancy complications, Anna leaves St. Petersburg with Vronsky and goes to live with him in Italy. Though Anna claims to be happy there, Vronsky's happiness is short-lived because he has nothing to do. They return to St. Petersburg, where Anna hopes to see her son again, but Karenin does not allow her to do so. Eventually Anna is allowed into the house by a servant and sees her child, who has been told she is dead, but Karenin discovers her and drives her away.

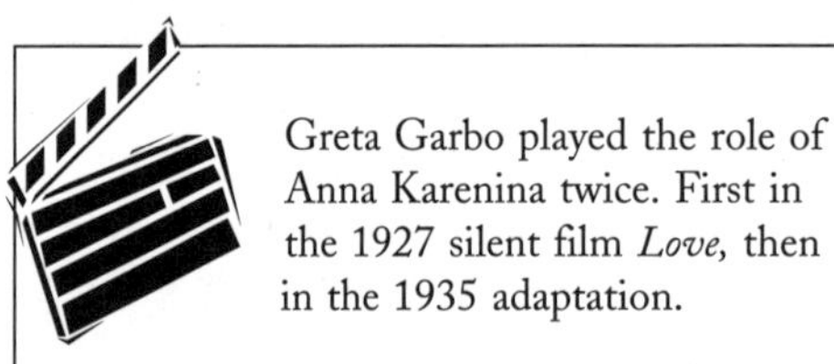

Greta Garbo played the role of Anna Karenina twice. First in the 1927 silent film *Love,* then in the 1935 adaptation.

Anna's life continues to spiral downhill as she finds herself separated from the love of her son and cooped up in the house by Vronsky, who does not let her go out with him for fear of what society will think. She becomes addicted to laudanum and throws frequent fits of anger, questioning Vronsky's love and accusing him of pursuing another woman. The count grows increasingly frustrated with her fits and warns her that his patience and tolerance are limited. Depressed and feeling unloved and betrayed, Anna goes to the train station and throws herself onto the tracks. Her death is accompanied by the image of a candle going out and her voice in the background whispering, "God, forgive me everything."

Following the death of Anna Karenina, Levin tries to discourage the depressed, self-loathing Vronsky from going to war. He tells the count that he has found answers to many of the difficult questions that have troubled him, and briefly touches on his philosophy of innate human goodness and morality. Unpersuaded, Vronsky says that it is too late for him to redeem himself. The film then ends with the musings of the narrator Levin, who speaks again of the philosophical contentment he has found in life by relying more on spiritual truths than human reason.

Filmed entirely in Russia, *Leo Tolstoy's Anna Karenina* boasts some wonderful photography. The beautifully filmed exteriors shot in St. Petersburg and Moscow are sweeping and majestic. Many of the exterior winter shots and even some indoor scenes are given a bluish hue that would seem to suggest an appropriate tone for the tragic story. The opening scene, combining the setting of a bluish, snow-covered vista with a smooth tracking crane shot of Levin fleeing from the wolves, is an interesting and promising one. Unfortunately, this engaging first scene and the wonderful photography that fills the film to follow are not accompanied by an equally crafted story or performances.

Although Levin's narration briefly attempts to explain Anna's needs and motivations, her development does not appear on-screen. The narrator says, once, that Anna needs love, that she is afraid of not having it. While in the novel Anna's needs are more complex than simply a need for love, it is strange that even this one need fails to be fully realized or demonstrated in this adaptation. Such a lack of development can be blamed in part on the film's gutting of the original story. The audience is not provided sufficient exposition to understand or see into Anna well enough to sympathize with whatever needs motivate her. The film does not reveal enough about her life with her husband to really make clear the reasons she may be unhappy with him, and the film does not show enough happening between Anna and Vronsky to really believe that anything truly resembling love occurs between them. This film moves too quickly through events that beg to be developed. Ironically, as a result of this missing development, the film actually seems longer than it is. Anna comes across as a spoiled, cold, amoral malcontent who hardly seems like she could be happy anywhere, and when she meets Vronsky there is no reason to believe that her attraction and subsequent affair are based on anything other than lust and perhaps a desire for adventure. When Anna is first introduced, arriving in Moscow via train, she immediately makes eye contact with Vronsky. When she next appears at the ball, she seems eager to dance with the count, so it is obvious that she is attracted to him, but that is all that is revealed about her. As Vronsky confronts her during the train stop, her discouragement seems only obligatory. Her resistance is brief, for within three scenes she allows him to seduce her, after she has quite clearly decided to begin an affair.

Sophie Marceau's performance only makes this very unsympathetic characterization worse. Where Tolstoy's Anna was passionate, originally kind and loving, and alluring, Marceau's interpretation of Anna is flat, whining, and simply unreadable at times. When she returns home after her visit to Moscow, Karenin tells her that he missed her presence while she was away. Anna replies that she missed him as well, but her statement lacks enthusiasm, and after her husband leaves the room, she sighs and pats her mouth, clearly bored. It is difficult to feel compassion for her, since the only portrait the film has provided of Karenin up to this point is rather sympathetic. The same kind of shallow characterization shows through when Karenin somewhat naively warns Anna about indiscretions. Almost pouting, Anna complains that Karenin doesn't want her to be dull but also does not like her to "go out and enjoy" herself. The response sounds like that of a child. Marceau's performance is possibly stilted by the lack of complexity afforded the character by the gutted story, but it is difficult to imagine ever finding much sympathy for a character who seems so shallow.

Likewise, Sean Bean's Vronsky gives little insight into the character's motivation. Tolstoy's count was a dashing, charming officer who never truly shared Anna's love or commitment, but Vronsky in this film seems little more than a man motivated by lust (and not even very dashing, at that). Bean's performance as a whole lacks passion, perhaps with the exception of the end of the film when he becomes extremely frustrated with Anna's hysterical fits, a sentiment the audience is likely to share. One scene that exemplifies the problem with Vronsky's portrayal and development occurs when his mother tells him that she wants him to end the affair because it is standing in the way of his career. Vronsky complains that his mother "has no idea what [he] feels." The trouble is that, while his words may be true of his mother, they are also true of the audience. He then proceeds to tell her that he finds lying and the deceit of the affair "intolerable," but his supposed frustration has not been visible in his actions, his words, or Bean's performance.

Alexi Karenin, as played by James Fox, elicits more sympathy than either of the two lovers, and although the film succeeds somewhat at portraying his befuddlement and hypocritical concern over social appearances, he tends to come out ahead and above his wife and Vronsky, as he is tolerant enough to actually think about putting up with Anna and does at one point forgive her. Karenin's most obvious flaws appear when he allows Lydia Ivanova (Fiona Shaw) to manage his house for him and essentially dictate his dealings with the estranged Anna—clearly, he feels incapable of making decisions on his own. However, even when Lydia insists that Anna should not be allowed to see her son, Karenin still reveals concern for his unfaithful wife by wondering whether he can refuse Anna's request.

Levin's story, enhanced by the occasional narration, could have been a strength in the film, for in Levin lie traces of a little more character complexity and the elements of a theme developing. One of the more interesting sections of the film occurs when Levin is in the country and begins to find inner peace through physical labor. A scene in which Levin takes a scythe and begins mowing alongside farm workers is rendered as an almost mystical experience that gives the questioning intellectual a magical sense of satisfaction and the awareness of an "external force," a spiritual reality guiding him. But, alas, Levin's story is not constructed to be, nor is it presented as, the focus of the film. Actually, given more development and a more enthusiastic perfor-

CREDITS

Anna Karenina: Sophie Marceau
Vronsky: Sean Bean
Levin: Alfred Molina
Kitty: Mia Kirshner
Karenin: James Fox
Lydia: Fiona Shaw
Stiva: Danny Huston
Vronskaya: Phyllida Law
Dolly: Saskia Wickham
Nikolai: David Schofield

Origin: USA
Released: 1997
Production: Bruce Davey for Icon; released by Warner Bros.
Direction: Bernard Rose
Screenplay: Bernard Rose; based on the novel by Leo Tolstoy
Cinematography: Daryn Okada
Editing: Victor Du Bois
Music director: Georg Solti
Production design: John Myhre
Art direction: Sergei Shemyakin
Costumes: Maurizio Millenotti
Sound: P. Glossop
MPAA rating: PG-13
Running Time: 108 minutes

mance by Alfred Molina, the film might be more interesting if it were the story of Levin rather than the story of Anna. Levin's experiences are meant to parallel Anna's, which they do to some extent, but so much of both stories is sacrificed that the purpose of drawing the parallel becomes muddled. Even Levin's philosophical musings at the end, which in the novel go to the heart of Tolstoy's themes, somehow seem disconnected from the story that has just unfolded. Had Anna been more developed, Levin's point would hit closer to home, as the audience would see that her life ended tragically because she did not discover the spiritual happiness that Levin himself did.

Perhaps the most significant lesson one can learn from a film like *Leo Tolstoy's Anna Karenina* is that some classic, epic tales are best left told in words on a page. The makers of this film obviously respect Tolstoy's novel, but the translation to a visual medium lasting under two hours has lost the power of the original story. One wonders if the filmmakers would have created a more convincing, interesting, and developed story if they had written their own original story instead of attempting to condense a Russian classic.

—David Flanagin

REVIEWS

Boxoffice. May, 1997, p. 62.
Entertainment Weekly. April 18, 1997, p. 50.
The Hollywood Reporter. April 1, 1997, p. 10.
Los Angeles Times. April 4, 1997, p. F14.
New York Times. April 4, 1997, p. B18.
People. April 14, 1997, p. 18.
Sight and Sound. June, 1997, p. 45.
Variety. April 7, 1997, p. 44.
Village Voice. April 15, 1997, p. 72.

Liar Liar

Trust Me.—Movie tagline

"Jim Carrey entertains himself mightily in *Liar Liar* and his enthusiasm is infectious."—Owen Glieberman, *Entertainment Weekly*

"*Liar Liar* proves one more time, there is probably no more consistently funny performer working in film today."—Kenneth Turan, *Los Angeles Times*

" . . . *Liar Liar* is not only surprisingly touching but also outrageously funny."—Michael Medved, *New York Post*

"Carrey is the current master of this brand of comedy and in *Liar Liar*, he's at the top of his game."—Jack Mathews, *Newsday*

"Two thumbs up!"—*Siskel & Ebert*

Box Office: $181,410,615

A birthday wish from his son curses attorney Fletcher Reede (Jim Carrey) to tell the truth for one day, which also leads to some abnormal antics in the courtroom by Reede in *Liar Liar*.

Hurt by his father's absence from his birthday party and a lifetime of other broken promises, 5-year-old Max Reede (Justin Cooper) makes a birthday wish that his father would have to tell the truth for one whole day. The plot is a reprise of Bob Hope's *Nothing But the Truth* (1941), in which the comedian got himself into major difficulties by betting he could tell the truth for a full 24 hours. The notable difference is that *Liar Liar* is loaded with profanity and sex-related humor even though it has a PG-13 rating, showing how sophisticated children have become—and how tolerant parents have become—since the forties. Screenplay writers Paul Guay and Stephen Mazur's idea of pairing a congenital liar with an innocent child was an improvement on the Hope movie because the contrast highlights how corrupt adults are capable of becoming in our greedy, anxiety-ridden modern society. The writers of *Liar Liar* have wisely given their lawyer-bashing story a leavening of social significance to keep it from being nothing but an 87-minute clown show.

The camera pans upward on the smoke billowing from Max's blown-out birthday candles to inform the audience in cinematic sign language that the gods or demons who rule movies are in the process of granting Max's wish. The audience has no trouble accepting this improbable premise without further ado. These wish-fulfillment stories, as old as "The Arabian Nights," have been used in movies since at least as far back as *Turnabout* (1940), a film based on a Thorne Smith novel about a mischievous Indian household god who fulfills the wishes of a bickering husband and wife that they could trade identities because each thinks the other has it so easy.

Max (making a funny face) asks his dad if it will freeze that way, Fletcher replies: "No. In fact, some people make a good living that way."

Max's father Fletcher Reede (Jim Carrey) is an ambitious lawyer who will say anything and do anything to win a partnership in his prestigious Los Angeles firm. He resembles the protagonist (Tom Cruise) of the very successful *Jerry Maguire* (1996) in being a workaholic who has sacrificed everything for success. He also resembles Robert Grant (Jason Alexander), the ambitious hotel manager in *Dunston Checks In* (1996), who eventually realizes that his kids are more important than money. Films about neglectful parents are very popular these days because they are made for highly lucrative family viewing, either at the multiplex or at home on videotape. Another such recent offering was *House Arrest* (1996), in which a group of neglected kids lock their parents in the basement to teach them a good lesson.

Fletcher has become so accustomed to lying that he doesn't know what the truth is until his 24-hour sentence to veracity forces him to realize how he has lost his wife and is losing his son by leading a life of lies. Much of the comedy is based on Carrey's struggle with himself as he tries to tell lies and finds it impossible. In one funny scene he tries the experiment of saying that a blue ballpoint pen is red and ends up with the word "BLUE" written all over his face in royal blue ink.

Fletcher's troubles begin on the elevator when he frankly expresses his admiration of the prominent bosom of a young woman who hauls off and slaps him. By the time he makes it from the elevator into his private office, he has angered many of his coworkers by impulsively blurting out his secret opinions of them. He then outrages and loses his devoted secretary by confessing that he had lied to her about being unable to get her a raise. Carrey is the most uninhibited comedian since Joe E. Brown, Danny Kaye, and Jerry Lewis. Joe Morgenstern of the *Wall Street Journal* called Carrey "the Jackie Chan of comedy." The only way director Tom Shadyac can try to keep the star from hogging the entire picture (which is just about what Carrey does anyway) is to turn the camera around and feature close-ups of the other members of the cast.

An Internet web site, http://www.lies.com, contained online surveys and information regarding lying and personal accountability.

Fletcher's immediate superior is Miranda (Amanda Donohoe), the stereotypical childless, slave-driving, sex-starved career woman who is becoming a stock figure in Hollywood films. She expects Fletcher to win a huge divorce settlement for Samantha Cole (Jennifer Tilly) in spite of this voluptuous client's flagrant and repeated breaches of a prenuptial agreement to relinquish her right to community property if she committed adultery. Samantha is busting out of her tight-fitting, low-cut dresses and bringing her latest stud right into the courtroom with her. Fletcher's involvement with his boss, repeatedly forces him to break promises to spend time with his son.

Fletcher's problems are brought to a head when his boss smugly asks him if he enjoyed having sex with her. He rolls over on his back with a complacent grin and finds himself candidly confessing, "I've had better." Miranda is so infuriated that she decides then and there to torpedo his career. Aware that for some perverse reason he has decided to tell nothing but the truth, she lures him into a big board meeting and asks him to express his opinion of the stone-faced president of their law firm. This precipitates the funniest scene in the movie. Fletcher goes around the enormous conference table telling all the bigwigs exactly what he thinks of them. But to Miranda's chagrin the president decides to take it as a hilarious "roast," and all the yes-men and women follow the big boss's lead. Instead of getting fired, Fletcher is in more solid than ever—but he still has to win the divorce settlement in order to win the partnership.

Fletcher's long-suffering ex-wife Audrey (Maura Tierney) has been asked by the wimpy Jerry (Cary Elwes) to marry him and move to Boston. She has been stalling because she is concerned about the psychological consequences of separating Max from his father. When she realizes that Max is never going to see much of his dad anyway, she accepts Jerry's proposal. She is aboard the Boston-bound plane with Max and Jerry before Fletcher comes to realize the film's message that human love is far more important than worldly success. He actually pursues the taxiing jet down the LAX runway on a motorized boarding-stairway in a 1920's-style slapstick chase scene that stretches credibility to the outer limit.

Since the days of Shirley Temple, children have been notoriously adept at stealing scenes (which was the reason W.C. Fields once quipped, "Anybody who hates kids can't be all bad"). Young Justin Cooper is the one person in the cast who stands a chance against the zany, irrepressible, and physically imposing Jim Carrey. Justin is not only adorable but sports what has come to be the standard adorable-little-boy haircut, which makes him look like a sheepdog. He has to keep tilting his head back in order to be able to see under his bangs.

There is another implicit moral in this story, which applies not only to parents but to adults in general. Most of us tell too many lies. We have gotten so accustomed to lying and so adept at it that we no longer even realize what we are doing. When the top executives of the Liggett Group recently admitted that, yes, cigarettes are addicting and will kill people if they smoke them, it was such an unprecedented example of honesty that the media hardly knew how to comment on it. Could it be that some sort of truth-telling mania is sweeping the country? Not very likely. Which of us could get through a whole 24-hours telling nothing but the truth without shutting off the phone and hiding under the covers?

Liar Liar's closing credits are interlaced with bloopers and outtakes in a style that has become a recent Hollywood vogue. The laughs accompanying the credits are better, because they are more spontaneous, than in the film itself. The time may come when some mogul conceives the hyper-modernistic idea of having a feature film that is nothing but bloopers and outtakes—leaving the main film on the cutting-room floor instead of the other way around. With their hair down, the supporting actors all seem exasperated with Carrey's shameless scene-stealing and overacting, but tolerant at the same time because they realize that this human dynamo is the star to which all their little wagons are hitched.

People who like Jim Carrey (and who liked Jerry Lewis's comedies) will like *Liar Liar.* There are enough Carrey fans to make it abundantly clear that he is on his way to becoming a superstar. His biggest problem, as it was for Danny Kaye and Jerry Lewis, will be to find suitable material.

—Bill Delaney

CREDITS

Fletcher Reede: Jim Carrey
Audrey Reede: Maura Tierney
Samantha Cole: Jennifer Tilly
Dana Appleton: Swoosie Kurtz
Miranda: Amanda Donohoe
Judge Marshall Stevens: Jason Bernard
Mr. Allan: Mitchell Ryan
Greta: Anne Haney
Max Reede: Justin Cooper
Kenneth Falk: Chip Mayer
Skull: Randall (Tex) Cobb
Jerry: Cary Elwes

Origin: USA
Released: 1997
Production: Brian Grazer for Imagine Entertainment; released by Universal Pictures
Direction: Tom Shadyac
Screenplay: Paul Guay and Stephen Mazur
Cinematography: Russell Boyd
Editing: Don Zimmerman
Music: John Debney
Production design: Linda DeScenna
Art direction: Richard A. Toyon
Set design: Thomas Betts, Colin de Rouin
Costume design: Judy L. Ruskin
Sound: Jose Antonio Garcia
MPAA rating: PG-13
Running Time: 87 minutes

REVIEWS

Chicago Tribune. March 21, 1997, p. 4.
Entertainment Weekly. March 28, 1997, p. 45.
Los Angeles Times. March 21, 1997, p. F1.
New York Times. March 21, 1997, p. B1.
New Yorker. March 31, 1997, p. 107.
People. March 31, 1997, p. 107.
Time. March 24, 1997.
USA Today. March 21, 1997, p. D1.
Variety. March 17, 1997, p. 52.
Wall Street Journal. March 21, 1997, p. A17.

A Life Less Ordinary

A comedy for anyone who's ever been in danger . . . of falling in love.—Movie tagline

"From the creators of *Trainspotting,* a romance as wild and witty as you'd expect, yet also surprisingly warm and wonderful."—Mike Cidoni, *ABC-TV*

"A profanely funny romance. The Marx Brothers meet the Coen boys. A valentine spiked with mirth and malice. *Life* leaves in what timid Hollywood movies leave out . . . Go on, see for yourself."—Peter Travers, *Rolling Stone*

"A twisted comedy. *A Life Less Ordinary* has wit and style."—Jeff Craig, *Sixty Second Preview*

Box Office: $4,333,829

A Life Less Ordinary is a fascinating failure. How could the team—director Danny Boyle, screenwriter John Hodge, and producer Andrew Macdonald—that made the uneven but engrossing *Shallow Grave* (1995) and the masterful *Trainspotting* make a film so at war with itself. Ostensibly a romantic comedy, *A Life Less Ordinary* is constantly sabotaged by darker, often violent elements. Watching the film is like seeing a train wreck in slow motion. The audience sits there helpless, wishing it could help these obviously talented filmmakers out of the hole they have dug for themselves.

Robert to Celine: "It's love. We were destined for one another."

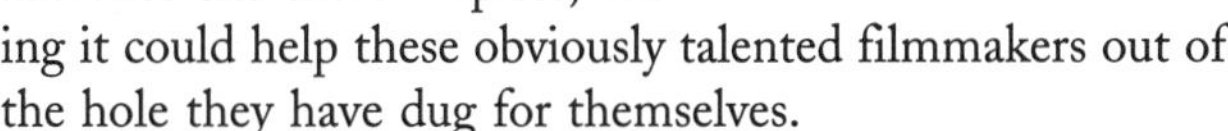

The convoluted plot is set in motion when the angel Gabriel (Dan Hedaya)—yes, that's right, the angel Gabriel—sends two of his operatives, O'Reilly (Holly Hunter) and Jackson (Delroy Lindo), down to earth to insure that certain two young people get together and fall in love. Gabriel is fed up with all the divorces and other romantic failures among mortals and is giving O'Reilly and Jackson, who have apparently been major bunglers, one last chance to succeed or else.

When Robert (Ewan McGregor), a janitor for a large corporation in a city somewhere in the American Southwest—the film was made in and around Salt Lake City—is fired, he charges into the office of the company's president, Mr. Naville (Ian Holm), manages to break away from a horde of security guards with one of their guns, and kidnaps Celine (Cameron Diaz), the boss's daughter. The epitome of spoiled rich girl, Celine is an all-too-willing hostage, given her boredom with Elliot (Stanley Tucci), her dentist suitor, and life in general. She sees Robert as a way of having fun while inflicting revenge on her father.

Much of the film's meager humor stems from Robert's ineptitude as a criminal: not knowing how much money to demand, composing a ransom note from letters cut out of newspapers even though everyone knows who the kidnapper is, being unable to reach Naville by telephone to make his demands, and not being taken seriously when he finally gets through. The considerably brighter Celine must take charge of the operation if it is to work, and she throws herself into it with relish. At one point, she even robs a bank—shades of Patty Hearst.

Meanwhile, Naville hires O'Reilly and Jackson to track down and kill Robert, with the angels planning to use this ruse to force the two to fall in love. That the couple meets and is thrown into unusual circumstances without any heavenly intervention is typical of the screenplay's fuzzy thinking. Comedy is supposed to ensue through the angels' efforts to appear threatening without actually posing any danger, but a narrow escape engineered by Celine develops through her initiative rather than anything O'Reilly and Jackson do or fail to do. When Jackson takes Robert into a wooded area to shoot him, the audience has no idea what would have happened had Celine not arrived in time, no thanks to O'Reilly, to whack Jackson on the head.

This confused plotting comes, however, at a point when many viewers will have long since tuned out for, among other reasons, repeated acts of explicit rather than comic violence. There is obviously nothing wrong with using violence in an essentially comic film. The violence in *Shallow Grave* when the protagonists turn against each other is fitting because the characters' selfishness is being ridiculed. The violence in *Trainspotting* is even more appropriate since it suits the film's manic anything-can-happen-at-any-moment tone. In *A Life Less Ordinary*, the violence seems to signal the filmmakers' uncertainty about the effect they are trying to achieve. One moment the film wants to be cute and cuddly, the next it is thumbing its nose at the audience.

To prepare for his first American film, director Danny Boyle drove across the United States in ten days to get a sense of what the country between New York and Los Angeles is like.

An additional problem is that the young lovers, especially Robert, are so uninteresting. Even the heroin-addicted, disloyal losers of *Trainspotting* are more sympathetic. The supposedly comic angels will be funny only to those who think crude physical comedy (getting hit in the head by a shovel, being knocked off a cliff by a pickup truck, etc.) is hilarious. Then there are other inconsistencies in the plot and tone of the film. The couple seek refuge with Elliot even though Celine despises him, and she engages in sexual role-playing with this creep, something completely out of character for this woman who must always be in control.

McGregor, the star of the filmmakers' two previous films, became Hollywood's flavor of the month after *Trainspotting*. Luckily, he was committed to several other projects before *A Life Less Ordinary* reared its pathetic little head. As Robert, he has no presence, no style, no charm, no sexuality. As a few reviewers pointed out, he becomes a Scottish Andrew McCarthy. It is amazing that this wet wimp is the same actor who, though in no way physically imposing, commands the screen in *Trainspotting*. McGregor, however, is not entirely at fault since Hodge's script does not give him much of a character to play. Robert has ambitions to write a cheap thriller about the illegitimate child of Marilyn Monroe and John F. Kennedy, an idea everyone ridicules, and that is all that is known about him. How a Scotsman becomes a janitor in cowboy country is never touched upon.

Hunter is an unusually inconsistent actress who can be very good, as in *Broadcast News* (1987) and *The Piano* (1993), but is irritating when she tries to be overly cute or eccentric, as in *Miss Firecracker* (1989). As O'Reilly, she adopts a different voice and persona in almost every scene for no apparent reason. She always seems to be imitating someone, but it is never clear whom. Likewise, Tucci is effective when he is most subtle, as in *Big Night* (1996), but can be embarrassing when he goes to the other extreme, as in *Undercover Blues* (1993). His dentist is constantly doing some unnecessary business to call attention to himself.

Holm, Lindo, and Hedaya have too little to do to make much of an impression. The only supporting performer to stand out is Maury Chalkin as Tod, a comically suspicious neighbor the protagonists encounter when they hide out in a remote cabin. Celine convinces him that Robert is a famous rock star seeking seclusion, and when Tod spots the couple at a country-western karaoke bar, he delightfully introduces Robert as his dear friend the superstar.

In this scene, Robert and Celine are called upon to sing "Beyond the Sea," and Diaz shows, as she did in a similar situation earlier in 1997 in *My Best Friend's Wedding*, that she cannot sing at all but is willing to try anything. Other than Chalkin, Diaz is the only person connected with *A Life Less Ordinary* who emerges from this disaster unscathed. Her confidence seems to grow with each film in her brief career, and she dominates the proceedings here with true star power. When Robert adds dancing to his singing and Celine crosses the room to join him, Diaz wears a look, a mixture of surprise, pride, and lust, that most people would wish their lovers would give them.

The worst element of *A Life Less Ordinary*, whose incredibly awkward title sounds like part of a quotation but apparently is not, is the music. In *Trainspotting*, the music comments on the action and underscores the mood. Here, it is simply here. The opening scene in heaven features Diana Ross and the Supremes singing "I Hear a Symphony," which has no clear connection to what is going on and does nothing to help set the film's tone. It is followed, in succession, by offerings from Sneaker Pimps, Elastica, Underworld, the Shirelles, Beck, Orbital, the Prodigy, Mel Tillis, Faithless, REM, Folk Implosion, Ash, the Cardigans, Elvis Presley, Squirrel Nut Zippers, Dusted, Gladys Knight, Oasis, and Luscious Jackson. Only Presley's "Always on My Mind," during a romantic interlude, seems to have anything to do with what is transpiring on the screen. The rest reflect a hodgepodge of periods and styles to no positive effect, like someone constantly changing radio stations. While popular music can be very effective in films, as *Trainspotting* illustrates, this misuse is an example of why some restraint should be shown.

CREDITS

Robert: Ewan McGregor
Celine Naville: Cameron Diaz
Mr. Naville: Ian Holm
O'Reilly: Holly Hunter
Jackson: Delroy Lindo
Elliot: Stanley Tucci
Mayhew: Ian McNeice
Gabriel: Dan Hedaya
Tod: Maury Chalkin
Al: Tony Shalhoub
Lily: K.K. Dodds
Celine's Mother: Judith Ivey

Origin: Great Britain
Released: 1997
Production: Andrew Macdonald for Figment Films; released by 20th Century Fox
Direction: Danny Boyle
Screenplay: John Hodge
Cinematography: Brian Tufano
Editing: Masahiro Hirakubo
Production design: Kave Quinn
Art direction: Tracey Lang Gallacher
Set design: Linden Snyder
Set decoration: Marcia Calosio
Costumes: Rachael Fleming
Music: David Arnold
Sound: Douglas Cameron
MPAA rating: R
Running Time: 104 minutes

Doyle has said in interviews that he showed the cast and crew Frank Capra's screwball comedy *It Happened One Night* (1934) and Michael Powell and Emeric Pressburger's fantasy *A Matter of Life and Death* (1946), also known as *Stairway to Heaven*, as preparation for this film. Both are well-made, charming films, but *A Life Less Ordinary* is clumsily constructed and has little charm beyond Diaz. It is fitting that producer Macdonald is the grandson of Pressburger since the Powell-Pressburger films vary wildly in their quality. For every over-the-top masterpiece like *Black Narcissus* (1947) and *The Red Shoes* (1948), there are bores such as *Gone to Earth* (1950) and *Oh Rosalinda!* (1955). Perhaps the team of Doyle-Hodge-Macdonald will be similarly inconsistent. The failure of *A Life Less Ordinary* is no reason not to look forward to their future efforts.

—*Michael Adams*

REVIEWS

Boxoffice. December, 1997.
Cinemafantastique. November, 1997, p. 12.
Entertainment Weekly. October 31, 1997, p. 74.
Los Angeles Times. October 24, 1997, p. F1.
Maclean's. November 3, 1997, p. 78.
The New York Times. October 24, 1997, p. E12.
The New Yorker. November 3, 1997, p. 114.
People. November 3, 1997, p. 21.
Rolling Stone. October 30, 1997, p. 72.
Sight and Sound. November, 1997, p. 47.
Time. November 3, 1997, p. 117.
USA Today. October 24, 1997, p. D6.
Variety. October 13, 1997, p. 77.
Village Voice. October 28, 1997, p. 79.

Lilies

"Artful, elegant & engrossing!"—*Time Out New York*

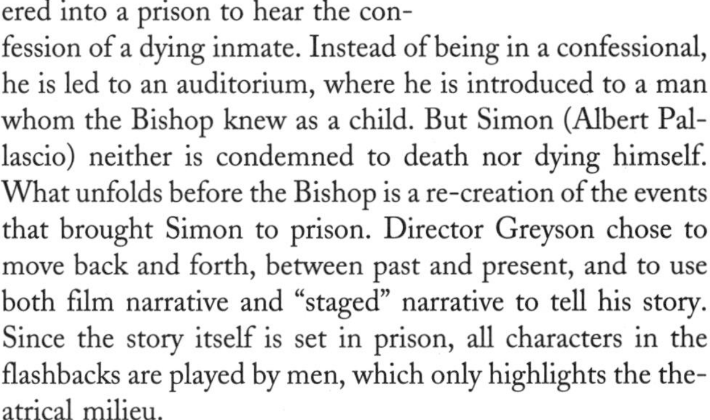

Lilies, director John Greyson's adaptation of Michel Marc Bouchard's play *Les Fleurettes ou La Repetition d'un Drame Romantique* (*Lilies,* or *The Revival of a Romantic Drama*), tells a story of betrayal, blackmail and repressed homosexuality in the turn of the century Quebec countryside. In the mid-1950's, Bishop Bilodeau (Marcel Sabourin) is ushered into a prison to hear the confession of a dying inmate. Instead of being in a confessional, he is led to an auditorium, where he is introduced to a man whom the Bishop knew as a child. But Simon (Albert Pallascio) neither is condemned to death nor dying himself. What unfolds before the Bishop is a re-creation of the events that brought Simon to prison. Director Greyson chose to move back and forth, between past and present, and to use both film narrative and "staged" narrative to tell his story. Since the story itself is set in prison, all characters in the flashbacks are played by men, which only highlights the theatrical milieu.

Director John Greyson: "The script was never meant to be sacrilegious. It was meant to be romantic. Its sensibility is romantic love."

Young Simon (Jason Cadieux) is a darkly handsome teenager, who is in love with pale, aristocratic Vallier (Danny Gilmore). They keep their love a secret (or so they think) from their parents, teachers, and friends. Yet one of their friends, an annoyingly superior young man, Bilodeau (Matthew Ferguson), suspects their relationship and it drives him mad, for he has a secret passion for Simon himself, which he camouflages under overbearing religious pomposity.

All three boys are graduating from high school and the question of what to do with their future looms large for all of them. Sweet, innocent Vallier wants nothing more than to lay down with his handsome Simon forever. Unlike Vallier, whose unstable mother, the Countess (Brent Carver), loves him unconditionally, Simon's overbearing father beats him when he suspects his son even entertains a "sissy" thought. Bilodeau, a nauseatingly earnest type, natters on and on to Simon about how the two of them have a great parochial future in front of them—they would be a winning team, sailing through theology school, all the way to Rome! Simon is torn apart by his desire for Vallier and the simple love he gives him,

AWARDS AND NOMINATIONS

Genie Awards 1996: Art direction, Costumes, Film, Sound
Nominations: Actor (Ferguson), Actor (Cadieux), Actor (Gilmore), Supporting Actor (Chapman), Cinematography, Director (Greyson), Editing, Score, Adapted Screenplay

and the accompanying hatred by society, and the promise of a dull life on the "straight and narrow."

In the midst of all this soul-searching, a catalyst for change literally drops into their lives. Parisian Lydie-Anne (Alexander Chapman) floats into town in a colorful hot air balloon, bringing the promise of wealth, luxury, and a life of heretofore unknown excitement into their small province. Lydie-Anne is instantly smitten with Simon and they begin a relationship. Simon reacts as if he is sucked into a whirlwind; all this new attention is both flattering and overwhelming. Vallier watches in hurt disbelief; Bilodeau smirks from the sidelines.

The only women shown in the film are in cameos by producer Anna Stratton and translator Linda Gaboriau.

Flash to present: the Bishop is appalled as the prisoners act out these scenes in front of him. The older Simon glares at the Bishop and challenges him to contradict the events—but sadly, the Bishop cannot.

The action flashbacks culminate in a series of events that lead to tragedy. Vallier assists his mother in a suicide act when she learns that Vallier's absent father has taken up with another woman in Paris. Bilodeau eavesdrops and sees this act. Simon finds Vallier to tell him that he is going away with Lydie-Anne. They are caught in an embrace by Bilodeau, who bursts forth with his love for Simon and the possibility of blackmail for Vallier. When Simon rebuffs him, Bilodeau, in a fit of humiliation, locks Simon and Vallier in an attic room and sets the room on fire. Within minutes, Bilodeau runs back and saves only Simon, leaving Vallier to die. Bilodeau deftly places the blame on Simon, who is convicted of the death of the only person he ever loved.

The Bishop faces Simon and the entire crew of prisoners. The prisoners are the gay outcasts from the rest of the prison population, and they face him squarely with the confidence of having the upper hand. Violence is not threatened, only implied, and indeed, more of an aura of overwhelming sadness prevails. As the men clear away the seats and props, the Bishop and Simon face each other. A lifetime of resentment, anger, pain, and hidden remorse are exchanged. The scene fades away as Simon and the others leave the Bishop to ponder his actions and his stance with his God.

Greyson gets uniformly wonderful performances from his actors; their performances only suffer from the theatrical conceit of so much artifice, time-switching, and narrative flip-flopping.

—*G.E. Georges*

CREDITS

The Countess: Brent Carver
Bishop Bilodeau: Marcel Sabourin
Older Simon: Albert Pallascio
Young Simon: Jason Cadieux
Vallier: Danny Gilmore
Young Bilodeau: Matthew Ferguson
Lydie-Anne: Alexander Chapman
Chaplain: Ian D. Clark

Origin: Canada
Released: 1996
Production: Anna Stratton, Arnie Gelbart, and Robin Cass for Triptych Media; released by Alliance Communications
Direction: John Greyson
Screenplay: Michel Marc Bouchard; based on his play *Les Feluettes ou La Repetition d'un Drame Romantique*
Cinematography: Daniel John
Editing: Andre Corriveau
Music: Myschael Danna
Production design: Sandra Kybartas
Costumes: Linda Muir
Art direction: Marie-Carole de Beaumont
Sound: Jane Tattersall
MPAA rating: Unrated
Running Time: 95 minutes

REVIEWS

Boxoffice. April, 1997, p. 180.
Los Angeles Times. October 17, 1997, p. F12.
New York Times. October 11, 1997, p. C16.
San Francisco Chronicle. October 10, 1997, p. C5.
San Francisco Examiner. October 10, 1997, p. C5.
Sight and Sound. January, 1998, p. 49.
Village Voice. October 21, 1997, p. 85.

The Locusts

Every betrayal begins with trust.—Movie tagline

Vince Vaughn does his best Paul Newman imitation as the drifter/stud with a secret past in John Patrick Kelley's allegorical cliche, *The Locusts*. The first-time writer-director attempts to imbue his tale of lust, liquor and lechery with Freudian symbolism, the trashy, smoke-filled milieu of Tennessee Williams and the sordid melodrama of William Faulkner. At least Kelley spares us the predictable sweaty Southern locale by transplanting the story to the sweaty Midwest.

Kitty to Clay: "So, now we're going to skip the sex part and go straight to the brooding?"

Family secrets are stirred up when a mysterious stranger drifts into the small 1950's cattle-ranching town of Sealy, Kansas. In search of work, Clay Hewitt (Vince Vaughn) lands a job at a ranch owned by sex-obsessed widow Delilah Potts (Kate Capshaw). Clay is one of those rugged men, adored in a plain white t-shirt with a pack of cigarettes rolled up in the one sleeve, who always seems to be posing in doorways, smoking seductively as he contemplates his next move. Delilah, in turn, is the alcoholic, nymphomaniacal, castrating older woman who beds all the young farmhands.

Before long, Clay is fending off Delilah's advances, preferring instead to practice all sorts of sexual acrobatics with Kitty (Ashley Judd), the local girl with the heart of gold. (The women characters are of the classic madonna/whore stereotype.) While Clay seems able to resist Delilah, he is inexplicably drawn to her emotionally-damaged son, Flyboy (Jeremy Davies of *Spanking the Monkey*, 1996). The boy stopped talking years earlier when his father committed suicide after catching Delilah in bed with another man, and Clay seems determined to teach fearful Flyboy how to be a man. As their friendship grows, the guarded family secrets come flooding to the surface.

Filmmaker Kelley succeeds in visually re-creating the 1950s; but the ultimate effect is curiously dated. Rather than strive to re-interpret the genre and transcend the melodrama, Kelley opts for the easier route of simply trying to emulate earlier films. The dialogue is stiff and loaded with innuendo, while the actors succumb to playing the period rather than the characters.

There are few sins that are not covered by *The Locusts*; revenge, incest, lust, and suicide all make an appearance sooner or later. Redemption, atonement and salvation are also present, along with the use of blatant metaphors—the castration of Flyboy's pet bull tops the list that also includes the characters' names and the film's title.

The casting of sometime-actress Kate Capshaw is quite savvy of director Kelley, not because of her talent, but more importantly because she is also the wife of Steven Spielberg. What better way to get a famous filmmaker to see your work? Unfortunately, it is this very casting that intensifies the flaws of *The Locusts*. Not necessarily known for her body of work—just witness her shrieking, weak heroine in Spielberg's *Indiana Jones and the Temple of Doom* (1984)—Ms. Capshaw has worked only sporadically over the past years.

Actor Vince Vaughn caught Hollywood's attention with his role in the independent feature *Swingers* (1997), then went on to more mainstream work in Spielberg's *Jurassic Park* sequel, *The Lost World* (1997). Ashley Judd played the young Marilyn Monroe in HBO's *Norma Jean and Marilyn* (1997), and recently appeared with Morgan Freeman in the dark thriller *Kiss the Girls* (1997).

The Locusts is nothing if not ambitious. But at over two hours, the film sags under the weight of its own preten-

CREDITS

Delilah Ashford Potts: Kate Capshaw
Clay Hewitt: Vince Vaughn
Flyboy: Jeremy Davies
Kitty: Ashley Judd
Earl: Paul Rudd
Joel: Daniel Meyer
Patsy: Jessica Capshaw

Origin: USA
Released: 1997
Production: Brad Krevoy, Steven Stabler and Bradley Thomas for Orion Pictures; released by MGM
Direction: John Patrick Kelley
Screenplay: John Patrick Kelley
Cinematography: Phedon Papmichael
Editing: Erica Flaum, Kathryn Himoff
Production design: Sherman Williams
Art direction: Roy Metcalf
Costumes: Gail McMullen
Music: Carter Burwell
Sound: Paul Cusack
MPAA rating: R
Running Time: 123 minutes

tiousness and predictability. John Patrick Kelley obviously had hoped to recreate one of those sordid tales of moral deprivation that were so popular in the late Fifties and early Sixties—Martin Ritt's *Hud* (1963) quickly comes to mind—where the characters oozed sex from every pore. What Mr. Kelley gave us, however, was an overwrought, though professionally-assembled, piece of regurgitated pulp.

—Patricia Kowal

REVIEWS

Boxoffice. December, 1997, p. 54.
Chicago Sun-Times. October 3, 1997.
Entertainment Weekly. October 14, 1997, p. 46.
Los Angeles Times. October 3, 1997, p. F14.
New York Times. October 3, 1997.
People. October 20, 1997, p. 21.
San Francisco Chronicle. October 3, 1997, p. C5.
San Francisco Examiner. October 3, 1997, p. C3.
USA Today. October 3, 1997, p. 8D.
Variety. September 8, 1997, p. 79.
Washington Post. October 3, 1997, p. B4.

Lost Highway

"Transfixing! Seriously spooky."—Janet Maslin, *New York Times*

"Hypnotic, sizzlingly erotic! Patricia Arquette gives off enough come-on carnality to singe the screen!"—Peter Travers, *Rolling Stone*

Box Office: $3,932,613

The suspicion that David Lynch has been gradually deconstructing American cinema is given ample evidence in *Lost Highway*, easily his most important work to date. *Lost Highway* takes off where *Wild at Heart* (1990) left off, pushing the limits of the road to the breaking point. While this film is not explicitly a road film, it reveals the point at which all films are road films. It does this by foregrounding narrative and disassembling the logic that guides plot and structure, a logic invested in a linear conception of time as moving from past to present to future. *Lost Highway* opts instead for a cyclical narrative that weaves back to its original point of departure, thus complicating the notion of beginning and ending, origin and destination. This cyclical pattern mirrors the reflexive nature of consciousness, revealing that it is in the mirror and the double that closure, coherence, and metaphysical binaries break apart. While Lynch has always made ample use of the flashback and parallel realities, incongruent points in space and time which exist simultaneously, in this film he takes them to their limit, permitting his characters the freedom to transverse the laws of logic and yet remain trapped in the grip of their existences. The result is a film of uncanny complexity and terror, demonstrating that there is nothing scarier than the double, the breakdown of logic, and the reappearance of something passed by miles ago.

Two worlds collide as one man tries to investigate the murder of his wife in David Lynch's surreal murder mystery *Lost Highway*.

Playing on classic film noir images and moods the film begins in the stylish retro interior of a sax player named Fred (Bill Pullman) who hears a strange message on his home intercom informing him that Dick Laurent is dead. But who is Dick Laurent? He looks out the window but there is no one. He and his wife Renee (Patricia Arquette) occupy their Los Angeles home like mutual suspects, double agents in a film noir script. He feels that he is not quite himself and that his wife is unfamiliar. Their silence locates the infinity between each unique, isolated individual. Each word that passes between them roars out into a void like a lighthouse beacon. On three successive days they find an anonymous unmarked envelope containing a video on their front steps. On the first day they watch the video together and it seems that a terrible secret involving one of them is about to be revealed to the other. But the first video is not yet narrative. It is merely a single shot of the exterior of their home. On the second day they watch with horror as narrative develops. The camera repeats the first image and follows with a second shot that has entered their interior, traveling up their staircase and into their bedroom where it looks down from an unlikely angle at the two of them sleeping.

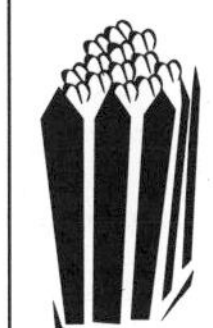

Fred: "I like to remember things my own way, how I remember them, not how they actually happened."

After informing the police they attend a party where Fred is approached by a sinister and ghastly man in black who claims to be both at the party and inside Fred's house simultaneously. When Fred resists the impossible, the nameless man (Robert Blake) pulls out a cellular phone and insists that he call to verify. When the nameless man answers on the other end followed by an echoing double laugh, Fred flees for home with Renee. On the third day the anonymous package has lost its sinister edge and become simply routine. Fred casually flicks the tape into the VCR before his wife can respond to his "aren't you going to watch the tape, honey?" To his horrified surprise the final image discloses a scene of himself over the bloody dismembered body of his wife. He's tried, condemned to death, and locked in a cell.

Co-screenwriter Barry Gifford is the author of *Wild at Heart,* which Lynch adapted for his 1990 film.

In his cell Fred suffers from excruciating head pain coupled with black-and-white memories of the murder scene that simply correspond to the video sequence. One night he reaches unbearable levels of pain and sees frantic images of the yellow dotted lines of the highway, a stranger approaching the road, and a windowless house in the desert that explodes and then miraculously implodes back into its original form. This is the scene of the first exchange. The following morning it is not Fred who sits in the cell. He has been replaced by a gentle young man named Pete (Balthazar Getty), who shows marks of a forgotten violence on his face and is uncertain how he got there or why. Pete is released to his parents, his mechanics job, and his girlfriend, but he is not quite himself.

At the auto shop Pete's most devoted patron, Mr. Eddy (Robert Loggia), leader of an underground sex ring, pays him a visit one day in his black Cadillac convertible accompanied by a blond bombshell named Alice (Patricia Arquette) who bears an uncanny resemblance to the dark haired Renee. Pete's first vision of Alice, emerging like a myth from the black Cadillac, is one of Lynch's privileged moments, a break into dream-time, music-time, enacting a moment of falling, into love, into an insatiable pursuit, a bottomless darkness, and into the web of the femme fatal. Their clandestine affair will slowly develop across a series of nights of hotel sex under the eyes of two laws: the police investigators and the sinister threat of Mr. Eddy and his friend the nameless man. As in *Wild at Heart* repeated episodes of gratifying sex merely highlight the perpetual gnaw, the itch that can never be scratched away.

As the threat encroaches the lovers are driven into flight. She concocts a plot whereby they will rob her pimp and flee with the cash. At the appointed time Pete enters the pimp's home and is accosted by an enormous obscene screen image of the naked Alice being fucked to the sound of industrial German music. They accidentally murder the pimp and hit the road but not before he glimpses a photo of Alice and Renee, blond and brunette, side by side in the same frame with the ring boys. Something is amiss, a mystery beckons to be resolved. Alice leads him to the house of a fence who will buy their goods, and oddly it is the same desolate house in the desert from Fred's mind. No one is home. They make love and when he cries out to her in anguish that he wants her she says in a roaring whisper "you will never have me," then walks toward the house and enters, becoming the receding destination of desire incarnate. The house is once again the site of exchange.

Pete transforms into Fred and rises to follow Alice to the house, but she has been displaced by the nameless man. Fred is chased to his car by the nameless man who films his flight with a video camera. Fred stops eventually at a motel along the road named the Lost Highway. In the adjoining room his wife Renee is fucking Mr. Eddy. She leaves and he enters and bludgeons Mr. Eddy and stuffs him in his trunk. Somewhere on the road he stops and with the aid of the nameless man, now configured as ally and double, he kills the man he now realizes to be the enigmatic Dick Laurent. He then rushes home to deliver into his intercom the original phantom message to himself that "Dick Laurent is Dead." The police are now waiting outside and a car chase commences. We leave Fred hurling down the lost highway toward yet another point of exchange.

The film's concluding credits mimic the opening ones, showing a vertical image of the broken yellow dotted lines of the highway flashing by chaotically in the darkness.

This film highlights three principal points of divisions: that which exists between one person and another, between the individual and itself, and between the thing and its representation. The nameless man can be understood as this vacant space between things. If the classic American road film transpires on a road that at first appears linear, as the path to California, the trip has always been the revelation that there is no destination. *Lost Highway* takes that discovery one mile further around the circle. Lynch has shown himself to be committed to a critique of the American dream, revealing the varmint that lay festering under the wax tulips. This interest is evident as early as his first feature *Eraserhead* (1978), which has become a cult classic. Many critics have been eager to insist that nothing has measured up to *Blue Velvet* (1986) and that everything since has been repetition and empty style. Lynch's exaggerated sense of style has divided his reception between critical dismissal and a devoted cult following. *Lost Highway* shows him developing those features most admired by his followers, the relationship between image and sound, surface and subterranean, link and totality. It will not disappoint those with strong visual tastes and metaphysical interests.

—Reni Celeste

CREDITS

Fred Madison: Bill Pullman
Renee Madison/Alice Wakefield: Patricia Arquette
Pete Drayton: Balthazar Getty
Mystery Man: Robert Blake
Mr. Eddy/Dick Laurent: Robert Loggia
Bill Dayton: Gary Busey
Sheila: Natasha Gregson Wagner
Arnie: Richard Pryor
Marian: Lisa Boyle
Andy: Michael Massee
Phil: Jack Nance

Origin: USA
Released: 1996
Production: Deepak Nayar, Tom Sternberg and Mary Sweeney for Ciby 2000, Asymetrical; released by October Films
Direction: David Lynch
Screenplay: David Lynch and Barry Gifford
Cinematography: Peter Deming
Editing: Mary Sweeney
Music: Angelo Badalamenti
Production design: Patricia Norris
Set decoration: Leslie Morales
Sound: Susumu Tokunow
MPAA rating: R
Running Time: 135 minutes

REVIEWS

Boxoffice. February, 1997, p. 56.
Chicago Tribune. February 28, 1997, p. 5.
Entertainment Weekly. February 21, 1997, p. 103.
The Hollywood Reporter. February 25, 1997, p. 16.
Los Angeles Times. February 21, 1997, p. F10.
New York Times. February 21, 1997, p. B1.
The New Yorker. March 10, 1997, p. 98.
People. March 3, 1997, p. 19.
Rolling Stone. March 6, 1997, p. 77.
Sight and Sound. September, 1997, p. 48.
Spin. March, 1997, p. 108.
Time. March 3, 1997.
USA Today. February 21, 1997, p. 4D.
Variety. January 20, 1997, p. 44.
Village Voice. February 25, 1997, p. 63.

The Lost World: Jurassic Park

Something has survived.—Movie tagline
"Thrilling."—Jack Mathews, *Newsday*
"Astonishing."—Joe Morgenstern, *Wall Street Journal*

Box Office: $229,086,679

Who wouldn't look forward to a sequel to director Steven Spielberg's megahit *Jurassic Park*? Especially knowing that the master himself would helm the project instead of farming it out to some second-string director. Expectations ran high, but disappointment seems the more common reaction. Of course, it's also a matter of degrees. Even a disappointing film from Spielberg is better than many a lesser director's magnum opus.

The expectation factor accounts for the fact that *The Lost World*—which opened on an incredible 6,000 screens across the U.S.—set an opening day record of $22 million, broke *Mission Impossible*'s Memorial Day weekend record with $90.2 million in box office receipts ($92.7 million if one counts Thursday night's sneak previews), and may go on to break George Lucas' *Star Wars* to be the biggest domestic moneymaker ever. But don't count *Star Wars* out yet, declining box office receipts, critical pans, and a slew of much-anticipated summer films could bury *Lost World* faster than a soldier under a T-rex's foot.

The dinosaurs are there, bigger and better than ever, so what went wrong? In one word: screenplay.

The premise to *Jurassic Park*'s sequel is that the park itself was Site A and that 80 miles away on another island is Site B—the location of the breeding area for the park's dinosaurs. However, since a hurricane destroyed the scientific station on Site B the dinos have freely roamed and created their own ecosystem.

Consequently, Jurassic Park creator John Hammond (Richard Attenborough) wants a small four-person scientific expedition to go to the island to see what's been going on. One of the people Hammond wants on the tour is chaos mathematician Ian Malcolm (Jeff Goldblum) who was in on the original Site A debacle. But Malcolm has had enough dinosaurs to last a lifetime . . . until Hammond tells him who the other three travellers will be. Also on the expedition is Nick Van Owen (Vince Vaughn), a video documentarian; Eddie Carr (Richard Schiff), a field equipment expert; and Sarah Harding (Julianne Moore), a paleontologist . . . who just happens to be Malcolm's girlfriend. Since Sarah is already at Site B, Malcolm has no choice but to go not to study the dinosaurs, but to rescue her.

However, when the team arrives at the island, they are not alone. For one thing, Malcolm's daughter, Kelly (Vanessa Lee Chester), has stowed away aboard the expedition's camp and science trailer. But she's not the only one. Not long afterward, an army of hunter/trapper mercenaries led by Hammond's nephew and INGEN corporate chief Peter Ludlow (Arliss Howard) arrive. Peter is out to boost INGEN's profit margin and compensate for the budgetary tumult created by Jurassic Park's failure. How is he going to do that? Well, if you can't get the people to Jurassic Park, why not bring the park to them. He plans on bringing dinosaurs back to San Diego in order to pocket a few tourist dollars. Of course, as Malcolm tells Ludlow, "in the history of bad ideas, this is the worst."

> Hammond: "I'm not making the same mistakes again." Malcolm: "No, you're making all new ones."

Ludlow's army is headed by a stereotypical "great white hunter," Roland Tembo (Pete Postlethwaite) who sees the T-rex as the ultimate trophy, and to get a chance at shooting it, he'd gladly help Ludlow round up a few dinosaurs for his tourist destination.

Of course, all does not go well—for hero and villain alike. First Sarah and Nick bring home a baby T-rex which Tembo had been using as bait in order to mend its fractured leg. However, Mom and Pop are a little angry about the whole thing and try to combine rescuing Jr. with snacking on a few humans who can be found by ripping apart the expedition trailer.

Now caught in the open with no shelter, Malcolm's ecologically-minded good guys are forced to link up with Ludlow's profit-minded soldiers of fortune. Needless to say, their combined ranks are soon depleted by the island's wide variety of predators.

Everyone concerned with the sequel admits that this film is much darker than the original. They must be referring not only to the high body count—including one dog!—but also to the number of scenes shot at night which gives the film a very grainy quality. (Cinematographer Janusz

AWARDS AND NOMINATIONS

Academy Awards 1997 Nominations: Visual Effects

Kaminski who did the B&W shooting on Spielberg's *Schindler's List* is the only member of *Lost World*'s tech staff who is not an alumnus of *Jurassic Park.*) But "darkness" would have been OK . . . if only the story had been better.

Interestingly enough, Spielberg and screenwriter David Koepp (*Mission Impossible*) developed their story ideas independently from the sequel written by *Jurassic Park*'s original writer, Michael Crichton. They conferred with Crichton, but ended up keeping little more than his original set up. Perhaps Koepp should have kept more. At least he could have checked his logic meter. Why are there bars on all the trailer's windows but the back one? And surely Sarah would *not* have continued to wear a jacket soaked in T-rex baby blood. Or couldn't he have distilled down the number of characters? There is virtually no chance to figure out who some of the people are, and eventually, as one moviegoer has said, "I didn't care who got eaten!"

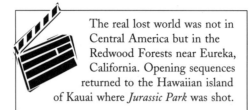

The real lost world was not in Central America but in the Redwood Forests near Eureka, California. Opening sequences returned to the Hawaiian island of Kauai where *Jurassic Park* was shot.

Lost World is Spielberg's first film in three years, since his Academy Award-winning *Schindler's List.* While he hasn't been idle, helping to cofound Dreamworks for example, he has publicly stated that he wanted to do the sequel to *Jurassic Park.* So why didn't he care more about the story and characters?

What he obviously *did* care about was the technology needed to make the sequel's dinosaurs even more realistic. And he even has added a few varieties. According to one interview, they were the ones kids most often requested when writing him letters about the original film. There are not only T-rexes and the menacing velociraptors, but also stegosauruses and some cute little devils called compies (Procompsognathus triassicus) who may just steal the show. Compies open the film and actually provide one of the most satisfying dino-death scenes. They scamper through the island's flora like funny, little green meerkats looking as if they want to play, but when you're not looking, the turn from meerkats to man-eaters. Consequently, when the vilest of the mercenaries, a sadist named Dieter (Peter Stormare of *Fargo* fame) who taunts anything living with an electric cattle prod, is "played with" by the compies, it is most gratifying . . . and wonderfully choreographed. However, the most anxiety-ridden scene in the entire film has no dinosaurs in it at all . . . only some cracking glass.

This is not to downplay the incredible technical feat done by the combination of awesome computer-generated effects of Industrial Light & Magic and the fantastic robotics of Stan Winston. *Lost World* far surpasses *Jurassic Park* just in terms of the interaction between the dinosaurs and

CREDITS

Ian Malcolm: Jeff Goldblum
Sarah Harding: Julianne Moore
Roland Tembo: Pete Postlethwaite
Peter Ludlow: Arliss Howard
John Hammond: Richard Attenborough
Nick Van Owen: Vince Vaughn
Kelly Curtis: Vanessa Lee Chester
Dieter Stark: Peter Stormare
Ajay Sidhu: Harvey Jason
Eddie Carr: Richard Schiff
Dr. Robert Burke: Thomas F. Duffy
Tim: Joseph Mazzello
Lex: Ariana Richards
Carter: Camilla Belle

Origin: USA
Released: 1997
Production: Gerald R. Molen and Colin Wilson for Amblin Entertainment; released by Universal Pictures
Direction: Steven Spielberg
Screenplay: David Koepp; based on the novel by Michael Crichton
Cinematography: Janusz Kaminski
Editing: Michael Kahn
Production design: Rick Carter
Art direction: Jim Teegarden
Set decoration: Gary Fettis
Full Motion Dinosaurs: Dennis Muren
Live Action Dinosaurs: Stan Winston
Special Dinosaur Effects: Michael Lantieri
Music: John Williams
MPAA rating: PG-13
Running Time: 134 minutes

REVIEWS

Boxoffice. July, 1997, p. 89.
Chicago Tribune. May 23, 1997, p. 4.
Cinemafantastique. June, 1997, p. 12.
Detroit News. May 23, 1997, p. F1.
Entertainment Weekly. May 30, 1997, p. 48.
Los Angeles Times. May 23, 1997, p. F1.
New York Times. May 23, 1997, p. B1.
The New Yorker. June 2, 1997, p. 91.
Newsweek. May 26, 1997, p. 74.
People. June 2, 1997, p. 21.
Rolling Stone. June 16, 1997, p. 60.
Sight and Sound. July, 1997, p. 44.
USA Today. May 23, 1997, p. D1
Variety. May 15, 1997, p. 48.
Village Voice. June 3, 1997, p. 65.

the humans and their environment. Even when the film picks up for a trite (and superfluous) final quarter with the T-rex rampaging the streets of San Diego, its blending with traffic and buildings is seamless.

Yes, *The Lost World is* entertaining and it *is* fun, but it could have been so much better, so much more satisfying. After all, one has come to expect only the best from Steven Spielberg.

—Beverley Bare Buehrer

Love Always

Between love and adventure . . . which would you choose?—Movie tagline

"A romantic adventure with a captivating performance by Marisa Ryan."—Scott Siegel, *Siegel Entertainment Syndicate*

"Utterly charming."—Jeffrey Lyons, *WNBC*

Love Always features the directing debut of Jude Pauline Eberhard, who also wrote the screenplay along with Sharlene Baker, the writer of the novel, *Finding Signs*, upon which it was based. Wannabe actress Julia (Marisa Ryan), who is currently waitressing in San Diego, receives a marriage proposal—via post card!—from her boyfriend Mark (Michael Reilly Burke) who has just passed the bar in Spokane. Not really sure if she wants to settle down with Mark (who adores her in puppy dog, slavish devotion) she decides to see him for "one last time," and then make her decision. Yet in a move that sets up Julia as the experience-seeking adventurer that she is, and to illustrate her hesitation about making a commitment to Mark, she hitchhikes from San Diego to Spokane. Not only does she hitchhike, she detours through Las Vegas, to Boston, to Minnesota and Seattle, before she finally heads up to her destination.

The film itself settles into a fairly straightforward "road" picture, with the one notable exception to the formula being that Julia is an attractive young woman who exhibits no paranoia as to the dangers or pitfalls that could befall a woman traveling alone. Julia, as evidenced from a few childhood stories, is the type that draws people towards her—she is hungry for life's experiences—and she attracts the same type of adventurers to her bosom. Along the way to Spokane, Julia encounters a man who claims he is Jim Morrison reincarnate; an AWOL Marine and an all female band called The Virgin Sluts.

First-time director Eberhard wants to illustrate the scattershot mind-set of someone like Julia—and she does this literally and figuratively; the amount of land territory that Julia covers is both liberating and dizzying. In an all too familiar scenario, Julia keeps moving rather than examine her innermost thoughts. After awhile, the elements which comprise most road movies wear thin—wacky characters in improbable situations, people who are meant to change your

CREDITS

Julia Bradshaw: Marisa Ryan
Mary Ellen: Moon Unit Zappa
Mark Righetti: Michael Reilly Burke
Sean: James Victor
Miranda: Beverly D'Angelo

Origin: USA
Released: 1997
Production: Isaac Artenstein for Persistence of Vision Films; released by Legacy Releasing
Direction: Jude Pauline Eberhard
Screenplay: Jude Pauline Eberhard and Sharlene Baker; based on her novel *Finding Signs*
Cinematography: Xavier Perez Grobet
Editing: Joel Goodman
Costumes: Judie Sarafian
Production design: Mauricio De Aguinaco
Music: Anton Sanko, Jaime Valle
Art direction: Eugenio Cabellero
MPAA rating: R
Running Time: 93 minutes

REVIEWS

Boxoffice. April, 1997, p. 191.
Los Angeles Times. October 10, 1997, p. F16.
New York Times. October 10, 1997, p. E20.
Variety. November 18, 1996, p. 62.
Village Voice. October 14, 1997, p. 96.

life with one exchange, the endless rolling highways and scenery. Ryan, best known as the eldest daughter on television's "Major Dad" is an exuberant personality, and she shines brightly throughout, making the long journey with her as pleasant as possible. Supporting characters such as Moon Unit Zappa, (who is also listed as a co-producer) and Beverly D'Angelo offer variety and charm as part of Ryan's travels.

—*G.E. Georges*

Love and Other Catastrophes

"A wryly hilarious portrait of lust, love, and library fines! Celebrates the poignant absurdities of courtship with sexual frankness and sparkling repartee."—Laura Winters, *Elle*

"Lively, spirited and unexpected!"—Kenneth Turan, *Los Angeles Times*

"Emma-Kate Croghan delivers a rip tide of hot, new faces and an off screen blast of high voltage talent."—Daphne Davis, *Movies & Videos*

"Hip! Attractive and intelligent!"—Thelma Adams, *New York Post*

"A delightful, charming screwball comedy!"—Jeff Craig, *Sixty Second Preview*

"Bursting with energy."—Andrew Johnston, *Time Out New York*

One of the more original and daring independents of late, the pursuit and knowledge of love is precisely what drives the main characters through *Love and Other Catastrophes*. Fast becoming known for churning out quirky, romantic comedies (*Strictly Ballroom* [1992], *Muriel's Wedding* [1994], *Hotel De Love* [1996]), Australia produces yet another young auteur safely within this idiom. First-time director, Emma-Kate Croghan, still faintly smacks of film school, but manages to make this brief, low-budget comedy memorable, with an appealing and talented cast of newcomers.

Co-written with Helen Bandis and Yael Bergman, Croghan's script focuses on two college students over the course of one day, Mia (Frances O'Connor) and Alice (Alice Garner), desperately searching for true love and a third roommate on their very own campus. The more self-centered and savvy Mia is bisexual and currently in a relationship with Danni (Radha Mitchell), the neglected girlfriend who patiently tries to give her space as Mia secretly pursues another man. Danni, although understanding Mia's confusion, overtly pals around with the ever silent Savita (Suzi Dougherty), who seems quietly on the verge of becoming Danni's new girlfriend. Conversely, Alice is Mia's kinder, gentler sidekick who doesn't take relationships lightly and yearns to find a left-handed man who shares her taste in movies. The two actors exhibit real chemistry in their roles as classic opposites, especially O'Connor, who manages to subtly convey her distinct personality and inner conflict without going over-the-top or seeming completely heartless.

Alice's job at the local cappuccino shop brings her into contact with Ari (Matthew Dyktynski), the campus (and the film's) heartthrob, for whom Alice falls. A casual acquaintance of his, Mia warns Alice against a romance with Ari, who has a reputation as a heartbreaker. Alice ignores her advice and the two strike up a friendship with possibilities of more. Ari, meanwhile, is engaged in another kind of search for love. A part-time gigolo, Ari is also surprisingly deep, an intellectual who wonders if his persistent coolness and detached kind of emotion isn't detrimental to his finding true love. His decision to pursue Alice is a conscious choice to get out of the emotional rut he's in and find his "opposite" in the innocent and slightly naive girl.

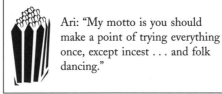

Ari: "My motto is you should make a point of trying everything once, except incest . . . and folk dancing."

The final piece of the romantic puzzle is Michael (Matt Day), a nice med student fed up with his party animal roommates. One of the best comedic scenes comes when Michael calls a number of roommate wanted ads and inadvertently speaks with every freak for miles around. Michael secretly pines for Alice and

AWARDS AND NOMINATIONS

Australian Film Institute 1996 Nominations: Film, Actress (O'Connor), Supporting Actress (Garner)

is able to meet her after inadvertently striking up a friendship with Ari who knows the girls are looking for someone to share the rent.

In an uninspired subplot, Mia desperately tries to switch majors to get into the same college as her newly beloved (who has no idea of her interest). As most college students and graduates can attest, the frantic running from building to building and from surly advisor to pompous professor Mia is forced to do to obtain the necessary permission is barely an exaggeration. Nonetheless, the bit goes on a little too long, is too predictable, and really not crucial to the story. A film major, Alice is similarly going to extremes, but in her case it's to avoid a nosy advisor for whom she's writing her thesis, "Doris Day as Feminist Warrior."

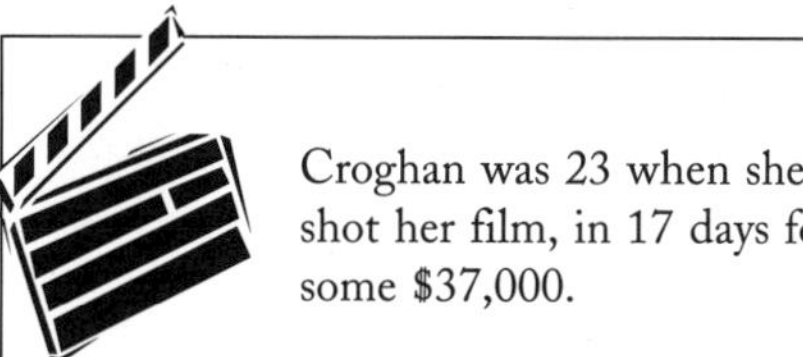

Croghan was 23 when she shot her film, in 17 days for some $37,000.

CREDITS

Alice: Alice Garner
Mia: Frances O'Connor
Michael: Matt Day
Ari: Matthew Dyktynski
Danni: Radha Mitchell
Savita: Suzi Doughtery
Prof. Leach: Kim Gyngell
Dr. Russell: Suzanne Dowling

Origin: Australia
Released: 1996
Production: Stavros Adonis Efthymiou for Beyond Films; released by Fox Searchlight
Direction: Emma-Kate Croghan
Screenplay: Emma-Kate Croghan, Yael Bergman, and Helen Bandis
Cinematography: Justin Brickle
Editing: Ken Sallows
Music: Oleh Witer
Sound: Martin Kier
MPAA rating: R
Running Time: 80 minutes

The six main characters have a unique and comic interaction with one another that culminates in the housewarming party the girls have been planning since the film opened. What keeps the viewer engaged until this point is the unpredictability of the characters, and this holds true throughout. Each actor turns in a worthy performance and definitely lends credibility to the somewhat wacky story line.

When the film is allowed to speak for itself, it is enjoyable. When the director injects unnecessary scenes to announce credibility as a filmmaker, it is not. In addition to injecting Alice with a vocal interest in film sprinkled throughout the movie, Croghan, in a rather self-conscious effort, also manages to pay homage to film's past and present great directors in a lecture scene with Mia's donut-scarfing professor. Although humorous, it seems to belong in another film and detracts from the engaging love stories being played out.

A cohesive story it is not, but nonetheless an entertaining and fresh one. Although visually it looks like what it cost to make, original music and interesting cover tunes from bands like Bellydancer, Swoop, Blue Mink, Died Pretty, and SPDFGH (not to mention a song written by lead O'Connor) add perfectly to the film's original, lowbrow appeal.

—Hilary Weber

REVIEWS

Boxoffice. August, 1996, p. 54.
Chicago Tribune. April 11, 1997, p. 5.
Entertainment Weekly. April 4, 1997, p. 68.
Hollywood Reporter. March 26, 1997, p. 6.
Los Angeles Times. March 31, 1997, p. F1.
Los Angeles Times. April 4, 1997, p. F1.
New York Times. March 27, 1997, p. B7.
People. April 21, 1997, p. 23.
Sight and Sound. May, 1997, p. 48.
Variety. May 20, 1996, p. 34.
Village Voice. April 1, 1997, p. 72.

love jones

Get together. Fall apart. Start over.—Movie tagline

"Sizzling, sexy and refreshing!"—Nicole Andrews, *ABC Radio Network*

"A smart, perceptive film."—Roger Ebert, *Chicago Sun-Times*

"Glamorous, romantic fun!"—Kenneth Turan, *Los Angeles Times*

"*love jones* has what the best romantic comedies all have, sensational chemistry between the two attractive leads."—Stephen Farber, *Movieline*

"A smart, sassy romantic comedy!"—Leah Rozen, *People*

"Finally, Hollywood is realizing that gangs are not the only African-American story."—Chris Hewitt, *St. Paul Pioneer Press*

"Genuinely passionate! *love jones* reminds you just how sweet love can be."—Dyani Sexton, *Vibe*

Box Office: $12,554,569

love jones is a love story, capturing the young black bohemian scene in Chicago. Writer/director Theodore Witcher describes it as "a modern version of the Harlem Renaissance." Following the romance of aspiring novelist Darius Lovehall (Larenz Tate) and upcoming photographer Nina Mosely (Nia Long), *love jones* depicts the couple connecting at the Sanctuary, a hip spot for poetry readings.

But Darius' pursuit, including a poem spontaneously dedicated to her on stage, is timed poorly, since Nina is on the rebound from a breakup with her fiance. Yet his charm and persistence finally melt her resistance. They enjoy an evening with friends, and reggae dancing. He admires her photography, and claiming he only wants to talk, Darius ends up spending the night, and greets her the next morning with breakfast.

Nina tells her friend Josie (Lisa Nicole Carson) about the evening, comparing their sex to a conversation, but insists they're just "kickin'"—it's casual. Darius also claims to friend Savon (Isaiah Washington) that "it ain't no love thing"—yet their emotions contradict their words. Savon, suffering from marital problems, warns of falling in love—"when the jones come down."

To test Darius' intentions and the seriousness of their relationship, Nina takes Josie's advice and heads to New York when her old boyfriend beckons her back with a train ticket. Darius acts cool, belying his hurt. Her trip ends badly, but when she returns he's seeing another. So Darius' smooth pal, Hollywood (Bill Bellamy), puts the moves on Nina, and when they all meet up at a party together, a confrontation clears the air of misunderstandings.

After they tentatively make-up, their previous flirtation turns into a real relationship. Yet issues of trust and communication still loom between them when Nina finds a girl's number on his wall. They haven't been as honest with each other, or themselves, as they are with friends about how they really feel. She leaves, and he willingly lets her go.

One year later, Nina has headed off to New York to start shooting professionally, while Darius publishes his book, *Gypsy Eyes*. It's dedicated to "the woman who helped me reach my level—she knows who she is." When back in Chicago for a photo shoot, she stops at the Sanctuary to read a poem about the memory of love, hoping he's there to receive it. Disappointed, Nina jumps into a taxi as Darius calls out—and they finally profess their love. With the separation of miles, however, it's bad timing again—though a hint of hope hangs between them.

CREDITS

Darius Lovehall: Larenz Tate
Nina Mosley: Nia Long
Savon Garrison: Isaiah Washington
Josie Nichols: Lisa Nicole Carson
Marvin Cox: Khalil Kain
Eddie Coles: Leonard Roberts
Sheila Downes: Bernadette L. Clarke
Hollywood: Bill Bellamy

Origin: USA
Released: 1997
Production: Nick Wechsler and Jeremiah Samuels; released by New Line Cinema
Direction: Theodore Witcher
Screenplay: Theodore Witcher
Cinematography: Ernest Holzman
Editing: Maysie Hoy
Music: Darryl Jones
Production design: Roger Fortune
Art direction: Cydney M. Harris
Costumes: Shawn Barton
Sound: Scott D. Smith
MPAA rating: R
Running Time: 108 minutes

The plot meanders, and although it's realistic, perhaps, little moves the story along, except your wish that these appealing characters would get together. There are lots of nice ideas on screen, interesting moments, sharp dialogue (too much of it), and a glimpse into the world of educated and creative African Americans that is rarely portrayed on film. If a "love jones" means finding "the one," this film may need a fix—and this couple too.

—Roberta Cruger

REVIEWS

Boxoffice. May, 1997, p. 63.
Chicago Tribune. March 14, 1997, p. 5.
Entertainment Weekly. March 14, 1997, p. 59.
Los Angeles Times. March 14, 1997, p. F1.
New York Times. March 14, 1997, p. B14.
People. March 17, 1997, p. 21
Sight and Sound. July, 1997, p. 46.
USA Today. March 14, 1997, p. 4D.
Variety. January 27, 1997, p. 75.
Village Voice. March 18, 1997, p. 69.

Love Serenade

Sisters will do anything to hook the right man. *Love Serenade* is a comedy that proves men are a whole other species.—Movie tagline

"A movie of fantastic originality!"—Elizabeth Weitzman, *Cover Magazine*

"Wickedly funny!"—Kenneth Turan, *Los Angeles Times*

"Hilarious and tantalizing!"—Stephen Farber, *Movieline*

"A wonderful comic invention!"—Janet Maslin, *The New York Times*

"A very funny movie with a very unexpected ending!"—David Ansen, *Newsweek*

Australian writer/director Shirley Barrett's first film, *Love Serenade*, sneaks up on you. In a deadpan style, Barrett depicts what happens when sleazy, urbane, pseudo-sophistication meets backwater desperation. This film's thin, deft story modestly points the way to larger truths about the impact of feral mass culture on vulnerable proletarian hearts. It's a lot of fun to watch, a real original, and never heavy-handed.

The Hurley sisters—love-starved, worldly-wise Vicki Ann (Rebecca Frith) and painfully shy, awkward, clueless Dimity (Mirando Otto)—have exhausted their romantic prospects in their shoddy outback hometown of Sunray, Australia. Dimity (whose very name seems to suggest how out of touch she is) has never even kissed a man. Vicki, who runs a hair salon, had a boyfriend, until he fell on his chain saw. Albert (John Alansu), the strange older man who owns the town's Chinese restaurant where Dimity works as a waitress, at one time took a shine to Vicki Ann, but she didn't like his habit of practicing nudism at home.

Ken on the radio: "Ever hear the expression 'Stop the world, I want to get off?' Well, my name is Ken Sherry. And I got off in Sunray."

For the sisters, there's nothing left to catch in Sunray except fish, and that's what they're trying to do when a beat-up Datsun speeds into town. Returning home with a huge cod in hand, they find the car in the driveway next door, and the vanity license plate announces: SHERRY. Vicki Ann is ecstatic: the legendary Brisbane disc jockey Ken Sherry (George Shevtsov) has arrived in town to become the local radio station's new one-man show, replacing an ancient record-spinner who died of a liver ailment.

Man-hungry Vicki Ann trains her sights on the new neighbor, hoping to woo him with chicken casseroles and batting eyelashes. Sherry is an aging, lanky, hook-nose hipster who looks like Ichabod Crane as a lounge lizard. He has wrecked three marriages and presumably his radio career by clinging to the outmoded 1970s-style free-love philosophy expressed in the reptilian Barry White songs he habitually plays. He's everything the tightly- permed, would-be sophisticate Vicki Ann has ever imagined she desires, namely, a man who does not hail from Sunray, and his B- grade celebrity intoxicates her. Sherry wears print shirts with the buttons undone, sports sunglasses, and preaches his vapid hedonism on the air, telling listeners: "Go placidly amidst the haste . . . You are a child of the universe." The locals are such yokels that they fall for his phony patter and antediluvian charms.

Shevtsov's Sherry is exactly what you'd expect a two-bit deejay whose career and life are on the downside to look and act like. He even practices tai chi in his backyard, drawing worshipful stares from Dimity. Sherry pretends his exile to the lowest rung of the radio world is a self-chosen embrace of the simple life, and on the air he alternately insults and woos his hick listeners, reveling in his new life as a big fish in a small pond. Shevtsov is dead-on and hilarious, and his performance really makes this chancy film go.

Sherry looks like a cat who's captured a canary when he finds his shopworn come-ons work like fairy dust on his dim neighbors. Barrett uses the disco-era songs—mostly White's outrageous seductions—to superb effect, especially the movie's title track, which begins with the command: "Take it off. I want to see you the way you came into the world." Sherry imagines himself Barry White's incarnation, and mimics his laid-back, take-charge style with women.

Barrett makes the situation work for viewers by stopping just short of ridicule. Those viewers who long ago graduated from a macho, jive-talking worldview can see Sherry's game as hopelessly lame, but Barrett and her two lead actresses insist that you believe that such people as the Hurleys still pine for the Ken Sherrys of the world. Compare *Love Serenade* to its contemporary *Austin Powers*. In the latter, Mike Myers puts the 1960s idea of a lady-killer in the 1990s and shows how silly he looks. Barrett puts the 1970s idea of a lady-killer in a place where the 1990s are still trying to catch up to the 1970s and shows how successful he can be.

It works because it's not hard to imagine places like Sunray and people like the Hurleys who inhabit such places. Barrett has you laughing at her characters at the same time you sympathize with them. They stop just short of caricature and remain recognizable human beings. Sherry's willing victims have not even heard of feminism. They're still trying to get in tune with the if-it-feels-good-do-it attitude that most of the civilized world rejected a generation ago. Perhaps the most likeable aspect of Barrett's fable is how it illustrates the durability of cultural artifacts long ago discarded in their centers of manufacture. Sherry with his Barry White tunes is like a capitalist bringing TV sets to rural China, except he's bringing outmoded attitudes, not goods, which the natives are eager to embrace.

In a style evocative of early David Lynch films, Barrett sets her story against the visual and aural background of semi-rural industrialism. A machine hum pervades the air; the sisters eat lunch in a scruffy city park next to a huge storage tank; the climatic scene is played out on a huge silo. The sound of Albert chopping up a chicken in his kitchen is so loud it makes Dimity shudder. A whistling teapot almost drowns out a kitchen-table conversation between the sisters. Everyday life is intrusive, relentless and menacing; Sunray is dull and oppressive. Barrett's tableau helps you understand why Sherry is like a breath of fresh air to the Hurley sisters.

The sisters represent opposite poles. Dimity, plain-dressed and socially inept, rides her bike aimlessly around the fields and roads of the town and its outskirts. She's totally out of it and doesn't really care that she's an odd duck. Despite her initial indifference, Dimity becomes fascinated with Sherry. With obvious effort she overcomes her shyness to approach him at the restaurant, and they begin to talk about fish, her favorite subject and the film's overused metaphoric tool. Ken invites her home to see his big fish—a lecherous-looking marlin mounted on the wall. Dimity announces she intends to relieve his loneliness, then performs what must be cinema's most inept striptease. Otto plays Dimity's sexual awakening with a frighteningly vacant and goofy grin plastered on her face.

When Sherry has Dimity eating out of his hand and Vicki Ann apoplectic with jealousy, he switches horses. Vicki Ann, on the surface the more tuned-in sister, immediately assumes that sex means love and marriage. Dimity turns out to be the more sensible of the two.

Love Serenade succeeds best as an out-and-out parody of Hollywood romances. In Barrett's world, seduction and sex are awkward, silly, crude and designed only for male satisfaction. Like a patriarch, Sherry lies on his couch and issues orders to his worshipers to do what pleases him. Without a hint of rhetoric, Barrett lets us see how ridiculous it all is, and even the Hurleys eventually understand that what's behind the Barry White lyrics and the accompanying airwaves philosophy is a bunch of hokum. It's like the curtain being pulled back to reveal the little man playing the Wizard of Oz. Barrett's gentle lampooning is much more effective than a raft of feminist manifestos.

Barrett, who won the 1996 Cannes Film Festival's prestigious prize for best first film, concocted a movie that is quirky without calling too much attention to itself. Everyone and everything is a little off-kilter, though not always to good effect. The most problematic character is restaurateur Albert, who breaks out suddenly and inexplicably with a reverential rendition of "The Wichita Lineman". Albert is chagrined when Sherry questions the freshness of his prawns and soon turns against the celebrity, lecturing him for playing too many songs "about procreation" over the radio. For no apparent reason, Albert seems to understand when Dimity tells him that Sherry might not be quite what he seems to be.

The numerous references to fish build to a climax in which Sherry, after finally being given his due, takes on mythic qualities. The film's climactic scenes, though highly original, are a little more obvious than what has come before, and the multiple metamorphoses don't really work. For the most part, though, *Love Serenade* succeeds on its own terms. Barrett's take on men and women is both caustic and compassionate, and the world she creates is both wacky and believable, right down to Sunray's welcome sign, which an-

AWARDS AND NOMINATIONS

Australian Film Institute 1996 Nominations: Production design, Costumes

CREDITS

Dimity Hurley: Miranda Otto
Vicki-Ann Hurley: Rebecca Frith
Ken Sherry: George Shevtsov
Albert Lee: John Alansu
Deborah: Jessica Napier

Origin: Australia
Released: 1996
Production: Jan Chapman; released by Miramax Films
Direction: Shirley Barrett
Screenplay: Shirley Barrett
Cinematography: Mandy Walker
Editing: Denise Haratzis
Production design: Steven Jones-Evans
Costumes: Anna Borghesi
Sound: Gary Wilkins
MPAA rating: R
Running Time: 101 minutes

nounces that the village won runner-up for Australia's "Tidy Town" award. Barrett has the look and feel of small-town, Anywhere, and its inhabitants down so right that she could make a franchise out of Sunray movies, like a Thornton Wilder gone daft.

—*Michael Betzold*

REVIEWS

Boxoffice. August, 1996, p. 54.
Cinema Papers. October, 1996, p. 42.
Entertainment Weekly. August 15, 1997, p. 50.
Harper's Bazaar. June 1997, p. 66.
Los Angeles Times. August 1, 1997, p. F4.
National Review. September 15, 1997, p. 80.
New York Times. August 1, 1997, p. B32.
Newsweek. July 28, 1997, p. 70.
Variety. May 20, 1996, p. 32.
Village Voice. August 5, 1997, p. 72.
Wall Street Journal. August 1, 1997, p. A12.

Love! Valour! Compassion!

One summer. Eight men. Figure it out.—Movie tagline

"A witty, buoyant comedy." Peter Travers, *Rolling Stone*

"Funny and moving. Don't miss it!"—Barbara Shulgasser, *San Francisco Examiner*

"Two thumbs up!"—*Siskel & Ebert*

"Hilarious! Jason Alexander is every bit as impressive as he is in *Seinfeld*."—Andy Seiler, *USA Today*

Box Office: $2,977,807

Gregory (Stephen Bogardus), a successful choreographer, lives with his blind and much younger lover, Bobby (Justin Kirk), in a beautiful turn-of-the-century Victorian home in the country. Gregory is very proud of his home and enjoys filling it with his friends, which is what he does for the three major summer holidays.

And so it is that we meet Gregory's circle of friends as they arrive for the first weekend, Memorial Day. First comes Arthur (John Benjamin Hickey) and Perry (Stephen Spinella), an accountant and a lawyer who have been together as a couple for fourteen years. Next comes the dour

Eight friends vacationing in an upstate New York house laugh, love, and accept the mortality of two of their HIV-positive friends in the comedy *Love! Valour! Compassion!*.

and angry British composer John (John Glover) and his latest romantic interest, the Hispanic, young, and very attractive dancer, Ramon (Randy Becker). Then there is Buzz (Jason Alexander), the most flamboyant and seemingly happy-go-lucky of the men, who lives for old Broadway musicals, but is also dying of AIDS. Buzz may present a happy exterior, but his impending death can't be far from his mind, and the fact that he arrives with no significant other attests to his loneliness.

This first weekend allows us to know and understand the characters and their relationships to each other, but the only real drama comes from the facts that John is disliked by several of the other guests, and that just about everyone is attracted to Ramon who makes a play for Bobby.

Buzz: "Life and Gregory's plumbing should be more like a musical—there was always a happy ending. . . . with plenty of hot water."

The second summer holiday weekend, the Fourth of July, marks the arrival of the final character, James (also John Glover), John's twin brother who, like Buzz, is also dying of AIDS. He may be John's physical twin, but in temperament they are poles apart. In fact, it doesn't take long for the house guests to start referring to them as James the Fair and John the Foul. Where John is embittered, James is giving. Where John is surly, James is loving. Where the men dislike John, they become devoted to James. And as the weekend develops, James and Buzz find solace in each other's companionship.

The only actor in the film who was not part of the original New York cast is Jason Alexander (Buzz). Nathan Lane played the role on stage.

By the Labor Day weekend, friendships have been strained and formed, personal lives challenged and strengthened, and the summer has been filled with show tunes, romance, skinny-dipping, jokes, and men in tutus.

CREDITS

Buzz Hauser: Jason Alexander
Ramon Fornos: Randy Becker
Gregory Mitchell: Stephen Bogardus
John and James Jeckyll: John Glover
Arthur Pape: John Benjamin Hickey
Bobby Brahms: Justin Kirk
Perry Sellars: Stephen Spinella

Origin: USA
Released: 1997
Production: Doug Chapin and Barry Krost; released by Fine Line Features
Direction: Joe Mantello
Screenplay: Terrence McNally; based on his play
Cinematography: Alik Sakharov
Editing: Colleen Sharp
Production design: Francois Seguin
Costumes: Jess Goldstein
Set decorator: Anne Galea
Music: Harold Wheeler
MPAA rating: R
Running Time: 115 minutes

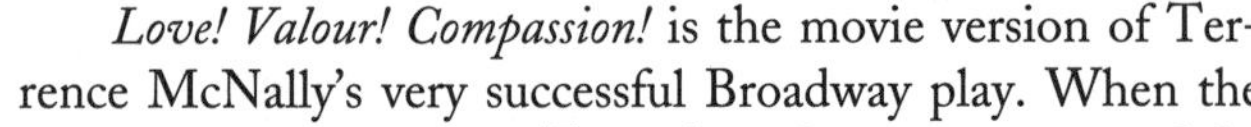

Love! Valour! Compassion! is the movie version of Terrence McNally's very successful Broadway play. When the Tony Awards were announced for 1994, it garnered more nominations than any other play for that year, and won both Best Play and Best Actor for John Glover.

On Broadway, the play was directed by Joe Mantello who here makes his film debut. The film also contains all but one of the original stage cast. The exception is Nathan Lane who played Buzz on Broadway, but who in the film is played by Jason Alexander. However, Alexander (best known for his work on TV's "Seinfeld"), seamlessly fits in with a well-integrated cast who really feel as if they have been friends for a long time.

But of all the actors, the real stand-out is John Glover's twin brothers who are opposite sides of the same coin. It is a bravura performance that understandably won Glover his Tony award.

In some ways, *Love! Valour! Compassion!* is more like *The Big Chill* than *The Boys in the Band* and other gay films to which it is often compared. Both are small, personal stories about loneliness, friendship, jealousy, mortality and coping. In *The Big Chill* the characters just happened to be baby boomers and put their particular spin on the subject matter. In *Love! Valour! Compassion!* the characters just happen to be gay and therefore put their own unique interpretation on the same material. Similarly, both films are filled with memorable, well-defined characters finely portrayed by skilled actors. This story's point is not so much about homosexuality, but about the fact that we all fight loneliness; find, lose and keep friends; and need love and laughter to get us through life. Not a bad message, and here it is told with great dialogue and gifted acting, and with wit and kindness.

—Beverley Bare Buehrer

REVIEWS

Boxoffice. March, 1997, p. 39.
Detroit Free Press. June 13, 1997, p. 3C.
Entertainment Weekly. May 23, 1997, p. 45.
Los Angeles Times. May 16, 1997, p. F6.
New York Times. May 16, 1997, p. B3.
People. May 26, 1997, p. 25.
Rolling Stone. May 29, 1997, p. 56.
Sight and Sound. September, 1997, p. 49.
USA Today. May 16, 1997, p. 2D.
Variety. February 3, 1997, p. 45.
Village Voice. May 20, 1997, p. 78.

Ma Vie en Rose; My Life in Pink

Sometimes you just have to be yourself.—Movie tagline

"An invitation that's all but impossible to resist! Certain to be a big crowd pleaser!"—Jay Carr, *Boston Globe*

"Deft and wildly colorful!"—Janet Maslin, *New York Times*

"Not to be missed!"—David Ansen, *Newsweek*

A suburban couple prepare to welcome guests to their new home, and the wife wiggles into her sheath dress and asks her husband to zip her up. The zipper sticks, but she doesn't stop her party preparations. All through the neighborhood, the game of dress up to meet the new neighbors continues. Husbands zip up their wives' dresses and a bit of fanny patting and innuendo follows. Pierre and Hanna Fabre (Jean-Philippe Escoffey and Michèle Laroque) count heads: all but one of their four children are here and then Hanna's mother arrives, a free spirit in a fast car. The guests troop across the lawn to meet the new family—we already know Pierre desperately wants to impress his boss, and that the boss, Albert (Daniel Hanssens) already approves of Pierre's large family. As Pierre introduces his children to murmurs of approval, a late arrival appears in the doorway. The neighbors smile: little girls love to dress up in mommy's clothes. The little figure in pink pumps, lipstick and taffeta dress is adorable. Shocked, Pierre and Hanna laugh it off—"Ludovic!" she scolds. She apologizes; it is all a game. He's so young and innocent. "It means nothing until they are seven—I read it in *Marie-Claire*," she says, brushing it off. The guests smile knowingly, but their discomfort shows. The perfect family has a problem.

Ludovic: "I'm a boy now, but one day I'll be a girl."

Alain Berliner's *Ma Vie en Rose* (*My Life in Pink*) is a gentle film with a big heart. Quietly, persistently, the film makes its case. Called by one critic "a plea for compassion," *Ma Vie en Rose* is never strident and often funny, full of unexpected joy. In less capable hands, the story would sag—weighed down by sadness, or veer into farce. Berliner's touch is sure and deft, all the more remarkable in this, his first feature film. In an interview with the *New York Times*, the director explained his approach: "I like films where the audience can identify with what they see on the screen, where there are emotions and you live simple and basic things. You can have all the technique in the world, but if you don't have a good story, the film is simply not interesting."

Seven-year-old Ludovic (Georges du Frene) is convinced that he should have been a little girl; that he will be a girl soon and all will be well. He has even decided on a future husband, a grave little boy named Jérôme (Julien Rivere), who just happens to be the son of Pierre's boss. A dark-eyed "gamine" with an androgynous bob, and like a changeling, slight and dark in a fair and robust family, Ludovic is frustrated by the inability of his family to understand him, but his sunny nature wins out. The young actor is an expressive, beautiful child with an innocence that puts to shame all the adults around him. Whatever Ludovic does, he does with single-minded determination, believing that God really did mistakenly drop his "X" chromosome and gave him a "Y" instead.

Enraptured by the romantic fantasies of his favorite television program, Ludovic looks to a Barbie-like character named Pam for life lessons. Pam is impossibly blonde and sweet, dressed in Day-Glo colors—her sweetheart Ben woos her with roses that magically bloom in his hand. These fantasies make us smile as Pam sings and flies about through the air, but they make a telling observation about the cloying way little girls learn about love, femininity and the ultimate, being a bride. Ludovic loves Pam so much he brings the doll to "Show and Tell" in his new school. Unaffected by the snickering of his classmates, he yearns to be with Jérôme, who is drawn to him as well. The situation becomes impossible for all concerned when Jérôme's stiff and dowdy mother finds the pair playacting a wedding. She keels over, and the inevitable reckoning brings the two families to a crisis.

Berliner and cinematographer Yves Cape create a world of vivid color, not just pink but shocking pink, oranges like fiery sunsets—the palette of Pam's plastic and crushed velour dollhouse. The little boy prefers his own world, only admitting his patient older sister and adoring grandmother. He's almost oblivious to the havoc he's caused. The parents grow increasingly more anxious to bring Ludo around. Pierre's tolerance snaps when Ludovic seems to step up his efforts to show them why he will become a girl, and very

AWARDS AND NOMINATIONS

Golden Globe Awards 1998: Foreign Language Film

soon. Hanna, taking a cue from her broad-minded mother, sticks to her assertion that Ludovic is only going through a phase. Exasperated by his stubborn refusal to conform, Pierre explodes in anger. Given the cold shoulder by his priggish boss and now worried about his job, he insists that Ludo visit a psychiatrist, which Hanna resists until she notices the boy even wears his boxer shorts turned around. This scene is a good example of Alain Berliner's understated style and eye for detail—Hanna's revelation is in her sunny kitchen, where she is happy and satisfied. Only Ludovic's "problem" spoils their happiness in suburbia—an open jar of "Bonne Mamman" jam is prominently displayed in the foreground as the parents earnestly confer.

Like a good mother, Hanna hauls the child to a doctor. Both the psychiatrist and Ludovic's teacher are kind and tolerant young women, and they alone refuse to force him to change. The psychiatrist asks if Hanna and Pierre wanted a girl, and after some protestations, they concur. Ludo's face is lit with a smile that says "of course!"

Eventually, conformity closes in on the Fabre family. The last straw is the school pageant, in which Ludovic finds a way to play "Snow White" to Jérôme's prince. Expelled from school after parents petition the principal, harassed and beaten by bullies at the soccer practice his father hopes will make him a boy like his other two sons, Ludovic is finally driven to despair. Pierre loses his job, the neighbors are cold and vengeful, and Hanna openly blames the boy. When Ludovic runs away, and Hanna finds him, martyr-like, clutching a crucifix inside a chest freezer, she finally understands what she must do for her son. Perhaps it is just a phase, as Berliner himself suggested in an interview. The Fabres defiantly crash a neighborhood barbecue, and once again, Ludovic is the talk of the neighborhood in a plaid skirt. The difference is that the family is a family again, and Ludovic is presented proudly, with no apologies.

Finally the Fabres embark on a new job and a new home in another town, a downscale development of shabby condominiums right on a busy highway. The working class neighbors are portrayed in far more flattering terms, since the refugees from bourgeois intolerance are welcomed in a genuinely friendly way. Ludovic's life takes an interesting turn when he meets a stocky tomboy named Christine (surely the child persona of *Ma Vie en Rose*'s Lesbian screenwriter, Christine vander Stappen) as Hanna at last sees into her son's dream life in a marvelous special effects sequence. The conclusion of the film invites us via a billboard, to "Enter the World of Pam" and if there can be such a thing as Belgian "magic realism" then this last gender-bending revelation must be it. Ludo's fairy godmother has changed the hearts of his family, and while the film makes no predictions about Ludovic's future, it simply asks for kindness and acceptance.

This award-winning film (Best Foreign Film - Golden Globe) and film festival favorite is far more than a sweet little fable or a family comedy, however much it resembles a TV movie in its dead-on portrayal of a noxious middle-class enclave. *Ma Vie en Rose* makes it clear everyone involved is touchy on the subject of sexual identity. Homosexuality is never really discussed, but the fear of it is always present for the adults. The film is not about sexual awareness; rather, it is about difference and the price to be paid for it. One key to the film's appeal may lie in the charming scene where Ludovic helps his young-thinking grandmother apply cucumber slices to her face for a facial. Ludo is her confidant as she passes on some hard truths to the child who clings to an identity as a "girl-boy." The rest of the family treat her as an eccentric for her pursuit of youth, and she ruefully muses that she yearns for a smooth and beautiful face and body again. Their bond is one of the soul—for wanting what you can't have and particularly acting on it can get you laughed at and worse. Yet she recklessly pursues her dream, shrugging off her daughter's disapproval and tacitly encouraging the child to do the same.

CREDITS

Ludovic: Georges Du Fresne
Hanna: Michele Laroque
Pierre: Jean-Philippe Ecoffey
Elisabeth: Helene Vincent
Jérôme: Jlien Rievere

Origin: France, Belgium, Great Britain
Released: 1997
Production: Carole Scotta for Haut et Court; released by Sony Pictures Classics
Direction: Alain Berliner
Screenplay: Alain Berliner and Chris Vander Stappen
Cinematography: Yves Cape
Editing: Sandrine Deegen
Music: Dominique Dalcan
Production design: Veronique Melery
Costumes: Karen Muller Serreau
Sound: Ludovic Henault
MPAA rating: R
Running Time: 88 minutes

REVIEWS

Boxoffice. August, 1997, p. 47.
Entertainment Weekly. January 23, 1998, p. 41.
Los Angeles Times. December 26, 1997, p. F1.
New York Times. October 3, 1997, p. E13.
People. February 2, 1998, p. 20.
Sight and Sound. November, 1997, p. 48.
Time. January 12, 1998.
Variety. May 19, 1997, p. 37.
Village Voice. December 30, 1997, p. 66.

So few films present the life of a child convincingly: most famously *The Red Balloon* (1956), *Hope and Glory* (1987) or 1997's *Ponette*. Fewer still convey what being "different" means to a child, when conformity rules absolute in the playground and classroom. Ludovic, unlike everyone else, knows who he is. He resists the panic and anger of adults with serenity and faith. Alain Berliner and Chris vander Stappen have created a unique and moving film, and Georges du Fresne as Ludovic is unforgettable. "Be yourself" is the simple truth of *Ma Vie en Rose.*

—*Mary Hess*

Mad City

One man will make a mistake. The other will make it a spectacle.—Movie tagline

"Hoffman and Travolta are sheer dynamite!"—Susan Stark, *Detroit News*

"Spellbinding performances. Breathlessly suspenseful."—Jeanne Wolf, *Jeanne Wolf's Hollywood*

"A galvanizing filmmaker and a splendid cast."—Janet Maslin, *New York Times*

"A must-see movie you'd be mad to miss!"—Barbara & Scott Siegel, *Siegel Entertainment Syndicate*

"Provocative, intelligent and well-crafted."—Jeff Craig, *Sixty Second Preview*

"The most challenging, dynamic, timely film of the year. Hoffman is astonishing, delivering another powerhouse, Oscar-quality performance, and Travolta stands out in what may be his best dramatic work."—*SSG Syndicate*

Box Office: $10,465,501

News hungry journalist Dustin Hoffman manipulates a hostage situation initiated by John Travolta in *Mad City.*

The latest film by Constantin Costa-Gavras, *Mad City* is a meditation on the ethics of journalism and raw ambition, as well as an exposé of media madness and mob psychology. It starts out with an attempt by a television reporter, Max Brackett (Dustin Hoffman), to ambush a banker suspected of mismanagement and wrongdoing. The reporter editorializes in his coverage, deemed unethical and unfair by his assignment editor (Robert Prosky), who refuses to air the story out of consideration for the banker, whose wife is dying of cancer. After a heated exchange in the news room, Max is put down by being sent out to cover an apparently mundane story concerning budget cuts at the local natural history museum.

The backstory on Max is that he was once a hotshot network reporter who clashed with the network's national news anchor and lost his job as a consequence. For two years, now, he has been working as a reporter for a local affiliate station in Madeline, California, but Max knows the business, and he is very good at what he does. Before Max gets out of the museum, he finds himself involved in a news story big enough to capture national attention, and since he is on the spot, the scoop appears to be his, and renewed fame awaits.

Just after Max interviews the museum director, Mrs. Banks (Blythe Danner), Sam Baily (John Travolta) comes into the museum to see her. Sam has recently been laid off as a result of the budget cuts and desperately wants to be rehired. How desperate is he? Well, he is armed and carrying a satchel filled with dynamite. Sam locks the museum doors and takes hostage a group of school children and their teacher. His shotgun accidently discharges and wounds another guard, who was standing outside the museum. From that point on, the situation escalates.

Max: "It's all show business today. It's not journalism."

Meanwhile, Max has stepped into the museum bathroom and is still miked for broadcasting, so that he can report from the inside what is taking place. Sam is surprised to see his story on television, and eventually finds Max, since it is clear that a reporter is in the building. Sam is none too bright, but he is not evil, merely confused, and he quickly takes advice from Max, who begins to control the situation and who recognizes the value of this opportunity to revive his own media career. Max advises Sam to release two of the children if the sheriff will allow Max to interview Sam on camera, so that people will better understand Sam's side of the story, which Max knows how to slant in Sam's favor, sympathetically. Almost immediately the story goes national and the network gets interested.

When the network then sends its popular national anchor, Kevin Hollander (Alan Alda), in to report from the scene of the crime, Kevin begins to consider this "his" story, even though Max is not willing to give it up. Max, unlike Kevin, has the ability to move in and out of the museum at will. Max has effectively put a favorable spin on Sam's dilemma, and national polls indicate that viewers are solidly on Sam's side. Kevin hates Max, however, and is even jealous of him. Kevin was responsible for getting Max fired from his network job. Kevin puts pressure on Max's assistant, Laurie Callahan (Mia Kirshner), who has the raw footage Max used to build sympathy for Sam. Kevin re-edits this footage and puts a reverse spin on the story in order to make Sam look unstable and dangerous. Ironically, Max's version of the story is closer to the truth, but Kevin is more interested in his own career than in reporting the truth, just as the network is more interested in the ratings than the truth.

Tom Matthews and fellow writer Eric Williams first came up with the story idea during 1993's Branch Davidian siege in Waco, Texas.

Events take a grim turn for the worse when the wounded museum guard dies at the hospital. Sam now appears to be a murderer, and the FBI is determined to take him out. The truth is that Sam is a good husband and father who becomes trapped in a situation that he cannot control. Finally, he releases the children, one of whom politely thanks him on the way out. Sam was kind to the children, who seemed to like him. He even entertained them with stories while they were held hostage. But gratitude and compassion will not finally govern Sam's fate.

Max is Sam's only advocate, but Max is involved in his own career struggle with the vindictive and ruthless Kevin. Sheriff Lemke (Ted Levine) is caught in the middle of this power struggle and also under pressure from the FBI, which is itching to send in its SWAT team. The fact that the sheriff is played by the same actor who played the awful serial killer Jame Gumb in *The Silence of the Lambs* (1990) surely works subconsciously with viewers to throw sympathy towards Sam, who must appear to be a relatively witless victim of his own stupidity.

The casting is brilliant. Nominated for six career Academy Awards, Dustin Hoffman is a two-time Oscar winner with a genius for choosing great roles. John Travolta has earned two Oscar nominations and a Golden Globe and has remade his image as one of Hollywood's hottest talents on the basis of smart recent role decisions. Alan Alda has earned six Golden Globes and 28 Emmy nominations. Beyond these movie and television stars, Tony Award-winner Blythe Danner has had three Tony Award nominations. Robert Prosky has two Tony nominations and has won the Helen Hayes Award for his work on stage. In brief, the acting couldn't be better.

The idea behind *Mad City* resembles Billy Wilder's *Ace in the Hole* (1951), in which a reporter played by Kirk Douglas capitalized on a story he was covering in New Mexico, with little regard for the victim. Wilder's film was originally entitled "The Big Carnival," and the carnival atmosphere certainly resembles the media circus that surrounds the hostage situation in *Mad City*, even though the Costa-Gavras film is less cynical. Hoffman's reporter at first seems to be the soul of cynicism, as when he reprimands his assistant Laura for becoming "part of the story" when she leaves her camera and goes to the assistance of the wounded museum guard. The irony, of course, is that if anyone becomes part of the story, it is the reporter himself, who gives Sam advice on how to handle the situation and what "demands" to make, but eventually the reporter seems to develop real sympathy for Sam and is able to convey that sympathy to the public.

As long as the reporter controls the situation, Sam is safe. The FBI will not move against Sam so long as public opinion is on Sam's side, but they are just waiting for him to screw up, as he is bound to do. Max becomes Sam's agent and mediator, but Max is bound to clash with his old network rival. Kevin Hollander, "the man America most trusts," is in fact a ruthless cynic who is determined to take over the story and discredit Max. His motive is revenge, because Max once embarrassed Kevin while broadcasting "live" coverage of an airline disaster. Max was devastated by the tragedy. Kevin seemed more interested in getting cover footage of body parts, and Max exposed Kevin for his thoughtlessness and tastelessness, even though it was Max who ended up getting fired from the network afterwards. Kevin hates Max and discredits Sam mainly to get at Max. Kevin will ruin Sam's life and reputation in order to ruin Max's career. Kevin is a media shark and the true villain of the piece.

Mad City should have done better with reviewers, some of whom responded with bored cynicism and were not attentive enough to get the details of the story right. Desson Howe of the *Washington Post Weekend* claimed, for example, that Sam "fires his gun in frustration," when in fact the weapon discharged accidentally when the nervous Sam first entered the museum. Gary Arnold of the *Washington Times* claimed Max was sent to the museum to do a "soft news" story "about a new exhibit," but there is no new exhibit in evidence. Stephen Hunter of the *Washington Post* seemed

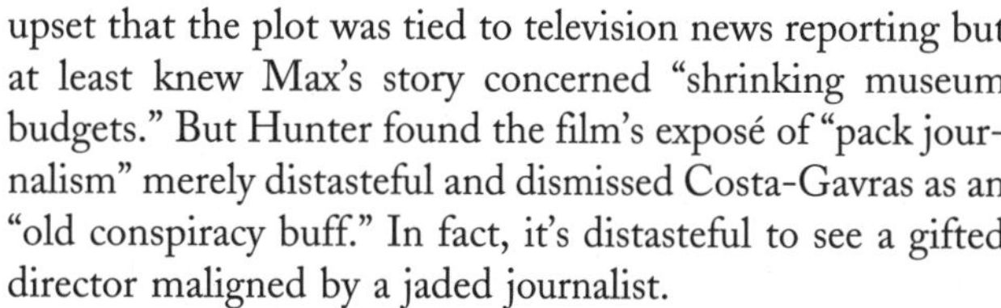

upset that the plot was tied to television news reporting but at least knew Max's story concerned "shrinking museum budgets." But Hunter found the film's exposé of "pack journalism" merely distasteful and dismissed Costa-Gavras as an "old conspiracy buff." In fact, it's distasteful to see a gifted director maligned by a jaded journalist.

Ann Hornaday of the *Baltimore Sun*, on the other hand, praised the film for its clarity and the director's "unswerving visual logic." For her, *Mad City* was "a surprisingly effective psychological drama." The film pushes a number of hot-button issues—paparazzi journalism, downsizing layoffs, arts funding, the militia movement's distrust of FBI tactics, for example, and the "venality, violence, and excess of the media." As far as offensive tabloid tactics on television are concerned, Costa-Gavras gets it right by making Larry King his poster-boy for talk-show excesses.

The story by Tom Matthews is flawlessly directed by Constantin Costa-Gavras, whose reputation rests upon Oscar-winning political thrillers based on actual events, such as *Z* (1969), based on a political assassination and attempted coup d'etat in Greece and its aftermath, and *Missing* (1982), concerning the attempt of Ed Horman, an American father, to locate his son, who turned up "missing" as a political prisoner in Latin America. Old enough and wise enough to remember who Costa-Gavras is, Janet Maslin of the *New York Times* was respectful of this "galvanizing" filmmaker's ability "to tell this story in style," and at "an entertaining clip." Costa-Gavras is one of a disappearing breed of distinctive directors who helped design the political thriller. He is still in excellent form, as this film and its talented cast certainly give evidence.

—James M. Welsh

CREDITS

Sam Baily: John Travolta
Max Brackett: Dustin Hoffman
Laurie: Mia Kirshner
Kevin Hollander: Alan Alda
Lou Potts: Robert Prosky
Mrs. Banks: Blythe Danner
Dohlen: William Atherton
Lemke: Ted Levine

Origin: USA
Released: 1997
Production: Arnold and Anne Kopelson for Punch Productions; released by Warner Bros.
Direction: Costa-Gavras
Screenplay: Tom Matthews
Cinematography: Patrick Bloosier
Editing: Francoise Bonnot
Music: Thomas Newman
Production design: Catherine Hardwicke
Art direction: Ben Morahan
Set decoration: Jan Pascale
Costumes: Deborah Nadoolman
Sound: John Coffey, Edward Tise
Special effects coordinator: David Kelsey
MPAA rating: PG-13
Running Time: 114 minutes

REVIEWS

The Baltimore Sun. November 7, 1997, p. E1.
Boxoffice. December, 1997, p. 14.
Chicago Tribune. November 7, 1997, p. 5.
Entertainment Weekly. November 14, 1997, p. 52.
New York Times. November 7, 1997, p. B14.
The New Yorker. November 17, 1997, p. 114.
People. November 17, 1997, p. 26.
USA Today. November 7, 1997, p. 8D.
Variety. October 27-November 2, 1997, p. 42.
The Washington Post. November 7, 1997, p. G7.
Washington Post Weekend. November 7, 1997, p. 49.
Washington Times Metropolitan Times. November 7, 1997, p. C17.

The Man Who Knew Too Little

He's on a mission so secret, even he doesn't know about it.—Movie tagline

"A funny, funny film! Bill Murray fans will rave!"—Ron Brewington, *American Urban Radio Networks*

"Bill Murray delivers his best comedy since *Groundhog Day*. Hysterically funny."—Jeff Craig, *Sixty Second Preview*

"Sidesplittingly funny! You'll love it."—Jules Peimer, *WKDM-AM*

"Relentlessly funny! No one can make you laugh like Bill Murray."—Jeffrey Lyons, *WNBC-TV*

Box Office: $13,520,636

With both title and plot sarcastically lifted from Alfred Hitchcock's *The Man Who Knew Too Much* (1934 and 1956), this Bill Murray vehicle has a lot to live up to. Fortunately, it does. Although the tongue-in-cheek title and disappointing trailers lead one to believe otherwise, this movie is actually a hilarious spy spoof that provides nonstop laughs and is a suitable showcase for Murray, no stranger to hilarious performances in comedies such as *Caddyshack* [1980], *Stripes* [1981], *Ghostbusters* [1984] and the more recent *Groundhog Day* [1993], and *Kingpin* [1996]. Murray proves he's still the man in *Man.*

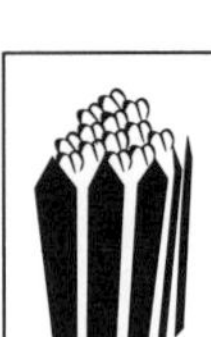

Bill Murray: "It was such a great premise for a movie—the idea of a guy thinking he's an actor in a theatrical performance that's actually real."

Murray plays Wallace Ritchie, an innocent video store clerk from Iowa who travels to London to celebrate his birthday with his wealthy younger brother, James Ritchie (Peter Gallagher, *sex, lies and videotape* [1989], *Short Cuts* [1993], *To Gillian on Her 37th Birthday* [1996]), and his British wife. Scheduled to host an important business dinner that night, James signs Wallace up for "Theater of Life," a night of trendy interactive drama where actors and "audience" play out different scenarios around the streets and apartments of London. Before Wallace is given his opening scene, however, he is mistaken for a mysterious hit man who is blackmailing corrupt British and Russian government officials seeking to bring back the Cold War and, unbeknownst to him, is sent out on a series of real assignments.

Writer Robert Farrar's inspiration came from the audience-participation theater performances that were popular in England in the 1980s.

Although the intricate conspiracy plot takes some time to fully understand, it is still pure enjoyment in the meantime, as Wallace meets "the girl," (Joanne Whalley) whom he thinks is an actress but is actually Lori, the savvy mistress of an important government official. As he plays along in what he thinks is a scene, he threatens to kill her if she doesn't help him in his mission to find some incriminating letters. The seemingly carefree nonchalance he employs in his threats is frightening to Lori, who thinks he is probably a psychopath, and is forced to do his bidding. The two bond, however, and team up to take on the international bad guys and get the multi-million dollar blackmail loot.

To guide him along his adventure, Wallace is outfitted with a communications device by panicked government officials who think he's the real killer and provide him with instructions, in code, on where to go and what to do. He hilariously interprets their "code" words literally, and while their order to "take the girl to the bathroom and make sure to flush," means kill her and get rid of the body, all they hear at the other end of the line is a flushing toilet. Wallace thinks this is all part of the elaborate "Theater of Life" staged action. As he stumbles through his misadventure with self-deluded delight at his acting ability and the thrill of the quest, he is unaware of the incredibly dangerous situations he's actually in. He is transformed from geeky clerk to super suave secret agent who wholly intimidates the cast of characters he encounters. As more characters enter the fray, the charade becomes more complex and the satire increasingly delightful.

The joy is that Wallace thinks everyone him and Lori encounter in London are in on the act—including the real police following him in a high speed chase while he and Lori tear down a London road. When Wallace finally pulls over, he gives the bewildered policeman such a hard time and so intimidates him with his phoney persona, that the cop ends up apologizing to Wallace. Murray is completely in his element with the sardonic pomposity and self-grandiosity he's allowed to unleash here while softening the portrayal with a naive innocence that makes the character so appealing.

Wallace eventually finds himself in a few situations that he may not be able to "act" his way out of—tied up

CREDITS

Wallace Ritchie: Bill Murray
James Ritchie: Peter Gallagher
Lori: Joanne Whalley
Boris: Alfred Molina
Sir Roger Daggenhurst: Richard Wilson
Dr. Ludmilla Kroptkin: Geraldine James
Embleton: John Standing

Origin: USA
Released: 1997
Production: Arnon Milchan, Michael Nathanson, and Mark Tarlov for Regency Enterprises; released by Warner Bros.
Direction: Jon Amiel
Screenplay: Robert Farrar and Howard Franklin; based on the novel *Watch That Man* by Farrar
Cinematography: Robert Stevens
Editing: Pamela Power
Music: Chris Young
Production design: Jim Clay
Art direction: Chris Seagers
Set decoration: Maggie Gray
Costumes: Janty Yates
Sound: Simon Kaye
MPAA rating: PG-13
Running Time: 94 minutes

and threatened with torture and shot at repeatedly on the ledge of a hotel balcony—but leave it to Murray to make these fun too. What is so satisfying is that throughout the film, to the writers and director's credit, Wallace never finds out that he isn't acting, as a fun twist at the end proves.

Gallagher is as appealing as Murray in his supporting role as the successful younger brother and Whalley provides pleasant, low-key appeal as Murray's love interest. Although director Amiel (*Copycat* [1995], *Sommersby* [1993]) keeps the action going at a fairly fast pace, critics were less than enthusiastic about this caper comedy. However, for good, silly fun, this cloak-and-dagger farce delivers the laughs, due in part to Murray's engaging and goofy performance.

—Hilary Weber

REVIEWS

Boxoffice. January, 1998, p. 46.
Entertainment Weekly. November 21, 1997, p. 99.
Los Angeles Times. November 14, 1997, p. F23.
New York Times. November 14, 1997, p. E22.
People. November 24, 1997, p. 20.
USA Today. November 14, 1997, p. 6D.
Variety. November 10, 1997, p. 40.

Margaret's Museum

She found a way to preserve her memories forever.—Movie tagline

"Searing and haunting. A surprise depth charge of a film."—Jay Carr, *Boston Globe*

Margaret's Museum is a movie dedicated to depicting the hardships of coal mining on Cape Breton Island, Nova Scotia, in the 1940s. It opens, however, with some stunning footage of the beautiful seascape of the island leading into a scene that verges on Grand Guignol. On a beautiful summer day, a couple of tourists drive up to a lonely shack bearing a sign that names it "Margaret's Museum." The female tourist asks to use the restroom and, shortly thereafter, emerges from the shack screaming her head off. The proprietor of the museum, Margaret MacNeil (Helena Bonham Carter), looks on, smiling contentedly.

The remainder of the film explains the mystery of what is exhibited in Margaret's Museum and the reasons for Margaret's odd response to the tourist's terror. Although much of what comes after the opening scene is grim, it casts an eccentric, quirky light on all that follows, lessening the gloom. *Margaret's Museum* is based on "The Glace Bay Miner's Museum" and other stories written by the contemporary Canadian writer, Sheldon Currie, who himself grew up in a mining family on Cape Breton. Director Mort Ransen, who tried for ten years to make Currie's tales into a film, has succeeded admirably in capturing the odd, independent spirit of the people who inhabit this isolated landscape.

When we next see Margaret, she is sitting in a booth at a down-at-the-heels diner wearing a dress that looks as if it had been made from a flour sack—this is plainly not the polished, cultured heroine Bonham Carter usually plays.

The time is some years earlier than that in the opening scene. As she sits there in all her dowdiness, she is spotted by Neil Currie, whom she does not know. Drunk as a lord, he proceeds to court her by playing his bagpipes for her. The effort seems a failure, as Margaret retains her sardonic attitude, and the noise Currie produces gets him thrown out of the restaurant.

Jimmy about his girlfriend: "They're not supposed to dance on Sunday." Margaret: "They're not supposed to work. Dancing's not work." Jimmy: "They're Protestant, aren't they? For them, it's work."

The tall, handsome Neil, however, has begun to work his magic on Margaret. Not only does he play the pipes, he speaks Gaelic. The most important thing about him from Margaret's point of view, however, is that unlike other men on the island, Neil does not work in the coal mines. She takes him home to meet her family.

Margaret's family consists of her mother, Catherine (Kate Nelligan), her adolescent brother, Jimmy (Craig Olejnik), and her grandfather, who is so debilitated by black lung disease that he needs to be pounded on the back periodically in order to keep on breathing. Two other members of the family, Margaret's father and a beloved older brother, have already been lost to the mines, like so many other Cape Bretoners. The losses have permanently warped Catherine, who casts a jaundiced eye on Neil only to predict that he, too, will return to the mines. Margaret, however, retains some sense of hope for the future, and it is this modest wish for a normal life that enables her to marry Neil. Catherine's only comment on the union is, "I'm sure you'll be happy or miserable, as the case may be. Fair enough?"

Still, the marriage begins promisingly enough. Neil, who objects on principle to working for the mine owners, pledges to Margaret that he will not go down into the pit. Instead, he works as a dishwasher at the Chinese diner where they first met and, after he is replaced by the owner's immigrant relative, he works at odd jobs. Margaret, for her part, labors as a scrubwoman at the local hospital, where she sees firsthand all the casualties the mine produces. The couple gets by, building a house out of discarded materials and living on love, until the day that Margaret insists they must begin using birth control, as they cannot afford to bring a child into the world. Neil, a traditionalist dedicated to family, is aghast at the notion of trying to prevent a pregnancy. He returns to the mines.

The mines, dangerous as they are, are nonetheless the only game in town. As one of the miners who is injured early on in the film tells Margaret, he misses the work his mangled legs keep him from pursuing. And despite Catherine's and Margaret's best efforts, underage Jimmy surreptitiously begins working there, too, through the reluctant offices of Uncle Angus (Kenneth Walsh), yet another miner.

Margaret's Museum follows a fairly predictable course. One day when the siren goes off as Margaret is scrubbing the hospital floors, it heralds the deaths of both Jimmy and Neil, felled by the same cave-in. Margaret's response to this tragedy is less foreseeable. While her uncle suffers a kind of breakdown, momentarily abandoning his stoicism as he sets fire to the company store, Margaret adopts more radical means of showing the world how the mine owners have ruined lives. Demanding that she be given Neil's and Jimmy's remains to prepare for burial, she shuts herself in the house with their corpses—and that of her grandfather who, left unattended during the recent crisis, succumbed to lack of oxygen—and she performs a kind of bizarre autopsy, in the course of which she removes what she regards as their most vital organs. Margaret is quickly committed, but she remains true to the impulse that drove her to commemorate her loved ones' deaths in such a singular fashion. Years later, after she is released, Margaret displays the items she removed from her men in her "museum" as mute testimony to the sad legacy of the coal mines. One of these exhibits—although not, in all probability, the one that causes her visitor to flee shrieking from her memorial—is her grandfather's shrunken black lungs, preserved for posterity in brine.

Like many works of regionalism, *Margaret's Museum* focuses on the local color of a far-flung place and on the oddities of its inhabitants. The benefit of this approach lies primarily in the detailed way in which the locale is represented and in the manner in which singular characters are explored. Its weakness, often, is the distance this strategy promotes between the audience and what happens on the page or on the screen. *Margaret's Museum* is indeed an odd little film, but one so winningly told—and so finely acted—that it arrives, finally, at some home truths with universal appeal. As one reviewer wrote, its sense of tragedy is as simple as a folk song. Like many of the tunes that grace the soundtrack, traditional Celtic ballads like "Jenny's Chickens" and "The Wedding Reel," the movie speaks to something deep, something almost atavistic, in the soul.

As played by Helena Bonham Carter, Margaret comes across as a young woman both deeply rooted in her place and time and deeply fearful of it. She seems to recognize that she, like her neighbors and family, is trapped by circumstances, but she rebels against them nonetheless. When Neil Currie comes into her life, she has the wit to recognize and seize upon an opportunity for happiness.

AWARDS AND NOMINATIONS

Genie Awards 1995: Best Actress (Bonham Carter), Supporting Actor (Welsh), Supporting Actress (Nelligan), Costumes, Music, Screenplay

Clive Russell's Neil, tall and fey and twinkling with Gaelic charm, manages to be at once irresistible and fallible. Perhaps the strongest performance in the film comes from Kate Nelligan, who conveys a sense of disappointment with life so powerful and of such long standing as to be almost palpable.

It is a relief, in the end, to see that Margaret has not become her mother. Employing some of the only methods of protest available to her in this land of scarcity, Margaret has become a survivor, albeit a rather strange one. The conclusion, which could have been merely gothic, is instead rendered oddly comic. When her museum visitor is repulsed by what she sees there, Margaret takes this reaction fully in stride. Isn't this effect the one she sought, after all? In displaying her wounds, isn't her purpose to demonstrate to the public in a visceral way the horror of what the mining company has wrought? Alone once more, Margaret settles into a rocking chair in the sunshine, the picture of equanimity.

Having the movie begin where it ends helps to promote the feeling that "Margaret's Museum" follows the logic of the folk tale. The fabulous quality of Margaret's life is by this means made apparent from the outset, and when we revisit her museum after seeing how she got there, we smile with her. In her own idiosyncratic way, she has prevailed against the odds.

—Lisa Paddock

CREDITS

Margaret: Helena Bonham Carter
Neil: Clive Russell
Jimmy: Craig Olejnik
Catherine: Kate Nelligan
Angus: Kenneth Welsh

Origin: Canada, Great Britain
Released: 1995, 1997
Production: Mort Ransen, Christopher Zimmer, Claudio Luca, and Steve Clark-Hall for Ranfilm/Imagex/Tele-Action/Skyline and Malofilm Communications; released by Cabin Fever Entertainment
Direction: Mort Ransen
Screenplay: Mort Ransen and Gerald Wexler; based on the short story "The Glace Bay Miner's Museum" by Sheldon Currie
Cinematography: Vic Sarin
Editing: Rita Roy
Music: Milan Kymlicka
Production design: William Fleming, David McHenry
Costumes: Nicoletta Massone
Art direction: Emanuel Jannasch
Set decoration: Ian Greig
MPAA rating: R
Running Time: 118 minutes

REVIEWS

Boxoffice. November, 1995, p. 108.
Los Angeles Times. March 14, 1997, p. F14.
New York Times. February 7, 1997.

Masterminds

The criminal mastermind of the century just met his match.—Movie tagline

"Patrick Stewart rocks and Vincent Kartheiser thrills in this witty cat and mouse."—Anne Brodie, *CFTO-Toronto*

"Fun, exciting and non-stop action. *Masterminds* is for the whole family. Patrick Stewart is fun to watch."—Don Stotter, *Entertainment Time Out*

"All the fun of *Home Alone* with a heart-stopping dose of *Die Hard* action. Patrick Stewart is fabulous as the bad guy you love to hate and Vincent Kartheiser is sure to score as America's new teen hero."—Jeanne Wolf, *Jeanne Wolf's Hollywood*

"This summer's thrill-packed cyberspace *Die Hard*!"—*Network One*

Box Office: $1,935,539

Think *Die Hard* without death or *Home Alone* with an older protagonist and less bumbling criminals and you'll have the essence of *Masterminds.* Sixteen-year-old Oswald "Ozzie" Paxton (Vincent Kartheiser) is a classic underachiever. A skinny, lank-haired teenager with an attitude, whose only natural ability (besides attracting trouble) is that he's a computer hacker par excellence and a MacGyver for ingenuity. Ozzie's resentful of stepmom Helen (Annabelle Gurwitch), annoyed by bratty young stepsister Melissa (Katie Stuart) and barely civil to corporate workaholic dad Jake (Matt Craven), who threatens his offspring with military school if there are anymore screw-ups.

Bentley about Ozzie: "He's the only worthy opponent among the whole bleeding lot."

But Ozzie's just about to skateboard into big trouble when he's forced to drop off Melissa at her private school, Shady Glen, or "Snotty Glen, home of over-privileged suck-ups" as Ozzie prefers to call it. A former student, Ozzie was banned from the premises for blowing up the science lab and a run-in with tough principal Claire Maloney (Brenda Fricker) only reinforces Ozzie's desire for one last prank against the school administration. Which is why Ozzie is lurking in the basement when unctuous security expert Ralph Bentley (Patrick Stewart) is ready to put his plan in motion.

Ralph and his security crew have been at Shady Glen for three weeks installing a new security system and he's ready to give Claire a demonstration—by shutting all the gates and locking everyone inside. Only Ozzie's already hacked into the system (thanks to an unguarded security room) and provided a little show of his own. So Bentley's boys bring out the "hard-core artillery" and offer a more graphic demonstration of firepower. And why - well, as Bentley says "Why does anyone do anything in this country, Claire, money." It seems a number of Shady Glen's students are the scions of very wealthy parents who will pay a great deal for their children's safety, $75 million (and a helicopter) is Bentley's first negotiating offer to the police. As Ozzie (who's viewing the situation) says: "We've got a *Die Hard* situation here."

Separating out the ten wealthiest kids (and getting Melissa in the bargain), Bentley's let the other children and teachers go as a good-faith gesture and received a $5 million down payment on the ransom. He's got a group of his cohorts drilling an escape route in the school's basement, which will hook-up to the city's underground sewer and power tunnels and he's cocky enough to believe everything's going fine. An ex-SAS man, Bentley's "not some sodding amateur" and is prepared for all likely police scenarios but he's not prepared for the quick-thinking Ozzie. Ozzie crawls through the school's air shafts and manages to overload the building's heating/cooling and electrical systems, temporarily disrupting Bentley's security, and causing the increasingly irascible kidnapper to send some of his men after the teen.

Bentley's also come out with his true ransom demand—$650 million in bearer bonds from his former employer, media mogul Miles Lawrence (Brad Whitford), whose daughter Bentley holds hostage. While Bentley's plan goes forward, so does Ozzie—he's managed to steal some dynamite from the drilling crew and, with the help of Ms. Maloney, he's gotten the kids safely out of Bentley's reach, except for his own stepsister, whom Bentley is holding as a bargaining chip. Bentley's bluffed his way into the final ransom and is leading his subordinates (and Melissa) into their basement escape route when Ozzie's (who has finally been caught and tied up) last prank literally explodes. Seems he's used the stolen dynamite to blow a hole in the school's pool, thus flooding the basement and washing away Bentley's men but, of course, not before Bentley escapes with Melissa in one of the All Terrain Vehicles he's stashed in the tunnels for his getaway.

Naturally, Ozzie manages to get free, get to the tunnels and another ATV, and drive off to rescue his bratty stepsister. Bentley briefly escapes, but having lost his way in the maze of tunnels, the exit he finally locates leads straight into the city's waste overflow pond and a quick pickup by the cops. Oh yes, since Ozzie is a hero (even

CREDITS

Ralph Bentley: Patrick Stewart
Ozzie Paxton: Vincent Kartheiser
Claire Maloney: Brenda Fricker
Miles Lawrence: Brad Whitford
Jake Paxton: Matt Craven
Helen Paxton: Annabelle Gurwitch
Melissa Randall: Katie Stuart
K-Dog: Jon Abrahams
Ollie: Callum Keith Rennie
Col. Duke: Michael David Simms
The Ferret: David Paul Grove
Capt. Jankel: Earl Pastko
Larry Mallard: Jim Byrnes

Origin: USA
Released: 1997
Production: Robert Dudelson, Floyd Byars for Pacific Motion Pictures; released by Columbia Pictures
Direction: Roger Christian
Screenplay: Floyd Byars
Cinematography: Nic Morris
Editing: Robin Russell
Music: Anthony Marinelli
Production design: Douglas Higgins
Art direction: Doug Byggdin
Costumes: Monique Sanchez, Derek Baskerville
Sound: Michael McGee
Digital design: Brian De Paoli
MPAA rating: PG-13
Running Time: 105 minutes

though he did blowup part of the school again), he manages to reconcile with his contrite dad and his stepmom, who promises to make them into a real family.

Although there's lots of firepower, no one dies in this PG-13 adventure. Bentley has his commandoes armed with tranquilizer guns (at least when they're aiming at people) and makes certain that the police are clear before he blows up their vehicles. And even though he's also mined the school grounds, it's with concussion mines that provide lots of noise but not much damage. Bentley threatens when things goes wrong—"I'm not a violent man but I really do think I'm going to have to kill someone here"—and one of his associates promises to make cat food of Ozzie, but the worst that happens to the teen (besides the constant terror of the situation) is some mild roughing up. Writer/producer Floyd Byars stated in the production notes that "moments like explosions and gun-fire are used as diversions rather than as tools of violence" and director Roger Christian also wanted to show that "Ozzie is not just an action hero—he's also a witty, mixed-up kid who is trying to figure out how to come together with his family. We wanted to show both sides of him in a film that is funny, entertaining, suspenseful and has something for audiences of all ages." Although adults may find the action only mildly diverting, the young teen audience will certainly take to a movie where, once again, the teen hero easily manages to outsmart all the adults.

Production designer Douglas Higgins built some 600 feet of tunnels in an old Vancouver plumbing factory for the climatic chase scene.

—Christine Tomassini

REVIEWS

Boxoffice. October, 1997, p. 43.
Los Angeles Times. August 22, 1997, p. F18.
New York Times. August 22, 1997, p. C5.
Variety. August 25, 1997, p. 74.

The Matchmaker

The most successful matchmaker in Ireland is about to hit a brick wall.—Movie tagline

"Janeane Garofalo proves she can do it all—romance and comedy!"—Don Stotter, *Entertainment Time-Out*

"A match made in heaven! The best date movie of the year! This is a real gem of a movie!"—Lloyd Gite, *KRIV-TV*

"Magical, visually breathtaking. Follow Janeane Garofalo on a magical trip to Ireland."—Jim Ferguson, *Prevue Channel*

"Two thumbs up!"—*Siskel & Ebert*

"Outrageously funny! Extraordinarily moving and utterly charming. Janeane Garofalo is brilliant!"—Paul Wunder, *WBAI Radio*

"Absolutely adorable! One sweetheart of a comedy. Janeane Garofalo confirms her status as comedy's leading screen queen."—Mike Cidoni, *WOKR-TV*

Box Office: $3,398,083

If nothing else, *The Matchmaker* could work well as a film for the Irish tourism bureau. Director Mark Joffe has his camera roam lovingly over the rocky ocean cliffs, the herds of sheep roaming over green hills, and the huge, gray, cloudy skies. Between that, the crumbling ancient stone buildings, and the bountiful friendly locals, it's enough to make anyone want to order up a few airline tickets for an Irish vacation.

Our heroine Marcy Tizard (Janeane Garofalo) is in Ireland not on a vacation, but on business. She is an all-business, yuppie type who is a political aide to a U.S. senator, Boston's John McGlory (Jay O. Sanders). McGlory is the type of style-over-substance politician who looks good, but doesn't seem to hold any political views. McGlory is down in the polls and what with the big election coming up, his sleazy chief of staff, Nick Ward (Denis Leary), cooks up the idea that Marcy should go to Ireland and dig up some McGlory ancestors. The rationale behind this is that it would make for a good photo op and help McGlory score a bit o' the Irish vote.

In the tradition of movies like *Local Hero* (1983) or *Brigadoon* (1954), where fast-paced yuppies go to charming Scotch/Irish towns, Marcy finds herself in the quaint small town of Ballinagra (actually small town Roundstone in

County Galway in the West of Ireland). The day Marcy arrives also happens to be the beginning of the town's annual Matchmaking Festival. Marcy tries to ignore the festivities and attempts to plow through her task of locating McGlorys. While trying to find these elusive McGlorys, she meets various townspeople, including two local matchmakers, Dermot (Milo O'Shea) and Millie (Rosaleen Linehan). As a nice-looking American, she's prime matchmaking fodder, but Marcy is not having any of it.

Marcy reacts to Sean's compliment: "Oh yes, I'm so *very* Mary Tyler Moore. Everybody says so."

While going about her unfruitful search for McGlorys, she meets an instantly annoying man, Sean (David O'Hara). It's not impossible to guess what's going to happen, but it's fun to watch the whole thing unfold nonetheless.

Gradually, Marcy begins to be seduced by the town and its gentle residents (more literally seduced by one in particular) and starts questioning her morals and her life as a senator's aide. Naturally, the transition isn't easy. There's the matter of a boyfriend back home (mentioned only once, strangely) and the more important roadblock of the surprise return of Sean's lovely wife (Saffron Burrows).

What with the cutesy matchmaking festival, the colorful locals and the none-too-surprising plot, this is a movie that could be pretty hokey, but somehow it's not. How is this story above being just a run-of-the-mill romantic comedy? A big part of it has to do with the setting. Any story, photographed under moody clouds and wide-open beautiful vistas is going to tend to seem a little better than others of a similar ilk.

The other aspect of the film that works is the casting. Janeane Garofalo, who was a charming everywoman in her debut lead role in *The Truth About Cats and Dogs* (1996), brings a similar regular gal energy to her part. Casting the ironic and cynical Garofalo in a romantic comedy is an interesting choice since she would be the first to mock any sappy missteps in the film. That she seems to be happy with the going-ons in the movie, gives it sort of a Gen-X seal of approval for the terminally ironic.

For Garofalo fans, she's actually at her best during the early part of the movie when she's still a quick-witted cynic rather than later when she starts to get more contented. She never completely loses her edge, though. When she and Sean are on a highly picturesque boat ride, Sean is explaining why a big city-type girl could never be happy in a small town like Ballinagra. "You're Mary Tyler Moore," he exclaims. Garofalo, bringing out her best sarcasm for the occasion, says: "Right, I am SO Mary Tyler Moore."

O'Hara's Sean also has an appealing regular guy quality to him. In fact, in the early scenes, it seems like he isn't going to be the love match at all. In one scene at the beginning of the movie, Sean sits, pale and, well, somewhat flabby in Marcy's bathtub. That they share a bathroom is yet another annoyance to Marcy about this slow-paced, backwards town and it seems more likely that Sean is going to be just another colorful local (a pale, colorful local, that is) instead of the love interest. Just like in real life, though, he somehow starts to look more appealing as Marcy gets to know him better. Sean is a strong match for Marcy. He's a lapsed journalist and can toss around the verbiage almost as quickly as she can. He also has the kind of bemused calm that Marcy could use in her life.

Because Garofalo and O'Hara aren't stars on the same level as Julia Roberts or Mel Gibson actually works well for the story. It's a change of pace in a romance film to see people who are certainly attractive but not freakishly attractive—it makes the whole thing seem more believable somehow and less a meeting of superstars.

As the amoral political henchman, Denis Leary is appropriately slimy. No matter how well Marcy is toeing the party line, Leary's Nick Ward makes sure to be condescending and dismissive of her. Sanders' politician John McGlory sports the right look of well-groomed, superficial cheeriness. There might be some real malice behind his

CREDITS

Marcy Tizard: Janeane Garofalo
Sean: David O'Hara
Dermot: Milo O'Shea
Sen. John McGlory: Jay O. Sanders
Nick: Denis Leary
Millie: Rosaleen Linehan
Sarah: Maria Doyle Kennedy

Origin: USA, Great Britain
Released: 1997
Production: Tim Bevan, Eric Fellner, and Luc Roeg for Working Title and Polygram Filmed Entertainment; released by Gramercy Pictures
Direction: Mark Joffe
Screenplay: Karen Janszen, Louis Nowra, and Graham Linehan
Cinematography: Ellery Ryan
Editing: Martin Smith
Music: John Altman
Production design: Mark Geraghty
Art direction: Terry Pritchard
Costumes: Howard Burden
Sound: Brendan Deasy
MPAA rating: R
Running Time: 96 minutes

pleasant facade, though. As he huddles in his limousine that's surrounded by the yelling press corps, he sneers "When I'm elected, I'll have you all killed," through a calculatedly guileless smile.

As the matchmaker looking to hook up Marcy and Sean, O'Shea's Dermot is elfishly endearing. He's half-romantic and half-huckster (his matchmaker clients get a discount at the local tanning salon—which he also happens to own.) Other locals, the friendly innkeeper, the genealogist/souvenir shop owner, a lovesick adolescent with a crush on Marcy, are all similarly picturesque and good-natured. Director Joffe, has the locals saying "feckin'" a lot, to show, presumably, that the Irish aren't just cheery leprechaun types.

One of the best parts about the "Irishness" of the film is the music. There's a soundtrack full of Irish music, including the duet "Haunted" with Sinead O'Connor and Shane MacGowan, formerly of the great Irish band the Pogues. In Ireland, music is a part of life, a big part. At one point Marcy, as the resident foreigner, judges a singing contest in a pub (the prize—a kiss). Although no one in the contest is going to be the next Shane MacGowan, it is charming to take part in the custom and hear the sound of each person sincerely singing his heart out into the dim light of the pub.

In comparing the two cultures, it's pretty clear which stance the movie is taking. The American, fast-paced lifestyle is frowned upon, while the Irish, small town life is revered. It may be unfairly black-and-white, but when the comparison involves idyllic life in a small town vs. big-city American politics, maybe it really is that clear-cut which way is the better way.

Despite the sweeping and grand scenery, *The Matchmaker* isn't *Dr. Zhivago* (1965). It's no epic saga, the angst is minimal, and the characters' problems are small and generally solvable. But as a modest, understated romantic comedy, it's a charming way to spend a couple of hours.

—*Jill Hamilton*

REVIEWS

Boxoffice. December, 1997, p. 54.
Detroit Free Press. October 3, 1997, p. 3D.
Entertainment Weekly. October 24, 1997, p. 46.
Los Angeles Times. October 3, 1997, p. F22.
New York Times. October 3, 1997, p. E16.
Variety. September 29, 1997, p. 66.
Village Voice. October 14, 1997, p. 94.
Washington Post Weekend. October 3, 1997, p. 48.

McHale's Navy

He's under siege and out-of-control.—Movie tagline

"Ship-shape comedy."—Jeff Strickler, *The Minneapolis Star-Tribune*

"Fun high-tech action."—Mari Cartel, *SW Network*

Box Office: $4,529,343

Like most television series, the original "McHale's Navy" stayed afloat because of its memorable characters, chiefly, Ernest Borgnine's McHale and Tim Conway's Ensign Parker. But when you turn a half-hour TV show into a feature-length motion picture, you need more than a few sketches featuring familiar characters. You need a plot. And that's where *McHale's Navy*, the movie, founders, as have so many other sitcom-to-film transplants.

The thin comedy centering around the Quinton McHale character, a happy-go-lucky ex-naval officer who supplies a laid-back Caribbean naval base on San Ysidro Island with brew, ice cream, stereos and pin-up calendars, among other items, might have been enough to sustain the early 1960s TV show, but screenwriter Peter Crabbe didn't count on the timid byplay to carry a film. Unfortunately, instead of adding just enough drama to keep things interesting, Crabbe overloaded on ridiculous plot elements that fit better in a James Bond movie than a silly remake of a silly old TV show. The result, as directed by Bryan Spicer, is a mess in which lame attempts at humor keep popping up amidst even lamer attempts at suspense.

There are characters enough to float any boat. Tom Arnold, his face seemingly stuck in a dumb grin, plays McHale as a sort of chief dimwit, kindly uncle, and good-hearted good old boy; it's a character with no depth and little charm. David Alan Grier, as a goofy Ensign Parker, is the one character who strikes perfectly the sought-after tone of inspired wackiness. Dean Stockwell, as the blowhard

Captain Binghamton, sounds mostly grating notes; he's silly but rarely funny, which is the curse of the entire movie. Debra Messing, as the straightlaced Lt. Penelope Carpenter, has hair that looks like it's plastered onto her head, a bullhorn for a voice, and absolutely nothing in the way of dialogue to work with. McHale's "crew" of professional sandbaggers consists of five sketchy personality stereotypes: a womanizer, a genius, a brutish dolt, a lazybones, and a fifth man who is ill-defined but turns out to be a poker wizard.

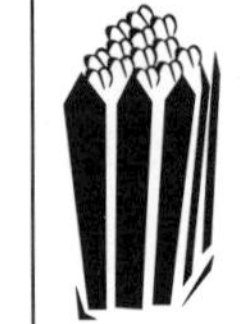

Binghampton: "Did we wake you up?" Willie: "No sir, we've been up since the crack of noon."

Laughs are supposed to ensue when Binghamton and Carpenter arrive to clean up the base and end McHale's reign of bootlegging and bartering. Parker gets caught in the middle, McHale has his eye on unstraightening Carpenter's laces, and McHale's men delight in puncturing Binghamton's pretentiousness. All that would be a fairly faithful remake of "McHale's Navy" the TV show, but unfortunately there is much more.

Three Communist world leaders have bankrolled the world's second-best terrorist, Vladakoff (Tim Curry), to set up a missile base on the remote island and help them regain power. They buy off the island's governor and leave Vladakoff, who wants to get to number one on the terror charts, in charge. Vladakoff burns down the village and takes over the baseball field for a missile site, repeatedly ignoring the pleas of his psychiatrist to channel his anger more constructively. The notion of a terrorist having a shrink as advisor is the only funny new element in the film.

Of course, Vladakoff and McHale have an old score to settle. Seems both were secret operatives in Panama, and Vladakoff betrayed McHale. Not only that, but McHale's best friend was killed because of Vladakoff, and that's why McHale moved to this island, to take care of his dead buddy's son, who is the star player on a youth baseball team McHale coaches. Of course, the kid is also an amateur spy who attempts to get revenge on Vladakoff.

All this is more than enough to sink a lighthearted comedy, but there's even more. When Binghamton learns about Vladakoff, he contacts his boss at the Pentagon, a guy known only by his code name, Cobra. Cobra is played by Borgnine with more grace and good humor in his small part than the rest of the cast can muster. Cobra puts McHale in charge of dismantling Vladakoff, although it's unclear why Cobra doesn't immediately call in the Pentagon's overwhelming power.

McHale, who's already had his house and boat blown to smithereens by Vladakoff's "stealth" cruiser, rounds up his crew to infiltrate and disarm Vladakoff. Through the thinnest of plot contrivances, they end up taking a detour to Cuba to get needed electronic parts, which McHale obtains from Ernesto (Tommy Chong). It's a sad commentary that Chong has probably the funniest character in the film. Then it's back to San Ysidro for a series of endings that go from absurd to worse.

With its recycled plot about Communist subversives, *McHale's Navy* tries to fit the happy-go-lucky lead character with the oversized mantle of American freedom fighter saving the world from destruction. The outdated patriotic fervor is even sillier than the various shenanigans. What's all this drumbeating and heavy-handed drama doing in the middle of the palm trees and alignering? It's a frighteningly ill-fitting coexistence. In the final chase seen, McHale tries to fire a torpedo, and out of the hole falls a bunch of cigars one of his men smuggled back from Cuba. McHale laughs, and then it's back to a battle for the future of the free world.

None of this is played with the kind of comic-book broad satire that worked for James Bond or Batman.

CREDITS

Lt. Cmdr. Quinton McHale Tom Arnold
Maj. Vladikov: Tim Curry
Capt. Wallace B. Binghampton: Dean Stockwell
Ensign Charles T. Parker: David Alan Grier
Lt. Penelope Carpenter: Debra Messing
Cobra: Ernest Borgnine
Armando/Ernesto: Tommy Chong
Virgil: Bruce Campbell
Happy: French Stewart
Christy: Brian Haley
Gruber: Danton Stone
Willie: Henry Cho
Roberto: Anthony Jesse Cruz
David: Scott Cleverdon

Origin: USA
Released: 1997
Production: Sid, Bill and Jon Sheinberg for the Bubble Factory; released by Universal Pictures
Direction: Bryan Spicer
Screenplay: Peter Crabbe
Cinematography: Buzz Feitshans IV
Editing: Russell Denove
Music: Dennis McCarthy
Production design: Gene Rudolf
Art direction: Kim Hix, Fernando Ramirez
Set decoration: Patrice Laure
Costumes: Michael T. Boyd
Sound: Fernando Camara
Marine coordinator: Ransom Walrod
MPAA rating: PG
Running Time: 108 minutes

Everyone in the film acts as if he or she is afflicted by sunstroke, and almost nothing makes sense. Still, there are a few good bits, mostly involving Grier. When McHale's crew members go AWOL and descend on a bar in Cuba, there's a pleasant amount of controlled mayhem. When they're hauled off to jail and Parker dresses up as Castro to order them freed, there's an engaging level of wackiness, and when he meets the real Fidel on the way out, *McHale's Navy* briefly approaches the level of the filler material in a Marx Brothers movie.

Universal Pictures released a film version of the TV show in 1964, also titled *McHale's Navy,* and a 1965 sequel, *McHale's Navy Joins the Air Force.*

Spicer's direction imbues the film with a sunny sort of "What-me-worry?" Caribbean attitude. At times this kind of *Mad* magazine approach to filmmaking, though devoid of that publication's satirical punch, does exert a certain appeal. There is much that is mildly amusing: McHale's Robinson-Crusoe-like hilltop home with its pet pig, pulley system for hauling goods, and its own pop machine; his brute crewman's ability to open a beer bottle with his eye; Grier's adventures in a wet suit. But there is nothing to produce out-loud laughter.

Arnold is amazingly unremarkable, as always. Worse is Curry, who rolls his eyes, bares his teeth, and snarls in a terrible Eastern European accent, and the plot, which is as welcome as a cockroach in a hammock. You can't go more than a minute or two in *McHale's Navy* without being jarred by the bad karma between a silly sitcom and an even sillier seriocomic drama overlaid with retro Cold War elements. Well, at least everyone appeared to be having fun, with the possible exception of Messing, stuck in that unbecoming sailor suit with the plastered-down hair. 

—Michael Betzold

REVIEWS

Chicago Tribune. April 18, 1997, p. 5.
Los Angeles Times. April 19, 1997, p. F6.
New York Times. April 19, 1997, p. 10.
People. May 5, 1997, p. 152.
Variety. April 21, 1997, p. 60.

Meet Wally Sparks

He's a menace to High Society.—Movie tagline

"Hilarious!"—Don Stotter, *Entertainment Time-Out*

"Rodney at his best! The laughs just keep coming."—Lloyd Gite, *FOX-TV, Houston*

"Deliciously naughty!"—Jeanne Wolf, *Jeanne Wolf's Hollywood*

Box Office: $4,073,582

If the body of world cinema was to be compared to a human body, movies in the vein of *It's A Wonderful Life* (1946) would probably represent the heart, while the films of Ingmar Bergman might correspond to various folds of the cerebral cortex, and *Top Gun* (1986) would almost certainly be instrumental in the production of adrenaline. Continuing this train of thought, the Rodney Dangerfield vehicle *Meet Wally Sparks* obviously belongs in the realm of the sex organs.

Besides verbally emboldening his privates, Dangerfield spends much of the film insulting the pride of other men. He also makes time to leer at women and generally be the life of the party. Rodney plays the title character, a TV talk show host with a penchant for creating three-ring circuses out of the parade of philanderers, porn stars, and undersexed housewives who march across his stage on a daily basis. As the film opens, the raunchiness has apparently gotten to the show's sponsors, who, though the show is a hit, threaten to pull out if Wally doesn't clean up his act. As a plot point, this doesn't make much sense, because if it has never occurred to the ratings board to crack down on "The Wally Sparks Show" (which features swearing and toplessness), then why would the people who are making money off the show care?

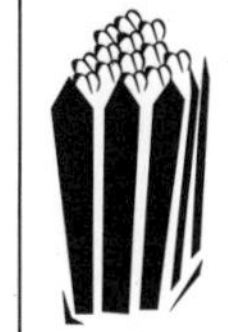

Wally: "Siskel and Ebert reviewed me and gave me one finger up."

Lenny Spencer (Burt Reynolds), the president of the network who also runs the show, gives Wally an ultimatum: Clean up or be canceled. Spencer is also being pressured by the governor of Georgia, Floyd Preston (David Ogden Stiers), who is leading a campaign to sanitize the airwaves. The governor has problems of his own, however, as allegations of extramarital affairs are popping up. So when Floyd's son invites Wally to the Governor's Ball, he and his producer (Debi Mazar) devise a plan: if they can get pictures of the governor in a compromising position, maybe they can expose him as a hypocrite and protect the "integrity" of their show.

Cameos include Michael Bolton, Jay Leno, Tim Allen, Roseanne, Jerry Springer, Sally Jessy Raphael, and Rolanda.

So it's off to the Ball, where distinguished southern gentlemen and buxom southern belles in hoop dresses mingle with politicians and other society types. What happens next pretty much fulfills the promise of the film's tag line: "He's a menace to high society." Rodney moves through the party like a hurricane, spewing unwholesome suggestions and groping at everything in a dress. This is a potentially hilarious situation, the kind Groucho Marx would have placed himself at the center of. The difference, of course, is in the quality of the one-liners, their delivery, and the direction. This brand of drunken insult humor came and went long ago, and Rodney's bug-eyed leer is now just a look of exhaustion.

Wally, after a drunken fall from a horse, ends up feigning injury and immobility, and so becomes a guest at the governor's mansion. Soon, the household is transformed as Wally systematically endears each family member to his philosophy of free sex and uninhibited flatulence. One scene in which Wally leads the governor's wife and her friends in a game of strip poker plays a little like "Golden Girls" uncensored.

If these vignettes—devoid of original thought as they are—seem dull, they can't hold a candle to the unbelievably protracted finale. Set in the governor's mansion where Wally is broadcasting live from the living room, the scene revolves around the possible future of Wally's show, and involves more than a dozen characters in its attempt to tie up twice as many loose ends. The director, Peter Baldwin, piles complication upon wild complication, yet somehow manages to generate zero energy from the situation. The same can be said of nearly every other element in *Meet Wally Sparks.*

—*David King*

CREDITS

Wally Sparks: Rodney Dangerfield
Sandy Gallo: Debi Mazar
Emily Preston: Cindy Williams
Lenny Spencer: Burt Reynolds
Gov. Floyd Preston: David Ogden Stiers
Judge Randall Williams: Alan Rachins

Origin: USA
Released: 1997
Production: Leslie Greif for Largo Entertainment; released by Trimark Pictures
Direction: Peter Baldwin
Screenplay: Rodney Dangerfield and Harry Basil
Cinematography: Richard Kline
Editing: Raul Davalos
Music: Michel Colombier
Production design: Bryan Jones
Art direction: Steve Karman
Costumes: Alexandra Welker
Sound: Stephen Halbert
Stunt choreography: Charles Picerni
MPAA rating: R
Running Time: 104 minutes

REVIEWS

Boxoffice. March, 1997, p. 44.
Detroit Free Press. February 2, 1997, p. 8G.
Los Angeles Times. February 3, 1997, p. F6.
San Francisco Chronicle. February 1, 1997, p. E1.
Variety. February 3, 1997, p. 43.

Men in Black

Protecting the Earth from the scum of the universe.—Movie tagline

"The most amazing film this summer. Fast, funny, futuristic and has a lot of soul."—*CBS-TV*

"This is it! This is the one! The one you'll want to see two or three times!"—Joel Siegel, *Good Morning America*

"Mr. Smith and Mr. Jones save the world in the summer's coolest, funniest movie."—*Newsweek*

"This summer's number one joy ride! A playfully hip and hilarious comedy! Director Barry Sonnenfeld loads the bases with action, fantasy, laughs and hits a grand-slam! Smith and Jones are a powerhouse pair!"—Peter Travers, *Rolling Stone*

"It's good enough to see twice! A snappy sci-fi hoot."—Susan Wloszczyna, *USA Today*

Covert government agents K (Will Smith) and J (Tommy Lee Jones) heavily arm themselves to rid the earth of vengeful aliens in *Men in Black.*

Box Office: $250,004,561

Basing movies on comic books often results in films that retain the original material's action, look, or atmosphere but lack strong characterization or well-developed storylines. Such films frequently look good as far as production design and special effects but fall short on substance. However, when director Barry Sonnenfield (*The Addams Family, Get Shorty*) and screenwriter Ed Solomon adapted the Marvel comic *Men in Black* (created by Lowell Cunningham) for the screen, they produced a film that is not only appropriately atmospheric but also rich in characterization and dark humor. One of the highest grossing films of the year and one of the more critically acclaimed films of an overall lackluster summer season, *Men in Black* stands apart from many similar comic book adaptations and/or science fiction films (1996's blockbuster *Independence Day*, for example) in that it benefits not only from interesting special visual effects but also a sophisticated and often wry sense of humor that basically refuses to take anything too seriously.

K to J: "At any given time, around fifteen hundred landed aliens are on the planet. The majority right here in Manhattan."

The plot of *Men in Black* follows a familiar pattern that in some ways recalls many other science fiction "alien invasion" films. The Men in Black (or MIB) are members of a secret agency that "monitors, licenses, and polices" the activities of extraterrestrial aliens that have relocated to Earth and assumed human identities. After his aging, tiring partner "D" realizes he is unable to perform his job satisfactorily, MIB secret agent "K" (Tommy Lee Jones) sets out to recruit a new partner, which he finds in brash young New York City police officer Edwards (Will Smith). K convinces Edwards that being a part of the agency is "worth it" even though it means changing one's identity and cutting off all previous ties to the world; subsequently, Edwards takes on the name "J" and joins K in investigating an encounter Edwards had with an alien who carried an illegal weapon and who warned that "Your world's going to end."

Meanwhile, a hostile alien called a "bug" arrives on Earth and assumes the identity of a farmer (Vincent D'Onofrio). The bug then heads to New York City in search of a jewel-like object called the "galaxy," a powerful source for subatomic energy, which is in the possession of the ambassador of the Arquillian Empire, a tiny alien who lives inside the mechanical replica of a human body and works as a jeweler. The alien bug finds and kills the Arquillian ambassador but does not find the galaxy. The death of the ambassador, along with the printed stories of a distressed farmer's wife who claims her husband was abducted by aliens, subsequently leads agents K and J to the realization that the planet has been invaded by a dangerous bug that "lives on carnage," and the two set out to find this alien before he causes more damage and death.

In the meantime, as the bug searches for the galaxy and agents K and J search for the bug, an Arquillian battleship appears in orbit over Earth and sends an ominous warning to the MIB headquarters, demanding that the galaxy be safely handed over (returned to its owners) or the planet will be destroyed. With little time to spare, J & K recall that, before his death, the Arquillian ambassador had made the cryptic statement that "To prevent war, the galaxy is on Orion's belt." J finally realizes that Orion was the ambassador's beloved cat, now in the company of Dr. Laurel Weaver (Linda Fiorentino) at the city morgue. K & J head for the morgue but there find that the alien bug has beat them to it; the bug takes Dr. Weaver hostage and, after retrieving the galaxy from the collar around Orion's neck, swallows the sought-after object for safekeeping.

Although the bug escapes with Dr. Weaver, K & J track them down to the world's fair grounds, where the alien hopes to procure an old abandoned spacecraft and leave the planet. When confronted by the two MIB agents, the bug sheds its human shell and is revealed to be a huge, insect-like creature; the slimy alien then swallows the weapons which K & J have brought with them. Determined to "get his gun back," K taunts the creature into swallowing him whole. Now alone, J attempts to keep the bug from reaching the spacecraft and leaving, ultimately resorting to stirring the creature's wrath by repeatedly stepping on some nearby insects and teasing the alien about losing its relatives. The alien attacks J but is soon stopped when K, inside its body, reaches his gun and fires it, sending the creature into countless slimy pieces.

As the story nears an end, K tells J that he is ready to retire and that he has actually been training a "replacement" rather than a partner. Reluctantly, J complies with K's wishes and uses one of the MIB's memory-erasing devices to clear K's memory of his life as a member of the Men In Black organization. K then returns to a normal life and a woman he once loved but had to leave many years before, while J finds himself a new partner in the person of Dr. Weaver.

One of the most enjoyable aspects of *Men in Black* is the ever-present humor which arises out of both ironic dialogue and intentionally ridiculous situations. In the film's first scene, an MIB unit headed by K intervenes after the border patrol picks up a group of illegal aliens from Mexico. "We'll take it from here," K says before letting all the aliens except one go. With humorous irony playing off the meaning of the word "alien," it turns out that this remaining individual is actually another *kind* of alien—an alien from outer space—who has disguised himself quite convincingly with a lifelike reproduction of a human head. "That's enough, Mikey," demands K, "give me that head." The line, delivered with deadpan seriousness by Tommy Lee Jones, is typical of the type of well-written, irony-laced dialogue found throughout the film, which often arises out of situations in which the strange and/or absurd is treated lightly.

In fact, the film revels in treating almost everything lightly, and the resultant irreverent humor pervades many enjoyable scenes, from aliens who regrow their heads to K's consulting tabloid "hotsheets" for news because they're more reliable than traditional periodicals like the *New York Times*. The film also pokes lighthearted fun at some contemporary public figures: as J discovers at MIB headquarters, the aliens who have settled on Earth and assumed human form include celebrities such as Steven Spielberg, George Lucas, Sylvester Stallone, Danny DeVito, and Newt Gingrich. Also humorous is a scene in which Edwards is tested as a potential candidate for the MIB alongside members of the navy and the marines; Edwards finds it odd that these other candidates are content simply to be tested even though they do not really know what they're being tested for, accepting with a blind loyalty and patriotism that they are there because the organization is "looking for the best of the best." Ultimately, of course, the irreverent Edwards is the one chosen. All these examples of the comedy in *Men in Black* demonstrate the film's refusal to take anything—most of all itself or the genre to which it belongs—too seriously.

Men in Black also features some strong performances from virtually every member of the cast, but particularly from the main players, and especially Tommy Lee Jones. Jones' deadpan portrayal of K is the source of much of the humor in the film, precisely because he comes across as the "straight man" in the middle of bizarre situations. His ability to deliver quirky dialogue with a straight face or to maintain a calm persona in the most ridiculous scenarios underscores the film's eccentric atmosphere. While the film itself does not take much of anything seriously, Jones' "serious" performance succeeds in contributing to *Men in Black*'s self-parodying tone. One of the most memorable examples of this occurs late in the film when K & J are on their way to the fairgrounds to stop the alien bug. As they approach a crowded tunnel, K instructs J to activate a red button and their car converts into a flying vehicle which turns upside down and cruises along the tunnel ceiling. While J, pressed against the roof of the car, seems on the verge of panic, K attempts to calm him. "You need to relax," he says, and then he inserts an eight-track tape of Elvis Presley and begins to sing along. Jones' character is also to some extent more fully developed than others, in that K often betrays a sense of growing tiredness and regret with his life, arising from the fact that many years before he had left behind the woman he loved in order to become a member of the MIB. Jones portrays the character's regret and longing for the life he left

AWARDS AND NOMINATIONS

Academy Awards 1997: Makeup
Nominations: Art Direction, Original Musical or Comedy Score
BAFTA 1997 Nominations: Special effects
Golden Globe Awards 1998 Nominations: Best Musical/Comedy

behind with complete believability, even though these feelings occur in the midst of incredible and outlandish surroundings.

Vincent D'Onofrio's portrayal of the alien villain is at once appropriately humorous and disgusting, and the actor convincingly distorts his voice, facial expressions, and bodily movements as an alien trying without much success to pose as a human. However, even though the portrayal is for a while humorous and consistently convincing, the character itself is actually one of the weakest elements of the film—that is, until the end of the story, when the "bug" appears in its true, deadly form. The problem with the character throughout much of the film is that this lone villain often comes across as not only disgusting but also stupid, and as a result the character's strange behavior may become tiresome and the character itself difficult to accept as a true threat.

Although enhanced by intriguing and often amusing special effects, *Men in Black* takes a different approach from many big-budget, visual-effects laden science fiction films and achieves a rare success as a sophisticated comedy by relying on an intentionally quirky story, irreverent humor, strong performances, and calculated self-parody. While certainly not the only one of its kind, the film is a welcome departure from many of the less substantive representatives of the various genres to which it belongs, and it demonstrates that, once in a while, sophisticated films can be derived even from comic books.

—David Flanagin

CREDITS

K: Tommy Lee Jones
J: Will Smith
Laurel: Linda Fiorentino
Edgar: Vincent D'Onofrio
Zed: Rip Torn
Jeebs: Tony Shalhoub

Origin: USA
Released: 1997
Production: Walter F. Parkes, Laurie MacDonald for Amblin Entertainment; released by Sony Pictures Entertainment
Direction: Barry Sonnenfeld
Screenplay: Ed Solomon; based on the Malibu Comic by Lowell Cunningham
Cinematography: Don Peterman
Editing: Jim Miller
Music: Danny Elfman
Production design: Bo Welch
Art direction: Thomas Duffield
Costumes: Mary E. Vogt
Sound: Peter F. Kurland
Alien makeup effects: Rick Baker
Visual effects supervisor: Eric Brevig
MPAA rating: PG-13
Running Time: 98 minutes

REVIEWS

Boxoffice. April, 1997, p. 30.
Boxoffice. August, 1997, p. 48.
Chicago Tribune. July 2, 1997, p. 1.
Cinemafantastique. April, 1997, p. 10.
Cinemafantastique. June, 1997, p. 10.
Detroit News. July 2, 1997, p. E1.
Entertainment Weekly. May 16, 1997, p. 53.
Entertainment Weekly. July 11, 1997, p. 38.
Hollywood Reporter. June 23, 1997, p. 8.
Los Angeles Times. July 1, 1997, p. F1.
Movieline. June, 1997, p. 51.
Newsweek. July 7, 1997, p. 58.
New York Times. July 1, 1997, p. C9.
People. July 14, 1997, p. 19.
Rolling Stone. July 10, 1997, p. 127.
Sight and Sound. August, 1997, p. 47.
USA Today. July 1, 1997, p. D1.
Variety. June 23, 1997, p. 93.
Village Voice. July 8, 1997, p. 69.

Metro

San Francisco's top police hostage negotiator is about to get more than he ever bargained for. *Metro.* Life is a negotiation.—Movie tagline

"Hilarious, tough and sexy!"—Cameron Turner, *Hangin' N Hollywood*

Box Office: $32,017,895

Eddie Murphy scored his first film success as Nick Nolte's reluctant buddy in the cop movie *48 Hours* (1990). Murphy was even more successful as a rogue cop in *Beverly Hills Cop* (1984), *Beverly Hills Cop 2* (1987), and *Beverly Hills Cop 3* (1994). He played with Nick Nolte again in *Another 48 Hours* (1990). Now Murphy, whose career has been noticeably shaky, is apparently trying to play it safe by starring in yet another cop flick as a fast-talking, wisecracking, street-smart defender of law and order.

In *Metro*, Murphy invades the picturesque streets of San Francisco, heretofore the bailiwick of Dirty Harry Callahan, as played by Clint Eastwood in five films between 1971 and 1988. In fact, *Metro* seems so much like a Dirty Harry film that the viewer often has the feeling of deja vu all over again. There is a lingering suspicion that the film was made from one of the hundreds of Dirty Harry scripts, treatments, proposals, and "concepts" that Eastwood rejected. Murphy seems a bit uncomfortable traipsing up and down the hills of the photogenic city by the bay—almost as if he were afraid of coming face to face with Dirty Harry holding an oversize automatic and challenging him to make his day.

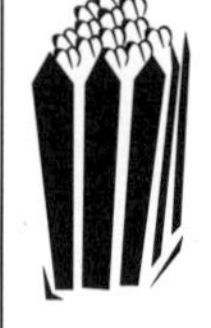

Eddie Murphy: "I tip my hat to Stallone, Schwarzenegger and Bruce Willis—I don't know how they can do movies like this all the time, because you really get beat up doing them."

Metro does not attempt to explain how Murphy's familiar cop character got from Beverly Hills to San Francisco. As Scott Roper, he has the highly specialized, occasionally unenviable, but more often enviable job of being a SFPD hostage negotiator. As such he has lots of leisure time interrupted by brief intervals of terrible tension. He has to go alone into situations where some drugged-out psychopath is holding terrified civilians at gunpoint and threatening to kill everybody.

Being a hostage negotiator seems like the ideal occupation for the character Eddie Murphy plays in cop dramas; a fun-loving fellow capable of violence when the chips are down. In fact, the one word that best describes Murphy is "disarming." He demonstrates his effectiveness in one of *Metro*'s early scenes by sweet-talking a would-be bank robber into a momentary lapse of caution and then shooting him right through the forehead.

After putting in ten minutes of highly specialized work, Roper can go back to pursuing the beautiful Ronnie Tate (British newcomer Carmen Ejogo). Most of their socializing seems to consist of preparing gourmet meals and drinking fine California wines, which is what Hollywood filmmakers seem to think is all San Franciscans ever do in their quaint, cozy city. Ronnie, however, has heard enough of Roper's sweet talk. Like everyone else who has become acquainted with the Eddie Murphy character, she never knows when he is jiving and when he is telling the truth. She has found another boyfriend, a professional athlete who earns millions and seems to have every advantage over Roper, including height and potential longevity.

The Dirty Harry aficionado will immediately suspect that Ronnie will eventually become a hostage herself—and he will not be disappointed. The script by Randy Feldman seems afraid to depart from the tried-and-true formulas of cop dramas, including maniacal chases up and down Nob Hill and Russian Hill with cars flying through the air and landing on the pavement with frame-bending impact.

Like lone wolf Dirty Harry, Roper gets saddled with a partner he does not want. His expressive face reveals his negative opinion of the square, white, college-educated, inexperienced Kevin McCall (Michael Rapaport), who quotes books like "Strategies and Countermeasures in Hostage Situations." These unwanted partners seem an indispensable element of cop films because they allow the star to explain his philosophy and methodology without engaging in Hamlet-like soliloquies. The new guy asks the questions, the contemptuous star gives laconic answers accompanied by hands-on demonstrations.

Enter the villain. As is often the case in these films, he is the most interesting character, even though his behavior often makes his supposedly acute intelligence very questionable. Michael Korda (Michael Wincott) makes an excellent foil to Murphy's Steve Roper because Korda is equally foxy and equally lethal. Korda proves how sadistic he can be by presenting Roper with a human ear and threatening to cut more pieces off his hostages unless he gets a free ride out of the jewelry store where the cops have him surrounded. This leads to what is probably the most spectacular chase scene ever filmed. It outdoes even the memorable chases through the streets of San Francisco in *Bullitt* (1968) and through the streets of New York in *The French Connection* (1971).

Korda is a hard man to catch. When his automobile is demolished he jumps aboard one of San Francisco's venerable cable cars and shoots the brakeman, who falls into the antiquated controls and sends the crowded car hurtling down the steep side of Nob Hill towards Market Street. Some of the passengers—probably natives—very judiciously jump off and roll like armadillos; others—probably tourists—cling to handrails and add to the pandemonium with shrieks of terror. Roper leaps aboard from the commandeered Cadillac convertible (which belongs to his chief!). He gets into a hand-to-hand fight with Korda while the cable car trashes one automobile after another and tears through intersections miraculously missing most but not all of the cross traffic. As might be expected, Roper's unwelcome sidekick, bent on proving he can be just as crazy as his partner, saves lives by turning the Cadillac in front of the cable car and bringing it to a halt after this outlandish juggernaut of fused Cadillac and cable car has plowed a path of destruction down several crowded blocks.

The mature viewer may be thinking that no villain could be so dedicated to villainy and no cop so dedicated to duty. Is it worth catching one jewelry store bandit if it means killing a dozen or so assorted civilians and creating untold property damage? Cop shows, of course, have a logic of their own. Roper's colleague was killed by Korda during the jewel heist. Naturally Roper is ordered off the case because he is too emotionally involved—but who ever heard of a movie cop laying off a case because his superior ordered him to do so?

The seething Korda soon ends up in a cell vowing revenge. He is the only lawbreaker who can make Roper lose his cool. Even behind bars the master criminal seems as dangerous as Hannibal the Cannibal (Anthony Hopkins) in *The Silence of the Lambs* (1991). Korda is an example of the kind of pathologically fixated criminal genius found only in the movies. What he has in mind—illogical as it might seem—is to kidnap the beautiful Ronnie and possibly cut off one of her ears. With Ronnie as hostage, he can force Roper to risk his career by appropriating the impounded bag of jewels and delivering it to one of those ominously silent, deserted rendezvous spots so familiar to fans of Dirty Harry. The rendezvous in this case is at a shipyard which appears to have gone out of business because of recent cutbacks in defense spending.

Roper knows he will be a sitting duck. He doesn't expect Korda to play straight with him, so he doesn't play straight with Korda. He brings along his partner McCall, who happens to be qualified as a SWAT sharpshooter. The greenhorn helps to turn the tables on Korda but leaves the derring-do and all the glory to Roper.

Rapaport is a competent actor but has no opportunities to be anything more than Roper's stooge. The dynamic contrast that existed between Eddie Murphy and Nick Nolte in their two cop-buddy outings is conspicuously absent in the relationship between Murphy and Rapaport, mainly because Rapaport lacks Nolte's charisma but also because Rapaport was given such an anemic part. Murphy really is a stand-up soloist at heart but needs to be balanced by strong supporting actors to prevent him from seeming like a runaway train. His egomania jeopardizes his popularity. Audiences may be getting too much of him—and too much of the same.

Since *Metro* seems so much like a Dirty Harry film, it is natural to compare Murphy with Clint Eastwood. Eastwood was unremittingly grim, while Murphy often tries to give his detective character another dimension by clowning it up with his specially patented style and what *New York Times* reviewer Stephen Holden calls "his twinkling-eyed barracuda grin." The clowning undermines Murphy's cop persona while his dominant cop persona makes his clowning seem like a psychotic reaction to stress. It is no wonder that his on-again off-again girlfriend doesn't know what to make of him.

Critics were mostly unkind to *Metro*, although they noted the solid direction by Thomas Carter, the good camera work by Fred Murphy, as well as the state-of-the-art production values. Kevin Thomas of the *Los Angeles Times* calls the film "a painfully derivative stale action thriller," while Stephen Holden calls it an aimless police drama which

CREDITS

Scott Roper: Eddie Murphy
Kevin McCall: Michael Rapaport
Michael Korda: Michael Wincott
Ronnie Tate: Carmen Ejogo
Capt. Frank Solis: Denis Arndt
Lt. Sam Baffert: Art Evans
Earl: Donal Logue
Clarence: Paul Ben-Victor

Origin: USA
Released: 1997
Production: Roger Birnbaum for Varavan Pictures; released by Touchstone Pictures
Direction: Thomas Carter
Screenplay: Randy Feldman
Cinematography: Fred Murphy
Editing: Peter E. Berger
Music: Steve Porcaro
Production design: William Elliott
Art direction: Greg Papalia
Costumes: Ha Nguyen
Sound: Willie Burton
Stunt Coordinator: Mickey Gilbert
MPAA rating: R
Running Time: 117 minutes

finds Murphy "back in the rut he appeared to have escaped" as Sherman Klump in the innovative and highly successful *The Nutty Professor* (1996). Howard Feinstein, writing in *Variety*, a magazine that tends to view movies strictly as commercial products, praised *Metro* with faint damns, predicting that "this runaway vanity production should scoop up some solid quick coin as a mainstream winter attraction." Eddie Murphy remains very bankable even though he often seems to be trying to sabotage his superstardom with look-alike scripts and stereotyped performances.

—*Bill Delaney*

REVIEWS

Boxoffice. March, 1997, p. 45.
Chicago Tribune. January 17, 1997, p. 5.
Entertainment Weekly. January 24, 1997, p. 36.
Los Angeles Times. January 17, 1997, p. F1.
New York Times. January 17, 1997, p. B3.
People. January 27, 1997, p. 22.
Time. January 27, 1997.
USA Today. January 17, 1997, p. 4D.
Variety. January 13, 1997, p. 151.
Village Voice. January 28, 1997, p. 70.

Midnight in the Garden of Good and Evil

"One of the best American movies of the year! *Midnight* is extremely funny!"—James Verniere, *Boston Herald*

"A beautifully realized treatment of the best-selling novel about high crimes and misdemeanors in Savannah, Georgia."—Gene Siskel, *Chicago Tribune*

"Marvelous! A terrific film. Great performances and brilliant direction by Clint Eastwood."—Larry King, *CNN*

"A fabulously assured and entertaining film. Come awards season, *Midnight* will be a formidable contender."—Susan Stark, *Detroit News*

"Eastwood's elegantly crafted *Midnight* preserves the tone of the book and brings its gorgeous moss-draped setting to life."—Jack Mathews, *Newsday*

"Beguiling. Unique. Haunting."—Carrie Rickey, *Philadelphia Inquirer*

"A mystery laced with class and sass."—Gene Shalit, *Today Show*

"A funky fusion of southern gentility and mojo melodrama that's always entertaining."—Desson Howe, *Washington Post*

"A smoky, southern murder mystery, packed with wit, old secrets and incredible characters."—Pat Collins, *WWOR-TV*

Box Office: $22,998,162

Journalist Jack Kelso (John Cusack) and Savannah socialite Jim Williams (Kevin Spacey) form an unlikely friendship when Williams is accused of killing his male lover in *Midnight in the Garden of Good and Evil.*

Making the leap from the printed page to the silver screen is almost always a precarious endeavor. Ask anyone who has watched a film after reading the text that preceded it what they thought. Invariably and without hesitation, they'll tell you that the book was better. Those who derive equal enjoyment from reading books and watching movies are generally disappointed when one of their favorite publications is transferred over to celluloid. People who don't read books find the movie versions of best-sellers to be a godsend. Two hours in the dark with a minimum of exertion and, just like that, you can hold your own in a conversation with well-versed people who actually like to read.

Transferring popular and acclaimed literary works into movies is a firmly established Hollywood tradition that is unlikely to change anytime soon; it is a process that presents a win-win situation for studios. People who have read the book will more than likely go to the movie simply to satisfy their curiosity. They can't wait to see if the images conjured up in their minds are anything like those of the director of the film. Non-readers, not familiar with the text and thus not having any kind of artistic barometer to compare the film to, are likely to go and pass judgment on the story without any preconceived notions. More often than not, they will like the film more than the readers of the book.

In very rare instances, movies made or "inspired by" literary works indeed adhere to the spirit of the text and reach the same level of respectability as their pulp predecessors. Two relatively recent releases, *The English Patient* (1996) and *The Silence Of The Lambs* (1990) were immensely successful adaptations (both won the Academy Award for Best Picture). The book *The Silence Of The Lambs*, written by Thomas Harris, was a riveting, richly-detailed work. Though director Jonathan Demme crafted an equally rewarding and thoughtful picture, Ted Tally's screenplay omitted huge chunks (actually entire chapters) of the novel and gave the story an altogether different ending. The film's ending wasn't necessarily better or worse than the book's, just different. But it came as a jarring surprise to the book's ardent and loyal following. For the most part, fans of Michael Ondaatje's *The English Patient* sang the praises of director Anthony Minghella's equally intricate, convoluted screenplay. Yet Minghella had two things going for him that Tally did not. He was both the screenwriter and the director and his film was three hours long. If Tally had been given the luxury of having an extra hour to work with, he might have found room for more details. Perhaps the most famous film in movie history, *Gone With The Wind* (1939), had a whopping 231 minutes to spin its yarn. Screenwriter Sidney Howard was able to adapt Margaret Mitchell's novel with a minimum of trimming and condensing. Does this mean that the only thing preventing a film from being a high quality adaptation is screen time? Not in the least. Proper trimming and thoughtful compression is the one, vital key.

Jim Williams: "Truth is in the eye of the beholder."

Having recently set a record for spending over three years on the *New York Times* bestseller list, John Berendt's *Midnight in the Garden Of Good and Evil* was a novel just begging to be made into a movie. It possessed all the dream elements: murder, money, sex, greed, deviancy, bitter legal wrangling and dark magic all set amid the placid backdrop of Savannah, Georgia; a lazy, coastal hamlet oozing with history and quirky, offbeat, Southern charm.

Considering the intricacies of the book that inspired it, this film directed by (but not including) Clint Eastwood is somewhat engaging and moderately thorough, considering the tangled nature of the original work. Purists will (for good reason) find fault with the inevitable omissions made to accommodate the 150 minute length. If Eastwood wanted the film to be absolutely true to the text, he would have had to flirt with the four hour mark.

Eastwood is no mere novice when it comes to adapting works with a rabid cult following. In 1995 he swept away the dust and obliterated the lacy frills of James Robert Walker's *The Bridges of Madison County*. Eastwood stripped the story down to its foundation and, with his trademark efficiency, produced a moving, albeit dry love story. Full of longing and what-could-have-been regrets, it remained faithful to Walker's intentions. In addition to his streamlined work habits, Eastwood's virtually flawless track record as a director lies in his ability to select material that fits his unassuming style. The *Midnight* book was anything but unassuming. Perhaps Eastwood saw the genteel upper-crust citizens of Savannah as low-key and on the surface, they were. But just below the facade of magnolias and warm breezes was a community that regularly strayed far from convention.

When initially presented with the task of writing the screenplay, John Lee Hancock (*A Perfect World* [1993]) turned it down. "This is an impossible adaptation," he said. Despite his prophetic vision, Hancock did adapt Berendt's book and took what some would call "extreme liberties" with the facts. There are four glaring discrepancies that completely erase the unique and off-center allure of the book. If Eastwood hadn't lucked out with some of his cast, the entire project could have been a disaster.

Hancock's first and most unfathomable mistake was in the creation of the film's only fictional character, a New York-based writer named John Kelso (played by John Cusack). Although Kelso is little more than a thinly-veiled substitute for Berendt, he eventually becomes an integral part of the story itself. While Berendt alternated between first and third person in the book, he was exclusively an observer to the goings-on. This single variation removes the voyeuristic feel of the book. Why not include a Berendt character or perhaps just a simple voice-over narrator in his stead? Hancock also creates a superfluous, tepid love affair between Kelso and a local beauty named Mandy (given a bland but passable interpretation by Eastwood's daughter Alison). Hancock also turns Kelso into a bit of a sleuth, having him discover some key evidence in a case that ends up exonerating the defendant, Jim Williams (Kevin Spacey).

The film opens as Kelso arrives in Savannah to report on an extravagantly ornate Christmas party given annually by Williams, an eccentric, retiring antiques dealer. On the same night of the party, Williams kills his much younger, volatile gay lover (Jude Law), supposedly in self-defense.

Glaring error number two. Forget the fact that in the book the murder doesn't take place until near the story's halfway point. For no apparent reason, Hancock changes the name of the victim from Danny Hansford to Billy Hanson. Although the murder took place on May 2, 1981, Hancock must have felt that the Christmas party would have provided a more vivid canvas. It didn't. As the saying goes, "truth is stranger than fiction." There was no need for Hancock to change these facts; nobody could have written anything better or more bizarre than these truths.

Concluding that a seedy murder story is a much bigger challenge than a lightweight, human interest/fluff piece, Kelso decides to stick around and observe the trial. During his stay he interacts with the resplendent townsfolk, whom he describes affectionately as "*Gone With The Wind* on mescaline." Just the type of line we've come to expect from John Cusack. He's an immensely talented actor who is just now coming into his own. He had a busy year in 1997 with three other projects, but here his trademark boyish charm comes across as little more than befuddlement.

Kelso soon begins to do his job as an investigative journalist by trying to blend in but is immediately pegged as an out-of-towner and, even worse, a Yankee. Instead of getting the expected cold shoulder, many of the citizens welcome him into the fold and freely offer their opinions of Williams, who is equally revered and reviled. A self-made millionaire, Williams has no problem walking the Southernly gentlemen walk. His vast antiques collection makes him the envy of the well-to-do. He also does things his own way. The Savannah community seems to share in the universal opinion that if one can afford it, they can be as eccentric as they please. Kevin Spacey wasn't the first choice to play Williams (both Jack Nicholson and Tommy Lee Jones turned it down), but his eerie resemblance to the real Williams, coupled with his substantial skills of understatement made him the best choice. For the most part, Eastwood wastes Spacey by regulating him to just another supporting player. Luckily for Eastwood, he found another supporting player to help pick up the slack.

Mercer House, the home of Jim Williams, was left to his sister who allowed Eastwood to film there.

Veteran Australian actor Jack Thompson is largely unfamiliar to American audiences, but his role here as Sonny Seiler, Williams' defense attorney, could change that. With equal parts bluster and a perfectly reproduced, sinewy Georgia charm, Thompson steps into Seiler's skin and subtly steals every scene in which he appears. Like many other foreign actors, Thompson has nailed down the Southern U.S. accent with stunning efficiency. As Seiler, he is fervent in his defense of Williams and despite overwhelming evidence (and his own suspicion of his client's guilt), he presents points so well, it's easy to see why the jury was eventually swayed by his arguments. But it didn't start out that way. In what is the most abhorrent of all of Hancock's blunders, he condenses Williams' *four* murder trials into just one. The first three trials all ended with guilty verdicts or hung juries which set the stage for the book's exhausting, emotionally draining finale. To add further insult to injury, Hancock and Eastwood bring in The Lady Chablis as the star defense witness which is, to put it mildly, questionable poetic license. The Lady Chablis never appeared as a witness at any of the trials.

From Atlanta originally, The Lady Chablis makes her living as a female impersonator and bawdy burlesque performer who plays herself in the movie. Eastwood's choice to cast Chablis was both good and bad. The unusual events that led to his casting decision aren't completely clear and eventually created a minor controversy. It is rumored that Berendt refused to sign over the film rights until it was stipulated that Chablis would indeed portray herself. Other sources report that Chablis threatened legal action over the use of her name and image if she wasn't included. What is clear is Chablis' boundless enthusiasm at playing herself onscreen (in the movies, your 15 minutes of fame can be relived endlessly). Once introduced, Chablis dominates every scene she's in and in most instances, overwhelms the story. The requisite swishing and tail-wagging are there, along with the most obvious double entendres. The Lady Chablis is definitely not wanting when it comes to leaving a memorable impression. Unfortunately, finding local success with a glittery, camp stage show does not equate to possessing formidable acting skills. Chablis' performance is far too pedestrian and self-serving to be taken seriously.

Beyond Chablis, Eastwood used many Savannah residents to appear in background scenes and even included the real Sonny Seiler as the judge in the murder trial. Due to an incredible misappropriation of time spent elsewhere and endless mugging by Chablis, two of the book's most endearing and memorable characters are given token, barely noticeable acknowledgment. Two piano players, one known simply as The Lady of 6,000 Songs and a nomadic con-artist named Joe Odom are barely mentioned.

Eastwood does redeem himself somewhat by giving adequate attention to Minerva, a mysterious voodoo priestess played with vigor by Irma P. Hall. Perhaps in a move to keep all of his spiritual bases covered during the trial, Williams sought out the services of Minerva. With Kelso in tow, Williams makes a late-night trek to a graveyard where Minerva attempts to clear the air, metaphysically speaking, and douse the trial with good karma. The book's title came from this particular meeting.

In what is arguably the film's only interesting original

scene, Williams is shown face down on the floor of his study, during a party given shortly after his acquittal. He's just had a heart attack and suddenly an apparition of his victim lies next to him, smiling. Only here does Eastwood ever come close in matching the book's Southern gothic tone. But even as his film draws to a close, readers of the book endure one final insult. As interesting as Hancock's one fleeting success is, it too never happened. Williams actually died of pneumonia long after the last trial ended. And it wasn't during a party.

The priestess Minerva is shown both at the beginning and at the end of the film as is the statue of a young girl holding what appears to be birdbaths in each hand. The statue stands guard at the cemetery where Williams and many other lesser-known Savannahns are permanent guests. The statue also adorns the cover for Berendt's book as well as the movie poster. When looking at the statue, it is tempting to compare it to the blindfolded lady who holds the scales of justice, the indelible icon of the often-questioned American judicial system. There is no doubt that Jim Williams committed murder—that much he admitted. It's unlikely that it was in self-defense. Did he eventually receive his proper justice? Probably. Did John Berendt's mesmerizing book receive its proper justice? Absolutely not.

—J.M. Clark

CREDITS

Jim Williams: Kevin Spacey
John Kelso: John Cusack
Sonny Seiler: Jack Thompson
The Lady Chablis: The Lady Chablis (as herself)
Mandy Nichols: Alison Eastwood
Minerva: Irma P. Hall
Billy Hanson: Jude Law
Joe Odom: Paul Hipp
Serena Dawes: Dorothy Loudon
Margaret Williams: Anne Haney
Betty Harty: Kim Hunter
Luther Driggers: Geoffrey Lewis

Origin: USA
Released: 1997
Production: Clint Eastwood and Arnold Stiefel for Malpaso; released by Warner Bros.
Direction: Clint Eastwood
Screenplay: John Lee Hancock; based on the book by John Berendt
Cinematography: Jack N. Green
Editing: Joel Cox
Music: Lennie Niehaus
Production design: Henry Bumstead
Art direction: Jack G. Taylor Jr., James J. Murakami
Sound: Willie Burton
Costumes: Debora Hopper
MPAA rating: R
Running Time: 155 minutes

REVIEWS

Entertainment Weekly. November 28, 1997, p. 48.
Los Angeles Times. November 21, 1997, p. F1.
New York Times. November 21, 1997, p. E1.
Newsweek. June 16, 1997, p. 52.
People. December 1, 1997, p. 29.
Sight and Sound. March, 1998, p. 52.
Time. December 1, 1997.
USA Today. November 21, 1997, p. 9D.
Variety. November 24, 1997, p. 63.
Village Voice. December 2, 1997, p. 84.

Mimic

For thousands of years, man has been evolution's greatest creation . . . until now.—Movie tagline

A bold experiment . . . A deadly mistake!—Movie tagline

"A heart-pounding, sci-fi thriller!"—Greg Procaccino, *ABC-TV*

"A smart, hip adrenaline rush! This is what going to the movies is all about."—Michael Calleri, *CBS-TV*

"The scariest movie this summer!"—Jeffrey Lyons, *NBC-TV*

"An elegant scare picture! A virtuoso at tension and atmosphere."—Ray Sawhill, *Newsweek*

"It works as both pulp and poetry! It gets scare shivers tickling the lay audience while connoisseurs nod sagely at the canonical resonance."—Richard Corliss, *Time*

Box Office: $25,514,166

In a review of *Mimic*, one critic wrote: "After seeing *Mimic*, you may go out of your way to kill any and all insects, annoying or not, just to stave off any unwelcome evolution." You may also not want to use the New York City subway system again, or even go to New York. *Mimic* is an old-fashioned scary movie, with plenty of premature deaths, monsters, and oozy guts.

The basic premise is that bugs attack everyone. The longer version is that scientist Susan Tyler (Mira Sorvino) and her husband Peter Mann (Jeremy Northam), the deputy director of the Center for Disease Control, are called to New York City to help with an epidemic. It seems that a new, incurable disease is spread by cockroaches, so entomologist Tyler is needed. Tyler screws around with bug DNA and creates a mutant species called Judas. This new species has a six-month life span and cannot reproduce, therefore solving that disease transmission problem. Tyler's a heroine and that's that. For awhile, at least.

Director Guillermo Del Toro: "When mankind allows its ego to balloon and schemes of gaining total control of the planet, nature steps in to remind us who's boss."

Three years later, some boys bring Tyler a big, weird bug they've found in the subway. Oh no, it's a Judas bug and it's only a baby! Meaning, Tyler has made one big-time mistake. Tyler has to find out what's happening with her insects, so she, Mann, and a few others end up in the subway system—often alone.

There they find that the Judas bugs have mutated into really giant bugs. The "mimic" part is that the bugs mimic their predators to protect themselves. Now the Judas bugs are starting to mimic their human predators. To do this the bugs have the pattern of a human-like face on their chest armor and they can fold their wings in a way that resembles a long, black overcoat. This mutation is never taken to its natural conclusion—that is, the Judas bugs never turn into anything realistically resembling a human, but then there's always *Mimic 2.*

Production designer Carol Spier based the subway station on photos of an extant disused station built in 1904 underneath New York's old city.

When the movie gets down to bug vs. human chaos, there are a lot of gross-out moments, most involving bug innards. Tyler operates on bugs, bugs get smashed, and people rub bug guts on themselves (the scent fools the bugs into thinking that the humans are one of their own species). All of these moments are accompanied by the appropriately sickening, gooey, and squishy sound effects. Director Guillermo Del Toro knows how to work an audience, especially with sound. The icky sound effects, the bugs' creepy clicking noises and the music is always menacing at the right time.

Del Toro (who directed the 1992 Mexican vampire flick *Cronos*) is also big on atmosphere. The tunnels of the New York City subway system, already plenty creepy on their own, are a labyrinth of twisting passages, old, forgotten staircases, and dark, wet rooms. In each of the subterranean rooms, there is a creepy water drip. The effect is overwhelmingly claustrophobic and the viewer gets no relief.

And what of the special effects? They work. It's hard to say exactly what nine-feet-tall bugs might look like, but probably pretty much like the bugs in *Mimic*. The Judas bugs swoop through the subway with a certain grace, like multi-legged vampires. Their larvae and eggs are similarly realistic and sticky-looking. The insects are really the stars of the movie. The Judas bugs' main character trait is that they want to kill humans, and they seem believable in this endeavor.

The humans in the film have deeper desires and motivations, but not much deeper. Sorvino does a good job playing the role of the beautiful, brainy entomologist. It's the kind of role where she has to say dialogue to herself for no other reason than to explain what's going on in the scene. When she comes across a giant bug in a subway tunnel, instead of being quiet to avoid attracting attention, she has to say to herself, "It's the male." Just the fact that she makes these lines sound reasonable is fine acting for this film. The other half of her role is standard scary movie girl victim, reacting to various threats. To her credit, Sorvino plays this character stronger than most and never lets the audience have any kind of prurient thrills of watching a girl in danger.

Jeremy Northam's Peter Mann is blandly yuppie-like and maybe a little wimpy while F. Murray Abraham is the voice of reason as Dr. Gates, Susan's mentor, who was against her meddling with the natural order of things. Others who get up-close-and-personal with the insects are Leonard (Charles S. Dutton), a subway cop; smart-alecky biologist Josh (Josh Brolin); and Italian shoeshine man Manny (Giancarlo Giannini) and his autistic grandson Chuy (Alexander Goodwin). Dutton's policeman is enjoyably grouchy while Brolin adds some comic relief, especially when he has to scrape a sample from a disgustingly large amount of bug waste and laments that he hadn't gone into dentistry because he thought it would be too gross.

There needs to be a character or two for the audience to care whether or not they're eaten by giant bugs and that's where Manny and Chuy come in. Manny is quietly touching as the old country grandfather who lives only to protect

CREDITS

Susan Tyler: Mira Sorvino
Peter Mann: Jeremy Northam
Josh: Josh Brolin
Manny: Giancarlo Giannini
Leonard: Charles S. Dutton
Chuy: Alexander Goodwin
Remy: Alix Boromzay
Dr. Gates: F. Murray Abraham

Origin: USA
Released: 1997
Production: Bob Weinstein, B.J. Rack, and Ole Bornedal; released by Dimension Films
Direction: Guillermo Del Toro
Screenplay: Guillermo Del Toro, Matthew Robbins, Matthew Greenberg, and John Sayles; based on the short story by Donald A. Wolheim
Cinematography: Dan Laustsen
Editing: Patrick Lussier
Music: Marco Beltrami
Production design: Carol Spier
Art direction: Tamara Deverell
Set decoration: Elinor Rose Galbraith
Costumes: Marie-Sylvie Deveau
Creature design: Rob Bottin, Ty Ruben Ellingson
Sound: Glen Gauthier
Visual effects supervisor: Brian M. Jennings
MPAA rating: R
Running Time: 105 minutes

his special charge. Though autistic, the big-eyed Chuy is a savant in matters involving shoes. "Mr. Funny Shoes," he says unemotionally of a bug, after watching it kill a man. Later, Chuy suddenly seems to discover his emotions, which doesn't make much sense but who's going to be a stickler for such things? If it's logic problems one is looking for there are plenty—the most jarring being that one character survives a gigantic gas explosion, burn-free no less, simply by diving into a small pool of water.

But horror movies don't ride on their logical purity; it's whether they're horrifying. And, by that measure, *Mimic* does the job, with critics generally liking the film. *Entertainment Weekly* called it a "stylish B-horror movie" and taken as that *Mimic* works. It's got bugs galore, it's scary, and it's gross. Or, pretty much just about everything anyone could hope for in a movie about bugs attacking humans.

—*Jill Hamilton*

REVIEWS

Boxoffice. August, 1997, p. 48.
Chicago Tribune. August 22, 1997, p. 5.
Entertainment Weekly. August 22, 1997, p. 107.
Los Angeles Times. August 22, 1997, p. F20.
Movieline. June, 1997, p. 55.
New York Times. August 22, 1997, p. C3.
People. September 1, 1997, p. 21.
Time. August 25, 1997, p. 70.
USA Today. August 22, 1997, p. 7D.
Variety. August 18, 1997, p. 30.

Mrs. Brown

Queen Victoria, the world's most powerful woman. John Brown, a simple Scottish Highlander. Their extraordinary friendship transformed an empire.—Movie tagline

"This is one of those great films. The special effects, great acting. I wish there were more movies like *Mrs. Brown.*"—Joel Siegel, *Good Morning America*

"Irresistible. A thoroughly enjoyable outing. Judi Dench's performance has a depth and fire that sets the tone for everything else in this smart production. Billy Connolly is a revelation."—Amy Dawes, *Los Angeles Daily News*

"Marvelous. Judi Dench gives a performance nothing short of titanic. Billy Connolly is sensational. A wonderful movie."—Jeffrey Lyons, *NBC-TV*

"*Mrs. Brown* seduces. This true story, deftly embellished by writer Jeremy Brock and directed at a bracing English trot by John Madden, is a splendid showcase for its three superb leads —Judi Dench, Billy Connolly and Antony Sher."—David Ansen, *Newsweek*

"Judi Dench and Billy Connolly have volatile chemistry!"—Bruce Williamson, *Playboy*

"A romantic treat. Judi Dench is flat-out wonderful. Billy Connolly is smashing."—Peter Travers, *Rolling Stone*

Box Office: $8,490,954

A small-scale film with a loose, episodic structure, *Mrs. Brown* selects a gallery of moments from the odd but nourishing friendship of Queen Victoria (Judi Dench) and her late husband's groom, John Brown (Billy Connolly). The irreverent Scotsman, who comes to represent all Victoria has left of Albert, manages in the years from 1864 to 1868 to return the Queen from her life of grief in Balmoral to the active life of London.

Henry Ponsonby (Geoffrey Palmer) has sent for Albert's groom on the hunch that riding might start to dispel Victoria's three years of mourning. All of Osborne House feels itself to be "prisoners of the Queen's grief." John Brown turns out to an outspoken man who stands like a statue next to Victoria's horse in full view of the Queen's window. Soon she agrees to ride to the spot where Albert intended to build a bench. Eventually, Brown's bluntness ("Lift your foot, woman") is accepted by Victoria, though his plainness always produces a gasp from any onlookers.

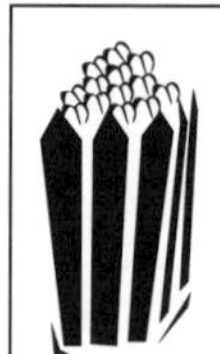

Sir Henry Ponsonby on Queen Victoria: "She is in a state of unfettered morbidity. We are all prisoners of the Queen's grief."

A collection of scenes from 1866 depicts the Queen and Brown becoming more companionable and the start of some disapproving gossip. While riding one day, she confides to Brown her intentions to publish portions of her journal. Director John Madden later crosscuts between a scene of Prime Minister Disraeli (Antony Sher) at a social gathering and the Queen and Brown dining with the humble Mr. and Mrs. Grant (Jimmy Chisholm and Jason Morell) at their simple cottage. When the two return late to Balmoral, Victoria's cheeks are flushed from Scotch whiskey. Over time, Brown grows more familiar, dancing with the Queen, high-handing other servants, scattering onlookers who might invade her privacy. By 1867, Parliament recognizes her need to come out of seclusion, and Brown's self-importance has produced some spats with Bertie (David Westhead), the Prince of Wales.

Queen Victoria had John Brown's room kept as it was from his death to her own, 18 years later. She also requested that she be buried with his photograph in her hand.

Judi Dench, whose distinguished career has focused primarily on the stage, has never before starred in a feature film. Her performance as Victoria requires her to convey at different times the "ferocious introspection" brought on by the grief that her household has noted as well as the delicately cautious attempts to reach out to a renewed interest in life.

Mrs. Brown reveals the true story of the unlikely friendship between Queen Victoria (Judi Dench) and Scottish servant John Brown (Billy Connolly).

In one scene Brown talks her into going swimming, and the royal dressing wagon is backed to the very edge of a pond. Dench emerges garbed from neck to ankles in a bathing costume with an iron look that dares anyone to intrude on her privacy. As she descends the stairs, wades into the water, and dog-paddles away, the indignities of immersing herself in water do not diminish her queenly rectitude. Another scene shows how Dench communicates the needs of Victoria, when she admits after a conversation with her cleric, "I know I do not have a subtle mind." Her advisor, thus prompted, is then able to tell her that a settled resignation can often be more proof of genuine affection than active grief. In a sense, the course of this episodic film takes Victoria from her active grief via the help of John Brown to a more settled resignation. Judi Dench effectively registers her many emotions in this difficult transition.

Other acting honors in the film belong to Antony Sher, who plays Disraeli as a cunning Machiavelli. Sher has a de-

AWARDS AND NOMINATIONS

Academy Awards 1997 Nominations: Actress (Dench), Makeup

BAFTA 1997 Nominations: Best Film, Best British Film, Original Screenplay, Actress (Dench), Actor (Connolly), Production design, Costumes, Make-up/Hair

Golden Globe Awards 1998: Drama Actress (Dench)

liciously sinister leer, and he either covers or unmasks this smirk in his scenes with the Queen or in various political gatherings. He strikes an interesting balance between these extremes toward the end in a hiking scene with Brown when he attempts to talk Brown into getting the Queen to return to London. When Brown later speaks to Victoria, a shouting match results over the subject of duty. Sher's work in the hiking scene is so nicely nuanced that he appears to the audience as he must to Brown, as if his concern for the country has momentarily overridden his love of political power. Billy Connolly's performance as John Brown does not show the same subtleties as Dench's or Sher's. He is stronger in the many moments of bravado than in those few times, as for example in some scenes with his brother (Richard Pasco), when he is required to show greater reason and calm.

In 1883, long after her return to London, John Brown lies dying of pneumonia and Victoria ends the longest hiatus in their friendship in a visit in which she makes amends. In its leisurely, sometimes undramatic manner, *Mrs. Brown* maps the private emotions in a public woman and the growth of an uncommon friendship.

—*Glenn Hopp*

CREDITS

Queen Victoria: Judi Dench
John Brown: Billy Connolly
Henry Ponsonby: Geoffrey Palmer
Disraeli: Antony Sher
Archie Brown: Gerald Butler
Doctor Jenner: Richard Pasco
Prince of Wales: David Westhead

Origin: Great Britain
Released: 1997
Production: Sarah Curtis for Ecosse Film; released by Miramax Films
Direction: John Madden
Screenplay: Jeremy Brock
Cinematography: Richard Greatrex
Editing: Robin Sales
Music: Stephen Warbeck
Production design: Martin Childs
Art direction: Charlotte Watts
Costumes: Deirdre Clancy
Sound: Alistair Crocker
MPAA rating: PG
Running Time: 103 minutes

REVIEWS

Boxoffice. August, 1997, p. 47.
Chicago Tribune. July 25, 1997, p. 5.
Entertainment Weekly. July 25, 1997, p. 54.
The Hollywood Reporter. May 12, 1997, p. 9.
Los Angeles Times. July 18, 1997, p. F12.
Movieline. August, 1997, p. 38.
New York Times. July 18, 1997, p. C5.
New Yorker. August 4, 1997, p. 77.
People. July 28, 1997, p. 22.
Sight and Sound. September, 1997, p. 50.
USA Today. July 18, 1997, p. 4D.
Variety. May 19, 1997, p. 58.
Village Voice. July 22, 1997, p. 65.

Mr. Magoo

You'll laugh so hard you'll see double!—Movie tagline

Box Office: $10,038,008

Seemingly, every show that was ever on television when Baby Boomers were growing up is being made into a movie for aging Boomers. Thus, we have *Mr. Magoo*, a live-action incarnation of a cartoon that in its own day was more wry than hilarious. The cartoon focused on a big-hearted, nearsighted, bumbling old man whose poor vision kept getting him into improbable situations that he escaped through even more improbable good luck.

The best thing about the cartoon Magoo was the mumbling, preoccupied, scatterbrained voice of Jim Backus. The new film version, directed by Hong Kong action director Stanley Tong, has none of the original's cool, laid-back feel but all of its preposterous silliness. The new Magoo is broadly drawn, hyperkinetic and extravagant, but it works reasonably well as a brainless entertainment confection.

Enthusiastically taking over the lead role is Leslie Nielsen, the comic star of *Airplane!* (1980), *Naked Gun* (1988) and their numerous spinoff spoofs. Nielsen, who is tall and angular, is an odd choice to play the squat, balding Magoo, but he does an admirable job, getting the voice down perfectly and keeping his character lovable and low-key.

Nielsen's Magoo is an amiable, befuddled, and well-intentioned mogul who runs a canned vegetable company. Nielsen perfectly conveys the impression of an old-fashioned gentleman lost in the maze of an increasingly complicated modern world. That befuddlement was the subtext of the original cartoon, which used a visual handicap as a metaphor for modern angst.

The first Mr. Magoo cartoon was released in 1949 and later became a syndicated TV series in 1960.

The credibility problem with Magoo is this: Why doesn't he get glasses? The explanation given here is that he's too stubborn to admit he can't see, and that very pigheadedness is part of what gets him in trouble constantly. The "sight gags" that carried the cartoon couldn't sustain a feature-length film, and in the film they are wisely kept to a minimum. Magoo mistakes a mummy's case for a telephone booth, a mandrill for a child on a swing, and, in the most successful instance of mistaken identity, the paddle wheel of a tourist boat for an escalator.

As produced by Disney studios, the Magoo update had to tackle the issue of avoiding offense to people with visual handicaps. Given the sensitivity of the era, it is surprising the film was made at all. A disclaimer at the end of the film notes that the movie in no way corresponds to the reality of visual impairment and maintains that the blind shouldn't be victimized. If the intent is to get Disney off the hook for making a movie that pokes fun at a character who can't see, it would have been better to put the notice at the beginning. Placed where it is, it's more laughable than effective.

The bigger problem was how to make a feature film out of a one-joke premise. The answers, supplied by director Tong and screenwriters Pat Proft and Tom Sherohman, were to create a high-energy stew of mayhem involving a jewel heist and to populate the film with a number of appealing minor characters. These techniques pad the story and take some of the comic burden off Nielsen and his impaired vision.

One of the most serviceable of the additions is a bulldog named Angus, who functions as Magoo's personal valet, guardian and savior. The resourceful mutt not only picks out Magoo's clothes for him in the morning, he acts swiftly when he sees trouble coming and pushes vacuum cleaners or footstools out of the way of his approaching master. Angus is also the only character who is effective in the many efforts to retrieve the stolen jewel. If one can speak of great performances by a dog, this is certainly one.

The real show-stealer, however, is Kelly Lynch, the attractive actress who has made an unusual career out of combining light comedy with playing strung-out women in films like *Drugstore Cowboy* (1989). Here, Lynch displays a great knack for comic timing and a superb ability to switch costumes, personas and disguises at will. Her arch-villain Luanne Leseur at various times impersonates an old lady, a reporter, an FBI agent, and a moll. Provocatively and smartly portrayed by Lynch, Leseur is a karate-kicking, coldhearted femme fatale in outrageous outfits who could have stepped right out of a James Bond movie. Lynch is wonderfully funny, purring like a kitten one second and then delivering a ruthless kick in the groin the next. Her face is a perfect mask for multiple role-playing and her body a supple arsenal of danger and seduction.

Lynch is at the center of most of the best action and comedy in the film. The other villainous sidekicks have much less impact. Malcom McDowell is steely-eyed, low-keyed and not nearly menacing enough as the criminal mastermind Austin Cloquet. The script gives his character very little to do. As Cloquet's underling Bob Morgan, Nick Chinlund is a bumbling, foolish, luckless agent who spends most of the film vainly pursuing Leseur and Magoo and getting clobbered in various ways.

On the side of justice are two feuding, inept government agents, the CIA's Gus Anders (Ernie Hudson) and the FBI's Chuck Stupak (Stephen Tobolowsky). They're a Mutt-and-Jeff duo. Hudson does a fine job portraying the publicity-hungry, trouble-shy CIA man. Tobolowsky is suitably buffoonish as the more daring of the duo, getting mashed and insulted left and right. Less interesting are Magoo's cherubic nephew Waldo (Matt Keeslar), who is something of a nebbish, and his unlikely love interest, the princess of the nation whose crown jewel was stolen, whose unlikely Western/Eastern combo name is Stacey Sampanahoditra. She is played by newcomer Jennifer Garner with a jarring eagerness.

Most of the film consists of the bad guys and the good guys chasing Magoo and one another. Magoo is being pursued because the government suspects him of being in on the jewel heist—an improbable assumption, to say the least, since Magoo was the museum benefactor who donated the jewel in the first place. But believability is not among director Tong's chief concerns here. Comic skullduggery is. Tong succeeds best with a scene in which almost all the characters skulk around Magoo's house, trying to find the jewel while avoiding bumping into one another. Agent Stupak at one point hides beneath a coat on a hook, suspending himself off the floor. Magoo tries to cook a chicken by means of an instructional TV show, unaware that various bumps to the remote control have changed the channel first to an exercise program, then to a home improvement show. So he makes the chicken legs do aerobics, then applies sandpiper and a drill according to the instructions he hears. The complicated scene ends in a chase in which Magoo, Waldo and Leseur end up in an eggplant-shaped car chasing Bob Morgan down busy streets. The car ends up flying off a cliff into a huge sewer pipe suspended from a crane.

Another amusing sequence occurs in a ski resort where Cloquet is trying to auction off the stolen jewel to a gallery of villains. Magoo impersonating a master villain is less funny than a chase scene down a snowy slope. Magoo seizes an inverted ironing board and sashays down the mountain in the middle of a snowboard race. The scene contains the film's best tongue-in-cheek line: when a policeman pulls a gun on an ice-encrusted Bob Morgan, stopped dead in his tracks on the verge of an icy abyss, and shouts: "Freeze!"

The last part of the film takes place in Brazil at the wedding of a master criminal to whom Leseur is selling the jewel. The capers involve Magoo impersonating a bride, jumping off a helicopter, and doing some impromptu white-water rafting. For such a thoroughly silly film, a lot of money has obviously been spent on elaborate action and chase scenes and some special effects. It's much too grand a canvas on which to paint a rather pedestrian story, but at least the action keeps things moving.

Mr. Magoo keeps its antics coming at a fairly breakneck pace. While it never reaches a lunatic fever pitch, it's often a lot of fun, especially with Lynch's multiple disguises. The film is not gross or offensive, which is a significant back-handed compliment in an era where the top stars of such mass-audience, light-brained comedies include Jim Carrey and Adam Sandler. All involved in *Mr. Magoo* seem to have had a very good time, as is illustrated in closing-credit out-takes. Bracketing the movie with newly animated Magoo sequences is a good choice, too. It emphasizes that, despite all the bells and whistles, this is merely a cartoon after all. And as a live-action cartoon, it succeeds better than one might expect from a feature-length remake of an old, thin, one-joke TV show.

—*Michael Betzold*

CREDITS

Mr. Magoo: Leslie Nielsen
Luanne Leseur: Kelly Lynch
Waldo: Matt Keeslar
Bob Morgan: Nick Chinlund
Agent Chuck Stupak: Stephan Tobolowsky
Agent Gus Anders: Ernie Hudson
Austin Cloquet: Malcolm McDowell
Ortega Peru: Miguel Ferrer
Stacey: Jennifer Garner

Origin: USA
Released: 1997
Production: Ben Myron for Walt Disney Pictures; released by Buena Vista Pictures
Direction: Stanley Tong
Screenplay: Pat Proft and Tom Sherohman
Cinematography: Jingle Ma
Editing: Stuart Pappe, David Rawlins, Michael R. Miller
Music: Michael Tavera
Production design: John Willett
Art direction: Doug Byggdin
Costumes: Tom Bronson
Sound: Rob Young
MPAA rating: PG
Running Time: 87 minutes

REVIEWS

Cinemafantastique. January, 1998, p. 10.
Cinemafantastique. April, 1998, p. 53.
Entertainment Weekly. January 9, 1998, p. 48.
New York Times. December 24, 1997.
Variety. December 22, 1997, p. 60.

Money Talks

"*Money Talks* pays off and Chris Tucker triumphs. He's funny in that cocky, freefall way that Jim Carrey and Jerry Lewis get away with: He's floating on inspiration and improvisation, like a musician."—Roger Ebert, *Chicago Sun-Times*

"A comedy action adventure that actually is funny (so many that are meant to be these days aren't). Tucker clearly knows how to showcase himself and make others look good too. Slam-bam action and knockout humor."—Kevin Thomas, *Los Angeles Times*

"In the Eddie Murphy role, Chris Tucker, the rising star, can be sweet and edgy, even tragic, while never losing the comic beat."—Thelma Adams, *New York Post*

Box Office: $40,922,619

Money Talks is a comedic buddy film about a street hustler and a TV news reporter who transform their antagonistic relationship into a beneficial bond while fighting off a gang of smugglers. Opening with a tour of the streets of Los Angeles, Franklin Hackett (Chris Tucker) drives a convertible Mercedes singing along to Barry White's lines, "You're my first, my last, my everything."

But *Money Talks* isn't a love story. Hackett stops at the L.A. Sports Arena to meet a ticket scalper and begins his jokey jabbering for the entire film. His next destination is the car wash where shoe shine customers anticipate delivery of his hot merchandise and the Mercedes owner has awaited impatiently. The KJLA newsman, James Russell (Charlie Sheen), also stands by counting on an interview to expose Hackett's covert activities.

Hackett on Russell's fiance Grace: "Phat! P-H-A-T. Pretty hot and tempting."

Between "beeps" in Franklin Hackett's foul-mouthed testimony, he excuses himself to deal with an irate loan shark, leaving reporter Russell with little material for his story on "our city and our crimes." On returning from the sleazy meeting, Hackett is greeted by cops arresting him. It was a set-up.

On an inmate transfer bus headed to the courthouse, Hackett's motormouth annoys the French-speaking prisoner he's handcuffed. Meanwhile, an ominous group of black-cloaked men in black vans and trucks jet about, blocking traffic, securing the bridge the bus travels over and blasting the vehicle in half, setting the orange-jumpsuited jailbirds on fire. Rescued by a helicopter, the Frenchman takes Hackett in tow. Hackett keeps blathering until he's cut loose, pushed out and into the ocean—but not before he notices a red camel stamp on the henchman's hand and hears the words "Auto Expo" among the foreign dialogue.

Russell is fired from Channel 12 for his lame story. As he's leaving the studio, he catches Hackett's photo on a news flash about the escape and then receives a phone call from the fugitive who's intent on revenge for the mess he's in. Russell has a better idea, and agrees to provide refuge to the two-bit criminal and guaranteed exoneration, in exchange for exclusive rights to the story during TV rating "sweeps" the next week. He gets his job back but must contain live-wire Hackett and endure the ensuing troubles all weekend. The other hitch is that Russell is getting married Saturday.

At the wedding rehearsal, Hackett poses as Russell's former college buddy—Vic Damone, the son of Vic Senior and Diahann Carroll. Russell's finance (Heather Locklear) and her dad (Paul Sorvino) swallow the tale and are touched by Junior's toast—"You're his first, his last, his everything," borrowing from the Barry White song.

The police are on Hackett's tail, staking out his girlfriend's apartment hoping for the escaped con to visit. While Hackett and Russell elude the cops, they discover the bad guys' Red Camel Club, attempting to gather evidence of Hackett's innocence and nail the offenders; they narrowly flee an assault. Hackett then enlists the support of a gun-running, pimp pal.

Back at the prospective in-laws, Hackett persuades the father that the parent's gift should be a super sports car instead of diamond studded watches. At the Auto Expo auction, the father and Hackett engage in a bidding war with the French thugs over a vintage Jaguar. In one of many absurd scenes, crude gestures are exchanged under the guise of raising the offers, until they reach a foolish $250,000. While Russell calls the cops during this fiasco, he ends up getting kidnapped.

Hackett screeches off in the Jaguar, with the French crooks in hot pursuit, and discovers the reason for the entire escapade—a hidden bagful of diamonds. He calls everybody—the cops, the loan shark, his gun-runner chum, and even the ticket scalper—to all meet at the Sports Arena for a showdown with the smugglers who demand the jewels in exchange for Russell.

The final confrontation has everyone involved—mobsters fighting the French bunch, bad cop against good—and every type of weapon—automatic arms, bombs and grenades blowing up the Coliseum. Suddenly Hackett decides to toss

CREDITS

Franklin Hatchett: Chris Tucker
James Russell: Charlie Sheen
Grace Cipriani: Heather Locklear
Guy Cipriani: Paul Sorvino
Raymond Villard: Gerard Ismael
Paula: Elise Neal
Detective Pickett: Paul Gleason
Connie Cipriani: Veronica Cartwright
Barclay: David Warner

Origin: USA
Released: 1997
Production: Walter Coblenz and Tracy Kramer; released by New Line Cinema
Direction: Brett Ratner
Screenplay: Joel Cohen and Alec Sokolow
Cinematography: Russell Carpenter, Robert Primes
Editing: Mark Helfrich
Music: Lalo Schifrin
Production design: Robb Wilson King
Art direction: John Marshall
Costumes: Sharen Davis
Sound: Kim Ornitz
Stunt coordinator: Buddy Joe Hooker
MPAA rating: R
Running Time: 95 minutes

the gems down the steps at his attackers because the fight isn't worth dying for. But the next day, the carat size on the wedding ring he hands over for Russell's new wife belies Hackett's gesture.

Full of the requisite shoot-outs, car chases, questionable language and explosions of an action picture, *Money Talks* follows the tradition of *48 Hours* and other Eddie Murphy vehicles, but Chris Tucker is unable to fit into the footsteps of his comic predecessor's success. Other performances are perfunctory, the script flimsy and gags only slightly amusing.

—*Roberta Cruger*

REVIEWS

Boxoffice. October, 1997, p. 43.
Entertainment Weekly. August 22, 1997, p. 106.
Los Angeles Times. August 22, 1997, p. F6.
New York Times. August 22, 1997, p. C5.
People. September 1, 1997, p. 21.
USA Today. August 22, 1997, p. 7D.
Variety. August 18, 1997, p. 33.

A Mongolian Tale; Hei Ma

"A graceful . . . timeless story!"—Dave Kehr, *Daily News*
"Beautiful."—Kevin Thomas, *Los Angeles Times*
"A moving tale of the strength of the spirit."—Bill Hoffman, *New York Post*
"Innocence, betrayal, sacrifice and redemption!"—Janet Maslin, *New York Times*

Chinese director Xie Fei brings a surprising degree of universality to the epic romance *A Mongolian Tale* (Hei Ma). Based on the 1982 novel *Black Steed* by Cheng-zhi Zhang (he also wrote the screen adaptation), the story dramatizes a thirty-year relationship between two star-crossed lovers in Outer Mongolia. It is a visually stunning and emotionally evocative film about love, longing, regret—emotions that know no cultural boundaries.

In the vast, sweeping plains of Mongolia, a benevolent Nai Nai, or Grandmother (Dalarsurong) raises two young abandoned children in a nomadic settlement of herders. They live in yurts, using dung for fuel; it is a simple life, but a happy one, and the children prove to be perfect playmates. There is even an orphaned wild black colt that wanders in and befriends the boy. And although the two are raised as brother and sister, it is Nai Nai's wish that her two foster children will someday marry.

But when they are older, Bayinbulag (played as an adult by Tengger) decides to return to the city to pursue an education. In his excitement, the young man brushes aside the suggestion of marriage to Someyer (Naranhuar), leaving her with the promise of his eventual return.

Bayinbulag, who now dreams of becoming a musician, remains in the city much longer than expected. When he does finally return, he finds Someyer, having been seduced by a drunken herdsman, pregnant with the other man's child. Bayinbulag is devastated. Unlike traditional Mongolians who revere children, Bayinbulag's modern education has conditioned him to spurn Someyer. His anger and disappointment drive him to once again leave, breaking all ties with both Nai Nai and Someyer.

Some ten years pass before Bayinbulag has the courage to again return to the steppes of Mongolia. He is now a popular musician; Someyer is a disillusioned wife and mother of five. As she relates the fates of both Nai Nai and the black horse, Bayinbulag realizes that Someyer will never be his wife, and that life will never be as uncomplicated, nor love as protected, as it was in his childhood. His voice-over narration tragically acknowledges, " . . . only when it was gone did I realize what I had lost."

A Mongolian Tale is a gentle and subtle film that utilizes a simple approach to explore the complexity of love. Shot on location in the remote terrain, its breathtaking scenery is captured in the artful compositions by cinematographer Jing Sheng Fu. In many ways, the Mongolian landscape is as much a character in the film as the people. Perhaps it is the thrill of experiencing a land that has yet to be exploited in the cinema and remains relatively untouched by commercialism.

The acting is accomplished throughout Xie's film. The role of Bayinbulag is played effectively and with restraint by Mongolia-born, Taiwan-based pop star, Tengger. He also is credited with writing the film's haunting score and sings on the soundtrack, as well. London-based Mongolian actress Naranhuar imbues Someyer with an implicit sensuality and tragic resignation. But it is veteran actress Dalarsurong who stands out in *A Mongolian Tale.* She gives a compelling performance as the grandmother, Nai Nai.

CREDITS

Bayinbulag: Tengger
Somiya: Naren Hau
Nai Nai (Grandmother): Dalarsurong
Dawasong: Gangbater
Qiqig: Aorjirdai

Origin: China, Hong Kong
Released: 1995, 1997
Production: Ma Fung-kwok and Wellington Fung; released by New Yorker Films
Direction: Xie Fei
Screenplay: Zhang Cheng-zhi; from his novel *Black Steed*
Cinematography: Jing Sheng Fu
Editing: Xie Fei, Zhao Xiu-qiu
Costumes: Wurtanasun
Music: Tengger
MPAA rating: Unrated
Running Time: 100 minutes

Filmmaker Xie Fei is one of China's lesser known "fourth generation" directors. To his credit, Xie has managed to tell a compelling, heart-wrenching story without falling victim to the potential melodrama inherent in such material. *A Mongolian Tale* is a stirring film that artfully conveys societal change, how modern life has begun to impinge on this ancient culture. It is a beautifully crafted tale of the vagaries of fate—and a reminder that both life and love wait for no one.

—*Patricia Kowal*

REVIEWS

Boxoffice. April, 1997, p. 185.
New York Times. May 16, 1997, p. F14.
San Francisco Chronicle. April 25, 1997, p. D3.
San Francisco Examiner. April 25, 1997, p. D5.
Toronto Sun. April 23, 1997.

Mortal Kombat: Annihilation

Destroy all expectations.—Movie tagline

Box Office: $34,543,875

Coming up with story ideas in Hollywood is getting harder. In 1996, works by William Shakespeare enjoyed their umpteenth revival. Lesser known (to movie audiences), more recent writers (Jane Austen, Henry James) are being mined *ad infinitum* and you can't swing a dead cat in Tinseltown without hitting an actor who starred in or is preparing to do a remake or a sequel. With baby boomers in control of not only the family purse strings but also what to see, producers have pillaged through countless '60s and '70s sitcoms and adapted them for the silver screen. Batman and Superman have paved the way for the X-Men and the Green Hornet. Coupled with the success of this year's *Men In Black*, you can bet that we haven't seen the last of comic book transformations. Just tap into those treasured, recessed, baby-boomer memories and they will surely come. What comic books were to the boomers, video games are to the Gen-Xers and beyond. Similar mindless boogie, different medium.

Considering the heavy market saturation and fertile consumer landscape of the interactive video market, there have been relatively few screen adaptations targeted at this huge audience. Perhaps what some shortsighted developers and producers have failed to notice is the basic appeal of interactive games; they require interaction. *Double Dragon* (1994), *Street Fighter* (1994) and *Super Mario Brothers* (1993), all perennial favorites in the interactive market, were adapted for the screen and all failed miserably at the boxoffice. It's easy to see why. The target audience had to sit there for two hours and do nothing but watch. As anyone with a prepubescent child will tell you, getting them to do anything while in a stationary position (save for perhaps sleep) for two hours is next to impossible.

The only interactive game to see any kind of profitable return as a movie was *Mortal Kombat* from 1995. Being smart enough to cash in while the getting was good, the producers of *Mortal Kombat* recognized they had a small-time window of opportunity and caught the wave. As the boxoffice receipts from the first weekend of *Annihilation*, the *Mortal Kombat* sequel proved, there is a dedicated, obsessed horde of *Mortal Kombat* followers who will blindly support anything with that franchise stamp on it. Call them

Trekkies: The Next Generation. However, the receipts for the second week fell off considerably.

For adults (and those not familiar with the many uses of a interactive joystick), sitting through the nearly two hours of the first *Mortal Kombat* was taxing enough. There was one moderately talented actor involved (Christopher Lambert) and the *Star Wars/Star Trek* special effects had their own guilty pleasure appeal. *Annihilation* throws any considerations for an adult audience (or anyone with an IQ above room temperature) out the window. Present is the same overblown, apocalyptic mishmash storyline and histrionics that would make a soap opera star blush. The glaring politically correct band of protagonists is in place; equal portions black, brown, white, yellow, male, female. Between the attempts at coherent dialogue are (admittedly well choreographed) martial arts fights scenes where nobody loses their '80s era, mousse-and-blow dryer hairdos or gets even a little bit soiled. Unless, of course, you count the scene where two of the female leads participate in the requisite catfight. In mud. Perhaps part of the adult audience can find something worth watching after all.

If you can overlook the overacting (which is hard to do) you'll find a movie that makes no claims to being anything more than it is—unrestrained eye-candy. PG-13 level sexual innuendo and bloodless violence where very few characters die or even suffer any permanent injury. Actors looking for any vehicle to get exposure and technical folks cutting their teeth before graduating to the big leagues. It's *Mighty Morphin Power Rangers* without the disco clothes meeting the cast of "The Young & The Restless" at Luke Skywalker's summer home during a meteor shower.

—J.M. Clark

CREDITS

Liu Kang: Robin Shou
Kitana: Talisa Soto
Shao-Khan: Brian Thompson
Sonya Blade: Sandra Hess
Jax: Lynn Red Williams
Jade: Irina Pantaeva
Sheeva: Marjean Holden
Shinnok: Reiner Schoene
Sindel: Musetta Vander
Nightwolf: Litefoot
Rayden: James Remar

Origin: USA
Released: 1997
Production: Lawrence Kasanoff for Threshold Entertainment; released by New Line Cinema
Direction: John R. Leonetti
Screenplay: Brent V. Friedman and Bryce Zabel; based on the video game
Cinematography: Matthew F. Leonetti
Editing: Peck Prior
Costumes: Jennifer L. Parson
Music: George S. Clinton
Production design: Charles Wood
Art direction: Nathan Schroeder
Sound: John Midgley
Visual effects supervisors: Chuck Comisky, Alison Savitch
Fight coordinator: Robin Shou
MPAA rating: PG-13
Running Time: 91 minutes

REVIEWS

Cinemafantastique. December, 1997, p. 14.
Detroit Free Press. November 22, 1997, p. 2A.
Entertainment Weekly. December 5, 1997, p. 54.
Los Angeles Times. November 24, 1997, p. F10.
New York Times. November 22, 1997, p. B10.
Variety. November 24, 1997, p. 64.

Most Wanted

Sometimes the most patriotic thing a Marine can do . . . is disobey orders.—Movie tagline

Box Office: $6,391,946

Most Wanted tells the story of Special Forces Marine Sgt. James Dunn, who was imprisoned for five years after refusing an extreme command while on duty in Iraq (the intended assassination target was a ten-year-old boy and Dunn refused). After serving his time in a military prison, Dunn is released into the care of General Adam Woodward (Jon Voight), a taunting, aggressive military madman. Woodward explains to Dunn and a small select group of other Marines that they are to assassinate a businessman, Donald Bickhart (Robert Culp), who is accused of trafficking in biological warfare for his own profit. He is to be killed while he is escorting The First Lady through a local hospital.

Dunn and the other soldiers are strategically placed outside the hospital; Dunn is especially nervous since he has been designated as the "kill shot." Yet, as Dunn watches in horror, the First Lady—not Bickhart—takes the fatal shot to the head. Dr. Victoria Constantini (Jill Hennessy) witnesses the shot, and also records it on videotape. She is interviewed on television talking about her tape, and when Dunn later sees her on TV, he knows she is the key to clearing his name.

Dunn: "I'm a Marine. We don't plan—we improvise."

CIA Director Kenny Rachmill (Paul Sorvino) spearheads the case to find the assassin; he relies on his second in command Spencer (Eric Roberts). A composite is sent all over Los Angeles, and Dunn finds himself pursued by the government, the CIA, and the general public. Dunn does find Constantini and convinces her that he has been framed and that she must help him get to the bottom of this mess.

CREDITS

Sgt. James Dunn: Keenen Ivory Wayans
General Adam Woodward/Lt Colonel Grant
Casey: Jon Voight
Dr. Victoria Constantini: Jill Hennessy
CIA Deputy Director Kenny Rackmill: Paul Sorvino
Donald Bickhart: Robert Culp
Assistant Deputy Director Spencer: Eric Roberts

Origin: USA
Released: 1997
Production: Eric Gold Ivory Way Productions; released by New Line Cinema
Direction: David Glenn Hogan
Screenplay: Keenen Ivory Wayans
Cinematography: Marc Reshovsky
Editing: Michael J. Duthie
Music: Paul Buckmaster
Art direction: Arlan Jay Vetter
Production Design: Jean-Phillippe Carp
Costumes: Ileane Meltzer
Sound: Michael Hogan
MPAA rating: R
Running Time: 99 minutes

Hennessy, a talented actress (known for her work on the superlative television drama "Law and Order") is given little to do but wait for Wayans at a safe house in a tight camisole. Other talented actors such as Sorvino and Voight are given little to work with beyond the most lackluster lines and stock characterizations. Wayans himself comes across as a most dull, insipid hero, without the occasional funny line tossed in to keep the ridiculous actions in check. Wayans actually falls so low as to include lines directed to the nervous Hennessy when he first corners her at her apartment: "mmm—looks so good, I need a piece. I can't tell you how long since I had a piece" and then reaches beyond her for a slice of pizza.

Without humor to buoy this into a *Die Hard* or a *Lethal Weapon*, the momentum falls back onto its confusing, uninteresting storyline. Dunn and Constantini piece together the cause for the First Lady's assassination; she was a tireless Veterans Right's Advocate and was scheduled to visit the nearby hospital to meet with the sick Vets there. Constantini informs Dunn that there was a virulent strain wrongly unleashed on a division led by Woodward. Hence, Woodward wanted the First Lady out of the picture before she and the ACLU began to sue the government and the Armed Forces on behalf of sick soldiers.

Dunn and Constantini manage to inform Rachmill, who also discovers that Spencer was a mole to Woodward. After an elaborate, explosive chase, Dunn hooks up with Rachmill and pulls the trigger on Woodward himself. Thanks to the Witness Protection Plan, Dunn slips off anonymously into the Los Angeles streets. Director David Hogan (*Barb Wire*, 1996) tries to infuse some action into this lifeless drama, but the turgid story overwhelms all concerned.

—*G.E. Georges*

REVIEWS

Boxoffice. December, 1997, p. 53.
Entertainment Weekly. October 24, 1997, p. 46.
Los Angeles Times. October 10, 1997, p. F8.
New York Times. October 10, 1997, p. E20.
People. October 27, 1997, p. 20.
Variety. October 13, 1997, p. 84.

Mouse Hunt

The squeak shall inherit the earth.—Movie tagline

Who's hunting who?—Movie tagline

"The hunt for family fun is over."—Gary Schendel, *KGTV*

"As adorable as *Babe* and as wickedly funny as the *Roadrunner*."—Jeanne Wolf, *Jeanne Wolf's Hollywood*

"The funniest, fastest, most dazzling family film of the year. The mouse is completely irresistible."—Amy Longsdorf, *Philadelphia Weekly*

"Feisty, fresh holiday fun for kids of all ages."—*SSG Syndicate*

"Loads of fun. The kids will love it."—Jeffrey Lyons, *WNBC-TV*

Brothers Lars (Lee Evans) and Ernie (Nathan Lane) become victims of one mouse's maliciousness when they decide to sell their inherited house in DreamWork's *Mouse Hunt*.

Box Office: $28,584,968

Rudolf Smuntz (William Hickey) is a man whose life was dedicated to his business, manufacturing string. This is unfortunate for his two hapless sons, Ernie (Nathan Lane) and Lars (Lee Evans), who seem to have made lives for themselves despite their father's inattention: Ernie owns his own restaurant and Lars is married to April (Vicki Lewis). When Pop dies, however, Ernie and Lars eagerly hope for a sudden increase in their bank accounts only to find themselves the owners of their father's archaic string factory, a ceramic egg, a half a box of Cuban cigars, and a collection of spoons. This is not the fortune they had hoped for, and there seems to be no payoff for them until the lawyer mentions one other item . . . a mansion.

> Caesar: "Normal people are not psychologically equipped to catch a mouse."

Of the entirety of their inheritance, only the gloomy and neglected house seems to hold any hope of being traded for cash. And when Ernie loses his restaurant because one of the cockroaches inhabiting that box of cigars makes its way into the mayor's lobster dinner causing him to die of a heart attack, and when Lars is kicked out of his home by his avaricious wife, then the two find that the only roof they can put over their head is that of the run-down mansion their father left them.

Their first goal is to try and rehab the house just enough to make a few thousand dollars from selling it, but when the brothers discover blueprints from 1876 that prove it is the famous lost house designed by architect Charles Lyle LaRue, they also discover that what they thought was worth a few thousand is now worth millions.

And so, with plans for renovation and a big payday, the two brothers move into their derelict and (assumedly) unoccupied legacy. But they are not alone in the house. The real "owner" of the home, as they soon realize, is a mouse. But a mouse would depreciate the value of the home, so Ernie and Lars do the obvious, set a few traps. But this is no ordinary mouse, and as much as the brothers want to get rid of him before the estate auction, so too does the mouse have plans for evicting Ernie and Lars.

When traps, a psychotic cat and even mailing him to Cuba fail to catch, kill or oust the pest, Ernie and Lars resort to calling an exterminator. Caesar (Christopher Walken), the most professional of vermin obliterators, also soon finds that he, too, is no match for the mouse. Now all the brothers can hope to do is prevent potential bidders from finding out that there's a mouse on the premises before they can walk off into the sunset with their bankrolls.

Mouse Hunt has a lot in common with another film, *Home Alone* (1990). Only instead of having intrusive burglars invade the domicile of a cute eight-year-old, it has two bungling brothers—the legal owners of the home—invading the living space of a cute, furry mouse. However, where the eight-year-old had to think of all sorts of diabolical ways to stop and maim the burglars, in *Mouse Hunt* the mouse never initiates the mayhem, he just turns the Smuntz brother's antagonistic acts back upon themselves.

For example, in one of their early yet desperate attempts to catch him they set the entire kitchen floor awash in mousetraps . . . only to find they've backed themselves into a corner. They must sit there for as long as it takes for just one of the traps to catch their prey. However, as mentioned before, this is no ordinary mouse. He even knows how to make a sandwich by toasting only one side of the bread so as not to wilt the arugula! So, it should come as no surprise when the mouse dances his way across the top of kitchen cupboards until he reaches a point where he can "toss" a cherry onto the floor touching off a tidal wave of trap action that only succeeds in catching Lars and Ernie. (This scene involved 1,000 hand-built mousetraps individually loaded with plastic cheese and olives then rigged to a master trigger panel creating a spiderweb of 5,000 yards of monofilament under the floor. Luckily, only one take was needed because it would have taken 3 days to re-rig the elaborate sequence.)

Final film for actor William Hickey who died on June 29, 1997, only weeks after completing his role.

Obviously, in a movie like this it's the believability of the mouse that will make or break the film's spell. As good as Nathan Lane (who stole *The Birdcage* [1995] from Robin Williams) and Lee Evans (the English actor who walked away with *Funny Bones* [1994]) are, there is no doubt that this is the mouse's film.

A cinematic composite of more than 60 trained live mice, computer-generated (CGI) mice, and an animatronic mouse for the closeups, the unnamed protagonist is a delight to watch onscreen, and only rarely is the spell broken by the realization that a real mouse can't possibly be doing what it's doing. The special effects are almost seamless.

Unfortunately, when the little guy is not onscreen, the movie slows down immensely. When he's walking a wheel of Gouda, or setting off a floor full of mousetraps, or sending the Smuntz's psychotic cat down the dumbwaiter, we are amazed and amused. When it's just the humans, all we want is to have the mouse back. This isn't saying that the actors aren't good; it's just that the mouse is even better.

Lane and Evans make interesting bunglers, and Christopher Walken as the exterminator uses his normally manic persona to an interesting comic effect, but without the mouse, who gets the best "lines," this would be little more than a third-rate Three Stooges film.

One amusing turn the human actors of the film have involves an in-joke cameo when Ernie and Lars go to the animal pound to obtain a suitably psychopathic cat. There they find actor Ernie Sabella who is more than glad to give them Catzilla. Sabella was the voice of Pumba to Lane's Timon in *The Lion King* (1994). A reference noted again when Lane greets an auction guest with a throwaway "Hakuna Matata."

There is also one sad note to the human performances in *Mouse Hunt*. William Hickey who plays Ernie and Lars' father, who garnered a Best Supporting Actor Oscar nomination for his role in *Prizzi's Honor* (1985), died just a few weeks after completing work on this film. That is why it is dedicated to him.

But the good performances by the real actors and the great performance by the combined mice actors (real and man-made) is the best part of the film. What doesn't help is its very dark, stylized look. It was meant to set the tone of theatricalness and of being anywhere and anytime, but instead it distances the viewer from the humor. It creates chilliness instead of warmth. It imparts an atmosphere of apprehension instead of amusement. This real-life cartoon (which even involves a genuine "Tom and Jerry" chase between Catzilla and the mouse) deserves a lighter, more colorful ambience. And while the Rube Goldberg string factory and the slapstick mouse hunt will

CREDITS

Ernie Smuntz: Nathan Lane
Lars Smuntz: Lee Evans
April Smuntz: Vicki Lewis
Alexander Falko: Maury Chaykin
The Lawyer: Eric Christmas
Quincy Thorpe: Michael Jeter
Ingrid: Debra Christofferson
Hilde: Camilla Soeberg
Auctioneer: Ian Abercrombie
Roxanne Atkins: Annabelle Gurwitch
The Banker: Eric Poppick
Maury: Ernie Sabella
Rudolf Smuntz: William Hickey
Caesar: Christopher Walken

Origin: USA
Released: 1997
Production: Alan Riche, Tony Ludwig and Bruce Cohen; released by DreamWorks Pictures
Direction: Gore Verbinski
Screenplay: Adam Rifkin
Cinematography: Phedon Papamichael
Editing: Craig Wood
Production design: Linda DeScenna
Art direction: James Nedza
Set decoration: Ric McElvin
Costumes: Jill Ohanneson
Music: Alan Silvestri
Visual effects supervisor: Charles Gibson
Animatronic effects: Stan Winston
MPAA rating: PG
Running Time: 95 minutes

appeal to children, this gloomy environment may put them off a bit.

Perhaps even more unsettling for the littlest ones will be the scene with a little girl being led from the animal pound, screaming about her kittens which we assume are being put to sleep. And was it really necessary to have Lars reach down—way down—the front of a woman's low-cut dress in search of the mouse who just escaped in that direction? It was disconcertingly uncomfortable in this "family film," not funny.

Mouse Hunt is one of those films that could not have been made just a few years ago. It is the epitome of today's special effects, and without them the film would have floundered. Thankfully the mouse has the intelligence, the creativity and the cuteness to carry the film.

—*Beverley Bare Buehrer*

REVIEWS

Cinemafantastique. January, 1998, p. 12.
Entertainment Weekly. January 9, 1998, p. 47.
People. January 19, 1998, p. 17.
Variety. December 22, 1997, p. 59.

Mouth to Mouth; Boca a Boca

Your fantasies are only a phone call away.
—Movie tagline

"Sexy and uproarious!"—Jim Svejda, *CBS Radio*

"Outrageously funny, witty and sexy!"—Jeffrey Lyons, *NBC-TV*

"A saucy burlesque with an extra screw loose!"
—Bruce Williamson, *Playboy*

It is a well known fact that struggling actors have been forced to take many odd and often demeaning jobs in order to survive. There's very little that these brave thespians haven't done to get by, prior to their "big breaks." There is nothing especially unique about their trials and tribulations, so it was a pleasant surprise that a film out of Spain titled *Boca a Boca* (*Mouth to Mouth*) was able to add a clever freshness to a somewhat unoriginal theme. It is a delightfully zany little comedy that deals with risque subject matter without becoming lewd and lascivious.

Manuel Gomez Pereira directed this Spanish romp as well as produced, along with Cesar Benitez and Joaquin Oristrell. In Spain, *Mouth to Mouth* was the nation's comedy hit of the winter and has been receiving favorable reviews in America. It is not "great filmmaking," but manages to entice audiences with its ribald sense of humor.

The story begins with a fairly standard "out of work" actor scenario. While singing and dancing his heart out at an audition, a young actor, Victor Ventura (Javier Bardem) gets his bicycle stolen. This is a disastrous situation, since he used the bike for his job as a pizza delivery man. Desperate for work, he takes a job as a caller for an erotic phone service called "The Hotline." He quickly becomes extremely proficient at this trade and soon establishes a recurring "hot" conversation with one of his callers. The caller, Ricardo (Josep Maria Flotats), gets a crush on him even though he's a married man. Victor happens to be straight, and one night he speaks to a very sexy and seductive female on the line who proceeds to excite and titillate young Victor. Breaking company rules, he makes a date with this mystery woman and ends up in bed with her. She happens to be a gorgeous creature named Amanda (Aitana Sanchez-Gijon) and also just happens to be the wife of Victor's phone admirer, Ricardo. The plot thickens as Amanda tries to lure Victor into a blackmail scheme to force Ricardo to divorce her for reasons of her own. All the while Victor is involved in this devious plot with Amanda, his agent is working feverishly hard on getting him the lead role in a major American film. If all goes well, he could very well become the next Antonio Banderas. What more could an aspiring actor ask for? Meanwhile, the naive Victor soon discovers that Amanda is not really Ricardo's wife and that his real wife, Angela (Maria Barranco) is out to kill her hopelessly confused husband. There were actually so many sub-plots going on simultaneously that it became somewhat exhausting trying to keep up with the action—a map would have helped.

Perhaps the most ingratiating thing about *Boca a Boca* was the offbeat appeal of the cast. They took their roles seriously, but seemed also to be in on the joke. Also the script, albeit slightly confusing and convoluted, had an originality

AWARDS AND NOMINATIONS

Independent Spirit Awards 1997 Nominations:
Foreign Film

to it. It took a well known topic (unemployed actors), added some sexy scenes and created a fresh sassiness to the subject matter. It also made some interesting points about the American film industry in choosing mostly stereotypes in casting minorities. In one funny scene where Victor meets with the American director for the first time, the director exclaims, "John Travolta looks more Spanish than you do!"

The film's success in large part depends upon the appeal of the central character, Victor Ventura. This part is the central character to which all the action revolves around, so it is essential that he be sexy, funny, sensitive and very appealing. Javier Bardem (*High Heels* [1991], *Jamon, Jamon* [1993]) is all of those things and much more. He displays a natural adeptness at comic timing plus sensitivity. In his past films he was always sexy and virile and macho, but in *Mouth to Mouth* he is able to build subtle shadings to his "machismo." The contrast is interesting and disarming, adding great appeal to young Victor. The entire cast give very funny and quirky performances, adding to the offbeat charm of the film. Amanda, played by Aitana Sanchez-Gijon (*A Walk in the Clouds* [1995]) is especially good and her performance is both alluring and touching.

"*Mouth to Mouth* combines high gloss production values, breathless plotting and a healthy lack of good taste," wrote Jonathan Holland in his *Variety* review. It is a funny and sexy farcical tale that delights in telling a familiar story in its own unique and, surprisingly, original way.

—Rob Chicatelli

CREDITS

Victor Ventura: Javier Bardem
Amanda: Aitana Sanchez-Gijon
Ricardo: Josep Maria Flotats
Angela: Maria Barranco
Raul: Fernando Guillen-Cuervo
David: Emilio Guiterrez Caba

Origin: Spain
Released: 1995, 1997
Production: Cesar Benitz, Joaquin Oristrell, Manuel Gomez Pereira for Sogotel, Bocaboca Producciones, and Starline; released by Miramax Films
Direction: Manuel Gomez Pereira
Screenplay: Joaquin Oristrell, Naomi Wise, Juan Luis Iborra, and Manuel Gomez Pereira
Cinematography: Juan Amoros
Editing: Guillermo Repressa
Music: Bernardo Bonezzi
Art direction: Luis Valles
Sound: Carlos Faruolo
MPAA rating: R
Running Time: 105 minutes

REVIEWS

New York Times. September 5, 1997, p. C8.
People. September 15, 1997, p. 28.
Variety. January 8, 1996, p. 73.
Village Voice. September 9, 1997, p. 86.

Murder at 1600

This address changes all the rules.—Movie tagline

"A gripping murder mystery with loads of heart-pounding action!"—Ron Brewington, *American Urban Radio Networks*

"This murder-thriller at the White House is a wild, high-tech ride—you'll love it!"—Jim Ferguson, *Prevue Channel*

"A solid whodunit, engrossing and engaging."—John Batlake, *Sacramento Bee*

"A winning performance from Wesley Snipes. He is hugely likeable as the cool detective. *Murder at 1600* is a well-crafted suspense thriller."—Gene Shalit, *Today Show*

Box Office: $25,842,024

The gradual emergence of a new film genre often seems to be linked to tried and true older ones. Recently a number of films have used the White House as a setting, perhaps because of the notoriety of the long-standing investigations that have troubled the Clinton Administration. The staples of this new subgenre of White House films have not yet become fixed, so each film so far has defined itself by drawing on elements from existing genres such as romantic comedy (*The American President* [1995]), the road film (*My Fellow Americans* [1996]), science-fiction/horror

(*Independence Day* [1996]), action-adventure (*Air Force One* [1997]), and thriller (*Absolute Power* [1997]). Now murder mystery can be added to the group with *Murder at 1600*, a whodunit with Wesley Snipes and Diane Lane set in the White House. Like the others, this film uses the White House for color, setting, and some satire, but it primarily adheres to the elements of older cinematic forms, in this case the whodunit, in spite of its presidential trappings.

Stengel to Regis: "What are you going to do? Put the president in a lineup?"

One of the strongest scenes is the credit sequence that opens the film. As a nighttime thunderstorm crashes overhead, director Dwight Little intercuts quick shots of a couple making love with shots that ironically identify the location as the oval office: the presidential seal in the carpet on which the lovers sprawl, the faces of the presidential portraits looking on in seeming disapproval. The woman glimpsed in this opening scene, Carla Town (Mary Moore), is found murdered later that night in a White House bathroom stall. Homicide detective Harlan Regis (Wesley Snipes) is assigned the case, and he immediately clashes with the chief of security Nick Spikings (Daniel Benzali) and Nina Chance (Diane Lane), the secret service agent Spikings appoints to assist Regis.

The smooth efficiency of the government moving into action can be seen in how quickly the administration has decided on what "punch words" ("appropriate," "timely") to emphasize in the upcoming statement to the press about the murder. Regis discovers when he gets to the victim's apartment and finds empty photo albums that potentially embarrassing evidence has also been whisked out of his grasp. Further confusing the matter is Agent Chance's contention that thirty people were in the White House at the time of the murder rather than the thirty-one Spikings had claimed. Regis's partner Detective Stengel (Dennis Miller) finds a claim check at Town's apartment for additional photographs, and he slips it to Regis when Chance is not looking.

This detail and the autopsy report provide Regis with his early leads as the political element begins to give way to the murder mystery. An enlarged negative from one of Town's unclaimed pictures reveals a security agent assigned to Kyle Neil (Tate Donovan), the president's son. Regis confirms that Neil, whose "one mission in life was to get laid in every room in the White House," was having an affair with the victim.

Red herrings and additional suspects proliferate. Agent Chance herself had been previously assigned to Kyle Neil, but she had requested a different posting after she had been ordered to cover up evidence of Kyle's violence toward a girlfriend. National security advisor Alvin Jordan (Alan Alda) tries to balance his cooperation in the murder investigation with his need to confer with the president (Ronny Cox) about the breaking story of American hostages in Korea. Agent Chance, suspecting a coverup in the murder case, sneaks the victim's dayplanner out of the national archives. She later meets with Regis in a diner to report her speculation that the president himself may not have been at Camp David on the night of the murder.

As these clues unravel, the filmmakers incorporate three chase scenes into the middle of the film. Intended to balance the footwork and conversation of the murder investigation with some action, these chase scenes depict Regis pursuing an intruder who tries to bug his apartment, Chance eluding secret service men who suspect her of tampering with evidence, and both Chance and Regis fleeing a sudden attack. To keep the mystery plot from resolving too early, however, none of these action scenes is allowed to uncover anything important to the plot. Regis fails to catch his intruder, Chance eludes her pursuers, and she shoots out the searchlight of the helicopter trailing her and Regis. Three such dead ends tease the audience needlessly. After the first of these scenes leads nowhere, the others give way to the predictable feeling that they too will fizzle.

The detection element is helped by the large cast of characters and the star performers who personalize their roles. In addition, each character seems to be identified by one key defining trait. With Regis, his interest in Washington during the Civil War has led him to recreate in his apartment a scaled replica of the Battle of Manassas. The filmmakers use this hobby twice as a tool for furthering the plot: Regis suspects an intruder when he notices one of the toy soldiers has fallen to the floor. This knowledge of the city also allows Regis secretly to invade the White House during the film's implausible climax by gaining access through an elaborate system of underground tunnels. Agent Chance's defining trait is her past competitions as an Olympic sharpshooter, a talent that helps her foil the pursuing helicopter. It also leads to one of the film's few jokes when Chance somehow repeatedly misses the security agents attacking her and Regis in a gun battle at Spikings' house. As the two finally escape after a lengthy fusillade, Regis's only comments to her is the droll, "Olympic sharpshooter, huh?" The president is defined by his spineless good intentions and desire to be liked, his son by his abusive treatment of women. Alvin Jordan is personalized by his long-standing association with the president as trusted advisor. Detective Stengel appears to be on hand for the comic relief of his caustic remarks, but after the first few scenes his occasions for sarcasm all but disappear.

Such a method for character presentation permits the filmmakers to keep the suspects clear in the mind of the audience without becoming too focused on the development of any one. This use of brush strokes rather than detail work to personalize characters turns up often in murder mysteries where the mechanics of the genre demand that the real motives of some characters be kept hidden until the resolution. This strategy for development also reveals the filmmakers' priorities. They care more about the misdirections of the murder plot than the potential seriousness of the White House and closed-door power struggles as a film subject. When the real killer is revealed and his motive becomes known, few will find it plausible. In the world of slim chances, his gambit is the power broker's equivalent of Regis's confident attempt to tunnel undetected into the White House. Both the murder story and the political story resolve themselves disappointingly.

One noticeable strength, however, is the look of the film. Both the set design and the photography reveal a consistent and effective plan. Production designer Nelson Coates supervised the construction on soundstages of a 30,000 square foot White House set that featured adjoining offices and hallways. Director of photography Steven Bernstein chose to film the set in a way that conveyed the menace and uncertainty of the murder plot: "The colors have been desaturated to achieve the effect of impending disaster. It's darker and more ominous than the real White House, with more subtle and somber tones. The compositions are based on heavy and claustrophobic interiors. . . . We used a lot of steadicam, weaving in and out of narrow corridors, to create tension. As the camera moves along the corridors, you never know what is around the next corner." The style that Bernstein describes adds suspense to some of the strategy sessions on the Korean hostage crisis. It also highlights the showdown in the White House during the climax after Regis has entered the building to arrest the killer.

Former presidential aide George Stephanopoulos addressed the recent popularity of the White House as a setting for films in an article for *Newsweek* magazine. Calling this new subgenre "presidential pulp," Stephanopoulos observed that these films share the assumption that "crime and corruption are routine at the highest levels." He questioned that assumption, however. In an age of intense media scrutiny, Stephanopoulos maintained that the current crop of films, lacking the more conventional villains of the Cold War, simply recruit their heavies from the familiar world of government and the White House. *Murder at 1600* illustrates his point. The filmmakers are less concerned with government and politics than with keeping the audience guessing about the identity of the culprit.

—Glenn Hopp

CREDITS

Detective Harlan Regis: Wesley Snipes
Nina Chance: Diane Lane
Nick Spikings: Daniel Benzali
Detective Stengel: Dennis Miller
Alvin Jordan: Alan Alda
President Jack Neil: Ronny Cox
Kitty Neil: Diane Baker
Kyle Neil: Tate Donovan
Carla Town: Mary Moore

Origin: USA
Released: 1997
Production: Arnold Kopelson and Arnon Milchan for Regency Enterprises; released by Warner Bros.
Direction: Dwight Little
Screenplay: Wayne Beach and David Hodgin
Cinematography: Steven Bernstein
Editing: Billy Weber, Leslie Jones
Music: Christopher Young
Production design: Nelson Coates
Art direction: Dan Yarhi
Set decoration: Tedd Kuchera
Costumes: Denise Cronenberg
Sound: Bruce Carwardine
Special effects coordinator: Neil Trifunovich
MPAA rating: R
Running Time: 107 minutes

REVIEWS

Chicago Tribune. April 18, 1997, p. 5.
Detroit News. April 18, 1997, p. C1.
Entertainment Weekly. April 25, 1997, p. 47.
New York Times. April 18, 1997, p. C23.
Newsweek. May 5, 1997, p. 34.
People. April 28, 1997, p. 19.
Sight and Sound. July, 1997, p. 49.
USA Today. April 18, 1997, p. 3D.
Variety. April 14, 1997, p. 91.
Village Voice. April 29, 1997, p. 82.

My Best Friend's Wedding

Julianne fell in love with her best friend the day he decided to marry someone else.—Movie tagline

A comedy about finding your heart and losing your head.—Movie tagline

"It's the year's best comedy! Sparkling, funny and absolutely delightful. You'll fall in love with the *Pretty Woman* all over again."—Kyle Osborne, *ABC-TV*

"It's marvelous!"—Jack Garner, *Gannett*

"The best romantic comedy of the year!"—Sara Edwards, *NBC News*

"Julia Roberts is back in glorious comic form!"—David Ansen, *Newsweek*

"Two thumbs up!"—*Siskel & Ebert*

Box Office: $126,713,608

Julianne Potter's (Julia Roberts) personal life is a lot like her professional life. As a food critic she samples an appetizer here, a soup there, and main course here and a dessert there. A full meal, eaten with gusto from first lettuce leaf to last cake crumb is not her style. Ditto for her love life. On the eve of her 28th birthday, she is unmarried and uncommitted. Instead she just tastes relationships and never devotes herself to any of them.

Oh, she's had a few delicious relationships, like the one with college pal Michael O'Neal (Dermot Mulroney), but she cut it short, too, by making him her best friend. In fact, they're such good friends that they've made a pact: if neither of them is married by the time they're 28, they'll marry each other.

Then one day Julianne finds a phone message from Michael, who is now a sports writer, waiting for her. Julianne fears the worse—he's now desperate at 28 and wants to marry her. How will she put him off? To her surprise however, she learns that Michael is far from resigned to marrying Julianne, instead he wants to invite her to his wedding . . . to Kimmy Wallace (Cameron Diaz), a junior at the University of Chicago whose wealthy father owns a cable empire and the Chicago White Sox.

Well, for Julianne, the food is always tastier on the other diner's table, and, God forbid, should someone take the last piece of beefcake on an overloaded dessert cart, Julianne absolutely must have it. Now she discovers her love for Michael but, in her words, she has "four days to break up a wedding, steal the bride's fellow, and I haven't a clue how to do it."

Julia Roberts plays Julianne Potter, a woman bent on stopping her best friend from marrying the wrong woman in *My Best Friend's Wedding*.

Upon her arrival in Chicago for that Sunday's wedding, Jules (as Michael calls her) is greeted not only by her long-lost love, but also by his new-found love. Kimmy is guileless, bubbly, sweet and unaffected. She welcomes Jules not with coolness and a handshake but with a giddy bear hug . . . and an invitation to be her bridesmaid. Unable to refuse, Jules accepts the unwanted honor.

However, from this position of trust Jules begins to plot ways to destroy the unsuspecting Michael and Kimmy's plans and advance her own. And what better way to do that than to pretend to go along with everything . . . while subverting from within.

AWARDS AND NOMINATIONS

Academy Awards 1997 Nominations: Original Musical or Comedy Score

BAFTA 1997 Nomination: Supporting Actor (Everett),

Golden Globe Awards 1998 Nominations: Best Musical/Comedy, Musical/Comedy Actress (Roberts), Supporting Actor (Everett)

Unfortunately for Jules, her every attempt to make Kimmy look bad backfires on her. When Kimmy admits she can't carry a tune, Jules takes her and Michael to a Karaoke bar where she sticks a mike in Kimmy's hands then sits back to watch Michael shrivel in horror as she sings. Her rendition of "I Just Don't Know What To Do With Myself" is enough to curdle a custard, but instead of making Michael crawl under the table in embarrassment, her spunk in attempting to overcome what she has to know is a handicap just makes him love her all the more.

"I knew one day we'd end up like this. Like some glittering Doris Day-Rock Hudson extravaganza."—George to Jules when he is asked to play her fiancee.

Knowing that Michael loves his itinerant sports writing job (for which Kimmy has promised to be supportive), Jules now schemes and connives a way for Kimmy's father (Philip Bosco) to offer him a job which would keep him in sports, but settle him down in Chicago. Believing his fiance put her father up to this —which proves she is not supportive at all of his career—he is at first angry at her. But when she empties her soul to him, once again love blossoms and Jules withers.

The only voice of sanity in Jules' life is her editor George Downes (Rupert Everett) who at first tells her that instead of plotting she should just come out and tell Michael how she feels. "Tell him you love him," he says. "Bite the bullet." Jules tries to do it, but the words just won't come out of her mouth. So, there's one last attempt at treachery: she fakes an e-mail from Kimmy's father to Michael's boss which should get him fired and make Michael so angry at Kimmy and her family that he will stomp off into the sunset with Jules.

But what Jules has failed to see, and what only George can make her realize, is that Michael truly loves Kimmy and Kimmy loves Michael. And that maybe Jules's motives are less than romantic. "Do you really love him or is this just about winning? Seriously?" he asks her. Now how will the heroine manage to end up with her love?

In the originally filmed ending, Julianne is shown dancing with a potential new beau (played by John Corbett) but because of the popularity of Rupert Everett's character, George, the ending was reshot.

What's interesting in this question is that we're really not too sure who the heroine is. Julianne is funny and pretty, but she's devious and ultimately mean. Kimmy is sweet and winsome, but she's not the star of the film.

This incertitude in light of what seems like a by-the-books romantic comedy is just one of the things that make *My Best Friend's Wedding* a summer delight amongst a herd of big-budget SFX monsters. Scriptwriter Ronald Bass (*Sleeping with the Enemy*, *Joy Luck Club*, *When a Man Loves a Woman*, *Dangerous Minds*, *Waiting to Exhale*) tips quite a few conventions on their heads in this film. It would have been so easy to make Kimmy stupid or her family mean. It would have been so facile to make Michael a fickle dolt. It would have been so stereotypical to make George a gay "bitch." But Bass avoids all of those cliches and instead delivers a surprising, satisfying, funny, and entertaining moviegoing experience.

Another plus is the quirky and whimsical touch of Australian director P.J. Hogan. Best known for the critical and popular hit *Muriel's Wedding*, Hogan admits that this, his second matrimonial film, does share two messages with its predecessor: the belief some people have that marriage will fulfill them and the belief that they have to trick people into loving them. These messages ring true in both films but they are bathed in such color, fun and music that they are eminently consumable.

Right from the start we know *My Best Friend's Wedding* will not be taking itself too seriously. Four girls looking like crinoline escapees from the fifties lip-synch their way through Burt Bacharach and Hal David's "Wishin' and Hopin'." They are the sweet icing on a cake made of styrofoam.

And speaking of music, the scene in which George leads an entire restaurant in an impromptu rendition of "I Say a Little Prayer for You," is seamlessly worked into the storyline and is one of the film's highlights. And, just as *Muriel's Wedding* revived the careers of '70s Swedish rock stars ABBA, this film—if we're all lucky—may revive Dionne Warwick's career enough to pull her from the clutches of the Psychic Friend's Network.

The final element in selling this film is Julia Roberts. Returning to her roots in romantic comedy (*Pretty Woman*), Roberts has a 100 watt smile guaranteed to raise even the sourest souffle, and a face that captures the most subtle emotions. Even when her character stoops to its lowest trick, we may not like her, but we care about her. Roberts alone could revive the screwball comedy. She's as likeable and smart, as tough and vulnerable a comedienne as Katharine Hepburn or Barbara Stanwyck. Just give her a good story, a solid supporting cast and stand back and watch her cook.

Luckily she does have a good story and a solid supporting cast in *My Best Friend's Wedding*. Cameron Diaz (*Mask*) is positively radiant as Kimmy who wears her love of Michael and her unconditional acceptance of Julianne on her sleeve. Mulroney, too, embodies the silent stalwartness and sincerity of a Jimmy Stewart or a Henry Fonda which, in typical screwball style, may give him little to do, but it makes him a good foil for the dueling women.

But, if the film belonged to anyone besides Roberts, it is Rupert Everett (*The Madness of King George*). When the film was first tested on audiences Rupert's George was so warmly accepted that the film was actually rewritten in order to beef up his role. As the voice of reason while never losing his sensitivity, George is the only one who can really rescue Jules from her own wickedness. He is the only one not caught up in the emotions of the love triangle, and that puts him in the position of seeing the obvious. But beyond that, George is also the source of much of the film's humor. He is the one elevating the laugh quotient when he is forced to play Jules' fiancee. He is the one stealing the restaurant sing-along scene. He is the one who walks off with the film's ending and makes it unexpected yet pleasing.

Although *My Best Friend's Wedding* is the summer's second entry in the "let's sabotage the romance" films after *Addicted to Love*, it is a kinder and gentler film. Its simple and traditional premise is originally dealt with and the characters are appealing. It is a film that leads us to laugh at and learn about ourselves. When Jules tries to explain to Kimmy why Michael should be with her in terms most familiar to the food critic, she compares herself to the more sophisticated and substantial creme brulee and Kimmy with the empty calories of Jell-O. This film has both the significance of the creme brulee without ever loosing the joy of Jell-O.

—*Beverley Bare Buehrer*

CREDITS

Julianne Potter: Julia Roberts
Michael O'Neal: Dermot Mulroney
Kimmy Wallace: Cameron Diaz
George Downes: Rupert Everett
Walter Wallace: Philip Bosco
Joe O'Neal: M. Emmet Walsh
Samantha Newhouse: Rachel Griffiths
Amanda Newhouse: Carrie Preston
Isabelle Wallace: Susan Sullivan
Scott O'Neal: Chris Masterson

Origin: USA
Released: 1997
Production: Jerry Zucker and Ronald Bass for Predawn; released by Tristar Pictures
Direction: P.J. Hogan
Screenplay: Ronald Bass
Cinematography: Laszlo Kovacs
Editing: Garth Craven, Lisa Fruchtman
Production design: Richard Sylbert
Art direction: Karen Fletcher Trujillo
Set decoration: William Kemper Wright
Costumes: Jeffrey Kurland
Music: James Newton Howard
Sound: Ed Novick
MPAA rating: PG-13
Running Time: 105 minutes

REVIEWS

Chicago Tribune. June 20, 1997, p. 5.
Entertainment Weekly. June 20, 1997, p. 40.
The Hollywood Reporter. June 11, 1997, p. 8.
Los Angeles Times. June 20, 1997, p. F1.
New York Times. June 20, 1997, p. B3.
Rolling Stone. July 10, 1997, p. 28.
Sight and Sound. September, 1997, p. 50.
USA Today. June 20, 1997, p. 4D.
Variety. June 16, 1997, p. 35.

My Mother's Courage

A uniquely perceptive view of one quiet woman's confrontation with the Nazi Holocaust is provided in *My Mother's Courage*, Michael Verhoeven's wry adaptation of a popular play by Hungarian author George Tabori. Totally unlike most films on this difficult subject, Verhoeven's movie is a richly detailed account of the quiet summer day in which Tabori's mother and hundreds of other Budapest Jews were rounded up and put on a train to a concentration camp. In this film, the victims are caught unaware, and the terror creeps in quietly, bit by bit, as normalcy slips slowly away.

In March 1944, the Nazis occupied Hungary and started secretly rounding up Jews in the countryside and herding them into concentration camps. Budapest remained a place of refuge, mostly because the Nazis were concerned about the connections that many Jews who lived there had with people in the West. In July 1944, when *My Mother's Courage* takes place, the Hungarian government still officially denied that Jews were being persecuted even as the Nazis quietly started removing them from the capital by the thousands.

George Tabori, a young man in his 20s, had gone to London with his brother. His father, a bookish newspaper editor, was rounded up in the spring of 1944 and sent to Auschwitz, which at the time had not yet earned any reputation beyond being a prison camp. His mother, Elsa, a woman who always trusted that things would turn out alright, visited her husband frequently and remained optimistic. Then, on a hot summer day, everything changed.

After the war, Elsa Tabori wrote the story of the events

of this remarkable day. Her son made the tale into a novel, then transformed it into a play which became popular in Europe. Verhoeven, best known for his harrowing *The White Rose* (1982), about a group of Munich students who resisted the Nazis, brings the story to film. The director employs great delicacy and a unique mix of stark realism, warm humanism, irony and surrealism.

Verhoeven takes pains at the beginning of *My Mother's Courage* to distance his film from the true events it is depicting. Tabori, now 80, appears both to introduce the film and to guide the telling of the story. He is both narrator and participant. We see the actors and the director actually involved in the filming. Tabori comes onto the set as a scene is being shot, and the Irish actress playing his mother, Pauline Collins, brings him a birthday cake. Another actor pastes on a fake Hitler-type mustache; when we next see him, he looks more like Charlie Chaplin doing a little comic sketch.

In a scene where his father is taken away, Tabori steps in to interrupt the action and point out the shoddiness of the Nazis' clothing and the mismatched boots worn by the officer who kicked his father. "We Hungarians had our own Nazis, but they were shabbier than the German Nazis," Tabori explains.

These are brilliant scenes which evoke both Bertolt Brecht and Fellini. Verhoeven seems to be launching a satiric, multi-leveled farce, but in fact he is doing something both less ambitious and more daring. He is exposing the fact that his film cannot pretend to capture the truth, but merely to approximate a rendition of a story. Though wry, satiric and artistic touches continue sporadically throughout the film, the movie soon becomes a more conventional piece of cinema as the day-in-the-life story unfolds.

Collins, best known for *Shirley Valentine* (1989), has her lines dubbed in Hungarian and then translated back to English in the subtitles. This is done so well it is not at all noticeable. Having an Irish woman play a Hungarian Jew is an indication of how Verhoeven attempts to make the events of the story universal. Collins' portrayal is magnificently understated, a masterpiece of nuances displayed in a placid face that attempts to maintain a look of normalcy come what may.

Tabori tells us of his mother: "She believed in a happy ending. She'd seen a lot of Douglas Fairbanks films." He also speaks of her "incomparably blue eyes" and "her Jewish sigh." Those eyes become our surrogate window on a world that turns slowly from sunshine to darkness, and that sigh is transformed from a commentary on the minor annoyances of everyday life to a deep comprehension of the human potential for evil.

My Mother's Courage is the cinematic equivalent of a lethal summer storm that arises out of a clear blue sky. Elsa Tabori goes out to visit her sister, but on the way she discovers a Jewish shopkeeper has been taken away and his shop defaced. Soon she is comically arrested by two apologetic, decrepit retirees from the local constabulary, who are so inept that they give her plenty of chances to escape. But Tabori, whose black dress is emblazoned with the yellow star marking her as a Jew, goes along dutifully, trusting no great harm will come if she is obedient. So bumbling are the men who arrest her that it adds to the false sense that there is no real danger.

As she arrives at a train station packed with other citizens wearing yellow stars, her sense of well-being is slow to be shaken. Since no one is aware of any atrocities in Hungary, and because they have been rounded up so quietly and gently, the crowd expects merely to be deported, and a rumor spreads that the train will take them to Sweden. Verhoeven casts a broad, ironic, humanitarian lens on the motley crowd. A devout man covers his head because he has lost his hat; another man loans him one. A grandfather reassures his grandson that there is nothing to fear. A man wipes toothpaste off the corner of a young man's mouth. It is a masterful sequence that provides us a detached yet sympathetic look at human hope, dignity and tragedy.

As the crowd is herded past a group of examining doctors and Nazi officers, the collective sense of self-assurance is gradually replaced by terror. A shrunken, paraplegic man who is wheeled about in a pram is separated from his father. Two beautiful twin girls are taken from their mother. A young man who dares to inquire about their true destination is taken into an office; a blanket is thrown over his head and he is knocked unconscious; his body falls to the floor, nudging a typist; she shudders, picks up a piece of paper that has been knocked to the floor, and goes back to her work. The cold, detached procedures of the Nazis come as a shock to people who don't expect such cruelty.

The group of Budapest Jews is herded into cattle cars, and the truth of what is happening finally begins to dawn on them. Elsa looks out through a crack in the train car, and the light of normalcy—the passing countryside, a train full of children on holiday, and golden visions from her childhood—shines softly against her blue eyes.

Elsa befriends a young woman, Maria (Natalie Morse), who explains that she is not a Jew. In flashback sequences, we see Maria with her Jewish friend, Olga, when Nazis break into their home; Olga is murdered and Maria is raped. On the train a young man befriends Maria. His name is Adolph, and he will be gunned down for trying to pick a flower to give to her.

Verhoeven intersperses views of Elsa and Marie with those of the ordinary soldiers and nurses in another car, who are boasting and joking as if nothing unusual is taking place. We are introduced to the officer in charge (Ulrich Tukur), a delicate beast who listens to waltzes on a phonograph, reads a book on astronomy, and is a strict vegetarian. He is a stark contrast to the other Nazis in positions of authority, who are caricatures: fat pigs with monocles surrounded by fleshy, whorish women. Those cartoonish Nazis are Verhoeven's only false step in the film, perhaps a concession to those who need monsters to explain monstrous events. The strength of *My Mother's Courage* is that quite ordinary people on a quite ordinary day are being taken on a ride into hell, and that is what makes the film terrifying.

Through good fortune and the inexplicable tolerance of the vegetarian officer, Elsa Tabori survives and is able to return to a world that is completely unaware of what has happened. That thousands of people can be taken off to die without notice creates a terrifying portrait of a society plagued by lack of awareness. Verhoeven feels no need to cast blame, only to observe, to depict the cataclysm that lurked beneath the sunny skies, bright architecture, and unshakable confidence of Budapest in the summer of 1944. Isn't this how it is in most places? People are so wrapped up in their ordinary lives that they do not notice the evil until it is too late, until it has enveloped them.

Verhoeven's wry approach to the Holocaust in *My Mother's Courage* has struck some reviewers as impolitic. But not every film about the most monstrously evil event in human history must approach the subject with rage. It is disturbing to suppose that something so systematic and brutal can be hidden, can come up out of nowhere, can catch its victims so unaware. It is precisely this capacity of the commonplace to mask the grotesque side of human nature that makes it imperative for people to live without delusions. Elsa Tabori's story does not belittle the tragedy that befell millions of others just because she was optimistic and was lucky enough to survive. It puts what happened to the others in even more powerful perspective. *My Mother's Courage* is a powerful, gentle, extraordinary, moving and wildly original film.

—*Michael Betzold*

CREDITS

Elsa Tabori: Pauline Collins
SS Officer: Ulrich Tukur
Maria: Natalie Morse
Kellerman: Heirbert Sasse
Cornelius Tabori: Robert Giggenbach
Rabbi: Buddy Elias
Moustache: Gunter Bothur

Origin: Germany, Great Britain
Released: 1995, 1997
Production: Michael Verhoeven for Sentana Film, Little Bear and Wega Filmproduktion; released by the National Center for Jewish Film
Direction: Michael Verhoeven
Screenplay: Michael Verhoeven; based on the memoir *Mutters Courage* by George Tabori
Cinematography: Michael Epp, Theo Bierkes
Editing: David Freeman
Music: Julian Nott, Simon Verhoeven
Production design: Wolfgang Hundhammer
Costumes: Rosemarie Hettmann
Sound: Johannes Rommel
MPAA rating: Unrated
Running Time: 88 minutes

REVIEWS

Boxoffice. October, 1996, p. 42.
New Republic. September 29, 1997, p. 26.
New York Times. September 10, 1997 p. C16.
Sight and Sound. January, 1998, p. 49.
Variety. September 25, 1995, p. 94.
Village Voice. September 16, 1997, p. 98.

The Myth of Fingerprints

"Wyle and Moore shine."—Oliver Jones, *Details*

"A very accomplished first feature."—Janet Maslin, *New York Times*

"A remarkable cast!"—Dennis Dermody, *Paper Magazine*

"Absorbing! A fascinating portrait of modern American Gothic angst."—Bruce Williamson, *Playboy*

"Vividly moving! Uncommon subtlety and grace. Noah Wyle is strikingly good. Julianne Moore is extraordinary. An engrossing blend of humor and heartbreak. Attention is richly rewarded."—Peter Travers, *Rolling Stone*

In his debut as a feature film director, Bart Freundlich focuses on the notion that the identities of individuals in a nuclear family—like their fingerprints—are not as unique as we suppose. He does this by setting his story in a repressed New England family that gets together, for the first time in several years, for a Thanksgiving reunion.

Freundlich has assembled a stellar cast to act out his tale of family troubles. Roy Scheider plays Hal, the lugubrious, eccentric father, while Blythe Danner plays Lena, the all-embracing mother figure who declines to look too closely into what is bothering her husband and her offspring. Something is clearly amiss with older daughter Mia (Julianne Moore), who is unaccountably cruel to all those around her, including her boyfriend, Elliot (Bruce Kerwin), whom she has brought home for the holidays. Older brother Jake (Michael Vartan) has also brought along his significant other, Margaret (Hope Davis). The youngest child, Leigh (Laurel Holloman) still lives at home. But we are invited to share the perspective of Warren (Noah Wyle), whom we first meet at his therapist's, discussing the upcoming reunion: "It's been long enough that I can't quite remember why I shouldn't go."

Warren to ex-girlfriend Daphne: "I never knew how I would ever get over you. And I still don't."

Warren is quickly reminded of why he has avoided this homecoming for so long. On his first night back, he is driven out of his bed and up into his kid sister's attic retreat by the sounds of lovemaking that make the old homestead creak and groan. The next day he is awakened by a telephone call from an old girlfriend, Daphne (Arija Bareikis), for whom he has been pining for years. The two broke up under somewhat mysterious circumstances that have traumatized Warren and seem to hold the key to what ails his entire family.

Blythe Danner and Roy Scheider previously worked together on Broadway in Harold Pinter's play "Betrayal."

Freundlich takes his time about revealing the series of events that have robbed Warren of his manhood. In the meanwhile, the writer/director demonstrates a gift for revealing character through nuanced interactions. Sometimes these interactions are not so nuanced, as when Hal takes off with his gun to perform the faux Thanksgiving ritual of killing the family turkey himself (in the end he purchases one at a store, then shoots the carcass). For the most part, however, we are left with a vague sense of unease as we watch the members of this dysfunctional unit do a good a job of differentiating themselves from one another. But why *is* Mia so angry at the world, and does her unhappiness have something to do with her mother's myopia, or with her brother Warren's inability to consummate his renewed relationship with Daphne? These problems share no conspicuously common element, yet we sense they spring from the same source.

Freundlich never tells us explicitly what is wrong with the picture he presents, and when the climactic moment comes, it seems almost anticlimactic. In a series of flashbacks, Daphne reveals that a few years earlier, Hal had attempted to corner and kiss her in an upstairs hallway while the rest of the family made merry below. And Warren remembers that, unbeknownst to Daphne, he witnessed the event, but was unable to bring himself to intervene. But is this the moment of revelation? Perhaps the more telling moment occurs when Hal calls after his disaffected younger son, only to hide so that Warren will not know for sure that his father has reached out for him.

The fact that we are never really shown the source of the trouble, but only, as it were, the fingerprints it has left behind, is both the principle flaw and the chief virtue of *The Myth of Fingerprints*. The sturm und drang of the family members can seem in the end to be much ado about nothing. (Don't all families have such difficulties? Aren't reunions always doomed to fail?) On the other hand, by focusing on character rather than events, Freundlich demonstrates just how affecting family problems can be. Tolstoy begins *Anna Karenina* by observing that while happy families are unique,

AWARDS AND NOMINATIONS

Independent Spirit Awards 1997 Nominations:
Supporting Actor (Scheider)

CREDITS

Lena: Blythe Danner
Margaret: Hope Davis
Warren: Noah Wyle
Mia: Julianne Moore
Hal: Roy Scheider
Leigh: Laurel Holloman
Elliott: Brian Kerwin
Cezanne: James LeGros
Jake: Michael Vartan
Daphne: Arija Bareikis

Origin: USA
Released: 1997
Production: Mary Jane Skalski, Im Perell, and Bart Freundlich for Eureka Pictures and Good Machine; released by Sony Pictures Classics
Direction: Bart Freundlich
Screenplay: Bart Freundlich
Cinematography: Stephen Kazmierski
Editing: Kate Williams, Ken J. Sackheim
Music: David Bridie, John Phillips
Costumes: Lucy W. Corrigan
Production design: Susan Bolles
Sound: Peter Schneider, Jesse Feigelman
MPAA rating: R
Running Time: 93 minutes

unhappy ones are all alike. Then he employs one of the tritest situations imaginable to tell a singular story of tragic inevitability. *The Myth of Fingerprints* isn't quite *Anna Karenina*, but it is, nonetheless, a worthwhile attempt to illustrate the truism that the elements that give rise to individual identity are all too common.

—*Lisa Paddock*

REVIEWS

Boxoffice. April, 1997, p. 178.
Entertainment Weekly. September 19, 1997, p. 60.
Los Angeles Times. September 26, 1997, p. F22.
New York Times. September 17, 1997, p. E5.
People. September 29, 1997, p. 20.
Rolling Stone. October 2, 1997, p. 61.
Sight and Sound. December, 1997, p. 48.
Variety. February 3, 1997, p.48.
Village Voice. September 23, 1997, p. 96.

Napoleon

He's boldly going where no house pet has ever gone before.—Movie tagline

Napoleon is the sweet and simple story of a golden retriever puppy named Muffin, who decides he wants to be brave and have adventures. Muffin gets his chance when he climbs over the wall at a birthday party, hops into a wicker basket that's tied with balloons, and accidentally lifts off.

He decides that a brave dog needs a brave name so he chooses "Napoleon." Soon he's flying over the Australian outback and when he lands, Napoleon meets a variety of interesting creatures who become both friends and foes. His mentor is the silly but friendly and loyal Birdo, a Galah, which are migratory birds native to Australia. One of his enemies is Cat, a black cat driven crazy by being lost in the wild, who thinks that Napoleon is a mouse she must hunt.

Napoleon finally finds some "relatives" in a family of dingos (wild dogs), and discovers he does have courage by surviving a stampede, fire, and a flood, where he even rescues one of the dingo pups. When he realizes he is brave, Napoleon decides it's time to go back home.

Napoleon is the first live-action feature film in Australia to use an all-animal cast. As in the live-action version of *101 Dalmatians* there was a continuous need for puppies of the right age and size during the 34-week shoot. Some 64 puppies between the ages of nine and twelve weeks were used and as director Andreacchio realized, you can't "expect the puppy to behave like a human." Which meant that, though the pup-

Napoleon to Cat: "I'm not a mouse. You are a deeply disturbed animal."

Director Andreacchio's three children inspired the film by asking him to make a movie that had no humans, only animals.

CREDITS

Napoleon: Jamie Croft (voice)
Birdo: Philip Quast (voice)
Owl: Brenton Whittle (voice)
Spider: Anne Lambert (voice)
Cat: Carol Skinner (voice)
Conan Penguin: Casey Siemaszko (voice)
Napoleon's Mom: Susan Lyons (voice)
Mother Penguin: Joan Rivers (voice)

Origin: Australia, Japan
Released: 1997
Production: Michael Bourchier and Mario Andreacchio for Herald Ace, Inc. and Australian Film Finance Corporation Ltd.; released by Goldwyn Entertainment Company
Direction: Mario Andreacchio
Screenplay: Mario Andreacchio, Michael Bourchier and Mark Saltzman
Cinematography: Roger Dowling
Editing: Edward McQueen-Mason
Music: Bill Conti
Production design: Vicki Niehus
MPAA rating: G
Running Time: 81 minutes

pies were trained to some extent, they couldn't be taught to "act." Andreacchio used the puppies' natural instincts to play and explore to obtain what was needed for a particular scene.

The production, the longest in Australian history, was filmed in locales in South Australia, New South Wales, the Northern Territory, Tasmania, and Kangaroo Island, which certainly adds to its unique look. Overall, *Napoleon* is a straightforward, earnest story that parents may find too simplistic but small children should find entertaining.

REVIEWS

Boxoffice. December, 1997, p. 53.
New York Times. October 11, 1997, p. B11.

Nenette and Boni

"Exhilarating."—Jay Carr, *Boston Globe*

" . . . Fluid and lyrical . . . An absorbing film that hefts quite an emotional kick . . . makes one feel as though caught in a strangely erotic dream . . ."—Kevin Courrier, *Boxoffice*

"Warm, tender and poetically vague. Vivid . . ." —Dave Kerr, *Daily News*

" . . . Another understated triumph for gifted French writer-director Claire Denis . . . exquisitely evoked . . . A tender, impassioned celebration of life . . ."—Kevin Thomas, *Los Angeles Times*

"Edgy, tender . . . risk taking cinema."—Janet Maslin, *New York Times*

"A blessedly unconventional coming-of-age movie . . ."—John Hartl, *Seattle Times*

"Remarkable . . . not to be missed."—Elliot Stein, *Village Voice*

Dreams and fantasies beautifully weave their way through director Claire Denis' tale of a brother and sister painfully growing up after their mother has died and their father all but abandoned them. Set in the seedy seaport town of Marseilles, we see little of the beauty of the famed French Riviera with Agnes Godard's camera remaining tightly focused, almost claustrophobically so, on the revealing faces of the title characters. This constant closeness creates an immediate bond with the 19-year-old Boniface (Gregoire Colin) for the first half of the film until rebellious 15-year-old Nenette (Alice Houri) makes her appearance. The talented duo also starred in Denis' 1994 television movie, "U.S. Go Home." Capturing powerful emotions lurking just underneath the seemingly indifferent surfaces of the characters, this film also recalls Denis' acclaimed 1988 debut, *Chocolat.*

Independent teenager Boniface (Boni) works making pizza out of a van and lives simply, with a few equally hapless friends, in the somewhat run-down house his family has abandoned. The three greatest joys in his life are his white pet rabbit, his new electronic coffee maker, and indulging in frequent fantasies about the local baker's blond wife (Valeria Bruni-Tedschi). These fantasies make up much of the film and are wonderfully and effectively done, creating a total sensory picture with a combination of unusual sounds and images. Food, a major theme, is filmed erotically, with the rich and lush delights in the bakery melding with Boni's lust. Boni seems contented with his life, which is weirdly cut off from intimacy. Notably absent of family or close friends, it seems Boni's fantasies are his attempts to find that closeness with another person.

Denis quietly draws the viewer into the daily routine of Boni's life for a good one-half of the movie. This serves to underscore the impact of the change when his long absent younger sister, away at boarding school, shows up at his doorway unannounced. Nenette, it seems, is pregnant and has nowhere else to go. Her sudden arrival after such an extended separation throws Boni off guard and brings out his pent-up anger at his sister for her absence when their mother died. The reemergence of Nenette in Boni's life also brings with it their estranged father (Jacques Nolot), a sometime gangster and lamp salesman, who tries to persuade Nenette to live with him. Unlike the loving relationship Boni had with his late mother, his resentment of his father is equally

AWARDS AND NOMINATIONS

Independent Spirit Awards 1997 Nominations:
Foreign Film

strong and his father's now frequent and uninvited visits to charm Nenette are a source of further irritation.

Nenette, for her part, also wants nothing to do with their no-good father. The break-up of their family has hardened her more than the self-reliant yet still vulnerable Boni and she coolly resents the growing life within her. After spending some time with his sister, who has more or less moved in, Boni seems to regain some of the softness he lost with his mother's death and now establishes a surprising bond with Nenette's unborn child, whose father she refuses to name. Nenette, now too far into her term for a legal abortion, grows more and more determined to rid herself of the child. Ironically, the first sign of hope for Boni is also a frightening glimpse of the future for Nenette.

Juxtaposing the troubled siblings are the American baker, played by Vincent Gallo, and his wife. They seem to have an ideal relationship and are the picture of happiness as they play together with their young children. Unlike Nenette and Boni's unhappily wed parents, the baker is an adoring husband, who is shown gazing lovingly at his radiantly happy wife as she works in their shop. The free-wheeling pair also add a healthy dose of humor to the rather serious and inward-looking picture.

An equally dreamy Tindersticks soundtrack complements the ongoing drama, in which dreams mix seamlessly with reality. Vibrant yet understated portrayals by the leads are exactly what is called for, dictated by the intimate cinematography and sparse dialogue. Supporting characters are solid as well. Overall, Denis succeeds with this tender and absorbing film.

—Hilary Weber

CREDITS

Boni: Gregoire Colin
Nenette: Alice Houri
Baker: Vincent Gallo
Baker's wife: Valeria Bruni-Tedeschi
Mr. Luminaire: Jacques Nolot

Origin: France
Released: 1996
Production: Georges Benayoun for Dacia Films, Ima Films, and La Sept Cinema; released by Strand Releasing
Direction: Claire Denis
Screenplay: Claire Denis and Jean-Pol Fargeau
Cinematography: Agnes Godard
Editing: Yann Dedet
Music: Tindersticks
Art direction: Arnaud de Moteron
Sound: Jean-Louis Ughetto
MPAA rating: Unrated
Running Time: 103 minutes

REVIEWS

Boxoffice. April, 1997, p. 197.
Detroit Free Press. January 18, 1998, p. 8G.
Los Angeles Times. October 24, 1997, p. F14.
New York Times. October 3, 1997, p. E18.
Variety. August 26, 1996, p. 62.
Village Voice. October 7, 1997, p. 80.

Nick and Jane

The meter is running . . . on a fare to remember.—Movie tagline

"A quirky cast of New York characters."—*Genre Magazine*

"Romantic, amusing and heartfelt."—Duane Byrge, *The Hollywood Reporter*

Nick and Jane winks at convention with its very title: this is a movie involving stock characters in a standard plot—but with a twist. Jane (Dana Wheeler-Nicholson) is the one who apparently holds the power: in the film's opening sequence we see this high-octane businesswoman balancing her notebook computer on her lap as she rides in the back of a limo while talking on her cell phone. Nick (James McCaffrey), on the other hand, is first seen cruising around New York behind the wheel of a battered checker cab.

These disparate worlds intersect when Jane, distraught at finding her executive boyfriend in bed with one of their co-workers, rushes out into the street and into a waiting taxi—which just happens to be Nick's. Their meeting seems the product of fate and the conventions of screwball comedy, as does much of the movie. A second chance encounter in a bar provides Jane with an opportunity to make her former boyfriend, John (John Dorsett), jealous by pretending that Nick is her new beau. After introducing Nick to John as "Nolan Miller," Jane offers the handsome but impoverished cabbie a thousand dollars to pose as her romantic interest at an upcoming corporate party. Nick, who is about to be evicted from his apartment, accepts.

More comedic conceits follow. In a scene taken straight from *Pretty Woman* (1990), Jane shepherds Nick through a make over. First, she suggests they visit a fancy salon, where Nick's goatee is shaved and his hair cut. Then she pays for a beautifully tailored suit. Nick is now unquestionably a knock-out; Jane always has been. They look absolutely terrific together.

Writer/director Richard Mauro first met David Johansen, who plays Carter, when he was a waiter at a restaurant Johansen patronized.

Nick fulfills his role admirably, making John so jealous that he begs Jane to marry him. The kicker, of course, is that Nick is not simply acting. He is more than just a taxi driver; he is an aspiring poet and artist. And he is in love with Jane. Jane, for her part, appreciates Nick's qualities, but continues to insist that she loves John. She and Nick, she says, come from two different worlds.

What Jane does not count on—but Nick does—is John's continuing perfidy. When he undermines Jane at work, Nick is there to step into the breach. In a scene borrowed from another screwball comedy that romantically pairs characters from disparate social strata, 1988's *Working Girl*, Nick makes a brilliant presentation to Jane's bosses that rescues her and her business plan at the eleventh hour from the trap John has set. Recognizing at last where her affections truly lie, Jane bolts from the meeting and rushes into Nick's waiting arms.

Unfortunately, this clincher comes at the very end of *Nick and Jane*. One of the best, most believable things about the film is the chemistry between its two leads, both of whom are very good to look at. Far too much screen time is spent on extraneous characters, such as Nick's foot fetishist poet/rapper roommate Enzo (Gedde Wantanabe) and his transvestite neighbor, Miss Coco (Clinton Leupp). These curiosities do little to further the story line and seem—like Las Vegas entr'acte performers—to be merely thrown in to keep the audience amused while the leading players prepare for their next scene.

Nick and Jane was director Richard Mauro's first feature film, and his inexperience often shows. But the movie's plot—the compelling tale of the male Cinderella, the frog who turns into a prince—comes not from screenwriting class, but directly from Mauro's own life. The director claims to have gotten the idea of *Nick and Jane* when he was himself hired and groomed to act as a surrogate boyfriend at a fancy wedding. Mauro did his job well, igniting jealousy in a former boyfriend and romance in the woman who engaged him. And he does a good job here of recreating his own experience. Surely this coincidence of real life and fairy tale—as well as good casting—helps to account for why the movie's seemingly hackneyed story is rendered so diverting.

Mauro has said that he made his film "for all the blue-collar guys who never seem to get the attention of girls on the wealthier side of the coin." In all likelihood, however, the audience for *Nick and Jane* will not be made up of blue collar guys—unless they're cut from the same fairy tale, diamond-in-the-rough romantic mold that produced the movie's hero.

—*Lisa Paddock*

CREDITS

Jane: Dana Wheeler-Nicholson
Nick: James McCaffrey
Vicki: Lisa Gay Hamilton
Carter: David Johansen
Enzo: Gedde Watanabe
John: John Dossett
Miss Coco: Clinton Leupp
Stephanie: Saundra Santiago

Origin: USA
Released: 1996
Production: Bill McCutchen III; released by Avalanche
Direction: Richard Mauro
Screenplay: Richard Mauro, Peter Quigley and Neil W. Alumkal
Cinematography: Chris Norr
Editing: Richard Mauro, Wendy Spanzler
Music: Mark Suozzo
Production design: Mark Helmuth
Art direction: Stacy Tanner
Costumes: Liz McCaffrey
MPAA rating: R
Running Time: 92 minutes

REVIEWS

Boxoffice. June, 1996, p. 56.
Cover. Vol. 11, #5, 1997, p. 52.
Los Angeles Times. November 14, 1997, p. F20.
New York Times. November 14, 1997, p. E33.
Variety. December 17, 1997, p. 64.
Village Voice. November 25, 1997, p. 102.

Night Falls on Manhattan

In a city of nine million people is there room for one honest man?—Movie tagline

"Powerful! Truly triumphant! Legendary director Sidney Lumet is in top form, a career high for Andy Garcia."—Mike Cidoni, *ABC-TV*

"A powerful, bluesy new film! Sidney Lumet remains a master of the morally complex American drama. It boasts several high-powered performances."—James Vernier, *Boston Herald*

"Boasts one of the best screen performances in recent memory. Ever dependable Ian Holm."—Howard Feinstein, *Detour Magazine*

"An intelligent, brilliantly acted, suspenseful morality play of a film."—John Corcoran, *KCAL-TV*

"One of Sidney Lumet's best! Expertly crafted. A screen full of strongly drawn, fully dimensional psychologically valid characters. Excellence in all aspects."—Kevin Thomas, *Los Angeles Times.*

"Full of surprises. Great performances."—Bobbie Wygant, *NBC-TV*

"One of those rare films with impact and insight that also keeps you riveted. Sidney Lumet is one of the most important filmmakers of our time."—Rex Reed, *New York Observer*

"Gripping and superbly well-acted, creating some of the most compelling characters we're likely to see this year."—Michael Medved, *New York Post*

"Andy Garcia leads a strong cast. His coiled intensity works well with the gifted Holm as the father whose conflict with his son gives *Night* its moments of hard truth. Dreyfuss is electric."—Peter Travers, *Rolling Stone*

"Filled with first-rate actors in a gripping story. Strong dialogue and forceful performances deliver a wallop of tough entertainment."—Gene Shalit, *Today Show*

Box Office: $9,889,670

Director Sidney Lumet's best films deal with police, criminals, and lawyers: *Serpico* (1973), *Dog Day Afternoon* (1975), *Prince of the City* (1981), and *The Verdict* (1982). All except the latter, set in Boston, take place in New York City, the milieu examined more closely by Lumet than by any other filmmaker, including Woody Allen and Martin Scorsese. Lumet's New York is often a world in which the corrupt are more likely to survive, in which the enforcers of the law are only slightly less vicious than its breakers. *Night Falls on Manhattan* presents Lumet's usual concerns quite effectively with a strange twist at the end, managing to be both sentimental and cynical at the same time. While the film is not on the level of Lumet's best work, principally because the protagonist is rather bland, it is an entertaining look at the complexities of the legal system.

Idealistic district attorney Sean Casey (Andy Garcia) grapples with tough choices when he accepts a case dealing with police corruption in New York City in the gritty crime drama *Night Falls on Manhattan.*

Sean Casey (Andy Garcia) is a former New York policeman who has slowly worked his way through law school and attained a junior position with the district attorney's office. Sean's father, Liam (Ian Holm), is veteran cop who, with his partner, Joey Allegretto (James Gandolfini), has been tracking a notorious drug dealer, Jordan Washington (Shiek Mahmud-Bey). When a tip leads them to the apartment where Washington is hiding, Liam is seriously wounded, and three other policemen are killed. Morgenstern (Ron Liebman), the publicity-conscious district attorney facing reelection, appoints the relatively inexperienced Sean to prosecute Washington. Lumet, who also wrote the screenplay based on Robert Daley's novel *Tainted Evidence*, ignores the likelihood of a prosecutor being assigned to a case in which a close relative is a victim.

From this relatively straightforward premise, all sorts of ramifications erupt. Sean's opponent is Sam Vigoda (Richard Dreyfuss), a high-powered attorney famous for taking cases involving civil-liberties issues. Vigoda defends Washington on the grounds of the police being his bagmen and accuses the law enforcers of setting up his client for assassination to prevent their exposure. Sean confronts his father about his and Joey's possible involvement in this corruption which Liam vehemently denies. Despite the self-defense pleas, Vigoda loses, and Sean becomes a hero. When Morgenstern suffers a debilitating heart attack, Sean is appointed his successor and then wins the election, another example of the film's pulp-fiction roots.

This happy ending becomes undermined when the investigation of an internal affairs officer (Jude Ciccolella) reveals that the backup Joey summons after the shooting of Liam was on its way before the policeman was wounded, that Vigoda's seemingly wild claim is true. In pressing this point with his father, Sean discovers that not only has Joey been lying to him but that Liam forged a judge's signature on the search warrant for Washington's apartment because the original warrant had expired and there was no time for a new one. This revelation is made more complicated by Sean's affair with Peggy Lindstrom (Lena Olin), a lawyer on Vigoda's staff who becomes torn over her loyalties to her lover, her boss, the law, and the truth.

> Vigoda to Sean: "Sometimes I just get so sick inside. So discouraged you know. I feel we have to just give up on an entire generation. Lock 'em up and throw away the key."

While films from the period when Lumet began directing find mushy, humane ways of resolving such crises, as with Lumet's *Twelve Angry Men* (1957), and films from the 1960s and 1970s take a more realistic, downbeat approach, as in the director's *The Hill* (1965) and *The Offence* (1973), the Lumet of the 1990s wants his audience to be confirmed in its suspicions about the legal system while feeling uplifted at the same time. To achieve this effect, Sean, Liam, Peggy, Vigoda, and the judge (Dominic Chianese) enter into a conspiracy of silence to keep Washington behind bars.

Such a resolution works because of how painstakingly Lumet has set up *Night Falls on Manhattan* as a morality tale about an innocent crusader's moral education. The film must show Sean—and the audience—that the law is a malleable institution that must be manipulated occasionally to achieve just outcomes. How a contemporary lawyer with a metropolitan police background could be as naive as Sean is another matter. Lumet sometimes strains to emphasize his hero's innocence, as when Sean, Peggy, and others gather for the announcement that Sean is to succeed Morgenstern and the new district attorney is seen wearing white socks with his black suit. And Vigoda's revelation that he is defending the subhuman Washington to expose the police involvement with drug dealers because his daughter died of a drug overdose is a tad trite.

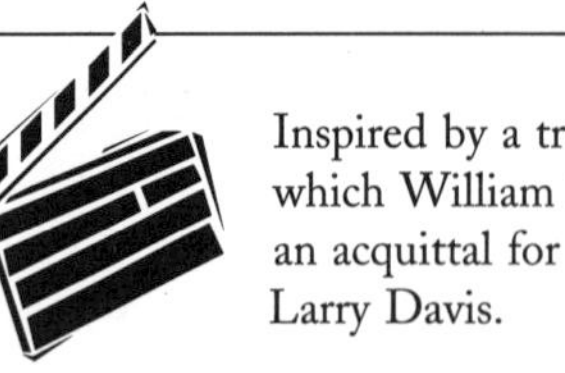

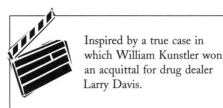

> Inspired by a true case in which William Kunstler won an acquittal for drug dealer Larry Davis.

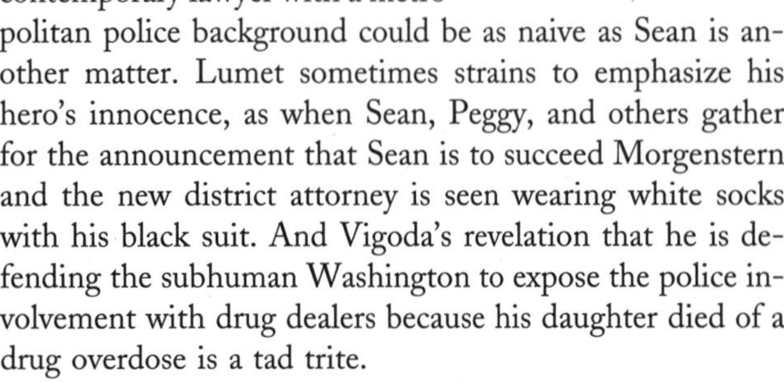

Despite such occasional hokey touches, *Night Falls on Manhattan* is an engrossing film in part because of Lumet's sheer professionalism. Though the director has made a few embarrassingly bad films, especially *The Last of the Mobile Hotshots* (1970) and *The Wiz* (1978), he knows how to push enough of the right buttons to keep viewers entertained and often enlightened. Even such lesser works as *A Stranger Among Us* (1992) and *Guilty as Sin* (1993) are generally so well made that they are more watchable than the material would seem to warrant.

Making Movies (1995), Lumet's fascinating account of the process of filmmaking, explains why he is able to achieve so much even with inferior material: because he treats all his projects as equally worthwhile endeavors and because he surrounds himself with like-minded craftsmen. In *Night Falls on Manhattan*, he is working for the first time with two of the best: editor Sam O'Steen, whose credits include *The Graduate* (1967), *Rosemary's Baby* (1968), and *Chinatown* (1974), and cinematographer David Watkin who shot *Help!* (1965), *Chariots of Fire* (1981), and *Out of Africa* (1985). The skills of these three are best displayed during the shootout with Washington because the scene is a well-staged action sequence during which the audience always knows what is going on even as chaos reigns on the screen. Though Lumet usually plays down showy visuals, this scene's most memorable moment comes when a large group of police outside the apartment think they are being fired on from above, fall on their backs, and begin blasting away, killing one of their own. The overhead shot of the panicked police is one of the most striking images in any of Lumet's films.

Lumet's films are perhaps most notable for their large number of remarkable performances: Marlon Brando in *The Fugitive Kind* (1960), Katharine Hepburn and Ralph Richardson in *Long Day's Journey Into Night* (1962), Henry Fonda in *Fail Safe* (1964), James Mason in *The Deadly Affair* (1967) and *The Verdict*, Sean Connery in *The Offence*, Al Pacino in *Serpico* and *Dog Day Afternoon*, Treat Williams in *Prince of the City*, Paul Newman in *The Verdict*, River Phoenix in *Running on Empty* (1988), Nick Nolte in *Q&A* (1990). While none of the actors in *Night Falls on Manhattan* reaches those levels, most of the performances are uniformly good.

While some might complain that Garcia is too bland to play Sean, the role calls for someone who can convey strength and weakness, innocence and wisdom, confusion and clarity, and Garcia does all this. His natural passivity is an advantage here since Sean is more an observer than a participant in these events. Holm is one of the greatest contemporary character actors because of his work in such films *The Homecoming* (1973), *Chariots of Fire*, *Dance with a Stranger* (1985), *Dreamchild* (1985), and, especially, *Big Night* (1996). While Liam Casey lacks the flamboyance of the restaurateur of *Big Night*, Holm ably conveys the conflicts raging in the policeman over trying to help his son protect his partner, and be true to his code of honor. Dreyfuss is famous for giving in to his fondness for excesses, but here, except for the scene of Vigoda escorting his client into hostile custody, he underplays the part, particularly in the two steamroom encounters with Sean. The film's only truly flashy performance comes from Leibman, another actor given to excesses. Leibman's shouting and arm waving are fitting given Morgenstern's smug confidence, cocky class consciousness, and heart-attack potential. He is at his best in a confrontation with Elihu Harrison (Colm Feore), the preppy assistant whose privilege he abhors. Olin, an excellent actress ill used in American films, fares less well since her poorly written role is more a plot device than a character.

Lumet's films are also notable for their generosity to all the performers, and in *Night Falls on Manhattan*, the best work comes from the actors in smaller roles. Feore, unrecognizable as the same actor who personifies neuroses in *Thirty-Two Short Films About Glenn Gould* (1993), makes a vivid impression as someone outraged that his divine right to a position of power has been denied. Ciccolella is notable for how quietly he makes his investigator stand out, hunching his shoulders, pausing often, to make the character even more threatening than he would be as a nasty bully. Best of all is the wonderful, ordinary-looking Paul Guilfoyle as the world-weary official who indoctrinates the new recruits of the district attorney's office. In the monologue at the beginning of the film, Guilfoyle perfectly embodies the cynicism Sean must overcome. The film ends most fittingly with this character stepping aside so that Sean can share his hard-earned wisdom with a new batch of innocents.

—*Michael Adams*

CREDITS

Sean Casey: Andy Garcia
Liam Casey: Ian Holm
Sam Vigoda: Richard Dreyfuss
Peggy Lindstrom: Lena Olin
Joey Allegretto: James Gandolfini
Morgenstern: Ron Liebman
Elihu Harrison: Colm Feore
Jordan Washington: Shiek Mahmud-Bey
McGovern: Paul Guilfoyle
Lieutenant Wilson: Jude Ciccolella
Judge Impelliteri: Dominic Chianese

Origin: USA
Released: 1997
Production: Thom Mount and Josh Kramer for Spelling Films; released by Paramount Pictures
Direction: Sidney Lumet
Screenplay: Sidney Lumet; based on the novel *Tainted Evidence* by Robert Daley
Cinematography: David Watkin
Editing: Sam O'Steen
Production design: Philip Rosenberg
Art decoration: Robert Guerra
Set decoration: Carolyn Cartwright
Costumes: Joseph G. Aulisi
Music: Mark Isham
Sound: Les Lazarowitz
MPAA rating: R
Running Time: 115 minutes

REVIEWS

Boxoffice. July, 1997, p. 88.
Chicago Tribune. May 16, 1997, p. 4.
Detroit Free Press. May 11, 1997, p. F1.
Entertainment Weekly. May 23, 1997, p. 46.
Los Angeles Times. May 16, 1997, p. F8.
The New Republic. June 16, 1997, p. 28.
New York. June 2, 1997, p. 53.
The New York Times. May 16, 1997, p. C3.
People. May 26, 1997, p. 20.
Rolling Stone. May 29, 1997, p. 56.
Sight and Sound. September, 1997, p. 51.
USA Today. May 16, 1997, p. D1.
Variety. May 12, 1997, p. 63.
The Wall Street Journal. May 16, 1997, p. A16.
The Washington Post. May 16, 1997, p. B1.

Nothing Personal

Loyalty has its price.—Movie tagline

The deadliest gangsters are those with a cause. —Movie tagline

"Riveting!"—*Detour*

"Exceptional!"—*Elle*

"*Nothing Personal* is especially good . . . A work that stands strongly on its own."—*Los Angeles Times*

"Powerful! Impressive! A wild, frightening fury. . . . A hint of *Mean Streets*."—*New York Times*

Nothing Personal shows what happens when innocence gets caught in the crossfire of unending violence. Over the opening credits of Thaddeus O'Sullivan's film are heard the sounds of clinking glasses, liquid pouring, and undistinguishable chatter. It's 1975 in a Belfast Protestant pub that's about to be ripped apart by an IRA-planted bomb. After seeing the patrons and watching the pub explode, the screen returns to more credits and the sound of people digging through rubble, looking for bodies and possible survivors. Among those helping the victims is Catholic single father of two, Liam Kelly (John Lynch). He returns home and warns his daughter Kathleen (Jeni Courtney, also seen with Lynch in *The Secret of Roan Inish*) to stay close to home, knowing there will be reprisals by Protestant Loyalists.

Eddie: "We're all on the same side here, sir." Leonard: "Christ, son, you've no idea how nervous that makes me."

The first act comes as Loyalist paramilitary unit leader Kenny (James Frain) waits in a car with mate Ginger (Ian Hart) outside a Catholic pub. Ginger's a trigger-happy sociopath who thinks the only good Catholic is a dead one and believes he can recognize an IRA man at a glance. A man finally exits the pub and Ginger kills him. A warehouse meeting is arranged between Loyalist leader Leonard (Michael Gambon) and his IRA counterpart Cecil (Gerard McSorley) to arrange a truce and for the removal of the barricades between the Protestant and Catholic neighborhoods. Cecil informs Leonard that the Catholic man killed was not in the IRA, although Leonard professes no knowledge of the act, except to say there's lots of "nutters" about. Cecil replies to him, sotto voce, that perhaps "it's about time we got the nutters off the streets." Leonard knows Kenny and Ginger were responsible and tells Kenny that he must bring the hotheaded Ginger under some kind of control.

Kenny tries to visit his estranged wife Ann (Maria Doyle Kennedy) and their two children, whom he left to dedicate his time to the cause. Ann rebuffs his attempts at conversation. Meanwhile, worried by the closeness of local street rioting, Liam goes out to see what he can do to help—his first, if unsafe, impulse. Kenny and his men, Ginger and Eddie (Gary Lydon) are also nearby. Petrol bombs are being thrown, as are rocks and bottles, one of which hits Liam in the head. When a firebomb sets a Protestant man on fire, a Catholic boy is caught and doused with gasoline, with a gleeful Ginger setting him ablaze. A furious Kenny shoots the youth to put him out of his misery and turns on Ginger telling him: "I can't trust you anymore to keep your head down and act sensible."

Escaping from the riots, Liam is still in a Protestant neighborhood, where he's attacked and beaten up in an alley. In the film's one blatant stretch of coincidence, Ann notices the injured Liam trying to make his way down her block and takes him inside to patch him up. Kathleen begins to worry over her father's continued absence and asks her older friend Michael (Gareth O'Hare) to ask around and see if anyone knows where Liam is. While asking some of the local IRA men, Michael manages to slip a gun from a man's pocket, believing he'll use it to get revenge for the local boy who's been killed.

Leonard and his bodyguards go to the club where Kenny lives in the back and has an altercation with the mouthy Ginger, who resents the older man's efforts to control the violence. Leonard privately informs Kenny that there's a truce, the barricades will start coming down, and the British will resume patrolling the neighborhoods. He also lets Kenny know that Ginger is a liability that the Loyalist's can't afford: "I don't want to hear his name mentioned again. I don't want to see his face again. . . . He's to be put to sleep, Kenny. You can take that as an order."

At the club, Kenny draws the worshipful attention of the teenaged Tommy (Ruaidhri Conroy). When Tommy takes care of a drunk, he draws Kenny's notice. Kenny gives the boy a gun, asking him to watch for trouble at the door. He also tries talking to Ginger, giving him a subtle warning about his out-of-control behavior. Heading out on patrol with Ginger and Eddie, Kenny invites Tommy to drive around the neighborhood with them. He's also let Eddie know that he's decided to break the ceasefire and the four shoot-up a Catholic pub, with Kenny nearly killing Ginger in the crossfire.

Kathleen decides to cross the barricade in search of Liam but finds out nothing and returns home. While patching up Liam, Ann and he discover how much they have in common. She worries he won't be able to get home safely, but Liam says he knows the streets, having played in the area as a child, before "The Troubles" truly began. But, of course, he doesn't get home safely.

In a horrifying turn of events, Liam's snatched up by Kenny and his men as a Catholic interloper. When Kenny hears his name, he realizes Liam is a childhood mate. This doesn't prevent Kenny from taking Liam to a warehouse and allowing Ginger (who of course believes Liam's with the IRA) and Eddie to brutalize him. Tommy watches in horror and runs out as Ginger plays Russian roulette with Liam. When Ginger and Eddie run after the boy, the bloodied Liam acknowledges also recognizing Kenny and the two have a somewhat surreal discussion about their childhood. Kenny admits to knowing that Liam isn't in the IRA and you realize that he's struggling to regain control of the situation.

A end credit line states: "The Director wishes to acknowledge Gilo Pontecorvo's *Battle of Algiers.*"

Cecil, who's been informed that Liam is missing, lets Leonard know that Liam is a family man and not involved. While Leonard again professes ignorance of the situation, he knows Kenny and his men are responsible and he decides, for the sake of the truce, to turn them in to the British.

Kenny informs a furious Ginger that they're taking Liam—alive—back to the barricade and setting him free. Kathleen and Michael see Kenny and Liam at the street corner and run to them, while Ginger pulls a gun and once again threatens to shoot Liam. Instead, Kenny shoots Ginger in the leg. While Liam steps towards Kathleen, Michael pulls his gun and threatens Kenny, who's amused and taunts the boy. Kathleen sees Michael's gun, she tries to snatch it, and it goes off, killing the girl. Liam and Kenny both stare in shock at the lifeless child, while Eddie urges his mates to get back in the car and get out the area. As they drive away, Liam cradles Kathleen in his arms.

When Ginger, riding in front with Eddie, exults at Kathleen's death, the shocked Tommy attacks him. Kenny prevents Ginger from shooting the boy and allows him to leave the car, while Eddie notices a British patrol has pulled around the corner. As Kenny and Ginger struggle for the gun, Ginger informs Kenny: "I regret the day I ever set eyes on you." When Kenny shoots Ginger, the patrol think they're being fired upon and start returning fire and the three die in a hail of bullets, although without the slow-motion brutality of *Bonnie and Clyde* (1967). Leonard comes upon the bloody scene, with the subtle acknowledgement of one problem solved.

Finally, at the city cemetery where Ann's buried Kenny, she sees Liam at the funeral of Kathleen. They briefly exchange sympathies and Liam watches as Ann walks away.

Nothing Personal may be the only film focusing on the violence that's perpetuated by the equally illegal Protestant paramilitary units, rather than showing only the IRA. And it's abundantly clear as poet Jacques Ellul wrote in "Laws of Violence" that "All kinds of violence are the same. Violence begets violence - *nothing else.*" And, as is so heartbreakingly common, it's often the true innocents who pay the steepest price.

While Kenny firmly believes that what he's doing is right, even though it causes the estrangement of his family, even he's appalled by the blatant pleasure that Ginger takes in killing. Though the deeply hateful Ginger spouts off all the correct rhetoric, it seems only too clear that he has no life without the violence continuing. Both Ginger, Kenny and their IRA counterparts are quick to condemn the weary old guard of Leonard and Cecil attempting to broker a truce. And Kenny's only too willing to be the one to deliberately break it. They've forgotten what peace is like—and maybe they just don't care.

English actor James Frain, who's probably not widely known in the U.S., does a strong job with Kenny, the leader whose loyalty to a cause is tested by his loyalty to his men, Ginger and Eddie, the only two people he believes he can

CREDITS

Liam Kelly: John Lynch
Kenny: James Frain
Ginger: Ian Hart
Leonard: Michael Gambon
Eddie: Gary Lydon
Kathleen: Jeni Courtney
Ann: Maria Doyle Kennedy
Tommy: Ruaidhri Conroy
Cecil: Gerald McSorley
Michael: Gareth O'Hare

Origin: Ireland, Great Britain
Released: 1995, 1997
Production: Jonathan Cavendish and Tracey Seaward for Little Bird, Channel Four Films, the Irish Film Board, and British Screen; released by Trimark Pictures
Direction: Thaddeus O'Sullivan
Screenplay: Daniel Mornin; based on his novel *All Our Fault*
Cinematography: Dick Pope
Editing: Michael Parker
Production design: Mark Geraghty
Costumes: Consolata Boyle
Music: Philip Appleby
Art direction: Fiona Daly
Sound: Peter Lindsay
MPAA rating: R
Running Time: 85 minutes

count on. While this has to seem familiar territory to Irish actor John Lynch, whose career has frequently encompassed innocent men caught in the middle of untenable situations, beginning with his first film role in 1984's *Cal.* Ian Hart's sociopathic Ginger was acknowledged with a best supporting actor award at the 1995 Venice Film Festival (the film was also nominated for a Golden Lion). Hart manages to keep Ginger at full boil, he's a character the viewer is never tempted to feel sorry for, yet Hart plays him as small and human enough that Ginger can't be dismissed as only a grotesque.

Filmed in Dublin, O'Sullivan and some of his actors did manage to do some research in Northern Ireland during a ceasefire, which had broken by the time the film was released. O'Sullivan was relieved to discover that reaction to the film in Northern Ireland was good and Belfast cinemas had no trouble with violence when showing the film. However, the film had only a short and limited release in the U.S., following slowly on the heels of 1996's *Michael Collins* and *Some Mother's Son*, though it was filmed before both. It deserves to have a second life on video—if not for the message at the very least for the strength of its performances.

—*Christine Tomassini*

REVIEWS

Boxoffice. July, 1996, p. 88.
Empire. November, 1996.
Hollywood Reporter. April 24, 1997, p. 10.
Los Angeles Times. April 27, 1997, p. 22.
Los Angeles Times. April 30, 1997, p. F1.
New York Times. April 25, 1997, p. C4.
San Francisco Chronicle. May 9, 1997, p. D3.
San Francisco Examiner. May 9, 1997, p. C3.
Sight and Sound. February, 1996, p. 50.
Variety. September 11, 1995, p. 107.
Village Voice. April 22, 1997, p. 77.

Nothing to Lose

One has no job. The other has no life. Together, they have everything to gain and . . . *Nothing to Lose.*—Movie tagline

"Absolutely hilarious!"—Ron Brewington, *American Urban Radio Networks*

"The funniest comedy of the year!"—Neil Rosen, *NY 1 News*

"Wildly, wonderfully, outrageously funny. Don't miss it!"—Paul Wunder, *WBAI Radio*

Box Office: $44,480,039

Mismatched buddy flicks must have their own unique place in the hearts of Hollywood casting agents. Let your imagination run wild and find two actors who not only have little in common artistically, but physically create such glaring, off-kilter contrasts, viewers can't help but laugh at their hair-brained escapades. Invariably, this genre works entirely within the framework of cops and robbers and inevitably pans out best (or at least receives the most favorable audience reception) when the two leads are racially balanced. What starts out with gargantuan clashes of culture, societal assumptions, off-color, testosterone-based bathroom humor and the occasional fisticuffs, eventually blossoms into a mutually rewarding, "tough love," co-existence where the two principals become better people as a result of their exposure to The Other Side. Some prime examples of this tried-and-true formula include *White Men Can't Jump* (1992) and *Money Train* (1995), both starring Woody Harrelson and Wesley Snipes, as well as both the *Lethal Weapon* and *48 Hours* franchises. *Nothing To Lose* captures all of the above elements and milks them for all their worth, which is very little.

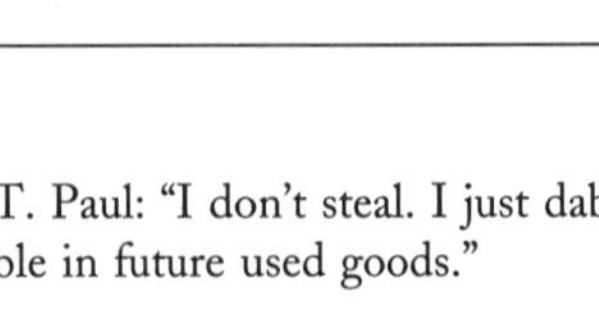

T. Paul: "I don't steal. I just dabble in future used goods."

As far as the two lead actors are concerned, the title itself couldn't be more ironic. It fits Tim Robbins like a glove. He's been nominated for a Best Director Oscar (*Dead Man Walking*, [1995]) and regularly displays his versatile acting chops. From light comedy (*Bull Durham*, [1988]) to dark comedy (*Bob Roberts* and *The Player* [both from 1992] and *Short Cuts* [1993]) to high drama (*Jacob's Ladder* [1990] and *The Shawshank Redemption* [1994]), Robbins has long since proven he deserves consideration as a major Hollywood talent. At this point, he can pretty much write his own ticket. Even a flop like this won't hurt his reputation. Here he plays Nick, an advertising executive, whose suburban home and suburban four-runner suggest all the comfortable surroundings of mindless suburban bliss. After a very bad day which concludes with him witnessing, what appears to be, his wife (Kelly Preston) having sex with his boss Michael McKean), he snaps.

Shaken, Nick jumps in his vehicle and drives aimlessly through the streets of Los Angeles. His little jaunt eventually finds him touring the streets of The Ghetto. While at a stoplight, a man bursts through the passenger door demanding his wallet and car keys. Enter Martin Lawrence. Compared to Robbins, who has little to lose, Lawrence has *everything* to lose. He regularly gets himself into bizarre skirmishes with the police (including an incident during the filming of this project where he was arrested for ranting and waving a loaded pistol in the middle of a busy L.A. intersection). "Martin," his long-running Fox series was cancelled at the peak of its popularity, due no doubt in part to a (since settled) sexual harassment suit brought on by a female co-star. Lawrence clearly has comic talent (some say genius), but like so many troubled souls before him, can't seem to handle the trappings of superstardom. Here he plays T, who is . . . ahem . . . a crazy man with a gun (true-to-life casting to say the least).

Writer/director Steve Oedekerk has a cameo as a disco-dancing night watchman.

Undaunted and completely unthreatened, Nick turns the tables, locks T in, and takes him hostage. The pair then speed through L.A., eventually winding up in a diner in the middle of nowhere. The next two hours are spent bonding, Hollywood style, raising hell and escaping one life threatening situation after another. One such scenario finds Nick and T potential victims of another racially balanced, male duo (played by Giancarlo Esposito and John C. McGinley). What brings Nick and T together (bonding-wise) is a half-baked burglary/vandalism scam Nick dreams up to get back at his boss. While in the boss' office, the two must wait patiently, lurking in the shadows while a night watchman exorcises all of his John Travolta/Danny Terrio dancing demons, gyrating through a painfully long solo performance augmented with only a flashlight. The part of the guard is played by Steve Oedekerk, who wrote and directed the project. The self-indulgence of this self-gratifying useless bit of adolescent posturing goes far to explain Oedekerk's shallow depth and narrow artistic range. The material here is as patently banal as his 1995 rookie effort, *Ace Ventura: When Nature Calls*. With his coupling of Robbins and Lawrence, Oedekerk is vainly grasping to rekindle the spark of the many semi-magical Richard Pryor/Gene Wilder capers (*Silver Streak* [1976], *Stir Crazy* [1980] and *See No Evil, Hear No Evil* [1989]). Yet another racially balanced team that found their success with an impeccable sense of timing.

While proving to be nothing more than an annoying pit-stop in Robbins' career, this film was a make-or-break venture for Lawrence. Luckily for him, the box office numbers were respectable. Oedekerk was fortunate enough to snare these actors—they made it barely tolerable. There's no telling how bad it might have been with less talented leading men.

—J.M. Clark

CREDITS

Nick Beame: Tim Robbins
T. Paul: Martin Lawrence
Davis Lanlow: John C. McGinley
Charlie Dunt: Giancarlo Esposito
Ann: Kelly Preston
Phillip Barrow: Michael McKean
Bertha: Irma P. Hall
Danielle: Rebecca Gayheart

Origin: USA
Released: 1997
Production: Martin Bregman, Dan Jinks, Michael Bregman for Touchstone Pictures; released by Buena Vista
Direction: Steve Oedekerk
Screenplay: Steve Oedekerk
Cinematography: Donald E. Thorin
Editing: Malcolm Campbell
Music: Robert Folk
Production design: Maria Caso
Art direction: James J. Murakami
Costumes: Elsa Zamparelli
Sound: Maury Harris
MPAA rating: R
Running Time: 97 minutes

REVIEWS

Boxoffice. September, 1997, p. 123.
Chicago Tribune. July 18, 1997, p. 4.
Entertainment Weekly. July 25, 1997, p. 52.
The Hollywood Reporter. July 7, 1997, p. 5.
Los Angeles Times. July 18, 1997, p. F1.
New York Times. July 18, 1997, p. C12.
People. July 28, 1997, p. 21.
Rolling Stone. August 7, 1997, p. 69.
Sight and Sound. November, 1997, p. 48.
USA Today. July 18, 1997, p. 4D.
Variety. July 14, 1997, p. 44.
Village Voice. July 22, 1997, p. 70.
Washington Post Weekend. July 18, 1997, p. 41.

Nowhere

Let the love feast begin.—Movie tagline

"Risky and confident, *Nowhere* is stylized to the max—yet its emotions are real."—Kevin Thomas, *Los Angeles Times*

"A surreal *American Graffiti* crossed with a kinky *Beverly Hills 90210*."—Stephen Holden, *New York Times*

"Sexy, psychedelic, dementedly funny, with a sensational soundtrack . . . it's like *Clueless* with nipple rings."—Dennis Dermody, *Paper*

CREDITS

Dark: James Duval
Mel: Rachel True
Montgomery: Nathan Bexton
Lucifer: Kathleen Robertson
Kriss: Chiara Mastroianni
Kozy: Debi Mazar
Egg: Sarah Lassez
The Teen Idol: Jaason Simmons
Dark's Mom: Beverly D'Angelo
Dingbat: Christina Applegate
Cowboy: Guillermo Diaz
Shad: Ryan Phillippe
Lilith: Heather Graham
Bart: Jeremy Jordan
Moses Helper: John Ritter

Origin: USA
Released: 1997
Production: Gregg Araki and Andrea Sperling for Why Not; released by Fine Line Features
Direction: Gregg Araki
Screenplay: Gregg Araki
Cinematography: Arturo Smith
Editing: Gregg Araki
Production design: Patti Podesta
Costumes: Sara Jane Slotnick
MPAA rating: R
Running Time: 82 minutes

Nowhere is not a good movie to watch if you're burned out on the fast-paced flood of information from the modern world, or have even the teeniest bit of a headache. Watching it probably closely mirrors the experience of having your eyes pried open and being forced around the tram at Disneyland at ten times the normal speed. Though *Nowhere* offers an offhand brutality that a sped-up version of a theme park does not, both share a tendency toward saturated colors, surrealism, and relentlessness.

In Gregg Araki's world, "L.A. is like nowhere—everybody who lives here is lost," as the main character, Dark (Araki favorite, James Duval), says in the movie's opening line. Despite this seemingly bleak beginning, the characters that people the film are not the sort to wallow in their unhappiness. They embrace the shallowness of their lives, using the tools of bulimia, promiscuity, and S&M. They are unfazed by the bizarre subjects of their high school classes (History of Lethal Epidemics and Thermonuclear Disasters)—but maybe that's because they never seem to actually attend school, anyway. They seek solace at "The Hole" where they chat about what bands will be playing at the Butt Crack, scarf down desserts they plan on vomiting up later, and experience youthful angst by hanging out with their girlfriends' alternate lovers. Even when one of the less savory members of their crowd pummels a guy to death with a tomato soup can, it is only slightly more horrible to these kids than the day-to-day reality of their grim lives—which is to say, horrible, but somehow bearable.

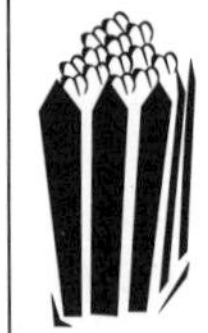

Egg: "Are we still in reality?"

There are a few real issues tackled in this stylized, purposefully shallow piece of celluloid. The main character, Dark, slogs through the movie on a quest for true love, a goal that's always easy to identify with. While this is something he'd like to extract from longtime girlfriend Mel (Rachel True), the notion of monogamous love clashes with her philosophy that everyone should have sex with as many people as possible before they get old and ugly and bumped from the A list. She practices what she preaches, frequently with companion Lucifer (Kathleen Robertson) and, to the chagrin of both Dark and Lucifer, with buff blonde twins Surf and Ski (Keith and Derek Brewer). Dark's plea to Mel—"Can't we just leave this planet behind . . . and be in love and stuff?"—seems as unlikely to come true as John Ritter showing up as a televangelist, so he turns to Montgomery (Nathan Bexton) to fulfill this role.

But wait . . . What was that about John Ritter? Pop culture references in *Nowhere* go far beyond just a few tired catch phrases. John Ritter does indeed appear as televangelist Moses Helper (1-800-GO-JEU). His character provides a message of hope for several traumatized teenagers, especially the lovely Egg (Sarah Lassez). After Egg meets a Teen Idol (Jaason Simmons) at the local hangout, they begin a seemingly sweet romance. The romance turns into a nightmare when the famed star brutally rapes her, and Egg crawls home, mesmerized by the commercialized version of God's love that Ritter's character offers.

The last of Araki's "Teen Apocalypse" trilogy, following *Totally F***ed Up* and *The Doom Generation.*

But the cameos don't stop there. Lauren Tewes, Julie McCoy of "Love Boat" fame, appears as a newscaster and former "Brady" kids Eve Plumb and Christopher Knight play odd couple Mr. & Mrs. Sigvatssohn, at which point the in-jokes get to be a little too much. Even Traci Lords and Shannon Doherty show up as Valley girls at the bus stop. After the space alien zaps them, all that's left is their retainers.

Yes, space aliens. A Godzilla-type creature roams L.A. randomly zapping unlucky teenagers. Talk about your multiple genre movie! In fact, at the near-conclusion of the film, recently abducted high schooler Montgomery returns to be with Dark, who he has just realized his true feelings for. But of course this is just too fortunate for those *Nowhere* kids, and Montgomery starts writhing around, until he explodes into a huge, disgusting bug. Yech!

Nowhere manages to effectively balance the superficiality of *Clueless* with the casual brutality of *Reservoir Dogs*. But, like both of those movies, *Nowhere* was never expected to have mainstream appeal. Hey, maybe it's not a movie for you. In the words of one *Nowhere* character, "whatev."

—*Nancy Matson*

REVIEWS

Entertainment Weekly. May 23, 1997, p. 46.
The Hollywood Reporter. May 9, 1997, p. 10.
Los Angeles Times. May 9, 1997, p. F14.
New York Times. May 9, 1997, p. B17.
Variety. February 10, 1997, p. 66.
Village Voice. May 13, 1997, p. 79.

Office Killer

Working here can be murder.—Movie tagline

Office Killer is photographer Cindy Sherman's first foray into filmmaking. Sherman is best known for her stunning series, "Untitled Film Stills," which were recently exhibited at New York's Museum of Modern Art, and which attracted high praise. Sherman was deemed one of the finest artists of the past three decades. She may be the quintessential postmodernist, if what is meant by that term includes a sensibility that portrays the way contemporary identity has been largely influenced by the media, especially film and television. Indeed, Sherman's photographs treat life like a media event. She usually uses herself, posed in a scene, in a costume, in an attitude that vaguely seems to recall not a specific film but rather memories of countless films that people now imitate. Whether Sherman is some creepy clone of a movie horror victim, a gun moll, or a sex doll, it is her "acting" that is striking. Identity, in her lens, is provisional and contextual; that is, it is made up for the occasion and derives its meaning from the setting the artist chooses for herself.

Cindy Sherman: "I like the fact that it's evoking horror film stereotypes, but not really scaring you. It's more psychological horror . . ."

Sherman's photographs are serious art, yet they are spoofs and satires. It is almost as if she is saying "how could we take the cinema so seriously when actually it is so silly, so contrived?" The photographs also suggest, however, that love of cinema is just another instance of the mimetic drive, the human impulse to create an identity out of copying and collecting images from media. Sherman's interest in freakishness and the Gothic, is a latter day kind of romanticism laced with irony. Her choice of subject matter is reminiscent of that great photographer Diane Arbus, whom Susan Sontag writes about so memorably in *On Photography*—although Arbus prefers to shoot her subject's head-on, forsaking the distorting techniques of horror films, since her subjects (dwarfs and giants, for example) simply have to present themselves in order to look freaky. Arbus seems to be employing obvious physical distortions as perhaps a metaphor for the inequalities and asymmetries of life. Sherman, on the other hand, works up her grotesqueries by means of makeup and whatever props and paraphernalia are necessary to establish a "scene." It is interesting that Sherman came to maturity as an artist at the same time as the word scenario entered into common usage via the Watergate hearings. People's stories were thought of as shooting scripts.

It is not surprising, then, that Sherman might wish to try her hand at a movie. But it is also not surprising that it has taken her a considerable time to actually produce one. There is a world of difference between films and photographs—even when the photographs are, like Sherman's, parodies of film stills. Photographs freeze a moment; they do not talk. They are enigmatic, elliptical, and fragmentary. The best photographs can repay hours of study; the multitudes of shots in a film flash by. Photographs are a static study; film is a narrative, even though it is made out of still pictures. Nevertheless, film has been such an inspiration to Sherman that she has to have wondered—as have her viewers—what she would do as a filmmaker.

Office Killer, not surprisingly, has some startling visual effects. There is, for example, the scene in the photocopy room. It is late at night, and the interrupted light from the photocopy machine casts shadows. The flickering light, and the mechanical back-and-forth action of the machine, evoke a sinister, closed-in atmosphere, and a controlling environment that produces considerable tension. It seems an inhuman kind of environment in which to work, a setting in which murder is all-too-likely. It is also a place where there are no originals, where everyone is copying or following orders, desperately trying to perform on deadline and ready a magazine for press.

The film has the atmosphere of a Gothic thriller/horror film but also the mundanity the characters in Sherman's photographs, are apparently escaping when they don their dramatic guises. For devotees of Sherman, there is a game to be played, identifying how close some of her movie scenes resemble her film stills. A recent article in *The New York Times*, for example, juxtaposes "Untitled, No. 180," a 1987 photograph against a scene in the film when Jeanne Tripplehorn sits in shock next to two corpses. The visual echoes suggest how involved and yet how removed Sherman is from her own creations. The film scene is ghastly, but it is also laughable because it goes so over-the-top in its layering of the grotesque. There have to be two corpses, one on each side of Tripplehorn, and they have been propped up so that they seem to be watching television. This is a good joke in itself because so much ink has been wasted on deploring the zombie-like trance that television is supposed to instill in its viewers.

Actually, there are more than two corpses in the room. Dorinne (the office killer played with aplomb by Carol Kane) has begun collecting dead bodies, the result of her unfortunate, accidental killing of her boss. She has been working overtime at night, for she senses that her job is in jeopardy. She is an extremely nervous, retiring soul who is easily spooked. She has almost no friends in the office, and she is rattled because she has to learn about the new computer she has just been given. What is worse, she is trying to please a cantankerous male who ridicules her intelligence and her modest manners. Indeed, he makes her sick, and she goes to the bathroom to vomit.

On her way back to her desk, Dorinne notices that the office lights are out. She does not know that her boss has shut off the circuit breaker in order to check the connections to her malfunctioning computer. As she cautiously advances, she trips and her hands hit the circuit switch, instantly electrocuting her obnoxious boss. In shock, Dorinne tries to awaken the man. When she realizes he is dead, she takes a moment to lecture him on his bad behavior. It is a comic but enormously satisfying scene both for Dorinne and for the audience. How many times have employees wanted to have Dorinne's opportunity? The fantasy of killing off the opposition must have occurred to millions of people, even to those who do not attend horror films. It is absurd to talk to a dead person, but of course such dialogues happen all the time—and not only in the movies.

The boss's death could easily be explained, but Dorinne (so tongue-tied in the office) decides to drag the body away. She takes it home, where her invalid mother is her only company. With the boss safely dead, he becomes Dorinne's confidant. She sets him up on the sofa and flirts with him. Later she tries to straighten up and clean him with some scotch tape and Windex. Her efforts are sincere, if hilarious. Kane does not camp it up. Her Dorinne is a straightforward, dedicated worker, who proves better at her job than anyone in the company expected. Indeed, as she embarks on a crime spree, killing anyone who crosses her or who might expose her crimes, she becomes more confident and better looking, letting down her hair and using makeup. She does get carried away, though, when she does in two little girls selling Girl Scout cookies. (Door-to-door solicitors beware!)

Flashbacks help to tell the reasons why Dorinne is so inhibited and full of latent hostility. A good deal of it is explained when her slimy father (played expertly by Eric Bogosian) turns up in several flashbacks. He is an oily child abuser who gets his comeuppance when he tries one time too many to fondle Dorinne in the family car. The child abuse excuse should be no more than a cliché that weakens Sherman's film, but it does not because so much of the action is stylized—a comment on such explanations, not an embrace of them.

Critics have been rather hard on this film. It was held up for some time while Sherman edited and re-edited it. It has been called murky and clunky, a far cry from Sherman's sophisticated photography. Certainly the plot is unoriginal. But the performances are dead-on, with no effort to exaggerate what is by definition satirical material. A New York audience found it engrossing and entertaining—if the unusual silence and clapping afterwards count as evidence.

Like Sherman's film stills, *Office Killer* is engaging because it raises questions about human identity in a sly, comic fashion. Sherman is fond of her subjects, even when she is questioning the importance we invest in them. She has real empathy for her characters, yet she retains her critical eye. Although she trades on the conventions of cinema and photographs, she also questions the suspension of disbelief we accord them. It is all rather ridiculous, her work seems to say, and yet we cannot live without these images, can we?

—*Carl Rollyson*

CREDITS

Dorine Douglas: Carol Kane
Kim Poole: Molly Ringwald
Norah Reed: Jeanne Tripplehorn
Virginia: Barbara Sukowa
Daniel: Michael Imperioli
Carlotta Douglas: Alice Drummond
Dorine's father: Eric Bogosian

Origin: USA
Released: 1997
Production: Christine Vachon and Pamela Koffler for Good Machine, Good Fear, and Kardana/Swinsky Films; released by Strand
Direction: Cindy Sherman
Screenplay: Elise MacAdam and Tom Kalin
Cinematography: Russell Fine
Editing: Merril Stern
Music: Evan Lurie
Production design: Kevin Thompson
Art direction: Ford Wheeler
Sound: Neil Danzinger
MPAA rating: Unrated
Running Time: 81 minutes

REVIEWS

Boxoffice. January, 1998, p. 46.
Cinemafantastique. December, 1997, p. 42.
Entertainment Weekly. December 5, 1997, p. 58.
Hollywood Reporter. September 9, 1997, p. 6.
Los Angeles Times. December 5, 1997, p. F4.
New York Times. December 3, 1997, p. E5.
San Francisco Chronicle. December 12, 1997, p. C3.
San Francisco Examiner. December 12, 1997, p. B3.
Variety. August 25, 1997, p. 76.

187

When schools become war zones and both sides start taking casualties, what then?—Movie tagline

"A scorching drama that will mesmerize you! Totally gripping and dramatically stunning! Stinging, cutting edge reality."—Ron Brewington, *American Urban Radio Networks*

"A riveting story, one that you'll never forget."—Sam Hallenbeck, *Fox 13/Tampa*

"Powerful and important."—Jeff Craig, *Sixty Second Preview*

Box Office: $5,747,802

The odd title *187* is a police codeword for homicide. The film begins with shots of a dedicated science teacher, Trevor Garfield (Samuel L. Jackson), racing across Brooklyn on a bicycle. He intends to use the bike for a classroom demonstration of centrifugal force for students that seem to be rude and, you know, disrespectful, but tolerate his attempts to amuse and instruct them. He knows that props are necessary for capturing the attention of his potentially rowdy ghetto students. He is a good teacher, a natural, and a good man.

But Trevor has not won over all of his students and has enemies, particularly one thuggish student at the high school where he teaches in Bedford-Stuyvesant. After the demonstration, Trevor picks up his physics textbook and finds "187" scrawled with a marker on page after page. He understands the code and knows that he is a marked man.

Trevor reports the warning, to unsympathetic administrators, but to no avail. Later that day he is attacked and stabbed in the back. The student is later apprehended and sent to a juvenile detention center. The criminal is underaged, and for that reason he can get away with attempted murder, but Trevor does not die.

Fifteen months later Garfield has recovered physically and has relocated to Los Angeles, where he is now working as a substitute teacher in the barrio of East L.A. under circumstances that are not much better. Substitute teachers are not taken seriously anywhere, especially in classrooms populated with hoodlums and gangbangers. The woman he replaces has been intimidated and brutalized by her students and is forced to take a leave of absence by a cowardly school principal who has never taught, but sides with the students because he fears litigation.

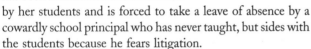

"Kids understand how dangerous the world of public schools is—some adults just don't get it."—Director Kevin Reynolds

Garfield is befriended by history teacher Dave Childress (John Heard), who was once a good teacher but has since become disillusioned, burnt-out and jaded. He packs a pistol to school for his own self-defense and has reason to regard students as the enemy. Garfield later tells Childress that they have nothing in common, though Childress regards him as a hero. Garfield also befriends Ellen Henry (Kelly Rowan), a young computer science teacher, who is far more upbeat and optimistic than Childress, but who, in the end, will also become disillusioned, to the point where she will throw her framed "excellence in teaching" certificate in the wastebasket and leave the profession. The film certainly has a point to make about good teachers who are not supported by cowardly administrators. Things are pretty grim in the classroom.

Although one of the walking wounded, Garfield does not give up easily. He has one student, a girl named Rita (Karina Arroyave), who is certainly street-wise and tough, but also smart. He discovers that she really wants to learn to become a writer, and he becomes her private tutor, meeting her at his home and at the school library to help her improve her grammar and spelling in order to get better marks in English. Only Garfield seems to take genuine personal interest in his students.

Verdugo Hills High School was utilized as the Los Angeles school where Garfield teaches.

The problem with Garfield is that his earlier attack has eroded his soul and driven him crazy, turning him into a vigilante who resembles the unnamed character known only as "DFENS" played by Michael Douglas in *Falling Down* (1993). His main antagonist is Benny Chacon (Lobo Sebastian), who has also been threatening the defenseless Ellen Henry. Lacking any reasonable support from the school system, Garfield takes the law into his own hands. Benny is a hard case and a murderer. The film shows him killing a rival gang member who has defiled Benny's spray-painted graffiti gang icon. Not long thereafter, Benny's body is found in the river. Eventually the viewer begins to suspect that Garfield might have had something to do with Benny's death.

Cesar (Clifton Gonzalez Gonzalez), one of Benny's sidekicks, is another troublemaker who is disrespectful of his teachers and who beats and brutalizes his own mother. Garfield takes it upon himself to teach Cesar a lesson. He drugs and disables the boy with a dart and chops his finger off. After Cesar wakes up and is taken to the hospital, the severed finger is sent to the hospital in an unmarked envelope and reattached, but Cesar knows who has mutilated him and is looking for payback. In this instance, Garfield underestimates his antagonist.

While recovering at home, Cesar is influenced by the Russian roulette sequence from Michael Cimino's *The Deer Hunter* (1978). He sees to it that Garfield loses his job, even though there is no evidence to link Garfield with his mutilation. Garfield cleans out his desk and walks to his car, and finds "187" scratched on the door. Garfield goes home and waits for Cesar's assassination gang to come calling, wanting to play Russian roulette. Cesar forces his teacher to play Russian roulette, but Garfield challenges Cesar's manhood and pride by making him out to be a coward if Cesar will not play the game himself. Both men end up blowing their brains out. Rita later gives a eulogy for Garfield at her graduation ceremony.

The film clearly has a political point to make, and that point is slammed home at the end by means of a subtitle that informs viewers that one out of every nine teachers is attacked by students every year, followed by the declaration that "A teacher wrote this movie." Scott Yagemann was the teacher who wrote the movie after working for seven years in the trenches of the Los Angeles public school system. "I had a kid threaten to kill me," Yagemann noted in the Warner Bros. Press release. "I later found out that he had stabbed a teaching assistant the semester before, and I was never told anything about this kid." Yagemann later discovered that in order to protect themselves, teachers personally had to research every student's file in order to find out which ones were dangerous and given to violence. This explains the screenplay's sense of anger and outrage.

The problem with the screenplay is Yagemann's inexperience, since *187* is his first feature film. His only previous writing credits had been for television series such as "Love Connection," "Jeopardy," and "The Liar's Club." Before that he had worked as a page for such Norman Lear comedies as "All in the Family" and "The Jeffersons"—hardly appropriate training for a serious message film. That may help to explain the scrambled nature of the screenplay, which lifts elements from earlier films such as *Falling Down* and *The Deer Hunter.*

The screenplay offers a reasonable characterization of Garfield, powerfully represented by Samuel L. Jackson, but one that takes an unexpected turn when the character turns to violence and angry payback in order to provide an action-packed conclusion. Overall it has the look and feel of a low-budget "B" movie, one that has the additional advantage of giving the film a sort of gritty, surface realism. It presents disturbing images of high-school violence, but it finally goes over the top.

It is interesting to compare *187* to *The Blackboard Jungle*, the model for the genre directed by Richard Brooks in 1955 and adapted from Even Hunter's novel. In that film Glenn Ford played the dedicated teacher attempting to reach and convert the disaffected student played by Sidney Poitier. But *Blackboard Jungle* sweetened its fable to prepare for a happy ending and is now remembered mainly for its music "Rock Around the Clock," as played by Bill Haley and the Comets, which popularized rock'n'roll for a new audience of white, middle-class teenagers.

The problem with *Blackboard Jungle* was that it sanitized the problem and solution of inner-city teaching. The problem with *187* is that it goes to the other extreme and is unrelentingly pessimistic, but it is far more convincing in the way it showcases the problem, even if it has no real solution to offer, other than madness and mayhem. The film was directed by Kevin Reynolds, best known for the silly Kevin Costner action-adventure epic *Robin Hood: Prince of Thieves* (1991) and the idiotic *Waterworld* (1995). At least to his credit in this picture Reynolds shows some skill in filming realistic settings.

Kevin Reynolds first read the script in Seattle, where he lives, and immediately struck a deal with the production executives for Icon, Mel Gibson's company. Originally Garfield was not an African-American but a middle-class Caucasian. According to *Movieline* magazine the script was shopped around to Nicolas Cage, Gary Sinise, and other actors who were "disturbed by the material" and turned it down, but Samuel L. Jackson was interested. "He understood the pitfalls of taking on a character who gets involved in situations that are not entirely sympathetic," Reynolds told the *Movieline* interviewer. The casting of Jackson almost compensates for the weakness of the script that turns a dedicated teacher into a vigilante and turns a potentially decent man into a murderer. Having Jackson in the role takes the edge of racism out of the picture, since an African-American is attacked and nearly killed by another, younger African-American. The violence that later ensues is not simply a matter of racist backlash, in other words.

Reviewing the picture favorably for *The Washington Times*, Gary Arnold noted that "the filmmakers borrow a notorious suspense device from *The Deer Hunter* in order to resolve their own portentous scenario." Arnold found an analogue for Garfield's "free-lance" vigilantism, "hidden even from a sympathetic audience to some extent," in Charles Bronson's *Death Wish* (1974), adapted by Michael Winner from Brian Garfield's novel, in which vigilantism as a deterrent to violent crime, unlike the film, was not seen as a solution but as another problem, as is the case in *187*. Arnold even suggested that screenwriter Scott Yagemann might "have had novelist Brian Garfield in mind when naming his protagonist." To its credit, as Arnold asserted, the film does not "solicit vicarious approval" as Garfield "makes things costly for the class thugs" and is, as a consequence, "demoralized by the effort."

Arnold rightly noted that even though the director "never quite harmonizes the social-problem elements with a mythic-tragic character study," Reynolds "reaffirms an aptitude for contemporary and realistic subject matter and showcases several impressive performances" from an ensemble headed by Jackson and "distinctively enhanced" by Kelly Rowan, John Heard, and Karina Arrayave. Not all reviewers were so generous, however. Stephen Farber called the film "ambitious but fatally misguided" in the way it "mutates from social realism to garish cartoon melodrama in the style of *Death Wish*." The film "so thoroughly dehumanizes Trevor's adolescent victims

CREDITS

Trevor Garfield: Samuel L. Jackson
Dave Childress: John Heard
Ellen Henry: Kelly Rowan
Cesar: Clifton Gonzalez Gonzalez
Garcia: Tony Plana
Rita: Karina Arroyave
Benny: Lobo Sebastian
Hyland: Jack Kehler

Origin: USA
Released: 1997
Production: Bruce Davey and Stephen McEveety for Icon; released by Warner Bros.
Direction: Kevin Reynolds
Screenplay: Scott Yagemann
Cinematography: Ericson Core
Editing: Stephen Semel
Production design: Stephen Storer
Art direction: Mark Zuelzke
Set design: Gary Sawaya
Costumes: Darryle Johnson
Sound: Geoffrey Patterson
MPAA rating: R
Running Time: 119 minutes

and so lovingly romanticizes his sadistic methods of torture that the message turns hopelessly muddled."

In the same vein Owen Gleiberman claimed that the film's "unruly delinquents" were not characterized but "visualized," and that "the prospect of a teacher driven to his students' level of sociopathic vengeance might have packed a ghoulish wallop had the film viewed it as tragic." The tragic potential is there, however, and effectively delivered through Jackson's acting. As Stephen Farber conceded, the film has "moments that capture the surreal flavor of the '90s blackboard jungle," as in the scene "in which a principal cowers because a student hoodlum threatens to sue." This scene has "real sting," but it also panders to the popular misconception that the legal system is designed to protect criminals rather than victims. Mixed signals are a problem here, suggesting that it may be justifiable for a victim to take the law into his own hands since the system is corrupt.

—*James M. Welsh*

REVIEWS

Boxoffice. September, 1997, p. 119.
Chicago Tribune. July 30, 1997, p. 1.
Entertainment Weekly. August 8, 1997, p. 51.
The Hollywood Reporter. July 28, 1997, p. 9.
Los Angeles Times. February 17, 1997, p. F1.
Los Angeles Times. July 30, 1997, p. F1.
Movieline. June, 1997, p. 55.
New York Times. July 30, 1997, p. C15.
People. August 11, 1997, p. 19.
Rolling Stone. August 21, 1997, p. 97.
Sight and Sound. September, 1997, p. 52.
USA Today. July 30, 1997, p. 5D.
Variety. July 28, 1997, p. 57.
Village Voice. August 12, 1997, p. 72.
Washington Times Metropolitan Times. July 30, 1997, p. C11.

One Night Stand

It was just one night that changed everything.—Movie tagline

"Director Mike Figgis is a master cinematic storyteller."—Stephen Farber, *Movieline*

Box Office: $2,642,983

Mike Figgis gained widespread critical acclaim in 1995 with *Leaving Las Vegas*, the wrenching story of an alcoholic who is determined to drink himself to death and the prostitute who befriends him in his final days. Figgis created two memorable characters and was able to mine a unique and honest love story out of the most desperate of situations.

Figgis's follow-up film, *One Night Stand*, is rather uneven by comparison. Like *Leaving Las Vegas*, it also tries to find redemption in a confrontation with death, but, while it displays flashes of brilliance and some excellent individual scenes, the disparate elements of the story do not coalesce into a satisfying whole. The movie opens with Max (Wesley Snipes) walking down the streets of New York and introducing himself to us directly—a bold introduction that immediately establishes an intimacy between the protagonist and the audience. He is a successful commercial director who has returned to New York to visit an old friend, Charlie (Robert Downey Jr.), who is HIV-positive. They had a fight several years ago, and Max, it seems, wants to make amends for past mistakes. He meets Charlie in a brief scene and offers financial help when the medical bills start rolling in.

While Max briefly re-establishes contact with Charlie, the bulk of the film's first section is concerned with Max's misadventures in New York. The opening plays like a little nightmare out of a film noir as Max finds himself trapped in the big city and unable to leave, no matter how hard he tries. (In a clever cameo, Mike Figgis plays the hotel clerk who checks Max out and thus leaves him stranded in the big city.) One scene depicts Max attempting to leave but boxed in by a United Nations parade, as if the whole world were conspiring to keep him from getting home. He must stay in New York an extra day and makes contact with a woman named Karen (Nastassja Kinski), whom he met earlier in the day. They enjoy a concert together, survive an attempted mugging, and end up spending the night together. Their sex scenes are soft and tender and are set against Figgis's own lush jazz score—the city, it seems, is dangerous, but Karen offers respite from Max's frustrating day.

The film's middle section, Max's return to Los Angeles, is its weakest as it illustrates in broad strokes what is wrong with Max's life. His wife, Mimi (Ming-Na Wen), is somewhat crude in contrast to the demure, sophisticated

Karen. Mimi, in a reversal of the common stereotype that depicts the wife as less sexually adventurous than the other woman (Adrian Lyne's *Fatal Attraction*, for example) goes for wild, rough sex and proudly tells her husband she has bought an instructional video to spice up their sex life.

On a professional level, Max finds the commercial business increasingly demeaning. He refuses to do a pickle commercial, and later (in an overly long scene) is obnoxious at a dinner party with colleagues. In a lengthy diatribe, he calls television, the source of his livelihood, a "frontal lobotomy." Given that television is generally an easy target, Max's sentiments do not come as a major revelation but rather as the trite criticism of a man who sees himself as a true artist trapped in a degrading business.

Broad humor also distinguishes the L.A. scenes. From the outset, we are constantly wondering if Mimi will discover Max's one night stand when she detects a different scent on him (even the family dog is suspicious). Later, just when we think she has discovered the truth about his infidelity, she instead accuses him of smoking on his trip. Such scenes are funny but belong in a sex comedy, not a supposedly serious film about the consequences of adultery.

The original script was written by Joe Eszterhas, but after reading Figgis' rewrite Eszterhas has removed his name from the credits deciding it was no longer his work.

This transitional sequence merely sets us up for the film's third (and best) act, which takes place a year later as Max returns to New York to see Charlie, who is now near death. The scenes between Max and Charlie are the most affecting in the film. We see a real love and friendship between them and also a sense of regret over the years that have been wasted. Their relationship is very strong emotionally and dramatically—a very honest and realistic depiction of a man comforting his friend as he faces the end. Moreover, Max's tenderness and compassion round out his character. Being a friend to Charlie brings out the best in Max and in essence frees him from the frustrations and tediousness of his daily life. Whereas he seems very self-absorbed and belligerent at home, with Charlie he is compassionate and generous.

Thus, Charlie's death does redeem Max. It is too bad, then, that Max's growing appreciation for the shortness and preciousness of life becomes a device to make him follow his heart and pursue Karen, who, in a remarkable coincidence that strains credulity, just happens to be Charlie's sister-in-law. Karen may be beautiful and smart (we eventually learn she is a rocket scientist), but ultimately she is a flat character.

Indeed, the central problem in *One Night Stand* is Karen, who remains a cipher throughout the film. The role is very underwritten, and so we are never able to grasp what makes her special to Max, beyond her beauty and some vague notion of sophistication that Mimi lacks. While the film justifiably focuses on Max, for the romance to work, we need a better sense of who Karen is. Because their relationship is tentative and sketchy at best, the audience has no rooting interest in the outcome.

By contrast, the quasi-love story between Max and Charlie is quite moving and really the centerpiece of the film. While Max tells us at the outset that he is not gay and even denies he is gay when Charlie presses him on the point, there is a sense that they could be lovers, that they share an intimacy no one else in the film does. This is especially evident in Charlie's death scene, in which he confesses his envy of Max and Max openly weeps for the friend he is losing. Their encounter is moving and tender without becoming maudlin.

Kyle MacLachlan brings some originality to the small role of Charlie's brother, Vernon. While he truly loves his brother, he makes an offhanded homophobic comment and is conspicuously the only person who wears latex gloves around Charlie. At the same time, though, he never becomes a stereotypical villain; rather, he is a man both well-intentioned and somewhat misguided and shallow. Vernon could have been played as a one-dimensional, middle-class jerk but instead is given a sympathetic side.

After Charlie's death, Max pursues Karen (he has a vision of Charlie encouraging him to find his happiness), and, in a surprising scene, when Max and Karen sneak away to have sex, they discover Vernon and Mimi doing the same—a surprising development that really comes out of nowhere and seems forced. It feels as if Figgis did not think the audience would accept Max and Karen cheating on their respective spouses (after all, Vernon and Mimi may be shallow, but they are not evil people who deserve to be betrayed), so having the spouses also cheat may be a way of making us feel better about Max and Karen's relationship. In a coda that takes place a year later, the foursome meet again for dinner, and, at the end, Karen and Max are together, while Mimi and Vernon leave together in a cab.

Wesley Snipes give a solid performance (he won the Best Actor prize at the Venice International Film Festival), and, given the sketchiness of the script, makes believable the wide range of emotions Max experiences. Robert Downey Jr. plays most of Charlie's scenes on his deathbed and convincingly conveys a man fighting the weakness of his body as he attempts to communicate with his friend. In struggling to breathe with his oxygen mask while trying to speak a few words at a time, he displays courage without begging for our sympathy.

Critical reaction to *One Night Stand* was mixed. Stephen Farber in *Movieline* was very enthusiastic and believed the

CREDITS

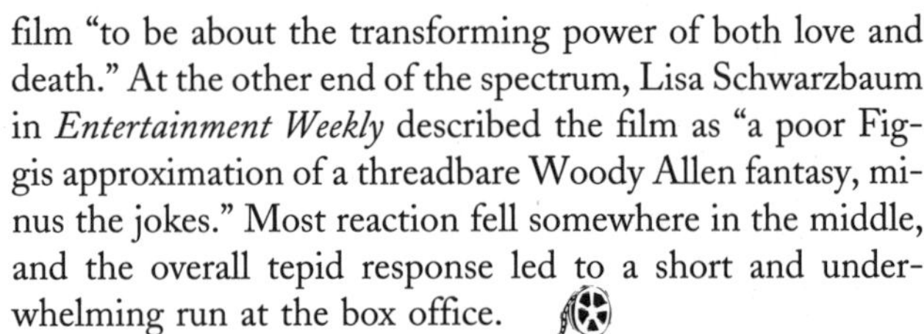

Max: Wesley Snipes
Karen: Nastassja Kinski
Mimi: Ming-Na Wen
Charlie: Robert Downey Jr.
Vernon: Kyle MacLachlan
George: Glenn Plummer
Margaux: Amanda Donohoe
Don: Thomas Hayden Church
Charlie's Nurse: Julian Sands

Origin: USA
Released: 1997
Production: Mike Figgis, Annie Stewart, and Ben Myron for Red Mullet; released by New Line Cinema
Direction: Mike Figgis
Screenplay: Mike Figgis
Cinematography: Declan Quinn
Editing: John Smith
Music: Mike Figgis
Production design: Waldemar Kalinowski
Art direction: Barry Kingston
Costumes: Laura Goldsmith, Enid Harris
Set decoration: Florence Fellman
Sound: Pawel Wdowczak
MPAA rating: R
Running Time: 103 minutes

film "to be about the transforming power of both love and death." At the other end of the spectrum, Lisa Schwarzbaum in *Entertainment Weekly* described the film as "a poor Figgis approximation of a threadbare Woody Allen fantasy, minus the jokes." Most reaction fell somewhere in the middle, and the overall tepid response led to a short and underwhelming run at the box office.

—Peter N. Chumo II

REVIEWS

Boxoffice. November, 1997, p. 120.
Detroit News. November 14, 1997, p. F1.
Entertainment Weekly. November 28, 1997, p. 54.
Los Angeles Times. September 6, 1996, p. F1.
Los Angeles Times. November 14, 1997, p. F2.
Movieline. December, 1997, p. 50.
New York Times. November 14, 1997, p. E19.
People. November 17, 1997, p. 22.
Rolling Stone. December 11, 1997, p. 86.
Sight and Sound. December, 1997, p. 49.
USA Today. November 14, 1997, p. 6D.
Variety. September 8, 1997, p. 77.
Village Voice. November 25, 1997, p. 91.
Washington Post Weekend. November 14, 1997, p. 50.

Operation Condor; Feiying Gaiwak; Armour of God 2

On his most dangerous mission ever, the world's toughest secret agent isn't going in alone.—Movie tagline

"A breathtaking ride! Jackie Chan is more fun to watch than all other movie action heroes put together."—Jay Carr, *Boston Globe*

"Exhilarating and jaw-dropping!"—Michael Wilmington, *Chicago Tribune*

"Dynamite entertainment!"—Gary Arnold, *Washington Times*

Box Office: $10,461,161

Jackie Chan, successor to Bruce Lee as the reigning Asian karate film star, is less handsome and formal than his predecessor but funnier, more acrobatic, and more democratic. Bruce Lee had a quirky and somewhat sadistic sense of humor, while Jackie Chan is a natural comedian. No one expects a karate film to make much sense, and *Operation Condor* is no exception. The difference is that the star himself does not take the whole business very seriously, even when he is being kicked, clubbed and tossed around by overwhelming numbers of assorted bad guys (who all happen to be karate experts too). The plot is something of a spoof of *Raiders of the Lost Ark* (1981), with the MacGuffin in question being a lost horde of stolen Nazi gold in place of the lost Ark of the Covenant.

Jackie, a secret agent for the American government, is called to the U.S. Embassy in Madrid where a U.N. representative spells out the nature of his assignment in an even more painfully static scene than such explanatory scenes usually are. (Jackie's code name is Condor, but it isn't worth much as a secret name because everybody keeps calling him Jackie.) When Jackie is not spinning around like a human pinwheel his limitations as an actor are glaringly apparent. Fortunately, there isn't much to understand. The time is the present. The gold, 240 tons of it worth around $150,000,000 on today's market, was stolen by the Nazis from the conquered nations of Europe and then hidden in the desert when it became obvious that Germany was going to lose the war. Who gets the gold if recovered is left a little vague. Presumably some effort will be made to return it to its rightful owners or their heirs.

Operation Condor is a remodeled version of a martial arts film titled *Armour of God II* (1990), a sequel to *The Armour of God* (1986), both of which were in Cantonese with English subtitles. *Armour of God II* has been streamlined and given a new musical score and sound design. The voices have all been dubbed in English. The dubbing was done exceptionally well—but it is dubbing nevertheless. Some viewers will be troubled by the fact that the actors' lips almost, but never completely, synchronize with their words. It is easy in such cases to become fascinated by the actors' lips and forget about where the story is supposed to be going. (Fortunately—or unfortunately—the plot is so derivative that the continuity is self-evident and could be followed by a viewer who was stone deaf.) There is also a troubling "distance" between the actors and their dubbed-in voices, making it obvious that substitutes are reading into microphones. Though Jackie Chan is becoming very popular with American audiences, these and other substandard production values should keep *Operation Condor* from becoming an outstanding box-office success. The human dynamo has yet to make the great leap forward of starring in an American big-budget production with a predominantly American cast and dialogue in English, but this development seems to be written in the tea leaves.

Jackie is assigned a Chinese partner named Ada (Carol Cheng), who naively believes she will be in charge of the operation and will be able to tell the volatile Jackie what to do. Along the road to Morocco they pick up blond Elsa (Eva Cobo de Garcia), who claims to have special knowledge about the whereabouts of the gold because it was being transported under the command of her German grandfather. These two young women and a third occasional companion named Momoko (Shoko Ikeda) provide eye appeal and a certain amount of PG-13 sex appeal but otherwise prove more of a liability than an asset to our hero. At one point he has to save them from being auctioned off as exotic concubines in an Arab slave market.

Operation Condor may be a secret mission but everybody on three continents seems to know about it. Jackie and his companions can never get forty winks without having thugs climbing through their windows or breaking down their doors. Jackie fights them off as best he can. His karate expertise, his dazzling speed, and his acrobatics are the heart and soul of the film. Getting into impossible situations and getting out of them are what Jackie Chan films are all about. He does amazing things like kicking a gun out of an opponent's hand, turning a somersault, and catching the weapon before it hits the floor. No one in the audience really worries about his safety, even when he is up against a dozen goons, because he is so versatile and so durable. His strategy seems to be to seek the high ground. He climbs up walls, scaffoldings, and anything else that is vertical with the agility of an orangutan. He gives the screen a dizzying new dimension because he seems capable of walking on walls and ceilings.

Jackie and his photogenic girlfriends are carrying a brass key that will open the vault full of gold—if they can ever find it among all those sand dunes. Their quest takes them out into the middle of the Sahara Desert, where they are still pursued by Arabic villains, German villains, and other villains of uncertain ancestry. Part of the confusion about ethnic identities and national affiliations is due to the fact that they are all speaking dubbed-in English, a language which few of them can really understand.

At last Jackie and his clinging female companions find themselves inside an vast, multi-level underground military installation where skeletons in old German army uniforms show that they have come to the right place. This complex World War II facility evidently served as a munitions storage depot as well as a testing site for buzz bombs which would be larger and more advanced than the V2 rockets that rained down on Great Britain in the closing years of World War II. The most spectacular scenes in the film involve Jackie and opponents being blown back and forth in a huge wind tunnel built to test the super buzz bomb. As always, Jackie does his own stunts and seems to be enjoying himself immensely. The big brain behind Jackie's assailants is Adolf (Alfred Brel Sanchez), the only surviving German soldier who took part in hiding the stolen gold. All the others had been ruthlessly executed by Elsa's grandfather on the precept that "dead men tell no tales."

Operation Condor is one of the new movies made in the spirit of non-violent violence to avoid an R rating and to make the film acceptable for future family viewing via television and videotapes. Although there is nothing but aggressive action from start to finish, no one gets killed on camera or even seriously bruised. In one scene, Elsa empties a machine gun inside a crowded hotel lobby and shreds all the furniture without killing or wounding any of the guests or staff. This new kind of pseudo-violence might be even more harmful to young minds than the old-fashioned kind full of blood and gore. The replacement might conceivably give youngsters the notion that violence is good fun and not really dangerous.

After the hero and heroines escape from the underground base, the whole place, quite predictably, explodes. The villain turns out to be a sort of latter-day Captain Nemo who elects to destroy everything and himself along with it. All those beautiful gold ingots are buried along with the villain and his henchmen. This, of course, is pretty violent stuff—but all the viewers see is a sand dune collapsing. There are no interior shots in which screaming men are smashed by falling objects made of balsa wood and papier-mache. The fact that Jackie failed to accomplish his mission is a disappointment. Many viewers, no doubt, would have preferred to see him bring back at least some of those 240 tons of gold ingots. However, such an ending might have presented a logistical problem which the filmmakers decided to evade by blowing up the whole set. (It would have taken 1,200 camels to haul all that gold.) After all, Harrison Ford did not manage to bring back the lost Ark of the Covenant either.

Operation Condor is a big-budget production for a karate film, but it still has the quality of a comic strip or an old Saturday matinee serial. Jackie Chan is becoming an international star because of his daredevil stunts, his comic spirit, and his winsome personality. He deserves to be given better scripts and may soon be in a position to demand them. Even though his knowledge of English may be extremely limited, he ought to be able to manage as well as superstar Arnold Schwarzenegger.

The closing credits are accompanied by outtakes showing Jackie flubbing some of his stunts. These bloopers and outtakes accompanying closing crawlers are an increasingly popular innovation. The intent seems to be to get the audience to stick around to see how many technicians were involved in the production. Consumers who buy or rent videotapes want to feel assured they are seeing a major feature film produced on a big budget. In the case of *Operation Condor*, the bloopers and outtakes also serve to reinforce the implicit message that this was just a movie and nobody really got seriously hurt.

—Bill Delaney

CREDITS

Jackie: Jackie Chan
Ada: Carol Cheng
Elsa: Eva Cobo de Garcia
Momoko: Shoko Ikeda
Adolf: Alfred Brel Sanchez

Origin: Hong Kong
Released: 1991, 1997
Production: Leonard Ho; released by Dimension Films
Direction: Jackie Chan
Screenplay: Jackie Chan and Edward Tang
Cinematography: Wong Ngok Tai
Editing: Cheung Yiu Chung
Music: Stephen Edelman
Sound: Glenn T. Morgan
Stunt coordinator: Jackie Chan
MPAA rating: PG-13
Running Time: 92 minutes

REVIEWS

Boxoffice. September, 1997, p.121.
Chicago Tribune. July 18, 1997, p. 5.
Entertainment Weekly. August 1, 1997,p. 50.
Los Angeles Times. July 18, 1997, p. F14.
New York Times. July 18, 1997, p. C14.
USA Today. July 18, 1997, p. 4D.

Oscar and Lucinda

They were two improbable dreamers who dare to play the game of love, faith, and chance.—Movie tagline

A Dream. A Lie. A Wager. Love.—Movie tagline

"The most adventuresome movie yet made by one of the best filmmakers of her time. A vibrant period piece with wit and style to burn."—Kevin Thomas, *Los Angeles Times*

"Exquisitely directed . . . gorgeously photographed. Offers a steady supply of visual surprises."—Janet Maslin, *New York Times*

"One of the most beautiful films. Cate Blanchett is a captivating presence."—John Anderson, *Newsday*

"Two thumbs up. Wonderful performances by Ralph Fiennes and Cate Blanchett."—*Siskel & Ebert*

"A rarity. One of the 10 best films of the year. A sight to behold . . . Turns sure-thing expectations into a game of chance. Ralph Fiennes and Cate Blanchett are fierce and funny."—Richard Schickel, *Time*

"A more rewarding costume drama than *The Piano* or *Wings of the Dove*."—Amy Taubin, *Village Voice*

Oscar (Ralph Fiennes), an Anglican priest, and Lucinda (Cate Blanchett), an Australian heiress, form an unusual friendship after they discover they share the same passion for gambling in *Oscar and Lucinda.*

Peter Carey's 1988 Booker Prize-winning novel, *Oscar and Lucinda*, would seem to be a challenge for adaptation to film. Running over 400 pages and telling the complex, intertwining stories of two misfits in mid-19th century England and Australia, the novel could easily have been turned into an unwieldy, meandering film. However, director Gillian Armstrong and screenwriter Laura Jones have done an admirable job of bringing to life the two protagonists and streamlining the plot. While some of the psychological depth of the characters is missing, the essence of the story remains in all of its offbeat charm.

We first meet Oscar Hopkins and Lucinda Leplastrier as children. Oscar grows up in Devon, England, where his father, Theophilus (Clive Russell) is the head of a strict religious sect called the Plymouth Brethren. Through a childhood game of chance, Oscar believes he is called to be an Anglican and rebels against his father by seeking out the local minister, Hugh Stratton (Tom Wilkinson). As a little girl in Australia, Lucinda receives a piece of glass known as a Prince Rupert's drop. Immune to the whack of a hammer, it shatters into smithereens when pliers are applied to it. Thus begins her obsession with the fragility and beauty of glass.

As a young adult studying to be a minister, Oscar (Ralph Fiennes) becomes fascinated with gambling at the racetrack. The wagering itself is the thrill—after all, he puts most of his winnings into the church's poor box. Meanwhile, Lucinda (Cate Blanchett) inherits a small fortune when her mother dies, and, inspired by her lifelong love of glass, buys the Prince Rupert's Glassworks in Sydney. The Reverend Dennis Hasset (Ciaran Hinds) aids her in the venture, and they become close friends. Lucinda, too, loves to gamble, especially in card games, and ultimately this passion brings the title characters together. Gambling for them becomes a metaphor for the larger idea of taking chances in life, of making a leap of faith, and finally of risking oneself for love.

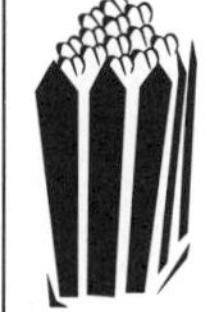

Narrator: "In order that I exist, two gamblers, one obsessive, one compulsive, must meet."

Lucinda goes to England to purchase equipment for her glassworks, and, on the return trip to Australia, Oscar is taking the same ship to do God's work in Sydney (he sees it as a penance for his gambling). They meet on board when Lucinda is looking for a card game and happens to run into Oscar. Feeling guilty, she asks him to hear her confession. As she confesses the sin of gambling, Oscar cannot control himself. He moans and fidgets upon seeing he has found a kindred spirit. Instead of absolving her, he justifies what she has done by comparing common wagering to betting on the existence of God: "Where is the sin? We bet. It is all in Pascal, you know. We bet that there is a God. We bet our life on it." Lucinda is stunned at what she is hearing but pleasantly surprised (Cate Blanchett's startled reaction is priceless), and she soon has a partner in card playing. This scene is wonderful in the way it lays out their passion in all its euphoria and giddiness as they come alive in each other's presence.

In Australia, things do not go well. The bishop sends Hasset away, and so Lucinda is left friendless. When she meets Oscar in a Chinese gambling establishment, they start to play cards again, which becomes a scandal when two people in his congregation catch them and Oscar is defrocked.

Fiennes gives a performance unlike any of his previous career highlights. Oscar is nervous and fidgety, oftentimes shy and timid like a little boy. He exhibits a childlike enthusiasm, an openness, and a sweet naiveté, especially in his very tentative courtship of Lucinda. As Gillian Armstrong remarked in an interview on PBS's "Charlie Rose" (Dec. 9, 1997), "I had to find this person that could be both a nerd who was odd and people laughed at him and yet at the same time he is ultimately a romantic hero and has inner strength and goodness." In the novel, Oscar is a much weaker, even pathetic creature oppressed by those in authority. For example, he holds a clerk's job, where he is scorned and demeaned. It becomes a major source of humiliation, and Lucinda feels sorry for him when she visits him there.

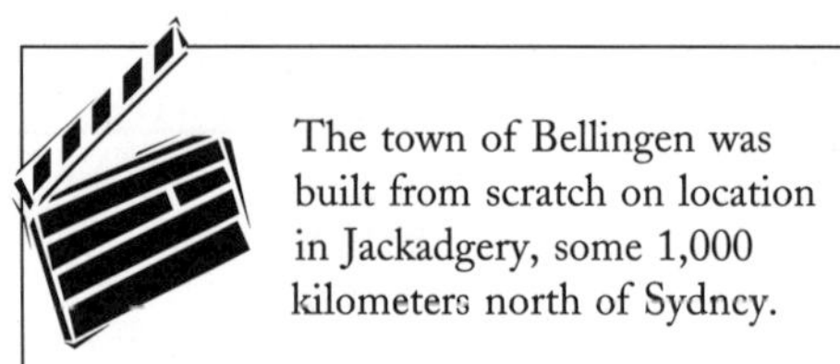
The town of Bellingen was built from scratch on location in Jackadgery, some 1,000 kilometers north of Sydney.

Cate Blanchett is a fine match as Lucinda. (She made her feature-film debut earlier in 1997 in Bruce Beresford's *Paradise Road.*) Lucinda is a determined and feisty woman, an entrepreneur, and a dreamer who is both strong-willed and vulnerable to her passions. Blanchett has a radiance that lights up her face when Lucinda is excited about her glassworks or when she is falling in love with Oscar.

While the script often fails to spell out character motivations that are clear in the novel—Oscar and Lucinda's complex feelings about each other, for example—it develops character through some stunning visual motifs, like Oscar and Lucinda's contrasting relationship to water. Oscar has a fear of water from his youth when Theophilus discards his departed wife's clothing into the sea, and, in a visually exciting scene, we experience his seasickness on board the voyage to Australia. Lucinda, on the other hand, embraces water. When we first see the adult Lucinda, she is immersed in water and blowing bubbles, and even her costume design reinforces this motif in the rich blues she wears.

There are no overt love scenes between Oscar and Lucinda. They share a tentative romance and some tender kisses, but, when Oscar sees all the letters Lucinda writes to Hasset, Oscar becomes discouraged. He mistakenly believes she is in love with Hasset and embarks on a mad plan to win Lucinda's love. He proposes building a glass church and transporting it to Hasset in Bellingen since he has no permanent church structure. The outrageous idea, of course, is captivating to Lucinda, whose love of glass makes her wager her inheritance on the scheme. "We are mad to think of it," Lucinda jubilantly declares in a line that sums up their passions.

The expedition is led by Jeffris (Richard Roxburgh), a tyrant who kills the natives in his way, mocks Oscar, and forces laudanum on him. However, he is actually far more mean-spirited in the novel, in which his mistreatment of Oscar starts when the defrocked Oscar works under him as a clerk. Oscar kills Jeffris after an altercation in a bar and ultimately finishes the journey with his expedition partner, Percy (Bille Brown). Because Oscar's job as a clerk is lost in the adaptation and the tension between Oscar and Jeffris is not very well-developed, the killing lacks the deeper resonance that it has in the novel and the sense that it is the culmination of a long and bitter relationship.

The end of the journey produces the film's most beautiful image—the glass church travelling down river. This is the fulfillment of Oscar and Lucinda's dream, the embodiment of all the passions that drive them—love of God, the beauty of glass, and the thrill of gambling. Oscar delivers the church to Hasset, now married and thus somewhat embarrassed to receive such a resplendent gift from a woman. Oscar is physically weak from the long journey and is cared for by Miriam Chadwick (Josephine Byrnes), a two-time widow working as a governess and looking for a husband. She practically forces herself sexually on the near-comatose, sunburned Oscar, and, in his naiveté, he feels obligated to marry her. Miriam is a minor character in the novel as well, but at least she is given more background story so we better understand her motivations. In the film, we are left with the awkward sense

CREDITS

Oscar Hopkins: Ralph Fiennes
Lucinda Leplastrier: Cate Blanchett
Rev. Dennis Hasset: Ciaran Hinds
Hugh Stratton: Tom Wilkinson
Mr. Jeffris: Richard Roxburgh
Theophilus Hopkins: Clive Russell
Percy Smith: Bille Brown
Miriam Chadwick: Josephine Byrnes
Wardley-Fish: Barnaby Kay
Jimmy D'Abbs: Barry Otto
Narrator: Geoffrey Rush

Origin: Australia
Released: 1997
Production: Robin Dalton and Timothy White for Dalton Films, Australian Film Finance Corp. and New South Wales Film & Television Offices; released by Fox Searchlight
Direction: Gillian Armstrong
Screenplay: Laura Jones; based on the novel by Peter Carey
Cinematography: Geoffrey Simpson
Editing: Nicholas Beauman
Music: Thomas Newman
Production design: Luciana Arrighi
Costumes: Janet Patterson
Sound: Ben Osmo
Special effects supervisor: Steve Courtley
MPAA rating: R
Running Time: 132 minutes

that a seemingly insignificant character has suddenly become crucial to the final turns of the plot.

Before they marry, however, Oscar dies. In a touching scene, he goes into the glass church to pray for forgiveness for all of his sins and soon becomes trapped in the church when it starts to sink and he is unable to open the door. This produces the haunting image of Oscar enveloped by water; he has a vision of his estranged father and then of Lucinda, who reaches out to him as he dies.

The film departs from the even harsher ending of the novel, in which Lucinda is ruined. The coldhearted Miriam, formally engaged to Oscar, is able to take Lucinda's fortune because of the wager agreement she had made with Oscar. In the film, however, Hasset burns the agreement before Miriam, who is pregnant with Oscar's child, discovers it.

In an epilogue, the narrator informs us of Miriam's death (after she has seen her child), and it is implied that Lucinda will raise the boy. Our last image of Lucinda is of her frolicking with the child in the sea. Thus, the film gives us a hopeful ending, but it does not feel like a cop-out. It does rely on Miriam's suddenly unexplained death (a departure from the novel), but since she is a minor character and since Oscar's death itself relies on chance, it does not feel forced but rather like one final tragedy. The film's ending is actually quite elegant in the way it brings closure to Lucinda's story and suggests, through its water imagery, that Lucinda will have a positive influence on Oscar's child, that the son will not be encumbered by the fears of his father.

Oscar and Lucinda received generally favorable, if not overwhelming reviews. *Time*'s Richard Schickel was perhaps the most enthusiastic major critic and called the film "genuinely eccentric yet deeply insinuating." Nonetheless, *Oscar and Lucinda* got lost in the onslaught of year-end releases, and this quirky, oddly beautiful, if somewhat uneven film never found the audience it deserved.

—*Peter N. Chumo II*

AWARDS AND NOMINATIONS

Academy Awards 1997 Nominations: Costume Design

REVIEWS

Chicago Tribune. January 23, 1998, p. 4.
Entertainment Weekly. January 16, 1998, p. 49.
Los Angeles Times. December 31, 1997, p. F8.
New York Times. December 31, 1997, p. E5.
New Yorker. January 12, 1998, p. 84.
People. January 19, 1998, p. 18.
Rolling Stone. January 22, 1998, p. 62.
San Francisco Chronicle. January 23, 1998.
Time. December 22, 1997.
Variety. December 8, 1997, p. 110.
Village Voice. January 6, 1998, p. 68.

Other Voices, Other Rooms

The heart is deceitful, who can know it?—Movie tagline

"Powerful . . . poetic . . . superby evokes 1930's life in the Deep South."—Emanuel Levy, *Variety*

Other Voices, Other Rooms, Truman Capote's first novel, has been made into a sensitive, if still slight film. It is set in the lush landscape of Louisiana, where Joel Sansom (David Speck), thirteen-years-old and lonely, has come to stay with his father after his mother's death. Joel's father, however, is nowhere to be seen. Instead Cousin Amy (Anna Thomson) and Cousin Randolph (Lothaire Bluteau) watch over him. They keep putting off Joel's questions about his father. Joel is only told that he will see his father after he recovers from his illness.

Joel finds company in Zoo (April Turner), a black cook, and Idabell (Aubrey Dollar), the local tomboy. Both characters, however, reinforce Joel's sense of alienation. He has nothing to do, really, and he has no grounding in reality. Even his education is taken over in a desultory way by the languid Randolph.

The setting evokes all the cliches about Southern Gothic and the special decadence of New Orleans and its surroundings. Gradually Joel is able to piece together what has happened to his father. It would be a shame to give away any of the details, though, because what little drama the film contains is wrapped up in Joel's slow, agonized understanding of his family history.

Neither plot nor theme are especially distinguished in the novel or the film. Randolph has charm, but it wears thin when all he has to offer is pleasant talk day after day. Even Cousin Amy, who is hopelessly enraptured with Randolph, complains that they have nothing to do, nowhere to go. All Randolph gives in reply are soothing words and also a brief dance with Amy when she is distraught.

Randolph: "Everything's going to be all right." Amy: "*When* is everything going to be all right?"

The movie is a pleasure to watch, thanks to the wonderful cinematography, direction, and editing. Nothing is hurried—which makes for a pleasant change from so many movies that depend on action scenes, jump cuts, and closeups to jazz up the drama. *Other Voices, Other Rooms* insists on a different sense of time, of a life that is leisurely with no point to it except to protect that sense of the leisurely. Without this lulling rhythm, Randolph would seem unbelievable.

Director David Rocksavage is a British peer: the Marquess of Cholmondeley and England's Lord Great Chamberlain.

Of course, in another sense Randolph is unreal. He is trying to stop time, to prevent Joel from growing up, and from learning what happened to his father. Cousin Amy abets him by confiscating the letters Joel writes to his aunt, thereby making the young boy's life even more claustrophobic.

Even though the setting of *Other Voices, Other Rooms* is exotic, Joel's plight is not as singular as might be supposed. His story is compelling when it dwells on that feeling that most children have—that adults are holding out on them, concealing the crucial facts that would make life more understandable. Joel would like some straight answers, and he cannot get them even when he arrives in town on a bus and asks the way to his father's plantation. The lady at the town eatery cannot resist teasing the boy and taking advantage of his ignorance.

Similarly, when Joel and Idabell decide to run away, they speak to feelings that many children have had—that there must be a way out, a new territory to explore—as Huckleberry Finn puts it at the end of Twain's novel. The friendship of Joel and Idabell might have been a stronger part of the film, for it provides a substantial counter to Randolph's effete vision. In writing the novel, Capote was drawing on his own friendship with the Southern novelist Harper Lee (author of the classic, *To Kill a Mockingbird*.

There are side issues in the film that are never developed. Why does Zoo, for example, leave the plantation and then return after she is raped? It is true that she is not treated very well by Cousin Amy, and that her flight parallels Joel's own itch to be gone. And it is understandable that Zoo would want to strike out for herself. She is smart and would like to be independent. But would she be fool enough to set off by herself on a road where she can be set upon by two white boys? Obviously, there is supposed to be a bond between Joel and Zoo, but somehow this black/white, servant/child relationship does not work the way it does in Carson McCuller's novel, *Member of the Wedding*.

It seems that *Other Voices, Other Rooms*, a first novel that is derivative of earlier Southern fiction, needed an adaptation that is not merely faithful but therapeutic, so to speak—taking the young author's work (Capote was twenty-four when the novel was published) not as a finished masterpiece but as a starting point for a more complex cinematic work.

—Carl Rollyson

CREDITS

Randolph: Lothaire Bluteau
Amy: Anna Thompson
Joel: David Speck
Zoo: April Turner
Idabell: Aubrey Dollar

Origin: USA
Released: 1995, 1997
Production: Peter Wentworth and David Rocksavage for Golden Eye Films; released by Artistic License Films
Direction: David Rocksavage
Screenplay: Sara Flanigan and David Rocksavage; based on the novel by Truman Capote
Cinematography: Paul Ryan
Editing: Cynthia Scheider
Music: Chris Hajian
Production design: Amy McGary
Costumes: Jane Greenwood
Sound: Jeffree Bloomer
MPAA rating: Unrated
Running Time: 98 minutes

REVIEWS

Boxoffice. January, 1998, p. 47.
Chicago Tribune. February 14, 1998, p. 32.
Los Angeles Times. December 19, 1997, p. F16.
New York Times. December 5, 1997, p. E10.
Variety. October 30, 1995, p. 74.
Village Voice. December 9, 1997, p. 79.

Out to Sea

Get ready to Rumba!—Movie tagline

"Hilarious!"—Mike Cidoni, *ABC-TV*

"In a summer overwhelmed with $100 million special effects pictures, here's a classic comedy with big laughs and a sweet story."—Roger Ebert, *Chicago Sun-Times*

"Lemmon and Matthau are a national treasure."—David Sheehan, *KCBS-TV*

"Don't miss it!"—Jim Ferguson, *KTTU-TV*

"Generates both laughter and emotion."—Kevin Thomas, *Los Angeles Times*

"Two thumbs up!"—*Siskel & Ebert*

Box Office: $29,016,459

Out to Sea is Jack Lemmon's and Walter Matthau's seventh outing as a comedy team, equaling the number (and to some degree the spirit) of the famous "Road" films starring Bing Crosby, Bob Hope and Dorothy Lamour. Lemmon and Matthau's first buddy film was *The Fortune Cookie* (1966), a box-office success which established their contrasting personas. Matthau would be the cynic and Lemmon the idealist, Matthau the grouch and Lemmon the patsy, Matthau the realist and Lemmon the dreamer. Matthau would be Bing and Lemmon would be Bob.

Lemmon and Matthau's biggest hit was *The Odd Couple* (1968), which their contrasting personalities and combined chemistry turned into a minor classic and spawned a long-running television series with the same title. *The Front Page* (1974), a remake of the Howard Hawks' classic *His Girl Friday* (1940), also had Lemmon and Matthau well cast as friendly enemies. *Buddy Buddy* (1981) was one they would prefer to gorget. Both had parts in Oliver Stone's controversial *JFK* (1991) but not as a comedy team. *Grumpy Old Man* (1993) successfully paired the now aging actors, but the sequel *Grumpier Old Men* (1995) lacked humor and might have been called "Sadistic Old Men" instead. It looked as if Lemmon and Matthau were getting too old to attract young viewers and had lost the magic they had together.

Charlie to Herb: "As dance hosts, it's our job to flirt with all the classy broads."

Now with *Out to Sea*, Lemmon and Matthau are right back in form. They look rejuvenated and are really funny again. All that was needed was the right script, the right situation. They have shuffled off the heavy coil of decrepit old age haunting them in *Grumpier Old Men*. They are not only funny again but appear to be eminently bankable again. In fact, they were working on a sequel to their classic *The Odd Couple* even before *Out to Sea* was released across the nation.

It takes awhile for the pair to get out to sea. The film opens at beautiful Santa Anita Racetrack in Arcadia, where Charlie (Matthau) cons a pari-mutuel clerk into comping him a ten-dollar bet on a very long longshot—which wins. Charlie's lucky day lasts only minutes before he bumps into a tough creditor who snatches his wad of hundred-dollar bills and tells him he still owes three thousand dollars more—or else. Deciding he needs a little vacation for his health, Charlie shows up at Herb's (Jack Lemmon's) house with a couple of "free" cruise tickets. Herb's quaint furnishings effectively characterize him as a thrifty, inhibited recluse—everything his brash, insensitive brother-in-law is not.

Herb and Charlie have nothing in common except their relationship to Herb's deceased wife. Herb, a retired Gimbel's department-store clerk, tolerates his sponging brother-in-law out of respect for the memory of the wife whom he still mourns. He is naturally suspicious of Charlie's "free" tickets but allows himself to get conned into the trip, only to discover once they are aboard that Herb has signed them up to work their passage by being "dance hosts." Herb is out to marry a rich widow and knows that a cruise ship is the ideal place to meet lonely women. When Charlie reminds Herb of the trivial fact that Herb can't dance, his brother-in-law reveals his motif for dragging Charlie along. Charlie is an excellent dancer who won contests with his wife when she was alive. Herb expects Charlie to give him a crash course in ballroom dancing in their stateroom. This leads to one funny scene in which the two men are caught dancing in each other's arms and are presumed to be a couple of closet queens.

The film's concept allows Lemmon and Matthau to be funny together as well as separate, unlike the situation in *Grumpier Old Men* in which they had little to do but harass each other. Predictably, both men become involved in shipboard romances. Charlie meets Liz (Dyan Cannon), a sexy divorcee, and Herb meets Vivian (Gloria De Haven), a sensitive widow who, like himself, had thought there was no more room for romance in her life. The love affairs are complicated by the fact that both men are trying to pass themselves off as big shots rather than members of the crew.

Critics were nearly unanimous in their praise of Brent Spiner, who plays Godwyn, the ambitious, unscrupulous cruise director who doubles as a crooner and drill sergeant for the identically dressed squadron of dance hosts. Kevin Thomas of the *Los Angeles Times* wrote that "Spiner is so hilarious he comes close to stealing the show"—quite a feat when up against old pros like Matthau and Lemmon. With his wide mustache and simpering manner, Spiner resembles the prissy, uptight character actor Franklin Pangborn who played similar roles in comparably silly, escapist Hollywood comedies of the 1930s and 1940s.

This is the 10th film that Lemmon and Matthau have done together.

Godwyn immediately recognizes Charlie and Herb as a couple of potential freeloading loafers. "I'm your worst nightmare," he tells them, "a song-and-dance man raised on an army base." If they fail to toe the line they will end up as paying passengers. The ultra-conservative Herb is horrified to learn that if he refuses to work as a sort of gigolo/taxi dancer he will have to pay the full fare—which amounts to over five thousand dollars. Like Charlie Chaplin in *Monsieur Verdoux* (1947), both Charlie and Herb have to conduct their love affairs on the run, sometimes diving for cover behind the furniture when in danger of being caught on the wrong deck at the wrong time.

By far the funniest scene is the one in which Herb is forced to give up his flagrant malingering and take to the dance floor. He ends up doing his impression of the rhumba with none other than Mrs. Carruthers (Rue McClanahan), owner of the cruise liner. He drags her back and forth across the dance floor like a cave man abducting an unwilling bride. There is no synchronism between the music and his relentless stalking gait. But the bedraggled lady, who resembles one of the snooty matrons the Marx Brothers loved to bedevil, believes his explanation that he is dragging her through the latest steps from Brazil.

Cinematographer Lajos Koltai's camera work gives the audience the illusion of being on a luxury cruise in tropical waters. In this respect the film hearkens back to some of Hollywood's oldest features, like *Flying Down to Rio* (1933). Many scenes were actually shot aboard the luxurious Westerdam while on a cruise. *Out to Sea* is pure escapism. It says nothing. It has no redeeming social significance. Older viewers might almost expect to see Eugene Pallette and Edward Everett Horton aboard the ship, dressed in immaculate white dinner jackets. Wide-angle shots across the tranquil blue ocean give *Out to Sea* an entirely different feel from that of chilly *Grumpy Old Men* and its depressing sequel. For an added touch of nostalgia, the filmmaker has found places for many old-timers, including Gloria De Haven, Hal Linden, Edward Mulhare, Rue McClanahan, Elaine Stritch, and the still agile dancer Donald O'Connor.

Both shipboard romances fizzle out when the women discover that their lovers are not what they intend to be. But it turns out that Liz was at least as big a phoney as Charlie. She was practically broke and had come on this cruise looking for a rich husband. The film ends like many of the old Hollywood comedies with a preposterous chase scene. The disillusioned ladies are taking a chartered seaplane back to the States, while the impassioned lovers are recklessly chasing the taxiing plane in a motor launch stolen from the cruise liner. (By this time these two loose cannons have pulverized poor Godwyn, who has lost his job and nearly lost his sanity.)

Charlie and Herb have undergone a sea change. The music, the dancing, the rocking of the waves, the moonlight, the atmosphere of leisure and luxury have all contributed to their transformation. Their characters have also rubbed off on each other. Charlie has become more of a romanticist, while Herb has become enough of a realist to relinquish his love affair with a ghost. Herb has discovered that he can fall in love again. Confirmed bachelor Charlie has discovered that he can fall in love at all.

CREDITS

Herb: Jack Lemmon
Charlie: Walter Matthau
Liz: Dyan Cannon
Vivian: Gloria DeHaven
Godwyn: Brent Spiner
Mavis: Elaine Stritch
Mac: Hal Linden
Jonathan: Donald O'Connor
Carswell: Edward Mulhare
Mrs. Carruthers: Rue McClanahan

Origin: USA
Released: 1997
Production: John Davis and David T. Friendly for Davis Entertainment Company; released by 20th Century Fox
Direction: Martha Coolidge
Screenplay: Robert Nelson Jacobs
Cinematography: Lajos Koltai
Editing: Anne V. Coates
Music: David Newman
Production design: James Spencer
Art direction: William F. Mathews
Costumes: Jane Robinson
Sound: Jim Webb
Choreography: Kim Blank
MPAA rating: PG-13
Running Time: 109 minutes

Robert Nelson Jacobs' classic shipboard farce is just what the doctor ordered to rejuvenate Matthau and Lemmon. There are no younger characters in the cast to make the principals seem older by contrast. In *Grumpy* and *Grumpier*, the young viewers were laughing at old people, but in *Out to Sea* they are laughing with them.

The long crawler of closing credits is accompanied by the bloopers and outtakes which are becoming a popular feature of Lemmon-Matthau films and may become standard for Hollywood films in general. The closing crawler is further enlivened with shots of all the principals dancing, including Matthau, who is obviously not as awkward as he pretended to be. These seemingly endless lists of credits, including everybody who moved a lamp or wielded a hammer, are something nobody reads anyways (except in Westwood Village, Century City, and a few other spots around Los Angeles). Evidently the calculating motive behind this amusing innovation is to impress upon viewers that these are "Big-Budget Feature Films," so that the products may enjoy greater longevity at the video outlets.

—Bill Delaney

REVIEWS

Boxoffice. September, 1997, p. 126.
Chicago Tribune. July 2, 1997, p. 2.
Entertainment Weekly. July 11, 1997, p. 44.
The Hollywood Reporter. June 30, 1997, p. 5.
Los Angeles Times. July 2, 1997, p. F12.
New York Times. July 2, 1997, p. B1.
People. July 14, 1997, p. 19.
San Francisco Chronicle. July 2, 1997, p. E1.
USA Today. July 2, 1997, p. 5D.
Variety. June 30, 1997, p. 65.

Paperback Romance; Lucky Break

Some fall in love the hard way.—Movie tagline

If she can hide her past, and he can hide his present, they just might have a future.—Movie tagline

"Hilarious!"—John Anderson, *Los Angeles Times*

"Gia Carides is a brilliant comic actress, and her sparkling performance is a triumph."—Louise Mae Reamoinn, *The Star-Ledger*

Screened at the Toronto Film Festival back in 1994, *Paperback Romance* starring Gia Carides and Anthony LaPaglia was originally called *Lucky Break*. Considering a good deal of the film's humor comes from the heroine's physical handicap, it seems a much more apropos title. Leave it to the Australians—a country proving itself to be the King of Screwball Comedy—to play polio for laughs.

Eddie to Sophie: "You're the most fascinating woman I'm ever likely to meet."

Sitting alone in the public library, the attractive Sophie (Gia Carides) reads her raunchy erotica aloud as she feverishly pens her latest entry. Fascinated by this tale of torrid sex is Eddie (Anthony LaPaglia), a charming rogue who seems to have a few secrets of his own.

Eddie's intrigued by this comely lass who has quite the way with words. At first tempted to just walk away without saying anything (or so he tells Sophie), he finds himself unable to leave. "You're the most fascinating woman I'm ever likely to meet," Eddie confesses. He asks her out for coffee and some undoubtedly great conversation, but she declines—despite her obvious attraction to this smooth stranger. When he is gone, we suddenly understand her shyness. She wears a leg brace, the result of childhood polio. The clanging of her crutches as she leaves the library underscores her fear of rejection.

Regretting her initial shyness, Sophie does some real-life detective work and discovers that her dream lover is a high-priced jeweler whose store is in the local mall. She is about to confront her fears when Eddie's brittle fiancee Gloria (Rebecca Gibney in a thankless role) shows up at the store. In her haste to flee, Sophie takes a bizarre tumble from a shopping mall balcony. With her leg now in a plaster cast, the spunky Sophie turns what could be disastrous for some less imaginative types into the perfect ruse.

Sophie decides to tell Eddie that she broke her leg skiing. When Gloria discovers the truth, Sophie pleads with her to not to tell because she is only hoping for a short-term fling with Eddie anyway. But things take on a bizarre turn when Eddie nearly slices off his tongue on Sophie's cast during a romantic interlude. It is puzzling as to how this really happens, but the end result is that Eddie then speaks in a garbled slur for a sizeable portion of the movie.

Paperback Romance relies far too heavily on sexual fantasy sequences that spring from Sophie's twisted imagination as she replays her misadventures as if they were yet another scenario for her books. They distract from the story and honestly, Ms. Carides is far more interesting to watch than some faux Greek God. She possesses a wonderful comedic timing, combined with a sweet vulnerability that is pleasing to watch. She is perhaps best known—but not necessarily easily identified—as the spiky-haired blonde rival from Baz Luhrmann's *Strictly Ballroom* (1992).

CREDITS

Sophie: Gia Carides
Eddie: Anthony LaPaglia
Gloria Wrightman: Rebecca Gibney
Kate: Sioban Tuke
Yuri: Jacek Koman
Benny: Michael Edward Stevens

Origin: Australia
Released: 1994, 1997
Production: Bob Weis for Generation Films; released by Goldwyn Entertainment Company
Direction: Ben Lewin
Screenplay: Ben Lewin
Cinematography: Vincent Monton
Editing: Peter Carrodus
Production design: Peta Lawson
Art direction: Victoria Hoboay
Costumes: Anna Borghesi
Music: Paul Grabowsky
MPAA rating: R
Running Time: 87 minutes

Anthony LaPaglia fares less well with his part as the shady dealer of stolen jewels. He tries and definitely has his moments, but his character is too thinly sketched. He is charming in a small screen way (which might explain his recent success on television's "Homicide"). With their obvious chemistry, it is no surprise to learn that Carides and LaPaglia share an off-screen personal involvement.

Paperback Romance is essentially a morality tale about honesty in relationships—and the disastrous results of withholding important parts of ourselves from our lovers. There are some genuinely funny moments, but overall the tone is uneven. In many ways this film is similar to *My Best Friend's Wedding* (1997), particularly in their preference for dark humor. Both Jules (the Julia Roberts character) and Sophie share some unsympathetic qualities, most notably their willingness to be deceitful while pursuing the men they desire. By the end of this tale, however, it is not at all a surprise that these two conniving and deceitful people seem like a match made in heaven, or rather, in hell.

Paperback Romance is replete with the kind of pratfall humor that has marked many Australian romantic comedies of late. Director/writer Ben Lewin, whose last film was *The Favor, the Watch, and the Very Big Fish* (1991), displays a willingness to find the humor in wearing leg braces that is audacious, and quite frankly, the real reason to see this otherwise formulaic romance.

—*Patricia Kowal*

REVIEWS

Los Angeles Times. August 15, 1997, p. F8.
New York Times. August 15, 1997, p. C8.
San Francisco Chronicle. August 29, 1997, p. D3.
San Francisco Examiner. August 29, 1997, p. D3.

Paradise Road

In a time of war, an extraordinary group of women turned a song of hope into a symphony of triumph.—Movie tagline

Courage echoes forever.—Movie tagline

"Unforgettable! A riveting performance by Glenn Close!"—Garrett Glaser, *CBS-TV*

"Not since *Schindler's List* or *The Bridge On the River Kwai* has there been so much power on the big screen!"—Don U. Stotter, *Entertainment Time-Out*

"Exceptional! A brilliant movie! Cate Blanchett and Jennifer Ehle are new faces to remember!"—Bruce Williamson, *Playboy*

Box Office: $2,007,100

A producer of Bruce Beresford's *Paradise Road* stated that much of the Australian writer/director's work "revolves around women." While this is not true of all his films, one need only remember characters like Miss Daisy Werthan (Jessica Tandy) in 1989's Oscar-winning *Driving Miss Daisy* or Lenny, Babe and Meg (Diane Keaton, Sissy Spacek and Jessica Lange, respectively) in *Crimes of the Heart* (1986) to understand what he meant. That is one of the reasons Beresford was approached with the true story of a group of women who found salvation in song while in an internment camp in Japanese-held Sumatra during World War II. While *Paradise Road* recalls *The Bridge On the River Kwai* (1957) among other films, the work that is immediately brought to mind is "Playing for Time," the excellent 1980 film made for television about a women's orchestra in Auschwitz. Beresford's film does not come close to reaching the heights of these two superb cinematic achievements, for while the events he recounts are admirable and interesting, they are not fashioned into a film which successfully sustains that interest.

Margaret: "I've tried, but I just can't bring myself to hate people. The worse they behave, the sorrier I feel for them."

Paradise Road begins with an elegant dinner party in Singapore's Raffles Hotel in February of 1942. As dancers swirl by the camera, Beresford begins introducing his film's main characters. Susan McCarthy (Cate Blanchett), a sweet young Australian country girl blushes when a soldier flirts with her, while Rosemary Leighton-Jones (Jennifer Ehle, daughter of the great Rosemary Harris), a beautiful English rose, beams in the arms of her adoring, adored husband. To underscore the latter couple's feelings for each other, a singer on stage croons about being "mad about the boy" and feeling deliriously happy and young. At a nearby table, immensely-noble Brit Adrienne Pargiter (Glenn Close) sits with her husband and other couples and listens to the men put down the Japanese in racist terms. They are certain that the enemy is doubtlessly inferior and utterly inept, and so, while the Japanese are not far away, there is no chance that they can outwit the Allies. Somehow, Beresford's set-up of his story seems to be presented too quickly and drawn too neatly, as the singer's words and the excessive, sweeping pomposity of the stuffed shirts seem like oversized, neon signs pointing to what is to come down *Paradise Road.* Sure enough, bombs immediately begin exploding near the hotel, and the partygoers are shocked to learn that the Japanese have ringed the city instead of being driven back as previously reported. Woman and children leave immediately by boat, and everything on board is almost as sunny as the weather, with passengers playing cards and games, reading and enjoying their afternoon tea. When the women are told that the boat will soon be out of range of the Japanese, the audience instantly scans the skies, recognizing this statement as another instance of rather obvious foreshadowing. The vessel is promptly sunk by the enemy, and the passengers that survive are forced to dive overboard.

Film was shot primarily in Penang, Malaysia.

Pargiter, McCarthy and Leighton-Jones swim to Sumatra. After struggling through muck and dense vegetation, they are picked up by the enemy, who initially does not seem especially sinister. When the women are dropped off, however, they are roughed up, herded together with the other survivors of their ship, and forced to make a long trek across the countryside to an internment camp. Once there, they endure beatings and humiliations like having to go to the bathroom side-by-side perched atop little pots. Some succumb to malaria and fatigue. When one character risks her life to get quinine for another, she is burned alive for her efforts by the Japanese secret police. The uneasy, enforced mixture of nationalities, cultures, languages and classes causes further problems, resulting in suspicions, accusations and confrontations amongst the women. Amidst it all, Pargiter copes by humming Sir Edward Elgar's Violin Concerto. She and missionary Margaret Drummond (Pauline Collins), who both studied music, decide to form a vocal orchestra which will perform great works of classical music by singing the notes instead of playing them. This is a dangerous endeavor, as even gatherings for religious services and classes for the camp's few children are angrily dispersed by their wary captors. They must also overcome the skepticism of their fellow captives. When American Topsy Merritt states flippantly that she is "not in the mood for a sing along," she is told that "that is the point." Also, some women, lured by the promise of hot water, soap and generally better conditions, leave to become "friends" with the Japanese officers. (Unfortunately, Beresford does not delve into this fascinating choice, or the outcome and consequences of it for these women.) Finally, the vocal orchestra performs the famous Largo movement (also known as "Goin' Home") from Antonin Dvorak's Symphony No. 9, and the guards put down their guns and listen in awed silence. While the women are still captive physically, their spirits have found an escape. (The film utilized the original, handwritten vocal scores which survived the real-life ordeal.) Having obtained a degree of respect from some of their captors, other concerts are permitted, until the women are no longer capable of performing. After Drummond dies, the exhausted women form a slow procession behind her body and express themselves by rhythmically striking stones together in a final, spirited show of defiance and unity. Shortly before the war ends and the surviving women are liberated,

Leighton-Jones dies of a broken heart after seeing her true love on his way to being executed.

Paradise Road received mixed reviews, and did not even break the $2 million mark in its first two months of release. According to *Variety*, it never opened wider than 350 theaters during that period. All the actors do an acceptable job playing the characters as Beresford has written them, and therein lies one of the film's problems. For all the time that we spend in the camp with these people, we never seem to get far below the surface to full-bodied, engaging characterization. It is therefore too easy for the audience to simply observe what happens to the women instead of rooting for them. Even when the vocal orchestra succeeds in performing, there is not much of an emotional payoff for the audience, and Beresford fails to elicit the welling-up of emotion that he doubtlessly expected—and needed—to achieve. Glenn Close may play her role with a bit too much saintliness and stiff upper lip, but she is here, as always, a commanding performer. Just as admirable, but more appealing, is the character played by—and the performance given by—Pauline Collins (1988's *Shirley Valentine*). Cate Blanchett, with her refreshing, luminously-pretty face, stands out, as well, and one can say with certainty that she will soon be an A-list performer in Hollywood. *Paradise Road* takes a relatively small story about people and an achievement undeniably worth remembering and tries to stretch it to feature length. What Beresford recounts, at least, does not have the richness nor the dramatic intensity to do so successfully.

—*David L. Boxerbaum*

CREDITS

Adrienne Pargiter: Glenn Close
Margaret Drummond: Pauline Collins
Susan McCarthy: Cate Blanchett
Dr. Verstak: Frances McDormand
Topsy Merritt: Julianna Margulies
Rosemary Leighton-Jones: Jennifer Ehle
Mrs. Roberts: Elizabeth Sprigg
Celia Robers: Tessa Humphries
Oggi: Susie Porter
Colonel Hiroyo: Sab Shimono

Origin: Australia, USA
Released: 1997
Production: Sue Milliken and Greg Coote for Village Roadshow Pictures; released by Fox Searchlight
Direction: Bruce Beresford
Screenplay: Bruce Beresford
Cinematography: Peter James
Editing: Tim Wellburn
Music: Ross Edwards
Production design: Herbert Pinter
Art direction: Ian Gracie
Set decoration: Brian Edmonds
Costumes: Terry Ryan
Sound: Gary Wilkins
Visual effects coordinator: Brian Cox
MPAA rating: R
Running Time: 115 minutes

REVIEWS

Boxoffice. May 1997, p. 57.
Chicago Tribune. April 18, 1997, p. A7.
Detroit News. April 25, 1997, p. F1.
Entertainment Weekly. April 25, 1997, p. 46.
Los Angeles Times. April 11, 1997, p. F12.
New York Times. April 11, 1997, p. C12.
New Yorker. April 14, 1997, p. 89.
People. April 21, 1997, p. 23.
Rolling Stone. May 1, 1997, p. 59.
Sight and Sound. December, 1997, p. 50.
Time. April 14, 1997, p. 96.
USA Today. April 18, 1997, p. D3.
Variety. April 7, 1997, p. 42.
Village Voice. April 15, 1997, p. 72.
Wall Street Journal. April 11, 1997, p. A12.
Washington Post. April 18, 1997, p. C7.

The Peacemaker

In the fall of 1997, every nuclear device in the world will be accounted for . . . Except one.—Movie tagline

"Great action! Great suspense!"—Joel Siegel, *Good Morning America*

"Quite simply the most thrilling, and plausible, thriller Hollywood has ever made."—Michael Medved, *The New York Post*

"A breathless thriller."—Janet Maslin, *The New York Times*

"A red-hot thriller."—Peter Travers, *Rolling Stone*

"White-knuckle tension with plenty of smarts."—Gene Shalit, *Today Show*

"Put it at the top of your must see list . . . One of the best, most intelligent thrillers you'll see this year."—Jeffrey Lyons, *WNBC*

Box Office: $41,263,140

On September 7, 1997, General Aleksandr Lebed, the former secretary of Boris Yeltsin's Security Council, was interviewed on "60 Minutes" on CBS television and claimed that over 100 portable nuclear bombs had gone missing in Russia. But was Lebed telling the truth, or was this a spectacular hoax perpetrated to hype *The Peacemaker*, the first release of Steven Spielberg's Dream Works studio operation, William M. Arkin wanted to know, writing in *The Nation* on September 29? So why would "60 Minutes" want to promote this film? Because CBS producer Leslie Cockburn had written with her husband Andrew the book on which the movie was based, entitled *One Point Safe*. Of course it was up to viewers to decide whether on not to believe General Lebed, but the idea that such "perfect terrorist weapons" could be missing is extremely disturbing, even though Lebed's claim was dismissed by the C.I.A. and the State Department and denied by Russian Prime Minister Viktor Chernomyrdin and the Moscow Defense Ministry.

Regardless of how real such a threat may be, *The Peacemaker* proved to be the top grossing box-office feature the weekend it opened. The main reason for the film's popularity may have more to do with the casting and direction than with public anxiety about nuclear politics. The film starred George Clooney, from the top-rated television show "ER," who seems to be making a far more successful transition to motion pictures than one-time TV heartthrob David Caruso, who bolted from stardom on the ABC police series "NYPD Blue" to try his luck as a movie star. After two unmemorable movies, *Kiss of Death* (1995) and *Jade* (1995), Caruso returned to television to restore his dignity. Perhaps some television talents are not so impressive on the large screen, but Clooney's prospects seemed to be more promising.

Clooney's co-star is Nicole Kidman. In the ridiculous *Days of Thunder* (1989), she played a brain surgeon in love with a greaseball racer on the NASCAR circuit. In *The Peacemaker* she plays a brainy nuclear scientist, Dr. Julia Kelly, who works with Lieutenant Colonel Thomas Devoe (Clooney) to keep the United Nations from getting nuked by a mad terrorist, whose motives seem to be scrambled. "What do you want?" they ask him, but he has no coherent answer. Nor does the screenplay by Michael Schiffer, working in a Tom Clancy mode. His earlier work includes *Crimson Tide* (1995), which broached the threat of nuclear war in telling its story of a mutiny on a U.S. Navy submarine.

None the less, *The Peacemaker* proved to be a popular pacemaker, even against such still competition as *L.A. Confidential*, hailed by some critics as the year's best movie. Although *The Peacemaker* is in fact pretty conventional, it is still a well made action thriller about nuclear warheads hijacked off a train in the Ural Mountains by a renegade Russian General willing to sell them to the highest bidder. The film begins with the hijacking, as one train overcomes and overpowers another, transfers its deadly cargo after wasting a trainload of guards, then sends the ghost train down the tracks to a spectacular head-on collision, with an armed nuclear device that is timed to explode after the collision. However, there is a four-minute lapse between the collision and the explosion, said to be more deadly than Chernobyl (the legacy of which should never be trivialized in a silly Hollywood movie). Spy satellite photos tip off the Americans that what happened was in fact a terrorist hijacking, and not merely an accident. The warheads seem to be a truck headed for Iran.

Army intelligence officer Thomas Devoe (George Clooney) doesn't actually go by the book when tracking down Russian terrorists who have stolen nuclear warheads in the action drama *The Peacemaker*.

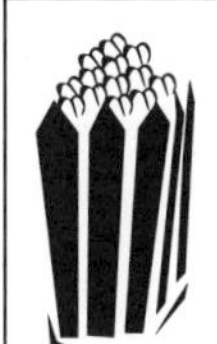

NSA Advisor Hamilton: "God, I miss the Cold War."

Devoe and Kelly trace the truck to a company in Vienna, where, after beating and brutalizing the company owner to get information about the truck's destination, they are chased by blackmarket thugs in BMWs that crash and burn. At this point Clooney could qualify for that demolition derby that was *Days of Thunder*, putting Kidman on familiar ground. But this is merely a prelude to more violence, when Clooney, leading a charge of choppers to intercept the truck, violates the airspace of the Federated Republics and has to outmaneuver a missile attack. But the choppers stop the truck and disable it on a bridge, so the mission is accomplished and the renegade Russian General killed, but one terrorist manages to escape with a warhead to former Yugoslavia. It is passed on to another terrorist who has managed to infiltrate the diplomatic service.

Feature film debut for veteran TV director Mimi Leder, who has been signed by DreamWorks for two more films.

That warhead is then smuggled from Sarajevo to New York City, hidden in diplomatically protected luggage by an angry terrorist named Dusan (Marcel Iures), who seems to want to nuke the United Nations headquarters, for reasons that are beyond comprehension, but seem to have something to do with the fact that Dusan's wife and daughter were killed by sniper fire on the streets of Sarajevo, another violation of good taste and good sense, since the film seems to trivialize the killing fields of former Yugoslavia and the agonies of "ethnic cleansing" and genocide. Dusan's politics, even his nationality, seems murky. He calls himself a Serb, a Croat, a Muslim, in an irrational videotaped statement he leaves behind, but whatever this anguished, demented terrorist is, he is a desperate man who intends to kill thousands of Americans as payback for his personal grief. How he came to negotiate with the Russian General Kodoroff (Alexander Balluev) to purchase the contraband warhead is never explained. How he came by the money to pay for it is never explained. How he managed to become part of the diplomatic mission to New York is suggested, but not really explained satisfactorily. Maybe it's only a movie? But one that seems to be dealing with extraordinarily important issues.

According to *Parade* magazine, the Kidman character "was modeled after Jessica Stern, 39, who headed the White House anti-nuclear-smuggling operation in the first Clinton Administration," but who bears no physical resemblance to Nicole Kidman. According to Stern the film does not provide "a realistic portrayal of what my job was." As a bureaucrat she did not go chasing after bombs, and, as a National Security Council official, she would not have been "capable of disabling a nuclear device."

On the other hand, Stern explained that the threat the film broaches is real: "The danger from loose nukes—illicit sales of nuclear materials or warheads—is very serious." She added that during her year with the NSC she did meet people willing "to risk their lives" in order to disable nuclear weapons. Moreover, she knew Special Forces intelligence officers who resembled the character played by George Clooney. And she warned that government "budget priorities do not reflect the fact that this is THE threat to international security."

The film was budgeted at $50 million, and reviewers were disappointed that this "doomsday suspenser," as *Variety* called it, was so utterly conventional. "Is It a Bomb?" Richard Corliss asked in the title of his *Time* magazine review. "No, but Dream Works' first film does misfire." *Entertainment Weekly* considered George Clooney merely a Bruce Willis clone, but praised director Mimi Leder's "pleasing flair for 'rhythmic' visual detail."

The producers would like viewers to believe that there is a serious political message behind this movie, but it's really just another action-adventure spectacle, shot in exotic locations such as Slovakia, Croatia, and Macedonia and featuring an international cast that includes Armin Mueller-Stahl from East Prussia and Marcel Iures from Romania, who gives the film's best performance as the crazed terrorist Dusan. "Next to Iures," Anthony Lane wrote in *The New Yorker*, "George Clooney looks ominously lightweight." Though the relationship between Clooney and Kidman is not exactly romantic (they are simply too busy trying to save the world), the chemistry is pretty good,

CREDITS

Thomas Devoe: George Clooney
Julia Kelly: Nicole Kidman
Dusan Gavrich: Marcel Iures
Alexsander Kodoroff: Alexander Baluev
Vlado Mirich: Rene Medvesek
Jerry Hamilton: Gary Werntz
Ken: Randall Batinkoff
General Garnett: Jim Haynie
CPN Beach: Michael Boatman
Dimitri Vertikoff: Armin Mueller-Stahl

Origin: USA
Released: 1997
Production: Walter Parkes and Branko Lustig; released by DreamWorks Pictures
Direction: Mimi Leder
Screenplay: Michael Schiffer
Cinematography: Dieter Lohmann
Editing: David Rosenbloom
Music: Hans Zimmer
Production design: Leslie Dilley
Costumes: Shelley Komarov
Sound: Tom Nelson, Brian Simmons
Stunt coordinator: G.A. Aguilar
MPAA rating: R
Running Time: 123 minutes

though one reviewer expected more "human spark."

The New Yorker considered *The Peacemaker* "a curious choice" as the début picture for Dream Works, "the thoroughbred studio set up by Steven Spielberg, David Geffen, and Jeffrey Katzenberg." The studio promised significance, but instead of taking the opportunity to break new ground, "they played it safe." As Desson Howe wrote in the *Washington Post*, this was not "the greatest movie to launch a would-be media empire," but "the jury is still out" on the new studio, awaiting the release of Steven Spielberg's *Amistad*, a "$38 million movie about slave revolt," scheduled for Christmas release. Even so *The Peacemaker* was competently directed by Mimi Leder, whose credentials are television-based, distinguished by the Emmy awards she has won for her work on "ER." Although political issues are simplified, the action sequences are well done.

—James M. Welsh

REVIEWS

Boxoffice. September, 1997, p. 32.
Boxoffice. October, 1997, p. 42.
Chicago Tribune. September 26, 1997, p. 4.
Detroit Free Press. September 26, 1997, p. 9C.
Detroit News. September 26, 1997, p. 5F.
Entertainment Weekly. October 3, 1997, p. 52.
Los Angeles Times. September 26, 1997, p. F1.
The Nation. September 29, 1997, p. 6.
The New York Times. September 26, 1997, p. B10.
The New Yorker. October 6, 1997, p. 125.
People. October 6, 1997, p. 25.
Rolling Stone. October 16, 1997, p. 116.
Sight and Sound. November, 1997, p. 49.
Time. September 29, 1997, p. 95.
Variety. September 22, 1997, p.37.
Village Voice. September 30, 1997, p. 84.
The Washington Post. September 26, 1997, p. C7.
Washington Post Parade. September 14, 1997, p. 14.
Washington Post Weekend. September 26, 1997, p. 49.

The Pest

What kind of freakazoid would let someone hunt him just to collect $50,000? Next question.—Movie tagline

"Outrageously funny! Get ready for some downright serious laughing, John Leguizamo is so crazy, this film should be certified pure wacky."—Ron Brewington, *American Urban Radio Networks*

"John Leguizamo is all the Marx Brothers rolled into one in *The Pest,* a rollicking, rude and politically incorrect comedy that's a non-stop laugh riot. 82 minutes of beautifully timed slapstick."—Bill Hoffman, *New York Post*

Box Office: $3,600,616

Like a Latino Bugs Bunny on speed, John Leguizamo (*Spawn* [1997], *William Shakespeare's Romeo and Juliet* [1996], *To Wong Foo, Thanks for Everything, Julie Newmar* [1995]) tears through this frenetic, fast-paced farce in record time, leaving a trail of scatological humor, tasteless parodies, and relentless raunch in his wake. Not for the faint of heart or squeamish of stomach, this vehicle for its talented comedian lead, at best, showcases Leguizamo's hilarious impersonations (a rabbi, a Chinese businessman, a blind charity case) and, at worst, is a never-ending parade of disgusting sight gags which, at the same time, equally denigrates just about every race, color and creed. Playing like a teen comedy, *The Pest* is best suited for those in the well under-30 crowd and hard-core Leguizamo fans.

The movie opens with Pestario "Pest" Vargas (Leguizamo) in the shower, dancing and doing a rap ode to his previously unsung talent as a con artist and first-class mimic. Pest's self-proclaimed "lovable" antics, paired with the crude humor packed into this brief scene (which is repeated again at the movie's end), plays like a music video version of the entire film. A small-time Miami scammer, Pest's unstoppable ego won't allow him to heed warnings from friends who tell him to lay low for awhile, at least until he repays the $50,000 he owes to the Scottish mob. The fearless Pest is soon out on the streets, looking for the next sucker he can scam with his rigged shell game. Meanwhile, also roaming the streets for suitable prey, is German eccentric Gustav Shank (Jeffrey Jones). In one of the film's most entertaining scenes, Gustav follows Pest, who flees his shell game when approached by two toughs in kilts, to a Chinese restaurant where Pest attempts to imitate an Oriental employee who is grieving over an accident with his pet duck.

Gustav orders out and is soon "entertaining" Pest at his spacious home, having convinced him that he is going to offer him a convenient $50,000 scholarship for college. In reality, Gustav is a "big-game" hunter looking to add a "Latinus Spicticus" to his human head collection in the movie's hackneyed plot straight from TV's "Gilligan's Island" (among others).

Once on Gustav's eerie island, where Pest thinks he is going to hunt with Gustav, Pest meets the bizarrely morbid Himmel (Edoardo Ballerini), Gustav's homosexual son. Himmel reveals an incident from his childhood in which Gustav locked him in a closet with his beloved pet snake and ordered Himmel to kill it. Himmel, who hates his father, befriends Pest and warns him that he's to be the hunted not the hunter. Soon, the chase is on, and Pest, on the run from the crazy German, has twenty-four hours to elude the bad guys and win the money or become a trophy on Gustav's wall. Some of the chase sequences are actually funny, but most are cliched and/or vulgar attempts at comedy. With Himmel's help, a boat, and plenty of vomiting, Pest gets off the island and the chase continues in Miami, where he meets up with buddies Ninja and Chubby and hides out at the house of his girlfriend Xantha's parents.

Posing as a radical black activist, a rabbi, and an Oriental businessman, Pest is chased by Gustav and the reluctant Himmel through a synagogue and nightclub. Desperate, Gustav brings the Scottish mob into the picture when he calls the Scottish "don" Angus (Charles Hallahan) and tells him Pest plans to skip town with the money he owes them. With everyone after him, the clever and wily Pest is never brought to his knees, and like a living cartoon, slithers out of every sticky situation unscathed. A furious Gustav finally kidnaps Pest's family, his girlfriend, and her parents, and the fast-thinking Pest must come to their rescue.

Extremely versatile, Leguizamo not only starred, but coproduced and co-created this story. Although perfectly cast as an impish con man, even Leguizamo's furious energy cannot keep this movie from sinking into lame parody, and is an unworthy vehicle for his considerable talents. Jones is the lone standout as the deranged Gustav, with supports Ballerini, Spears, and Hallahan doing as much as can be done with the little material they are given. What's really flawed is the over-the-top caricatures and overdone plot, which relies entirely too much on Leguizamo's talent to carry it. Pluses include the colorful Miami background (which gives the film an appropriate look), deft cinematography, and thankfully, the short run time, which makes the experience painful, but quick.

—Hilary Weber

CREDITS

Pestario Vargas: John Leguizamo
Gustav Shank: Jeffrey Jones
Himmel Shank: Edoardo Ballerini
Ninja: Freddy Rodriguez
Xantha Kent: Tammy Townsend
Mr. Kent: Joe Morton
Chubby: Aries Spears
Angus: Charles Hallahan

Origin: USA
Released: 1997
Production: Sid, Jon and Bill Sheinberg for The Bubble Factory; released by TriStar Pictures
Direction: Paul Miller
Screenplay: David Bar Katz
Cinematography: Roy H. Wagner
Editing: Ross Albert, David Rawlins
Music: Kevin Kiner
Production design: Rodger E. Maus
Art direction: Suzette Ervin
Costumes: Tom McKinley
Sound: Mark Ulano
MPAA rating: PG-13
Running Time: 82 minutes

REVIEWS

Boxoffice. April, 1997, p. 200.
Hollywood Reporter. February 11, 1997, p. 10.
Los Angeles Times. February 10, 1997, p. F4.
Variety. February 10, 1997, p. 64.

Picture Perfect

She was prepared for anything until love stormed in.—Movie tagline

"Smart, sharp, funny and wonderful. Jennifer Aniston has big-screen presence for days."—Mike Cidoni, *ABC-TV, Rochester*

"A warm, witty and wonderful romantic comedy. Jennifer is Hollywood's newest leading lady."—David Sheehan, *CBS-TV*

"Jennifer Aniston proves she is indeed a movie star. *Picture Perfect* is my favorite romantic comedy of the year."—Kathryn Kinley, *WPIX-TV, New York*

"This summer's perfect romantic comedy."—Don Stotter, *Entertainment Time-Out*

Kate (Jennifer Aniston) creates a fictitious relationship with Nick (Jay Mohr) in order to make the man of her dreams jealous in *Picture Perfect.*

Box Office: $31,404,556

Out of the entire cast of TV's "Friends," Jennifer Aniston seems to have enjoyed the most success in making the leap from the small screen to the movies (excluding Courteney Cox's appearances in the ensemble horror hits *Scream* (1996) and *Scream 2* (1997). After acclaimed supporting roles in two films (*She's the One* (1996) and *'Til There Was You*) (1997), Aniston gets top billing in the lightweight romantic comedy *Picture Perfect.*

Ms. Aniston stars as Kate Mosley, an ambitious and talented young woman who finds out that her career at a New York ad agency will go no further until she gets some personal commitments in her life (mortgage, kids, etc.). Her boss won't consider her for a promotion because he fears that with no tangible responsibilities, she could just pick up and leave the firm any time she feels like it. Even though she's come up with the winning slogan for the Gulden's mustard account, Kate is cut out of the actual campaign, until her co-worker Darcy (Illeana Douglas) fabricates a fiance from a Polaroid snapshot of Kate and a stranger. The random guy in the photo is Nick (Jay Mohr), a nice Boston-based videographer, who Kate met at a friend's wedding.

Pretending she's engaged to Nick, Kate not only gets her much deserved promotion, but she also wins the attention of the office lothario, Sam Mayfair (Kevin Bacon), who's only attracted to unavailable women. The caddish exec finds Kate's engaged status to be a major turn-on, but things get complicated when Nick accidentally becomes an overnight celebrity and her boss insists upon meeting him.

At this point Kate has to track Nick down, convince him to go along with the deception, and then stage a public breakup at the dinner with her boss. Of course, nothing goes as planned, and Nick finds himself actually falling for Kate.

Director and co-writer Glenn Gordon Caron (TV's "Moonlighting" keeps *Picture Perfect* moving with a light, breezy touch. Although the film has its share of TV moments and the premise is far-fetched, Caron infuses the film with enough wit and energy to make it all seem fresh and funny.

Aniston easily carries the picture with her expert comedic timing and surefire one-liners, not to mention her equally adoring wardrobe (featuring many teensy dresses with plunging necklines). Costumes and comedy aside, Aniston is also able to convey the vulnerable and wistful side of her character. Taking the role of Kate was a smart choice for Aniston in her first leading turn, as it's much in the same vein as her "Friends"' character Rachel. *Picture Perfect* allows Aniston to do what she does best and she definitely delivers the goods. Her TV fans won't be disappointed.

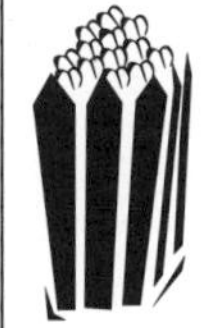

Kate: "I'm looking into getting some eggs frozen." Rita: "Wonderful. I can tell everyone I'm having a grandsicle."

Previously seen as Tom Cruise's rival in *Jerry Maguire* (1996), Mohr is likeable and disarming as the nice-guy hero. Bacon is perfectly sleazy as the roguish playboy and Douglas gets laughs as her long-married colleague. Other secondary characters include Olympia Dukakis as Kate's over-

CREDITS

Kate: Jennifer Aniston
Nick: Jay Mohr
Sam: Kevin Bacon
Rita: Olympia Dukakis
Darcy: Illeana Douglas
Mr. Mercer: Kevin Dunn
Mrs. Mercer: Faith Prince
Sela: Anne Twomey

Origin: USA
Released: 1997
Production: Erwin Stoff for 3 Arts; released by 20th Century Fox
Direction: Glenn Gordon Caron
Screenplay: Arleen Sorkin, Paul Slansky and Glenn Gordon Caron
Cinematography: Paul Sarossy
Editing: Robert Reitano
Music: Carter Burwell
Production design: Larry Fulton
Art direction: John Wright Stevens
Set decoration: Debra Schutt
Costumes: Jane Robinson
Sound: Les Lazarowitz
MPAA rating: PG-13
Running Time: 100 minutes

bearing mother and Kevin Dunn as the boss whose logic about climbing the corporate ladder (in real life) would most likely get him slapped with a discrimination lawsuit.

Even if you don't buy into the film's slight premise, you can still enjoy this film for what it is: a cute and refreshing romantic comedy. Overall, most critics found Ms. Aniston and the movie to be a pleasant surprise. Compared often to that other summer romantic comedy, *My Best Friend's Wedding*, *Picture Perfect* is actually the more appealing and engaging of the two.

—*Beth Fhaner*

REVIEWS

Boxoffice. September, 1997. p. 118.
Chicago Tribune. August 1, 1997, p. 4.
Entertainment Weekly. August 1, 1997, p. 44.
The Hollywood Reporter. July 28, 1997, p. 9.
Los Angeles Times. August 1, 1997, p. F18.
New York Times. August 1, 1997, p. C10.
People. August 4, 1997, p. 19.
Rolling Stone. August 21, 1997, p. 116.
Sight and Sound. December, 1997, p. 51.
Time online. August 11, 1997, Vol. 150, No. 6.
USA Today. August 1, 1997, p. 3D.
Variety. July 28, 1997, p. 98.
Village Voice. August 12, 1997, p. 74.

The Pillow Book

From the creator of *The Cook, the Thief, His Wife and Her Lover* comes a sensuous tale of passion, obsession and revenge.—Movie tagline

"Stunning! Gorgeous! Voluptuous! A boldly erotic explosion . . . taken to places no film has ever gone before."—Jay Carr, *Boston Globe*

"Visually dazzling."—Oliver Jones, *Details*

"Thrilling! Style and story mesh exquisitely in *The Pillow Book*."—Graham Fuller, *Interview*

"A masterpiece."—F.X. Feeney, *Los Angeles Weekly*

"Richly sensual. Rapturously perverse."—Janet Maslin, *New York Times*

"Gorgeous. Sumptuous. An epic erotic poem. Mysterious and operatic and intoxicatingly mad."—Dennis Dermody, *Paper*

"A masterpiece of erotic and political intrigue. Text and texture meet so exquisitely."—Richard Corliss, *Time*

"An exquisite, extremely sexy film."—John Powers, *Vogue*

Box Office: $2,372,744

Shaved ice in a silver bowl, plum blossoms covered in snow, indigo-colored silk . . . these are only a few of the items taken from a tenth-century Japanese text called *The Pillow Book* of Sei Shonagon that Peter Greenaway includes in his film of the same name. True to his training as a painter, Greenaway illustrates voice-over readings from

Shonagon's diary-like collection with color-rich shots evoking still life. In addition to over 100 lists enumerating "splendid things," "poetic subjects," and "things that make the heart beat faster," Shonagon's text includes character sketches and anecdotes from her life as a lady in waiting in the Heian court. Yet the quotations from Shonagon's text and scenes recreating tenth-century Japan provide more than visual imagery. To a certain extent, Greenaway's heroine Nagiko (Vivian Wu) represents a contemporary version of Sei Shonagon, a literary lady for whom writing provides a source of sensual pleasure and self-definition. In this way, Greenaway's *The Pillow Book* offers us a late twentieth-century cinematic translation of Shonagon's work, while his choice of text and method of adaptation pose questions about the timeliness of East Asia (the film's American release nearly coincided with the transfer of Hong Kong to the People's Republic of China) and the timelessness of writing as subjects for film.

Although a plot description in no way does justice to the film, *The Pillow Book* is organized around a fairly simple narrative. Each year, Nagiko's father (Ken Ogata) paints a birthday blessing on her face. On her fourth birthday, her aunt (Hideko Yoshida) gives her a copy of Shonagon's *Pillow Book* and begins reading it aloud to her. Despite an arranged marriage to a boorish husband (Ken Mitsuishi), Nagiko escapes an unhappy fate by fleeing to Hong Kong and becoming a fashion model. While there, she engages in a series of affairs with calligraphers who agree to write on her body. A young English translator named Jerome (Ewan McGregor) convinces her to take up the ink brush herself, and she ultimately composes a series of thirteen books on the bodies of men. By becoming an author in her own right, Nagiko manages to do honor to her father, while at the same time claiming heir to Shonagon's legacy of empowerment through writing.

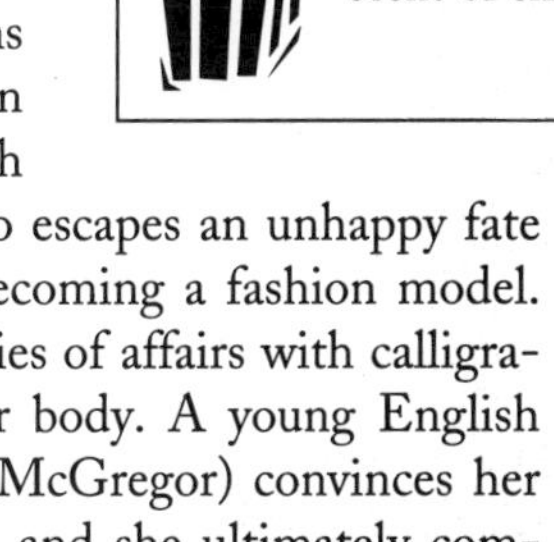

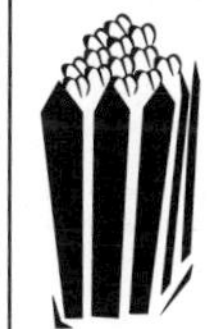

Nagiko: "I like the smell of paper - all kinds. It reminds me of the scent of skin."

The 28 years of Nagiko's life that *The Pillow Book* chronicle raise a number of intriguing questions. In the first place, her development from text to author suggests that sexual preferences and occupations are dictates, not only by our family histories, but by the broader cultures of which our families are also a part. Despite the glamour of high fashion, Nagiko would rather be a writer (like her father and Sei Shonagon) than a model. At the same time, *The Pillow Book* effectively blurs the distinction between determinism and choice, between dominance and submission. Does Nagiko's desire for calligrapher lovers who will write on her body indicate an obsession with her father? of her female passivity? Or is there something downright aggressive in her demands? By the film's end, positions like dominance and submission seem less important than pleasure—and pleasure, at least in *The Pillow Book,* is always grounded in something other than sex itself. Sex, Greenaway would have us believe, isn't really sexy. It is only an artful mixture of memory, history, and aesthetic appeal that makes it thus. In this way, *The Pillow Book,* like David Cronenberg's *Crash* (1997), radically challenges what we find sexy, why we do, and how we judge anyone's preferences, including our own.

Those familiar with Greenaway's work will find that, although *The Pillow Book*'s Asiatic setting and motifs represent a cultural and geographical shift, it is thematically and stylistically consistent with his earlier films. Like *The Draughtsman's Contract* (1982), *Drowning By Numbers* (1987), and *The Cook, the Thief, His Wife, and Her Lover* (1989), *The Pillow Book* intertwines sexual contracts and revenge. Not only does the young Nagiko witness her father's sexual submission to his publisher (Yoshi Oida), but she ultimately seeks revenge against the publisher for her father's humiliation. The sexual contract in *The Pillow Book,* however, touches on another theme found consistently in Greenaway's work: writing and texts. Like *The Cook* and *Prospero's Books* (1991), literal books and other representations of writing appear throughout *The Pillow Book.* Japanese calligraphy is artfully penned on beautiful bodies; French song lyrics float across the screen; diaries are written and burned; and a human body is turned into the ultimate pillow book.

But *The Pillow Book* uses these images of writing as more than mere decoration. Its fixation on texts and calligraphy calls to mind sayings like "It's written all over your face" and "Your life is an open book." Everything from the characters' use of the human body as a blank page to the film's own narrative as an overt translation of a prior text suggests, not only that we do read people and their lives as if they were books, but that we can only make sense of the world because books and the stories they contain govern our ways of seeing. Nagiko pointedly emphasizes this idea when among her own list of "Things That Make the Heart Beat Faster" she includes, "Writing of love and finding it," and not the reverse.

Ironically, for all its emphasis on books, the film represents Greenaway's most cinematically experimental project yet. Despite the fact that it gains structure through the story of Nagiko's life, *The Pillow Book* progresses in a manner that is both dischronic and disjunctive. The film shifts back and forth between the Heian court, Nagiko's early childhood in Japan, and her adult life in Hong Kong. These shifts in place and time are marked through the manipulation of cinematic technique. For instance, both imperial Japan and contemporary Hong Kong are shot in color whereas scenes from Nagiko's childhood are, for the most part, presented in black and white. Greenaway compounds this difference both by using an outdated Cinemascope aspect ration (ratio of width to height of the frame) in the black and white footage and by shooting much of the Hong Kong scenes in a style evocative of martial-arts movies. The use of these techniques supports the sense that the different phases of Nagiko's life take place in very different worlds, but the resulting lack of visual continuity draws attention to film itself as a subject.

Greenaway's use of inset frames and multiple screens is more visually striking but more difficult to assess. The inset frame—a smaller picture within a picture—provides a commentary within the primary scene, for instance, by juxtaposing the past and the present. Although the film borrows this technique from the Asian tradition of "chop signatures" (cartouche-like stamps used to sign calligraphic works of art), movie audiences will no doubt associate it with multiple-channel televisions and sports playbacks. Likewise, Greenaway's use of multiple screens (several scenes presented in checkerboard fashion) recalls Cubism and other modernist movements because it allows him to show the same event from different perspectives simultaneously. But here again, the similarity between multiple screens and computer windows is unmistakable. In fact, even the use of Cinemascope ration, which is intended to recall earlier Japanese cinema, actually results in a screen image that looks like it has already been letterboxed for video playback. Thus the various technical innovations featured in *The Pillow Book* allude both backward towards established forms of higher art and sidelong to artifacts of popular culture, ultimately suggesting that the boundary between high and low culture is as artificial as that between active and passive personalities.

Because many of the film's characters are Japanese, American movie audiences will not be familiar with most of the actors. Even the two principles, Vivian Wu and Ewan McGregor, were not particularly well known at the time of the film's American release. Both actors deliver credible performances, but this is not a film that depends upon acting strength for its effects. In typical Greenaway fashion, *The Pillow Book* is rife with nudity, and it is clear that these actors were chosen as much for their bodies as for their talent. With its fixation on the decorative potential of the human form, *The Pillow Book* lays more emphasis on physical spectacle than on character development. For this reason, moviegoers attuned to a novelistic viewing experience may find themselves confused and even disappointed. But those who are interested in seeing film itself pushed to new limits will find that Greenaway has spoken for the future—and what a brave and beautiful new world it is.

—Jacqui Sadashige

CREDITS

Nagiko: Vivian Wu
Jerome: Ewan McGregor
The Publisher: Yoshi Oida
The Father: Ken Ogata
The Mother: Judy Ongg
The Aunt/The Maid: Hideko Yoshida
The Husband: Ken Mitsuishi

Origin: Great Britain, France, Netherlands
Released: 1996
Production: Kees Kasander for Kasander & Wigman Productions, Woodline Films and Alpha Films; released by Cinepix Film Properties
Direction: Peter Greenaway
Screenplay: Peter Greenaway
Cinematography: Sacha Vierny
Editing: Chris Wyatt, Peter Greenaway
Production design: Wilbert van Dorp, Andree Putman
Costumes: Dien van Straalen, Emi Wada
Calligraphy: Brody Neuenschwander, Yukki Yaura
Sound: Garth Marshall, Nigel Heath
MPAA rating: Unrated
Running Time: 126 minutes

REVIEWS

American Cinematographer. December, 1996, p. 99.
Boxoffice. July, 1996, p. 84.
Chicago Tribune. July 4, 1997, p. 5.
Entertainment Weekly. June 20, 1997, p. 43.
Los Angeles Times. June 6, 1997, p. F11.
New York Times. June 6, 1997, p. B10.
People. June 30, 1997, p. 20.
Sight and Sound. November, 1996, p. 14.
Sight and Sound. November, 1996, p. 57.
Variety. May 20, 1996, p. 32.
Village Voice. June 10, 1997, p. 69.

Pink Flamingos

At Fine Line Features, we're proud to recycle our trash.—Movie tagline

"One of the most vile, stupid and repulsive films ever made."—*Daily Variety*

"Like a septic tank explosion, it has to be seen to be believed."—*Detroit Free Press*

"Lewd! Shameless! May God forgive its makers for concocting such a vulgar, offensive mess! And may audiences the world over be forever grateful."—*Philadelphia Daily News*

Who's the filthiest person in the world? If you don't know the answer to that one, you obviously haven't seen the vilest, most disgusting, trashiest piece of American cinema to ever survive 25 years of cult worship. John Waters' 1972 opus *Pink Flamingos* has been censored, ruled obscene, and even banned. Armed with a 16mm camera, a script featuring kinky sex, cannibalism, feces (and the ingesting of), drugs, murder, incest, castration, and any other revolting thing you can think of, Waters made the movie that he will be most remembered for, the Bible of bad taste, the ultimate punk movie years before punk. We laughed at every revolting act committed on the screen. We snickered at every obscene line said. And we marveled at Divine, that 300-pound transvestite who seemed to really enjoy every piece of filth thrown at her.

"Even if I discovered a cure for cancer, *Pink Flamingos* would be above it in my obituary."—John Waters on the popularity of his film.

Whatever derogatory label may be attached to the film ("vulgar, offensive mess" "vile, stupid and repulsive") *Pink Flamingos* is, at its core, a comedy. In fact, it was included in the 1976 Bicentennial Salute to American Film Comedy at the Museum of Modern Art in New York. The film is a parody of exploitation, intended by Waters as "terrorism against the politically correct hippie culture." The plot centers around Bab Johnson (Divine), her traveling companion Cotton (Mary Vivian Pearce), Bab's son, Crackers (Danny Mills), and Bab's mother, Edie (Edith Massey), the "egg lady"—a group that proudly considers themselves to be "the filthiest people alive." Living in a pink and grey trailer with leopard print wallpaper (and, of course, a pink flamingo on its lawn), Babs and company practice what they preach: stealing steaks by hiding them between her thighs, sex involving a live chicken, cannibalism, incestuous oral sex. But across town, baby-brokers Connie and Raymond Marble (Mink Stole and David Lochary) are enraged at the threat of competition to what they feel is their own claim to fame (the Marbles keep women imprisoned in a basement pit so that their "rather fertile" servant Channing can impregnate them in order that they may sell the babies to lesbian couples to finance their drug operations). The Marbles set out to do battle for the title, and their salvo is "the filthiest gesture alive": sending Babs human excrement through the mail. This act foreshadows surely the real-life filthiest celluloid moment in film: Divine following a dog down the street, and in one medium shot without cuts, scooping up the freshly excreted doggy doo and actually eating it. With a grin and a wink to cover her gag.

Don't find that funny? Many a viewer, so repulsed by the audacity of the auteur's filth, has missed the film's humor. There is comedic justice when Raymond Marble, who enjoys flashing women in the park, is "outflashed" by a woman who bares (to his delight) her breasts, and then (to his horror) lifts her skirt to reveal male genitalia. (The part was played by a transsexual in mid-procedure.) The movie mocks itself when the Marble's servant, Channing, furtively dresses in his master's and mistress' clothing and parodies their bedroom dialogue, unable to make it sound any more ridiculous in his disdain than they did in their sincerity. Waters' choice of music to foreshadow filth is also good for a grin; the tune of "How Much Is That Doggy in the Window" is heard while Divine stalks the soon-to-defecate dog; "Happy Birthday" plays when Divine opens the aforementioned excremental birthday gift; and strains of "The Girl Can't Help It" introduce a scene where Divine sashays down the street and passersby turn to stare. (This scene is particularly effective, since the passersby are not extras, but innocent people gawking at a 300-pound transvestite out window shopping.)

Some might question the restoration and theatrical re-release of this 25-year-old masterpiece of trash cinema. Celebrating their 30th anniversary, New Line Cinema (who are re-issuing it through their subsidiary company, Fine Line Features), claims that their motive was a return-to-their-roots exercise in the preservation of an American classic. And what better retrospective of a now-successful filmmaker than to showcase his penultimate work, while at the same time giving advance publicity to the video release of a new and improved version of a long out-of-print videotape title. *Pink Flamingos* is one of those rarities, a title that, at both the mainstream (those that dare to carry it) and the cult stores, has "legs," meaning that it sells consistently and rents over and over again.

Looking at *Pink Flamingos* now, it not only holds up, but is actually more topical than when first released. In 1972, the tabloids existed and most people probably picked one up while in line at the supermarket at least once in awhile. But *Pink Flamingos* depicted a world rampant with sleazy sensationalism, foreshadowing the '90s, when the line between journalism and tabloidism becomes very blurred. We are first introduced to Babs/Divine on the cover of *Midnight,* a tabloid of the time that rivaled *The Enquirer* in popularity. A short while later Raymond Marble is looking at an actual copy of *The Enquirer* with the shockingly truthful headline, "The People Around You Can Make You Sick." And when Babs is in danger of losing her title as the "filthiest person alive," she calls a press conference of sleazoid reporters; she knows the best way to rid herself of her arch rivals the Marbles is to kill them, and how better to shoot to tabloid stardom than to hold an outrageously staged trial, tar and feathering, and an actual execution, all in front of the reporters? In 1972, *Pink Flamingos* foreshadowed the themes used in 1993's *Man Bites Dog* and 1994's *Natural Born Killers* and *Love and a .45.*

Director Waters provides the film's narration.

In *Pink Flamingos,* the fact that the reporters do nothing to stop the murder is part of the film's hyperbole; today, that behavior is sadly very close to the truth. These days, it is almost impossible to avoid the mark of tabloidism even if you want to watch or read some "real" news—which bombards us for a year with all the grizzly details of the O.J. murder case after interrupting prime time to present the most amazingly slow "car chase" ever filmed. War brews in Iraq, yet the pervading story on every media outlet is President Clinton's "intern-al affairs." The morning newspaper works hard to put out headlines that with just a little stretch could go head-to-head with the most exploitative rags in the business. Talk shows present the best of white trash, Nazis, husband-stealing-pregnant daughters, and interviews with our favorite convicted serial killers. Waters refers to the characters in *Pink Flamingos* as "publicity hags" whose "unquenchable thirst for notoriety" can't help but give the public what it wants.

Seeing the 25th Anniversary Edition is not just an experience in nostalgia (although the adolescent appreciation of the ultra-disgusto potty humor certainly finds itself easily revived), the added footage and the superb quality of the new prints make it a *Pink Flamingos* like you've never seen. The theatrical presentation opens up with a "public service announcement" by John Waters himself discouraging smoking in the theaters while puffing up a storm. Then comes the movie itself, boasting a much clearer and easier to understand dialogue track re-mastered from the original 16mm mag stripe. The music, originally recorded from scratchy 45s from Waters' personal collection, have been re-recorded from digital sources, providing a crisp, undistorted, scratch-free soundtrack.

As for the visuals themselves, the new 35mm print is extremely sharp with more vibrant colors, and is in every way an improvement over memories of past theatrical viewings, much less the video that we have been watching for years. Following the film is 13 minutes of "bonus" footage—scenes shot but not used—with John Waters giving an onscreen narration to previously unseen sequences including murder, nudity, Patty Hitler, eggs, and even a pig-Latin chant of "we are the filthiest people alive" by Babs, Cotton, and Crackers.

A year after *Pink Flamingos* screened at Sundance in 1997, a documentary on the making of the movie, *Divine Trash,* won the Sundance Filmmakers Trophy for best documentary. Director Steve Yeager was producing a series of documentaries on local artists for Maryland Public Television at the time Waters was filming *Pink Flamingos*; 25 years later—in time for the reissue—Yeager finished weaving together behind-the-scenes footage and interviews with Waters, Waters' mother, cast members, and the head of the Maryland Censor Board during the '70s (Waters'

CREDITS

Divine/Babs: Divine
Connie Marble: Mink Stole
Raymond Marble: David Lochary
Cotton: Mary Vivian Pearce
Cracker: Danny Mills
Mama Edie: Edith Massey
Channing: Channing Wilroy
Cookie: Cookie Mueller
Egg Man: Paul Swift

Origin: USA
Released: 1972, 1997
Production: John Waters for Dreamland Productions; released by New Line Cinema
Direction: John Waters
Screenplay: John Waters
Cinematography: John Waters
Editing: John Waters
Production design: Vincent Peranio
Art direction: Vincent Peranio
Costumes: Van Smith
MPAA rating: NC-17
Running Time: 93 minutes

particular nemesis) into a superb low-budget documentary of a low-budget midnight classic. (Scenes from *Divine Trash* are included in the Criterion laserdisc release of *Pink Flamingos.*)

And where will *Flamingos* fly from here? Waters did write a sequel—*Flamingos Forever*—intended as a $600,000 reprise of male rape, necrophilia, child kidnapping, and communism. However, the deaths of Edith Massey and then Divine—as well the lack of any backers—rendered the project what Waters' refers to as "my first abortion."

—*Jim Olenski* and *Carol Schwartz*

REVIEWS

Detroit Free Press. May 2, 1997.
Washington Post. April 6, 1997.

Plan B

When life gives you lemons, pucker up.—Movie tagline

"*Plan B* is engaging . . . Jon Cryer is outstanding!"—Kevin Thomas, *Los Angeles Times*

Plan B concerns a small group of friends in Los Angeles approaching their thirties, accepting the reality that not every part of their lives seem to be working out according to plan. Stuart Winer (Jon Cryer) gets nothing but rejection letters for the novel he spent two years writing; Clare Sadler (Lisa Darr) can't seem to get pregnant and her husband Jack's eyesight (Lance Guest) is not good enough to pass the airline pilot exam. Stuart's actor roommate Ricky (Mark Matheisen) can't get arrested for a part and is losing his luck with the ladies. And while Clare's sister Gina (Sara Mornell) has enjoyed great success with her designer career, she can't seem to find a decent guy.

The group is close-knit; Stuart and Jack were roommates at Penn, and Clare worries about her sister's lack of stability and wishes that she would settle down. The entire group knows that Clare is obsessed with her ovulation times and often catch her post-lovemaking with her legs up in the air, savoring the fertilization experience.

Stuart sees his novel, *Saranoya Sucker* (the story of a serial killer who is tracked by the police and a professor of Japanese history) rejected right and left by publishers. Gina, who has nursed a crush on Stuart since she first met him, encourages him to write about his real feelings and experiences—not what he thinks will just sell. Meanwhile, Ricky freaks out at his graying hair; his only salvation comes when he scores a lead—the new "Ty-De Bowl Man" in a commercial.

As Clare fails to conceive month after month, she and Jack consider adoption. But Jack is going through his own heartbreak; his eyes are not good enough to pass him through the airlines' pilot's test and he's dreamed of nothing but commercial flying all his life. Due to Ricky's insatiable sexual appetite, Jack hits upon a more productive and lucrative business. When Jack takes Ricky and his latest girl up for a "mile-high club" adventure, he realizes that Ricky is not the only one who would enjoy this. Soon Jack is ferrying people constantly for a "ride of love."

When Gina abandons all efforts to find a mate (she even tries dating women), she finds herself spending more time with Stuart. She consoles Stuart when even his own self-published books come back to him unsold. But other trouble is brewing within the group; at a Christmas party, Ricky passes out. He had taken a handful of pills, trying to

CREDITS

Stuart Winer: Jon Cryer
Clare Sadler: Lisa Darr
Jack Sadler: Lance Guest
Ricky Stone: Mark Matheisen
Gina Ferris: Sara Mornell

Origin: USA
Released: 1997
Production: Lulu Baskins-Leva, Nancy Joslin, and Gary Leva for Puny But Loud Productions; released by Curb Entertainment
Direction: Gary Leva
Screenplay: Gary Leva
Cinematography: Yoram Astrakhan
Editing: Jane Allison Fleck
Costumes: Kelly Knutzen
Production Design: Carol Strober
Music: Andrew Rose
MPAA rating: Unrated
Running Time: 102 minutes

commit suicide. Luckily, Stuart gets him to the hospital in time. Ricky confesses that with his 30th birthday just around the corner, he feels like a failure. Stuart convinces him that he—like everyone else—is just beginning.

Stuart and Gina realize their attraction and move in together. Clare and Jack receive their adorable adopted baby. Ricky settles into a career as a "working" character actor. All realize that life may be going according to "Plan B," but that plan is pretty sweet in itself.

Writer-director Gary Leva explores familiar, cliched territory with an adequate, but not spectacular storyline. Cryer and Darr stand out among the actors, with Darr in particular catching one's attention. Production values are mediocre at best; the Los Angeles locale is not very well utilized. If not for the "acting" angle, the story could very well be set anywhere.

—*G.E. Georges*

REVIEWS

Detroit News. November 14, 1997, p. 10F.
Los Angeles Times. October 17, 1997, p. F16.

Playing God

It's about power. It's about survival. It's about . . . *Playing God.*—Movie tagline

A game with no rules.—Movie tagline

"Exciting and action-packed."—Roger Rose, *Entertainment Asylum*

"David Duchovny is a powerfully sympathetic anti-hero."—Michael Medved, *New York Post*

"Smart, sexy, clever!"—Dr. Joy Browne, *WOR Radio*

Box Office: $4,166,918

In the highly successful TV series "The X-Files," actor David Duchovny's character is constantly finding and fighting conspiracies. In Duchovny's latest film, *Playing God*, the only conspiracy his character faces is that created by his own self-destructive demons.

As a talented young surgeon who plays god every day when he saves peoples' lives, Eugene Sands (Duchovny) has thrown his career away by operating on a patient while under the influence of drugs. When his patient dies, his medical license is revoked. His life now no longer has a purpose.

Eugene: "Being a slave in heaven or a star in hell is a choice many men have to make. And on a good day, hell can look a lot like L.A."

And so it is that Eugene aimlessly wanders through his days and spends his nights buying drugs from seedy pushers whose offices are in even seedier bars. Then one night, a bar patron standing next to Eugene is shot, and the doctor is once again in business. Using the bar as a makeshift emergency room, a nearby beautiful woman as his operating nurse, and coat hangars and pop bottles as instruments, Eugene saves the man's life . . . and changes his own.

Eugene's "nurse" is none other than Claire (Angelina Jolie), the pouty-lipped girlfriend of the very wealthy crook Raymond Blossom (Timothy Hutton). Raymond specializes in counterfeit goods which he sells to former second world countries. Currently he is trying to sell his Calvin Clone version of the American dream to the Chinese. As it also turns out, Eugene's barroom patient was one of Raymond's boys, and Raymond is very impressed. So this exporter of knock off goods offers Eugene money ($10,000), praise ("for using your considerable medical skills to save one of my friends"), and fun times (court side seats at a Lakers' basketball game). But he also offers Eugene something even more important, a chance to be a doctor again. Of course his patients will all be people who can't take their ills and injuries to a hospital where too many questions would be asked, but is that really a problem if it lets Eugene practice the craft he loves?

It's a tempting—if morally ambiguous—offer, especially when Eugene finds himself attracted to Claire. But it is also made more difficult when his first "house call" takes him to some flipped out hippie beach bums who want Eugene to "fix" their dead friend and threaten him with severe bodily harm if he fails to do so. Want more factors to perplex our hero? The FBI wants Eugene to accept Raymond's offer just so they can use him to catch Raymond and his corrupt Chinese diplomatic contact.

It's an intriguing and philosophically challenging tale told with style and wit. *Playing God*'s storytelling technique is very reminiscent of film noir brought up to date with a '90s setting. From Duchovny's opening and continuing voice-overs which set up his character's personal melancholy and despair to the between-scenes wipes which aren't seen much these days, *Playing God*'s mood and setting is well established as retro gloom and shadows within Los Angeles' sun and colors. One of the most interesting scenes—although perhaps a tad overdone—is that in which Raymond attempts to convince Eugene to operate on a Russian gangster, Vlad (Peter Stormare), who has been shot by Raymond's own henchmen. Vlad is all prepped and waiting in a luxurious downtown LA apartment, but Eugene is having ethical and practical qualms. Their discussion takes place in a mirrored hallway where both characters are seen as multiple fragments, their exchange of ideas seen through the prism of the mirrors, symbolic of their shattered lives.

It's interesting that this awareness of Hollywood's noirish past has been revived by a British director. Andy Wilson, who is making his feature film debut here, is probably best known for his CableACE award-winning British television series "Cracker." In *Playing God*, Wilson shows an adeptness for storytelling technique that should garner him many more job offers.

Luckily, the story he tells is a seductive one of people who seemingly can only regain their self-worth through less than ethical means. And also, luckily, Wilson has two crack performers to make this dilemma believable.

David Duchovny's famed deadpan delivery of lines during even the most tense of situations is effectively used to accentuate his character's loss of interest in everything in his post-license life. When Eugene wakes up from a night of drug dreams only to find FBI agents in his room, he uninterestedly asks, "What are you going to do? Arrest me for failure to live up to my potential?" The movie should have offered Duchovny more opportunities to use this sly persona, it is what makes his silently desperate character believable, interesting, and ultimately sympathetic.

Also turning in a fascinating performance is Timothy Hutton as the initially likable criminal who begins to show more and more tendencies toward villainous behavior. More often associated with "nice guy" characters (*Daniel*, *Made in Heaven*, *Ordinary People*), Hutton here shows an edge the other roles never allowed. With his bleach-blonde hair, snaky clothes, and winning smile, Hutton's Raymond is genial (when he wants to be) but can just as easily be intensely terrifying. He is a mesmerizing, quixotic villain, and we can see how Eugene would be seduced by him.

Of less interest is Claire whose underwritten part gives Angelina Jolie (daughter of actor Jon Voight) little motivation for her actions. Her character is an enigma. Does she or doesn't she love Raymond? Why? How did they ever hook up? There is no history, so there is little curiosity.

In the end, *Playing God* is an attractive combination of style, story and performance. It plants a thoughtful plot within the more audience-grabbing genre of crime and violence. Unfortunately, its distributor, Touchstone Pictures, didn't give it the support it was due and limited its runs to cineplexes of eight screens or more. That leaves a lot of Duchovny fans out there in smaller venues stuck watching reruns of "The X-Files" and *Kalifornia* and having to wait for *Playing God* to hit video before they'll be allowed to see it.

—Beverley Bare Buehrer

CREDITS

Eugene Sands: David Duchovny
Raymond Blossom: Timothy Hutton
Claire: Angelina Jolie
Gage: Michael Massee
Vladimir: Peter Stormare
Cyril: Andrew Tiernan
Yates: Gary Dourdan
Flick: John Hawkes
Perry: Will Foster Stewart
Casey: Philip Moon
Andrei: Pavel D. Lynchnikoff
Jim: Tracey Walter
Sue: Sandra Kinder

Origin: USA
Released: 1997
Production: Marc Abraham and Laura Bickford for Beacon Communications Corp; released by Touchstone Pictures
Direction: Andy Wilson
Screenplay: Mark Haskell Smith
Cinematography: Anthony B. Richmond
Editing: Louise Rubacky
Production design: Naomi Shohan
Art direction: Troy Sizemore
Set decoration: Evette Frances Knight
Costumes: Mary Zophres
Music: Richard Hartley
Sound: Mark Weingarten
MPAA rating: R
Running Time: 93 minutes

REVIEWS

Entertainment Weekly. October 24, 1997, p. 42.
Los Angeles Times. October 17, 1997, p. F14.
New York Times. October 17, 1997, p. E18.
People. October 27, 1997, p. 19.
Variety. October 20, 1997, p. 71.
Village Voice. October 28, 1997, p. 84.

Ponette

"Lovely and heartbreaking . . . the film immerses itself in a childlike innocence that emerges as transcendently pure!"—Janet Maslin, *The New York Times*

"Absolutely stunning!"—Jack Mathews, *Newsday*

"A major film portrait of the world of a child . . . with an astonishing performance by 4-year-old Victoire Thivisol!"—David Stratton, *Variety*

"Enchanting . . . an authentic tour de force!" —J. Hoberman, *Village Voice*

Box Office: $1,530,354

No plot description could make *Ponette* into a film most audiences would rush to see. The story of a four-year-old girl struggling to come to terms with the death of her mother can't help but sound depressing. And *Ponette* does have its excruciating moments. But this remarkable film also holds humor and rare insight. It is one of the bravest, most uplifting and most honest films ever made.

Ponette to her aunt, regarding Jesus's resurrection: "Daddy said that's not true. It's not nice to lie to me."

The fact that it's also reasonably entertaining from time to time is astounding for a film that has no action and has more than 90 percent of its dialogue performed by children, almost always in close-up. Even more remarkable is the almost total absence of the kind of cloying, pretentious precociousness that infects most filmmakers when they deal with child actors.

French director Jacques Dillon isn't interested in cuteness. In this intensely personal story, he delves deeply into the sorrows and the horrors of childhood, as visited upon young Ponette (Victoire Thivisol) by an unfathomable event—the death of her mother in an automobile accident—and subsequent unfathomable attempts by adults to teach her how to make sense of the situation.

Determined not to be overly maudlin despite his subject matter, Dillon initially handles the tragedy in matter-of-fact fashion. Ponette is immediately burdened not just with the grief of her loss, but with the responsibility of taking care of her anguished father (Xavier Beauvois) and his volatile emotions. First there is his anger at her mother for being reckless. The scared little girl, cowering in close-up in the huge front seat of her daddy's car, must defend her mother: "It's not her fault," Ponette says. "She's not stupid." Then her father demands reassurance: "Will you make me a promise, Ponette?" he asks. "Never die." Responds the child: "Even when we're old?"

Ponette is a sensible child but highly impressionable, especially in her grief. Her cousin Matiaz (Matiaz Bureau), who knows all about zombies, makes sure Ponette understands her mother can't rise from the dead. But then her Aunt Claire (Claire Nebout) tells her the story of Jesus Christ's resurrection, which makes Ponette believes her mother also can come back to Earth, at least for a visit. She waits, pathetically. She tries invoking nonsense magic words her cousins have used in play. She aches when her mother does not come to her in dreams. Then, when her father returns and discovers her situation, Ponette is severely upbraided for indulging in nonsense.

One of the best things about *Ponette* is how unsparingly it reveals the way adults, even when trying to be helpful, can send a child into deeper confusion and despair. Her father can't stand the religious consolations of her aunt. "Live in a world of the living!" he barks at her. His anger at Ponette is cruel, but Doillon makes it easy to understand that it's his imperfect way of dealing with grief. So, too, are Aunt Claire's attempts at spiritual comfort, which go badly awry.

When Ponette and her cousins are placed in a boarding school, her efforts to understand her situation and her hopes for her mother's return are further complicated by the often contradictory advice of her schoolmates and teachers. What Dillon accomplishes in this middle part of the film is the seemingly impossible. He takes the viewer on a profound spiritual journey, through Ponette's eyes and mind, an attempt to decipher the meaning of life and death. It's accomplished with the sometimes fantastic but mostly believable dialogue of children at play.

Ponette is referred by her schoolmates to an older girl who is a self-proclaimed "child of God." Ponette's cousin Delphine (Delphine Schiltz) explains that the wise schoolmate is a Jew and thus knows more than anyone about Jesus because Jesus was Jewish. Thus begins Delphine's wacky, half-baked explanation of the difference between Jews,

AWARDS AND NOMINATIONS

New York Film Critics Circle 1997: Foreign Language Film

Christians, and Arabs. It's one of the many hilarious pieces of a script that plunges audiences into a remorseless child's world and never leaves to pass judgment on that world's own peculiar logic. It's not long before the viewer begins to understand how that logic is no more twisted or inconsistent than the adults' tortured, facile and inadequate explanations of death, life after death, and God.

Victoire Thivisol was the youngest (and controversial) Best Actress winner at the 1996 Venice Film Festival.

The "child of God," who claims she not only can talk to God but can get him to shut up once in awhile because "sometimes he talks too much," gets Ponette to undergo several trials, mostly involving difficult playground leaps, in an attempt to connect Ponette spiritually to the deity and thus to her mother. It doesn't work. Nothing helps. In the face of mounting confusion and despair, Ponette's persistence in trying to get her mother back, if only for a few words of comfort, is both admirable and pathetic. Eventually, after a bully informs her that her mother's death was all her fault, Ponette nearly succumbs to despair. It is just when you think Doillon has crossed the line into morose and unbearable anguish that the tone of the picture changes magically from nihilistic to miraculous. But even then, this unique and remarkable film manages to keep its bearings.

At times, Doillon's script indulges in the typically French capacity for terribly precious language and impossibly trenchant philosophical comment. But most of the time, what the children say is just what children would say: brutally blunt, unvarnished, and taking adult logic to its illogical extreme. To his credit, Doillon does not pontificate on the spiritual instructions Ponette receives, which are inadequate to give her the comfort she needs. The searching itself, he suggests, the effort she puts forth to comprehend her situation and receive direction from others—adults, her cousins, her schoolmates, God—is admirable and ultimately rewarding.

What lends the film its tremendous power are the remarkably unaffected performances of the children. Thivisol received a best actress award at the Venice Film Festival for her unflinching, disturbing, deeply moving, and totally authentic portrayal, and it was well-deserved. It is not just one of the best juvenile performances in many years, it is one of the top performances in any age category. The way her emotions register on her face is not something that can be taught, and there is not one place in the film where Thivisol—or any other of the children, for that matter—seem transparent in their acting. They are wonderfully real in a way that only the youngest performers can be when they are not directed to act precociously. Young Matiaz Bureau, playing the role of Ponette's confidant and would-be swain, is every bit Thivisol's match, and the other children are wondrous as well.

Much credit must go to a script that manages to put profound thoughts in the mouths of children in the most natural and unaffected way, and to Doillon's direction for pausing unhurriedly to indulge in telling and funny conversations. Particularly amusing is one scene in which the three young girls talk about romance, and another in which Matiaz and Ponette discuss disease and medical treatment. "Suppositories are the worst," Matiaz says, but Ponette contends she likes them.

The only other film I've ever seen that achieves this kind of authentic children's perspective is the obscure Australian drama, *Careful He Might Hear You* (1984), which also deals with tragedy and loss. It seems that to get into the truth of childhood, films most depict the depths of sorrow and fear that children can plumb. For those who have lost a parent at a young age, *Ponette* is especially poignant and uplifting. There is more truth about growing up in this one quiet, unusual film than in dozens of Disney extravaganzas.

CREDITS

Ponette: Victoire Thivisol
Father: Xavier Beauvois
Aunt: Claire Nebout
Matthias: Matiaz Bureau
Delphine: Delphine Schlitz
Mother: Marie Trintignant

Origin: France
Released: 1996
Production: Alain Sarde; released by Arrow Releasing Inc.
Direction: Jacques Doillon
Screenplay: Jacques Doillon
Cinematography: Caroline Champetier
Editing: Jacqueline Fano
Music: Philippe Sarde
Production design: Henri Berthon
Costumes: Astrid Traissac
MPAA rating: Unrated
Running Time: 92 minutes

REVIEWS

Detroit News. May 9, 1997, p. 3D.
Entertainment Weekly. June 13, 1997, p. 40.
Los Angeles Times. June 20, 1997, p. F10.
New York Times. May 23, 1997, p. B14.
USA Today. June 27, 1997, p. 3D.
Village Voice. May 27, 1997, p. 22.

Ponette is too daunting and quirky to hope to win a wide audience. But for viewers with the maturity to abandon their presumptions about what childhood ought to be and the courage to follow little Ponette on her painful journey of self-discovery, there is ample reward. Doillon ought to win an award of some sort for traveling an emotional landscape that few, if any, filmmakers have dared to venture, and for having the sense to look at children through their own eyes.

—*Michael Betzold*

The Postman

The year is 2013. One man walked in off the horizon and hope came with him.—Movie tagline

"A most extraordinary film. An unforgettable adventure."—Ron Brewington, *American Urban Radio Networks*

"*The Postman* delivers!"—Jay Carr, *Boston Globe*

"An epic filled with adventure, excitement and hope."—David Sheehan, *CBS-TV*

"A thoroughly entertaining movie filled with action, adventure, humor and romance. *The Postman* is Costner's best work since *Dances With Wolves*."—Neil Rosen, *NY 1 News*

"An epic filled with passion."—Kathryn Kinley, *WPIX-TV*

Box Office: $9,373,991

"The year is 2013," the audience is informed. "There is no order. There is no peace." What is most surprising about this post-apocalyptic futurist fantasy directed by Kevin Costner and adapted by Eric Roth and Brian Helgeland from David Brin's 1985 novel is the speculative timetable which allows the United States of America to become utterly disunited in something like fifteen years. Is our civilization so fragile, our governmental infrastructure so weak, that the whole country could be reduced to ruin and rubble so quickly?

Kevin Costner: "I think that films have to have a heartbeat. If you're going to fight in a movie, you have to have something to fight for. If you're going to kill somebody, there has to be a reason why. If someone's going to have to die, it must hurt."

The film makes no attempt to explain what has reduced the country to such a sorry state, and that's a weakness. Apparently there has been nuclear devastation of some sort and a civil war of some kind that has destroyed the central government, leaving behind disconnected and miserable little city states, pillaged by a cruel and despotic feudal army of "Holnists," commanded by the barbaric General Bethlehem (Will Patton).

A nameless drifter (Kevin Costner) is first seen as an itinerant trouper travelling with his mule from one fortress town to another, giving garbled monologue performances of Shakespeare's *MacBeth* on the basis of partly remembered lines. When the Army invades the town to exact tribute and conscript soldiers, he is captured and recruited into Bethlehem's army against his will, put through basic training, and branded with the number "8," the army's insignia. His faithful mule is killed and eaten. He is a loner who values his freedom, however, and he manages to escape.

After escaping, the drifter discovers an abandoned mail truck and a sack of undelivered mail. Donning the driver's uniform, he invents an identity for himself to help him gain entry, food, and shelter from such towns as he encounters. He calls himself the Postman and poses as a representative of what he calls "the restored government of the United States," which he claims is now operating from Minneapolis and has sent him to Oregon to deliver the mail. At the first town he visits, Pineview, Oregon, he is challenged by a skeptical sheriff and nearly shot, until he finds a letter for a blind woman who lives there. The townspeople want to believe he is what he claims to be.

The Postman is then accepted for what he says he is and his bogus claim gives him a privileged status. A comely lass named Abby even asks him sweetly to father her child, since her husband is sterile. Abby is played by Hollywood newcomer Olivia Williams, trained at Cambridge University, the Bristol Old Vic, and the Royal Shakespeare Company, who may be too good for this movie, but improves it by her presence. Her husband is later killed and she is taken as a concubine by General Bethlehem. The Postman is captured in the same raid. Abby enables him to escape with her and they spend the winter in an abandoned cabin high in the mountains, where the Postman can heal himself and ponder his destiny.

Come spring, they descend from the mountain to find a changed world. They first encounter a girl on horseback (played by Costner's real-life daughter Annie), delivering the mail. She has been deputized by an African-American with the unlikely name of Ford Lincoln Mercury (Larenz Tate), who had himself been deputized by the Postman and who seems to have started a movement that will eventually challenge General Bethlehem's army and restore peace and happiness. Eventually the two armies will meet and the Postman will challenge Bethlehem to single combat. But by then the General knows he cannot defeat an idea, the idea of freedom and unity.

The Postman could most accurately be described as an Oregonian New Age Western disguised as a futurist fantasy. Author David Brin has explained that *The Postman* was written "as an answer to all those post-apocalypse books and films that seem to revel in the idea of civilization's fall. Instead," he claims, "this is a story about how much we take for granted—and how desperately we would miss the little, gracious things that connect us today." He sees the central character as "the last idealist in a fallen America. A man who cannot let go of a dream we all once shared, who sparks restored faith that we can recover—and perhaps; even become better than we once were." Brin hopes to remind us, through his fable, "of the decency that lies within."

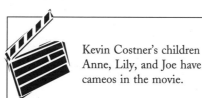

Kevin Costner's children Anne, Lily, and Joe have cameos in the movie.

Will Patton as General Bethlehem perfectly embodies indecency and the anti-government hostility of the fringe militia mentality. He is a megalomaniac who spends his spare time painting self-portraits and misquoting Shakespeare out of context. ("Cry havoc and unleash the dogs of war!" is one of his favorites.) When he hears the Postman's claim that President Richard Starkey is governing the "Restored United States of America," he is skeptical and unbelieving, since he witnessed the burning of the White House at the Battle of Georgetown, but the Postman effectively counters with the fabrication that the country is now being run from the Metrodome in Minneapolis. The tall-tale tradition came out of the west in American literature, and the Postman, a kind of actor who pretends to do Shakespeare, has something in common with those reprobate charlatans, the King and the Duke, in Mark Twain's *The Adventures of Huckleberry Finn*. The people believe the Postman, however, because he seems so genuine and sincere and because they desperately need to believe in something. He delivers hope, and the daughter Abby bears him is later to be named Hope. The film ends in 2043, with Hope dedicating a statue to her father, on horseback, plucking a letter from a young boy's hand. The viewer has seen this pose, earlier in the film, but there is no way the sculptor could have. The boy was played by Costner's son Joe. Daughters Annie and Lily, who sings "America the Beautiful," are also in the cast. The picture is loaded with family values.

The best that Warner Bros. could hope for is that audiences might forget Kevin Costner's last disaster movie, the spectacularly expensive and awful *Waterworld* (1995). In fact, *The Postman* is more closely related to *Dances With Wolves* (1990), which had its moments, was outrageously popular (though not so popular with Native Americans, really), and won seven Academy Awards, including Best Director and Best Picture. At nearly three hours running time, *The Postman* stretches for epic significance but will not do so well in the Oscar competition. It is too often sententious and begs to be taken seriously, but at least it looks to the future rather than the past, like James Cameron's *Titanic*, which swamped it at the box office when both pictures opened.

Some critics scoffed at the idea of America being saved by the postal service, a bureaucracy that has driven some of its workers crazy—a postal worker took hostages in real-life America, for example, the week before the film was released. Costner has done excellent work for Oliver Stone (*JFK*, 1991), Brian De Palma (*The Untouchables*, 1987), and Clint Eastwood (*A Perfect World*, 1993); he has had lovable roles in *Bull Durham* (1988) and *Field of Dreams* (1989); but he has also played stupidly in the films he made with Kevin Reynolds—*Robin Hood: Prince of Thieves* (1991), and the *Waterworld* fiasco, for example, in 1995. Some critics therefore had their knives sharpened and were waiting to attack *The Postman*. After *Waterworld* Costner cannot afford many more mistakes, and directing a film as well as acting in it simply makes him a bigger target. Early returns were not too promising. On Christmas Day *The Postman* grossed $1.6 million, ahead of *Mr. Magoo* ($1.3 million) and *Amistad* ($1.26 million), but far behind *Tomorrow Never Dies* ($5.8 million) and the box-office leader, *Titanic* ($8.5 million), in a market glutted with product.

Reviews were mixed, to be sure. Critics made all sorts of comparisons while attempting to define *The Postman*, looking both forward and backward. As a post-apocalyptic epic it resembled *The Road Warrior* (1981) and *Waterworld*, to an extent. It does not really resemble Akira Kurosawa's *Yojimbo* (1961), as one misguided reviewer claimed, because the Postman is not really a hired gun. In that respect it more closely resembles *Shane* (1953), for some critics THE archetypal Western, but Kevin Costner is neither Alan Ladd or John Wayne. As Betsy Sharkey wrote in the *New York Times*, Costner's hero is heroic in spite of himself, a "flawed, solitary man who tries unsuccessfully to dodge his destiny rather than swagger into it." Costner's Postman carries his mythic burden awkwardly and uneasily. It is conferred on him by others, not something he has courted. He wears a postal cap rather than a white hat. He is a quiet American, an ordinary guy who somehow muddles through a bad situation, but, when cornered, will do the right thing. Costner is perfectly fitted for this role and plays it well.

The movie is basically an allegory for our own cynical times and it could strike a responsive chord with some millennium-minded viewers. The production design by Ida Random was praised by Rick Lyman in the *New York Times* for its texture and depth. She was attracted to the post-apocalyptic production because Costner's concept was "down to earth," rather than "spacey and bizarre." To visualize that concept, she worked with two art directors and one assistant. The film was shot in 80 separate locations, extending from Arizona, to Idaho and Washington State. Producer Steve Tisch told the *New York Times* that the budget was "less than half of the $200 million reportedly spent on *Titanic.*" The photography orchestrated by Stephen Window is spectacular. The film is much longer than it needed to be, however, and the treatment is profoundly eccentric.

—*James M. Welsh*

CREDITS

The Postman: Kevin Costner
Bethlehem: Will Patton
Abby: Olivia Williams
Ford: Larenz Tate
Idaho: James Russo
Sheriff Briscoe: Daniel von Bargen
Bridge City Mayor: Tom Petty
Luke: Scott Bairstow
Bandit #20: Giovanni Ribisi
Irene March: Roberta Maxwell
Ellen March: Peggy Lipton
Getty: Joe Santos

Origin: USA
Released: 1997
Production: Jim Wilson, Steve Tisch, and Kevin Costner for Tig; released by Warner Bros.
Direction: Kevin Costner
Screenplay: Eric Roth and Brian Helgeland; based on the novel by David Brin
Cinematography: Stephen Windon
Editing: Peter Boyle
Music: James Newton Howard
Production design: Ida Random
Art direction: Scott Ritenour
Costumes: John Bloomfield
Sound: Kirk Francis
Stunt coordinator: Norman Howell
MPAA rating: R
Running Time: 177 minutes

REVIEWS

Cinemafantastique. December, 1997, p. 14.
Cinemafantastique. April, 1998, p. 36.
Entertainment Weekly. January 9, 1998, p. 43.
The New York Times. November 9, 1997, p. B1.
The New York Times. December 21, 1997, p. B17.
The New Yorker. December 8, 1997, p.40.
People. January 12, 1998, p. 25.
Premiere. January, 1997, p. 22.
Variety. December 22, 1997, p. 57.
The Washington Post. December 25, 1997, p. C10.
Washington Post Weekend. December 26, 1997, p.35.

Prefontaine

He ran for his country, for the gold . . . for himself.—Movie tagline

"*Prefontaine* is exciting, uncompromising, and unforgettable."—Jim Svejda, *KNX/CBS/Radio*

"Two thumbs up!"—*Siskel & Ebert*

Although there is something essentially appealing about a footrace—no complicated rules, no elaborate equipment, no placard-waving subjective judges—the greatest achievements of American runners have been virtually ignored in the United States. And while some fine films have been made about athletes in other sports, like *Pride of the Yankees* (1942) or *Raging Bull* (1980), most sport films have been relatively trivial efforts targeted towards a specific audience so interested in the subject that any distinctive cinematic feature were almost incidental. Nonetheless, the primal appeal of running—its purity as a form of athletic competition, its inherent expression of the beauty of the human body in motion—has led to a few compelling if obscure films such as *On the Edge* (1985) or *Chariots of Fire* (1981), which won the Academy Award for Best Picture, and captured the imagination of such an extensive audience that it was a significant factor in the running boom of the 1980s.

Producer Irby Smith: "I actually saw Pre run several times, and was profoundly amazed by how strongly people responded to him on such a passionate, personal level. That connection between the person that he was and people from all walks of life was very emotional."

The life of the great American distance runner Steve Prefontaine, who died at 24 when his golden MG overturned on a windy Oregon road as he was coming home from a party celebrating a final victory, contained some of the elements which made *Chariots of Fire* such a captivating film. Prefontaine (or "Pre" as he was known, a working title for the film) was a fierce competitor with a rebel's refusal to conform to any rules he didn't agree with, a gifted runner willing to work with a cantankerous, iconoclastic coach in order to challenge every distance record on the books, an idealist ready to confront a self-serving athletic establishment which enforced an absurd "shamateur" code that degraded America's Olympic champions, and a thoughtful, brooding young man whose brashness camouflaged his sensitive, introspective nature. These attributes, plus the turbulent times of the sixties when Pre grew toward greatness, and the terrorist assault at the Munich Olympics in 1972 just prior to the 5000 meter run where Pre was favored to win and came in fourth, provided the ingredients for the kind of film which, as *Runner's World* put it in an article on the film's production, had "a chance to galvanize the American public." The fact that *Prefontaine* opened to mixed reviews and miniscule grosses, vanished almost immediately from the screen, and may eventually find an appreciative audience on video of running aficionados and fans of Jared Leto (who plays Pre superbly) is a product of the film's limitations as well as a result of the somewhat convoluted path the original idea took on its way toward *two* entirely separate versions of Pre's life.

As *Runner's World* describes it, the project took shape when two producers based in Eugene, Oregon, where Bill Bowerman built an extraordinarily successful track program at the University of Oregon, purchased the rights to Pre's story from his family. They asked Kenny Moore, fourth in the Olympic marathon in Munich, a very accomplished writer for *Sports Illustrated* and a close friend of Pre's, to work on a screenplay. Moore had a small part in Robert Towne's *Personal Best* (1982) and contacted Towne about directing the film. At this point, accounts differ, as is often the case with the development of a film, but eventually some kind of schism occurred. The producers sold the rights to Disney, and the partnership that made the highly praised documentary *Hoop Dreams* (1994), Steve James and Peter Gilbert, were hired to produce and direct the film. Towne and Moore embarked on a separate project for Warner Bros.—their film *Without Limits*, with Billy Crudup as Prefontaine, has been budgeted at 25 million dollars and is scheduled for release in March, 1998.

A second film biography on the runner, *Without Limits* starring Billy Crudup, is scheduled for release in early 1998.

The documentary technique that worked so well for James and Gilbert in *Hoop Dreams*, unfortunately, is ill-suited to the story they are trying to dramatize in *Prefontaine*. Their instinct for historical accuracy is laudable, but misplaced. While their regard for the tiny contingent of track freaks who know the details and care about every iota of authenticity is suitable as a kind of basis for recreating the incidents of Pre's life and his magnificent "failure" in Munich, there are much more important matters to be considered if the film is to appeal to a general audience. It does no harm that Leto looks so much like Pre and has learned to run duplicating Pre's characteristic head-tilted slant to such an extent that Pre's father said of the resemblance, "My wife cried and so did my daughter. When he came around the field, looking up at the clock like Steve did, it was hard to take." And Leto, perhaps most familiar for his role on TV's "My So-Called Life," fully conveys not only the rock-star aura (the BBC once called Pre "the athletic Beatle") but also the smoldering intensity which Leto describes as " . . . prideful one moment, insecure the next. Charismatic, then cocky. He had great confidence, and yet he doubted himself." Leto holds the screen with the forceful presence of a man who the camera likes, a quality not exactly crucial to acting but very useful on the screen, and the intelligence and sympathy he brings to the role is an indication of his preparation and of his growing ability as an actor. Leto's performance, and those of R. Lee Ermey as the sardonic Bowerman, Pre's mentor and guru to many great runners, and Ed O'Neill (familiar as Al Bundy from "Married . . . with Children") as the Oregon coach Bill Dellinger, are solid and convincing, as are the portrayals of Pre's first girlfriend Nancy Alleman (Amy Locane) and his main flame Elaine Finley (Laurel Holloman).

These competent performances and the efforts at authenticity, however, are not enough to capture the core of Pre's magnetism, the qualities which touched so many people who knew him. In Oregon, people felt the film failed to express the almost mystic aspects of Pre's personality and the docudrama technique that James and Gilbert employ, with its quasi-objective location of the camera as, primarily, an observer of the action, tends to create a kind of distance that dulls the power of the physical that is at the heart of extraordinary athletic ability and will. This is a story about a racer, not just a man who loved to run and found in running the truest expression of his being. There are snippets of Pre running from the start, and the climactic race in Munich is covered in considerable detail, interspersed with fleeting (and tantalizing) footage of the actual contest, but most of this is from the outside. As *Runner's World* commented, "There will be no swooping camera angles, no intricate special effects in Disney's production." James and Gilbert are sticking to a method that worked once, but here, much more is required. The kind of super slow-motion filming and radically enhanced sound mixes that made *Chariots of Fire*'s race scenes so gripping are a kind of cliché in sports photography, but that doesn't mean they can be dispensed with. From the beginning of the film, the various historical figures speaking to the camera about their recollections juxtaposed with shots of Pre running here or there establish a mood of rational examination when an ethos of passionate participation is needed to grab the audience at the start. The most effective dramatic moments, Pre's defiance of dictatorial authority, his moments of doubt at Munich, his last race, his very moving funeral (a hearse circling the track with the scoreboard clock counting back from 13:13, the then world-record at 5000 meters) occur after too many opportunities have been lost.

There is nothing like the gorgeous scene of runners near the ocean from *Chariots of Fire*, although the Oregon hillsides offer many possibilities for linking landscape and human passage. The way in which crucial races in Pre's career can be anchor-points and dramatic highlights is ignored. The sense of what it is like to be *in* a race with world-class runners is absent in spite of the Munich footage. Towne has said he "wants the viewer to experience a world 99.9 percent of them don't understand, much as Martin Scorsese did by putting us inside the boxing ring in *Raging Bull*," and while it remains to be seen how successful he will be, the absence of this experience is a major flaw in *Prefontaine*. Too much of the photography, serviceable at best, is predictable and pedestrian, and the lighting is almost relentlessly bright, even in the darkness at Munich, rarely taking advantage of the many ways in which mood can be manipulated through variations in hue and shade.

During the years after the race in Munich, the film begins to find its footing—Leto's character now clearly established and maturing, the fragmentary pseudo-documentary

CREDITS

Steve Prefontaine: Jared Leto
Bill Bowerman: R. Lee Ermey
Bill Dellinger: Ed O'Neil
Pat Tyson: Breckin Meyer
Elfriede Prefontaine: Lindsay Crouse
Nancy Alleman: Amy Locane
Elaine Finley: Laurel Holloman
Ray Prefontaine: Peter Anthony Jacobs
Mac Wilkins: Brian McGovern

Origin: USA
Released: 1997
Production: Irby Smith, Mark Doonan, Peter Gilbert, and Jon Lutz for Hollywood Pictures; released by Buena Vista Pictures
Direction: Steve James
Screenplay: Steve James and Eugene Corr
Cinematography: Peter Gilbert
Editing: Peter C. Frank
Production design: Carol Winstead Wood
Art direction: Gregory Weimerskirch
Music: Mason Daring
Costumes: Tom Bronson
Sound: Peter Marts
MPAA rating: PG-13
Running Time: 106 minutes

format giving way to scenes that flow, and Pre's perseverance and decency in a hard time impressive. The conclusion, using Bob Dylan's "Forever Young" and "I Shall Be Released," leaves an impression that exceeds the general effect of the film. The sense of loss and admiration which is its final point is palpable, and suggests just what might have been (and still might be) done with the life of an unusual man and his brief struggle toward magnificence.

—*Leon Lewis*

REVIEWS

Boxoffice. March, 1997, p. 44.
Entertainment Weekly. January 31, 1997, p. 34.
Los Angeles Times. January 24, 1997, p. F1.
Los Angeles Times. January 31, 1997, p. F14.
New York Times. January 24, 1997, p. C12.
People. February 10, 1997, p. 21.
Running Journal. February, 1997, p. 21.
USA Today. January 24, 1997, p. 3D.
Variety. January 27, 1997, p. 75.
Washington Post. January 30, 1997, p. E1.
The Winston-Salem Journal. January 30, 1997, p. C5.

Prisoner of the Mountains; Kavkazsky Plennik; Prisoner of the Caucasus

An extraordinary story of hope, courage and humanity.—Movie tagline

"Passionate . . . Powerful . . . Compelling."—Tom Meeks, *The Boston Phoenix*

"An emotional and visual feast laced with moments of magical realism."—Ella Taylor, *LA Weekly*

"A strong and affecting pacifist fable."—Janet Maslin, *New York Times*

"Two thumbs up!"—*Siskel & Ebert*

"Crowd-pleasingly exotic."—Jim Hoberman, *Village Voice*

"One of the very best films you'll see in 1997."—John Powers, *Vogue*

Russian soldiers Vania (Sergei Bodrov, Jr.) and Sacha (Oleg Menshikov) are kidnapped by a Muslim who hopes this action will bring his own captured son back in *Prisoner of the Mountains.*

Box Office: $790,078

Prisoner of the Mountains is a Russian film set in the midst of the Chechen war. Two Russian soldiers, a sergeant and a private, are captured in a Chechen ambush. The sergeant (played with panache by Oleg Menshikov, who resembles Kevin Kline) is sublimely nonchalant. He tells the young raw recruit Gilin (Sergei Bodrov Jr., the director's son) that he is a bad soldier because he did not get a chance to fire a shot at the Chechens. The sergeant seems to be the perfect example of a soldier turned into a killing machine. He went to war, he tells Gilin, because he needed the money and wanted the adventure. At first, he hated the army, then he grew to love it. In the first scenes he is shown wielding his automatic rifle with abandon. He has the arrogance of a matinee idol. His treatment of Gilin is rather like a hazing.

> Russian Captain to Vanya's Mother: "You can't trust anyone here. Soldiers traded grenades for hash, and kids threw the grenades back at them."

But Gilin is stubbornly his own man. He neither accepts nor rejects the sergeant's insults. He merely hangs in, trying to understand the situation, probing the sergeant for information. The sergeant has his fun making up scenarios about what will happen to the two men. At one point, he suggests that he will be ransomed for Abdul-Murat's son. Abdul-Murat is their captor and a village elder. When Gilin asks what will happen to him, the sergeant replies that he will surely be killed. Who would want such an inexperienced soldier? Then he asks Gilin if he has ever had sex with a woman. Gilin says yes, and the sergeant replies that things are all right. At least Gilin has had that pleasure.

> Film was shot in the village of Arecha, in the republic of Dagestan, along the border with Chechnya.

Gradually the sergeant drops his pose of superiority and treats Gilin decently. They are still not equals, and he orders Gilin around, but Gilin is perfectly willing to learn from his more experienced comrades, and Gilin is no coward. He bears his suffering without whining and keeps his fear under control. The sergeant relents and says he will make sure that both men are exchanged for Abdul-Murat's son.

What is striking about both of these characters is their well-rounded humanity. The sergeant is a killer, but he has a sympathetic side, winning the affection of the dour Chechen guard who has had his tongue cut out by Russians. The guard is a fascinating study: a hard man, but one who loves music and used to sing. Now he hums tunes and is softened by the sergeant's gift of sunglasses—a souvenir, the sergeant says, as if the Russians are on holiday in the guard's country. Such moments are moving and seem absolutely authentic. Human beings, no matter what their differences, find it hard not to recognize the humanity in each other—even as those same people will kill each other when they believe the circumstances call for it.

Gilin, however, is in a unique position. He is captured before he has had a chance to fire a shot. He gets to know the Chechens before he has time to develop any hatred of them. He is a draftee, and he has gone to war for his country, singing patriotic songs. But he does not know what the war is about, and he cannot commit himself to it with any fervor once he is there. He is too fixed on staying alive. Although he is shackled and confined to a dirty, stinking cellar, he has, in a sense, the comforts of home: plenty of food, companionship, and even a beautiful young Chechen girl Dina (Abdul-Murat's daughter) played by Susanna Mekhralieva. She waits on him, and he flirts with her.

Abdul-Murat himself is a complex study in humanity. He is a devout Muslim. He does not seem involved in the war, except to the extent of trying to get his son out of the local prison. He has staged the ambush of the Russians in order to have a hostage. He seems implacable. He will kill the men if he does not get his son back. Yet he allows his daughter to wait on the men, and he does not object when the men are taken on the roof and are allowed to dance and cavort. He nods in appreciation when Gilin fixes his wristwatch. Abdul-Murat is no murderer by nature. Indeed, he faces community criticism for harboring the Russians. He is told repeatedly they should be killed immediately. He is waiting to arrange the exchange and even meets with Gilin's mother who has received a letter from her son.

One of the film's finest scenes is the confrontation between Gilin's mother and the Russian commanding officer. He tells her the Chechens cannot be trusted and implies that the exchange will not work. As he blithely suggests that there is nothing he can do for her son, she attacks him—not once, but twice, evincing not merely a mother's rage but the viewer's anger at all such facile explanations in times of war, explanations that mean the death of countless individuals.

When Gilin's mother meets Abdul-Murat, she tries to reach him by saying that like his son she is a teacher. He cuts her off. Such similarities mean nothing now, he curtly tells her. "How do I know I can trust you?" she asks him. "You don't," he replies. "But you have to." It is a brutal scene, but later it is apparent that Gilin's mother has had more of an impact on Abdul-Murat than he can allow himself to show.

Almost every scene in *Prisoner of the Mountains* shows how in war individuals are constantly making choices that reflect or stifle their humanity. When the sergeant and Gilin escape, and their guard catches up with them, the sergeant does not hesitate to kill him. The guard is holding on to Gilin's arm as he dangles off a cliff. It is the sergeant who comes up and shakes the guard off Gilin's arm as the two Russians watch him clutch at the air falling into the precipice.

On the run, the Russian fugitives find a shepherd with a rifle and, again, it is the sergeant who stabs and kills the man for his weapon. Moments later, the Chechens recapture the Russians and ask which one killed the shepherd. Unhesitatingly, the sergeant says "Ja." While Gilin is taken back to Abdul-Murat, the sergeant is taken out to a tree and his throat is cut.

The film's final scenes show Gilin facing almost certain death. The exchange has been thwarted because Abdul-Murat's son has been shot trying to escape. Gilin asks Abdul-

AWARDS AND NOMINATIONS

Academy Awards 1996 Nomination: Best Foreign Language Film
Cannes Film Festival 1997: International Critics Prize

Murat's daughter to set him free. The two have formed a close bond and joked about marrying, although the girl solemnly informs Gilin that she could never marry him. She also says she cannot free him, but that she will make sure he has a decent burial. Usually dead Russians are fed to the jackals, she tells him. Later, she relents and throws to him the keys to his shackles. When he climbs out of his prisoner pit, she urges him to flee. But he just sits with her, pointing out that she will be blamed for allowing him to escape. Abdul-Murat returns and sternly reminds his daughter that she should be mourning for her brother. He tells her that Gilin must die.

Gilin gets up and Abdul-Murat walks him at gunpoint into the mountains. The men walk and walk. Why is Abdul-Murat taking so much time to kill Gilin? This Muslim has not been sadistic, and it is not likely that he is drawing out the prisoner's suffering. Finally, he stops and tells Gilin to keep walking and not to turn back. The camera focuses on the back of Gilin's neck. He is obviously awaiting the fatal shot, and he stands there without flinching. The shot comes but Gilin remains standing as Abdul-Murat turns and walks back to his home.

Like so many moments in *Prisoner of the Mountains*, the scene could be sentimental; it could seem unrealistic, a concession to the desire for a happy ending. But this is hardly the case with this scene or any other in the film. It is too complex for simplistic solutions. Some of the most charming people in this film are killers. Abdul-Murat has not lost his hatred, but he cannot shoot the man who has befriended his daughter, made a toy for her, and shown nothing but his humanity. One more murder is pointless.

For Gilin this denouement is devastating. In a voice-over coda to the film, he speaks of the Chechens, and how he would like them to visit them, but even in memory they remain elusive. His longing for them and his sense of guilt are keenly balanced. He has indeed become a prisoner of the mountains, as has the whole Russian nation.

Prisoner of the Mountains is a haunting film. Its director, Sergei Bodrov, claims it may have influenced Boris Yeltsin's decision to end the war. In any case, in the film's documentary-like revelation of Chechen life, its humor, and its compassion, it ranks among the great anti-war films such as *All Quiet on the Western Front* and *Grand Illusion.*

—Carl Rollyson

CREDITS

Sacha: Oleg Menshikov
Vanya: Sergei Bodrov Jr.
Abdul-Mourant: Djemal Sikharulidze
Dina: Susanna Mekhralieva
Hassan: Alexander Burejev
Russian Captain: Alexei Zharkov
Vanya's Mother: Valentia Fedotova

Origin: Russia
Released: 1996
Production: Boris Giller and Sergei Bodrov for Caravan Co.; released by Orion Classics
Direction: Sergei Bodrov
Screenplay: Sergei Bodrov, Boris Giller and Arif Aliev
Cinematography: Pavel Lebeshev
Editing: Olga Grinshpun, Leonid Desyatnikov
Production desgin: Valery Kostrin
Costumes: Vera Romanova
Sound: Yekaterina Popova
Music: Leonid Desyatnikov
MPAA rating: R
Running Time: 98 minutes

REVIEWS

Boxoffice. February, 1997, p. 59.
Entertainment Weekly. March 7, 1997, p. 50.
Los Angeles Times. February 7, 1997, p. F2.
New York Times. January 31, 1997, p. B3.
Sight and Sound. March, 1998, p. 55.
Variety. May 20, 1996, p. 38.
Village Voice. February 4, 1997, p. 69.

Private Parts; Howard Stern's Private Parts

Never before has a man done so much with so little.—Movie tagline

"A wild and outrageous good time!"—Sara Edwards, *NBC*

"Makes you laugh! A lot. Out loud."—Leah Rozen, *People*

"A comic firecracker with a surprising human touch."—Peter Travers, *Rolling Stone*

"Two thumbs up! A comic valentine."—*Siskel & Ebert*

"Very funny!"—Richard Corliss, *Time*

Box Office: $41,230,799

Private Parts had a slew of publicity, tested well with preview audiences, and received glowing reviews. It opened well, then its ticket sales inexplicably and quickly dropped off. It's possible that the film suffered from the same problem as the biopic *The People vs. Larry Flynt*—moviegoers were too offended by the subject of the film to see it. In the end, it turned out that not as many people as expected were interested in hearing all the details about Stern's *Private Parts.*

The opening scene shows Stern, who plays himself, at the MTV Music Awards. He is being lowered with ropes from the ceiling, dressed in the character Fartman. The moment is, in a sense, a microcosm of the whole movie. Howard does something daring (playing a superhero whose superpower is flatulence), reveals something embarrassing about himself (some very white and untoned butt cheeks), is revered by the public (the unrealistically delighted awards show audience), and misunderstood (the musicians backstage all sneer in disgust).

Howard Stern: "The idea that Alison fell in love with me and then stayed with me through the failure and then put up with me through the success is ridiculous. This whole thing, my success, our life together is about beating the odds."

So goes *Private Parts,* the 109-minute movie version of Stern's best-selling book. Stern has said that he envisioned the movie as being a kind of *Rocky,* where a man overcomes the odds to become a success. Instead of battling Apollo Creed, Rocky, er, Stern, overcomes idiotic radio station management, a high whiny voice, and the FCC to become the self-proclaimed "King of All Media."

Directed with a light, pop culture-savvy touch by Betty Thomas, *Private Parts* traces Stern's rise from quiet boy to famous shock jock. The movie's framing device is Stern telling his story to his airline seatmate, Gloria (Carol Alt). By the end of the movie, Gloria is so charmed that her attitude turns from disgust to lustful admiration for Stern. Her newfound respect is embarrassingly overdone, probably having to do with the fact that the ego-driven Stern was a major creative force in the movie.

But Stern's story does have a certain charm. He shows how he became THE Howard Stern with quick snippets from his youth until the present. The young Stern has a father (Richard Portnow) who continually tells him to shut up, a penchant for anarchy (he livens up a boyhood puppet show by adding some puppet sex), and a strong desire to be on the radio.

The movie isn't trying to be *Citizen Kane* and sticks with a light touch when showing the influential moments in Stern's life. One scene suggests that Stern might have picked up his proclivity for wild, off-the-cuff remarks from his mother (Kelly Bishop). Mrs. Stern is shown driving the young Howard and a couple of his friends somewhere. When the friends complain about blacks moving into the neighborhood, she shushes them. "I'm black," Mrs. Stern says to the shocked boys. "And Howard's half-black," she adds, making it up as she goes along.

Of the collection of moments that shaped Stern's life, his biggest epiphany comes after an almost-adulteress affair with an actress. Although he doesn't actually cheat on wife Alison (Mary McCormack), he is wracked with guilt. When Alison finds some telltale damp underwear, she walks out on him. A downtrodden Stern goes to his new job in Detroit alone and one day, depressed, he starts talking about his private life on the air. He decides then that everything he feels that he shouldn't say on the air is exactly what he should say.

One by one, Stern adds the elements that make his show what it is today: naked women on the air, jokes about his notoriously small penis, and plenty of talk about lesbians. This kind of stuff makes for great ratings—and trouble with the FCC, which makes up the drama in the latter part of the film. When Stern is called to be morning man on NBC's flagship station, WNBC in New York City, the powers-that-be are shocked when they hear Stern's raunchy show and one of their henchmen, Kenny (Paul Giamatti), volunteers to make certain Stern tones down the program. Stern takes his battles with Kenny, whom he dubs "Pig Vomit," to the airwaves. He turns his show into a vehicle designed to torment Kenny, including putting a live fight with Kenny on the air.

Stern's life in *Private Parts* is depicted as a black and white battle between Stern and the outside world. Stern is good, his enemies are bad. The good include his sidekicks, his fans, lesbians, and naked women. The bad are those who don't "get" him, uptight radio management, Don Imus, and the FCC. Stern needs to have enemies and gets his energy and focus from vanquishing his real or imagined foes. His fight with Kenny propels him to his highest ratings ever and his battles with the FCC inspire him to new heights of outrageousness.

Surprisingly, it's not the battles that make the movie, it's the performances. The movie is packed with cameos and most of the main characters play themselves. Stern does a great job portraying himself as a nerdy college student who does a terrible radio show and winds up with the lovely Alison. Donning a big curly wig, a dorky moustache and glasses, he doesn't really look like a college kid, but as he explains in a voice-over, "In this movie, you've got to suspend disbelief."

Stern seems to relish playing himself in the geeky years and it's fun to watch him decked out in '70s garb and being an unconfident loser. When he makes a mistake during one live radio broadcast, he panics and starts whining in a way that might even be taken for crying. A brave move for a person who makes a living pointing out the weaknesses in others. Stern's team of sidekicks, Robin Quivers, Fred Norris, and Jackie Martling (all playing themselves), seem to be having a great time; Quivers evens sports her own embarrassing old hairstyle, a small blast-from-the-past Afro.

Although the movie is ostensibly about Stern's rise to top shock jock, a big part of the film is devoted to Stern's relationship with his wife. Through it all, Alison is the one who stands by him, encourages him, and believes in him. Howard never seems to get over the fact that this lovely woman fell in love with a geek like him and some critics consider *Private Parts* to be a tribute to Alison, a kind of public (could it be anything else) love letter.

But their relationship is also shown to be somewhat less than idyllic. Alison considers Stern's radio persona to be "just an act," but still, the reality of hearing about her sex life on the air is a continual sore spot. The tension between private and public comes to a head when Stern jokes about his wife's miscarriage on the air. Although Stern, to cheer Alison up, made her laugh with jokes privately at home, Alison is furious when Howard does a tasteless radio skit about it the next day. The conflict is clear: Stern thinks that if he doesn't say whatever comes into his mind, he is not being true to himself and his art; Alison thinks some things should remain private. The movie doesn't try to solve the problem, it just lets it exist, like a problem in real life.

Real life, or at least the appearance of real life, is what Stern is aiming for here. Not content to simply be famous for his radio persona, Stern also wants us to love the "real" him, the shy, lovable family man. To get to know that kinder, gentler image, a lot of Stern's most offensive behavior isn't mentioned at all. According to the movie, Stern's just a funny, slightly naughty guy and anyone who doesn't like him is an uptight prig. It's not exactly a fair picture, but, hey, it is Stern's film.

Still, he could have gone for a cheap-shot movie that would please his fans, like a longer, visual version of his radio show. Instead Stern gets credit for trying to do something more daring, making a surprisingly softhearted tale of growing up geeky, trying to do a good job, and loving your wife.

—Jill Hamilton

CREDITS

Howard Stern: Howard Stern (as himself)
Robin Quivers: Robin Quivers (as herself)
Alison Stern: Mary McCormack
Fred Norris: Fred Norris (as himself)
Kenny: Paul Giamatti
Gloria: Carol Alt
Jackie Martling: Jackie Martling (as himself)
Mr. Stern: Richard Portnow
Mrs. Stern: Kelly Bishop

Origin: USA
Released: 1997
Production: Ivan Reitman for Rysher Entertainment; released by Paramount Pictures
Direction: Betty Thomas
Screenplay: Len Blum and Michael Kalesniko; based on the book by Howard Stern
Cinematography: Walt Lloyd
Editing: Peter Teschner
Music: Van Dyke Parks
Production design: Charles Rosen
Art direction: Rick Butler
Set decoration: Beth Kushnick
Costumes: Joseph G. Aulisi
Sound: Tod A. Maitland
MPAA rating: R
Running Time: 109 minutes

REVIEWS

Chicago Tribune. March 11, 1997, p. 78.
Entertainment Weekly. March 14, 1997, p. 53.
The Hollywood Reporter. February 25, 1997, p. 12.
Los Angeles Times. March 7, 1997, p. F1.
New York Times. March 7, 1997, p. B1.
People. March 10, 1997, p. 19.
Rolling Stone. March 20, 1997, p. 89.
Sight and Sound. July, 1997, p. 49.
Time. March 10, 1997.
USA Today. March 7, 1997, p. 1D.
Variety. March 3, 1997, p. 67.

La Promesse; The Promise

"Extraordinary! Energetic! A story told straight, and with great intensity."—David Denby, *New York Magazine*

"A breathless, cinema-verite roller-coaster ride."—Thelma Adams, *New York Post*

"Devastating! One of the saddest and scariest father-son confrontations ever filmed."—Stephen Holden, *The New York Times*

"Remarkable!"—David Ansen, *Newsweek*

"An absolute stunner! A work of great power."—Joe Morgenstern, *The Wall St. Journal*

Luc and Jean-Pierre Dardenne's *La Promesse* is a richly-faceted film, a tale of economic misery, criminal exploitation and childhood gone terribly awry.

The film concerns the daily experiences of Igor (Jeremie Renier), an energetic 15-year-old who is being schooled in the ways of criminality by his father, Roger (Olivier Gourmet), a small-time hustler who has recently carved a lucrative niche for himself by providing falsified documents and temporary safe houses to an ever-changing panoply of illegal immigrants.

As the story begins, Igor is torn between his real job as an apprentice in a car repair garage and his increasingly demanding role as Roger's juvenile partner in crime. Playing the Artful Dodger to Roger's malicious and mostly incompetent Fagin, Igor is, in his way, a marvel of industry and efficiency, as sharply-focused as any respectable bourgeois businessman. He handles much of the money, dodges the local immigration authorities, circulates forged passports, and keeps lists of who comes and goes, adroitly shuffling the human freight of exhausted, terrorized immigrants through an array of makeshift hiding places. He is a misused but fundamentally intelligent boy. His activities on his father's behalf require a great deal of daring, but there is nothing especially picaresque about his daily routine. His only genuine amusement is derived from occasional jaunts on a go-kart that he is building, in bits and pieces, with the help of a few friends. This represents the only time we see him engaging in genuinely childlike behavior.

The last vestiges of Igor's childhood innocence seem well on their way to extinction, but his finer qualities are suddenly enlivened by Assita (Assita Ouedraogo), a native of Guinea-Bissau who has recently immigrated to Belgium with her husband, Amidou (Rasmane Ouedraogo), in hopes of making a better life. Arriving on the scene with little money and exaggerated expectations, Assita and Amidou soon fall prey to Roger's manipulations and moneymaking schemes. Roger is more like a jailer than a benefactor to the immigrants, who are kept under lock and key for days at a time and are forever being told that they owe still more money for his dubious "services." The improvised flophouses into which Roger corrals these distraught people often double as shooting galleries for local drug addicts.

The immigrants, who come from every place imaginable, are beset by language difficulties. They are also half-crazed with fatigue, and so overwrought from the strain of navigating their way through a foreign (and mostly hostile) culture that they cannot adequately defend themselves against Roger's petty degradations and extortion schemes. They have no rights under the law, so they live with the constant threat of betrayal and exposure to local immigration authorities, who are themselves highly corrupt and easily bought. When Assita's husband falls to his death in a scaffolding accident—the unforeseen and bloody outcome of a sudden police raid—Igor's carefully-tended routine begins to fall apart. Roger compels Igor to help him hide the body, but before Amidou dies he extracts a pledge from Igor to look after his wife and child.

The story concerns Igor's fitful efforts to wrest himself away from his malevolent father whose capacity for cruelty is matched only by his galloping stupidity. After Amidou's death, Roger wants nothing more than to rid himself of Assita and tries various means to drive her away. Assita struggles to survive and solve the mystery of her husband's disappearance. Her instincts tell her that her husband has not simply disappeared voluntarily. Her native beliefs, which are deeply important to her, are depicted in scattered scenes throughout the film. They oblige her to search out the truth. Igor is reluctant to reveal what he knows, partly because he is being terrorized by Roger and fears criminal prosecution, but also because he fears losing contact with Assita, who is the only sympathetic adult figure he knows.

Without actually intending to, Assita comes to serve as a surrogate mother to Igor, who has clearly not known much in the way of genuine parental affection. Although she has a baby of her own and is naturally concerned for her child's welfare, she allows Igor to display his anxieties in a way that would never be possible under Roger's dubious tutelage. A brief moment in which Igor clings to the startled Assita as

AWARDS AND NOMINATIONS

Los Angeles Film Critics Association 1997: Foreign Language Film

National Society of Film Critics 1997: Foreign Language Film

though she were his mother indicates just how childlike Igor still is.

Stymied by her experience in Belgium, Assita begins to ponder the idea of migrating yet again and taking refuge with relatives in Italy, but she continues to be consumed by the unanswered question of her husband's whereabouts. The film ends with Igor's disclosure that her husband is in fact dead. Although Igor displays the beginnings of a moral transformation in the film's final scenes, and clearly forms an alliance with Assita, there is no indication that the material circumstances under which they live will improve significantly.

The frenetic camera work of Alain Marcoen reflects the constant state of upheaval in which Assita and the other immigrants are forced to live. The brothers Dardenne scrupulously avoid making the setting seem unduly glamorous or even hospitable. The nation of Belgium has never looked so unrelentingly gray and dismal. Hailed in recent years as the glittering capital of the emerging European Community, the Belgium we see in *La Promesse* looks instead like a disreputable quagmire, the epicenter of all the world's misery.

The "promise" to which the title refers has several layers of meaning in addition to the one Igor makes to Amidou. It refers to the promise of a new life, which the immigrants soon discover is a mirage, as well as Assita's personal vow, made long ago to her husband, that he will receive a proper and dignified burial in his own country. On a more positive note the title also refers to the promise of renewal and redemption which Igor and Assita pursue.

The brothers Dardenne show great skill in dramatizing Igor's and Assita's particular difficulties, but they are also very mindful of the larger picture—that of a formerly "civilized" society which has been cast precipitously into a state of economic upheaval and decline. *La Promesse* could be described as a deeply political film, even though the characters themselves spend very little time engaging in overtly political discussion or pondering the deeper meaning of their situation. The filmmakers are astute enough to avoid editorializing about the social implication of their characters' predicament. They let Assita's many degrading experiences speak for themselves. This is especially true when she is being hustled for money by Roger, dodging a potential rape or being urinated upon by a marauding gang of right-wing biker types.

The upsurge of bourgeois triumphalism in the aftermath of the collapse of the Soviet Union has allowed the ruling classes of Europe to wink at these degraded conditions, creating an illusion of prosperity where there is none, and perpetuating the foul conditions under which Igor, Assita and their contemporaries are forced to live.

Through the experience of Igor and Assita, Luc and Jean-Pierre Dardenne's *La Promesse* presents a searing portrait of post-Cold War Europe in a state of decline. Visual evidence alone tells us that the glorious social transformation, which was supposed to result from the fall of the Berlin Wall, is little more than an elaborate pack of lies. What we see instead, through the daily experiences of Assita and her family, is the revival of inter-ethnic rivalries, the resurgence of racist violence against a mostly helpless immigrant population, and the generalization of misery.

La Promesse tells the story of two ordinary people, from vastly different backgrounds, who find themselves thrown together as the world around them disintegrates. Igor and Assita differ from one another in every conceivable way, and they play opposite roles in the cycle of exploitation which Roger helps to perpetuate. They are eventually united by their sense of being victimized and exploited, as well as their raw determination to succeed in the face of impossible circumstances.

This is a film of rare intelligence and complexity. It is personally affecting but also rich in political subtext. The brothers Dardenne prove that they are fine storytellers. They succeed in creating much sympathy for Igor and Assita, but they also present a clear and unflinching picture of a world that continues to slide precipitously into a state of moral, physical, and political decline.

—Karl Michalak

CREDITS

Igor: Jeremie Renier
Roger: Olivier Gourmet
Assita: Assita Ouedraogo
Amidou: Rasmane Ouedraogo

Origin: France, Belgium, Luxembourg
Released: 1996
Production: Luc Dardenne and Hassen Daldoul for Les Films du Fleuve, Touza Productions, and Samsa Films; released by New Yorker Films
Direction: Jean-Pierre Dardenne, Luc Dardenne
Screenplay: Jean-Pierre and Luc Dardenne
Cinematography: Alain Marcoen
Editing: Marie-Helene Dozo
Music: Jean-Marie Billy, Denis M'Punga
Art direction: Igor Gabriel
Sound: Jean-Pierre Duret
MPAA rating: Unrated
Running Time: 94 minutes

REVIEWS

Boxoffice. July, 1997, p. 90.
Los Angeles Times. May 30, 1997, p. F14.
Variety. May 27, 1996, p. 75.
Village Voice. May 20, 1997, p. 71.

The Quiet Room

"So simple and so honest, it's shattering."—Jay Carr, *Boston Globe*

"Striking, original, compelling and unsentimental."—Dave Kehr, *Boston Phoenix*

"*The Quiet Room* is fascinating, moving and unusual."—Michael Wilmington, *The Chicago Tribune*

There is power in silence. And for a seven-year-old little girl watching her parents' marriage fall apart, silence is the only weapon she can wield against them. Australia-based filmmaker Rolf de Heer has written and directed a heart-wrenching study of one small child's turmoil in *The Quiet Room*.

The seven-year-old girl about her parents: "You'll speak to each other before I'll speak again."

Through a chillingly detached voice-over narration, the Girl (Chloe Ferguson), an only child, allows us to be privy to her stream of consciousness, to share in her observations and frustrations, and to understand why she refuses to speak. This use of an unconventional voice-over narration that focuses on present events rather than reminiscences of the past helps to subvert our expectations and to draw us intimately inside the Girl's world. It is a technique that attempts to capture the disjunctive thinking that a child employs while processing information. It is replete with naughty jokes and rhymes, moments of sorrow and longing, and confusion.

The Girl longs for a return to the way things were four years earlier, when her parents (Celine O'Leary and Paul Blackwell) would embrace her with warm "family hugs" and roughhouse on their bed, eliciting joyful squeals of laughter from the three-year old (played by Miss Ferguson's younger sister, Phoebe). These flashbacks are in direct contrast to the present, where the Girl silently pleads for a hug and the estranged couple can only tensely go through the motions.

Brooding alone in her blue bedroom, with its collection of Barbie dolls, crayons and a goldfish swishing around in its glass bowl, the Girl attempts to convey her anxiety and anger through primitive drawings depicting the erosion of her familial security. She longs to live in the country and to have a dog; and she firmly believes that her silence will trigger enough worry to lead to a reconciliation for her parents. Her infuriating refusal to speak therefore becomes an extreme form of protest against her parents' incessant arguments. "Why can't they simply love each other?," she asks.

In many ways the film turns the viewer into the Girl's surrogate confidante to whom she is free to reveal all the darkness and pain of seeing her tiny little world fall apart. The Girl is ever watchful. At times she accurately assesses situations, while on other occasions she misinterprets the events. She struggles with her vulnerability and attempts to mask her insecurities with a deliberate detached deportment.

The young Miss Ferguson gives an impressive, understated performance as the Girl. Her poker-faced expression and detached narration dramatically reinforce the Girl's emotional blackmail of her parents. There is nary a hint of forced emotionalism in the young actress's performance.

Director/writer Rolf de Heer creates a compassionate reminder of the emotional and mental vulnerability of children. He shows us the harm that a careless word or a casual dismissal can do to a small child. The power of this film is derived from the Girl's solitude; while her parents' arguments become more aggressive, the Girl retreats to the sanctity of her belief that she can make things right again within the family. De Heer refrains from condescension towards this young girl's perspective throughout the film, but succumbs to a jarring sentimentality in an abrupt happy ending.

The Quiet Room may be seen by some as a departure for the Dutch-born de Heer, best known for the graphic and controversial film *Bad Boy Bubby* (1993), which won both the Critics' and Jury Prizes at the Venice Film Festival. Yet

CREDITS

Mother: Celine O'Leary
Father: Paul Blackwell
Child Aged 7: Chloe Ferguson
Child Aged 3: Phoebe Ferguson

Origin: Australia, Italy
Released: 1996
Production: Domenico Procacci and Rolf de Heer for Vertigo and Fandango; released by Fine Line Features
Direction: Rolf de Heer
Screenplay: Rolf de Heer
Cinematography: Tony Clark
Editing: Tania Nehme
Production design: Fiona Paterson
Art direction: Beverley Freeman
Costumes: Beverly Freeman
Music: Graham Tardif
Sound: Peter D. Smith
MPAA rating: PG
Running Time: 98 minutes

both films have an unwavering point of view: one from a child-man who is suddenly unleashed into the world after thirty-five years of isolation within the walls of his apartment; the other from a child who arrogantly believes she has the power to save her parents' marriage.

Despite a unique, albeit idiosyncratic style, de Heer is perhaps one of the lesser-known filmmakers working out of Australia. He made his debut in 1980 with the children's film *Tail of a Tiger*, yet his work has remained relatively unseen in the United States. Only *Bad Boy Bubby* and *Dingo* (1991) have been screened at film festivals in this country.

The Quiet Room, an official selection of the 1996 Cannes Film Festival, is a challenging, yet ultimately rewarding viewing experience. At times disturbing and emotionally wrenching, the film contains some insightful observations about adults and children, as well as the futility of words—and their power to wound. Critics were generally enthusiastic about the film, although many made a point of criticizing its sentimental ending.

—*Patricia Kowal*

REVIEWS

Boxoffice. March, 1997, p. 42.
Entertainment Weekly. April 4, 1997, p. 68.
Los Angeles Times. May 2, 1997, p. F17.
New York Times. March 21, 1997, p. B3.
Variety. May 6, 1996, p. 81.
Village Voice. March 25, 1997, p. 84.

Red Corner

Leniency for those who confess. Severity for those who resist.—Movie tagline

"Shocking and compelling!"—Bill Diehl, *ABC Radio Network*

"Fascinating . . . Gere and Bai Ling are electric."—David Sheehan, *KCBS*

"An explosive performance by Richard Gere."—Bobbie Wygant, *KXAS TV*

"A highly suspenseful and provocative thriller. Don't miss it!"—Paul Wunder, *WBAI Radio*

Box Office: $22,201,291

The corrupt Chinese judicial system is examined when American businessman Jack Moore (Richard Gere) is falsely accused of killing a Chinese woman in the political thriller *Red Corner*.

American businessman Jack Moore (Richard Gere) goes to the People's Republic of China to cut a deal with the Chinese government and to sell American television programming. He is a lawyer who represents an entertainment conglomerate that controls American satellite technology. His main competition is from Germany, but Jack has the superior product.

Taken to a decadent nightclub that features Western music, Jack meets a beautiful Chinese girl who ends up in his bed back at his hotel room. The next morning he is slapped awake by Chinese soldiers, who arrest him for the murder of the girl. Jack has no memory of what happened, but the evidence points toward him as the murderer. He apparently has been framed. He is immediately brought to trial under a legal system he does not understand conducted in a language he does not know.

The American Embassy is unable and unwilling to help Jack in order to avoid an international "incident" that might complicate Sino-American relations. The American ambassador therefore declines to visit Jack in prison. His captors and the judge advise him to plead guilty. So does his state-appointed attorney, at least initially. Being a naive American, Jack considers himself innocent until proven guilty, but that's not the way things work in China, where the presumption of guilt takes precedence. If Jack pleads innocent and is found guilty, he will be executed within days.

Clearly, Jack has been set up by people in high places, and this courtroom procedural takes its time in sorting things out. Jack has no apparent motive for the murder. The woman was a stranger, apparently sent to set Jack up for a scandal. She takes pictures of him undressed, and he takes pictures of her. The police hold the film as evidence. Hotel records indicate that two bottles each of scotch and champagne were sent to the room. Though Jack denies having ordered so much booze, his fingerprints are on all the bottles and on the murder weapon. The dead woman's father is a powerful general who demands swift justice.

Shen Yuelin on why she's helping Jack: "I no longer wish to be silent."

This is the ultimate nightmare for any American who has travelled in an exotic and potentially unfriendly country. Jack does not know the language, nor does he have any friends who are able to help him. The Embassy turns a deaf ear. Jack's only chance is his attorney, who, fortunately, turns out to be intelligent and open-minded. She lived through the Cultural Revolution and feels profound guilt because she stood in silence as ideological thugs humiliated her father. In the present circumstance, she will not stand by silently while a man who may be innocent is railroaded through a Communist kangaroo court. She is willing to put her own career and reputation on the line in order to defend her client.

The film is less static than one might have guessed. Of course there are shots of Jack being interrogated and in his cell and long sequences in the courtroom. Eventually his lawyer gets permission to take him to the scene of the crime to help him remember what happened. While being transported back to prison, the police car gets stalled in traffic. For no apparent reason the driver leaves the car and locks Jack and his lawyer inside. Suddenly, an assassin dressed in a military uniform appears. After a struggle, Jack manages to disarm the man and escapes, enabling the camera to bolt into action as Jack bolts for the American Embassy seeking refuge, while pursued over rooftops by the police.

Since the filmmakers couldn't shoot in China, they recreated Beijing locations at Culver Studios in Culver City, California.

Jack actually gets to the Embassy, but learns that his lawyer will be held responsible for his escape. Amazingly, to save her reputation and career, he leaves the security of the Embassy and surrenders himself to the Chinese so that the trial may continue. Jack's fate is left hanging until the very end, when the mystery is solved. Jack was betrayed by the very people he came to China to do business with. One young hotshot wanted Jack discredited because he knew he could cut a better deal with the competing German firm, which would also reward him with a lucrative position in media management. The woman who was supposed to set Jack up had second thoughts after spending the night in his hotel room. Jack remembers that she had made a call on her cell phone from his room, but he can only remember bits and phrases of her side of the conversation, when she in fact was calling to say the deal was off. When the conspirators try to go ahead as planned and chloroform Jack into unconsciousness, she attempts to intercede, and that was how she got killed.

Finally, the plot of the film works well enough. After the pieces of the puzzle finally fall into place, the movie ultimately makes sense. China looks like a complicated and corrupt place, and of course official China objected to the film, sight unseen, even though the villainy represented is not caused by the government, but by greedy Chinese businessmen who have influence in high places. By some miracle (or quirk in the screenplay), it turns out that justice is possible in the People's Republic, a far more positive message than one might have expected. Even so, the Chinese were clearly upset that the release of this film coincided with President Jiang Zemin's state visit to Washington, D.C. in November, as evidenced by a threatened boycott against the studio that released the film, since the film seemed to reflect badly on human rights in the People's Republic.

The film is critical of Chinese totalitarianism, and the legal system certainly does seem harsh and repressive by Western standards. On the other hand, in defense of the Chinese system, Jack's lawyer points out that China, with a population six times larger than the United States, has a crime rate that is only one-tenth as large. So the repression seems to yield social results, at the expense of individual rights. It is nearly impossible to make bail there, and it is more logical to plead guilty and to hope for lenience than to argue innocence. Once decided, the death sentence will be carried out within a week of its being uttered, and the family of the accused will be billed for the cost of the bullet used to execute the convicted criminal.

In her *New York Times* review, Janet Maslin questioned the credibility of Robert King's screenplay for the way it allows Moore's lawyer, Shen Yuelin (Bai Ling) to continue her investigation of the case unimpeded. Her successful defense involves rather too many "Hollywood miracles." For example, she somehow finds a locket the murder victim had been wearing, and that locket contains a photograph that enables her to solve the mystery and to learn who was behind the set-up.

The movie belongs to Richard Gere and to the lovely Bai Ling, who plays his lawyer. She is a Chinese citizen who in real life took part in the Tiananmen Square demonstrations but is now pursuing her acting career outside China. "Like the character she embodies," Gary Arnold wrote of the 27-year-old Bai Ling, "the performer may have left herself in a vulnerable position in her own country." She still has family in China—her parents, a sister, and an elderly grandmother who lives in Beijing. Both Gere and director Jon Avnet "were soliciting support from the press in case the Chinese government decides to take imprudent and probably self-defeating reprisals against Miss Ling," Arnold noted in the *Washington Times*. Arnold thought her performance was "astute enough" to merit an Academy Award nomination. But there are other strong performances here as well. Tsai Chin, who played Antie Lindo so memorably in Amy Tan's *The Joy Luck Club* (1993), for example, plays the no-nonsense judge who presides over Jack Moore's trial.

CREDITS

Jack Moore: Richard Gere
Shen Yuelin: Bai Ling
Bob Ghery: Bradley Whitford
Lin Dan: Byron Mann
David McAndrews: Peter Donat
Chairman Xu: Tsai Chin
Lin Shou: James Hong

Origin: USA
Released: 1997
Production: Jon Avnet, Jordan Kerner, Charles B. Mulvehill, and Rosalie Swedlin; released by Metro Goldwyn Mayer
Direction: Jon Avnet
Screenplay: Robert King
Cinematography: Karl Walter Lindenlaub
Editing: Peter E. Berger
Music: Thomas Newman
Production design: Richard Sylbert
Art direction: Virginia Randolph-Weaver
Costumes: Albert Wolsky
Sound: Jeffrey Wexler
Visual effects supervisor: Kevin Mack
Stunt coordinator: Buddy Joe Hooker
MPAA rating: R
Running Time: 122 minutes

Reviews were mixed. Dismissing the film as "a Hollywood liberal movie at its most sanctimonious," Stephen Hunter's *Washington Post* review, entitled "Ego Trip to China," was mainly an ad hominem attack on Richard Gere. Hunter charged that this "trivialized melodrama," filled with "the poison vapor of vanity," could "never find room to accommodate both the head of its anger toward China's government and the radiance of its star's self-regard." From Hunter's corrosive perspective the movie had to be flawed because Richard Gere played the central character, but in fact it is Gere's energy that makes the film work.

Gary Arnold of the *Washington Times* was far more tolerant of Gere, whom he described as the "celebrity lightning rod of protest about Chinese imperialism and cultural intolerance in Tibet," though, of course, *Red Corner* has nothing directly to do with Tibet. According to Janet Maslin of the *New York Times*, *Red Corner* "shows an earnest, committed interest in criticizing Chinese totalitarianism." Richard Gere told *Movieline* magazine that it was Bai Ling's line, "I will not be silent anymore," that first captured his interest. Maslin judged Gere's performance to be "forceful" and thought that as anti-Chinese propaganda the film was "certainly way ahead of the clumsier *Seven Years in Tibet*." The direction by Jon Avnet is excellent. The film is well-paced and expertly made. Although some reviewers were critical of Gere's indulgence, there is nothing really wrong with his performance. In fairness, the film should be judged by that performance, and not by the actor's presumed political motives for making it.

—James M. Welsh

REVIEWS

Chicago Tribune. October 31, 1997, p. 4.
Entertainment Weekly. November 11, 1997, p. 60.
Los Angeles Times. October 31, 1997, p. F1.
Movieline. November, 1997, p. 48.
New York Times. October 31, 1997, p. B20.
People. November 10, 1997, p. 23.
USA Today. October 31, 1997, p. 1D.
Variety. November 3, 1997, p. 97.
Village Voice. November 4, 1997, p. 84.
The Washington Post. October 31, 1997, p. B1.
Washington Post Weekend. October 31, 1997, p. 53.
The Washington Times Metropolitan Times. October 31, 1997, p. C13.

The Relic

The next evolution in terror.—Movie tagline

"An absolute shocker! White knuckles until the very last minute!"—Doug Moore, *Fox-TV*

"A thrill ride!"—John Anderson, *Los Angeles Times*

"Thrills, chills and non-stop terror!"—Bill Swecker, *NBC-TV*

"An out-of-your-seat suspense thriller."—Jim Ferguson, *Prevue Channel*

Box Office: $33,956,608

The beast lurking in the basement of Chicago's Field Museum of Natural History rips out and devours part of the brains of its human prey. If you leave most of your brain behind when you watch *The Relic*, but keep the part that controls the fear response, you might get quite a kick out of this shamelessly derivative, gory, silly, and grandly entertaining monster mash.

With no big-name stars to steal the show or inflate the payroll, the loathsome beast is the center of this $65 million production. Oscar-winning creature creator Stan Winston (who worked on *Jurassic Park* and *Alien*) designed the monster, an amalgam of lizard, tiger, kangaroo, mastodon, and alien. It also has a Satanic connection, being the living embodiment of a primitive Brazilian tribe's devil-god, Kothoga.

True to horror-flick conventions, we get only glimpses of the beast's leathery body at first. It lurks in the shadows, breathes heavily, growls menacingly, and strikes rapidly with unimaginable force. Gradually, we see more and more of the thing, as it decapitates victims—museum workers, guests, policemen—at a rapidly increasing pace.

The Relic would have been nothing but great goofy fun if director Peter Hyams and a foursome of scriptwriters hadn't bothered to try to document the beast's pedigree with a bothersome barrage of sometimes contradictory explanations. It's always a bad sign when a team of writers get screenwriting credit; it signals a script that's been worked-over again and again. Based on a respected horror novel by Douglas Preston and Lincoln Child, the plot of *The Relic* is a bunch of hokum that takes itself far too seriously.

It starts with a boiling cauldron and chanting natives, a white guy in an Indiana Jones hat, and a bunch of crates on a cargo ship. You know there's a monstrous presence inside the crates because the obvious musical score starts thumping and screeching whenever the camera zooms in on the box. So it's no surprise when a ship full of decapitated corpses shows up floating on Lake Michigan. Alert geographers, however, may wonder how the ship got there from Brazil; does the beast know how to navigate the St. Lawrence Seaway boat locks? Best not to ask such questions; you need to react to *The Relic* with a primitive brain.

The monster next shows up in the bowels of the famed South Side museum, where it attacks a black security guard as he smokes dope in a lavatory after hours. But as soon as you spot Dr. Margo Green (Penelope Ann Williams), a spunky, sassy, serious-minded evolutionary biologist with fashion-model looks and a sexy wardrobe of chic short skirts and heels, you know who the monster would really like to tongue-lash. And when Lt. Vincent D'Agosto (Tom Sizemore) takes the case, you know he and Dr. Green are destined to play the opposites-attract hero/heroine roles. She despises superstition; he carries around a lucky bullet that should have killed him but didn't explode, and he never steps over corpses. He asks her, "Are we still evolving?" and she barks back, "Some of us are."

Vincent: "Are we still evolving?"
Margo: "Some of us."

The museum is all set to host a gala opening of a major exhibit on, you guessed it, superstition. The museum director, Dr. Cuthbert (Linda Hunt, a talented actress wasted in a pedestrian role), insists the show must go on, as does the shallow, vain mayor (Robert Lesser). D'Agosta, of course, is a straight-arrow cop who isn't satisfied when a homeless ex-con is caught and identified as the killer. Reluctantly, he agrees to let the exhibit proceed, but as it opens he's taking a team of dogs down into sub-basements to sniff out the monster he suspects is still there. He soon realizes that the beast took a tunnel from the lake to the museum.

Annoyingly inconsequential plot diversions include Dr. Green's battle with another scientist, Greg Lee (Chi Muoi Lo), to get a grant from some tony museum benefactors. The rivalry only serves to make Lee into monster-food that the audience might enjoy seeing devoured.

As D'Agosta stalks the overgrown gecko god, Margo analyzes odd-looking fungi on leaves left in crates delivered to the museum by her professional enemy, Dr. John Whitney. Also in the crate is a stone relic of Kothoga. Plot twists leave Dr. Green and the wheelchair-bound museum curator, Dr. Frock (James Whitmore), alone in a sealed-off laboratory wing pecking away at computers which are helping to unravel the mystery of the monster. Dr. Frock's theory is that evolutionary gaps may have produced genetic freaks; when he meets the creature face-to-face, he is glad to have his theory confirmed by the most tangible of all evidence; his supposition devours him!

All this computer work and scientific theorizing keeps getting in the way of the action. Do we really care why the creature likes to munch on the human hypothalamus? Hardly, though the notion does provide a grotesquely black-comic cameo by a wisecracking, sex-crazed coroner (Audrey Lindley, the sex-crazed Mrs. Roper on TV's "Three's Company"); it's the first movie autopsy you've ever seen complete with tasteless gags.

When decapitated bodies start raining down on the gala guests, and the beast (who seems to be everywhere) chews some cables and shuts down the museum's power, the film's all set up for a haunted-house, thriller ending. Ceiling sprinklers are raining on dignitaries in tuxes and minks, it's dark and dank, the beast is picking off people and even tracking dogs one by one, and Dr. Green and Lt. D'Agosto are thrown together to confront the monster. It's great fun, except when the heroic pair have to take time out for yet another go at the computer.

CREDITS

Dr. Margo Green: Penelope Ann Miller
Lt. Vincent D'Agosta: Tom Sizemore
Dr. Ann Cuthbert: Linda Hunt
Dr. Albert Frock: James Whitmore
Detective Hollingsworth: Clayton Rohner
Greg Lee: Chi Muoi Lo
John Whitney: Lewis Van Bergen

Origin: USA
Released: 1997
Production: Sam Mercer and Gale Anne Hurd for Cloud Nine Entertainment; released by Paramount Pictures
Direction: Peter Hyams
Screenplay: Amy Jones, John Raffo, Rick Jaffa, and Amanda Silver; based on the novel by Douglas Preston and Lincoln Child
Cinematography: Peter Hyams
Editing: Steven Kemper
Music: John Debney
Production design: Philip Harrison
Art direction: Eric Orbom, James Murakami
Costumes: Dan Lester
Sound: Gene S. Cantamessa
Creature effects: Stan Winston
MPAA rating: R
Running Time: 110 minutes

Though at times the techno-monster looks fake, this film is not for the queasy. It's genuinely scary and very bloody. Hyams doesn't flinch from going for cheap thrills (the early part of the movie is filled with phony scares), and *The Relic* ups the ante with plenty of furious and loud ambushes. It's a sort of kitchen-sink approach to the thriller genre, with everything from flood to fire, Satanism to giant insects, and even the obligatory pseudo-rape scene of Dr. Green by the monster, which makes not a bit of sense.

Thankfully, *The Relic* downplays the flirting, and both Sizemore and Miller are noticeably restrained. It suffices for D'Agosta to give Green his lucky bullet at the key moment of crisis, and for her to thrust it into the bosom of her cocktail dress—that's all the sexual innuendo needed. And instead of damsel in distress, Miller gets to play the more resourceful, courageous, and athletic of the heroic duo when it comes to showdown time. It's a nice twist.

For all its throw-everything-at-the-audience verve, *The Relic* stops short of being truly nightmarish. Subtlety is crucial to producing chills, and Hyams seems incapable of subtlety. With *The Relic*, you always know you're watching a movie that is making an all-out, unsophisticated effort to frighten you. Far more frightening is a movie that draws its audience unwittingly into its web.

Even by the standards of the rock-faced action-hero stereotype, Sizemore's beefy D'Agosta is remarkably nondescript. All we know about him is that he's lost his dog in a custody battle with his ex-wife (a mediocre joke that's repeated too often) and that he's an old-fashioned guy. Just as pedestrian is the scripting of Green as the sexy super-scientist who can keyboard her way through a specimen analysis while wearing a killer dress and being stalked by a demon beast. This pair just doesn't have enough heart and blood to make the audience care about what happens to them. Both Miller and Sizemore act as if they were birds with their wings clipped; they're afraid to go to emotional extremes, shy back from opportunities to camp it up or vamp it up, and seem better suited to light comedy than to gut-wrenching drama. The many minor characters have more personality and have more fun with their roles, and the script has more fun with them, especially the mayor, who pressures D'Agosta to let the opening gala go on by noting that

REVIEWS

Boxoffice. March, 1997, p. 45.
Entertainment Weekly. January 24, 1997, p. 41.
Los Angeles Times. January 10, 1997, p. F6.
New York Times. January 10, 1997, p. C1.
Rolling Stone. February 6, 1997, p. 54.
Sight and Sound. June, 1997, p. 97.
USA Today. January 10, 1997, p. 4D.
Variety. January 13, 1997, p. 151.

his wife is wearing a dress with great cleavage and "that cleavage got me elected."

The advantage of *The Relic* is that, if you're the type of moviegoer who sees a horror film only once in a while, you get a heavy dose of just about everything at once here: mutation, mutilation, and demonic pursuit down dark, wet tunnels. And the climactic confrontation between Miller and the reptilian/mammalian amalgam is a blockbuster. *The Relic* has all the tooth-marks of a cult favorite but absolutely no chance of biting the heads off any Oscars.

—*Michael Betzold*

The Return of the Jedi

Box Office: $45,471,742

Originally directed by Richard Marquand from a screenplay by George Lucas and Lawrence Kasden in 1983, *The Return of the Jedi* is the last and arguably the weakest segment of the *Star Wars* Trilogy. It brings back the characters who were more fully developed in *The Empire Strikes Back* and places them in the toy factory of Jabba the Hutt, the slimiest villain of the trilogy, and a disgusting icon for Capitalist greed. Later on it turns into a fabulously furry creature-feature with the introduction of the Ewoks, carebears with bows and arrows cavorting in the forests of Northern California. It depends too heavily on special effects. As Stephen Holden remarked in *The New York Times*, this is the only movie in the trilogy that feels as much like a video game as a film.

The cliffhanger resumes with a mission to Tatooine to rescue Han Solo (Harrison Ford), frozen in carbon and captured by Jabba the Hutt. The plot divides into two parts: the rescue of Han Solo and the destruction of the newly activated Death Star and the defeat of the Empire. The latter conflict far supersedes the former in significance, but the second part can only follow if the heroes can be re-assembled, and both parts are given equal weight. Solo has to be free if he is to lead the attack on the moon of Endor to dismantle the Death Star's deflector shield. Rather too much time is spent on the rescue and its spectacle of strange and fabulous disgusting creatures in the Fortress of Jabba the Hutt. This spectacle far outdoes the earlier cantina sequence in the original *Star Wars*, and one wonders why Lucas wanted to extend it. At least in the presence of the Empire all the characters are recognizable humanoids and more believable, even if they are dressed like Nazi soldiers and speak English with vaguely sinister European accents.

The creature workshop must have worked overtime for this movie. The heroic creatures of the latter part consist mainly of cuddly Ewoks, who regiment themselves to assist Solo and Leia (Carrie Fisher) in overcoming legions of Star Troopers and Imperial Walkers on the moon of Endor. The Rebels are first captured by the Ewoks, who at first seem interested in cooking them, until they discover C-3PO and decide to worship "him" as a deity. C-3PO at first has problems with this because he has not been programmed to function as a droid-god, but he quickly adjusts in order to help his friends.

In this finale feature all relationships are clarified. Luke Skywalker (Mark Hamill) and Princess Leia (Carrie Fisher) turn out to be twins, both inheriting those Jedi genes, removing the obstacle of her divided love for Luke and Han Solo so that the galactic buccaneer and his princess may be united. This would be quite touching if the story were not so blatantly foolish. The finale has its moments as Luke confronts Darth Vader and the Emperor (Ian McDiarmid), but audiences will already have seen the Rebel fleet attack the Death Star and the second attack here seems conveniently indulgent.

Young Luke, growing older, pays a return visit to the Jedi Master Yoda, only to find that 900-year-old Zen gnome at death's door, able to give advice but not further instruction, which Luke apparently thinks he needs. The spirit of Obi Wan Kanobi appears to Luke, who confronts him about his failure to inform Luke that Darth Vader was really Luke's father, but Ben answers that once the Jedi Knight who was Luke's father turned to the dark side, he ceased to be Luke's father: "He is more machine than man, twisted and evil." Even so, Luke senses some goodness in Vader and resolves to change him back to what he was.

The film ends with a furry flurry of activity. Solo and Leia and the droids are trying to get to the deflector shields on the moon of Endor. The Rebel fleet is trying to hold its own until the deflector shields are down. And Luke and Darth Vader duel with their light sabers in the presence of the Emperor. When Luke refuses to convert, his father is ordered to kill him, but Luke has grown strong and deals Vader a fatal blow. Like an evil sorcerer, the Emperor then turns on Luke and seems about to kill him, but Vader has a final change of heart and attacks the Emperor to save his son, killing the Evil One. Knowing his death is near, Vader asks Luke to remove his helmet so that he may look on Luke with his own eyes before he dies. This is one of the film's few effective human moments.

CREDITS

Luke Skywalker: Mark Hamill
Princess Leia: Carrie Fisher
Han Solo: Harrison Ford
Lando Calrissian: Billy Dee Williams
C-3PO: Anthony Daniels
Chewbacca: Peter Mayhew
Darth Vader: David Prowse
Darth Vader: James Earl Jones (voice)
Yoda: Frank Oz (voice)
Wicket: Warwick Davis

Origin: USA
Released: 1983; 1997
Production: Howard Kazanjian, Robert Watts, Jim Bloom for Lucasfilm; released by 20th Century Fox
Direction: Richard Marquand
Screenplay: Lawrence Kasdan and George Lucas
Cinematography: Alan Hume, Jack Lowin, Jim Glennon
Editing: Sean Barton, Marcia Lucas, Duwayne Dunham, Arthur Repola
Music: John Williams
Production design: Norman Reynolds
Art direction: Fred Hole, James Schoppe, Joe Johnston
Costumes: Aggie Guerard Rodgers, Nilo Rodis, Jamero
MPAA rating: PG
Running Time: 133 minutes

So what's new here in this "special edition" re-release? The musical orgy at Jabba the Hutt's fortress adds new footage shot seventeen years later of Femi Taylor as Oola, the dancing slave girl, as truly strange creatures play and sing an anachronistic bluesy tune. There is more definition given to the sand monster Sarlacc awaiting human sacrifices from Jabba the Hutt. There are scenes of jubilation after the final victory in Tatooine, Cloud City, and the Imperial headquarters planet Coruscant. Stephen Holden accurately criticized the trilogy's "troubled dialogue about filmmaking and the relationship between technology and storytelling." The story potential gets seriously shorted in *The Return of the Jedi*; characters are diminished, as is the dialogue (neither Jabba the Hutt nor the Ewoks speak a language that can be understood), and spectacle reigns supreme. This is a film that will only delight diehard fans. The plot has run its course, and all that is left is spectacular escapism that can lead only to other contrived escapist spectacles, such as *Warriors of Virtue*. One hopes that in planning the next trilogy George Lucas will remember to emphasize the human component and maybe give the special effects a rest. Except for the conflict between Vader and Luke, the last sequel is hardly more interesting than an episode of one of the *Star Trek* spin-offs on television, offering little more than nostalgia for the true believers.

—*James M. Welsh*

REVIEWS

The Baltimore Sun. March 14, 1997, p. E1.
Entertainment Weekly. March 28, 1997, p. 46.
The New York Times. March 14, 1997, p. B3.
The Philadelphia Inquirer Weekend. March 14, 1997, p. 4.
The Washington Post. March 14, 1997, p. G1.
Washington Post Weekend. March 14, 1997, p. 44.

Rhyme & Reason

Box Office: $1,608,277

With his ambitious documentary *Rhyme & Reason*, director Peter Spirer attempts the definitive guide to the world of rap music. It is a serious and noble effort to introduce the uninitiated to an African-American cultural phenomenon, but most likely it plays more like a refresher course for an audience that is already heavily immersed in this self-contained universe.

While superficially engaging and ofttimes quite amusing, the film is an unwieldy oral history that lacks the in-depth analysis that might have helped those perplexed viewers who cannot even begin to decipher the differences between rap and hip-hop. (The explanation that "Rap is something that is being done, while hip-hop is something that is being lived" is not particularly enlightening.) Spirer presents a cornucopia of talking-head interviews with such rap luminaries as Ice-T, the late Tupac Shakur and the female duo Salt-N-Pepa. But he employs a scattershot technique that only the already-converted will embrace, while further alienating the mainstream.

Rhyme & Reason starts out promising as it attempts to delineate the history of rap music. It is traced back to the South Bronx in the mid-1970s, where outdoor block parties provided a competitive forum for the free-floating street culture—but claims are often merely unsubstantiated hearsay not necessarily based in fact. No comparison is made, however, to the earlier emergence of early-Sixties doo-wop, nor is the connection between and the significance of record "scratching," break-dancing, and graffiti clearly articulated.

Peter Spirer: " . . . the media had completely written off this culture, had misunderstood it and ignored it. It was time somebody really documented it for what it is and let the artists speak for themselves."

Spirer's film has a tendency to ramble; far too much ground is covered in its ninety-three minute time span, with too many artists included. (According to the press materials, some eighty artists were interviewed for the film.)

It is obvious that Peter Spirer viewed this film as a forum for social commentary, a broader platform for those inner-city denizens who view themselves as the oppressed masses. Yet his lack of perspective and narrow agenda fail to place this commentary within a broader social context. It might have been interesting to contrast the ways in which the mainstream media portrays and interprets the hip-hop culture with the rappers' perspective.

And therein lies perhaps the greatest weakness of *Rhyme & Reason* as a social document. The rap industry has been accused of pervasive misogyny—men routinely refer to women in such degrading terms as "bitch" and "ho" (street slang for whore)—and of promoting violence, guns, and drugs. Yet Spirer's documentary pays mere lip-service to these accusations, dismissing the use of such labels as not being automatically demeaning when taken in the context of tough street language. This is particularly noticeable in the way that the female rappers gingerly dance around the issue, diplomatically downplaying any possible sexism.

Of all the male rappers who appear in *Rhyme & Reason*, Los Angeles-born and based Ice-T is undoubtedly the most articulate, and would have served as an impressive guide through this confusing maze. Ensconced in his palatial home high in the prestigious Hollywood Hills—complete with its own private shark tank!—the ultra-successful recording artist blasts those critics who accuse him of betraying his "homies" by moving out of "the 'Hood." "There is no 'black community,'" he angrily declares to the camera, "There is a poor community, and I don't choose to live there." He expresses his belief that his indulgence in an opulent lifestyle sends a positive and reinforcing message to aspiring rappers, as well as ghetto youths, that it is possible to achieve success on one's own terms using a unique voice.

The captivating Ice-T goes on to vehemently accuse the dominant white culture of racial intolerance and reminds the viewer that, "I've got six gold records and my music's never been on the radio." With a startling insouciance, the West Coast rapper describes the allure of a violent gang lifestyle as he attempts to outline the origins of controversial "gangsta rap" and how it differs from the more lightweight and party-oriented East Coast music.

In the end, director Peter Spirer—a 1994 Oscar nominee for his documentary *Blood Ties: The Life and Work of Sally Mann*—resorts to too many superficial MTV video tricks of the trade while failing to adequately demonstrate the musical and lyrical nuances that define the individual artists.

—Patricia Kowal

CREDITS

Origin: USA
Released: 1997
Production: Charles X. Block, Peter Spirer and Daniel Sollinger for City Block Films and Aslan Pictures; released by Miramax Films
Direction: Peter Spirer
Cinematography: Peter Spirer, Daniel Sollinger, George Mitas, Sean Adair, Brennan McClean, Alex Rappaport, Adam Vardy, Antonio Ponti
Editing: Andy Robertson, David Wilson
Music supervisors: Happy Walters, Andrew Shack
MPAA rating: R
Running Time: 93 minutes

REVIEWS

Chicago Tribune. March 5, 1997, p. 1.
Los Angeles Times. March 5, 1997, p. F4.
New York Times. March 7, 1997.
San Francisco Chronicle. March 5, 1997, p. E5.
San Francisco Examiner. March 5, 1997, p. C3.
Variety. March 10, 1997, p. 80.

Ripe

No one stays innocent forever.—Movie tagline

"Utterly compelling. Daisy Eagan and Monica Keena give career-making performances."—Kevin Thomas, *Los Angeles Times*

"Strikingly original."—Manohla Dargis, *LA Weekly*

"Remarkable! An almost primeval vision of budding female sexuality."—Stephen Holden, *New York Times*

"A fabulous first feature."—Amy Holden, *Village Voice*

The feature debut of director Mo Ogrodnik, *Ripe* tells the story of fraternal twins Rosie (Daisy Eagan) and Violet (Monica Keena), who have fashioned an unusual "twin" bond, primarily to escape their brutish father and ineffectual mother. Throughout their childhood, their father was not above pointing loaded rifles at the girls in the guise of a "game." Understandably, when dad swerves away from a deer on the road and runs into a tree, killing himself and the twins' mother, they are far from upset. They hit the road, ready to seek their fortune. Rosie has convinced Violet that their lives will be infinitely better in Kentucky, so off to the Bluegrass State it is.

> Rosie about Violet: " . . . I made her promise me no boys—just the two of us—forever."

Tomboyish Rosie is the tougher of the two, madly in love with her more attractive sister. Although Rosie seems slightly more strange than Violet, both girls display aggressiveness in various ways—flirting, shoplifting, or lying to get what they want.

They encounter a greasy drifter, Pete (Gordon Currie), who has just taken a job as a handyman on the rundown local Army base. Rosie notices that Pete and Violet are attracted to one another (the fact that Violet is only 14 obviously holds no taboo for Pete at all). Soon the girls are ensconced on the shabby base, helping Pete with odd jobs, letting everyone think that he is their uncle. Disgusted and distraught at the burgeoning sexual feelings between Violet and Pete, Rosie finds a friend in straight-arrow Ken (Ron Brice), a former juvenile delinquent who has found discipline and meaning in the Army's rigorous life. Oblivious to Rosie's twisted personality, Ken shows Rosie how to shoot guns at the pistol range.

Writer/director Ogrodnik successfully shows how frighteningly vulnerable unhappy teens are to any and all kinds of attention—particularly the wrong kinds. Although it is all too painfully obvious that Rosie and Violet are careening down a dangerous path, Keena and Eagan are such wonderful, naturalistic actors that they wring pathos out of every scene. Ogrodnik has created characters so achingly real that one can almost see them flailing around on a sleazy daytime talk show, discussing their parental abuse, sisterly resentments, and problems with their dim-witted, unreliable men. Several scenes are so poignant and painfully ugly that one can both empathize and cringe in horror as the sisters lay themselves open for love, but find only more abuse. These girls are desperate to grow up and find their place in the adult world, and the only ticket they have in hand is their sexuality. Scenes of budding sexuality, such as Pete comforting Violet about her first period, are contrasted with the ugliness of Rosie's near-rape after a dance.

Rosie is seething with anger and jealousy when Pete and Violet start sleeping together. She begs Violet to help her pull together all their resources, which would enable them to get closer to Kentucky. Tragedy beckons when Rosie finds a stash of cash in Pete's belongings. She entices Pete and Violet to play their "game" from childhood and shoots Pete while they are alone in the closet. Stunned, Violet sees her sister for the out-of-control disturbed soul she really is and makes tracks with Pete's cash. As impossible as it was to imagine these two sisters alone

CREDITS

Violet: Monica Keena
Rosie: Daisy Eagan
Pete: Gordon Currie
Ken: Ron Brice
Jimmy: Vincent Laresca
Janet Wyman: Karen Lynn Gorney

Origin: USA
Released: 1996
Production: Suzy Landa and Tom Razzano for C&P Productions; released by Trimark Pictures
Direction: Mo Ogrodnik
Screenplay: Mo Ogrodnik
Cinematography: Wolfgang Held
Editing: Sarah Durham
Production design: Sally Petersen
Music: Anton Sanko
Art direction: Hannah Moseley
Costumes: Katherine Jane Bryant
Sound: Jonathan S. Gaynor
MPAA rating: R
Running Time: 93 minutes

without family to guide them, it is unfathomable to imagine what these two girls will do without each other. Ken seemed to be the only adult figure that had genuine and appropriate concern, coupled with normal restraint, in their lives, but he was no match for the dangerous pull of sexuality for these girls. Ogrodnik and her talented cast offer up a disturbing portrait of a family torn apart again and again, with no sign of a moral or rational compass in sight.

—G.E. Georges

REVIEWS

Entertainment Weekly. May 16, 1997, p. 89.
Filmmaker. Spring 1997, p. 47.
Los Angeles Times. May 30, 1997, p. F4.
New York Times. May 2, 1997, p. B16.
Variety. April 22, 1996, p. 92.
Village Voice. May 6, 1997, p. 86.

Rocket Man

He's just taking up space.—Movie tagline

Box Office: $15,435,096

If there is life on Mars, it's bound to be more intelligent than *Rocket Man*, a real spacey movie from Walt Disney's Caravan Pictures. It's the preposterous story of what happens when NASA decides to send a goofy computer geek named Fred Randall (Harlan Williams) on the first manned mission to Mars. Williams is a fairly funny guy with a rubbery face and a gift for imitation, but he's stuck in a film that is inane and instantly forgettable.

Rocket Man peaks in its opening scene, in which seven-year-old Fred pretends to be an astronaut by hiding inside a drier. "Houston, we have a problem," the boy intones as the drier starts to spin. Flash-forward 23 years later, and Randall is a programming wizard who drives an orange car that looks like an oversized golf cart, wears orange pants and likes to get to work five minutes early so he can play shoot-'em-up computer games. He's still a little boy who likes to pretend he's an astronaut.

Fred's constant cry when things go wrong: "It wasn't me!"

The unenviable task of scriptwriters Greg Erb and Craig Mazin is to get this moron into space. Since the target audience for this film is 11 and under, plausibility is no concern.

The mission's flight director (Jeffrey DeMunn) and two of his crew members visit Randall, who wrote the mission's landing program, to ask him about a glitch. During the visit, one of the astronauts suffers a skull fracture when Randall's table-top landing simulator hits his head. That leaves an opening for a computer specialist, and for no good reason Randall is considered a candidate.

The film's only concession to logic — and one of its funnier lines — comes when crew member Julie Ford (Jessica Lundy) questions Randall's candidacy by asking: "Because we're going to Mars, we should take along a guy who's from Mars?" The answer, improbably, is yes. Randall has to beat out only one competitor. Director Stuart Gillard has some fun with the training competitions. Yet even here, the film cheats. When Fred and his competitor have to spend 24 hours in side-by-side isolation chambers, Fred drives the other guy crazy by loudly singing nonsense songs and reciting dialogue from sock-puppets plays he invents. An isolation chamber that can admit noise only from an adjacent isolation chamber? Even kids can figure out there's something wrong with that premise.

Though *Rocket Man* is silly, it's at least agreeably so in the early going. Williams has more comic range than Jim Carrey, the comedian whom he most resembles in physique and style. Williams isn't laugh-out-loud funny, but he's clever at mimicry, at facial expressions, and at sheer goofiness. When the flight is on its way to Mars and the crew chimp Ulysses steals Randall's place in a sleep chamber, Fred has to get through eight months of insomnia while the other two crew members, Ford and Commander Wild Bill Overbeck (William Sadler), are hibernating. It's Gillard's best sequence, as he gives us rapid looks at Randall painting with space food, dancing with an empty space suit, and doing his own take on bits from old B-movies.

Another positive is that most of *Rocket Man*'s brand of humor isn't offensive. In family films these days, that's a blessing. There is one bit involving flatulence and shared oxygen, but it's actually pretty funny. Apart from that, there is nary any potty humor or sexual innuendo, so this film is safer for children than those of Carrey or Adam Sandler.

But Gillard and his screenwriters aren't content to stay merely silly. They feel compelled to give Randall some redeeming qualities, and that's where the film goes badly awry. It starts when, during a live global broadcast feed, Randall speaks of his childlike awe of outer space and starts leading millions of viewers around the globe in singing "He's got the whole world in his hands." The goofball suddenly has become a warm and fuzzy goofball. It gets worse when Julie Ford's gruff exterior suddenly evaporates and she too falls for Fred's juvenile whimsy. Looking out a spaceship porthole at the stars, Ford says to Fred: "For all the research I've done, I don't really understand what's out there." Right. Female astronauts are really weak-kneed little girls at heart. Lundy doesn't fare well in pulling off this difficult transition from hard-bitten researcher to someone ditzy enough to fall for an overgrown little boy. Throughout the film, she is more maternal than romantic, which is probably appropriate since Randall is a momma's boy.

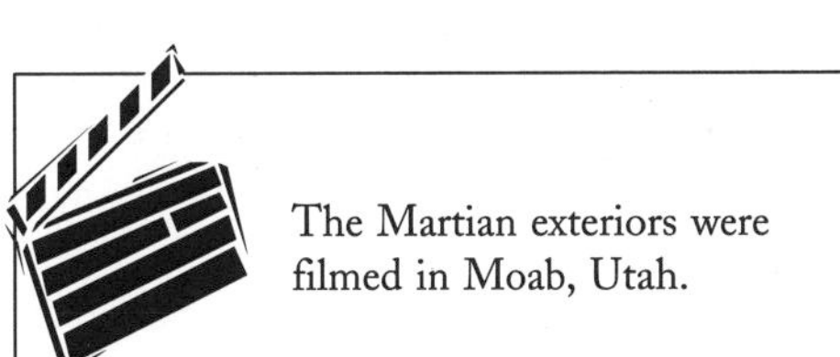

The Martian exteriors were filmed in Moab, Utah.

The nutty space traveler also forms an improbable alliance with Bud (Beau Bridges), an ex-astronaut blamed for messing up the ill-fated Apollo 13 mission. Bridges, a serious actor, looks like he's wandered into the wrong movie. He shuffles around in a plaid shirt with a cup of coffee in-hand, speaking softly, and apparently hoping not to be recognized. Bud is redeemed because he, too, for some unfathomable reason, believes in Randall, though Fred's given him no reason to do so.

So even though he's an imbecile, Fred Randall is revealed as a gentle, lovable guy with a deep love for the universe and a refreshing belief in the goodness of all mankind. Worse still, the last 30 minutes of the film endows him with superhuman courage, nerves of steel, and genius under pressure. Single-handedly, Randall saves the Mars mission from disaster. All the while, he keeps acting like an idiot.

The tone of *Rocket Man* is flagrantly inconsistent. Randall starts out being laughable and ends up being laudable, and what held promise of being a wacky farce turns into a maudlin sermon. One minute Randall is dropping the American flag into a Martian crater and fashioning a new one out of his stars-and-stripes underpants, the next he is lifting a land rover off Overbeck in the middle of a blinding sandstorm.

It's typical for something that bears the Disney imprimatur to try to combine goofiness with tugs at the heartstrings. In this film, though, the formula simply doesn't work. In the midst of a slapstick, senseless film, audiences must bear Harland Williams crooning "When You Wish Upon A Star" with his starstruck astronaut girlfriend staring dreamily into his eyes. *Rocket Man*'s central character is alternately held up for ridicule, because he is ridiculous, and then hailed as heroic, which is even more ridiculous.

As it churns predictably to its paint-by-numbers conclusion, *Rocket Man* becomes embarrassingly bad. Adults might want to look away, and children will be, at best, mildly amused. Its worst feature might be a cameo by the once-promising comic actress Shelley Duvall, who looks and acts ghastly. That she shared top billing with Bridges shows the paucity of material here for marketers to promote.

Another problem for *Rocket Man* is that in an era filled with outer-space films that are loaded with fantastic special effects, this film looks chintzy. That would be fine if the movie was played strictly for laughs, but it's not. It aspires to being pretentious, and that's fatal. If *Rocket Man* had sim-

CREDITS

Fred Z. Randall: Harland Williams
Julie Ford: Jessica Lundy
"Wild Bill" Overbeck: William Sadler
Paul Wick: Jeffrey DeMunn
Ben Stevens: James Pickens Jr.
Bud Nesbitt: Beau Bridges
Gary Hackman: Peter Onorati

Origin: USA
Released: 1997
Production: Roger Birnbaum for Caravan Pictures and Walt Disney Pictures; released by Buena Vista
Direction: Stuart Gillard
Screenplay: Craig Mazin and Greg Erb
Cinematography: Steven Poster
Editing: William D. Gordean
Music: Michael Tavera
Production design: Roy Forge Smith
Art direction: Michael Rizzo, Joseph Hodges
Sound: Pud Cusack
Costumes: Daniel Orlsndi
MPAA rating: PG
Running Time: 94 minutes

REVIEWS

Boxoffice. December, 1997, p. 52.
Cinemafantastique. November, 1997, p. 116.
Entertainment Weekly. October 14, 1997, p. 46.
Los Angeles Times. October 10, 1997, p. F14.
New York Times. October 10, 1997, p. E14.
USA Today. October 10, 1997, p. 4D.
Variety. October 13, 1997, p. 78.

ply been content to lampoon the whole astronaut business, it might have had a chance to go into orbit. Failing that, however, it has the look and feel of a throwaway — a film made by people with limited talent and limited vision who are almost cynical in their estimation of how much preposterous stuff a juvenile audience will tolerate. Yes, kids will consume anything, but they're not likely to remember *Rocket Man* as one of their favorite cinematic meals.

—*Michael Betzold*

Romy and Michele's High School Reunion

The blonde leading the blonde.—Movie tagline

"More fun than a trip to the mall!"—Gayl Murphy, *ABC Radio*

"Totally irresistible!"—Ron Brewington, *American Urban Radio*

"An all-out hoot with a huge heart!"—Alan Silverman, *Voice of America*

"Sorvino and Kudrow are brilliant!"—Paul Wunder, *WBAI Radio*

Box Office: $29,235,353

When the reunion committee sends out invitations, every generation of Americans faces the prospect of re-examining their high school years. For some they evoke nostalgia, happiness and laughter. For others they bring forth loneliness, anger, sorrow, or hate. And since art imitates life, it's no surprise that reunion movies pop up in the theaters each time a generation checks their mailboxes and finds the past beckoning to them.

Earlier this year *Grosse Pointe Blank* had John Cusack returning to his Michigan hometown worried about how to answer the inevitable question, "What are you doing now?" Since he was a professional hit man, it posed quite a dilemma. Luckily, Cusack had a canny script to help audiences breeze through the film. And where *Grosse Pointe Blank*'s script made for a good black comedy, *Romy and Michele's High School Reunion*'s actresses and unforgettable characters make for a highly entertaining light comedy.

"All we really need are, like, better jobs and boyfriends, right?"—Romy, about changing their lives before going to the reunion.

Everybody was insecure and made someone else's life miserable in high school is the first message of *Romy and Michele*. For Romy (Mira Sorvino) and her best friend Michele (Lisa Kudrow), it was the A-list girls. A quartet of bitches led by Christie (Julia Campbell) whose idea of a joke is to stick refrigerator magnets onto Michele's body brace which she wears to cure her scoliosis. Michele, in turn, made high school hell for resident geeks Sandy Frink (Alan Cumming) who had an unrequited crush on her, and on Heather (Janeane Garofalo) who had an unrequited crush on the oblivious Sandy.

But *Romy and Michele* is not a film about insecurity and revenge—although there is the necessary retaliation against Christie and her self-absorbed boyfriend/husband Billy (Vincent Ventresca) on whom Romy has always had a crush. Believe it or not, this airy comedy goes deeper than that. Because behind the self-doubt is the question of our basic identity. Who were we in high school, who are we now, and how do we want to present ourselves when we revisit our past? What's truly incredible is that we come to this realization through two characters who could easily be stereotyped as dumb blondes. But are they?

Well, yes and no. There certainly seems to be a reality filter on the world-views of these leggy beauties, but in a way, it all makes sense in their world—and their world, in essence, is a happy one. The two late twenty-something women live comfortably in a Venice Beach, California apartment. Michele is currently unemployed and Romy works as a cashier at a Jaguar dealership. But when re-examining their lives in preparation for the reunion, it comes as a genuine surprise to them that, as Romy notes, "our lives don't look as impressive as I thought." Consequently, in the two weeks they have, they decide to make a few drastic changes in their lives. "All we really need are, like, better jobs and boyfriends, right?" says Romy. But as Michele reminds her, "if they were that easy to get wouldn't we have them by now?"

But, that doesn't stop our reality-challenged heroines. If you can't be the real thing, pretend. So, they borrow a Jaguar, put on Michele-made little black suits to pass themselves off as successful businesswomen, and drive off to Tucson. On the way there it occurs to them that they don't know what business they're in. So they decide they invented Post-It Notes. Eventually, though, the weight of creating and maintaining this deception is a burden that strains their friendship to the breaking point. It also provides the basis for a hilarious fantasy sequence in which Michele provides a very convincing explanation of how she discovered Post-It glue but also for yet another Christie-inspired public embarrassment for the two.

Eventually, however, Romy and Michele decide to just be themselves, and with this discovery comes an empowerment that gives the film a satisfying, feel-good ending.

CREDITS

Romy: Mira Sorvino
Michele: Lisa Kudrow
Heather: Janeane Garofalo
Sandy Frink: Alan Cumming
Christie: Julia Campbell
Cheryl: Mia Cottet
Kelly: Kristin Bauer
Lisa: Elaine Hendrix
Billy: Vincent Ventresca
Toby: Camryn Manheim
Cowboy: Justin Theroux
Ramon: Jacob Vargas

Origin: USA
Released: 1997
Production: Laurence Mark for Bungalow 78 Productions; released by Touchstone Pictures
Direction: David Mirkin
Screenplay: Robin Schiff; adapted from her play *Ladies Room*
Cinematography: Reynaldo Villalobos
Editing: David Finfer
Production design: Mayne Berke
Set decoration: Jackie Carr
Costumes: Mona May
Music: Steve Bartek
Sound: David Ronne
MPAA rating: R
Running Time: 91 minutes

Interestingly enough, the characters of Romy and Michele first appeared in writer Robin Schiff's play *Ladies' Room*, which featured a pre-"Friends" Kudrow in the part she also plays here. At the time they were minor characters, but audiences responded so favorably to them that a story featuring them was inevitable.

Although first-time feature film director David Mirkin does an assured job with the interweaving of high school past with reunion present, kudos really belong to editor David Finfer and costume designer Mona May (*Clueless*). From prom dresses a la Madonna to reunion gowns of shine and fluff, May's costumes help to bring out the essential characters of Romy and Michele: two beauties hidden behind blonde assumptions and skin-tight kookiness.

Not since Bill and Ted had a few excellent adventures have two dimwits been played so lovably and to perfection. Sorvino, hot off her Oscar for *Mighty Aphrodite*, is a perfect counterpart for TV's "Friends" star Lisa Kudrow. They feed off each other's shallowness and silliness and make for a great comic team. We laugh at them, but we care about them.

It is left to Janeane Garofalo to provide some much needed wickedness within all the sweetness. Chain-smoking and wisecracking, the hard-boiled Heather provides us yet another pair of eyes through which to experience the realities of self-doubt and image.

Romy and Michele is a charming, light comedy that doesn't mind being slyly intelligent when presenting a message that might seem trite in any less goofy or entertaining context.

—Beverley Bare Buehrer

REVIEWS

Boxoffice. July, 1997, p. 94.
Chicago Tribune. April 25, 1997, p. 5.
Entertainment Weekly. May 2, 1997, p. 42.
Los Angeles Times. April 25, 1997, p. F4.
New York Times. April 25, 1997, p. C5.
People. May 5, 1997, p. 21.
Sight and Sound. September, 1997, p.54.
USA Today. April 25, 1997, p. 4D.
Village Voice. May 6, 1997, p. 79.

Rosewood

In 1923, a black town was burned to the ground, its people hunted and murdered because of a lie. This film is for them.—Movie tagline

"Touching and emotionally explosive. Makes an impact that won't soon be forgotten."—David Sheehan, *CBS-TV*

"A terrific film. A gripping story."—Roger Ebert, *Chicago Sun-Times*

"It is an impressive, epic production."—Gene Siskel, *Chicago Tribune*

"A great film. A superb cast."—Bob Strauss, *Los Angeles Daily News*

"*Rosewood* is an impressive film - significant and powerful."—Kenneth Turan, *Los Angeles Times*

"One of the most important films you will see this year!"—Sara Edwards, *NBC News*

"Don't miss it! Jon Voight and Ving Rhames are superb. Brilliant."—Paul Wunder, *WBAI Radio*

"An unforgettable film. Superior performances."—Pat Collins, *WWOR-TV*

Box Office: $13,177,005

Mann (Ving Rhames) and Beulah (Elise Neal) seek shelter as a false accusation of rape by a white woman causes a white mob to burn down the small black town in Florida in *Rosewood.*

If America now recognizes a shameful weave in its historical tapestry—that of slavery—this does not mean that every fiber in that weave has been revealed to the light of day. Around 60 years following the abolition of slavery, in the early 1920s, a black town called Rosewood was consumed in a conflagration of hatred. Director John Singleton and screenwriter Gregory Poirier's involving effort in *Rosewood* illuminates the horrible true story of a modern American massacre.

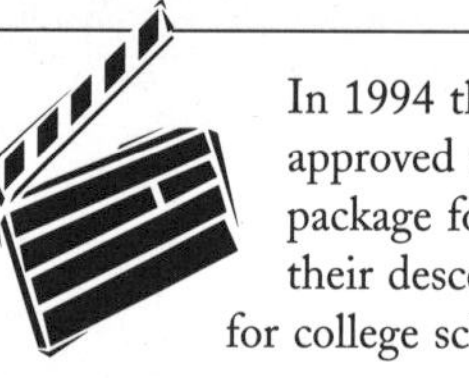

In 1994 the Florida legislature approved a compensation package for living survivors, their descendants, and money for college scholarships.

Although the record is not clear as to exactly how many victims perished, what is certain is that Rosewood's presence as an independent town for African Americans in Florida came, in essence, to a terrible end.

In this long picture, Singleton begins by presenting a bucolic tranquility—at least on the surface. In Rosewood, houses and their crops are well-ordered, and people are gainfully employed and doing well. On a distasteful note, store owner John Wright (Jon Voight) is having sex with his young black employee, thereby cheating on his wife and taking advantage of his worker, and all the while he is looking for opportunities to increase his wealth. The early casual references to "niggers" and "crackers" provide early hints of the strife to come.

It is December 31, 1923, when Mann (Ving Rhames) rides into town. His horse needs re-shoeing, and he is forced to spend a night there. School teacher Scrappie (Elise Neal), the cousin of the town's music teacher Sylvester Carrier (Don Cheadle), catches Mann's eye; Carrier has already warned one of the white men in neighboring Sumner not to be disrespectful of Scrappie and her beauty. Mann is invited to dinner at the Carriers, and is particularly made welcome by the matriarch of the family, Aunt Sarah (Esther Rolle), who declares that "crackers" cannot change their attitude towards "colored folk."

Mann is immediately attracted not only to the prosperous town and the lot adjacent to Wright's that is up for sale, he and Scrappie are drawn together. We learn that he is a veteran of the Great War, that he was wounded, and that he volunteered for action. Meanwhile, Wright's intention to purchase the vacant land is to the chagrin of his new wife Mary (Kathryn Meisel). Not only does she want to move from the town, she realizes that her husband has not recovered from the death of his first wife, and that his two boys do not want her to be their mother.

At the auction, Mann and a surprised Wright go head-to-head in bidding. Elsewhere, Fanny Taylor (Catherine Kellner) is being beaten by her lover (Robert Patrick), watched silently and helplessly by Aunt Sarah. Rather than accuse her white lover of the crime, and thereby expose her infidelity to her husband James (Loren Dean), she staggers out in the street and cries for help. She insists to the sheriff (Michael Rookner) that she has been raped by a black man, and at once a crowd of white people gather.

As Aunt Sarah looks on, Fanny begins to retract her story when the sheriff insists on the truth. She wilfully proclaims she was beaten, and this is enough to set off some of the men—people disgruntled at their inferior quality of life compared to the more affluent inhabitants of Rosewood. The mob's greed and prejudice is soon aflame.

A notion runs that the perpetrator is an escaped convict, and perhaps the stranger who rode into town the day before. The auction is called off when news spreads of Fanny's claim and the assault on two members of the black community subsequent to the false accusation.

The evening finds the black community in the church assessing the situation. Wright turns up but is asked to leave. Mann is saddling his horse, only to be intercepted by Scrappie. He tells her that he will return when the trouble has subsided, and asks her to keep his war medal for him until that time. In turn, she hands over her scarf for him to wear. It is a rare moment of tenderness in an inexorably tragic situation.

The following day, a judge appears in town and orders the capture of the culprit. Aunt Sarah laments that "nigger—it's just another word for guilty." By evening, trying to affix to a semblance of normalcy, Sylvester and his family hold a birthday party for his son. But a mob advances on the house, is deaf to Sarah's pleas, and a renegade shooter murders her. Clambering beyond Sarah's body, the assaulters try to take the cottage. Sylvester orders the children evacuated into the nearby woods while he takes a stand alongside his cousin. Fire soon overtakes the house, and as the mob enters, what looks like Sylvester's corpse lies on the stairs.

A pained John Wright supplies ammunition to the blood-thirsty whites while remonstrating with them. But the senseless hatred grows, with men in KKK hoods now appearing, blacks lynched and hung from trees, the church burned, and the hiding children retreating further into the woods—now under the guidance of Mann, who has returned to do what he can.

Forced to choose sides, Wright supplies Mann with bullets. Slowly he is impelled onto the just road, and he and his wife begin to shelter blacks in their house. He forms a plan to reroute the local train to scoop up the surviving children and whisk them to Gainesville. Mann senses danger in the tactic, but Wright insists they have no choice.

Wright then persuades the two sympathetic train drivers to carry out his proposal, only for the train to break down under the duress of its excessive speed. In what is left of Rosewood, Mary Wright fends off attackers, and Mann marshals his charges until being captured. Upon his horse, a noose is set on his neck, and he seems to be hanged, but in a touch of Hollywood corn, he survives, pulls the rope away, and gets back onto his faithful animal.

With the train fixed, it races onto its rendezvous, and the children are rescued. Mann fights off their pursuers, boards, exchanges a salute with Wright, and takes his leave, promising to meet up with Scrappie. And, like a resurrection of the dead, the brave Sylvester appears on horseback.

An exhausted Wright returns to his wife, and his two boys acknowledge her as their rightful new mother. The train plows on to freedom. But it leaves behind a ruined Rosewood and many, many dead. A final shot reveals untouched white-owned houses on one side of the railway track, and devastation on the other.

John Singleton's film is a mainstream Hollywood effort, boasting accomplished cinematography by Johnny E. Jensen and editing by Bruce Cannon, a swelling John Williams score, detailed production design courtesy of Paul Sylbert, set design by Mark Garner, and acrobatic stunts coordinated by Glenn Randall Jr.

In its review, *Variety* admitted that although the film "increasingly succumbs to a tendency towards conventional movie heroics . . . [it] tells a story of rare interest and tragedy." The *Los Angeles Times* called the film "impressive," but also pointed to the fact that it was "broader and more simplistic than it needs to be." Critic Kenneth Turan praised "the sequences of torture and violence" as having "undeniable force," but disliked the "few show-biz plot twists," near the end.

Indeed, the chase to catch the train to freedom does have a familiar Hollywood feel to it, yet it does work to spur the audience's hopes that some will escape the massacre. Performances are satisfying throughout the large cast. As the plucky Scrappie, Elise Neal makes a favorable impression, and the underrated Don Cheadle turns in a portrait of quiet pride and erupting anger as the defiant Carrier. Set against Ving Rhames's straightforwardly stalwart Mann—someone who has seen horrors on the battlefield and naturally wishes to do everything to avoid witnessing them afresh—is an intriguingly flawed John Wright. As written, and acted by Voight, shopkeeper Wright is first and foremost a neo-bourgeois citizen who is not particularly racist: Whomever he can make money from, black or white, is equal in his eyes. His slow arousal to take the steps towards some kind of justice are the most interesting aspects of *Rosewood.*

Rightly choked by rage at the thought of such a hideous occurrence on 20th-century American soil, writer Poirier and director Singleton channel their fury into creating a fairly gripping depiction of that incident. Poirier sketches

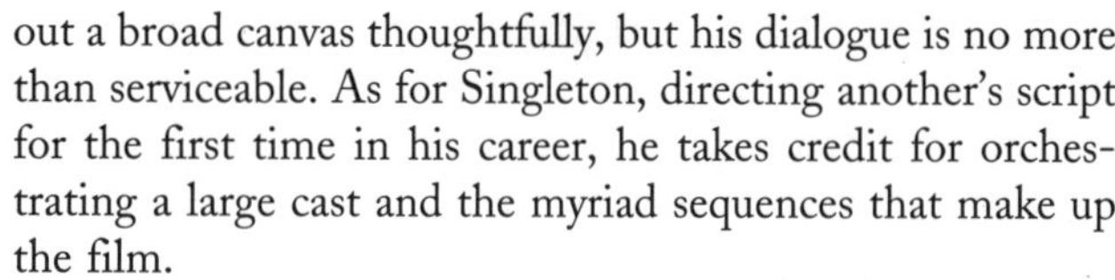

CREDITS

John Wright: Jon Voight
Mann: Ving Rhames
Sylvester Carrier: Don Cheadle
Duke: Bruce McGill
James Taylor: Loren Dean
Sarah Carrier: Esther Rolle
Scrappie: Elise Neal
Fannie Taylor: Catherine Kellner
Sheriff Walker: Michael Rooker

Origin: USA
Released: 1997
Production: Jon Peters for New Deal Productions; released by Warner Brothers
Direction: John Singleton
Screenplay: Gregory Poirier
Cinematography: Johnny E. Jensen
Editing: Bruce Cannon
Music: John Williams
Production design: Paul Sylbert
Art direction: Chris Gorak
Set decoration: Dan May
Costumes: Ruth E. Carter
Sound: Veda Campbell
MPAA rating: R
Running Time: 140 minutes

out a broad canvas thoughtfully, but his dialogue is no more than serviceable. As for Singleton, directing another's script for the first time in his career, he takes credit for orchestrating a large cast and the myriad sequences that make up the film.

When the credits roll, one cannot be filled with anything less than sorrow at the tragedy of *Rosewood.* The motion picture bearing the lost town's blood-drenched name is not, ultimately, memorable. Yet if it etches the history of that place into the American consciousness a little deeper, it has done a noble, and necessary, job.

—*Paul B. Cohen*

REVIEWS

Boxoffice. April 1997, p. 198.
Chicago Tribune. February 21, 1997, p. 5.
Detroit News. February 21, 1997, p. D1.
Entertainment Weekly. March 7, 1997, p. 46.
The Los Angeles Times. February 21, 1997, p. F15.
New York Times. December 28, 1996, p. 11.
New York Times. February 21, 1997, p. B18.
People. March 3, 1997, p. 19.
Rolling Stone. March 20, 1997, p. 90.
Time. March 3, 1997.
USA Today. February 21, 1997, p. 4D.
Variety. February 17, 1997, p. 68.
Village Voice. March 4, 1997, p. 76.

Rough Magic

In the world of magic, the hand is quicker than the eye and love is the wild card.—Movie tagline

"Charming, witty, fetching and full of twists."—Jonathan Rosenbaum, *Chicago Reader*

"*Rough Magic* is distinguished by its solid performances, excellent cinematography and dazzling production design"—Maria Garcia, *Film Journal*

"There's fun surprising trickery here."—Sarah Miller—*Philadelphia Weekly*

Rough Magic tells the story of Myra Shumway (Bridget Fonda), a tough cookie by all accounts. Orphaned at an early age, she has grown into a lovely woman, working as a magician's assistant in 1950s Los Angeles. She is used to having knives tossed at her, and being sawed in half by her mentor, magician Ivan (Kenneth Mars). Myra is an assistant who would make any magician proud; she has an innate feel for any trick or situation—a natural. Ivan is concerned that her impending marriage to slick, aspiring politician Cliff Wyatt (D.W. Moffett) is doomed, and he is determined to stop the wedding. Ivan is correct; Wyatt is in love with Myra more for her status as an orphan (and voter sympathy) than with Myra herself. In a twisted bit of business, Myra takes a picture of Wyatt accidentally shooting Ivan. Fearing for her life, and realizing that the roll of film is the only thing between her safety and the wrong end of a .45, Myra escapes to Mexico with Wyatt right behind her.

Once in Mexico, Myra cannot leave her magic roots behind. Hooking up with snake oil salesman Doc Ansell (Jim Broadbent), they decide to join forces and hatch a plan to seek out a famous medicine woman and get the recipe for her powerful elixir.

However, Wyatt is not done with Myra; he sends handsome Alex Ross (Russell Crowe) after her, with an equally handsome price on her head. Alex is a typical down-and-out reporter who hides a heart of gold under his gruff exterior. When he and Myra meet they court and spark in classic hard-boiled Hollywood repartee—"You're a tough girl." "I'm smooth for the right pair of hands—a girl's gotta keep her knuckles nimble." After a disastrous encounter with surly Mexican mechanic Diego (Paul Rodriguez), Myra, Alex, and Doc find an Indian guide who takes them to the medicine woman, Tojola (Euva Anderson).

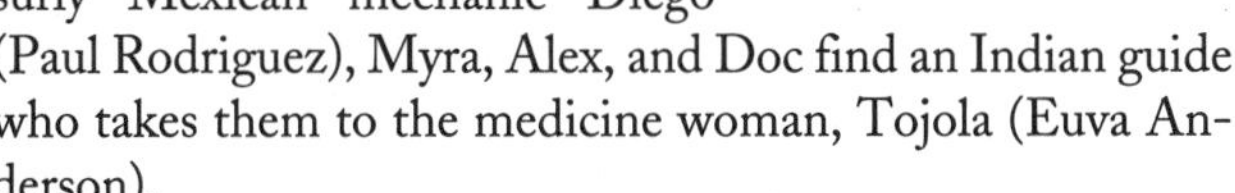

Ivan the magician to Myra: "Magic, my dear, comes from the heart, not the head."

Myra is extremely affected by her visit with Tojola. She goes in and out of trances, sees visions, and ultimately passes out, remaining unconscious until Alex, crazy with concern for her safety, finds her and brings Myra back to a hotel. At this point Alex and Myra cannot conceal their attraction, and kiss. Suddenly, Wyatt enters, ready to take over possession of his wayward fiancee. Sickened, Myra rushes to the bathroom where she vomits up what appears to be her trusting and loving heart. Even though Myra doesn't trust Wyatt and knows that the incriminating roll of film she still has is her only ticket to safety, she is so furious at Alex that she goes back to Los Angeles with Wyatt.

Back home, Myra has consistent visions and hallucinations. Alex tracks her down and tries to win her back, but he is shocked to hug her and feel that she has no pulse—no heart! She callously sends him away and prepares to marry Wyatt.

The day of the wedding, Myra breaks down and confesses her misery to Wyatt's assistant. She realizes that she must follow her heart, and leaves Wyatt at the altar. Surprisingly, Wyatt finds his (male) assistant suddenly irresistible, and the two men embrace. Leaving the church Myra is shocked to find Ivan the magician alive and well and driving a cab! He admits he disappeared in order to show her the way to find her own true love. Myra heads home and finds Alex waiting for her. After a close examination, Alex is overjoyed to discover that Myra has her heart back and they retire to practice their own magic.

Director Clare Peploe tries her best to fashion this rambling story into a quirky romantic comedy, but she cannot reign in the wildly disparate plot and ragtag group of characters. Fonda tries her best but the stilted faux film noir dialogue falls flat. Crowe fared much better with the fifties time period in the 1997 critically acclaimed *L.A. Confidential.* Peploe has a fondness for different images dropped into the story to symbolize the elusiveness of magic, but by the final shot of two bunnies fornicating, it is obvious that this technique hasn't worked. Peploe tries for whimsy but doesn't succeed.

—G.E. Georges

CREDITS

Myra Shumway: Bridget Fonda
Alex Ross: Russell Crowe
Doc Ansell: Jim Broadbent
Cliff Wyatt: D.W. Moffett
Diego: Paul Rodriguez
Tojola: Euva Anderson
Ivan: Kenneth Mars

Origin: Great Britain
Released: 1995, 1997
Production: Laurie Parker and Declan Baldwin for UGC Images and Recorded Picture Company; released by Goldwyn Entertainment Company
Direction: Clare Peploe
Screenplay: Clare Peploe, William Brookfield, and Robert Mundy; based on the novel *Miss Shumway Waves a Wand* by James Hadley Chase
Cinematography: John J. Campbell
Editing: Suzanne Fenn
Music: Richard Hartley
Production design: Waldemar Kalinowski
Costumes: Richard Hornung
MPAA rating: PG-13
Running Time: 104 minutes

REVIEWS

Boxoffice. May, 1997, p. 55.
Chicago Tribune. May 30, 1997, p. 5.
Los Angeles Times. May 30, 1997, p. F4.
New York Times. May 30, 1997, p. B12.
New Yorker. June 2, 1997, p. 92.
Sight and Sound. April, 1996, p. 52.
USA Today. June 6, 1997, p. 12D.
Variety. September 11, 1995, p. 108.

Rudyard Kipling's The Second Jungle Book: Mowgli and Baloo; The Second Jungle Book: Mowgli and Baloo; Jungle Book 2

Journey back to a magical place where the adventure all began.—Movie tagline

"The entire family will love it!"—Elayne Blythe, *Film Advisory Board*

"A thrilling jungle adventure for children of all ages."—Ted Baehr, *Movie Guide Magazine*

Rudyard Kipling, British journalist, poet, fiction writer, jingoist, published *The Jungle Book* in 1894 and *The Second Jungle Book* in 1895. No filmmaker has ever done justice to the books as they were written. The two previous major screen adaptations are *The Jungle Book* (1942), starring Sabu, and Walt Disney's animated feature *The Jungle Book* (1967), in which Kipling's wise and sober animals are shown singing and dancing to songs like "Trust in Me," "I Wanna Be Like You," and "Bare Necessities."

Harrison: "I'll be a monkey's uncle, the animals are cooperating with each other."

Most people take it for granted that all the stories in *The Jungle Book* and its sequel are about Mowgli. Many editions titled "The Jungle Book" contain nothing but Mowgli stories. Actually, Kipling included seven other stories in the two books, the best known being about Rikki-Tikki-Tavi, the brave little mongoose who kills deadly cobras. Two other stories were about seals in the Arctic. *Rudyard Kipling's the Second Jungle Book*, like its predecessors, is outrageously unfaithful to the stories of Kipling. As in previous productions, this latest borrowing focuses on Mowgli and incorporates elements from "Letting in the Jungle," "The King's Ankus," "Tiger! Tiger!" and "Kaa's Hunting."

This new film adaptation is distinguished from its predecessors by being given a title that will be impossible to fit on any marquee: *Rudyard Kipling's the Second Jungle Book: Mowgli and Baloo.* When the title appears on the screen it also includes the subtitle *Kaa's Hunting*. In the Kipling story he is one of Mowgli's principal animal friends. In the film version, however, the enormous python is used against Mowgli and spends most of his time wrapped around the neck of Karait (Dyrk Ashton), a tracker who uses the snake as a bloodhound. Kaa is so lethargic that he seems present mainly for visual interest, all sixteen feet of him.

Mowgli's chief animal enemy is the tiger Shere Khan, who has sworn to kill the little wild boy and devour him. Fortunately, Mowgli has plenty of friends in the animal kingdom, especially Baloo, a wise brown bear who teaches Mowgli the Law of the Jungle and the languages of all the animals; Grey Wolf, one of Mowgli's wolf cub "brothers"; and Bagheera, a black panther who also acts as Mowgli's guardian and tutor. Shere Khan appears in the film but is only a minor threat to Mowgli. The main threat comes from Harrison (Bill Campbell), an American hunter who collects wild animals for the P.T. Barnum circus.

Harrison immediately realizes that the wild boy would be a stellar attraction in America. He drops everything and sets out after Mowgli through the jungle, accompanied by Karait and two others. The local potentate Buldeo (Gulshan Grover), who volunteers to join the posse, soon makes it obvious that he has no intention of helping bring Mowgli back alive. Buldeo believes, probably correctly, that Mowgli is actually his own nephew and the rightful heir to his lands and fortune. On more than one occasion he is on the point of murdering the little boy but is thwarted by one of Mowgli's animal friends. Buldeo, like the other human characters in the film, did not appear in any of Kipling's stories but was created out of whole cloth by the screenwriters.

The other human in the hunting party is Chuchundra (David Paul Francis), who is along to provide comic relief. This Indian con-artist, posing as an organ grinder, has trained a little monkey to steal for him. The monkey, dressed in a bellhop uniform, sees an opportunity to escape from a life of crime and unnatural living conditions and runs off with Mowgli. Chuchundra's comedy is based largely on the fact that he is a city man totally out of place in a jungle setting. Chuchundra is torn between fear and greed, always hoping to recapture his talented little monkey. He is terrified by all the animals he encounters, especially by Baloo the enormous black bear and Bagheera the black panther with the glowing green eyes.

There are only two women in the film, and they have minimalistic parts. Emily Reece (Cornelia Hayes O'Herlihy) and Molly Ward (Amy Robbins) are wives of British colonial officers. These fair ladies wear long skirts and blouses with muttonchop sleeves, helping to lend the film a note of historical authenticity, as do the uniforms of the officers and enlisted men.

This low-budget film should appeal to children because the real stars, except for Mowgli, are the trained animals. The tiger, the black panther, and the young wolves are all beautiful animals. Baloo the bear is also impressive, although his acting talents are limited to rearing back and growling while walking on his hind legs. These animals give the film a feeling of freedom and wildness which is the main appeal of Kipling's stories. Adolfo Bartoli's camera work enlivens the film. Director Duncan McLachlan does a creditable job considering that he is working with animals and inexperienced actors in the outdoors. The script by Bayard Johnson and Matthew Horton relies heavily on voice-over narration to fill viewers in on Mowgli's history and what the animals are supposedly doing.

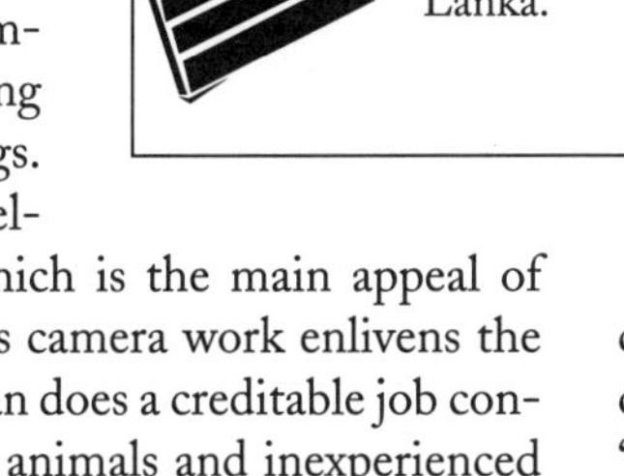

Filmed on location in Sri Lanka.

The little Indian boy who was lost in the jungle of Central India as an infant is played by cute, precocious James Williams. Unlike Sabu, Williams does not have any dialogue. He sometimes howls and snarls like a wolf, but human language is unknown to the character he plays. When he is captured in the jungle he puts up an amazing fight for a child who could not be much more than nine years old. He is also as agile as a monkey. In fact, he outruns, outclimbs and outleaps the two chimpanzees who were trying to capture him before he ran into the trainload of British soldiers and colonizers.

Chimpanzees obviously do not belong in India but make better actors than the Indian monkeys who inhabit the forgotten city. The monkey people want to make Mowgli their prisoner so that they can "learn the ways of humans." They already have one human captive who is under the delusion that he is their king. This is King Murphy (Roddy McDowall), who still wears the familiar red coat of a British soldier and has been AWOL for many years. Murphy is no longer useful to the monkey people, however, because he is old and crazy. As the talented Roddy McDowall portrays him, Murphy resembles old Ben Gunn who went insane from being marooned by himself in *Treasure Island* (1934). McDowall, who was a popular child actor back in the early 1940s when he appeared in such films as *How Green Was My Valley* (1941) and *Lassie, Come Home* (1943), is the only "name" in the film and he gives it a lift that none of the other adults can provide. It seems appropriate that he should be cast as king of the monkey people, since he is best remembered as one of the talking simians in *Planet of the Apes* (1968) and its sequels.

The story is a succession of chases and narrow escapes. The monkeys are chasing Mowgli to make him a prisoner. Harrison is chasing the little boy to make him a circus attraction. Buldeo is hoping to kill Mowgli and, if possible, to make it look like an accident. Shere Khan is chasing Mowgli because he has sworn to kill him. Chuchundra is chasing his fugitive monkey, who sticks close to the jungle boy. On more than one occasion Mowgli is actually caught and tied up or imprisoned in a wooden cage, but he always manages to escape, usually with a little help from one of his animal friends—and the chase begins all over again.

Although Mowgli spends much time in the forgotten city now inhabited by the monkey people, he does not discover a fabulous treasure guarded by a cobra, as he did in "The King's Ankus." He does, however, encounter plenty of cobras in one deserted chamber. Fortunately, Harrison arrives and lowers a rope by which the agile lad can climb to safety. By this point, Harrison has changed. He has come to realize that bringing Mowgli back to live in a traveling circus like a caged animal would be tantamount to killing him. After Buldeo gets his well-deserved comeuppance, Harrison sets Mowgli free to roam through the jungle with the wild animals.

Although there is plenty of chasing, some shooting, and many confrontations with animals, nobody gets seriously hurt in this low-budget PG-rated production. When Buldeo

CREDITS

Mowgli: James Williams
Harrison: Bill Campbell
King Murphy: Roddy McDowall
Chuchundra: David Paul Francis
Buldeo: Gulshan Grover
Karait: Dyrk Ashton

Origin: USA
Released: 1997
Production: Raju Patel for MDP Worldwide; released by TriStar Pictures
Direction: Duncan McLachlan
Screenplay: Baynard Johnson and Matthew Horton; based on the book by Rudyard Kipling
Cinematography: Adolfo Bartoli
Editing: Marcus Manton
Music: John Scott
Production design: Errol Kelly
Art direction: Paul Takis, Sunil Wijeratne
Costumes: Ann Hollowood
Animal coordinator: Brian McMillan
MPAA rating: PG
Running Time: 88 minutes

is finally disposed of, he is shot out of an ancient cannon by the two chimpanzees; he is not killed, however, but only flies through the air howling in terror. Mowgli probably does not kill and skin Shere Khan in this production, as in Kipling's original story, because the filmmakers were minimizing violence in order to appeal to the youngest possible viewers.

In the old days before videotapes this film would have been called a "four-waller," a low-budget production intended to reap a quick profit on a single weekend from families with young children after being given intensive local promotion. Nowadays such a feature is being called "straight-to-video." *Rudyard Kipling's the Second Jungle Book* had only token engagements in a few movie theaters and was quickly released on videotape. As reviewer Leonard Klady of *Variety* writes: "The monkeyshines and other animal antics promise strong cassette sales and reasonable response from cable outings." Because it is a period piece, this modest, fairly entertaining little film will not become dated and can continue to make money for years to come in the booming homevideo market.

—Bill Delaney

REVIEWS

Boxoffice. July, 1997, p. 90.
Chicago Tribune. May 16, 1997, p. 5.
Hollywood Reporter. May 13, 1997, p. 13.
Los Angeles Times. May 16, 1997, p. F8.
New York Times. May 16, 1997, p. B3.
Variety. May 12, 1997, p. 64.

The Saint

Never reveal your name. Never turn your back. Never surrender your heart.—Movie tagline

"Non-stop spy thrills laced with a wonderful sense of humor. Val Kilmer is terrific!"—George Pennacchio, *ABC-TV*

"Loads of nail-biting excitement. You'll really love this film!"—Ron Brewington, *American Urban Radio Networks*

"Move over James Bond. Here comes *The Saint.*"—Diane Kaminsky, *CBS-TV*

"Val Kilmer delivers brilliantly. See it and believe it!"—Bonnie Churchill, *National News Syndicate*

Box Office: $61,363,304

Simon Templar, code named *The Saint,* protects beautiful scientist Emma Russell (Elisabeth Shue) from Russian industrialists hot on their trail.

Val Kilmer sheds his Batsuit in favor of a halo in Philip Noyce's *The Saint.* Remotely based on the character created in 1928 by Leslie Charteris that was later interpreted on television in the Sixties by suave ex-James Bond, Roger Moore, this latest incarnation of the thief with a streak of goodness, does away with the halo and the self-acknowledged wink of the eye. In its place is a muddled and preposterous tale that rivals *Mission Impossible* (1996) in its willingness to abscond with the bare rudiments of its source material while fashioning a blatant star-vehicle designed more as a franchise than a cohesive narrative whole.

Emma: "Who are you?"
Simon: "No one has a clue. Least of all me."

Simon Templar was the subject of more that fifty novels and some fourteen films, but British author Leslie Charteris never explained how this charming rogue became the Saint. For the film, screenwriters Jonathan Hensleigh (*Die Hard With a Vengeance* (1995) and Wesley Strick (*Cape Fear* (1991) have fashioned a romantic prologue in the Far East in which an abused orphan (Adam Smith as a believable young Val Kilmer) masterminds an escape that results in the death of his pretty young sweetheart. It is suggested that this childhood trauma has transformed the orphan into a cipher with no sense of his own identity.

> The film is dedicated to casting director Elisabeth Leustig, who was killed when hit by a car in Moscow while doing preliminary work on the picture in December 1995.

In a clever variation of the dissolve technique, little Simon's face morphs into that of the adult (Val Kilmer), a mercenary thief, an "independent contractor" with a fondness for disguises and aliases that are all names of Catholic saints. In Moscow, Templar is about to break into a safe to steal a very important microchip. He has been hired by former Russian commissar Ivan Tretiak (Rade Serbedzija of *Before the Rain* [1994] and *Broken English* [1997]), a billionaire with a devious plan to manipulate a heating-oil crisis to his advantage. Tretiak wants Templar to steal the formula for cold fusion that has been developed by Albert Einstein's successor, U.S. scientist Dr. Emma Russell (the ludicrously cast Elisabeth Shue), so that Tretiak can then deliver cheap energy to his country. Tretiak would wind up a hero, not to mention an even potentially richer man.

Templar agrees to the job when Tretiak offers enough money to put Simon's retirement fund at fifty million dollars. What Templar does not count on, however, is that he would start to have romantic stirrings over the comely Dr. Russell which cause him to have second thoughts over his job. Not only is she brilliant, Emma has a poet's romantic soul and longing. "I'm in love with a man named Percy," she wistfully sighs as she explains her fondness for Byron. She also literally has a bad heart.

Emma Russell is pure naive goodness incarnate, "an angel," as Templar describes her, who just happens to keep her Nobel Prize-worthy scribblings in her bra. She gets all giddy whenever she speaks of serving humankind and she falls instantly for Templar when he appears as the South African hippie poet (who bears a striking resemblance to Jim Morrison). When she learns of Templar's betrayal, she brokenheartedly asks, "Who are you?" When he replies, "No one has a clue . . . least of all me," shades of a full-blown identity crisis worthy of the equally confused Bruce Wayne in *Batman* (1989) comes rushing to the forefront.

Australian director Phillip Noyce, known for maintaining a kinetic pace in such films as *Patriot Games* (1992) and *Clear and Present Danger* (1994), aided by cinematographer Phil Meheux, makes great use of the stunningly beautiful Moscow scenery, particularly the Kremlin at night. But *The Saint* quickly disintegrates into a mundane cat-and-mouse chase.

It had been reported in the industry trades that *The Saint* originally had a very different—and much darker—ending in which the good doctor Emma is poisoned and dies. Test audiences apparently refused to accept anything less than a happy ending, despite the fact that the resolution as originally scripted was not only tragic and much more in keeping with Templar's character, it also made more sense if the filmmakers were hoping for a franchise.

There is no doubt that actress Elisabeth Shue is talented, she garnered an Academy Award nomination for her

CREDITS

Simon Templar: Val Kilmer
Dr. Emma Russell: Elisabeth Shue
Ivan Tretiak: Rade Serbedzija
Ilya Tretiak: Valery Nikolaev
Dr. Lev Botvin: Henry Goodman
Chief Inspector Teal: Alan Armstrong
Vereshagin: Michael Byrne
President Karpov: Evgeny Lazarev
Frankie: Irina Apeximova

Origin: USA
Released: 1997
Production: David Brown, Robert Evans, William J. Macdonald, Mace Neufeld for Rysher Entertainment; released by Paramount Pictures
Direction: Phillip Noyce
Screenplay: Johnathan Hensleigh, Wesley Strick; based on a character created by Leslie Charteris
Cinematography: Phil Meheux
Editing: Terry Rawlings
Production design: Joseph Nemec III
Art direction: Lucy Richardson, Nick Palmer
Costumes: Marlene Stewart
Music: Graeme Revell
Sound: Ivan Sharrock
Visual effects supervisor: Robert Grasmere
Supervising makeup artist: Paul Engelen
Stunt coordinator: Greg Powell
MPAA rating: PG-13
Running Time: 116 minutes

performance in *Leaving Las Vegas* (1996); still, it is a challenge believing her as the brilliant physicist. She is indeed soulful, but she and Val Kilmer, who turned down a repeat performance as the Caped Crusader following *Batman Forever* (1995) often seem to be acting in two separate films: while he plays it rather tongue-in-cheek, she is all sincerity and earnestness.

While some may be quick to compare *The Saint* to James Bond, there is one very blatant difference: Agent 007 never had a moment of not knowing exactly who *he* was. Reviews for the film were decidedly mixed, but *The Saint* failed to generate much excitement at the box office.

—*Patricia Kowal*

REVIEWS

Boston Globe. April 4, 1997, p. E5.
Chicago Tribune. April 4, 1997, p. 4.
Entertainment Weekly. April 11, 1997, p. 58.
Los Angeles Times. April 4, 1997, p. F1.
The New Times. April 3, 1997, p. 24.
New York Times. April 14, 1997, p. B24.
The New Yorker. April 14, 1997, p. 88.
People. April 14, 1997, p. 18.
Rolling Stone. April 17, 1997, p. 83.
Sight and Sound. May, 1997, p. 52.
USA Today. April 3, 1997, p. 6D.
USA Today. April 4, 1997, p. 4D.
Variety. March 31, 1997, p. 103.
Village Voice. April 8, 1997, p. 88.
Washington Post. April 4, 1997, p. B01.

Saint Clara

It is hard to characterize *Saint Clara*. Superficially, the plot concerns a thirteen-year-old Russian immigrant attending junior high school in a grimy industrial Israeli backwater in 1999. The immigrant, Clara Chanov (Lucy Dubinchik), has compelling violet eyes and the ability to see into the future. Her clairvoyance runs the gamut, from being able to intuit the answers to a math test to foreseeing the anarchy of the millennium. Her abilities seem to be inherited from her family of former bear hunters. But whereas her gift seems to render her serene, the rest of her family seems wildly eccentric—as does every other grown-up in the picture. The only hitch is that Clara's ability to see into the future will be erased the first time she falls in love. Given her beauty and the raging hormones of her male classmates, it is only a matter of time.

The odd admixture that is *Saint Clara* owes a great deal to its origins. The film began as a screenplay written in the early 1960s by Yelena Machinova when she was a student of the Czech writer Milan Kundera at the Prague Film Academy. Czechoslovakia was still under Soviet rule at the time, and the original screenplay is fraught with the black humor that characterized much of the art coming out of the Eastern bloc during that era. This brand of humor became even more pronounced when the screenplay inspired Machinova's husband, Pavel Kohout, to adapt it as a novel in the last 1960s after the couple was exiled to Austria (Kohout was the coauthor, with playwright Vaslav Havel, of the dissident manifesto, *Charter 77*).

The novel, *Napady Svate Klara*, was first published in German in 1980, and was subsequently translated into a dozen other languages—including Hebrew. In 1993, first-time Israeli filmmakers Ari Folman and Ori Sivan won the film rights to Kohout's novel—but only if they agreed to keep the original story line. At the time, both Folman and Sivan were thirty years old, and although both had lived in Israel since childhood (Folman was born in Warsaw, Poland, and Sivan in San Francisco), they managed to see many connections between the Eastern Europe of the 1960s and post-modern Israel. Both had grown up in Haifa, a gray industrial port city with a strong communist orientation. They remembered the skies of their childhood as gray and orange smoke-filled tableaux, which they translated onto the screen. In *Saint Clara*, as in their lives, the harshness of the setting resulted in hostility and aggression.

But what could be an oppressive atmosphere is lightened by the looniness of the adults—especially those who hold sway at Golda Meir School. The headmaster, Tissona (Yigal Naor) brags of having slept with the French singer Edith Piaf and constantly spouts nonsense French phrases. Given such authority figures, is it any wonder that the kids turn to Clara for leadership? She is beautiful *and* she can give them the answers to their tests in advance. Her ability to see into the future—a rather frightening, anarchic world where teenagers run amok—renders her worthy of sainthood in their eyes.

Clara is played by a fourteen-year-old girl who is herself a Russian immigrant to Israel. By the time she had been in her new homeland for two years, Lucy Dubinchik was supporting her family with income she made from television commercials. The preternatural poise she developed shows up clearly in this, her first feature film role. Dubinchik was one of over 1,000 young girls who auditioned for the lead in *Saint Clara*, but she knew from the outset that she would get the part. Indeed, when she was offered the job, Dubinchik seemed already to embody Clara's serene supernatural abilities, telling the directors: "I've never been to an audition where I didn't get the part. And the one time I didn't get the part on a TV series, the show was a huge failure and was canceled after two months."

With Israel on the brink of the millennium, when it seems that aggressive, destructive teenagers will rule a world gone mad, *Saint Clara* manages to redeem all with love. When Clara falls for one of her schoolmates, Eddie Tikel (played by the Israeli rock star Halil Elohev), her frightening vision of the life that is to come is replaced with a more humane view of the world. Clara's first kiss in essence robs her of her otherworldly status and brings her back to earth, where life goes on as it always has.

Saint Clara had a long theatrical run in Israel, where it won a number of major awards, including best picture of 1996.

—*Lisa Paddock*

CREDITS

Clara Chanov: Lucy Dubinchek
Eddie Tikel: Halil Elohev
Tissona: Yigal Naor

Origin: Israel
Released: 1997
Production: Marek Rozenbaum and Yuri Sabag; released by Kino
Direction: Ari Fulman, Ori Sivan
Screenplay: Ari Fulman and Ori Sivan; adapted from the novel by Yelena Machinova and Pavel Kohout
MPAA rating: PG
Running Time: 85 minutes

REVIEWS

Boxoffice. March, 1997, p. 39.
Cinemafantastique. November, 1997, p. 124.

Schizopolis

Come early! Come often!—Movie tagline

Schizopolis is an apt title for this venture from Steven Soderbergh, director of the famous Sundance discovery *sex, lies and videotape* (1989). He has spun an intriguing, if not entirely accessible, story that has enough time, character and story shifts to keep anyone guessing.

Shot in realistic, wobbly docudrama style (cinematography by Soderbergh himself) the story ostensibly concerns Fletcher Munson (Steven Soderbergh), a harried advertising executive assigned the dubious task of assembling a speech for arrogant L. Ron Hubbard clone T. Azimuth Schwitters (Mike Malone), whose self-actualization cult is called Eventualism.

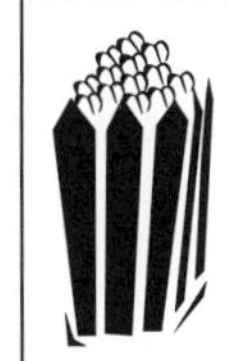

Angry Elmo: "No more of this mayonnaise!"

This storyline is the anchor for a wild array of other characters and their own plotlines. Halfway through the film, Soderbergh materializes in the role of Dr. Jeffrey Korchek, a dentist who is having an affair with Munson's wife (Betsy Brantley, who happens to be Soderbergh's ex-wife). In another odd twist, Korchek is wildly attracted to a patient, Attractive Woman No. 2, who is also played by Brantley.

Add to this mix a character who dresses in orange jumpsuits and alternately beds women and sprays for bugs in their homes, Elmo Oxygen (David Jensen). Elmo also speaks in a farcical language half the time, and ordinary English the rest of the time. Elmo's whimsical use of words is different from the laconic word use that Munson and his wife employ: "Generic greeting." "Generic greeting returned." "Inquiry as to dinner?" "Overdramatic answer as to meal's imminent arrival."

Soderbergh goes to town with every aural and visual device available to a director. He cross-cuts with grainy home movies, jump-cuts, and routinely has people answer phones that aren't ringing. He obviously wants to jolt the very conventions of film language and this, coupled with his wry observations of life's everyday observations and exchanges, make for sporadic—but big—laughs. Whether or not Soderbergh has ever worked in any kind of office he perfectly captures the time-wasting, paranoia-fueled gossip that can often eclipse work and take up the majority of one's day.

As Munson/Korchek are concerned with their separate dramas, Schwitters is arriving in town for his local book appearance. Munson's speech for Schwitters is finally approved and he meets the lauded author/pitchman. To Munson's dismay, Schwitters turns out to be a rude, selfish boor. In front of Schwitter's rapt audience, Elmo tries to assassinate the leader but only succeeds in wounding him.

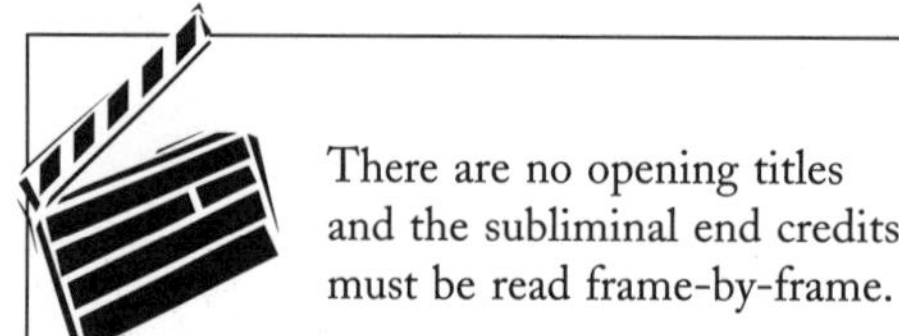
There are no opening titles and the subliminal end credits must be read frame-by-frame.

In a final tag scene, Munson is seen sitting in a crowded shopping mall, while the other shoppers whirl past him. In voice-over he relays how his wife will leave him and he will eventually die in a snowbank, after passing out drunk. Dry, understated humor is the norm here, and one gets a good glimpse of what Soderbergh's personality offers beyond his dramatic films such as *sex, lies and videotape* and *Kafka* (1991). Although it is a device that wears thin at times, Soderbergh often has people speak in brutally honest ways that underscore what people really are thinking (one particularly hysterical scene at a funeral comes to mind).

In conclusion, this is not a film for everyone, nor the kind of independent film that could find a broad—or even sustaining—audience. Yet it is always a pleasure to discover a filmmaker's unknown, untapped potential—even if the film is not entirely successful.

—*G.E. Georges*

CREDITS

Fletcher Munson/Dr. Jeffrey Korchek: Steven Soderbergh
Mrs. Munson/Attractive Woman No. 2: Betsy Brantley
Elmo Oxygen: David Jensen
T. Azimuth Schwitters: Mike Malone
Attractive Woman No. 1: Katherine LaNasa
Nameless Numberheadman: Eddie Jemison
Right-Hand Man: Scott Allen

Origin: USA
Released: 1996
Production: John Hardy for Point 406 Ltd.; released by Northern Arts Entertainment
Direction: Steven Soderbergh
Screenplay: Steven Soderbergh
Cinematography: Steven Soderbergh
Editing: Sarah Flack
Sound: Mark A. Mangini
MPAA rating: Unrated
Running Time: 96 minutes

REVIEWS

Boxoffice. April, 1997, p. 196.
Entertainment Weekly. April 4, 1997, p. 66.
Los Angeles Times. May 23, 1997, p. F18.
New York Times. April 9, 1997.
San Francisco Chronicle. June 13, 1997, p. C3.
Variety. May 27, 1997, p. 66.

Scream 2

Someone has taken their love of *sequels* one step too far.—Movie tagline

"Stunningly scary! You'll scream even louder with *Scream 2*!"—*ABC-TV*

"Finally a sequel that's an equal!"—*CBS-TV*

"Entertaining and way more energizing!"—Terry Lawson, *Detroit Free Press*

"Clever, hip and sophisticated!"—*Entertainment Weekly*

"One hell of a fun movie!"—*Newsweek*

"Delicious, diabolical and fun!"—*Rolling Stone*

"The best sequel in years! Wes Craven has done it again!"—*UPN*

"Twice as hip, scary and entertaining as the original!"—*WBAI Radio*

Box Office: $75,631,806

Shortly after 1996's original *Scream* became a financial and critical success, director Wes Craven and writer Kevin Williamson announced that the film would be followed by a second installment in a planned *Scream* trilogy. The first film was praised by critics for the way it transcended the "slasher" horror genre popularized in the 1980s in movies such as the *Friday the 13th* and *Nightmare on Elm Street* series (the latter of which was initiated by Wes Craven himself). Craven's *Scream* elevated the B-picture "slasher" to a more sophisticated level by playfully commenting on the genre itself. In addition to featuring well-known (and better) actors, clever dialogue, and a more plausible plot, the film reveled in self-references and self-parody. Throughout the story, horror movies and the "rules" of the "slasher flick" become the topics of discussion and to some degree even guide the direction of the plot. As a result, *Scream* is not merely a horror film but a film about horror films. With the sequel *Scream 2*, the filmmakers take the approach one step further. Craven and Williamson's second film includes even more playful self-commentary than the original, and as a result works quite enjoyably as a postmodern work of metafiction as well as a frequently intense thriller. Taking quite literally the postmodernist ideas that all stories are retellings of others and that all fiction is actually self-referential, *Scream 2* is intentionally a retelling of *Scream*, which the film openly acknowledges and which makes for one of the more enjoyable elements of the film.

The Killer: "What's your favorite scary movie?" Randy: "*Showgirls.*"

Set in the town of Woodsboro, the original *Scream* told the story of a crazed killer who committed a number of grisly murders but focused his attention on one potential victim, the true object of his homicidal quest, high school student Sidney Prescott (Neve Campbell). Ultimately the killer was revealed to be Sidney's boyfriend, aided by an accomplice, who sought revenge because Sidney's mother (now deceased) had had an affair with his father. Now Sidney has moved on to Windsor College, along with high school friend Randy (Jamie Kennedy), a film aficionado who spent much of his time in *Scream* discussing the "rules" of horror movies. As the story of *Scream 2* begins, a new horror movie titled *Stab* has been released, based on the killings in Woodsboro as described in a book by reporter Gale Weathers (Courteney Cox). The troubles (and the self-references) start when a killer wearing the same ghostly "scream" costume as the original Woodsboro murderer gruesomely slays two of the movie's audience members. As victims begin accumulating it becomes clear that a copycat killer is on the loose, a killer who also targets Sidney in the same way as the original murderer. Like the first killer, this new one also often calls his victims on the phone and questions them about their favorite scary movies. As the unfolding story of this new killing spree hits the news, some people question whether the culprit is imitating the events from *Stab*, a controversy over life imitating art that soon involves reporter Gale Weathers, whom Sidney blames for capitalizing on the earlier tragedy.

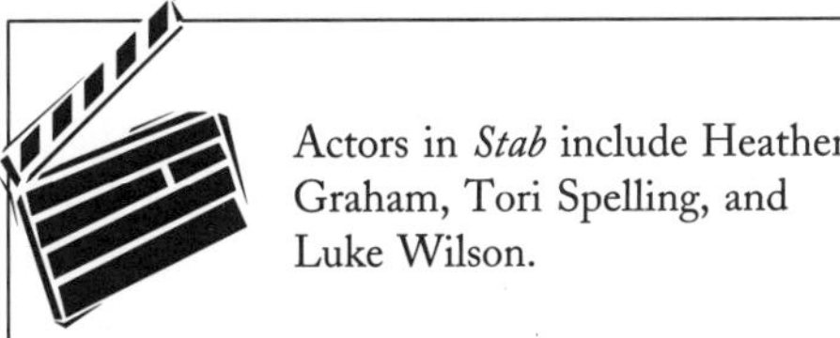

Actors in *Stab* include Heather Graham, Tori Spelling, and Luke Wilson.

Reporter Gayle Weathers (Courteney Cox) and friend Dewey Riley (David Arquette) are looking out for a crazed killer in *Scream 2.*

Meanwhile, Sidney's friend Randy speculates that someone is trying to create a "real-life sequel" to *Stab* and ponders the rules of horror movie sequels in trying to guess who the killer might be. He duly notes that everyone, including himself, could be a suspect. After Sidney meets the killer face-to-face inside a house and narrowly escapes outside, her boyfriend (Jerry O'Connell) suddenly shows up and runs into the house to confront him, but the murderer gets away. Sidney then begins to wonder if her boyfriend might actually be the killer, just as her boyfriend was the guilty party the first time around. She also wonders if it could be Cotton Weary (Liev Schreiber), the strange young man she had wrongly accused of killing her mother years before and who has returned to persuade Sidney to help him redeem his good name.

After the death of more victims, including Randy, Sidney eventually finds herself pursued by the killer once again. In a manner not unlike the first movie, the murderer traps Sidney and unmasks himself. The killer turns out to be one of Randy's fellow film students, who declares that it is the movies that are to be blamed, not him, for he was imitating what he saw on the screen. However, he is soon joined unexpectedly by a woman who had claimed to be a local reporter but who now reveals that she was the mother of Sidney's old boyfriend. She was the one, in fact, who orchestrated this killing spree, with the intent of exacting revenge on the young woman who had killed her son. The film student/killer is then shot and Sidney finds herself in a fight with the crazed mother—a fight Sidney almost loses until Cotton Weary shows up on the scene to save her.

Scream 2 succeeds quite well in places as an intense horror movie and can be genuinely enjoyed on that level. The film includes a number of memorably suspenseful scenes, beginning with the initial murders in the movie theater. Also equally suspenseful is a scene in which Sidney and her girlfriend are trapped in a car with the unconscious murderer and are forced to climb over his body to get through the window, as well as a scene in which Gale Weathers is chased by the killer into a sound-proofed television production room on the college campus. Unlike many of the "slasher" movies which it in many ways spoofs, *Scream 2* achieves its intense moments more often with genuine suspense than with blood and gore, though there is plenty of blood to be seen. However, although the element of suspense and fear is certainly an aspect of the film that would appeal to many audience members, the suspense alone does little on its own to elevate the film above most other well-made representatives of the genre. Just as with its predecessor, what makes *Scream 2* enjoyable on a more sophisticated level is the permeating presence of playful metadrama.

While *Scream* was a horror film about horror films, *Scream 2* is a film sequel about sequels—and thus, by extension, a film about itself. As such, the film's self-consciousness interestingly and effectively blurs the lines between reality and drama. Using the fiction-within-fiction of the movie *Stab* to parallel the real-life fictional movie *Scream*, *Scream 2* allows itself to break through the dramatic "fourth wall" and acknowledge to the audience its own status as a work of fiction. In doing so, the film discusses the conventions of the genre to which it belongs and then proceeds to both violate and fulfill those conventions. One of the soon-to-be victims at the movie theater, played by Jada Pinkett, tells her boyfriend that horror movies like *Stab* always limit their victims to white women; she then becomes the second person to die in *Scream 2*. The film also invites the audience to consider itself as fiction through Randy's discussions of horror sequel "rules." In sequels, he says, the body count is always higher, there is more blood, and established characters are more likely to perish. *Scream 2* follows the first two rules and, ironically, Randy himself becomes a victim and fulfills the third.

The self-consciousness of the story is especially entertaining, and perhaps most pertinent, in scenes in which film students and other characters debate whether all film sequels are inferior to the originals. Randy opines that sequels always "suck" and supports his claim with numerous examples. The student who is later revealed as the killer insists that sequels can be equal to or even improve upon their predecessors (he gives *The Empire Strikes Back* as an example, but Randy replies that the second *Star Wars* film was not technically a sequel). These discussions, of course, point to the status of *Scream 2* itself and invite the audience to compare the film to its predecessor. Also, the careful viewer may realize that some foreshadowing is also involved in such self-conscious discussions, for the student who defends sequels is the one who is actually creating and living out a "real-life sequel" as the killer (his insisting that sequels can be better than the originals also hints, on a metadramatic level, that he is the culprit). Thus, while this character in the story attempts to improve upon his predecessor, the story itself prompts the viewer to wonder whether *Scream 2* can improve upon *Scream*. Finally, the discussions in the film about whether life imitates art raise age-old questions but the story offers only ambiguous answers because *Scream 2* intention-

CREDITS

Sidney Prescott: Neve Campbell
Dewey Riley: David Arquette
Gale Weathers: Courteney Cox
Cici Cooper: Sarah Michelle Gellar
Randy Meeks: Jamie Kennedy
Debbie Salt: Laurie Metcalf
Hallie: Elise Neal
Derek: Jerry O'Connell
Maureen: Jada Pinkett
Mickey: Timothy Olyphant
Cotton Weary: Liev Schreiber
Phil: Omar Epps
Gus Gold: David Warner
Chief Louis Hartley: Lewis Arquette
Joel: Duane Martin

Origin: USA
Released: 1997
Production: Cathy Konrad and Marianne Maddalena for Craven/Maddalena Films and Konrad Pictures; released by Dimension Films
Direction: Wes Craven
Screenplay: Kevin Williamson
Cinematography: Peter Deming
Editing: Patrick Lussier
Music: Marco Beltrami
Production design: Bob Ziembicki
Art direction: Ted Burner
Set design: Martin Roy Mervel
Costumes: Kathleen Detoro
Special makeup effects: Kamar Bitar
Sound: Jim Stuebe
MPAA rating: R
Running Time: 120 minutes

ally, and effectively, blurs the lines between life and art and suggests that the two can often be closely intertwined.

While *Scream 2* may not be a great work of film art, or even the best example of a suspenseful thriller when compared to some of the classic works of the genre, its complex layering of fictional levels and its intentional self-consciousness, refusing to take itself too seriously, combine with convincing performances, suspenseful plotting, and witty dialogue to elevate the film above the many mediocre and artless movies that populate its genre.

—David Flanagin

REVIEWS

Entertainment Weekly. December 12, 1997, p. 49.
Los Angeles Times. December 12, 1997, p. F20.
New York Times. December 12, 1997, p. E16.
People. December 22, 1997, p. 22.
Rolling Stone. December 25, 1997, p. 174.
Time. December 15, 1997.
USA Today. December 12, 1997, p. D1.
Variety. December 8, 1997, p. 111.
Washington Post. December 12, 1997, p. C1.

Selena

For one brilliant, shining moment the American Dream came true.—Movie tagline

The story of a girl who had the spirit to believe in a dream and the courage to make it come true.—Movie tagline

"*Selena* is deeply moving! Jennifer Lopez explodes across the screen."—Jeffrey Lyons, *NBC-TV*

"*Selena* deserves a standing ovation! A poignant, heartwarming movie. Lopez and Olmos are brilliant!"—Jules Peimer, *WKDM Radio*

Box Office: $35,450,113

Selena is the dramatized biography of Selena Quintanilla Perez, the phenomenally popular "Queen of Tejano Music" who was murdered by a disgruntled subordinate in Corpus Christi, Texas, in 1995. The film is in the tradition of *Lady Sings the Blues* (1972), *The Rose* (1979), *What's Love Got to Do With It* (1993), *La Bamba* (1987), and a number of other rags-to-riches musical biopics. The title role is played by the beautiful Jennifer Lopez, who lip-synchs to the real Selena's recorded vocals.

Lopez bears an uncanny resemblance to Selena. Fully half the film features performances in front of frenzied Latino audiences packed so tightly together that they have to applaud by holding their hands over their heads. Selena was ready to conquer the larger and more lucrative English-language market with a so-called "crossover album" when assassin's bullets ended her meteoric career at the age of only twenty-three. She thus joined a whole galaxy of stars, including Elvis Presley, Marilyn Monroe and John Lennon, who seem to have been martyred by adulation.

Selena's real-life father, Abraham Quintanilla Jr., was the film's executive producer. He had script approval and control of Selena's music. It is not surprising, therefore, that his counterpart in the film (portrayed by Edward James Olmos) is shown playing a crucial role in his daughter's success from its earliest beginnings up until the very end.

Abraham is one of the many ex-musicians who never achieved the stardom of his dreams. He works for a living at unskilled jobs which give him no creative satisfaction. He blames his failure on the fact that he was a Mexican American trying to play gringo music of the doo-wop variety. His paranoia points in both directions: he suspects gringos of prejudice because he is a Mexican, and he suspects Mexicans of prejudice because he is a Chicano. Occasionally throughout the film he will lecture his children on the problems of being a Mexican American. When he realizes that his nine-year-old daughter (played by winsome Becky Lee Meza) has inherited his talent and love of music, he becomes obsessed with motivating her to achieve the stardom he never could achieve himself. Ultimately this neurotic, ambitious man opens a Mexican restaurant and dragoons his family into running the ill-fated enterprise. His wife supervises the kitchen; the children provide musical entertainment.

The whole Quintanilla family—father, mother, sister, and brother—are soon involved in little Selena's career. The amateurishness of the whole ensemble, with brother trying to pick out chords on the guitar and sister reluctantly beating on the drums, makes it evident that their climb to the top is going to be a steep one. Little Selena loves music, loves dancing, and loves admiration. Her coltish coquetry will remind viewers of the doomed JonBenet Ramsey, inadvertently providing a little of the foreshadowing the film otherwise conspicuously lacks. Aside from her unusual voice, little Selena is a fairly ordinary kid who would obviously never have gotten far in the brutally competitive, heartbreaking entertainment world without the coaching of her obsessive stage father. At least this is the film's dominant theme.

Olmos is perfect in his role as Selena's father. He makes the grown-up Selena shine brighter by contrast. He is as homely as she is beautiful, as apprehensive as she is self-confident, as greedy as she is generous, as paranoid as she is trusting. He is a frog who knows she could change him into a prince if only she could understand how badly he wanted that metamorphosis. Lopez is perfect too as a girl who has never known disillusionment. She would have to be that kind of person to put such unbridled enthusiasm into her upbeat music, which is a democratic mixture of polkas, country-and-western, traditional Mexican folk music, and elements of rock-and-roll. Between the explosive father and the tempestuous daughter, the frog and the princess, there is little elbow room left for the other actors, whose roles are rudimentary.

Abraham to Selena: "You have to sing who you are."

Like Loretta Lynn (Sissy Spacek) of *The Coal Miner's Daughter* (1980), Selena tours the South and Southwest in an old converted bus, singing standard pop and rock music in English. In time the little girl blossoms into a young woman bursting with a sexuality that appeals to audiences while causing her conservative father no end of concern. Abraham is horrified when his daughter begins appearing onstage in the sequined bustier which was to become her trademark. Like many another father, Abraham realizes he will soon be losing his place as the most important man in her life, but he is determined not to lose his place as her mentor and business manager.

It does not take long before Selena is heavily involved with a young man. In fact, given Selena's beauty and sexuality, it is surprising that it takes as long as it does for this to happen. The only thing that has delayed it was the fact that the family is perpetually on the move. The lover is handsome, brooding heavy-metal guitarist Chris Perez (Jon Seda), who is picked up along the way and gives the group the raunchy musical inspiration it has been needing.

Much of the dramatic conflict in the story involves Abraham's violent objections to the relationship, even though—at least from the viewer's perspective—that relationship never becomes horizontal. Abraham wants more for his daughter than a match with a traveling musician of dubious morals. He was a traveling musician himself, so he knows what they are like. (Reviewers have complained that the story has been "sanitized"; there is only one scene in which Perez misbehaves. Stephen Holden, writing for the *New York Times*, says that Selena herself has been "all but canonized.") Abraham fires Chris from the group, but the lovers keep prearranged assignations at every tour stop. Eventually Selena takes the radical step of defying her father and marrying the man she loves.

At this point the dramatic interest starts to fade because there is little, after all, that the father can do but accept the "fait accompli." There is no conflict left. The film has to be carried by the torrid music and the star's dynamic personality. Selena's charm, talent and optimism overcome all obstacles. When the question arises of whether she can succeed with audiences in Mexico who might object to her imperfect Spanish, that problem proves to be just another straw man.

Everyone falls in love with Selena on sight. It would appear that the young woman's personality, her loving spirit and lovability are more responsible for her success than her voice. She is a bit like Evita Peron in this respect. People love her because she loves them and wants them to love her—and somehow she manages to put this across from the wire-strewn, floodlighted stages to the masses of ignominious humanity who need idols to worship. She is filling a role people seem to need; she is assuming a place about halfway between humanity and divinity, becoming a sort of demi-goddess through whom the masses can vicariously experience all the things they never will experience in their own humble lives. She conquers audiences in the U.S. and Mexico. This is almost too much to believe; the film has a fairy tale quality about it like the stories of Cinderella and Snow White.

Selena displays another whole dimension of talent by opening a chain of fashion boutiques bearing the magical name of "Selena." Viewers may consider the fashions rather garish, if not actually absurd, but nothing succeeds in this film like success. Money pours in. Selena is about to make the quantum leap of becoming an international singing star, rather than a Tex-Mex tejano singer, by putting out a English-language album which seems certain to succeed.

Selena's death in the film does not come as a shocking climax but more as a non sequitur, a jolt, as if someone pulled the plug and the joyful music expired with a discordant decrescendo. Any viewer unfamiliar with the facts of Selena's death will be left puzzled at the end. Yolanda Saldivar (Lupe Ontiveros), president of her fan club and entrusted with handling her money, is exposed as an embezzler. She is psychologically traumatized by disgrace and loss of her privileged relationship with the employer she idolizes. She shoots Selena in the middle of a performance and then turns the revolver on herself.

Abraham always dreaded something happening to ruin everything for his daughter and himself. His suspicions pointed in every direction except the direction from which the fatal blow finally came. The event lacks the dramatic impact it might have had in the film because there was no foreshadowing and no explanation of the assassin's motives. As a story *Selena* does not deserve a high rating; its charming star who is rarely off camera and its always exhilarating music compensate for its deficiencies.

The film ends with documentary footage of the real Selena performing before a huge audience, symbolizing that her music and reputation will live long after her. Her untimely death contributed to her fame. She is becoming a legendary figure like Elvis Presley. Her posthumous crossover album, "Dreaming of You," made No. 1 on the charts as soon as it was released. The film, bursting at the seams with more than thirty tunes throughout its two-hour running time, will enjoy lucrative longevity on home video.

—Bill Delaney

CREDITS

Selena Quintanilla: Jennifer Lopez
Abraham Quintanilla: Edward James Olmos
Chris Perez: Jon Seda
Marcela Quintanilla: Constance Marie
Abie Quintanilla: Jacob Vargas
Yolanda Saldivar: Lupe Ontiveros

Origin: USA
Released: 1997
Production: Moctesuma Esparza and Robert Katz for Q Productions, Inc.; released by Warner Bros.
Direction: Gregory Nava
Screenplay: Gregory Nava
Cinematography: Edward Lachman
Editing: Nancy Richardson
Music: Dave Grusin
Production design: Cary White
Art direction: Ed Vega
Set decoration: Jeanette Scott
Costumes: Elisabetta Beraldo
Sound: Bayard Carey
Choreography: Miranda Garrison
MPAA rating: PG
Running Time: 127 minutes

REVIEWS

Boxoffice. May, 1997, p. 62.
Chicago Tribune. March 21, 1997, p. 5.
Detroit News. March 21, 1997, p. 3F.
Entertainment Weekly. March 28, 1997, p. 47.
Los Angeles Times. March 21, 1997, p. F1.
New York Times. March 21, 1997, p. C16.
People. March 31, 1997, p. 21.
Rolling Stone. April 17, 1997, p. 86.
Time. March 24, 1997.
USA Today. March 21, 1997, p. 1D.
Variety. March 24, 1997, p. 33.
Village Voice. April 1, 1997, p. 70.

A Self-Made Hero; Un Heros Tres Discret; A Very Discreet Hero

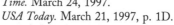

Hero . . . Imposter . . . Lover—Movie tagline

" . . . Fascinating to watch . . ."—Jay Carr, *Boston Globe*

"One of the year's best movies!"—Ernest Hardy, *LA Weekly*

"One of the top ten films of the year! A delicious piece of work . . . Smart and provocative."—Kenneth Turan, *Los Angeles Times*

"Irresistible."—Dave Kehr, *New York Daily News*

"A gem . . . audacious moviemaking."—Larry Worth, *New York Post*

"Smart."—John Anderson, *Newsday*

"A deadpan comedy cloaked in noir atmosphere . . . Leaves an indelible taste, somehow both bitter and savory."—Richard Corliss, *Time*

" . . . the pleasure, rewards, and fascination of pretending . . . an amusing and finely crafted exercise in the betrayal of history."—Leslie Camhi, *Village Voice*

The French will always have a bad conscience about World War II. The country could not withstand Hitler's onslaught and collapsed in a shockingly short time. Even worse, the Vichy regime was set up to collaborate with the

Nazis. The French turned in Jews, who were sent to concentration camps. There was a Resistance, but its impact was negligible—except to soothe troubled French consciences after the war, when it seemed that every Frenchman had been a stout anti-Fascist.

Albert: "The best lives are invented, someone said that. I think it was me."

Many literary and historical works have attempted to confront this shameful legacy. Jean-Francois Deniau's novel, for example, recounts the story of a fantasizing nobody who builds his career on fabricating a story about his exploits in the Resistance. *A Self Made Hero*, written and directed by Jacques Audlord, adapts the novel into a riveting film. Albert Dehousse (Mathieu Kassovitz) abandons his French provincial family out of shame. He has spent the entire war on the sidelines only to learn that his wife's family has been active in the Resistance. He cannot stay married to her, and he cannot stay at home, because he suddenly realizes that he has spent a trivial and meaningless life.

Jean-Louis Trintignant and Mathieu Kassovitz were also the stars of Jacques Audiard's first film, 1994's *Regarde Les Hommes Tomber/See How They Fall.*

What to do? He arrives penniless in Paris and is reduced to begging from passersby. They ignore him. A French Captain (Albert Dupontel) observes the inept Dehousse and gives him basic lessons in begging. He teaches Dehousse to go after handouts with style, opening car doors and extending his hand with confidence. Dehousse soon learns about the Resistance from the Captain, who imparts a sense that the Resistance was a kind of confidence game, a pretending and a process of deception in order to lead people, to gain power, and to dominate one's environment. Suddenly Dehousse realizes that his fantasizing is not merely a private penchant; rather, the making up of stories is exactly what many successful people do. They contrive a front for themselves, a persona, a mix of identities that depend on the situations in which they find themselves.

Since Dehousse has precious little identity to dispose of, he readily takes to making up his entire life. He studies the history of the Resistance, begins attending meetings of Resistance veterans, and then assumes the persona of a Resistance fighter. What he learns is that people want to see him as a hero and that their need coincides with his own. In this sense, he is self-made.

What makes the film riveting is that Dehousse is not merely presented as a fraud. On the contrary, he has learned his tricks from the Resistance fighters. When the Captain passes Dehousse on a road and realizes that the former beggar has promoted himself into a war hero, the Captain is delighted—perhaps because, after all, the Resistance was about Frenchmen believing they could alter the course of history long after Hitler had seized control of it. The Resistance, in other words, spoke to people's imaginations. They needed to believe in the illusion that they could still topple the Nazis. Similarly, Servanne (Anouk Grinberg), a female sergeant in the Resistance, falls in love with Dehousse even though she suspects he is a phony. When he confesses as much (after having had to shoot a group of French deserters), she does not reject him. Instead, she tries to lessen his sense of inauthenticity.

In effect, Dehousse is an extreme example of a bifurcated national sensibility. On the one hand, the French thought of themselves as Resisters; on the other hand, they knew the talk of resistance was largely that: talk. Even those who did more than talk realized that they had to magnify their exploits and to have others, who did practically nothing or worse than nothing, also claim a heroic part. The paradox the film presents is of a nation without any illusions about itself indulging in illusions about itself. In effect, this is how life went on in France, contradicting itself. The French experience is reminiscent of Keats's definition of negative capability, of the poet's ability to keep two contradictory ideas in a state of fruitful tension.

CREDITS

Albert Dehousse (young): Mathieu Kassovitz
Servante: Anouk Grinberg
Yvette: Sandrine Kimberlain
Dionnet: Albert Dupontel
Albert Dehousse (old): Jean-Louis Trintignant

Origin: France
Released: 1995, 1997
Production: Patrick Godeau for Aliceleo and Lumiere; released by Strand Releasing
Direction: Jacques Audiard
Screenplay: Jacques Audiard and Alain Le Henry; based on the novel by Jean-Francois Deniau
Cinematography: Jean-Marc Fabre
Editing: Juliette Welfling
Music: Alexandre Desplat
Production design: Michel Vandestien
Set design: Dominique Douret
Costumes: Caroline De Vivaise
Sound: Jean-Pierre Duret, Dominique Gaborieau
MPAA rating: Unrated
Running Time: 105 minutes

Servanne does not want Dehousse to give up on himself—to merely expose himself as a charlatan. For as an imposter he has been able to do great things—perhaps because he knows he is an imposter and feels a special loyalty to the role he plays. This attitude may seem farcical but it is genuinely French. It accounts for the country's longevity and its ability to live with its own faults. As if to underscore that fact, the film includes scenes with Dehousse as an old man (played by Jean-Louis Trintignant) wryly recounting his posturing. The astringent Trintignant and the quasi-documentary interviews with others about Dehousse's remarkable career also provide a complex, musing, coda on the vexing relationship between reality and illusion.

—*Carl Rollyson*

REVIEWS

Boxoffice. March, 1997, p. 42.
Los Angeles Times. October 3, 1997, p. F10.
Sight and Sound. April, 1997, p. 47.
Variety. May 20, 1996, p. 32.
Village Voice. September 16, 1997, p. 98.

Seven Years in Tibet

"Exhilarating, gorgeous, important - filmmaking at its very best! This magnificently told story will be remembered and loved forever."—Anne Brodie, *BBS/CTV*

"Exquisite! Jean-Jacques Annaud delivers a beautiful film."—Steve Oldfield, *FOX-TV*

"A film of grand proportions! The kind of movie you can't wait to see again."—Bobbie Wygant, *KXAS-TV*

"Astonishing! An unforgettable, sweeping epic."—Jeffrey Lyons, *NBC-TV*

"An epic masterpiece! This is Brad Pitt's finest role. Don't miss it."—Neil Rosen, *NY1 News*

"An epic adventure on a grand scale . . . Annaud steps into David Lean territory with this one."—Bob Healy, *Satellite News Network*

"Spectacular! Brad Pitt delivers an Oscar-caliber performance."—Susan Granger, *SSG Syndicate*

"A mesmerizing motion picture epic! Important, moving and visually stunning."—Paul Wunder, *WBAI Radio*

Box Office: $37,602,068

As renowned explorer Heinrich Harrer, actor Brad Pitt dons a dubious Austrian accent and heads for the Himalayans in Jean-Jacques Annaud's tedious *Seven Years in Tibet*. More of a travelogue than a drama, the film paints some beautiful pictures while simultaneously explaining Buddhism, reincarnation and the Chinese takeover of Tibet. It fails miserably, due largely to its tendency towards oversimplification.

Austrian mountain climber, Heinrich Harrer (Brad Pitt), befriends a young Dalai Lama and experiences a spiritual awakening in *Seven Years in Tibet*.

Based on Harrer's memoir, *Seven Years in Tibet* was mired in controversy prior to its release when reports surfaced of a shocking secret from the famous mountain climber's past: Harrer was a member of Hitler's elite SS. In addition, the film was hampered by the additional burden

AWARDS AND NOMINATIONS

Golden Globe Awards 1998 Nominations: Original Score

of having an unsympathetic central character who abandons his pregnant wife and unborn son for the sake of adventure. The filmmakers chose to downplay Harrer's Nazi involvement by adding two lines of voice-over to the film in post-production, while sentimentally excusing the protagonist's moral ambiguity.

Set in the mid-1940s through early 1950s, *Seven Years in Tibet* sets out to chronicle the true story of Harrer's spiritual journey from self-centered arrogance to peaceful enlightenment through his friendship with the young Dalai Llama. The tale begins as Harrer (Brad Pitt) joins an Aryan expedition to the Himalayan peak of Nanga Parbat led by Peter Aufschnaiter (David Thewlis). An avalanche eventually leads to the team's imprisonment in a British prisoner-of-war camp in India. Harrer must temporarily abandon his alienating tendencies and join the others in order to effect their escape. Despite their mutual contempt, Aufschnaiter and Harrer succeed in breaching the forbidden kingdom of Tibet and become friends.

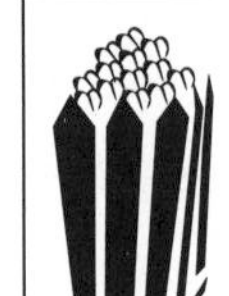

Dalai Lama to Harrer: "Do you think some day people will look at Tibet on the movie screen and wonder what happened to us?"

Harrer left Tibet in 1951 and has remained friends with the Dalai Lama.

Thirsty for knowledge of the outside world, the Dalai Lama (Jamyang Jamtsho Wangchuk), Tibet's spiritual leader, befriends the worldly stranger. The wise and articulate young boy easily senses Harrer's spiritual alienation and in turn sets out to imbue the foreigner with some humanity before the Chinese invade Tibet in the 1950s.

Political problems forced Annaud and company to film in Argentina at the foothills of the Andes, rather than in Tibet. But the director's obsession with authenticity led to the importation of nearly one hundred Tibetan monks from a monastery in India, as well as herds of yaks from Montana (reportedly at a cost of nearly four thousand dollars apiece!). While meticulous attention to detail is important to a degree, so is the need for a compelling story and more than a modicum of character development.

Written by Becky Johnston (*The Prince of Tides*, 1991), the script is burdened not only by its egomaniacal protagonist, but by its preachy tone and inexplicable character transformation. Ms. Johnston seems overwhelmed by the task of condensing the story's time frame and resorts to glossing over Harrer's motivations for change. Even the title is misleading; it takes longer to get to Tibet than the time spent there.

Jean-Jacques Annaud, director of *Quest for Fire* (1981) and *The Bear* (1989), here gives us what easily could have

CREDITS

Heinrich Harrer: Brad Pitt
Peter Aufshnaiter: David Thewlis
Ngawang Jigme: B.D. Wong
Kungo Tsarong: Mako
Great Mother: Jetsun Pema
Pema Lhaki: Victor Wong
Dalai Lama, aged 14: Jamyang Wang Chuck
Dalai Lama, aged 8: Tenzin Wang Chuck

Origin: USA
Released: 1997
Production: Jean-Jacques Annaud, Iain Smith and John H. Williams for Mandalay Entertainment, Reperage, Vanguard Films and Applecross; released by TriStar Pictures
Direction: Jean-Jacques Annaud
Screenplay: Becky Johnston; based on the book by Heinrich Harrer
Cinematography: Robert Fraisse
Editing: Noelle Boisson
Production design: At Hoang
Set decoration: Jim Erickson
Costumes: Enrico Sabbatini
Music: John Williams
MPAA rating: PG-13
Running Time: 139 minutes

REVIEWS

Boxoffice. November, 1997, p. 123.
Chicago Sun-Times. October 10, 1997.
Chicago Tribune. October 10, 1997, p. 4.
Detroit News. October 10, 1997.
Entertainment Weekly. October 10, 1997, p. 64.
Los Angeles Times. July 16, 1997, p. F1.
Los Angeles Times. August 15, 1997, p. F1.
Los Angeles Times. October 8, 1997, p. F1.
New York Times. January 4, 1997, p. 13.
New York Times. June 21, 1997, p. 18.
New York Times. October 8, 1997, p. E1.
Newsday. October 10, 1997.
People. October 13, 1997, p. 19.
Rolling Stone. October 30, 1997, p. 71.
San Francisco Chronicle. October 10, 1997, p. C1.
San Francisco Examiner. October 10, 1997, p. C1.
Sight and Sound. December, 1997, p. 53.
Time. September 15, 1997.
Toronto Sun. October 8, 1997.
Variety. September 22, 1997, p. 37.
Village Voice. October 14, 1997, p. 96.
Washington Post. October 10, 1997.

been a Disney film. It is a sanitized account of a complex journey of epic proportions complicated further by Brad Pitt's limited acting range. The actor practically sleepwalks through his role, relying heavily on his photogenic good looks and dazzling smile that he perfected in Ridley Scott's *Thelma and Louise* (1991). Pitt simply lacks the depth of some of his contemporaries (Johnny Depp, in particular)—a flaw that is underscored even further by the casting of the talented English actor David Thewlis (Mike Leigh's *Naked*, 1993). Watching their scenes together, we are constantly reminded that Thewlis is indeed an accomplished actor, while Pitt is a star.

—Patricia Kowal

The Shadow Conspiracy

Life. Liberty. And the pursuit of absolute power.—Movie tagline

Box Office: $2,315,743

The Shadow Conspiracy is a paranoid Washington political thriller that forgot one thing: the thrills. It is ill-conceived and utterly simplistic with nearly every cliched situation and character imaginable. The film died a quick death at the box office—and rightfully so. There is nary an actor who does not sleepwalk his or her way through this preposterous elongated chase sequence masquerading as a plot. A more apt title might have been "See Bobby Run."

Bobby: "He who gets the first sound bite wins."

Charlie Sheen stars as Bobby Bishop, a fast-on-his-feet, basketball-playing, Corvette-driving, idealistic presidential aide who is drawn into a clandestine plot to assassinate the President (Sam Waterston). It seems that the Commander-in-Chief has become too liberal for the comfort of some of his fellow government officials. Bishop learns of the involvement of several high placed officials from some Eastern bloc intellectual known as The Professor (Theodore Bikel) working out of some sort of government-monitoring institute. Before he can reveal the coveted info, the source is shot down and Bishop finds himself the next target of a robotic assassin known only as The Agent (Stephen Lang). Before long, Bishop finds that the only one he can trust appears to be his mentor, Conrad (the ghastly Donald Sutherland).

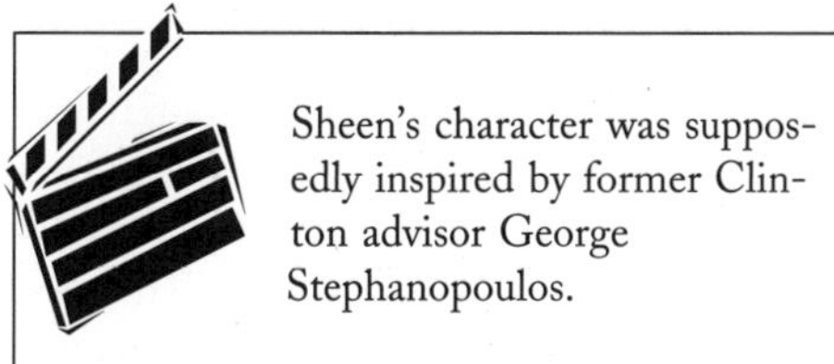

Sheen's character was supposedly inspired by former Clinton advisor George Stephanopoulos.

As Bishop tries to figure out who is behind this evil assassination plot, he is aided by a cynical investigative journalist with the worst taste in hats imaginable, Amanda Givens (Linda Hamilton), who, of course, has a history with Bishop. The two dash around the nation's capital, trying to elude The Agent (who seems to be able to hit everyone but Bishop), pausing just long enough for several photo-ops in front of some of the most famous sights in Washington, D.C.

The cast is uniformly uninspired; one suspects the actors all just needed the money. It certainly could not have been the one-dimensional characters that populate *The Shadow Conspiracy*. It is sad to witness the continual transformation of Donald Sutherland into a virtual caricature of himself. The mere casting of this once interesting actor telegraphs the character's ultimate evilness; no need to even suspect that Conrad might be a stand-up guy. Mr. Sutherland has strayed far from his earlier, more challenging work in such films as Robert Altman's *M.A.S.H.* (1970) and Fellini's *Casanova* (1976). As for Charlie Sheen, he, too, seems content to take the laziest way to characterization. Unlike some actors, Mr. Sheen simply does not possess a strong enough on-screen charisma to allow him to gloss over the work involved in generating—and sustaining—an interesting character.

This first chase sequence comes far too early in the film, undercutting the suspense and grinding the plot to a near standstill. Director George P. Cosmatos—whose other work includes the more interesting *Tombstone* (1995), as well as the dreadful *Cobra* (1986) and the insipid *Rambo II* (1985)—stages the chases in such a perfunctory manner that they become mere physical exercises engineered to get Charlie Sheen in shape. It is interesting to note that the cinematographer on *The*

Shadow Conspiracy was also one of the Executive Producers, which might help to explain why this project is little more than frenetic camerawork and ornate art direction. Someone obviously forgot to tell Mr. Cosmatos that there is more to constructing a taut thriller than staging chase scenes. There is no attempt, for example, to justify the conspirators' motivations, while Bishop is simply taken at face value.

The film lacks intrigue and the single most element that will kill any thriller: suspense. The masterful director Alfred Hitchcock believed that suspense is far better than mystery. While the latter withholds some piece of vital information from the audience—good examples are *No Way Out* (1987) and *The Usual Suspects* (1996), both ending with an unexpected "twist"—suspense, on the other hand, generates the tension through the discrepancy that exists between what the viewer knows and the protagonist's ignorance. In a good suspense thriller, the audience, theoretically, should be on the edge of their seats, waiting for the good guy to catch on. In *The Shadow Conspiracy*, the ending is so ludicrous, so preposterous that one cannot help but howl with laughter; it no longer matters whether the bad guys are stopped or not. At least they succeeded in eliciting some response from the audience.

—Patricia Kowal

CREDITS

Bobby Bishop: Charlie Sheen
Amanda Givens: Linda Hamilton
Conrad: Donald Sutherland
The Agent: Stephan Lang
President: Sam Waterston
Vice-President Saxon: Ben Gazzara
Treasury Secretary Murphy: Henry Strozier
General Blackburn: Charles Gioffi
Grasso: Nick Turturro
Congressman Page: Gore Vidal (cameo)

Origin: USA
Released: 1997
Production: Terry Collis for Cinergi and Hollywood Pictures; released by Buena Vista
Direction: George P. Cosmatos
Screenplay: Adi Hasak and Ric Gibbs
Cinematography: Buzz Feitshans IV
Editing: Robert A. Gerretti
Production design: Joe Alives
Art direction: Bill Hiney
Costumes: April Ferry
Music: Bruce Broughton
Sound: Keith A. Wester
MPAA rating: R
Running Time: 94 minutes

REVIEWS

Boxoffice. April, 1997, p. 203.
Chicago Tribune. January 31, 1997, p. 5.
Entertainment Weekly. February 14, 1997, p. 44.
The Hollywood Reporter. January 3, 1997, p. 10.
Los Angeles Times. January 31, 1997, p. F10.
New York Times. January 31, 1997, p. B6.
People. February 10, 1997, p. 21.
Sight and Sound. July, 1997, p. 7.
USA Today. January 31, 1997, p. 3D.
Variety. February 3, 1997, p. 43.

Shall We Dance?

"Enormously entertaining!"—Roger Ebert, *Chicago Sun-Times*

"A world-class charmer . . . like *Cinema Paradiso* and *Like Water for Chocolate.* Don't sit this one out!"—Kevin Thomas, *Los Angeles Times*

"An enchanting invitation that's impossible to resist!"—Michael Medved, *New York Post*

"Rich in humor and heart, *Shall We Dance* is sweet magic!"—Peter Travers, *Rolling Stone*

Box Office: $9,527,507

Dancing as performance in films has functioned as an escapist release, as much for the film's characters, constrained to serve what has often been a mere excuse for a storyline, as much as for us, as an audience, seeking gratification in limited but instant doses. When Astaire and Rogers break into 'The Continental,' we couldn't care less about the fictional characters they are portraying for those few minutes. Even so, the repetitive drudgery behind their perfection remains masked. The dancing ends; the film's narrative resumes.

It should come as no surprise that a film that exposes the backbreaking trial-and-error behind just such a form of dancing should come from a distant film culture steeped in radically different narrative customs. Film historians inform us that the first Japanese film audiences were as much taken up by the mechanics of film projection as by the images they were supposed to look at. Traditionally therefore, the protagonist in a Japanese film is viewed not so much as a psychologically individuated character, but rather someone controlled by the political, cultural and even metaphysical processes at work in society. Unlike us, the Japanese audience is not expected to identify with an individual predicament or desire, but rather relate it to those wider processes uncovered by the film, and in turn, to a concomitant set of values. In short, the narrative dilemma isn't so much resolved at the end of the film, as put into perspective.

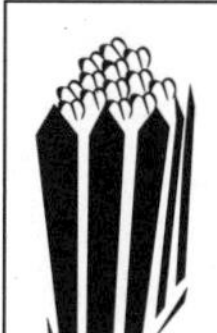

Shohei to Mai on learning to dance: "At my age, it's embarrassing to say so, but every day I feel so alive."

Thus, Masayuki Suo's brilliantly original *Shall We Dance?* opens with a viewpoint of its own on the recent Japanese craze for ballroom dancing. We are informed by the film's brief introductory narration that the overtness of abandon which the western dance form requires opposes native social custom founded on intuitive understanding, one which forbids even married couples to exchange "I love you's" in public. The film's bird's-eye view is thus established, along with its overall purpose: to chart the liberating effect of such a fad, as well as the schizoid rifts it is bound to create in Japanese society.

The film affirms its omniscience by opening in faraway Blackpool, England. Suo's camera subserviently tracks along the ceiling of the Winter Garden dance hall upon which has been inscribed a quotation from Shakespeare: "Bid me discourse, and I will enchant thine ear." As if enchanted itself, the camera then pans down to reveal couples dressed in their finest formals, twirling, entranced under the spotlight, lost in each other's arms. We will learn later that this isn't just any dance hall, but the mecca of all ballrooms, the world-renowned arena for the crowning of virtuosos.

Winner of 13 Japanese Academy Awards in 1996.

The film then begins to tell its story. On a deserted street strewn with bars and awash in neon, Shohei (Koji Yakusyo), a humble nondescript office worker in his early 40's, takes leave of his colleagues, wanting to call it a night. On the train home, he dozes off, but is jolted awake at a station long enough to catch sight of beautiful Mai (Tamiyo Kusakari), a young dance instructor, who is looking out the window of a dance school, a forlorn expression on her face. The train speeds on, to carry Shohei to his stop, where he clambers onto his bicycle and pedals to his functionally modest suburban house.

Early the next morning, Shohei eats breakfast by himself, ready to start his routine all over again. His wife, Masako (Hideko Hara), steeped in her household chores, and his young daughter, Natsuko (Misa Shimizu), lost in her interactive pursuits, excuse his absence from their lives, content that he has ensconced them in a new home. Shohei's high-tech office scene renders him even more anonymous in a setting of computers and modems, where efficiency is gauged by an ability to master the latest software. However, it is here that Aoki (Naoto Takenaka), a systems analyst, confides to Shohei about his newfound passion for ballroom dancing.

That evening, Shohei makes it a point to look up from the train at the dance school window, and sees Mai dancing with a partner. After that, a magazine ad is all the prodding it takes for Shohei to get down at the stop and make his way hesitantly to the dance school. Despite his secret desire to take individual instruction from Mai, Shohei's conscience allows him to invest only in group lessons supervised by the congenial, but much older, Tamako (Reiko Kusamura). These turn out to be a motley affair. Shohei lags behind, finding even a simple 'quick-quick-slow' routine too painful to emulate. Moreover, his steps remain comically militaristic, and too wide.

The film then makes clear the dichotomy behind this alien social custom: the feet have to move as if stirred by the heart. This dictate then becomes extended not just to Shohei's personal life, but into the film's many little subplots . In so doing, the film astutely comments on the all too familiar Japanese urge to outdo the west as a striving unable to fill a void at the heart of a society torn between the traditional and the modern. Shohei, like his countrymen, finds that excessive diligence is no substitute for feeling.

For example, we soon learn that romance is missing from Mai's life as well, that Shohei's secret heartthrob was once a semi-finalist at the Winter Garden, but that, through no fault of her own, a mere misstep brought her dreams to an end, leaving her to teach at her father's dance school. Surprisingly, even when Shohei sees her by herself, he keeps his distance, as if trusting some intuitive force to do his work for him.

When Mai eventually deigns to treat him to an individual lesson, Shohei extends his hand in mid-air, which she grasps in a close-up. As could be foreseen, Shohei's feet now move as they should. His passion stirred by this first con-

AWARDS AND NOMINATIONS

National Board of Review 1997: Foreign Language Film

tact, Shohei waits outside the school that evening. After thanking Mai for the lesson, he invites her for dinner, but she cannot accept, claiming that the school doesn't allow any private contact with students. She then adds, "I take dancing very seriously. This is a classroom, not a disco." Even so, the meeting marks a turning point for Shohei, providing just that missing element to fuel his aspirations. We see him practicing by himself during every spare moment: on the platform while waiting for a train, in the deserted station courtyard at night, and even in the office washroom.

It is when his daughter spies him practicing at home that she reports to her mother about her father acting strange. Herself unable to understand the recent bounce in her husband's step, Masako decides to hire a costly private investigator. "He makes strange body movements," she confides to him. "His shirts smell of perfume. He might be caught up in something weird." Soon, the detective shows her photos of Shohei dancing with Mai, then remarks, "He's keeping it a secret because he's ashamed." Shame then, resulting from the interpersonal contact necessary in ballroom dancing, no doubt incomprehensible to the film's western audience, provides the film's narrative thrust with its second major dichotomy.

As Mai pulls Shohei's body against hers, while teaching him the rumba, her instructions remains forthright: "It's important your right side remains firmly pressed against your partner's." As if ashamed, Shohei turns to stone. Sensing his earnestness however, Mai agrees to tutor him and another instructor, the plump but attractive Toyoko (Eriko Watanabe) for the Amateur Dance Competition.

It is during a private moment that Shohei at last shares his feelings with Mai. "I married at 28, had a child at 30 and bought a house at 40, but it is only now that I feel so alive." Mai in turn responds by admitting, "It's been a long time since I've felt so enthusiastic," and fills Shohei in on her past, thereby explaining the melancholy look on her face that Shohei glimpsed from the train.

It is the contest however, which Masako, her daughter and the detective also decide to attend, that brings matters to a head for Shohei. With rigorous practice behind him, and dressed in his formal best, Shohei sweeps Toyoko across the dance floor with surefire grace, even drawing applause, until his daughter breaks his concentration by crying out: "Dad!" The mere sight of his wife and daughter is enough to send Shohei into a tailspin, resulting in his stepping on Toyoko's dress, which comes off as the audience watches in shocked silence. Mortified, Shohei salvages his domestic life by promising Masako that he will never dance again.

The film's final sequence shows how circumstances draw the circumspect Shohei out of his shell long enough to attend a farewell party thrown for Mai at a local dance hall. For 'Ladies' Choice', as Mai has to choose a partner, the spotlight roams all over the darkened hall, but she chooses no one. Shohei then appears just in time, his briefcase in hand. Mai then walks in a straight line across the darkened floor, an overhead spot following her, until she stands in front of Shohei and utters the words from a foreign language, in her foreign accent, but which the film has by now imbued with magic: "Shall we dance?" As if to commemorate their momentary romance, the film returns to the dancers at the Winter Garden in Blackpool much as we saw them at the start of the film.

Critics have been unanimous in relating to the film's transcultural idealism and overall cheer. Amy Taubin's assessment in *The Village Voice* could be taken to sum up critical response to the film: "Combining conservative sexual politics with a liberating vision of self-expression through the mastery of a form, *Shall We Dance?* is an arthouse *Saturday Night Fever* (1977)." Michael Medved in the *New York Post* felt it fitting that the film swept all 13 Japanese Academy Awards.

—Vivek Adarkar

CREDITS

Shohei Sugiyama: Koji Yakusho
Mai Kishikawa: Tamiyo Kusakari
Tomio Aoki: Naota Takenaka
Toyoko Takahashi: Eriko Watanabe
Toru Miwa: Akira Emoto
Tokichi Hattori: Yu Tokui
Masahiro Tanaka: Hiromasa Taguchi

Origin: Japan
Released: 1996
Production: Yasuyoshi Tokuma for Altamira Pictures; released by Miramax Films
Direction: Masayuki Suo
Screenplay: Masayuki Suo
Cinematography: Naoki Kayano
Editing: Junichi Kikuchi
Production design: Kyoko Heya
Music: Yoshikazu Suo
MPAA rating: PG
Running Time: 118 minutes

REVIEWS

Boxoffice. May, 1997, p. 62.
Chicago Tribune. July 18, 1997, p. 5.
Chicago Tribune. July 20, 1997, p. 7.
Entertainment Weekly. July 18, 1997, p. 52.
Hollywood Reporter. July 10, 1997, p. 8.
Los Angeles Times. July 11, 1997, p. F13.
New York Post. July 11, 1997.
New York Times. April 5, 1997, p. 16.
New York Times. July 6, 1997, p. H9.
People. July 21, 1997, p. 18.
Rolling Stone. May 29, 1997, p. 56.
USA Today. July 10, 1997, p. 2D.
Village Voice. July 15, 1997, p. 68.

She's So Lovely

The story of one outrageous woman. Caught between two men. Both of them certain of one thing . . . *She's So Lovely.*—Movie tagline

"This roller-coaster romance summons the Cassavetes spirit with daring and affection! Sean Penn gives a boisterous, tender performance! John Travolta is terrific!"—Janet Maslin, *New York Times*

"*She's So Lovely* is a gift! Sean Penn and Robin Wright Penn could not be better! John Travolta is dynamite!"—Peter Travers, *Rolling Stone*

"Brilliant, funny and completely unpredictable!"—John Powers, *Vogue*

Box Office: $7,281,450

Eddie's (Sean Penn) release from a mental institution creates a love triangle for his ex-wife Maureen (Robin Wright), who has remarried in the offbeat romance *She's So Lovely.*

Whenever the name John Cassavetes is mentioned, it inevitably evokes strong feelings of either praise and admiration or harsh negative criticism. Many view him as having been a bold, creative, rebel force who paved the way for today's independent filmmakers. Others are far less complimentary and view him as a rather self-indulgent, improvisational bore. Love him or hate him—he has undeniably made an impact on the art of filmmaking.

She's So Lovely is a Miramax Films presentation of Hachette Premier Productions in association with Clyde Is Hungry Productions, Inc. This recently released film is based on a script that John Cassavetes wrote twenty years ago. The senior Cassavetes originally planned to direct the project, but his death in 1989 prevented it from coming to fruition. Sean Penn had also expressed interest early on and Hal Ashby had been set to direct. Tragically, he, too, passed away before production ever started. Finally, John's son, Nick, succeeded in getting the film produced and took over the directorial duties. This esoteric piece is the younger Cassavetes' second outing as director (the first being *Unhook the Stars*, starring his mother, Gena Rowlands). *Rolling Stone Magazine* called *Lovely*, "a valentine from father to son." It was labeled by *Variety* as a "serio-comic meditation on the various forms of love and madness." It stars Sean Penn, Robin Wright-Penn, and John Travolta.

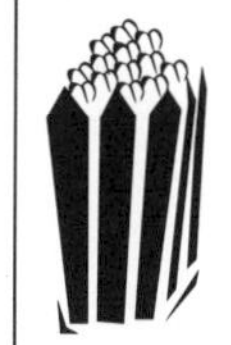

Eddie to Miss Green: "You're a very beautiful woman, and I haven't been around the kindness of women in some time."

It opens with an aerial view, as the camera moves slowly into the heart of a major city. It is a visual invitation to the audience to enter the lives of the film's major characters. They are first introduced to Maureen (Wright-Penn), lying on a bed, in a sleazy flophouse, looking haggard, hungover and hard-core. The harshness of the lighting exposes her dissipated, but still beautiful face. This fallen angel is feverishly searching for her absentee husband, Eddie (Sean Penn), who has been missing for three days. This is not unusual for Eddie, but these unexplained absences drive Maureen to distraction. She naively seeks solace by having a few drinks with her insistent boozy neighbor Keifer (realistically played by James Gandofini). What starts out being a flirtatious romp becomes a brutally graphic rape attempt. Suffice it to say that the world which these characters inhabit is not a pretty one. The situation becomes even more sordid when it is revealed that this smoking, drinking, battered creature is pregnant. Following her "bout" with not-so-neighborly Keifer, Maureen stumbles around in the rain and finally finds the "long-lost Eddie" (in a bar, naturally). "Get her in the back before her brain freezes altogether," is Eddie's first response to her rain-

AWARDS AND NOMINATIONS

Cannes Film Festival 1997: Actor (Penn)

drenched appearance. Upon closer examination, he takes her to a hospital to find her relatively undamaged by her ordeal. Since Eddie is somewhat "emotionally unstable," Maureen decides to keep him from knowing the truth. Her fear is that he would retaliate and kill Keifer. These events all take place during a dark and shadowy evening, giving the film an ominous and foreboding atmosphere. The scenes seem submerged in liquor and seediness, reminiscent of *Bar Fly*. This 1987 film was based on the auto-biographical writings of cult favorite, Charles Bukowski. Eventually, the truth of what happens emerges and results in a drunken rampage. A violent and seriously disturbed Eddie loses control and winds up killing an officer. This outburst lands the incoherent father-to-be in a mental institution for "observation."

John Cassavetes wrote the script in the late '70s, intending to cast himself and wife Gena Rowlands in the lead roles.

Abruptly, it's ten years later and how things have changed. Eddie is still locked up, but Maureen has made a 180-degree turn. She now lives in the suburbs with new husband, Joey (John Travolta) and her three children. Joey is a contractor, possesses a rough-edged charm, and loves Maureen. Actually, Joey seems almost like a grown-up Vinnie Barbarino—the character that Travolta played on TV's "Welcome Back Kotter." Things seem to be going relatively well for the couple, with one major exception—Eddie is about to be released from the institution. Knowing of Maureen's lingering feelings for her former lover, Joey wants a resolution to this long-standing obsession. He wants her to face the past and decide the future. He sets up a meeting with Eddie and angrily declares, "You can't take a shit on my life." Eddie defiantly responds, "I love Maureen. I don't care if you love her or not. If I come to dinner, I'm taking her with me!" The line is drawn in the sand and the showdown begins between the two determined adversaries.

The second part of this film catapults the audience into an entirely different style of film. Suddenly, the situation is less dark (although still serious) and switches to a comedic scenario between two men fighting over one woman. It's an interesting choice with minimal results. At this point, the dialogue becomes contrived and mannered. Travolta to his daughter, "You haven't lived long enough for me to argue with you. You're just a glorified piece of blue sky." It's hard to imagine a suburban contractor talking like this—it's born from the writer's pen, not the character. Eddie doesn't seem to have improved much at all after ten years of being locked up and Maureen (although cleaned up a lot) still seems a little shaky. After much shouting and gnashing of teeth, a decision is reached. Maureen abandons the last ten years of her life and drives off into the sunset with her weather-beaten prince.

Emanuel Levy, who reviewed the film at the Cannes Film Festival said that "twenty years ago, the triangle played by Penn, Wright and Travolta would have been cast with Peter Falk, Gena Rowlands and Ben Gazzara." The comparisons are certainly obvious, considering the script is by John Cassavetes, and perhaps that's the problem. It seems that Cassavetes is trying to "duplicate" his father's style, rather than create one of his own. The "maestro's" shadow looms over this entire production and consequently the film looks like an imitation of the real thing. Whether a fan or not, vintage Cassavetes serves up an assortment of enviable traits. The quality of acting is uniformly good, if not exceptional. There seems to be an urgency to the characters who live life on the edge, making them extremely fascinating to watch. It's as if the audience is peering into their bedrooms as they expose their raw, uncensored emotions. It takes a certain commitment by the actors to "go for broke" and unveil their flaws and vulnerabilities. *She's So Lovely* contains some of these characteristics, but fails to evoke the immediacy and originality of a Cassavetes film twenty years earlier. The script does appear dated and, in some scenes, Robin Wright-Penn seems to be imitating Gena Rowlands in *Woman Under the Influence*. She falls dangerously close to excessive self-indulgence. Also, the writing needed to be coherent and structured. The viewer needed to know some details about Mau-

CREDITS

Eddie: Sean Penn
Maureen: Robin Wright Penn
Joey: John Travolta
Shorty: Harry Dean Stanton
Georgie: Debi Mazar
Kiefer: James Gandolfini
Miss Green: Gena Rowlands
Jeanie: Kelsey Mulrooney

Origin: USA
Released: 1997
Production: Rene Cleitman for Clyde Is Hungry Productions and Hachette Premiere; released by Miramax Films
Direction: Nick Cassavetes
Screenplay: John Cassavetes
Cinematography: Thierry Arbogast
Editing: Petra Von Oelffen
Music: Joseph Vitarelli
Production design: David Wasco
Costumes: Beatrix Aruna Pasztor
Sound: Jim Stueve
MPAA rating: R
Running Time: 97 minutes

reen's new life with Joey. Although the story is about irrational, obsessive love, more information was needed to justify her walking out on her family— the *first day* Eddie was released. It needed to be supported by a more thorough character development. The film also needed a third act. As it is, it leaves the audience feeling incomplete and dissatisfied.

So, when all is said and done, the controversy continues—it's part of the Cassavetes' legacy. Individuality and boldness were trademarks of the senior Cassavetes' style. His son, Nick, needs to be just as bold and step out of his father's shadow. Perhaps his own individuality will forge exciting new trails in today's cinema and even surpass his illustrious father.

—*Rob Chicatelli*

REVIEWS

Boxoffice. August, 1997, p. 46.
Chicago Tribune. August 29, 1997, p. 4.
Details. September, 1997, p. 113.
Entertainment Weekly. September 5, 1997, p. 47.
Los Angeles Times. August 29, 1997, p. F10.
New York Times. August 27, 1997, p. C9.
People. September 8, 1997, p. 18.
Rolling Stone. September 4, 1997, p. 74.
Time. August 25, 1997.
USA Today. August 29, 1997, p. 3D.
Variety. May 26, 1997, p. 64.
Village Voice. September 2, 1997, p. 73.

Sick: The Life and Death of Bob Flanagan, Supermasochist

"Fascinating! A work of genius."—Hillel Italie, *Associated Press*

"Amazing! Extraordinarily rich and haunting."—Owen Gleiberman, *Entertainment Weekly*

"Unforgettable! Groundbreaking. Among the most intimate love scenes ever filmed."—Stephen Holden, *New York Times*

"The movie of the year!"—John Anderson, *Newsday*

"Hilarious!"—Jack Kroll, *Newsweek*

"Astonishing!"—Peter Travers, *Rolling Stone*

Nary a word in the English language is more open to selective interpretation than "art." It means so many things to so many people. Luckily (for artists), there is no "wrong" definition; all viewpoints conjured up in one's mind when referencing art of any kind are completely subjective and selective. What one pair of eyes finds visually pleasing or enriching can often turn-off or even repulse someone else. The cycle of art imitating life turning into life imitating art seems to overlap more now than it ever has before. Very often, someone's life and lifestyle can serve as an easel to display their art. After watching *Sick*, you might find it difficult to consider Bob Flanagan an appealing, likable, endearing or mentally balanced individual. What cannot be disputed was Flanagan's unique ability to provoke, educate, stimulate and, to a very select few, entertain.

Bob Flanagan: "I've learned to fight sickness with sickness."

Not in recent memory has film been so visceral in its execution. Diagnosed at birth with cystic fibrosis, Bob Flanagan wasn't expected to make it through infancy. Amazingly, he lived to the age of 43 while making his living as a performance artist, balancing comedic jabs at his crippling affliction with deviant self-mutilation. Recognized shortly after Flanagan's birth, cystic fibrosis causes a breakdown in the exocrine glands which leads to faulty digestion due to a deficiency of pancreatic enzymes. Other symptoms include an inordinately high build-up of mucus in the lungs resulting in inhibited breathing. Flanagan chose to deal with this area of his life by making light of his situation much in the manner of a stand-up comedian. In the latter stages of his life he actually delivered his material while lying flat on his back on a hospital gurney. Another scene in the movie shows him explaining the workings of "Invisible Man," a clear plastic model that pretty much served as a metaphor for his life. In what is easily the film's lightest moment, Flanagan pumps various concoctions through the model to simulate the oral extrication of mucus, the act of defecating, and penile ejaculation. Flanagan's entire life was one of continuous, protracted pain; he knew little else. This could go far to explain his attraction to sadomasochism. His need for humiliation and pain in the bedroom paralleled the rest of his existence. That need was in plentiful supply, courtesy of Sheree Rose, his girlfriend/dominatrix.

The many scenes of Flanagan and Rose in all of their leather and rubber regalia are moments best saved for the privacy of their own chamber or a specialized porno flick. The time devoted to Flanagan and Rose's intimate relations borders on the excessive and often comes across as gratuitous. Watching the pair work with oversized butt plugs, high heels, and body mutilation educates to a point. In what has to be one of the most disturbing acts ever captured for use in a non-pornographic film, Flanagan is seen driving a nail through the head of his own penis into a board. This one scene takes close to a minute from beginning to end, but audience members, particularly men, will view it as a lifetime. Even audiences who appreciate the most visceral of documentary features will find this footage disconcerting.

Director Kirby Dick divides time equally between Flanagan's life with Rose, his stage performances, and his slow, spiraling physical deterioration. As documentary films go, it is near perfect. Flanagan's ability to make light of his disease is admirable. However, mixing his plight with S&M diminishes its impact and validity and often makes him look like nothing more than an exhibitionist and circus sideshow freak. Flanagan died while the project was nearing completion and Dick includes footage of his subject on his deathbed, his corpse, and subsequent memorial service. Dick's objective, documentarian eye temporarily makes way for an engaging and truly moving image. Rose, surrounded by Flanagan's brother and parents, bids him a tearful farewell. Flanagan lived longer than he should have and managed to find a way to educate and entertain those who would listen. This is a daring project, nothing like it has ever been made before and probably for good reason. Is it art? Without a doubt. Is it entertaining? It will be immensely entertaining to anyone who prefers or identifies with a lifestyle similar to that of Flanagan and Rose. Does it benefit society? Does it have "redeeming social value?" Yes. A resounding yes. Its only glaring problem is that only a fraction of the population has the stomach to sit through it. With *Sick*, Kirby Dick has paved the way for other documentary filmmakers to break even more boundaries. For that reason alone, Dick's film is one of the most important releases of 1997.

—J.M. Clark

CREDITS

Origin: USA
Released: 1997
Production: Kirby Dick; released by Cinepix Film Properties
Direction: Kirby Dick
Cinematography: Jonathan Dayton, Kirby Dick, Sheree Rose, Geza Sinkovics
Editing: Kirby Dick, Dody Dorn
Music: Blake Leyh
Sound: Alan Barker, Kip Glynn
MPAA rating: Unrated
Running Time: 89 minutes

REVIEWS

Entertainment Weekly. November 11, 1997, p. 98.
Los Angeles Times. November 7, 1997, p. F19.
Premiere. December, 1997, p. 52.
Rolling Stone. December 11, 1997, p. 86.
Village Voice. November 11, 1997, p. 86.
Village Voice. November 18, 1997, p. 27.

A Simple Wish

Anabel made a wish. Murray made a mess.—Movie tagline
Your wish is his command . . . sort of—Movie tagline
"Magical. The funniest family film of the summer."—Joanna Levenglick, *Kids News Network*
"Martin Short . . . as funny a performance as the year will see."—Kenneth Turan, *Los Angeles Times*
"A charming family picture, witty and sophisticated."—Laoise Mac Reamoinn, *Newark Star-Ledger*
"Mara Wilson is a delight."—Michael H. Price, *Philadelphia Daily News*
"Martin Short is hysterical."—Jeff Craig, *Sixty Second Preview*

Box Office: $8,333,283

The current release of Universal's Bubble Factory film, *A Simple Wish* starring Martin Short and Mara Wilson, simply fell short of the promising expectations of the trailers and the opening ten minutes. In those opening shots showing Martin Short (Murray) taking an exam to become a certified fairy godmother, the audience is introduced to the star's considerable and unique talents. His rubbery-faced brand of humor reminds the viewers as to why he's become so popular. The comic actor has come a long way since his Ed Grimley days on the hilarious Canadian-based SCTV comedy series. Unfortunately, those funny ten minutes go by much too quickly and then the story begins—"Once upon a time—three months ago."

Mara Wilson (*Matilda* [1996]) plays Anabel, a sweet kid who loves her father Oliver (Robert Pastorelli) very much. Oliver longs to become an actor and singer on Broadway. In the meantime, he works as a hansom cab driver in New York's picturesque Central Park. In an attempt to help him fulfill his dream, Anabel conjures up a fairy godmother in the form of Murray. She accomplishes this in the usual fashion, by placing one of her baby teeth under her pillow. Much to her chagrin, Murray is not only the wrong gender, but it appears that his magic wand is on the fritz—it's broken! Nevertheless, she tells Murray about her dad's dream and he begins to come up with a plan to get Dad on Broadway. In reality, Dad is a pretty good singer and lands an audition for a musical based on *A Tale of Two Cities.* Upon finishing his singing audition for the show's composer, Lord Richard (played wonderfully by Jonathan Hadary), even comments that his chances look good. Meanwhile, there happens to be a convention of the National Fairy Godmothers Association going on in a hotel on the other side of town. Things aren't going smoothly at this gathering due to the fact that Claudia (Kathleen Turner), who is an outcast-turned-witch, is trying to crash the party. In revenge, she wants to steal all of the magic wands from the kindly old fairy godmothers. Claudia is neither kindly nor old, in fact she finds herself rather drop-dead gorgeous. At one point while passing by a mirror, she stops to take a closer look and says, "I love this mirror," while adjusting one of her long golden tresses.

Murray: "One wish per customer and no wishes for more wishes. They plugged that loophole up years ago. In past years there were abuses."

Murray and Anabel are getting into all sorts of mischief by this time due to Murray's incompetence as a fairy godmother. They inadvertently land somewhere in Nebraska, looking down the nose of a double-barreled shotgun. A maniacal redneck is not readily amused by the unlikely pair and is about to blow them to smithereens. Their untimely death is halted when Murray turns the clod into a giant rabbi—that's right, rabbi. It was supposed to be a rabbit. Things ain't looking very good for Oliver, back on Broadway. It looks like the producers have decided to cast a smug superstar, Tony Sable, played by a preening Alan Campbell, in spite of Murray's attempt at sabotage. He turned poor Tony into a leaping-frog machine when he started clearing his throat while auditioning. Murray keeps on trying, but bungles again and turns dear old Dad into a statue in Central Park. Claudia and her assistant, Boots (Amanda Plummer, looking like a cast member from *Cats*), are still collecting magic wands in her castle, which is quietly nestled under what looks like the George Washington Bridge. If the spell on Oliver is not undone by midnight it seems that he will be a pigeon perch forever. The suspense builds right up to the last second until the power of love saves the day.

There is little confusion as to why Martin Short was cast in this fantasy film geared towards children. He has an elfin quality about him and he's goofy enough to generate laughs with his physical comedy. He was quite wonderful in the *Father of the Bride* films, co-starring with Steve Martin and Diane Keaton. The question is, can his crazy antics carry a film completely on their own? Perhaps, but it needs to be a far better project than *A Simple Wish.* He works tirelessly to make it work, but the film's meandering script and threadbare special effects undermine his efforts. In some of Short's scenes with Kathleen Turner, he actually works too hard.

Michael Ritchie (*The Candidate* [1972], *Fletch* [1985], *The Bad News Bears* [1976]) directs this film with a fair amount of good judgment. The scenes that occur in the theater are actually very entertaining and well done. The musical "Two Cities," for which Pastorelli's character is auditioning, looks quite interesting and credible. However, when the leaping frogs and special effects are added, it all seems misplaced and oddly inappropriate to the action. Also, in its attempt to appeal to both children and adults, *A Simple Wish* lacked an identity. It seemed to flip-flop back and forth. If individual scenes were viewed on their own, they looked fine. When they were woven together there was a disjointed effect. Another weakness was the unwillingness to follow through with an idea to its satisfying completion. For example, when the camera entered into the fairy godmothers convention hall it was a dazzling and quite spectacular set. Well, that was it—the audience was never allowed back in again. Instead, the action for this sequence ended up taking place in the drab hotel lobby. *Variety*'s Todd McCarthy stated that this missed opportunity prevented the film from "mining what would seem to have been considerable comic gold."

Mara Wilson, called "child actress supreme" by *USA Today*, is an accomplished professional. She possesses a straightforwardness to her acting and manages to avoid the pitfalls of many child actors—cuteness and coyness. When Anabel puts one of her teeth under her pillow she simply announces that "the money from the tooth fairy is really going to come in handy." Her matter-of-fact delivery makes her all the more engaging and charming. It was a wise casting choice by Rick Pagano. It also served to counterbalance Short's over-the-top zaniness.

Kathleen Turner's career, like many other actors, has been a series of hits and misses. In 1981 she set the screen on fire in *Body Heat* with William Hurt. Her long hair, sultry good looks and husky voice led many critics to call her the next Lauren Bacall. After this debut film she starred in a diverse number of roles, in such films as *Romancing the Stone* (1984), *Prizzi's Honor* (1985), *The Jewel of the Nile* (1985), *Peggy Sue Got Married* (1986), and *War of the Roses* (1989). Her career was most definitely on the fast track, moving at an accelerated speed. She then appeared in a film titled *V.I. Warshawski* (1991), which received terrible reviews and bombed at the box office. It seems that her career began to stall after this rather dismal failure. She certainly was taken off of Hollywood's notorious "A-list." In her latest project, *A Simple Wish*, she plays the evil Claudia. Formerly a fairy godmother, she's now a witch. She looks great, decked out in glamorous costumes by Luke Reichle. She seems to have maintained the trappings of a star. Many of her scenes with Martin Short are awkwardly written and ill-conceived. In spite of this, she plays the "witchiness" of her character to the hilt. When she plays her scenes with Short she has a tendency to overact. Perhaps this is the only way not to get swallowed up by his performance. It is at these moments that she falls into the category of high camp. In context of the fantasy nature of this film, her work is appropriate.

Robert Pastorelli as Anabel's father, Oliver, turns in a solid and well-conceived performance. He is completely convincing as an honest man with a dream of supporting his family. He adds a nice touch of truth and reality to a film that is based on a magical theme. His subtle charm and humor overlays his character. While being admonished for being incredibly late for his audition by his agent, he astonishingly queries, "Since when is six minutes incredibly late?"

As mentioned earlier, the special effects were adequate, but sparse. Although they were created by Blue Sky Studios and Matte World Digital and well executed, there just wasn't enough of them. It would seem that a film trying to compete with some of the summer's blockbusters would pull out all the stops in order to dazzle the audience. Perhaps it was the budget or just an unfortunate miscalculation. The message of the film was basically one that depicts love and perseverance—the "love will conquer all" theme. This may be an admirable story line, but the young audiences of today are accustomed to the modern technological wizardry of animation and computerized graphics. The audiences of today are used to being astounded by the likes of *The Lost World* (1997), *The Lion King* (1994), *Aladdin* (1992), *E.T.* (1982) and many, many more. *A Simple Wish* seemed drab by comparison. Maybe it's not a simple thing to create magic in these ever-changing days of technical wonderment, but it takes much more than a wish.

—*Rob Chicatelli*

CREDITS

Murray: Martin Short
Anabel: Mara Wilson
Oliver: Robert Pastorelli
Claudia: Kathleen Turner
Boots: Amanda Plummer
Charlie: Francis Capra
Hortense: Ruby Dee
Rena: Teri Garr

Origin: USA
Released: 1997
Production: Sid, Bill and Jon Sheinberg for Bubble Factory; released by Universal Pictures
Direction: Michael Ritchie
Screenplay: Jeff Rothberg
Cinematography: Ralf Bode
Editing: William Scharf
Music: Bruce Broughton
Production design: Stephen Hendrickson
Set decoration: Jaro Dick
Costumes: Luke Reichle
Sound: Doug Hanton
Visual effects producer: Tim Healy
MPAA rating: PG
Running Time: 89 minutes

REVIEWS

Boxoffice. September, 1997, p. 125.
Chicago Tribune. July 11, 1997, p. 5.
The Hollywood Reporter. July 7, 1997, p. 11.
Los Angeles Times. July 11, 1997, p. F18.
New York Times. July 11, 1997, p. C18.
People. July 28, 1997, p. 23.
Sight and Sound. November, 1997, p. 51.
USA Today. July 11, 1997, p. 8D.
Variety. July 14, 1997, p. 44.
Washington Post. July 11, 1997, p. B7.

The Sixth Man

They're lifting the game to a higher level.—Movie tagline

"A first-rate comedy!"—Henry Cabot Beck, *Star-Ledger*

"Utterly irresistible!"—Kathryn Kinley, *WPIX-TV*

Box Office: $14,772,788

Antoine Tyler (Kadeem Hardison), basketball star at the University of Washington, suffers a fatal heart attack on the court, leaving his younger brother Kenny (Marlon Wayans) to be team leader. Coach Pederson (David Paymer), who has his heart set on getting to the Final Four in New York City, knows Kenny can do it—but Kenny is plagued by self-doubt. All his life he has lived in his older brother's shadow. Without Antoine he is lost. He is not accustomed to calling the plays and taking the three-point shots. He has always left the starring role up to Antoine—which partially explains why big brother, although likeable, had developed an ego comparable to that of real-life basketball superstar Dennis Rodman.

Without Antoine the Washington Huskies go into a mid-season slump. They had been on their way to winning the Pac 10 Conference but are suddenly in danger of not even getting to the NCAA. Finals. Under pressure from the fans, from his teammates, and from his coach, Kenny sends up a prayer to his dead brother to do something to help him. Such prayers rarely go unanswered in Hollywood movies. The ghost of Antoine appears after hours in the dark locker room, scaring poor Kenny out of his wits in the funniest scene in the film.

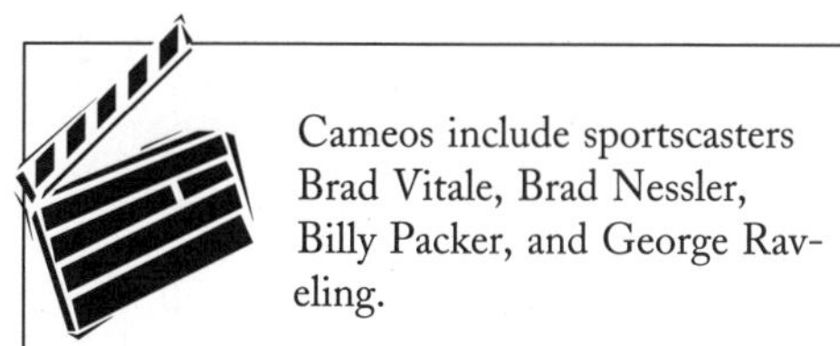

Cameos include sportscasters Brad Vitale, Brad Nessler, Billy Packer, and George Raveling.

Antoine, who always appears in a blue Huskies uniform and emitting a supernatural glow, can only be seen and heard by his brother. This is a convention with which movie audiences are thoroughly familiar, but it can be traced back as least as far as Shakespeare's *Hamlet.* ("Alas, how is't with you,/That you do bend your eye on vacancy/And with the incorporeal air do hold discourse?") Antoine's putative invisibility will allow for many funny scenes in which teammates and coach see Kenny apparently talking to himself, wrestling with himself, and doing impossible acrobatics. Wayans is indeed a gifted comedian and is at his best in scenes such as these. *The Sixth Man* is better when it is content to be funny rather than melodramatic or sententious. Antoine promises that he is going to become "the sixth man" on the team and lead the Huskies to victory.

Much of the film is taken up with bizarre happenings on the court in the heat of crucial games. The opponents' shots are blocked by outrageous invisible goaltending, while the Huskies' shots go into the basket even when they should have missed by yards. Seven-foot center Zigi Hrbacek (Vladimir Cuk), who has never made a three-point shot in his life, is making them easily, while diminutive Danny O'-Grady (Travis Ford), who has never even tried to slam dunk, now finds that he can fly through the air like Superman with the assistance of the invisible Antoine. As critic Joe Leydon, writing for *Variety* points out: "College basketball players haven't had so much help on the court since Fred MacMurray attached Flubber to their shoes in *The Absent-Minded Professor* [1961]."

As in most films about games—football, poker, billiards, or whatever—the situations are oversimplified for the benefit of those viewers who know nothing about the rules. Typically, with only a few seconds left on the game clock, the Huskies are down two points and have to make a long-distance three-point shot to win the game. Coach Pederson occasionally draws a few lines and crosses on his clipboard to diagram plays he is calling, but most of his instructions are abstract and inspirational. He tells the youngsters that they have to have team spirit and play from their hearts. As Coach Pederson, Paymer does a creditable job in his pivotal role of explaining what is happening on the court and how things are stacking up in the play-offs, while verbalizing the emotions being experienced by the team, the rooters, and presumably the entire University of Washington.

With the indispensable help of Antoine's dirty tricks, the Huskies make it all the way to the Final Four. Although the other four starters cannot see Antoine, they have become well aware of his ghostly presence. They are beginning to realize, however, that winning by cheating is not really winning at all. Not only is it cheating to make impossible shots happen, but it is cheating to have a sixth man on a five-man team, even if nobody can see him.

Kenny, of course, cannot conceal Antoine's presence from his teammates indefinitely. They know that when a ball is flying out of bounds it cannot suddenly make a 180-degree turn and drop into the basket. They know that they cannot normally defy gravity the way they have been doing while making some of their fantastic slam-dunks. Not even Nijinski could have stayed up in the air that long. At first they welcome Antoine's assistance. Gradually, however, the invisible Antoine undergoes a psychological transformation similar to the character change exhibited by another invisible man, Griffin (Claude Rains), in *The Invisible Man* (1933).

Like Griffin, Antoine is becoming criminally insane. His dirty tricks become more dangerous, as well as more outrageous. Finally, he alienates everyone on the Huskies team by injuring one of their star opponents so badly that the young player has to be taken out of the game. This change in Antoine's character is the most interesting feature in a mostly superficial plot because it illustrates a truth about human psychology. Power corrupts. Antoine is even more powerful than Griffin because Antoine is dead and cannot be touched, whereas Griffin is still very vulnerable to the police and double pneumonia. The corruption seems especially sinister in Antoine's case because he is still just a kid wearing a basketball uniform. Kenny's character change, when it comes, is less intriguing because Kenny clowns around so much of the time that it is hard to take him seriously when he finally does become serious.

Kenny is pressured by his four teammates to make Antoine go back into the spirit world he came from. This forces a confrontation between the two loving brothers in which Kenny is at a disadvantage. He is the younger brother. He has always followed Antoine's lead. He has never stood up to him in the past and finds it especially difficult to do so now because of Antoine's supernatural status as a ghost. There is no question of Kenny's using physical force. Computer-generated special effects show that blows either pass right through Antoine's body or stretch it out like molten plastic—and painful retribution inevitably follows.

Kenny has a girlfriend. The beautiful R.C. St. John (Michael Michele) happens to be a shrewd reporter who is trying to find out what is really sparking the now unbeatable Huskies. Antoine is justifiably opposed to this blossoming love relationship and does his best to sabotage it. He realizes that the sportswriter is too beautiful and too smart, while his naive little brother is too susceptible to her blandishments. While Kenny and R.C. are having dinner, the invisible Antoine forces his little brother to behave like an idiot, pouring a whole bottle of steak sauce on his fish and spilling ice water all over the table.

It is this interference with his love life that finally triggers Kenny's rebellion. In an acrimonious showdown he makes it clear that he is his own man and intends to be the team leader from now on. The Huskies will either win the NCAA championship game against the University of Massachusetts honestly or they will go down trying. Antoine is made to realize that he has lost his brother's heart to the beautiful sportswriter. He reluctantly accepts the fact that he has no place on the team and no place on earth. He walks back into the void still carrying a basketball and wearing his Huskies uniform.

Randall Miller previously directed *Houseguest* (1994) and *Class Act* (1991) for Disney. In this new Disney feature he has a harder task making sense of a story that contains much fast action, an invisible star, impossible happenings, and real-life people mixed in with fictitious ones. Writers Christopher Reed and Cynthia Carle know the ins and outs of college basketball but neither they nor Miller have been able to overcome the problems arising from the story's premise. A super-protagonist needs to be pitted against a super-antagonist or else there is no suspense, just as there is no excitement in watching a game in which the teams are grossly mismatched. Antoine can hardly have conflict with anyone but his brother because nobody else can see him, and his conflict with Kenny is undercut from the beginning because the two brothers love each other. The coach and his players may want very badly to win the championship, but this feeling does not infect most members of the audience who are not already Huskies fans because there is no real contest.

Critics have pointed out that the viewer is troubled by all the dirty tricks on the basketball court long before the players begin to catch on to the fact that what the Huskies players are doing is called cheating. It may be that the intended thesis of *The Sixth Man* was, "It matters not if you win or lose but how you play the game." If so, the film is a very bizarre and complicated illustration of a platitude that fails to make its point. There is something unfair about get-

CREDITS

Kenny Tyler: Marlon Wayans
Antoine Tyler: Kadeem Hardison
Coach Pederson: David Paymer
R.C. St. John: Michael Michele
Mikulski: Kevin Dunn
James Tyler: Harold Sylvester
Zigi Hrbacek: Vladimir Cuk
Danny O'Grady: Travis Ford

Origin: USA
Released: 1997
Production: David Hoberman for Mandeville Films; released by Touchstone Pictures
Direction: Randall Miller
Screenplay: Christopher Reed and Cynthia Carle
Cinematography: Michael Ozier
Editing: Eric Sears
Music: Marcus Miller
Production design: Michael Bolton
Art direction: Eric Fraser
Sound: Rick Patton
Special effects coordinator: Stewart Bradley
MPAA rating: PG-13
Running Time: 107 minutes

ting the audience to root for a team that is cheating and then informing that audience that cheating is shameful. It is the cinematic equivalent of what criminal lawyers call "entrapment." Lawrence Van Gelder of the *New York Times* called the film "a technical foul."

—*Bill Delaney*

REVIEWS

Chicago Tribune. March 28, 1997, p. 4.
Los Angeles Times. March 28, 1997, p. F14.
New York Times. March 28, 1997, p. C21.
USA Today. March 28, 1997, p. 4D.
Variety. March 31, 1997, p. 86.

Slaves to the Underground

Love. Sex. Insanity. Thank god you're only young once.—Movie tagline

"Sexy. Contemporary."—Francesca Miller, *Female FYI*

"A buoyant, high-spirited romp."—Anne Markowski, *Sojourner: The Women's Forum*

Slaves to the Underground is a first attempt by director Kristine Peterson to break out of the type of male-oriented work which fills her resume. A veteran of such low-budget and obviously cloned films as *Body Chemistry* (1990) and *Critters* 3 (1992), Ms. Peterson longed to make a "more personal" film. While its intentions are in the right direction, *Slaves* turns out to be yet another ill-conceived clone with a great—but misleading—title.

Shelly (newcomer Molly Gross) is a sulky twenty-year-old guitar player in a Seattle "riot grrrl" band named the No Exits who suddenly moves out on her passive male lover Jimmy (Jason Bortz), a struggling "zine" (slang for magazine) publisher, and in with Suzy (Marisa Ryan), the band's volatile lesbian lead singer. Obviously, Shelly is a bit confused about her sexual orientation—and in search of her own identity.

There is very little that is fresh or original about *Slaves to the Underground*, whose title suggests a satire on the self-declared bohemian sub-culture of faddish Nineties' "slackers." The film, however, does not appear to have that particular take on its agenda. Rather, it is in many ways more like a mock documentary, but without any irony or self-consciousness. Pity, since the subject held such rich potential for divine mockery.

What Peterson does seem interested in conveying is the freedom that this generation of women has in dictating their own lifestyles. They are no longer held prisoner to rigid sexual expectations and demands; they are pilots of their own destiny. And it is possible to also infer that Peterson regards all relationships as a constant re-negotiation of the power structure—one in which the male does not necessarily have all the power nor makes all the choices, especially when it involves sex. This is particularly obvious in a scene in which Shelly asks Jimmy to masturbate in front of her and he complies, establishing Shelly as the sexually dominant partner.

That said, it is also possible to argue that Shelly is selfish, manipulative and prone to inflicting devastating emotional pain indiscriminately on her lovers. Needless to say, it is difficult, if not impossible, to understand her appeal and to appreciate her power over every one with whom she comes in contact.

The Seattle scene, with its coffeehouses and Generation-X angst, was captured much more effectively in Cameron Crowe's *Singles* (1992), while the lesbian-sexually ambivalent-Nineties-riot grrrl-tale was handled with

CREDITS

Shelley: Molly Gross
Suzy: Marisa Ryan
Jimmy: Jason Bortz
Big Phil: Bob Neuwirth
Zoe: Natacha La Ferriere
Brenda: Claudia Rossi

Origin: USA
Released: 1997
Production: Kristine Peterson, Bill Coc, and Taquel Caballes Maxwell for Neo Motion Pictures; released by First Look Pictures
Direction: Kristine Peterson
Screenplay: Bill Cody
Cinematography: Zoran Hochstatter
Editing: Eric Vizents
Music: Mike Martt
Production design: Michael Moran
Costumes: Maggie Brown
MPAA rating: R
Running Time: 93 minutes

warm sensitivity in Alex Sichel's overlooked *All Over Me* (1997).

Ms. Peterson's film succumbs to the very stereotypes it so desperately tries to lampoon. There are the politically obtuse men, and of course, the tough, castrating lesbian who looks for any excuse to punch out men. There is impassioned talk of "the cause," but we are never quite sure what that actually is.

The acting of Seattle natives Molly Gross and Jason Bortz is strictly amateur, which combined with extremely poor editing and uninspired cinematography, give the film a decidedly film-school look and feel. Only actress Marisa Ryan, known perhaps for her work on the television show "Major Dad," fares well as the angry activist. She manages to elicit our sympathy despite a weakly-written role.

Ultimately, *Slaves to the Underground* tries so hard to be politically correct that it ends up saying relatively little about its politics, its characters or the youth culture at large. Bill Cody's script is unfocused with a weak narrative, but it does have some amusing moments, particularly when Shelly offers up a scathing analysis of Benjamin in *The Graduate* (1967), a movie embraced by her parents.

—Patricia Kowal

REVIEWS

Boxoffice. April, 1997, p. 181.
San Francisco Chronicle. November 14, 1997, p. C14.
San Francisco Examiner. November 14, 1997, p. C4.
Variety. January 27, 1997, p. 79.
Village Voice. November 18, 1997, p. 85.

A Smile Like Yours

The shortest distance between two people is a certain smile.—Movie tagline

"Funny, intelligent and stylish. The entire cast shines."—Kevin Thomas, *Los Angeles Times*

Box Office: $3,330,352

A Smile Like Yours is a dubious romantic comedy about a couple attempting to have a baby. Danny Robertson (Greg Kinnear) and wife Jennifer (Lauren Holly) enjoy lots of sex, thanks to an aphrodisiac she created at her aromatherapy shop. However, after the "spontaneous" dates around San Francisco that Jennifer plans, she secretly tests the results for pregnancy. The fragrance isn't a fertility drug too.

Danny to Jennifer: "I can't be dangling loose in boxer shorts—I work around power tools!"

The co-owner of the perfumery, wisecracking Nancy (Joan Cusack), begs for the concoction to help snag a mortician she has a crush on. She offers her partner alternative methods to improve conception chances, such as switching briefs with boxers—but Danny, a construction foreman specializing in elevator shafts (metaphor intended, no doubt), doesn't like "hanging out" around power tools. He also prefers that nature take its course so getting pregnant doesn't consume their lives.

Jennifer withholds her desperate efforts and continued disappointment while she determines the reason for their problem, fearful she's infertile. Practicing to deceive—not conceive—she sneaks a semen sample and learns that Danny's "lazy swimmers" are the source of the difficulty and she must finagle her unsuspecting husband into a fertility clinic. Embarrassed that his zygotes travel too slowly to her eager eggs, he's the butt of a series of somewhat amusing gags at the masturbatorium, including the nurse's suggestion that he watch the "Romancing the Bone" video.

A montage to the Paul Anka song "You're Having My Baby" graphically shows several unsuccessful in vitro fertilization procedures using gynecological equipment resembling torture devices. The emotional strain and pain are overcome by their persistence but finally the couple agree to take time off.

To pay for the expensive process, Jennifer considers an offer to buy her best-selling aroma, neglecting to tell Danny when he announces he's accepting a job in Seattle—apparently to protect his wounded sensibility. In parallel restaurant scenes, Jennifer takes the lucrative bid for the 7th Scent and overtures from cosmetic company CEO, Richard Halstrom (Christopher McDonald), while Danny confirms the deal with his client, alluring architect Lindsay Hamilton (Jill Hennessy), whose advances he holds at bay.

Further problems set in as Danny and Jennifer detach during their break. Seeing his wife enter a limo with handsome Halstrom, Danny turns suspicious, discovering her other falsehood, and confronts her before his business trip. Showing up at the airport to apologize, Jennifer is surprised to find leggy Lindsay. Detecting trouble at home, the architect executes her seduction but the estranged-though-tempted husband remains faithful, returning home. With his wife missing, he visits her mother (Shirley MacLaine, in a cameo appearance), who seeks a confession of his affair, while playfully peeling a banana.

Danny's work buddy Steve (Jay Thomas) proffers one of his children for adoption, jokingly describing kids as both the best and worst moments of his life. During another contemplative interlude set to music (a too convenient device), the Robertsons examine their issues of trust, as well as, presumably, whether they're ready for parenthood and the purpose of bringing a child into the world. Jennifer arranges a meeting up the elevator at Danny's building site for a carnal reconciliation and they both reveal their desire for a baby with "a smile like yours"—ending up with more than they bargain for.

Although finding humor in this premise is challenging, the supporting cast, Joan and Jay, deliver most of the laughs. Nancy, spritzing a scent called "Clearing Apprehension," sends an appropriate message to the audience. Despite a few madcap situations, *Smile* smells more romantic than comedic.

There's not much sympathetic about a perky, pregnancy-obsessed liar and a sex-crazed, carriage-shy guy whose nice one-dimensional yuppiedom only seems just short of perfect. Nancy marrying an undertaker elicits more compassion than the tears Jennifer musters watching Ricky Ricardo realize Lucy is carrying Little Ricky.

Their dilemma in spawning a progeny is less realistic than a "Mad About You" episode—whose characters viewers know and care about. *A Smile Like Yours* is a formula film from first-time director (and co-writer) Keith Samples (the former head of production company, Rysher Entertainment). With "a smirk like his," Kinnear's appeal lies in cynical roles, as seen in his other screen duet with Holly, *Sabrina,* not the sort of sappy stuff echoed in the film's theme song by Natalie Cole.

—Roberta Cruger

CREDITS

Danny Robertson: Greg Kinnear
Jennifer Robertson: Lauren Holly
Nancy Tellen: Joan Cusack
Steve Harris: Jay Thomas
Lindsay Hamilton: Jill Hennessy
Richard Halstrom: Christopher McDonald
Dr. Felber: Donald Moffat
Dr. Chin: France Nuyen
Martha: Shirley MacLaine

Origin: USA
Released: 1997
Production: David Kirkpatrick and Tony Amatullo for Rysher Entertainment; released by Paramount Pictures
Direction: Keith Samples
Screenplay: Keith Samples and Kevin Meyer
Cinematography: Richard Bowen
Editing: Wayne Wahrman
Music: William Ross
Production design: Garreth Stover
Art direction: Chris Cornwell
Set design: Larry Dias
Costumes: Jill Ohanneson
Sound: Doug Axtell
MPAA rating: R
Running Time: 98 minutes

REVIEWS

Boxoffice. September, 1997, p. 115.
Los Angeles Times. August 22, 1997, p. F10.
New York Times. August 22, 1997, p. C5.
People. September 8, 1997, p. 19.
San Francisco Chronicle. August 22, 1997, p. D3.
San Francisco Examiner. August 22, 1997, p. C9.
Variety. August 25, 1997, p. 74.
Village Voice. September 2, 1997, p. 82.

Smilla's Sense of Snow

"An uncommonly intelligent adult thriller!"—Thelma Adams, *New York Post*

"Elegant . . . Sleek and good looking. Miss Ormond plays Smilla in a chic, alert, unsmiling fashion . . . She brings considerable glamour to this stoney heroine."—Janet Maslin, *The New York Times*

"Mesmerizing! Julia Ormond radiates a cool intelligence! Hooks you in with insinuating power from the first scene."—Peter Travers, *Rolling Stone*

"Brilliant . . . A great performance! Great writing! Julia Ormond does a brilliant job!"—Roger Ebert, *Siskel & Ebert*

"Truly haunting. Julia Ormond gives a searing performance."—Richard Schickel, *Time*

Box Office: $2,372,903

Smilla's Sense of Snow is a smart adaptation of Danish author Peter Hoeg's riveting novel. Julia Ormond is a credible Smilla Jasperson, which is saying a lot, because the novel's main character/narrator is not easy to envision on-screen. The novel's Smilla is surely not as beautiful as Ormond, and Hoeg's creation is an obsessed, hardened woman with no sentimentality about her fellow men and women—only a conviction that the young Inuit boy, Isaiah (Clipper Miano), who has died jumping off a roof is a murder victim. What makes the novel work is Smilla's narrative voice. It has a clipped Hemingwayesque quality and an extraordinary sense of irony. These are not the winning traits of a movie heroine. Playing Smilla on-screen exactly as she appears in the novel would make her look (from the outside) forbidding indeed. Smilla tells her own story in the novel, and the film cannot be a first person narrative. So Ormond and the filmmakers have to find a way to use Ormond's beauty—not as a passive attraction but as a facet of her intelligence and dedication to her project.

Smilla: "The only thing that makes me truly happy is mathematics. Snow, ice, and numbers."

In one sense, *Smilla's Sense of Snow* is a classic detective thriller. In this case, the female detective (she is the scientist daughter of an American father and a Greenlandic-Inuit mother) has to penetrate the Danish bureaucracy and the coverup of the circumstances of Isaiah's death. Like the classic detective, she exposes society's corruption, and she stands for the principle of the lone individual with enough integrity to withstand the threats that the collective authority of government poses. In another sense, however, she is a feminist and multicultural heroine. Because of her Greenlandic childhood, she knows too well how the majority culture victimizes minorities, and she is not fooled by official explanations of how Isaiah jumped off the roof.

Smilla knows that Isaiah was afraid of heights, and that the tracks on the roof suggest he was being chased. What made this boy afraid? Smilla pursues this question doggedly, and Ormond's cool personality gives just the right edge to Smilla's prying questions and ruses (at one point she masquerades as a cleaning woman to get into a government official's office). Smilla, by the way, is no bleeding heart. Flashbacks show that her own relationship with Isaiah began badly. Neglected by his alcoholic mother, Isaiah latches onto Smilla, who rejects him, telling him he smells. But the boy persists and Smilla gradually accepts his presence and begins to care for him. His death, then, strikes directly at her, and it arouses her sense of a society that conspires against individuals and considers them expendable.

What is today's most common news story that demonstrates how vulnerable individuals are? It is, of course, the repeated exposures of people to scientific experiments, and via the media to the awareness that they are the targets of governmental and scientific manipulation. Smilla's training as a scientist is in part what leads her to linking Isaiah with the experiments done in Greenland. The boy is part of an experiment gone awry, and he is part of the evidence that must be destroyed.

Like the novel, the movie has a love interest. Gabriel Byrne plays Smilla's neighbor, the Mechanic. He makes no secret of his attraction to Smilla, which she initially rebuffs just as she rebuffed Isaiah. Smilla wants no lover or co-detective. She is suspicious, and rightly so, since the Mechanic seems to be a double agent. Why does he follow her? Is it just love? Hardly. She sees him in a restaurant conversing with Tork (Richard Harris), the organizer (Smilla will learn) of the experiment that resulted in the events leading to Isaiah's death. But the Mechanic is not the villain, and he stands for the ambiguity of events and human nature, showing Smilla that life is not as clear-cut as she wants it to be.

With actors as physically appealing as Byrne and Ormond it is hard not to respond cynically. Aren't they in the movie so that they can fall in love, so that the conventions of romance will capture the largest possible audience? Judging by the reviewers responses, however, this does not happen—and the movie pays a price: some reviewers fault Ormond for being too aloof and Byrne for being too mysterious. Yet these are exactly the film's strengths; its main characters refuse to be movie stars and to emote. They play, instead, difficult personalities who are hard to read. The acting, in other words, complements both the novel's and the film's sense of an elliptical reality. It is not just the mystery, the plot, that has to be unraveled. The mystery is the human personality itself, of how a Smilla can reject and then become attracted first to Isaiah, and then to the Mechanic.

There is one role in the film, however, that seems misplaced or poorly acted. The surprising weak link is Smilla's father, played by the usually superb veteran actor Robert Loggia. His lines make him too avuncular and Loggia does nothing to tone down the sentimentality of his performance. In the novel, Smilla has a much edgier relationship with her father. He is, after all, the white man, the Dane, who marries her Inuit mother. He has the scientist's arrogance, though he is attracted to the native land and personality. He wants to help Smilla, but he is also part of the problem. She needs his counsel, but she also resents what he represents. A part of this dilemma does surface in the movie, but there is simply not enough friction between father and daughter. Instead, the film incomprehensibly puts Smilla in conflict with her father's new young woman. Of course Smilla resents such a woman in her father's life, but what is the point really? By replacing the father/daughter conflict with a jealous, territorial fight between two women, the film psychologizes Smilla's plight—making it merely some kind of grievance over her father's love life (her mother died several years ago anyway). Part of Smilla's problem may be psychological, but she is also confronting major issues. When the film loses sight of that fact, it behaves crudely, as though stopping the story to watch a catfight.

As in the novel, the film builds up a fascinating contrast between modern, antiseptic Copenhagen and the stark beauty of Greenland. In the city, criminal conspiracies are easily papered over; in the glacial world of Greenland Smilla is in her element and can see quite clearly the forces opposed to her—to any individual who does not conform to official reality.

Reviewers have rightly credited Hoeg's fellow Dane, director Bille August, for giving *Smilla's Sense of Snow* the right look and feel. His lighting is exquisite—no matter whether it is playing off of Ormond's cold beauty or Greenland's landscape. Jorgen Persson's cinematography unifies the film's emotional tone of a cold world that requires Smilla's excellence sense of interpretation. She has to open people up. And yet she herself is one of the cold ones. What makes her different from the other characters is her ability to empathize. She identifies with Isaiah not only because he is a fellow solitary but because he has helped her regain her humanity. She might easily have become an Isaiah herself. Like Smilla, his mother is an Inuit. He loses his father (whose death is part of the Byzantine plot Smilla has to unravel), and like her has to make his way in modern Copenhagen.

It would not do to reveal too many of the plot details of *Smilla's Sense of Snow*—not only because it is a thriller that depends on suspense but because of the film's conception of modern life as a plot against the individual. At least since Kafka modern literature has been making precisely that point. Part of this film's achievement is its fusion of this modernist theme of paranoia and alienation with what several reviewers have called James Bondish stylistic effects. They fault the film for becoming, in its last third, an action picture. It comes a little to easily to closure, given its murky, troubling beginnings. True enough, although this is a hazard of the detective/mystery genre that almost no one has successfully negotiated. Mystery stories are designed to clear up mysteries. There is almost always a feeling of letdown after the big buildup. The novel, no less than the film, has to reckon with this problem, and with its tendency to make

CREDITS

Smilla Jasperson: Julia Ormond
Mechanic: Gabriel Byrne
Tork: Richard Harris
Elsa Lubing: Vanessa Redgrave
Moritz Jasperson: Robert Loggia
Lagermann: Jim Broadbent
Isaiah: Clipper Miano
Ravn: Bob Peck
Dr. Loyen: Tom Wilkinson
Benja: Emma Croft

Origin: Denmark, Germany, Sweden
Released: 1997
Production: Bernd Eichinger, Martin Moszkowicz for Constantin Film Produktion, Greenland Film Production and Bavaria Film; released by Fox Searchlight
Direction: Bille August
Screenplay: Ann Biderman; based on the novel by Peter Hoeg
Cinematography: Jorgen Persson
Editing: Janus Billeskov Jansen
Music: Harry Gregson-Williams, Hans Zimmer
Production design: Anna Asp
Costumes: Barbara Baum
Sound: Chris Munro
Special effects: Peter Hutchinson
MPAA rating: R
Running Time: 121 minutes

Smilla an action-heroine who time-after-time escapes serious injury.

The way to read the novel and film, however, is as myth that trades on reality. Smilla and the other characters are real enough, but they are deployed in the service not of a naturalistic novel or documentary film. On the contrary, they speak to the zeitgeist, the spirit of the times that questions the people who are in control and suspects that our individual lives are no longer our own.

—Lisa Paddock

REVIEWS

Entertainment Weekly. March 7, 1997, p. 48.
Los Angeles Times. February 28, 1997, p. F1.
The New Yorker. March 10, 1997, p. 99.
People. March 10, 1997, p. 19.
Rolling Stone. March 20, 1997, p. 90.
Sight and Sound. November, 1997, p. 52.
Time. March 10, 1997.
USA Today. February 28, 1997, p. 3D.
Variety. February 17, 1997, p. 68.
Village Voice. March 4, 1997, p. 72.

Soul Food

"An ever-so-tasty comedy with very, very big laughs."—Joel Siegel, *Good Morning America*

"A hot ticket. *Soul Food* has a heart and soul that will strike a chord with audiences everywhere."—Steve Oldfield, *KSTU-TV*

"A warm and embracing family drama."—Kevin Thomas, *Los Angeles Times*

"*Soul Food* is honest, humorous and heartfelt."—Thelma Adams, *New York Post*

"This movie has appealing stars, family values and down-home atmosphere."—Janet Maslin, *New York Times*

"Just a beautiful story. *Soul Food* is definitely food for thought. Wonderful."—Jim Ferguson, *Prevue Channel*

"Two thumbs up for a big-hearted family drama and for its strong ensemble acting."—*Siskel & Ebert*

"Inspiring! Don't miss this movie! Rarely do we get to see families portrayed so accurately and lovingly."—Patty Spitler, *WISH-TV*

Box Office: $43,234,423

Three sisters (Vanessa Williams, Nia Long and Vivica A. Fox) are about to stir up some trouble at their youngest sister's wedding in the family drama/comedy *Soul Food.*

The title of the movie *Soul Food* pretty much explains it all. This is a film about soul and about food.

First, the food. There's soul food, and plenty of it. There are huge tables of ham hocks, fried catfish, black-eyed peas, biscuits and heaps of other artery-busting dishes, all lovingly photographed in vivid color. As in other food-heavy movies like *Tampopo* (1986), *Eat Drink Man Woman* (1994) or *Big Night* (1996), the food in *Soul Food* is the thing that gives people something to bond over and helps hold families together. It's almost one of the characters (and as such, gives a fine performance).

The food also helps provide a framework for the soul of the movie. Every Sunday for forty years, Big Mother Joe, aka Big Mama, (Irma P. Hall) has been hosting a big Southern-cookin' dinner for her brood, including the local reverend, in her big old-fashioned Chicago house. It's the kind of event where the women stay in the kitchen, shucking corn and checking the roast and the men hide in the den watching TV and drinking beer. In Mother Joe's mind, it's what holds the family together. And maybe it does.

When Mother Joe goes into a coma after complications from a diabetes-related leg amputation, the family starts falling apart. First, the oldest daughter Teri (singer and actress Vanessa L. Williams), an uptight, workaholic, successful lawyer, starts clashing with her attorney husband, Miles (Michael Beach) who wants to work on his piano playing full-time. Miles finds solace from Teri's rejection in the arms of cousin Faith (Gina Ravera), a somewhat flaky, former exotic dancer looking to make the switch to Broadway dancer.

Teri also fights with her younger sister Maxine played by Vivica A. Fox (*Independence Day*, 1996). The two haven't been getting along since the roller disco days when Maxine stole Teri's boyfriend and married him. Teri strikes out at the family by constantly reminding them of the money she has provided for the family. This includes barbs directed at the youngest sister Bird (Nia Long of *love jones*, 1997) who can't seem to get through a family gathering without hearing about how Teri put up the money for Bird's successful beauty shop.

Mother Joe: "See, soul food cookin' is about cookin' from the heart!"

And it's not like the bubbly Bird doesn't have enough problems of her own. Her husband Lem (Mekhi Phifer) is an ex-con who gets fired from his job because he lied about his past on his job application.

Sound like a soap opera? It is, and that's part of what's nice about *Soul Food*. It's refreshing to see a movie about middle-class African Americans that's not a wild comedy or a violent gang film. The movie doesn't gloss over the family's troubles—it spends a good deal of time on Lem when he loses his job and finds it impossible to get a second chance as a black man with a prison background—but it doesn't reduce African-American life to the usual stereotypes. Lem's problems are all just part of life's ups and downs, or as Mother Joe puts it, "if you don't get though the bad parts, you're not around for the good parts."

Twenty-eight year old writer-director, George Tillman Jr., based the story on the big family dinners that his own grandmother cooked in Milwaukee. Tillman wanted to show a more personal, Midwestern, middle-class look at African-American life than what has been portrayed previously. The recent success of other African-American, family-based, personal movies like *Waiting To Exhale* (1995) and *love jones* (1997) helped pave the way for *Soul Food*.

With at least nine major characters in the film, one of the young narrator's biggest jobs is just explaining who everyone is, and what their respective situations are. At the beginning of the movie, it's kind of confusing sorting out all the characters, but one soon begins to feel like part of the group. Director Tillman choreographs the big ensemble well and they seem like a genuine family.

The movie gives the actors some meaty roles and they're up to the challenge. Hall as the matriarch Mother Joe is a big booming woman, all strong love and full of sayings like "One finger pointing blame can't make no impact. But five fingers balled up can deliver a mighty blow. This family got to be that fist." She's that one relative who makes everyone feel special for who they are. Although a character like that sounds like she could be annoying or flat, Hall's character is no goody-goody pushover. Mother Joe has a sharp tongue and an iron will, making her character three-dimensional and believable.

Also good is Michael Beach as Teri's husband, Miles, who provides a fine breakaway from the usual African-American male film role. He has a good job, plus he's loving and family-oriented. Beach plays Miles as a strong, quiet man who knows himself and wants to do what's right.

Williams' Teri is the most problematic character, not because of Williams' acting, but because of how the character is written. She is a go-getter who lords it over others and a career woman who puts career in front of family. Teri is unbelievably petty, especially about money. She knows to the cent how much of the money is hers in her and her husband's joint checking account. Because the character is written to be the bad guy in practically every situation, it seems to be suggesting that to be successful and to have career goals, a woman has

CREDITS

Teri: Vanessa L. Williams
Maxine: Vivica A. Fox
Bird: Nia Long
Miles: Michael Beach
Lem: Mekhi Phifer
Kenny: Jeffrey D. Sams
Mother Joe: Irma P. Hall
Ahmad: Brandon Hammond
Faith: Gina Ravera

Origin: USA
Released: 1997
Production: Tracey E. Edmonds and Robert Teitel for Edmonds Entertainment and Fox 2000 Pictures; released by 20th Century Fox
Direction: George Tillman Jr.
Screenplay: George Tillman Jr.
Cinematography: Paul Elliott
Editing: John Carter
Music: Wendy Melvoin, Lisa Coleman
Production design: Maxine Shepard
Art direction: Cydney M. Harris
Costumes: Salvador Perez
Sound: David Obermeyer
MPAA rating: R
Running Time: 114 minutes

to be non-maternal and hard. That said, with her steely blue eyes and perfect hair, Williams is great at playing the cold-hearted go-getter.

While Williams' Teri is too harsh, Fox's Maxine might just be too good. She has an ideal marriage (her husband still lusts after her even after three kids), a loving, maternal way about her and well-behaved kids. But Fox makes the character believable by playing her as a person who approaches life with a ready smile and a genuine sense of excitement and anticipation.

One of the standout performances in the film comes from Brandon Hammond, who plays Ahmad, Maxine's oldest boy and the favorite grandchild of Mother Joe. The film is seen through Ahmad's eyes as he narrates the film. Hammond is smart and sweet as the young boy, with none of the "cute kid" affectations that child movie actors often possess. He shares Mother Joe's inherent ability to understand human nature and is the one who keeps the family together while she is out of commission.

Music plays a big part in the film as evidenced by a strong soundtrack filled with R & B songs like "A Dream" by DeBarge and headed by the omnipresent producer Kenneth "Babyface" Edmonds. R & B fans might want to take note that in a nightclub scene where Miles' band is playing, his group happens to include Babyface, plus K-Ci Halley of Jodeci. Having an R & B supergroup playing a bar band probably has something to do with the fact that Babyface's company, YabYum Entertainment, produced the film.

Soul Food is a sentimental movie, but not in the sappy sense. It's a movie about family and a movie with heart. While it pulls at some heartstrings, it's never done in a manipulative way. In *Soul Food*, sisters fight, spouses stray, people get in trouble with the law, babies are born and people eat (a lot). In the end, things work out, but not perfectly, and life goes on. Kind of like real life.

—Jill Hamilton

REVIEWS

Boxoffice. November, 1997, p. 132.
Detroit News. September 27, 1997, p. C1.
Entertainment Weekly. October 3, 1997, p. 58.
Los Angeles Times. September 26, 1997, p. F20.
New York Times. September 26, 1997, p. E10.
People. October 6, 1997, p. 28.
Rolling Stone. October 16, 1997, p. 116.
Variety. September 22, 1997, p. 38.
Village Voice. September 30, 1997, p. 80.

Sous-Sol; Not Me!

French-Canadian director Pierre Gang's *Sous-Sol* is a coming-of-age story in more ways than one. The plot unfolds at a time when the province of Quebec attracted the world's attention to an unprecedented degree, due largely to the opening of Expo '67, an extraordinarily ambitious cultural exhibition, which was viewed at the time as French-speaking Canada's grande entree onto the world stage.

The film's narrative concludes nine years later with the opening of the Montreal Summer Olympics of 1976, an event that did even more to bolster the visibility of French-Canadian culture in the world abroad. These transformative events serve as a very appropriate framework for the story Gang chooses to tell—that of Rene (Richard Moffatt), an eleven-year-old boy who is struggling toward adulthood under very difficult circumstances.

The title is a reference to the basement apartment from which Rene's mother manages their building. From an adult point of view, it is a time of great change and excitement, but for Rene these momentous events are only a cause for bewilderment. The world as he sees it is not colorful and enticing, but only strange, chaotic and unmanageable. At the outset, Rene's chances of success seem as bleak as the view of the local cemetery, which he sees from his front door.

The first section of the film presents Rene in a series of potentially traumatic situations. One evening at home, he accidentally interrupts his parents while they are having sex. This classic "primal scene" is followed almost immediately by the death of his father, Raymond (Daniel Gadouas), from an unfortunate heart attack. Rene's understanding of these events is influenced by his barely acknowledged desire to see the older man expunged from the familial picture.

The father's sudden death comes as a result of a moderately outre bondage scene in which he and his wife were engaged. Because Rene witnesses only a part of this erotic ritual, and has no basis from which to judge its meaning, he assumes that his mother, Reine (Louise Portal), has indeed killed his father, an idea that dovetails with his own secret wishes. The son's desire to eliminate the father as a source of competition for the mother's love is a well-known tenet of Freudian psychology, and probably common enough in boys Rene's age, but it is also scandalous, and not one which he is evenly remotely prepared to recognize.

For her part, the mother learns to view her sudden descent into widowhood as a source of liberation. She engages in a respectable period of mourning, but in relatively short order Reine is shown packing away her dead husband's clothes and dyeing her hair blonde. His demise gives her a rare opportunity to experiment with herself, to be adventurous and to try new things. Depicted throughout as a warm, sensual woman, Reine makes no effort to conceal her vigorous interest in sex, but she is not so adept at explaining its more troublesome ramifications to her guilt-ridden young son, who continues to believe that he "wished" his father dead in some mysterious way. The mother joyously sets about exploring the boundaries of her new world, but she is also deeply concerned about Rene, who fumbles his way through this transition with an air of complete unease.

Evidence of adult sexual activity and its messy after-effects is everywhere: Reine takes up with a series of forgettable, short-term boyfriends before settling down with Roch (Patrice Godin), a hunky longshoreman several years her junior who delights her with his insatiable appetites. Rene's teenage older brother gets his girlfriend pregnant and ends up married and with a child while still living at home. Francoise (Isabelle Pasco), the kindly young neighbor who is visiting from France, befriends Rene but soon develops a social life of her own, leaving him to feel more abandoned than ever. And in the evening, prostitutes and sex-hungry young couples prowl the neighborhood, using the local cemetery as their preferred cruising ground.

"I'll never have sex! I'll never do that!," insists Rene, who has quickly become convinced that such activity always has diabolical consequences. To underline this point, Gang presents a series of complications that may or may not serve to push Rene over the edge into delinquency and psychosis. Rene clearly suffers as he stumbles through a world of adults whose desires are always running at full steam. He is too painfully lacking in guidance to understand whether the turmoil which surrounds him is part of "normal" life or an aberration of some kind.

There are several moments in the early stages of the film in which Rene's awareness of older people's erotic antics may end up having deeply ominous repercussions. This is especially true during a Christmas scene in which Rene gives his mother a number of scarves not unlike those she used to bind her husband in the moments before his death. He also presents her with a large butcher knife, which he hopes she will use to dispatch her new and mostly unwelcome boyfriend. When this tactic fails, Rene cajoles Roch into a game of "Cowboys and Indians" that comes close to having genuinely murderous intentions. The viewer rightfully expects these sinister elements to culminate in some significant way, but they are never explored to their fullest dramatic potential.

Sous-Sol is reminiscent of, but fares badly in comparison to, a number of other well-known films which concern a young boy's treacherous passage into sexual maturity. The most notable of these is Louis Malle's *Murmur of the Heart* (*Le Souffle au Coeur*) (1971), a film that was considered shocking in its time for its frank, non-judgmental view of mother-son incest, but which was also deeply infused with warmth and a genuine sympathy for the dilemmas faced by its young male protagonist.

Sous-Sol ends with Rene's inadvertent exposure to yet another scene in which his mother and stepfather are shown engaging in a rollicking sex act. However, an abrupt reverse angle reveals that Rene is now nine years older and mostly unfazed by such displays. The film's greatest failure lies in Gang's refusal to explain just how and why Rene ultimately manages to make an accommodation to the highly-charged atmosphere in which he was raised.

In his public statements about the film, director Pierre Gang has insisted that Rene's positive adjustment is owed to "the mysteries of sexuality and the process of growing up." This is a vague and inadequate answer to the film's central question. Like a play with no discernible third act, *Sous-Sol* starts with a number of dramatic possibilities, presents a series of tantalizing developments, then ends with a thud, its most urgent issues left maddeningly unresolved. This lapse keeps *Sous-Sol* from being a fully successful film.

It is not unreasonable to expect a more satisfying denouement, since Gang spends a great deal of time in the film's early stages hinting at the darker implications of Rene's subjection to other people's erotic escapades. Will Rene end up killing his mother's new boyfriend, as one initially suspects? Will his imagined rejection by Francoise have far-reaching psychological effects? Gang dodges all of these questions in the film's final moments. He merely presents us with the image of Rene as an older, presumably well-adjusted adolescent, and asks us to accept this transformation on faith. Essentially, Gang has succeeded in making two-thirds of an engaging movie about the emotional perils of childhood. The film is full of keen social observations and nuances of character, but the tacked-on ending is neither mysterious nor thought-provoking—it's just incoherent, a symptom of lazy storytelling.

Sous-Sol is rather like a jigsaw puzzle with several crucial pieces missing. Gang displays a great deal of sympathy for his love-starved, working-class characters. He has a sharp visual sense that allows us to appreciate the look and feel of

AWARDS AND NOMINATIONS

Genie Awards 1996: Original Screenplay
Nominations: Actress (Portal)

CREDITS

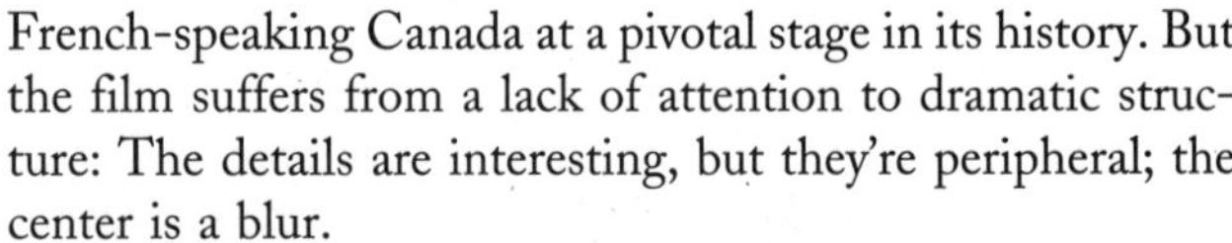

Reine: Louise Portal
Francoise: Isabelle Pasco
Roch: Patrice Godin
Raymond: Daniel Gadouas
Rene: Richard Moffatt

Origin: Canada
Released: 1996
Production: Roger Frappier for Max Films; released by Malofilm International
Direction: Pierre Gang
Screenplay: Pierre Gang
Cinematography: Pierre Mignot
Editing: Florence Moreaux
Music: Anne Bourne, Ken Myrh
Production design: Francois Laplante
Costumes: Suzanne Harel
MPAA rating: Unrated
Running Time: 90 minutes

French-speaking Canada at a pivotal stage in its history. But the film suffers from a lack of attention to dramatic structure: The details are interesting, but they're peripheral; the center is a blur.

"What will become of my little man?," asks Rene's mother in the aftermath of her husband's death. It is a heart-wrenching question, and one which we long to see answered in a more complete fashion. It is gratifying to learn, in the film's final scenes, that Rene's story does indeed have a happy ending. One merely wishes that director Gang had illuminated a few more of the steps along the way.

—*Karl Michalak*

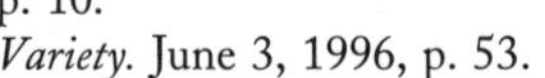

REVIEWS

The Hollywood Reporter. February 11, 1996, p. 10.
Variety. June 3, 1996, p. 53.

Spawn

Born in darkness. Sworn to justice.—Movie tagline

"*Spawn* is by far the best movie of the summer!"—Darcel Rockett, *Arizona Republic*

"*Spawn* rules! It's the ultimate summer thrill ride!"—Jim Wilson, *Fox-TV*

"*Spawn* is a super-hero for the millennium!"—David Ramsey, *KMLE-FM*

"*Spawn* delivers action, intensity and one heck of a kick!"—Leo Quinones, *KRS-FM*

Box Office: $54,879,992

The expression, "You've come a long way, baby!" could certainly apply to comic books. The popularity of such comic books as *Archie, Blondie,* and *Little Lulu* are long gone and have been surpassed by those with superhuman heroes like *Superman, Spiderman, Batman, The Phantom,* and others. Now, there's a new kid on the block named *Spawn* (short for Hellspawn), so 'draconian' in its concept that it makes the others and their world seem like a trip to Oz in comparison. The interesting thing about *Spawn* (the comic book) is that it's only four-years-old and has a huge following, mostly among young males.

Created in 1992 by Todd McFarlane, *Spawn* was launched by Image Comics, a company that was formed by previous employees of Marvel Comics. These young innovators broke new ground and *Spawn* has become the best-selling comic book in the United States. It was just a matter of time before the film studios took notice of this success and images of *Batman* profits began to dance through their heads. New Line Cinema made the most appealing bid and *Spawn,* the motion picture, became a reality. There was already a video game, HBO series, and a line of toys. Simply put *Spawn* is a phenomenal success story.

The tastes of today's younger audiences seem to be changing as rapidly as computer technology. *Spawn* is by far, the darkest, most malevolent tale of any comic book hero, to date. He starts out as a government agent, Al Simmons (Michael Jai White). He's brutally set on fire by his boss, Jason Wynn (Martin Sheen), and then is literally blown to Hell where he spends the next five years. He is offered the chance to return to earth to do the devil's bidding. In return, he gets to see his wife, Wanda (Theresa Randle) and daughter, Cyan (Sydni Beaudoin). All he needs to do for that privilege is to lead Satan's army to take over the world. To insure that he will carry out these duties, Satan sends his emissary, a fat, disgusting, vitriolic character named Clown (John Leguizamo). Clown also has the ability to morph into a 12-foot monster at the slightest provocation. So, a badly scarred Spawn returns to earth to reunite with his family. Not exactly welcomed, due to his grotesque appearance, Spawn feels spurned by the earthlings. Along the way, he encounters a mysterious conjurer by the name of Cogliostro (Nicol Williamson) who greets him with "You're welcome to join us." Clown, on the other hand, greets him with "Bad crispy, bad crispy."

Todd McFarlane on why Spawn is black: "I got tired of Clark Kent and Superman and Batman and everyone all being good-looking little white guys. It didn't make any sense to me."

Alan McElroy's screenplay becomes increasingly complicated when Martin Sheen's character, in collusion with Clown, has his own scheme to take over the beleaguered planet. Meanwhile, Wanda, after all this time, has taken up with Spawn's former partner and best friend. Feeling angry and betrayed, Spawn sets out to avenge his own fiery death and go after Wynn. His wrath is intense, recalling the old adage "Hell hath no fury, like a Spawn scorned."

If all of this seems somewhat muddled and confusing, it's because much of it is. Todd McCarthy commented in *Daily Variety,* "Rarely has there been a film so loaded with effects at the expense of character or narrative coherence."

First-time director, Mark Dippe, who worked on the special effects for *The Flintstones* (1994) and *Jurassic Park,* (1993) seemed to forget that special effects should revolve around the plot—not the other way around. Both he and his partner, visual effects supervisor, Steve Williams (affectionately known as Spaz), are masters of their craft. They needed to focus more on a seemingly neglected craft, that of "writing."

One of the film's more successful components was the casting of Michael Jai White as the Al Simmons/Spawn character. White was previously seen in the HBO telefilm "Tyson," playing the title character. He possessed the necessary physical prowess required for the strenuous role, as well as the acting capabilities. It was refreshing to see an African-American portraying a superhero. However, when he returned to earth as Spawn, it was difficult to ascertain what species he was, let alone race. His special effects makeup was quite elaborate and extremely well-done. In speaking about the role, White said, "To me, Spawn deals with contemporary times. Superman or The Phantom were cool way back in their day, but Spawn reflects more of what society is now."

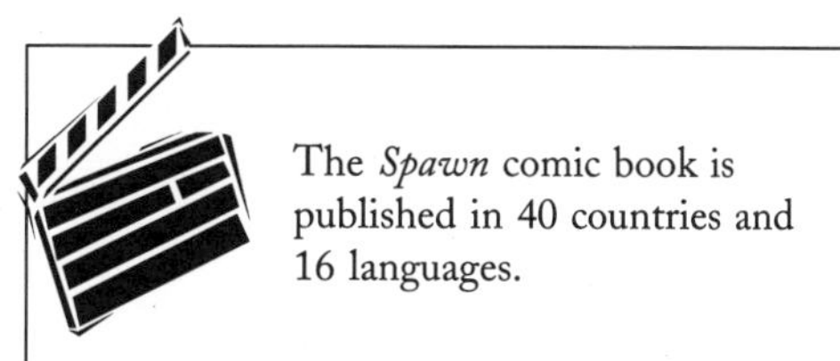

The *Spawn* comic book is published in 40 countries and 16 languages.

It is questionable as to whether all of society is dealing with Satanic clowns and madmen trying to take over the planet. However, in a metaphoric sense, there is an element of accuracy to White's comment. The character of Spawn is ultimately waging his own personal moral battle between good and evil. Once he returns to planet earth and finds it polluted with corruption, riddled by a myriad of vices and consumed by an insatiable appetite for power, he breaks his pact with the devil—after all, his beloved daughter, Cyan, has to grow up in this world. With the help and encouragement of Cogliostro, who reminds him that "the war between heaven and hell depend on the choices we make," Spawn chooses to wage his own personal battle with the master of evil himself—Satan. The demonic force in the universe proves to be a fierce adversary and "the games begin."

John Leguizamo, a well-known character actor, plays the role of the flatulent, corpulent Clown from hell. He has played a wide variety of unusual roles from a heavy in *William Shakespeare's Romeo and Juliet* (1996) to a transvestite in *To Wong Foo, Thanks for Everything, Julie Newmar* (1995). He is completely unrecognizable as Clown, wearing a fat suit and grotesque makeup, including a full set of rotting teeth. The Clown character, an icon of repulsiveness, spews forth vulgarities such as "You can be James Stewart and I'll be Clarence. (referring to Frank Capra's film *It's a Wonderful Life* [1946]). Every time somebody passes gas, a demon gets his wings." Leguizamo may have wanted to make this his "over-the-top" signature role in the company of such performances as Michael Keaton in *Beetlejuice* (1988) or Jack Nicholson as The Joker in *Batman* (1989). This performance gives new meaning to the phrase "over-the-top" and borders on hysteria.

"All that high-tech razzle dazzle doesn't make for great entertainment. It makes for a headache and a new eye-glass prescription. *Spawn* doesn't seem so much directed as programmed," wrote Andy Seller in *U.S.A. Today.* This somewhat caustic review certainly makes a valid point. The basic story of *Spawn* is actually a good premise. The title character does make a shift in his thinking and, with the influence of Cogliostro, wages a war with an extremely evil force. Also, the target audience made up of mostly young, male viewers have grown up with computer technology. All summer long they have

CREDITS

Al Simmons/Spawn: Michael Jai White
Clown: John Leguizamo
Jason Wynn: Martin Sheen
Wanda: Theresa Randle
Jessica Priest: Melinda Clarke
Zack: Miko Hughes
Cyan: Sydni Beaudoin
Cogliostro: Nicol Williamson
Terry Fitzgerald: D.B. Sweeney

Origin: USA
Released: 1997
Production: Clint Goldman for Todd McFarlane Entertainment; released by New Line Cinema
Direction: Mark A.Z. Dippe
Screenplay: Alan McElroy; based on the comic book by Todd McFarlane
Cinematography: Guillermo Navarro
Editing: Michael N. Knue
Music: Graeme Revell
Production design: Philip Harrison
Art direction: Eric W. Osborn
Costumes: Dan Lester
Sound: Jim Thornton
Visual effects supervisor: Steve Williams
Visual effects producer: Tom Peitzman
Stunt coordinator: Charles Croughwell
MPAA rating: PG-13
Running Time: 97 minutes

been exposed to massive doses of violence, action-adventure, computerized special effects and a virtual blitz of technological gimmickry. So, why not pull out all the stops? The last twenty minutes or so of *Spawn,* did just that to the detriment of the film's effectiveness. It transformed the film into a CD-Rom extravaganza that overpowered every other element of the piece.

It would be interesting to see what the possibilities would have been if *Spawn*'s creators had opted to make a more balanced film, to devote more energy into constructing a screenplay that was more coherent, to work on some kind of emotional life for the characters, and to tone down some of the vulgarities in the script. Then, they could add in the "pyrotechnic wizardry." Perhaps by doing these things it might have appealed to a broader, more discerning audience.

—Rob Chicatelli

REVIEWS

Boxoffice. September, 1997, p. 118.
Chicago Tribune. August 1, 1997, p. 4.
Cinemafantastique. July, 1997, p. 14.
Entertainment Weekly. August 15, 1997, p. 46.
Los Angeles Times. August 1, 1997, p. F20.
New York Times. August 1, 1997, p. C10.
People. August 18, 1997, p. 21.
USA Today. August 1, 1997, p. 2D.
Variety. August 4, 1997, p. 34.
Village Voice. August 12, 1997, p. 74.

Speed 2: Cruise Control

Rush hour hits the water.—Movie tagline

"Hold-your-breath action. A great summer film."—Joel Siegel, *Good Morning America*

"Enough action for two movies."—Gene Siskel, *Chicago Tribune*

"Spectacular, it never stops moving, and man, it's fun."—Amy Dawes, *L.A. Daily News*

"Two thumbs up!"—*Siskel & Ebert*

Box Office: $48,608,066

Speed 2: Cruise Control was supposed to be one of the biggest of the mega-budget hits of the summer of 1997. Well, it has a big budget all right (reportedly $125 million), but big hit? I don't think so.

Right from the start, this movie is insulting to the moviegoer's intelligence. Remember Annie Porter (Sandra Bullock) the woman who took charge of that racing bus in the first *Speed* film? She maneuvered, she swerved, she dodged, she did everything—including keeping a cool head—while the LAPD tried to unload then diffuse the booby-trapped bus? Well, for some reason, between that bus and this movie, Annie has become such a poor, distracted driver that she can't even pass a driving test given by Tim Conway. The film just goes downhill from there.

Turns out Annie's new significant other is another LAPD cop, Alex Shaw (Jason Patric), who to compensate for the fact that he never told Annie he was a SWAT cop—Annie hates risk takers—now takes her on a Caribbean cruise with an engagement ring in his pocket.

> "I swear I am never leaving the house again."—Annie, after being hijacked again.

However, on the ship with them is a disgruntled former cruise line employee, John Geiger (Willem Dafoe) who has gone postal in the most subtle way. Since he designed all the ship's computer systems, he now takes control of them, tosses the captain overboard, heads the ship on a suicide path into the rocks off the island of St. Martin, steals diamonds from the ship's safe, and makes for his escape.

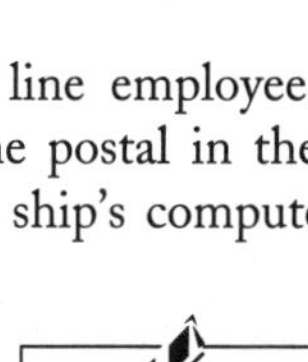

> UB40 is featured as the lounge band in a couple of movie scenes as well as on the soundtrack.

Of course, all this counts on everyone being as stupid as can be—with the obvious exceptions of Annie and Alex who must, according to the script but no logic, save the few passengers left on the ship after it was evacuated. (It should come as no surprise that this effort is the first feature for scriptwriters Randall McCormick and Jeff Nathanson who rely far too heavily on cliches and stereotypes instead of intelligence.)

Adding to the groanability of this film is the Batman-style music and a complete lack of chemistry between stone-faced Patric and everygirl Bullock. But worst of all are the overblown special effects and the continuously annoying camera work. Director de Bont (of the first *Speed* film and *Twister*) goes out of his way to replace story, dialogue and character development with explosions, floods and fires. They are a poor substitute. In what one can only assume is his attempt to provide the audience with a sense of panic, he relies heavily on darkness, flashing lights, and hand-held cameras which, unfortunately, don't heighten viewer involvement, but instead makes one seasick!

It gets to the point where one begins to divorce oneself from the film and mentally discuss which is worse, the stupidity of the action a character is about to take or the wobbly closeup of a passenger's forehead.

Speed 2 will undoubtedly garner good box office attendance for the first week or two as those who loved the first *Speed* go back for more, but generally bad reviews—both from critics and moviegoers—may send this film to video fairly quickly.

If he had a chance to read the script, it should be pretty obvious why Keanu Reeves opted out of this sequel. Saying he wanted to spend more time with his rock band, Dogstar, may just be a polite way of saying "you've got to be kidding."

—Beverley Bare Buehrer

CREDITS

Annie Porter: Sandra Bullock
Alex Shaw: Jason Patric
John Geiger: Willem Dafoe
Maurice: Glenn Plummer
Juliano: Temuera Morrison
Merced: Brian McCardie
Drew: Christine Firkins
Capt. Pollard: Bo Svenson
Mr. Kenter: Tim Conway

Origin: USA
Released: 1997
Production: Jan De Bont for Blue Tulip; released by 20th Century Fox
Direction: Jan De Bont
Screenplay: Randall McCormick, Jeff Nathanson, and Jan De Bont
Cinematography: Jack N. Green
Editing: Alan Cody
Production design: Joseph Nemec III, Bill Kenney
Music: Mark Mancina
Art direction: Bill Skinner
Costumes: Louise Frogley
Sound: Robert Janiger
Special effects coordinator: Al Disarro
MPAA rating: PG-13
Running Time: 125 minutes

REVIEWS

Chicago Tribune. June 13, 1997, p. 4.
Entertainment Weekly. April 25, 1997, p. 8.
Entertainment Weekly. June 25, 1997, p. 41.
The Hollywood Reporter. June 12, 1997, p. 2.
Los Angeles Times. June 13, 1997, p. F1.
Movieline. June, 1997, p. 52.
New York Times. June 13, 1997, p. B12.
Sight and Sound. August, 1997, p. 53.
Time. June 23, 1997.
USA Today. April 2, 1997, p. 6D.
USA Today. June 13, 1997, p. 4D.
Variety. June 16, 1997, p. 34.
Village Voice. June 24, 1997, p. 75.

Sprung

Way past whipped!—Movie tagline

"Packed with humor, wild sex, and romance."—Dwayne E. Leslie, *Boxoffice*

Box Office: $7,597,941

Rusty Cundieff, director of the hilarious *Fear of a Black Hat* (1994), a documentary send-up of contemporary rap culture, has struck again with *Sprung*, a romantic comedy aimed at satirizing both extreme views of African-American urban dating and romantic comedies in general.

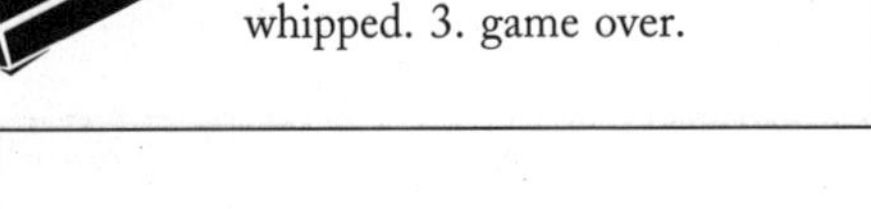

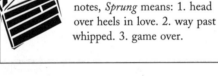

According to the production notes, *Sprung* means: 1. head over heels in love. 2. way past whipped. 3. game over.

Sprung opens up with Montel (Rusty Cundieff), an aspiring young photographer, dressed to the nines in a tuxedo, sprinting to a wedding. As he meets up with his best pal, Clyde (Joe Torry), Montel's voice-over begins to ruminate on the mysterious ups and downs of modern-day love, and we are transported back in time a year. Montel and Clyde arrive at a party, dressed to kill. In his own fashion, Montel, the more low key, easygoing of the two, is hoping to meet a nice girl—someone he can talk with and get to know. On the other hand, Clyde, the gold-chain red-suit wearing "poseur," is looking to score; to assure that result, he flaunts a pilfered ATM receipt as his own. Adina (Paula Jai Parker), a classic gold digger dressed in eye-popping fashion, casts her calculating eye over the room full of available men. An instantaneous computer readout in her brain scans men and labels them as "dog," "crackhead," "nerd," "unemployed," or "gay"—but stops on a dime when Clyde deliberately drops his bogus receipt. After a bumbling start, Clyde whisks Adina away to Clyde's apartment for a night of wildness, assuring her that this shabby abode is his "down" city digs.

When Adina and Clyde engage in "extreme" sex, Montel and Adina's friend, Brandy (Tisha Campbell), get off to a rocky start. A law clerk who aspires to lawyer status, Brandy is recovering from too many cads, geeks, and bores to take Montel seriously. In the middle of the night, after many wrong turns trying to get Montel home, Brandy and Montel run into an amusing sight: a nude Clyde, stranded on the street after Adina discovered the truth about his identity—and wallet size. Unable to stop the police from hauling Clyde in for questioning, Brandy and Montel can only wait together in the police station.

Adina shows up dressed as demurely as a schoolgirl, and proceeds to humiliate Clyde in a criminal lineup. By the time Montel drives a chastised Clyde back home, he and Brandy have sufficiently warmed up to each other. The next day, Montel meets Brandy at her office and takes her for a pleasant, charming walk and talk by a lake. They end the night by slow-dancing and watching the stars together.

Soon, Adina and Montel are dismayed to find out that their friends are engaged in a hot and heavy passionate affair of the heart and soul—they are "kootchy-koo" in love; their love irritates the former two enough to unite with one cause—break up Brandy and Montel!!

After a few hits and misses that serve only to drive Montel and Brandy further into each other's arms, Adina and Clyde panic when their friends announce that they are moving in together. This news prompts the duo to pull out the big guns; they arrange for Brandy to catch Montel in a compromising situation with an old high school girlfriend. It works; a tearful break-up results.

But soon Adina and Clyde realize the error of their ways and arrange a nifty reunion for their friends at a posh ho-

CREDITS

Brandy: Tisha Campbell
Montel: Rusty Cundieff
Adina: Paula Jai Parker
Clyde: Joe Torry
Detective: John Witherspoon
Veronica: Jennifer Lee
Grand Daddy: Clarence Williams III

Origin: USA
Released: 1997
Production: Darin Scott; released by Trimark Pictures
Direction: Rusty Cundieff
Screenplay: Darin Scott and Rusty Cundieff
Cinematography: Joao Fernandes
Editing: Lisa Bromwell
Music: Stanley Clarke
Production design: Terrence Foster
Set decoration: Melanie Paizis
Costumes: Tracey White
Sound: Oliver L. Moss
MPAA rating: R
Running Time: 105 minutes

tel. But Montel and Brandy are not in such a hurry to utilize the plush suite and retreat for a long talk—leaving Clyde and Adina to test out the Jacuzzi and bedsprings.

Cut back to the wedding at the beginning of the film—it is not Brandy and Montel's wedding, but Clyde and Adina's. It seems that our two lovebirds are taking things slow and learning more about what they need and need to give in a relationship.

Cundieff lays the satire on heavy—the men are draped in gold chains and the women are scantily clad in club-hopping outfits that are barely legal, ultra-long nails, and enough hairspray to shellac a boat. Although the stereotypes are present, the emotions and situations that these characters experience are universal—and cross all cultural and social boundaries. The main experience that actor/writer/director Cundieff brings to the table is a lighthearted approach to the story; when Adina looks at herself in the mirror after discovering Clyde's ruse, she sees a lollipop labeled "sucker." When Brandy and Adina look at all the men at the party, they visualize life-size men with big dog heads. Cundieff's writing and directing style is perfectly matched to this lighthearted treatment, yet if it were to be stretched further, it would surely snap.

—*G.E. Georges*

REVIEWS

Boxoffice. June, 1997, p. 52.
The Hollywood Reporter. May 15, 1997, p. 5.
New York Times. May 19, 1997, p. B4.
People. May 26, 1997, p. 25.
Variety. May 19, 1997, p. 49.
Village Voice. May 20, 1997, p. 80.

Squeeze

Only the strong survive these streets. One tough city. Three extraordinary kids.—Movie tagline
"Fresh, raw and vigorous!"—*Boston Globe*

Three inner-city teenagers, experiencing the violence of their environment, are caught on the threshold between the enticements of crime and the conflicts of a straight life. Although this independent film by newcomer writer/director Robert Patton-Spruill received attention in film festival circles, it opened and closed too quickly for its realistic portrayal and critical message to reach audiences.

> Robert Patton-Spruill: "Most people don't see kids like these as human, but kids who've seen the stuff they see every day are unstable, and even the ones who come through without getting into trouble may have been badly damaged inside."

Fourteen-year-old Tyson (Tyrone Burton) pumps gas for spare change with friends Hector (Eddie Cutanda) and Bao (Phuong Duong) in a Boston area ghetto, encountering grateful though ungenerous drivers as well as gang members' taunts. Tyson works instead of attending school, while he holds onto dreams of playing professional basketball someday. When the local community center director, J.J. (Geoffrey Rhue), offers the boys "red shirt" jobs cleaning up the neighborhood, they don't seriously consider it.

Angered by the gang harassment, the youths jump a member, beat him and rob him. A torn Tyson considers flushing the money down the toilet, and filled with fear of repercussions he heads to the center to apply for work. Tommy's Pathfinder full of gangsters stalks the boys, so Hector seeks protection with a rival drug dealer. Admitting they're tired of being called the PG13 crew, they accept the arrangement to peddle drugs. Hector's philosophy "when you go, you go" doesn't sit well with Tyson, but he's afraid for his life and too scared to tell J.J. the truth.

Clearing up a park with other "red shirts," Tyson and his friends juggle two disparate lives. At night, they sell dope on the streets. Although Tyson enjoys the financial rewards, he has to hide his activity from J.J. and deny it to his confrontational aunt and hospitalized mother. Meanwhile, Tommy and his thugs continue keeping track of the boys.

While fishing with the community center group, Vietnamese Bao catches a crab, leading J.J. to a rap about scav-

AWARDS AND NOMINATIONS

Independent Spirit Awards 1997 Nominations: Debut Performance (Burton/Cutanda/Duong)

engers and his "old school" days "before crack, knives and 45s." Tyson realizes his boss has earned respect in their community but Hector's influence is strong. The three drive over to visit a girl Tyson likes from the center, however she suspects they've stolen the car and walks off. Bao jumps out to graffiti a wall only to get stopped by a cop.

Hector and Tyson escape. Sleeping at Hector's place, the boys witness Hector's mother, who has AIDS, shoot herself in an insane rage. Tyson runs to a phone booth to call 911 and keeps running. While Bao reaches out to J.J. for help, Tyson finds cover in a center van, then hears gunshots and peeks out to discover Tommy's killed someone. The warnings continue, yet he refuses to learn his lesson.

Tyson and Hector sleep in an abandoned church and plan to depart for New York. On the corner that night conducting a drug transaction, they are found by Tommy's boys. Hector flees the gunfire but the gang grabs Tyson to torture him and take his stash before tossing him back onto the street. The boy's drug connection seeks revenge, shooting Tommy and another, putting the teenagers at further risk. The series of dangerous situations become too intense for the overwhelmed Tyson, but as he attempts to jump in front of a bus, J.J. saves him.

A hospital psychiatrist helps the young man through his paranoid breakdown. When Hector can't persuade his pal to run off to Manhattan, he reconsiders and decides to go clean, reaching out to J.J. The story concludes with Tyson practicing basketball, reclaiming his dream. Although a challenging choice showing maturity, the decision to reject a violent lifestyle allows the boys' survival and opens up their possibilities.

This story relates the critical dilemma that impressionable youth face in a chaotic world that appears to offer few options. Full of spirited moments between the boys and honest performances with authentic language, the worthwhile message comes through strong without seeming self-righteous. The "squeeze" the three feel is painfully realized and resolved hopefully.

While teaching at a youth center, Patton-Spruill met the three teens he cast in the starring roles. Finding their natural talents, he directed them well—perhaps proving the film's point in real life, and garnering nominations for Tyrone and Eddie from the Independent Spirit Awards. *Squeeze* could have been preaching to the choir if the story were whitewashed, and achieved more box-office success, ironically, if it were more violent.

—Roberta Cruger

CREDITS

Tyson: Tyrone Burton
Hector: Eddie Cutanda
Bao: Phuong Duong
J.J.: Geoffrey Rhue

Origin: USA
Released: 1997
Production: Ari Newman, Garen Topalian, Stephanie Danan, and Patricia Moreno for ca.thar.tic filmWorks and Danan/Moreno Films; released by Miramax Films
Direction: Robert Patton-Spruill
Screenplay: Rober Patton-Spruill
Cinematography: Richard Moos
Editing: Richard Moos
Music: Bruce Flowers
Production design: Macimilian Cutler
Art direction: Ben Dulong
MPAA rating: R
Running Time: 105 minutes

REVIEWS

Los Angeles Times. June 13, 1997, p. F8.
New York Times. June 13, 1997, p. B8.

Star Maps

In Hollywood every dream has a price.—Movie tagline

"Outstanding! One of the most engrossing, original movies!"—Michele Shapiro, *Glamour*

"A hard edged comic film!"—Karen Durbin, *Mirabella*

"A California *Midnight Cowboy*!"—Janet Maslin, *New York Times*

"Striking and sexy!"—David Ansen, *Newsweek*

Independent films have received a great deal of attention over the last several years. Many have become box-office hits such as *Sling Blade* (1996), *Secrets and Lies* (1995), and *The Crying Game* (1992), to mention a few. The era of the "indies" has arrived and is bringing creativity back to filmmaking. This trend should certainly be appreciated by film buffs. Audiences now have a large assortment of product to choose from ranging from big studio blockbusters to fascinating documentaries. One of the most famous showcases for these creative celluloids is the Sundance Film Festival. Originally conceived by mega-movie star Robert Redford, it is a great arena for young and sometimes-gifted filmmakers to show their wares. A good word or "buzz" can transform a formerly unknown film into a heralded hit. It is indeed an excellent environment for creativity to flourish. However, not all of the films that garner praise at festivals deserve the accolades they receive. There was a lot of talk about *Star Maps* (directed by newcomer Miguel Arteta) but, unfortunately, it turns out to be a misguided disappointment.

Carlos on his work: "Listen, I'm an actor. I know how to put on a show."

Nearly three decades ago, *Midnight Cowboy* (1969), a film by the talented John Schlesinger, was released. It was an emotionally shattering dramatization of James Leo Herlihy's novel and deservedly won Oscars for best picture, director and screenplay. It was an intensely keen and complex character study of a young man, Joe Buck (Jon Voight), who comes to New York City to make it big as a hustler. It was a gritty, bold and intelligent portrait of misplaced values and painful disillusionment. *Cowboy* bears mentioning because in her review in the *New York Times*, Janet Maslin called *Star Maps* a "California *Midnight Cowboy*!" Putting it mildly, this comment is a gross exaggeration. The main comparison between the two films is the subject matter but the similarity stops at this point.

Douglas Spain (Carlos) is an eighteen-year-old, Latino youth who is on his way back from Mexico to his family in Los Angeles. It becomes immediately apparent that he has aspirations to become an actor. He fantasizes about winning an Oscar throughout much of his bus ride back to Hollywood. Once ensconced back into the family unit, it doesn't take long to realize that his family gives new meaning to the word "dysfunctional." His mother, Teresa (Martha Velez) is not-so-successfully trying to recover from a nervous breakdown. Upon seeing her son, she plaintively remarks, "You were always like the moon, sad and beautiful." Actually, she spends a great deal of her time talking to the moon. It seems that Cantinflas (a well-known Mexican comedian) has taken up residence there and she happens to be a big fan. This is not the worst of it! Carlos' father Pepe (Efrain Figueroa), who runs a business selling maps to the stars' homes, is really a pimp. The maps are merely a front for the peddling of young flesh on various corners of Tinseltown. Naturally, he wants to bring his handsome son into the family business and enlists Carlos into his army of young, male prostitutes. In his naivete, Carlos sees this as a stepping stone to making it big as an actor. He reluctantly endures all sorts of sexual encounters with both men and women, much like a sacrificial lamb.

Miraculously, one day, a very successful T.V. star named Jennifer (Kandeyce Jordan) pulls up and propositions Carlos, the Antonio Banderas "wannabe." She breathlessly drives him to her palatial estate in Beverly Hills and Carlos begins to realize that he's in the presence of a celebrity. Wide-eyed he asks, "What's it like to be famous?" Jennifer simply looks bored and changes the topic of conversation to one that suits her better—sex. One romantic afternoon while lying in bed, the Latino Lothario begins reciting Chance Wayne's lines from *Sweet Bird of Youth* to Miss Jennifer. She asks Carlos if he just made that up. When Carlos divulges the source, Jennifer, in amazement, responds, "You really can act!" She then offers him a small part on one of her T.V. shows. Equally awestruck, Carlos doesn't believe her at first. He is pleasantly surprised when he finds that the lady is, in

AWARDS AND NOMINATIONS

Independent Spirit Awards 1997 Nominations: First Feature, Debut Screenplay, Supporting Actor (Figueroa), Debut Performance (Flores), Debut Performance (Spain)

fact, telling the truth. However, his good fortune doesn't sit well with the other "star-map boys." Surprisingly, Carlos' father, Pepe, doesn't take well to the idea, either.

Undaunted, Carlos shows up to rehearse on the set with Jennifer. In the heat of the moment, they opt to have sex instead of going over the lines and blocking. Things become more and more complicated until Jennifer's jealous husband has Carlos replaced by none other than Pepe himself. Infuriated and enraged by years of pent-up anger, Carlos nearly decapitates dear old Dad with a shovel. No one dies in this debacle, but ultimately nothing really gets resolved in the end.

Although the film's heart and soul were in the right place, because of inexperience and lack of strong technical "know-how," these elements did not translate onto the screen. The issues of fame, fortune, morality, family values, and racism are certainly worthy of exploring. The film's weakness comes from a lack of commitment to what it wants to be. Is it comedy, black comedy, tragedy, or satire? It needed to know in order for an audience to comprehend it.

Miguel Arteta made some wise choices which enhanced the film's quality. Chuy Chavez, a leading Mexican cinematographer, captured the sunny sleaziness of an amoral Los Angeles. Also, the musical score under the direction of Lysa Flores has a Latino rock'n'roll style which keeps the action and pace moving. It was actually better than some of the scenes that is underscored.

There were also some solid performances from certain cast members that are worth mentioning. Efrain Figueroa as Pepe captured the "machismo" and false bravado of an insensitive man who brutalizes his entire family. If he had added some more shadings to his performance, his character may have been more sympathetic. Martha Velez's character is poignant and touching as a woman slowly retreating into madness. Witnessing the dynamics within her family certainly explained the cause of this decline. Annette Murphy (Letti) turns in a tough portrayal of Pepe's streetwise girlfriend. Although Douglas Spain possessed a sweetness to his personality, he lacked the skill and technique to be convincing as Carlos. It was a limited and self-conscious performance. Kandeyce Jordan was as bland and wooden as her superficial character, Jennifer. Since Spain and Jordan were two pivotal characters, their inadequacies were glaring and distracting.

Success is always built to some degree on prior failure. The beauty of independent films is their willingness to be experimental and take risks. They may not always be successful but should be applauded for their efforts. Missing the mark is sometimes a means to getting back on track. It will be interesting to see when this happens to Miguel Arteta.

—Rob Chicatelli

CREDITS

Carlos: Douglas Spain
Pepe: Efrain Figueroa
Jennifer: Kandeyce Jensen
Teresa: Martha Velez
Maria: Lysa Flores
Letti: Anette Murphy
Juancito: Vincent Chandler

Origin: USA
Released: 1997
Production: Matthew Greenfield for King Films and Flan de Coco Films; released by Fox Searchlight
Direction: Miguel Arteta
Screenplay: Miguel Arteta
Cinematography: Chuy Chavez
Editing: Jeff Betancourt, Tom McArdle, Tony Selzer
Production design: Carol Strober
Costumes: Melanie Stavinski
Sound: Yehuda Maayan
MPAA rating: R
Running Time: 86 minutes

REVIEWS

Boxoffice. September, 1997, p. 121.
Entertainment Weekly. August 1, 1997, p. 50.
Hollywood Reporter. July 23, 1997, p. 9.
Los Angeles Times. July 23, 1997, p. F1.
New York Times. July 23, 1997, p. C11.
New Yorker. July 28, 1997, p. 78.
Variety. February 3, 1997, p. 49.
Village Voice. July 29, 1997, p. 76.

Star Wars; Star Wars, Episode IV: A New Hope

A long time ago in a galaxy far, far away . . .
—Movie tagline

Box Office: $138,257,865

The 20th anniversary of *Star Wars* was celebrated by a rerelease of the hugely successful film.

Film production was up last year and more titles than ever will go into release during 1997, but the prize for the largest opening ever in January went not to a new film, but to one made twenty years ago, a film that has been available in video markets, a film that millions of people have seen but that millions more apparently want to see again and again. By now *Star Wars* has few surprises, other than the "new" footage that George Lucas prepared for the 20th anniversary rerelease, but this science fiction extravaganza took the nation by storm. In Washington, D.C., crowds waited all night in the cold for the box office to open at the large-screen Cineplex Odeon Uptown Theatre Friday morning to sell afternoon and evening tickets, and some waited in vain. No one anticipated the overwhelming response to this rereleased classic. By the time the weekend was over, *Star Wars* had grossed nearly $36 million, doing more business than all of the other current releases combined.

The story is familiar, though a bit retrograde as sci-fi, since, after all, it begins "Long, long ago in a galaxy far, far away" and concerns the past, not the future. The sci-fi concept behind *Star Trek* (1979) and its futuristic gadgetry was, after all, far more sophisticated, but the mythic and human potential of *Star Wars* compensates adequately. (No doubt Paramount will think about dressing up *Star Trek: The Motion Picture*, directed by Robert Wise two years after the success of *Star Wars*, even though the *Star Trek* series seems to have exhausted itself through too many worn out sequels). The film borrowed shamelessly from American pop culture while working out a larger mythic structure. The most recent paperback edition of Joseph Campbell's *Hero With a Thousand Faces* has Luke Skywalker on its cover.

Luke: "I'm Luke Skywalker. I'm here to rescue you." Leia: "This is some rescue!"

The mythic framework was carefully considered and gives the film a kind of significance that cannot be easily dated (unlike the absurd sideburns of some of the rebel pilots). Rebel Princess Leia Organa (Carrie Fisher) is a captive hostage of the Evil Empire ruled by the lapsed Jedi knight Darth Vader, garbed in black as emblematic of his dark side, whose voice sounds like James Earl Jones on a respirator. She manages to send lovable robot R2-D2 to the planet Tatooine, seeking help from the Jedi knight Obi-Wan Kenobi (Alec Guinness), who lives there in seclusion and disguise. The robot is captured by salvaging Jawas, who sell it to farm boy Luke Skywalker (Mark Hamill), who is able to play back part of the robot's holograph message from the Princess. He discovers that the message is for Obi-Wan Kenobi, and speculates that it might be for Ben Kenobi, to whom he takes it. Meanwhile, the Empire Storm Troopers trace the robot to Luke's aunt and uncle, whom they destroy (recalling the destruction of the rancher's family in John Ford's *The Searchers* [1956] by Scar's ruthless, renegade Comanchee).

Luke, now homeless, joins forces with Ben and takes instructions from the wise Jedi knight, who teaches him how to duel with light sabers and how to draw upon the inner power of "The Force." With the help of the mercenary interplanetary pirate Han Solo (Harrison Ford) and his sidekick, the fur-bearing Wookie, Chewbacca (Peter Mayhew), Ben and Luke commission the Millennium Falcon to undertake a dangerous rescue mission. They track the Empire's Death Star—the ultimate battleship, capable of destroying whole planets—and manage to rescue the Princess, though Ben Kenobi falls while doing battle with Darth Vader. The rebels then organize their fleet to do battle with the Death Star, and Luke, with the help of Ben's spirit and Solo's Millennium Falcon, saves the day.

What explained the phenomenal success of this "special edition" rerelease of *Star Wars*? The film is a remade toy enhanced by magic, Industrial Light & Magic, the company director George Lucas founded when he turned his talents to creating special effects for others after the initial success of the Star Wars Trilogy. ILM went on to do pioneering work in digital technology, creating the special effects for such films as *Twister* (1996). Lucas tinkered with the film, enhancing it with effects that were not possible to achieve twenty years ago. His mythical beasts of burden in the Tatooine desert now actually move for the first time, for example, and the entrance into the city of Mos Eisley, the spaceport, with its Western-style cantina filled with very strange creatures, is far more spectacular.

Lucas also added new footage. In this version, for example, Han Solo faces Jabba the Hutt in person, not one of the creature's henchmen, and buys time on the loan Jabba wants to call in. "Let's get outta here!" Solo says after the exchange, but the new footage makes his need to escape rather less urgent than the first time around, even though the spectacle is enhanced by giving the previously stationary Jabba, originally introduced in the soon-to-be rereleased sequel the ability to move in a slithering, sluglike fashion. "I wanted to connect the first film with the next two, the way it was meant to be," Lucas explained, apparently unconcerned that the new footage created a problem of diegesis interruptus, as the heavyweight critics might say.

This computer-generated creature spectacle in itself is not worth rushing to the multiplex to witness in person, but

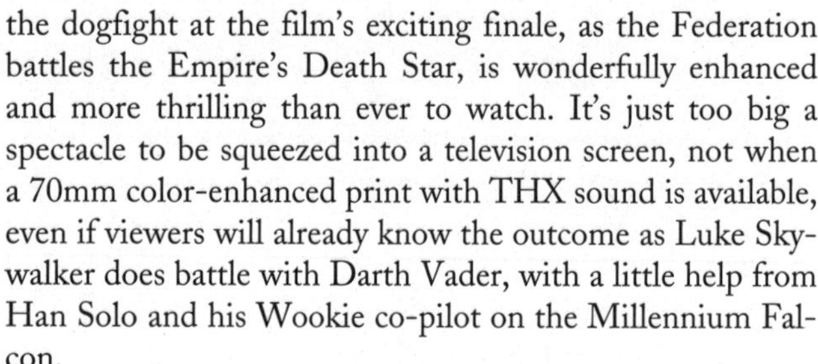

the dogfight at the film's exciting finale, as the Federation battles the Empire's Death Star, is wonderfully enhanced and more thrilling than ever to watch. It's just too big a spectacle to be squeezed into a television screen, not when a 70mm color-enhanced print with THX sound is available, even if viewers will already know the outcome as Luke Skywalker does battle with Darth Vader, with a little help from Han Solo and his Wookie co-pilot on the Millennium Falcon.

In fact, the original release of *Star Wars* preceded the introduction of the THX sound systems in theatres. "We went back to some of the original tracks," Lucas explained, "and obtained the cleanest copy. We then re-mastered it digitally, so that this will be the first time the film has been released in digital sound."

The reason for rereleasing the Trilogy is surely to drum up interest in the long-awaited "prequel" trilogy, the first increment of which is currently in production, perhaps to be released in 1999. As for the Special Edition, Lucas began several years ago to think about the forthcoming anniversary. "I suggested we try to release all three films as a trilogy," he explained, "one right after the other, and within a few weeks of each other; this would allow audiences to experience them like Saturday matinee serials, which they closely resemble. Because I've always seen the three films as one epic story, this seemed to be a very appropriate way of celebrating the twentieth anniversary." In other words, Lucas was not thinking purely in terms of profit.

What is encouraging about the rerelease is that it demonstrated that huge profits could be made by investing in refurbishing a classic. To restore *Star Wars* to its current state required an additional investment of $15 million, an investment that more than doubled itself during the film's opening weekend. *Star Wars* was a benchmark in film history and quite subversive, in the way it encouraged pure escapist cinema to come back into vogue. This, after all, was the movie that reminded audiences that movies could be fun, shifting attention away from more serious pictures that had messages and attempted to treat adult problems. It also opened the floodgates for the action-adventure special-effects spectacles that have become so dominant in current markets.

In short, then, *Star Wars* represented a paradigm shift in American popular culture by marking the end of the Vietnam era, the end of intelligent political cinema, the rebirth

CREDITS

Luke Skywalker: Mark Hamill
Han Solo: Harrison Ford
Princess Leia: Carrie Fisher
Grand Moff Tarkin: Peter Cushing
Ben (Obi-Wan) Kenobi: Alec Guinness
C-3PO: Anthony Daniels
R2-D2: Kenny Baker
Chewbacca: Peter Mayhews
Darth Vader: David Prowse
Darth Vader: James Earl Jones (voice)

Origin: USA
Released: 1977, 1997
Production: Gary Kurtz for Lucasfilm Ltd.; released by 20th Century Fox
Direction: George Lucas
Screenplay: George Lucas
Cinematography: Gilbert Taylor
Editing: Richard Chew, Paul Hirsch, Marcia Lucas
Music: John Williams
Production design: John Barry
Costumes: John Mollo
MPAA rating: PG
Running Time: 125 minutes

REVIEWS

Entertainment Weekly. February 14, 1997, p. 6.
The New York Times. January 26, 1997, p. C11.
The New York Times. January 31, 1997, p. C16.
The Washington Post. January 31, 1997, p. C1.
Washington Post Weekend. January 31, 1997, p. 45.
The Washington Times Metropolitan Times. January 31, 1997, p. C14.

of trivial escapism. It was the film industry's gift to Ronald Reagan, for it gave him rhetorical notions of an Evil Empire that he later put effectively to political use. It spawned an industry of toys to be merchandized. Nostalgia cycles are said to run in twenty-year increments as the children of a new generation attempt to understand the enthusiasms and the culture of their parents. To underestimate the drawing power of *Star Wars* would be to underestimate the power of toys, mythic memories, childhood fantasies, and nostalgia.

—James M. Welsh

Starship Troopers

A new kind of enemy. A new kind of war.—Movie tagline

"A must-see!"—Robert Hoffler, *Buzz Weekly*

"One of the best science fiction movies ever!"—Maria Salas, *CBS Telenoticicas*

"One of the year's most physically exciting movies."—Michael Wilmington, *Chicago Tribune*

"Sensationally exciting! Like *Star Wars* it's ground zero for a new generation of thrill seekers!"—Owen Gleiberman, *Entertainment Weekly*

"One hell-of-a-rock-and-roll rocket ride! A real blast!"—Sam Hallenbeck, *FOX-TV, Tampa*

"A jaw-dropping experience."—Kenneth Turan, *Los Angeles Times*

"Extraordinarily dynamic special effects creatures on a nonstop rampage, shrieking, stampeding, breathing fire, these bizarre monsters are really something to see!"—Janet Maslin, *New York Times*

"The battles are magnificent!"—Jeff Giles, *Newsweek*

"The year's most brazen blockbuster!"—Mike Clark, *USA Today*

"An eye-popping, explosively entertaining epic!"—Paul Wunder, *WBAI Radio*

Box Office: $54,208,270

If the flawless representation of violent death was the highest standard for a film then *Starship Troopers* would be a 10. Luckily, that is not yet the case. And yet director Paul Verhoeven has used computer-generated effects for more than just simulated carnage. He has created a spectacular panorama of warring giant soldier bugs marching wave upon wave across the screen.

Based on Robert A. Heinlein's 1959 novel of the same name, *Starship Troopers* is the story of four young people who find themselves caught up in a war between earth's World Federation and the monster bugs of the Klendathu System. Although Verhoeven mesmerizes the viewer with effects that create a rich visual tapestry, the lack of any substance to the plot or the characters soon makes even the most spectacular effects fall flat.

Starship Troopers opens in the distant future with a news report from behind the Arachnid Quarantine Zone, the AQZ, where the Federation's Mobile Infantry has landed to take on an army of giant bugs who have firebombed Buenos Aires, killing millions. During the report, the infantry is overtaken and one of the spider-like bugs skewers the war correspondent like a kebab, as the camera mercifully falls to the ground in the ensuing melee of battle.

The film then returns to one year earlier, in a high school in Buenos Aires, where Johnny Rico (Casper Van Dien) is trying to win the heart of the beautiful Carmen Ibanez (Denise Richards). They are both seniors and in the process of planning their futures. Carmen is going on to Fleet Academy after graduation, to become a pilot, and Rico decides to join the Mobile Infantry in order to win Ibanez's heart.

His best friend, Carl Jenkins (Neil Patrick Harris), is interested in mind reading and decides to enter Intelligence. The last of the foursome, Dizzy Flores (Dina Meyer), who carries a torch for the indifferent Rico, has also joined the infantry.

Rasczak to his troops: "Kill anything that has more than two legs."

There are not a lot of career choices in this new world, because there are basically only two tracks, civilian or citizen. Citizens are anyone who has worked in the armed forces. After military service they are awarded citizenship and the basic rights, because "a citizen has the courage to make the safety of the human race his responsibility." Civilians are residents of the federation who have not served in the military, and therefore have none of the rights of citizenship, excluding them from entering government positions or even having children without governmental permission.

Visual effects artist Phil Tippett also designed *Return of the Jedi*'s Jabba the Hutt, the robots in *RoboCop*, and the T-Rex in *Jurassic Park.*

The teachers in the school, obviously citizens, all have some injury, either blindness or amputations of some sort, inferring an earlier confrontation with the "bugs." One of the teachers, Mr. Rasczak (Michael Ironside), spouts fascist propaganda and tries to recruit students into the military, while bitterly rubbing the stump of his missing arm. His words seem to move Rico, giving him new resolve to defy his parents and become an infantryman.

But it's now a time of peace, where football games and proms are the only battlegrounds. After graduation, as Rico and Dizzy are completing boot camp, a fireball from the AQZ takes Buenos Aires off the map, and the Mobile Infantry is sent into the Klendathu System to fight the giant bugs.

Whole armies of spider-like creatures, beetles, dragonflies, and the big brain bugs, who have organized all the other critters, are waiting for them. Battles ensue, friends are lost, bugs are splattered everywhere, and humans are decapitated, cut in half, impaled, and squished. Some soldiers even have their brains sucked out by the brain bug, who can somehow synthesize the grey matter to learn of the Federation's plans.

By the end of the film, the war rages on, but it has reached a vital and hopeful turning point. A brain bug has been captured, and now the Federation will be able to learn "how they think," and possibly conquer them.

In *Starship Troopers,* Verhoeven, who directed *RoboCop* (1987), *Basic Instinct* (1992), and *Showgirls* (1995), offers the viewer a feast for the eyes, while he leaves the heart and mind famished. The characters, although attractive, are so lacking in humanity that when one character says, "We're in this for the species," one wonders just what subspecies they might fall under. The truly believable characters are the bugs, rendered painstakingly perfect.

Next to the four main characterless players, Michael Ironside's performance as Rasczak stands out in bold relief. Ironside gives a passionate portrayal of the rabid-yet-bitter teacher turned rabid-yet-bitter lieutenant and leader of "Rasczak's Roughnecks."

Although the film courts the teenage audience, with its tattoo parlor scene, its shower scene, the sophomoric dialogue, and more violence than anyone could ever want, this film is not for children. It has received criticism for its violence, going down in the record books as the film that used more ammunition than any other film to date.

But it has received even more criticism for its glorification of a fascist future. Verhoeven's mimicry of the Hitler propaganda film style in his simulated computer ads for the Mobile Infantry, and his sets and uniforms that use the symbols of the Third Reich have offended those who see it as promoting a fascist utopia.

Yet there are those who see it as Verhoeven's ironic sense of humor, cautioning the very people who are his market to be wary of being seduced into a media-hyped nationalism that desensitizes the viewer and dehumanizes the "enemy" of the hour. The film's comicbook characters can hardly persuade anyone to the fascist dream, or any other dream for that matter.

CREDITS

Johnny Rico: Casper Van Dien
Dizzy Flores: Dina Meyer
Carmen Ibanez: Denise Richards
Carl Jenkins: Neil Patrick Harris
Ace Levy: Jake Busey
Sgt. Zim: Clancy Brown
Zander Baraclow: Patrick Muldoon
Sugar Watkins: Seth Gilliam
Jean Rasczak: Michael Ironside
General Owen: Marshall Bell

Origin: USA
Released: 1997
Production: Jon Davison and Alan Marshall for TriStar and Touchstone Pictures; released by Sony Pictures
Direction: Paul Verhoeven
Screenplay: Ed Neumeier; based on the novel by Robert A. Heinlein
Cinematography: Jost Vacano
Editing: Mark Goldblatt, Caroline Ross
Music: Basil Poledouris
Production design: Allan Cameron
Art direction: Steve Wolff, Bruce Robert Hill
Set decoration: Bob Gould
Costumes: Ellen Mirojnick
Sound: Joseph Geisinger
Creature visual effects supervisor: Phil Tippett
Spaceship visual effects supervisor: Scott E. Anderson
Special effects supervisor: John Richardson
MPAA rating: R
Running Time: 129 minutes

AWARDS AND NOMINATIONS

Academy Awards 1997 Nominations: Visual Effects

The last hour of *Starship Troopers* is relentless, almost nonstop, violence. When the house lights come on, any stirrings of blind nationalism that might have been evoked during the film cannot help but be replaced by sheer exhaustion by the film's end. Verhoeven has succeeded in creating a rich, if visceral, three-dimensional future world, but he fails his audience by peopling it with two-dimensional characters.

—*Diane Hatch-Avis*

REVIEWS

Boxoffice. November, 1997, p. 18.
Boxoffice. January, 1998, p. 47.
Chicago Tribune. November 7, 1997, p. 4.
Detroit News. November 7, 1997, p. F1.
Entertainment Today. November 7, 1997, p. 19.
Entertainment Weekly. November 7, 1997, p. 53.
Hollywood Reporter. October 27, 1997, p. 6.
LA Weekly. November 7, 1997, p. 41.
Los Angeles Times. September 23, 1996, p. F1.
Los Angeles Times. November 7, 1997, p. F1.
New York. November 17, 1997, p. 72.
New York Times. November 7, 1997, p. E14.
People. November 17, 1997, p. 21.
Rolling Stone. November 27, 1997, p. 113.
Sight and Sound. January, 1998, p. 53.
Time. November 10, 1997.
Variety. November 3, 1997, p. 98.
Village Voice. November 11, 1997, p. 77.

Steel

Heroes don't come any bigger. *Steel* Man. Metal. Hero.—Movie tagline

Box Office: $1,734,074

Steel is the second starring vehicle for Shaquille O'Neal, the gigantic African-American basketball star and sometime rapper who is trying to carve out a third career as an actor. He first played the genial genie in the moderately successful *Kazaam* (1996). Shaq is one inch over seven feet tall. He is no string bean either but perfectly proportioned at some 300 pounds of bone and muscle. Nature has further endowed him with good looks and a warm personality. His enormous size is at once an asset and a handicap. It makes him a formidable basketball player for the Los Angeles Lakers but makes it hard to find suitable parts in films. When he appears with ordinary actors they all look like tourists gawking up at the Empire State Building or the Statue of Liberty. Shaq seems destined to play larger-than-life fantasy figures like Kazaam the genie or the RoboCop-lookalike of *Steel.*

Director Kenneth Johnson on the character: "Our guy is sort of a blue-collar Batman who works out of Uncle Joe's junkyard and has to piece things together as best he can."

The film was inspired by the DC Comics superhero Steel and has a typical comic-strip plot. Shaq, as John Henry Irons, is trying to stop super-villain Nathaniel Burke (Judd Nelson), a disgraced former Army officer, from selling stolen high-tech weapons to gangsters, terrorists, revolutionaries, and hostile foreign powers. To finance his international skullduggery, Burke arms and masterminds a gang of black youths who terrorize Los Angeles, robbing banks with stun guns, missile launchers, and a laser weapon that can cut through steel doors. They even have the temerity to attack a federal depository where hundreds of transparent packages of brand-new greenbacks are piled from floor to ceiling.

The police are outgunned. Only Irons, who knows as much about advanced weaponry as Burke, can hope to deal with him. With the help of friendly junkyard owner Uncle Joe (Richard Roundtree), Irons fashions a suit of steel armor and emerges as the Man of Steel. As in the comic strip, he carries a huge weapon that looks like a sledgehammer but can fire missiles from the handle and snatch opponents' weapons out of their hands with its electromagnetic force.

Electronic genius Susan Sparks (Annabeth Gish) was an ambitious Army lieutenant until an accident deliberately caused by Burke left her a paraplegic confined to a wheelchair and staring despondently out the dirty window of a V.A. hospital. Irons carries her off to Uncle Joe's junkyard—wheelchair and all—because he loves her and needs her help. She can use remote monitoring gadgetry to provide him with the kind of supersensory intelligence the U.S. displayed so dramatically during the Gulf War.

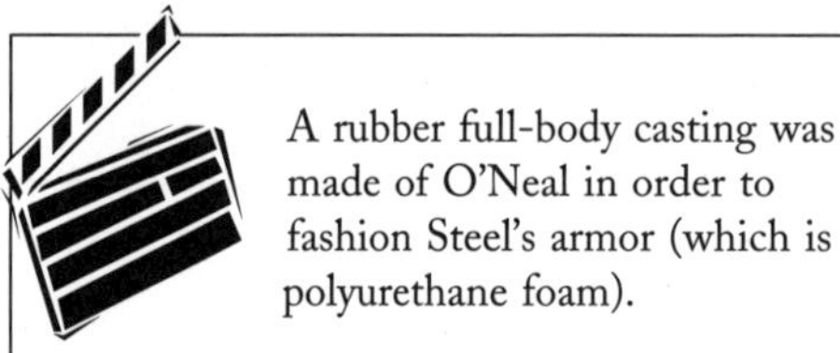

A rubber full-body casting was made of O'Neal in order to fashion Steel's armor (which is polyurethane foam).

Even a giant like Shaquille O'Neal would be slowed down by all the weight he has to lug around. His big hammer alone is about as much as an ordinary man could lift. This concept might be digestible in a comic strip, but in a film it tends to make the hero hopelessly sluggish. This is one of the drawbacks to the story by writer-director Kenneth Johnson. Steel often stands rooted to one spot while the bullets bounce off him. He may be well protected, but he makes a perfect target.

Inevitably all the fireworks attract wailing squad cars with flashing lights. The bad guys, who are much quicker on their feet, flee the scene and leave poor Steel to pick up the tab for all the property damage. Steel spends more of his time fleeing from the cops on his gadget-equipped motorcycle than chasing the crooks. In his flight he is aided by Susan, whose radar and other devices enable her to tell him how to elude pursuit and even turn all the stoplights green. Uncle Joe has converted his junkyard into a fortress with secret entrances and a command center disguised as a mound of junk. But eventually Burke discovers Steel's hideaway and kidnaps Susan, leading to a violent climax with lots of thrills for immature viewers of all ages.

Since Shaquille dominates the film, both by his size and his celebrity status, its success or failure depend on his performance. (The film was even advertised as *Shaq Steel.*) Critics generally recognized the star's charming personality but did not think much of his acting talents. Lawrence Van Gelder, writing for the *New York Times,* diagnosed the problem succinctly: "Once again Mr. O'Neal displays an endearing smile, a genial personality and an almost total lack of the charisma and acting skills that his role call for . . . Despite his gifts as a basketball player, Mr. O'Neal seems ungainly in the action sequences."

Variety critic Leonard Klady, who called the film "strictly kids' stuff," reported: "Warner Bros.' not-so-super *Steel* was an immediate casualty with a tarnished $1.3 million opening sputter . . ." By the third week it had disappeared from *Variety*'s Box Office Chart.

—Bill Delaney

CREDITS

John Henry Irons: Shaquille O'Neal
Susan Sparks: Annabeth Gish
Nathaniel Burke: Judd Nelson
Uncle Joe: Richard Roundtree
Grandma Odessa: Irma P. Hall
Martin: Ray J.
Col. David: Charles Napier
Senator Nolan: Kerrie Keane

Origin: USA
Released: 1997
Production: Quincy Jones, David Salzman and Joel Simon; released by Warner Bros.
Direction: Kenneth Johnson
Screenplay: Kenneth Johnson; based on characters created by Louise Simonson and Jon Bogdanove
Cinematography: Mark Irwin
Editing: John F. Link
Music: Mervyn Warren
Production design: Gary Wissner
Art direction: Gershon Gingsburg
Costumes: Catherine Adair
Visual effects supervisor: Mark Franco
Stunt coordinator: M. James Arnett, Jon Epstein
Sound: Susumu Tokunow
MPAA rating: PG-13
Running Time: 97 minutes

REVIEWS

Boxoffice. November, 1997, p. 135.
Cinemafantastique. July, 1997, p. 7.
Los Angeles Times. August 18, 1997, p. F4.
New York Times. August 16, 1997, p. 16.
Variety. August 8, 1997, p. 33.

subUrbia

"A compelling and important film!"—Marshall Fine, *Gannett News Service*

"Wonderful! A winning cast. Elegantly directed."—Janet Maslin, *New York Times*

"Fierce and funny! Hotblooded, haunted and blisteringly comic . . . a fireball."—Peter Travers, *Rolling Stone*

"Two thumbs up!"—*Siskel & Ebert*

Box Office: $727,571

Richard Linklater is a director concerned with the mundane, with the way life is lived on a daily basis. That's not to say his movies are boring, though boredom works as a theme in both *Slacker* (1991), and *Dazed and Confused* (1993). Those films are about characters living a life devoid of structure. They're without hope for the future; maybe because they've no confidence there will even be a future. The way they see it, the world around them is going to hell, so they might as well just relax and mark the time by chatting with others in the same boat. 1995's *Before Sunrise* limited this scenario to a pair of educated young tourists hoofing it through Vienna, but the two still fit easily into Linklater's roster of slackers and societal misfits, having many of the same insecurities as the characters in his earlier films.

Like all Linklater's films, *subUrbia* confines its story to a period of about twenty-four hours. It takes place in the fictional town of Burnfield, Texas, and covers a day and night in the life of a group of . . . friends? It's hard to say, though they might have been at one time. Now, they seem more like the walking dead, drawn to the Circle-A food mart at the edge of the suburban sprawl seeking nourishment, or what passes for it, inside.

There is Jeff (Giovanni Ribisi), Sooze (Amie Carey), Bee-Bee (Dina Spybey), Buff (Steve Zahn), and Tim (Nicky Katt). Jeff is intelligent, sensitive, and the closest thing the film has to a hero. He is also a bit of a loser, refusing to use his intelligence to make a difference in anyone's life, his own included. Sooze is his girlfriend, a somewhat hyperactive performance artist. Bee-Bee works as a medical assistant and has a drinking problem. Buff is simply a round-the-clock drunk. Tim used to be in the Air Force, but now appears to spend a good deal of time (most of the movie, anyway) harassing immigrants and anyone else he doesn't feel belongs in this country.

These kids are a product of their little city, and Burnfield is depicted as the average suburb: not much wealth, not much outright poverty—though certainly there's an overwhelming lack of imagination present. A town like this often seems to straddle urban and rural, being not quite one or the other, existing instead as a curious mixture of both. This can result in a kind of cultural confusion for the inhabitants, and that is the case for the characters who populate Burnfield.

The film is based on a play by Eric Bogosian, but Linklater makes the story his own, taking Burnfield out of New York and placing it in his home state of Texas. Linklater thankfully has not tried to open the play up, instead keeping it limited to a handful of locations. This helps to underline the sense of entrapment these characters feel, in that although they could, in theory, drift anywhere within the wide-open expanses of Texas, it never

AWARDS AND NOMINATIONS

Independent Spirits Awards 1997 Nominations:
Actor (Naidu)

CREDITS

Jeff: Giovanni Ribisi
Sooze: Amie Carey
Erica: Parker Posey
Buff: Steve Zahn
Tim: Nicky Katt
Pony: Jayce Bartok
Bee-Bee: Dina Spybey
Pakeesa: Samia Shoaib
Nazeer: Ajay Naidu

Origin: USA
Released: 1996
Production: Anne Walker-McBay for Castle Rock Entertainment; released by Sony Pictures Classics
Direction: Richard Linklater
Screenplay: Eric Bogosian; based on his play
Cinematography: Lee Daniel
Editing: Sandra Adair
Production design: Catherine Hardwicke
Art direction: Seth Reed
Costumes: Melanie Armstrong
Sound: Jennifer Murphy
MPAA rating: R
Running Time: 118 minutes

occurs to them to consider anyplace other than the few areas they know.

The film begins as a series of random occurrences, many of them funny, as when Sooze performs her one-woman sketch, which apparently is about what she'd put in a manifesto, if she had one. Then, midway through the movie, a limo arrives at the Circle-A, carrying their old friend Pony (Jayce Bartok), now an alternative rock star, come back to relive his past for a night, possibly out of guilt over not keeping up with the gang over the years. He and his rich and snotty publicist, Erica (Parker Posey), wind up being the source of much of the drama for the rest of the film. But the film's plot turns out to be not nearly as important as the character revelations that Linklater and his cast are able to bring out.

Jeff: "I don't need a limousine to know who I am. At least I know I don't know."

The opening credits sequence is set to the Gene Pitney song "Town Without Pity."

In one incident, Tim squares off with his rival in the film, a Pakistani convenience store owner (Samia Shoaib). They find themselves deadlocked, each looking down the barrel of the other's pistol (it's Texas, remember, where it's legal to carry a concealed weapon). Jeff, to his own surprise, finds he can be a voice of reason in a tense situation, as he begs the both of them to each ask the other's name. That's a good moment, and there are more, though most of them are a good deal bleaker, as in the scene where Tim uses his veteran's checks to buy whiskey, and when Jeff crawls out of a tent (his home) in his parents' garage. The movie unfolds the same way these characters go through life: moment by moment.

If the film has a weakness, it's in its handling of the constantly inebriated Buff, who Linklater has allowed to be portrayed as a caricature of drunkenness. Buff spends the film careening in and out of the frame, slowing only to hump the legs of his friends and the hoods of cars. The overacting here seriously threatens to affect more than one scene's credibility, though the fact that it never does might be the best measure of Linklater's skill as a filmmaker.

—*David King*

REVIEWS

Entertainment Weekly. February 7, 1997, p. 51.
Los Angeles Times. February 7, 1997, p. F4.
New York Times. October 11, 1996, p. C16.
New Yorker. February 10, 1997, 85.
Sight and Sound. October, 1997, p. 59.
Spin. March, 1997, p. 108.
USA Today. February 7, 1997, p. 4D.
Variety. October 14, 1996, p. 58.
Village Voice. February 11, 1997, p. 70.

Sudden Manhattan

Actress Adrienne Shelly, best known for her work in Hal Hartley's *Trust* (1991) and *The Unbelievable Truth* (1990), takes a stab at writing and directing her first feature film, the madcap urban comedy, *Sudden Manhattan*. Like her mentor, Shelly brings a quirkiness to this absurd tale of zany young lower Manhattanites in search of the meaning of life.

Donna (Adrienne Shelly) is an aimless young New Yorker concerned about her lack of employment, love, and direction. Only in her twenties, the neurotic Donna is having trouble getting out of bed in the morning. She feels her life has no meaning. She lives rent-free in a building in Greenwich Village owned by an ardent, but unrequited admirer, eccentric Englishman Murphy (Roger Rees), who is also her professor, and is in a relationship with impotent lover Adam (Tim Guinee) who would much rather just read Dostoyevsky aloud in bed.

One day Donna hears ominous rumbling emanating from her scrambled eggs, then witnesses a murder that is scoffingly dismissed by the police. Fearing that she might be going insane, Donna heads for some psychic guidance from a doom-and-gloom gypsy fortune-teller named Dominga (Louise Lasser).

Donna's recently jilted best friend Georgie (Hynden

Walch) and a pair of equally wacky men round out the eccentric cast of characters who accompany Donna as she desperately tries to negotiate her descent into existential whimsy.

While *Sudden Manhattan* is often amusing, it is not necessarily successful as a well-plotted story. There is no denying that Shelly brings her own brand of offbeat vision to her film; she certainly has a firm grasp on deadpan delivery of countless non-sequiturs, wacky characters, and existential madness. But as is often the case with the films of Woody Allen, Shelly tends to be more observational than insightful. She is good with "the moments," those little bits of business that comedians like Jerry Seinfeld have parlayed into somewhat of a fine art. But Shelly's script is too reminiscent of Martin Scorsese's *After Hours* (1985), as well as David Lynch's often inaccessible body of work. Furthermore, she is not able to navigate the similar pitfalls that plagued Susan Seidelman's *Desperately Seeking Susan* (1985), another offbeat comedy that could not sustain its buoyant rhythm through to the end.

The world of low-budget independent filmmaking is teeming with tales of Generation-X angst and ennui, which makes Shelly's outrageous urban romp a tad more tolerable. However, acting zany and being funny are not necessarily the same thing. Characters careen off each other and encounter a succession of bizarre situations; but once Shelly has introduced this motley crew, she loses her footing. The film is allowed to degenerate into inconsequential surrealism that ultimately culminates in a totally unsatisfying resolution.

To her credit, Ms. Shelly directs with a self-assurance not often found in novices, and she maintains a breezy pace throughout. But the paper-thin characters and contrived hipness of *Sudden Manhattan* give the film a superficiality that contrasts sharply to its loftier pretentiousness. It is not enough to write eccentric characters—they must have movement, as well as a story to move through.

In an interview, actor Kiefer Sutherland remarked how shocked he was when shown some old home movies of himself and friends. His memories of the time were so strikingly different than the reality. At the time he thought he was so profound, but the truth was that he was pretty idiotic. What does this have to do with *Sudden Manhattan*? Aside from sharing a rather insightful anecdote, it is a somewhat circuitous way of suggesting that Adrienne Shelly might want to save all that searching for answers to life's more profound issues until she's lived enough of life to know what questions to ask.

—Patricia Kowal

CREDITS

Donna: Adrienne Shelly
Adam: Tim Guinee
Murphy: Roger Rees
Dominga: Louise Lasser
Georgie: Hynden Walch
Alex: Jon Sklaroff
Ian: Paul Cassell

Origin: USA
Released: 1996
Production: Marcia Kirkley for Homegrown Pictures; released by Phaedra Cinema
Direction: Adrienne Shelly
Screenplay: Adrienne Shelly
Cinematography: Jim Denault
Editing: Jack Haigis
Production design: Teresa Mastropierro
Art direction: Tina Khayat
Costumes: Cherish Cullison
Music: Pat Irwin
Sound: Bill Kozy
MPAA rating: R
Running Time: 85 minutes

REVIEWS

Boxoffice. September 9, 1997, p. 122.
New York Times. March 7, 1997, p. B12.
Variety. April 29, 1997, p. 135.
Village Voice. March 11, 1997, p. 74.

Sunday

"A bold piece of filmmaking. One resonant performance after the next. It's Antonioni in Long Island City."—Michael Agovino, *Esquire*

"*Sunday* shimmers with mystery and beauty."—Richard Jameson, *Film Comment*

"A lovingly crafted romantic mystery!"—Robert Dominquez, *New York Daily News*

"Crisply written and luminously acted. David Suchet and Lisa Harrow give deeply, finely etched performances."—Stephen Holden, *New York Times*

The myriad ways in which one's everyday identity can be abruptly lost, stolen or even destroyed are the subject of Jonathan Nossiter's *Sunday,* an exceptionally sophisticated first feature which was shown to great acclaim at the Sundance Film Festival in January 1997 and scored a similar success this spring as part of the "New Directors/New Films" series at the New York Museum of Modern Art.

The spectacle at hand is horrible but nonetheless fascinating. Set in a particularly degraded section of Queens, the film traces one dreary, aimless Sunday in the lives of a group of neighborhood misfits. These include Oliver (David Suchet), a former IBM functionary who has recently been downsized into oblivion. Suddenly bereft of a job, not to mention the wife and family which were once crucial components of his sense of self, Oliver has been reduced to the ignominy of inhabiting a borrowed bed in a dingy men's shelter.

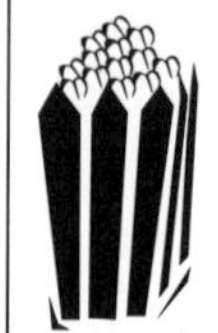

Oliver: "No work, no hope for work, like every day's Sunday."

Thanks to the cinematographic contributions of Michael Barrow, John Foster and Daniel Lerner, the borough of Queens has never looked so relentlessly dismal. The film's initial, early morning scenes are bathed in a hazy, blue light, so that the setting becomes a kind of "non-place," vague, featureless and not immediately recognizable. The sense of dislocation is accentuated by the director's use of an old Edith Piaf song, rendered in French and concerning the bedraggled street people of Paris, over the opening credits. The seemingly incongruous musical reference also causes us to wonder exactly where we are. This highly stylized introduction has a surreal, even soothing effect, but it soon gives way to a string of boisterous, unrelentingly noisy scenes depicting the daily wake-up routine at the men's shelter.

Like his cohorts, Oliver is faced with the ignominious task of finding a way to pass the time on "Sunday, the most empty of all days." House rules dictate that the men be cast out of their digs during the daylight hours, so that their daily routine becomes an exercise in improvisation, one which usually consists of attempts at panhandling, not to mention long hours spent hiding out on highway overpasses, snowy street corners and filthy subway platforms.

This particular Sunday morning, like all others of its kind, finds Oliver on the loose. Suddenly he quite literally collides with Madeleine Vesey (Lisa Harrow), an unemployed British actress who has "crash-landed" in Queens as a result of her marriage to an American. Madeleine instantly mistakes Oliver for one Matthew Delacorta, a world-renowned film director whom she claims to have met during better days in London. Within minutes, these two very misplaced persons latch onto one another, each seeing in the other an avenue of escape from the pointless, dreary day, or perhaps even a way of reclaiming a former way of life.

Eager to make a lasting impression, Madeleine insists on giving "Matthew" an impromptu tour of the neighborhood. The excursion is a comical misfire: it includes a trip to such dubious local "landmarks" as a greasy-spoon diner where Oliver suffers through a meal of irksome fast food. The stakes are raised considerably when Madeleine invites "Matthew" home. They exchange pleasantries about matters of show business, but Madeleine is also secretly hoping that this chance meeting will result in the offer of a film role.

Oliver's wish to be delivered from the torment of being himself, if only for one day, dovetails ominously with Madeleine's tendency to fantasize. At the early stages of their encounter, Oliver has several opportunities to correct Madeleine's mistake, but he is too lonely, and perhaps too intrigued by the idea of "being" a famous person with a distinct and meaningful identity, to tell the whole truth. (She also offers him food and shelter for the day, which is no small thing to a person in Oliver's straitened circumstances.)

"Tell me a story," says Madeleine, who is perhaps too accustomed to the invented world of the theater for her own good. Although she is initially charming, she also seems dangerously disconnected from reality, sometimes even hostile. "Matthew" complies as best he can, presenting her with a "story" about a former IBM executive who becomes unemployed, loses his home and family and ends up in a men's shelter. Madeleine is unaware, or at least, unwilling to acknowledge, that Oliver is attempting to communicate the real truth about himself. She simply assumes "Matthew" is describing the plot of an upcoming film project.

The sudden appearance of "Matthew" serves to inject an element of excitement into Madeleine's routine. As we learn from her description of her daily life, she is very much at a loss when she is not actively working. During the long periods of unemployment that are the lot of most actresses, her life seems vague, empty and improvised. Exiled at least temporarily from the privileged world of working actors, Madeleine compensates for her sense of isolation and failure by turning daily life into a kind of performance. Like Blanche Dubois, she "pretends" compulsively, even when such behavior is damaging and uncalled for: we see her pretending to be happy, pretending to be kind, pretending to be fulfilled by her role as a mother. In truth, she leads a joyless, monotonous life based on an elaborate web of lies.

Jonathan Nossiter's previous film was the documentary *Resident Alien,* about Quentin Crisp.

Oliver and Madeleine have one great trait in common. They both feel the need to glamorize, to make their daily lives seem much more colorful and exiting than they really are. To varying degrees, both characters lie compulsively, not in order to inflict damage, but to save face in a hostile world. This is their greatest failing, but it is also their way of saving themselves from an onslaught of deeply-felt pain and anguish.

Despite their shared tendency toward self-delusion, the viewer feels moved to grant Madeleine and Oliver a certain measure of sympathy. Her aimlessness stems from the fact that, personally and professionally, she depends on others to provide her with a role in the world. She appears to have genuine ability as an actress, as is evidenced by her constant repetition at home of a videotape in which she is shown playing a key role in an Elizabethan drama. But since that brief glimmer of success, Madeleine seems to have been cut adrift, both socially and professionally. By virtue of his sudden descent into the realm of the unemployed, Oliver has also become a "de-classed" person, someone who no longer has a respectable role in the world. His willingness to discard his own identity in order to fulfill Madeleine's expectations is initially understandable, given the blighted circumstances in which he lives.

Throughout the afternoon, the strange dance of misunderstanding continues. Opportunities to tell the unvarnished truth appear at every turn, but Oliver remains reluctant to break the spell, since Madeleine's very mistaken notion of who he is offers him some respite from the horrible indignity of being homeless and unemployed. The afternoon culminates in an impulsive and perfunctory sexual episode. This encounter, which unfolds on a stair landing in Madeleine's home, is viewed from a distance and from a strangely skewed angle. It is remarkably lacking in passion or feeling, which is perhaps the point.

Events become even more complicated when Madeleine receives a visit from her estranged husband, Ben (Larry Pine), a wild-eyed, passive/aggressive type who takes great pleasure in attempting to explode her illusion about her new friendship. As it turns out, Ben has many lies of his own to tell: Although he has recently undergone open-heart surgery, and has the appropriate scars to prove it, he insists upon telling "Matthew" that these were caused by a crazed knife attack by Madeleine.

Once Ben appears, Oliver realizes that he has become entangled with an entire family whose sense of reality is deeply, even dangerously confused. As Madeleine and Ben continue to argue, Oliver rushes away from the scene, only to realize that he has left behind his winter coat—a highly significant item, one which, for a genuinely destitute person, represents not only warmth and safety but a crucial link with the "normal," civilized world. Oliver returns to Madeleine, and their peculiar encounter resumes in earnest.

Because it concerns a transitory, but highly-charged, romance, *Sunday* has been compared to David Lean's *Brief Encounter* (1946), but this comparison is slightly mistaken. *Sunday* actually has much more in common with Alfred Hitchcock's *Vertigo* (1958), a film that also turns on the notions of mistaken identity, the sometimes dangerous allure of role playing, and the difficulty of reconciling dull, everyday reality with a more romanticized view of the self. (In the scenes involving the men's shelter, there is even a minor character named "Scottie Elster," an amalgamation of character names from Hitchcock's famous film.) Madeleine Vesey may in fact be considered a direct cinematic descendant of another "Madeleine"—the Madeleine Elster/Judy Barton character played by Kim Novak in *Vertigo,* a woman whose willingness to assume another identity and discard her own, in order to fulfill the wishes of a man she barely knows, has strange and terrible consequences.

The central performances in *Sunday* are excellent. As Oliver, David Suchet offers a characterization which is worlds removed from his recurring role as Hercule Poirot in the British "Agatha Christie Mysteries" series. He is very well-matched by Lisa Harrow. She is not especially well-known to the American moviegoing public, but in *Sunday* she radiates an intellectual complexity, as well as a kind of

AWARDS AND NOMINATIONS

Independent Spirit Awards 1997 Nominations: Actress (Harrow), Cinematography
Sundance Film Festival 1997: Grand Jury Prize, Screenplay

world-weary, middle-aged sensuality, which ought to win her a wider audience in this country.

The film ends with the strong implication that, because of Ben's malicious game-playing, Madeleine is about to be confronted with irrefutable evidence of Oliver's "real" identity. But given her previous willingness to see only what she wants to see, it is by no means clear that this new material—an article about the real Matthew Delacorta from a recent issue of a major magazine—will do much to alter her view of Oliver, or cause her to rethink the imaginary role she has assigned to him.

Jonathan Nossiter's *Sunday* is an intellectually rich film. It succeeds best as a study of human communication gone completely and utterly wrong. No film in recent memory does a better job of depicting the very real psychological terror of the homeless and the unemployed, or the precipitous crash in self-esteem which comes with falling on hard times. Some viewers may be put off by *Sunday*'s rather detached style of observation—the film sometimes seems as cold and impersonal as an autopsy report—but it is never less than compelling. Although *Sunday* takes the viewer on a deeply disturbing psychological journey, it is an experience not to be missed.

—*Karl Michalak*

CREDITS

Oliver/Matthew: David Suchet
Madeleine Vesey: Lisa Harrow
Ben: Larry Pine
Ray: Jared Harris
Scottie Elster: Joe Grifasi
Andy: Arnold Barkus

Origin: USA
Released: 1996
Production: Jonathan Nossiter and Alix Madigan for Goatworks, Sunday Productions and Double A Films; released by Cinepix Film Properties
Direction: Jonathan Nossiter
Screenplay: Jonathan Nossiter and James Lasdun
Cinematography: Michael Barrow, John Foster, Daniel Lerner
Editing: Madeleine Gavin
Costumes: Kathryn Nixon
Music: Jonathan Nossiter
Sound: David Ellinwood
Art direction: Stephen Beatrice
Production design: Deana Sidney
MPAA rating: Unrated
Running Time: 93 minutes

REVIEWS

Boxoffice. July, 1997, p. 80.
Entertainment Weekly. August 22, 1997, p. 110.
Los Angeles Times. August 22, 1997, p. F16.
New York Times. April 4, 1997, p. B12.
The New Yorker. September 15, 1997, p. 94.
People. September 15, 1997, p. 27.
Rolling Stone. September 4, 1997, p. 76.
Variety. February 3, 1997, p. 42.
Village Voice. August 26, 1997, p. 84.

Supercop; Police Story 3: Supercop

After *First Strike* (1997) and *Rumble in the Bronx* (1995), Jackie Chan achieved a kind of comic cachet among camp action-adventure fans, so the quest was on to find more product from the Jackie Chan Hong Kong archives. *Supercop* is recycled Chan, originally released in 1992 as *Police Story III.* Jackie plays Detective Kevin Chan, known as Supercop of the Royal Hong Kong Police, sent to Mainland China on an undercover assignment while posing as Fu Sheng, a member of a football team. Jackie rescues a prisoner named Panther (Yuen Wah) from a prison compound work camp. After the prisoner takes Jackie to his gang and kills the stooge who betrayed him, he then offers Jackie $100,000 to go with him to Hong Kong to meet his Big Brother, Chaibat (Ken Tsang), a drug kingpin and a dangerous criminal.

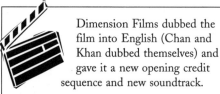

> Dimension Films dubbed the film into English (Chan and Khan dubbed themselves) and gave it a new opening credit sequence and new soundtrack.

On the way to Hong Kong, Jackie is taken to his "home," the village where he claims to come from, for a reunion with his undercover "family," but Chinese Chief of Security Yang (Michelle Khan), has anticipated this complication and sets up a false "family." She goes undercover herself by posing to be his sister, Hana, in this comic diversion. Arriving in Hong Kong, Chan is introduced to Chaibat and recruited at once on a mission to the Thai-Cambodian border, where Chaibat cuts a heroin deal with a corrupt Thai general (Law Lit) after a violent firefight in which Chaibat manages to kill all of his competitors.

The next mission takes them to Kuala Lumpur Prison in Malaysia, where Big Brother's wife, Madame Chaibat (Josephene Koo) is being held under a death sentence. Since she has the required codes for his husband's Swiss bank accounts, it is imperative that they rescue her. At the resort hotel in Kuala Lumpur where undercover Chan is staying with Panther and Chaibat's gang, he accidently runs into his girlfriend May (Maggie Cheung), who is there as a tour leader. He does his best to avoid her but finally has to explain that he is there on an undercover mission. May is relieved, but she foolishly shares this information with her girlfriend in a crowded elevator, and she is overheard by one of Chaibat's gangsters, who warns Panther.

As a result, Chaibat takes May hostage in order to force Chan to rescue Madame Chaibat after she has been sentenced to death. In order to rescue Madame Chaibat, Chan creates a diversion with a runaway truck, enabling him to take control of the armored truck that contains the prisoner. Chan then threatens to kill Madama Chaibat unless her husband, now in a helicopter circling overhead with May, releases her. After May is released in this prisoner exchange, Chan and Hana go quickly in pursuit in order to recapture the prisoner in a well orchestrated chase involving cars, motorcycles, trains, and the helicopter. When the helicopter lowers a ladder to the escaped prisoner to pluck Madame Chaibat off a rooftop, Jackie leaps to catch the tail end of the dangling ladder and attempts to follow her.

One goes to a Jackie Chan movie for the stunts and the outtakes edited into the final credits to demonstrate that Jackie performs his own dangerous stunts, not for the story, which is flimsy and episodic. Chan's earlier Hong Kong movies were directed by John Woo, who has now gone Hollywood. *Supercop* was directed by former Hong Kong stuntman Stanley Tong, who also directed *Rumble in the Bronx* (1995) and *First Strike: Police Story IV* (1997). Tong, born in Hong Kong, worked as a stunt-double for the Shaw Brothers, then, after multiple fractures, established his own film company, Golden Gate, in 1989.

Born in Hong Kong in 1954 and famous for his impressive comic stuntwork, Jackie Chan has appeared in over 40 films and is not only a supercop, but an international superstar in Hong Kong, where he had been featured in nine of the top ten all-time highest grossing films. His first starring role was in *A Stranger in Hong Kong* (1974). He went on to become the most popular kung fu star since Bruce Lee.

Jackie Chan proves why he is a *Supercop* as he performs his martial arts skills.

In *Supercop* Chan's co-star Michelle Khan (a.k.a. Michelle Yeoh), in the words of one reviewer, "seems every bit his equal when it comes to martial-arts prowess and fool-

CREDITS

Detective Kevin Chan/Fu Sheng: Jackie Chan
Director Yang/Hana: Michelle (Yeoh) Khan
May: Maggie Cheung
Chaibat/Big Brother: Ken Tsang
Panther: Yeun Wah
Madame Chaibat: Josephine Koo

Origin: Hong Kong
Released: 1992, 1996
Production: Willie Chan and Edward Tang for Golden Harvest Productions; released by Dimension Films
Direction: Stanley Tong
Screenplay: Edward Tang, Fibe Ma, and Lee Wai Yee
Cinematography: Ardy Lam
Editing: Cheung Yu Chung, Cheung Kar Fei
Music: Joel McNeely
Production design: Wong Yue Man
MPAA rating: R
Running Time: 93 minutes

hardy daredevilry." Born Yeo Choo Kheng in Ipoh, Malaysia, and later trained in ballet at the Royal Academy of Dance in London, she was crowned Miss Malaysia in 1983 before going to Hong Kong to work in a television commercial with Jackie Chan. Maggie Cheung, one of Asia's most popular stars and the winner of the Hong Kong Film Award for Best Actress, has appeared regularly as Jackie Chan's girlfriend in the Police Story series.

Reviewing the film for the *New York Times*, Lawrence van Gelder defined it as a "moving comic book" about which only one question should be asked: "Once the action begins to accelerate, how's the ride?" The answer for van Gelder was "dumb but delightful." The stunts also accelerate from Panther's escape from prison by way of a high-wire cable line spanning a valley far below to the Golden Triangle opium-war shoot-out to the final chase in which Jackie leaps from a ten-story building to a rope ladder dangling from a helicopter that has rescued Madame Chaibat, then is dragged aloft and crashed through a billboard. The film excels in harebrained derring-do. The film is dubbed, "and wonderfully badly," in the words of one reviewer, but in fact the wretched dubbing only enhances the movie's camp charm, since in any Jackie Chan feature, actions speak much louder than words.

—*James M. Welsh*

REVIEWS

Entertainment Weekly. August 2, 1996.
The New York Times. July 26, 1996, p. C8.
San Francisco Chronicle. July 26, 1996, p. D1.
The Washington Post. July 26, 1996, p. D6.

The Sweet Hereafter

There is no such thing as the simple truth.—Movie tagline

"*The Sweet Hereafter* is hypnotic and jolting. It has integrity that few films even try for, let alone match."—Jay Carr, *Boston Globe*

"*The Sweet Hereafter* is a brilliant powerhouse full of searing images and performances."—Michael Wilmington, *Chicago Tribune*

"*The Sweet Hereafter* is spellbinding!"—Owen Gleiberman, *Entertainment Weekly*

"Astonishing! The best film of this year, or any year."—Karen Durbin, *Mirabella*

"*The Sweet Hereafter* is a powerful, emotionally charged work."—Thelma Adams, *New York Post*

"*The Sweet Hereafter* is an exhilarating and eloquent film."—Janet Maslin, *New York Times*

"Resonant and tender. Indelibly stamped with soul & style."—John Anderson, *Newsday*

"*The Sweet Hereafter* is mesmerizing. Ian Holm is superb!"—David Ansen, *Newsweek*

"A luminous masterpiece."—Harlan Jacobson, *USA Today*

"Egoyan has made a smolderingly personal adaptation of Russell Banks' novel."—Georgia Brown, *Village Voice*

Box Office: $1,540,443

Adapted from Russell Banks's highly acclaimed novel, Atom Egoyan's *The Sweet Hereafter* centers around the small town of Sam Dent, British Columbia—a community facing the aftermath of a school-bus accident that wiped out many of its children. It is a haunting film in which the accident is the catalyst for a larger meditation on the splintering of community, the loss of children, and the ways in which people cope with the unexplained tragedies of life. The novel employs four narrators who tell us how the accident has affected them, and these characters form the core of the film: Dolores Driscoll (Gabrielle Rose), the bus driver; Billy Ansel (Bruce Greenwood), a widower who lost two children; Mitchell Stephens (Ian Holm), a big-city lawyer who comes to town to file a negligence suit; and Nicole Burnell (Sarah Polley), a teenager who survives the accident but can no longer walk. The movie beautifully explores the overarching themes of loss and recovery and shows how some lives can be redeemed in the most unexpected way.

The main narrative thread involves Stephens's investigation of the accident and his attempt to get the townspeople to sign on for a negligence suit. As he probes into the events of the fateful day, we seem to be in a detective yarn or maybe a legal thriller; then, as we learn of the town's secrets, including Billy's adulterous affair with Risa Walker (Alberta Watson) and Nicole's incestuous relationship with her father, Sam (Tom McCamus), the movie looks like a melodrama like *Peyton Place* or TV's "Twin Peaks". However, *The Sweet Hereafter* ultimately eschews traditional narrative for an exploration of character. How do different people respond to tragedy and try to make sense of it?

> Mitchell: "I can help you."
> Billy: "Not unless you can raise the dead."

A secondary narrative strand concerns the tragedy of Stephens's daughter, Zoe (Caerthan Banks, the author's daughter), who has been addicted to drugs for years and is constantly calling him for help. In the latest of the film's many time frames, Stephens is flying on an airplane, talking to a woman named Allison (Stephanie Morgenstern), a girlhood friend of Zoe, and revealing all the struggles he has undergone with his daughter. In one sense, Allison is simply a device, a sounding board for Mitchell to say the things that he narrates in his portion of the novel. However, because Allison is the daughter of Mitchell's former partner and now works with her father, she is in a way a surrogate daughter—the ideal child who was not lost and maybe the daughter Mitchell wishes he had.

The movie employs a free-floating time structure in which various time frames, both pre- and post-accident, alternate. The movie does not make an issue of where we are in time—only once is it made explicit for us—and yet the film, while challenging, is not hard to follow. Sometimes we move back in time because someone is telling a story. At other times, we move to an event without any narrative motivation; the movie simply connects scenes that follow a certain mood or theme.

One complex example of cutting across time occurs with the presentation of the accident itself in the middle of the film. We see the bus go off the road and moments later simply fall through the partially frozen ice as Billy Ansel, who had been following the bus, watches helplessly. The film then cuts to a family in bed (also seen in the opening credits but now identified as a young Stephens, his wife, and three-year-old Zoe) and Stephens telling Allison about the time Zoe nearly died—Mitchell and his wife had to rush her to the hospital while he had to be ready to perform an emergency tracheotomy should Zoe stop breathing. It is a harrowing story that produces an indelible image of the little girl in Mitchell's lap and the knife beside her ready to be plunged in at any moment. We then cut back to the immediate aftermath of the accident as Billy Ansel looks on, presumably at the bodies of his children. Using the bus accident to frame Stephens's story is a brilliant move because both are stories of the unexpected dangers that can befall a child—a nest of baby black widow spiders or a wayward bus. While Mitchell does not have to use the knife and Zoe survives, we know she is not a survivor in the long run—she is a lost child like those on the bus.

Ian Holm's Stephens is a complex character. When he interviews the parents of the dead children, he seems to empathize with their suffering, and yet he also exhibits the worst traits of an ambulance chaser. "Judges like adopted Indian boys," he declares when he learns the identity of one of the victims. At the same time, he is a wounded father, and his mission seems at least in part motivated by his desire to avenge the loss of his daughter. "We've all lost our children. They're dead to us," he mournfully states in a line that sums up the burden he carries. Ian Holm shows us the torment Mitchell is feeling for his daughter's condition even while working his cunning skills on the bereaved families. "Let me direct your rage," he tells Billy in one of many lines that seem both genuine and yet calculated.

Billy Ansel does not respond to Stephens's persuasion. He rejects the lawsuit because he does not feel the need to assign blame where no one is apparently blameworthy. He tries in vain to get Nicole's father, Sam, to drop the lawsuit by evoking a time when the people of the community helped each other instead of retaining lawyers to wage court battles. Despite his adulterous affair with Risa, Billy becomes the conscience of the town, and finally Nicole becomes its voice.

One of the key additions from novel to film is the brilliant use of Robert Browning's poem, "The Pied Piper of Hamelin." In the poem, the pied piper leads away the rats that are infesting Hamelin, but, when he is not paid, he gets revenge by leading away the town's children. A lame child is left behind, and this child becomes identified with Nicole. On the night before the accident, Nicole reads the poem aloud to Billy's children as a bedtime story, but her voice-over of parts of the poem is subsequently employed at key moments in the film and gives certain scenes an eerie, almost fairy tale-like quality. However, the poem does not become a heavy-handed metaphor. Rather, it fits the general theme of the loss of children but is open to interpretation. When Sam leads Nicole into a barn to make love, he is the piper, as is Mitchell when he is trying to lead the town in

AWARDS AND NOMINATIONS

Academy Awards 1997 Nominations: Director (Egoyan), Adapted Screenplay
Genie Awards 1997: Best Film, Director (Egoyan), Actor (Holm), Cinematography, Editing, Sound, Sound Editing, Original Score
Independent Spirit Awards 1997: Foreign Film

his proposed lawsuit. At the climax of the film, though, Nicole becomes the piper.

When Nicole is deposed by the opposing attorney, she claims the bus was going 72 miles per hour—a lie that ends the possibility of a lawsuit. She is in essence rejecting her father, putting an end to their illicit relationship, and thus reclaiming her right to childhood. She also is saving the town from the further trauma that numerous lawsuits would bring. Most interestingly, when she speaks her lines suggesting her lie was a punishment of her father, they are in the rhythm of the poem, as if she were rewriting Browning's work or at least adding her voice to it and leading the town to a place where, in the poem, "everything was strange and new"—the last spoken words of the film. Sarah Polley's performance is excellent in its subtlety, its understated directness, especially in this climactic scene, in which Nicole's chance at redemption merges with the future of the town.

Russell Banks' novel was inspired by accounts of a real-life school bus accident in south Texas in the late 1980s.

Perhaps the most important change from novel to film is a subtle shift in emphasis from Dolores to Nicole. Dolores opens and closes the novel; we see the accident from her point of view and finally the ramifications of Nicole's lie on her life. The novel ends at the county fair's demolition derby, where Dolores's former car is entered and where she learns of the lie the town believes. The crowd goes from rooting against her car to rooting for her car in the derby, and she has the epiphany that it does not really matter, that people will project onto her what they need to. In the film, all of this is lost—we last see Dolores at her new job driving a hotel shuttle. She has lost her old job and community, but we can only imagine how this has affected her. Interestingly enough, the titular notion of "the sweet hereafter"—what the film's press kit defines as "a realm reserved for those who are at peace with their fate"—is transferred from Dolores in the novel to Nicole in the movie, where it is incorporated into her last "Pied Piper" voice-over. This illustrates the transfer of sympathy from Dolores to Nicole—Nicole has found this state of peace, but Dolores's future is less certain.

The Sweet Hereafter beautifully examines how lives torn apart can somehow be redeemed, how people like Billy and Nicole can find, however uneasily, a state of grace, whereas a figure like Mitchell goes searching in vain for solutions he may never find. It was one of the best films of 1997, and this was reflected in the glowing reviews it received. In his *Los Angeles Times* review, Kenneth Turan called it an "exquisite and overwhelming emotional tapestry" and later declared it the best film of the year, as did Stephen Holden of *The New York Times*. *The Sweet Hereafter* is a rare film in which all of the elements work together. The performances are excellent, the cinematography of the snow-covered town both beautiful and frightening, the editing innovative, and the music, anchored by Sarah Polley's gorgeous soprano on several beautiful songs, a stunning final touch.

—*Peter N. Chumo II*

CREDITS

Mitchell Stephens: Ian Holm
Nicole Burnell: Sarah Polley
Billy Ansell: Bruce Greenwood
Sam Burnell: Tom McCamus
Risa Walker: Alberta Watson
Dolores Driscoll: Gabrielle Rose
Wanda Otto: Arisnee Khanjian
Wendell Walker: Maury Chaykin
Zoe: Caerthan Banks

Origin: Canada
Released: 1997
Production: Atom Egoyan and Camelia Frieberg for Ego Film Arts and Alliance Communications; released by Fine Line Films
Direction: Atom Egoyan
Screenplay: Atom Egoyan; based on the novel by Russell Banks
Cinematography: Paul Sarossy
Editing: Susan Shipton
Music: Mychael Danna
Production design: Phillip Barker
Sound: Steve Munro
Costumes: Beth Pasternak
MPAA rating: R
Running Time: 110 minutes

REVIEWS

Boxoffice. August, 1997, p. 45.
Entertainment Weekly. November 28, 1997, p. 56.
Hollywood Reporter. May 16, 1997, p. 10.
New York Times. October 3, 1997, p. E13.
New Yorker. November 24, 1997, p. 137.
Rolling Stone. December 11, 1997, p. 85.
Sight and Sound. October, 1997, p. 60.
Time. December 1, 1997.
USA Today. November 21, 1997, p. 9D.
Variety. May 19, 1997, p. 54.
Village Voice. November 25, 1997, p. 91.
Village Voice. December 9, 1997,p. 74.

SwitchBack

The hunter is tracking the killer. But the killer is setting the trap.—Movie tagline

"A pulse-pounding keep-you-guessing thrill ride!"—Mason Woods, *CBS-TV*

"A cat and mouse game that will have you guessing. An action thriller, with a powerful touch of mystery and suspense."—Jim Ferguson, *Prevue Channel*

Box Office: $6,504,442

Danny Glover gives an intriguing, against-the-grain performance in *SwitchBack*, a meandering, predictable movie about a serial killer. Glover's Bob Goodall, an ingratiating, seemingly trustworthy drifter with a yen for thrills and a few other quirks, brings life to a script that otherwise would be dead on arrival. Screenwriter Jeb Stuart, who conquered the action-movie genre with *Die Hard* (1988) and *The Fugitive* (1993), falls flat on his face here in his first directorial effort, trundling out a mess of an old script from his school days.

SwitchBack covers up for a lack of real tension and intrigue with a bloated cast of characters, most of whom are unnecessary. The central tension, between the mysterious killer and his dogged pursuer, FBI agent Frank LaCrosse (Dennis Quaid), is not fully fleshed out. And Quaid doesn't help matters with a stony-faced, underplayed performance that is practically lifeless.

So many films have been made about serial killers that screenwriters no longer feel required to explain the rationale behind their acts. That's part of the trouble here. LaCrosse reveals that this killer acts out of a thirst for power and publicity—so what's new? The murderer also ups the ante whenever he is actively pursued, for reasons never made clear. LaCrosse headed an FBI investigation that seemed to exacerbate the killer's bloodlust. Then, just as the feds were closing in on him, the killer murdered LaCrosse's baby-sitter and kidnapped his two-year-old son, then mysteriously stopped killing for several months.

Unlike serial killers with complicated psychological profiles, *SwitchBack*'s villain is generic; he's saved from being completely colorless only by Glover's personality. Beyond his yen for fame, which almost all film serial killers possess, no explanation is ever offered for his rampage. He's a guy who seems to have a lot of friends and have done a lot of good deeds, and his turn to violence is an implausible mystery. We also never find out why he kills by slashing his victims' femoral artery with a knife. If you don't fall asleep in a key scene early in the film, you'll identify the killer by this trademark method, yet Stuart for the next hour keeps manufacturing lame red herrings.

Viewers can figure out what's going on long before the cops in the film catch on. Stuart gives everything away early on. You see the baby-sitter/killer's face in the opening scene, but it's soon clear he's not the real killer. Suspicion comes to focus on Glover's character, Goodall, and a young hitchhiker, Lane Dixon (Jared Leto). Dixon is initially repelled by Goodall because he drives a Cadillac upholstered with pinup photos. But Goodall rescues him from a barroom brawl and later again proves his worth by saving him from falling off a mountain. Leto is poster-boy handsome, blue-eyed and genteel, and his character is a doctor who's abandoned his profession after one of his patients dies. It's not hard to figure out who's the killer.

Stuart clutters up the first half of the film with a subplot about a political rivalry between straight-arrow, small-town Texas Sheriff Buck Olmstead (R. Lee Ermey) and his oily electoral rival, Amarillo police chief Jack McGinnis (William Fichtner). The killer, inexplicably, has struck again in a motel room in Olmstead's jurisdiction on the eve of the election. When a man with a knife and a car linked to the motel killing shows up in an Amarillo hostage situation, McGinnis thinks he's found the killer, but LaCrosse knows better.

The politics offers nothing to the plot but distraction. LaCrosse slowly unburdens himself to Olmstead, who then protects him from his FBI superiors who want him off the case. LaCrosse warns McGinnis not to announce he's found the killer because that will set off the real killer. McGinnis wants to win the election so badly he doesn't care about that. Olmstead sacrifices his career to protect LaCrosse from his FBI superiors and keep him on his case.

The theme of *SwitchBack* is about trust and honesty among "real," uncorrupted men. Olmstead and LaCrosse form a bond because they are selfless and dedicated to the truth. Their rivals and superiors are corrupt, selfish and ruthless. In a parallel fashion, Goodall and Leto also engage throughout the film is a testing of each other's mettle and confidence. Leto earns Goodall's respect by performing a counter-top tracheotomy on a customer in a diner who is choking to death.

Set in the Texas plains and the Rockies, *SwitchBack* is really an updated Western. Its main characters all show they are willing to sacrifice anything—their career, even their life—for truth and friendship. The catch is that one of the four characters is a serial killer. But that hardly seems to matter in this homage to traditional male values. In fact, as

LaCrosse says at the end of the villain: "He was a killer, but he wasn't a liar." And the killer does prove as good as his word.

SwitchBack has one of those familiar plots where the cops and the criminals have a grudging admiration for each other's expertise, creativity and persistence. They are equally virtuous, equally loyal, equally devoted to the truth, and their battle is a kind of blood sport. This is why the killer has no marked psychological quirks, because he's morally akin to the other three men.

Stuart is trodding on dangerous territory. On the one hand it's terrifying to suppose that a serial killer is just like the rest of us. But the concept also trivializes the killing itself. Viewers need villains to be distinguishable from the good guys. And even when the killer looks and acts the same as the rest of us, at least by the end of the film we need to understand why he's not, what went wrong inside him to set him off the wrong path. There's absolutely no hint of that in *SwitchBack*.

Morally, the film makes no sense. If there is merit in being honest, generous and loyal, then how can someone who embodies all those characteristics secretly be a ruthless killer who at heart betrays all the principles he seems to embody? The killer here plays a role akin to those legendary Western outlaws, yet he is no modern Robin Hood and populist hero, but a totally gratuitous murderer.

Other than LaCrosse's kidnapped son, there is disturbingly little attention paid to the killer's victims. They are generic, random, faceless people, except for the babysitter and a store owner who has a bit part late in the film. The killer doesn't seem to select any particular type of victim, but simply slices whomever is convenient and accessible. The killing is merely an excuse for the game he's playing with the cops. The absence of motive and empathy makes the film vacuous.

Besides the performance of Glover, who pulls off the film's most demanding role with almost effortless grace, there is little to recommend in *SwitchBack*. Even Stuart's knack for high-octane action comes only in spurts. Almost all the tension in the film is telegraphed in advance by Basil Poledouris's formulaic score. And most of the action seems contrived. Not once, but twice, do main characters plunge off snow-covered mountain roads and miraculously survive. The mountain setting and the railroad motif that dominate the last half of the film also seem arbitrary. The killer is luring his pursuer there, but apparently for no particular reason than to facilitate the fight-aboard-a-speeding-train sequences. Throughout the film LaCrosse puzzles over a cryptic message from the killer. It turns out to refer to nothing but a railroad stop.

Stuart has capitalized on his success by making a film that is lazy and illogical. Stuart reveals key plot points, in pedestrian fashion, long after viewers have already grasped them. Despite the suggestion of the film's title, there are no surprising twists and turns in the film, which lurches ahead like a freight train to its inevitable destination. In style and manner, *SwitchBack* keeps suggesting there must be something more to its characters and the plot, some revelation that will explain the killer's motivation. But there's nothing except that well-executed but predictable fight on the train. By then, viewers have been taken for a long ride that leads absolutely nowhere.

—*Michael Betzold*

CREDITS

Frank LaCrosse: Dennis Quaid
Bob Goodall: Danny Glover
Lane Dixon: Jared Leto
Sheriff Buck Olmstead: R. Lee Ermey
Dep. Nate Booker: Ted Levine
Chief Jack McGinnis: William Fichtner
Shorty: Leo Burmester

Origin: USA
Released: 1997
Production: Gale Ann Hurd for Pacific Western and Rysher Entertainment; released by Paramount Pictures
Direction: Jeb Stuart
Screenplay: Jeb Stuart
Cinematography: Oliver Wood
Editing: Conrad Buff
Music: Basil Poledouris
Production design: Jeff Howard
Art direction: Carl Stensel
Costumes: Betsy Heiman
Sound: David Kelson
Stunt coordinator: Gary Hymes
MPAA rating: R
Running Time: 118 minutes

REVIEWS

Boxoffice. January, 1998, p. 48.
Entertainment Weekly. November 14, 1997, p. 62.
The Hollywood Reporter. October 28, 1997, p. 20.
Los Angeles Times. October 31, 1997, p. F12.
New York Times. October 31, 1997, p. E20.
People. November 10, 1997, p. 23.
USA Today. October 31, 1997, p. 4D.
Variety. October 27, 1997, p. 42.
Village Voice. November 4, 1997, p. 84.

The Tango Lesson

"What a breath of fresh air! Women unite and go see *The Tango Lesson*!"—Donna Gianell, *Dance and the Arts*

"An edge-of-your-seat dance fest! Pablo Veron has the feet of a god!"—Brandon Judell, *Detour*

"Unfolds with the silent grace of a dream!"—Ray Pride, *New City*

"Astonishing! This is a wonderful film! One of those magical and completely unexpected experiences that renews your faith in the movies. The music is fabulous too!"—Roger Ebert, *Siskel & Ebert*

"Provocative and passionate entertainment!"—Paul Wunder, *WBAI Radio*

With her first effort in over four years, the obscure yet infinitely talented English writer/director Sally Potter (*Orlando*, 1993) has created an ethereal potpourri that literally defies categorization. It is shot in clearly defined, striking black and white that recalls European efforts from the late '40s and early '50s which lend it a lyrical, romantic nuance. Bits and pieces of vibrant color footage are tossed in at various points and initially create confusion and appear out of place, but in retrospect, make complete sense. Potter has made a film that looks like a dream and has the lingering effects of one. It is a crafty and subtle work that will confuse many and hypnotize others. Love it or hate it, it's hard to dispute its originality and nerve.

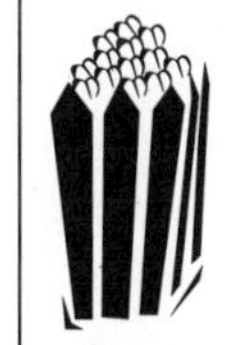

Pablo to Sally during rehearsal: "You're doing it alone; wait for me!"

Potter plays a character named Sally who, for all intents and purposes, is Potter herself. We see that she is a screenwriter who is suffering from either writer's block or has grown dissatisfied with her current work-in-progress. Between several fits and starts, the aforementioned color shots are injected to show her artistic vision; a murder/mystery film about the fashion industry entitled *Rage*.

Conceding that she is making little progress, Sally travels to Paris for a break. After watching Pablo Veron (as himself) give a performance of the Tango, she becomes obsessed with learning it and asks Pablo to teach her. Sally presents Pablo with a *quid pro quo* proposition: if he's successful in his instructional tasks, she will let him star in her next film. Their professional and personal lives wind up intersecting, as their arrangement soon blossoms into a romance. As is often the case in romances with two A-type personalities, the inevitable power struggle surfaces. Potter makes a sly acknowledgment of this through dance. Sally and Pablo begin feuding, ostensibly because their timing is off. In reality, she is trying to dance the lead. Obviously, two people cannot lead at once and Potter resolves the problem with a compromise. Whether intended or not, Potter's film is an allegory for relationships. People need to not only hear, but to *listen* and anticipate their partner's wants and needs. At various points, it's also apparent that Sally and Pablo are involved in this arrangement solely for their own benefit and are using each other as a simple means to an end. Potter volleys the onus of guilt back and forth, never making a final judgment or declaring a clear winner, loser or user. Issues of respect, responsibility, humility, and love become blurred. Sally and Pablo eventually forget their peripheral interests and realize that the survival and success of their partnership is of paramount importance. The needs of the collective body outweigh those of the individual.

In addition to his understated turn as the romantic lead, Veron also serves as the film's choreographer. Veron flirts with well over a half dozen different styles and tempos, often solo, and is a marvel to watch. He seems to be a fan of modern ballet; while borrowing the grace and fluidity of a Mikhail Baryshnikov or Rudolf Nureyev, he has removed some of the reserved, often stoic air of the classic demonstrative art form and injected it with playful humor. He also gives a respectful nod to America with tap and ballroom by pulling off some steps that could

CREDITS

Sally: Sally Potter
Pablo: Pablo Veron

Origin: Great Britain
Released: 1997
Production: Christopher Sheppard for Adventure Pictures; released by Sony Pictures Classics
Direction: Sally Potter
Screenplay: Sally Potter
Cinematography: Robby Muller
Editing: Herve Schneid
Production design: Carlos Conti
Costumes: Paul Minter
Sound: Jean-Paul Mugel, Gerard Hardy
Choreography: Pablo Veron
MPAA rating: PG
Running Time: 101 minutes

challenge the likes of Gregory Hines and Gene Kelly (he even includes a small homage to *Singin' in the Rain*, 1952).

The Tango Lesson is also something of a return to Potter's roots. In the 1970s, she was trained as a dancer at the London School Of Contemporary Dance before embarking on her film career. Perhaps she has stumbled on a cure for writer's block. If you find yourself pushing too hard or trying to a force a piece that doesn't feel natural, go back to the beginning. Don't overthink it and it will come back to you.

While female directors are becoming more commonplace in modern cinema, Potter has pushed the boundaries even further by not only writing this piece, but by also being perhaps the first female (save for Ida Lupino) who has directed herself in a feature. For this project, Potter assembled the soundtrack, co-wrote five of the instrumental pieces and sings the film's closing track. Where many before her have tried and (mostly) failed to mesh life with art, Potter has done so with an original, unerring grace.

—J.M. Clark

REVIEWS

Boxoffice. November, 1997, p. 120.
Chicago Tribune. December 21, 1997, p. 6.
Entertainment Weekly. November 28, 1997, p. 58.
New York Times. November 14, 1997, p. E19.
Sight and Sound. December, 1997, p. 54.
Variety. September 8, 1997, p. 78.
Washington Post. December 25, 1997, p. C14.

Telling Lies in America

Dress sharp. Drive fast. Look cool. Laugh last.—Movie tagline

Just don't get caught.—Movie tagline

"Real and touching."—Kenneth Turan, *Los Angeles Times*

"Loaded with heart! Mr. Bacon's role as Billy Magic is one of the juiciest of his career."—Stephen Holden, *New York Times*

"A surprise! Played to perfection by Kevin Bacon and sensitively directed by Guy Ferland. Eszterhas brings a fresh, immigrant's-eye perspective to his tale."—David Ansen, *Newsweek*

"Bacon is brilliant."—Peter Stack, *San Francisco Chronicle*

"Bacon is dazzling."—John Hartl, *Seattle Times*

"I loved this movie!"—Roger Ebert, *Siskel & Ebert*

"Touching, absorbing and wonderfully acted."—Jeffrey Lyons, *WNBC-TV*

Telling Lies in America is a wonderfully told fable, concentrating on a very specific time and place, illuminating one immigrant teenager's experiences in Cleveland, Ohio in the early 1960s. Written by Joe Eszterhas, better known for violence and sex-filled films such as *Basic Instinct* (1992), *Showgirls* (1995) and Jagged Edge (1985), *Lies* travels terrain that is somewhat cliched, but ultimately works, due to the heartfelt performances by the three leads.

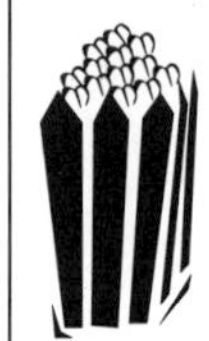

Billy to Karchy: "You lie real good, kid. Stick around."

Karchy Jonas (Brad Renfro) is a 17-year-old Hungarian immigrant who lives with his father Dr. Istvan Jonas (Maximilian Schell). They are both struggling to acclimate themselves to American life and both also miss Karchy's mother (who passed away a few years before in a work camp in Europe). Karchy suffers from the desire to impress people and win friends, but he is stymied by the fact that he and his father are poor (he attends his tony Catholic school on scholarship) and that he cannot lose his European accent (he is unable to master the "th" sound). He especially tries to impress Diney (Calista Flockhart of TV's "Ally McBeal"), a slightly older girl with whom he works after school, but she gravitates more towards her American boyfriend who is older and has a car.

Change steps into Karchy's life in the form of Billy Magic (Kevin Bacon). Magic is a flashy, sharkskin-suited Disc Jockey for a local AM station who regularly awards local high schoolers with token awards. When Karchy manages to get Magic's attention, his bravado and bluster lead the DJ to hire him as his assistant. Karchy will get to drive Magic's shiny red Cadillac, juggle the phone calls from the DJ's various girlfriends, and receive and deliver mysterious envelopes for Magic.

Thus begins a relationship that will shape and define Karchy, his view of America and finally, his view of himself. At first, Karchy cannot believe his luck. He sees Billy Magic as the embodiment of all good things that America has to offer—money, women, and power. He ignores the pleas of his father and Father Norton (Paul Dooley) to shape up and take school seriously. The presence of Billy in Karchy's life only serves to exaggerate his most misguided instincts. He manages to woo Diney out on a date, where he spikes her drink with "Spanish fly"—only to see her get deathly ill. Seeing his slavish devotion to her only dissipates her anger.

Kevin Bacon and Brad Renfro also worked together on *Sleepers* (1996).

Soon, Karchy finds out that all that glitters is not gold about Magic. He is dismayed to learn that a very affectionate woman with whom he lost his virginity was, in fact, a hooker hired by Magic. He is shocked when the police come to investigate Magic about mysterious "payoffs" regarding certain artists and the frequency with which their songs are played. And Magic himself turns off Karchy when he confesses that he is twice divorced, barely makes his alimony and child care payments and doesn't own a thing—not a car or a house. Magic's own self-deprecation sends Karchy reeling.

Director Guy Ferland infuses the best parts of this picture—the core stories of the feeling of being an outsider, the yearning to belong, and the realization of one's own code of right and wrong—with a firm hand. Although some of the situations border on cliché, the actors carry on with aplomb.

Karchy finds himself at a moral crossroads that most 17-year-olds couldn't fathom, much less handle: when the police begin to question him about his "activities" with Magic, Karchy realizes that his job has been primarily to be the buffer and "mule" between Magic and any illegal actions. His eager enthusiasm has been exploited and it is up to Karchy to clear his own name and turn Magic in, or continue to support him and cover up for him. In a climax that (almost too) neatly ties up all the elements that he has been struggling with, Karchy breaks free of Magic's hold on his psyche, says good-bye to his crush on Diney and realizes the strength of his father. Eszterhas has created a deceptively simple situation that illustrates right and wrong, and woven it into a rich tapestry of his youth in the 1960s.

—*G.E. Georges*

CREDITS

Billy Magic: Kevin Bacon
Karchy Jonas: Brad Renfro
Dr. Istvan Jonas: Maximilian Schell
Diney Majeski: Calista Flockhart
Father Norton: Paul Dooley
Kevin Boyle: Jonathan Rhys Meyers
Henry: Luke Wilson

Origin: USA
Released: 1997
Production: Ben Myron and Fran Rubel Kuzui; released by Banner Entertainment
Direction: Guy Ferland
Screenplay: Joe Eszterhas
Cinematography: Reynaldo Villalobos
Editing: Jill Savitt
Costumes: Laura Cunningham
Production design: James A. Gelarden
Set design: Thomas Paul
Music: Nicholas Pike
Sound: Jonathan Andrews
MPAA rating: R
Running Time: 101 minutes

REVIEWS

Chicago Tribune. October 24, 1997, p. 5.
Detroit News. November 7, 1997, p. 5F.
Entertainment Weekly. November 7, 1997, p. 60.
Los Angeles Times. October 24, 1997, p. F12.
New York Times. October 9, 1997, p. E5.
New York Times. October 12, 1997, p. 24.
People. October 27, 1997, p. 19.
Variety. September 15, 1997, p. 78.
Village Voice. October 21, 1997, p. 94.

Temptress Moon; Feng Yue

Behind closed doors . . . a world of forbidden desire.—Movie tagline

A brilliant criminal specializing in blackmail is about to seduce China's most powerful woman.—Movie tagline

What the heart hides, the moon reveals.—Movie tagline

"One of the most sensuous love stories you'll ever see!"—Howard Feinstein, *New York Post*

"Beautiful and sensuous! A Chinese *Gone With the Wind*!"—Stephen Holden, *New York Times*

"A ravishing tale of decadence!"—David Ansen, *Newsweek*

"Mesmerizing."—Richard Corliss, *Time*

"Enthralling."—Geoff Andrew, *Time Out*

Box Office: $1,117,181

CREDITS

Yu Zhongliang: Leslie Cheung
Pang Ruyi: Gong Li
Pang Duanwu: Kevin Li
Yu Xiuyi: He Saifei

Origin: Hong Kong
Released: 1996
Production: Tong Cunlin and Hsu Feng for Tomson Films Co. and Shanghai Film Studio; released by Miramax Films
Direction: Chen Kaige
Screenplay: Shu Kei
Cinematography: Christopher Doyle
Editing: Pei Xiao-nan
Music: Zhgao Jiping
Art direction: Huang Qiagui
Costumes: William Chang, Chen Changmin
Sound: Lai Qizhen
MPAA rating: R
Running Time: 115 minutes

"In Shanghai, men and women are at war. One side will win; one side will lose." This is the predominant theme of Chen Kiage's lush but ultimately rather unsatisfying film, *Temptress Moon*. Kiage, best known for the wonderful *Farewell, My Concubine* (1993), once again shows his interest in the changes brought to China after the Revolution in the early part of the 20th century. Like many Chinese filmmakers, Kiage uses personal relationships to symbolize the volcanic changes in his country. As a history, *Temptress Moon* doesn't serve particularly well, however, because it is more potboiler than epic saga: the symbolism and history take a backseat to the melodramatic story.

Miramax had director Chen Kaige cut some 15 minutes from the original release and resubtitled the film.

In 1911, Zhongliang, a young boy, is orphaned and joins his older sister and her wealthy husband on his family estate. Almost immediately, Zhongliang becomes a servant to his sister and brother-in-law, both of whom are opium addicts. Director Kiage takes the audience through some rather confusing moments during this early part of the story: the gist of it is that something horrible happens and Zhongliang has to leave the Pang Estate. The story then jumps ten years and Zhongliang (Kevin Lin) is a cardsharp and gangster in Shanghai, a city greatly influenced by Western culture, most specifically by opium trade.

The plot mostly turns on Zhongliang's return to the Pang Estate to take money from the young cousin now ruling it, Ruyi (Gong Li). In the course of the story, Zhongliang faces his inner demons and resolves the horrible events of the past as he falls in love with Ruyi and returns to Shanghai.

Much of *Temptress Moon* plays like a Chekhov play. There are distracted and bored characters frightened by the future and by changing cultural values. They are fearful and uncertain about tomorrow, falling into foolish schemes and love triangles in vain attempts to hide their pain and fear. An important distinction between this story and, say *Three Sisters*, is that *Temptress Moon* feels less like a commentary on human nature than a very well lit "Movie-of-the-Week," Chinese style. Perhaps that is harsh, but Chen Kiage is up to the task of doing better. Perplexing, for example, is Kiage's use of corny music every time we see the beautiful Ruyi. Another example is his off-putting use of intermittent stares from principal actors directly into the camera.

Still, he chooses some fine camera work, particularly in the numerous love scenes, and a vivid and well-chosen use of slow-motion for a near-rape scene. The still waters surrounding the Pang family estate are lit beautifully and shot with sensitive detail by cinematographer Christopher Doyle. Kiage is quite adept at providing exciting crowd scenes, as shown by a fine scene portraying young Zhongliang's escape from the Pang family home by train.

Gong Li is as gorgeous as ever, but doesn't have a chance to show her range. Mostly called upon to look love-starved and cry a lot, the character of Ruyi doesn't seem to change as much onscreen as the story seems to indicate. There might be more harshness to Ruyi after her painful encounters with Zhongliang than Gong Li and Kiage have allowed her. But with all the beautiful music surrounding her each time she is photographed, it is hard to think of anything other than sweetness about a character that emotionally endures much more than that.

Kevin Lin is excellent and up to the task of displaying Zhongliang's descent and redemption. His is the most well-rounded role, and Lin keenly shows the pain behind the steely eyes of his cardsharp. Never once do we as an audience believe him when he says he doesn't care about love, and that is just as it should be.

The Moon remains ever-glowing and luminous in this picture as well, filmed beautifully by Kiage, but just like the film, rather ill-defined as to why it is there.

—Kirby Tepper

REVIEWS

Boxoffice. May, 1997, p. 58.
Detroit News. June 20, 1997, p. 2D.
Entertainment Weekly. June 27, 1997, p. 96.
Hollywood Reporter. April 23, 1996.
Los Angeles Times. June 13, 1997, p. F1.
New York Times. October 5, 1996, p. 19.
Sight and Sound. March, 1996, p. 10.
Sight and Sound. October, 1997, p. 61.
Variety. May 20, 1996, p. 56.

That Darn Cat

This FBI agent is putting his life on the line. Fortunately, he's got nine.—Movie tagline

Box Office: $18,301,828

The new Walt Disney feature film *That Darn Cat* is a remake, not a sequel, of the 1965 Disney hit with the same title. Both are based on the novel *Undercover Cat* by Mildred and Gordon Gordon, who co-wrote the screenplay for the first version in collaboration with Bill Walsh. As with so many sequels and remakes, the original outshines the copy. *That Darn Cat* (1965) is so far superior to *That Darn Cat* (1997) that the Disney people might have been better advised to offer the still entertaining Technicolor original as a rerelease with the kind of lavish promotion they always put into rereleases of their classic animated films.

Mom Judy: "Why do you always wear black?" Patti: "Because it matches my soul."

The new version received dismal reviews, perhaps because the remake seemed even weaker by contrast with the popular original. Joe Leydon, writing for *Variety*, predicted accurately that "this overbearing comedy isn't likely to pussyfoot very long in theaters before it hightails to homevideo." Kevin Thomas wrote in the *Los Angeles Times*: "Disney's reworking of its beloved 1965 *That Darn Cat* is too contrived and drawn out to have much appeal for audiences beyond small children." Laurel Graeber, in a short review for the *New York Times*, suggested that children ages 7-12 represented "the perfect audience" and that younger children could not follow the plot while older children "will probably find Patti's environment as stupefying as she does." Peter Stack in the *San Francisco Chronicle* praised "the cool charm" of 16-year old Christina Ricci but concluded: "*That Darn Cat* is darn tedious."

What is missing in the remake is just what was so appealing in the original: good casting. The 1965 version featured charismatic character actors like Roddy McDowall, Elsa Lancaster, and William Demarest (who played the crabby housekeeping uncle in the long-running 1960s television sitcom "My Three Sons"). The original *That Darn Cat* even had a part for legendary comedian Ed Wynn. These professionals seemed to understand exactly what sort of spirit was required for such a lightweight story. Director Robert Stevenson's job must have been fairly easy. Hayley Mills, the young British star, was already a veteran herself and took to her airhead role like a duck to water.

The remake, scripted by Scott Alexander and Larry Karazewski, follows the same story line with only minor changes. Yet the whole show seems flat. Perhaps the biggest disappointment is Doug E. Doug as Zeke, the FBI agent.

Dean Jones, who played Zeke in the 1965 outing, portrayed his character as the stereotypical uptight FBI agent stamped out by a cookie-cutter. Doug E. Doug, an African American, seems compelled to mug his way through the film like a second-rate Eddie Murphy. Doug E. Doug is burdened with the impossible task of providing all the comedy that was provided in the original version by such really funny professionals as McDowall, Lancaster, Demarest, Wynn, and other lesser-known Hollywood character actors. Zeke, as portrayed by Doug E. Doug, acts like such a zany office clown that it is hard to understand how he ever made it into the FBI. Instead of ridiculing the FBI, as was original version's main intent, the remake inadvertently seems to be ridiculing African Americans.

In keeping with the spirit of the 1990s, brunette Christina Ricci, who takes over as amateur detective Patti, has a far more complicated role than the 1960s blond California cheerleader played by Hayley Mills. The new Patti is tortured by 1990s angst. Instead of being a typical American teenager, this introverted, latchkey Patti is a loner who despises her clueless parents and hates the small town she is stuck in.

For some reason the producers have moved the story clear across the continent. The original was set in California; the remake is supposedly set in Massachusetts, although it was actually shot in the picturesque town of Edgefield, South Carolina. Perhaps the idea was to make everything a little different while keeping everything pretty much the same. The cat in the original film was Siamese; the new D.C. looks like pure American alley cat. The kidnap victim in the original version was a bank teller; the new victim is a housemaid who was kidnapped by a couple of incompetent novices who thought she was the wife of a wealthy businessman. The situation does not ring true. In this tiny town, the kidnappers, who are locals, should know the difference between the housemaid and the businessman's wife. In the original version, both the kidnappers and their victim were strangers just traveling through. Like Seth and Richard Gecko (George Clooney and Quentin Tarantino) in *From Dusk Till Dawn* (1995), Dan and Iggy (Neville Brand and Frank Gorshin) were bank robbers who had taken a hostage.

D.C. ("Darn Cat") makes his rounds every night at the same time, stealing food to appease his insatiable appetite. This nosy feline intrudes into the shed where the victim sits bound and gagged. She replaces the cat's collar with her wristwatch after scratching the first three letters of the word "HELP" on the back. Eventually Patti discovers the watch and deduces that it belongs to the missing housemaid, who is the object of a multi-state search. Patti manages to interest the FBI sufficiently to get Zeke and a crew of assistant agents assigned to the case. As in the original version, the whole problem revolves around trying to shadow an elusive cat who can leap over fences, climb trees, and squeeze through tiny openings. J. Edgar Hoover's G-Men may have been better targets for satire in the liberal-activist 1960s; in the late 1990s their Keystone-Cop antics fail to arouse much mirth.

When Patti and Zeke finally track D.C. to the captive and her abductors, the climax comes as a disappointment. As far as the audience is concerned, the kidnappers are total strangers. In crime films it is common for the villain to be anonymous and invisible for awhile, but usually by the second act his identity has to be revealed to the audience, if not to the detective. Otherwise the unmasking and apprehension fail to have an emotional impact. In the original version of *That Darn Cat*, Dan and Iggy are generously featured throughout the film. They provide some real menace while generating a few laughs at the same time. In the remake it is hard to understand who the perpetrators are or what their motive was. One of the two bungling novices is Pa, played by the talented Peter Boyle, who is probably best remembered as the tap-dancing monster in Mel Brooks' *Young Frankenstein* (1974). The other is Pa's wife (Rebecca Schull). Boyle could have been much more of an asset to this disappointing remake of *That Darn Cat* if he had been used more extensively throughout the film. Like so many of the other supporting players, including George Dzundza and Estelle Parsons, Boyle is not given much to do. The climax devolves into an old-fashioned 1920s car chase embellished with 1990s state-of-the-art pile-ups and voluptuously blossoming gasoline explosions.

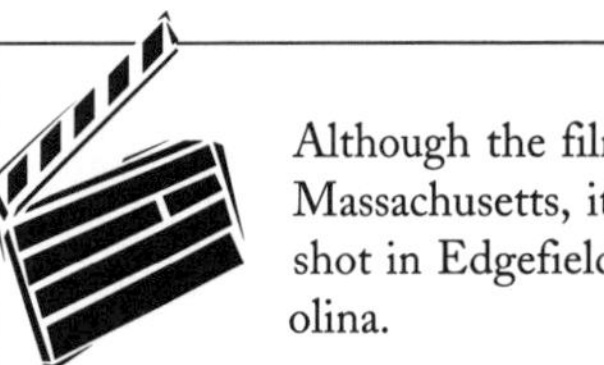

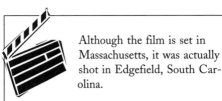

Although the film is set in Massachusetts, it was actually shot in Edgefield, South Carolina.

The new, brunette Patti undergoes a character change that was hardly thought necessary with the 1960s blond Patti in the original. This complicated, sophisticated 1990s Patti comes to realize that small-town life and small-town values are not so bad after all. Instead of being such a militant loner, she decides to become integrated with the teenagers she thought she despised. Instead of regarding her parents as a couple of jailers, she decides to accept them with all their grown-up deficiencies. How her radical character change comes about is hard to understand—but there are more puzzles in this film than are worth the trouble of investigating. Patti's 180-degree character change may have been due to her new status as the town heroine, or perhaps all the excitement and property damage cheered her up.

In the original version, Patti's parents were away from home and Patti was sharing the big home with her beautiful, sexy older sister Ingrid (Dorothy Provine). A love in-

CREDITS

Patti: Christina Ricci
Zeke: Doug E. Doug
Mr. Flint: Dean Jones
Boetticher: George Dzundza
Pa: Peter Boyle
Peter Randall: Michael McKean
Judy Randall: Bess Armstrong
Mrs. Flint: Dyan Cannon
Dusty: John Ratzenberger
Old Lady McCracken: Estelle Parsons
Ma: Rebecca Schull
Lizzie: Rebecca Koon
D.C.: Elvis

Origin: USA
Released: 1997
Production: Robert Simonds for Walt Disney Pictures; released by Buena Vista
Direction: Bob Spiers
Screenplay: S.M. Alexander and L.A. Karaszewski; based on the novel *Undercover Cat* by Mildred and Gordon Gordon
Cinematography: Jerzy Kielinski
Editing: Roger Barton
Music: Richard Kendall Gibbs
Production design: Jonathan Carlson
Art direction: Jeremy A. Cassells
Costumes: Marie France
Sound: Walter Anderson
MPAA rating: PG
Running Time: 89 minutes

terest developed between Ingrid and Zeke. Meanwhile Patti had her own puppy-love involvement with the good-looking, happy-go-lucky Canoe (Tom Lowell). Although both relationships were totally chaste, they provided a romantic interest which is conspicuously lacking in the remake. Since there is no equivalent of teenage Canoe in the new Patti's life, she is cast, by default, as an unhappy loner, adding an unnecessary note of pathos to what should have been a lightweight comedy about a goofy cat.

Both the original and the remake of *That Darn Cat* are sprinkled with "colorful" characters. The idea was to give the audience a voyeuristic treat by shooting scenes from the cat's point of view. The effect was somewhat similar to what was done in Alfred Hitchcock's classic *Rear Window* (1954). But the characters in the original really were colorful, while the characters in the remake are, unfortunately, colorless. The fault may lie at least in part with director Bob Spiers, a British television director whose main credits include the sitcom "Fawlty Towers." But more likely the corpse should be laid at the door of the Disney executives who tried to cut corners on the casting.

—*Bill Delaney*

REVIEWS

Chicago Tribune. February 14, 1997, p. 5.
Los Angeles Times. February 14, 1997, p. F16.
New York Times. February 14, 1997, p. C12.
San Francisco Chronicle. February 14, 1997, p. D3.
USA Today. February 14, 1997, p. 4D.
Variety. February 17, 1997, p. 69.

That Old Feeling

It was the perfect wedding except for two things . . . the bride's parents.—Movie tagline

"A hilarious, romantic comedy!"—Bill Diehl, *ABC Radio*

"Bette Midler is at her entertaining best."—David Sheehan, *KCBS*

"Laugh-packed! Bette Midler reaches new heights of hilarious comedy."—Bobbie Wygant, *KXAS*

"Outrageous, side-splittingly funny. Wonderfully written, acted and directed."—Paul Wunder, *WBAI Radio*

"Hysterical! Bette Midler and Dennis Farina are hysterical!"—Omar Lugones, *WSVN*

Box Office: $16,575,739

Bette Midler fans will love *That Old Feeling,* a raucous romantic comedy in which she stars as Lily, a flamboyant but lovable movie star, who, years after a messy divorce, encounters her ex-husband Dan (Dennis Farina) at their daughter's wedding.

CREDITS

Lily Leonard: Bette Midler
Dan De Mora: Dennis Farina
Molly De Mora: Paula Marshall
Rowena: Gail O'Grady
Alan: David Rasche
Keith Marks: Jamie Denton
Joey Donna: Danny Nucci

Origin: USA
Released: 1997
Production: Leslie Dixon and Bonnie Bruckheimer for Boy of the Year, All Girl Productions and the Bubble Factory; released by Universal Pictures
Direction: Carl Reiner
Screenplay: Leslie Dixon
Cinematography: Steve Mason
Editing: Richard Halsey
Music: Patrick Williams
Production design: Sandy Veneziano
Art direction: Alicia Keywan
Costumes: Robert De Mora
Sound: Bruce Carwardine
MPAA rating: PG13
Running Time: 105 minutes

Exes Lilly (Bette Midler) and Dan (Dennis Farina) hate each other but their daughter's wedding brings them together again in *That Old Feeling.*

When daughter Molly (Paula Marshall) becomes engaged to Keith (Jamie Denton), an up-and-coming politician, the couple plan an elaborate, formal wedding and invite both of Molly's parents.

Even though the divorce was years before, there is still a lot of bad blood between the ex-spouses, and even more hostility toward their current spouses. Dan married Rowena (Gail O'Grady), who was the "other woman" in Lilly and Dan's marriage. Lilly married Dan and Lilly's marriage counselor Alan (David Rasche), a psycho-babble pop psychologist with a string of best-sellers.

The premise allows for plenty of funny lines as Lilly dishes on the younger new wife, and Dan taunts Lilly. Dan tells Rowena that Lilly has radar for any cosmetic changes, and, with a single raised eyebrow from Lilly during the wedding ceremony, we are made aware of Rowena's overly upturned nose and lips that are perhaps a touch too full.

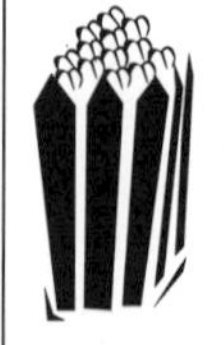

Lily to daughter Molly: "Don't you know what your twenties are for? They're for having sex with all the wrong people!"

The jibes exchanged by Dan and Lilly escalate into a full-blown shouting match at the reception, and they are told to take it outside. But their heated argument turns into just plain heat, and, in the best scene in the film, Lilly and Dan are reconciled in a very big way in a very small sports car. They return to the reception and conceal their rekindled passion from their spouses, only to meet again that night, when they decide to run away together "like in the old days."

When Molly's new husband Keith finds out about his in-laws liaison, he is afraid that the press will publicize the scandal and that it will put his campaign in jeopardy. Molly, in an attempt at damage control, goes off in search of her parents.

To find them, she turns to an unlikely source. She contacts Joey (Danny Nucci), the paparazzo who has tracked Lily for the past few years, making a living from taking unflattering photos of her for the tabloids. As the debutante Molly and the streetwise Joey come together to track down Molly's parents, the structure of the film begins to fall apart. Despite Molly and Joey's rushing hither and thither, the momentum is gone, and the budding romance between the two lacks credibility.

Directed by Carl Reiner and written by Leslie Dixon, who wrote *Outrageous Fortune* (1987), *That Old Feeling* is funny, witty, and romantic—until the wedding ends. And although the actors continue to give splendid performances, after Dan and Lilly flee from their partners, the plot becomes forced and contrived.

After Molly and Joey find the couple by following their credit card purchases, they track them down to the hotel where Lilly manages to lock the two of them in a room overnight, so that Dan and she can have just one more romantic evening together.

As the parents rekindle the magic of their love, they begin to infect their daughter with this same sense of freedom and trust in passion. But when Dan and Lilly finally succeed in bringing Molly and Joey together, their total lack of chemistry makes the ending a little uncomfortable.

That Old Feeling showcases the comedic talents of Gail O'Grady, who is a perfect shrew as Rowena, and David Rasche's very funny portrayal of a neurotic psychologist. But the most delightful surprise of the film is the wonderfully talented performance of Dennis Farina, who plays Dan.

Farina, who usually plays heavies, has the machismo to match Midler's "come up and see me sometime" sort of lustiness, along with a twinkle in his eye that adds to the sexy playfulness of the film, and together Farina and Midler send out more sparks than an old muffler dragging along a highway.

Although the film showcases many excellent and talented actors, after the wedding reception scene, the script underutilizes those talents, leading us on a contrived chase that does nothing to further the plot except to replace Molly and Keith's odd relationship with an utterly inconceivable one.

The power of the very funny first half of the film is not enough to make up for the weaknesses in the second half. And although Farina and Midler are still strong presences on the screen, they can't carry the film.

That Old Feeling is a mild sex farce in which the actors are more interesting than the storyline, but the film is saved by the infectious passion of Lilly and Dan, not to mention a glorious rendition of "Somewhere Along the Way" by Midler.

—*Diane Hatch-Avis*

REVIEWS

Detroit News. April 4, 1997, p. D1.
Entertainment Weekly. April 19, 1997, p. 50
The Hollywood Reporter. March 31, 1997, p. 10.
Los Angeles Times. April 4, 1997, p. F10.
The New York Times. April 4, 1997, p. C22.
People. April 14, 1997, p. 16
Sight and Sound. September, 1997, p. 56.
Variety. April 7, 1997, p. 43.

This World, Then the Fireworks

Meet Marty and Carol. Two people who are very good at being very bad.—Movie tagline

This World, Then the Fireworks is the latest screen adaptation of the pulp writer Jim Thompson's works—others include the recent, more successful *The Grifters* (1990), directed by Stephen Frears. For years Hollywood directors and producers have anxiously sought to duplicate the legions of film noirs that were released by the dozens in the years following World War II. Because of audience sophistication (most people can spot a cliché a mile away these days) and because of the different standards of movie morality, most modern noirs fail to pack the punch of a *The Killers* (1964) or *Gun Crazy* (1949), or *Double Indemnity* (1944). Director Michael Oblowitz vainly tries to rein in his actors and fashion this outrageous story into a cohesive tale, but the resulting film fails to gel into an emotionally affecting story. The characters are all so self-involved, humorless and downright despicable that they fail to connect on a visceral level.

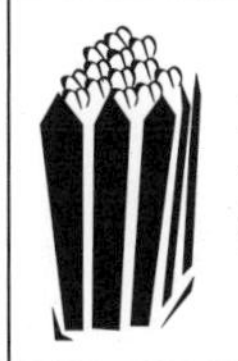

Marty's come-on to Lois: "Are you blonde all over or just where it shows?"

Marty (Billy Zane) and Carol Lakewood (Gina Gershon) are darkly handsome fraternal twins. As children they witnessed a terrible tragedy that mentally scarred both of them; their father and his mistress were murdered before their eyes in their home. Their mother (Rue McClanahan), her face marred by a blast of gun pellets, mentally cracks and pulls the children from their hometown, and embarks on years of traveling, finally settling down in a small town in California.

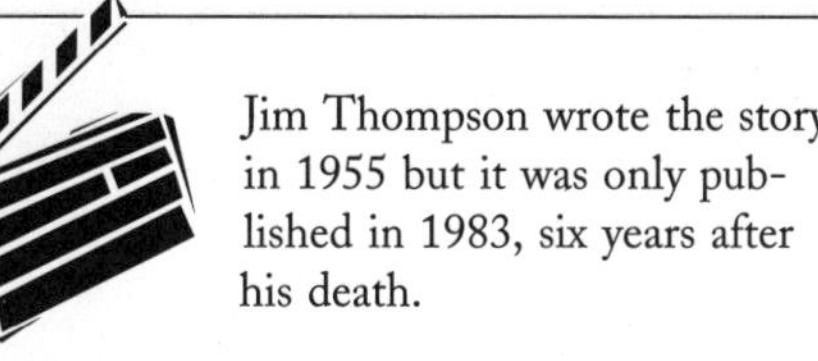

Jim Thompson wrote the story in 1955 but it was only published in 1983, six years after his death.

Both Marty and Carol carry emotional problems from their unusual childhood; it is quickly obvious that their love is incestuous, a fact which incenses their deeply religious mother. Marty, who glibly narrates the story, has become an investigative reporter, and has also married a mousy woman with elephantiasis. Miserable in his marriage and with various pissed off city officials on his heels, Marty decided to head home to visit his sister and mother.

Mother Lakewood warily greets him. Carol, on the other hand, warmly welcomes him into her bed. Carol is on the rebound from a bad marriage and has taken to hooking out of the local bar. Gershon is a steamy, sensuous beauty; dolled up in wide brim hats and garish red lips. She's a low-rent Ava Gardener, and Zane is a pasty version of Fred MacMurray in *Double Indemnity*; he thinks he's in control, but alas, the future is controlling him.

CREDITS

Marty Lakewood: Billy Zane
Carol Lakewood : Gina Gershon
Lois Archer: Sheryl Lee
Mother Lakewood: Rue McClanahan
Police Detective Harris: Seymour Cassel
Police Lt. Morgan: Will Patton
Joe: Richard Edson

Origin: USA
Released: 1996
Production: Larry Gross, Chris Hanley and Brad Wyman for Largo Entertainment; released by Orion Classics
Direction: Michael Oblowitz
Screenplay: Larry Gross; based on the story by Jim Thompson
Cinematography: Tom Priestley Jr.
Editing: Emma Hickox
Music: Pete Rugolo
Costumes: Dan Moore
Production design: Maia Javan
Sound: Coll Anderson
Makeup: Brad Boles
Special effects coordinator: Michael Schorr
MPAA rating: R
Running Time: 100 minutes

In true noir fashion, the combustible combination of Marty and Carol leads them down their own private path to hell. Marty meets and seduces detective Lois Archer (Sheryl Lee), a perfect blond counterpart to his sultry dark sister. Archer is a dichotomy in both her personal and professional life; she is a competent policewoman, but begs Marty to abuse and humiliate her. They enjoy decadent "Lost Weekends" at her private beach cottage. Marty learns that her absent husband owns the cabin with Archer, and soon begins to plot to get the cabin for himself and Carol.

Meanwhile, Carol exhibits her own cold-blooded business sense by poisoning a pair of local gangsters who try to muscle into her hooking business. She knows Marty is having a relationship and it kills her. All of the signs point to the inevitable downward spiral for all characters involved. Yet the ending, abrupt and senseless, involving Carol dying from a botched abortion in Mexico, alone and without the brother she loves so much, is much more vintage Thompson than classic film noir.

The film has a lush look (by cinematographer Tom Priestley Jr.) and calls up a languid feel by using vintage tunes by Chet Baker, but the film in its entirety never coalesces into the powerful, affecting drama it aspires to be.

—G.E. Georges

REVIEWS

Boxoffice. September, 1997, p. 125.
Hollywood Reporter. July 14, 1997, p. 5.
Los Angeles Times. July 11, 1997, p. F14.
New York Times. July 11, 1997.
People. July 21, 1997, p. 18.
Sight and Sound. December, 1997, p. 55.
Variety. January 27, 1997, p. 76.
Village Voice. July 15, 1997, p. 65.

A Thousand Acres

Best friends. Bitter rivals. Sisters.—Movie tagline

"Lange and Pfeiffer's exquisite performances should earn them both Oscar nominations!"—David Sheehan, *CBS-TV*

"*A Thousand Acres* should receive a thousand Oscars!"—Mose Persico, *CFCF-TV*

"Anyone who wants to see two of the juiciest performances of the year shouldn't miss it!"—David Ansen, *Newsweek*

"The best drama of the year!"—Bill Zwecker, *WMAQ-TV*

Box Office: $7,936,780

Despite the promotional chatter, viewers should not expect to find a modernized *King Lear* in this movie. There are no kings in Iowa these days, where the story is set, or in Illinois, where the film was made. Though Jane Smiley's 1991 novel lifts its plot design from Shakespeare's greatest play, the weight placed on the characters in the film is far different, and the millionaire farmer, Larry Cook (Jason Robards), who makes a bad decision and later becomes a crazed and pathetic image of his former self, is not really the central character. Something is seriously amiss here if this story is merely a reworking of the Lear plot, which works better in the novel than in the dramatized and flattened-out version the film provides.

The plot is set in motion when Larry gives away the farm, dividing it between his two daughters, Ginny Cook Smith (Jessica Lange) and Rose Cook Lewis (Michelle Pfeiffer), who are made far more sympathetic when they later turn against their father than Goneril or Reagan could ever be. In Shakespeare's play the daughters are evil and uncaring, defined by their greed and ambition and by their lust not only for power, but for Edmund, the bastard son of the Earl of Gloucester. In Smiley's modern-day version, they are daughters, not tigers, and abused daughters at that. Both have been victims of incest, sexually molested by their father while they were growing up. Rose, moreover, is a victim of cancer. Since they have been clearly wronged by their father, they have motives for treating him as they do.

Larry proposes, quite unexpectedly, to turn the family farm—the largest in the area, encompassing 1000 acres—into a corporation that will be split three ways among his daughters, Ginny and Rose and their husbands Ty Smith (Keith Carradine) and Peter Lewis (Kevin Anderson) and Caroline Cook (Jennifer Jason Leigh), the youngest, and Cordelia's counterpart. Caroline has left the farm to become a lawyer, and, and, unlike her sisters who think Larry's scheme is a "great idea," she ever so quietly expresses reservations about her father's intentions. That's Cordelia's fatal flaw, but in Smiley's story it's not fatal at all, merely bothersome.

All Caroline says is "I don't know." The father, who has had too much to drink at a pig roast given by his neighbor Harold Clark (Pat Hingle) in honor of the return of his prodigal son Jess (Colin Firth), responds in anger "You don't want it, my girl, you're out! It's as simple as that." And she is disinherited on the spot. "My father's pride, always touchy, had been injured to the quick," Ginny explains in the novel, but in neither the novel nor the film does Larry's anger approximate the rage of Shakespeare's Lear. Caroline spends the night with Rose after her run-in with her father. When she goes to see Larry the next day, he closes the door in her face. So she returns to Des Moines.

After he has given up the farm, Larry becomes moody and despondent and drinks himself into dementia. Ginny and Rose worry about him, and Ginny threatens to take away the keys to his pick-up truck after a drunken outing. A storm is brewing that night and Larry walks away from his house into the storm, vowing to live with his friend and neighbor Harold Clark. Before long, Jess Clark, the prodigal hippie, moves into Larry's house and has affairs first with Ginny, then with Rose. Jess turns out to be a "bastard," but he is not illegitimate. He doesn't betray his father as Edmund does Gloucester in the Shakespeare play. He doesn't have Edmund's motives. He is simply a self-indulgent, manipulative jerk and homewrecker. Aware that he has been cuckolded, Rose's husband gets drunk, wrecks his truck, and dies. No great loss, since he had been an abusive husband (and a very shadowy character in the film).

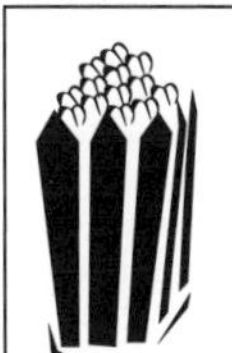

Rose: "We're not going to be sad. We're going to be angry till we die."

Ginny's husband Ty goes to Des Moines and tells Caroline that her sisters have treated their father badly. So Caroline takes her father to court to sue Ginny and Rose—litigation replacing the warfare of Shakespeare's play. The judge rules that Larry's case is not justified after Larry reveals himself to be quite insane and incoherent when giving his testimony, but the litigation bankrupts Ty, and after Ginny's infidelity is revealed, Ginny goes to the city to work as a waitress, while Rose stays on to look after the failing farm. Ultimately the farm fails and Rose dies, falling victim to cancer. Families are destroyed, and the kingdom is in ruins.

The film attempts a faithful adaptation of the novel as Jessica Lange's voice-over narration leads the viewer through the story. According to *USA Today* "Smiley's book was the bible on the set," but Lange expected criticism from readers "because key scenes are deleted and the male roles are downplayed." Both Lange and Pfeiffer "committed to the film before deciding which sister each would play." Lange knew and respected the novel and understood that "certain things have to go" when a novel is reduced to a two-hour movie, but she hoped the picture would not "be dismissed as a woman's film in which all the men are 'crummy' and the women 'heroic.'" Those hopes were soon dashed after the film's release.

Jane Smiley's 1991 novel won the Pulitzer Prize and a National Book Critics Circle Award.

Despite the filmmakers' good intentions to be true to the book, reviewers were not impressed. Rita Kempley of the *Washington Post* objected to the "skeletal litany of miscarriages, mastectomies, sexual abuse, public humiliations and private betrayals." Although New Zealand screenwriter Laura Jones preserves much of the novel's dialogue and some of Smiley's prose through the narration, the film, directed by Australian Jocelyn Moorhouse, flattens the narrative into what Kempley called "a feminist screed" and turned Larry Cook into what *Washington Times* critic Gary Arnold called a "demented patriarch." Sister Caroline is hardly made endearing by being transformed into a big-city lawyer.

Comparisons were made to *The English Patient* (1996), which took a different approach to the problem of translating an award-winning novel to the screen by transforming the story into an equally powerful work of art, as Ann Hornaday protested in the *Baltimore Sun*: "Rather than make Smiley's story their own, Moorhouse and screenwriter Laura Jones settle for a tepid, visually static re-hash, wherein the social issues the author wove into her book are pressed with hot-button force." Janet Maslin of the *New York Times* believed that once the characters of Ginny and Rose became dramatically central, the "talk-show subtext" gives the story "an all-too-modern aspect." Owen Gleiberman of *Entertainment Weekly* objected to the "tangle of 'issues' that includes miscarriage, breast cancer, and spousal abuse (as if incest weren't enough!)" He also objected to the film's manipulation and its "emotional structure, which asks us to see Lange and Pfeiffer caught in a complex storm of sympathy and rage" that is "undercut at every turn by Robards' odious, one-dimensional performance."

David Ansen of *Newsweek* was not so hostile. He conceded that the film does not do justice to the book, but "anyone in search of a powerful emotional experience, and anyone who wants to see two of the juiciest performances of the year shouldn't miss it," he advised. Moreover, the film does carry a disclaimer pointing out that "dialogue and certain credits and characters contained in the film were created for the purposes of dramatization." Finally, it should be noted that the producers hired an outside editor to rework the film after rejecting the director's cut, which upset Moorhouse to the extent that she threatened to take her name off the film. In other words, the faults of the film might not be the faults of the director.

Although, as one reviewer noted, the filmmakers are occasionally able to make "a family in pain come into vivid focus," in general the film takes the material of high tragedy and reduces it to a cornfield soap opera. The novel does a better job of establishing Larry's dignity and his honored standing in the community, and that is utterly

CREDITS

Rose Cook Lewis: Michelle Pfeiffer
Ginny Cook Smith: Jessica Lange
Larry Cook: Jason Robards
Caroline Cook: Jennifer Jason Leigh
Jess Clark: Colin Firth
Ty Smith: Keith Carradine
Peter Lewis: Kevin Anderson
Harold Clark: Pat Hingle
Ken LaSalle: John Carroll Lynch

Origin: USA
Released: 1997
Production: Marc Abraham, Lynn Arost, Steve Golin, Kate Guinburg, and Sigurjon Sighvatsson for Via Rosa, Prairie Films, Beacon Pictures, Propaganda Films; released by Touchstone Pictures
Direction: Jocelyn Moorhouse
Screenplay: Laura Jones; based on the novel by Jane Smiley
Cinematography: Tak Fujimoto
Editing: Maryann Brandon
Music: Richard Hartley
Production design: Dan Davis
Art direction: James F. Truesdale
Costumes: Ruth Meyers
Sound: Richard Lightstone
MPAA rating: R
Running Time: 105 minutes

necessary if one is to appreciate the man's decline and fall. The film moves the Lear figure too quickly to the background, while it slathers pity, sympathy and understanding on Ginny and Rose, both of whom are excellently portrayed by Pfeiffer and Lange. Reviewing the film for *Variety*, Godfrey Cheshire singled out Keith Carradine as Ginny's husband Ty for the film's "standout performance." *Variety* saw Shakespeare as being left "stranded in the high corn" since the film owes more to "the spirit of Oprah than to the Bard." There is a twinned transformation at work here as Shakespeare's play becomes Smiley's Pulitzer Prize-winning novel, which is then in turn dramatized on film. But the resonance is lost in this pale imitation of art imitating life. The film is well worth seeing for the performances of Lange and Pfeiffer, but viewers should also read the novel, which will make more sense than this film ever could.

—*James M. Welsh*

REVIEWS

The Baltimore Sun. September 19, 1997, p. E1.
Boxoffice. November, 1997, p. 132.
Chicago Tribune. September 19, 1997, p. 5.
Entertainment Weekly. September 26, 1997, p. 51.
The Hollywood Reporter. September 9, 1997, p. 10.
Los Angeles Times. September 19, 1997, p. F1.
The New York Times. December 8, 1996, p. H22.
The New York Times. September 19, 1997, p. B12.
The New Yorker. September 29, 1997, p. 86.
Newsweek. September 22, 1997, p. 82.
People. September 29, 1997, p. 20.
The Philadelphia Inquirer. September 19, 1997, p. 4.
Rolling Stone. October 16, 1997, p. 116.
USA Today. September 18, 1997, p. D1.
Variety. September 15, 1997, p. 69.
Village Voice. September 30, 1997, p. 84.
The Washington Post. September 19, 1997, p. C7.
Washington Post Weekend. September 19, 1997, p. 51.
Washington Times Metropolitan Times. September 19, 1997, p. C15.

'Til There Was You

It took them twenty years to fall in love at first sight.—Movie tagline

"Witty and warm!"—Don Stotter, *Entertainment Time-Out*

"An inventive and emotionally enthralling movie. It's consistently enterprising."—Stephen Farber, *Movieline*

"A fresh, fascinating perspective on the story of love at first sight."—Michael Medved, *New York Post*

"Sexy Sarah Jessica Parker is pure comic gold."—Peter Travers, *Rolling Stone*

"Delightfully charming . . . this season's most enjoyable romantic comedy."—Bob Healy, *Satellite News Syndicate*

Box Office: $3,525,125

'Til There Was You, a confused romantic comedy, sat on Hollywood's shelf for over a year waiting for a theatrical debut. After viewing this film, it's not difficult to understand why. This trite, modern-day love story is the first feature for writer Winnie Holzman and director Scott Winant (both alums from TV's "thirtysomething" and "My So-Called Life"), and would have been far better suited for life on the small screen.

The jumbled plot revolves around three young professionals looking for love in the '90s. Dwelling on the mysteries of destiny, the storyline follows two lonely people, Gwen Moss (Jeanne Tripplehorn) and Nick Dawkan (Dylan McDermott) through their separate lives in Los Angeles until the fateful encounter finally takes place. Although their lives are intertwined, they don't actually meet until the very end of the film and therein lies the main problem.

The premise of a romance that doesn't begin until the movie ends is a difficult idea to execute, and only a few filmmakers have successfully pulled it off—most notably Nora Ephron in *Sleepless in Seattle* (1993) and French director Claude Lelouch's *And Now My Love* (1974). Both of these films used the same contrivance with considerably more narrative skill. *'Til There Was You* spends most of its time cutting back and forth between Gwen and Nick's affairs while several other stories and characters are introduced that never get fully realized.

The threads linking the intended couple together are many: Gwen is working on the autobiography of Nick's girlfriend, Francesca, a former child TV star (Sarah Jessica Parker) fresh out of drug rehab, and architect Nick designs a condo development that threatens to demolish La Fortuna,

Gwen's beautiful, vintage rental complex. And who happens to own La Fortuna? None other than Francesca herself. To make a long story short, Gwen fights to save her historic apartment complex from being torn down. She pleas to the City Council and writes letters to the editor of the local paper to spare La Fortuna. Somehow, Nick is so touched by these letters that he visits the old building and he too is charmed by not only its romance, but by the residents—especially one elderly lady—as well. It is only then that he's worthy enough to meet and marry Gwen.

Screenwriter Winnie Holzman: "Any time it looks like people fell in love at first sight, the truth is that there was a whole history which made that happen."

Although the leads are quite attractive, there is nothing particularly likeable about these characters. Aside from the fact that they're weakly drawn, both Tripplehorn and McDermott give bland performances. They just don't generate any excitement and even when they finally get together at the end, there is still no chemistry. At this point, the viewer could care less whether Gwen and Nick find true love.

The one performer who manages to bring some life to the screen is Sarah Jessica Parker as the neurotic, sexy, recovering child star. By far the film's most enjoyable character, Ms. Parker is hilarious in her portrayal as a seductive woman with a take-charge attitude. Having been the star of a "Brady Bunch"-type series, Francesca is still trying to cope with the fact that people still think of her as "Taffy". Although Parker's character is clearly the highlight of the film, even she gets stuck with lame, uninspired lines like, "God, I love amphetamines more than life itself."

Also popping up briefly in *'Til There Was You* is Jennifer Aniston as Gwen's best friend; Michael Tucker and Christine Ebersole, as Gwen's parents; Karen Allen as Nick's mother; Alice Drummond as La Fortuna's aging movie actress, and Ken Olin as a bisexual professor who breaks young Gwen's heart. Unfortunately, these minor characters all lack development and none of these roles are flattering. Aniston appears so infrequently in the film that one wonders what she's doing there at all. (Her talent is put to much better use in her other '97 release, *Picture Perfect*). With the exception of Parker's amusing turn, all the actors in this movie deserve a much better vehicle.

Perhaps the most bizarre aspect of *'Til There Was You* is the frequency of scenes that take place at the Awful Truth, a harsh, industrial deco restaurant designed by Nick. So many scenes are set here it seems as if this must be the only restaurant in town. This trendy, yet dangerous spot comes complete with post-modern decor—triangular tables, metal sculptures and spiky chairs. And every time Gwen enters the restaurant she hits her head on a metal sculpture suspended from the ceiling. If the director was hoping for big laughs with this obvious gimmick, he didn't get it. By the second or third time this gag is repeated, it's downright irritating.

Overall, critics were negative in their reviews of this convoluted romantic comedy, although a few noted its small charms. Ultimately, *'Til There Was You* fails to draw us in because the storyline is too rambling and we never care about the leads. There are just too many threads running throughout this script. If writer Holzman and director Winant had opted for a simpler story, this could have had a much stronger picture.

—Beth Fhaner

CREDITS

Gwen Moss: Jeanne Tripplehorn
Nick Dawkan: Dylan McDermott
Francesca Lanfield: Sarah Jessica Parker
Debbie: Jennifer Aniston
Gregory Haas: Ken Olin
Jon: Craig Berko
Sophie Monroe: Nina Foch
Beebee Moss: Christine Ebersole
Saul Moss: Michael Tucker
Timo: Patrick Malidhide

Origin: USA
Released: 1997
Production: Penney Finkelman Cox, Tom Rosenberg, and Alan Poul for Lakeshore Entertainment; released by Paramount Pictures
Direction: Scott Winant
Screenplay: Winnie Holzman
Cinematography: Bobby Bukowski
Editing: Richard Marks, Joanne Cappuccilli
Music: Miles Goodman, Terence Blanchard
Production design: Craig Stearns
Art direction: Randy Moore
Sound: Bo Harwood
MPAA rating: PG-13
Running Time: 113 minutes

REVIEWS

Boxoffice. July 7, 1997, p. 88.
Chicago Tribune. May 30, 1997, p. 5.
Detroit News. May 30, 1997, p. 3H.
Entertainment Weekly. June 6, 1997, p. 48.
Los Angeles Times. May 30, 1997, p. F6.
New York Times. May 30, 1997, p. B10.
People. June 9, 1997, p. 20.
Rolling Stone. May 1, 1997, p. 59.
USA Today. May 30, 1997, p. 9D.
Variety. April 21, 1997, p. 60.

Timothy Leary's Dead

When sixties iconoclastic psychedelic guru Dr. Timothy Leary learned he was dying of inoperable prostate cancer, he claimed to be thrilled. Death was for him the ultimate adventure, the greatest trip of all. He planned to broadcast his last moments from his deathbed over the Internet, followed by his bizarre intention to have his head surgically removed and cryogenically preserved.

In real life, Leary—the man Richard Nixon once called "the most dangerous man in America"—dismissed the cryogenics team from his bedside. He reportedly scoffed at the whole idea of being able to freeze, then later thaw, human brain tissue. A bit of a disappointment coming from such a hell-raiser as Dr. Timothy Leary, the man who coined the slogan, "Turn On, Tune In, Drop Out."

With that said, be aware that the end of *Timothy Leary's Dead*, a documentary from Paul Davids and co-writer Todd Easton Mills (son of actor John), contains a fabricated fantasy sequence that is shockingly graphic. If only it were true.

By the time ex-Harvard professor of philosophy Timothy Leary reached the end of what many would describe as a full life, he had pretty much become a faded memory, little more than a dusty remnant of a counterculture long since gone by. It's doubtful that most of today's Generation-Xers even know his name, short of being a refrain in some old Moody Blues tune. Still, Timothy Leary is *the* reason—the only reason—to see this shoddy and haphazardly constructed documentary.

At a slight eighty minutes *Timothy Leary's Dead* lacks a clear-eyed perspective that is generally considered one of the marks of a good documentary. Novice filmmaker Paul Davids—whose previous work includes the novelizations of such *Star Wars* stories as "The Glove of Darth Vader"—engages in some serious hero worship and pays mere lip service to objectivity by giving only a quick, halfhearted acknowledgement to Leary's critics.

It seems obvious that Leary was a major icon to Davids and Mills. But it is practically a cardinal sin in the world of documentary filmmaking to succumb to such idolatry. Yes, it is true that Timothy Leary was somewhat of a legend in his time. He got to hang out in his pajamas with John and Yoko when they had their famous sleep-in. He dropped out in exile in Algiers with Eldridge Cleaver. And he tuned in to the jabbering of a madman when he was imprisoned in the cell next to Charlie Manson. But even with all that, hard as it might seem to believe, not everyone necessarily finds Timothy Leary all that interesting.

What Davids fails to do is argue convincingly for Leary's place in American history. The director seems unable to grasp what it was about Timothy Leary that made him significant, what the essence of the man was, and why or how he managed to speak to an entire generation. Plenty of people took drugs in the Sixties, but few did so with Leary's commitment to exploration. He claims to have tried LSD over five hundred times, yet by the end of his life, he still seemed articulate and mentally alert.

The film does have some startling revelations, such as, most incredibly, when it is revealed that Leary's father, a dentist, inadvertently introduced his young son to the thrills of a chemically-induced high when he gave him nitrous oxide. Leary also claims that President John F. Kennedy took LSD, that Watergate burglar G. Gordon Liddy led the raid on his New York commune in the Sixties, and that his first wife killed herself on his thirty-fifth birthday. Prison, he tells us, was great because he had no rent to pay. But overall, *Timothy Leary's Dead* has a difficult time seeing past the cultural icon to the man.

A good deal of the eighty minutes is spent preparing for Leary's eventual demise. The rest centers on recollections, primarily by Leary's Harvard and LSD colleague, Dr. Richard Alpert—later known to many as the spiritual leader Ram Dass—and to a lesser degree, Beat Poet Allen Ginsberg, (who just recently found himself On The Road to the great beyond).

CREDITS

Origin: USA
Released: 1997
Production: Paul Davids and Todd Easton Mills for Davids & Mills Productions; released by Strand Releasing
Direction: Paul Davids
Screenplay: Paul Davids and Todd Easton Mills
Cinematography: Paul Helling
Editing: David J. Watson, Mark Deimel
Sound: Ted Gordon
MPAA rating: Unrated
Running Time: 80 minutes

REVIEWS

Entertainment Weekly. June 6, 1997, p. 43.
The Hollywood Reporter. June 6, 1997, p. 10.
Los Angeles Times. June 6, 1997, p. F8.
New York Times. June 6, 1997, p. B20.
People. June 9, 1997, p. 19.
San Francisco Chronicle. June 27, 1997, p.C3.
San Francisco Examiner. June 27, 1997, p. C6.

The dying Timothy Leary comes across as the prototype for the Heaven's Gate group, or at the very least a fanatical viewer of television's "The X-Files", when he talks of death as the ultimate trip and his body as a vehicle.

Confronted with death, Leary, that "Prophet of Perception" as Alpert calls him, decided to make it the biggest adventure of all. He wanted to go out with an iconoclastic big bang. But in the end, Dr. Timothy Leary died a much more orthodox death than his vivid life would have prepared us for.

—Patricia Kowal

Titanic

Nothing on earth could come between them. —Movie tagline

"*Titanic* has the sweep and scope of the greatest epics ever made."—Rod Lurie, *ABC*

"An overwhelming journey that takes you from romantic delight to tragic drama."—David Sheehan, *CBS*

"*Titanic* grabs hold of you and doesn't let go!"—Leonard Maltin, *Entertainment Tonight*

"Prepare to be blown away!"—Sam HaBenbeck, *Fox-TV*

"Lush romanticism and sweeping emotional force!"—Stephen Farber, *Movieline*

"One of the greatest motion pictures of all time!"—Bobbie Wygant, *NBC-TV*

"Visually spectacular and timeless. *Titanic* lives up to its title!"—Rex Reed, *New York Observer*

"Jim Cameron's *Titanic* is grand. There are sights here that no other film director would have the nerve to stage."—Anthony Lane, *New Yorker*

"*Titanic* is epic! Big, bold, touchingly uncynical filmmaking."—David Ansen, *Newsweek*

"It's a blockbuster! DiCaprio and Winslet both deliver star-making performances."—Leah Rozen, *People*

"A cinematic spectacular!"—Bruce Williamson, *Playboy*

"*Titanic* is thrilling in ways that no other movie in 1997 dares to be! It's the movie event of the year. Jaw-dropping! It'll get to you."—Peter Travers, *Rolling Stone.*

"A glorious Hollywood epic!"—Roger Ebert, *Siskel & Ebert*

"DiCaprio is simply extraordinary!"—John Powers, *Vogue*

Jack (Leonardo DiCaprio) and Rose (Kate Winslet) are young lovers who share one last embrace before tragedy strikes aboard the doomed *Titanic.*

Box Office: $112,594,173

With a cost of well over 200 million dollars to film earning it the distinction of one of the most expensive films ever made to date, *Titanic* arrived in theaters amidst speculation over whether its box office performance might bear some resemblance to the dreadful fate of its seaborne namesake. After all, a number of grand-scale, over-budget films released over the past few years met disastrous ends, both critically and commercially. As *Titanic*'s production and post-production stretched months past the film's original targeted completion and release dates, some industry observers half-jokingly, half-seriously drew comparisons to another over-budget, ocean-faring spectacle, the ill-fated Kevin Costner film *Waterworld* (1995), and wondered aloud whether this latest project helmed by director James Cameron (*Aliens* 1986, *Terminator 2* 1991, *The Abyss* 1989, *True Lies* 1994) would likewise "sink" at the box office. However, the long-awaited release of the film proved such omens to be premature, as *Titanic* received glowing critical reviews and lured huge audiences into theaters. The movie, its director, its story, and its stars were soon named as strong contenders for Oscar nominations, while the film's commercial success promised to qualify *Titanic* a genuine blockbuster rather than a "bomb." As a film about a story that's been told and retold numerous times, *Titanic* could have easily been simply more of the same, just another "disaster" movie with a tragic, but also very predictable, ending. However, under Cameron's skilled direction, and with powerful performances by its cast, *Titanic* works on almost every critically important level as a sophisticated, well-rounded drama, principally because the film focuses on the development of its two main characters and the way their lives affect one another rather than the historical tragedy that serves as the story's backdrop.

> Old Rose on seeing her youthful nude portrait: "Wasn't I a dish?"

The drama in *Titanic* revolves around two characters from two very different worlds, Jack Dawson (Leonardo DiCaprio) and Rose DeWitt Bukater (Kate Winslet). It is from the point of view of the aged, present-day Rose that the story of *Titanic* is told. A group of treasure-hunters looking for a long-lost diamond known as the Heart of the Ocean, which supposedly went down with the Titanic in 1912, discover that Rose, a passenger on the ill-fated ship, is still alive and may hold a key to the diamond's location. Before an intrigued audience that includes her granddaughter, Rose then relates her tale.

When the Titanic sets sail in 1912, Rose boards the ship with her mother and her fiance, Caledon (Cal) Hockley (Billy Zane), a wealthy, arrogant, self-absorbed member of high society. Unfortunately, Rose is not happily engaged, and she is very unhappy in the shallow, upper crust society which is her world. She feels "trapped" and "enslaved" by the constraining conventions and expectations that shape a young woman's "place" in such a society. Her relationship with Cal, who seems bent on controlling her (he does not approve of her reading Freud and makes fun of her fascination with the paintings of an "unknown" artist named Picasso), lacks any true love, and in fact her engagement has apparently been arranged in part by her mother, whose late husband squandered the family's riches. Believing that the voyage to America aboard the Titanic is a path to her doom, she heads in despair to the ship's stern with the intention of casting herself into the ocean.

Her halfhearted attempt at suicide is halted by the intervention of Jack Dawson, a poor, homeless, wandering artist who won a ticket to board the Titanic in a poker game. Jack convinces Rose not to take her life, and a bond between the two is quickly forged. Just as Jack is drawn to her, Rose becomes fascinated by Jack, his drawings, and the adventuresome freedom of his life. He promises her that one day he will teach her to ride a horse "like a man" rather than sidesaddle, that he will show her the west coast of America, and that the two of them will ride a roller coaster until they get sick. Jack teaches Rose how to spit and takes her to a party among the third-class passengers, which she thoroughly enjoys. Unfortunately, of course, her mother and her fiance do not approve. For awhile Rose is torn between both worlds, but she realizes she loves Jack and tells him she will go away with him when they get to America.

Fate does not allow their dream to become realized, however, as Titanic strikes an iceberg and begins to sink. The drama of Rose and Jack's story merges with the unfolding tragic drama of the ship's demise as passengers and crew, increasingly overcome with panic, face impending doom. After being pursued by the obsessed Cal, who seems fixated on not losing Rose, Jack and Rose make their way to the ship's deck, where the crew is initially allowing only first-class women and children into the limited number of lifeboats. Rose first boards a lifeboat but then proclaims that she will not leave Jack, and she returns to the ship. Ulti-

AWARDS AND NOMINATIONS

Academy Awards 1997: Best Picture, Director (Cameron), Cinematography, Art Direction, Song ("My Heart Will Go On"), Film Editing, Original Dramatic Score, Visual Effects, Sound Effects Editing, Sound, Costume Design

Nominations: Best Actress (Winslet), Best Supporting Actress (Stuart), Makeup

BAFTA 1997 Nominations: Best Film, Director (Cameron), Music, Cinematography, Production design, Costumes, Editing, Sound, Special effects, Make-up/Hair

Broadcast Film Critics Association 1997: Director (Cameron)

Directors Guild of America 1997: (Cameron)

Golden Globe Awards 1998: Best Drama, Director (Cameron), Original Score, Song ("My Heart Will Go On")

Nominations: Drama Actress (Winslet), Drama Actor (DiCaprio), Supporting Actress (Stuart), Screenplay

Los Angeles Film Critics Association 1997: Production design

Screen Actors Guild Awards 1997: Supporting Actress (Stuart)

mately, as the Titanic is sinking beneath them, the rear half of the ship moving upward into a vertical position, Jack leads Rose to the stern of the ship, staying on board as long as possible, to await the vessel's complete disappearance into the sea.

James Cameron, a former art director, drew the nude sketch of Rose from photos of a clothed Kate Winslet.

Once the ship goes under, Jack helps Rose onto a floating piece of debris, while he holds on in the water beside her. As they and the many other survivors in life jackets around them wait for the lifeboats to come to the rescue, they begin to freeze. When Rose seems on the verge of giving up hope, Jack tells her not to give up, that she is not going to die here. She will one day have children and live to an old age, he says, and she will die comfortably in bed, not here in this way. She promises not to give up. Eventually, one lone lifeboat does return to look for survivors, but it is too late. Everyone but Rose has frozen to death in the water. Realizing that Jack has perished as well, Rose tearfully tells him that she will never let go, and then she procures a whistle from a nearby corpse and signals to the lifeboat.

As the story returns to the present, the old Rose explains that when she reached America, she took the name Rose Dawson. She then lived a very fruitful and fulfilling life, pursuing the many dreams she wished to accomplish. Her audience, deeply moved by her tale, realizes what the sinking of the Titanic was really about. Her personalized, emotional account helps them to see the human drama of the tragedy, the story of people rather than the story of a sinking ship. That night, while lying peacefully in bed, Rose passes away, her tale having been told for the first time.

While the intense drama of the sinking of the Titanic provides an emotionally powerful context for the story, *Titanic* is at its heart a rich, well-developed dramatic tale of a man and woman who fall in love and change each other's lives. Jack's life is shortened tragically, but before he dies he finds happiness and fulfillment with Rose. As he awaits what will be his death in the freezing water, Jack tells Rose that the day he won the ticket for the Titanic was the luckiest and best day of his life. Having found true love, he is undaunted by the prospect of losing his life as a result of boarding the ship. What is important to him is Rose's survival, and her living life to its fullest.

Even moreso, though, *Titanic* is Rose's story, and not merely in the sense that she is the film's narrator. The growth of her character lies at the heart of the tale, for the impact that Jack Dawson has on her life enables her to emerge from the tragedy as a victorious human being. She boarded the Titanic a frustrated, entrapped woman who saw no place for herself to go except into tighter imprisonment, but Jack shows her a way into a new world of freedom and love. Rose learns Jack's philosophy of "make each day count" and applies it to her life; in so doing, she finds life itself. There is an interesting irony underlying this drama, for Rose boarded Titanic with expectations of death while everyone else marveled at the majesty of the mighty "unsinkable" ship, yet in the midst of all the tragic death with which the voyage of the Titanic ends, Rose discovers life. The death of the Titanic is, in a sense, the beginning of a new life for her. Rose's personal renewal and victory in the face of tragedy is one of the most satisfying elements of the film, for somehow, in the middle of great disaster, there is also an uplifting story of hope.

While dramatically secondary to the story of Jack and Rose, the sinking of the Titanic does of course play a major role in the film, and the intense yet personal manner with

CREDITS

Jack Dawson: Leonardo DiCaprio
Rose DeWitt Bukater: Kate Winslet
Cal Hockley: Billy Zane
Molly Brown: Kathy Bates
Ruth DeWitt Bukater: Frances Fisher
Old Rose: Gloria Stuart
Brock Lovett: Bill Paxton
Captain Smith: Bernard Hill
Thomas Andrews: Victor Garber
Bruce Ismay: Jonathan Hyde
Spicer Lovejoy: David Warner
Fabrizio: Danny Nucci
Lizzy Calvert: Suzy Amis
Col. Archibald Gradie: Bernard Fox

Origin: USA
Released: 1997
Production: James Cameron and Jon Landau for Lightstorm Entertainment; released by Paramount Pictures and 20th Century Fox
Direction: James Cameron
Screenplay: James Cameron
Cinematography: Russell Carpenter
Editing: Conrad Bluff, Richard A. Harris, James Cameron
Music: James Horner
Production design: Peter Lamont
Art direction: Martin Laing
Set design: Marco Niro, Dominic Masters, Peter Francis
Costumes: Deborah L. Scott
Sound: Mark Ulano
Visual effects supervisor: Robert Legato
Special effects: Thomas L. Fisher
MPAA rating: PG-13
Running Time: 194 minutes

which the tragedy is rendered builds dramatic effect upon dramatic effect. The special effects in the film are astoundingly realistic, and the actual manner in which the ship sank is depicted with fascinating accuracy, but the realism is not an end in itself; instead, it serves the personal, human drama being depicted. From the noble sorrow of the ship's designer, who knew all along the ship was not invulnerable, to the quiet confusion and despair of the captain whose years of experience did not prepare him for this tragedy, to the third-class passengers who struggle futilely to reach the remaining lifeboats, the human element of the drama is foregrounded. This element, which enables the film's audience to identify with the real story unfolding just as the aged Rose's audience learns the true meaning of the sinking of the Titanic, is what makes *Titanic* a powerful, emotionally satisfying film rather than just another disaster movie.

—*David Flanagin*

REVIEWS

Boxoffice. January, 1998, p. 45.
Detroit News. December 19, 1997, p. 1D.
Entertainment Weekly. December 19, 1997, p. 49.
Los Angeles Times. March 11, 1997, p. F1.
Los Angeles Times. April 19, 1997, p. F1.
Movieline. June, 1997, p. 51.
New York Times. December 19, 1997, p. E1.
Newsweek. November 25, 1996, p. 73.
People. December 22, 1997, p. 21.
Rolling Stone. December 25, 1997, p. 172.
Time. November 25, 1996.
Time. December 8, 1997.
USA Today. December 19, 1997, p. 1D.
Variety. November 3, 1997, p. 7.
Village Voice. December 23, 1997, p. 79.

Tomorrow Never Dies

"Absolutely incredible!"—Patty Spitler, *CBS-WISH TV*
"Spectacular!"—David Sheehan, *KCBS-TV*
"Pulse pounding and brilliant!"—Jason Miller, *KDNL-ABC-TV*
"The best Bond film ever!"—Bonnie Churchill, *National News Syndicate*
"Non-stop thrills!"—Bill Zwecker, *NBC-TV*
"A bullseye!"—Jim Ferguson, *Prevue Channel*

Box Office: $73,307,122

Tomorrow Never Dies is the latest James Bond film. It's a catchy title, sounds phonetically concise for announcers and fits nicely in the obligatory Bond theme song (sung by Sheryl Crow). But it also holds no meaning to this film whatsoever. This and several other factors merely prove that the 18th installment of the James Bond series is a less memorable action film and more expensive marketing campaign. The film is also an attempt by the Bond film producers to further bring this middle-aged, secret-agent man into the next millennium. Ironically, their efforts to further modernize Bond smack of deja vu of a recipe developed over 30 years ago, which is quickly showing its age.

James Bond (Pierce Brosnan) gets some help from Chinese agent Wai Li (Michelle Yeoh) to foil the plans of an evil media mogul in the 18th Bond film *Tomorrow Never Dies.*

Hardly straying from its basic formula, the film opens with an exhilarating opening sequence. Set at the Russian border, a huge arms deal (nuclear weapons, fighter jet planes and maybe some handguns) is about to take place. Our dashing spy is sent undercover to foil the plans of these ominous Russian cretins. Tension and suspense (two elements you will never experience again during this film) come into play when it looks as if Bond (played again by

Pierce Brosnan) has met his demise and is faced with total annihilation from a top British military officer who would much rather see the area nuked before any of these lethal weapons en route to smugglers' row get past that border. But just in the nick of time, Bond steals one of the elite fighter aircrafts and saves the day by bombing the area himself.

Media mogul Elliott Carver: "There's no news like bad news."

Bond's return to headquarters is greeted with congratulations and a debriefing on his next assignment. A British submarine was destroyed by what military officials in Great Britain detected as a Chinese missile. Such actions would no doubt bring about hostilities, even war among these countries, yet a premature retaliation by England would do just that when China denies any involvement. Coincidentally, at the same time the British ship went down, a suspicious satellite transmission was picked up from a dish owned by media mogul Elliot Carver (Jonathan Pryce), who turns out to have a materialistic and sadistic connection to this military attack. Bond has been given orders from M (Judi Dench) to investigate Carver and his multimedia empire. Bond's meddling reveals that Carver's (newspaper and television baron that he is) involvement with these attacks results in his thirst for domination over the world's perception of the truth and of the news. He wants to control the news right up to the point where he makes up the news. Who else would have the latest, most up-to-date, and accurate information on a war, than the man who actually started it? Carver would wipe out his competition as people would flock to Carver-owned newspapers and cable news services. More subscriptions mean more money for Carver, at least that's what he thinks.

Thailand stands in for China. The film also shot in Mexico, Germany, Florida, and outside London.

All of Bond's nemeses are wealthy, intelligent, greedy, and powerful masterminds. Their plots to take over the world are brilliant plans to create a new world order, but are foiled by the even more brilliant James Bond. But in the instance of Carver, enemies have never developed schemes that would backfire on them. Carver doesn't seem to realize that if war is to be declared, a certain amount of destruction will render people either homeless or jobless, which in turn, makes it quite difficult to watch t.v. or buy newspapers. Instead of an evil genius, Carver comes across as a very rich man with a little too much time on his hands. This image is further reinforced by Pryce's uninspired performance to give Carver any dimension, conviction, or menace. He's evil because he wears nothing but black, starts a war for profit, and sells tainted computer software to customers who will need to buy his upgrades in two years. A pseudo Bill Gates on an ego trip may make for interesting drama, but certainly not for high-octane adventure drama.

James Bond's intent to intercept Carver's scheme has a personal bent when one of his lost loves, Paris (played by a shallow Teri Hatcher), turns out to be Mrs. Elliot Carver. Paris's former relationship with Bond rekindles some sparks between the two but is quickly squelched when a jealous Elliot kills Paris. This relationship is baffling due to the lack of onscreen chemistry between Brosnan and Hatcher, and you wonder what Bond ever saw in Paris in the first place. What makes this relationship/connection even more trying, is how Paris initially lies to Elliot on the conditions of how she met Bond. "He dated my roommate from college," fibs Paris. Bond on a college campus. It doesn't take an evil genius to see through that ridiculous untruth. Maybe she wasn't killed for cheating on Elliot, but because she's such a lousy liar and couldn't fake enough passion for a role that was otherwise unnecessary.

As the film was being promoted, it advertised that Ms. Hatcher was one of two Bond girls. Her ten minutes of screen time doesn't quite qualify her as a Bond girl or any significant cast member. But the title of latest Bond girl (Bond girl of the nineties) does belong to Hong Kong import and martial arts queen Michelle Yeoh. Yeoh plays Chinese agent Wai Lin, who partners up with Bond to fight Carver and his henchmen. Yeoh is the only bright point in this film and the only diversion to the Bond formula. Yeoh is more than a mere Bond girl—she's a Bond equivalent, both elegant and lethal. As she reveals her prowess in kung fu fighting, she also demonstrates that she could have accomplished her mission quicker than Bond and with less gadgets.

But when the action lags, you do have the gadgets to look forward to and *Tomorrow Never Dies* tops its previous films with a unique high-tech BMW. It can be controlled by a remote control panel that's small enough to fit in a coat pocket. The interesting spin on this car is that's involved in a thrilling high-speed chase with driver Bond in the backseat, holding a remote control instead of the steering wheel.

AWARDS AND NOMINATIONS

Golden Globe Awards 1998 Nominations: Song ("Tomorrow Never Dies")

Starting with *Goldeneye*, with Brosnan's arrival as the new James Bond coinciding with a new BMW, this car has gained some significant clout in the Bond series and is always featured in the best scenes. Along with a car, a BMW motorcycle is also put to good use during a scene in Thailand in *Tomorrow Never Dies*. But this obvious product placement pays off, for both parties. After *Goldeneye*'s release, these one of a kind BMWs netted the car company millions of dollars. Hoping to reap the rewards of such product placement, *Tomorrow Never Dies* became a marketing magnet for various other consumer-based businesses. Companies that sold such products as beer (Heineken), credit cards (Visa), vodka (Smirnoff), watches (Omega), cellular phones (Ericcson) and even cosmetics (L'Oreal) rushed to get their products associated with the film. These companies paid collectively $100 million dollars for their products to be included in a special-effects laden James Bond film. Advertising has replaced entertainment in a James Bond film.

Brosnan has proven, with *Goldeneye*, that he has the looks and the accent to fill the shoes of such previous Bonds as Sean Connery and Roger Moore. But his acting range in these films has yet to prove that Brosnan is more than just a pretty face dressed in an impeccable wardrobe. As succeeding Bond films might prove, acting becomes secondary when your role is being reduced to a video arcade game character. It's not how you feel, it's how you look and on the surface, *Tomorrow Never Dies* looks sleek and spectacular. With location shots in France, Mexico, Thailand, and Germany, the film is shot with picture-postcard scenery.

Tomorrow Never Dies has become the highest grossing Bond film to date. It has grossed over $100 million dollars domestically and perhaps it will double that overseas. With this kind of business, the next Bond film (Bond #19) has a lot riding on it and a lot to live up to. But as the story and villain in *Tomorrow* indicates, creativity is slowly waning in the Bond camp. It certainly doesn't help much when a lightweight and visionless director such as Roger Spottiwoode from *Stop! Or My Mother Will Shoot* (1992) fame is brought along to follow the assembly-line approach to filmmaking and when a script is sent through many rewrites, which was the case during *Tomorrow*'s pre-production hell. Alas, if the plot for Bond #19 does become a bothersome enigma for the Bond camp, they could always work in James Bond driving his sporty BMW through a McDonald's drive-thru to order a Big Mac. At least the producers can make their money back from product placements.

—Michelle Banks

CREDITS

James Bond: Pierce Brosnan
Elliot Carver: Jonathan Pryce
Wai Lin: Michelle Yeoh
Paris Carver: Teri Hatcher
Wade: Joe Don Baker
Henry Gupta: Ricky Jay
Stamper: Gotz Otto
M: Judi Dench
Q: Desmond Llewelyn
Dr. Kaufman: Vincent Schiavelli
Admiral Roebuck: Geoffrey Palmer
Robinson: Colin Salmon
Moneypenny: Samantha Bond

Origin: USA
Released: 1997
Production: Michael G. Wilson and Barbara Broccoli for Eon Productions; released by United Artists
Direction: Roger Spottiswoode
Screenplay: Bruce Feirstein
Cinematography: Robert Elswit
Editing: Dominique Fortin, Michael Arcand
Music: David Arnold
Production design: Allan Cameron
Costumes: Lindy Hemming
Sound: Chris Munro
Special effects supervisor: Chris Coubould
Stunt supervisor: Dickey Beer
Aerial coordinator: Marc Wolff
MPAA rating: PG-13
Running Time: 119 minutes

REVIEWS

Boxoffice. November, 1997, p. 13.
Chicago Sun-Times. December 12, 1997.
Cinemafantastique. January, 1998, p. 16.
Cinemafantastique. April, 1998, p. 55.
The Detroit News. December 19, 1997, p. 3D.
Entertainment Weekly. January 9, 1998, p. 43.
The New York Times. December 19, 1997, p. E18.
Variety. December 15, 1997, p. 57.
Village Voice. December 30, 1997, p. 72.

Touch

A gripping comedy.—Movie tagline

"Wonderfully wicked!"—Susan Granger, *CRN International*

"Ace performances."—Graham Fuller, *Interview*

"One pleased smile from start to finish!"—Kenneth Turan, *Los Angeles Times*

"Smart and funny."—Jeff Craig, *Sixty Second Preview*

It's difficult to figure out how to take *Touch*, an unlikely collaboration between writer Elmore Leonard and director Paul Schrader. Leonard, whose quirky crime novels have also spawned the movies *Get Shorty* and *52 Pickup*, has produced in *Touch* one of his most atypical stories. While it is characteristically character driven, here crime takes a back seat to religion. Written in 1977 and originally set in Detroit, it has been updated by Schrader to the present day and moved to Los Angeles, but the story remains basically the same.

But was the serious Schrader the best one to bring out the ironies of Leonard's words and worlds? Originally making his name as a screenwriter (*Taxi Driver*, *Raging Bull*), Schrader graduated to directing such unusual films as *Mishima* and *Hard Core*. The risks he has taken in the subject matter of his films as a director continues with *Touch*, the story of a young man with the ability to heal with the laying on of his hands.

Touch opens with a fascinating scene. Elwin Worrell (John Doe) is abusing his blind wife Virginia (Conchata Ferrell) in a drunken rage. Into the melee comes Bill Hill (Christopher Walken), a one-time preacher in whose church Virginia played the organ. Now a recreational vehicle salesman, the sharkskin-suited Bill tries to calm down Elwin, but he will not be deterred from destroying all the dishes in the kitchen.

Now coming to the rescue is Juvenal (Skeets Ulrich), a one-time Franciscan priest who currently works for Alcoholics Anonymous at Sacred Heart Rehabilitation Center where he has befriended Elwin. The innocent-faced Juvenal soon quiets Elwin and begins asking Bill about Virginia's blindness. But as Juvenal places a wet cloth on Virginia's bleeding head, she suddenly stands up and begins to sweep up the china shards . . . she can see.

Bill is more than stunned at the miracle. He immediately begins to scheme how to exploit Juvenal's skills for his own enrichment. But Bill is not the only one who wants to capitalize on Juvenal's powers.

Lynn to Juvenal as she washes his clothes: "Do you think it's all right? Stigmata blood going through the wash?"

CREDITS

Juvenal: Skeet Ulrich
Bill Hill: Christopher Walken
Lynn Faulkner: Bridget Fonda
August Murray: Tom Arnold
Kathy Worthington: Janeane Garofalo
Antoinette Baker: Lolita Davidovich
Artie: Paul Mazursky
Debra Lusanne: Gina Gershon
Father Donahue: Anthony Zerbe
Virginia Worrel: Conchata Ferrell
Father Navaroli: Don Novello

Origin: USA
Released: 1997
Production: Lila Cazes, Fida Attieh for Lumiere International; released by United Artists
Direction: Paul Schrader
Screenplay: Paul Schrader; based on the novel by Elmore Leonard
Cinematography: Ed Lachman
Editing: Cara Silverman
Production design: David Wasco
Art direction: Daniel Bradford
Set decoration: Sandy Reynolds Wasco
Costumes: Julie Weiss
Music: David Grohl
MPAA rating: R
Running Time: 97 minutes

Reporter Kathy Worthington (Janeane Garofalo) wants his exclusive story, tabloid TV host Debra Lusanne (Gina Gershon) wants him to perform miracles on prime time, and most of all, religious purists and militant August Murray (Tom Arnold) wants Juvenal to promote his cause, "Outrage," to restore the traditional mass to the Catholic Church.

At first Bill tries to use an old friend of his, a one-time baton-twirler in his church and current assistant record promoter, Lynn Faulkner (Bridget Fonda), to find out more about Juvenal. By having her pretend to be an alcoholic and thereby gain entry to the inner rooms of Sacred Heart she does manage to meet him, but Lynn is so attracted to him that they become lovers—a sin the woman-hating August can't bear.

In *Touch*, Juvenal is an innocent who can't help but lay his hands on the infirm which cures them but results in his bleeding from the five wounds of Christ (the stigmata). And Ulrich (*Scream*) is believable and even charismatic as someone who is accepting of his gift and not corrupted by it. But while the story presents him as a man who has no goal of profiting from his gifts, it also never explains why he eventually throws in with Bill. Has he plans of his own and he's using Bill? Does he believe his being chosen of God preserves him from being exploited? Is he naive? Stupid? Totally passive? We never know.

Director Paul Schrader was raised in a strict and religious home and didn't see his first movie until he was 17.

Equally as puzzling is his relationship with Lynn. As played by Fonda, Lynn is a simpering airhead. One thinks she should be a bit of a hustler herself just from her years with Bill (which would also make her more typical of a Leonard character), but she is played as an innocent equal to Juvenal. Maybe that's the only way Schrader can explain his attraction to her, for motives are never clear here. Neither is our understanding of if this is a comedy or a drama. Sometimes it's one and sometimes it's the other.

Touch is Schrader's first feature since *Light Sleeper* which he made five years ago and *Witch Hunt* which he made for HBO, but it is too unconvincing and confused in tone to be truly satisfying.

—*Beverley Bare Buehrer*

AWARDS AND NOMINATIONS

Independent Spirit Awards 1997 Nominations:
Director (Schrader), Screenplay

REVIEWS

Chicago Tribune. February 21, 1997.
Cinefantastique. February, 1997, p. 12.
Los Angeles Times. February 14, 1997, p. F2.
New York Times. February 14, 1997, p. B5.
People. March 10, 1997, p. 19.
Time. February 24, 1997.
Variety. February 10, 1997, p. 63.
Village Voice. February 25, 1997, p. 70.

Traveller

Swindlers. Scammers. Con-men. As American As Apple Pie.—Movie tagline

"Great! It will touch your heart!"—Bill Diehl, *ABC-Radio*

"Stunning! Dangerous! Sexy!"—Donald Lyons, *Film Comment*

"A hot little sleeper! Made with a sharp, appealing simplicity that has all but gone out of style!"—Janet Maslin, *New York Times*

Irish-American gypsies who practice con games somewhere in the southern United States are the focus of *Traveller*, a film with several puzzle pieces missing. The early going of the movie, which stars and is produced by Bill Paxton, promises to be an exploration of a shady sort of workaday subculture. But first-time director Jack Green never seems to settle on a mood, toying with whimsical comedy, sappy melodrama and, finally, a shocking descent into egregious violence.

Green was the Oscar-winning cinematographer of *Twister* (1996), in which Paxton also starred. Here, the screenplay by Jim McGlynn appears to have been blown apart by a tornado. The movie has a randomness to it, yet its action still feels forced. The dialogue is the kind in which characters speak the obvious and telegraph their feelings. When young initiate Pat (Mark Wahlberg) corners the object of his desires, who happens to be the daughter of the gypsy clan's boss, she tells him: "If this is something you really want, you gotta go for it with everything you got." She's ostensibly talking about the lifestyle, but we know what else is on her mind, as we do about every character.

The premise of the film makes little sense. An entire clan of scam artists is headquartered in a compound deep in the backwoods. Members regularly fan out to practice their con games and pay a portion of their ill-gotten gain to the head man, Jack Costello (Luke Askew). When Pat asks Paxton's character, Bokky, why Jack gets this tribute, Bokky explains: "He's minding the store." What store?

Wearing a suit and a look of bewilderment, Pat arrives at the travellers' headquarters for the funeral of his father, who was one of the clan but committed the cardinal sin of marrying an outsider. No sooner is the dirt placed over the casket than Costello roughly tells Pat he's no longer welcome in the extended gypsy family. But Paxton, after consulting with his wise, blind grandmother, decides to take the lad under his wing. Of course, the greenhorn proves to be tougher than his mentor.

Bokky on learning Jean is divorced: "Bet your husband's kickin' himself." Jean: "He was good at kickin' things."

For a film about scam artists to hold your interest, there ought to be a variety of delightful scams. Bokky, however, practices only two, and neither of them is particularly clever. One is to apply phony driveway or roof sealant which is really just some black oil. Another is to buy chintzy mobile homes for $5,000 and sell them for $10,000. If these two cons are the only things this clan knows how to do, it's a wonder they're still around. Such lack of invention dooms the script.

Green lingers over these con games as if he is mining treasures. The result is a film which pays meticulous attention to the mundane. Neither the clan nor what they do is exotic or ingenious enough to deserve the attention asked of the viewer. Playing some Irish music and employing a word or two of special lingo does not make these folks seem authentic or interesting.

Pat makes some rookie mistakes but also hits a few home runs to show that he's got what it takes. It's in his blood, as we're continually reminded. Soon he proves himself Bokky's superior, both in nerve and creativity. Together they practice a bait-and-switch scam on a foxy bartender, Jean (Julianna Margulies of the television series "ER"). Wearing tight jeans and flashing bedroom eyes, Margulies is far too movie-star-sexy to be working in such a sleazy backwoods bar. Of course, she's recently divorced, to boot. She tries hard to make her character believable, without much success. It's hard to believe she's as desperate as she appears to be.

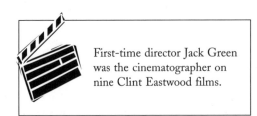

First-time director Jack Green was the cinematographer on nine Clint Eastwood films.

Bokky falls hard for her, to the disgust of Pat, who fears a repeat of his father's apostasy. We find out Bokky has an emotional tragedy in his past which has left a huge void that his life as a con artist cannot fill. The film, which at first tried for a touch of wry comedy and failed, now tries to pull at the heartstrings, and also fails. A favorite device of the plot-starved writer rears its ugly head: Jean has a daughter who needs an operation to save her from going deaf, and she must raise $35,000 to pay for it. Bokky jumps at a chance to rescue her.

Throughout the film, Bokky has been stalked by a shadowy, annoying character named Double D (James Gammon), a con artist in a cowboy hat who talks of "vision" and "opportunity" and wants to recruit Bokky for a big scam he's plotting in Nashville. The film never answers the question Bokky keeps asking, which is why Double D doesn't just find another partner. Now, blinded by love, Bokky jumps in over his head, and Pat, eager to belong, comes along too.

The last part of the film shifts focus two more times. The new trio of partners gets involved in a complicated game with another trio of ruthless con artists led by a bald, fat gangster named Bimbo (delightfully played by Vincent Chase). Double D executes a bewildering series of double-dealing betrayals which involve counterfeit money, and Bokky gets the money for Jean's daughter. Then, inexplicably, the film, which for all its doldrums has at least been innocuous, turns inexplicably ugly, ending in gruesome torture scenes and a hail of gunfire.

Up to that point, *Traveller* is simply a misdirected, misfiring little film which aspires to be an ironic slice-of-life but consistently fails to arouse much excitement. In its climax, the film turns dreadful. It's like playing for 90 minutes with a wind-up toy that suddenly turns lethal.

The most redeeming aspect of the film is Wahlberg's performance. He's surly, edgy, and likeable all at once. Far more than Paxton, whose portrayal is simply bland, Wahlberg's simmering energy seems close to the temperament of an Irish vagabond. Wahlberg is an actor who's not afraid to take risks—he mumbles, deadpans, sulks and smirks at unexpected moments—but he does so in a quiet, non-grandstanding way. His Pat has a hot-tempered mystery about him. You find yourself watching Wahlberg in a sort of trance and then wondering how he's just stolen a scene by doing nothing really extraordinary. *Traveller* is worth renting to see what Wahlberg did just before bursting into stardom with his acclaimed lead role in *Boogie Nights* (1997, reviewed in this volume).

Some of the smaller performances, especially those of Gammon and Chase, are also splendidly done. Paxton is suitable but lacks flash; his character seems mostly forlorn,

CREDITS

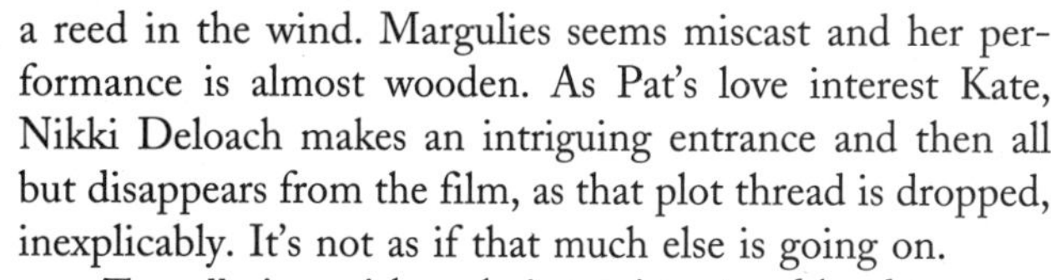

Bokky: Bill Paxton
Pat: Mark Wahlberg
Jean: Julianna Margulies
Double D: James Gammon
Boss Jack: Luke Askew
Kate: Nikki Deloach

Origin: USA
Released: 1997
Production: Bill Paxton, Brian Swardstrom, Mickey Liddell, and David Blocker for Banner Entertainment; released by October Films
Direction: Jack Green
Screenplay: Jim McGlynn
Cinematography: Jack Green
Editing: Michael Ruscio
Music: Andy Paley
Production design: Michael Helmy
Set decoration: Steve Davis
Costumes: Douglas Hall
Sound: Carl Rudisill
MPAA rating: R
Running Time: 100 minutes

a reed in the wind. Margulies seems miscast and her performance is almost wooden. As Pat's love interest Kate, Nikki Deloach makes an intriguing entrance and then all but disappears from the film, as that plot thread is dropped, inexplicably. It's not as if that much else is going on.

Traveller is a mishmash, inconsistent and hard to warm up to. It lacks the sharpness required for a perceptive glance on an unusual subculture, it has way too few entertaining or comic moments for a film about con artists, it indulges in sappy sentimentalism, and it goes seriously awry in the last half. If you want a mesmerizing, authentic film about the Irish "travellers," rent *Into the West* (1992) instead.

—*Michael Betzold*

REVIEWS

Boxoffice. May, 1997, p. 59.
Entertainment Weekly. May 2, 1997, p. 43.
Entertainment Weekly. May 9, 1997, p. 55.
Los Angeles Times. April 25, 1997, p. F11.
New York Times. April 18, 1997, p. C3.
People. April 21, 1997, p. 23.
USA Today. May 1, 1997, p. 3D.
Variety. March 17, 1997, p. 53.

Trial and Error

The 2nd most outrageous trial of the century.—Movie tagline

What's a courtroom circus without a couple of clowns?—Movie tagline

"You'll be guilty of laughing yourself silly in this wacky comedy!"—Jeanne Wolf, *Jeanne Wolf's Hollywood*

"The verdict is in . . . hilarious!"—Joanna Langfield, *The Movie Minute*

"Richards and Daniels play a wonderful comic team!"—Janet Maslin, *The New York Times*

"Two thumbs up!"—*Siskel & Ebert*

"Michael Richards proves himself to be a comic genius!"—Paul Wunder, *WBAI Radio*

"*Trial and Error* is inspired lunacy!"—Bill Bregoli, *Westwood One Radio*

Box Office: $13,602,831

Trial and Error boasts a robust cast, proficient in both comedy and drama, but the film ultimately crumbles under the weight of both weak direction and a reluctance to let one of its lead stars cut loose and show off his considerable comedy teeth. Directed by Jonathan Lynn (*My Cousin Vinny*), this film is heralded as the first leading man role for Michael Richards, the loose-limbed, spastic-mannered comic from the phenomenally successful television sitcom, "Seinfeld;" yet this vehicle falls short of the wonderful smaller role that Richards inhabited in the heartbreaking drama, laced with poignant comedy, *Unstrung Heroes.* Here, Richards stars as actor Richard Rietti, who inadvertently switches places with his lawyer best friend Charles Tuttle (Jeff Daniels) for what he thinks will only be the continuance of a highly important trial.

Charlie seemingly has it all—the corner office in a prestigious law firm, his engagement to the spoiled but beautiful Tiffany Whitfield (Alexandra Wentworth), who coincidentally is the daughter of the head (Lawrence Pressman) of the Whitfield law firm. Whitfield throws him a curveball by asking Charlie to go to a small, dusty Nevada cow town to defend a relative, Benny Gibbs (Rip Torn), who has been accused of bilking people with a mail-order business that promises buyers their own copper artwork engraved with Lincoln's presidential image—in other words, investors paid $19.99 for a shiny copper penny. Charlie winces, but he will do all for his father-in-law-to-be. Richard arranges for Charlie's bachelor party to take in the small town's honky-tonk bar, replete with cowboys, bikers and tough-talking babes.

Richard to Charlie about his trial appearance: "It was just one line. It was a walk-on."

Charlie imbibes so much that he is completely blotto by the dawn's early light, completely unable to appear at Benny's continuance hearing. Richard, at the ready as the Actor's actor, agrees to merely show up, request the continuance, and postpone the rest of the trial until Charlie has sobered up. But Judge Paul Z. Graff (Austin Pendleton) and sharp prosecutor Elizabeth Gardner (Jessica Steen) are more than a match for him. Richard returns to Charlie's room to tell him that the trial is on, and the court thinks that he, Richard, is Charles Tuttle. Charlie freaks out; he accompanies Richard to court the next day and pretends to be an accomplished associate, but the judge will hear none of this. It appears that Richard will have to carry the weight of this trial himself.

Charlie seeks comfort from the serene waitress Billie Tyler (Charlize Theron), a luminous breath of fresh air in this arid town. She is a free spirit, a waitress who lives on the edge of town, content with the simple things in life—a stark contrast to Tiffany, who manages to harangue Charlie about the wedding plans long distance. Meanwhile, Richard manages to offend both the judge and the prosecutor with almost every statement that comes from his mouth. Even though Charlie and Richard set up an elaborate scheme in which Charlie, wired to Richard, beeps coded messages with his car horn, the trial seems a lost cause to the defense. Richard tries to sweet-talk prosecutor Gardner into cutting a deal for them, but to no avail.

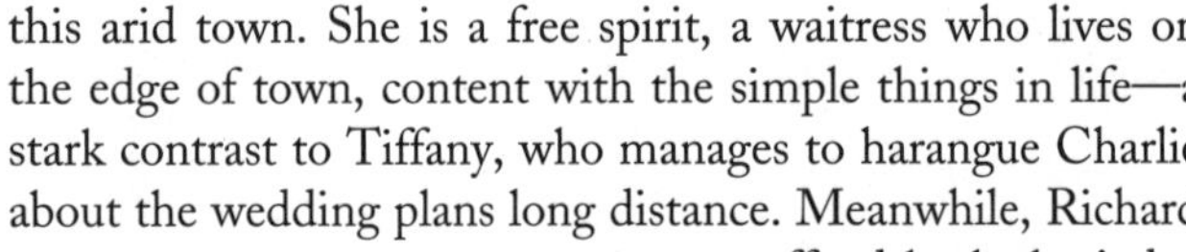

Meanwhile, Charlie and Billie have consummated their flirtation; Charlie is enchanted by this warm, genuine creature. He is stunned to come into his cabin to find another creature—Tiffany! (The hilarious Wentworth is woefully underused in this greedy, grasping girlfriend role.) Billie is so understanding that she doesn't make a scene, she understands his involvement and backs graciously away. Theron shines in this otherwise thankless role; she breathes life and warmth into the most ordinary dialogue.

Richard resorts to the most extraordinary defense tactic; he tries to wring sympathy from the jury by citing ridiculous, trumped-up stories of Benny's abusive childhood. By this time, even Richard is repulsed and advises Benny to plea bargain. Benny refuses and not surprisingly, he is found guilty.

All loose ends are successfully wrapped up; Charlie spurns his obnoxious fiance and invites Billie to come to Los Angeles where they can both start anew; Richard turns prosecutor Gardner's antipathy towards him into a bona-fide attraction—they ride off into the desert sunset on her Harley. What is so disappointing about this movie is not only the flat, forced nature of the courtroom scenes, the uninspired familiar plotline, but more so the waste of the accomplished cast. From Rip Torn (flawless as the acid-tongued producer on HBO's "The Larry Sanders Show"), to Michael Richards, to the winsomely charming Wentworth ("In Living Color"), the actors are mere caricatures, barely fleshed out past the most rigid outlines. Only Theron manages to steal every scene she's in. The overall effect is of a marginally passable comedy, aching with unused potential.

—G.E. Georges

CREDITS

Richard Rietti: Michael Richards
Charles Tuttle: Jeff Daniels
Billie Tyler: Charlize Theron
Elizabeth Gardner: Jessica Steen
Judge Paul Z. Graff: Austin Pendleton
Benny Gibbs: Rip Torn
Tiffany Whitfield: Alexandra Wentworth
Whitfield: Lawrence Pressman

Origin: USA
Released: 1997
Production: Gary Ross and Jonathan Lynn for Larger Than Life; released by New Line Cinema
Direction: Jonathan Lynn
Screenplay: Sarah Bernstein and Gregory Bernstein
Cinematography: Gabriel Beristain
Editing: Tony Lombardo
Music: Phil Marshall
Production design: Victoria Paul
Art direction: Philip Messina
Costumes: Shay Cunliffe
Sound: Joseph Urbanczyk
MPAA rating: PG-13
Running Time: 98 minutes

REVIEWS

Chicago Tribune. May 30, 1997, p. 4.
Entertainment Weekly. June 6, 1997, p. 46.
Los Angeles Times. May 30, 1997, p. F12.
People. June 9, 1997, p. 19.
Sight and Sound. January, 1998, p. 54.
USA Today. May 30, 1997, p. 9D.
Variety. May 26, 1997, p. 64.

Trojan Eddie

Dying for love is one thing. Living to tell the tale is another.—Movie tagline

"Compelling! Two of the finest screen performances of the year."—*Time Out*

Stephen Rea is spectacular in the role of Trojan Eddie, a seemingly hapless Irish loser whose wife leaves him and whose partners in crime constantly let him down. Eddie is likeable, but his get along attitude disgusts his hard-edged wife and his associates in crime, who make fun of him. But Eddie is not stupid, and he has the gift of gab. He makes a wonderful salesman, delighting crowds who come to hear his spiel but leave having coughed up fifty pounds a piece for his stolen goods. Eddie dreams of making the big strike and going off on his own, but he is betrayed by both of his partners.

Equally impressive is Eddie's boss, John Power, played with ruthless veracity by Richard Harris. Harris is now at a venerable age in which every line and crack in his face expresses character. Sometimes all the camera has to do is linger on the fissures of Harris's face to reveal the splits in this man's personality. On the one hand, he is a gangster backed up by his thuggish son. On the other hand, he is an old man weeping at his wife's grave and mooning over a young woman whom he hopes to marry as his next queen.

The film soon settles into a battle between these two men. Is John Power right? Is Eddie just a pathetic minion who will never amount to anything? It seems so. Eddie lets his wayward wife stay with him any time she pleases, even though he goes out with other men right in front of him. Eddie lets his younger partner seduce Power's intended, even though Power is likely to find out and blame Eddie. Eddie never appears to put up a fight for what he wants. He always seems to be left holding the bag—getting neither the girl nor the money, as his wife points out.

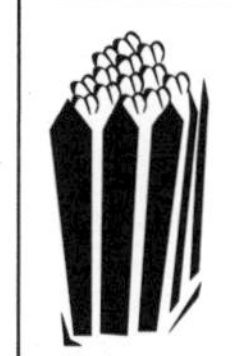

Shirley to Eddie: "You just keep getting left behind."

Stephen Rea's face is a study of alternate moods—primarily patience and exasperation. He goes out of his way to avoid trouble and puts up with Power's constant ragging of him. But at one point he also tells Power "Do you think people aren't laughing at you?" Eddie is referring to the way Power's young love has cheated on him, married him, and then stolen his money, while Power still yearns for her, telling Eddie that he will take her back no questions asked.

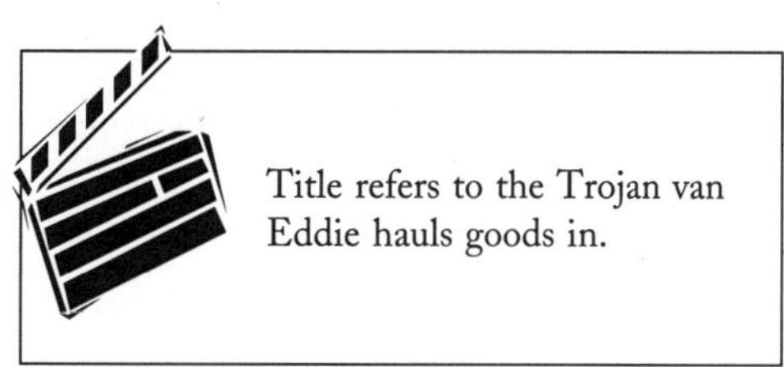

Title refers to the Trojan van Eddie hauls goods in.

Rea's Eddie realizes that no one is as independent or as tough as Power makes himself out to be. Indeed, in a drunken pub scene Power confronts the room, telling off everyone about how they don't have the slightest idea of how to live or to be successful. His bragging is pathetic, though he instills fear with the sheer force of his violent will. Eddie just watches him. Indeed he is always watching and waiting for his opportunity. Rea's face is as fascinating as Harris's. Eddie can lie smoothly and evenly. He just stands his ground and placidly prevaricates. Power suspects Eddie has been disloyal, but he cannot prove it. And Eddie's docility is too useful for Power to forsake.

CREDITS

Trojan Eddie: Stephen Rea
John Power: Richard Harris
Ginger: Brendan Gleeson
Raymie: Sean McGinley
Shirley: Angeline Ball
Betty: Brid Brennan
Dermont: Stuart Townsend
Kathleen: Aislin McGuckin

Origin: Great Britain, Ireland
Released: 1996
Production: Emma Burge for Initial Films, The Irish Film Board, and Channel Four Films; released by Castle Hill Productions
Direction: Gilles MacKinnon
Screenplay: Billy Roche
Cinematography: John de Borman
Editing: Scott Thomas
Music: John Keane
Production design: Frank Conway
Art direction: John Paul Kelly
Costumes: Consolata Boyle
Sound: Simon Willis
MPAA rating: Unrated
Running Time: 105 minutes

Power's kingdom begins to tumble when his thuggish son crosses the line—not merely beating up Eddie's partner but murdering him. Power's violence has threatened all along to bring him down, because it isolates him from others. The film emphasizes this separateness by placing Power atop the second floor of an antique shop and garage. The camera often catches him inside his gaudy kingdom, looking out and sneering at the world below. Whenever he leaves his lair, he seems older and vulnerable. At the graveyard he is positively maudlin, whereas Eddie straightens up. It is the one place where he gives Power a little lip. Power is astonished but helpless. All he can do is splutter as Eddie walks away, saying to Eddie that he cannot survive without Power and that he will come begging back to him.

The film ends with an extraordinary image. Power is in a movie theater with his young wife who has indeed come back to him. But on the screen he sees Trojan Eddie hawking his goods in a commercial. Eddie has always dreamed of making it big—and now it has happened because he has found the stash of cash that his dead partner had stolen from Power's young wife and lover. Power stares at the screen, his mouth open—looking like an old fish out of water. Power does not comment; his expression doesn't change. He simply sits in front of the screen staring—like a fish in a fishtank, separated from any knowledge of the world that Eddie inhabits, a world now much bigger than Power's, whose power, in other words, is waning.

—*Carl Rollyson*

REVIEWS

Boxoffice. April, 1997, p. 197.
Los Angeles Times. September 12, 1997, p. F14.
New York Times. August 29, 1997, p. C3.
Sight and Sound. April, 1997, p. 53.
Variety. September 16, 1997, p. 72.
Village Voice. September 2, 1997, p. 73.

Troublesome Creek: A Midwestern

Where one family takes a stand.—Movie tagline
"Filmmaking at its finest!"—*Boston Globe*
"Superb!"—*Rolling Stone*
"Stunning!"—*Time-Out*

Troublesome Creek: A Midwestern, is named for a switchback creek that runs through the Iowa farm director June Jordan's family has worked since 1867. In 1990, when Jordan and her husband and co-director, Steven Ascher, learned that her family might lose the farm, the couple left their home in Cambridge, Massachusetts, for the Midwest. Amid the haunting, hardscrabble landscape of northwestern Iowa, Jordan and Ascher spent a year and a half documenting the end of one chapter of the Jordan family saga.

The demise of the family farm has, almost from the nation's birth, been a staple of American popular culture, and following the long, difficult recession of the late 1970s and early 1980s, several feature films were made chronicling the drama that inevitably ensues when bankers call in the loans they have made to overextended independent farmers. Never, though, has this archetypal saga been so well filmed. Jordan's parents, the bushy browed Russell, who once won an Abraham Lincoln look-alike contest, and Mary Jane, a former 4-H club president, could not be more perfectly cast. They are salt of the earth, no nonsense individuals who like to spend their few hours of relaxation watching old westerns such as *Red River* on television. Their dilemma, too, could not be more American: after years of following the custom of borrowing from the local bank in order to work the farm, the elder Jordans find themselves $200,000 in debt with the bank's new owners calling in their markers.

Troublesome Creek may follow a standard scenario, but it is not a melodrama; like the eponymous creek, its course can be unpredictable. Russell and Mary Jane decide that what matters most is that the farm stay in the family. Without much ado, they resolve to sell off all but the bare necessities of living in order to pay back the bank and give the land to one of their sons, Jim, who works a nearby rented property. This process could be heartbreaking, but the Jordans maintain an air of stoic dignity. Only occasionally does Mary Jane object to the sale of certain knickknacks or bemoan the loss of her prized Ethan Allen furniture.

AWARDS AND NOMINATIONS

Sundance Film Festival 1996: Grand Jury Prize-Documentary, Audience Award-Documentary

The composed but elegiac tone of the film owes a great deal to the somewhat wry voice-over narration supplied by Jeanne Jordan, who also makes an occasional appearance on-screen. This is, we are reminded, her story, too. On auction day, as scores of people gather in the snow and blistering wind, we see the director hug a family friend who has driven 150 miles not to bid on possessions, but to offer moral support: neither of these persons is simply fulfilling a role. The moment is not dramatized or highlighted in any way, and for this very reason it serves to underscore the bittersweet message that is the burden of *Troublesome Creek*. As Jordan's voice-over tells us, in the past 30 years, the numbers of Americans who make their living by farming has dwindled from 6 million to 2 million. America is changing, and not necessarily for the better. And yet, the Jordans do manage, through sheer willpower it seems, to keep the family farm in the family—at least for the time being. At the end of *Troublesome Creek*, we are uncertain whether Jim and his family will be able to make a go of it, and "home" has been reduced to a tiny bungalow in Wiota, Iowa, where the senior Jordans have taken up residence. They don't seem to mind—but we do, and so does Jeanne Jordan. We, like Jeanne—and indeed, like her parents—may have moved on, but something clearly has been lost forever. The point is underscored when Jeanne and her parents visit a former family home, now sitting empty in the middle of an Iowa hamlet so unpeopled it appears to be almost a ghost town.

But *Troublesome Creek* is, as its subtitle implies, not a classic western with good guys and bad guys and a neat conclusion. Instead, it is something more modest, a "midwestern," a kind of home movie about the loss not of a home per se, but more of a sense of home. Jeanne Jordan's documentary, by focusing on a particular place and time and group of individuals, manages to capture an emblematic moment and create a small, quiet elegy to a way of life that is vanishing before our eyes.

—Lisa Paddock

CREDITS

Origin: USA
Released: 1996
Production: Jeanne Jordan, Steven Ascher for West City Films Inc.; released by Artistic License/Forensic Films
Direction: Jeanne Jordan, Steven Ascher
Screenplay: Jeanne Jordan and Steven Ascher
Cinematography: Steven Ascher
Editing: Jeanne Jordan
Music: Sheldon Mirowitz
Sound: Victoria Garvin Davis
MPAA rating: Unrated
Running Time: 88 minutes

REVIEWS

Entertainment Weekly. February 14, 1997, p. 44.
New York Times. January 24, 1997, p. C6.
Variety. February 5, 1996, p. 61.

Truth or Consequences, N.M.

Life's harsh. Why behave?—Movie tagline

"A solid directing bow for actor Keifer Sutherland."—*Film Journal*

"A fresh, exciting and thoroughly involving thriller. A strong first directorial outing for Kiefer Sutherland. *Truth or Consequences* delivers the action goods with welcome intelligence."—Kevin Thomas, *Los Angeles Times*

"The action is fast and furious. Sutherland is off to a flying start."—Bill Hoffman, *New York Post*

"Gritty and suspenseful. A top notch thriller!"—Alan Silverman, *Voice of America*

"A superb, fast-paced drama of love, murder and mayhem."—*WBAI Radio*

"A potent cocktail of love and bullets."—*Westwood One*

The studio's hyphenated description of this "action-comedy-thriller" indicates that this is a movie that cannot decide what it wants to be and ends up, like bad Tarantino, being a failed experiment in postmodern, postgenre confusion, tilting between a gangster film and an updated Western, being neither fish nor fowl, but tending toward the foul in its violent excesses. It's a little surprising that the actor Kiefer Sutherland (who is also prominent in the cast, of course, armed and dangerous), working from a derivative screenplay by Brad Mirman, would choose this project for his debut as film director. Later in the year Alicia Silverstone would make a similar debut miscalculation when she produced and starred in *Excess Baggage*, which alienated both fans and critics. Both would discover that bad decisions may have unforeseen consequences, but at least *Excess Baggage* went into wide distribution, as Sutherland's film did not.

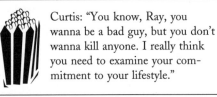

Curtis: "You know, Ray, you wanna be a bad guy, but you don't wanna kill anyone. I really think you need to examine your commitment to your lifestyle."

Truth or Consequences begins with petty criminal Raymond Lebecke (Vincent Gallo) being paroled from prison in a nicely photographed title sequence. He desperately loves Addy Monroe (Kim Dickens) and wants nothing more than to escape with her to a new life after his release from prison, but he lacks resources, both financial and intellectual. Ray thinks maybe one more caper will do the trick, and then he can go straight, but after he gets involved in a botched drug heist, things go seriously wrong and people get killed, including an undercover cop. Ray has the bad judgment to join forces with former prisonmate Curtis Freley (Sutherland) and his sidekick Marcus Weans (Mykelti Williamson), who turns out to be an undercover narcotics agent. Attempting to flee to Mexico, they take a detour to Las Vegas and pick up two yuppie hostages along the way for no clear reason, Gordon Jacobson and Donna Moreland (Kevin Pollack and Grace Phillips) "found picnicking in the middle of nowhere," in the words of one reviewer. Gordon owns a recreational vehicle, and it is a potentially amusing comment on middle-class America to show gangsters on the lam in a Winnebago.

Feature film directorial debut for Keifer Sutherland.

The plot then quickly disintegrates into psychopathic antics, with the Sutherland character front and center, guns blazing when they attempt to sell the stolen drugs to mob lord Tony Vaga (Rod Steiger) in Vegas. Tony knows they stole the heist from Eddie Grillo, but they did not know that Eddie worked for Tony. Curtis has two revolvers concealed in the suitcase that holds the drugs, and manages to kill Tony and his two bodyguards. Well, it turns out that Tony works for Franco Giannino, an old-fashioned gangster who believes in vendettas and who sends his enforcer, known only as "Sir" (Martin Sheen), after Curtis and Ray, with an army of hit men. On their way to Ray's brothers house in Truth or Consequences, New Mexico, Ray crashes with Wayne (Max Perlich), his former cellmate now on parole. "Sir" and his assassins call on Wayne, who is tortured into telling them where Ray is headed, then killed.

Gordon becomes so fascinated with his captors that he is converted to Curtis's ranting about how life is just a game. Gordon is stupid, and Gordon is a loser, but in the final shootout, it is Gordon who manages to save Donna's life by shooting the Mafia assassin played by Martin Sheen. As Stephen Holden noted in his *New York Times* review, the only new twist this film brings to the genre is the "unconvincing suggestion that in the breast of every mild-mannered yuppie beats the heart of a would-be killer," but this is hardly "new." Gordon proves to be a natural born killer, just like the television reporter in Oliver Stone's film. What was really new was Oliver Stone's suggestion that we are all, at heart, natural born killers.

But what is the genre at issue here? Holden argues that the Western did not simply fade away but "merely curdled into a cynical new genre in which the alienated progeny of Bonnie and Clyde gallivant through the American heartland, wreaking death and destruction until they are mowed down." The idea of misguided degenerates on the run is hardly a new one in the American cinema. It can be traced from *Bonnie & Clyde* (1967) to *Bad Company* (1972) to *Natural Born Killers* (1994), in descending order of taste and excess. In

CREDITS

Raymond Lembecke: Vincent Gallo
Marcus Weans: Mykelti Williamson
Curtis Freley: Keifer Sutherland
Gordon Jacobson: Kevin Pollack
Addy Monroe: Kim Dickens
Donna Moreland: Grace Phillips
Frank Thompson: Rick Rossovich
Eddie Grillo: John C. McGinley
Wayne: Max Perlich
Tony Vago: Rod Steiger
Sir: Martin Sheen

Origin: USA
Released: 1997
Production: J. Paul Higgins, Kevin J. Messick and Hilary Wayne for Triumph Films; released by Sony Pictures Entertainment
Direction: Keifer Sutherland
Screenplay: Brad Mirman
Cinematography: Ric Waite
Editing: Lawrence Jordan
Music: Jude Cole
Production design: Anne Stuhler
Art direction: Rowell Hamrick
Costumes: Susan Bertram
Sound: Walter Anderson
MPAA rating: R
Running Time: 106 minutes

the final shootout in Truth or Consequences, New Mexico, Curtis and Ray first have to face down the Mafia assassins, then the FBI, and it's a no-win situation, demonstrating that most banal of conclusions, crime doesn't pay.

Lisa Schwarzbaum of *Entertainment Weekly* criticized the film's pointless violence, the "moronic" love affair between Raymond and Addy, and the "derivative" and "hackneyed" script, and she was right on all points. "To paraphrase one of the posse's description of Sutherland's character," she concluded, *Truth or Consequences* "is as bad as they come." The only emotion one feels for these doomed lovers, according to Stephen Holden, "is contempt for their stupidity in teaming up with an obvious nut case." In brief, this certainly was not an auspicious beginning for Kiefer Sutherland's directorial debut.

Sutherland gave himself the film's meatiest role. In their cameo roles, both Rod Steiger as the Las Vegas drug lord and Martin Sheen as a ghastly mob enforcer, overplay their roles for comic effect, as Stephen Holden noted. Even so, Holden did not consider the film a comedy; instead he wrote that it "aspires to be an all-American romantic tragedy," but it is not at all convincingly done. Poisoned by negative reviews, the film did not go into wide release and died aborning at the box office. Ignored or ridiculed by the critics, it appeared to be quickly destined for video markets, where it arrived in November. This film was more about consequences than truth, the consequences of idiots on a spree, and the consequences of both characters and filmmakers making bad choices.

—James M. Welsh

REVIEWS

Boxoffice. May, 1997, p. 56.
Entertainment Weekly. May 16, 1997, p. 89.
Entertainment Weekly. November 7, 1997, p. 92.
The Hollywood Reporter. May 2, 1997, p. 10.
Los Angeles Times. May 2, 1997, p. F19.
The New York Times. May 2, 1997, p. C33.
People. May 12, 1997, p. 23.
Variety. April 28, 1997, p. 100.
Village Voice. May 6, 1997, p. 86.

Turbo: A Power Rangers Movie

Shift into Turbo!—Movie tagline
The Power is Back!—Movie tagline
" . . . a high-spirited fantasy adventure . . ."
—Daniel Hunter, *Hollywood Reporter*

Box Office: $8,363,899

Turbo: A Power Rangers Movie lacks everything a movie aimed at kids should have, except for high energy, which it's got to spare. The film, which takes the legendary Mighty Morphin Power Rangers and pits them against a crew of nasty space pirates, is a headache of hyper-kinetic movement. Conceived and executed by ruthless profiteers for sure, the film is joyless, and a trial to sit through—made worse by the adult viewer's knowledge that eventually millions of very young children will have been duped into seeing it in one format or another.

Turbo begins with scrolling narration a la *Star Wars*, explaining of a good wizard from a distant planet who is the key to an energy prison located inside one of Earth's volcanoes. Inside the volcano is a bad deity named Maligore who has been kept there for centuries, separated from his beloved wife, Divatox. Their union would mean chaos for the universe. So Divatox plans to kidnap the wizard and open the gate.

Lerigot is the name of the Great Wizard. He looks pretty much like an Ewok and purrs *just* like E.T. During the film's unintentionally hilarious opening scenes, the filmmakers go to great pains to establish that Lerigot is a family man who cares nothing about intergalactic wars and only wants to provide for his Ewok-looking wife and child. As the film opens, Divatox's fellow space pirates have landed on Lerigot's home planet and are in the process of tracking him down. A hunt ensues, but the wizard is too clever, using magic to transport himself off the planet just as the pirates are bearing down on him.

Down here on earth, Rocky (Steve Cardenas), aka The Blue Ranger, is participating in a kickboxing match. In the audience are the other Rangers. There is Tommy, the Red Ranger (Jason David Frank), Katherine, the Pink Ranger (Catherine Sutherland), Tanya, the Yellow Ranger (Nakia Burrise), and Adam, the Green Ranger (Johnny Yong Bosch). Also watching Rocky fight is the whiny Justin (Blake Foster), a 10-year-old friend of the Rangers who doesn't know their identities, but who hangs around with them when they're just being regular teenagers (uh-huh).

Suddenly, Rocky goes down. He's hurt. Bad. Later, as he's waking up, he starts talking Ranger talk. Of course,

Justin is right there to hear. Realizing who his friends really are, Justin somehow convinces Rocky and the other Rangers to let him be the new Blue Ranger. Later on in the film, he will don Rocky's Blue Ranger outfit and fight alongside the other Rangers. This is the kind of plot point that the term "suspension of disbelief" was created for. Otherwise, how could anyone buy the fact that there's not a single objection raised by any of the Rangers to this 10-year-old boy being placed in the kinds of peril they face everyday?

Meanwhile, deep in the Pacific, Divatox and her pirates have commandeered a submarine. Inside, Divatox and her crew conspire to capture Lerigot, who has transported himself to earth. One of the most frustrating things about the movie is what's left unexplained. For example, why did Lerigot transport himself to earth? Wouldn't he want to get as far away from Maligore's prison as he possibly could, being the key and all? And what does Divatox need a submarine for, except to add another toy to the product line? The whole movie is like that, shamelessly tossing in potential toy after potential toy.

Back at the Power Rangers' hideout, Zordon, the Power Rangers' leader, who in this film is supposed to be a being of infinite wisdom, is alerted that Lerigot has entered earth's atmosphere. He summons the Rangers, minus Rocky but including Justin, and explains to them that they must stop Divatox and her goons at all costs. But this will be no easy task, he warns, and explains that he has decided to upgrade their Morphin powers (apparently he's been holding out on them all these years).

To further aid them in their quest, Zordon has provided them each with a brand new vehicle called Turbo Zords. In addition to a few super-charged extras, it seems that these Turbo Zords can be combined to create one giant Turbo Megazord, which is basically just a giant human-shaped transportation vehicle that eventually will do battle against one of Divatox's similarly composed enemy vehicles. So the Rangers, including Justin, set out to find and confront Divatox.

While four of the Rangers seek out Divatox, two others, Tommy and Katherine, search the jungles of South America for Lerigot, who somehow has found himself face-to-face with a well-trained lion. Back down in the sub, Divatox instructs her minion creatures to go out and find two earthlings of exceptional purity for use in the upcoming ceremony designed to free Maligore. Naturally, the minions decide to abduct chaste citizens Tommy and Katherine. Imprisoned in the sub's cargo hold alongside Lerigot, the two devise an elaborate plan to break free.

Meanwhile, the other four Rangers have commandeered an old Spanish galleon and are sailing towards the sub. What happens is that Divatox captures the whole lot of them and takes them all to the island of Muranthias, home to the active volcano-prison in which resides Maligore. The finale centers around Tommy and Katherine, who are the conduits through which Maligore takes physical form. Only their strengths of mind can keep Maligore from altering their personalities—but they also employ a lot of karate kicks and back flips. The noisy conclusion resembles a four ring circus as the good guys fight scores of bad guys around a pit of bubbling lava.

The movie is full of injustices, chief among them being the wasting of talent. For example, Catherine Sutherland projects smarts and a likable personality in her performance as Katherine, the Pink Ranger, but the scripting and the direction conspire to keep her personality subdued. None of the rest of the Rangers even register on the personality meter; they seem almost to be sleepwalking through their performances. On the other hand, the cinematographer, Ilan Rosenberg, has done a fine job; the film looks good. Sadly, his talents have been wasted on an inferior screenplay.

Turbo: A Power Rangers Movie seems like it just might be the last gasp of a dying franchise, and not because of its awfulness (pretty much every project and product associated with the Power Rangers is of a similar quality), but because the generation of kids who were raised on these color-coded heroes are getting older, and the new generation doesn't seem

CREDITS

Tommy Oliver: Jason David Frank
Rocky DeSantos: Steve Cardenas
Adam Park: Johnny Yong Bosch
Tanya Sloan: Nakia Burrise
Katherine Hillard: Catherine Sutherland
Justin: Blake Foster
Farkus "Bulk" Bulkmeir: Paul Schrier
Eugene "Skull" Skullovich: Jason Narvy
Jason Lee Scott: Austin St. John
Kimberly Hart: Amy Jo Johnson
Divatox: Hillary Shepard
Ernie: Richard Genelle
Lerigot: Jon Simanton

Origin: USA
Released: 1997
Production: Jonathan Tzachor for Saban Entertainment; released by 20th Century Fox
Direction: Shuki Levy, David Winning
Screenplay: Shuki Levy and Shell Danielson
Cinematography: Ilan Rosenberg
Editing: Henry Richardson, B.J. Sears
Production design: Yuda Ako
Costumes: Danielle Baker
Car Customizer: George Barris
Music: Shuki Levy
Sound: Neil Spritz
MPAA rating: PG
Running Time: 99 minutes

interested in taking its place. That's definitely an encouraging sign. The Power Rangers are faceless, conformist, bland. None of them reveals even a single identifiable personality trait. The only way to tell them apart is by the color of their outfits. It seems that one of the messages that the Mighty Morphin Power Rangers have been sending to our kids these past few years is that individuality is something to be repressed. If that's the case, then good riddance to them.

—*David King*

REVIEWS

Chicago Tribune. March 28, 1997, p. 5.
New York Times. March 29, 1997, p. 17.
People. April 7, 1997, p. 20.
Variety. March 31, 1997, p. 85.

Turbulence

Fear is in the air.—Movie tagline
It's a killer ride.—Movie tagline
"Over the top action!"—Jim Ferguson, *Fox-TV*
"A wild ride!"—Steve Oldfield, *KSTU-TV*
"Non-stop entertainment!"—Mike Cidoni, *WOKR-TV*

Box Office: $11,538,235

Disaster films have an effect on the viewer in a manner that is akin to a bloody traffic accident. Nobody wants to be involved in one, but everyone wants to stop and gawk at the carnage. The most successful disaster movies of the past (*Earthquake* [1974], *Independence Day* [1996], *The Poseidon Adventure* [1972], *The Towering Inferno* [1974]) have been big-budget, larger-than-life affairs. Style takes a commanding presence over substance. *Twister* [1996] and *Daylight* [1996], despite their many technical advances, drew blanks from the majority of the pundits due to a complete lack of any real story. *Daylight* was so unoriginal, many critics jokingly referred to it as "The Poseidon Inferno," referring to its blatant pilfering of ideas from those films. Dazzling explosions, computer generated effects and thunderous soundtracks have been implemented by producers and directors as decoys to divert audiences' attention away from the utter lack of substantial script. Setting a disaster film in the air always provides a (slightly) more interesting premise: filmmakers can take their little bags of peripheral tricks and combine the public's deep-seeded fear of flying and come up with some top-notch, exploitative, terror-fests. The "best" films of this genre include *Airport* [1970], *Die Hard 2: Die Harder* [1990], *Executive Decision* [1996] and *Fearless* [1993]. Although it used an air disaster as its central theme, the success of *Hero* [1992] is credited more to its scathing sarcasm of the media than to its sensational special effects.

Scheduled for release in late July 1996, MGM delayed the premiere of *Turbulence*, allegedly citing many unsavory similarities to the TWA flight 800 tragedy in New York. The studio decided that showing a film about terrorism in the air so soon after a real-life catastrophe would not only be bad timing, it would also be in bad taste. They were right, but for all the wrong reasons. This movie is thoroughly lacking in anything resembling taste. Any correlation to the TWA calamity is negligible, the situations are completely dissimilar. The studio simply recognized this hackneyed project couldn't possibly compete with the much stronger summer fare. They decided to cut their losses and instead waited for a January release. Often regarded as the ugly stepchild by the studios, January regularly proves to be the cinematic dumping ground for movies that they wish would just go away.

Ray Liotta stars as murderer Ryan Weaver, whose unexplained crimes and subsequent vaguely shady conviction was secured by an ethically challenged cop (Hector Elizondo). During a Christmas Eve air transport, Weaver heroically rescues the passengers and crew when another prisoner wipes out his inept police escorts. Without any warning, rhyme or reason, Weaver himself goes nuts. Deciding he has nothing to live for and wishing to go out in a "blaze of glory," he decides he's going to crash the plane then starts to browbeat a recently heartbroken flight attendant (Lauren Holly). Holly is plucky and cute, but in a by-the-numbers manner. After the remainder of the crew and passengers have been locked away by Liotta, Holly makes radio contact with authorities on the ground who begin instructing her on how to land the plane. Growing crazier and more demented by the minute, Liotta flushes Holly out of the cockpit by starting a fire in the cabin. After the pair tussle and tangle for awhile, Holly scrapes her way back into the pilot's chair and Liotta finds his way to the part of the

CREDITS

Ryan Weaver: Ray Liotta
Teri Halloran: Lauren Holly
Stubbs: Brendan Gleeson
Lt. Aldo Hines: Hector Elizondo
Capt. Sam Bowen: Ben Cross
Rachel Taper: Rachel Ticotin
Brooks: Jeffrey DeMunn
Sinclair: John Finn
Maggie: Catherine Hicks

Origin: USA
Released: 1997
Production: Martin Ransohoff and David Valdes for Rysher Entertainment; released by MGM/UA
Direction: Robert Butler
Screenplay: Jonathan Brett
Cinematography: Lloyd Ahern II
Editing: John Duffy
Music: Shirley Walker
Production design: Mayling Cheng
Art direction: Donald B. Woodruff
Costumes: Robert Turturice
Visual effects supervisor: Mark Vargo
Sound: David MacMillan
MPAA rating: R
Running Time: 100 minutes

aircraft that houses the electronics. He disables the automatic pilot mechanism, forcing Holly to land the plane manually. After a failed first attempt, Holly makes a second pass and brings the plane in for a near perfect landing.

Liotta is a very talented actor who is one of a very select few who can play protagonists and antagonists with equal success and believability. With *Something Wild* [1986] and *Unlawful Entry* [1992], he embodied truly credible menace and terror. Steely, penetrating blue eyes and a healthy dose of synthetic charm made his characters eerily foreboding. The careful restraint he showed in those films has been replaced by a cartoonish, absolutely over-the-top posturing. The fact that his character has no real motive for his actions makes the performance even more disappointing. Painfully pedestrian dialogue, bombastic sound and dizzying visuals are blended together with such slipshod ineptitude, you don't know whether to laugh or quickly reach for an airsick bag.

—J.M. Clark

REVIEWS

Boxoffice. March, 1997, p. 46.
Los Angeles Times. January 10, 1997, p. F4.
New York Times. January 10, 1997, p. C3.
People. January 20, 1997, p. 18.
USA Today. January 10, 1997, p. 4D.
Variety. January 6, 1997, p. 179.

Twin Town

An extreme comedy.—Movie tagline

"Fresh, twisted, fun!"—Oliver Jones, *Details*

"Very funny! The boys' perverted antics are hysterically insane."—Dwight Brown, *Emerge Magazine*

"Wild entertainment! A gleefully anarchic comedy. The performances are excellent."—Lawrence Van Gelder, *The New York Times*

"You'll laugh in horror."—Dennis Dermody, *Paper*

"Wildly enjoyable."—Tom Gliatto, *People*

Actor and TV documentarist Kevin Allen makes his feature-film directorial debut with the blacker than black comedy *Twin Town*, a raucous and perversely hilarious romp through the post-mining landscape of the Welsh industrial town of Swansea—a place once described by poet Dylan Thomas as "the graveyard of ambition."

Allen and co-writer Paul Durden seem determined to blast the cultural ball-and-chain notion of Wales as idyllic pastoral existence to smithereens, effectively juxtaposing pure sentimentality with really raunchy humor.

One of the film's running gags is that the trailer trash Lewis Twins are not even really twins. Like the actors that play them, Llyr Evans and Rhys Ifans (Welsh for Evans), they are actually only brothers. The unemployed and perpetually stoned duo joy-ride around town in a variety of stolen cars while rolling joints and wrecking havoc in a town rife with class tensions and corruption.

And what better a target than the pretentious local bigwig contractor Bryn Cartwright (William Thomas). Cartwright is trafficking in drugs on the side with two corrupt cops. Greyo (Dorien Thomas) has it bad for the twins' sister, a "receptionist at an executive health spa" or more precisely, a massage parlor hooker. The younger, volatile Terry (Dougray Scott), is a thug ambitious about his corruption. After all, the town motto is "Ambition is Critical."

While Thomas described Swansea as an "ugly, lovely town," Terry prides himself in his own little riff on the relative nature of the town's beauty: "Pretty, shitty city." Hey, he reminds us, at least his version rhymes.

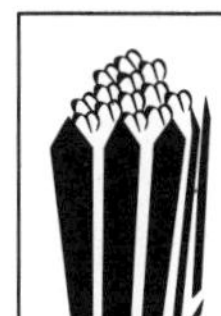

Filmed on location in Swansea, South Wales.

When their father is injured while working on the sly for Cartwright, the Twins demand compensation for dear old Fatty. Cartwright sneers at the suggestion and sooner than you can say, Geez I can't understand a word these guys are saying, things have escalated into some absurdly satisfying acts of revenge. It may not be very PC to laugh at the brutality, but one should at least appreciate such a twisted sense of humor.

Twin Town is one of the year's funniest films—but that does not give it universal appeal. It is hip, unwaveringly harsh and edgy without having to rely on the obvious grossness of heroin abuse of films such as *Trainspotting* (1996), the film directed and produced by *Twin Town*'s Exec Producers Danny Boyle and Andrew MacDonald. While the Lewis Twins are serious potheads, most of this film's scathing humor flows out of its social commentary, of which drug abuse is but one issue.

Twin Town's intensity comes from its observations about the decay of a once-thriving city and the moral corruption and ambition of both the pseudo-powerful and the nouveau riche. Allen and Durden harpoon everything from the class-conscious anarchy of post-Thatcher Britain, Welsh men's choral groups, and yes, even karaoke as an art form. And lest those Brits think they can get away with their well-known fondness for canine companions, there is even a really sick homage to *The Godfather* (1972).

When the Lewis Twins turn to revenge, the film takes what might be considered its own tonal U-turn from quirky to ruthless. But in a brilliant exercise of form equaling content, the filmmakers have managed to visually articulate the Evil Twin of Swansea. When the noirish nightmare of pervasive evil takes firm hold, there is nary a Good Guy left standing. Or so it might seem.

What is particularly interesting in *Twin Town*'s complicated structure is the final morality play. The Lewis Twins may seem to be immoral, hedonistic slackers, but by the end, they have succeeded in righting a terrible wrong. They have avenged the deaths of their family and meted out a little karmic justice along the way.

Scotsman Dougray Scott stands out in a uniformly vital cast as the crooked cop Terry. He is a darkly engaging presence that captivates the screen and although his character is quite the lout, Scott manages to imbue him with these subtle little chinks in his armor, fleeting moments of pain beneath the swagger. They are surprisingly honest in the midst of such mayhem.

While in many ways inspired by Allen's BBC experience covering the Glasgow, Scotland Ice Cream Wars—a turf dispute between ice cream vendors that resulted in the deaths of five people—he insists that *Twin Town* is in no way meant as social realism. Attempting to put any further speculation to rest, Allen reminds us, "People do not wear Hawaiian shirts in Swansea."

—Patricia Kowal

CREDITS

Julian: Llyr Evans
Jeremy: Rhys Ifans
Terry: Dougray Scott
Greyo: Dorien Thomas
Lucy: Sue Roderick
Fatty: Hugh Ceredig
Adie: Rachel Scorgie

Origin: Great Britain
Released: 1997
Production: Peter McAleese for Agenda, Figment Films and Polygram Filmed Entertainment; released by Gramercy Pictures
Direction: Kevin Allen
Screenplay: Kevin Allen and Paul Durden
Cinematography: John Mathieson
Editing: Oral Norrie Ottey
Music: Mark Thomas
Production design: Pat Campbell
Art direction: Jean Kerr
Costumes: Rachael Fleming
Sound: Colin Nicholson, Mike Harris
MPAA rating: Unrated
Running Time: 99 minutes

REVIEWS

Boxoffice. May, 1997, p. 63.
Detroit News. May 30, 1997, p. H1.
Los Angeles Times. May 16, 1997, p. F14.
New York Times. May 12, 1997, p. B5.
People. May 12, 1997, p. 24.
Sight and Sound. April, 1997, p. 53.
Variety. February 10, 1997, p. 67.
Village Voice. May 13, 1997, p. 86.

Ulee's Gold

The story of a family on the edge, and the man who brought them back.—Movie tagline

"One of the year's best and richest films!"—Jay Carr, *Boston Globe*

"A quiet masterpiece!"—Graham Fuller, *Interview*

"Moving and emotional."—Kenneth Turan, *Los Angeles Times*

"A quietly powerful drama."—Jack Mathews, *New York Newsday*

"*Ulee's Gold* is beautiful and heartfelt. The finest work of Peter Fonda's career."—Janet Maslin, *New York Times*

"Peter Fonda gives the performance of his career!"—David Ansen, *Newsweek*

"A triumph!"—Peter Travers, *Rolling Stone*

"One of the year's best films."—Gene Siskel, *Siskel & Ebert*

Box Office: $8,671,423

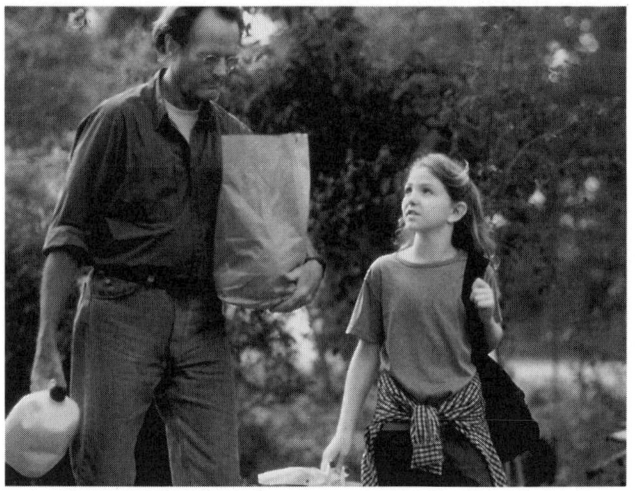

A request from his incarcerated son to protect his wife and daughters gets Ulee Jackson (Peter Fonda) involved with some unscrupulous thugs in the celebrated independent film *Ulee's Gold.*

During the dullest summer season in recent memory, *Ulee's Gold* was a welcome surprise. This film, written and directed by Victor Nunez, was pure gold, a wholly unexpected drama about real people, told in a carefully measured style and pace and committed to confounding viewer expectations. Ulysses Jackson (Peter Fonda) is a beekeeper in the tupelo marshes of the Florida Panhandle. He's a chilly and rather remote person who seems more comfortable prowling among his hives than caring for the two granddaughters left in his care.

Ulee: "The bees and I have an understanding. I take care of them, and they take care of me."

Gradually, the viewer begins to piece together the situation. Ulee has seen a world of hurt during his fifty-odd years: He was the sole survivor of the massacre of his unit in Viet Nam; his wife died unexpectedly, six years before the film starts; his son Jimmy (Tom Wood) is in jail for theft; his daughter-in-law Helen (Christine Dunford) split and left him with her two children, Penny (Vanessa Zima) and Casey (Jessica Biel); and he faces ruination unless he can get that specialty honey in from the hives.

As bad as all this seems, things get worse. A telephone call from his incarcerated son leads him on a trip to retrieve the errant wife, who's currently being "kept" by the son's former accomplices, Eddie Flowers (Steven Flynn) and Ferris Dooley (Dewey Weber). Ulee goes to Orlando to get Helen and is given an ultimatum at gunpoint: Unless he delivers to them the money his son has hidden away after the theft, they will come to Ulee's house and kill his granddaughters (or worse!). In something of a daze, Ulee returns home with the addlepated, struggling daughter-in-law. While she gradually recovers and reestablishes a relationship with her daughters who hardly know her, Ulee makes his plans to deliver the swag, but first he needs to harvest his honey, or face ruination.

The two hoods arrive earlier than expected at Ulee's place. He agrees to show them where the money is hidden. They leave, after tying the girls to chairs, bound and gagged. To protect the women, Ulee talks both of them into going into the swamp with him, where Jimmy left the money in a cooler under the cab of an abandoned truck. The money is recovered, but not before Ulee manages to kick the hoods' revolver into the swamp. He is stabbed in retaliation, but minutes later the local sheriff picks up the two punks and discovers the bag of money.

Ulee later recovers from his wound, and the sheriff tacitly agrees to look the other way, pretending that Ulee did not know about the hidden loot. The film ends with Ulee back at his hives, only by now some things have changed: the girls have reconciled with their mother, and the winsome nurse across the road, Connie Hope (Patricia Richardson), has begun to win his heart. Even Jimmy seems to have reformed in prison and plans to return home and carry on the family tradition of beekeeping.

Ulee's Gold takes its time to measure deliberately the Florida swamp locations, Ulee's beekeeping procedures, and the slowly evolving relationships among the characters. Fonda, who, in his steel-rimmed glasses looks more than ever like his father, is convincing as a burned-out, slow-talking, distrustful relic of bad times (if anything, at times he is too laconic and maddeningly stoic, to a fault). Patricia Richardson plays Connie, the nurse next door who manages to crack through his weathered facade and helps to care for the addicted daughter-in-law. One might protest that the film's reconciliation of family members at the end is too hasty and contrived, but, no, *Ulee's Gold* has far too much going for it to quibble.

The title refers to Tupelo honey, which is produced from the tupelo gum tree that grows along the Chipola and Apalachicola rivers of northwest Florida.

Janet Maslin called Peter Fonda's performance in *Ulee's Gold* "The great surprise at this year's Sundance Film Festival." Once a counterculture icon as a result of *Easy Rider* (1969, considered by *Time* magazine as "one of the 10 most important motion picture events of the decade"), Fonda seemed to be in hibernation for nearly 30 years, eclipsed by the political activism and celebrity status of his sister Jane, whose star set during the 1990s after her marriage to Ted Turner. But while Jane was playing politics with Jean-Luc Godard after her stint with Roger Vadim, Peter's star was rising. He not only starred with Dennis Hopper "looking for America" and finding it unfriendly in *Easy Rider*, but came up with the story concept and shared screenwriting credits with Dennis Hopper and Terry Southern. He told James Brady that his celebrity father Henry Fonda once kept bees on his nine-acre ranch and "produced something called 'Fonda's Bel Air Honey.'"

The young Peter Fonda of the trippy '60s who experimented with LSD once would have been cast as Ulee's ne'er-do-well son Jimmy or as one of the two hoods that threaten Ulee, but the mature Peter Fonda has grown into the role that his own father might have played. "I think it was therapeutic for Peter to play a character like his father," director Victor Nunez told Jamie Diamond of the *New York Times*: "His ability to understand that person from the inside, as well as to understand him from the receiving end, is part of Mr. Fonda's growing up."

Ulee is defined by his composure and control. "You have to be very calm," Fonda told the *New York Times*, in order to handle bees bare-handed: "I'm not out of control at all with my life or body. It's just that my father thought I was." In the film, as Janet Maslin remarked, "Every measured movement counts for a great deal, as Ulee's wariness and understatement set the drama's overall tone." For Fonda, as Maslin noted in a later piece on atypical summer films, this was a "career-resuscitating role" that was "sure to be remembered at year's end," in other words, when the Academy Award nominations are decided.

Stanley Kauffmann described Victor Nunez as a "stubborn and gifted independent filmmaker" who has "personal objectives in mind," centered in northern Florida, and interested in making films "in and about his native heath, in a range of themes." A total filmmaker, Nunez "not only wrote, directed and edited the film but also served as camera operator" for director of photography Virgil Marcus Mirano, as Stuart Klawans noted in *The Nation*. Like Klawans, Kauffmann was impressed by the director's feelings for and "evocation of the landscape." Despite Billy Bob Thornton's success with *Sling Blade* (1996), which told an oddly affective, low-keyed story of rural Arkansas, it is rare for a regional filmmaker to succeed in a Hollywood-dominated atmosphere that usually centers upon urban violence and corruption, usually found in New York or Los Angeles. Clearly, there are other stories to be told and other voices need to be heard, and Nunez makes a strong case for a portion of Florida that is usually not much in the public eye. He shows evidence of being a fresh and original talent. As Desson Howe remarked, as if instructing his readers how to view this film, "in independent movies such as this, where good intentions and offbeat creative instincts meet with modest budgets, there's a pact between filmmaker and audience. If things are a little slow, ponderous or tentative, the audience helps things along by a collective act of goodwill." In the films of Victor Nunez, he added, "it's the characters—not the events—that take us through to the other side." As Terrence Rafferty noted in *The New Yorker*, *Ulee's Gold* was very typical of Nunez's previous work, *Gal Young 'Un* (1979), *A Flash of Green* (1984), and *Ruby in Paradise* (1993), in which the director's pace, "at its speediest, could be described as ruminative." In this context Fonda's "very deliberate style seems appropriate." It was both unusual and refreshing to see an American film so highly praised for its "sluggishness" and slow pace.

Certainly, one has to get used to the careful rhythms of this film. Especially impressive is the film's refusal to reward viewer expectations, since one might expect those buzzing bees to intervene and kill off the bad guys. But, no, this movie is made of tougher stuff. In a telling conversation Ulee

AWARDS AND NOMINATIONS

Academy Awards 1997 Nominations: Actor (Fonda)
Golden Globe Awards 1998: Drama Actor (Fonda)
Independent Spirit Awards 1997 Nominations: Feature, Director (Nunez), Actor (Fonda), Screenplay, Supporting Actress (Richardson)
New York Film Critics Circle 1997: Actor (Fonda)

CREDITS

Ulee Jackson: Peter Fonda
Connie Hope: Patricia Richardson
Casey Jackson: Jessica Biel
Sheriff Bill Floyd: J. Kenneth Campbell
Helen Jackson: Christien Dunford
Jimmy Jackson: Tom Wood
Penny Jackson: Vanessa Zima
Eddie Flowers: Steven Flynn
Ferris Dooley: Dewey Weber

Origin: USA
Released: 1997
Production: Victor Nunez for Clinica Estetico; released by Orion Classics
Direction: Victor Nunez
Screenplay: Victor Nunez
Cinematography: Virgil Mirano
Music: Charles Engstrom
Production design: Robert Garner
Art direction: Debbie Devilla
Set decoration: Charles Kulsziski
Costumes: Marily Wall-Asse
Sound: Pete Winter
MPAA rating: R
Running Time: 111 minutes

thanks the goons for reminding him that not all weakness is evil. His apparent passivity and stoicism is ultimately stronger than the brutal aggression of the thieves, which is another way of describing the movie's virtues in the face of the overproduced, blustering, confused movies surrounding it at the theatres. This movie was about ordinary people, not about car-chases or airplane crashes, or cartoon violence. It was simply too good for the summer season, which usually does not feature the year's best films.

—*James M. Welsh* and *John C. Tibbetts*

REVIEWS

The Baltimore Sun. June 27, 1997, p. E1.
Boxoffice. April, 1997, p. 176.
Entertainment Weekly. June 6, 1997, p. 42.
Los Angeles Times. June 13, 1997, p. F1.
The Nation. July 14, 1997, p. 34.
The New Republic. July 7, 1997, p. 26.
The New York Times. June 13, 1997, p. B3.
The New Yorker. June 16, 1997.
Newsweek. June 16, 1997, p. 57.
Parade Magazine. June 15, 1997, p.14.
Rolling Stone. June 26, 1997, p. 59.
USA Today. June 13, 1997, p. 4D.
Variety. February 3, 1997, p. 42.
Village Voice. June 17, 1997, p. 66.
The Washington Post Weekend. June 20, 1997, p. 37.

Underworld

Sometimes revenge is the best therapy.—Movie tagline

Johnny Alt (aka Johnny Crown, played by Denis Leary) has been released after seven years in prison and is out to avenge his father's murder at the hands of mobsters. Two years have passed since Johnny's father was attacked and rendered brain-dead by Ned Lynch (Larry Bishop), a cold-blooded killer who pays Johnny's now comatose father a visit at the hospital and shoots him through the head. Johnny holds several mobsters and gunsels responsible for what has happened to his father and manages to kill them all in a series of "Father's Day Massacres." But the two Johnny suspects are most responsible are Ned Lynch and Richard Essex (aka Frank Gavilan, aka Frank Cassady, played by Joe Mantegna). One problem with this plot is that the major characters are also known by other aliases. Neo-noir plots are supposed to be confusing, but this is ridiculous.

Johnny to Frank: "I want to be frank about your frankness and, frankly, I don't give a damn."

The film opens with shots of Johnny's red stretch limo (he seems to have two of them, not a bad trick for a man just released from prison) as it drives from massacre to massacre intercut with shots of a stripper performing for Frank (Mantegna) at a private Father's Day party (though there is no evidence, really, that Frank is a father). A poster seems to say it all and announces the theme: "Sex and Death." Johnny picks up Frank and begins playing an extended cat-and-mouse game with him. First, he murders three other hoods who are in the limo with him; then he takes Frank to a shrink, Dr. Diane Leah (Annabella Sciorra), for sex therapy. The two men seem to be (or have been) friends, but it later turns out that Johnny is testing Frank to determine if Frank indeed ordered his father's shooting.

While Frank gets "therapy" from the doctor, Johnny continues his psychotic killing spree. Hearing that Johnny is on the rampage, Ned Lynch behaves psychotically, as do almost all of the twisted characters in this perverse movie. Ned concludes that he is "back to nothing again." He shoots his drop-dead blonde lover, torches his Rolls Royce, throws all of his money away, goes to the hospital, and kills Johnny's father, all for no apparent reason, other than Ned claims that he functions best when he is "back to nothing." This doesn't really make sense, but, then, almost nothing does in this neo-noirish screenplay by Larry Bishop, who plays Ned. It's little more than recycled, imitation Quentin Tarantino, right up to the final confrontation, executed in *Reservoir Dogs*-style. The best Roger Christian's film can do is to provide an increasingly repulsive violent spectacle of sadistic and psychotic behavior, murder and mayhem.

The hit-men are all caricatures, but, then, the main characters are, too. They have colorful names, such as Wild Man Palmer (Ken Roberts), Dan "Iceberg" Eagan (James Tolkan), and Todd Streeb, aka Smilin' Phil Fox, played with wicked-cool, evil detachment by Jimmie F. Skaggs. Johnny certainly talks too much. He claims to have read too many books while in prison, but his ranting is nearly incoherent. One major goal for him is to find out if Richard Essex was involved in his father's death, and once that issue is solved in a Mexican stand-off at the "Underworld" sports arena, to reconcile Richard Essex/Frank Cassady with Frank's father, Will Cassady (Abe Vigoda), who mysteriously appears at the "Underworld" after the shooting is over. Why Frank and his father are estranged and have not been speaking to one another is never satisfactorily explained.

As Johnny, Dennis Leary has some charisma and might be interesting, if only he could keep his mouth shut. In contrast, the merely reactive Mantegna has all the charm of a cigar-store Indian. The lines of Larry Bishop's screenplay are so awful that one wonders how the actors could speak them with a straight face. The film is stylishly shot, but this cannot compensate for the lack of sense and substance. The only idea that holds the script together beyond Johnny's bloodlust for revenge is the Father's Day theme, but that is not enough to hang a movie on. *Underworld* was one of the year's most remarkable failures and deserved to go straight to video. There is nothing in this picture to redeem or justify the effort or the expense. This movie was as bad as they come.

—James M. Welsh

CREDITS

Johnny Crown/Johnny Alt: Denis Leary
Frank Gavilan/Richard Essex: Joe Mantegna
Dr. Leah: Annabella Sciorra
Ned Lynch: Larry Bishop
Will Cassady: Abe Vigoda
Stan: Robert Costanzo
Anna: Traci Lords
Smilin' Phil Fox/Todd Streeb: Jimmie F. Skaggs

Origin: USA
Released: 1997
Production: Robert and William Vince for Keystone Pictures Inc.; released by Trimark Pictures
Direction: Roger Christian
Screenplay: Larry Bishop
Cinematography: Steven Bernstein
Editing: Robin Russell
Music: Anthony Marinelli
Production design: John Ebden
Sound: Bill Sheppard
MPAA rating: R
Running Time: 95 minutes

REVIEWS

Boxoffice. April, 1997, p. 188.

U-Turn

Sex. Murder. Betrayal. Everything that makes life worth living.—Movie tagline

"A really powerful, original film! A definite don't miss."—Ron Brewington, *American Urban Radio Networks*

"An overdue event! Dazzling and sexy."—Owen Gleiberman, *Entertainment Weekly*

"Suspense and humor! Sean Penn, Jennifer Lopez and Nick Nolte are terrific."—Steve Oldfield, *FOX TV*

"Brutally hilarious and emotionally gripping."—Bob Strauss, *Los Angeles Daily News*

"*U-Turn* is a showcase for the filmmaker's terrific arsenal of visual mannerisms and free association imagery!"—Janet Maslin, *The New York Times*

"Provocative! Dazzling, stylish and truly unique entertainment."—Paul Wunder, *WBAI Radio*

Box Office: $6,665,606

The idea of Oliver Stone, the master of unsubtle cinema, making a black comedy version of a film noir sounds as if it should at least result in something memorable. While the best films noir have their subdued moments when an actor, director, screenwriter, or cinematographer conveys considerable meaning with an economical gesture, line, or use of shadow, the genre also lends itself to the overblown as with the endings to *Out of the Past* (1947) and *Chinatown* (1974), the marriage between Elisha Cook, Jr., and Marie Windsor in *The Killing* (1956), and just about everything in *Kiss Me Deadly* (1955) and *Touch of Evil* (1958). Poking fun at such excesses, however, could easily result in disaster, but with *U-Turn*, Stone does a commendable job of finding the right balance between the violent, sexy, and strange sides of film noir.

Bobby: "Is everybody in this town on drugs?"

Driving to Las Vegas to pay off a gambling debt that has already cost him two fingers, Bobby Cooper (Sean Penn) is sidetracked when the radiator hose of his vintage Mustang convertible blows apart. Bobby and steed limp into the nearest excuse for a town, Superior, Arizona, and he leaves the car in the dubious care of Darrell (Billy Bob Thornton), the greasy, potbellied proprietor of a classically rundown garage. From this humble beginning, Bobby's dilemma escalates into the ridiculous.

He meets beautiful young Grace McKenna (Jennifer Lopez) and falls instantly into lust. She invites him to her home and keeps sending him obvious sexual signals, but when he tries to act, she puts him off until finally her seedy middle-aged husband, Jake (Nick Nolte), charges in. Bobby retreats only for Jake to follow him and ask the stranger to murder his wife. After Bobby stumbles into a convenience-store robbery and the $30,000 he needs to save his life is first stolen and then blown apart by the storekeeper (Aida Linares), he begins taking Jake's offer seriously. Then Grace makes a counteroffer of the stash hidden in Jake's safe.

Others complicating Bobby's Superior visit include a suspicious sheriff (Powers Boothe), who seems unusually protective of Grace; Jenny (Claire Danes), a horny teenager; Toby N. Tucker (Joaquin Phoenix), her excitable, jealous boyfriend; and a blind half-Indian beggar (Jon Voight) with an apparently dead dog and lots of half-baked advice. Meanwhile, Darrell does not seem to be making much progress repairing the Mustang, leading to several angry confrontations. Are Bobby and Grace in love, or are they just using each other? Do they even know how they feel? As hilariously bizarre complications continue to rain down on the hapless Bobby, he decides to forget about his car, Grace, and money and simply get out of Superior alive. As production designer Victor Kempster pointed out in an interview in *American Cinematographer*, Bobby is a corrupt Alice lost in Wonderland, but unlike Alice, he will not escape.

Screenwriter John Ridley, adapting his novel *Stray Dogs*, borrows the stranger lured into killing the older husband of a hot young wife plot from *Double Indemnity* (1944) and *The Postman Always Rings Twice* (1946) and plays comic variations on it by exaggerating Bobby's desperation, Grace's seeming innocence, and Jake's viciousness. Grace's resentment of her husband stems in part from his having been her Apache mother's lover and his responsibility for the mother's death. Even a half-alert viewer can spot the incest possibility long before the payoff. While not central to film noir, incest appears, of course, in *Chinatown* and in the noirish fiction of Jim Thompson. *U-Turn* could almost be a parody of the desperate straits Thompson's characters always find themselves in. The film also expertly merges the film noir tradition with the western, bringing the antagonists to a ludicrous showdown in homage to the wonderfully bizarre ending to King Vidor's great western *Duel in the Sun* (1947).

Ridley and Stone keep matters lively with numerous quirky touches. One of the thugs who robs Bobby has a tatoo reading "Dry Clean Only." Toby N. Tucker's initials are shaved into the back of his skull. Jenny wonders why Patsy Cline does not release any new records. Bobby catches Darrell, in his underwear, preparing for a date with dance-step diagrams. The beggar, who wears black-and-white saddle oxfords, keeps changing his story about the cause of his blindness. Is his dog really dead? The film's best humor comes during the arguments between Bobby and the duplicitous Darrell. Ridley apparently recognizes, as T. Coraghessan Boyle has shown in his brilliant short story "The Big Garage," that having a vehicle repaired or even serviced can be one of life's most humiliating experiences.

Sean Penn replaced Bill Paxton in the role of Bobby Cooper four days before shooting began.

That many reviewers greeted *U-Turn* with some bewilderment is not surprising. Because Stone's earlier films, notably *Platoon* (1986) and *Born on the Fourth of July* (1989), were somewhat overrated by reviewers, audiences, and those who bestow awards, some of his later works, particularly *JFK* (1991), *Natural Born Killers* (1994), and *Nixon* (1995), have been underrated. Another factor in the critical response to Stone's films may be that in interviews he comes across as an arrogant jerk, and reviewers look for reasons not to like his films. The film was released at the same time a highly unflattering portrait of the director was published in Jane Hamsher's *Killer Instinct: How Two Young Producers Took on Hollywood and Made the Most Controversial Film of the Decade*. Stone is also a Stanley Kramer or Richard Attenborough with talent: a filmmaker who sees himself as daring to tackle large historical, political, or social subjects no one else will touch. As a result, some reviewers have been puzzled that *U-Turn* is, in Stone's usual sense, not about anything. (American audiences apparently felt the same because the film barely registered at the box office.)

What it is about, of course, is having fun with the medium. Like Francis Ford Coppola's *Bram Stoker's Dracula* (1992), *U-Turn* is about the love of filmmaking. Stone, with the help of Ridley's script, takes some characters and situations that can be seen as either hackneyed, because of overexposure, or mythopoeic, as a result of their centrality to an enduring part of popular culture, and tries to give them a new twist. The result may not be brilliant filmmaking on the level of Stone's best efforts, but this head-on collision of id, greed, and survival instincts, executed with a vigorous visual style, makes for considerable entertainment.

U-Turn has several similarities to *Natural Born Killers*. Both films employ grainy film stock, stark, washed-out images, excessive use of jump cuts, and loud popular music with the American Southwest as a backdrop to depravity. (Cinematographer Robert Richardson, working with Stone for the eleventh time, told *American Cinematographer* that he overexposed images to emphasize what he considers the film's bleak romanticism.) But while the earlier film perhaps takes its anti-media message too seriously, Stone, whose sense of humor may be a tad underdeveloped, seems to get the joke about *U-Turn*'s torrent of overindulgence.

The film also works because of its excellent cast. While Danes and Phoenix have been little more than too-sensitive adolescents in most of their previous roles, they throw themselves headlong into the comic spirit of *U-Turn*, gleefully overemphasizing the sexual awakening of Jenny and the macho posturing of "TNT," both characters all talk and no action. The often stoic Boothe is good at displaying the confused passion beneath the sheriff's calm surface. Nolte eschews his usual leading-man aura for a character part in the Harry Dean Stanton tradition. Gaunt, stubbled, his face like a death mask, Nolte creates a memorable convergence of greed, paranoia, and sexual desire. Lopez, playing a more sinister version of her earlier 1997 role in *Blood and Wine*, has probably the meatiest part of her brief career. Her Grace is credible as innocent victim, sex goddess, and schemer much smarter than the men she manipulates. Voight continues his wholly unexpected transformation from bland leading man to gritty, comic character actor, offering subtle variations on the blind man's crazy/prophetic ravings.

The best of the many good performances in *U-Turn* are by Thornton and Penn. Thornton has portrayed characters maliciously sinister, as in *One False Move* (1992), which he also wrote; sinister but sentimental, as in *Sling Blade* (1996), which he wrote and directed; and, finally, comically sinister with Darrell, whose costumes he created and much of whose dialogue he improvised, as Stone praised in an interview on *Charlie Rose*. Darrell's toothy grimace of redneck ignorance belies a cunning that springs forth whenever his livelihood is threatened. Darrell is both the scariest and funniest character in *U-Turn*. Stone and Ridley, a former standup comedian who clearly knows something about timing, pace the film so that the focus returns to Darrell whenever his peculiar brand of meanness is needed to make Bobby's Superior day even worse.

Penn has made a career of playing different versions of cruel characters: the psychopath, as in *Casualties of War* (1989), the cunning manipulator, as in *Carlito's Way* (1993),

CREDITS

Bobby Cooper: Sean Penn
Grace McKenna: Jennifer Lopez
Jake McKenna: Nick Nolte
Darrell: Billy Bob Thornton
Sheriff Potter: Powers Boothe
Blind man: Jon Voight
Jenny: Claire Danes
Toby N. Tucker: Joaquin Phoenix
Flo: Julie Haggerty
Ed: Bo Hopkins
Jamilla: Aida Linares
Bus station clerk: Laurie Metcalf
Girl in bus station: Liv Tyler
Biker #1: Abraham Benrubi

Origin: USA
Released: 1997
Production: Dan Halsted and Clayton Townsend for Phoenix Pictures, Illusion Entertainment Group, and Clyde Is Hungry Films; released by TriStar Pictures
Direction: Oliver Stone
Screenplay: John Ridley; based on his novel *Stray Dogs*
Cinematography: Robert Richardson
Editing: Hank Corwin, Thomas J. Nordberg
Production design: Victor Kempster
Art direction: Dan Webster
Set decoration: Merideth Boswell
Costumes: Beatrix Aruna Pasztor
Sound: Gary Alper
Music: Ennio Morricone
Makeup: John Blake
Stunt coordinator: Tierre Turner
MPAA rating: R
Running Time: 125 minutes

and the deadly yet sensitive soul, as in *Dead Man Walking* (1995). His Bobby Cooper is not particularly stupid or smart, neither a victim nor an anti-hero. He is more a Kafkaesque everyman who would like to triumph but will simply settle for surviving. While most film noir protagonists are cool and calculating, Bobby grows increasingly desperate, and Penn is adept at showing Bobby's initial cockiness, when he thinks he can easily con these Arizona hicks, and his insecurity. Penn is at his best when Bobby reaches his lowest point, begging a bus station clerk (Laurie Metcalf) for compassion when he has lost so much he cannot even pay for a bus ticket. This scene encompasses the blend of melodramatic excess, realistic human pain, and dark humor that defines *U-Turn*.

—*Michael Adams*

REVIEWS

Boxoffice. November, 1997, p. 125.
Chicago Tribune. October 3, 1997, p. 4.
Entertainment Weekly. October 10, 1997, p. 63.
Los Angeles Times. October 3, 1997, p. F1.
New York Times. October 3, 1997, p. E18.
People. October 13, 1997, p. 19.
Rolling Stone. October 30, 1997, p. 73.
Time. October 6, 1997, p. 109.
USA Today. October 3, 1997, p. D8.
Variety. September 1, 1997, p. 74.
Village Voice. October 7, 1997, p. 73.
Washington Post Weekend. October 3, 1997, p. 48.

The Van

They got soul in *The Commitments*, and a scandal in *The Snapper*. Finally they're getting their act together and taking it on the road.—Movie tagline

A comedy about friends, family and fish.—Movie tagline

"Radiates an intimate humor and humanity! Colm Meaney is excellent!"—Richard Rayner, *Harper's Bazaar*

"Hilarious! Funny! Warm-hearted!"—Anne Marie O'Connor, *Mademoiselle*

"Full-blooded new comedy!"—Stephen Holden, *The New York Times*

"A perfect follow-up to *The Commitments* and *The Snapper*."—Bruce Williamson, *Playboy*

"Two thumbs up! Funny and energetic!"—*Siskel & Ebert*

Box Office: $712,095

European films present working-class characters as sentimentalized figures with touches of nobility, as crass caricatures, or, more often, some better-balanced level between these extremes. (With the notable exception of the work of writer-director Victor Nunez, American films generally ignore blue-collar characters unless they are involved in crime.) Among the more balanced portrayals of the working class have been the first two films adapted from Roddy Doyle's Barrytown Trilogy about the inhabitants of a North Dublin neighborhood: Alan Parker's *The Commitments* (1991) and Stephen Frears' *The Snapper* (1993). Frears and Doyle have again collaborated, but *The Van*, the final installment of Doyle's trilogy, unlike its warmhearted, perceptive, and funny predecessors, offers two crude, tiresome protagonists.

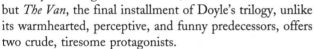

Larry reassures a customer who's just found a disposable diaper in his food: "Is it a used one? No? Then it's all right."

While *The Commitments* and *The Snapper* present events from the lives of a single family, *The Van* moves on to two households very similar to that of the earlier films. After Bimbo (Donal O'Kelly) is laid off from his job in a bakery, he joins his long-unemployed pal Larry (Colm Meaney) in looking for ways to occupy their time. Bimbo soon realizes the slack existence Larry has become reconciled to is not for him and purchases a grease-encrusted rattletrap and tries, with Larry's bumbling aid, to convert it into a successful business selling burgers and fish and chips.

The Van is set in 1990 when Ireland advanced to the semifinals of the World Cup. Bimbo and Larry set up their enterprise in a parking lot outside their favorite pub in hopes that hungry football fans will storm their mobile kitchen after communally watching their national team. After a few anxious moments, their wait is rewarded, and Bimbo's inspiration is an instant success. Once Ireland is eliminated, however, business suffers, and the duo are off to a seedy beach in search of new customers. Even with the help of Larry's daughter, Diane (Neili Conroy), and son, Kevin (Ruaidhuri Conroy), the business fails to flourish, and when a health inspector comes calling, Bimbo's Burgers is shut down.

During a moment of exhilaration, Larry yelps like the cowboys at the start of the cattle drive in Howard Hawks' *Red River* (1948). Stephen Frears is the narrator of *Howard Hawks: American Artist* (1997), a BBC/British Film Institute documentary about the filmmaker which includes the scene to which Hawks' British admirer pays homage.

There are a few amusing moments during these misadventures. Kevin converts to vegetarianism and refuses to cook any meat. A diaper (unused) of Diane's infant is accidentally fried and served in a sandwich. Before acquiring the van, Larry and Bimbo try to sneak in a few rounds of golf at the local course without paying any fees, once in a downpour with Diane's baby in tow.

For the most part, however, the humor in *The Van* is uncomfortably flat. *The Commitments* is funny because of a group of young Dubliners daring to try to create an authentic soul band in the Wilson Pickett tradition, and *The Snapper* finds gentle laughs in a working-class father's bewilderment over his beloved unmarried daughter's pregnancy. In these two films, the comedy is inseparable from character and situation. *The Van* does not manage to locate much amusement in Larry, Bimbo, and their plight.

Paddy Clarke Ha Ha Ha (1994) and *The Woman Who Walked Into Doors* (1996), Doyle's two most recent, highly praised novels, abandon the comedy of his earlier works for more serious themes. *The Van* can be seen, in retrospect, as the work in which Doyle began to make the transition from comic writer to serious chronicler of his country's malaise. What he apparently intends in *The Van* is showing that no matter how a typical Irish working-class man may appear on the surface, humanity, even dignity, lurks beneath. The problem is that Larry and Bimbo are boors. Larry is constantly doing and saying stupid things for which he instantly apologizes. After his tenth "I'm sorry," this expression has become much more annoying than fingernails on a blackboard could ever be. Bimbo is an irritable and irritating presence from the very beginning, and even he adopts the "I'm sorry" mantra.

The tiresomeness of these two is increased by the contrast with their wives. Maggie (Ger Ryan) knows from the beginning that Bimbo's venture will fail but supports him anyway. Even though Mary (Caroline Rothwell) is taking college courses about writers Larry has never heard of, such as George Eliot, she refuses to look down at her husband. And how does Doyle reward these women for overlooking their men's many flaws? By having Larry and Bimbo go out for a night on the town and try to pick up young women—and almost succeed. Doyle is apparently trying to show how such people can be redeemable despite their stupidity and insensitivity, but in this case, the latter qualities are so pronounced that the men become completely unsympathetic.

The most surprising side of the failure of *The Van* to achieve any of its goals is that it is directed by Frears. The director has made a few bad films, but the much-reviled

Hero (1992) and *Mary Reilly* (1996) are more interesting than *The Van*. While Frears' best and best-known films are *Dangerous Liaisons* (1988) and *The Grifters* (1990), he has specialized in perceptive, quirky, extremely well-acted films about people from working-class backgrounds: *Gumshoe* (1972), *The Hit* (1984), *My Beautiful Laundrette* (1985), *Prick Up Your Ears* (1987), and *The Snapper*. Frears never seems to find the right tone for *The Van*, never seems certain of what could be funny or poignant. The film's rhythms are off, especially in the scene in which Bimbo's bedraggled van is towed into his neighborhood and dozens of children begin following it as if the circus has come to town. The scene reveals nothing about this milieu and goes on for at least a minute too long. It may be the most awkwardly staged scene in any of Frears' films.

Even Frears' skill at directing actors—exemplified by the performances of Albert Finney in *Gumshoe*, Terence Stamp in *The Hit*, Daniel Day-Lewis in *My Beautiful Laundrette*, Alfred Molina and Gary Oldman in *Prick Up Your Ears*, Glen Close and Michelle Pfeiffer in *Dangerous Liaisons*, and Angelica Huston and Annette Bening in *The Grifters*—fails him here. O'Kelly plays Bimbo as a one-note whiner, and Meaney, a wonderful comic actor who gives his best performance as the flustered father in *The Snapper*, never finds a handle on Larry. Meaney wants to make him charming, but Doyle's script keeps getting in the way. In *The Commitments*, Meaney's character is comically obsessed with Elvis Presley, and his Larry comes alive when doing imitations of John Wayne. Such moments, however, are rare.

Frears and Doyle want these characters' humanity to be clear despite their circumstances, but production designer Mark Geraghty and costume designer Consolata Boyle give them such tacky homes and pathetically trashy clothes that they are reduced even more to a condescending caricature level. Cinematographer Oliver Stapleton, who has shot six previous Frears films, makes both the interiors and exteriors equally drab, emphasizing how inescapable is the characters' fate. Only in the final shot of a beach sunset does Stapleton allow any visual beauty to appear, with the image showing how Bimbo and Larry have missed their chance. The rock/blues/jazz score by Eric Clapton and Richard Hartley and performed by Clapton is too similar to the music Mark Knopfler has composed for Bill Forsyth films. The concluding piece sounds just like the ending of *Local Hero* (1983).

The titular character of *The Van* seems to offer salvation for the protagonists at first, but by the end of the film, it has become, for Bimbo at least, a symbol of their failure. He drives it to the beach and fails in an attempt to drown it. Bimbo has come to see it as some unearthly creature, like a monster out of a horror film. This conceit, though it seems to come out of nowhere, is a good attempt on Doyle's part to illustrate how these characters feel they exist at the whim of forces over which they have no control. But all this comes a bit too late for *The Van* whose real monsters are, unfortunately, a pair of shouting, whining louts.

—Michael Adams

CREDITS

Larry: Colm Meaney
Bimbo: Donal O'Kelly
Maggie: Ger Ryan
Mary: Caroline Rothwell
Diane: Neili Conroy
Kevin: Ruaidhuri Conroy
Weslie: Brendan O'Carroll
Sam: Stuart Dunne

Origin: Great Britain, Ireland
Released: 1996
Production: Lynda Myles for Deadly Films and BBC Films; released by Fox Searchlight
Direction: Stephen Frears
Screenplay: Roddy Doyle; based on his novel
Cinematography: Oliver Stapleton
Editing: Mick Audsley
Production design: Mark Geraghty
Art direction: Fiona Daly
Costumes: Consolata Boyle
Music: Eric Clapton, Richard Hartley
Casting: Leo Davis
MPAA rating: R
Running Time: 105 minutes

REVIEWS

Los Angeles Times. May 30, 1997, p. F15.
New York. May 19, 1997, p. 78.
New York Times. May 16, 1997, p. C19.
New Yorker. May 26, 1997, p.89.
People. May 26, 1997, p. 20.
Sight and Sound. December, 1996, p. 56.
USA Today. June 5, 1997, p. 12D.
Variety. May 20, 1996, p. 36.
Village Voice. May 20, 1997, p. 76.

Vegas Vacation

This time the Griswolds are on a roll.—Movie tagline

Box Office: $36,470,465

Vegas Vacation is the fourth and least inspired installment of the Griswold Holiday Chronicles, a series that has been looking a little road-weary since the late '80s. It's been 14 years since Chevy Chase first imposed an unwanted holiday on his big-screen family in *National Lampoon's Vacation* (1983), and a lot has changed since then. Mostly, Chevy has changed, to the point where he has now lost whatever made him a star in the first place. It's all gone: the timing, the physicality, even his ability to deliver lines with any sense of conviction. Is it irretrievable? It's hard to say, though certainly he has made little effort to get any of it back. What's left is the empty shell of a formerly brilliant comic who used to dominate every scene and sketch he appeared in. It's telling, then, that Chase has been spending the last few years trading in whatever legitimacy he has left to appear in bad movies for big paychecks. It's like he knows he's on his way out, and had better grab all that he can, and fast.

Clark: "Eddie, don't you know you're bad luck?" Eddie: "Those were my mother's dying words. But I guess if your body's covered in third degree burns, and your foot's caught in a bear trap, you tend to start talkin' crazy."

Vegas Vacation has Clark W. Griswold (Chase) and his Chicago-based clan vacationing in the city of glitter under the pretense that it has become a wholesome, family-oriented getaway spot: sort of like a Wally World that's open all the time. No doubt the real reason the Griswolds are here is so their little unit can get pulled apart in every direction, as each member succumbs to old-fashioned Las Vegas wish fulfillment. Will Clark be able to pull the members of the family back into the fold? It's happened three times before, so yeah, probably.

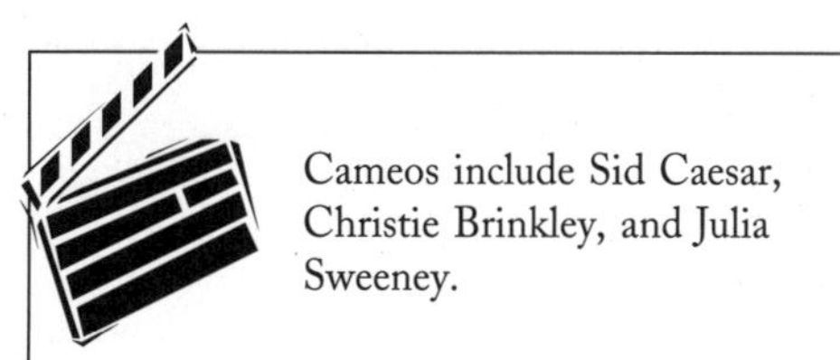

Cameos include Sid Caesar, Christie Brinkley, and Julia Sweeney.

The film begins as Clark comes home from work after receiving a promotion (he creates chemical additives for foods), and proclaims that the whole family is going to Vegas. Race ahead to when they first step foot in a casino: Clark rushes right up to a blackjack table and starts blowing all their money. In fact, he spends the rest of the film throwing down his cash like a fiend. Now, this could lead one to believe that the man is a gambling addict, and only planned the family vacation to Vegas so as to feed his addiction. Later in the film, there's a scene where he explains he never intended to gamble more than a few dollars, only the bug got him. He seems sincere enough, so why did the filmmakers have him march right up and plunk down his bucks in that earlier scene? This particularly dissatisfying plot thread is just the tip of the iceberg of what's wrong with *Vegas Vacation*.

Anyway, Clark embarks on a seemingly endless losing streak, which is overseen by an abrasive blackjack dealer (Wallace Shawn), who basically taunts him into playing the fool and gambling away the family's nest egg. Soon, he's so deeply in debt he starts making huge credit card withdrawals. His teenage son, Rusty (Ethan Embry), has got problems of a different sort, having fallen in with a family of mobsters enamored with the fact that he's apparently incapable of losing at craps. Soon, the kid is painting the town red. There's also a subplot about some security guards trying to crack down on the underage Rusty, but it never goes anywhere (certainly nowhere funny) and seems like it could easily have been cut.

So, Russ and his newfound friends somehow manage to avoid Clark and Ellen Griswold (Beverly D'Angelo) for a good three quarters of the movie. No matter, as the folks have their own problems to keep them occupied. Besides Clark's gambling, there's Ellen's infatuation with Wayne Newton (played by Newton himself), who reciprocates her interest. During one performance, he actually invites her on stage to sing with him. They're able to harmonize perfectly, to Clark's horror. It gets worse, as Wayne invites the two to lunch with him at his table, then asks Ellen to dinner at his home—just the two of them. In an interesting twist, Clark lets her go, being so far gone in his gambling problem that he sees his wife's absence merely as an opportunity to gamble more.

He's the same way with the kids: he lets Rusty out of his sight for days on end, then lets his teenage daughter, Audrey (Marisol Nichols), become seduced by the very attractive world of cage dancing. The family's problems, then, are rooted in Clark's addiction. Hey, anything can be made to be funny, but apparently not by these filmmakers.

As a last-ditch effort to save the movie from being a total wash, the screenwriters march out that old standby,

Cousin Eddie, played as always by a supremely trashy Randy Quaid. Quaid had some truly wonderful moments in the original *Vacation*, as when, beer in hand, he asked "Hows about an ice cold one, Clark?" and Clark replied "Now you're talkin', Eddie" and Eddie handed Clark his half-empty beer while popping open a new one for himself. This time, Eddie and his family have settled down on a desolate acre of the nearby Nevada desert, undeterred by the fact that it was formerly an H-bomb testing site—it's okay, because the atmosphere seems to agree with the plate in Eddie's head. Eddie's wife, Cousin Catherine (Miriam Flynn,) works as a fertility drug tester to pay the bills. Eddie's teenage son has gone and pierced his ears, nose, eyebrows, cheeks, forehead, chin, and even his lips, which are actually pierced shut. That's good for a laugh.

Then there's Vickie (Shae D'Lyn), the really wild cousin. Being Audrey's age, Vickie takes her under her wing and shows her how to really party. And that's how the cage dancing comes about. These scenes, set in sleazy, pulsating dance clubs, represent the absolute low point of the proceedings, and caused a portion of the audience this reviewer saw the film with to head for the exits.

To help pad this formulaic clunker out to its current 91 minutes, the filmmakers have thrown in a long, puzzling scene involving Siegfried & Roy and their stage show. What happens is that Clark is called up to the stage and, during a magic act, is made to disappear. Only, he doesn't come back. Ellen starts to get worried. Minutes pass as the act continues with a tiger. Ellen becomes *really* worried. Suddenly, Clark emerges from behind a stage prop. The on-screen audience cheers. It's as pointless as it sounds.

The energy level in *Vegas Vacation*, generally, is low—really, really low. There's Chase, not even pretending to try, and D'Angelo, putting forth the minimal effort required to ensure a paycheck. The casting for the kids is just as uninspired and their roles as unmemorable as in the last two films, *European Vacation* (1985) and *Christmas Vacation* (1989). Rusty and Audrey Griswold haven't been played by any two actors twice, and the only time anyone's made a real impression in either of the roles was when Anthony Michael Hall played Rusty back in the original outing. Here, Embry and Nichols act so snotty, so sure of themselves, that by the end, it's a wonder their parents don't just ditch the kids in Vegas. Quaid has nothing new to bring to the Cousin Eddie character, save for one single funny moment where the plate in his head starts picking up all sorts of signals. Wayne Newton is the only one who manages to get through this mess with his integrity still intact, by poking fun at his own famous ego—something Chevy seems incapable of doing at this point in his career.

Vegas Vacation ends on a particularly despicable note: After Clark loses somewhere in the neighborhood of $22,000, and the family is destitute, they come together in front of a Keno board, having bet their last two dollars against a $20,000 jackpot. They loose, but despite this (maybe because of it) they become closer. Then, just as it seemed that the filmmakers would have the courage to stick with the plot's new, realistic direction, the old man sitting in the seat next to them has a heart attack and dies, dropping the winning ticket at their feet. They cash it in. Lucky, too, that unbeknownst to the rest of the family, Rusty has kept four of the luxury cars from his mobster days. Each of the Griswolds gets to drive back to Chicago in style, though why they didn't leave one car for their poverty-stricken cousins is a question no one involved in the making of this film must have felt comfortable asking.

—David King

CREDITS

Clark Griswold: Chevy Chase
Ellen Griswold: Beverly D'Angelo
Cousin Eddie: Randy Quaid
Rusty Griswold: Ethan Embry
Audrey Griswold: Marisol Nichols
Cousin Catherine: Miriam Flynn
Cousin Vickie: Shae D'Lyn
Marty: Wallace Shawn
Wayne Newton: Wayne Newton (as himself)

Origin: USA
Released: 1997
Production: Jerry Weintraub; released by Warner Bros.
Direction: Stephen Kessler
Screenplay: Elisa Bell
Cinematography: William A. Fraker
Editing: Seth Flaume
Production design: David L. Snyder
Art direction: Tom Valentine
Costumes: Carole Brown-James
Sound: Andy Wiskes
Music: Joel McNeely
MPAA rating: PG
Running Time: 91 minutes

REVIEWS

Chicago Tribune. February 17, 1997, p. 8.
Detroit Free Press. February 15, 1997, p. 2A.
Los Angeles Times. February 17, 1997, p. F4.
Variety. February 17, 1997, p. 71.

Volcano

The coast is toast.—Movie tagline

"Non-stop excitement and suspense."—Don Stotter, *Entertainment Time-Out*

"Truly spectacular!"—Thelma Adams, *New York Post*

"A radiant gusher of movie magma!"—David Ansen, *Newsweek*

"Tommy Lee Jones takes on the forces of nature, and wins."—Jim Ferguson, *Prevue Channel*

"You'll have a hell-lava time."—Richard Corliss, *Time*

"Explosively entertaining. An-eye-popping thriller."—Paul Wunder, *WBAI Radio*

Box Office: $49,323,468

Volcano is a gusher of empty moralism that promises more disaster, social commentary and entertainment than it delivers. Perhaps never has a film with such a bloated budget (reportedly nudging $100 million), such a gargantuan set (the largest ever constructed in the United States) and such an explosive premise (a volcano erupts in the middle of Los Angeles) produced such a whimper. After 90 minutes of fire and brimstone and heroic responses to a monstrous threat, *Volcano* dissolves into mush. Until then, it's merely preposterous.

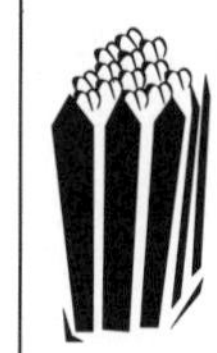

Mike: "Lava? Here in L.A.?"

The idea is certainly an explosive one, if scientifically far-fetched. Volcanoes usually don't pop up in a matter of hours from underneath a city where there's been no volcanic activity for millions of years, and if they did, they wouldn't be nearly as tame as this one. But the laudable notion of the Jerome Armstrong and Billy Ray script seems to be to take the typical southern California anxiety, the constant worry about the Big One, and give it an even more hellish twist.

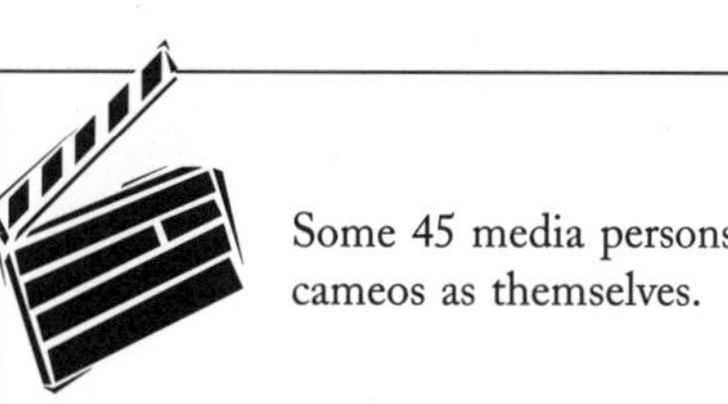

Some 45 media persons make cameos as themselves.

There's much about this disaster that is decidedly diabolical. At first the threat is a sneaky, elusive, almost serpentine subterranean demon that fries a group of construction workers, then clutches with white-hot steamy figures at the legs of disaster experts and scientists seeking its source in underground tunnels. It's a monster from the deep stalking the city's sewers and subway lines. When the top finally blows off, the demon becomes a fireball-belching rain of terror from the sky, and it metes out its flaming punishment mostly on those icons and individuals worthy of damnation, starting with a billboard of an oversized bimbo.

Although it's a bit hokey right from the start, *Volcano* is engaging, entertaining and suspenseful through the point at which the lava bombs start to rocket, the ash starts to fall, and the fiery rivers begin to gush down Wilshire Boulevard (actually a set at 80 percent size of the real Wilshire Boulevard, reconstructed in nearby Torrance). It's an apocalyptic scenario that seems to be unfolding, posing almost unbearable peril to the stranded protagonists, emergency management director Mike Roark (Tommy Lee Jones) and his daughter (Gaby Hoffmann), who are stranded at the epicenter.

Roark, a by-the-book guy who takes his job seriously even though most other officials in quake-jaded L.A. don't, is taking care of daughter Kelly after a recent marital separation. We don't know enough about Roark or his personality; in fact, we don't much about any of the character's pre-disaster motives or conflicts. But we can surmise that others, including his daughter and his co-workers, might doubt that Roark would be up to the task of handling a real disaster, since he can't even handle a phone call from his ex-wife. Jones, getting the most mileage he can out of his character, as he always does, makes it clear that Roark is a serious and careful person who cares deeply about his responsibilities to the people he serves. But when the volcano blows, he's caught in the middle of it with Kelly, a superficially jaded 13-year-old who's actually a frightened child, and he is soon forced to choose between his familial duties and his responsibility to millions of others.

It's a harrowing scene as Roark sees people everywhere in need of rescue, and when he leaves the car to attend to a crisis, Kelly ends up with her leg burned by lava. Jones precisely conveys the sense of a human being whose judgment is temporarily overwhelmed by terrifying events, and when he decides to send his frightened daughter off to a hospital in the care of a heroic doctor, Jaye Calder (Jacqueline Kim), it's a wrenching scene. As Kelly, young Hoffmann, in this and every scene, is absolutely convincing.

The violence, terror and chaos of the unfolding disaster are frequently gut-churning even when the plot is nonsensical. The impossibly media-savvy, brainy and witty seismologist, Amy Barnes (Anne Heche) does an impossibly stupid thing by venturing down a tunnel with a luckless comrade, who's sucked down to her death. There's a great shot of her upraised hand disappearing in a cloud of steam. Director Mick Jackson is supple and powerful in this early going. Heche's character, losing her co-worker and friend, is caught in a vise between deeply personal emotion and compelling professional duty, much as Roark is.

Heche is an intriguing actress—wiry, sassy, earthy and unusually casual in speech, manner and appearance for a Hollywood beauty. More miraculous than her character's heroics is the way she and Jones overcome their stereotypical characters and the plot devices that you know will have them mutually clashing and then attracting. It's become an indispensable formula: slightly macho man meets brainy beauty, she proves more than his equal in intelligence, bravery and physical prowess, and the flying sparks turn into sizzling chemistry. Fortunately, the attraction is only suggested, never realized. And Heche makes her impossible attributes seem almost possible. If anyone can be this perfect and this natural, she can. And Jones, himself the perfect Everyman who becomes the hero, never stops being human.

But then, with this fever burning, *Volcano* begins to belch preposterousness. The lava, instead of flowing in every direction, moves menacingly but obediently down a single street and later, down a single subway tunnel. The rocketing firebombs stop spewing, but not before Barnes has improbably instructed disaster workers in how to avoid them by tracking their projectory until the last second, and then running, like an outfielder judging a fly ball. The ash, which by all rights should be burning and clogging everything, becomes no more than a constant substitute for dandruff. *Volcano*'s mayhem looks like a nuclear disaster and feels like a nuclear disaster, but it all turns out to be quite manageable.

In fact, the volcano is merely a sort of fiery cauldron in which the mettle of ordinary human beings is tested. Most emerge as savior material. While it's unexpected and refreshing to find recognition of such vast human potential in the midst of cynical, jaded Los Angeles, the moral object lessons soon turn didactic. After levelling that huge, tawdry billboard, the volcano visits its wrath on other symbols of materialism. Its cleansing lava washes away racism and class differences with a kind of simplistic, fairy-tale moralism.

Roark, with Barnes as his sidekick, performs Herculean tasks of ingenuity. He's not only rescuing people left and right, he's directing the city's disaster response from the scene, while his second-in-command, the opportunistic Emmit Reese (Don Cheadle), is reduced to a sort of gopher at office headquarters. Somehow they commander concrete freeway dividers, on short order, and erect a barrier across the street. A stereotyped white racist cop and a stereotyped black cop-baiter from the 'hood join forces lifting one of the blockers into place. The lava docilely flows against the barrier, then fails to climb it, while firefighters and helicopters hose it into a nice crust.

The disaster seems contained, but Barnes warns of much bigger worries, noting that Mt. St. Helen's eruption equalled the force of 70 Hiroshima A-bombs. Yet the threat becomes confined to a stream of lava racing down a subway tunnel towards the medical center where Kelly Roark is learning heroism from Dr. Calder. Roark calculates that the only way to send the lava flowing out a storm drain to the sea is to knock down a building (the one built by Calder's greedy, selfish architect husband) across its path.

By then, as the disaster grows increasingly meek, the eruption of egregious moralism has long since raged out of control. A subway boss who was more concerned with money than safety (John Carroll Lynch) turns suddenly into a man willing to give his life to save an employee. Calder,

CREDITS

Mike Roark: Tommy Lee Jones
Dr. Amy Barnes: Anne Heche
Kelly Roark: Gaby Hoffmann
Emmit Reese: Don Cheadle
Dr. Jaye Calder: Jacqueline Kim
Lt. Ed Fox: Keith David
Norman Calder: John Corbett
Gator Harris: Michael Rispoli
Stan Olber: John Carroll Lynch

Origin: USA
Released: 1997
Production: Neil H. Moritz and Andrew Z. Davis for Shuler Donner/Donner and Moritz Original; released by 20th Century Fox
Direction: Mick Jackson
Screenplay: Jerome Armstrong and Billy Ray
Cinematography: Theo van de Sande
Editing: Michael Tronick, Don Brochu
Music: Alan Silvestri
Production design: Jackson DeGovia
Art direction: Scott Rittenour, Tom Reta, William Cruse, Donald Woodruff
Set decoration: K.C. Fox
Costumes: Kirsten Everberg
Sound: Jim Tanenbaum
Visual effects supervisor: Mat Beck
Stunt coordinator: Mic Rodgers
MPAA rating: PG-13
Running Time: 102 minutes

a Samaritan superwoman, chooses her humanitarian vocation over her marriage. Kelly learns to be brave and responsible. Reese learns his boss really deserves his adulation. Countless police and fire officials and ordinary citizens turn into wartime superheroes. And, at the end, an innocent boy emerges from the rubble to pronounce that the era of human equality has dawned, and a cleansing rain falls.

What seemed an unspeakable apocalypse degrades into a minor disaster; impossibly, only 100 people have died. And the movie, lurching back into chic cynicism, ends with a sarcastic Randy Newman song, "I Love L.A." For all its special effects and apocalyptic pretense, *Volcano* has the emotional scope of a 30-second television commercial.

It's too bad *Volcano* didn't have courage in its convictions equal to the size of its backers' investment. Then, with the talents of this director and this cast, the End of the World As We Know It might have lived up to its billing. *Volcano*'s ads promised: "The Coast Is Toast." Naw, just a mere singe.

—*Michael Betzold*

REVIEWS

Chicago Tribune. April 25, 1997, p. 4.
Entertainment Weekly. May 2, 1997, p. 40.
Los Angeles Times. April 25, 1997, p. F1.
New York Times. April 25, 1997, p. C1.
People. May 5, 1997, p. 21.
Sight and Sound. October, 1997, p. 62.
USA Today. April 25, 1997, p. 4D.
Variety. April 21, 1997, p. 59.
Village Voice. April 29, 1997, p. 71.

Waco: The Rules of Engagement

"Two thumbs up for the shocking documentary *Waco: Rules of Engagement,* a special motion picture."—*Siskel & Ebert*

On April 19, 1995 convicted terrorist Timothy McVeigh blew up the Oklahoma federal building. It was on the second anniversary of the burning of the Branch Davidian compound, referred to as Mount Karmel, in Waco, Texas. Many theorists insist McVeigh's actions were a retaliatory response to the AFT's and FBI's calculated annihilation of Vernon Howell (aka David Koresh) and the bulk of his followers. Even to this day, the Justice department maintains that Koresh led a mass suicide and its agents never fired a shot in anger into the building. Unless directors William Gazacki and Dan Gifford went through the arduous task of staging events that took place during the 51 day standoff and hired actors to rerecord phone conversations between negotiators and Davidian intermediates, the government is flat-out lying.

The intricate and exhausting 165 minute film leaves no stone unturned, every detail revealing that not only did AFT and FBI underlings plan and carry out these heinous crimes, their boss, Janet Reno, categorically denied any wrongdoing on their part. Several key pieces of evidence, turned over to the agencies by the media and medical examiners were conveniently lost or misplaced. The two strongest bits of proof against the government lie in video and audio recordings that only the most ignorant person could ignore.

In phone conversations with Koresh, FBI negotiators stumble, fumble, and contradict themselves with numbing consistency as they supposedly try to end the skirmish peacefully. It is easy to understand why the government handled Koresh in the haphazard manner they did. A religious extremist, steadfast and unwavering, leading followers into spiritual Armageddon like so many lambs to the slaughter. Koresh was heading in the direction of Jonestown leader Jim Jones and the idea of a mass suicide in the face of overwhelming adversity was an easy sell to the American public. Another point the government conveniently glossed over: The Branch Davidians weren't some new upstart fringe group searching out free publicity or wanting to die for a cause. The Davidians were actually part of the Seventh Day Adventists that broke off in 1938 and settled in Waco. As non-conforming as they were (it is said that Koresh, who truly believed he was Jesus Christ, fathered 24 children who lived at Mount Karmel), they weren't doing anything illegal. Religious fanaticism coupled with a (perfectly legal) stockpiling of assault weapons made for any easy call on the part of Reno and the many agencies at her disposal: take them out and leave no witnesses.

The government's second and fatal mistake was forgetting the existence of aerial shots of the compound. Tanks which rammed through the back of the building (far removed from the view of the banks of television cameras) unloaded liberal amounts of CS, a highly combustible form of tear gas. With a dried-out wooden structure, a flammable gas and ventilation conducive to fire, all that was needed was a spark. Say from an errant gun shot from outside of the building.

In *JFK* [1991], conjecture was fortuitously mixed with fact, leading viewers to make knee-jerk, passion-influenced judgments. But *JFK* was a dramatic production. The Kennedy debacle had few live witnesses and even less physical evidence. *Waco* could have gone in the direction of the far right; building a case on biased propaganda that, while pleasing the legions of devoted, dogmatists who would have believed literally anything they were told. But luckily, a Zapruder tape was found. Gazecki and Gifford instead did what all great documentarians must do: keeping their emotions in close check, they took cold hard facts, mixed them with an endless supply of minutia and testimony from experts and witnesses (from both sides of the fence) and built an all-encompassing, riveting film that lends considerable credence to the doctrine of the nation's many fringe groups. Our government is far from the lily-white humanitarian entity it claims to be. What is worse (and far more unsettling) is the government's unwavering belief that information this damning would never leak out. But it did.

Traditionally, even the best and most newsworthy documentaries fail to raise the ire of an American public whose thirst for blood and unseemly titillation is legendary. Whatever it may be; OJ, Lady Di, Monica Lewinsky, you name it, there never seems to be anything resembling overkill or a saturation point. As a people we just love witnessing the pitfalls of others. If you want to squash a budding rumor, try presenting your case in documentary form. It will sink quicker than a stone.

—*J.M. Clark*

CREDITS

Origin: USA
Released: 1997
Production: William Gazecki and Michael McNulty; released by SomFord Entertainment
Direction: William Gazecki
Cinematography: William Gazecki, David Hamilton
Editing: William Gazecki
Music: David Hamilton
MPAA rating: Unrated
Running Time: 136 minutes

REVIEWS

Chicago Tribune. September 22, 1997, p. 5.
Los Angeles Times. August 7, 1997.
New York Times. June 13, 1997.
San Francisco Chronicle. February 28, 1997.
San Francisco Examiner. February 28, 1997.
Village Voice. June 17, 1997.

Wag the Dog

A Hollywood producer. A Washington spin-doctor. When they get together, they can make you believe anything.—Movie tagline

A comedy about truth, justice and other special effects.—Movie tagline

"A gloriously cynical black comedy. A wicked, smart satire!"—Kenneth Turan, *Los Angeles Times*

"A scalding satire on the politics of spin. So good it hurts!"—Karen Durbin, *Mirabella*

"Swift, hilarious and impossible to resist!"—Janet Maslin, *New York Times*

"*Wag the Dog* is the most wickedly entertaining movie of the season!"—David Ansen, *Newsweek*

"A comic triumph!"—Leah Rozen, *People*

"Outrageous fun!"—Peter Travers, *Rolling Stone*

"Two thumbs up! Way up! One of the year's best films!"—*Siskel & Ebert*

A Hollywood film producer (Dustin Hoffman), a presidential publicist (Anne Heche), and a Washington spin-doctor (Robert De Niro) create a fictitious war in the political satire *Wag the Dog.*

Satire, in the well-worn theatrical saying, is what closes on Saturday night, suggesting that the genre is too sophisticated for mass audiences. The prevailing Hollywood attitudes toward satire have been either to ignore the genre as unworkable or to make its few satires too obvious to insure that the folks in Bangor, Baton Rogue, and Boulder get the joke. While American filmmakers have occasionally created satirical treatments of politics, the media, and Hollywood itself, the results, including such efforts as *The Loved One* (1965), *The President's Analyst* (1967), and *Network* (1976), have been rather disheartening, with three clumsy moves for every graceful one. Although a handful of such films have been noteworthy, as with *Nothing Sacred* (1937), *Dr. Strangelove* (1964), and *The Player* (1992), each Hollywood example of the genre should be greeted with low expectations.

Motss to Brean: "You want me to produce your war?"

Even with a director such as Barry Levinson, whose films since *Rain Man* (1988) have been inconsistent, a screenwriter like David Mamet, who, though brilliant, did write *We're No Angels* (1989) and *Hoffa* (1992), and actors the caliber of Dustin Hoffman and Robert De Niro, who have been, for the most part, cruising through the 1990s, there is no overwhelming reason to expect *Wag the Dog* to be any different. But it is. It is a triumph of sophisticated filmmaking and one of the funniest films of the decade. *Wag the Dog* takes realistic situations and exaggerates them just enough to be effective without turning cartoonish. It is a masterful blending of subtle wit and black humor.

Wag the Dog features cameos by James Belushi, as a spokesman for Albanian-American concerns; Merle Haggard, and Jay Leno.

The problems begin when the President of the United States (Michael Belson) is accused of a sexual indiscretion with a teenaged girl in the Oval Office eleven days before he hopes to be reelected. (The film was released a month before the Bill Clinton-Monica Lewinsky scandal broke.) The mysterious Conrad Brean (Robert De Niro), with a reputation for solving such dilemmas, and Presidential aide Winifred Ames (Anne Heche) are engaged to create a diversion. Brean eventually decides to create the appearance of a war with Albania by leaking to the press pieces of innocuous information that seem to add up to something. He also solicits the help of Stanley Motss (Dustin Hoffman), a well-known film producer, to create a visual sense of the war.

Motss' first major contribution is creating a videotape, to be fed to the television news outlets, of a young Albanian fleeing the bombing of her village. The footage is created on a Hollywood soundstage by combining an actress (Kirsten Dunst) with computer technology that changes the bag of Tostitos the girl is carrying into a cat. Motss wants a calico; the President prefers a white one. (Ironically, while Motss' technicians can impose the images of a cat, a bridge, and explosions onto a videotape, Levinson's real-life film crew cannot put leaves on the barren trees outside Motss' mansion supposedly in sunny Southern California.)

Wag the Dog is wonderful in the way the deception grows slowly as Motss, Brean, Ames, and their co-conspirators come up with a germ of an idea, kick it around, take action, and then take counteraction when something unexpected develops. Motss brings in a team of show-business types, including someone known only as the Fad King (Dennis Leary), for his ability to spot trends, and Johnny Green (Willie Nelson), a singer-songwriter. Motss decides the project, which Brean terms a "pageant," needs an anthem, and Green comes up with a pompously patriotic tune which he records with an all-star choir. This parody of "We Are the World" is too easy but funny nevertheless for puncturing the entertainment industry's zeal for showing its sentimental side.

When the President's opponent (Craig T. Nelson) halts the war fury simply by going on television and declaring the imaginary conflict over, Motss invents a hero, an American left behind the lines, forgotten like an old shoe. Green and a blues singer (Pops Staples) improvise a 1930s-style song, "Good Old Shoe," and Brean arranges for a scratchy recording of it to be smuggled into the Library of Congress where it can be found by the media hungry to celebrate heroism. That a blunder by the Fad King gives them a psychotic rapist, Sgt. William Schumann (Woody Harrelson), to pass off as the hero only causes Motss and Brean to do more fancy embroidering on the soldier's legend.

Levinson's best films are character studies with comic overtones: *Diner* (1982), *Tin Men* (1987), *Rain Man*. He also has a tendency toward sentimentality and pomposity that works sometimes, as in the latter film and *The Natural* (1984), but not always: *Good Morning, Vietnam* (1987), *Avalon* (1990), *Bugsy* (1991), *Sleepers* (1996). Levinson attempts a slightly satirical treatment of Hollywood and the media in the underrated *Jimmy Hollywood* (1994), whose ef-

AWARDS AND NOMINATIONS

Academy Awards 1997 Nominations: Actor (Hoffman), Adapted Screenplay

fectiveness is undercut by its sentimentality. While *Wag the Dog* may not be the savage look at its subjects that they deserve, it is decidedly unsentimental.

Levinson displays his directorial talents primarily in the film's headlong pace. It keeps charging relentlessly toward its goal in the same way that Ames, Brean, and Motss do. Some scenes in which the protagonists toss ideas back and forth occur at a breakneck speed reminiscent of Howard Hawks' immortal farce *His Girl Friday* (1940). Levinson shot the film in an amazingly brief twenty-nine days when his special-effects production *Sphere* (1998) was delayed. (A minimum of sixty days is normal for studio films.) *Wag the Dog* betrays the quickness of its creation only with the frequently pointless close-ups that may have resulted from not having time to shoot the actors from enough angles.

Much of the credit for *Wag the Dog* has been given to Mamet, one of the greatest American playwrights and an excellent screenwriter. There is some controversy over the film's screenwriting credits because Levinson has said in interviews that he filmed a screenplay written by Mamet, and Mamet is reported to have read neither the novel by Larry Beinhart upon which, according to the credits, the film is based nor an earlier screenplay by Hilary Henkin, best known for the flawed black comedy *Romeo is Bleeding* (1993), who shares screen credit with him. (Beinhart's 1993 satire suggests that George Bush manufactured the Persian Gulf war to increase his approval ratings.) Mamet's plays and screenplays are generally darker than *Wag the Dog*, but they always have solid comic moments. And he is known for writing biting, realistic, often profanely funny dialogue, of which *Wag the Dog* has an abundance. Regardless of who actually wrote what, the film is an example of what can happen when a talented director, two great actors, and a good supporting cast come together with an excellent script.

From *The Graduate* (1967) through *Tootsie* (1982), Hoffman was the greatest American film actor, a chameleon who created a distinctly different character in almost every film, and Motss is his best creation since *Tootsie*. Considerable publicity has been given to Motss' similarity to Robert Evans, former head of production at Paramount, producer of *Chinatown* (1974), and legendary egotist. A videotape was unearthed of Hoffman imitating Evans when they were making *Marathon Man* (1976). Hoffman's oversized eyeglasses and slick hairstyle resemble those of Evans, and Motss' ego can match the one Evans immortalizes in his autobiography, *The Kid Stays in the Picture* (1994): Motss wants the President to stay on hold while he completes an anecdote about Cecil B. DeMille.

What Hoffman offers, however, is considerably more than an impression for Hollywood insiders. He, Mamet, and Levinson combine to create a truly memorable character. Motss progresses from lack of interest to mild interest to agreement to working with Brean and Ames to commander of a major operation. He constantly whines about how unappreciated producers are, how the public does not understand what splendid work they do, and even though common sense—and Brean—tells him that no one can ever know what he has done, he convinces himself that he deserves credit for the best work he has ever done.

Motss could easily become a larger-than-life caricature, but Hoffman delineates the character with great subtlety, rarely raising his voice, communicating with small gestures. The collaborative nature of filmmaking—acting, directing, and writing blending perfectly—is captured when a character is shot off-camera, Motss enters the left corner of the frame and reports that the person is only wounded, a second shot is heard, and Hoffman, pausing briefly, utters, "Check that" in the calm way Motss would correct his dictation to a secretary. Ironically, Motss emerges as an admirable, even moral, character because of his unrelenting positive outlook—"This is nothing" is his mantra—and the joy he takes in his work. Hoffman, Levinson, and Mamet make Motss an engagingly tainted example of American idealism.

CREDITS

Conrad Brean: Robert De Niro
Stanley Motss: Dustin Hoffman
Winifred Ames: Anne Heche
The Fad King: Dennis Leary
Liz Butsky: Andrea Martin
Johnny Green: Willie Nelson
Tracy Lime: Kirsten Dunst
Sgt. William Schumann: Woody Harrelson
Agent Young: William H. Macy
Senator John Neal: Craig T. Nelson
Blues singer: Pops Staples
President: Michael Belson

Origin: USA
Released: 1997
Production: Jane Rosenthal, Robert De Niro, and Barry Levinson for Tribeca Productions, Punch Productions, and Baltimore Pictures; released by New Line Cinema
Direction: Barry Levinson
Screenplay: David Mamet and Hilary Henkin; based on the novel *American Hero* by Larry Beinhart
Cinematography: Robert Richardson
Editing: Stu Linder
Production design: Wynn Thomas
Art direction: Mark Worthington
Set decoration: Robert Greenfield
Costumes: Rita Ryack
Music: Mark Knopfler
Sound: Steve Cantamessa
MPAA rating: R
Running Time: 120 minutes

Many reviewers of *Wag the Dog* observed that De Niro acts primarily as Hoffman's straight man, but he is much more than that. (The admirable Heche generously helps set up bits of business by her costars.) Brean, supposedly inspired by former Clinton advisor Dick Morris, is an amoral man who throws himself completely into an assignment once he accepts it. If his goal is to distract a gullible public and even more gullible press from a Presidential scandal, he will do anything necessary to achieve his objective. Because Brean rations the emotions that would get in his way, De Niro creates the character with small gestures: a raised eyebrow, a slight, tight smile. Faced with a life-and-death decision, De Niro allows Brean only a flicker of remorse.

Like these characters, *Wag the Dog* propels forward without worrying too much about insignificant trivia, like the fact that such a phony war could never fly for long in the age of media overkill. The result, again like the work of Brean and Motss, is slick American enterprise at its finest.

—Michael Adams

REVIEWS

Boxoffice. February, 1998, p. 52.
Entertainment Weekly. January 16, 1998, p. 40.
The New York Times. December 26, 1997, p. B29.
The New Yorker. January 5, 1998, p. 73.
Newsweek. December 22, 1997, p. 84.
People. January 12, 1998, p. 21.
Rolling Stone. January 22, 1998, p. 62.
Sight and Sound. March, 1998, p. 57.
Time. December 22, 1997, p. 82.
USA Today. December 23, 1997, p. D3.
Variety. December 15, 1997, p. 58.

Waiting for Guffman

A new comedy from the lead guitarist of *Spinal Tap.*—Movie tagline

There's a good reason some talent remains undiscovered.—Movie tagline

"It's very funny right up to and including the credits!"—Roger Ebert, *Chicago Sun-Times*

"Kitschy cleverness and inspired lunacy!"—Susan Granger, *CRN International*

"Start your year off laughing! One of the funniest films in years!"—Steve Oldfield, *FOX-TV*

"Hilarious! A work of brilliance!"—Jeffrey Lyons, *WNBC-TV*

Box Office: $3,002,691

At first glance, Christopher Guest's *Waiting for Guffman* is reminiscent of such Depression-era "backstage" musicals as *Love Finds Andy Hardy* (1938) and *Babes In Arms* (1939). Imagine what those films might have been like if Judy Garland and Mickey Rooney had been allowed to ingest huge amounts of hallucinogenic substances, and you'll get a pretty clear idea of the effect that is created by this deeply farcical film.

The premise is as American as apple pie. The residents of Blaine, Missouri are engaged in plans to commemorate their town's 150th anniversary. In honor of this occasion, the city fathers decide to stage "Red, White and Blaine," a preposterously ambitious musical celebration of their town's history. Borrowing a motif from the long-running stage production of "A Chorus Line," *Waiting for Guffman* traces every step in the development of this show, from the grueling audition process to the frantic opening night. The ringleader of this production is Corky St. Claire (Christopher Guest), an effete prodigal son who returns to his hometown after an undistinguished assault upon the big stages of New York.

Every small town in America has a Corky St. Claire, a semi-closeted homosexual misfit with artistic pretensions who is looked upon by the local townspeople with a strange combination of revulsion, admiration and just plain bewilderment. No one in the cultural backwater of Blaine knows or even cares that Corky scored a resounding flop on the Great White Way: failure is certainly undesirable, but failure in New York has its own particular cachet. Corky knows this, and plays up his dubious theatrical achievements for all they're worth. (These include a catastrophically ill-considered stage version of the recent disaster film, *Backdraft.*)

The production generates a wave of excitement not seen in Blaine since the town received an impromptu visit from the soon-to-be-assassinated President William McKinley. The gung-ho citizens are undaunted by the fact that, in terms of dramatic historical incident, they don't have much to work with. They are anxious to celebrate the town's burgeoning footstool industry, but due attention must also be given to a 1946 Roswell-style UFO sighting that is the town's other great claim to fame. (In a series of comic asides, several local citizens gleefully share the intimate details of the "alien probes" to which they were subjected during the Martians' visit.)

Everybody who is anybody in the beleaguered town tries out for the Big Show. Although the "audition sequence" is played for laughs, it is clear that the town's aspiring thespians are deadly serious about the theatrical opportunity that has been placed before them. Early front runners for the show's most glamorous roles are Ron (Fred Willard) and Sheila (Catherine O'Hara) Albertson, local travel agents who are known for their towering devotion to the theater. The Albertsons' limitless enthusiasm is undimmed by the fact that neither of them is particularly talented: their audition piece is a horrendous, cabaret-style rendition of Maria Muldaur's "Midnight at the Oasis."

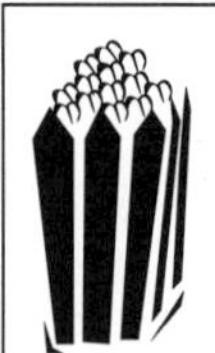

Mrs. Pearl: "We don't associate with the creative types. We have a Scrabble club. We associate with people with babies."

Eugene Levy of "SCTV" fame scores a comic bull's-eye as Dr. Allan Pearl, a dangerously nearsighted orthodontist who harbors an unfulfilled yearning for a life on the stage. The show's great new discovery is Libby Mae Brown (Parker Posey), a rather shopworn "ingenue" who might otherwise have spent her life slaving away at the local Dairy Queen. The principal cast is rounded out by Johnny Savage (Matt Keeslar), a hunky if somewhat dim-witted local mechanic, and Clifford Wooley (Lewis Arquette), a crusty senior citizen who has previously been famous around town for his rather mangled taxidermy experiments.

Corky's ego is so enormous that he feels he must put his unique personal stamp, Barbra Streisand-style, on every aspect of the production. These include some peculiar experiments in choreography that would make Agnes De Mille spin in her grave. Nevertheless, the Blaineans are thrilled with Corky, whom they perceive as an accomplished, big-city artiste. The film's one great in-joke is that the rather dense citizens never seem to recognize that a flamboyant homosexual has entered their midst; as far as they're concerned, he's not gay, he's simply "artistic." Indeed, Corky himself seems to be somewhat clueless when it comes to his own thinly-veiled homosexual longings. These come to light at hilariously inopportune times, such as when he is trying to cajole Johnny Savage into trying out for the show's romantic male lead.

Shot on location in Austin and Lockhart, Texas.

"Red, White and Blaine" is composed of a variety of musical numbers, some of which are so bad they're almost good. These include an obligatory tribute to the local footstool-making industry, as well as "Nothing Ever Happens on Mars," which features Levy as a cranially-challenged visiting alien. And, of course, there's "A Penny for Your Thoughts," a hilariously implausible romantic interlude featuring the very miscast Corky and the sweetly inept Libby Mae Brown.

The Blaineans' enthusiasm reaches a fever pitch when they receive word that their show is to be viewed by one "Mister Guffman," who is supposedly an honest-to-God New York talent scout. ("I think this means we may be heading to Broadway," says the ever self-deceiving Corky.) The Big Night arrives, and the show does indeed go on, but the mythical Mr. Guffman fails to materialize.

Despite the cast's disappointment, the citizens of Blaine consider Corky's production a resounding triumph. The final section of the film traces the ways in which the lives of the show's "stars" are radically transformed. Spurred on by their continued success as "the Lunts of Blaine," Ron and Sheila Albertson pull up stakes and run off to Hollywood, where they are thrilled to embark on matching careers as film and television extras. Libby Mae Brown moves on to a "better" Dairy Queen in Alabama, and Dr. Allan Pearl, now fully convinced that he is indeed funny, migrates to Florida, where he augments his career as an orthodontist with stand-up gigs at a variety of local senior citizens' homes.

Guest's Corky St. Claire very nearly manages to steal the show, which is saying a great deal considering the comic talents of the rest of the cast. The foremost of these is another "SCTV" alumnus Catherine O'Hara, who is priceless as Sheila Albertson, the local travel agent turned patroness of the arts. Sheila is so eager to please that she discloses much more than anyone really wants to know about her innermost feelings. She offers long explanations of her breathlessly serious approach to acting, as well as the gory details of her husband's recent "penis reduction" surgery.

More of an irrepressible diva than ever, Corky returns to New York to take a second stab at big-time success. Foiled in very short order, he ends up running a touristy film and

AWARDS AND NOMINATIONS

Independent Spirit Awards 1997 Nominations:
Feature, Actor (Guest), Screenplay

theater memorabilia shop whose curiosities include *My Dinner with Andre* "action figures" and *The Remains of the Day* lunch boxes. To the bitter end, he remains impervious to the idea that he might be better suited for some other line of work.

Waiting for Guffman is a direct descendant of *This Is Spinal Tap* (1983), a surprise cult favorite, which was directed by Rob Reiner and co-written by Guest, Harry Shearer and Michael McKean. That pseudo-serious "mockumentary" followed the progress of a truly awful rock 'n' roll band as they worked their way across the country in search of fame and fortune. Like the grandly self-deluded residents of Blaine, the aging, spandex-clad performers in *Spinal Tap* are so enthralled by the glitz and glamour of show business that they never seem to realize just how stunningly untalented they are.

Aspiring actors, dancers, and writers who are presently doing dinner theater gigs in New Jersey while they wait for their Big Break on Broadway will probably be made slightly nervous by the premise of *Waiting for Guffman.* But not to worry, at its core, *Guffman* is a sweet-natured movie. To director Guest's great credit, the film traces the funny consequences of the characters' grandiose self-delusions without ever seeming unduly mean-spirited or condescending.

That being said, *Waiting for Guffman* is not exactly a Restoration comedy—it feels like a hyper-extended "Saturday Night Live" sketch. The film's deeper meaning, to the extent it pretends to have any, may be that all human beings have the right to dream, no matter how outlandish those dreams are. Guest and his gifted co-stars clearly have a ball exploring the comic implications of this idea.

The starry-eyed residents of Blaine may be utterly devoid of talent, but they are never less than charming. Despite their show business deficiencies, which are considerable, they manage to infuse *Waiting for Guffman* with a great number of well-earned laughs.

—*Karl Michalak*

CREDITS

Corky St. Claire: Christopher Guest
Allan Pearl: Eugene Levy
Ron Albertson: Fred Willard
Sheila Albertson: Catherine O'Hara
Libby Mae Brown: Parker Posey
Clifford Wooley: Lewis Arquette
Johnny Savage: Matt Keeslar
Lloyd Miller: Bob Balaban
Mrs. Allan Pearl: Sally Wingert

Origin: USA
Released: 1996
Production: Karen Murphy for Pale Morning Dun and Castle Rock Entertainment; released by Sony Pictures Classics
Direction: Christopher Guest
Screenplay: Christopher Guest and Eugene Levy
Cinematography: Roberto Schaefer
Editing: Andy Blumenthal
Production design: Joseph T. Garrity
Art direction: John Frick
Costumes: Julie Carnahan
Music: Christopher Guest, Michael McKean, Harry Shearer
Sound: Jennifer Murphy
MPAA rating: R
Running Time: 84 minutes

REVIEWS

Boxoffice. November, 1996, p. 135.
Entertainment Weekly. February 14, 1997, p. 43.
Film Threat. February, 1997, p. 55.
Los Angeles Times. January 31, 1997, p. F1.
New York Daily News. January 31, 1997.
New York Times. January 31, 1997, p. B6.
Newsweek. February 10, 1997, p. 66.
People. March 17, 1997, p. 21.
USA Today. January 31, 1997, p. 3D.
Variety. September 16, 1996, p. 71.

The War at Home

"A stunning achievement! Unforgettable performances by Martin Sheen and Kathy Bates propel this gripping drama straight into your heart!"—Jeanne Wolf, *Jeanne Wolf's Hollywood*

"A magnificent tour de force for director Emilio Estevez and his splendid cast!"—Paul Wunder, *WBAI Radio*

A generation after the generation-gap turmoil of the Vietnam era, it remains horrifying to reopen the wounds of that troubled time. That's probably why *The War at Home*, a splendidly acted and excruciatingly painful domestic drama, got shelved after a very brief theatrical run.

Reflecting America's inability to look honestly at the dirty, divisive war, Hollywood was late to dramatize the Vietnam drama. The monumental and controversial allegorical films, *The Deer Hunter* (1978) and *Apocalypse Now* (1979), were followed belatedly by more straightforward efforts such as *Platoon* (1986), *Full Metal Jacket* (1987), and *Born on the Fourth of July* (1989). By the time Emilio Estevez traded his agreement to play in a third "Mighty Ducks" films in exchange for Disney Studios' backing of James Duff's 1984 Broadway play about the implosion of the family of a young Vietnam veteran, Hollywood had long since finished with Vietnam. But the fact is that all camps in that conflict live in an uneasy truce, content with smug but unsatisfying half-truths.

Mom Maurine: "I wasn't screaming, I was using my loud voice."

Estevez's third directorial effort, *The War at Home* blows that pretense to shreds. Watching the movie is like trying to pick up the shards of the shattered mirror of recent history. Duff's screenplay has the cracks and thuds of Asian firefights echoing in the lethal grenades of the everyday conversations of an archetypical American family.

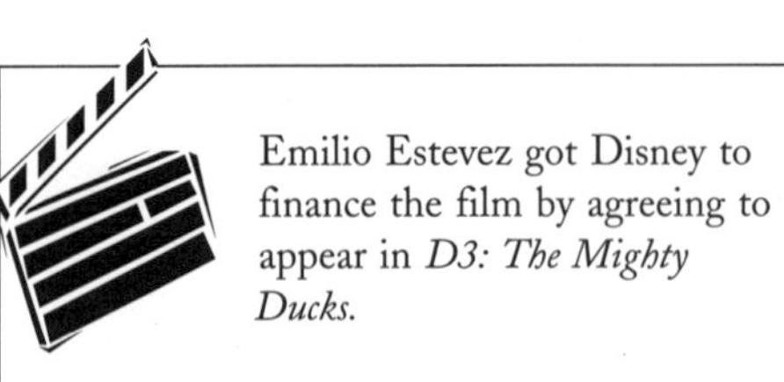

Emilio Estevez got Disney to finance the film by agreeing to appear in *D3: The Mighty Ducks*.

To those deaf to the muffled sounds of this domestic battle, *The War at Home* might seem strained, overdone or nonsensical. One reviewer suggested that Duff's theory is that Americans' inner rage caused the war in Southeast Asia. But the screenplay is more subtle than that. The Collier family, deep in the heart of Texas, is more a metaphor for the war than an explanation of it.

The War at Home isn't really about the deep divisions the conflict caused in American families. In fact, there is no discussion in the film about the morality of the war. The story is about how the Vietnam war made it impossible to carry on business as usual in some families. *The War at Home* wouldn't be such a frightening film if it truly was about a conflict that ended long ago. Estevez's trite reliance on Crosby, Stills & Nash counter-culture anthems is the only nostalgic element in it. Estevez was just a toddler, and his father, Martin Sheen, a draft-age man when the war raged. Here, a generation later, they play a father and son with a raging friction that could only come from plumbing the depths of real-life experience.

Vietnam is little more than a peg on which to hang this wrenching examination of interfamilial warfare. For Duff and Estevez are more interested in what went wrong in the American family than in America's horrible war.

The movie's opening sequence, a recounting of the Collier family's long history of service to America, is a reminder of how Vietnam veterans met with abuse rather than the adulation given to veterans of other wars. Estevez dispenses with any more explanation, and wisely so. Americans over 35 certainly need no primer in the issues of those days; they remain indelibly etched in memory even after 25 years.

When this slice-of-life drama opens, Jeremy Collier (Estevez) is not being spat upon by protesters. But he is being disconnected from everyone who once mattered. His former girlfriend, Melissa (Carla Gugino), explains that she never responded to his letters because they were too scary, so now she's living with someone else. His sister, Karen (Kimberly Williams), who's immersed in her shallow world, is repulsed by her suddenly weird and uncool brother.

Jeremy is fragile and forlorn, and rejections push him further into his bunker of guilt and shame. His very self is permeable, subject to periodic war flashbacks. Estevez films these sequences brilliantly. Jeremy is in his parents' yard, and hears the sound of exploding rockets; he turns, and the yard has become a jungle of smoke and fire; he crawls through it, still in civilian clothes. Then, in the middle of battle, he hears his mother's voice; he turns around, there's the house, and the jungle dissolves. The suggestion is not only that the war is still raging in Jeremy's psyche, but that it has merged with the war he is fighting with his family, a war that is every bit as bewildering and unwinnable as the one in Vietnam.

Kathy Bates makes his mother, Maureen, into a monster of bombast, self-pity and manipulation. Played brilliantly and frighteningly as only Bates can, Maureen Collier is a devout Baptist who won't watch Ingrid Bergman movies because she lived in sin. She conducts a non-stop campaign of emotional terrorism within her family that is thinly disguised as long-suffering maternal duty. She is blithely capable of lying and betrayal, of doling out blame and playing the martyr. Yet we also see glimpses of truth behind the constant theatrics, as when she announces she is going to bed, and, ignored by her husband and daughter, allows her face a used-up look. Bates is terrific, all her words and gestures Texas-sized, turning on and off her various tactics like a precision bombardier.

As Bob Collier, Sheen at first appears as putty, a husband who has found it easier to humor and avoid his wife than confront her. But with a finely understated performance, Sheen becomes much more than that. He is the icon of a crumbling patriarch, who ineptly tries to rule his roost while battling powerlessness. His bumbling attempts to reach his son are both heartfelt and pathetic.

Everyone in the family wants Jeremy to go back to being the perfect little boy they once cherished, but that Jeremy has been destroyed. Try as they might, Jeremy's parents and sister don't have a clue as to why Jeremy can't just shrug off his wartime experiences. They take his funk and his rejection of their overtures as an insult, and denounce him for no longer being willing to play the game of getting along.

His mother is like a squawking hen trying to get her chick back in the fold. Alternately pleading and cajoling, Maureen hopes to get Jeremy interested in playing piano, watching TV, doing something, anything. But the more she tries, the more he retreats. His father, himself an emotional loner, insists that Jeremy just needs to be left alone. Karen, who's taking psychology classes, pretends to understand his emotional needs but then rejects him when he doesn't want to talk to her.

Deadly sarcasm, covert threats, and emotional brinkmanship are this family's conversational staples. To the others, the only thing wrong is that Jeremy has changed. Yet the land mines that explode at a decisive Thanksgiving dinner had been waiting to go off long before. There's brilliance in Duff's script, as little issues over sequestered peanut brittle and mealtime blessings turn into major squabbles, just as they do in real families. The script sees no need to manufacture mountains; it just makes them out of molehills, and the dialogue rings horrifyingly true, even when the constant pecking spins out of control.

To Jeremy, his emotions raw, his family has become very much like Vietnam. The landscape is confusing, with traps lurking everywhere and alliances constantly shifting. It is not clear who is friend and who is enemy. If he has learned one thing from the war, it is not to trust. On the surface, he seems cold or crazy when he rejects his family's ill-conceived but sincere attempts to help him. But it soon becomes clear that he has been taught a code of dishonor and distrust that is only thinly masked by an appearance of honor and civility.

Apart from the sterling performances, what's remarkable about *The War at Home* is how it tears asunder the facade of normal family life and reveals the barbarism within. Like Vietnam itself, the film is all raw and jangled nerves and lurking insanity poking through the rituals of accepted behavior. It's intense, excruciating, disturbing and powerful.

It is also somewhat muddled. The shift at the film's climax to a showdown between father and son is disturbing, because most of the movie suggests the fundamental problem is between mother and son.

Both as director and actor, Estevez shows remarkable maturity, resisting the temptation to make his character into an icon. As is the case for so many veterans of wartime and domestic strife, there is no sappy ending, no forgiveness; mirrors that break into a thousand pieces can't be put back together. Going against the grain, Estevez takes the risk of pointing out that deep wounds cannot be papered over with uneasy half-truths, that America is still fighting the war at home, one that continually erupts into violence. Not many viewers, unfortunately, will be willing to take that tour.

—Michael Betzold

CREDITS

Jeremy Collier: Emilio Estevez
Bob Collier: Martin Sheen
Maurine Collier: Kathy Bates
Karen Collier: Kimberly Williams
Melissa: Carla Gugino
Donald: Corin Nemec

Origin: USA
Released: 1996
Production: Emilio Estevez, Brad Krevoy, Steve Stabler, and James Duff for Motion Picture Corp. of America and Avatar Entertainment; released by Touchstone Pictures
Direction: Emilio Estevez
Screenplay: James Duff; based on his play *Home Front*
Cinematography: Peter Levy
Editing: Craig Bassett
Music: Basil Poledouris
Production design: Eve Cauley
Costumes: Grania Preston
Sound: Jennifer Murphy
MPAA rating: R
Running Time: 124 minutes

REVIEWS

Entertainment Weekly. December 13, 1996, p. 60.
New York Times. November 22, 1996, p. C18.
Variety. September 16, 1996, p. 66.

Warriors of Virtue

In a world beyond your wildest imagination a battle for the universe has begun.—Movie tagline

"Move over Ninja Turtles, the kangaroos are here!"—*The Hollywood Channel*

"A kids' movie that is irresistible!"—*Siegel Entertainment Syndicate*

Box Office: $6,524,454

Heavily promoted in theaters in the early part of 1997, *Warriors of Virtue* looked like the next big adventure film for kids. Complete with a tie-in line of action figures, *Warriors* was enjoying saturation marketing a la Disney. But a funny thing happened on the way to the bank: The movie flopped because kids just didn't like it. Released in the late spring of 1997, it played only briefly in the multiplexes.

In the movie business, with an increasing number of both big-studio and independent releases, word of mouth is becoming more and more crucial. What happened to *Warriors of Virtue* shows that the children's action-film market is also dangerously close to saturation. Toys tied to films in 1997 included lines for *Batman and Robin*, *The Lost World*, *Spawn*, *Men in Black*, *Hercules*, and *Space Jam*. All were overwhelmed by the revival of *Star Wars*. And the one-two-three punch of the trilogy's re-release in early 1997 also may have doomed *Warriors of Virtue*.

Komodo: "The center cannot hold; things fall apart."

Judging by the reaction from my 12-year-old son and seven-year-old daughter, *Warriors of Virtue* succumbed to bad word-of-mouth from its intended audience. My children were mesmerized by *Star Wars* and saw *Warriors of Virtue* as pedestrian in comparison. *Warriors* is not very clever or inventive and its characters are distinctly unsympathetic. Its heroes—a group of kangaroo-people—are neither cuddly nor sufficiently endowed with superpowers. They are merely strange and funny-looking and their frequent battles looked too obviously staged.

The first-time producers of *Warriors of Virtue*, the four Law brothers, are Colorado doctors who were born into a prominent family of toy manufacturers in Hong Kong. Apparently they were out to marry their knowledge of children's products with an interest in film. The interiors of the film were shot in Beijing, and the production credits are heavy with Chinese contributors. There was also a Vancouver crew.

No expense seemed to be spared in mounting the film, with elaborate sets by Eugenio Zanetti depicting an underground fantasy kingdom, ruled by a overly familiar Asian guru named Master Chung (Chao-Li Chi) and protected by the five Warriors in their kangaroo outfits: Yun (Jack Tate), Yee (Doug Jones), Lai (Don W. Lewis), Chi (J. Todd Adams) and Tsun (Adrienne Corcoran). It is a dreamlike, naturalistic world where leaves are always blowing, a River of Life is flowing, and the villagers live in primitive structures.

Their enemy is Komodo (Angus Macfayden), an evil seeker of perpetual youth who is mining a life-preserving mineral from the river. Komodo has a castle and a huge army which is sometimes seen marching from the castle across an open plain. At all other times his minions are sneaking around the underground world. It is puzzling how the two landscapes are connected, and that is but one of the film's many disjunctures.

Everything in *Warriors of Virtue* seems derivative. Hong Kong director Ronny Yu is most attentive to fight scenes, which borrow heavily from kung fu movies. The characters can defy gravity, spinning and flying through the air, and occasionally propelling other creatures and objects as well. Yu relies way too much on slow-motion and quick cuts that fail to cover up the physical improbabilities of the fight scenes, which look cartoonish. Bodies yank up and down like yo-yos on strings, or do flips like mechanical toys. The five warriors themselves, known as the Roos, represent the natural forces of earth, water, fire, wood, and metal, and are reminiscent of the Power Rangers, though less campy.

Screenwriters Michael Vickerman and Hugh Kelley have cobbled together a story that borrows from many sources. As in countless children's adventures, from *The Wizard of Oz* through *A Kid in King Arthur's Court* (1996), the fantasy is framed as a reverie that provides a lesson in life for a typical child. In the film's first 15 minutes, we learn that Ryan Jeffers (Mario Yedidia) has a passion for comic-book fantasies, a mom who can't cook and leaves him unattended day and night, a father who's away somewhere, a bad leg, and something of a psychic gift that allows him to call the winning play for the high school football team. Improbably, he also has a friendship with an acrobatic cook in a Chinese restaurant, Ming (Dennis Dun), who not only can throw rice into a bowl at long distances but can keep a straight face while spouting corny aphorisms about "letting go of your limitations." Ming gives Ryan the Tao, an ancient Chinese manuscript that certainly will reveal the secret to life if only someone can read it.

Wanting to prove himself cool so he can hang with

older kids, Ryan accepts a dare from the quarterback to walk across a whirlpool in an underground sewer, but is sucked down into the world of the Roos. Not surprisingly, the book that he is carrying in his backpack holds many prophecies, and both Master Chung and the evil Komodo need to know the Tao's secrets. Of course, only Ryan has the power to read the manuscript.

Ryan, whose bad leg works perfectly in this world, is befriended by a fetching princess-like girl, Elysia (Marley Shelton). It's not clear why she is the only other inhabitant who seems human. She's seemingly on the side of the Roos, but it's eventually revealed that her brother has been killed by Yun. The warriors had vowed never to take a life, so Yun, ashamed of his deed, has given up his sword and his will to fight. Ryan soon convinces him to return to action.

The rest of the movie consists of Komodo's efforts to have his imbecilic and highly caricatured underlings capture Ryan and the book, efforts that are thwarted by Chung and the warriors. Elysia turns out to be a traitor who is in thrall to Komodo's life-force drug. There are plenty of pointless fight scenes, but they don't establish the Warriors of Virtue as interesting enough to capture the attention of young moviegoers used to heroes with superhuman powers. This despite Ryan's frequent pronouncements that the warriors are "cool," which are too-obvious attempts to get the audience to agree.

The film's biggest problem is that the five Roos are really not all that cool. Their human voices, speaking in stereotypically heavy-breathing hero style, don't match their animal costumes, and they sound like bad actors trapped in bad costumes. Their various abilities, which seem to come and go, are rather lame and consist mostly of gravity-defying leaps and bounds and kung-fu-type twists and turns.

The action, while frequently preposterous, is intense and frenetic, but the story is dragged down by the script's frequent heavy doses of pseudo-profound mysticism. Macfayden chews a lot of scenery as a sort of cross between a Tim Curry type of villain and a rock star a la Kiss. His Komodo is more foppish than menacing. As a bad guy, Macfayden's not so bad at all, but this kind of film needs a more physically threatening nemesis.

If boys think the warriors and the fights are lame or phony, the audience for the film evaporates. Though one of the warriors is ostensibly female, she doesn't have much of a role, and the princess character, Elysia, turns out to be a harlot and a turncoat, so young girls don't have anything to relate to. The film doesn't hold the attention of adults; the script doesn't provide any clever winks or nods to the parental audience.

The plot turns confusing and nonsensical as the film approaches its climax. Back and forth the balance between good and evil swings, with disparate scenes following one after another, and no tension building. Worst of all, what the Tao ends up revealing is nothing more than the mystical gobbledygook which infects the whole movie. At the end, Ryan has learned how to avoid "negative kung" and how to marshall his "positive kung."

To be fair, *Warriors of Virtue* is not that much worse than the many films it imitates, and it is immeasurably better than the crude *Mighty Morphin Power Rangers*. A lot of effort was put into making the film, and a lot of money too. The performances aren't bad; Yedidia is a little too earnest, but sympathetic enough, and Macfayden is sometimes a hoot. The sets are terrific, the action heated if not dazzling. But children, given so much to choose from in the entertainment business of the late 1990s, seem to have taken a pass on this one.

In the end, there's nothing remarkable about this film other than the expectations it tried to generate for itself. If the film had sneaked up unannounced, it might have done better. But even kids these days get jaded by promotional efforts, and many of them apparently decided, just from watching the previews and seeing the toys, that the Warriors weren't really as cool as Ryan Jeffers thinks.

—*Michael Betzold*

CREDITS

Komodo: Angus Macfadyen
Ryan Jeffers: Mario Yedidia
Master Chung: Chao-Li Chi
Elysia: Marley Shelton
Ming: Dennis Dun

Origin: USA
Released: 1997
Production: Dennis, Ronald, Christopher, and Jeremy Law and Patricia Ruben; released by MGM
Direction: Ronny Yu
Screenplay: Michael Vickerman and Hugh Kelley
Cinematography: Peter Pau
Editing: David Wu
Music: Don Davis
Production design: Eugenio Zanetti
Costumes: Shirley Chan
Visual effects supervisor: John Gajdecki
Makeup and animatronic effects: Tony Gardner
Action coordinator: Siuming Tsui
MPAA rating: PG
Running Time: 101 minutes

REVIEWS

Boxoffice. July, 1997, p. 94.
Entertainment Weekly. May 9, 1997, p. 92.
The Hollywood Reporter. May 2, 1997, p. 10.
New York Times. May 2, 1997, p. B10.
People. May 19, 1997, p. 26.
Sight and Sound. August, 1997, p. 57.
Variety. May 5, 1997, p. 67.
Village Voice. May 13, 1997, p. 86.

Washington Square

He was beautiful, passionate and penniless. For a lonely young heiress, the promise of his love was worth any price.—Movie tagline

"A triumph! Jennifer Jason Leigh delivers a masterful Oscar-caliber performance."—Bill Diehl, *ABC Radio*

"One of the year's finest movies. Brimming with cinematic energy and packed with superb performances."—Michael Wilmington, *Chicago Tribune*

"Elegant, intelligent, and abundance of rich performances."—Terry Lawson, *Detroit Free Press*

"Brilliant, moving and beautifully acted. One of the year's best films."—Jim Svejda, *KNX-AM*

"The most passionate motion picture of the year! Beautiful and heartbreaking. The Oscar race begins."—Michael Medved, *New York Post*

"Bracing and perfectly cast."—Janet Maslin, *The New York Times*

"A film that both respects James's complexities and bitter ironies and adds a visceral kick all its own."—David Ansen, *Newsweek*

"*Washington Square* is ravishingly done."—Peter Travers, *Rolling Stone*

"A film for everyone to see and savor. It's elegant."—Jeffrey Lyon, *WNBC-TV*

Handsome-but-poor Morris's (Ben Chaplin) intentions toward wealthy Catherine (Jennifer Jason Leigh) are suspect in the period love story *Washington Square.*

Box Office: $1,654,534

Washington Square is not a remake of William Wyler's *The Heiress* (1949) but a reinterpretation of Henry James's short novel "Washington Square," published in 1880 but harkening back to the elegant upper-class New York of the 1850s. Both film adaptations, though admirably acted, leave the viewer still wondering about the principal characters' motivations. One of the most perplexing questions is: Did Morris Townsend care anything at all about Catherine Sloper or was he solely interested in her fortune? But this raises another question: Even if he was only after her money, might she not have been happier married to a handsome man rather than spending the rest of her life a lonely spinster?

Austin to daughter Catherine: "How obscene—that your mother should give her life so you can inhabit space on this earth."

Catherine Sloper (Jennifer Jason Leigh), the only child of socially prominent Dr. Austin Sloper (Albert Finney), is homely, awkward and shy. In the early scenes the talented Leigh overplays her character's clumsiness to such an extent that she almost rivals Kramer on the television comedy series "Seinfeld." Viewers may laugh at Kramer, but Catherine's gaucheness only makes them wince. She is continuously dropping things, bumping into doors, and even falling down. Critic Todd McCarthy wrote in *Daily Variety:* "Leigh . . . pushes her character's clumsiness and skittishness when faced with masculine attention to an almost embarrassing degree, making Catherine seem more a buffoon than a wallflower." Fortunately, her deportment improves after she thinks she has had the unbelievable good luck of finding in Morris Townsend (Ben Chaplin) a handsome young man who truly loves her.

Unlike *The Heiress,* the new film makes it clear that Catherine is shy, self-conscious, and miserable in social situations because of her father. She displeases him with her inhibitions, and she is inhibited because of her terror of displeasing him. The filmmakers have adequate justification for reading this interpretation into James's story. James writes in his inimitable fashion: " . . . it is a literal fact that he [Dr. Sloper] almost never addressed his daughter save in the ironical form. Whenever he addressed her he gave her pleasure; but she has to cut her pleasure out of the pieces, as it were." Both Ralph Richardson in *The Heiress* and Albert Finney in *Washington Square* pick up that cruel, mocking, distancing tone that James describes as "the ironical form." The opening scenes of *Washington Square,* which do not occur in the book, show the body of Catherine's mother who has just died in childbirth. Dr. Sloper never can forgive his adoring daughter for being the cause of his wife's death nor bring himself to accept his daughter as a replacement for his wife.

The 1949 film *The Heiress* was actually based on the successful stage adaptation by Ruth and Augustus Goetz rather than directly from the Henry James novel.

Dr. Sloper, who thinks he can see right through his unworldly daughter's handsome, impetuous suitor (and probably can), warns her that Townsend will squander all her money and leave her destitute. (She already has an income of $10,000 a year from her mother's estate and will receive another $20,000 a year when her father dies.) The warning is delivered in a frightening setting in the Swiss Alps at the edge of a cliff. The doctor has taken Catherine to Europe for a year, hoping she will be distracted from her infatuation by all the castles, cathedrals, museums, and romantic scenery associated with famous books and paintings. Even though the viewer fears the angry doctor might actually push his daughter off the cliff if she continues to defy him, she remains loyal to her lover. She may not have inherited her mother's beauty or charm, but she has inherited her father's strength of will.

The makers of *Washington Square* have taken every opportunity to open the story up for the screen, except in the case of the European interlude. Evidently they felt that the Europe scenes would have been too much of a distraction as well as a strain on their budget. James was not happy with his novella and omitted it from his *New York Edition,* although F.O. Matthiessen quipped that it "has frequently been James' favorite novel with readers who don't really like James." One of its faults, in James's view, may have been that it lacks a "second act." Townsend proposes, Catherine accepts. Dad says he will disinherit her if she marries this lazy fortune-hunter. There is a stalemate. The trip to Europe fills up space but does nothing to advance the story. Then Townsend, having concluded that the doctor really intends to carry out his threat, reveals himself as a total cad by running off to California on the day he has promised Catherine they will elope.

Both film versions also raise many questions about Dr. Sloper. Does he have an unconscious incestuous attraction to his daughter? Is he concerned about losing control of the capital she inherited from her mother? Is he afraid of being left all alone in his old age? Does he hate to see his hard-earned money and his beautiful house full of treasures fall into the clutches of a fortune-hunter who never did a day's work in his life? Or, as they say in college multiple-choice exams, is the correct answer "All of the above?" James himself is too subtle to provide much help. He is better at raising questions about human character than answering them. People are still wondering whether the heroine in his *The Turn of the Screw* (which has several film adaptations) is really seeing ghosts or experiencing hallucinations induced by sexual frustration. At least *Washington Square* will leave audiences thinking and debating, which can hardly be said for the current deluge of blockbusters, shoot-em-ups, and mindless comedies.

Critics have emphasized that the big difference between *The Heiress* and the 1997 film version of the novella is the feminist spin that screenwriter Carol Doyle and director Agnieszka Holland have given the story. This spin is not blatant but pervasive. The most glaring difference is in the endings. In *The Heiress,* after Dr. Sloper's death Catherine becomes the stereotypical lonely, embittered spinster in a gloomy mansion, almost like Miss Havisham in Charles Dickens's *Great Expectations* or Miss Emily Grierson of William Faulkner's short story, "A Rose for Emily." In the new film, however, Catherine ends up smiling and playing a merry tune on the piano. She seems better off without any men in her life—insensitive men who are incapable of true love and only want to use women for one purpose or another. Men are not much good and women can get along just fine without them.

This is the feminist angle the filmmakers have read into James—and it did not require much stretching of the old master's material. James himself wrote of his homely heroine: "She was greatly liked, and as time went on she grew to be a sort of kindly maiden aunt to the younger portion of society. Young girls were apt to confide to her their love affairs . . . and young men to be fond of her without knowing why." As mistress of a beautiful mansion with an income that would be equivalent to at least $100,000 a year in our inflated dollars, Catherine is hardly to be pitied. She has no children of her own, but she has many friends, all female, and is surrounded by adoring and adorable surrogate nieces and nephews. She can entertain on a lavish scale, and she has a staff of servants to make all the preparations and do the cleaning up. When Morris Townsend presents himself after eight years in a last-ditch effort to rekindle her affection, Catherine has the added pleasure of telling him in the most ladylike fashion that he can go straight to hell. The fact that both the men and women in the audience enjoy seeing the slick, selfish Morris receive what James calls "the retribution of time" would seem to prove that Dr. Sloper was dead right about the man's character and that Catherine is much better off without him.

As Aunt Lavinia Penniman, Maggie Smith gives a fine performance as a romanticizing woman whose mind has been shaped by poets like Keats, Shelley, Byron, and Tennyson. She is not only useful to the dramatic purposes of the film, serving as go-between, trouble-maker, and confidante, but she symbolizes the old-fashioned type of woman who believed the only happiness to be hoped for was to be found in love and devotion to a man.

The Heiress was shot in black-and-white, which acclaimed director William Wyler deemed appropriate to a somber story of the horse-and-buggy era. *Washington Square,* however, was shot in bright, beautiful colors and the soundtrack is full of rich music. Much camera attention is lavished on the plush interior of the house in Washington Square. Color seems appropriate to upbeat *Washington Square* as black-and-white did to downbeat *The Heiress.* The feminist spin required the filmmakers to highlight how much there was in Catherine's life without the presence of a lord and master.

There is perhaps a deeper meaning to be read into *Washington Square*, the film, as well as *Washington Square*, the novel. Anyone, man or woman, who hopes to attain happiness and self-realization through being loved by another human being is waiting for Godot. Or as latter-day New Yorkers are fond of saying: "You want love? Buy a dog!"

—Bill Delaney

CREDITS

Catherine Sloper: Jennifer Jason Leigh
Dr. Austin Sloper: Albert Finney
Morris Townsend: Ben Chaplin
Aunt Lavinia Penniman: Maggie Smith
Mrs. Elizabeth Almond: Judith Ivey
Mrs. Montgomery: Betsy Brantley

Origin: USA
Released: 1997
Production: Roger Birnbaum and Julie Bergman Sender for Caravan Pictures and Alchemy Filmworks; released by Hollywood Pictures
Direction: Agnieszka Holland
Screenplay: Carol Doyle; based on the novel by Henry James
Cinematography: Jerzy Zielinksi
Editing: David Siegel
Music: Jan A.P. Kaczmarek
Production design: Allan Starski
Set decoration: William A. Cimino
Costumes: Anna Sheppard
Sound: Michael Barosky
MPAA rating: PG
Running Time: 115 minutes

REVIEWS

Boxoffice. October, 1997, p. 37.
Chicago Tribune. October 10, 1997, p. 5.
Entertainment Weekly. October 17, 1997, p. 41.
Los Angeles Times. October 10, 1997, p. F1.
New York Times. October 3, 1997, p. E13.
People. October 6, 1997, p. 26.
Rolling Stone. October 30, 1997, p. 72.
Time. October 20, 1997.
USA Today. October 3, 1997, p. 8D.
Variety. September 15, 1997, p. 76.
Village Voice. October 7, 1997, p. 80.
Wall Street Journal. October 10, 1997, p. A20.

Wedding Bell Blues

Micki, Tanya and Jasmine have 24 hours to get divorced. There's just one problem . . . They're still single.—Movie tagline

"Paulina Porizkova is bewitching, Julie Warner is a pint-sized comic treasure and Illeana Douglas is getting to be a celluloid addiction."—*Critic's Choice*

"Well acted and entertaining."—*Movieline*

"A very modern romantic comedy."—*Sixty Second Preview*

" . . . a sly, romantic romp . . . fiercely funny!"—*SSG Syndicate*

Wedding Bell Blues is a slow-moving, annoying, and obvious would-be romantic comedy about three single roommates—Jasmine (Illeana Douglas), Tanya (Paulina Porizkova), and Micki (Julie Warner)—who are about to turn thirty. Exactly how these three very disparate personalities ever got together is never explained (they apparently share Jasmine's house—maybe she needs the rent). Jasmine and Tanya actively seem to dislike each other and they both treat the emotional Micki like a little girl. Why they're concerned about each other and why the viewer should be is one of the film's first problems.

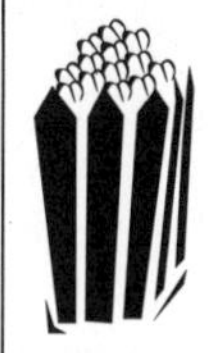

Jasmine: "I didn't know turning 30 was terminal."

Tiny Jewish Micki, who has the prototypical meddling mother (Liz Sheridan) that she's constantly talking to on the phone, is about to be married when her mensch fiance, Jeff (Joseph Urla), calls off the wedding. She's "the nicest girl he ever met" but there's "no passion" between them. Before leaving, Jeff hands Micki his credit card to pay off the wedding expenses.

Tall, thin, beautiful Tanya has taken every home pregnancy test on the market (a scene that opens the film) and they all come out positive. Upset and uncertain of her future, she manages to get fired from her sales clerk job, and then discovers boyfriend Tom (Richard Edson) "isn't ready" to get married and doesn't want the baby.

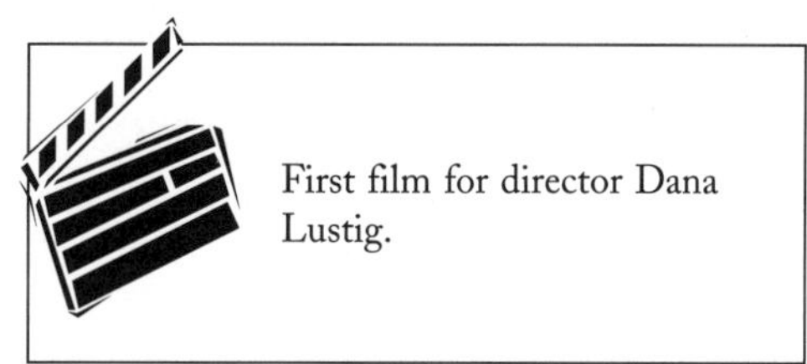

First film for director Dana Lustig.

Meanwhile, cynical Jasmine, who likes sex (and bad boys) but apparently not commitment, must attend the wedding of her younger sister. She reluctantly dresses in a frou-frou bridesmaid's dress and is subjected to her large Armenian family's constant (and unsubtle) concern about her single status.

When Tanya and Jasmine discover Micki eating and drinking herself into a coma over her cancelled nuptials, they have a bonding chat. Jasmine declares they should all "find a guy—some stranger—marry him, then get divorced the next day, and then just mail their families the marriage certificate and just tell them to shove it." Drunk Micki says there's no waiting period in Vegas and they should just do it.

So the threesome head for a weekend in Las Vegas (on Jeff's credit card). Micki has a makeover (deciding that blondes do have more fun) and winds up returning to the wrong hotel room. Who should answer her knock but a wet, towel-clad, tall, and very attractive (single) guy, Cary (John Corbett), who's in town for the rodeo (a cowboy no less!), and the duo wind up making a date for the evening.

Tanya puts her assets on display poolside, having decided to take her equally beautiful mother's advice to get a "nice rich man to look after you." She makes a date with divorced, middleaged businessman Oliver (Charles Martin Smith) and persuades Jasmine to double with Oliver's younger friend, nice guy Matt (Jonathan Penner).

When Micki and Cary become winners at blackjack, she decides her luck is changing for the better and suddenly proposes to him—a one-night wedding—and he laughingly agrees. In keeping with tradition with movies that have Vegas settings, the wedding chapel has an Elvis impersonator who serenades the newlyweds with the apropo "Crying in the Chapel." Micki's determined to experience her first orgasm and she and Cary spend their wedding night in the stables, pursuing sexual nirvana. (All you see are the horses outside their stalls—it's really quite a passionless movie). Micki achieves the big O, and is grateful to Cary, who tells her to send the divorce papers to his home in Wyoming. (Corbett's cowboy charm is definitely missed).

Meanwhile, Jasmine discovers Tanya's pregnant and that she plans to trick Oliver into thinking the baby's his after Tanya marries him. She leaves in disgust (with Matt following her) as Tanya and Oliver head for a wedding chapel. Oh yeah, Oliver also thinks it's a hoot to get married for a night, especially if he can send a picture of his new bride to the ex that dumped him. But Tanya's conscience finally gets the better of her and she 'fesses up to her deception before the ceremony.

Jasmine and Matt spend the remainder of the evening drinking and playing true confessions on a hotel rooftop. When they wake up the next morning in the back of Jasmine's old, convertible Cadillac, she finds a marriage certificate in her hand. They also apparently had great sex (they don't remember the wedding but they do remember the sex), thus fulfilling Jasmine's belief that sex is all she's good at (and for). Yes, beneath Jasmine's tough exterior beats the heart of a girl who doesn't like being "different"—and just wants a "normal" life.

CREDITS

Jasmine: Illeana Douglas
Tanya: Paulina Porizkova
Micki: Julie Warner
Cary: John Corbett
Matt: Jonathan Penner
Oliver: Charles Martin Smith
Tom: Richard Edson
Jeff: Joseph Urla
Tanya's mother: Stephanie Beacham
Micki's mother: Liz Sheridan
Debbie Reynolds: Debbie Reynolds (as herself)

Origin: USA
Released: 1996
Production: Mike Curb, Carole Curb Nemoy, Ram Bergman, and Dana Lustig for Bergman Lustig Productions and Curb Entertainment; released by BMG Independents
Direction: Dana Lustig
Screenplay: Annette Goliti Gutierrez
Cinematography: Kent Wakeford
Editing: Caroline Ross
Music: Paul Christian Gordon, Tal Bergman
Production design: Shay Austin
Costumes: Dana Allyson
MPAA rating: R
Running Time: 101 minutes

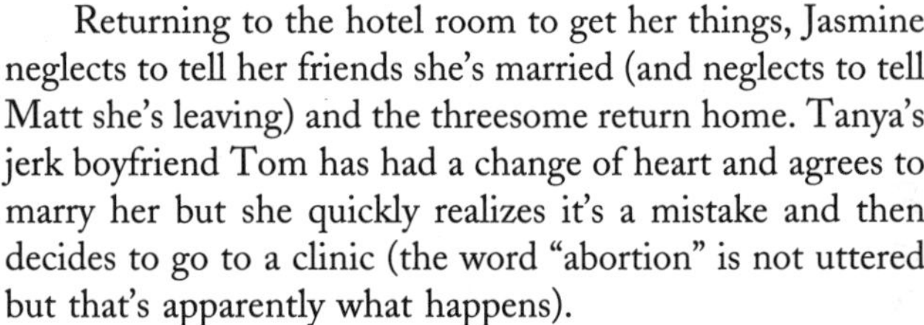

Returning to the hotel room to get her things, Jasmine neglects to tell her friends she's married (and neglects to tell Matt she's leaving) and the threesome return home. Tanya's jerk boyfriend Tom has had a change of heart and agrees to marry her but she quickly realizes it's a mistake and then decides to go to a clinic (the word "abortion" is not uttered but that's apparently what happens).

In a role reversal Micki is hitting the town every night with some "mystery man" and coming home disheveled every morning while previous "nightclub babe" Jasmine is pining for Matt, without doing anything concrete about her feelings. When he finally sends her divorce papers (which is how Tanya and Micki find out about Jasmine's weekend escapade), an angry Jasmine goes to return them in person. She then blames Matt for wanting a divorce (which makes no sense), the two have a brief heart-to-heart and, voila, decide to stick together.

The final scene shows Micki (several months later) once again preparing for a wedding. It turns out her "mystery man" has been former fiance Jeff, who's eager to get married now that Micki's discovered what "passion" is all about. You wonder if she ever told him exactly how she learned to have great sex. And to make things tackier, if that's possible, Tanya's even invited the good advice-giving Oliver to Micki's wedding and he arrives with his ex/and future wife. Seems Tanya did send the missus a picture of her and Oliver as a couple and she got jealous enough to give Oliver another try.

The entire movie is enough to give marriage a bad name—though it gives lip service to the importance of love and commitment, it does nothing to show it with its trio of unsatisfied, unhappy, and self-deluding women (the men are no prize-winners either). And it certainly does nothing for the careers of any of the actors involved in the production.

—Christine Tomassini

REVIEWS

Boxoffice. July, 1997, p. 82.
Variety. October 28, 1996, p. 68.

Welcome to Sarajevo

For this celebrated, outrageous, adrenaline-loving bunch of reporters, home is the latest war zone. Now, one of them is about to do the unthinkable - get emotionally involved.—Movie tagline

They're a group of celebrated, fun-loving reporters about to do the unthinkable - mount an impossible escape to freedom. The true story of an extraordinary act of courage.—Movie tagline

"Triumphant, compelling and utterly inspirational!"—Tom Meek, *Boston Phoenix*

"A brilliantly crafted film! No other movie this year can match its power to absorb an audience."—Michael Medved, *New York Post*

While it was beginning, the majority of the rest of the world refused to take heed of the civil unrest and tactical genocide being waged on the citizens of Bosnia. The United States was busy with a presidential election and the subsequent changing of the guard. On a daily basis, all of the major networks were showing us images that smacked of an equally dark chapter that occurred some fifty years earlier. But nobody seemed to be doing much about it.

Flynn: "This place is like a virus you can't get rid of."

With prison camps that could rival the degradations of Nazi Germany and a Gestapo police force that would murder entire villages on a whim, it's amazing that the enlightened, politically correct society of the '90s remained so complacent and unaware of this three-way civil war that virtually destroyed the former Yugoslavia. President Clinton recently informed American service personnel stationed in Bosnia that they would be kept in place indefinitely. If the US and international peace keepers presence was stronger when these skirmishes had initially blossomed, the bulk of all the unnecessary carnage could have been alleviated. Clinton's rejuvenated conscience, while admirable, seems to be too little too late.

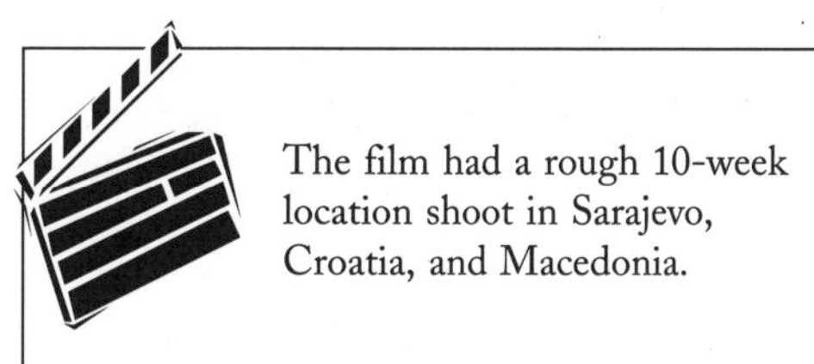

The film had a rough 10-week location shoot in Sarajevo, Croatia, and Macedonia.

Director Michael Winterbottom (*Jude*, 1996) wastes no time in showing the relative rapid decline of one of Europe's most glamorous and romantic cities. Black bordered images of a newscast by a British reporter are shown at the start of the siege. Winterbottom then reverts to stock footage of the 1984 Winter Olympics showing the heavy economic windfalls experienced by host cities. Then he cuts again to the present. A family is seen inside a beauty parlor preparing for a daughter's wedding when the generator goes down. The mother pulls the generator chord and suddenly everything is back to relative normalcy. Van Morrison is on the radio and people are putting on their Sunday best for a special event. Citizens are fully aware of the chaos going on around them but are determined to make the best of it. Laughing and dancing and dressed to the nines, the family begins sauntering down the street on the way to ceremony and the mother is shot dead by a sniper. A band of international journalists who huddle together waiting for carnage like so many ambulance chasing lawyers, converge on the scene and begin filming. The success or failure of their craft is totally dependent on the misfortunes of the people with which they cohabitate.

In what is viewed by many as selfish grandstanding, the American reporter Flynn (Woody Harrelson) throws caution to the wind and helps to remove the corpse from the street. Motivations aside, his actions are seen later that evening through a worldwide feed. Winterbottom creates the first of many conflicts with this scene. Flynn is regarded as a pariah by his contemporaries. Henderson (Stephen Dillane), his principal rival, is disgusted by Flynn's actions. Henderson is there to report, not beef up his resume. While Flynn is celebrating his coup at one of the local watering holes, Henderson removes himself from the revelry. Soon enough, however, Henderson will lose his own objectivity.

The morning after finds Flynn nursing a hangover while the remaining journalists wait by ready for the day's upcoming bloodshed. Interrupting breakfast, word arrives and everyone quickly departs into waiting vans that scurry them to a marketplace full of casualties. It's not revealed whether or not they were the victims of snipers or a bomb. The how doesn't really seem to matter as much as the what. Amidst the dead are people and pieces of people in a state of shock. The documentarians instruct their cameramen on where to point the cameras. It's clear Henderson is shaken but must go about his business by getting the shots that contain the greatest shock value. Henderson's perspective changes forever after he's forced to inform a little girl that both of her parents were killed in the attack. While editing his footage,

Henderson is informed that his story won't be the lead for that day's broadcast. Instead, his superiors have determined that a story announcing the separation of the Duke and Duchess of York is more important. Henderson is now permanently jaded.

Perhaps in an effort to make his work carry more meaning, Henderson decides to visit a local orphanage. Receiving little or no coverage, the orphanages house the true victims of the hostilities. Very few external wounds are visible, but the daily exposure to the barbaric violence and the loss of their families have created a tribe of weary, battle-scarred bystanders who desperately want out. Winterbottom then dons what is perhaps his most acerbic tone. Shots of makeshift headstones and pictures of bloody toddlers on hospital beds are interwoven with clips of British prime minister John Major delivering a speech to Parliament appearing to show immediate concern for the children. The sarcasm hits a fever pitch as Bobby McFerrin's "Don't Worry, Be Happy" begins playing in the background.

Evidently, Henderson's report hit home. Immediately airplanes carrying several foreign dignitaries and United Nations delegates land in Sarajevo. This, of course, causes a media frenzy. During a impromptu press conference, one of the delegates states matter-of-factly that the world's problems must be handled in order of importance. There are 13 other world countries that are suffering worse than Sarajevo. Not missing a beat, Flynn inquires as to what those other 13 countries might be and whether or not Sarajevo is sliding up or down the scale.

Many people have criticized the casting of Woody Harrelson in the role of Flynn. Some have sighted Harrelson's considerable marquee value as a reason for his inclusion, which is understandable. Many people who might stay away from a picture about death and war could be persuaded to attend if they recognize a familiar name in the credits. This point was not lost on Winterbottom. Harrelson has a knack for playing smart-alecks and dimwits and his Flynn is definitely a self-absorbed, self-serving narcissist (although later in the film, Flynn contradicts himself making a monumentally touching gesture). Covering a civil war ain't no picnic. Remaining stoic, taciturn and unflappable is not the way to make it through intact. Sarcasm (and a heavy bending of the elbows) provides a much-needed release valve for pressure and stress. Winterbottom's choice of Harrelson makes all the sense in the world.

Henderson's coverage of the orphans continues. Even his producer Jane (Kerry Fox), the one who alerted him of the children's plight, begins to question his decisions. They've already done that story, it's time to move on. Henderson retorts by stating that they've just started. He begins to film each child individually, overdubbing their Bosnian with the details on each one's individual journey. Suddenly, they're no longer a group of nameless vagabonds, but a collection of unnerved individuals. "That's not news, that's a campaign," his producer remarks. Henderson is unfazed. "I don't care what it is, we're going to get those kids out of here. What's the problem? Big guns, little children, evil men, it's great television." Henderson's outwardly cynical facade is in overdrive, but inside it's apparent that his heart is simultaneously melting and breaking over the plight of the children. He is now fully committed to getting them out of the country.

Henderson soon hooks up with Nina (Marisa Tomei), a recent arrival from America who has done the bulk of the busy work and arranged the necessary credentials to start the children's "temporary" evacuation. However, she cannot remove all of the children, just infants. This presents a sizable conundrum for Henderson. During one of his visits to the orphanage, he strikes up a conversation (through an interpreter) with Emira (Bosnian native Emira Nusevic). He shows her a photo of his home in England. Emira says she'd like to see it in person. In a half-serious, half-patronizing tone, done mostly to oblige her request, Henderson says he'll take her. Not satisfied, she coerces a concrete promise out of him. When the time comes to evacuate, Emira is told she can't go because she is too old. In tears, she reminds Henderson of his covenant and simply will not take no for an answer. Against Nina's advice, Henderson decides to honor his promise to the young girl. Without the knowledge of any of his contemporaries and at the risk of losing not only his career but also his life, Henderson joins the caravan with Emira in tow. Henderson and Emira make it back to England but not after some close calls along the way.

Finding a new beginning in England, Emira adjusts well to her new home, experiencing the simple joys denied to her in her homeland. Her journey is near completion but her new father's fight has just begun. Henderson must travel back to Bosnia. Nine years after she abandoned her, Emira's birth mother wants her back. Henderson runs a reverse gauntlet into hostile territory in an effort to convince Emira's mother that her daughter is better off with him.

The Henderson character is based on real-life journalist Michael Nicholson who spent time in Bosnia and wrote about his experiences in the book *Natasha's Story*, on which the film is based. Winterbottom adapted Nicholson's work, adding fictional elements along the way and the result was something more than a war picture. It is both tragic and uplifting, savagely brutal and heartbreakingly tender. In a year that delivered a minuscule amount of truly outstanding films, Winterbottom's effort rose to the very top. Whether it wins any awards or sets any boxoffice records is completely irrelevant. It was assuredly the most human and humane film of 1997, and should be considered a masterpiece.

CREDITS

Henderson: Stephen Dillane
Flynn: Woody Harrelson
Nina: Marisa Tomei
Emira: Emira Nusevic
Jane Carson: Kerry Fox
Risto: Goran Visnjic
Gregg: James Nesbitt
Annie McGee: Emily Lloyd
Helen Henderson: Juliet Aubrey

Origin: USA, Great Britain
Released: 1997
Production: Graham Broadbent and Damian Jones for Dragon Pictures and Channel Four Films; released by Miramax Films
Direction: Michael Winterbottom
Screenplay: Frank Cottrell Boyce; based on the book *Natasha's Story* by Michael Nicholson
Cinematography: Daf Hobson
Editing: Trevor Waite
Music: Adrian Johnston
Production design: Mark Geraghty
Art direction: David Minty
Costumes: Janty Yates
Sound: Martin Trevis
MPAA rating: R
Running Time: 100 minutes

With Nicholson's blueprint, Winterbottom tackled an issue that constantly plagues reporters: don't get personally involved with the story; keep your distance at all costs. But even the strongest willed individuals would find it impossible not to get emotionally involved when surrounded by such mounting, visible despair. Michael Henderson put his high-profile career on the back burner in order to save the lives of those much less fortunate than he and became a better man in the process.

—*J.M. Clark*

REVIEWS

Boxoffice. July, 1997, p. 82.
Boxoffice. October, 1997, p. 22.
Entertainment Weekly. November 28, 1997, p. 42.
GQ. November, 1997, p. 135.
Hollywood Reporter. May 12, 1997, p. 6.
Los Angeles Times. November 26, 1997, p. F1.
New York Times. November 26, 1997, p. E5.
New Yorker. December 1, 1997, p. 101.
Rolling Stone. December 11, 1997, p. 85.
Sight and Sound. November, 1997, p. 56.
Time. December 1, 1997.
USA Today. November 26, 1997, p. 9D.
USA Today. December 2, 1997, p. 8D.
Variety. May 12, 1997, p. 64.
Washington Post. January 9, 1998, p. D1.

When the Cat's Away; Chacun Cherche Son Chat; Everyone's Looking for Their Cat

This is a story about a girl who loses her cat but finds her heart.—Movie tagline

No man. No job. No cat.—Movie tagline

"It's a heart warmer par excellence!"—Graham Fuller, *Interview*

"A gentle breeze of a Parisian film by the refreshing new filmmaker Cedric Klapisch . . . charged with the energy of everyday life. Nimble and adventurous . . . it's a pleasure!"—Janet Maslin, *The New York Times*

"Charming!"—David Ansen, *Newsweek*

"Who would imagine that a French film about a young woman who loses her cat would be such a delight."—Dennis Dermody, *Paper Magazine*

"Rich and poignant!"—Steven Rea, *The Philadelphia Inquirer*

"Wonderfully funny, touching and unforgettable!"—Joe Morgenstern, *Wall Street Journal*

Box Office: $1,594,482

A young Parisian woman who is unsure of herself and going nowhere socially is the unlikely heroine of *When the Cat's Away*, a minimalist but pleasant and perceptive film from French writer-director Cedric Klapisch. With a wisp of a story and a very light touch, Klapisch is a master of understatement and milks plenty of insight out of a very thin story.

Many independent films of this era are called "small," but few are as limited in their ambitions and as claustrophobic in their scope as *When the Cat's Away*. Klapisch's first feature film (he made several shorts while studying in New York) is about Chloe (Garance Clavel), a twenty-something makeup artist who, while looking for her lost cat, slowly awakens to her run-down city neighborhood and its inhabitants, and to the possibility of falling in love.

For reasons not sufficiently explained, Chloe is socially inept, a little shy, and a step out of fashion. It would help if Clavel was as plain and unappealing as Chloe's character seems scripted to be. But Clavel is not really all that mousy, and what she wears doesn't seem more than slightly out of tune with her contemporaries. Though she's quiet, her personality isn't all that awkward. So it's a genuine puzzlement why Chloe is such a wet rag.

Part of the problem, apparently, is a lack of assertiveness. Chloe has little confidence, but enough to stand up on occasion to her co-workers and her browbeating bosses at her job, where she makes up saucy models for high-fashion shoots. Klapisch suggests that Chloe is a little lost soul in the big, frightening city, but it would be helpful if we knew more about her background.

Mme. Renee: "Men have often let me down, but cats never."

Such exposition is not, however, Klapisch's style. His characters, his scenes, are determinedly what they appear to be, and nothing more. Complexity is not this filmmaker's cup of tea. Fortunately, subtlety and characterization are.

Chloe lives with Michel (Olivier Py), a gay man, in a cluttered apartment. They engage in a lackluster competition to see who can land a lover first. Michel wins. He is more than a bit of a pain, though he's a reliable shoulder in a pinch. He not only refuses to take care of Chloe's black cat, Gris-Gris, while Chloe goes on vacation, he also suggests putting it in a plastic bag and dropping it out of a moving car. When the cat later turns up missing, he only reluctantly helps Chloe put up posters and is almost caught throwing them in the trash. Like everyone else in the film, Michel is human, with good qualities and bad.

Chloe's quest to find a cat-sitter leads her from the apartment out into her cramped Bastille district neighborhood. By the contacts that ensue, Klapisch suggests that this excursion is a considerable widening of Chloe's world, which previously must have been spent mostly in her apartment and at her job. Inquiries at local shops lead her to an elderly neighbor, Madame Renee (Renee Le Calm), who has a menagerie of felines and is eager to help. "Men have often let me down, but cats never," she explains.

In one of the more interesting directorial choices in an otherwise straightforward film, Klapisch dispenses Chloe's vacation in a quick three-shot sequence: a shot of her walking to the train station, a shot of her swimming in the ocean and looking bored, and a shot of her walking back from the train station, carrying a souvenir. Not only does the sequence suggest that the world beyond her Paris neighborhood is inconsequential, it deftly underlines the universal problem with vacations: once they end, it's as if you never left.

Chloe's tiny universe is shattered upon her return, however, when she learns that Renee has lost Gris-Gris, the pet that appears to be Chloe's emotional anchor. Renee tells Chloe that she left her kitchen window open and the cat disappeared, over the connected rooftops. Renee, who's never lost a pet before, is at least as distraught as Chloe. Le Calm, who is almost a dead ringer for Woody Allen in grandmotherly drag, is a great presence in the film, both prickly and endearing, resourceful and helpless. Amazingly enough, she is an amateur actress, a real neighborhood cat lady.

Renee introduces Chloe into an ever-expanding circle of kindly widows (also played by real inhabitants of Paris) who unleash their own kind of dragnet in the neighborhood to try and snare Gris-Gris. Why they are so interested is a bit opaque until one telling sequence. An elderly woman calls Chloe to give her the latest news on the search for Gris-Gris, which is simply that there is no news. Clearly, the widow is lonely and uses the phone call as an excuse to talk about the weather. Her life is as empty as the bare wall Klapisch places behind her. It's this kind of moment that defines the film and illustrates Klapisch's ability to give resonance to the simplest scenes and most incidental characters. It's much more effective than a later comic scene in which Chloe meets a woman who talks to her deceased husband's urn as if the ashes were still a live person.

Through the indulgence of the matrons, Chloe also meets Djamel (Zinedine Soualem), a kind but dimwitted man who is the butt of cruel jokes at the local bar. Djamel, who helps the matrons with errands and odd jobs, willingly joins in the search for the cat, chaperoning Chloe on day and night walks around the neighborhood. Djamel (splendidly portrayed with great sympathy by Soualem) tells Chloe that he fell off a roof when he was a child, which explains his feeble brain. He also contends he could move quickly through the city if he had a bike, which he does not, and that he sees things others cannot see and would take wonderful pictures if he only had a camera. Obviously, Djamel is being likened to a cat, and Chloe treats him much as she treated Gris-Gris. To Chloe, Djamel provides welcome companionship but is incapable of providing much more. Djamel is smitten with Chloe but unable to offer her what she needs.

The closest thing to high drama in the movie occurs when Djamel, who is determined to win Chloe's affections by retrieving her cat, clambers over a rooftop to pursue a black feline suspect. Suggesting the terror of a fall that would harken back to Djamel's childhood tragedy, Klapisch quickly eschews the possible drama to return to the mundane. That's his choice, repeatedly, and it keeps *When the Cat's Away* focused on the little, everyday foibles of people, rather than on the big events of cinema.

Eventually, the focus of the film veers away from the increasingly futile search for the cat and towards Chloe's seemingly equally futile search for a man. She keeps running into a mysterious young Bohemian type (Romain Duris), who turns out to be the drummer that is annoying the whole neighborhood, but their attempts to meet are continually thwarted. When Michel takes a lover and Chloe is awakened by the sounds of their sexual play, she becomes more determined in her quest; but her bar prowling proves fruitless. Wearing a slightly provocative dress, Chloe has a disastrous night in which she is chatted up in a bar by a man who claims he's dreamed about her, accosted in the bathroom by the man's girlfriend, assaulted outside the bar by other drunken men, and then chaperoned home by the female bartender, who also tries to put the make on her. This is the most eventful sequence in the film, but it's also the least believable. Chloe concludes she'll never wear a dress again, as if her fairly modest outfit were screaming for attention. Klapisch can't have it both ways with Chloe: she can't be as mousy as most of the film suggests *and* be as seductive as this sequence makes her out to be.

The ending, which suggests that Chloe's searching has overlooked something right under her nose, manages to be both a little too tidy and a little disquieting. It's bittersweet because Chloe discards Djamel, who concludes "Life isn't fair," and falls for a sullen painter, Bel Canto (Joel Brisse), who is one of the least interesting characters in the film. An unexpectedly exuberant ending suggests that Chloe, a late bloomer, has fallen in love for the first time in her life. It also suggests that Klapisch might be as skeptical about that as he is about Chloe's brutally sad fling with the mysterious drummer.

In some ways, *When the Cat's Away* is a metaphor for what's happening to old Paris. Renee and her matron friends complain the little shops are being leveled for ugly new stores selling ugly new products, and the older inhabitants are being evicted. Clearly, such "progress" is a disturbing prospect to Klapisch, whose characters move in a dissonant world in which they never quite seem to fit. With his skills at painting his little pictures of such a world and its inhabitants, Klapisch has a deft feel for how the world changes from one moment to the next, and for the importance of paying careful attention to life and love.

—*Michael Betzold*

CREDITS

Chloe: Garance Claval
Djamel: Zinedine Soualem
Michel: Olivier Py
Mme. Renee: Renee Le Calm

Origin: France
Released: 1996
Production: Farid Lahouassa, Aissa Djabri, and Manuel Munz for Vertigo Productions and France 2 Cinema; released by Sony Pictures Classics
Direction: Cedric Klapisch
Screenplay: Cedric Klapisch
Cinematography: Benoit Delhomme
Editing: Francine Sandberg
Production design: Francois Emmanuelli
Costumes: Pierre Yves Gayraud
Sound: Olivier Le Vacon
MPAA rating: Unrated
Running Time: 95 minutes

REVIEWS

Boxoffice. February, 1997, p. 72.
Entertainment Weekly. July 18, 1997, p. 56.
Los Angeles Times. July 3, 1997, p. 16.
National Catholic Reporter. August 1, 1997, p. 17.
New Republic. June 30, 1997, p. 27.
New York Times. March 21, 1997, p. B22.
People. July 7, 1997, p. 20.
Sight and Sound. November, 1996, p. 62.
Variety. March 26, 1996, p. 73.
Village Voice. June 24, 1997, p. 75.
Wall Street Journal. June 20, 1997, p. A16.
Washington Post. July 11, 1997, p. B7.
Washington Post Weekend. July 11, 1997, p. 37.

When We Were Kings

The untold story of the Rumble in the Jungle.—Movie tagline

"One of the most passionate celebrations of a hero ever assembled!"—Jack Mathews, *Newsday*

"An exuberant and remarkable film."—David Ansen, *Newsweek*

"A great, enthralling and poignant pageant."—Richard Corliss, *Time*

Box Office: $2,764,051

Reviewers have called *When We Were Kings*, the Academy Award-winning documentary, a time capsule. Certainly the scenes with Muhammed Ali in his heyday in the 1970s have a nostalgic feel. It is quaint and touching to see him poke fun at the late pontificating Howard Cosell, calling him a phony with a toupee he got from the tail of a pony. Ali's rhymes come as fast as his jabs. As a boxer, though, he was already past his prime, entering his mid-thirties when he could no longer dance like a butterfly or sting like a bee. Yet he was a king, lionized not merely by the people of Zaire, where he would challenge a young, awesome George Foreman for his heavyweight title, but by an entourage and a core following at home that recognized his greatness.

Muhammad Ali: "If you think the world was surprised when Nixon resigned, wait till I kick Foreman's behind."

Although Ali was a great clown and enjoyed jousting with reporters, he never lost his dignity—in part because his wit had a bite and his humor had a message. He wanted to fight in Zaire so that he could talk about Africa and the greatness of the African people, so that he could say not only to the overwhelmingly white reporters but also to his fellow African Americans that they needed to take pride in their identities and understand their roots. A Black Muslim, Ali had suffered ostracism from boxing for several years because of his religious and political beliefs—he would not serve in the army during the Vietnam War—and a barrage of criticism in the press that treated him as unpatriotic. But Ali was willing to risk everything, saying simply that no North Vietnamese had ever called him a nigger.

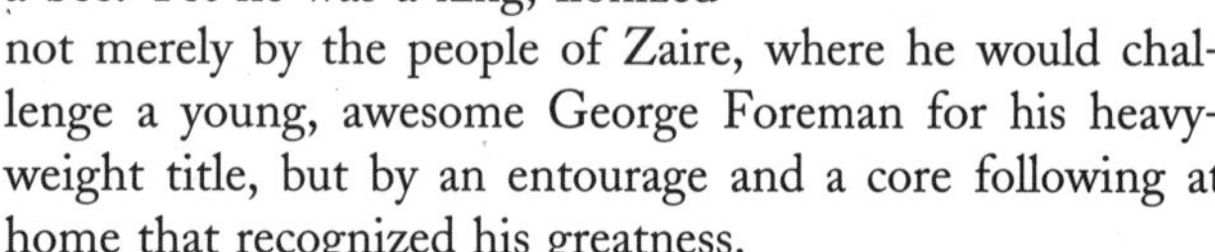

The video version includes exclusive interviews with Leon Gast on making the film and bringing it to the screen.

Yet *When We Were Kings* is no simple paean to Ali or to the black power movement. The fight in Zaire is shadowed by the sinister figure of Mobutu, a dictator who still tyrannizes over his country even as he battles cancer. While Ali speaks of the greatness of Africans and the African past, Mobutu degrades his own people in torture chambers underneath the stadium platform where Ali and Foreman will pummel each other.

AWARDS AND NOMINATIONS

Academy Awards 1996: Best Documentary Feature

There is one mystery that the film cannot fathom, an enigma that the commentators cannot penetrate. Behind the cockiness, the fooling, the shrewd criticism of the press and the American psyche that Ali served up daily with unflagging energy, was he afraid? Foreman had destroyed his other opponents, humiliating the seemingly invincible Joe Frazier who had given Ali so much trouble. Foreman was younger and stronger, and if not quite as fast as Ali, he had surprisingly good moves for a big puncher. When he hits the heavy bag the air vibrates ominously. More than one journalist expresses the fear that Ali will not merely lose the fight, he will be permanently injured, if not killed.

Foreman spends his training period practicing ways of cutting down the ring space, so that Ali won't be able to dance away from his deadly blows. The champion seems coldly confident, saying little. Ali talks all the time, of course, as if psyching himself up as he urges the people of Zaire into a frenzy of support for him. He is not especially sharp in his sparring rounds, but it is clear that he is training hard. In sober moments, he chastises the press for underestimating him—pointing out that he is no raw kid and that his experience will prevail over the twenty-five-year-old Foreman.

Not a single commentator in the film predicts an Ali victory. Even when the fight begins they do not have a clue about Ali's strategy. The first round is amazing. As Norman Mailer observes, Ali delivers a series of scoring punches with a right hand lead—a dangerous gambit since it takes twice as long to deliver as a left. Foreman has not seen such a maneuver in two years, Mailer points out, and he has not trained for it. Indeed, the punch is a kind of insult because it means that Ali has left himself open to a counterpunch. Foreman does retaliate, but the speed of Ali's hands keeps him busy, and Ali's accuracy is improved by not dancing and moving away from Foreman—as Foreman expected him to do.

Much of the first round is shown in the film—a wise choice because it shows Ali's daring and courage. He stands toe-to-toe with the bigger man and beats him to the punch. Mailer observes that it look as though Ali is the one going for a knockout. But Foreman presses ahead, losing points, but not hurt by Ali's attack.

A curious dynamic is at play as commentary cascades over the violent action in the ring. The discussion of the fighters' ring style is illuminating, yet it is almost beside the point. What is happening inside the ring is as mysterious as what was happening inside Ali's head before the fight. Is Mailer right? Did Ali have to confront his fear and find an inner fortitude that carried him into the fight? Ali himself suggests a different explanation: underneath his loud mouthing lay the cool plans of the professional. He was setting Foreman up, allowing him to think that the main thing to concentrate on was catching Ali: then body blows and head shots would soften and crush his opponent.

After the first round, Foreman has much less trouble tagging his older opponent. Time after time he drives Ali into the ropes, bashing him from head to stomach, with Ali covers his head and mid section with his gloves, forearms, and elbows. Outside the ring it appears that Ali is taking a terrific beating. Inside he is taunting Foreman to hit harder. And after seven rounds of heavy hitting, the champion is exhausted—an easy mark for Ali who finishes himself with a few well-timed blows.

The moment of Foreman's fall is the climax of the film. Ali pulls himself back from taking another punch as Foreman goes down. Mailer suggests Ali is concerned with esthetics—not wanting to ruin the scene by a clumsy blow that would interfere with Foreman's descent. Perhaps. Like so much of the talk in the film, Mailer's can only guess at what Ali really feels.

If Ali seems to be in perfect control of himself and of events, *When We Were Kings* reveals that he will not always be so. Reference is made to his subsequent fights, some of them creditable jobs and others rather embarrassing. He fought longer than he should have, and Parkinson's Disease has destroyed his motor skills, making him appear to be a shell of his former self. Although his mental ability has not deteriorated, years of boxing have clearly taken their toll, giving the film's title poignancy.

But of course the film has "we" in its title, which seems to imply that not just Ali but "we" have lost a certain greatness. There is a buoyancy to the fight scene in Zaire, of people who act like they are on top of the world, that probably could not be duplicated today. Leon Gast, the film's chief producer who labored for more than twenty years to clear the rights and to assemble the footage, seems to be suggesting that his film is a lament for lost youth and exuberance. Ali stood for all that: a poet in his youth who liked to fight. The film mourns a lost elegance and ease. It has the middle-aged man's grief over waning powers.

Next to Ali, the star of the film is Norman Mailer. Those who see *When We Were Kings* without a sense of his history will be missing half the fun and the melancholy of the film. Mailer was once the enfant terrible of American literature—a huge popular success with his World War II novel, *The Naked and the Dead*, and later an eccentric, rebellious, and controversial figure in the late 1950s and 1960s with a penchant for violence. He too was a poet in his youth who liked to fight. Mailer is good on Ali, but he is also constantly turning Ali into Mailer, into a writer who feared but also welcomed every test of his manhood.

Like Ali, Mailer has mellowed. He is fat, white-haired, and almost grandfatherly. Audiences who do not know him may wonder why this character is given so much screen time. The answer is surely in his final wry comments, which sum up why Ali was able to cause such a stir and to gain the affection of so many people, black and white. Mailer recounts running into Ali some ten years after the Foreman fight. Ali asks him how old he is. When he learns that Mailer is over sixty, Ali enthuses that he hopes he will look as good when he reaches Mailer's age. Mailer compares himself to a happy dog who has to go off to urinate after a compliment while Ali, looking hard at Mailer's much younger wife, says (out of Mailer's hearing) "Are you still married to that old man?" Mailer looks at the camera and grins. "That's Ali," he concludes, making clear that you have to love him even when he has just skewered you.

—Carl Rollyson

CREDITS

Origin: USA
Released: 1996
Production: David Sonenberg, Leon Gast, Taylor Hackford for DASFilms; released by Gramercy Pictures
Direction: Leon Gast
Cinematography: Maryse Alberti, Paul Goldsmith, Kevin Keating, Albert Maysles, Roderick Young
Editing: Leon Gast, Taylor Hackford, Jeffrey Levy-Hinte, Keith Robinson
MPAA rating: Unrated
Running Time: 92 minutes

REVIEWS

Boxoffice. February, 1997, p. 58.
Entertainment Weekly. February 21, 1997, p. 105.
The Hollywood Reporter. October 29, 1996, p. 9.
Los Angeles Times. October 25, 1996, p. F18.
People. February 24, 1997, p. 19.
USA Today. February 13, 1997, p. 4D.
Village Voice. February 18, 1997, p. 80.

The Whole Wide World

A true story about the true love of the greatest pulp fiction writer of all time.—Movie tagline

"One of the year's most remarkable screen achievements! Zellweger and D'Onofrio begin with the right chemistry, spark and sizzle with the right electricity, and part with all the splendor of a glorious sunset!"—Andrew Sarris, *New York Observer*

"D'Onofrio delivers a career-topping performance!"—Howard Karren, *Premiere*

"A beautiful, moving romance. Lush yet confined; mannered yet free from form, it's a vivid and deeply affecting tale of love unconsummated."—Jeff Craig, *Sixty Second Preview*

"Terrific. Accomplished and most emotionally exquisite! A touching and new flawless love story."—William Arnold, *Seattle Post Intelligencer*

"The year's most heartfelt love story!"—John Hart, *Seattle Times*

"Totally absorbing and a complete surprise!"—Jeffrey Lyons, *WNBC*

In the mid-1970s, science fiction and fantasy literature began to experience a resurgence of interest in the United States. For the first time, "pulp" fiction was being looked at from an academic point of view. Scholars, of course, ultimately turned to the works of Robert E. Howard, who, in the 1930s, was author of, among other dime-store fanzine characters, Conan the Barbarian.

About this time, Novalyne Price Ellis, a Texas schoolteacher, married and raising a family in her native state, became angered by the discussion of this man; people were forming opinions of him that she knew were wrong. After all, she had known this man more intimately than any other person ever had.

So, in 1985, determined to set the record straight, Ellis wrote a book about Robert E. Howard, the man whom she called "the greatest pulp fiction writer in the whole wide world," and she called that memoir *One Who Walked Alone*. Eleven years after the book was published, Ellis's story was made into a film, *The Whole Wide World*.

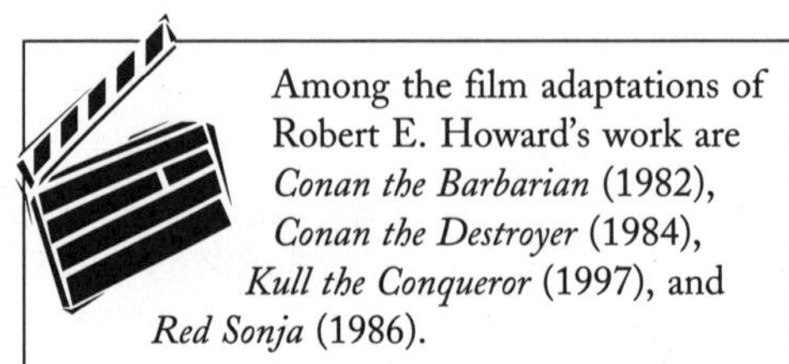

Among the film adaptations of Robert E. Howard's work are *Conan the Barbarian* (1982), *Conan the Destroyer* (1984), *Kull the Conqueror* (1997), and *Red Sonja* (1986).

Robert E. Howard was a legend in his small Texas hometown in 1934, well before his pulp/science-fiction tales of Kull the Conqueror and Conan the Barbarian brought him fame many years later. To his neighbors, he was a strange, brash young man who could be heard acting out his "yarns" of savagery, survival, and sexuality as he wrote them. A societal outsider and an imposing physical presence, Howard seemed more suited to his imagination than he did to his quiet, Depression-era surroundings.

Given his reputation, an unlikely thing happens: Novalyne Price, a curious and intelligent young schoolteacher and aspiring writer, becomes drawn to Howard and those same qualities most others have found repellent, if not frightening. Attracted by his creativity and passion for writing, Novalyne begins to see something gentler behind his bravado, and the two begin a stormy three-year relationship that seems always fatefully balanced just short of romance.

Before tackling *The Whole Wide World* as a first-time director, Dan Ireland had worn many hats in the filmmaking profession. Aside from producing 15 feature films, among them John Huston's *The Dead* (1987) and three Ken Russell films, Ireland also owned and operated The Egyptian Theater in Seattle, and is co-founder of The Seattle International Film Festival, one of the most highly respected festivals in the country. He was shown Novalyne Price Ellis's book by colleague Benjamin Mouton, a former student of Ellis's who had since begun writing the screenplay with another friend, Michael Scott Myers. Ireland fell for the script immediately, recalling, "The love between the two characters was so incredible. I thought it was the most beautiful tale of unrequited love."

Not content to just film the book, Ireland met with Novalyne often in 1992 as part of his research and kept her involved throughout the filmmaking process. Actor Vincent D'Onofrio, also captivated by her story, was brought onto the film early in order for him to meet with Novalyne as well. Ireland's commitment to the story and respect for the real lives of its characters comes through in the film: it is a well-told story, made with a touch of appropriate sentimentality.

Actors Vincent D'Onofrio and Renee Zellweger, though quite suitable as Howard and Ellis respectively, take an enormously passionate and enveloping story and seem to feel obligated to act accordingly. In their "playing it up," the viewer is left feeling almost self-conscious about the actors' performances. D'Onofrio (*Mystic Pizza* [1988], *Full Metal Jacket* [1987])

CREDITS

Robert E. Howard: Vincent D'Onofrio
Novalyne Price: Renee Zellweger
Mrs. Howard: Ann Wedgeworth
Dr. Howard: Harve Presnell
Clyde Smith: Benjamin Mouton
Enid: Helen Cates
Truett: Chris Shearer

Origin: USA
Released: 1996
Production: Carl-Jan Colpaert, Dan Ireland, Vincent D'Onofrio, and Kevin Reidy for Kushner-Locke and Cineville; released by Sony Pictures Classics
Direction: Dan Ireland
Screenplay: Michael Scott Myers; based on the memoir *One Who Walked Alone* by Novalyne Price Ellis
Cinematography: Claudio Rocha
Editing: Luis Colina
Music: Harry Gregson-Williams, Hans Zimmer
Production design: John Frick
Set decoration: Terri L. Wright
Costumes: Gail McMullen
Sound: Ken Segal
MPAA rating: PG
Running Time: 105 minutes

imbues his character with all the heaviness and energy of Howard the man, yet there is something that is just not quite believable. And Zellweger, who played opposite Tom Cruise in the heartwarming *Jerry Maguire* (1996), seems to be so in awe of her role, that she also comes off slightly less than perfect.

Even so, *The Whole Wide World* is a film to see, both for the rare story it presents, and for the enthusiasm and respect obviously shared by both cast and crew for the story's real-life players.

—*Jeffrey Hermann* and *Lynne Konstantin*

REVIEWS

Boxoffice. November, 1996, p. 136.
Chicago Tribune. February 7, 1997, p. 5.
Entertainment Weekly. January 17, 1997, p. 48.
Hollywood Reporter. November 4, 1996, p. 9.
Los Angeles Times. December 23, 1996, p. F4.
New York Times. December 27, 1996, p. C22.
New Yorker. January 27, 1997, p. 82.
USA Today. January 17, 1997, p. 4D.
Variety. January 22, 1996, p. 98.
Village Voice. January 7, 1997, p. 57.

Wild America

Take a ride on the wild side.—Movie tagline

"A rugged adventure that really soars."—Ron Brewington, *American Urban Radio Networks*

"Splendid! Thrilling! An abundance of humor, excitement, heart and soul. A movie for any and all ages."—Michael Medved, *New York Post*

"Terrific. Rollicking humor. Sharp thrills and delightful fun."—Peter Stack, *San Francisco Chronicle*

"A fascinating and entertaining film."—Paul Wunder, *WBAI Radio*

Box Office: $7,365,417

Making the transition from child to adult star isn't easy. In fact, it's damn near impossible. Shirley Temple, the most successful child actor of all-time, gave it a good try. She made a handful of films during her teen years, but couldn't generate the same spark that enamored her to the hearts of an entire nation when she was toddler. With alarming frequency, many former child actors, spoiled at too young of an age and unaware of the harshness of the real world, stumble through puberty, having nary a clue of how to make the often bumpy transition. Danny Bonaduce, Anthony Michael Hall and virtually the entire cast of TV's "Diff'rent Strokes" not only failed to carry the glory of their youth into adulthood, many met with the wrong end of the law in the process.

Teen heartthrob Jonathan Taylor Thomas is now at a point in his own career where he must decide if he wants to enter his awkward bridge years in the public eye. Having spent seven plus seasons on one of television's highest rated shows ever, "Home Improvement," Thomas has already participated in a number of feature films. In 1995, he received top billing over Chevy Chase in the lackluster *Man Of the House* and put a modern spin on Mark Twain with

Tom & Huck. He was an important component in 1994's box office champ *The Lion King* and did mostly voice work for another impressive children's effort, *The Adventures Of Pinocchio* (1996). In a recent interview, Thomas indicated he might quit show business altogether in order to pursue a college education away from the glitz, much like one of his idols and role models Jodie Foster did when she attended Yale. Thomas is a young man wise beyond his years and has obviously been raised with expert life and career guidance that keeps him humble and grounded, putting an accent on manners and common sense. His role of Marshall in *Wild America*, seems to mirror his offstage upbringing.

Screenwriter David Michael Wieger: "Marty, Mark and Marshall [Stouffer] left home one summer as kids in search of their dream. And they ended up finding it."

The Stouffer brothers continued their documentary career with the nature series, "Marty Stouffer's Wild America."

Marshall is the youngest of the three Stouffer brothers, children of a real-life family who lived in Arkansas during the 1960s. Their parents are no-nonsense folks. With a strong work ethic and something of a domineering nature, their dad Marty, Sr. (Jamie Sheridan) wants all of the boys to eventually take over the family auto and truck parts business. Having a penchant for nature and things that go fast, the boys spend most of their spare time chronicling woodland creatures, racing in anything with wheels and trying to impress the local female population. After a handful of toe-to-toe standoffs with Marty, Sr., the two eldest brothers Marty, Jr. (Scott Bairstow) and Mark (Devon Sawa) get hold of a (relatively) expensive camera and convince their parents to let them make a cross-country journey to document a number of endangered species. Marshall isn't included in their plans, but he secretly hides himself aboard the boys' van. After discovering him, an irritated Marty, Jr. wants to send him back home, but Marshall convinces his mother Agnes (Frances Fisher) to let him remain part of the crew and together the trio of brothers head westward.

During filming, they almost get killed by many of their subjects and fall into one calamity or another which would seem completely ludicrous if it weren't all true. Their adventures were edited down to an hour-long home movie that eventually aired in 1977 on a national network special narrated by Robert Redford. As adults, all three brothers pursued separate careers as noted documentarians and they all served as technical consultants on the production. The film has charm, bite, humor, fantastic scenery and a unique ability to hold the attention of children, teens, and adults. It is directed by William Dear who has helmed many other quality, family oriented projects in the past (*Harry & The Hendersons* [1987] and *Angels In The Outfield* [1994]). Think of it as a "National Geographic" special with equal parts *Stand By Me* (1986) and *Easy Rider* (1969).

If Thomas decides to "retire" at the end of his "Home Improvement" run, he will have left behind a short but admirable body of work, unblemished by anything resembling controversy. If he decides to continue on, or even take just a brief hiatus for educational purposes, it will be a good thing

CREDITS

Marshall Stouffer: Jonathan Taylor Thomas
Mark Stouffer: Devon Sawa
Marty Stouffer: Scott Bairstow
Agnes Stouffer: Frances Fisher
Marty Stouffer, Sr.: Jamey Sheridan
Leon: Tracey Walter
Stango: Don Stroud

Origin: USA
Released: 1997
Production: James G. Robinson, Irby Smith, Mark Stouffer for the Steve Tisch Company and Morgan Creek; released by Warner Bros.
Direction: William Dear
Screenplay: David Michael Wieger
Cinematography: David Burr
Editing: O. Nicholas Brown, Stuart Pappe
Music: Joel McNeely
Production design: Steve Jordan
Art direction: Jack Ballance
Costumes: Mary McLeod
Sound: Mary H. Ellis
MPAA rating: PG
Running Time: 106 minutes

REVIEWS

Chicago Tribune. July 2, 1997, p. 1.
Detroit News. July 2, 1997, p. 2E.
Entertainment Weekly. July 18, 1997, p. 56.
The Hollywood Reporter. July 2, 1997, p. 5.
Los Angeles Times. July 2, 1997, p. F11.
Movieline. June, 1997, p. 53.
New York Times. July 2, 1997, p. C22.
People. July 14, 1997, p. 20.
USA Today. July 2, 1997, p. 5D.
Variety. July 14, 1997, p. 44.

for the entertainment industry. Up to this point, he has made all the right career moves and has his priorities in order better than most people twice his age. He very well could end up mirroring the career of the two-time Academy Award winner Jodie Foster or opting to move behind the camera like one of his other idols, child star turned Oscar-nominated director Ron Howard.

—J.M. Clark

The Wind in the Willows

Go wild in the country!—Movie tagline

"An unequivocal delight! An enchanting book has become an enchanting film."—Lawrence Van Gelder, *New York Times*

Writer-director Terry Jones's live-action version of Kenneth Grahame's *The Wind in the Willows* is an imaginative, if somewhat dark, adaptation of the 1908 children's classic. Employing a host of fine English actors, the film creatively brings to life the beloved characters from the original story and highlights selected parts of the novel to emphasize action and adventure. While the original story focuses on the relationships between the characters, especially Mole and Rat's friendship, the film turns on a conflict of good versus evil, of Toad and his pals versus the weasels, a gang of dapper, wild animals who want to take away Toad Hall. As Jones himself admits in the film's press kit, *The Wind in the Willows* "is very picaresque" and "lacks within itself the dramatic conflict between the characters which is vital in a screenplay. I realized that in order to make it into a 90-minute film I needed to inject it with danger and conflict."

Filmed at Kentwell Hall, the house where Kenneth Grahame based his story, located in Melford, Suffolk.

The actors play their animal roles with very little makeup. Terry Jones wears light green makeup to play Toad, and Eric Idle wears buckteeth, whiskers, and a tail to denote Rat. For the most part, though, the actors focus more on the psychological traits of the characters. Mole (Steve Coogan), for example, is shy, while Badger (Nicol Williamson) is imperious.

Toad is the most colorful character in the novel, and, as played by Jones, he dominates the film with his sly, cunning personality and entertaining misadventures. Boastful, brash, and wealthy, Toad is an egomaniac who is nonetheless loved by his friends, even when he irritates them. As in the novel, his obsession with motorcars gets him into trouble. In the film, though, this problem is more excessive. He sells property to the weasels so he can afford motorcars, which he is constantly wrecking. At the beginning of the film, Mole's home is bulldozed because Toad has sold the meadow to the weasels, and later Toad's theft of a motorcar lands him in court, where his own lawyer, played in a funny cameo by John Cleese, basically admits his guilt.

Toad's outrageous antics in the novel, though, are balanced by stories reflecting the themes of camaraderie, friendship, and the leisurely life along the river. Without these interludes, the film is very frenetic and loses the gentle spirit of the novel.

The movie also has an overall darker tone. The villainous weasels are a major force at the end of the novel, but they are present throughout the film in their quest to take over Toad Hall. More importantly, in the novel, they simply take over the mansion for reckless carousing; in the film, their evil plans center on the creation of a dog food factory, in which the river-dwelling animals will be the main ingredients in its product. The tone grows especially dark in the final scenes. The weasels' excessive military reinforcements (including barbwire and searchlights), their huge banners inside the banquet hall, and arm insignias on their leather jackets suggest the look of a Nazi rally.

In the end, the film devolves into a standard action film. Toad makes his hilarious escape from prison in women's clothing, but finally he and his friends are captured and almost ground up into mincemeat in the factory until Mole stops the machines, saves the day at the last minute, and becomes the hero. It is a rather routine cliffhanger ending (reminiscent of the ending of Robert Zemeckis's *Who Framed Roger Rabbit*) among the giant machinery of the factory. The great irony is that, while the novel is a paean to the natural world, the film's climax is in love with the workings of the cogs, butcher's hooks, and conveyor belts of the factory.

Nonetheless, there are some lighthearted touches. The film's design contains many whimsical details, including

CREDITS

Mole: Steve Coogan
Rat: Eric Idle
Toad: Terry Jones
Chief Weasal: Anthony Sher
Badger: Nicol Williamson
Mr. Toad's Lawyer: John Cleese
Judge: Stephen Fry
Engine Driver: Bernard Hill
The Sun: Michael Palin

Origin: Great Britain
Released: 1996
Production: John Goldstone and Jake Eberts for Allied Filmmakers; released by Columbia Pictures
Direction: Terry Jones
Screenplay: Terry Jones; based on the novel by Kenneth Grahame
Cinematography: David Tattersall
Editing: Julian Doyle
Music: John Du Prez
Production design: James Acheson
Costumes: James Acheson
Visual effects supervisor: Peter Chiang
Special effects supervisor: Peter Hutchinson
Makeup: Jan Sewell
Choreography: Arlene Phillips
Sound: Bob Doyle
MPAA rating: PG
Running Time: 90 minutes

Mole's talking clock, Rat's rippling whiskers, and Michael Palin's cameo as the Sun. While the film includes a few musical interludes, only Toad's exuberant celebration of himself in court is very memorable. The movie is also peppered with dashes of sophisticated humor to appeal to the adult audience. When one of the weasels is trapped during the climax and pretends to be a friend, Mole reminds him that he once boasted there is no such thing; "Come on," the weasel slyly responds, "that was just an intro to a song"—a reference to the weasels' big musical number early in the film.

Terry Jones's adaptation of *The Wind in the Willows* takes a very specific point of view on this children's classic. In its focus on the character of Toad, broad comedy, and action, the film succeeds as a fast-paced romp through some of the highlights of the original story. On another level, it is a satire of industrialization's encroachment on the natural world. However, many delightful and memorable episodes from the novel, like Mole and Rat picnicking on the river bank or finding Otter's lost son, are left out of the movie, and thus, in a way, the heart of the original work is lost.

—Peter N. Chumo II

REVIEWS

Boxoffice. January, 1998, p. 48.
Cinemafantastique. April, 1998, p. 56.
Los Angeles Times. November 1, 1997, p. F2.
New York Times. October 31, 1997, p. E24.
People. November 17, 1997, p. 25.
Sight and Sound. November, 1996, p. 63.
Variety. November 3, 1997, p. 99.

The Wings of the Dove

A couple with everything but money. An heiress with everything but love. A temptation no one could resist.—Movie tagline

"A class act! The film swims in voluptuous intensity, is gorgeous to look at and is passionately acted!"—Jay Carr, *Boston Globe*

"With this film, the autumn Oscar derby is under way!"—Roger Ebert, *Chicago Sun-Times*

"A revelation! Beautifully photographed and marvelously acted. An exceedingly fine adaptation from director Iain Softley and screenwriter Hossein Amini."—Terry Lawson, *Detroit Free Press*

"A great film! *The Wings of the Dove* confirms the arrival of major screen talents. Helena Bonham Carter and Linus Roache create a dazzlingly intimate chemistry. The film is saturated with visual and dramatic beauty. Grade: A!"
—Owen Gleiberman, *Entertainment Weekly*

"Bold and sensual! Helena Bonham Carter and Linus Roache are heaven-sent. A visual swoon."—Thelma Adams, *New York Post*

"Magnificent and spellbinding! Helena Bonham Carter gives the performance of her career."
—Stephen Holden, *New York Times*

"Ravishing! Helena Bonham Carter, Alison Elliott and Linus Roache give flawless performances. They take your breath away . . . brilliant."—Carrie Rickey, *Philadelphia Inquirer*

"Mesmerizing! Helena Bonham Carter's thrilling performance blends defiant sexuality with delicate feeling. Linus Roache is superb."—Peter Travers, *Rolling Stone*

"Two thumbs up!"—*Siskel & Ebert*

Box Office: $8,193,833

W*ings of the Dove* is a beautifully acted and quietly emotional film about a romantic triangle "inspired by" (according to the production notes) the 1902 novel by Henry James. Director Iain Softley slightly updated the film to 1910 and he and screenwriter Hossein Amini make more explicit for moviegoers what James implies in his dense prose. But unlike both Jane Campion's *Portrait of a Lady* (1996) or Agnieska Holland's *Washington Square* (1997, reviewed in this volume), Softley allows James' characters to speak—or not—for themselves in all their confused, calculating, and heartwrenching glory.

Kate Croy (Helena Bonham Carter) has become the ward of her wealthy, snobbish, and domineering Aunt Maude (Charlotte Rampling) upon her mother's death, having finally been wrenched away from her "wretched" father (Michael Gambon), who spends his time with drink and opium. Maude expects Kate to marry well and entices her with clothes, jewelry and society parties—and the expectations of her money if Kate will do as Maude commands. "I won't let you make the same mistakes as your mother"—apparently marrying a penniless man, only to find love fading because of poverty. Kate also learns that Maude pays her father a small stipend to stay away and allow her to manage Kate's life.

But Kate is already in love—with poor-but-handsome journalist Merton Densher (Linus Roache). He's asked her to marry him but Kate doesn't want to be poor and has resisted: "I'd be penniless, cast out of society, and I'd be stuck with you." She says it facetiously but also means it more than a little.

Maude has introduced Kate to Lord Mark (Alex Jennings)—who has a title but no money—as a possible husband and a proper society escort. Maude has also discovered Kate's rendezvous with Merton and forced her to break things off by threatening to withdraw her father's allowance. Merton's hurt and angry by what will turn out to be the first of Kate's betrayals.

A dinner party introduces the third member of the coming romantic triangle, American heiress Millie Theale (Alison Elliott), the "world's richest orphan," who's traveling to Venice with her companion, Susan (Elizabeth McGovern). Unpretentious Millie quickly befriends Kate, who wonders why her new "best friend of the day" is visiting a radiology clinic and seeing a blood specialist.

After several months, Merton turns up at the same party Millie and Kate are attending. Millie's immediately attracted to Merton, who has eyes only for Kate, despite the suffering her actions have caused them. Kate notices Millie's interest and downplays her connection to Merton, referring to him as an old family friend. Kate has also learned from Lord Mark that the heiress is seriously ill. When he says he needs to marry Millie for her money, you can see the light of a very unpleasant idea slowly dawn in Kate's eyes.

Millie invites Kate to summer with her in Venice and even invites Merton to join them. He declines but is persuaded by Kate's letters and soon turns up. Kate tells Merton that Millie loves him—and that she's dying (from what is never quite clear, there's a lot of coughing involved). As the three see the beauties of Venice, it's clear Kate is pushing Merton at Millie but when Millie impulsively kisses Merton during a dance, Kate quickly pulls him away to re-establish her claims to his love.

Kate to Merton: "I'm not good at being impulsive."

However, Kate is equally quick to decide to return to London on her own. "You want me to seduce a dying girl? And you really think she'll leave me all her money?" Kate admits to her plan and to her certainty of Millie's love for Merton. She even tells Millie she doesn't love Merton and that it will be fine if they stay on together (like a good companion, Susan has faded into the background). You can see Merton's feelings for Millie change the longer they remain together. She's eager to experience life and pleasure, is open in her affections, and is an ego boost to the weary Merton, who believes in neither his work nor his future: "I don't believe in any of the things I write about. I fake passion. I fake conviction." Millie tells him "I believe in you. I have a good feeling."

Back in London, Kate is getting more frantic over Merton, writing that she loves him more than Millie ever could.

AWARDS AND NOMINATIONS

Academy Awards 1997 Nominations: Actress (Bonham Carter), Cinematography, Costume Design, Adapted Screenplay
BAFTA 1997 Nominations: Adapted Screenplay, Actress (Bonham Carter), Cinematography, Costumes, Make-up/Hair
Broadcast Film Critics Association 1997: Actress (Bonham Carter)
Golden Globe Awards 1998 Nominations: Drama Actress (Bonham Carter)
Los Angeles Film Critics Association 1997: Actress (Bonham Carter)
National Board of Review 1997: Actress (Bonham Carter)

Despite Merton's reassurances, Kate's insecurity leads her to a terrible impulse. She goes to Lord Mark and tells him about her and Merton, knowing he'll go immediately to Venice and tell Millie everything. Millie, who's become increasingly weak, lets Merton know that she can't fool herself forever. And it is not just about her health but also Kate and Merton's unspoken plotting—still she tells him: "I love you. Both of you."

When in Venice, Henry James stayed in the Palazzo Leporelli for several months. The filmmakers used the same palazzo as Millie's home.

After Millie's death and funeral in Venice, Merton returns to London. Kate visits him and he asks why she tried to destroy her own plans; Kate replies she was more scared of losing him. Merton holds out a letter from Millie's lawyer—she has indeed left him a fortune, but, guilt-ridden, Merton tells Kate he can't accept the money. Although the two make love, they realize that their love has changed irrevocably. Still, Merton tells Kate he wants to marry her—without Millie's money. But Kate has her own condition, she asks Merton to give her his word of honor that he's not in love with Millie's memory. And when all she receives is a long silence, she has her bitter answer.

This isn't a film with good guys and bad guys, despite Kate's constant manipulations (she's actually much more cold-blooded in the novel). Kate is obviously intelligent and hasn't been brought up with money so why can't she support herself? However, she is attracted to the carefree leisure and position in society her aunt's money provides and while she truly loves Merton, Kate's also willing to do whatever it takes to have it all. Even if that means taking advantage of the friendship of a naive, dying American heiress. But Kate is always sabotaging her own coldhearted plan by her jealous actions. She doesn't believe Merton could fall in love with Millie but any closeness she sees between them, she tries to interrupt in some manner.

Merton is not quite the easily maneuvered pawn he first seems. He's contemptuous of Kate's desire for money but desperate in his passion for her. He despises himself for playing along with Kate's schemes and can't help but recognize that Millie's a decent, good-hearted woman who deserves better from them both.

This is a movie filled with silences—although the score by Gabriel Yared is beautiful, Softley isn't afraid to let scenes be silent, without any background musical punctuation accompanying the onscreen emotions of the characters. This is also a magnificent film to look at. The actors are wonderfully costumed and Venice looks both beautiful and mysterious—even in the rain.

The leads also do fine work. Although another in her line of costume/period pieces, the perennially youthful Bonham Carter finally registers as an adult—a woman with a lot of conflicting emotions going on behind her beautiful dark eyes. The handsome Roache, probably best known on these shores for his lead role in Antonia Bird's 1994 film *Priest,* is equally expressive as a man lead by his desires. Only Alison Elliott is somewhat subdued in the no-doubt thankless role of the noble heiress. Millie doesn't get angry and she doesn't get even at Kate and Merton's betrayal—she truly does understand and love each of them—but her very acceptance destroys them both.

—*Christine Tomassini*

CREDITS

Kate Croy: Helena Bonham Carter
Merton Densher: Linus Roache
Millie Theale: Alison Elliott
Susan: Elizabeth McGovern
Lord Mark: Alex Jennings
Aunt Maude: Charlotte Rampling
Kate's father: Michael Gambon

Origin: Great Britain
Released: 1997
Production: David Parfitt and Stephen Evans for Renaissance Films; released by Miramax Films
Direction: Iain Softley
Screenplay: Hossein Amini; based on the novel by Henry James
Cinematography: Eduardo Serra
Editing: Tariq Anwar
Music: Gabriel Yared
Production design: John Beart
Art direction: Martyn John
Costumes: Sandy Powell
Sound: Sallie Jaye
MPAA rating: R

REVIEWS

Boxoffice. November, 1997, p. 121.
Chicago Tribune. November 14, 1997, p. 5.
Detroit News. November 14, 1997, p. F1.
Entertainment Weekly. November 7, 1997, p. 55.
Los Angeles Times. November 7, 1997, p. F2.
Movieline. December, 1997, p. 50.
New York Times. November 7, 1997, p. E16.
People. November 17, 1997, p. 21.
Rolling Stone. November 27, 1997, p. 116.
San Francisco Chronicle. November 14, 1997, p. C3
San Francisco Examiner. November 14, 1997, p. C1.
Sight and Sound. January, 1998, p. 55.
Time. November 10, 1997.
USA Today. November 7, 1997, p. 8D.
Variety. September 8, 1997, p. 76.
Village Voice. November 11, 1997, p. 88.

The Winner

Even losers get lucky sometimes.—Movie tagline

The Winner appears to derive in many ways from *Pulp Fiction* (1994). Its characters are the same lowlifes and hoodlums that dwell at the fringe of Las Vegas life. Its offbeat sense of humor mixes with violence and a constant feeling of danger. Its indirect plotting momentarily obscures cause and effect. Though these elements do not cohere as effectively in *The Winner* as in its more famous model and though its unresolved ending confuses and mars the film, *The Winner* contains some interesting characters and scenes.

The film concerns the plotting and counterplotting of a group of seedy characters attracted to Philip (Vincent D'Onofrio), a man who for five Sundays has been winning at the tables in Las Vegas and giving his money away. One of the predators drawn to Philip is Louise (Rebecca De Mornay), who sings in a casino. She tells her partner Jack (Billy Bob Thornton) that she is waiting for the magic words "I love you" from Philip to indicate that she will become the permanent recipient for his cash. Jack reminds Louise about her own $50,000 debt to Kingman (Delroy Lindo), the owner of the Paradise casino.

Unknown to Louise, Jack meets with Kingman, who from his office overlooking the gaming tables at the casino has been observing Philip. He tells Jack that there is no sport in killing a winner: "Losers take care of themselves—they lose. But a winner, Jack, you have to destroy. To bring to their knees." This advice sends Jack back to Louise. To help elicit Philip's declaration of love, Louise asks Jack to trash her house so that she can then convincingly inform Philip of her debts and hope for his financial protection.

Other characters round out the gallery of crooks. Joey (Frank Whaley) and two dimwit companions (Richard Edson, Saverio Guerra) pick up Philip on the strip and try to convince him that they are writing a magazine article about his lucky streak. Philip openly confides to Joey that he first gambled when he felt depressed. He was lost in the crowd of the world, Philip admits, and was planning to commit suicide. Winning, he suspects, is what it is like to be happy. Joey's view of Philip begins to change after this unexpected revelation.

This offbeat morality also links *The Winner* to *Pulp Fiction*. In both films the least likely characters are suddenly given to moments of moral speculation. In his first scene, Kingman is established as a ruthless mob leader, but then he admits to Jack that he is grieved over the chaos and violence in the world. Joey refuses to commit to the plan to rob Philip until he receives a sign from above. Philip's reason for turning to the gambling tables as well as his openness and innocence about life also suggest that the struggle between corrupting and protecting good in the world may underlie the developing plot. As Joey and his fellow hoods try on their rubber masks at the Par-a-dice Motel and map out their attempt to rob Philip next Sunday night, Joey concedes that he likes him. But then he says that the robbery is not about "a two-bit win [but] about changing our lives." As their plan proceeds, however, Joey eventually decides to protect Philip from the others who seek to betray him. "Saviors always get betrayed," Joey comes to believe. He alludes to God's destruction of the world in the days of Noah: "I will be the rain."

Some of the film's black humor and circuitous plotting can be illustrated by following the trail of information surrounding a mysterious severed hand. When Louise and Philip return to her ransacked house, they are shocked to find a human hand in her aquarium. At home that night, Philip is visited by his brother Johnny (Michael Madsen), who carries a lumpy sleeping bag that he says contains the body of their father, a Vegas drifter. Johnny explains that their father was shot in the head and that the killers took his hand. Later, Louise angrily confronts Jack about the hand in the aquarium, which was not part of the plan to trash her house. Jack vaguely refers to the contact who did the job: "I had to throw him a piece of meat." Predictably, in a later scene with Kingman, Jack contradicts this explanation by admitting to the father's murder himself. Meanwhile, Johnny begins touring the bars with a picture of his father to see if he can turn up some clues. As he searches his brother's house for money to pay off some of his own debts, Johnny welcomes Louise who comes by unannounced. Their past relationship again clouds the characters' motives. Does Louise love Philip or Jack? Or does her past with Johnny suggest a hidden motive? Part of the enjoyment of the film is watching it reverse itself and attach to various events a range of possible motives. Such red herrings and dead ends keep the audience alert.

Other examples of the film's quirky humor are less gruesome. Many of these involve sudden shifts of tone that are again reminiscent of *Pulp Fiction*. After a long argument with Philip about who will pay her debts, Louise suddenly opens the freezer of his refrigerator. "And you don't have any ice cream, either," she shouts, suddenly sending him off for some rocky road so that she can search for his cash box. In the middle of one of their meetings, Kingman inexplicably asks Jack, "You talk about water a lot. You like water?" Louise and Philip's visit to the Liberace museum suddenly turns into a passionate kiss as she sprawls back against a piano keyboard. A piano roll starts playing the minute waltz, and Philip and Louise begin to make love in this incongruous setting. In another scene, Joey's solicitous concern for Philip suddenly turns to rage when a panhandler approaches Philip for some pocket change. Joey's violent attack on the bum not only signals another sudden shift of emotion in this consistently off-balance film, but also reveals his own sense of conflict over his plan to rob Philip.

The ending of the film may take the cryptic blurring of cause and effect too far. Philip obtains a loan from Kingman that he gives to Louise to settle her debts. When she reads Philip's goodbye letter, she turns her car around and heads back to the casino. Jack, who was waiting for Louise to show with the money, angrily drives to the casino afraid that Louise is now in love with Philip. Joey and his two henchmen also arrive at the casino. A fusillade of gunshots goes off in the darkened room. When the lights come back on, Philip is one of the few still alive. He redeems the suitcase of money Louise returned to him for an enormous poker chip that glows in the dark. As he places this monumental bet on the roulette table, Kingman, watching from his office above, reaches over to throw a switch. The final shot of the film is a bird's-eye view of Las Vegas at night as block by block all of the lights in the city black out.

One way that director Alex Cox parts company with *Pulp Fiction* is the visual style of the film and his reliance on long takes. Many of the scenes are filmed in sequence shots, in which an entire action is presented with no editing. Some of these shots in *The Winner* last for over three minutes, an uncommonly long duration for a feature film. In addition, some of the lengthy takes playfully shift the dramatic action from one location to another while the moving camera all the while follows the characters.

The scene in which Louise asks Jack to wreck her house provides a good example. In a single unbroken shot of over three minutes, Louise leads Jack from the lobby of the casino down a flight of stairs to a table. They sit and she tells Jack about Philip's cash box, hidden under his bed. She hopes to be able to entice him to bet all of his $5000, which if his luck holds, would bring in enough to pay her debts. A character named Gaston (played in a cameo role by director Alex Cox) suddenly flops down in the chair next to Louise, and Jack and Louise rise again to find some privacy. The camera, still continuing the shot from the start of the scene, now precedes Louise and Jack down more stairs into a roomful of chorus girls rehearsing a number. After getting Gaston to take the girls away, Jack and Louise find two chairs and complete their plans for the evening, after which the camera moves in for a close-up of a satisfied Louise. The cut to the next scene occurs only then.

Of course, such virtuoso displays of camera work will begin to seem obtrusive and distracting if the context provides no good justification for them. Even in the most style-conscious films, the logic of the style usually derives in some fashion from the content rather than appears solely for the purpose of self-display. Sooner rather than later in *The Winner*, the audience is ready for all of the teasing of content and style to release its meaning. The film fails to deliver a payoff as good as its tantalizing build-up.

—*Glenn Hopp*

CREDITS

Philip: Vincent D'Onofrio
Louise: Rebecca DeMornay
Wolf: Michael Madsen
Jack: Billy Bob Thornton
Joey: Frank Whaley
Kingman: Delroy Lindo
Frankie: Richard Edson
Paulie: Saverio Guerra

Origin: USA, Australia
Released: 1996
Production: Kenneth Schwenker for Village Roadshow and Clipsal Film Partnership; released by Live Entertainment
Direction: Alex Cox
Screenplay: Wendy Riis; based on her play *A Darker Purpose*
Cinematography: Denis Maloney
Editing: Carlos Puente
Music: Daniel Licht
Costumes: Nancy Steiner
Production design: Cecilia Montiel
MPAA rating: R
Running Time: 90 minutes

REVIEWS

Boxoffice. September, 1997, p. 119.
Los Angeles Times. July 25, 1997, p. F20.
New York Times. July 25, 1997, p. C10.
Sight and Sound. February, 1998, p. 55.
Variety. September 23, 1996, p. 127.
Village Voice. August 5, 1997, p. 67.

The Winter Guest

A film about walking on thin ice and coming in out of the cold.—Movie tagline

"*The Winter Guest* is a beautiful, emotionally generous film with shining performances by real-life mother and daughter Phyllida Law and Emma Thompson."—Jay Carr, *Boston Globe*

"Poetic and hearthwarming. Emma Thompson is radiant."—Richard Rayner, *Harper's Bazaar*

"Astonishing!"—Simon Brennan, *Premiere*

Estranged mother and daughter (played by real-life mother and daughter Phyllida Law and Emma Thompson) spend an unexpected weekend together in actor Alan Rickman's directorial debut *The Winter Guest.*

A talented cast and beautiful cinematography help to elevate *The Winter Guest* above its metaphor-laden material. The film is accomplished British character actor Alan Rickman's directorial debut and as expected, it is the acting that provides the impetus to see this bleak and emotionally chilly comedy-drama.

Emma Thompson is the recently widowed Frances; her real-life mother, Phyllida Law, is her meddlesome mother, Elspeth. It is winter in this coastal town in Scotland, so poetically cold that the sea has frozen over. Dressed in her fur coat, Elspeth makes her way over the icy landscape for an unannounced—and unwelcomed—visit to the withdrawn Frances (Thompson) and her son, Alex (Gary Hollywood). Elspeth worries that Frances may move in an attempt to escape her grief.

Elspeth to Frances: "A person needs to be needed. And if you don't need me, you could lie."

Frances and Elspeth have a tenuous relationship, and the casting of Thompson and Law brings a kind of emotional shorthand, a comfortable familiarity with all the inherent nuances of people who have known each other a very long time. The always impressive Emma Thompson can convey more with a wry glance than most lines of dialogue. Frances and Elspeth jab and spar throughout, wounding then retracting until their inevitable warming. "I don't need you," Frances snarls. "I know you don't," replies her mother, "but you could lie."

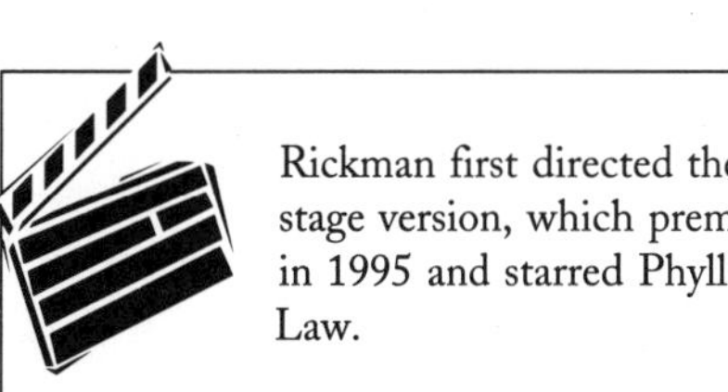

Rickman first directed the stage version, which premiered in 1995 and starred Phyllida Law.

Interspersed with this main storyline are three other tales. Frances' son, Alex confronts his nascent sexuality and the tentative flirtation with tomboyish Nita (Arlene Cockburn); two elderly woman, Lily (Sheila Reed) and Chloe (Sandra Voe), spend their days "comparison shopping" at funerals of people they have never known; and finally, in the most amusing segment, the errant, pubescent schoolboys, Tom (Sean Biggerstaff) and Sam (Douglas Murphy), scour the rocky coastline looking for adventure.

Mr. Rickman is perhaps best known to American audiences as what could be argued as two of film's best villains, the terrorist in *Die Hard* (1988) and the off-the-wall Sheriff of Nottingham in Kevin Costner's *Robin Hood: Prince of Thieves* (1991). His other work, such as Anthony Minghella's *Truly, Madly, Deeply* (1991) and the military suitor in *Sense and Sensibility* (1996), displays an impressive range.

As a director, Rickman brings a droll sense of humor and an artist's aesthetics to *The Winter Guest.* The landscape is stunningly monochrome, pierced only by the occasional person's presence. Rickman maximizes the intensity of the physical surroundings and manages, to a large degree, to transcend the limitations of Sharman MacDonald's stage play, which he helped to adapt.

Although fairly devoid of plot, *The Winter Guest* is an actor's dream piece, a rich character study that offers meaty scenes where they get to peel off the emotional layers in search of their character's humanity. But the episodic nature of the film is at times confusing and frustrating, and dilutes the intensity of the core mother-daughter relationship. It demands a good deal of patience waiting for Rickman to unveil the connection between the vignettes of the four disparate pair of characters, and he has a tendency to let scenes linger too long, undoubtedly in deference for his actors. The dialogue is stilted and far too insightful at times, while the symbolism is blatantly obvious—each pair represents a stage of life and the title most probably refers to death. Yet there are small moments where Rickman unearths a current of emotion by using something as simple as a flicker of candlelight to convey the power and fragile nature of death.

The young boys are perhaps the film's biggest surprise. Sean Biggerstaff displays a startling sensuality in his scenes with Ms. Thompson (In retrospect, it is hard to escape the irony of his last name, particularly given the scene during which the boys discuss penis size!) The Scottish accents of these two are particularly challenging, but their delivery of such bawdy laments as "My balls are never going to drop" is wickedly funny.

Alan Rickman closes his film with a powerfully existential ending which may leave some viewers feeling left out in the cold. But the more burning question: why does no one wear gloves? Reviews for *The Winter Guest* were decidedly mixed.

—*Patricia Kowal*

CREDITS

Elspeth: Phyllida Law
Frances: Emma Thompson
Alex: Gary Hollywood
Nita: Arlene Cockburn
Lily: Sheila Reid
Chloe: Sandra Voe
Sam: Douglas Murphy
Tom: Sean Biggerstaff

Origin: Great Britain, USA
Released: 1997
Production: Ken Lipper, Edward Pressman and Steve Clark-Hall for Capitol Films, Channel Four Films and The Scottish Arts Council Lottery Fund; released by Fine Line Features
Direction: Alan Rickman
Screenplay: Sharman MacDonald and Alan Rickman; based on the play by Sharman MacDonald
Cinematography: Seamus McGarvey
Editing: Scott Thomas
Production design: Robin Cameron Don
Sound: Colin Nicholson
Costumes: Joan Bergin
Music: Michael Kamen
MPAA rating: R
Running Time: 110 minutes

REVIEWS

Boxoffice. December, 1997, p. 12.
Detroit News. January 16, 1998, p. 3D.
Entertainment Weekly. January 16, 1998, p. 49.
New York Times. December 23, 1997, p. E5.
New Yorker. January 5, 1998, p. 74.
People. January 26, 1997, p. 22.
San Francisco Chronicle. January 16, 1998, p. D3.
San Francisco Examiner. January 16, 1998, p. C3.
Sight and Sound. January, 1998, p. 56.
Variety. September 8, 1997, p. 78.
Village Voice. December 30, 1997, p. 66.

Wishmaster; Wes Craven's Wishmaster

Be careful what you wish for.—Movie tagline

"It may be the best original independent horror film since George A. Romero's *Dawn of the Dead.*"—Mark Price, *Ft. Worth Star Telegram*

"A creepy crowd pleaser worthy of the prized imprimatur of horror honcho Wes (*Scream*) Craven."—The Phantom of the Movies, *New York Daily News*

Box Office: $15,738,769

Wishmaster is a horror movie that's chock-full of thrills, chills and special effects, but even though director Robert Kurtzman manages to keep the action moving along at a steady pace, the film's storyline is just not new or different enough to distinguish itself from the crowded horror pack.

Alexandra Amberson (Tammy Lauren) is an attractive, intelligent gemologist at the local university. Having just gotten over a rocky relationship, she is somewhat wary of getting involved with her best friend, handsome scientist Josh (Tony Crane). Josh is disappointed, but remains friendly with her, hoping for more.

Concurrently, Anthony Beaumont (Robert Englund) is

watching as an ancient statue is unloaded at the docks. Beaumont has pursued this ancient treasure for years and is anxious to showcase it at his yearly gala. But when a drunken longshoreman causes the statue to crash, it cracks open and The Djinn (Andrew Divoff) escapes into a large, semi-precious gem. A worker steals the gem and pawns it to slick dealer Nick Merritt (Chris Lemmon). Merritt cannot fathom what kind of jewel this is, so he farms it out to Josh to ascertain its value. Unfortunately for Josh, the Djinn is not a benevolent spirit; when disturbed he reacts violently. He kills Josh and disappears into the night.

Executive producer Wes Craven: "We all grew up dreaming of finding that stray lamp on the beach and having all of our wishes come true. Not in this movie!"

Besides Robert "Freddy Kreuger" Englund, the cast includes *Friday the 13th*'s "Jason," Kane Hodder, and *The Candyman,* Tony Todd.

Alexandra is devastated and vows to track down Josh's killer. She has her work cut out for her—she is chasing a form of ancient genie. These genies are deadly and cunning, offering people their wildest wishes, then granting them in a twisted manner (e.g. a beautiful woman who wants to live forever is changed into a mannequin). The Djinns' goals are to be able to grant three wishes for an earthbound human, which then allows them to take permanent human form on earth, where they presumably will be able to wreck havoc unchecked.

The Djinn leaves a trail of blood and carnage, yet manages to elude Alexandra in her hunt. Alexandra is an extremely capable woman, having raised her younger sister Shannon (Wendy Benson) after their parents died in a fire. She sets out to learn as much as she can about this mysterious Djinn; she canvases the victims' situations and comes to the conclusion that this villain is not of this world.

Alexandra turns for help to Wendy Derleth (Jenny O'Hara), an anthropologist who clues her into the modus operandi of Djinns—their devious, shape-shifting ways. Before Alexandra can turn around, the Djinn presents himself to her, practically begging to grant her every wish. Like all smart heroines before her Alexandra resists—until she realizes the Djinn has a bead on Shannon.

Although Alexandra tries to warn her, Shannon accepts an invitation to Beaumont's annual society bash—the very same bash where Beaumont intends to present his ancient statue. But the Djinn enters and turns the entire party into a bloody carnage, including Shannon, whose human form is trapped in a mural. Although she deftly escapes her own death, Alexandra is heartbroken over her sister—another loved one lost to the evil genie.

She banters with the Djinn, and realizes that she has one last wish. After careful consideration, Alexandra comes up with the brilliant answer that will end all of the Djinn's plans; Alexandra wishes that the longshoreman that unloaded the statue that contained the Djinn had not been drinking the morning of the accident. The Djinn gasps; all accidents and deaths reverse themselves and he himself is once again locked into his jewel—for eternity. Content with her reality, Alexandra does change one thing in her life, she accepts the affections of Josh.

Even though the special effects snap, crackle and pop, and there is enough blood, guts and gore to spread around

CREDITS

Alexandra Amberson: Tammy Lauren
The Djinn: Andrew Divoff
Anthony Beaumont: Robert Englund
Johnny: Tony Todd
Shannon: Wendy Benson
Josh: Tony Crane
Nick Merritt: Chris Lemmon
Wendy Derleth: Jenny O'Hara
Merritt's Guard: Kane Hodder

Origin: USA
Released: 1997
Production: Pierre David, Clark Peterson, and Noel A. Zanitsch; released by Live Entertainment
Direction: Robert Kurtzman
Screenplay: Peter Atkins
Cinematography: Jacques Haitkin
Editing: Dorian Vernacchio
Music: Harry Manfredini
Costumes: Karyn Wagner
Production design: Deborah Raymond, Dorian Vernacchio
Sound: James Hilton
Visual effects supervisor: Thomas C. Rainone
Special makeup effects: Howard Berger, Robert Kurtzman, Gregory Nicotero
MPAA rating: R
Running Time: 90 minutes

REVIEWS

Boxoffice. December, 1997, p. 54.
Entertainment Weekly. October 3, 1997, p. 58.
Los Angeles Times. September 22, 1997, p. F6.
New York Times. September 20, 1997, p. B11.
Variety. September 29, 1997, p. 67.

for everyone, this film falls short of establishing itself as memorable. The Djinn is too reserved, almost courtly, to inspire horror. In fact, he baits people to practically request their own demise, and they are all done in by their own sense of vanity and greed. The pleasant surprise is the character of Alexandra, a tough cookie who can hold her own mentally and physically with the Djinn, and never resort to whining or waiting for someone to rescue her.

—*G.E. Georges*

Year of the Horse

"Rip-snorting . . . Great sound and a good-humored tribute to Neil Young's 30 years of maverick rock and roll."—Janet Maslin, *The New York Times*

"A fine-tuned avalanche. Captures as well as any other music movie the natural untethered essence of live rock."—John Anderson, *Newsday*

"Electrifying!"—Dennis Dermody, *Paper Magazine*

"Dynamite!"—David Fricke, *Rolling Stone*

"A celebration of the collaboration of Young and his walloping band Crazy Horse!"—Joel Selvin, *San Francisco Chronicle*

Commenting on his film *Year of the Horse* about Neil Young and Crazy Horse, indie-type director Jim Jarmusch has said: "It's not even a documentary, really. It's just a rock and roll film."

The film is part-documentary, part-rock and roll concert film, and combines scenes of onstage jams and backstage footage from tours in 1976, 1986 and 1996. It's less a definitive biography than an impressionistic look at this band.

Although Neil Young has jumped from band to band and style to style throughout his erratic career, Crazy Horse has been the one constant. There's just something that happens when Young, guitarist Frank "Poncho" Sampedro, bassist Billy Talbot and drummer Ralph Molina get together and play. Their sound is raw, emotional and rough—some have called them the best garage band in the country. What is the Crazy Horse magic? None in the band can explain it, but over the course of the film it seems like it has something to do with just being together for so long, living through so much, and the sort of sixth sense they've developed about each other's playing.

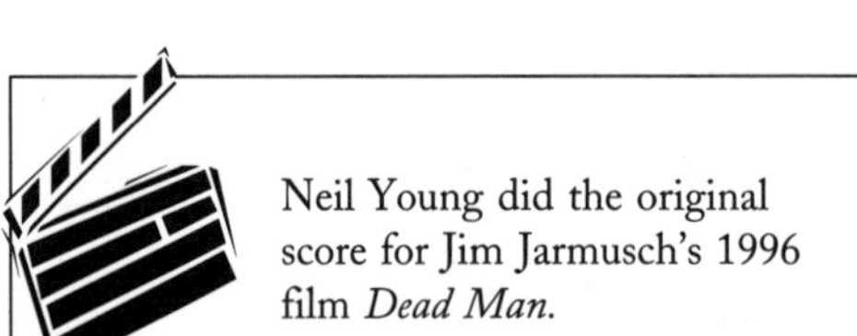

Neil Young did the original score for Jim Jarmusch's 1996 film *Dead Man.*

To make the point that Crazy Horse is mainly about this musical bond, Jarmusch just lets the band play for much of the film. Seeing the four men onstage, now older, hunched over their instruments and lost in the music, it's easy to see how they all need each other to create their musical altered state.

People who aren't into long, extended jams would do well to steer clear of this film because most of it is just that. We see Neil grimacing with intensity and doing his off-rhythmic dance while the band improvises on songs like "Like A Hurricane" and "Tonight's the Night."

Some of the most fun in the film comes from the backstage footage. We see the band go from young stoners accidentally setting some fake flowers on fire in their hotel room (it takes them several minutes to get it together enough to extinguish the flames) to older men who comment on the toll drugs have taken on their friends and associates.

The four men talk about long gone band members, how the band started and what a "year of the horse" is. (It's any time Crazy Horse gets together). There's even some commentary from Neil Young's dad, who looks eerily like Neil, but older and more conservative. Young's dad assesses that Young got some of his drive when his parents separated while Neil was a young teen.

One of the best surprises of the film is Neil Young's sense of humor. At one point, in some old footage, a not particularly sane flower child talking to Young backstage calls himself the resurrected Jesus. "Be careful, you know what happened last time," says Young. Another time Young is trying to understand some Bible passages about a vengeful God. "You mean he's mad because he created man and they were. . . . man," he says. And when Young is talking about how he stole some of his band members from another band, he dryly comments of the "trail of destruction" of his life.

The film begins with the words "Proudly filmed in Super 8." It was definitely the hipster choice for Jarmusch to use grainy film stock, but it can be looked at two ways. One is that Super 8 is too grainy, blurry and imprecise. Sometimes it's hard to even make out what's going on in the film. The other way to look at it, maybe, is to accept the rough, ragged film type as being the perfect way to capture the rough, ragged nature of Crazy Horse. (Jarmusch also used some Hi-8 and 16mm film.)

The film has a dreamy, haphazard feel. Even the way it came together was a bit haphazard. Jarmusch had approached Young to do some music for the film *Dead Man*. Young made no commitments, but after seeing a screening of the film, cut some tracks for it. The director ended up doing two videos for Crazy Horse. Young then called on Jarmusch to make a tour film of Crazy Horse's world tour. That's what ended up as this film.

Jarmusch won Young's heart, but maybe not the hearts of everyone in the band. Three times in the film guitarist Sampedro berates Jarmusch for being a "hip, trendy kind of New York artsy-fartsy film producer" (for the record, Jarmusch is a director, not a producer) who wants to ask "a couple of cute questions" and is only scratching "the tip of the iceberg" of all that is Crazy Horse.

Sampedro is right, but that's not the point. Jarmusch is just trying to create an impression of what Crazy Horse does and, in the ragged glory of *Year of the Horse*, he does just that.

—*Jill Hamilton*

CREDITS

Origin: USA
Released: 1997
Production: L.A. Johnson; released by October Films
Direction: Jim Jarmusch
Screenplay: Jim Jarmusch
Cinematography: L.A. Johnson, Jim Jarmusch
Editing: Jay Rabinowitz
Sound: Tim Mulligan
MPAA rating: R
Running Time: 108 minutes

REVIEWS

Boxoffice. October, 1997, p. 38.
Los Angeles Times. October 17, 1997, p. F20.
San Francisco Chronicle. October 31, 1997, p. C3.
San Francisco Examiner. October 31, 1997, p. C3.

Zeus and Roxanne

A friendship no one ever thought possible. An adventure no one ever will forget.—Movie tagline

Box Office: $7,233,275

Dog and dolphin meet and become fast friends in *Zeus and Roxanne*. This odd couple animal story is a kid-pleasing variation on a common premise, complete with villain and exotic Caribbean setting.

A scruffy dog barks at the end of a pier, fascinated by a playful dolphin squeaking back. The pooch, Zeus, runs home to wreak havoc in the neighbor's yard by chasing a cat up a tree. The dog's young owner, Jordan (Miko Hughes), takes photos of the incident, as his father, Terry (Steve Guttenberg), apologizes.

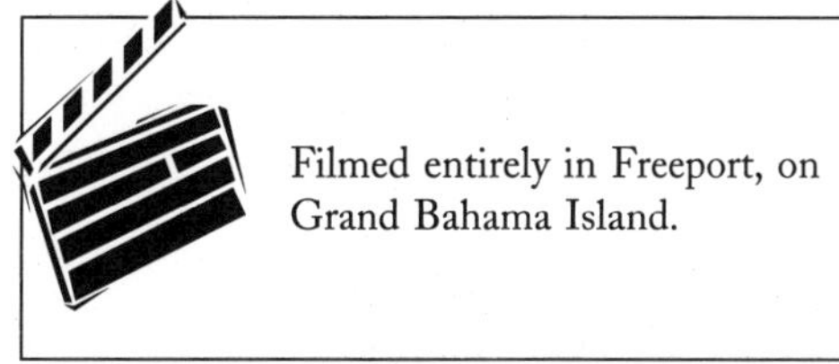

Filmed entirely in Freeport, on Grand Bahama Island.

The neighbor, Mary Beth (Kathleen Quinlan), rides off to work, followed by the canine who sneaks onto her boat, further annoying the marine biologist, who's stuck with him onboard as she conducts her studies. He barks hello to his new buddy through a porthole—as Roxanne the dolphin swims away. The scientist speeds off in search of her subject and Zeus slips off the deck into the sea. Back on land, Jordan searches all over town for his missing mongrel.

The dolphin butts a menacing shark combing the waters for the dog, and lifting Zeus onto her back, gives him a ride back to the boat—surprising Mary Beth, who's puzzled by their behavior. Her fellow researcher, Claude (Arnold Vosloo), keeps an eye on her work with binoculars. He suggests they combine their efforts to secure grant money—but Mary Beth passes on his proposition, questioning his practices.

Back home, she explains the phenomenon of the dog and the dolphin, asking her neighbor's permission for Zeus to join her research effort. Considering Roxanne doesn't socialize with other dolphins, it will provide companionship they both enjoy and help Mary Beth's work on dolphin communication. Meanwhile, her daughters and Terry's son conspire to bring their single parents together.

Terry, a composer, is on a vacation retreat for a couple months to jump-start his songwriting. As Terry crosses the street to ask Mary Beth out, Claude zooms along and barely misses hitting him. Secretly suspecting his associate will snag the research grant from him with her remarkable data, Claude offers her the use of his snazzy submersible vehicle as a gesture of working together and combining their efforts. She accepts the offer, but calls him on his motives.

Terry takes Mary Beth out and they enjoy each other's company, gradually growing closer. She inspires him to write songs again. However, time is running out on his house rental. The kids devise a plan to move him into her place.

Claude snags her notebook, but Zeus foils his attempt, sending him overboard. Despite trying to replicate Mary Beth's work, he can't match the special relationship between Zeus and Roxanne. So he devises another plot to subvert her activity.

The scheme to bring the couple together goes south when they question their motives—for the kids, the grant or us? Terry has second thoughts when he sees a photo of his dead wife and packs off to another island. But the dog and dolphin miss each other and make every effort to reunite—as the kids continue their strategy to mate their parents.

Roxanne is in danger of being trapped by Claude, while Mary Beth searches for her dolphin in the mini-submarine. Zeus arrives back on the docks seeking his friend, but Claude snatches him. Roxanne isn't easily captured and tricks the evil scientist into his own net.

Mary Beth snarls the underwater vehicle in illegal netting, and is unable to escape from the bottom of the sea, with leaking water filling the tank. Terry and the children frantically look for all their loved ones missing in action and finally find the boat anchored. Roxanne appears to lead Terry to Mary Beth, and he dives down to rescue her in the nick of time.

With Zeus guarding the boat, the police arrive to arrest Claude, after his assistants have spilled the beans on his unscrupulous practices. As Terry and Mary Beth marry the next Sunday, a telegram arrives with her grant award. Roxanne catches the bride's bouquet and Zeus barks "Congratulations!"

In this "Rin Tin Tin" meets "Flipper" scenario, accepting the corny storyline requires a giant leap of belief. Since the intended audience is young children, it's not much of a stretch since they're rooting for the kids and the creatures anyway—the parents are just a parallel device. "Dull spin on *101 Dalmatians* . . . for kids only" says Desson Howe of the *Washington Post*. There's no payoff with a song, so at least we're spared one cliché.

—*Roberta Cruger*

CREDITS

Terry: Steve Guttenberg
Mary Beth: Kathleen Quinlan
Claude Carver: Arnold Vosloo
Becky: Dawn McMillan
Jordan: Miko Hughes
Judith: Majandra Delfino

Origin: USA
Released: 1997
Production: Frank Price, Gene Rosow, Ludi Boeken for Rysher Entertainment; released by MGM
Direction: George Miller
Screenplay: Tom Benedek
Cinematography: David Connell
Editing: Harry Hitner
Music: Bruce Rowland
Production design: Bernt Capra
Art direction: Alfred Kemper
Set decoration: Beth Jushnick
Costumes: Marion Boyce
Sound: Shirley Libby
Underwater camera: Paul Mockler
MPAA rating: PG
Running Time: 98 minutes

REVIEWS

Boxoffice. April, 1997, p. 203
Chicago Tribune. January 29, 1997, p. 10.
Detroit Free Press. January 25, 1997, p. 2A.
Los Angeles Times. January 27, 1997, p. F4.
New York Times. January 25, 1997, p. 18.
Variety. January 17, 1997, p. 82.

List of Awards

Academy Awards

Best Picture: *Titanic*

Direction: James Cameron (*Titanic*)

Actor: Jack Nicholson (*As Good As It Gets*)

Actress: Helen Hunt (*As Good As It Gets*)

Supporting Actor: Robin Williams (*Good Will Hunting*)

Supporting Actress: Kim Basinger (*L.A. Confidential*)

Original Screenplay: Ben Affleck and Matt Damon (*Good Will Hunting*)

Adapted Screenplay: Brian Helgeland and Curtis Hanson (*L.A. Confidential*)

Cinematography: Russell Carpenter (*Titanic*)

Editing: Conrad Buff, James Cameron and Richard A. Harris (*Titanic*)

Art Direction: Peter Lamont (*Titanic*)

Visual Effects: Robert Legato, Mark Lasoff, Thomas L. Fisher and Michael Kanfer (*Titanic*)

Sound Effects Editing: Tom Bellfort and Christopher Boyes (*Titanic*)

Sound: Gary Rydstrom, Tom Johnson, Gary Summers and Mark Ulano (*Titanic*)

Makeup: Rick Baker and David LeRoy Anderson (*Men In Black*)

Costume Design: Deborah L. Scott (*Titanic*)

Original Music or Comedy Score: Anne Dudley (*The Full Monty*)

Original Dramatic Score: James Horner (*Titanic*)

Original Song: "My Heart Will Go On" (*Titanic:* music by James Horner, lyrics by Will Jennings)

Foreign-language Film: *Character* (The Netherlands)

Short Film, Animated: Jan Pinkava (*Geri's Game*)

Short Film, Live Action: Chris Tashima and Chris Donahue (*Visas and Virtues*)

Documentary, Feature: Rabbi Marvin Hier and Richard Trank (*The Long Way Home*)

Documentary, Short Subject: Donna Dewey and Carol Pasternak (*A Story of Healing*)

Directors Guild of America Award

Director: James Cameron (*Titanic*)

Writers Guild of America Awards

Original Screenplay: Ben Affleck and Matt Damon (*Good Will Hunting*)

Adapted Screenplay: Mark Andrus and James L. Brooks (*As Good As It Gets*)

New York Film Critics Awards

Best Picture: *L.A. Confidential*

Direction: Curtis Hanson (*L.A. Confidential*)

Actor: Peter Fonda (*Ulee's Gold*)

Actress: Julie Christie (*Afterglow*)

Supporting Actor: Burt Reynolds (*Boogie Nights*)

Supporting Actress: Joan Cusack (*In & Out*)

Screenplay: Brian Helgeland and Curtis Hanson (*L.A. Confidential*)

Foreign Film: *Ponette* (France)

Cinematography: Roger Deakins (*Kundun*)

First Film: Neil LaBute (*In the Company of Men*)

Nonfiction Film: Errol Morris (*Fast, Cheap & Out of Control*)

Los Angeles Film Critics Awards

Best Picture: *L.A. Confidential*

Direction: Curtis Hanson (*L.A. Confidential*)

Actor: Robert Duvall (*The Apostle*)

Actress: Helena Bonham Carter (*Wings of the Dove*)

Supporting Actor: Burt Reynolds (*Boogie Nights*)

Supporting Actress: Julianne Moore (*Boogie Nights*)

Screenplay: Curtis Hanson and Brian Helgeland (*L.A. Confidential*)

Cinematography: Dante Spinotti (*L.A. Confidential*)

Foreign Film: *La Promesse* (Belgium)

Outstanding Documentary: Michael Uys and Lexy Lowell (*Riding the Rails*)

National Society of Film Critics Awards

Best Picture: *L.A. Confidential*

Direction: Curtis Hanson (*L.A. Confidential*)

Actor: Robert Duvall (*The Apostle*)

Actress: Julie Christie (*Afterglow*)

Supporting Actor: Burt Reynolds (*Boogie Nights*)

Supporting Actress: Julianne Moore (*Boogie Nights*)

Screenplay: Curtis Hanson and Brian Helgeland (*L.A. Confidential*)

Cinematography: Roger Deakins (*Kundun*)

Foreign Film: *La Promesse* (Belgium)

Documentary: Errol Morris (*Fast, Cheap & Out of Control*)

National Board of Review Awards

Best Picture: *L.A. Confidential*

Direction: Curtis Hanson (*L.A. Confidential*)

Actor: Jack Nicholson (*As Good As It Gets*)

Actress: Helena Bonham Carter (*Wings of the Dove*)

Supporting Actor: Greg Kinnear (*As Good As It Gets*)

Supporting Actress: Anne Heche (*Donnie Brasco* and *Wag the Dog*)

Foreign Film: *Shall We Dance?* (Japan)

Documentary: Errol Morris (*Fast, Cheap & Out of Control*)

Golden Globes

Best Picture, Drama: *Titanic*

Best Picture, Comedy or Musical: *As Good As It Gets*

Direction: James Cameron (*Titanic*)

Actor, Drama: Peter Fonda (*Ulee's Gold*)

Actress, Drama: Judi Dench (*Mrs. Brown*)

Actor, Comedy or Musical: Jack Nicholson (*As Good As It Gets*)

Actress, Comedy or Musical: Helen Hunt (*As Good As It Gets*)

Supporting Actor: Burt Reynolds (*Boogie Nights*)

Supporting Actress: Kim Basinger (*L.A. Confidential*)

Screenplay: Ben Affleck and Matt Damon (*Good Will Hunting*)

Original Score: James Horner (*Titanic*)

Original Song: "My Heart Will Go On" (*Titanic:* music by James Horner, lyrics by Will Jennings)

Foreign Film: *My Life In Pink* (Belgium)

Life Achievement Award

Robert Wise

Robert Wise, the twenty-sixth recipient of the American Film Institute's Life Achievement Award, differs from many of his predecessors in that the thirty-nine features he has directed reveal no unifying vision or signature cinematic style. Like many of the last generation of directors who learned their craft during the final days of the studio system, Wise seems mostly to regard moviemaking as a forum for well-crafted, commercial properties rather than as an opportunity for personal, artistic expression. His selection as the AFI's 1998 honoree confirms that a consistent body of quality motion pictures can be created through the hard work of a talented man who becomes a master craftsman.

Wise himself is often the first to acknowledge the absence of a single artistic vision and the emphasis on storytelling in his work: "I'm not a man who has just one theme to express through his art. I have different interests and I like to try different things. My first reaction in reading a piece of material is if it grabs me as a reader. The second thought is if there's an audience for it. The third is what is the theme, or the by-product, as I always call it." Sergio Leemann, the author of the only book-length study of Wise's films to date, describes the director this way: "Wise is not the author of his films the way an Ingmar Bergman or a Federico Fellini is. He is a film storyteller par excellence; one who translates into purely cinematic terms the stories of others that he makes his own."

Wise was born September 10, 1914, in Winchester, Indiana. After a year at Franklin College studying journalism, he was sent by his parents to Los Angeles, where his older brother, working as an accountant for RKO Pictures, helped Wise find work to ease the financial hardships of the Depression. Wise started at RKO as a film porter—someone who carried prints to the projection booth and checked them later for damage—and then worked in the shipping room for seven months before T.K. Wood, the head sound-effects editor, took Wise on as an apprentice. His next advance came when Wise became the assistant to film editor William Hamilton, who involved Wise closely in every project beginning with their first film, *Winterset* (1936). Eventually, Hamilton let Wise assemble the first cuts of features himself. He also generously gave Wise his first screen credits, as co-editor of *The Hunchback of Notre Dame* (1939) and *Fifth Avenue Girl* (1939).

Wise's work as an editor forms an important early part of his career. In 1977, *Film Comment* magazine polled 100 film editors in the U.S. and Europe for lists of both respected editors and directors whose films consistently revealed superb editing. Wise appeared on the first list as one of the best all-time editors, and only David Lean ranked higher than Wise on the second. Wise's most famous editing credit came on *Citizen Kane* (1941). An excellent example of Wise's work may be seen in the celebrated breakfast table sequence that depicts in a few seconds of screen time the disintegration of Kane's first marriage. The brilliant idea was Welles's (adapted, he divulged, from an old one-act play by Thornton Wilder, *The Long Christmas Dinner*), but Wise and Mark Robson devoted weeks to timing and perfecting the wipes, the pans, and the overlapping voices on the soundtrack before the completed sequence was shown to Welles for final approval.

The politics and production behind Wise's editing of Welles's second film has become part of motion picture lore. After finishing a 130-minute version of *The Magnificent Ambersons* (1942), Welles flew to South America to work on his next project. While he was gone, *Ambersons* was previewed to two audiences with almost uniformly negative reaction cards. RKO wanted the film shortened considerably, but a wartime embargo on civilian flights abroad kept Wise from meeting Welles in Brazil and trapped him in the horrible spot between the studio and Welles, between the demands of art and commerce. Wise obeyed the closer boss. He cut the film to its current 88-minute length, work that required Wise and others to shoot new scenes and a new ending to make the shortened film cohere. This coverage was Wise's inauspicious directorial debut. Since the excised footage was destroyed, the alterations have always been controversial, but Wise has always been diplomatic about his work on *Ambersons*: "As a work of art and a cinematic achievement, it was undoubtedly a better film in its original length, but it just didn't play. . . . I think the fact that it has come down through the years as a classic in its own right means that we didn't destroy everything that Orson did. I would be the first to say it."

After editing four more films, including *The Devil and Daniel Webster* (1941), RKO gave Wise his first official chance to direct when producer Val Lewton had to fire Gunther Fritsch for slowness in completing *The Curse of the Cat People* (1944). Wise finished this job in the ten days that Lewton allotted him and then apprenticed, like many of his peers, by directing a string of B movies. Another project Wise directed for producer Lewton, *The Body Snatcher* (1946), shows the psychological tension and moody atmosphere Lewton was known for. Wise has often singled this film out as his favorite among his early motion pictures. The finale showcases rich photography and superb editing as a hearse races through a stormy night. The driver (Henry Daniell) imagines the corpse he carries to be one of his previous victims, and his growing terror eventually causes the fatal crash that concludes the film. Years later, Wise returned to the atmospheric horror film in *The Haunting* (1963), a first-rate work that shows Wise's experience as a sound editor in its evocative use of sound effects.

When Wise graduated to bigger budgets, he showed his versatility by making fine films in a series of genres. *The Set-Up* (1949), one of Wise's best films and his last project for RKO, presents 72 minutes in the life of aging boxer Stoker Thompson (Robert Ryan) as he prepares for what will be his last fight. Although his manager has sold him out, in the ring Thompson refuses to take a dive, and he eventually musters the strength to knock out his younger opponent. He pays for his integrity, however. The handlers who arranged the fix crush Thompson's hand after the fight, leaving him and his wife to face an uncertain future. Wise's preparation for this film was meticulous: it was the first film he pre-planned with storyboard drawings, and he also frequented local arenas to soak up the flavor of small-time boxing. Covering the carefully choreographed fight scenes with three cameras, he used footage from the hand-held camera to cut together a tricky portion of the climactic fight. He later reported that this was the last time he worked at the editing bench. Wise returned to the fight genre in 1956 with his biographical film about Rocky Graziano, *Somebody Up There Likes Me*.

Another genre growing in popularity at the time was the film set among corporate boardrooms. Wise's big business drama was *Executive Suite* (1954), still an underrated film. It stands out for Wise's ability to work effectively with an ensemble cast and for the suspense of the climactic board meeting, in which William Holden challenges the corporate leaders over routinely compromising the quality of the furniture they manufacture in favor of easy profits. Jean-Pierre Coursodon, in an insightful essay-length study of Wise's career, sees this final scene as a symbol of the director's gift for making quality, commercial films: "The ideal of good craftsmanship it expresses is best represented in the motion picture industry by products like *Executive Suite*. Unlike the chair Holden breaks to make his point, the film has been crafted never to fall to pieces."

Wise also directed one of the landmarks of the science-fiction genre, *The Day the Earth Stood Still* (1952). At a time when science fiction in the movies dwelt on the horrific by-products of nuclear testing (in films like *The Beast from 20,000 Fathoms* [1953], *Tarantula* [1955], and *The Incredible Shrinking Man* [1957]), Wise de-emphasized special effects and concentrated primarily on the ideas and the characters in his story. His admired and respected film concerns a flying saucer arriving on Earth with the anti-nuclear message that mankind must learn to live in peace with one another and with the universe. The alien visitor Klaatu assumes human form, moves anonymously into a boarding house, and befriends a mother and her son. In addition to depicting (mostly) benevolent aliens long before Steven Spielberg did in *Close Encounters of the Third Kind* (1977), Wise faithfully balances both the developing drama of the human element and the suspense of the grim alien warning. The scene in which Patricia Neal hurries from the wounded Klaatu with the crucial words she has memorized ("Klaatu barada nikto") to prevent the robot Gort from destroying the world has become one of the cinema's most memorable moments. Wise later returned to the genre of science fiction with the films *The Andromeda Strain* (1971) and *Star Trek: The Motion Picture* (1979).

Wise's most honored and most popular work has been in the musical. His two Academy Awards have come for his work on *West Side Story* (1961—a directing credit he shared with choreographer Jerome Robbins, who directed the musical on Broadway) and on *The Sound of Music* (1965). The critical and commercial popularity of both films helped to continue in the 1960s an emphasis on screen adaptations of stage musicals. It is not often recalled that Wise and his collaborators during pre-production worked to reduce the sentimentality in *The Sound of Music* (this was also Julie Andrews's first request to the director when they met). Three songs from the stage musical were dropped, and screenwriter Ernest Lehman conceived the idea for the new song "I Have Confidence" as a lively transition from the convent to the Captain's Salzburg estate. Richard Rodgers agreed to compose the new music. Wise also talked a reluctant Christopher Plummer into appearing in the film because Wise felt that Plummer could bring warmth and depth to the wooden stage character Captain von Trapp. *The Sound of Music* became the biggest-grossing film to that time, though many critics still faulted its saccharine elements. Wise counters: "We really diminished a lot of it from the stage show. We made every effort to find ways of not getting too cute." The failure of occasional Broadway revivals of the stage musical, one as recent as 1998, may bear him out.

As the preceding remarks suggest, Wise is not a director who personally selected most of the projects for his films. The consistent quality of the resulting motion pictures has come about through his professionalism, perfectionism, humility, and craftsmanship. This humility may be seen in his reaction to Harold Mirisch's request that he accept Jerome Robbins as a co-director on *West Side Story*. Wise had already established himself in the industry, but as he now says: "I went home and started to think about it. I took off my directing hat and put on my producer's hat and asked myself, 'What's the best thing for the film?' The answer was that if there's any possible way to get Robbins on the film, that would be the best thing." Combining good craftsmanship and the best commercial qualities has always been the best thing for the films of Robert Wise.

—Glenn Hopp

Obituaries

William Alland (March 4, 1916-November 10, 1997). Alland was an actor and producer who worked with Orson Welles's Mercury Theater. He was the reporter and narrator of *Citizen Kane* (1941). He also appeared in Welles's *The Lady From Shanghai* (1948) and *Macbeth* (1948). In 1942, he became a producer, specializing in low budget science fiction films. His production credits include *The Black Castle* (1952), *It Came From Outer Space* (1953), *The Creature From the Black Lagoon* (1954), *This Island Earth* (1955), *The Mole People* (1957), *Look in Any Window* (1961, which he also directed), and *The Lively Set* (1964).

John Ashley (December 25, 1934-October 4, 1997). Ashley was an actor and producer who worked both in film and television. As an actor, he played second leads in low budget exploitation films such as *Hot Rod Gang* (1958) and *Frankenstein's Daughter* (1959) in the 1950s. He began producing in the 1970s, most notably in television, where he was involved with such hits as "The A-Team" and "Walker, Texas Ranger." His additional screen credits include *How to Make a Monster* (1958), *Muscle Beach Party* (1964), *Bikini Beach* (1964), *Beach Blanket Bingo* (1965), *Beyond Atlantis* (1973), and *Savage Sisters* (1974).

Hy Averback (1924-October 14, 1997). Averback was an actor turned director who specialized in comedy. He was perhaps best known for his work in television, directing popular situation comedies such as "The Flying Nun" and "M*A*S*H." His film acting credits include *The Benny Goodman Story* (1956), *Four Girls in Town* (1957), and *How to Succeed in Show Business Without Really Trying* (1967). His film directing credits include *Chamber of Horrors* (1966), *I Love You Alice B. Toklas!* (1969), *Suppose They Gave a War and Nobody Came* (1970), and *Where the Boys Are* (1984).

John Beal (August 13, 1909-April 26, 1997). Born J. Alexander Bieldung, Beal began his film career playing juvenile leads in such films as *Another Language* (1933) and *The Little Minister* (1934). As he matured, he gradually moved to supporting roles. In a career that spanned six decades, his screen credits included *Les Miserables* (1935), *Madame X* (1937), *Key Witness* (1947), *The Sound and the Fury* (1959), *The Funhouse* (1981), and *The Firm* (1993).

Marjorie Best (1904-June 14, 1997). Best was a costume designer who won an Academy Award for her work on *Adventures of Don Juan* (1948), and was nominated for the Award for *Giant* (1956), *Sunrise at Campobello* (1960), and *The Greatest Story Ever Told* (1965). Her additional screen credits include *The Nun's Story* (1959), *Rio Bravo* (1959), *Tender Is the Night* (1962), and *State Fair* (1962).

Sally Blane (1910-August 27, 1997). Blane was an actress whose career thrived during the Silent Era. She appeared in her first film, *Sirens of the Sea* (1907) at the age of seven, and went on to make scores of additional films. Her screen credits include *Rolled Stockings* (1927), *Casey at the Bat* (1927), *Dead Man's Curve* (1928), and *Vagabond Lover* (1929).

June Carlson (1925-December 9, 1997). Carlson was an actress best known for the role of the teenage Lucy Jones in all seventeen of the Jones Family films (a "typical American family," a la the Andy Hardy series, albeit not as popular) in the 1930s and early 1940s. Her screen credits include *Every Saturday Night* (1936), *The Jones Family in Big Business* (1937), *A Trip to Paris* (1938), *The Jones Family in Hollywood* (1939), and *Young as You Feel* (1940).

Thelma Carpenter (1922-May 14, 1997). Carpenter was an African-American swing era jazz singer who also acted on stage, radio, television, and in film. Her screen credits include *The Wiz* (1978), *The Cotton Club* (1984), and *New York Stories* (1989).

Adriana Caselotti (May 6, 1916-January 19, 1997). Caselotti was an actress best known for providing the voice of Snow White in Walt Disney's first feature-length animated cartoon, *Snow White and the Seven Dwarfs* (1937). Her additional screen credits include *The Bride Wore Red* (1937) and *The Wizard of Oz* (1939).

Saul Chaplin (February 12, 1912-November 15, 1997). Born Saul Kaplan, Chaplin was a composer, musical director, and producer. He won three Academy Awards for his scoring and orchestration work on *An American in Paris* (1951), *Seven*

Brides for Seven Brothers (1954), and *West Side Story* (1961). His additional screen credits include *Manhattan Merry-Go-Round* (1937), *Meet Me on Broadway* (1946), *On the Town* (1949), *Jolson Sings Again* (1950), *Kiss Me Kate* (1953), *High Society* (1956), *Can-Can* (1960), *The Sound of Music* (1965), *Star!* (1968), and *That's Entertainment Part 2* (1976).

Shirley Clarke (1925-September 23, 1997). Born Shirley Brimberg, Clarke was a documentary film director who applied her training in choreography to filmmaking. She co-directed *Skyscraper* (1959), which earned an Academy Award as Best Live-Action Short. She also won an Academy Award for co-directing the feature length documentary *Robert Frost: A Lover's Quarrel With the World* (1963). She changed styles with *The Connection* (1963), *The Cool World* (1963), and *A Portrait of Jason* (1967), controversial cinema verite looks at heroin addiction, Harlem gangs, and male prostitution, respectively. After an attempt at working in Hollywood ended in frustration, Clarke experimented with video and taught film at UCLA. Her additional screen credits include *Bridges-Go-Round* (1959), *Man in the Polar Regions* (1967), and *Ornette: Made in America* (1986).

Robert Clouse (1928-February 4, 1997). Clouse was a director, best known for his work on Bruce Lee's breakthrough film, *Enter the Dragon* (1973). Two of his short films, *The Cadillac* (1962) and *The Legend of Jimmy Blue Eyes* (1964), were nominated for Academy Awards. His additional screen credits include *Darker Than Amber* (1970) and *Golden Needles* (1974).

Jacques-Yves Cousteau (June 11, 1910-June 25, 1997). Cousteau was an oceanographer and director. As a French naval officer, he helped design the aqualung, a self-contained underwater breathing apparatus which enabled humans to swim underwater for extended periods of time. He also developed an underwater film camera, and his documentaries of sea life did much to popularize the sport of scuba diving. Two of his films won Academy Awards as Best Documentary: *The Silent World* (1956) and *World Without Sun* (1964). In the 1960s, he also did some underwater documentary work for ABC television. Cousteau's additional screen credits include *Voyage to the Edge of the World* (1976).

Eliot Daniel (1908-December 6, 1997). Daniel was a composer whose best known work was probably the theme song from the popular 1950s television show "I Love Lucy." In film, he co-wrote two songs which were nominated for Academy Awards: "Lavender Blue," from the Disney film *So Dear to My Heart* (1949), and "Never," from *Golden Girls* (1951).

Gail Davis (October 5, 1925-March 15, 1997). Davis was an actress who specialized in B westerns; she was famous for doing her own trick riding and shooting stunts. Her work in a series of Gene Autry films led to a starring role in the 1950s children's television series "Annie Oakley." Her screen credits include *Cow Town* (1950), *Indian Territory* (1950), *Texans Never Cry* (1951), *Yukon Manhunt* (1951), *Blue Canadian Rockies* (1952), and *On Top of Old Smoky* (1953).

Giuseppe De Santis (February 11, 1917-May 16, 1997). De Santis was an Italian director, and one of the founders of the postwar neorealism movement. His earliest involvement with film was as a critic, and from there he began writing screenplays. After World War II, he began directing. His best known film is *Bitter Rice* (1949), which made a star of Sylvia Mangano. His additional film credits include *Under the Olive Tree* (1950), *Rome 11 O'Clock* (1952), *A Husband for Anna* (1953), and *Days of Love* (1954).

David Doyle (December 1, 1925-February 27, 1997). Doyle was an actor best known for his stint as John Bosley on the popular 1970s television series "Charlie's Angels." His screen credits include *Act One* (1963), *Coogan's Bluff* (1968), *Vigilante Force* (1976), and *Capricorn One* (1978).

David Doyle

Harry Essex (November 29, 1910-February 6, 1997). Essex was a screenwriter and director best known for his work in the action and science fiction genres. He wrote or co-wrote screenplays for *Boston Blackie and the Law* (1943), *Dragnet* (1947), *Kansas City Confidential* (1952), *It Came From Outer Space* (1953), *The Creature From the Black Lagoon* (1954), and *The Sons of Katie Elder* (1963). He directed as well as wrote three films: *I the Jury* (1953), *Mad at the World* (1955), and *Octaman* (1971); and directed and produced *The Cremators* (1972).

Chris Farley (February 15, 1964-December 18, 1997). Farley was a comic actor who rose to fame on television's "Saturday Night Live." He idolized former "Saturday Night Live" star John Belushi, and like Belushi, Farley had a self-destructive lifestyle; both men died of drug overdoses. Farley had starring roles in *Tommy Boy* (1995), *Black Sheep* (1996), and *Beverly Hills Ninja* (1997), films which met with box office success despite being generally panned by critics.

Chris Farley

George Fenneman (November 11, 1919-May 29, 1997). Fenneman was a radio and television announcer and actor. He is best remembered as Groucho Marx's announcer and straight man on the comedy game show "You Bet Your Life," which was both a radio and television hit from 1947 to 1959. His film credits include *The Thing* (1951), *How to Succeed in Show Business Without Really Trying* (1967), and *Once You Kiss a Stranger* (1969).

Marco Ferreri (May 11, 1928-May 9, 1997). Ferreri was an Italian director and screenwriter whose films were often satirically allegorical treatments of social problems. His best known film was *La Grande Bouffe* (1973), in which a group of people eat themselves to death. His additional film credits include *The Wheelchair* (1960), *The Ape Woman* (1964), *Dillinger Is Dead* (1969), *Liza* (1972), *The Last Woman* (1976), and *Tales of Ordinary Madness* (1981).

Gabriel Figueroa (April 24, 1907-April 27, 1997). Figueroa was a Mexican cinematographer who worked extensively in both American and Mexican films. He studied with famed cinematographer Gregg Toland before returning to Mexico to embark upon his own career. In Mexico, he worked with director Emilio Fernandez on *Maria Candelaria* (1943), *The Pearl* (1946), and *Rio Escondido* (1947); and with Luis Bunuel on *Los Olvidados* (1950), *The Young One* (1961), and *The Exterminating Angel* (1962). In the United States, he shot John Ford's *The Fugitive* (1947) and John Huston's *Under the Volcano* (1984). He was nominated for an Academy Award for his cinematography in Huston's *The Night of the Iguana* (1964). His additional film credits include *Alla en el Rancho Grande* (1936), *The Young and the Damned* (1950), *El* (1953), *Nazarin* (1959), *Simon of the Desert* (1965), *Two Mules for Sister Sara* (1970), and *Kelly's Heroes* (1970).

Frances Foster (1924-June 17, 1997). Foster was an African-American actress who won awards for her theater work. She also appeared in three Spike Lee films: *Malcolm X* (1992), *Crooklyn* (1994), and *Clockers* (1996).

Sam Fuller (August 12, 1911-October 20, 1997). Fuller was a screenwriter, actor, producer and director, best known for his hard-hitting B action films of the 1950s and 1960s. As a young man, Fuller saw the rough side of life as a crime reporter, as a hobo during the Depression, and as a soldier during World War II. He began writing pulp novels and then screenplays in the 1930s, for films such as *Gangs of New York* (1938) and *Bowery Boys* (1940). After the war, he returned to Hollywood, where he began translating his experiences into films as a screenwriter-director. Films such as *I Shot Jesse James* (1949), *Pickup on South Street* (1953), *China Gate* (1957), *Merrill's Marauders* (1962), and *Shock Corridor* (1962) earned him the respect of critics, especially in France, where he was revered as one of the greatest filmmakers of the postwar era. After a hiatus of several years, Fuller made a film based on his experiences in the Army's First Infantry Division in World War II. *The Big Red One* (1980), which starred Lee Marvin as a grizzled combat veteran, reestablished Fuller's reputation and is considered the capstone of his career. Fuller usually wrote his own scripts; his additional writing and directing credits include *Fixed Bayonets* (1951), *Hell and High Water* (1954), *Underworld U.S.A.* (1961), *The Naked Kiss* (1965), *Dead Pigeon on Beethoven Street* (1972), *White Dog* (1982), *Thieves After Dark* (1984), and *Street of No Return* (1989).

Will Hare (1919-August 28, 1997). Hare was a character actor who worked extensively on stage, in television, and in film. His screen credits include *The Wrong Man* (1957), *Heaven Can Wait* (1978), *The Effects of Gamma Rays on Man-in-the-Moon Marigolds* (1979), *The Rose* (1979), *The Electric Horseman* (1979), and *Pennies From Heaven* (1981).

William Hickey (1928-June 29, 1997). Hickey was a veteran character actor whose film career spanned four decades. He was perhaps best known for his role as the aged Mafia leader in *Prizzi's Honor* (1985), for which he earned an Academy Award nomination as Best Supporting Actor. His additional film credits include *A Hatful of Rain* (1957), *Something Wild* (1961), *The Producers* (1968), *Little Big Man* (1970), *The Name of the Rose* (1986), *Puppet Master* (1989), and *Mouse Hunt* (1997).

William Hickey

Joseph Hoffman (1909-May 25, 1997). Hoffman was a screenwriter who worked in film in the decade following World War II and in television for many years after that. His screenwriting credits include *China Sky* (1945), *And Baby Makes Three* (1949), *Against All Flags* (1952), and *Has Anybody Seen My Gal* (1952).

Jennifer Holt (November 10, 1920-September 21, 1997). Born Elizabeth Marshall Holt, Holt was an actress who was featured opposite such B Western stars as Johnny Mack Brown and Rod Cameron in the 1940s. Her father Jack Holt and her brother Tim Holt were also actors. Holt's film credits include *Deep in the Heart of Texas* (1942), *Cowboy Buckaroo* (1942), *Lone Star Trail* (1943), *Cowboy in Manhattan* (1943), *Gun Smoke* (1945), *Moon Over Montana* (1946), *Buffalo Bill Rides Again* (1947), and *The Hawk of Powder River* (1948).

King Hu (April 29, 1931-January 14, 1997). Born Hu Chin-ch'uan, Hu was a Chinese director who landed in Hong Kong after the communist takeover of mainland China. He worked in a variety of capacities in the Hong Kong film industry, including acting and screenwriting. In 1958, he began directing for the prolific Shaw Brothers, where he brought a high level of imagination and technique to their traditional action films. His screen credits include *Sons of the Good Earth* (1964), *Dragon Gate Inn* (1966), *A Touch of Zen* (1969), *Legend in the Mountains* (1979), and *Swordsman* (1990).

Richard Jaeckel (October 10, 1926-June 14, 1997). Jaeckel was an actor who played a wide variety of character roles in a career that spanned four decades. He was nominated for an Academy Award as Best Supporting Actor for his work in *Sometimes a Great Notion* (1971; later rereleased as *Never Give an Inch*). He also worked in television, with regular roles on "Spenser: For Hire" and "Baywatch." His additional film credits include *Guadalcanal Diary* (1943), *Sands of Iwo Jima* (1949), *3:10 to Yuma* (1957), *Platinum High School* (1960), *Town Without Pity* (1961), *The Dirty Dozen* (1967), *Chisum* (1970), *Pat Garrett and Billy the Kid* (1973), *Twilight's Last Gleaming* (1977), *...All the Marbles* (1981), and *The King of the Kickboxers* (1991).

Richard Jaeckel

Paul Jarrico (January 12, 1915-October 28, 1997). Jarrico was a screenwriter who worked extensively in the 1940s and 1950s. He earned an Academy Award nomination for his work on *Tom, Dick, and Harry* (1941). But his career was disrupted when he ran afoul of the blacklist after being identified as a member of the Communist Party in 1951. Unapologetic, he worked only sporadically thereafter, either in Europe or in an uncredited role in Hollywood productions. He died in an automobile accident on his way home from a ceremony to honor surviving victims of the blacklist. Jarrico's screen credits include *No Time to Marry* (1938), *Thousands Cheer* (1943), *Song of Russia* (1944), *The Search* (1948), *The White Tower* (1950), *Salt of the Earth* (1954, as producer), *The Day the Hot Line Got Hot* (1969), *The Day That Shook the World* (1976), and *Messenger of Death* (1988).

Stubby Kaye (November 11, 1918-December 14, 1997). Kaye was a singer and actor who specialized in comic character roles. The short, rotund Kaye is best remembered for his role as Nicely-Nicely Johnson in both the Broadway and screen versions of *Guys and Dolls* (1955). His additional film credits include *Taxi* (1953), *Li'l Abner* (1959), *Cat Ballou* (1965), *The Way West* (1967), *Sweet Charity* (1969), *The Cockeyed Cowboys of Calico County* (1970), and *Who Framed Roger Rabbit?* (1988).

Brian Keith (November 14, 1921-June 24, 1997). Keith was an actor who worked extensively in both film and television. He appeared in his first film, *Pied Piper Malone* (1924), at the age of three; as an adult, he at first specialized in action films such as *Arrowhead* (1953) and *Five Against the House* (1955). His role as Haley Mills' father in Disney's *The Parent Trap* (1961) was a big breakthrough for Keith, who was also featured in several television series, most notably "Family Affair" and "Hardcastle & McCormick." His additional film credits include *Storm Center* (1956), *Run of the Arrow* (1957), *The Young Philadelphians* (1959), *Ten Who Dared* (1960), *The Russians are Coming, the Russians are Coming* (1966), *Reflections in a Golden Eye* (1967), *The Wind and the Lion* (1975), *Hooper* (1978), *Moonraker* (1978), *Sharkey's Machine* (1981), and *Young Guns* (1988).

Brian Keith

Dorothy Kingsley (October 14, 1909-September 26, 1997). Kingsley was a screenwriter who got her start writing radio comedy for Bob Hope and Edgar Bergen. Her film career spanned over a quarter of a century, and she specialized in light comedies. Her screen credits include *Girl Crazy* (1943), *Broadway Rhythm* (1944), *A Date With Judy* (1948), *Angels in the Outfield* (1951), *Kiss Me Kate* (1953), *Seven Brides for Seven Brothers* (1954), *Pal Joey* (1957), *Can-Can* (1960), *Valley of the Dolls* (1967), and *Half a Sixpence* (1967).

Burton Lane (February 2, 1912-January 5, 1997). Born Burton Levy, Lane was a composer/songwriter whose best known musicals were the Broadway and film versions of *Finian's Rainbow* (1968) and *On a Clear Day You Can See Forever* (1970). He earned Academy Award nominations for his songs "How About You," from *Babes on Broadway* (1942) and "Too Late Now," from *Royal Wedding* (1951). His additional screen credits include *Artists and Models* (1937), *Thousands Cheer* (1943), *Hollywood Canteen* (1944), and *Jupiter's Darling* (1955).

Frank Launder (1907-February 23, 1997). Launder was a British screenwriter, director, and producer. He partnered with Sidney Gilliat in all these capacities. The Launder-

Gilliat duo's best remembered contribution was probably their St. Trinian's films, a long-running series of comedies about the misadventures of the students at a school for girls. Launder's screenwriting credits include *Hobson's Choice* (1931), *The Lady Vanishes* (1938), *The Young Mr. Pitt* (1942), and *The Green Man* (1956). As writer, director, and producer, his credits include *I See a Dark Stranger* (1946), *The Blue Lagoon* (1949), *The Happiest Days of Your Life* (1950), *The Belles of St. Trinian's* (1954), *Geordie* (1955), *Blue Murder at St. Trinian's* (1957), *The Pure Hell of St. Trinian's* (1960), *The Great St. Trinian's Train Robbery* (1966), and *The Wildcats of St. Trinian's* (1980).

Rosina Lawrence (1914-June 23, 1997). Lawrence was an actress who specialized in comedy in the early years of sound pictures. She appeared in at least two Little Rascals films, playing the "new teacher," Miss Lawrence, most notably in *Bored of Education* (1936), which won an Academy Award as Best Short Subject. She was also featured opposite Laurel and Hardy in *Way Out West* (1937). Her additional film credits include *Music Is Magic* (1935), *General Spanky* (1936), *The Great Ziegfeld* (1936), *Nobody's Baby* (1937), and *Pick a Star* (1937).

Sheldon Leonard (February 22, 1907-January 11, 1997). Born Sheldon Leonard Bershad, Leonard was a character actor in the 1940s who became a successful television producer in the 1950s, producing such hits as "Make Room For Daddy," "The Andy Griffith Show," "The Dick Van Dyke Show," "I Spy," and "Gomer Pyle." As an actor, he is perhaps best remembered for his role in *It's a Wonderful Life* (1946), in which he played the bartender who ejected James Stewart from his bar. Leonard's additional film credits include *Another Thin Man* (1939), *Tortilla Flat* (1942), *Hit the Ice* (1943), *To Have and Have Not* (1944), *Somewhere in the Night* (1946), *Guys and Dolls* (1955), *Pocketful of Miracles* (1961), and *The Brinks Job* (1978).

Robert Lewis (1909-November 23, 1997). Lewis was an acting coach and an actor who worked on Broadway and in film. He was a founder of Actor's Studio; among his students were Marlon Brando, Faye Dunaway, Martin Sheen, and Meryl Streep. His film credits include *Dragon Seed* (1944), *Son of Lassie* (1945), *Ziegfeld Follies* (1945), and *Monsieur Verdoux* (1947).

Audra Lindley (September 24, 1918-October 16, 1997). Lindley was an actress best known for her work on the television series "Three's Company." In addition to her television and Broadway work, she also appeared in a number of films, including *Taking Off* (1971), *The Heartbreak Kid* (1972), *Best Friends* (1975), *Cannery Row* (1982), *Desert Hearts* (1985), *Troop Beverly Hills* (1989), and *Sudden Death* (1995).

Dietrich Lohman (1943-November 13, 1997). Lohman was a German cinematographer, best known for his work with filmmaker Rainer Werner Fassbinder, with whom he made *Love Is Colder Than Death* (1969), *Katzelmacher* (1969), and *Gods of the Plague* (1970). His additional screen credits include *Why Does Herr R Run Amok?* (1970), *Merchant of the Four Seasons* (1972), *Effi Briest* (1974), *Hitler—A Film From Germany* (1977), *Germany in Autumn* (1978), and *The Lover* (1990).

Jean Louis (October 5, 1907-April 20, 1997). Louis was one of the preeminent costume designers of Hollywood's postwar golden age. He designed looks for, among others, Lana Turner, Rita Hayworth, and Doris Day. He won an Academy Award for his work on *The Solid Gold Cadillac* (1956), and was nominated for his contributions to ten other films, including *Born Yesterday* (1951), *Affair in Trinidad* (1952), *From Here to Eternity* (1953), *A Star Is Born* (1954), *It Should Happen To You* (1954), *Queen Bee* (1955), *Pal Joey* (1957), *Bell, Book and Candle* (1958), *Back Street* (1961), *Judgment at Nuremberg* (1961), *Ship of Fools* (1965), *Gambit* (1966), and *Thoroughly Modern Millie* (1967).

Elizabeth McBride (1954-June 16, 1997). McBride was a costume designer who was involved with several popular films of the 1980s and 1990s. She was nominated for an Academy Award for her work on *Driving Miss Daisy* (1989). Her additional screen credits include *Tender Mercies* (1983), *True Stories* (1986), *Thelma and Louise* (1991), *Fried Green Tomatoes* (1992), and *Michael* (1996).

Catherine McLeod (July 2, 1921-May 11, 1997). McLeod was an actress who was a leading lady in a number of films in the 1940s and 1950s. Her screen credits include *The Courage of Lassie* (1946), *I've Always Loved You* (1946), *That's My Man* (1947), *The Fabulous Texan* (1947), *So Young, So Bad* (1950), *My Wife's Best Friend* (1952), *A Blueprint for Murder* (1953), *The Outcast* (1954), *Tammy Tell Me True* (1961), and *Ride the Wild Surf* (1964).

Burgess Meredith (November 16, 1908-September 9, 1997). Born George Meredith, Meredith was an actor who appeared in a wide variety of lead and character roles in a career that spanned nearly six decades. Meredith began acting on stage in the 1920s, and by 1932 he had appeared on Broadway. His breakthrough role was in Maxwell Anderson's *Winterset*, in 1935. He reprised his performance in the Hollywood version of *Winter-*

Burgess Meredith

set (1936), and from there enjoyed a prolific career. As he grew older, he moved into supporting roles, in theater, film and on television, where he is remembered as The Penguin, one of the classic villains in the mid-1960s "Batman" series. His screen career peaked again with *The Day of the Locust* (1975) and *Rocky* (1976), when his work in both films earned him Academy Award nominations as Best Supporting Actor. He repeated his role as Sylvester Stallone's trainer, Mickey, in *Rocky II* (1979), *Rocky III* (1982), and *Rocky V* (1990). He directed two films, *The Man on the Eiffel Tower* (1949) and *James Joyce's Women* (1985). He was married for a time to actress Paulette Goddard. Meredith's additional screen credits include *There Goes the Groom* (1937), *That Uncertain Feeling* (1941), *Magnificent Doll* (1946), *Advise and Consent* (1962), *A Big Hand for the Little Lady* (1966), *The Hindenburg* (1975), *Clash of the Titans* (1981), *True Confessions* (1981), *Twilight Zone—The Movie* (1983), *Santa Claus—The Movie* (1985), and *Grumpy Old Men* (1993).

Toshiro Mifune (April 1, 1920-December 24, 1997). Mifune was a Japanese actor who worked extensively with director Akira Kurosawa. He came to occupy a position in Japanese cinema similar to that of John Wayne in American film; he embodied all of the manly virtues which Japanese culture valued, and like Wayne, is best remembered for his period roles, samurai to Wayne's cowboy. His breakthrough came when he caught the attention of Kurosawa, who cast him in a supporting role in *Drunken Angel* (1948), and then in the lead in *Rashomon* (1950), a performance which made him a star. He was featured in other Kurosawa samurai epics such as *The Seven Samurai* (1954) and *Yojimbo* (1960), and as Kurosawa's films became popular in Europe and America, Mifune's fame spread to the West. He and Kurosawa had a falling out after *Red Beard* (1965), and Mifune set out on his own. He appeared in several non-Japanese productions, including *Hell in the Pacific* (1969), a World War II drama in which he starred opposite Lee Marvin. In 1981, his performance in a featured role in the television miniseries "Shogun" earned him an Emmy nomination. Mifune's additional screen credits include *These Foolish Times* (1946), *Stray Dog* (1949), *Eagle of the Pacific* (1953), *Throne of Blood* (1957), *The Bad Sleep Well* (1960), *The Legacy of the Five Hundred Thousand* (1964, which he also directed), *Samurai Assassin* (1965), *Grand Prix* (1966), *Red Sun* (1971), *Paper Tiger* (1975), *Midway* (1976), *The Bushido Blade* (1979), *1941* (1979), *Inchon* (1982), and *The Death of a Tea Master* (1989).

Toshiro Mifune

Pilar Miro (1940-October 19, 1997). Miro was a Spanish director whose work went in and out of favor with the post-Franco democratic Spanish government. Her expose of the Civil Guard, *El Crimen de Cuenca* (1979), was banned in her native country, but she was rehabilitated sufficiently to be named head of Spain's national television and direct the coverage of two royal weddings. She was a feminist who was often frustrated by her country's attitude toward women, and her *Gary Cooper Who Art in Heaven* (1980) was a satirical look at Spanish machismo. Her additional film credits include *La Peticion* (1976), *Let's Talk Tonight* (1982), and *Werther* (1986).

Robert Mitchum (August 6, 1917-July 1, 1997). Mitchum was an actor whose bad boy reputation did nothing to detract from his screen success. He worked at a variety of exotic jobs as a teenager before marrying young and developing an interest in acting. He was cast as a villain in several Hopalong Cassidy Westerns, making eighteen films in 1943 alone. His first starring role was in *The Story of G.I. Joe* (1945), for which he earned an Academy Award nomination as Best Supporting Actor. After a brief stint in the military, he returned to Hollywood and resumed his career. He acquired an aura of controversy in 1949 when he spent time in jail for possession of marijuana, but his popularity remained unaffected. He made well over 100 films, not all of them memorable. But his heavy-lidded gaze and rugged good looks, combined with his seemingly careless attitude translated into screen charisma, and when he got the right parts, his star quality shone through. He starred opposite Marilyn Monroe in *River of No Return* (1954), and made the noir classics *The Night of the Hunter* (1955) and *Cape Fear* (1962). Mitchum even enjoyed some success as a singer in the 1950s and early 1960s; he wrote the title song for *Thunder Road* (1958), in which he starred with his son, Jim Mitchum. He continued to command leading roles into the 1970s, portraying private eye Philip Marlowe in *Farewell My Lovely* (1975) and *The Big Sleep* (1978). Towards the end of his career, he worked in television, enjoying success in the miniseries "Winds of War" and "War and Remembrance." One of his last screen appearances was in a cameo role in Martin Scorsese's remake of *Cape Fear* (1991). Mitchum's additional screen credits include *Hoppy Serves a Writ* (1943), *Cry Havoc* (1943), *Till the End of Time* (1946), *Blood on the Moon* (1948), *The Red Pony* (1949), *White Witch Doctor* (1953), *Track of the Cat* (1954), *Heaven Knows Mr. Allison* (1957), *The Angry Hills* (1959), *The Longest Day* (1962), *El Dorado* (1967), *Ryan's Daughter*

Robert Mitchum

(1970), *The Friends of Eddie Coyle* (1973), *The Yakuza* (1975), *That Championship Season* (1982), *Scrooged* (1988), and *Tombstone* (1993).

Michael O'Herlihy (April 1, 1928-June 14, 1997). O'Herlihy was an Irish-born director who immigrated to the United States and worked extensively in film and television. He directed several Disney features, including *The Fighting Prince of Donegal* (1966), *The One and Only Genuine, Original Family Band* (1967), and *Smith!* (1969).

Denver Pyle (May 11, 1920-December 23, 1997). Pyle was a veteran character actor who worked extensively in television and film, where he specialized in westerns. He is probably best remembered for his role as Uncle Jesse Duke in the 1979-1985 television series "The Dukes of Hazzard." Pyle's film credits include *The Guilt of Janet Ames* (1947), *Horse Soldiers* (1959), *The Alamo* (1960), *The Man Who Shot Liberty Valence* (1962), *Bonnie and Clyde* (1967), and *Cahill, United States Marshall* (1973).

John Rawlins (June 9, 1902-May 20, 1997). Rawlins was a director who specialized in low budget action films, both features and serials, during his most prolific period in the 1940s. His film credits include *State Police* (1938), *The Green Hornet Strikes Again* (1940), *Junior G-Men* (1940), *Six Lessons From Madame La Zonga* (1941), *Raiders of the Desert* (1941), *Sherlock Holmes and the Voice of Terror* (1942), *Dick Tracy's Dilemma* (1947), *Dick Tracy Meets Gruesome* (1947), *Arizona Ranger* (1948), *Rogue River* (1950), *Shark River* (1953), and *Lost Lagoon* (1958).

Marjorie Reynolds (August 12, 1921-February 1, 1997). Born Marjorie Goodspeed, Reynolds was an actress whose career had several facets. She broke into film during the Silent Era as Marjorie Moore, in *Scaramouche* (1923), and changed her name to Reynolds in 1937. Her early films were low budget action pictures, but in the 1940s, she dyed her hair blonde and won roles opposite Bing Crosby in *Holiday Inn* (1942), and Ray Milland in *Ministry of Fear* (1944). In the 1950s, she starred in the title role of the long-running situation comedy "I Married Joan." Her additional screen credits include *Collegiate* (1935), *Six-Shootin' Sheriff* (1928), *Racketeers of the Range* (1939), *Dixie* (1943), *Duffy's Tavern* (1945), *Monsieur Beaucaire* (1946), *Heaven Only Knows* (1947), *Mobs Inc.* (1955), and *Juke Box Rhythm* (1959).

Marjorie Reynolds

William Reynolds (1910-July 16, 1997). Reynolds was a film editor whose film career spanned five decades. He worked on some of the most popular American films of the 1960s and 1970s, including *The Sound of Music* (1965) and *The Sting* (1973), for which he earned Academy Awards. His additional film credits include *The Farmer Takes a Wife* (1935), *Give My Regards to Broadway* (1948), *The Day the Earth Stood Still* (1951), *Three Coins in the Fountain* (1954), *South Pacific* (1958), *Hello, Dolly!* (1969), *The Godfather* (1972), *The Turning Point* (1977), and *The Little Drummer Girl* (1984).

Robert Ridgely (1931-February 8, 1997). Ridgely was a character actor who worked frequently in comedy films, including Mel Brooks' *Blazing Saddles* (1974), *High Anxiety* (1977), *Life Stinks* (1991), and *Robin Hood: Men in Tights* (1993). His additional film credits include *Melvin and Howard* (1980), *Beverly Hills Cop II* (1987), and *That Thing You Do!* (1996).

Alexander Salkind (1915-March 8, 1997). Born in Poland and raised in Germany, Salkind was a producer who was best known for his blockbuster action film *Superman* (1978) and its sequels. His additional film credits include *The Battle of Austerlitz* (1960), *The Trial* (1962), *The Light at the Edge of the World* (1971), *Bluebeard* (1972), *The Three Musketeers* (1974), *The Four Musketeers* (1975), *Superman II* (1981), *Superman III* (1983), *Supergirl* (1984), and *Santa Claus: The Movie* (1985).

George Schaefer (December 16, 1920-September 10, 1997). Schaefer was a director best known for his distinguished television work, where he directed over fifty productions of the "Hallmark Hall of Fame" series. His screen credits include *Macbeth* (1963), *Pendulum* (1969), *Generation* (1969), *Doctors' Wives* (1971), *Once Upon a Scoundrel* (1974), and *An Enemy of the People* (1978).

Red Skelton (July 18, 1910-September 17, 1997). Born Richard Bernard Skelton, Skelton was a comedian who achieved popularity in three media—radio, television, and film. Known as "Red" for his red hair, Skelton was the son of a circus clown, and worked in medicine shows, circuses, and vaudeville from the time he was ten years old. He parlayed a successful radio show into a film career. He started in supporting roles in films such as *Having a Wonderful Time* (1938), and by *Whistling in the Dark* (1941) he began assuming lead roles. Films such

Red Skelton

as *I Dood It* (1943) and *The Fuller Brush Man* (1948) continued his popularity. In 1951, he made the transition to the medium of television, then in its infancy, and "The Red Skelton Show," a variety show built around Skelton's comic sketches, was one of the most popular series in television history, running through 1971. Skelton's additional screen credits include *Whistling in Dixie* (1943), *Du Barry Was a Lady* (1943), *Whistling in Brooklyn* (1943), *Bathing Beauty* (1944), *A Southern Yankee* (1948), *The Yellow Cab Man* (1950), *The Clown* (1953), *Public Pigeon No. 1* (1957), and *Those Magnificent Men in Their Flying Machines* (1965).

James Stewart (May 20, 1908-July 2, 1997). Stewart was an actor who became an American archetype, the Everyman of American cinema. He was born in Indiana and educated at Princeton, where he appeared in some theatrical revues. He joined Josh Logan's University Players, where he met actress Margaret Sullivan, who helped Stewart's early career by insisting that he be cast in several of her films. His gangly frame and hesitant midwestern drawl made him an oddity among leading men, but he caught on with audiences and directors alike. By the late 1930s, he was starring in such films as *Destry Rides Again* (1939) and Frank Capra's *Mr. Smith Goes to Washington* (1939); he earned an Academy Award nomination for his work as an earnest neophyte politician in the latter film. The next year, he was featured alongside Cary Grant and Katharine Hepburn in *The Philadelphia Story* (1940), for which he won the Academy Award as Best Actor. In 1941, Stewart entered the Army, where he rose through the ranks from private to colonel, flying bombing missions in Europe. He attained the highest rank achieved by any entertainer during World War II, and stayed active in the Air Force Reserve until 1968. After the war, Stewart teamed up again with Frank Capra to make what has become one of the most beloved American films of all time, the Christmas classic *It's a Wonderful Life* (1946). Ironically, the film was not considered a classic when it was first released, although it did earn Stewart another Academy Award nomination, as did the gentle comedy of manners *Harvey* (1950). In the 1950s, Stewart began to turn his attention to westerns and thrillers, in which he revealed a darker, grittier screen presence than his audiences had been accustomed to. From *Winchester 73* (1950) and *Broken Arrow* (1950) through *The Man Who Shot Liberty Valance* (1962), *Cheyenne Autumn* (1964) and *The Cheyenne Social Club* (1970), Stewart's westerns were enormously popular. His work with Alfred Hitchcock gave him an opportunity to work in the thriller genre in *Rope* (1948), *Rear Window* (1954), *The Man Who Knew Too Much* (1956), and *Vertigo* (1958). His final Academy Award nomination came for Otto Preminger's *Anatomy of a Murder* (1959). By the early 1970s, Stewart had dramatically reduced his workload, appearing in the occasional film and starring in two short-lived television series in the early 1970s. In 1984, Stewart was honored with a special Academy Award "for his fifty years of memorable performances and for his high ideals both on and off the screen, with the respect and affection of his colleagues." His additional screen credits include *The Murder Man* (1935), *After the Thin Man* (1936), *You Can't Take It With You* (1938), *It's a Wonderful World* (1939), *The Shop Around the Corner* (1940), *Call Northside 777* (1948), *The Stratton Story* (1949), *The Glenn Miller Story* (1954), *The Man From Laramie* (1955), *The Spirit of St. Louis* (1957), *Bell, Book and Candle* (1958), *How the West Was Won* (1962), *Shenandoah* (1965), *Fools' Parade* (1971), *The Shootist* (1976), *Airport 77* (1977), and *An American Tail 2: Fievel Goes West* (1991).

James Stewart

Tomoyuki Tanaka (1920-April 2, 1997). Tanaka was a Japanese producer with more than 200 films to his credit. He is best known for producing all of the Godzilla films. Known in Japan as "Gojira," a combination of the words "gorilla" and "kujira," the Japanese word for whale, Godzilla was a prehistoric, radioactive sea monster who ravaged Japan in a series of films including *Godzilla, King of the Monsters* (1954; released in the United States with additional scenes in 1956), *Godzilla vs. the Thing* (1965), and *Godzilla vs. the Smog Monster* (1971).

Bo Widerberg (June 8, 1930-May 1, 1997). Widerberg was a Swedish director who started as a film critic and began making films to illustrate his points. He wrote his own screenplays and edited his films personally. His best known film in the United States is *Elvira Madigan* (1967), a lyrical study of a tragic romance. Three of his films earned Academy Award nominations as Best Foreign Film: *Raven's End* (1963), *The Adalen Riots* (1969), and *All Things Fair* (1996). His additional film credits include *The Baby Carriage* (1963), *The White Game* (1968), *Joe Hill* (1971), *Man on the Roof* (1977), *The Serpent's Way* (1986), and *Up the Naked Rock* (1988).

Bo Widerberg

Mary Lillian Wills (1914-February 7, 1997). Wills was a much honored costume designer during the 1950s and 1960s. She was nominated for Academy Awards, often in collaboration with Charles Lemaires, for her work on *Hans Christian Andersen* (1952), *The Virgin Queen* (1955), *Teenage Rebel* (1956), *A Certain Smile* (1958), *The Diary of Anne Frank* (1959), and *The Passover Plot* (1976). She won the Academy Award for *The Wonderful World of the Brothers Grimm* (1962). Her additional film credits were *Song of the South* (1946), *Carousel* (1956), *Cape Fear* (1962), and *Camelot* (1967).

Alexander Zarkhi (1908-January 27, 1997). Zarkhi was a Russian director best known for his collaborations in the 1930s and 1940s with Josef Heifitz. These included *Facing the Wind* (1930), *Red Army Days* (1935), *Baltic Deputy* (1937), *The Great Beginning* (1937), and *In the Name of Life* (1947). His solo directing credits include *Pavlinka* (1952), *Men on the Bridge* (1960), *My Younger Brother* (1962), *Anna Karenina* (1967), and *Towns and Years* (1973).

Fred Zinneman (April 29, 1907-March 14, 1997). Born in Austria, Zinneman was a director who worked extensively in Hollywood, scoring his greatest successes in the 1950s and 1960s. After he finished college, he worked as an assistant cameraman in Vienna and Paris, and emigrated to the United States in 1929. After working in various capacities for a variety of filmmakers, he was hired by MGM to make short subjects in 1937, and quickly won an Academy Award for his medical documentary *That Mothers Might Live* (1938). He won a second short subjects Academy Award for *Benjy* (1951), another health-related film. Although Zinneman directed several B pictures, *The Seventh Cross* (1944), with Spencer Tracy, was his first important feature length film. Having established himself as a successful filmmaker, Zinneman proceeded to create hits, some of which provided major actors with their screen debuts. *The Search* (1948) introduced Montgomery Clift to the screen, and earned Zinneman an Academy Award nomination for Directing; *The Men* (1950) likewise introduced Marlon Brando to film audiences. Zinneman hit his stride with the psychological western *High Noon* (1952), for which both the film and Zinneman received Academy Award nominations. His adaptation of *From Here to Eternity* (1954) won Best Film and Directing. At this point in his career, however, Zinneman, never a prolific director, began to slow the pace of his filmmaking. He made only three more films in the 1950s, and directed only twenty features in nearly four decades of filmmaking. *Oklahoma!* (1955) was a successful adaptation of the hit Broadway musical, and *The Nun's Story* (1959) earned Academy Award nominations for Best Picture and Directing. But his next huge hit was *A Man for All Seasons* (1966), another stage adaptation, which Zinneman also produced; the film was named Best Picture, and Zinneman won the Academy Award for Directing. His last success was *Julia* (1977), which earned Zinneman his final Academy Award nomination for Directing. The critical reception of *Five Days One Summer* (1982), was poor, and Zinneman, concluding that his time had passed, retired from filmmaking to work on his autobiography, which was published in 1992. Though never acclaimed as a great director, Zinneman was acknowledged to have been a master craftsman who was able to bring out the best in the actors with whom he worked. His additional feature film credits include *Act of Violence* (1949), *The Member of the Wedding* (1953), *A Hatful of Rain* (1957), *The Sundowners* (1960), *Behold a Pale Horse* (1964), and *The Day of the Jackal* (1973).

Fred Zinneman

—*Robert Mitchell*

Selected Film Books of 1997

Ames, Christopher. *Movies About Movies: Hollywood Reflected.*
Lexington, Kentucky: University Press of Kentucky, 1997.

Ames examines the cultural meaning of Hollywood by analyzing fifteen films, from the 1930s to the 1990s, which take Hollywood and filmmaking as their narrative subject.

Andreychuk, Ed. *The Golden Corral.*
Jefferson, North Carolina: McFarland, 1997.

Andreychuk devotes a chapter each to an extended discussion of fourteen classic Hollywood Westerns, from *Stagecoach* in 1939 to *Unforgiven* in 1992.

Atkins, Rick. *Let's Scare Em!*
Jefferson, North Carolina: McFarland, 1997.

Atkins offers a collection of interviews with a variety of filmmakers associated with the horror genre, as well as a filmography of horror films released between 1930 and 1961.

Baxter, John. *Stanley Kubrick: A Biography.*
New York: Carroll & Graf, 1997.

Interviewing a wide range of Kubrick's associates, Baxter's biography focuses on the details of the reclusive filmmaker's life as well as his career.

Benshoff, Harry M. *Monsters in the Closet.*
Manchester, United Kingdom: Manchester University Press, 1997.

Benshoff studies the theme of homosexuality in horror films, from the classic era to contemporary films.

Billman, Larry. *Film Choreographers and Dance Directors.*
Jefferson, North Carolina: McFarland, 1997.

Billman has produced an illustrated biographical encyclopedia with filmographies, for important figures in dance-related cinema from 1893-1995.

Blackwell, Marilyn Johns. *Gender and Representation in the Films of Ingmar Bergman.*
Columbia, South Carolina: Camden House, 1997.

Blackwell presents a scholarly feminist analysis of the work of the great Swedish filmmaker, discussing five of his major films in detail.

Bogdanovich, Peter. *Who the Devil Made It.*
New York: Alfred A. Knopf, 1997.

Filmmaker Bogdanovich presents interviews with sixteen Hollywood directors, collected over more than a quarter century, with filmographies for each man.

Brill, Lesley. *John Huston's Filmmaking.*
Cambridge, United Kingdom: Cambridge University Press, 1997.

Brill offers a detailed critical analysis of thirteen of Huston's films and argues that the director deserves to be ranked among America's most important filmmakers.

Brode, Douglas. *Denzel Washington: His Films and Career.*
Secaucus, New Jersey: Birch Lane Press, 1997.

Brode offers one of the first book length examinations of the life and work of the popular African American actor.

Bryant, Wayne M. *Bisexual Characters in Film: From Anais to Zee.*
New York: Haworth Press, 1997.

Recent years have seen numerous works on gay and lesbian characters in film, but Bryant offers the first analysis of the cinematic portrayal of bisexuals.

Burgoyne, Robert. *Film Nation: Hollywood Looks at U.S. History.*
Minneapolis, Minnesota: University of Minnesota Press, 1997.

Burgoyne analyzes seven recent American historical films which challenge, and in the process, rewrite, traditional United States history.

Burns-Bisogno, Louisa. *Censoring Irish Nationalism.*
Jefferson, North Carolina: McFarland, 1997.

Burns-Bisogno analyzes the ways in which the depiction of the Irish Republican movement has been suppressed or distorted in British, American, and Irish film since 1909.

Byrne, Terry. *Power in the Eye: An Introduction to Contemporary Irish Film.*
Lanham, Maryland: Scarecrow Press, 1997.

Byrne examines Irish films of the past quarter century in the context of national expression and self-definition.

Cameron, Kenneth M. *America on Film: Hollywood and American History.*
New York: Continuum, 1997.

Cameron offers a decade by decade review of Hollywood's treatment of American history, looking for the relationship between good films and good history.

Cohen, Karl F. *Forbidden Animation: Censored Cartoons and Blacklisted Animators in America.*
Jefferson, North Carolina: McFarland, 1997.

Cohen presents a history of the censorship of animated cartoons from the Silent Era through modern times, for sexual, racial, or political content.

Cones, John W. *The Feature Film Distribution Deal.*
Carbondale, Illinois: Southern Illinois University Press, 1997.

Cones calls the distribution deal the "single most important film industry agreement" in this study of the business of filmmaking.

Cripps, Thomas. *Hollywood's High Noon.*
Baltimore, Maryland: Johns Hopkins University Press, 1997.

Cripps examines Hollywood filmmaking at its zenith, from the advent of sound, through the heyday of the studio era, until the coming of television.

Custen, George F. *Twentieth Century's Fox.*
New York: Basic Books, 1997.

Custen offers this biography of Darryl F. Zanuck, influential producer and studio head, one of the founders of 20th Century-Fox at the beginning of the sound era.

D'Lugo, Marvin. *Guide to the Cinema of Spain.*
Westport, Connecticut: Greenwood Press, 1997.

D'Lugo presents a lengthy analysis of the national cinema of Spain, with chapters on the country's major films, directors, and actors.

Dannen, Frederic, and Barry Long. *Hong Kong Babylon.*
New York: Hyperion, 1997.

Dannen offers an inside look at the Hollywood of the East and Long adds a filmography with plot summaries of over 300 major Hong Kong films of the past two decades. The book also features twenty critics' "Best of Hong Kong cinema" lists.

Day, David Howard. *A Treasure Hard to Attain.*
Lanham, Maryland: Scarecrow Press, 1997.

Day examines the image of archaeology in popular film, with essays on 120 films, most of them American, some of which date back to the Silent Era.

Dick, Bernard F. *City of Dreams: The Making and Remaking of Universal Pictures.*
Lexington, Kentucky: University Press of Kentucky, 1997.

Dick offers a history of Universal Pictures, focusing primarily on the films made by the studio after the advent of sound and before its absorption into MCA in 1962.

Dukore, Bernard F., editor. *Bernard Shaw on Cinema.*
Carbondale, Illinois: Southern Illinois University Press, 1997.

Dukore collects the film-related criticism and commentary of the illustrious British playwright in this volume.

Dunne, John Gregory. *Monster: Living Off the Big Screen.*
New York: Random House, 1997.

Dunne tells the story of how he and his wife, Joan Didion, came to write the screenplay for *Golden Girl*, and how that screenplay came to diverge so substantially from the details of the life of its subject, newswoman Jessica Savitch.

Ebert, Roger. *Roger Ebert's Book of Film.*
New York: W.W. Norton, 1997.

Ebert has put together a collection of film commentary from various sources, "From Tolstoy to Tarantino," as the subtitle proclaims.

Eyman, Scott. *The Speed of Sound.*
New York: Simon & Schuster, 1997.

Eyman offers an detailed examination of Hollywood in the years 1926 to 1930, when talking films first emerged and then dominated the cinematic landscape.

Farrow, Mia. *What Falls Away: A Memoir.*
New York: Doubleday, 1997.

Farrow tells the story of her life and loves. She is generous to most of the men in her life, with the notable exception of ex-companion Woody Allen.

Fisher, James. *Eddie Cantor: A Bio-Bibliography.*
Westport, Connecticut: Greenwood Press, 1997.

Cantor was a vaudeville, radio, recording, and film star in the 1920s and 1930s. This volume offers a brief biographical sketch, along with a bibliography, discography, and filmography of his career.

Flom, Eric L. *Chaplin in the Sound Era.*
Jefferson, North Carolina: McFarland, 1997.

Flom offers a detailed analysis of the seven films made by Charlie Chaplin after the advent of sound, including biographical sketches of the filmmaker's life at the time each film was made.

Foster, Buddy. *Foster Child.*
New York: E.P. Dutton, 1997.

Jodie Foster's older brother describes his family as highly dysfunctional; most of the anger is directed at his mother, while sister Jodie is generally portrayed affectionately.

Friedman, Lawrence S. *The Cinema of Martin Scorsese.*
New York: Continuum, 1997.

Friedman analyzes Scorsese's films through *The Age of Innocence*, noting the religious passion that underpins all of the filmmaker's work.

Gehring, Wes D. *Personality Comedians as Genre: Selected Players.*
Westport, Connecticut: Greenwood Press, 1997.

Gehring analyzes seven prominent screen clowns, from John Bunny and Charlie Chaplin in the early days of film, to Bob Hope and his contemporary disciple, Woody Allen.

Gentry, Clyde III. *Jackie Chan: Inside the Dragon.*
Dallas, Texas: Taylor Publishing, 1997.

Hong Kong actor Chan has recently enjoyed success with American audiences; Gentry's critical biography is the best of several recent works on the action comedy star.

Gevinson, Alan, editor. *Within Our Gates: Ethnicity in American Feature Films, 1911-1960.*
Berkeley, California: University of California Press, 1997.

This catalog from the American Film Institute provides plot summaries plus information on cast and credits for over 2,400 American films which focus on issues relating to ethnicity.

Goldberg, Whoopi. *Book.*
New York: Rob Weisbach, 1997.

The African-American actress/comedian mixes autobiography with random, often scatological, observations and philosophizing as she tells her life story.

Goldman, Herbert G. *Banjo Eyes: Eddie Cantor and the Birth of Modern Stardom.*
New York: Oxford University Press, 1997.

Goldman argues that Cantor, an enormously popular figure in films, vaudeville, and music during the 1920s and early 1930s, was the prototype of the contemporary celebrity, a star whose personal life as well as his art was a part of his image.

Good, Howard. *Diamonds in the Dark.*
Lanham, Maryland: Scarecrow Press, 1997.

Combining the personal and the scholarly, Good examines films about baseball and baseball's place in American culture.

Griffith, James. *Adaptations as Imitations: Films from Novels.*
Neward, Delaware: University of Delaware Press, 1997.

Griffith offers a scholarly analysis of the process of adapting novels to the screen, arguing that while film cannot duplicate the novel that does not necessarily diminish the narrative pleasure to be found in the film.

Hamsher, Jane. *Killer Instinct.*
New York: Broadway Books, 1997.

Hamsher tells the irreverent story of how she and her friend Don Murphy came to produce Oliver Stone's controversial film *Natural Born Killers* from Quentin Tarantino's script, savaging both men along the way.

Harwood, Sarah. *Family Fictions.*
New York: St. Martin's Press, 1997.

Harwood examines the representation of families in Hollywood films of the 1980s, a time in which "family values" became a symbolic cultural and political battle cry.

Henabery, Joseph E. *Before, In and After Hollywood.*
Lanham, Maryland: Scarecrow Press, 1997.

This is the autobiography of a man who directed scores of feature films and shorts in the Silent and early sound eras; it includes a chapter in which Henabery notes errors in some of the popular biographies of Silent Era notables.

Holston, Kim R. *Science Fiction, Fantasy and Horror Film Sequels, Series and Remakes.*
Jefferson, North Carolina: McFarland, 1997.

The authors offer an illustrated filmography, with plot synopses and critical commentary, of sound era science fiction, fantasy, and horror films which generated some sort of sequel or remake.

Jenkins, Greg. *Stanley Kubrick and the Art of Adaptation.*
Jefferson, North Carolina: McFarland, 1997.

Jenkins focuses on Kubrick's adaptation of three novels into the films *Lolita*, *The Shining*, and *Full Metal Jacket.*

Johnson, Tom. *Censored Screams.*
Jefferson, North Carolina: McFarland, 1997.

Johnson's work examines the British censorship of American horror films during the 1930s, and the role this played in the decline of the genre during the latter part of the decade.

Keller, Gary D. *A Biographical Handbook of Hispanics and United States Film.*
Tempe, Arizona: Bilingual Press, 1997.

This reference work offers brief biographical entries, along with filmographies, for Hispanics working in American film and television.

Kelly, Andrew, James Pepper, and Jeffrey Reynolds, editors. *Filming T.E. Lawrence: Korda's Lost Epics.*
London: I.B. Tauris, 1997.

This is the story of British producer Alexander Korda's unsuccessful attempts during the 1930s to film the life of the man who became known as "Lawrence of Arabia."

Kinder, Marsha, editor. *Refiguring Spain: Cinema/Media/Representation.*
Durham, North Carolina: Duke University Press, 1997.

Kinder collects thirteen essays and an annotated bibliography on mass media, and particularly cinema, in post-Franco Spain.

Kirby, Lynne. *Parallel Tracks: The Railroad in Silent Cinema.*
Durham, North Carolina: Duke University Press, 1997.

Kirby's book is a scholarly study of Silent Era filmmakers' uses of the railroad train, literally and symbolically, in their work; the study is international in scope.

Klotman, Phyllis R., and Gloria J. Gibson. *Frame By Frame II: A Filmography of the African American Image, 1978-1994.*
Bloomington, Indiana: Indiana University Press, 1997.

This annotated filmography of films about African Americans updates the first volume on the series which was published in 1979.

Konigsberg, Ira. *The Complete Film Dictionary.*
New York: Penguin, 1997.

This is the second edition, much revised, of Konigsberg's useful compilation of definitions of film terminology.

Kramer, Stanley, with Thomas M. Coffey. *A Mad, Mad, Mad, Mad World.*
New York: Harcourt Brace, 1997.

Filmmaker Kramer, known for his "message" pictures, reviews his life and work in this straightforward autobiography.

Lambert, Gavin. *Nazimova: A Biography.*
New York: Alfred A. Knopf, 1997.

Lambert offers a biography of Alla Nazimova, the Russian born actress who was an American stage and screen star during the Silent Era.

Lawrence, Amy. *The Films of Peter Greenaway.*
Cambridge, United Kingdom: Cambridge University Press, 1997.

Lawrence offers a scholarly analysis of the films of one of the leading British filmmakers of the past two decades.

Lebo, Harlan. *The Godfather Legacy.*
New York: Fireside, 1997.

Lebo examines Coppola's *The Godfather Trilogy* individually and collectively, in this illustrated twenty-fifth anniversary commemoration.

Lee, Betty. *Marie Dressler: The Unlikeliest Star.*
Lexington, Kentucky: University Press of Kentucky, 1997.

Lee offers a biography of an actress who, despite her girth and plain looks, was one of Hollywood's most popular stars during the late Silent Era and into the 1930s.

Lee, Sander H. *Woody Allen's Angst.*
Jefferson, North Carolina: McFarland, 1997.

Subtitled "Philosophical Commentaries on His Serious Films," this book gives short shrift to Allen's early comedies and offers detailed analyses of his post-*Annie Hall* work.

Leider, Emily Wortis. *Becoming Mae West.*
New York: Farrar Straus Giroux, 1997.

This scholarly biography of the notorious vaudeville and film actress focuses on the first half of her life, through the 1930s, the period in which West created her persona.

Locke, Sondra. *The Good, the Bad & the Very Ugly: A Hollywood Journey.*
New York: William Morrow, 1997.

The actress who was once Clint Eastwood's paramour describes the breakup of that relationship and her battle with breast cancer in this autobiography.

Louvish, Simon. *Man on the Flying Trapeze: The Life and Times of W.C. Fields.*
New York: W.W. Norton, 1997.

In this first extended biographical examination of the comic actor in decades, Louvish exposes many myths about Fields, most of which Fields created himself.

Lynn, Kenneth S. *Charlie Chaplin and His Times.*
New York: Simon & Schuster, 1997.

Lynn offers a biography of the great American comic actor, with a subtext involving the rise of Hollywood as the center of the film industry.

Lu, Sheldon Hsiao-peng, editor. *Transnational Chinese Cinemas.*
Honolulu, Hawaii: University of Hawaii Press, 1997.

This is a collection of fourteen scholarly essays examining issues of nationality in Chinese cinema from China, Taiwan, and Hong Kong.

MacCann, Richard Dyer. *The Silent Screen.*
Lanham, Maryland: Scarecrow Press, 1997.

Film historian MacCann offers a history of American Silent film, focused on the personalities—studio executives, directors, and actors—of the era.

McBride, Joseph. *Steven Spielberg: A Biography.*
New York: Simon & Schuster, 1997.

McBride grounds his biography of Spielberg in the renowned director's shifting relationship to his Jewish roots.

McCabe, John. *Cagney.*
New York: Alfred A. Knopf, 1997.

McCabe was the ghostwriter for Cagney's autobiography; he draws upon that experience in this biography of the late actor.

McCarthy, Todd. *Howard Hawks: The Grey Fox of Hollywood.*
New York: Grove Press, 1997.

McCarthy provides the first detailed biography of Hawks, perhaps the least well-known giant of American cinema.

McGilligan, Pat. *Backstory 3.*
Berkeley, California: University of California Press, 1997.

McGilligan's third collection of screenwriter interviews offers conversations with fourteen writers whose careers began in the 1960s.

Mair, George. *The Barry Diller Story.*
New York: John Wiley & Sons, 1997.

Mair adds a chapter to the history of the economics of film with this study of the life of Barry Diller, powerful mogul of Paramount, Fox, and QVC.

Malden, Karl, with Carla Malden. *When Do I Start?*
New York: Simon & Schuster, 1997.

Malden, with the help of his daughter, tells the engaging story of his life and career in show business.

Marion, Donald J. *The Chinese Filmography.*
Jefferson, North Carolina: McFarland, 1997.

This massive filmography offers plot summaries plus information on cast and credits for 2,444 feature films produced in the People's Republic of China between 1949 and 1995.

Martin, Michael T., editor. *New Latin American Cinema.*
Detroit: Wayne State University Press, 1997.

This two volume work is a scholarly study of modern Latin American film, focusing both on national cinemas and on broader thematic and aesthetic issues.

Meyers, Jeffrey. *Bogart: A Life in Hollywood.*
Boston: Houghton Mifflin, 1997.

Meyers presents a straightforward popular biography of the legendary actor's life and career.

Mielke, Randall G. *Road to Box Office.*
Jefferson, North Carolina: McFarland, 1997.

Mielke offers an appreciation of the seven Road comedies made between 1940 and 1962 and featuring Bing Crosby, Bob Hope, and Dorothy Lamour.

Moon, Spencer. *Reel Black Talk.*
Westport, Connecticut: Greenwood Press, 1997.

Moon provides extended biographical entries on fifty African-American directors, from the pioneering Oscar Micheaux to contemporary filmmakers.

Nadel, Alan. *Flatlining on the Field of Dreams.*
New Brunswick, New Jersey: Rutgers University Press, 1997.

Nadel uses the Hollywood films of the 1980s to illuminate the cultural climate in the United States during the Reagan presidency.

Oller, John. *Jean Arthur: The Actress Nobody Knew.*
New York: Limelight Editions, 1997.

Oller's work is the first biography of the actress who was a popular leading lady of the 1930s and 1940s, and whose difficult personal life made her a deeply private person.

Petrie, Ruth. *Film and Censorship.*
London: Cassell, 1997.

This collection of essays from *Index on Censorship* offers a worldwide perspective on attempts to suppress various films for political or other reasons.

Pinedo, Isabel Cristina. *Recreational Terror.*
Albany, New York: State University of New York Press, 1997.

This is a scholarly examination of how the postmodern horror/slasher film provides female viewers with a pleasurable encounter with violence.

Pitts, Michael R. *Poverty Row Studios, 1929-1940.*
Jefferson, North Carolina: McFarland, 1997.

Pitts offers a history, including filmographies, of 53 low budget, independent film studios which operated from the inception of the sound era into the 1940s.

Puttnam, David, with Neil Watson. *The Undeclared War.*
London: HarperCollins, 1997.

Puttnam has produced films in America and Britain; this is his look at the century-long struggle between Hollywood and various national cinemas for worldwide market share.

Quirk, Lawrence J. *James Stewart: Behind the Scenes of a Wonderful Life.*
New York: Applause Books, 1997.

Quirk offers an affectionate and respectful look at the life and loves of one of America's most beloved actors.

Rhodes, Gary Don. *Lugosi.*
Jefferson, North Carolina: McFarland, 1997.

Rhodes' work includes a biographical sketch of the actor forever associated with the film *Dracula*, along with analyses of his film and television appearances.

Rossellini, Isabella. *Some of Me.*
New York: Random House, 1997.

The actress offers this lavishly illustrated volume of autobiographical observations on her life and career, warning readers early on that she embellishes the truth on occasion.

Rothman, William. *Documentary Film Classics.*
New York: Cambridge University Press, 1997.

Rothman offers detailed analyses of six classic documentary films, from *Nanook of the North* to *Don't Look Back.*

Salwolke, Scott. *The Films of Michael Powell and the Archers.*
Lanham, Maryland: Scarecrow Press, 1997.
"The Archers" were Powell and Emeric Pressburger, Britons who wrote, produced, and directed sixteen films between 1942 and 1957; Salwolke analyzes their work, together and separate.

Schultz, Margie. *Ann Sheridan: A Bio-Bibliography.*
Westport, Connecticut: Greenwood Press, 1997.

Known as the "Oomph Girl" to her fans, Sheridan was a popular actress of the 1940s. This volume offers a brief biographical sketch, along with a filmography, discography, and bibliography on her career.

Schwartz, Ronald. *Latin American Films, 1932-1994.*
Jefferson, North Carolina: McFarland, 1997.

Schwartz offers brief commentaries on 301 sound era films produced in Latin America, or in the United States, if the film had significant Latin American themes.

Segrave, Kerry. *American Films Abroad.*
Jefferson, North Carolina: McFarland, 1997.

Segrave offers a comprehensive analysis of the impact of Hollywood films in foreign countries, from the late 19th century to the present day.

Sperber, A.M., and Eric Lax. *Bogart.*
New York: William Morrow, 1997.

Ann Sperber did most of the basic research on this massive popular biography prior to her death; her manuscript was completed by Eric Lax.

Spoto, Donald. *Notorious: The Life of Ingrid Bergman.*
New York: HarperCollins, 1997.

Bergman was known as much for her affair with Roberto Rossellini as for her work in such films as *Casablanca*. Spoto's biography maintains a balanced focus on the actress's personal life and public career.

Stevens, Donald F., editor. *Based on a True Story.*
Wilmington, Delaware: SR Books, 1997.

Stevens presents this collection of a dozen scholarly essays on the cinematic treatment of various aspects of Latin American history.

Stevens, Jon. *Actors Turned Directors.*
Los Angeles: Silman-James Press, 1997.

Stevens offers ten lengthy interviews with actors such as Jodie Foster, Leonard Nimoy, and Mel Gibson, who have also directed films, on the subject of successful filmmaking.

Stock, Ann Marie, editor. *Framing Latin American Cinema.*
Minneapolis, Minnesota: University of Minnesota Press, 1997.

Stock collects a dozen scholarly critical essays on various aspects of contemporary national cinema in Latin America.

Strada, Michael, and Harold Troper. *Friend of Foe?*
Lanham, Maryland: Scarecrow Press, 1997.

The authors study the changing American view of Russia and its citizens by comparing American foreign policy and film from 1933 to 1991, after the demise of the Soviet Union.

Swenson, Karen. *Greta Garbo: A Life Apart.*
New York: Scribner, 1997.

Swenson offers an exhaustively detailed biography of the reclusive actress, portraying her as often irritated and bored with life.

Thomson, David. *Beneath Mulholland.*
New York: Alfred A. Knopf, 1997.

Film critic Thomson offers a collection of essays written over the past twenty years, imagining alternatives for the lives of actors and their characters in these thought provoking meditations on what might have been.

Tudor, Deborah V. *Hollywood's Vision of Team Sports.*
New York: Garland, 1997.

Tudor examines issues of athletic heroism, race, and gender in this feminist critique of sports icons on the field and on the screen.

Vasey, Ruth. *The World According to Hollywood, 1918-1939.*
Madison, Wisconsin: University of Wisconsin Press, 1997.

Vasey offers a scholarly study of the forces that shaped Hollywood's view of the world in the years between the First and Second World Wars.

Vertrees, Alan David. *Selznick's Vision.*
Austin, Texas: University of Texas Press, 1997.

Vertrees argues that, contrary to his popular image, producer Selznick's vision was the guiding intelligence behind the success of *Gone With the Wind* (1939).

Warren, Bill. *Set Visits.*
Jefferson, North Carolina: McFarland, 1997.

Warren collects interviews with 32 filmmakers who have worked on five recent films in the horror or science fiction genre, including *Bram Stoker's Dracula* and *Jurassic Park.*

Weiss, Ken. *To the Rescue.*
San Francisco: Austin & Winfield, 1997.

Weiss examines American cinema between 1906 and 1912 and argues that working class immigrants exerted a tremendous influence on the development of motion pictures during this period.

Whitfield, Eileen. *Pickford: The Woman Who Made Hollywood.*
Lexington, Kentucky: University Press of Kentucky, 1997.

Mary Pickford was one of the most popular and powerful figures of the Silent Era, but, as Whitfield notes in this critical biography, her refusal to properly preserve her work has led to her career being undervalued by film historians.

Willis, Sharon. *High Contrast: Race and Gender in Contemporary Hollywood Film.*
Durham, North Carolina: Duke University Press, 1997.

Willis offers a scholarly study of the process by which Hollywood takes America's fascination with race and sex and fashions it into entertainment.

Wills, Garry. *John Wayne's America: The Politics of Celebrity.*
New York: Simon & Schuster, 1997.

Wills argues that Wayne became an American icon because the characters he played embodied the virtues of the frontiersman, virtues which have been lost in modern America.

Windeler, Robert. *Julie Andrews: A Life on Stage and Screen.*
Secaucus, New Jersey: Birch Lane Press, 1997.

Windeler argues that Andrews' success in the saccharine *Mary Poppins* and *The Sound of Music* set her career back until the 1980s, when she broke through the stereotypes in films with her husband, Blake Edwards.

Wyke, Maria. *Projecting the Past.*
New York: Routledge, 1997.

Wyke offers a scholarly study of the portrayal of ancient Rome in cinema, focusing on the recurring themes of Spartacus, Cleopatra, Nero, and Pompeii.

Xavier, Ismail. *Allegories of Underdevelopment.*
Minneapolis, Minnesota: University of Minnesota Press, 1997.

Xavier offers a scholarly analysis of issues surrounding aesthetics and politics in Brazilian cinema from 1964-1970.

—Robert Mitchell

Magill's Cinema Annual 1998
Indexes

Directors

Screenwriters

Cinematographers

Editors

Art Directors

Music Directors

Performers

Subjects

Subjects

Title Index

This cumulative index is an alphabetical list of all films covered in the seventeen volumes of the *Magill's Cinema Annual.* Film titles are indexed on a word-by-word basis, including articles and prepositions. English and foreign leading articles are ignored. Films reviewed in this volume are cited in bold with an arabic number indicating the page number on which the review begins; films reviewed in past volumes are cited with the year in which the film was originally released. Film sequels are indicated with a roman numeral following the film title. Original and alternate titles are cross-referenced to the American release title. Titles of retrospective films, as well as those cited in the Life Achievement Award section are followed by the year, in brackets, of their original release.